The Python Library Reference

Release 3.6.4

Book 2 of 2
Chapters 19-37

**Guido van Rossum
and the Python development team**

February 03, 2018

Python Software Foundation
Email: docs@python.org

CONTENTS

1	Introduction	3
2	Built-in Functions	5
3	Built-in Constants	27
	3.1 Constants added by the `site` module	28
4	Built-in Types	29
	4.1 Truth Value Testing	29
	4.2 Boolean Operations — `and`, `or`, `not`	29
	4.3 Comparisons	30
	4.4 Numeric Types — `int`, `float`, `complex`	30
	4.5 Iterator Types	36
	4.6 Sequence Types — `list`, `tuple`, `range`	37
	4.7 Text Sequence Type — `str`	43
	4.8 Binary Sequence Types — `bytes`, `bytearray`, `memoryview`	53
	4.9 Set Types — `set`, `frozenset`	73
	4.10 Mapping Types — `dict`	75
	4.11 Context Manager Types	79
	4.12 Other Built-in Types	80
	4.13 Special Attributes	82
5	Built-in Exceptions	85
	5.1 Base classes	85
	5.2 Concrete exceptions	86
	5.3 Warnings	92
	5.4 Exception hierarchy	92
6	Text Processing Services	95
	6.1 `string` — Common string operations	95
	6.2 `re` — Regular expression operations	105
	6.3 `difflib` — Helpers for computing deltas	125
	6.4 `textwrap` — Text wrapping and filling	135
	6.5 `unicodedata` — Unicode Database	139
	6.6 `stringprep` — Internet String Preparation	141
	6.7 `readline` — GNU readline interface	142
	6.8 `rlcompleter` — Completion function for GNU readline	146
7	Binary Data Services	149
	7.1 `struct` — Interpret bytes as packed binary data	149
	7.2 `codecs` — Codec registry and base classes	154

8 Data Types — 173
- 8.1 `datetime` — Basic date and time types 173
- 8.2 `calendar` — General calendar-related functions 203
- 8.3 `collections` — Container datatypes 206
- 8.4 `collections.abc` — Abstract Base Classes for Containers 222
- 8.5 `heapq` — Heap queue algorithm 226
- 8.6 `bisect` — Array bisection algorithm 230
- 8.7 `array` — Efficient arrays of numeric values 232
- 8.8 `weakref` — Weak references 235
- 8.9 `types` — Dynamic type creation and names for built-in types 242
- 8.10 `copy` — Shallow and deep copy operations 246
- 8.11 `pprint` — Data pretty printer 247
- 8.12 `reprlib` — Alternate `repr()` implementation 252
- 8.13 `enum` — Support for enumerations 254

9 Numeric and Mathematical Modules — 273
- 9.1 `numbers` — Numeric abstract base classes 273
- 9.2 `math` — Mathematical functions 276
- 9.3 `cmath` — Mathematical functions for complex numbers 281
- 9.4 `decimal` — Decimal fixed point and floating point arithmetic 285
- 9.5 `fractions` — Rational numbers 311
- 9.6 `random` — Generate pseudo-random numbers 313
- 9.7 `statistics` — Mathematical statistics functions 320

10 Functional Programming Modules — 327
- 10.1 `itertools` — Functions creating iterators for efficient looping 327
- 10.2 `functools` — Higher-order functions and operations on callable objects . 341
- 10.3 `operator` — Standard operators as functions 347

11 File and Directory Access — 355
- 11.1 `pathlib` — Object-oriented filesystem paths 355
- 11.2 `os.path` — Common pathname manipulations 371
- 11.3 `fileinput` — Iterate over lines from multiple input streams 376
- 11.4 `stat` — Interpreting `stat()` results 378
- 11.5 `filecmp` — File and Directory Comparisons 383
- 11.6 `tempfile` — Generate temporary files and directories 385
- 11.7 `glob` — Unix style pathname pattern expansion 389
- 11.8 `fnmatch` — Unix filename pattern matching 390
- 11.9 `linecache` — Random access to text lines 391
- 11.10 `shutil` — High-level file operations 392
- 11.11 `macpath` — Mac OS 9 path manipulation functions 400

12 Data Persistence — 401
- 12.1 `pickle` — Python object serialization 401
- 12.2 `copyreg` — Register `pickle` support functions 414
- 12.3 `shelve` — Python object persistence 415
- 12.4 `marshal` — Internal Python object serialization 417
- 12.5 `dbm` — Interfaces to Unix "databases" 418
- 12.6 `sqlite3` — DB-API 2.0 interface for SQLite databases 422

13 Data Compression and Archiving — 443
- 13.1 `zlib` — Compression compatible with `gzip` 443
- 13.2 `gzip` — Support for `gzip` files 446
- 13.3 `bz2` — Support for `bzip2` compression 449
- 13.4 `lzma` — Compression using the LZMA algorithm 452

13.5	`zipfile` — Work with ZIP archives	457
13.6	`tarfile` — Read and write tar archive files	465

14 File Formats **477**
14.1	`csv` — CSV File Reading and Writing	477
14.2	`configparser` — Configuration file parser	483
14.3	`netrc` — netrc file processing	501
14.4	`xdrlib` — Encode and decode XDR data	502
14.5	`plistlib` — Generate and parse Mac OS X `.plist` files	505

15 Cryptographic Services **509**
15.1	`hashlib` — Secure hashes and message digests	509
15.2	`hmac` — Keyed-Hashing for Message Authentication	519
15.3	`secrets` — Generate secure random numbers for managing secrets	520

16 Generic Operating System Services **525**
16.1	`os` — Miscellaneous operating system interfaces	525
16.2	`io` — Core tools for working with streams	570
16.3	`time` — Time access and conversions	582
16.4	`argparse` — Parser for command-line options, arguments and sub-commands	590
16.5	`getopt` — C-style parser for command line options	621
16.6	`logging` — Logging facility for Python	623
16.7	`logging.config` — Logging configuration	639
16.8	`logging.handlers` — Logging handlers	649
16.9	`getpass` — Portable password input	662
16.10	`curses` — Terminal handling for character-cell displays	662
16.11	`curses.textpad` — Text input widget for curses programs	680
16.12	`curses.ascii` — Utilities for ASCII characters	681
16.13	`curses.panel` — A panel stack extension for curses	684
16.14	`platform` — Access to underlying platform's identifying data	685
16.15	`errno` — Standard errno system symbols	688
16.16	`ctypes` — A foreign function library for Python	694

17 Concurrent Execution **727**
17.1	`threading` — Thread-based parallelism	727
17.2	`multiprocessing` — Process-based parallelism	739
17.3	The `concurrent` package	781
17.4	`concurrent.futures` — Launching parallel tasks	781
17.5	`subprocess` — Subprocess management	787
17.6	`sched` — Event scheduler	802
17.7	`queue` — A synchronized queue class	804
17.8	`dummy_threading` — Drop-in replacement for the `threading` module	806
17.9	`_thread` — Low-level threading API	807
17.10	`_dummy_thread` — Drop-in replacement for the `_thread` module	808

18 Interprocess Communication and Networking **811**
18.1	`socket` — Low-level networking interface	811
18.2	`ssl` — TLS/SSL wrapper for socket objects	832
18.3	`select` — Waiting for I/O completion	862
18.4	`selectors` — High-level I/O multiplexing	869
18.5	`asyncio` — Asynchronous I/O, event loop, coroutines and tasks	872
18.6	`asyncore` — Asynchronous socket handler	932
18.7	`asynchat` — Asynchronous socket command/response handler	936
18.8	`signal` — Set handlers for asynchronous events	938
18.9	`mmap` — Memory-mapped file support	943

19 Internet Data Handling — 949
- 19.1 `email` — An email and MIME handling package 949
- 19.2 `json` — JSON encoder and decoder 1007
- 19.3 `mailcap` — Mailcap file handling 1016
- 19.4 `mailbox` — Manipulate mailboxes in various formats 1017
- 19.5 `mimetypes` — Map filenames to MIME types 1035
- 19.6 `base64` — Base16, Base32, Base64, Base85 Data Encodings 1038
- 19.7 `binhex` — Encode and decode binhex4 files 1041
- 19.8 `binascii` — Convert between binary and ASCII 1042
- 19.9 `quopri` — Encode and decode MIME quoted-printable data 1044
- 19.10 `uu` — Encode and decode uuencode files 1044

20 Structured Markup Processing Tools — 1047
- 20.1 `html` — HyperText Markup Language support 1047
- 20.2 `html.parser` — Simple HTML and XHTML parser 1047
- 20.3 `html.entities` — Definitions of HTML general entities 1052
- 20.4 XML Processing Modules 1052
- 20.5 `xml.etree.ElementTree` — The ElementTree XML API 1054
- 20.6 `xml.dom` — The Document Object Model API 1069
- 20.7 `xml.dom.minidom` — Minimal DOM implementation 1079
- 20.8 `xml.dom.pulldom` — Support for building partial DOM trees 1084
- 20.9 `xml.sax` — Support for SAX2 parsers 1085
- 20.10 `xml.sax.handler` — Base classes for SAX handlers 1087
- 20.11 `xml.sax.saxutils` — SAX Utilities 1092
- 20.12 `xml.sax.xmlreader` — Interface for XML parsers 1093
- 20.13 `xml.parsers.expat` — Fast XML parsing using Expat 1097

21 Internet Protocols and Support — 1107
- 21.1 `webbrowser` — Convenient Web-browser controller 1107
- 21.2 `cgi` — Common Gateway Interface support 1109
- 21.3 `cgitb` — Traceback manager for CGI scripts 1116
- 21.4 `wsgiref` — WSGI Utilities and Reference Implementation 1117
- 21.5 `urllib` — URL handling modules 1126
- 21.6 `urllib.request` — Extensible library for opening URLs 1126
- 21.7 `urllib.response` — Response classes used by urllib 1144
- 21.8 `urllib.parse` — Parse URLs into components 1144
- 21.9 `urllib.error` — Exception classes raised by urllib.request 1151
- 21.10 `urllib.robotparser` — Parser for robots.txt 1152
- 21.11 `http` — HTTP modules 1153
- 21.12 `http.client` — HTTP protocol client 1155
- 21.13 `ftplib` — FTP protocol client 1161
- 21.14 `poplib` — POP3 protocol client 1166
- 21.15 `imaplib` — IMAP4 protocol client 1169
- 21.16 `nntplib` — NNTP protocol client 1176
- 21.17 `smtplib` — SMTP protocol client 1182
- 21.18 `smtpd` — SMTP Server 1189
- 21.19 `telnetlib` — Telnet client 1192
- 21.20 `uuid` — UUID objects according to RFC 4122 1195
- 21.21 `socketserver` — A framework for network servers 1198
- 21.22 `http.server` — HTTP servers 1206
- 21.23 `http.cookies` — HTTP state management 1211
- 21.24 `http.cookiejar` — Cookie handling for HTTP clients 1215
- 21.25 `xmlrpc` — XMLRPC server and client modules 1223
- 21.26 `xmlrpc.client` — XML-RPC client access 1223

21.27 `xmlrpc.server` — Basic XML-RPC servers 1231
21.28 `ipaddress` — IPv4/IPv6 manipulation library 1236

22 Multimedia Services 1249
22.1 `audioop` — Manipulate raw audio data 1249
22.2 `aifc` — Read and write AIFF and AIFC files 1252
22.3 `sunau` — Read and write Sun AU files 1254
22.4 `wave` — Read and write WAV files 1257
22.5 `chunk` — Read IFF chunked data 1260
22.6 `colorsys` — Conversions between color systems 1261
22.7 `imghdr` — Determine the type of an image 1262
22.8 `sndhdr` — Determine type of sound file 1262
22.9 `ossaudiodev` — Access to OSS-compatible audio devices 1263

23 Internationalization 1269
23.1 `gettext` — Multilingual internationalization services 1269
23.2 `locale` — Internationalization services 1277

24 Program Frameworks 1285
24.1 `turtle` — Turtle graphics 1285
24.2 `cmd` — Support for line-oriented command interpreters 1319
24.3 `shlex` — Simple lexical analysis 1324

25 Graphical User Interfaces with Tk 1331
25.1 `tkinter` — Python interface to Tcl/Tk 1331
25.2 `tkinter.ttk` — Tk themed widgets 1342
25.3 `tkinter.tix` — Extension widgets for Tk 1359
25.4 `tkinter.scrolledtext` — Scrolled Text Widget 1364
25.5 IDLE 1364
25.6 Other Graphical User Interface Packages 1373

26 Development Tools 1375
26.1 `typing` — Support for type hints 1375
26.2 `pydoc` — Documentation generator and online help system 1390
26.3 `doctest` — Test interactive Python examples 1391
26.4 `unittest` — Unit testing framework 1415
26.5 `unittest.mock` — mock object library 1442
26.6 `unittest.mock` — getting started 1477
26.7 2to3 - Automated Python 2 to 3 code translation 1496
26.8 `test` — Regression tests package for Python 1501
26.9 `test.support` — Utilities for the Python test suite 1504

27 Debugging and Profiling 1511
27.1 `bdb` — Debugger framework 1511
27.2 `faulthandler` — Dump the Python traceback 1515
27.3 `pdb` — The Python Debugger 1517
27.4 The Python Profilers 1523
27.5 `timeit` — Measure execution time of small code snippets 1531
27.6 `trace` — Trace or track Python statement execution 1536
27.7 `tracemalloc` — Trace memory allocations 1539

28 Software Packaging and Distribution 1549
28.1 `distutils` — Building and installing Python modules 1549
28.2 `ensurepip` — Bootstrapping the `pip` installer 1549
28.3 `venv` — Creation of virtual environments 1551

  28.4 `zipapp` — Manage executable python zip archives 1559

29 Python Runtime Services   **1563**
  29.1 `sys` — System-specific parameters and functions 1563
  29.2 `sysconfig` — Provide access to Python's configuration information 1578
  29.3 `builtins` — Built-in objects 1582
  29.4 `__main__` — Top-level script environment 1582
  29.5 `warnings` — Warning control 1583
  29.6 `contextlib` — Utilities for `with`-statement contexts 1588
  29.7 `abc` — Abstract Base Classes 1599
  29.8 `atexit` — Exit handlers 1604
  29.9 `traceback` — Print or retrieve a stack traceback 1605
  29.10 `__future__` — Future statement definitions 1611
  29.11 `gc` — Garbage Collector interface 1612
  29.12 `inspect` — Inspect live objects 1615
  29.13 `site` — Site-specific configuration hook 1630
  29.14 `fpectl` — Floating point exception control 1633

30 Custom Python Interpreters   **1637**
  30.1 `code` — Interpreter base classes 1637
  30.2 `codeop` — Compile Python code 1639

31 Importing Modules   **1641**
  31.1 `zipimport` — Import modules from Zip archives 1641
  31.2 `pkgutil` — Package extension utility 1643
  31.3 `modulefinder` — Find modules used by a script 1645
  31.4 `runpy` — Locating and executing Python modules 1647
  31.5 `importlib` — The implementation of `import` 1649

32 Python Language Services   **1667**
  32.1 `parser` — Access Python parse trees 1667
  32.2 `ast` — Abstract Syntax Trees 1671
  32.3 `symtable` — Access to the compiler's symbol tables 1676
  32.4 `symbol` — Constants used with Python parse trees 1678
  32.5 `token` — Constants used with Python parse trees 1679
  32.6 `keyword` — Testing for Python keywords 1680
  32.7 `tokenize` — Tokenizer for Python source 1681
  32.8 `tabnanny` — Detection of ambiguous indentation 1684
  32.9 `pyclbr` — Python class browser support 1685
  32.10 `py_compile` — Compile Python source files 1686
  32.11 `compileall` — Byte-compile Python libraries 1687
  32.12 `dis` — Disassembler for Python bytecode 1690
  32.13 `pickletools` — Tools for pickle developers 1703

33 Miscellaneous Services   **1705**
  33.1 `formatter` — Generic output formatting 1705

34 MS Windows Specific Services   **1711**
  34.1 `msilib` — Read and write Microsoft Installer files 1711
  34.2 `msvcrt` — Useful routines from the MS VC++ runtime 1716
  34.3 `winreg` — Windows registry access 1718
  34.4 `winsound` — Sound-playing interface for Windows 1726

35 Unix Specific Services   **1729**
  35.1 `posix` — The most common POSIX system calls 1729

35.2	`pwd` — The password database	1730
35.3	`spwd` — The shadow password database	1731
35.4	`grp` — The group database	1732
35.5	`crypt` — Function to check Unix passwords	1732
35.6	`termios` — POSIX style tty control	1734
35.7	`tty` — Terminal control functions	1735
35.8	`pty` — Pseudo-terminal utilities	1736
35.9	`fcntl` — The `fcntl` and `ioctl` system calls	1737
35.10	`pipes` — Interface to shell pipelines	1739
35.11	`resource` — Resource usage information	1740
35.12	`nis` — Interface to Sun's NIS (Yellow Pages)	1744
35.13	`syslog` — Unix syslog library routines	1745

36 Superseded Modules — **1747**

36.1	`optparse` — Parser for command line options	1747
36.2	`imp` — Access the import internals	1773

37 Undocumented Modules — **1779**

37.1	Platform specific modules	1779

A Glossary — **1781**

Bibliography — **1793**

B About these documents — **1795**

B.1	Contributors to the Python Documentation	1795

C History and License — **1797**

C.1	History of the software	1797
C.2	Terms and conditions for accessing or otherwise using Python	1798
C.3	Licenses and Acknowledgements for Incorporated Software	1801

D Copyright — **1813**

Python Module Index — **1815**

Index — **1819**

While reference-index describes the exact syntax and semantics of the Python language, this library reference manual describes the standard library that is distributed with Python. It also describes some of the optional components that are commonly included in Python distributions.

Python's standard library is very extensive, offering a wide range of facilities as indicated by the long table of contents listed below. The library contains built-in modules (written in C) that provide access to system functionality such as file I/O that would otherwise be inaccessible to Python programmers, as well as modules written in Python that provide standardized solutions for many problems that occur in everyday programming. Some of these modules are explicitly designed to encourage and enhance the portability of Python programs by abstracting away platform-specifics into platform-neutral APIs.

The Python installers for the Windows platform usually include the entire standard library and often also include many additional components. For Unix-like operating systems Python is normally provided as a collection of packages, so it may be necessary to use the packaging tools provided with the operating system to obtain some or all of the optional components.

In addition to the standard library, there is a growing collection of several thousand components (from individual programs and modules to packages and entire application development frameworks), available from the Python Package Index.

CHAPTER
NINETEEN

INTERNET DATA HANDLING

This chapter describes modules which support handling data formats commonly used on the Internet.

19.1 `email` — An email and MIME handling package

Source code: Lib/email/__init__.py

The *email* package is a library for managing email messages. It is specifically *not* designed to do any sending of email messages to SMTP (RFC 2821), NNTP, or other servers; those are functions of modules such as *smtplib* and *nntplib*. The *email* package attempts to be as RFC-compliant as possible, supporting RFC 5233 and RFC 6532, as well as such MIME-related RFCs as RFC 2045, RFC 2046, RFC 2047, RFC 2183, and RFC 2231.

The overall structure of the email package can be divided into three major components, plus a fourth component that controls the behavior of the other components.

The central component of the package is an "object model" that represents email messages. An application interacts with the package primarily through the object model interface defined in the *message* sub-module. The application can use this API to ask questions about an existing email, to construct a new email, or to add or remove email subcomponents that themselves use the same object model interface. That is, following the nature of email messages and their MIME subcomponents, the email object model is a tree structure of objects that all provide the *EmailMessage* API.

The other two major components of the package are the *parser* and the *generator*. The parser takes the serialized version of an email message (a stream of bytes) and converts it into a tree of *EmailMessage* objects. The generator takes an *EmailMessage* and turns it back into a serialized byte stream. (The parser and generator also handle streams of text characters, but this usage is discouraged as it is too easy to end up with messages that are not valid in one way or another.)

The control component is the *policy* module. Every *EmailMessage*, every *generator*, and every *parser* has an associated *policy* object that controls its behavior. Usually an application only needs to specify the policy when an *EmailMessage* is created, either by directly instantiating an *EmailMessage* to create a new email, or by parsing an input stream using a *parser*. But the policy can be changed when the message is serialized using a *generator*. This allows, for example, a generic email message to be parsed from disk, but to serialize it using standard SMTP settings when sending it to an email server.

The email package does its best to hide the details of the various governing RFCs from the application. Conceptually the application should be able to treat the email message as a structured tree of unicode text and binary attachments, without having to worry about how these are represented when serialized. In practice, however, it is often necessary to be aware of at least some of the rules governing MIME messages and their structure, specifically the names and nature of the MIME "content types" and how they identify multipart documents. For the most part this knowledge should only be required for more complex applications, and even then it should only be the high level structure in question, and not the details of how those structures are represented. Since MIME content types are used widely in modern internet software (not just email), this will be a familiar concept to many programmers.

The following sections describe the functionality of the *email* package. We start with the *message* object model, which is the primary interface an application will use, and follow that with the *parser* and *generator* components. Then we cover the *policy* controls, which completes the treatment of the main components of the library.

The next three sections cover the exceptions the package may raise and the defects (non-compliance with the RFCs) that the *parser* may detect. Then we cover the *headerregistry* and the *contentmanager* sub-components, which provide tools for doing more detailed manipulation of headers and payloads, respectively. Both of these components contain features relevant to consuming and producing non-trivial messages, but also document their extensibility APIs, which will be of interest to advanced applications.

Following those is a set of examples of using the fundamental parts of the APIs covered in the preceding sections.

The forgoing represent the modern (unicode friendly) API of the email package. The remaining sections, starting with the *Message* class, cover the legacy *compat32* API that deals much more directly with the details of how email messages are represented. The *compat32* API does *not* hide the details of the RFCs from the application, but for applications that need to operate at that level, they can be useful tools. This documentation is also relevant for applications that are still using the *compat32* API for backward compatibility reasons.

Changed in version 3.6: Docs reorganized and rewritten to promote the new *EmailMessage/EmailPolicy* API.

Contents of the *email* package documentation:

19.1.1 email.message: Representing an email message

Source code: Lib/email/message.py

New in version 3.6:[1]

The central class in the *email* package is the *EmailMessage* class, imported from the *email.message* module. It is the base class for the *email* object model. *EmailMessage* provides the core functionality for setting and querying header fields, for accessing message bodies, and for creating or modifying structured messages.

An email message consists of *headers* and a *payload* (which is also referred to as the *content*). Headers are RFC 5322 or RFC 6532 style field names and values, where the field name and value are separated by a colon. The colon is not part of either the field name or the field value. The payload may be a simple text message, or a binary object, or a structured sequence of sub-messages each with their own set of headers and their own payload. The latter type of payload is indicated by the message having a MIME type such as *multipart/** or *message/rfc822*.

The conceptual model provided by an *EmailMessage* object is that of an ordered dictionary of headers coupled with a *payload* that represents the RFC 5322 body of the message, which might be a list of sub-**EmailMessage** objects. In addition to the normal dictionary methods for accessing the header names and values, there are methods for accessing specialized information from the headers (for example the MIME content type), for operating on the payload, for generating a serialized version of the message, and for recursively walking over the object tree.

The *EmailMessage* dictionary-like interface is indexed by the header names, which must be ASCII values. The values of the dictionary are strings with some extra methods. Headers are stored and returned in case-preserving form, but field names are matched case-insensitively. Unlike a real dict, there is an ordering to

---

[1] Originally added in 3.4 as a *provisional module*. Docs for legacy message class moved to *email.message.Message: Representing an email message using the compat32 API*.

the keys, and there can be duplicate keys. Additional methods are provided for working with headers that have duplicate keys.

The *payload* is either a string or bytes object, in the case of simple message objects, or a list of *EmailMessage* objects, for MIME container documents such as *multipart/** and *message/rfc822* message objects.

class email.message.EmailMessage(*policy=default*)
> If *policy* is specified use the rules it specifies to update and serialize the representation of the message. If *policy* is not set, use the *default* policy, which follows the rules of the email RFCs except for line endings (instead of the RFC mandated \r\n, it uses the Python standard \n line endings). For more information see the *policy* documentation.
>
> **as_string**(*unixfrom=False, maxheaderlen=None, policy=None*)
>> Return the entire message flattened as a string. When optional *unixfrom* is true, the envelope header is included in the returned string. *unixfrom* defaults to **False**. For backward compatibility with the base *Message* class *maxheaderlen* is accepted, but defaults to **None**, which means that by default the line length is controlled by the **max_line_length** of the policy. The *policy* argument may be used to override the default policy obtained from the message instance. This can be used to control some of the formatting produced by the method, since the specified *policy* will be passed to the *Generator*.
>>
>> Flattening the message may trigger changes to the *EmailMessage* if defaults need to be filled in to complete the transformation to a string (for example, MIME boundaries may be generated or modified).
>>
>> Note that this method is provided as a convenience and may not be the most useful way to serialize messages in your application, especially if you are dealing with multiple messages. See *email.generator.Generator* for a more flexible API for serializing messages. Note also that this method is restricted to producing messages serialized as "7 bit clean" when *utf8* is **False**, which is the default.
>>
>> Changed in version 3.6: the default behavior when *maxheaderlen* is not specified was changed from defaulting to 0 to defaulting to the value of *max_line_length* from the policy.
>
> **__str__**()
>> Equivalent to *as_string(policy=self.policy.clone(utf8=True))*. Allows **str(msg)** to produce a string containing the serialized message in a readable format.
>>
>> Changed in version 3.4: the method was changed to use **utf8=True**, thus producing an RFC 6531-like message representation, instead of being a direct alias for *as_string()*.
>
> **as_bytes**(*unixfrom=False, policy=None*)
>> Return the entire message flattened as a bytes object. When optional *unixfrom* is true, the envelope header is included in the returned string. *unixfrom* defaults to **False**. The *policy* argument may be used to override the default policy obtained from the message instance. This can be used to control some of the formatting produced by the method, since the specified *policy* will be passed to the *BytesGenerator*.
>>
>> Flattening the message may trigger changes to the *EmailMessage* if defaults need to be filled in to complete the transformation to a string (for example, MIME boundaries may be generated or modified).
>>
>> Note that this method is provided as a convenience and may not be the most useful way to serialize messages in your application, especially if you are dealing with multiple messages. See *email.generator.BytesGenerator* for a more flexible API for serializing messages.
>
> **__bytes__**()
>> Equivalent to *as_bytes()*. Allows **bytes(msg)** to produce a bytes object containing the serialized message.

is_multipart()
   Return True if the message's payload is a list of sub-*EmailMessage* objects, otherwise return False. When *is_multipart()* returns False, the payload should be a string object (which might be a CTE encoded binary payload). Note that *is_multipart()* returning True does not necessarily mean that "msg.get_content_maintype() == 'multipart'" will return the True. For example, is_multipart will return True when the *EmailMessage* is of type message/rfc822.

set_unixfrom(*unixfrom***)**
   Set the message's envelope header to *unixfrom*, which should be a string. (See *mboxMessage* for a brief description of this header.)

get_unixfrom()
   Return the message's envelope header. Defaults to None if the envelope header was never set.

The following methods implement the mapping-like interface for accessing the message's headers. Note that there are some semantic differences between these methods and a normal mapping (i.e. dictionary) interface. For example, in a dictionary there are no duplicate keys, but here there may be duplicate message headers. Also, in dictionaries there is no guaranteed order to the keys returned by *keys()*, but in an *EmailMessage* object, headers are always returned in the order they appeared in the original message, or in which they were added to the message later. Any header deleted and then re-added is always appended to the end of the header list.

These semantic differences are intentional and are biased toward convenience in the most common use cases.

Note that in all cases, any envelope header present in the message is not included in the mapping interface.

__len__()
   Return the total number of headers, including duplicates.

__contains__(*name***)**
   Return true if the message object has a field named *name*. Matching is done without regard to case and *name* does not include the trailing colon. Used for the in operator. For example:

```
if 'message-id' in myMessage:
    print('Message-ID:', myMessage['message-id'])
```

__getitem__(*name***)**
   Return the value of the named header field. *name* does not include the colon field separator. If the header is missing, None is returned; a *KeyError* is never raised.

   Note that if the named field appears more than once in the message's headers, exactly which of those field values will be returned is undefined. Use the *get_all()* method to get the values of all the extant headers named *name*.

   Using the standard (non-compat32) policies, the returned value is an instance of a subclass of *email.headerregistry.BaseHeader*.

__setitem__(*name***, ***val***)**
   Add a header to the message with field name *name* and value *val*. The field is appended to the end of the message's existing headers.

   Note that this does *not* overwrite or delete any existing header with the same name. If you want to ensure that the new header is the only one present in the message with field name *name*, delete the field first, e.g.:

```
del msg['subject']
msg['subject'] = 'Python roolz!'
```

If the `policy` defines certain headers to be unique (as the standard policies do), this method may raise a *ValueError* when an attempt is made to assign a value to such a header when one already exists. This behavior is intentional for consistency's sake, but do not depend on it as we may choose to make such assignments do an automatic deletion of the existing header in the future.

__delitem__(*name*)

Delete all occurrences of the field with name *name* from the message's headers. No exception is raised if the named field isn't present in the headers.

keys()

Return a list of all the message's header field names.

values()

Return a list of all the message's field values.

items()

Return a list of 2-tuples containing all the message's field headers and values.

get(*name*, *failobj=None*)

Return the value of the named header field. This is identical to *__getitem__*() except that optional *failobj* is returned if the named header is missing (*failobj* defaults to `None`).

Here are some additional useful header related methods:

get_all(*name*, *failobj=None*)

Return a list of all the values for the field named *name*. If there are no such named headers in the message, *failobj* is returned (defaults to `None`).

add_header(*_name*, *_value*, ***_params*)

Extended header setting. This method is similar to *__setitem__*() except that additional header parameters can be provided as keyword arguments. *_name* is the header field to add and *_value* is the *primary* value for the header.

For each item in the keyword argument dictionary *_params*, the key is taken as the parameter name, with underscores converted to dashes (since dashes are illegal in Python identifiers). Normally, the parameter will be added as `key="value"` unless the value is `None`, in which case only the key will be added.

If the value contains non-ASCII characters, the charset and language may be explicitly controlled by specifying the value as a three tuple in the format (`CHARSET`, `LANGUAGE`, `VALUE`), where `CHARSET` is a string naming the charset to be used to encode the value, `LANGUAGE` can usually be set to `None` or the empty string (see RFC 2231 for other possibilities), and `VALUE` is the string value containing non-ASCII code points. If a three tuple is not passed and the value contains non-ASCII characters, it is automatically encoded in RFC 2231 format using a `CHARSET` of `utf-8` and a `LANGUAGE` of `None`.

Here is an example:

```
msg.add_header('Content-Disposition', 'attachment', filename='bud.gif')
```

This will add a header that looks like

```
Content-Disposition: attachment; filename="bud.gif"
```

An example of the extended interface with non-ASCII characters:

```
msg.add_header('Content-Disposition', 'attachment',
               filename=('iso-8859-1', '', 'Fußballer.ppt'))
```

replace_header(*_name*, *_value*)

Replace a header. Replace the first header found in the message that matches *_name*, retaining header order and field name case of the original header. If no matching header is found, raise a `KeyError`.

get_content_type()
Return the message's content type, coerced to lower case of the form *maintype/subtype*. If there is no *Content-Type* header in the message return the value returned by `get_default_type()`. If the *Content-Type* header is invalid, return `text/plain`.

(According to RFC 2045, messages always have a default type, `get_content_type()` will always return a value. RFC 2045 defines a message's default type to be *text/plain* unless it appears inside a *multipart/digest* container, in which case it would be *message/rfc822*. If the *Content-Type* header has an invalid type specification, RFC 2045 mandates that the default type be *text/plain*.)

get_content_maintype()
Return the message's main content type. This is the *maintype* part of the string returned by `get_content_type()`.

get_content_subtype()
Return the message's sub-content type. This is the *subtype* part of the string returned by `get_content_type()`.

get_default_type()
Return the default content type. Most messages have a default content type of *text/plain*, except for messages that are subparts of *multipart/digest* containers. Such subparts have a default content type of *message/rfc822*.

set_default_type(*ctype*)
Set the default content type. *ctype* should either be *text/plain* or *message/rfc822*, although this is not enforced. The default content type is not stored in the *Content-Type* header, so it only affects the return value of the `get_content_type` methods when no *Content-Type* header is present in the message.

set_param(*param, value, header='Content-Type', requote=True, charset=None, language='', replace=False*)
Set a parameter in the *Content-Type* header. If the parameter already exists in the header, replace its value with *value*. When *header* is Content-Type (the default) and the header does not yet exist in the message, add it, set its value to *text/plain*, and append the new parameter value. Optional *header* specifies an alternative header to *Content-Type*.

If the value contains non-ASCII characters, the charset and language may be explicitly specified using the optional *charset* and *language* parameters. Optional *language* specifies the RFC 2231 language, defaulting to the empty string. Both *charset* and *language* should be strings. The default is to use the `utf8` charset and `None` for the *language*.

If *replace* is `False` (the default) the header is moved to the end of the list of headers. If *replace* is `True`, the header will be updated in place.

Use of the *requote* parameter with `EmailMessage` objects is deprecated.

Note that existing parameter values of headers may be accessed through the **params** attribute of the header value (for example, `msg['Content-Type'].params['charset']`.

Changed in version 3.4: `replace` keyword was added.

del_param(*param, header='content-type', requote=True*)
Remove the given parameter completely from the *Content-Type* header. The header will be rewritten in place without the parameter or its value. Optional *header* specifies an alternative to *Content-Type*.

Use of the *requote* parameter with `EmailMessage` objects is deprecated.

get_filename(*failobj=None*)

    Return the value of the `filename` parameter of the *Content-Disposition* header of the message. If the header does not have a `filename` parameter, this method falls back to looking for the `name` parameter on the *Content-Type* header. If neither is found, or the header is missing, then *failobj* is returned. The returned string will always be unquoted as per *email.utils.unquote()*.

get_boundary(*failobj=None*)

    Return the value of the `boundary` parameter of the *Content-Type* header of the message, or *failobj* if either the header is missing, or has no `boundary` parameter. The returned string will always be unquoted as per *email.utils.unquote()*.

set_boundary(*boundary*)

    Set the `boundary` parameter of the *Content-Type* header to *boundary*. *set_boundary()* will always quote *boundary* if necessary. A *HeaderParseError* is raised if the message object has no *Content-Type* header.

    Note that using this method is subtly different from deleting the old *Content-Type* header and adding a new one with the new boundary via *add_header()*, because *set_boundary()* preserves the order of the *Content-Type* header in the list of headers.

get_content_charset(*failobj=None*)

    Return the `charset` parameter of the *Content-Type* header, coerced to lower case. If there is no *Content-Type* header, or if that header has no `charset` parameter, *failobj* is returned.

get_charsets(*failobj=None*)

    Return a list containing the character set names in the message. If the message is a *multipart*, then the list will contain one element for each subpart in the payload, otherwise, it will be a list of length 1.

    Each item in the list will be a string which is the value of the `charset` parameter in the *Content-Type* header for the represented subpart. If the subpart has no *Content-Type* header, no `charset` parameter, or is not of the *text* main MIME type, then that item in the returned list will be *failobj*.

is_attachment()

    Return `True` if there is a *Content-Disposition* header and its (case insensitive) value is `attachment`, `False` otherwise.

    Changed in version 3.4.2: is_attachment is now a method instead of a property, for consistency with *is_multipart()*.

get_content_disposition()

    Return the lowercased value (without parameters) of the message's *Content-Disposition* header if it has one, or `None`. The possible values for this method are *inline*, *attachment* or `None` if the message follows RFC 2183.

    New in version 3.5.

The following methods relate to interrogating and manipulating the content (payload) of the message.

walk()

    The *walk()* method is an all-purpose generator which can be used to iterate over all the parts and subparts of a message object tree, in depth-first traversal order. You will typically use *walk()* as the iterator in a `for` loop; each iteration returns the next subpart.

    Here's an example that prints the MIME type of every part of a multipart message structure:

```
>>> for part in msg.walk():
...     print(part.get_content_type())
multipart/report
text/plain
```

```
message/delivery-status
text/plain
text/plain
message/rfc822
text/plain
```

walk iterates over the subparts of any part where *is_multipart()* returns **True**, even though `msg.get_content_maintype() == 'multipart'` may return **False**. We can see this in our example by making use of the **_structure** debug helper function:

```
>>> for part in msg.walk():
...     print(part.get_content_maintype() == 'multipart',
...           part.is_multipart())
True True
False False
False True
False False
False False
False True
False False
>>> _structure(msg)
multipart/report
    text/plain
    message/delivery-status
        text/plain
        text/plain
    message/rfc822
        text/plain
```

Here the **message** parts are not **multiparts**, but they do contain subparts. **is_multipart()** returns **True** and **walk** descends into the subparts.

get_body(*preferencelist=('related', 'html', 'plain')*)

Return the MIME part that is the best candidate to be the "body" of the message.

preferencelist must be a sequence of strings from the set **related**, **html**, and **plain**, and indicates the order of preference for the content type of the part returned.

Start looking for candidate matches with the object on which the **get_body** method is called.

If **related** is not included in *preferencelist*, consider the root part (or subpart of the root part) of any related encountered as a candidate if the (sub-)part matches a preference.

When encountering a **multipart/related**, check the **start** parameter and if a part with a matching *Content-ID* is found, consider only it when looking for candidate matches. Otherwise consider only the first (default root) part of the **multipart/related**.

If a part has a *Content-Disposition* header, only consider the part a candidate match if the value of the header is **inline**.

If none of the candidates matches any of the preferences in *preferencelist*, return **None**.

Notes: (1) For most applications the only *preferencelist* combinations that really make sense are ('plain',), ('html', 'plain'), and the default ('related', 'html', 'plain'). (2) Because matching starts with the object on which **get_body** is called, calling **get_body** on a **multipart/ related** will return the object itself unless *preferencelist* has a non-default value. (3) Messages (or message parts) that do not specify a *Content-Type* or whose *Content-Type* header is invalid will be treated as if they are of type **text/plain**, which may occasionally cause **get_body** to return unexpected results.

iter_attachments()
   Return an iterator over all of the immediate sub-parts of the message that are not candidate "body" parts. That is, skip the first occurrence of each of text/plain, text/html, multipart/related, or multipart/alternative (unless they are explicitly marked as attachments via Content-Disposition: attachment), and return all remaining parts. When applied directly to a multipart/related, return an iterator over the all the related parts except the root part (ie: the part pointed to by the start parameter, or the first part if there is no start parameter or the start parameter doesn't match the Content-ID of any of the parts). When applied directly to a multipart/alternative or a non-multipart, return an empty iterator.

iter_parts()
   Return an iterator over all of the immediate sub-parts of the message, which will be empty for a non-multipart. (See also *walk()*.)

get_content(**args, content_manager=None, **kw*)
   Call the *get_content()* method of the *content_manager*, passing self as the message object, and passing along any other arguments or keywords as additional arguments. If *content_manager* is not specified, use the content_manager specified by the current *policy*.

set_content(**args, content_manager=None, **kw*)
   Call the *set_content()* method of the *content_manager*, passing self as the message object, and passing along any other arguments or keywords as additional arguments. If *content_manager* is not specified, use the content_manager specified by the current *policy*.

make_related(*boundary=None*)
   Convert a non-multipart message into a multipart/related message, moving any existing Content- headers and payload into a (new) first part of the multipart. If *boundary* is specified, use it as the boundary string in the multipart, otherwise leave the boundary to be automatically created when it is needed (for example, when the message is serialized).

make_alternative(*boundary=None*)
   Convert a non-multipart or a multipart/related into a multipart/alternative, moving any existing Content- headers and payload into a (new) first part of the multipart. If *boundary* is specified, use it as the boundary string in the multipart, otherwise leave the boundary to be automatically created when it is needed (for example, when the message is serialized).

make_mixed(*boundary=None*)
   Convert a non-multipart, a multipart/related, or a multipart-alternative into a multipart/mixed, moving any existing Content- headers and payload into a (new) first part of the multipart. If *boundary* is specified, use it as the boundary string in the multipart, otherwise leave the boundary to be automatically created when it is needed (for example, when the message is serialized).

add_related(**args, content_manager=None, **kw*)
   If the message is a multipart/related, create a new message object, pass all of the arguments to its *set_content()* method, and *attach()* it to the multipart. If the message is a non-multipart, call *make_related()* and then proceed as above. If the message is any other type of multipart, raise a *TypeError*. If *content_manager* is not specified, use the content_manager specified by the current *policy*. If the added part has no Content-Disposition header, add one with the value inline.

add_alternative(**args, content_manager=None, **kw*)
   If the message is a multipart/alternative, create a new message object, pass all of the arguments to its *set_content()* method, and *attach()* it to the multipart. If the message is a non-multipart or multipart/related, call *make_alternative()* and then proceed as above. If the message is any other type of multipart, raise a *TypeError*. If *content_manager* is not specified, use the content_manager specified by the current *policy*.

add_attachment(**args, content_manager=None, **kw*)

If the message is a `multipart/mixed`, create a new message object, pass all of the arguments to its `set_content()` method, and `attach()` it to the `multipart`. If the message is a non-`multipart`, `multipart/related`, or `multipart/alternative`, call `make_mixed()` and then proceed as above. If *content_manager* is not specified, use the `content_manager` specified by the current `policy`. If the added part has no `Content-Disposition` header, add one with the value `attachment`. This method can be used both for explicit attachments (`Content-Disposition: attachment` and `inline` attachments (`Content-Disposition: inline`), by passing appropriate options to the `content_manager`.

clear()
Remove the payload and all of the headers.

clear_content()
Remove the payload and all of the `Content-` headers, leaving all other headers intact and in their original order.

`EmailMessage` objects have the following instance attributes:

preamble
The format of a MIME document allows for some text between the blank line following the headers, and the first multipart boundary string. Normally, this text is never visible in a MIME-aware mail reader because it falls outside the standard MIME armor. However, when viewing the raw text of the message, or when viewing the message in a non-MIME aware reader, this text can become visible.

The *preamble* attribute contains this leading extra-armor text for MIME documents. When the `Parser` discovers some text after the headers but before the first boundary string, it assigns this text to the message's *preamble* attribute. When the `Generator` is writing out the plain text representation of a MIME message, and it finds the message has a *preamble* attribute, it will write this text in the area between the headers and the first boundary. See `email.parser` and `email.generator` for details.

Note that if the message object has no preamble, the *preamble* attribute will be `None`.

epilogue
The *epilogue* attribute acts the same way as the *preamble* attribute, except that it contains text that appears between the last boundary and the end of the message. As with the *preamble*, if there is no epilog text this attribute will be `None`.

defects
The *defects* attribute contains a list of all the problems found when parsing this message. See `email.errors` for a detailed description of the possible parsing defects.

class email.message.MIMEPart(*policy=default*)
This class represents a subpart of a MIME message. It is identical to `EmailMessage`, except that no *MIME-Version* headers are added when `set_content()` is called, since sub-parts do not need their own *MIME-Version* headers.

19.1.2 `email.parser`: Parsing email messages

Source code: Lib/email/parser.py

Message object structures can be created in one of two ways: they can be created from whole cloth by creating an `EmailMessage` object, adding headers using the dictionary interface, and adding payload(s) using `set_content()` and related methods, or they can be created by parsing a serialized representation of the email message.

The *email* package provides a standard parser that understands most email document structures, including MIME documents. You can pass the parser a bytes, string or file object, and the parser will return to you the root *EmailMessage* instance of the object structure. For simple, non-MIME messages the payload of this root object will likely be a string containing the text of the message. For MIME messages, the root object will return **True** from its *is_multipart()* method, and the subparts can be accessed via the payload manipulation methods, such as *get_body()*, *iter_parts()*, and *walk()*.

There are actually two parser interfaces available for use, the *Parser* API and the incremental *FeedParser* API. The *Parser* API is most useful if you have the entire text of the message in memory, or if the entire message lives in a file on the file system. *FeedParser* is more appropriate when you are reading the message from a stream which might block waiting for more input (such as reading an email message from a socket). The *FeedParser* can consume and parse the message incrementally, and only returns the root object when you close the parser.

Note that the parser can be extended in limited ways, and of course you can implement your own parser completely from scratch. All of the logic that connects the *email* package's bundled parser and the *EmailMessage* class is embodied in the `policy` class, so a custom parser can create message object trees any way it finds necessary by implementing custom versions of the appropriate `policy` methods.

FeedParser API

The *BytesFeedParser*, imported from the `email.feedparser` module, provides an API that is conducive to incremental parsing of email messages, such as would be necessary when reading the text of an email message from a source that can block (such as a socket). The *BytesFeedParser* can of course be used to parse an email message fully contained in a *bytes-like object*, string, or file, but the *BytesParser* API may be more convenient for such use cases. The semantics and results of the two parser APIs are identical.

The *BytesFeedParser*'s API is simple; you create an instance, feed it a bunch of bytes until there's no more to feed it, then close the parser to retrieve the root message object. The *BytesFeedParser* is extremely accurate when parsing standards-compliant messages, and it does a very good job of parsing non-compliant messages, providing information about how a message was deemed broken. It will populate a message object's *defects* attribute with a list of any problems it found in a message. See the *email.errors* module for the list of defects that it can find.

Here is the API for the *BytesFeedParser*:

class email.parser.BytesFeedParser(*_factory=None*, ***, *policy=policy.compat32*)

    Create a *BytesFeedParser* instance. Optional *_factory* is a no-argument callable; if not specified use the *message_factory* from the *policy*. Call *_factory* whenever a new message object is needed.

    If *policy* is specified use the rules it specifies to update the representation of the message. If *policy* is not set, use the *compat32* policy, which maintains backward compatibility with the Python 3.2 version of the email package and provides *Message* as the default factory. All other policies provide *EmailMessage* as the default *_factory*. For more information on what else *policy* controls, see the *policy* documentation.

    Note: **The policy keyword should always be specified**; The default will change to *email.policy.default* in a future version of Python.

    New in version 3.2.

    Changed in version 3.3: Added the *policy* keyword.

    Changed in version 3.6: *_factory* defaults to the policy `message_factory`.

    feed(*data*)

        Feed the parser some more data. *data* should be a *bytes-like object* containing one or more lines. The lines can be partial and the parser will stitch such partial lines together properly. The lines can have any of the three common line endings: carriage return, newline, or carriage return and newline (they can even be mixed).

close()
> Complete the parsing of all previously fed data and return the root message object. It is undefined what happens if *feed()* is called after this method has been called.

class email.parser.FeedParser(*_factory=None*, *, *policy=policy.compat32*)
> Works like *BytesFeedParser* except that the input to the *feed()* method must be a string. This is of limited utility, since the only way for such a message to be valid is for it to contain only ASCII text or, if utf8 is True, no binary attachments.
>
> Changed in version 3.3: Added the *policy* keyword.

Parser API

The *BytesParser* class, imported from the *email.parser* module, provides an API that can be used to parse a message when the complete contents of the message are available in a *bytes-like object* or file. The *email.parser* module also provides *Parser* for parsing strings, and header-only parsers, *BytesHeaderParser* and *HeaderParser*, which can be used if you're only interested in the headers of the message. *BytesHeaderParser* and *HeaderParser* can be much faster in these situations, since they do not attempt to parse the message body, instead setting the payload to the raw body.

class email.parser.BytesParser(*_class=None*, *, *policy=policy.compat32*)
> Create a *BytesParser* instance. The *_class* and *policy* arguments have the same meaning and semantics as the *_factory* and *policy* arguments of *BytesFeedParser*.
>
> Note: **The policy keyword should always be specified**; The default will change to *email.policy.default* in a future version of Python.
>
> Changed in version 3.3: Removed the *strict* argument that was deprecated in 2.4. Added the *policy* keyword.
>
> Changed in version 3.6: *_class* defaults to the policy `message_factory`.
>
> **parse**(*fp*, *headersonly=False*)
>> Read all the data from the binary file-like object *fp*, parse the resulting bytes, and return the message object. *fp* must support both the *readline()* and `read()` methods.
>>
>> The bytes contained in *fp* must be formatted as a block of RFC 5322 (or, if utf8 is True, RFC 6532) style headers and header continuation lines, optionally preceded by an envelope header. The header block is terminated either by the end of the data or by a blank line. Following the header block is the body of the message (which may contain MIME-encoded subparts, including subparts with a `Content-Transfer-Encoding` of 8bit.
>>
>> Optional *headersonly* is a flag specifying whether to stop parsing after reading the headers or not. The default is False, meaning it parses the entire contents of the file.
>
> **parsebytes**(*bytes*, *headersonly=False*)
>> Similar to the *parse()* method, except it takes a *bytes-like object* instead of a file-like object. Calling this method on a *bytes-like object* is equivalent to wrapping *bytes* in a *BytesIO* instance first and calling *parse()*.
>>
>> Optional *headersonly* is as with the *parse()* method.
>
> New in version 3.2.

class email.parser.BytesHeaderParser(*_class=None*, *, *policy=policy.compat32*)
> Exactly like *BytesParser*, except that *headersonly* defaults to True.
>
> New in version 3.3.

class email.parser.Parser(*_class=None*, *, *policy=policy.compat32*)
> This class is parallel to *BytesParser*, but handles string input.
>
> Changed in version 3.3: Removed the *strict* argument. Added the *policy* keyword.

Changed in version 3.6: *_class* defaults to the policy `message_factory`.

parse(*fp*, *headersonly=False*)
Read all the data from the text-mode file-like object *fp*, parse the resulting text, and return the root message object. *fp* must support both the `readline()` and the `read()` methods on file-like objects.

Other than the text mode requirement, this method operates like `BytesParser.parse()`.

parsestr(*text*, *headersonly=False*)
Similar to the `parse()` method, except it takes a string object instead of a file-like object. Calling this method on a string is equivalent to wrapping *text* in a `StringIO` instance first and calling `parse()`.

Optional *headersonly* is as with the `parse()` method.

class email.parser.**HeaderParser**(*_class=None*, ***, *policy=policy.compat32*)
Exactly like `Parser`, except that *headersonly* defaults to `True`.

Since creating a message object structure from a string or a file object is such a common task, four functions are provided as a convenience. They are available in the top-level `email` package namespace.

email.**message_from_bytes**(*s*, *_class=None*, ***, *policy=policy.compat32*)
Return a message object structure from a *bytes-like object*. This is equivalent to `BytesParser().parsebytes(s)`. Optional *_class* and *strict* are interpreted as with the `BytesParser` class constructor.

New in version 3.2.

Changed in version 3.3: Removed the *strict* argument. Added the *policy* keyword.

message_from_binary_file(*fp*, *_class=None*, ***, *policy=policy.compat32*)
Return a message object structure tree from an open binary *file object*. This is equivalent to `BytesParser().parse(fp)`. *_class* and *policy* are interpreted as with the `BytesParser` class constructor.

New in version 3.2.

Changed in version 3.3: Removed the *strict* argument. Added the *policy* keyword.

email.**message_from_string**(*s*, *_class=None*, ***, *policy=policy.compat32*)
Return a message object structure from a string. This is equivalent to `Parser().parsestr(s)`. *_class* and *policy* are interpreted as with the `Parser` class constructor.

Changed in version 3.3: Removed the *strict* argument. Added the *policy* keyword.

email.**message_from_file**(*fp*, *_class=None*, ***, *policy=policy.compat32*)
Return a message object structure tree from an open *file object*. This is equivalent to `Parser().parse(fp)`. *_class* and *policy* are interpreted as with the `Parser` class constructor.

Changed in version 3.3: Removed the *strict* argument. Added the *policy* keyword.

Changed in version 3.6: *_class* defaults to the policy `message_factory`.

Here's an example of how you might use `message_from_bytes()` at an interactive Python prompt:

```
>>> import email
>>> msg = email.message_from_bytes(myBytes)
```

Additional notes

Here are some notes on the parsing semantics:

- Most non-*multipart* type messages are parsed as a single message object with a string payload. These objects will return `False` for *is_multipart()*, and *iter_parts()* will yield an empty list.

- All *multipart* type messages will be parsed as a container message object with a list of sub-message objects for their payload. The outer container message will return `True` for *is_multipart()*, and *iter_parts()* will yield a list of subparts.

- Most messages with a content type of *message/** (such as *message/delivery-status* and *message/rfc822*) will also be parsed as container object containing a list payload of length 1. Their *is_multipart()* method will return `True`. The single element yielded by *iter_parts()* will be a sub-message object.

- Some non-standards-compliant messages may not be internally consistent about their *multipart*-edness. Such messages may have a `Content-Type` header of type *multipart*, but their *is_multipart()* method may return `False`. If such messages were parsed with the *FeedParser*, they will have an instance of the `MultipartInvariantViolationDefect` class in their *defects* attribute list. See *email.errors* for details.

19.1.3 `email.generator`: Generating MIME documents

Source code: Lib/email/generator.py

One of the most common tasks is to generate the flat (serialized) version of the email message represented by a message object structure. You will need to do this if you want to send your message via *smtplib.SMTP.sendmail()* or the *nntplib* module, or print the message on the console. Taking a message object structure and producing a serialized representation is the job of the generator classes.

As with the *email.parser* module, you aren't limited to the functionality of the bundled generator; you could write one from scratch yourself. However the bundled generator knows how to generate most email in a standards-compliant way, should handle MIME and non-MIME email messages just fine, and is designed so that the bytes-oriented parsing and generation operations are inverses, assuming the same non-transforming *policy* is used for both. That is, parsing the serialized byte stream via the *BytesParser* class and then regenerating the serialized byte stream using *BytesGenerator* should produce output identical to the input[1]. (On the other hand, using the generator on an *EmailMessage* constructed by program may result in changes to the *EmailMessage* object as defaults are filled in.)

The *Generator* class can be used to flatten a message into a text (as opposed to binary) serialized representation, but since Unicode cannot represent binary data directly, the message is of necessity transformed into something that contains only ASCII characters, using the standard email RFC Content Transfer Encoding techniques for encoding email messages for transport over channels that are not "8 bit clean".

class `email.generator.BytesGenerator`(*outfp*, *mangle_from_=None*, *maxheaderlen=None*, ***, *policy=None*)

Return a *BytesGenerator* object that will write any message provided to the *flatten()* method, or any surrogateescape encoded text provided to the *write()* method, to the *file-like object* *outfp*. *outfp* must support a `write` method that accepts binary data.

If optional *mangle_from_* is `True`, put a > character in front of any line in the body that starts with the exact string `"From "`, that is `From` followed by a space at the beginning of a line. *mangle_from_* defaults to the value of the *mangle_from_* setting of the *policy* (which is `True` for the *compat32* policy and `False` for all others). *mangle_from_* is intended for use when messages are stored in unix mbox format (see *mailbox* and WHY THE CONTENT-LENGTH FORMAT IS BAD).

---

[1] This statement assumes that you use the appropriate setting for `unixfrom`, and that there are no `policy` settings calling for automatic adjustments (for example, `refold_source` must be `none`, which is *not* the default). It is also not 100% true, since if the message does not conform to the RFC standards occasionally information about the exact original text is lost during parsing error recovery. It is a goal to fix these latter edge cases when possible.

If *maxheaderlen* is not `None`, refold any header lines that are longer than *maxheaderlen*, or if 0, do not rewrap any headers. If *manheaderlen* is `None` (the default), wrap headers and other message lines according to the *policy* settings.

If *policy* is specified, use that policy to control message generation. If *policy* is `None` (the default), use the policy associated with the `Message` or `EmailMessage` object passed to `flatten` to control the message generation. See `email.policy` for details on what *policy* controls.

New in version 3.2.

Changed in version 3.3: Added the *policy* keyword.

Changed in version 3.6: The default behavior of the *mangle_from_* and *maxheaderlen* parameters is to follow the policy.

flatten(*msg, unixfrom=False, linesep=None*)

> Print the textual representation of the message object structure rooted at *msg* to the output file specified when the `BytesGenerator` instance was created.
>
> If the `policy` option `cte_type` is `8bit` (the default), copy any headers in the original parsed message that have not been modified to the output with any bytes with the high bit set reproduced as in the original, and preserve the non-ASCII `Content-Transfer-Encoding` of any body parts that have them. If `cte_type` is `7bit`, convert the bytes with the high bit set as needed using an ASCII-compatible `Content-Transfer-Encoding`. That is, transform parts with non-ASCII `Content-Transfer-Encoding` (`Content-Transfer-Encoding: 8bit`) to an ASCII compatible `Content-Transfer-Encoding`, and encode RFC-invalid non-ASCII bytes in headers using the MIME `unknown-8bit` character set, thus rendering them RFC-compliant.
>
> If *unixfrom* is `True`, print the envelope header delimiter used by the Unix mailbox format (see `mailbox`) before the first of the RFC 5322 headers of the root message object. If the root object has no envelope header, craft a standard one. The default is `False`. Note that for subparts, no envelope header is ever printed.
>
> If *linesep* is not `None`, use it as the separator character between all the lines of the flattened message. If *linesep* is `None` (the default), use the value specified in the *policy*.

clone(*fp*)

> Return an independent clone of this `BytesGenerator` instance with the exact same option settings, and *fp* as the new *outfp*.

write(*s*)

> Encode *s* using the ASCII codec and the `surrogateescape` error handler, and pass it to the *write* method of the *outfp* passed to the `BytesGenerator`'s constructor.

As a convenience, `EmailMessage` provides the methods `as_bytes()` and `bytes(aMessage)` (a.k.a. `__bytes__()`), which simplify the generation of a serialized binary representation of a message object. For more detail, see `email.message`.

Because strings cannot represent binary data, the `Generator` class must convert any binary data in any message it flattens to an ASCII compatible format, by converting them to an ASCII compatible `Content-Transfer_Encoding`. Using the terminology of the email RFCs, you can think of this as `Generator` serializing to an I/O stream that is not "8 bit clean". In other words, most applications will want to be using `BytesGenerator`, and not `Generator`.

class email.generator.Generator(*outfp, mangle_from_=None, maxheaderlen=None, *, policy=None*)

> Return a `Generator` object that will write any message provided to the `flatten()` method, or any text provided to the `write()` method, to the *file-like object* *outfp*. *outfp* must support a `write` method that accepts string data.
>
> If optional *mangle_from_* is `True`, put a `>` character in front of any line in the body that starts with the exact string `"From "`, that is `From` followed by a space at the beginning of a line. *mangle_from_*

defaults to the value of the *mangle_from_* setting of the *policy* (which is True for the *compat32* policy
and False for all others). *mangle_from_* is intended for use when messages are stored in unix mbox
format (see *mailbox* and WHY THE CONTENT-LENGTH FORMAT IS BAD).

If *maxheaderlen* is not None, refold any header lines that are longer than *maxheaderlen*, or if 0, do
not rewrap any headers. If *manheaderlen* is None (the default), wrap headers and other message lines
according to the *policy* settings.

If *policy* is specified, use that policy to control message generation. If *policy* is None (the default),
use the policy associated with the *Message* or *EmailMessage* object passed to flatten to control the
message generation. See *email.policy* for details on what *policy* controls.

Changed in version 3.3: Added the *policy* keyword.

Changed in version 3.6: The default behavior of the *mangle_from_* and *maxheaderlen* parameters is
to follow the policy.

flatten(*msg, unixfrom=False, linesep=None*)
>   Print the textual representation of the message object structure rooted at *msg* to the output file
>   specified when the *Generator* instance was created.
>
>   If the *policy* option *cte_type* is 8bit, generate the message as if the option were set to 7bit.
>   (This is required because strings cannot represent non-ASCII bytes.) Convert any bytes with
>   the high bit set as needed using an ASCII-compatible *Content-Transfer-Encoding*. That is,
>   transform parts with non-ASCII *Cotnent-Transfer-Encoding* (*Content-Transfer-Encoding:
>   8bit*) to an ASCII compatibile *Content-Transfer-Encoding*, and encode RFC-invalid non-
>   ASCII bytes in headers using the MIME **unknown-8bit** character set, thus rendering them RFC-
>   compliant.
>
>   If *unixfrom* is True, print the envelope header delimiter used by the Unix mailbox format (see
>   *mailbox*) before the first of the RFC 5322 headers of the root message object. If the root object
>   has no envelope header, craft a standard one. The default is False. Note that for subparts, no
>   envelope header is ever printed.
>
>   If *linesep* is not None, use it as the separator character between all the lines of the flattened
>   message. If *linesep* is None (the default), use the value specified in the *policy*.
>
>   Changed in version 3.2: Added support for re-encoding **8bit** message bodies, and the *linesep*
>   argument.

clone(*fp*)
>   Return an independent clone of this *Generator* instance with the exact same options, and *fp* as
>   the new *outfp*.

write(*s*)
>   Write *s* to the *write* method of the *outfp* passed to the *Generator*'s constructor. This provides
>   just enough file-like API for *Generator* instances to be used in the *print()* function.

As a convenience, *EmailMessage* provides the methods *as_string()* and **str**(aMessage) (a.k.a.
__str__()), which simplify the generation of a formatted string representation of a message object. For
more detail, see *email.message*.

The *email.generator* module also provides a derived class, *DecodedGenerator*, which is like the *Generator*
base class, except that non-*text* parts are not serialized, but are instead represented in the output stream
by a string derived from a template filled in with information about the part.

class email.generator.DecodedGenerator(*outfp, mangle_from_=None, maxheaderlen=None, fmt=None, *, policy=None*)
>   Act like *Generator*, except that for any subpart of the message passed to *Generator.flatten()*, if
>   the subpart is of main type *text*, print the decoded payload of the subpart, and if the main type is
>   not *text*, instead of printing it fill in the string *fmt* using information from the part and print the
>   resulting filled-in string.

To fill in *fmt*, execute `fmt % part_info`, where `part_info` is a dictionary composed of the following keys and values:

- `type` – Full MIME type of the non-*text* part
- `maintype` – Main MIME type of the non-*text* part
- `subtype` – Sub-MIME type of the non-*text* part
- `filename` – Filename of the non-*text* part
- `description` – Description associated with the non-*text* part
- `encoding` – Content transfer encoding of the non-*text* part

If *fmt* is None, use the following default *fmt*:

"[Non-text (%(type)s) part of message omitted, filename %(filename)s]"

Optional *_mangle_from_* and *maxheaderlen* are as with the *Generator* base class.

19.1.4 `email.policy`: Policy Objects

New in version 3.3.

Source code: Lib/email/policy.py

The `email` package's prime focus is the handling of email messages as described by the various email and MIME RFCs. However, the general format of email messages (a block of header fields each consisting of a name followed by a colon followed by a value, the whole block followed by a blank line and an arbitrary 'body'), is a format that has found utility outside of the realm of email. Some of these uses conform fairly closely to the main email RFCs, some do not. Even when working with email, there are times when it is desirable to break strict compliance with the RFCs, such as generating emails that interoperate with email servers that do not themselves follow the standards, or that implement extensions you want to use in ways that violate the standards.

Policy objects give the email package the flexibility to handle all these disparate use cases.

A *Policy* object encapsulates a set of attributes and methods that control the behavior of various components of the email package during use. *Policy* instances can be passed to various classes and methods in the email package to alter the default behavior. The settable values and their defaults are described below.

There is a default policy used by all classes in the email package. For all of the *parser* classes and the related convenience functions, and for the *Message* class, this is the *Compat32* policy, via its corresponding pre-defined instance *compat32*. This policy provides for complete backward compatibility (in some cases, including bug compatibility) with the pre-Python3.3 version of the email package.

This default value for the *policy* keyword to *EmailMessage* is the *EmailPolicy* policy, via its pre-defined instance *default*.

When a *Message* or *EmailMessage* object is created, it acquires a policy. If the message is created by a *parser*, a policy passed to the parser will be the policy used by the message it creates. If the message is created by the program, then the policy can be specified when it is created. When a message is passed to a *generator*, the generator uses the policy from the message by default, but you can also pass a specific policy to the generator that will override the one stored on the message object.

The default value for the *policy* keyword for the *email.parser* classes and the parser convenience functions **will be changing** in a future version of Python. Therefore you should **always specify explicitly which policy you want to use** when calling any of the classes and functions described in the *parser* module.

The first part of this documentation covers the features of *Policy*, an *abstract base class* that defines the features that are common to all policy objects, including *compat32*. This includes certain hook methods that are called internally by the email package, which a custom policy could override to obtain different behavior. The second part describes the concrete classes *EmailPolicy* and *Compat32*, which implement the hooks that provide the standard behavior and the backward compatible behavior and features, respectively.

Policy instances are immutable, but they can be cloned, accepting the same keyword arguments as the class constructor and returning a new *Policy* instance that is a copy of the original but with the specified attributes values changed.

As an example, the following code could be used to read an email message from a file on disk and pass it to the system **sendmail** program on a Unix system:

```
>>> from email import message_from_binary_file
>>> from email.generator import BytesGenerator
>>> from email import policy
>>> from subprocess import Popen, PIPE
>>> with open('mymsg.txt', 'rb') as f:
...     msg = message_from_binary_file(f, policy=policy.default)
>>> p = Popen(['sendmail', msg['To'].addresses[0]], stdin=PIPE)
>>> g = BytesGenerator(p.stdin, policy=msg.policy.clone(linesep='\r\n'))
>>> g.flatten(msg)
>>> p.stdin.close()
>>> rc = p.wait()
```

Here we are telling *BytesGenerator* to use the RFC correct line separator characters when creating the binary string to feed into **sendmail's stdin**, where the default policy would use \n line separators.

Some email package methods accept a *policy* keyword argument, allowing the policy to be overridden for that method. For example, the following code uses the *as_bytes()* method of the *msg* object from the previous example and writes the message to a file using the native line separators for the platform on which it is running:

```
>>> import os
>>> with open('converted.txt', 'wb') as f:
...     f.write(msg.as_bytes(policy=msg.policy.clone(linesep=os.linesep)))
17
```

Policy objects can also be combined using the addition operator, producing a policy object whose settings are a combination of the non-default values of the summed objects:

```
>>> compat_SMTP = policy.compat32.clone(linesep='\r\n')
>>> compat_strict = policy.compat32.clone(raise_on_defect=True)
>>> compat_strict_SMTP = compat_SMTP + compat_strict
```

This operation is not commutative; that is, the order in which the objects are added matters. To illustrate:

```
>>> policy100 = policy.compat32.clone(max_line_length=100)
>>> policy80 = policy.compat32.clone(max_line_length=80)
>>> apolicy = policy100 + policy80
>>> apolicy.max_line_length
80
>>> apolicy = policy80 + policy100
>>> apolicy.max_line_length
100
```

class email.policy.Policy(***kw*)

This is the *abstract base class* for all policy classes. It provides default implementations for a couple of trivial methods, as well as the implementation of the immutability property, the *clone()* method, and the constructor semantics.

The constructor of a policy class can be passed various keyword arguments. The arguments that may be specified are any non-method properties on this class, plus any additional non-method properties on the concrete class. A value specified in the constructor will override the default value for the corresponding attribute.

This class defines the following properties, and thus values for the following may be passed in the constructor of any policy class:

max_line_length

> The maximum length of any line in the serialized output, not counting the end of line character(s). Default is 78, per RFC 5322. A value of 0 or *None* indicates that no line wrapping should be done at all.

linesep

> The string to be used to terminate lines in serialized output. The default is \n because that's the internal end-of-line discipline used by Python, though \r\n is required by the RFCs.

cte_type

> Controls the type of Content Transfer Encodings that may be or are required to be used. The possible values are:

7bit	all data must be "7 bit clean" (ASCII-only). This means that where necessary data will be encoded using either quoted-printable or base64 encoding.
8bit	data is not constrained to be 7 bit clean. Data in headers is still required to be ASCII-only and so will be encoded (see *fold_binary()* and *utf8* below for exceptions), but body parts may use the 8bit CTE.

> A cte_type value of 8bit only works with BytesGenerator, not Generator, because strings cannot contain binary data. If a Generator is operating under a policy that specifies cte_type=8bit, it will act as if cte_type is 7bit.

raise_on_defect

> If *True*, any defects encountered will be raised as errors. If *False* (the default), defects will be passed to the *register_defect()* method.

mangle_from_

> If *True*, lines starting with *"From "* in the body are escaped by putting a > in front of them. This parameter is used when the message is being serialized by a generator. Default: *False*.
>
> New in version 3.5: The *mangle_from_* parameter.

message_factory

> A factory function for constructing a new empty message object. Used by the parser when building messages. Defaults to None, in which case *Message* is used.
>
> New in version 3.6.

The following *Policy* method is intended to be called by code using the email library to create policy instances with custom settings:

clone(**kw*)**

> Return a new *Policy* instance whose attributes have the same values as the current instance, except where those attributes are given new values by the keyword arguments.

The remaining *Policy* methods are called by the email package code, and are not intended to be called by an application using the email package. A custom policy must implement all of these methods.

handle_defect(*obj*, *defect*)

> Handle a *defect* found on *obj*. When the email package calls this method, *defect* will always be a subclass of Defect.

The default implementation checks the *raise_on_defect* flag. If it is `True`, *defect* is raised as an exception. If it is `False` (the default), *obj* and *defect* are passed to *register_defect()*.

register_defect(*obj*, *defect*)

Register a *defect* on *obj*. In the email package, *defect* will always be a subclass of `Defect`.

The default implementation calls the `append` method of the `defects` attribute of *obj*. When the email package calls *handle_defect*, *obj* will normally have a `defects` attribute that has an `append` method. Custom object types used with the email package (for example, custom `Message` objects) should also provide such an attribute, otherwise defects in parsed messages will raise unexpected errors.

header_max_count(*name*)

Return the maximum allowed number of headers named *name*.

Called when a header is added to an *EmailMessage* or *Message* object. If the returned value is not 0 or `None`, and there are already a number of headers with the name *name* greater than or equal to the value returned, a *ValueError* is raised.

Because the default behavior of `Message.__setitem__` is to append the value to the list of headers, it is easy to create duplicate headers without realizing it. This method allows certain headers to be limited in the number of instances of that header that may be added to a `Message` programmatically. (The limit is not observed by the parser, which will faithfully produce as many headers as exist in the message being parsed.)

The default implementation returns `None` for all header names.

header_source_parse(*sourcelines*)

The email package calls this method with a list of strings, each string ending with the line separation characters found in the source being parsed. The first line includes the field header name and separator. All whitespace in the source is preserved. The method should return the (`name`, `value`) tuple that is to be stored in the `Message` to represent the parsed header.

If an implementation wishes to retain compatibility with the existing email package policies, *name* should be the case preserved name (all characters up to the ':' separator), while *value* should be the unfolded value (all line separator characters removed, but whitespace kept intact), stripped of leading whitespace.

sourcelines may contain surrogateescaped binary data.

There is no default implementation

header_store_parse(*name*, *value*)

The email package calls this method with the name and value provided by the application program when the application program is modifying a `Message` programmatically (as opposed to a `Message` created by a parser). The method should return the (`name`, `value`) tuple that is to be stored in the `Message` to represent the header.

If an implementation wishes to retain compatibility with the existing email package policies, the *name* and *value* should be strings or string subclasses that do not change the content of the passed in arguments.

There is no default implementation

header_fetch_parse(*name*, *value*)

The email package calls this method with the *name* and *value* currently stored in the `Message` when that header is requested by the application program, and whatever the method returns is what is passed back to the application as the value of the header being retrieved. Note that there may be more than one header with the same name stored in the `Message`; the method is passed the specific name and value of the header destined to be returned to the application.

value may contain surrogateescaped binary data. There should be no surrogateescaped binary data in the value returned by the method.

There is no default implementation

fold(*name, value*)

The email package calls this method with the *name* and *value* currently stored in the Message for a given header. The method should return a string that represents that header "folded" correctly (according to the policy settings) by composing the *name* with the *value* and inserting *linesep* characters at the appropriate places. See RFC 5322 for a discussion of the rules for folding email headers.

value may contain surrogateescaped binary data. There should be no surrogateescaped binary data in the string returned by the method.

fold_binary(*name, value*)

The same as *fold()*, except that the returned value should be a bytes object rather than a string.

value may contain surrogateescaped binary data. These could be converted back into binary data in the returned bytes object.

class email.policy.EmailPolicy(***kw*)

This concrete *Policy* provides behavior that is intended to be fully compliant with the current email RFCs. These include (but are not limited to) RFC 5322, RFC 2047, and the current MIME RFCs.

This policy adds new header parsing and folding algorithms. Instead of simple strings, headers are **str** subclasses with attributes that depend on the type of the field. The parsing and folding algorithm fully implement RFC 2047 and RFC 5322.

The default value for the *message_factory* attribute is *EmailMessage*.

In addition to the settable attributes listed above that apply to all policies, this policy adds the following additional attributes:

New in version 3.6:[1]

utf8

If **False**, follow RFC 5322, supporting non-ASCII characters in headers by encoding them as "encoded words". If **True**, follow RFC 6532 and use **utf-8** encoding for headers. Messages formatted in this way may be passed to SMTP servers that support the **SMTPUTF8** extension (RFC 6531).

refold_source

If the value for a header in the Message object originated from a *parser* (as opposed to being set by a program), this attribute indicates whether or not a generator should refold that value when transforming the message back into serialized form. The possible values are:

none	all source values use original folding
long	source values that have any line that is longer than **max_line_length** will be refolded
all	all values are refolded.

The default is **long**.

header_factory

A callable that takes two arguments, **name** and **value**, where **name** is a header field name and **value** is an unfolded header field value, and returns a string subclass that represents that header. A default **header_factory** (see *headerregistry*) is provided that supports custom parsing for the various address and date RFC 5322 header field types, and the major MIME header field stypes. Support for additional custom parsing will be added in the future.

content_manager

An object with at least two methods: get_content and set_content. When the *get_content()* or *set_content()* method of an *EmailMessage* object is called, it calls the corresponding method

---

[1] Originally added in 3.3 as a *provisional feature*.

of this object, passing it the message object as its first argument, and any arguments or keywords that were passed to it as additional arguments. By default `content_manager` is set to *raw_data_manager*.

New in version 3.4.

The class provides the following concrete implementations of the abstract methods of *Policy*:

header_max_count(*name*)
    Returns the value of the *max_count* attribute of the specialized class used to represent the header with the given name.

header_source_parse(*sourcelines*)
    The name is parsed as everything up to the ':' and returned unmodified. The value is determined by stripping leading whitespace off the remainder of the first line, joining all subsequent lines together, and stripping any trailing carriage return or linefeed characters.

header_store_parse(*name, value*)
    The name is returned unchanged. If the input value has a **name** attribute and it matches *name* ignoring case, the value is returned unchanged. Otherwise the *name* and *value* are passed to **header_factory**, and the resulting header object is returned as the value. In this case a `ValueError` is raised if the input value contains CR or LF characters.

header_fetch_parse(*name, value*)
    If the value has a **name** attribute, it is returned to unmodified. Otherwise the *name*, and the *value* with any CR or LF characters removed, are passed to the **header_factory**, and the resulting header object is returned. Any surrogateescaped bytes get turned into the unicode unknown-character glyph.

fold(*name, value*)
    Header folding is controlled by the *refold_source* policy setting. A value is considered to be a 'source value' if and only if it does not have a **name** attribute (having a **name** attribute means it is a header object of some sort). If a source value needs to be refolded according to the policy, it is converted into a header object by passing the *name* and the *value* with any CR and LF characters removed to the **header_factory**. Folding of a header object is done by calling its **fold** method with the current policy.

    Source values are split into lines using *splitlines()*. If the value is not to be refolded, the lines are rejoined using the **linesep** from the policy and returned. The exception is lines containing non-ascii binary data. In that case the value is refolded regardless of the **refold_source** setting, which causes the binary data to be CTE encoded using the **unknown-8bit** charset.

fold_binary(*name, value*)
    The same as *fold()* if *cte_type* is **7bit**, except that the returned value is bytes.

    If *cte_type* is **8bit**, non-ASCII binary data is converted back into bytes. Headers with binary data are not refolded, regardless of the **refold_header** setting, since there is no way to know whether the binary data consists of single byte characters or multibyte characters.

The following instances of *EmailPolicy* provide defaults suitable for specific application domains. Note that in the future the behavior of these instances (in particular the `HTTP` instance) may be adjusted to conform even more closely to the RFCs relevant to their domains.

email.policy.default
    An instance of `EmailPolicy` with all defaults unchanged. This policy uses the standard Python \n line endings rather than the RFC-correct \r\n.

email.policy.SMTP
    Suitable for serializing messages in conformance with the email RFCs. Like `default`, but with `linesep` set to \r\n, which is RFC compliant.

email.policy.SMTPUTF8
    The same as SMTP except that *utf8* is True. Useful for serializing messages to a message store without using encoded words in the headers. Should only be used for SMTP transmission if the sender or recipient addresses have non-ASCII characters (the *smtplib.SMTP.send_message()* method handles this automatically).

email.policy.HTTP
    Suitable for serializing headers with for use in HTTP traffic. Like SMTP except that `max_line_length` is set to None (unlimited).

email.policy.strict
    Convenience instance. The same as `default` except that `raise_on_defect` is set to True. This allows any policy to be made strict by writing:

    ```
    somepolicy + policy.strict
    ```

With all of these *EmailPolicies*, the effective API of the email package is changed from the Python 3.2 API in the following ways:

- Setting a header on a *Message* results in that header being parsed and a header object created.
- Fetching a header value from a *Message* results in that header being parsed and a header object created and returned.
- Any header object, or any header that is refolded due to the policy settings, is folded using an algorithm that fully implements the RFC folding algorithms, including knowing where encoded words are required and allowed.

From the application view, this means that any header obtained through the *EmailMessage* is a header object with extra attributes, whose string value is the fully decoded unicode value of the header. Likewise, a header may be assigned a new value, or a new header created, using a unicode string, and the policy will take care of converting the unicode string into the correct RFC encoded form.

The header objects and their attributes are described in *headerregistry*.

class email.policy.Compat32(**kw*)
    This concrete *Policy* is the backward compatibility policy. It replicates the behavior of the email package in Python 3.2. The *policy* module also defines an instance of this class, *compat32*, that is used as the default policy. Thus the default behavior of the email package is to maintain compatibility with Python 3.2.

    The following attributes have values that are different from the *Policy* default:

    mangle_from_
        The default is True.

    The class provides the following concrete implementations of the abstract methods of *Policy*:

    header_source_parse(*sourcelines*)
        The name is parsed as everything up to the ':' and returned unmodified. The value is determined by stripping leading whitespace off the remainder of the first line, joining all subsequent lines together, and stripping any trailing carriage return or linefeed characters.

    header_store_parse(*name, value*)
        The name and value are returned unmodified.

    header_fetch_parse(*name, value*)
        If the value contains binary data, it is converted into a *Header* object using the `unknown-8bit` charset. Otherwise it is returned unmodified.

    fold(*name, value*)
        Headers are folded using the *Header* folding algorithm, which preserves existing line breaks in the

value, and wraps each resulting line to the **max_line_length**. Non-ASCII binary data are CTE encoded using the **unknown-8bit** charset.

fold_binary(*name, value*)
Headers are folded using the *Header* folding algorithm, which preserves existing line breaks in the value, and wraps each resulting line to the **max_line_length**. If **cte_type** is **7bit**, non-ascii binary data is CTE encoded using the **unknown-8bit** charset. Otherwise the original source header is used, with its existing line breaks and any (RFC invalid) binary data it may contain.

email.policy.compat32
An instance of *Compat32*, providing backward compatibility with the behavior of the email package in Python 3.2.

19.1.5 email.errors: Exception and Defect classes

Source code: Lib/email/errors.py

The following exception classes are defined in the *email.errors* module:

exception email.errors.MessageError
This is the base class for all exceptions that the *email* package can raise. It is derived from the standard *Exception* class and defines no additional methods.

exception email.errors.MessageParseError
This is the base class for exceptions raised by the *Parser* class. It is derived from *MessageError*. This class is also used internally by the parser used by *headerregistry*.

exception email.errors.HeaderParseError
Raised under some error conditions when parsing the RFC 5322 headers of a message, this class is derived from *MessageParseError*. The *set_boundary()* method will raise this error if the content type is unknown when the method is called. *Header* may raise this error for certain base64 decoding errors, and when an attempt is made to create a header that appears to contain an embedded header (that is, there is what is supposed to be a continuation line that has no leading whitespace and looks like a header).

exception email.errors.BoundaryError
Deprecated and no longer used.

exception email.errors.MultipartConversionError
Raised when a payload is added to a *Message* object using **add_payload()**, but the payload is already a scalar and the message's *Content-Type* main type is not either *multipart* or missing. *MultipartConversionError* multiply inherits from *MessageError* and the built-in *TypeError*.

Since **Message.add_payload()** is deprecated, this exception is rarely raised in practice. However the exception may also be raised if the *attach()* method is called on an instance of a class derived from *MIMENonMultipart* (e.g. *MIMEImage*).

Here is the list of the defects that the *FeedParser* can find while parsing messages. Note that the defects are added to the message where the problem was found, so for example, if a message nested inside a *multipart/alternative* had a malformed header, that nested message object would have a defect, but the containing messages would not.

All defect classes are subclassed from **email.errors.MessageDefect**.

- **NoBoundaryInMultipartDefect** – A message claimed to be a multipart, but had no *boundary* parameter.

- **StartBoundaryNotFoundDefect** – The start boundary claimed in the *Content-Type* header was never found.

- `CloseBoundaryNotFoundDefect` – A start boundary was found, but no corresponding close boundary was ever found.

    New in version 3.3.

- `FirstHeaderLineIsContinuationDefect` – The message had a continuation line as its first header line.

- `MisplacedEnvelopeHeaderDefect` - A "Unix From" header was found in the middle of a header block.

- `MissingHeaderBodySeparatorDefect` - A line was found while parsing headers that had no leading white space but contained no ':'. Parsing continues assuming that the line represents the first line of the body.

    New in version 3.3.

- `MalformedHeaderDefect` – A header was found that was missing a colon, or was otherwise malformed.

    Deprecated since version 3.3: This defect has not been used for several Python versions.

- `MultipartInvariantViolationDefect` – A message claimed to be a *multipart*, but no subparts were found. Note that when a message has this defect, its `is_multipart()` method may return false even though its content type claims to be *multipart*.

- `InvalidBase64PaddingDefect` – When decoding a block of base64 encoded bytes, the padding was not correct. Enough padding is added to perform the decode, but the resulting decoded bytes may be invalid.

- `InvalidBase64CharactersDefect` – When decoding a block of base64 encoded bytes, characters outside the base64 alphabet were encountered. The characters are ignored, but the resulting decoded bytes may be invalid.

19.1.6 email.headerregistry: Custom Header Objects

Source code: Lib/email/headerregistry.py

New in version 3.6:[1]

Headers are represented by customized subclasses of `str`. The particular class used to represent a given header is determined by the `header_factory` of the `policy` in effect when the headers are created. This section documents the particular `header_factory` implemented by the email package for handling RFC 5322 compliant email messages, which not only provides customized header objects for various header types, but also provides an extension mechanism for applications to add their own custom header types.

When using any of the policy objects derived from `EmailPolicy`, all headers are produced by `HeaderRegistry` and have `BaseHeader` as their last base class. Each header class has an additional base class that is determined by the type of the header. For example, many headers have the class `UnstructuredHeader` as their other base class. The specialized second class for a header is determined by the name of the header, using a lookup table stored in the `HeaderRegistry`. All of this is managed transparently for the typical application program, but interfaces are provided for modifying the default behavior for use by more complex applications.

The sections below first document the header base classes and their attributes, followed by the API for modifying the behavior of `HeaderRegistry`, and finally the support classes used to represent the data parsed from structured headers.

class `email.headerregistry.BaseHeader`(*name*, *value*)

    name and *value* are passed to `BaseHeader` from the `header_factory` call. The string value of any header object is the *value* fully decoded to unicode.

---

[1] Originally added in 3.3 as a *provisional module*

This base class defines the following read-only properties:

name
> The name of the header (the portion of the field before the ':'). This is exactly the value passed in the *header_factory* call for *name*; that is, case is preserved.

defects
> A tuple of `HeaderDefect` instances reporting any RFC compliance problems found during parsing. The email package tries to be complete about detecting compliance issues. See the *errors* module for a discussion of the types of defects that may be reported.

max_count
> The maximum number of headers of this type that can have the same `name`. A value of `None` means unlimited. The `BaseHeader` value for this attribute is `None`; it is expected that specialized header classes will override this value as needed.

`BaseHeader` also provides the following method, which is called by the email library code and should not in general be called by application programs:

fold(*, *policy*)
> Return a string containing *linesep* characters as required to correctly fold the header according to *policy*. A *cte_type* of `8bit` will be treated as if it were `7bit`, since headers may not contain arbitrary binary data. If *utf8* is `False`, non-ASCII data will be RFC 2047 encoded.

`BaseHeader` by itself cannot be used to create a header object. It defines a protocol that each specialized header cooperates with in order to produce the header object. Specifically, `BaseHeader` requires that the specialized class provide a *classmethod()* named `parse`. This method is called as follows:

```
parse(string, kwds)
```

`kwds` is a dictionary containing one pre-initialized key, `defects`. `defects` is an empty list. The parse method should append any detected defects to this list. On return, the `kwds` dictionary *must* contain values for at least the keys `decoded` and `defects`. `decoded` should be the string value for the header (that is, the header value fully decoded to unicode). The parse method should assume that *string* may contain content-transfer-encoded parts, but should correctly handle all valid unicode characters as well so that it can parse un-encoded header values.

`BaseHeader`'s `__new__` then creates the header instance, and calls its `init` method. The specialized class only needs to provide an `init` method if it wishes to set additional attributes beyond those provided by `BaseHeader` itself. Such an `init` method should look like this:

```python
def init(self, *args, **kw):
    self._myattr = kw.pop('myattr')
    super().init(*args, **kw)
```

That is, anything extra that the specialized class puts in to the `kwds` dictionary should be removed and handled, and the remaining contents of `kw` (and `args`) passed to the `BaseHeader init` method.

class email.headerregistry.UnstructuredHeader
> An "unstructured" header is the default type of header in RFC 5322. Any header that does not have a specified syntax is treated as unstructured. The classic example of an unstructured header is the *Subject* header.
>
> In RFC 5322, an unstructured header is a run of arbitrary text in the ASCII character set. RFC 2047, however, has an RFC 5322 compatible mechanism for encoding non-ASCII text as ASCII characters within a header value. When a *value* containing encoded words is passed to the constructor, the `UnstructuredHeader` parser converts such encoded words into unicode, following the RFC 2047 rules for unstructured text. The parser uses heuristics to attempt to decode certain non-compliant encoded words. Defects are registered in such cases, as well as defects for issues such as invalid characters within the encoded words or the non-encoded text.

This header type provides no additional attributes.

class email.headerregistry.DateHeader

RFC 5322 specifies a very specific format for dates within email headers. The `DateHeader` parser recognizes that date format, as well as recognizing a number of variant forms that are sometimes found "in the wild".

This header type provides the following additional attributes:

datetime

If the header value can be recognized as a valid date of one form or another, this attribute will contain a *datetime* instance representing that date. If the timezone of the input date is specified as -0000 (indicating it is in UTC but contains no information about the source timezone), then *datetime* will be a naive *datetime*. If a specific timezone offset is found (including *+0000*), then *datetime* will contain an aware `datetime` that uses *datetime.timezone* to record the timezone offset.

The `decoded` value of the header is determined by formatting the `datetime` according to the RFC 5322 rules; that is, it is set to:

```
email.utils.format_datetime(self.datetime)
```

When creating a `DateHeader`, *value* may be *datetime* instance. This means, for example, that the following code is valid and does what one would expect:

```
msg['Date'] = datetime(2011, 7, 15, 21)
```

Because this is a naive `datetime` it will be interpreted as a UTC timestamp, and the resulting value will have a timezone of -0000. Much more useful is to use the *localtime()* function from the *utils* module:

```
msg['Date'] = utils.localtime()
```

This example sets the date header to the current time and date using the current timezone offset.

class email.headerregistry.AddressHeader

Address headers are one of the most complex structured header types. The `AddressHeader` class provides a generic interface to any address header.

This header type provides the following additional attributes:

groups

A tuple of *Group* objects encoding the addresses and groups found in the header value. Addresses that are not part of a group are represented in this list as single-address `Groups` whose *display_name* is `None`.

addresses

A tuple of *Address* objects encoding all of the individual addresses from the header value. If the header value contains any groups, the individual addresses from the group are included in the list at the point where the group occurs in the value (that is, the list of addresses is "flattened" into a one dimensional list).

The `decoded` value of the header will have all encoded words decoded to unicode. *idna* encoded domain names are also decoded to unicode. The `decoded` value is set by *join*ing the *str* value of the elements of the `groups` attribute with ', '.

A list of *Address* and *Group* objects in any combination may be used to set the value of an address header. `Group` objects whose `display_name` is `None` will be interpreted as single addresses, which allows an address list to be copied with groups intact by using the list obtained from the `groups` attribute of the source header.

class email.headerregistry.SingleAddressHeader

A subclass of *AddressHeader* that adds one additional attribute:

address

The single address encoded by the header value. If the header value actually contains more than one address (which would be a violation of the RFC under the default *policy*), accessing this attribute will result in a *ValueError*.

Many of the above classes also have a `Unique` variant (for example, `UniqueUnstructuredHeader`). The only difference is that in the `Unique` variant, *max_count* is set to 1.

class email.headerregistry.MIMEVersionHeader

There is really only one valid value for the *MIME-Version* header, and that is 1.0. For future proofing, this header class supports other valid version numbers. If a version number has a valid value per RFC 2045, then the header object will have non-`None` values for the following attributes:

version

The version number as a string, with any whitespace and/or comments removed.

major

The major version number as an integer

minor

The minor version number as an integer

class email.headerregistry.ParameterizedMIMEHeader

MIME headers all start with the prefix 'Content-'. Each specific header has a certain value, described under the class for that header. Some can also take a list of supplemental parameters, which have a common format. This class serves as a base for all the MIME headers that take parameters.

params

A dictionary mapping parameter names to parameter values.

class email.headerregistry.ContentTypeHeader

A *ParameterizedMIMEHeader* class that handles the *Content-Type* header.

content_type

The content type string, in the form `maintype/subtype`.

maintype

subtype

class email.headerregistry.ContentDispositionHeader

A *ParameterizedMIMEHeader* class that handles the *Content-Disposition* header.

content-disposition

`inline` and `attachment` are the only valid values in common use.

class email.headerregistry.ContentTransferEncoding

Handles the *Content-Transfer-Encoding* header.

cte

Valid values are `7bit`, `8bit`, `base64`, and `quoted-printable`. See RFC 2045 for more information.

class email.headerregistry.HeaderRegistry(*base_class=BaseHeader, default_class=UnstructuredHeader, use_default_map=True*)

This is the factory used by *EmailPolicy* by default. `HeaderRegistry` builds the class used to create a header instance dynamically, using *base_class* and a specialized class retrieved from a registry that it holds. When a given header name does not appear in the registry, the class specified by *default_class* is used as the specialized class. When *use_default_map* is `True` (the default), the standard mapping of header names to classes is copied in to the registry during initialization. *base_class* is always the last class in the generated class's `__bases__` list.

The default mappings are:

> **subject** UniqueUnstructuredHeader
>
> **date** UniqueDateHeader
>
> **resent-date** DateHeader
>
> **orig-date** UniqueDateHeader
>
> **sender** UniqueSingleAddressHeader
>
> **resent-sender** SingleAddressHeader
>
> **to** UniqueAddressHeader
>
> **resent-to** AddressHeader
>
> **cc** UniqueAddressHeader
>
> **resent-cc** AddressHeader
>
> **from** UniqueAddressHeader
>
> **resent-from** AddressHeader
>
> **reply-to** UniqueAddressHeader

`HeaderRegistry` has the following methods:

map_to_type(*self, name, cls*)
> *name* is the name of the header to be mapped. It will be converted to lower case in the registry. *cls* is the specialized class to be used, along with *base_class*, to create the class used to instantiate headers that match *name*.

__getitem__(*name*)
> Construct and return a class to handle creating a *name* header.

__call__(*name, value*)
> Retrieves the specialized header associated with *name* from the registry (using *default_class* if *name* does not appear in the registry) and composes it with *base_class* to produce a class, calls the constructed class's constructor, passing it the same argument list, and finally returns the class instance created thereby.

The following classes are the classes used to represent data parsed from structured headers and can, in general, be used by an application program to construct structured values to assign to specific headers.

class email.headerregistry.Address(*display_name=", username=", domain=", addr_spec=None*)
> The class used to represent an email address. The general form of an address is:

```
[display_name] <username@domain>
```

> or:

```
username@domain
```

> where each part must conform to specific syntax rules spelled out in RFC 5322.

> As a convenience *addr_spec* can be specified instead of *username* and *domain*, in which case *username* and *domain* will be parsed from the *addr_spec*. An *addr_spec* must be a properly RFC quoted string; if it is not `Address` will raise an error. Unicode characters are allowed and will be property encoded when serialized. However, per the RFCs, unicode is *not* allowed in the username portion of the address.

display_name
    The display name portion of the address, if any, with all quoting removed. If the address does not have a display name, this attribute will be an empty string.

username
    The username portion of the address, with all quoting removed.

domain
    The domain portion of the address.

addr_spec
    The username@domain portion of the address, correctly quoted for use as a bare address (the second form shown above). This attribute is not mutable.

__str__()
    The str value of the object is the address quoted according to RFC 5322 rules, but with no Content Transfer Encoding of any non-ASCII characters.

To support SMTP (RFC 5321), Address handles one special case: if username and domain are both the empty string (or None), then the string value of the Address is <>.

class email.headerregistry.Group(*display_name=None, addresses=None*)
    The class used to represent an address group. The general form of an address group is:

```
display_name: [address-list];
```

As a convenience for processing lists of addresses that consist of a mixture of groups and single addresses, a Group may also be used to represent single addresses that are not part of a group by setting *display_name* to None and providing a list of the single address as *addresses*.

display_name
    The display_name of the group. If it is None and there is exactly one Address in addresses, then the Group represents a single address that is not in a group.

addresses
    A possibly empty tuple of *Address* objects representing the addresses in the group.

__str__()
    The str value of a Group is formatted according to RFC 5322, but with no Content Transfer Encoding of any non-ASCII characters. If display_name is none and there is a single Address in the addresses list, the str value will be the same as the str of that single Address.

19.1.7 email.contentmanager: Managing MIME Content

Source code: Lib/email/contentmanager.py

New in version 3.6:[1]

class email.contentmanager.ContentManager
    Base class for content managers. Provides the standard registry mechanisms to register converters between MIME content and other representations, as well as the get_content and set_content dispatch methods.

get_content(*msg, *args, **kw*)
    Look up a handler function based on the mimetype of *msg* (see next paragraph), call it, passing through all arguments, and return the result of the call. The expectation is that the handler will

---
[1] Originally added in 3.4 as a *provisional module*.

extract the payload from *msg* and return an object that encodes information about the extracted data.

To find the handler, look for the following keys in the registry, stopping with the first one found:

- the string representing the full MIME type (`maintype/subtype`)
- the string representing the `maintype`
- the empty string

If none of these keys produce a handler, raise a *KeyError* for the full MIME type.

set_content(*msg*, *obj*, **args*, ***kw*)

If the `maintype` is `multipart`, raise a *TypeError*; otherwise look up a handler function based on the type of *obj* (see next paragraph), call `clear_content()` on the *msg*, and call the handler function, passing through all arguments. The expectation is that the handler will transform and store *obj* into *msg*, possibly making other changes to *msg* as well, such as adding various MIME headers to encode information needed to interpret the stored data.

To find the handler, obtain the type of *obj* (`typ = type(obj)`), and look for the following keys in the registry, stopping with the first one found:

- the type itself (`typ`)
- the type's fully qualified name (`typ.__module__` + `'.'` + `typ.__qualname__`).
- the type's qualname (`typ.__qualname__`)
- the type's name (`typ.__name__`).

If none of the above match, repeat all of the checks above for each of the types in the *MRO* (`typ.__mro__`). Finally, if no other key yields a handler, check for a handler for the key `None`. If there is no handler for `None`, raise a *KeyError* for the fully qualified name of the type.

Also add a *MIME-Version* header if one is not present (see also *MIMEPart*).

add_get_handler(*key*, *handler*)

Record the function *handler* as the handler for *key*. For the possible values of *key*, see *get_content()*.

add_set_handler(*typekey*, *handler*)

Record *handler* as the function to call when an object of a type matching *typekey* is passed to *set_content()*. For the possible values of *typekey*, see *set_content()*.

Content Manager Instances

Currently the email package provides only one concrete content manager, *raw_data_manager*, although more may be added in the future. *raw_data_manager* is the *content_manager* provided by *EmailPolicy* and its derivatives.

email.contentmanager.raw_data_manager

This content manager provides only a minimum interface beyond that provided by *Message* itself: it deals only with text, raw byte strings, and *Message* objects. Nevertheless, it provides significant advantages compared to the base API: `get_content` on a text part will return a unicode string without the application needing to manually decode it, `set_content` provides a rich set of options for controlling the headers added to a part and controlling the content transfer encoding, and it enables the use of the various `add_` methods, thereby simplifying the creation of multipart messages.

email.contentmanager.get_content(*msg*, *errors='replace'*)

Return the payload of the part as either a string (for `text` parts), an *EmailMessage* object (for `message/rfc822` parts), or a `bytes` object (for all other non-multipart types). Raise a *KeyError* if called on a `multipart`. If the part is a `text` part and *errors* is specified, use it as the error handler when decoding the payload to unicode. The default error handler is `replace`.

email.contentmanager.**set_content**(*msg, <'str'>, subtype="plain", charset='utf-8' cte=None, disposition=None, filename=None, cid=None, params=None, headers=None*)

email.contentmanager.**set_content**(*msg, <'bytes'>, maintype, subtype, cte="base64", disposition=None, filename=None, cid=None, params=None, headers=None*)

email.contentmanager.**set_content**(*msg, <'EmailMessage'>, cte=None, disposition=None, filename=None, cid=None, params=None, headers=None*)

email.contentmanager.**set_content**(*msg, <'list'>, subtype='mixed', disposition=None, filename=None, cid=None, params=None, headers=None*)

Add headers and payload to *msg*:

Add a `Content-Type` header with a `maintype/subtype` value.

- For `str`, set the MIME `maintype` to `text`, and set the subtype to *subtype* if it is specified, or `plain` if it is not.

- For `bytes`, use the specified *maintype* and *subtype*, or raise a `TypeError` if they are not specified.

- For `EmailMessage` objects, set the maintype to `message`, and set the subtype to *subtype* if it is specified or `rfc822` if it is not. If *subtype* is `partial`, raise an error (`bytes` objects must be used to construct `message/partial` parts).

- For `<'list'>`, which should be a list of `EmailMessage` objects, set the `maintype` to `multipart`, and the `subtype` to *subtype* if it is specified, and `mixed` if it is not. If the message parts in the `<'list'>` have `MIME-Version` headers, remove them.

If *charset* is provided (which is valid only for `str`), encode the string to bytes using the specified character set. The default is `utf-8`. If the specified *charset* is a known alias for a standard MIME charset name, use the standard charset instead.

If *cte* is set, encode the payload using the specified content transfer encoding, and set the `Content-Transfer-Encoding` header to that value. Possible values for *cte* are `quoted-printable`, `base64`, `7bit`, `8bit`, and `binary`. If the input cannot be encoded in the specified encoding (for example, specifying a *cte* of `7bit` for an input that contains non-ASCII values), raise a `ValueError`.

- For `str` objects, if *cte* is not set use heuristics to determine the most compact encoding.

- For `EmailMessage`, per RFC 2046, raise an error if a *cte* of `quoted-printable` or `base64` is requested for *subtype* `rfc822`, and for any *cte* other than `7bit` for *subtype* `external-body`. For `message/rfc822`, use `8bit` if *cte* is not specified. For all other values of *subtype*, use `7bit`.

Note: A *cte* of `binary` does not actually work correctly yet. The `EmailMessage` object as modified by `set_content` is correct, but `BytesGenerator` does not serialize it correctly.

If *disposition* is set, use it as the value of the `Content-Disposition` header. If not specified, and *filename* is specified, add the header with the value `attachment`. If *disposition* is not specified and *filename* is also not specified, do not add the header. The only valid values for *disposition* are `attachment` and `inline`.

If *filename* is specified, use it as the value of the `filename` parameter of the `Content-Disposition` header.

If *cid* is specified, add a `Content-ID` header with *cid* as its value.

If *params* is specified, iterate its `items` method and use the resulting (`key, value`) pairs to set additional parameters on the *Content-Type* header.

If *headers* is specified and is a list of strings of the form `headername: headervalue` or a list of `header` objects (distinguished from strings by having a `name` attribute), add the headers to *msg*.

19.1.8 `email`: Examples

Here are a few examples of how to use the *email* package to read, write, and send simple email messages, as well as more complex MIME messages.

First, let's see how to create and send a simple text message (both the text content and the addresses may contain unicode characters):

```python
# Import smtplib for the actual sending function
import smtplib

# Import the email modules we'll need
from email.message import EmailMessage

# Open the plain text file whose name is in textfile for reading.
with open(textfile) as fp:
    # Create a text/plain message
    msg = EmailMessage()
    msg.set_content(fp.read())

# me == the sender's email address
# you == the recipient's email address
msg['Subject'] = 'The contents of %s' % textfile
msg['From'] = me
msg['To'] = you

# Send the message via our own SMTP server.
s = smtplib.SMTP('localhost')
s.send_message(msg)
s.quit()
```

Parsing RFC822 headers can easily be done by the using the classes from the *parser* module:

```python
# Import the email modules we'll need
from email.parser import BytesParser, Parser
from email.policy import default

# If the e-mail headers are in a file, uncomment these two lines:
# with open(messagefile, 'rb') as fp:
#     headers = BytesParser(policy=default).parse(fp)

# Or for parsing headers in a string (this is an uncommon operation), use:
headers = Parser(policy=default).parsestr(
        'From: Foo Bar <user@example.com>\n'
        'To: <someone_else@example.com>\n'
        'Subject: Test message\n'
        '\n'
        'Body would go here\n')

# Now the header items can be accessed as a dictionary:
print('To: {}'.format(headers['to']))
print('From: {}'.format(headers['from']))
```

```python
print('Subject: {}'.format(headers['subject']))

# You can also access the parts of the addresses:
print('Recipient username: {}'.format(headers['to'].addresses[0].username))
print('Sender name: {}'.format(headers['from'].addresses[0].display_name))
```

Here's an example of how to send a MIME message containing a bunch of family pictures that may be residing in a directory:

```python
# Import smtplib for the actual sending function
import smtplib

# And imghdr to find the types of our images
import imghdr

# Here are the email package modules we'll need
from email.message import EmailMessage

# Create the container email message.
msg = EmailMessage()
msg['Subject'] = 'Our family reunion'
# me == the sender's email address
# family = the list of all recipients' email addresses
msg['From'] = me
msg['To'] = ', '.join(family)
msg.preamble = 'Our family reunion'

# Open the files in binary mode.  Use imghdr to figure out the
# MIME subtype for each specific image.
for file in pngfiles:
    with open(file, 'rb') as fp:
        img_data = fp.read()
    msg.add_attachment(img_data, maintype='image',
                                 subtype=imghdr.what(None, img_data))

# Send the email via our own SMTP server.
with smtplib.SMTP('localhost') as s:
    s.send_message(msg)
```

Here's an example of how to send the entire contents of a directory as an email message:[1]

```python
#!/usr/bin/env python3

"""Send the contents of a directory as a MIME message."""

import os
import smtplib
# For guessing MIME type based on file name extension
import mimetypes

from argparse import ArgumentParser

from email.message import EmailMessage
from email.policy import SMTP
```

---

[1] Thanks to Matthew Dixon Cowles for the original inspiration and examples.

```python
def main():
    parser = ArgumentParser(description="""\
Send the contents of a directory as a MIME message.
Unless the -o option is given, the email is sent by forwarding to your local
SMTP server, which then does the normal delivery process.  Your local machine
must be running an SMTP server.
""")
    parser.add_argument('-d', '--directory',
                        help="""Mail the contents of the specified directory,
                        otherwise use the current directory.  Only the regular
                        files in the directory are sent, and we don't recurse to
                        subdirectories.""")
    parser.add_argument('-o', '--output',
                        metavar='FILE',
                        help="""Print the composed message to FILE instead of
                        sending the message to the SMTP server.""")
    parser.add_argument('-s', '--sender', required=True,
                        help='The value of the From: header (required)')
    parser.add_argument('-r', '--recipient', required=True,
                        action='append', metavar='RECIPIENT',
                        default=[], dest='recipients',
                        help='A To: header value (at least one required)')
    args = parser.parse_args()
    directory = args.directory
    if not directory:
        directory = '.'
    # Create the message
    msg = EmailMessage()
    msg['Subject'] = 'Contents of directory %s' % os.path.abspath(directory)
    msg['To'] = ', '.join(args.recipients)
    msg['From'] = args.sender
    msg.preamble = 'You will not see this in a MIME-aware mail reader.\n'

    for filename in os.listdir(directory):
        path = os.path.join(directory, filename)
        if not os.path.isfile(path):
            continue
        # Guess the content type based on the file's extension.  Encoding
        # will be ignored, although we should check for simple things like
        # gzip'd or compressed files.
        ctype, encoding = mimetypes.guess_type(path)
        if ctype is None or encoding is not None:
            # No guess could be made, or the file is encoded (compressed), so
            # use a generic bag-of-bits type.
            ctype = 'application/octet-stream'
        maintype, subtype = ctype.split('/', 1)
        with open(path, 'rb') as fp:
            msg.add_attachment(fp.read(),
                               maintype=maintype,
                               subtype=subtype,
                               filename=filename)
    # Now send or store the message
    if args.output:
        with open(args.output, 'wb') as fp:
            fp.write(msg.as_bytes(policy=SMTP))
    else:
        with smtplib.SMTP('localhost') as s:
            s.send_message(msg)
```

```python
if __name__ == '__main__':
    main()
```

Here's an example of how to unpack a MIME message like the one above, into a directory of files:

```python
#!/usr/bin/env python3

"""Unpack a MIME message into a directory of files."""

import os
import email
import mimetypes

from email.policy import default

from argparse import ArgumentParser


def main():
    parser = ArgumentParser(description="""\
Unpack a MIME message into a directory of files.
""")
    parser.add_argument('-d', '--directory', required=True,
                        help="""Unpack the MIME message into the named
                        directory, which will be created if it doesn't already
                        exist.""")
    parser.add_argument('msgfile')
    args = parser.parse_args()

    with open(args.msgfile, 'rb') as fp:
        msg = email.message_from_binary_file(fp, policy=default)

    try:
        os.mkdir(args.directory)
    except FileExistsError:
        pass

    counter = 1
    for part in msg.walk():
        # multipart/* are just containers
        if part.get_content_maintype() == 'multipart':
            continue
        # Applications should really sanitize the given filename so that an
        # email message can't be used to overwrite important files
        filename = part.get_filename()
        if not filename:
            ext = mimetypes.guess_extension(part.get_content_type())
            if not ext:
                # Use a generic bag-of-bits extension
                ext = '.bin'
            filename = 'part-%03d%s' % (counter, ext)
        counter += 1
        with open(os.path.join(args.directory, filename), 'wb') as fp:
            fp.write(part.get_payload(decode=True))
```

```
if __name__ == '__main__':
    main()
```

Here's an example of how to create an HTML message with an alternative plain text version. To make things a bit more interesting, we include a related image in the html part, and we save a copy of what we are going to send to disk, as well as sending it.

```
#!/usr/bin/env python3

import smtplib

from email.message import EmailMessage
from email.headerregistry import Address
from email.utils import make_msgid

# Create the base text message.
msg = EmailMessage()
msg['Subject'] = "Ayons asperges pour le déjeuner"
msg['From'] = Address("Pepé Le Pew", "pepe", "example.com")
msg['To'] = (Address("Penelope Pussycat", "penelope", "example.com"),
             Address("Fabrette Pussycat", "fabrette", "example.com"))
msg.set_content("""\
Salut!

Cela ressemble à un excellent recipie[1] déjeuner.

[1] http://www.yummly.com/recipe/Roasted-Asparagus-Epicurious-203718

--Pepé
""")

# Add the html version.  This converts the message into a multipart/alternative
# container, with the original text message as the first part and the new html
# message as the second part.
asparagus_cid = make_msgid()
msg.add_alternative("""\
<html>
  <head></head>
  <body>
    <p>Salut!</p>
    <p>Cela ressemble à un excellent
        <a href="http://www.yummly.com/recipe/Roasted-Asparagus-Epicurious-203718">
            recipie
        </a> déjeuner.
    </p>
    <img src="cid:{asparagus_cid}" />
  </body>
</html>
""".format(asparagus_cid=asparagus_cid[1:-1]), subtype='html')
# note that we needed to peel the <> off the msgid for use in the html.

# Now add the related image to the html part.
with open("roasted-asparagus.jpg", 'rb') as img:
    msg.get_payload()[1].add_related(img.read(), 'image', 'jpeg',
                                     cid=asparagus_cid)

# Make a local copy of what we are going to send.
with open('outgoing.msg', 'wb') as f:
```

```python
    f.write(bytes(msg))

# Send the message via local SMTP server.
with smtplib.SMTP('localhost') as s:
    s.send_message(msg)
```

If we were sent the message from the last example, here is one way we could process it:

```python
import os
import sys
import tempfile
import mimetypes
import webbrowser

# Import the email modules we'll need
from email import policy
from email.parser import BytesParser

# An imaginary module that would make this work and be safe.
from imaginary import magic_html_parser

# In a real program you'd get the filename from the arguments.
with open('outgoing.msg', 'rb') as fp:
    msg = BytesParser(policy=policy.default).parse(fp)

# Now the header items can be accessed as a dictionary, and any non-ASCII will
# be converted to unicode:
print('To:', msg['to'])
print('From:', msg['from'])
print('Subject:', msg['subject'])

# If we want to print a preview of the message content, we can extract whatever
# the least formatted payload is and print the first three lines. Of course,
# if the message has no plain text part printing the first three lines of html
# is probably useless, but this is just a conceptual example.
simplest = msg.get_body(preferencelist=('plain', 'html'))
print()
print(''.join(simplest.get_content().splitlines(keepends=True)[:3]))

ans = input("View full message?")
if ans.lower()[0] == 'n':
    sys.exit()

# We can extract the richest alternative in order to display it:
richest = msg.get_body()
partfiles = {}
if richest['content-type'].maintype == 'text':
    if richest['content-type'].subtype == 'plain':
        for line in richest.get_content().splitlines():
            print(line)
        sys.exit()
    elif richest['content-type'].subtype == 'html':
        body = richest
    else:
        print("Don't know how to display {}".format(richest.get_content_type()))
        sys.exit()
elif richest['content-type'].content_type == 'multipart/related':
    body = richest.get_body(preferencelist=('html'))
```

```
        for part in richest.iter_attachments():
            fn = part.get_filename()
            if fn:
                extension = os.path.splitext(part.get_filename())[1]
            else:
                extension = mimetypes.guess_extension(part.get_content_type())
            with tempfile.NamedTemporaryFile(suffix=extension, delete=False) as f:
                f.write(part.get_content())
                # again strip the <> to go from email form of cid to html form.
                partfiles[part['content-id'][1:-1]] = f.name
else:
    print("Don't know how to display {}".format(richest.get_content_type()))
    sys.exit()
with tempfile.NamedTemporaryFile(mode='w', delete=False) as f:
    # The magic_html_parser has to rewrite the href="cid:...." attributes to
    # point to the filenames in partfiles.  It also has to do a safety-sanitize
    # of the html.  It could be written using html.parser.
    f.write(magic_html_parser(body.get_content(), partfiles))
webbrowser.open(f.name)
os.remove(f.name)
for fn in partfiles.values():
    os.remove(fn)

# Of course, there are lots of email messages that could break this simple
# minded program, but it will handle the most common ones.
```

Up to the prompt, the output from the above is:

```
To: Penelope Pussycat <penelope@example.com>, Fabrette Pussycat <fabrette@example.com>
From: Pepé Le Pew <pepe@example.com>
Subject: Ayons asperges pour le déjeuner

Salut!

Cela ressemble à un excellent recipie[1] déjeuner.
```

Legacy API:

19.1.9 `email.message.Message`: Representing an email message using the `compat32` API

The *Message* class is very similar to the *EmailMessage* class, without the methods added by that class, and with the default behavior of certain other methods being slightly different. We also document here some methods that, while supported by the *EmailMessage* class, are not recommended unless you are dealing with legacy code.

The philosophy and structure of the two classes is otherwise the same.

This document describes the behavior under the default (for *Message*) policy *Compat32*. If you are going to use another policy, you should be using the *EmailMessage* class instead.

An email message consists of *headers* and a *payload*. Headers must be RFC 5233 style names and values, where the field name and value are separated by a colon. The colon is not part of either the field name or the field value. The payload may be a simple text message, or a binary object, or a structured sequence of sub-messages each with their own set of headers and their own payload. The latter type of payload is indicated by the message having a MIME type such as *multipart/** or *message/rfc822*.

The conceptual model provided by a *Message* object is that of an ordered dictionary of headers with additional methods for accessing both specialized information from the headers, for accessing the payload, for generating a serialized version of the message, and for recursively walking over the object tree. Note that duplicate headers are supported but special methods must be used to access them.

The *Message* pseudo-dictionary is indexed by the header names, which must be ASCII values. The values of the dictionary are strings that are supposed to contain only ASCII characters; there is some special handling for non-ASCII input, but it doesn't always produce the correct results. Headers are stored and returned in case-preserving form, but field names are matched case-insensitively. There may also be a single envelope header, also known as the *Unix-From* header or the **From_** header. The *payload* is either a string or bytes, in the case of simple message objects, or a list of *Message* objects, for MIME container documents (e.g. *multipart/** and *message/rfc822*).

Here are the methods of the *Message* class:

class email.message.Message(*policy=compat32*)

If *policy* is specified (it must be an instance of a *policy* class) use the rules it specifies to update and serialize the representation of the message. If *policy* is not set, use the *compat32* policy, which maintains backward compatibility with the Python 3.2 version of the email package. For more information see the *policy* documentation.

Changed in version 3.3: The *policy* keyword argument was added.

as_string(*unixfrom=False, maxheaderlen=0, policy=None*)

Return the entire message flattened as a string. When optional *unixfrom* is true, the envelope header is included in the returned string. *unixfrom* defaults to **False**. For backward compatibility reasons, *maxheaderlen* defaults to 0, so if you want a different value you must override it explicitly (the value specified for *max_line_length* in the policy will be ignored by this method). The *policy* argument may be used to override the default policy obtained from the message instance. This can be used to control some of the formatting produced by the method, since the specified *policy* will be passed to the **Generator**.

Flattening the message may trigger changes to the *Message* if defaults need to be filled in to complete the transformation to a string (for example, MIME boundaries may be generated or modified).

Note that this method is provided as a convenience and may not always format the message the way you want. For example, by default it does not do the mangling of lines that begin with **From** that is required by the unix mbox format. For more flexibility, instantiate a *Generator* instance and use its *flatten()* method directly. For example:

```
from io import StringIO
from email.generator import Generator
fp = StringIO()
g = Generator(fp, mangle_from_=True, maxheaderlen=60)
g.flatten(msg)
text = fp.getvalue()
```

If the message object contains binary data that is not encoded according to RFC standards, the non-compliant data will be replaced by unicode "unknown character" code points. (See also *as_bytes()* and *BytesGenerator*.)

Changed in version 3.4: the *policy* keyword argument was added.

__str__()

Equivalent to *as_string()*. Allows **str(msg)** to produce a string containing the formatted message.

as_bytes(*unixfrom=False, policy=None*)

Return the entire message flattened as a bytes object. When optional *unixfrom* is true, the envelope header is included in the returned string. *unixfrom* defaults to **False**. The *policy* argument may be used to override the default policy obtained from the message instance. This can be used to control some of the formatting produced by the method, since the specified *policy* will be passed to the `BytesGenerator`.

Flattening the message may trigger changes to the *Message* if defaults need to be filled in to complete the transformation to a string (for example, MIME boundaries may be generated or modified).

Note that this method is provided as a convenience and may not always format the message the way you want. For example, by default it does not do the mangling of lines that begin with **From** that is required by the unix mbox format. For more flexibility, instantiate a *BytesGenerator* instance and use its *flatten()* method directly. For example:

```
from io import BytesIO
from email.generator import BytesGenerator
fp = BytesIO()
g = BytesGenerator(fp, mangle_from_=True, maxheaderlen=60)
g.flatten(msg)
text = fp.getvalue()
```

New in version 3.4.

__bytes__()

Equivalent to *as_bytes()*. Allows `bytes(msg)` to produce a bytes object containing the formatted message.

New in version 3.4.

is_multipart()

Return **True** if the message's payload is a list of sub-*Message* objects, otherwise return **False**. When *is_multipart()* returns **False**, the payload should be a string object (which might be a CTE encoded binary payload. (Note that *is_multipart()* returning **True** does not necessarily mean that "msg.get_content_maintype() == 'multipart'" will return the **True**. For example, **is_multipart** will return **True** when the *Message* is of type `message/rfc822`.)

set_unixfrom(*unixfrom***)**

Set the message's envelope header to *unixfrom*, which should be a string.

get_unixfrom()

Return the message's envelope header. Defaults to **None** if the envelope header was never set.

attach(*payload***)**

Add the given *payload* to the current payload, which must be **None** or a list of *Message* objects before the call. After the call, the payload will always be a list of *Message* objects. If you want to set the payload to a scalar object (e.g. a string), use *set_payload()* instead.

This is a legacy method. On the **EmailMessage** class its functionality is replaced by *set_content()* and the related **make** and **add** methods.

get_payload(*i=None, decode=False***)**

Return the current payload, which will be a list of *Message* objects when *is_multipart()* is **True**, or a string when *is_multipart()* is **False**. If the payload is a list and you mutate the list object, you modify the message's payload in place.

With optional argument *i*, *get_payload()* will return the *i*-th element of the payload, counting from zero, if *is_multipart()* is **True**. An *IndexError* will be raised if *i* is less than 0 or greater than or equal to the number of items in the payload. If the payload is a string (i.e. *is_multipart()* is **False**) and *i* is given, a *TypeError* is raised.

Optional *decode* is a flag indicating whether the payload should be decoded or not, according to the *Content-Transfer-Encoding* header. When **True** and the message is not a multipart, the payload will be decoded if this header's value is `quoted-printable` or `base64`. If some other encoding is used, or `Content-Transfer-Encoding` header is missing, the payload is returned as-is (undecoded). In all cases the returned value is binary data. If the message is a multipart and the *decode* flag is `True`, then `None` is returned. If the payload is base64 and it was not perfectly formed (missing padding, characters outside the base64 alphabet), then an appropriate defect will be added to the message's defect property (`InvalidBase64PaddingDefect` or `InvalidBase64CharactersDefect`, respectively).

When *decode* is `False` (the default) the body is returned as a string without decoding the `Content-Transfer-Encoding`. However, for a `Content-Transfer-Encoding` of 8bit, an attempt is made to decode the original bytes using the `charset` specified by the `Content-Type` header, using the `replace` error handler. If no `charset` is specified, or if the `charset` given is not recognized by the email package, the body is decoded using the default ASCII charset.

This is a legacy method. On the `EmailMessage` class its functionality is replaced by *get_content()* and *iter_parts()*.

set_payload(*payload, charset=None*)

Set the entire message object's payload to *payload*. It is the client's responsibility to ensure the payload invariants. Optional *charset* sets the message's default character set; see *set_charset()* for details.

This is a legacy method. On the `EmailMessage` class its functionality is replaced by *set_content()*.

set_charset(*charset*)

Set the character set of the payload to *charset*, which can either be a *Charset* instance (see `email.charset`), a string naming a character set, or `None`. If it is a string, it will be converted to a *Charset* instance. If *charset* is `None`, the `charset` parameter will be removed from the `Content-Type` header (the message will not be otherwise modified). Anything else will generate a *TypeError*.

If there is no existing *MIME-Version* header one will be added. If there is no existing *Content-Type* header, one will be added with a value of *text/plain*. Whether the `Content-Type` header already exists or not, its `charset` parameter will be set to *charset.output_charset*. If *charset.input_charset* and *charset.output_charset* differ, the payload will be re-encoded to the *output_charset*. If there is no existing `Content-Transfer-Encoding` header, then the payload will be transfer-encoded, if needed, using the specified *Charset*, and a header with the appropriate value will be added. If a `Content-Transfer-Encoding` header already exists, the payload is assumed to already be correctly encoded using that `Content-Transfer-Encoding` and is not modified.

This is a legacy method. On the `EmailMessage` class its functionality is replaced by the *charset* parameter of the `email.emailmessage.EmailMessage.set_content()` method.

get_charset()

Return the *Charset* instance associated with the message's payload.

This is a legacy method. On the `EmailMessage` class it always returns `None`.

The following methods implement a mapping-like interface for accessing the message's RFC 2822 headers. Note that there are some semantic differences between these methods and a normal mapping (i.e. dictionary) interface. For example, in a dictionary there are no duplicate keys, but here there may be duplicate message headers. Also, in dictionaries there is no guaranteed order to the keys returned by *keys()*, but in a *Message* object, headers are always returned in the order they appeared in the original message, or were added to the message later. Any header deleted and then re-added are always appended to the end of the header list.

These semantic differences are intentional and are biased toward maximal convenience.

Note that in all cases, any envelope header present in the message is not included in the mapping interface.

In a model generated from bytes, any header values that (in contravention of the RFCs) contain non-ASCII bytes will, when retrieved through this interface, be represented as *Header* objects with a charset of *unknown-8bit*.

`__len__()`
> Return the total number of headers, including duplicates.

`__contains__(`*name*`)`
> Return true if the message object has a field named *name*. Matching is done case-insensitively and *name* should not include the trailing colon. Used for the `in` operator, e.g.:
> ```
> if 'message-id' in myMessage:
>     print('Message-ID:', myMessage['message-id'])
> ```

`__getitem__(`*name*`)`
> Return the value of the named header field. *name* should not include the colon field separator. If the header is missing, `None` is returned; a *KeyError* is never raised.
>
> Note that if the named field appears more than once in the message's headers, exactly which of those field values will be returned is undefined. Use the *get_all()* method to get the values of all the extant named headers.

`__setitem__(`*name*, *val*`)`
> Add a header to the message with field name *name* and value *val*. The field is appended to the end of the message's existing fields.
>
> Note that this does *not* overwrite or delete any existing header with the same name. If you want to ensure that the new header is the only one present in the message with field name *name*, delete the field first, e.g.:
> ```
> del msg['subject']
> msg['subject'] = 'Python roolz!'
> ```

`__delitem__(`*name*`)`
> Delete all occurrences of the field with name *name* from the message's headers. No exception is raised if the named field isn't present in the headers.

`keys()`
> Return a list of all the message's header field names.

`values()`
> Return a list of all the message's field values.

`items()`
> Return a list of 2-tuples containing all the message's field headers and values.

`get(`*name*, *failobj=None*`)`
> Return the value of the named header field. This is identical to *__getitem__()* except that optional *failobj* is returned if the named header is missing (defaults to `None`).

Here are some additional useful methods:

`get_all(`*name*, *failobj=None*`)`
> Return a list of all the values for the field named *name*. If there are no such named headers in the message, *failobj* is returned (defaults to `None`).

`add_header(`*_name*, *_value*, ***_params*`)`
> Extended header setting. This method is similar to *__setitem__()* except that additional header parameters can be provided as keyword arguments. *_name* is the header field to add and *_value* is the *primary* value for the header.

For each item in the keyword argument dictionary *_params*, the key is taken as the parameter name, with underscores converted to dashes (since dashes are illegal in Python identifiers). Normally, the parameter will be added as `key="value"` unless the value is None, in which case only the key will be added. If the value contains non-ASCII characters, it can be specified as a three tuple in the format (CHARSET, LANGUAGE, VALUE), where CHARSET is a string naming the charset to be used to encode the value, LANGUAGE can usually be set to None or the empty string (see RFC 2231 for other possibilities), and VALUE is the string value containing non-ASCII code points. If a three tuple is not passed and the value contains non-ASCII characters, it is automatically encoded in RFC 2231 format using a CHARSET of utf-8 and a LANGUAGE of None.

Here's an example:

```
msg.add_header('Content-Disposition', 'attachment', filename='bud.gif')
```

This will add a header that looks like

```
Content-Disposition: attachment; filename="bud.gif"
```

An example with non-ASCII characters:

```
msg.add_header('Content-Disposition', 'attachment',
               filename=('iso-8859-1', '', 'Fußballer.ppt'))
```

Which produces

```
Content-Disposition: attachment; filename*="iso-8859-1''Fu%DFballer.ppt"
```

replace_header(*_name*, *_value*)
  Replace a header. Replace the first header found in the message that matches *_name*, retaining header order and field name case. If no matching header was found, a *KeyError* is raised.

get_content_type()
  Return the message's content type. The returned string is coerced to lower case of the form *maintype/subtype*. If there was no *Content-Type* header in the message the default type as given by *get_default_type()* will be returned. Since according to RFC 2045, messages always have a default type, *get_content_type()* will always return a value.

  RFC 2045 defines a message's default type to be *text/plain* unless it appears inside a *multipart/digest* container, in which case it would be *message/rfc822*. If the *Content-Type* header has an invalid type specification, RFC 2045 mandates that the default type be *text/plain*.

get_content_maintype()
  Return the message's main content type. This is the *maintype* part of the string returned by *get_content_type()*.

get_content_subtype()
  Return the message's sub-content type. This is the *subtype* part of the string returned by *get_content_type()*.

get_default_type()
  Return the default content type. Most messages have a default content type of *text/plain*, except for messages that are subparts of *multipart/digest* containers. Such subparts have a default content type of *message/rfc822*.

set_default_type(*ctype*)
  Set the default content type. *ctype* should either be *text/plain* or *message/rfc822*, although this is not enforced. The default content type is not stored in the *Content-Type* header.

get_params(*failobj=None, header='content-type', unquote=True*)
   Return the message's `Content-Type` parameters, as a list. The elements of the returned list are 2-tuples of key/value pairs, as split on the `'='` sign. The left hand side of the `'='` is the key, while the right hand side is the value. If there is no `'='` sign in the parameter the value is the empty string, otherwise the value is as described in *get_param()* and is unquoted if optional *unquote* is `True` (the default).

   Optional *failobj* is the object to return if there is no `Content-Type` header. Optional *header* is the header to search instead of `Content-Type`.

   This is a legacy method. On the `EmailMessage` class its functionality is replaced by the *params* property of the individual header objects returned by the header access methods.

get_param(*param, failobj=None, header='content-type', unquote=True*)
   Return the value of the `Content-Type` header's parameter *param* as a string. If the message has no `Content-Type` header or if there is no such parameter, then *failobj* is returned (defaults to `None`).

   Optional *header* if given, specifies the message header to use instead of `Content-Type`.

   Parameter keys are always compared case insensitively. The return value can either be a string, or a 3-tuple if the parameter was RFC 2231 encoded. When it's a 3-tuple, the elements of the value are of the form (CHARSET, LANGUAGE, VALUE). Note that both CHARSET and LANGUAGE can be `None`, in which case you should consider VALUE to be encoded in the `us-ascii` charset. You can usually ignore LANGUAGE.

   If your application doesn't care whether the parameter was encoded as in RFC 2231, you can collapse the parameter value by calling *email.utils.collapse_rfc2231_value()*, passing in the return value from *get_param()*. This will return a suitably decoded Unicode string when the value is a tuple, or the original string unquoted if it isn't. For example:

   ```
   rawparam = msg.get_param('foo')
   param = email.utils.collapse_rfc2231_value(rawparam)
   ```

   In any case, the parameter value (either the returned string, or the VALUE item in the 3-tuple) is always unquoted, unless *unquote* is set to `False`.

   This is a legacy method. On the `EmailMessage` class its functionality is replaced by the *params* property of the individual header objects returned by the header access methods.

set_param(*param, value, header='Content-Type', requote=True, charset=None, language='', replace=False*)
   Set a parameter in the `Content-Type` header. If the parameter already exists in the header, its value will be replaced with *value*. If the `Content-Type` header as not yet been defined for this message, it will be set to `text/plain` and the new parameter value will be appended as per RFC 2045.

   Optional *header* specifies an alternative header to `Content-Type`, and all parameters will be quoted as necessary unless optional *requote* is `False` (the default is `True`).

   If optional *charset* is specified, the parameter will be encoded according to RFC 2231. Optional *language* specifies the RFC 2231 language, defaulting to the empty string. Both *charset* and *language* should be strings.

   If *replace* is `False` (the default) the header is moved to the end of the list of headers. If *replace* is `True`, the header will be updated in place.

   Changed in version 3.4: `replace` keyword was added.

del_param(*param, header='content-type', requote=True*)
   Remove the given parameter completely from the `Content-Type` header. The header will be re-

written in place without the parameter or its value. All values will be quoted as necessary unless *requote* is `False` (the default is `True`). Optional *header* specifies an alternative to `Content-Type`.

set_type(*type, header='Content-Type', requote=True*)
Set the main type and subtype for the `Content-Type` header. *type* must be a string in the form *maintype/subtype*, otherwise a `ValueError` is raised.

This method replaces the `Content-Type` header, keeping all the parameters in place. If *requote* is `False`, this leaves the existing header's quoting as is, otherwise the parameters will be quoted (the default).

An alternative header can be specified in the *header* argument. When the `Content-Type` header is set a `MIME-Version` header is also added.

This is a legacy method. On the `EmailMessage` class its functionality is replaced by the `make_` and `add_` methods.

get_filename(*failobj=None*)
Return the value of the `filename` parameter of the `Content-Disposition` header of the message. If the header does not have a `filename` parameter, this method falls back to looking for the `name` parameter on the `Content-Type` header. If neither is found, or the header is missing, then *failobj* is returned. The returned string will always be unquoted as per `email.utils.unquote()`.

get_boundary(*failobj=None*)
Return the value of the `boundary` parameter of the `Content-Type` header of the message, or *failobj* if either the header is missing, or has no `boundary` parameter. The returned string will always be unquoted as per `email.utils.unquote()`.

set_boundary(*boundary*)
Set the `boundary` parameter of the `Content-Type` header to *boundary*. `set_boundary()` will always quote *boundary* if necessary. A `HeaderParseError` is raised if the message object has no `Content-Type` header.

Note that using this method is subtly different than deleting the old `Content-Type` header and adding a new one with the new boundary via `add_header()`, because `set_boundary()` preserves the order of the `Content-Type` header in the list of headers. However, it does *not* preserve any continuation lines which may have been present in the original `Content-Type` header.

get_content_charset(*failobj=None*)
Return the `charset` parameter of the `Content-Type` header, coerced to lower case. If there is no `Content-Type` header, or if that header has no `charset` parameter, *failobj* is returned.

Note that this method differs from `get_charset()` which returns the `Charset` instance for the default encoding of the message body.

get_charsets(*failobj=None*)
Return a list containing the character set names in the message. If the message is a *multipart*, then the list will contain one element for each subpart in the payload, otherwise, it will be a list of length 1.

Each item in the list will be a string which is the value of the `charset` parameter in the `Content-Type` header for the represented subpart. However, if the subpart has no `Content-Type` header, no `charset` parameter, or is not of the *text* main MIME type, then that item in the returned list will be *failobj*.

get_content_disposition()
Return the lowercased value (without parameters) of the message's `Content-Disposition` header if it has one, or `None`. The possible values for this method are *inline*, *attachment* or `None` if the message follows RFC 2183.

New in version 3.5.

walk()
> The *walk()* method is an all-purpose generator which can be used to iterate over all the parts and subparts of a message object tree, in depth-first traversal order. You will typically use *walk()* as the iterator in a `for` loop; each iteration returns the next subpart.
>
> Here's an example that prints the MIME type of every part of a multipart message structure:
>
> ```
> >>> for part in msg.walk():
> ...     print(part.get_content_type())
> multipart/report
> text/plain
> message/delivery-status
> text/plain
> text/plain
> message/rfc822
> text/plain
> ```
>
> walk iterates over the subparts of any part where *is_multipart()* returns True, even though msg.get_content_maintype() == 'multipart' may return False. We can see this in our example by making use of the _structure debug helper function:
>
> ```
> >>> for part in msg.walk():
> ...     print(part.get_content_maintype() == 'multipart'),
> ...           part.is_multipart()
> True True
> False False
> False True
> False False
> False False
> False True
> False False
> >>> _structure(msg)
> multipart/report
>     text/plain
> message/delivery-status
>     text/plain
>     text/plain
> message/rfc822
>     text/plain
> ```
>
> Here the **message** parts are not **multiparts**, but they do contain subparts. is_multipart() returns True and walk descends into the subparts.

Message objects can also optionally contain two instance attributes, which can be used when generating the plain text of a MIME message.

preamble
> The format of a MIME document allows for some text between the blank line following the headers, and the first multipart boundary string. Normally, this text is never visible in a MIME-aware mail reader because it falls outside the standard MIME armor. However, when viewing the raw text of the message, or when viewing the message in a non-MIME aware reader, this text can become visible.
>
> The *preamble* attribute contains this leading extra-armor text for MIME documents. When the *Parser* discovers some text after the headers but before the first boundary string, it assigns this text to the message's *preamble* attribute. When the *Generator* is writing out the plain text representation of a MIME message, and it finds the message has a *preamble* attribute, it will write this text in the area between the headers and the first boundary. See *email.parser* and *email.generator* for details.

19.1. email — An email and MIME handling package

Note that if the message object has no preamble, the *preamble* attribute will be None.

epilogue
    The *epilogue* attribute acts the same way as the *preamble* attribute, except that it contains text that appears between the last boundary and the end of the message.

    You do not need to set the epilogue to the empty string in order for the *Generator* to print a newline at the end of the file.

defects
    The *defects* attribute contains a list of all the problems found when parsing this message. See *email.errors* for a detailed description of the possible parsing defects.

19.1.10 email.mime: Creating email and MIME objects from scratch

Source code: Lib/email/mime/

This module is part of the legacy (Compat32) email API. Its functionality is partially replaced by the *contentmanager* in the new API, but in certain applications these classes may still be useful, even in non-legacy code.

Ordinarily, you get a message object structure by passing a file or some text to a parser, which parses the text and returns the root message object. However you can also build a complete message structure from scratch, or even individual *Message* objects by hand. In fact, you can also take an existing structure and add new *Message* objects, move them around, etc. This makes a very convenient interface for slicing-and-dicing MIME messages.

You can create a new object structure by creating *Message* instances, adding attachments and all the appropriate headers manually. For MIME messages though, the *email* package provides some convenient subclasses to make things easier.

Here are the classes:

class email.mime.base.MIMEBase(*_maintype, _subtype, *, policy=compat32, **_params*)
    Module: `email.mime.base`

    This is the base class for all the MIME-specific subclasses of *Message*. Ordinarily you won't create instances specifically of *MIMEBase*, although you could. *MIMEBase* is provided primarily as a convenient base class for more specific MIME-aware subclasses.

    _maintype is the Content-Type major type (e.g. text or image), and *_subtype* is the Content-Type minor type (e.g. plain or gif). *_params* is a parameter key/value dictionary and is passed directly to *Message.add_header*.

    If *policy* is specified, (defaults to the *compat32* policy) it will be passed to *Message*.

    The *MIMEBase* class always adds a Content-Type header (based on *_maintype*, *_subtype*, and *_params*), and a MIME-Version header (always set to 1.0).

    Changed in version 3.6: Added *policy* keyword-only parameter.

class email.mime.nonmultipart.MIMENonMultipart
    Module: `email.mime.nonmultipart`

    A subclass of *MIMEBase*, this is an intermediate base class for MIME messages that are not *multipart*. The primary purpose of this class is to prevent the use of the *attach()* method, which only makes sense for *multipart* messages. If *attach()* is called, a *MultipartConversionError* exception is raised.

class email.mime.multipart.MIMEMultipart(*_subtype='mixed', boundary=None, _subparts=None, *, policy=compat32, **_params*)
    Module: `email.mime.multipart`

A subclass of *MIMEBase*, this is an intermediate base class for MIME messages that are *multipart*. Optional *_subtype* defaults to *mixed*, but can be used to specify the subtype of the message. A `Content-Type` header of *multipart/_subtype* will be added to the message object. A `MIME-Version` header will also be added.

Optional *boundary* is the multipart boundary string. When `None` (the default), the boundary is calculated when needed (for example, when the message is serialized).

_subparts is a sequence of initial subparts for the payload. It must be possible to convert this sequence to a list. You can always attach new subparts to the message by using the *Message.attach* method.

Optional *policy* argument defaults to *compat32*.

Additional parameters for the `Content-Type` header are taken from the keyword arguments, or passed into the *_params* argument, which is a keyword dictionary.

Changed in version 3.6: Added *policy* keyword-only parameter.

class email.mime.application.MIMEApplication(*_data*, *_subtype='octet-stream'*, *_encoder=email.encoders.encode_base64*, *, *policy=compat32*, ***_params*)

Module: `email.mime.application`

A subclass of *MIMENonMultipart*, the *MIMEApplication* class is used to represent MIME message objects of major type `application`. *_data* is a string containing the raw byte data. Optional *_subtype* specifies the MIME subtype and defaults to `octet-stream`.

Optional *_encoder* is a callable (i.e. function) which will perform the actual encoding of the data for transport. This callable takes one argument, which is the *MIMEApplication* instance. It should use `get_payload()` and `set_payload()` to change the payload to encoded form. It should also add any `Content-Transfer-Encoding` or other headers to the message object as necessary. The default encoding is base64. See the *email.encoders* module for a list of the built-in encoders.

Optional *policy* argument defaults to *compat32*.

_params are passed straight through to the base class constructor.

Changed in version 3.6: Added *policy* keyword-only parameter.

class email.mime.audio.MIMEAudio(*_audiodata*, *_subtype=None*, *_encoder=email.encoders.encode_base64*, *, *policy=compat32*, ***_params*)

Module: `email.mime.audio`

A subclass of *MIMENonMultipart*, the *MIMEAudio* class is used to create MIME message objects of major type `audio`. *_audiodata* is a string containing the raw audio data. If this data can be decoded by the standard Python module *sndhdr*, then the subtype will be automatically included in the `Content-Type` header. Otherwise you can explicitly specify the audio subtype via the *_subtype* argument. If the minor type could not be guessed and *_subtype* was not given, then *TypeError* is raised.

Optional *_encoder* is a callable (i.e. function) which will perform the actual encoding of the audio data for transport. This callable takes one argument, which is the *MIMEAudio* instance. It should use `get_payload()` and `set_payload()` to change the payload to encoded form. It should also add any `Content-Transfer-Encoding` or other headers to the message object as necessary. The default encoding is base64. See the *email.encoders* module for a list of the built-in encoders.

Optional *policy* argument defaults to *compat32*.

_params are passed straight through to the base class constructor.

Changed in version 3.6: Added *policy* keyword-only parameter.

class email.mime.image.MIMEImage(*_imagedata*, *_subtype=None*, *_encoder=email.encoders.encode_base64*, ***, *policy=compat32*, ***_params*)

Module: `email.mime.image`

A subclass of *MIMENonMultipart*, the *MIMEImage* class is used to create MIME message objects of major type *image*. *_imagedata* is a string containing the raw image data. If this data can be decoded by the standard Python module *imghdr*, then the subtype will be automatically included in the `Content-Type` header. Otherwise you can explicitly specify the image subtype via the *_subtype* argument. If the minor type could not be guessed and *_subtype* was not given, then *TypeError* is raised.

Optional *_encoder* is a callable (i.e. function) which will perform the actual encoding of the image data for transport. This callable takes one argument, which is the *MIMEImage* instance. It should use `get_payload()` and `set_payload()` to change the payload to encoded form. It should also add any `Content-Transfer-Encoding` or other headers to the message object as necessary. The default encoding is base64. See the *email.encoders* module for a list of the built-in encoders.

Optional *policy* argument defaults to *compat32*.

_params are passed straight through to the *MIMEBase* constructor.

Changed in version 3.6: Added *policy* keyword-only parameter.

class email.mime.message.MIMEMessage(*_msg*, *_subtype='rfc822'*, ***, *policy=compat32*)

Module: `email.mime.message`

A subclass of *MIMENonMultipart*, the *MIMEMessage* class is used to create MIME objects of main type *message*. *_msg* is used as the payload, and must be an instance of class *Message* (or a subclass thereof), otherwise a *TypeError* is raised.

Optional *_subtype* sets the subtype of the message; it defaults to `rfc822`.

Optional *policy* argument defaults to *compat32*.

Changed in version 3.6: Added *policy* keyword-only parameter.

class email.mime.text.MIMEText(*_text*, *_subtype='plain'*, *_charset=None*, ***, *policy=compat32*)

Module: `email.mime.text`

A subclass of *MIMENonMultipart*, the *MIMEText* class is used to create MIME objects of major type *text*. *_text* is the string for the payload. *_subtype* is the minor type and defaults to `plain`. *_charset* is the character set of the text and is passed as an argument to the *MIMENonMultipart* constructor; it defaults to `us-ascii` if the string contains only `ascii` code points, and `utf-8` otherwise. The *_charset* parameter accepts either a string or a *Charset* instance.

Unless the *_charset* argument is explicitly set to `None`, the MIMEText object created will have both a `Content-Type` header with a `charset` parameter, and a `Content-Transfer-Encoding` header. This means that a subsequent `set_payload` call will not result in an encoded payload, even if a charset is passed in the `set_payload` command. You can "reset" this behavior by deleting the `Content-Transfer-Encoding` header, after which a `set_payload` call will automatically encode the new payload (and add a new `Content-Transfer-Encoding` header).

Optional *policy* argument defaults to *compat32*.

Changed in version 3.5: *_charset* also accepts *Charset* instances.

Changed in version 3.6: Added *policy* keyword-only parameter.

19.1.11 `email.header`: Internationalized headers

Source code: Lib/email/header.py

This module is part of the legacy (`Compat32`) email API. In the current API encoding and decoding of headers is handled transparently by the dictionary-like API of the *EmailMessage* class. In addition to uses in legacy code, this module can be useful in applications that need to completely control the character sets used when encoding headers.

The remaining text in this section is the original documentation of the module.

RFC 2822 is the base standard that describes the format of email messages. It derives from the older RFC 822 standard which came into widespread use at a time when most email was composed of ASCII characters only. RFC 2822 is a specification written assuming email contains only 7-bit ASCII characters.

Of course, as email has been deployed worldwide, it has become internationalized, such that language specific character sets can now be used in email messages. The base standard still requires email messages to be transferred using only 7-bit ASCII characters, so a slew of RFCs have been written describing how to encode email containing non-ASCII characters into RFC 2822-compliant format. These RFCs include RFC 2045, RFC 2046, RFC 2047, and RFC 2231. The *email* package supports these standards in its *email.header* and *email.charset* modules.

If you want to include non-ASCII characters in your email headers, say in the *Subject* or *To* fields, you should use the *Header* class and assign the field in the *Message* object to an instance of *Header* instead of using a string for the header value. Import the *Header* class from the *email.header* module. For example:

```
>>> from email.message import Message
>>> from email.header import Header
>>> msg = Message()
>>> h = Header('p\xf6stal', 'iso-8859-1')
>>> msg['Subject'] = h
>>> msg.as_string()
'Subject: =?iso-8859-1?q?p=F6stal?=\n\n'
```

Notice here how we wanted the *Subject* field to contain a non-ASCII character? We did this by creating a *Header* instance and passing in the character set that the byte string was encoded in. When the subsequent *Message* instance was flattened, the *Subject* field was properly RFC 2047 encoded. MIME-aware mail readers would show this header using the embedded ISO-8859-1 character.

Here is the *Header* class description:

class email.header.Header(*s=None, charset=None, maxlinelen=None, header_name=None, continuation_ws=' ', errors='strict'*)

Create a MIME-compliant header that can contain strings in different character sets.

Optional *s* is the initial header value. If None (the default), the initial header value is not set. You can later append to the header with *append()* method calls. *s* may be an instance of *bytes* or *str*, but see the *append()* documentation for semantics.

Optional *charset* serves two purposes: it has the same meaning as the *charset* argument to the *append()* method. It also sets the default character set for all subsequent *append()* calls that omit the *charset* argument. If *charset* is not provided in the constructor (the default), the us-ascii character set is used both as *s*'s initial charset and as the default for subsequent *append()* calls.

The maximum line length can be specified explicitly via *maxlinelen*. For splitting the first line to a shorter value (to account for the field header which isn't included in *s*, e.g. *Subject*) pass in the name of the field in *header_name*. The default *maxlinelen* is 76, and the default value for *header_name* is None, meaning it is not taken into account for the first line of a long, split header.

Optional *continuation_ws* must be RFC 2822-compliant folding whitespace, and is usually either a space or a hard tab character. This character will be prepended to continuation lines. *continuation_ws* defaults to a single space character.

Optional *errors* is passed straight through to the *append()* method.

append(*s*, *charset=None*, *errors='strict'*)

Append the string *s* to the MIME header.

Optional *charset*, if given, should be a `Charset` instance (see `email.charset`) or the name of a character set, which will be converted to a `Charset` instance. A value of `None` (the default) means that the *charset* given in the constructor is used.

s may be an instance of `bytes` or `str`. If it is an instance of `bytes`, then *charset* is the encoding of that byte string, and a `UnicodeError` will be raised if the string cannot be decoded with that character set.

If *s* is an instance of `str`, then *charset* is a hint specifying the character set of the characters in the string.

In either case, when producing an RFC 2822-compliant header using RFC 2047 rules, the string will be encoded using the output codec of the charset. If the string cannot be encoded using the output codec, a UnicodeError will be raised.

Optional *errors* is passed as the errors argument to the decode call if *s* is a byte string.

encode(*splitchars=';, \t'*, *maxlinelen=None*, *linesep='\n'*)

Encode a message header into an RFC-compliant format, possibly wrapping long lines and encapsulating non-ASCII parts in base64 or quoted-printable encodings.

Optional *splitchars* is a string containing characters which should be given extra weight by the splitting algorithm during normal header wrapping. This is in very rough support of RFC 2822's 'higher level syntactic breaks': split points preceded by a splitchar are preferred during line splitting, with the characters preferred in the order in which they appear in the string. Space and tab may be included in the string to indicate whether preference should be given to one over the other as a split point when other split chars do not appear in the line being split. Splitchars does not affect RFC 2047 encoded lines.

maxlinelen, if given, overrides the instance's value for the maximum line length.

linesep specifies the characters used to separate the lines of the folded header. It defaults to the most useful value for Python application code (`\n`), but `\r\n` can be specified in order to produce headers with RFC-compliant line separators.

Changed in version 3.2: Added the *linesep* argument.

The `Header` class also provides a number of methods to support standard operators and built-in functions.

__str__()

Returns an approximation of the `Header` as a string, using an unlimited line length. All pieces are converted to unicode using the specified encoding and joined together appropriately. Any pieces with a charset of `'unknown-8bit'` are decoded as ASCII using the `'replace'` error handler.

Changed in version 3.2: Added handling for the `'unknown-8bit'` charset.

__eq__(*other*)

This method allows you to compare two `Header` instances for equality.

__ne__(*other*)

This method allows you to compare two `Header` instances for inequality.

The `email.header` module also provides the following convenient functions.

email.header.decode_header(*header*)

Decode a message header value without converting the character set. The header value is in *header*.

This function returns a list of (`decoded_string, charset`) pairs containing each of the decoded parts of the header. *charset* is `None` for non-encoded parts of the header, otherwise a lower case string containing the name of the character set specified in the encoded string.

Here's an example:

```
>>> from email.header import decode_header
>>> decode_header('=?iso-8859-1?q?p=F6stal?=')
[(b'p\xf6stal', 'iso-8859-1')]
```

email.header.make_header(*decoded_seq*, *maxlinelen=None*, *header_name=None*, *continuation_ws=' '*)

Create a *Header* instance from a sequence of pairs as returned by *decode_header()*.

decode_header() takes a header value string and returns a sequence of pairs of the format (`decoded_string, charset`) where *charset* is the name of the character set.

This function takes one of those sequence of pairs and returns a *Header* instance. Optional *maxlinelen*, *header_name*, and *continuation_ws* are as in the *Header* constructor.

19.1.12 email.charset: Representing character sets

Source code: Lib/email/charset.py

This module is part of the legacy (`Compat32`) email API. In the new API only the aliases table is used.

The remaining text in this section is the original documentation of the module.

This module provides a class *Charset* for representing character sets and character set conversions in email messages, as well as a character set registry and several convenience methods for manipulating this registry. Instances of *Charset* are used in several other modules within the *email* package.

Import this class from the *email.charset* module.

class email.charset.Charset(*input_charset=DEFAULT_CHARSET*)

Map character sets to their email properties.

This class provides information about the requirements imposed on email for a specific character set. It also provides convenience routines for converting between character sets, given the availability of the applicable codecs. Given a character set, it will do its best to provide information on how to use that character set in an email message in an RFC-compliant way.

Certain character sets must be encoded with quoted-printable or base64 when used in email headers or bodies. Certain character sets must be converted outright, and are not allowed in email.

Optional *input_charset* is as described below; it is always coerced to lower case. After being alias normalized it is also used as a lookup into the registry of character sets to find out the header encoding, body encoding, and output conversion codec to be used for the character set. For example, if *input_charset* is `iso-8859-1`, then headers and bodies will be encoded using quoted-printable and no output conversion codec is necessary. If *input_charset* is `euc-jp`, then headers will be encoded with base64, bodies will not be encoded, but output text will be converted from the `euc-jp` character set to the `iso-2022-jp` character set.

Charset instances have the following data attributes:

input_charset
The initial character set specified. Common aliases are converted to their *official* email names (e.g. `latin_1` is converted to `iso-8859-1`). Defaults to 7-bit `us-ascii`.

header_encoding
If the character set must be encoded before it can be used in an email header, this attribute will be set to `Charset.QP` (for quoted-printable), `Charset.BASE64` (for base64 encoding), or `Charset.SHORTEST` for the shortest of QP or BASE64 encoding. Otherwise, it will be `None`.

body_encoding
> Same as *header_encoding*, but describes the encoding for the mail message's body, which indeed may be different than the header encoding. `Charset.SHORTEST` is not allowed for *body_encoding*.

output_charset
> Some character sets must be converted before they can be used in email headers or bodies. If the *input_charset* is one of them, this attribute will contain the name of the character set output will be converted to. Otherwise, it will be `None`.

input_codec
> The name of the Python codec used to convert the *input_charset* to Unicode. If no conversion codec is necessary, this attribute will be `None`.

output_codec
> The name of the Python codec used to convert Unicode to the *output_charset*. If no conversion codec is necessary, this attribute will have the same value as the *input_codec*.

Charset instances also have the following methods:

get_body_encoding()
> Return the content transfer encoding used for body encoding.
>
> This is either the string `quoted-printable` or `base64` depending on the encoding used, or it is a function, in which case you should call the function with a single argument, the Message object being encoded. The function should then set the `Content-Transfer-Encoding` header itself to whatever is appropriate.
>
> Returns the string `quoted-printable` if *body_encoding* is `QP`, returns the string `base64` if *body_encoding* is `BASE64`, and returns the string `7bit` otherwise.

get_output_charset()
> Return the output character set.
>
> This is the *output_charset* attribute if that is not `None`, otherwise it is *input_charset*.

header_encode(*string*)
> Header-encode the string *string*.
>
> The type of encoding (base64 or quoted-printable) will be based on the *header_encoding* attribute.

header_encode_lines(*string*, *maxlengths*)
> Header-encode a *string* by converting it first to bytes.
>
> This is similar to `header_encode()` except that the string is fit into maximum line lengths as given by the argument *maxlengths*, which must be an iterator: each element returned from this iterator will provide the next maximum line length.

body_encode(*string*)
> Body-encode the string *string*.
>
> The type of encoding (base64 or quoted-printable) will be based on the *body_encoding* attribute.

The *Charset* class also provides a number of methods to support standard operations and built-in functions.

__str__()
> Returns *input_charset* as a string coerced to lower case. `__repr__()` is an alias for `__str__()`.

__eq__(*other*)
> This method allows you to compare two *Charset* instances for equality.

__ne__(*other*)
> This method allows you to compare two *Charset* instances for inequality.

The `email.charset` module also provides the following functions for adding new entries to the global character set, alias, and codec registries:

email.charset.add_charset(*charset, header_enc=None, body_enc=None, output_charset=None*)
   Add character properties to the global registry.

   charset is the input character set, and must be the canonical name of a character set.

   Optional *header_enc* and *body_enc* is either `Charset.QP` for quoted-printable, `Charset.BASE64` for base64 encoding, `Charset.SHORTEST` for the shortest of quoted-printable or base64 encoding, or `None` for no encoding. `SHORTEST` is only valid for *header_enc*. The default is `None` for no encoding.

   Optional *output_charset* is the character set that the output should be in. Conversions will proceed from input charset, to Unicode, to the output charset when the method `Charset.convert()` is called. The default is to output in the same character set as the input.

   Both *input_charset* and *output_charset* must have Unicode codec entries in the module's character set-to-codec mapping; use `add_codec()` to add codecs the module does not know about. See the `codecs` module's documentation for more information.

   The global character set registry is kept in the module global dictionary `CHARSETS`.

email.charset.add_alias(*alias, canonical*)
   Add a character set alias. *alias* is the alias name, e.g. `latin-1`. *canonical* is the character set's canonical name, e.g. `iso-8859-1`.

   The global charset alias registry is kept in the module global dictionary `ALIASES`.

email.charset.add_codec(*charset, codecname*)
   Add a codec that map characters in the given character set to and from Unicode.

   charset is the canonical name of a character set. *codecname* is the name of a Python codec, as appropriate for the second argument to the *str*'s `encode()` method.

19.1.13 email.encoders: Encoders

Source code: Lib/email/encoders.py

This module is part of the legacy (`Compat32`) email API. In the new API the functionality is provided by the *cte* parameter of the `set_content()` method.

The remaining text in this section is the original documentation of the module.

When creating *Message* objects from scratch, you often need to encode the payloads for transport through compliant mail servers. This is especially true for *image/** and *text/** type messages containing binary data.

The *email* package provides some convenient encodings in its **encoders** module. These encoders are actually used by the *MIMEAudio* and *MIMEImage* class constructors to provide default encodings. All encoder functions take exactly one argument, the message object to encode. They usually extract the payload, encode it, and reset the payload to this newly encoded value. They should also set the *Content-Transfer-Encoding* header as appropriate.

Note that these functions are not meaningful for a multipart message. They must be applied to individual subparts instead, and will raise a *TypeError* if passed a message whose type is multipart.

Here are the encoding functions provided:

email.encoders.encode_quopri(*msg*)
   Encodes the payload into quoted-printable form and sets the *Content-Transfer-Encoding* header to `quoted-printable`[1]. This is a good encoding to use when most of your payload is normal printable data, but contains a few unprintable characters.

---
[1] Note that encoding with *encode_quopri()* also encodes all tabs and space characters in the data.

email.encoders.encode_base64(*msg*)

    Encodes the payload into base64 form and sets the `Content-Transfer-Encoding` header to `base64`. This is a good encoding to use when most of your payload is unprintable data since it is a more compact form than quoted-printable. The drawback of base64 encoding is that it renders the text non-human readable.

email.encoders.encode_7or8bit(*msg*)

    This doesn't actually modify the message's payload, but it does set the `Content-Transfer-Encoding` header to either `7bit` or `8bit` as appropriate, based on the payload data.

email.encoders.encode_noop(*msg*)

    This does nothing; it doesn't even set the `Content-Transfer-Encoding` header.

19.1.14 email.utils: Miscellaneous utilities

Source code: Lib/email/utils.py

There are a couple of useful utilities provided in the *email.utils* module:

email.utils.localtime(*dt=None*)

    Return local time as an aware datetime object. If called without arguments, return current time. Otherwise *dt* argument should be a *datetime* instance, and it is converted to the local time zone according to the system time zone database. If *dt* is naive (that is, `dt.tzinfo` is None), it is assumed to be in local time. In this case, a positive or zero value for *isdst* causes `localtime` to presume initially that summer time (for example, Daylight Saving Time) is or is not (respectively) in effect for the specified time. A negative value for *isdst* causes the `localtime` to attempt to divine whether summer time is in effect for the specified time.

    New in version 3.3.

email.utils.make_msgid(*idstring=None, domain=None*)

    Returns a string suitable for an RFC 2822-compliant `Message-ID` header. Optional *idstring* if given, is a string used to strengthen the uniqueness of the message id. Optional *domain* if given provides the portion of the msgid after the '@'. The default is the local hostname. It is not normally necessary to override this default, but may be useful certain cases, such as a constructing distributed system that uses a consistent domain name across multiple hosts.

    Changed in version 3.2: Added the *domain* keyword.

The remaining functions are part of the legacy (`Compat32`) email API. There is no need to directly use these with the new API, since the parsing and formatting they provide is done automatically by the header parsing machinery of the new API.

email.utils.quote(*str*)

    Return a new string with backslashes in *str* replaced by two backslashes, and double quotes replaced by backslash-double quote.

email.utils.unquote(*str*)

    Return a new string which is an *unquoted* version of *str*. If *str* ends and begins with double quotes, they are stripped off. Likewise if *str* ends and begins with angle brackets, they are stripped off.

email.utils.parseaddr(*address*)

    Parse address – which should be the value of some address-containing field such as *To* or *Cc* – into its constituent *realname* and *email address* parts. Returns a tuple of that information, unless the parse fails, in which case a 2-tuple of (`''`, `''`) is returned.

email.utils.formataddr(*pair, charset='utf-8'*)

    The inverse of *parseaddr()*, this takes a 2-tuple of the form (`realname, email_address`) and returns the string value suitable for a *To* or *Cc* header. If the first element of *pair* is false, then the second element is returned unmodified.

Optional *charset* is the character set that will be used in the RFC 2047 encoding of the `realname` if the `realname` contains non-ASCII characters. Can be an instance of `str` or a `Charset`. Defaults to `utf-8`.

Changed in version 3.3: Added the *charset* option.

email.utils.**getaddresses**(*fieldvalues*)

This method returns a list of 2-tuples of the form returned by `parseaddr()`. *fieldvalues* is a sequence of header field values as might be returned by `Message.get_all`. Here's a simple example that gets all the recipients of a message:

```
from email.utils import getaddresses

tos = msg.get_all('to', [])
ccs = msg.get_all('cc', [])
resent_tos = msg.get_all('resent-to', [])
resent_ccs = msg.get_all('resent-cc', [])
all_recipients = getaddresses(tos + ccs + resent_tos + resent_ccs)
```

email.utils.**parsedate**(*date*)

Attempts to parse a date according to the rules in RFC 2822. however, some mailers don't follow that format as specified, so `parsedate()` tries to guess correctly in such cases. *date* is a string containing an RFC 2822 date, such as `"Mon, 20 Nov 1995 19:12:08 -0500"`. If it succeeds in parsing the date, `parsedate()` returns a 9-tuple that can be passed directly to `time.mktime()`; otherwise `None` will be returned. Note that indexes 6, 7, and 8 of the result tuple are not usable.

email.utils.**parsedate_tz**(*date*)

Performs the same function as `parsedate()`, but returns either `None` or a 10-tuple; the first 9 elements make up a tuple that can be passed directly to `time.mktime()`, and the tenth is the offset of the date's timezone from UTC (which is the official term for Greenwich Mean Time)[1]. If the input string has no timezone, the last element of the tuple returned is `None`. Note that indexes 6, 7, and 8 of the result tuple are not usable.

email.utils.**parsedate_to_datetime**(*date*)

The inverse of `format_datetime()`. Performs the same function as `parsedate()`, but on success returns a `datetime`. If the input date has a timezone of -0000, the `datetime` will be a naive `datetime`, and if the date is conforming to the RFCs it will represent a time in UTC but with no indication of the actual source timezone of the message the date comes from. If the input date has any other valid timezone offset, the `datetime` will be an aware `datetime` with the corresponding a `timezone tzinfo`.

New in version 3.3.

email.utils.**mktime_tz**(*tuple*)

Turn a 10-tuple as returned by `parsedate_tz()` into a UTC timestamp (seconds since the Epoch). If the timezone item in the tuple is `None`, assume local time.

email.utils.**formatdate**(*timeval=None, localtime=False, usegmt=False*)

Returns a date string as per RFC 2822, e.g.:

```
Fri, 09 Nov 2001 01:08:47 -0000
```

Optional *timeval* if given is a floating point time value as accepted by `time.gmtime()` and `time.localtime()`, otherwise the current time is used.

---

[1] Note that the sign of the timezone offset is the opposite of the sign of the `time.timezone` variable for the same timezone; the latter variable follows the POSIX standard while this module follows RFC 2822.

The Python Library Reference, Release 3.6.4

Optional *localtime* is a flag that when `True`, interprets *timeval*, and returns a date relative to the local timezone instead of UTC, properly taking daylight savings time into account. The default is `False` meaning UTC is used.

Optional *usegmt* is a flag that when `True`, outputs a date string with the timezone as an ascii string `GMT`, rather than a numeric -0000. This is needed for some protocols (such as HTTP). This only applies when *localtime* is `False`. The default is `False`.

email.utils.format_datetime(*dt, usegmt=False*)

Like `formatdate`, but the input is a *datetime* instance. If it is a naive datetime, it is assumed to be "UTC with no information about the source timezone", and the conventional -0000 is used for the timezone. If it is an aware `datetime`, then the numeric timezone offset is used. If it is an aware timezone with offset zero, then *usegmt* may be set to `True`, in which case the string `GMT` is used instead of the numeric timezone offset. This provides a way to generate standards conformant HTTP date headers.

New in version 3.3.

email.utils.decode_rfc2231(*s*)

Decode the string *s* according to RFC 2231.

email.utils.encode_rfc2231(*s, charset=None, language=None*)

Encode the string *s* according to RFC 2231. Optional *charset* and *language*, if given is the character set name and language name to use. If neither is given, *s* is returned as-is. If *charset* is given but *language* is not, the string is encoded using the empty string for *language*.

email.utils.collapse_rfc2231_value(*value, errors='replace', fallback_charset='us-ascii'*)

When a header parameter is encoded in RFC 2231 format, *Message.get_param* may return a 3-tuple containing the character set, language, and value. *collapse_rfc2231_value()* turns this into a unicode string. Optional *errors* is passed to the *errors* argument of `str`'s *encode()* method; it defaults to `'replace'`. Optional *fallback_charset* specifies the character set to use if the one in the RFC 2231 header is not known by Python; it defaults to `'us-ascii'`.

For convenience, if the *value* passed to *collapse_rfc2231_value()* is not a tuple, it should be a string and it is returned unquoted.

email.utils.decode_params(*params*)

Decode parameters list according to RFC 2231. *params* is a sequence of 2-tuples containing elements of the form (`content-type, string-value`).

19.1.15 email.iterators: Iterators

Source code: Lib/email/iterators.py

Iterating over a message object tree is fairly easy with the *Message.walk* method. The *email.iterators* module provides some useful higher level iterations over message object trees.

email.iterators.body_line_iterator(*msg, decode=False*)

This iterates over all the payloads in all the subparts of *msg*, returning the string payloads line-by-line. It skips over all the subpart headers, and it skips over any subpart with a payload that isn't a Python string. This is somewhat equivalent to reading the flat text representation of the message from a file using *readline()*, skipping over all the intervening headers.

Optional *decode* is passed through to *Message.get_payload*.

email.iterators.typed_subpart_iterator(*msg, maintype='text', subtype=None*)

This iterates over all the subparts of *msg*, returning only those subparts that match the MIME type specified by *maintype* and *subtype*.

Note that *subtype* is optional; if omitted, then subpart MIME type matching is done only with the main type. *maintype* is optional too; it defaults to `text`.

Thus, by default `typed_subpart_iterator()` returns each subpart that has a MIME type of `text/*`.

The following function has been added as a useful debugging tool. It should *not* be considered part of the supported public interface for the package.

`email.iterators._structure`(*msg*, *fp=None*, *level=0*, *include_default=False*)

Prints an indented representation of the content types of the message object structure. For example:

```
>>> msg = email.message_from_file(somefile)
>>> _structure(msg)
multipart/mixed
    text/plain
    text/plain
    multipart/digest
        message/rfc822
            text/plain
        message/rfc822
            text/plain
        message/rfc822
            text/plain
        message/rfc822
            text/plain
        message/rfc822
            text/plain
    text/plain
```

Optional *fp* is a file-like object to print the output to. It must be suitable for Python's `print()` function. *level* is used internally. *include_default*, if true, prints the default type as well.

See also:

Module `smtplib` SMTP (Simple Mail Transport Protcol) client

Module `poplib` POP (Post Office Protocol) client

Module `imaplib` IMAP (Internet Message Access Protocol) client

Module `nntplib` NNTP (Net News Transport Protocol) client

Module `mailbox` Tools for creating, reading, and managing collections of messages on disk using a variety standard formats.

Module `smtpd` SMTP server framework (primarily useful for testing)

19.2 `json` — JSON encoder and decoder

Source code: Lib/json/__init__.py

JSON (JavaScript Object Notation), specified by RFC 7159 (which obsoletes RFC 4627) and by ECMA-404, is a lightweight data interchange format inspired by JavaScript object literal syntax (although it is not a strict subset of JavaScript[1]).

`json` exposes an API familiar to users of the standard library `marshal` and `pickle` modules.

Encoding basic Python object hierarchies:

---

[1] As noted in the errata for RFC 7159, JSON permits literal U+2028 (LINE SEPARATOR) and U+2029 (PARAGRAPH SEPARATOR) characters in strings, whereas JavaScript (as of ECMAScript Edition 5.1) does not.

```
>>> import json
>>> json.dumps(['foo', {'bar': ('baz', None, 1.0, 2)}])
'["foo", {"bar": ["baz", null, 1.0, 2]}]'
>>> print(json.dumps("\"foo\bar"))
"\"foo\bar"
>>> print(json.dumps('\u1234'))
"\u1234"
>>> print(json.dumps('\\'))
"\\"
>>> print(json.dumps({"c": 0, "b": 0, "a": 0}, sort_keys=True))
{"a": 0, "b": 0, "c": 0}
>>> from io import StringIO
>>> io = StringIO()
>>> json.dump(['streaming API'], io)
>>> io.getvalue()
'["streaming API"]'
```

Compact encoding:

```
>>> import json
>>> json.dumps([1, 2, 3, {'4': 5, '6': 7}], separators=(',', ':'))
'[1,2,3,{"4":5,"6":7}]'
```

Pretty printing:

```
>>> import json
>>> print(json.dumps({'4': 5, '6': 7}, sort_keys=True, indent=4))
{
    "4": 5,
    "6": 7
}
```

Decoding JSON:

```
>>> import json
>>> json.loads('["foo", {"bar":["baz", null, 1.0, 2]}]')
['foo', {'bar': ['baz', None, 1.0, 2]}]
>>> json.loads('"\\"foo\\bar"')
'"foo\x08ar'
>>> from io import StringIO
>>> io = StringIO('["streaming API"]')
>>> json.load(io)
['streaming API']
```

Specializing JSON object decoding:

```
>>> import json
>>> def as_complex(dct):
...     if '__complex__' in dct:
...         return complex(dct['real'], dct['imag'])
...     return dct
...
>>> json.loads('{"__complex__": true, "real": 1, "imag": 2}',
...     object_hook=as_complex)
(1+2j)
>>> import decimal
>>> json.loads('1.1', parse_float=decimal.Decimal)
Decimal('1.1')
```

Extending *JSONEncoder*:

```
>>> import json
>>> class ComplexEncoder(json.JSONEncoder):
...     def default(self, obj):
...         if isinstance(obj, complex):
...             return [obj.real, obj.imag]
...         # Let the base class default method raise the TypeError
...         return json.JSONEncoder.default(self, obj)
...
>>> json.dumps(2 + 1j, cls=ComplexEncoder)
'[2.0, 1.0]'
>>> ComplexEncoder().encode(2 + 1j)
'[2.0, 1.0]'
>>> list(ComplexEncoder().iterencode(2 + 1j))
['[2.0', ', ', '1.0', ']']
```

Using *json.tool* from the shell to validate and pretty-print:

```
$ echo '{"json":"obj"}' | python -m json.tool
{
    "json": "obj"
}
$ echo '{1.2:3.4}' | python -m json.tool
Expecting property name enclosed in double quotes: line 1 column 2 (char 1)
```

See *Command Line Interface* for detailed documentation.

Note: JSON is a subset of YAML 1.2. The JSON produced by this module's default settings (in particular, the default *separators* value) is also a subset of YAML 1.0 and 1.1. This module can thus also be used as a YAML serializer.

19.2.1 Basic Usage

json.dump(*obj*, *fp*, ***, *skipkeys=False*, *ensure_ascii=True*, *check_circular=True*, *allow_nan=True*, *cls=None*, *indent=None*, *separators=None*, *default=None*, *sort_keys=False*, ***kw*)

Serialize *obj* as a JSON formatted stream to *fp* (a .write()-supporting *file-like object*) using this *conversion table*.

If *skipkeys* is true (default: False), then dict keys that are not of a basic type (str, int, float, bool, None) will be skipped instead of raising a *TypeError*.

The *json* module always produces str objects, not bytes objects. Therefore, fp.write() must support str input.

If *ensure_ascii* is true (the default), the output is guaranteed to have all incoming non-ASCII characters escaped. If *ensure_ascii* is false, these characters will be output as-is.

If *check_circular* is false (default: True), then the circular reference check for container types will be skipped and a circular reference will result in an *OverflowError* (or worse).

If *allow_nan* is false (default: True), then it will be a *ValueError* to serialize out of range float values (nan, inf, -inf) in strict compliance of the JSON specification. If *allow_nan* is true, their JavaScript equivalents (NaN, Infinity, -Infinity) will be used.

If *indent* is a non-negative integer or string, then JSON array elements and object members will be pretty-printed with that indent level. An indent level of 0, negative, or "" will only insert newlines.

None (the default) selects the most compact representation. Using a positive integer indent indents that many spaces per level. If *indent* is a string (such as "\t"), that string is used to indent each level.

Changed in version 3.2: Allow strings for *indent* in addition to integers.

If specified, *separators* should be an (item_separator, key_separator) tuple. The default is (', ', ': ') if *indent* is None and (',', ': ') otherwise. To get the most compact JSON representation, you should specify (',', ':') to eliminate whitespace.

Changed in version 3.4: Use (',', ': ') as default if *indent* is not None.

If specified, *default* should be a function that gets called for objects that can't otherwise be serialized. It should return a JSON encodable version of the object or raise a *TypeError*. If not specified, *TypeError* is raised.

If *sort_keys* is true (default: False), then the output of dictionaries will be sorted by key.

To use a custom *JSONEncoder* subclass (e.g. one that overrides the default() method to serialize additional types), specify it with the *cls* kwarg; otherwise *JSONEncoder* is used.

Changed in version 3.6: All optional parameters are now *keyword-only*.

json.dumps(*obj*, *, *skipkeys=False*, *ensure_ascii=True*, *check_circular=True*, *allow_nan=True*, *cls=None*, *indent=None*, *separators=None*, *default=None*, *sort_keys=False*, **kw*)
Serialize *obj* to a JSON formatted *str* using this *conversion table*. The arguments have the same meaning as in *dump()*.

> **Note:** Unlike *pickle* and *marshal*, JSON is not a framed protocol, so trying to serialize multiple objects with repeated calls to *dump()* using the same *fp* will result in an invalid JSON file.

> **Note:** Keys in key/value pairs of JSON are always of the type *str*. When a dictionary is converted into JSON, all the keys of the dictionary are coerced to strings. As a result of this, if a dictionary is converted into JSON and then back into a dictionary, the dictionary may not equal the original one. That is, loads(dumps(x)) != x if x has non-string keys.

json.load(*fp*, *, *cls=None*, *object_hook=None*, *parse_float=None*, *parse_int=None*, *parse_constant=None*, *object_pairs_hook=None*, **kw*)
Deserialize *fp* (a .read()-supporting *file-like object* containing a JSON document) to a Python object using this *conversion table*.

object_hook is an optional function that will be called with the result of any object literal decoded (a *dict*). The return value of *object_hook* will be used instead of the *dict*. This feature can be used to implement custom decoders (e.g. JSON-RPC class hinting).

object_pairs_hook is an optional function that will be called with the result of any object literal decoded with an ordered list of pairs. The return value of *object_pairs_hook* will be used instead of the *dict*. This feature can be used to implement custom decoders that rely on the order that the key and value pairs are decoded (for example, collections.OrderedDict() will remember the order of insertion). If *object_hook* is also defined, the *object_pairs_hook* takes priority.

Changed in version 3.1: Added support for *object_pairs_hook*.

parse_float, if specified, will be called with the string of every JSON float to be decoded. By default, this is equivalent to float(num_str). This can be used to use another datatype or parser for JSON floats (e.g. *decimal.Decimal*).

parse_int, if specified, will be called with the string of every JSON int to be decoded. By default, this is equivalent to int(num_str). This can be used to use another datatype or parser for JSON integers (e.g. *float*).

parse_constant, if specified, will be called with one of the following strings: `'-Infinity'`, `'Infinity'`, `'NaN'`. This can be used to raise an exception if invalid JSON numbers are encountered.

Changed in version 3.1: *parse_constant* doesn't get called on 'null', 'true', 'false' anymore.

To use a custom *JSONDecoder* subclass, specify it with the `cls` kwarg; otherwise *JSONDecoder* is used. Additional keyword arguments will be passed to the constructor of the class.

If the data being deserialized is not a valid JSON document, a *JSONDecodeError* will be raised.

Changed in version 3.6: All optional parameters are now *keyword-only*.

json.loads(*s*, **, encoding=None, cls=None, object_hook=None, parse_float=None, parse_int=None, parse_constant=None, object_pairs_hook=None, **kw*)

Deserialize *s* (a *str*, *bytes* or *bytearray* instance containing a JSON document) to a Python object using this *conversion table*.

The other arguments have the same meaning as in *load()*, except *encoding* which is ignored and deprecated.

If the data being deserialized is not a valid JSON document, a *JSONDecodeError* will be raised.

Changed in version 3.6: *s* can now be of type *bytes* or *bytearray*. The input encoding should be UTF-8, UTF-16 or UTF-32.

19.2.2 Encoders and Decoders

class json.JSONDecoder(**, object_hook=None, parse_float=None, parse_int=None, parse_constant=None, strict=True, object_pairs_hook=None*)

Simple JSON decoder.

Performs the following translations in decoding by default:

JSON	Python
object	dict
array	list
string	str
number (int)	int
number (real)	float
true	True
false	False
null	None

It also understands `NaN`, `Infinity`, and `-Infinity` as their corresponding `float` values, which is outside the JSON spec.

object_hook, if specified, will be called with the result of every JSON object decoded and its return value will be used in place of the given *dict*. This can be used to provide custom deserializations (e.g. to support JSON-RPC class hinting).

object_pairs_hook, if specified will be called with the result of every JSON object decoded with an ordered list of pairs. The return value of *object_pairs_hook* will be used instead of the *dict*. This feature can be used to implement custom decoders that rely on the order that the key and value pairs are decoded (for example, *collections.OrderedDict()* will remember the order of insertion). If *object_hook* is also defined, the *object_pairs_hook* takes priority.

Changed in version 3.1: Added support for *object_pairs_hook*.

parse_float, if specified, will be called with the string of every JSON float to be decoded. By default, this is equivalent to `float(num_str)`. This can be used to use another datatype or parser for JSON floats (e.g. *decimal.Decimal*).

parse_int, if specified, will be called with the string of every JSON int to be decoded. By default, this is equivalent to `int(num_str)`. This can be used to use another datatype or parser for JSON integers (e.g. *float*).

parse_constant, if specified, will be called with one of the following strings: `'-Infinity'`, `'Infinity'`, `'NaN'`. This can be used to raise an exception if invalid JSON numbers are encountered.

If *strict* is false (`True` is the default), then control characters will be allowed inside strings. Control characters in this context are those with character codes in the 0–31 range, including `'\t'` (tab), `'\n'`, `'\r'` and `'\0'`.

If the data being deserialized is not a valid JSON document, a *JSONDecodeError* will be raised.

Changed in version 3.6: All parameters are now *keyword-only*.

decode(*s***)**
> Return the Python representation of *s* (a *str* instance containing a JSON document).
>
> *JSONDecodeError* will be raised if the given JSON document is not valid.

raw_decode(*s***)**
> Decode a JSON document from *s* (a *str* beginning with a JSON document) and return a 2-tuple of the Python representation and the index in *s* where the document ended.
>
> This can be used to decode a JSON document from a string that may have extraneous data at the end.

class json.JSONEncoder(*, skipkeys=False, ensure_ascii=True, check_circular=True, allow_nan=True, sort_keys=False, indent=None, separators=None, default=None***)**
Extensible JSON encoder for Python data structures.

Supports the following objects and types by default:

Python	JSON
dict	object
list, tuple	array
str	string
int, float, int- & float-derived Enums	number
True	true
False	false
None	null

Changed in version 3.4: Added support for int- and float-derived Enum classes.

To extend this to recognize other objects, subclass and implement a *default()* method with another method that returns a serializable object for o if possible, otherwise it should call the superclass implementation (to raise *TypeError*).

If *skipkeys* is false (the default), then it is a *TypeError* to attempt encoding of keys that are not *str*, *int*, *float* or `None`. If *skipkeys* is true, such items are simply skipped.

If *ensure_ascii* is true (the default), the output is guaranteed to have all incoming non-ASCII characters escaped. If *ensure_ascii* is false, these characters will be output as-is.

If *check_circular* is true (the default), then lists, dicts, and custom encoded objects will be checked for circular references during encoding to prevent an infinite recursion (which would cause an *OverflowError*). Otherwise, no such check takes place.

If *allow_nan* is true (the default), then `NaN`, `Infinity`, and `-Infinity` will be encoded as such. This behavior is not JSON specification compliant, but is consistent with most JavaScript based encoders and decoders. Otherwise, it will be a *ValueError* to encode such floats.

If *sort_keys* is true (default: `False`), then the output of dictionaries will be sorted by key; this is useful for regression tests to ensure that JSON serializations can be compared on a day-to-day basis.

If *indent* is a non-negative integer or string, then JSON array elements and object members will be pretty-printed with that indent level. An indent level of 0, negative, or "" will only insert newlines. `None` (the default) selects the most compact representation. Using a positive integer indent indents that many spaces per level. If *indent* is a string (such as "\t"), that string is used to indent each level.

Changed in version 3.2: Allow strings for *indent* in addition to integers.

If specified, *separators* should be an (`item_separator`, `key_separator`) tuple. The default is (', ', ': ') if *indent* is `None` and (',', ': ') otherwise. To get the most compact JSON representation, you should specify (',', ':') to eliminate whitespace.

Changed in version 3.4: Use (',', ': ') as default if *indent* is not `None`.

If specified, *default* should be a function that gets called for objects that can't otherwise be serialized. It should return a JSON encodable version of the object or raise a `TypeError`. If not specified, `TypeError` is raised.

Changed in version 3.6: All parameters are now *keyword-only*.

default(*o*)

Implement this method in a subclass such that it returns a serializable object for *o*, or calls the base implementation (to raise a `TypeError`).

For example, to support arbitrary iterators, you could implement default like this:

```python
def default(self, o):
    try:
        iterable = iter(o)
    except TypeError:
        pass
    else:
        return list(iterable)
    # Let the base class default method raise the TypeError
    return json.JSONEncoder.default(self, o)
```

encode(*o*)

Return a JSON string representation of a Python data structure, *o*. For example:

```python
>>> json.JSONEncoder().encode({"foo": ["bar", "baz"]})
'{"foo": ["bar", "baz"]}'
```

iterencode(*o*)

Encode the given object, *o*, and yield each string representation as available. For example:

```python
for chunk in json.JSONEncoder().iterencode(bigobject):
    mysocket.write(chunk)
```

19.2.3 Exceptions

exception `json.JSONDecodeError`(*msg, doc, pos*)

Subclass of `ValueError` with the following additional attributes:

msg

The unformatted error message.

doc

The JSON document being parsed.

pos
    The start index of *doc* where parsing failed.

lineno
    The line corresponding to *pos*.

colno
    The column corresponding to *pos*.

New in version 3.5.

19.2.4 Standard Compliance and Interoperability

The JSON format is specified by RFC 7159 and by ECMA-404. This section details this module's level of compliance with the RFC. For simplicity, *JSONEncoder* and *JSONDecoder* subclasses, and parameters other than those explicitly mentioned, are not considered.

This module does not comply with the RFC in a strict fashion, implementing some extensions that are valid JavaScript but not valid JSON. In particular:

- Infinite and NaN number values are accepted and output;
- Repeated names within an object are accepted, and only the value of the last name-value pair is used.

Since the RFC permits RFC-compliant parsers to accept input texts that are not RFC-compliant, this module's deserializer is technically RFC-compliant under default settings.

Character Encodings

The RFC requires that JSON be represented using either UTF-8, UTF-16, or UTF-32, with UTF-8 being the recommended default for maximum interoperability.

As permitted, though not required, by the RFC, this module's serializer sets *ensure_ascii=True* by default, thus escaping the output so that the resulting strings only contain ASCII characters.

Other than the *ensure_ascii* parameter, this module is defined strictly in terms of conversion between Python objects and *Unicode strings*, and thus does not otherwise directly address the issue of character encodings.

The RFC prohibits adding a byte order mark (BOM) to the start of a JSON text, and this module's serializer does not add a BOM to its output. The RFC permits, but does not require, JSON deserializers to ignore an initial BOM in their input. This module's deserializer raises a *ValueError* when an initial BOM is present.

The RFC does not explicitly forbid JSON strings which contain byte sequences that don't correspond to valid Unicode characters (e.g. unpaired UTF-16 surrogates), but it does note that they may cause interoperability problems. By default, this module accepts and outputs (when present in the original *str*) code points for such sequences.

Infinite and NaN Number Values

The RFC does not permit the representation of infinite or NaN number values. Despite that, by default, this module accepts and outputs `Infinity`, `-Infinity`, and `NaN` as if they were valid JSON number literal values:

```
>>> # Neither of these calls raises an exception, but the results are not valid JSON
>>> json.dumps(float('-inf'))
'-Infinity'
>>> json.dumps(float('nan'))
'NaN'
>>> # Same when deserializing
```

```
>>> json.loads('-Infinity')
-inf
>>> json.loads('NaN')
nan
```

In the serializer, the *allow_nan* parameter can be used to alter this behavior. In the deserializer, the *parse_constant* parameter can be used to alter this behavior.

Repeated Names Within an Object

The RFC specifies that the names within a JSON object should be unique, but does not mandate how repeated names in JSON objects should be handled. By default, this module does not raise an exception; instead, it ignores all but the last name-value pair for a given name:

```
>>> weird_json = '{"x": 1, "x": 2, "x": 3}'
>>> json.loads(weird_json)
{'x': 3}
```

The *object_pairs_hook* parameter can be used to alter this behavior.

Top-level Non-Object, Non-Array Values

The old version of JSON specified by the obsolete RFC 4627 required that the top-level value of a JSON text must be either a JSON object or array (Python *dict* or *list*), and could not be a JSON null, boolean, number, or string value. RFC 7159 removed that restriction, and this module does not and has never implemented that restriction in either its serializer or its deserializer.

Regardless, for maximum interoperability, you may wish to voluntarily adhere to the restriction yourself.

Implementation Limitations

Some JSON deserializer implementations may set limits on:

- the size of accepted JSON texts
- the maximum level of nesting of JSON objects and arrays
- the range and precision of JSON numbers
- the content and maximum length of JSON strings

This module does not impose any such limits beyond those of the relevant Python datatypes themselves or the Python interpreter itself.

When serializing to JSON, beware any such limitations in applications that may consume your JSON. In particular, it is common for JSON numbers to be deserialized into IEEE 754 double precision numbers and thus subject to that representation's range and precision limitations. This is especially relevant when serializing Python *int* values of extremely large magnitude, or when serializing instances of "exotic" numerical types such as *decimal.Decimal*.

19.2.5 Command Line Interface

Source code: Lib/json/tool.py

The *json.tool* module provides a simple command line interface to validate and pretty-print JSON objects.

If the optional `infile` and `outfile` arguments are not specified, `sys.stdin` and `sys.stdout` will be used respectively:

```
$ echo '{"json": "obj"}' | python -m json.tool
{
    "json": "obj"
}
$ echo '{1.2:3.4}' | python -m json.tool
Expecting property name enclosed in double quotes: line 1 column 2 (char 1)
```

Changed in version 3.5: The output is now in the same order as the input. Use the `--sort-keys` option to sort the output of dictionaries alphabetically by key.

Command line options

infile

The JSON file to be validated or pretty-printed:

```
$ python -m json.tool mp_films.json
[
    {
        "title": "And Now for Something Completely Different",
        "year": 1971
    },
    {
        "title": "Monty Python and the Holy Grail",
        "year": 1975
    }
]
```

If *infile* is not specified, read from `sys.stdin`.

outfile

Write the output of the *infile* to the given *outfile*. Otherwise, write it to `sys.stdout`.

--sort-keys

Sort the output of dictionaries alphabetically by key.

New in version 3.5.

-h, --help

Show the help message.

19.3 `mailcap` — Mailcap file handling

Source code: Lib/mailcap.py

Mailcap files are used to configure how MIME-aware applications such as mail readers and Web browsers react to files with different MIME types. (The name "mailcap" is derived from the phrase "mail capability".) For example, a mailcap file might contain a line like `video/mpeg; xmpeg %s`. Then, if the user encounters an email message or Web document with the MIME type *video/mpeg*, `%s` will be replaced by a filename (usually one belonging to a temporary file) and the **xmpeg** program can be automatically started to view the file.

The mailcap format is documented in RFC 1524, "A User Agent Configuration Mechanism For Multimedia Mail Format Information," but is not an Internet standard. However, mailcap files are supported on most Unix systems.

mailcap.findmatch(*caps, MIMEtype, key='view', filename='/dev/null', plist=[]*)

> Return a 2-tuple; the first element is a string containing the command line to be executed (which can be passed to *os.system()*), and the second element is the mailcap entry for a given MIME type. If no matching MIME type can be found, (`None, None`) is returned.
>
> *key* is the name of the field desired, which represents the type of activity to be performed; the default value is 'view', since in the most common case you simply want to view the body of the MIME-typed data. Other possible values might be 'compose' and 'edit', if you wanted to create a new body of the given MIME type or alter the existing body data. See RFC 1524 for a complete list of these fields.
>
> *filename* is the filename to be substituted for `%s` in the command line; the default value is `'/dev/null'` which is almost certainly not what you want, so usually you'll override it by specifying a filename.
>
> *plist* can be a list containing named parameters; the default value is simply an empty list. Each entry in the list must be a string containing the parameter name, an equals sign (`'='`), and the parameter's value. Mailcap entries can contain named parameters like `%{foo}`, which will be replaced by the value of the parameter named 'foo'. For example, if the command line `showpartial %{id} %{number} %{total}` was in a mailcap file, and *plist* was set to `['id=1', 'number=2', 'total=3']`, the resulting command line would be `'showpartial 1 2 3'`.
>
> In a mailcap file, the "test" field can optionally be specified to test some external condition (such as the machine architecture, or the window system in use) to determine whether or not the mailcap line applies. *findmatch()* will automatically check such conditions and skip the entry if the check fails.

mailcap.getcaps()

> Returns a dictionary mapping MIME types to a list of mailcap file entries. This dictionary must be passed to the *findmatch()* function. An entry is stored as a list of dictionaries, but it shouldn't be necessary to know the details of this representation.
>
> The information is derived from all of the mailcap files found on the system. Settings in the user's mailcap file `$HOME/.mailcap` will override settings in the system mailcap files `/etc/mailcap`, `/usr/etc/mailcap`, and `/usr/local/etc/mailcap`.

An example usage:

```
>>> import mailcap
>>> d = mailcap.getcaps()
>>> mailcap.findmatch(d, 'video/mpeg', filename='tmp1223')
('xmpeg tmp1223', {'view': 'xmpeg %s'})
```

19.4 `mailbox` — Manipulate mailboxes in various formats

Source code: Lib/mailbox.py

This module defines two classes, *Mailbox* and *Message*, for accessing and manipulating on-disk mailboxes and the messages they contain. *Mailbox* offers a dictionary-like mapping from keys to messages. *Message* extends the *email.message* module's *Message* class with format-specific state and behavior. Supported mailbox formats are Maildir, mbox, MH, Babyl, and MMDF.

See also:

Module *email* Represent and manipulate messages.

19.4.1 Mailbox objects

class mailbox.Mailbox

A mailbox, which may be inspected and modified.

The `Mailbox` class defines an interface and is not intended to be instantiated. Instead, format-specific subclasses should inherit from `Mailbox` and your code should instantiate a particular subclass.

The `Mailbox` interface is dictionary-like, with small keys corresponding to messages. Keys are issued by the `Mailbox` instance with which they will be used and are only meaningful to that `Mailbox` instance. A key continues to identify a message even if the corresponding message is modified, such as by replacing it with another message.

Messages may be added to a `Mailbox` instance using the set-like method `add()` and removed using a `del` statement or the set-like methods `remove()` and `discard()`.

`Mailbox` interface semantics differ from dictionary semantics in some noteworthy ways. Each time a message is requested, a new representation (typically a `Message` instance) is generated based upon the current state of the mailbox. Similarly, when a message is added to a `Mailbox` instance, the provided message representation's contents are copied. In neither case is a reference to the message representation kept by the `Mailbox` instance.

The default `Mailbox` iterator iterates over message representations, not keys as the default dictionary iterator does. Moreover, modification of a mailbox during iteration is safe and well-defined. Messages added to the mailbox after an iterator is created will not be seen by the iterator. Messages removed from the mailbox before the iterator yields them will be silently skipped, though using a key from an iterator may result in a `KeyError` exception if the corresponding message is subsequently removed.

> **Warning:** Be very cautious when modifying mailboxes that might be simultaneously changed by some other process. The safest mailbox format to use for such tasks is Maildir; try to avoid using single-file formats such as mbox for concurrent writing. If you're modifying a mailbox, you *must* lock it by calling the `lock()` and `unlock()` methods *before* reading any messages in the file or making any changes by adding or deleting a message. Failing to lock the mailbox runs the risk of losing messages or corrupting the entire mailbox.

`Mailbox` instances have the following methods:

add(*message*)

Add *message* to the mailbox and return the key that has been assigned to it.

Parameter *message* may be a `Message` instance, an `email.message.Message` instance, a string, a byte string, or a file-like object (which should be open in binary mode). If *message* is an instance of the appropriate format-specific `Message` subclass (e.g., if it's an `mboxMessage` instance and this is an `mbox` instance), its format-specific information is used. Otherwise, reasonable defaults for format-specific information are used.

Changed in version 3.2: Support for binary input was added.

remove(*key*)
__delitem__(*key*)
discard(*key*)

Delete the message corresponding to *key* from the mailbox.

If no such message exists, a `KeyError` exception is raised if the method was called as `remove()` or `__delitem__()` but no exception is raised if the method was called as `discard()`. The behavior of `discard()` may be preferred if the underlying mailbox format supports concurrent modification by other processes.

__setitem__(*key, message*)

> Replace the message corresponding to *key* with *message*. Raise a `KeyError` exception if no message already corresponds to *key*.
>
> As with `add()`, parameter *message* may be a `Message` instance, an `email.message.Message` instance, a string, a byte string, or a file-like object (which should be open in binary mode). If *message* is an instance of the appropriate format-specific `Message` subclass (e.g., if it's an `mboxMessage` instance and this is an `mbox` instance), its format-specific information is used. Otherwise, the format-specific information of the message that currently corresponds to *key* is left unchanged.

iterkeys()
keys()

> Return an iterator over all keys if called as `iterkeys()` or return a list of keys if called as `keys()`.

itervalues()
__iter__()
values()

> Return an iterator over representations of all messages if called as `itervalues()` or `__iter__()` or return a list of such representations if called as `values()`. The messages are represented as instances of the appropriate format-specific `Message` subclass unless a custom message factory was specified when the `Mailbox` instance was initialized.

> **Note:** The behavior of `__iter__()` is unlike that of dictionaries, which iterate over keys.

iteritems()
items()

> Return an iterator over (*key*, *message*) pairs, where *key* is a key and *message* is a message representation, if called as `iteritems()` or return a list of such pairs if called as `items()`. The messages are represented as instances of the appropriate format-specific `Message` subclass unless a custom message factory was specified when the `Mailbox` instance was initialized.

get(*key, default=None*)
__getitem__(*key*)

> Return a representation of the message corresponding to *key*. If no such message exists, *default* is returned if the method was called as `get()` and a `KeyError` exception is raised if the method was called as `__getitem__()`. The message is represented as an instance of the appropriate format-specific `Message` subclass unless a custom message factory was specified when the `Mailbox` instance was initialized.

get_message(*key*)

> Return a representation of the message corresponding to *key* as an instance of the appropriate format-specific `Message` subclass, or raise a `KeyError` exception if no such message exists.

get_bytes(*key*)

> Return a byte representation of the message corresponding to *key*, or raise a `KeyError` exception if no such message exists.
>
> New in version 3.2.

get_string(*key*)

> Return a string representation of the message corresponding to *key*, or raise a `KeyError` exception if no such message exists. The message is processed through `email.message.Message` to convert it to a 7bit clean representation.

get_file(*key*)

> Return a file-like representation of the message corresponding to *key*, or raise a `KeyError` exception

if no such message exists. The file-like object behaves as if open in binary mode. This file should be closed once it is no longer needed.

Changed in version 3.2: The file object really is a binary file; previously it was incorrectly returned in text mode. Also, the file-like object now supports the context management protocol: you can use a **with** statement to automatically close it.

> **Note:** Unlike other representations of messages, file-like representations are not necessarily independent of the *Mailbox* instance that created them or of the underlying mailbox. More specific documentation is provided by each subclass.

`__contains__(`*key*`)`
> Return **True** if *key* corresponds to a message, **False** otherwise.

`__len__()`
> Return a count of messages in the mailbox.

`clear()`
> Delete all messages from the mailbox.

`pop(`*key, default=None*`)`
> Return a representation of the message corresponding to *key* and delete the message. If no such message exists, return *default*. The message is represented as an instance of the appropriate format-specific *Message* subclass unless a custom message factory was specified when the *Mailbox* instance was initialized.

`popitem()`
> Return an arbitrary (*key*, *message*) pair, where *key* is a key and *message* is a message representation, and delete the corresponding message. If the mailbox is empty, raise a *KeyError* exception. The message is represented as an instance of the appropriate format-specific *Message* subclass unless a custom message factory was specified when the *Mailbox* instance was initialized.

`update(`*arg*`)`
> Parameter *arg* should be a *key*-to-*message* mapping or an iterable of (*key*, *message*) pairs. Updates the mailbox so that, for each given *key* and *message*, the message corresponding to *key* is set to *message* as if by using *__setitem__()*. As with *__setitem__()*, each *key* must already correspond to a message in the mailbox or else a *KeyError* exception will be raised, so in general it is incorrect for *arg* to be a *Mailbox* instance.

> **Note:** Unlike with dictionaries, keyword arguments are not supported.

`flush()`
> Write any pending changes to the filesystem. For some *Mailbox* subclasses, changes are always written immediately and *flush()* does nothing, but you should still make a habit of calling this method.

`lock()`
> Acquire an exclusive advisory lock on the mailbox so that other processes know not to modify it. An *ExternalClashError* is raised if the lock is not available. The particular locking mechanisms used depend upon the mailbox format. You should *always* lock the mailbox before making any modifications to its contents.

`unlock()`
> Release the lock on the mailbox, if any.

`close()`
> Flush the mailbox, unlock it if necessary, and close any open files. For some *Mailbox* subclasses,

this method does nothing.

Maildir

class `mailbox.Maildir`(*dirname, factory=None, create=True*)

A subclass of *Mailbox* for mailboxes in Maildir format. Parameter *factory* is a callable object that accepts a file-like message representation (which behaves as if opened in binary mode) and returns a custom representation. If *factory* is `None`, *MaildirMessage* is used as the default message representation. If *create* is `True`, the mailbox is created if it does not exist.

It is for historical reasons that *dirname* is named as such rather than *path*.

Maildir is a directory-based mailbox format invented for the qmail mail transfer agent and now widely supported by other programs. Messages in a Maildir mailbox are stored in separate files within a common directory structure. This design allows Maildir mailboxes to be accessed and modified by multiple unrelated programs without data corruption, so file locking is unnecessary.

Maildir mailboxes contain three subdirectories, namely: `tmp`, `new`, and `cur`. Messages are created momentarily in the `tmp` subdirectory and then moved to the `new` subdirectory to finalize delivery. A mail user agent may subsequently move the message to the `cur` subdirectory and store information about the state of the message in a special "info" section appended to its file name.

Folders of the style introduced by the Courier mail transfer agent are also supported. Any subdirectory of the main mailbox is considered a folder if '.' is the first character in its name. Folder names are represented by *Maildir* without the leading '.'. Each folder is itself a Maildir mailbox but should not contain other folders. Instead, a logical nesting is indicated using '.' to delimit levels, e.g., "Archived.2005.07".

Note: The Maildir specification requires the use of a colon (':') in certain message file names. However, some operating systems do not permit this character in file names, If you wish to use a Maildir-like format on such an operating system, you should specify another character to use instead. The exclamation point ('!') is a popular choice. For example:

```
import mailbox
mailbox.Maildir.colon = '!'
```

The `colon` attribute may also be set on a per-instance basis.

Maildir instances have all of the methods of *Mailbox* in addition to the following:

`list_folders()`
: Return a list of the names of all folders.

`get_folder`(*folder*)
: Return a *Maildir* instance representing the folder whose name is *folder*. A *NoSuchMailboxError* exception is raised if the folder does not exist.

`add_folder`(*folder*)
: Create a folder whose name is *folder* and return a *Maildir* instance representing it.

`remove_folder`(*folder*)
: Delete the folder whose name is *folder*. If the folder contains any messages, a *NotEmptyError* exception will be raised and the folder will not be deleted.

`clean()`
: Delete temporary files from the mailbox that have not been accessed in the last 36 hours. The Maildir specification says that mail-reading programs should do this occasionally.

Some *Mailbox* methods implemented by *Maildir* deserve special remarks:

add(*message*)
__setitem__(*key*, *message*)
update(*arg*)

> **Warning:** These methods generate unique file names based upon the current process ID. When using multiple threads, undetected name clashes may occur and cause corruption of the mailbox unless threads are coordinated to avoid using these methods to manipulate the same mailbox simultaneously.

flush()
All changes to Maildir mailboxes are immediately applied, so this method does nothing.

lock()
unlock()
Maildir mailboxes do not support (or require) locking, so these methods do nothing.

close()
Maildir instances do not keep any open files and the underlying mailboxes do not support locking, so this method does nothing.

get_file(*key*)
Depending upon the host platform, it may not be possible to modify or remove the underlying message while the returned file remains open.

See also:

maildir man page from qmail
The original specification of the format.

Using maildir format
Notes on Maildir by its inventor. Includes an updated name-creation scheme and details on "info" semantics.

maildir man page from Courier
Another specification of the format. Describes a common extension for supporting folders.

mbox

class mailbox.mbox(*path*, *factory=None*, *create=True*)
A subclass of *Mailbox* for mailboxes in mbox format. Parameter *factory* is a callable object that accepts a file-like message representation (which behaves as if opened in binary mode) and returns a custom representation. If *factory* is None, *mboxMessage* is used as the default message representation. If *create* is True, the mailbox is created if it does not exist.

The mbox format is the classic format for storing mail on Unix systems. All messages in an mbox mailbox are stored in a single file with the beginning of each message indicated by a line whose first five characters are "From ".

Several variations of the mbox format exist to address perceived shortcomings in the original. In the interest of compatibility, *mbox* implements the original format, which is sometimes referred to as *mboxo*. This means that the **Content-Length** header, if present, is ignored and that any occurrences of "From " at the beginning of a line in a message body are transformed to ">From " when storing the message, although occurrences of ">From " are not transformed to "From " when reading the message.

Some *Mailbox* methods implemented by *mbox* deserve special remarks:

get_file(*key*)
Using the file after calling **flush()** or **close()** on the *mbox* instance may yield unpredictable results or raise an exception.

lock()
unlock()
> Three locking mechanisms are used—dot locking and, if available, the `flock()` and `lockf()` system calls.

See also:

mbox man page from qmail
> A specification of the format and its variations.

mbox man page from tin
> Another specification of the format, with details on locking.

Configuring Netscape Mail on Unix: Why The Content-Length Format is Bad
> An argument for using the original mbox format rather than a variation.

"mbox" is a family of several mutually incompatible mailbox formats
> A history of mbox variations.

MH

class mailbox.MH(*path*, *factory=None*, *create=True*)
> A subclass of *Mailbox* for mailboxes in MH format. Parameter *factory* is a callable object that accepts a file-like message representation (which behaves as if opened in binary mode) and returns a custom representation. If *factory* is `None`, *MHMessage* is used as the default message representation. If *create* is `True`, the mailbox is created if it does not exist.
>
> MH is a directory-based mailbox format invented for the MH Message Handling System, a mail user agent. Each message in an MH mailbox resides in its own file. An MH mailbox may contain other MH mailboxes (called *folders*) in addition to messages. Folders may be nested indefinitely. MH mailboxes also support *sequences*, which are named lists used to logically group messages without moving them to sub-folders. Sequences are defined in a file called `.mh_sequences` in each folder.
>
> The *MH* class manipulates MH mailboxes, but it does not attempt to emulate all of **mh**'s behaviors. In particular, it does not modify and is not affected by the `context` or `.mh_profile` files that are used by **mh** to store its state and configuration.
>
> *MH* instances have all of the methods of *Mailbox* in addition to the following:

list_folders()
> Return a list of the names of all folders.

get_folder(*folder*)
> Return an *MH* instance representing the folder whose name is *folder*. A *NoSuchMailboxError* exception is raised if the folder does not exist.

add_folder(*folder*)
> Create a folder whose name is *folder* and return an *MH* instance representing it.

remove_folder(*folder*)
> Delete the folder whose name is *folder*. If the folder contains any messages, a *NotEmptyError* exception will be raised and the folder will not be deleted.

get_sequences()
> Return a dictionary of sequence names mapped to key lists. If there are no sequences, the empty dictionary is returned.

set_sequences(*sequences*)
> Re-define the sequences that exist in the mailbox based upon *sequences*, a dictionary of names mapped to key lists, like returned by *get_sequences()*.

pack()
> Rename messages in the mailbox as necessary to eliminate gaps in numbering. Entries in the sequences list are updated correspondingly.

    Note: Already-issued keys are invalidated by this operation and should not be subsequently used.

Some `Mailbox` methods implemented by `MH` deserve special remarks:

remove(*key*)
__delitem__(*key*)
discard(*key*)
    These methods immediately delete the message. The MH convention of marking a message for deletion by prepending a comma to its name is not used.

lock()
unlock()
    Three locking mechanisms are used—dot locking and, if available, the `flock()` and `lockf()` system calls. For MH mailboxes, locking the mailbox means locking the `.mh_sequences` file and, only for the duration of any operations that affect them, locking individual message files.

get_file(*key*)
    Depending upon the host platform, it may not be possible to remove the underlying message while the returned file remains open.

flush()
    All changes to MH mailboxes are immediately applied, so this method does nothing.

close()
    `MH` instances do not keep any open files, so this method is equivalent to `unlock()`.

See also:

nmh - Message Handling System Home page of **nmh**, an updated version of the original **mh**.

MH & nmh: Email for Users & Programmers A GPL-licensed book on **mh** and **nmh**, with some information on the mailbox format.

Babyl

class `mailbox.Babyl`(*path, factory=None, create=True*)
    A subclass of `Mailbox` for mailboxes in Babyl format. Parameter *factory* is a callable object that accepts a file-like message representation (which behaves as if opened in binary mode) and returns a custom representation. If *factory* is `None`, `BabylMessage` is used as the default message representation. If *create* is `True`, the mailbox is created if it does not exist.

    Babyl is a single-file mailbox format used by the Rmail mail user agent included with Emacs. The beginning of a message is indicated by a line containing the two characters Control-Underscore (`'\037'`) and Control-L (`'\014'`). The end of a message is indicated by the start of the next message or, in the case of the last message, a line containing a Control-Underscore (`'\037'`) character.

    Messages in a Babyl mailbox have two sets of headers, original headers and so-called visible headers. Visible headers are typically a subset of the original headers that have been reformatted or abridged to be more attractive. Each message in a Babyl mailbox also has an accompanying list of *labels*, or short strings that record extra information about the message, and a list of all user-defined labels found in the mailbox is kept in the Babyl options section.

    `Babyl` instances have all of the methods of `Mailbox` in addition to the following:

get_labels()
    Return a list of the names of all user-defined labels used in the mailbox.

Note: The actual messages are inspected to determine which labels exist in the mailbox rather than consulting the list of labels in the Babyl options section, but the Babyl section is updated whenever the mailbox is modified.

Some `Mailbox` methods implemented by `Babyl` deserve special remarks:

get_file(*key*)
> In Babyl mailboxes, the headers of a message are not stored contiguously with the body of the message. To generate a file-like representation, the headers and body are copied together into an `io.BytesIO` instance, which has an API identical to that of a file. As a result, the file-like object is truly independent of the underlying mailbox but does not save memory compared to a string representation.

lock()
unlock()
> Three locking mechanisms are used—dot locking and, if available, the `flock()` and `lockf()` system calls.

See also:

Format of Version 5 Babyl Files A specification of the Babyl format.

Reading Mail with Rmail The Rmail manual, with some information on Babyl semantics.

MMDF

class `mailbox.MMDF`(*path*, *factory=None*, *create=True*)
> A subclass of `Mailbox` for mailboxes in MMDF format. Parameter *factory* is a callable object that accepts a file-like message representation (which behaves as if opened in binary mode) and returns a custom representation. If *factory* is `None`, `MMDFMessage` is used as the default message representation. If *create* is `True`, the mailbox is created if it does not exist.
>
> MMDF is a single-file mailbox format invented for the Multichannel Memorandum Distribution Facility, a mail transfer agent. Each message is in the same form as an mbox message but is bracketed before and after by lines containing four Control-A (`'\001'`) characters. As with the mbox format, the beginning of each message is indicated by a line whose first five characters are "From ", but additional occurrences of "From " are not transformed to ">From " when storing messages because the extra message separator lines prevent mistaking such occurrences for the starts of subsequent messages.
>
> Some `Mailbox` methods implemented by `MMDF` deserve special remarks:
>
> **get_file**(*key*)
> > Using the file after calling `flush()` or `close()` on the `MMDF` instance may yield unpredictable results or raise an exception.
>
> **lock**()
> **unlock**()
> > Three locking mechanisms are used—dot locking and, if available, the `flock()` and `lockf()` system calls.

See also:

mmdf man page from tin A specification of MMDF format from the documentation of tin, a newsreader.

MMDF A Wikipedia article describing the Multichannel Memorandum Distribution Facility.

19.4.2 Message objects

class mailbox.Message(*message=None*)

A subclass of the *email.message* module's *Message*. Subclasses of *mailbox.Message* add mailbox-format-specific state and behavior.

If *message* is omitted, the new instance is created in a default, empty state. If *message* is an *email.message.Message* instance, its contents are copied; furthermore, any format-specific information is converted insofar as possible if *message* is a *Message* instance. If *message* is a string, a byte string, or a file, it should contain an RFC 2822-compliant message, which is read and parsed. Files should be open in binary mode, but text mode files are accepted for backward compatibility.

The format-specific state and behaviors offered by subclasses vary, but in general it is only the properties that are not specific to a particular mailbox that are supported (although presumably the properties are specific to a particular mailbox format). For example, file offsets for single-file mailbox formats and file names for directory-based mailbox formats are not retained, because they are only applicable to the original mailbox. But state such as whether a message has been read by the user or marked as important is retained, because it applies to the message itself.

There is no requirement that *Message* instances be used to represent messages retrieved using *Mailbox* instances. In some situations, the time and memory required to generate *Message* representations might not be acceptable. For such situations, *Mailbox* instances also offer string and file-like representations, and a custom message factory may be specified when a *Mailbox* instance is initialized.

MaildirMessage

class mailbox.MaildirMessage(*message=None*)

A message with Maildir-specific behaviors. Parameter *message* has the same meaning as with the *Message* constructor.

Typically, a mail user agent application moves all of the messages in the **new** subdirectory to the **cur** subdirectory after the first time the user opens and closes the mailbox, recording that the messages are old whether or not they've actually been read. Each message in **cur** has an "info" section added to its file name to store information about its state. (Some mail readers may also add an "info" section to messages in **new**.) The "info" section may take one of two forms: it may contain "2," followed by a list of standardized flags (e.g., "2,FR") or it may contain "1," followed by so-called experimental information. Standard flags for Maildir messages are as follows:

Flag	Meaning	Explanation
D	Draft	Under composition
F	Flagged	Marked as important
P	Passed	Forwarded, resent, or bounced
R	Replied	Replied to
S	Seen	Read
T	Trashed	Marked for subsequent deletion

MaildirMessage instances offer the following methods:

get_subdir()

Return either "new" (if the message should be stored in the **new** subdirectory) or "cur" (if the message should be stored in the **cur** subdirectory).

Note: A message is typically moved from **new** to **cur** after its mailbox has been accessed, whether or not the message is has been read. A message `msg` has been read if `"S" in msg.get_flags()` is `True`.

---

set_subdir(*subdir*)
: Set the subdirectory the message should be stored in. Parameter *subdir* must be either "new" or "cur".

get_flags()
: Return a string specifying the flags that are currently set. If the message complies with the standard Maildir format, the result is the concatenation in alphabetical order of zero or one occurrence of each of `'D'`, `'F'`, `'P'`, `'R'`, `'S'`, and `'T'`. The empty string is returned if no flags are set or if "info" contains experimental semantics.

set_flags(*flags*)
: Set the flags specified by *flags* and unset all others.

add_flag(*flag*)
: Set the flag(s) specified by *flag* without changing other flags. To add more than one flag at a time, *flag* may be a string of more than one character. The current "info" is overwritten whether or not it contains experimental information rather than flags.

remove_flag(*flag*)
: Unset the flag(s) specified by *flag* without changing other flags. To remove more than one flag at a time, *flag* maybe a string of more than one character. If "info" contains experimental information rather than flags, the current "info" is not modified.

get_date()
: Return the delivery date of the message as a floating-point number representing seconds since the epoch.

set_date(*date*)
: Set the delivery date of the message to *date*, a floating-point number representing seconds since the epoch.

get_info()
: Return a string containing the "info" for a message. This is useful for accessing and modifying "info" that is experimental (i.e., not a list of flags).

set_info(*info*)
: Set "info" to *info*, which should be a string.

When a *MaildirMessage* instance is created based upon an *mboxMessage* or *MMDFMessage* instance, the *Status* and *X-Status* headers are omitted and the following conversions take place:

Resulting state	*mboxMessage* or *MMDFMessage* state
"cur" subdirectory	O flag
F flag	F flag
R flag	A flag
S flag	R flag
T flag	D flag

When a *MaildirMessage* instance is created based upon an *MHMessage* instance, the following conversions take place:

Resulting state	*MHMessage* state
"cur" subdirectory	"unseen" sequence
"cur" subdirectory and S flag	no "unseen" sequence
F flag	"flagged" sequence
R flag	"replied" sequence

When a *MaildirMessage* instance is created based upon a *BabylMessage* instance, the following conversions take place:

Resulting state	*BabylMessage* state
"cur" subdirectory	"unseen" label
"cur" subdirectory and S flag	no "unseen" label
P flag	"forwarded" or "resent" label
R flag	"answered" label
T flag	"deleted" label

mboxMessage

class mailbox.mboxMessage(*message=None*)

A message with mbox-specific behaviors. Parameter *message* has the same meaning as with the *Message* constructor.

Messages in an mbox mailbox are stored together in a single file. The sender's envelope address and the time of delivery are typically stored in a line beginning with "From " that is used to indicate the start of a message, though there is considerable variation in the exact format of this data among mbox implementations. Flags that indicate the state of the message, such as whether it has been read or marked as important, are typically stored in *Status* and *X-Status* headers.

Conventional flags for mbox messages are as follows:

Flag	Meaning	Explanation
R	Read	Read
O	Old	Previously detected by MUA
D	Deleted	Marked for subsequent deletion
F	Flagged	Marked as important
A	Answered	Replied to

The "R" and "O" flags are stored in the *Status* header, and the "D", "F", and "A" flags are stored in the *X-Status* header. The flags and headers typically appear in the order mentioned.

mboxMessage instances offer the following methods:

get_from()
> Return a string representing the "From " line that marks the start of the message in an mbox mailbox. The leading "From " and the trailing newline are excluded.

set_from(*from_*, *time_=None*)
> Set the "From " line to *from_*, which should be specified without a leading "From " or trailing newline. For convenience, *time_* may be specified and will be formatted appropriately and appended to *from_*. If *time_* is specified, it should be a *time.struct_time* instance, a tuple suitable for passing to *time.strftime()*, or True (to use *time.gmtime()*).

get_flags()
> Return a string specifying the flags that are currently set. If the message complies with the conventional format, the result is the concatenation in the following order of zero or one occurrence of each of 'R', 'O', 'D', 'F', and 'A'.

set_flags(*flags*)
> Set the flags specified by *flags* and unset all others. Parameter *flags* should be the concatenation in any order of zero or more occurrences of each of 'R', 'O', 'D', 'F', and 'A'.

add_flag(*flag*)
:   Set the flag(s) specified by *flag* without changing other flags. To add more than one flag at a time, *flag* may be a string of more than one character.

remove_flag(*flag*)
:   Unset the flag(s) specified by *flag* without changing other flags. To remove more than one flag at a time, *flag* maybe a string of more than one character.

When an *mboxMessage* instance is created based upon a *MaildirMessage* instance, a "From " line is generated based upon the *MaildirMessage* instance's delivery date, and the following conversions take place:

Resulting state	*MaildirMessage* state
R flag	S flag
O flag	"cur" subdirectory
D flag	T flag
F flag	F flag
A flag	R flag

When an *mboxMessage* instance is created based upon an *MHMessage* instance, the following conversions take place:

Resulting state	*MHMessage* state
R flag and O flag	no "unseen" sequence
O flag	"unseen" sequence
F flag	"flagged" sequence
A flag	"replied" sequence

When an *mboxMessage* instance is created based upon a *BabylMessage* instance, the following conversions take place:

Resulting state	*BabylMessage* state
R flag and O flag	no "unseen" label
O flag	"unseen" label
D flag	"deleted" label
A flag	"answered" label

When a *Message* instance is created based upon an *MMDFMessage* instance, the "From " line is copied and all flags directly correspond:

Resulting state	*MMDFMessage* state
R flag	R flag
O flag	O flag
D flag	D flag
F flag	F flag
A flag	A flag

MHMessage

class mailbox.MHMessage(*message=None*)
:   A message with MH-specific behaviors. Parameter *message* has the same meaning as with the *Message* constructor.

MH messages do not support marks or flags in the traditional sense, but they do support sequences, which are logical groupings of arbitrary messages. Some mail reading programs (although not the standard **mh** and **nmh**) use sequences in much the same way flags are used with other formats, as follows:

Sequence	Explanation
unseen	Not read, but previously detected by MUA
replied	Replied to
flagged	Marked as important

MHMessage instances offer the following methods:

get_sequences()
    Return a list of the names of sequences that include this message.

set_sequences(*sequences*)
    Set the list of sequences that include this message.

add_sequence(*sequence*)
    Add *sequence* to the list of sequences that include this message.

remove_sequence(*sequence*)
    Remove *sequence* from the list of sequences that include this message.

When an *MHMessage* instance is created based upon a *MaildirMessage* instance, the following conversions take place:

Resulting state	*MaildirMessage* state
"unseen" sequence	no S flag
"replied" sequence	R flag
"flagged" sequence	F flag

When an *MHMessage* instance is created based upon an *mboxMessage* or *MMDFMessage* instance, the **Status** and **X-Status** headers are omitted and the following conversions take place:

Resulting state	*mboxMessage* or *MMDFMessage* state
"unseen" sequence	no R flag
"replied" sequence	A flag
"flagged" sequence	F flag

When an *MHMessage* instance is created based upon a *BabylMessage* instance, the following conversions take place:

Resulting state	*BabylMessage* state
"unseen" sequence	"unseen" label
"replied" sequence	"answered" label

BabylMessage

class mailbox.**BabylMessage**(*message=None*)
    A message with Babyl-specific behaviors. Parameter *message* has the same meaning as with the *Message* constructor.

    Certain message labels, called *attributes*, are defined by convention to have special meanings. The attributes are as follows:

Label	Explanation
unseen	Not read, but previously detected by MUA
deleted	Marked for subsequent deletion
filed	Copied to another file or mailbox
answered	Replied to
forwarded	Forwarded
edited	Modified by the user
resent	Resent

By default, Rmail displays only visible headers. The *BabylMessage* class, though, uses the original headers because they are more complete. Visible headers may be accessed explicitly if desired.

BabylMessage instances offer the following methods:

get_labels()
  Return a list of labels on the message.

set_labels(*labels***)**
  Set the list of labels on the message to *labels*.

add_label(*label***)**
  Add *label* to the list of labels on the message.

remove_label(*label***)**
  Remove *label* from the list of labels on the message.

get_visible()
  Return an *Message* instance whose headers are the message's visible headers and whose body is empty.

set_visible(*visible***)**
  Set the message's visible headers to be the same as the headers in *message*. Parameter *visible* should be a *Message* instance, an *email.message.Message* instance, a string, or a file-like object (which should be open in text mode).

update_visible()
  When a *BabylMessage* instance's original headers are modified, the visible headers are not automatically modified to correspond. This method updates the visible headers as follows: each visible header with a corresponding original header is set to the value of the original header, each visible header without a corresponding original header is removed, and any of *Date*, *From*, *Reply-To*, *To*, *CC*, and *Subject* that are present in the original headers but not the visible headers are added to the visible headers.

When a *BabylMessage* instance is created based upon a *MaildirMessage* instance, the following conversions take place:

Resulting state	*MaildirMessage* state
"unseen" label	no S flag
"deleted" label	T flag
"answered" label	R flag
"forwarded" label	P flag

When a *BabylMessage* instance is created based upon an *mboxMessage* or *MMDFMessage* instance, the *Status* and *X-Status* headers are omitted and the following conversions take place:

Resulting state	*mboxMessage* or *MMDFMessage* state
"unseen" label	no R flag
"deleted" label	D flag
"answered" label	A flag

When a *BabylMessage* instance is created based upon an *MHMessage* instance, the following conversions take place:

Resulting state	*MHMessage* state
"unseen" label	"unseen" sequence
"answered" label	"replied" sequence

MMDFMessage

class mailbox.MMDFMessage(*message=None*)

>A message with MMDF-specific behaviors. Parameter *message* has the same meaning as with the *Message* constructor.
>
>As with message in an mbox mailbox, MMDF messages are stored with the sender's address and the delivery date in an initial line beginning with "From ". Likewise, flags that indicate the state of the message are typically stored in *Status* and *X-Status* headers.
>
>Conventional flags for MMDF messages are identical to those of mbox message and are as follows:

Flag	Meaning	Explanation
R	Read	Read
O	Old	Previously detected by MUA
D	Deleted	Marked for subsequent deletion
F	Flagged	Marked as important
A	Answered	Replied to

>The "R" and "O" flags are stored in the *Status* header, and the "D", "F", and "A" flags are stored in the *X-Status* header. The flags and headers typically appear in the order mentioned.
>
>*MMDFMessage* instances offer the following methods, which are identical to those offered by *mboxMessage*:
>
>**get_from()**
>>Return a string representing the "From " line that marks the start of the message in an mbox mailbox. The leading "From " and the trailing newline are excluded.
>
>**set_from**(*from_*, *time_=None*)
>>Set the "From " line to *from_*, which should be specified without a leading "From " or trailing newline. For convenience, *time_* may be specified and will be formatted appropriately and appended to *from_*. If *time_* is specified, it should be a *time.struct_time* instance, a tuple suitable for passing to *time.strftime()*, or True (to use *time.gmtime()*).
>
>**get_flags()**
>>Return a string specifying the flags that are currently set. If the message complies with the conventional format, the result is the concatenation in the following order of zero or one occurrence of each of 'R', 'O', 'D', 'F', and 'A'.
>
>**set_flags**(*flags*)
>>Set the flags specified by *flags* and unset all others. Parameter *flags* should be the concatenation in any order of zero or more occurrences of each of 'R', 'O', 'D', 'F', and 'A'.

add_flag(*flag*)

Set the flag(s) specified by *flag* without changing other flags. To add more than one flag at a time, *flag* may be a string of more than one character.

remove_flag(*flag*)

Unset the flag(s) specified by *flag* without changing other flags. To remove more than one flag at a time, *flag* maybe a string of more than one character.

When an *MMDFMessage* instance is created based upon a *MaildirMessage* instance, a "From " line is generated based upon the *MaildirMessage* instance's delivery date, and the following conversions take place:

Resulting state	*MaildirMessage* state
R flag	S flag
O flag	"cur" subdirectory
D flag	T flag
F flag	F flag
A flag	R flag

When an *MMDFMessage* instance is created based upon an *MHMessage* instance, the following conversions take place:

Resulting state	*MHMessage* state
R flag and O flag	no "unseen" sequence
O flag	"unseen" sequence
F flag	"flagged" sequence
A flag	"replied" sequence

When an *MMDFMessage* instance is created based upon a *BabylMessage* instance, the following conversions take place:

Resulting state	*BabylMessage* state
R flag and O flag	no "unseen" label
O flag	"unseen" label
D flag	"deleted" label
A flag	"answered" label

When an *MMDFMessage* instance is created based upon an *mboxMessage* instance, the "From " line is copied and all flags directly correspond:

Resulting state	*mboxMessage* state
R flag	R flag
O flag	O flag
D flag	D flag
F flag	F flag
A flag	A flag

19.4.3 Exceptions

The following exception classes are defined in the *mailbox* module:

exception mailbox.Error

The based class for all other module-specific exceptions.

exception `mailbox.NoSuchMailboxError`
   Raised when a mailbox is expected but is not found, such as when instantiating a *Mailbox* subclass with a path that does not exist (and with the *create* parameter set to `False`), or when opening a folder that does not exist.

exception `mailbox.NotEmptyError`
   Raised when a mailbox is not empty but is expected to be, such as when deleting a folder that contains messages.

exception `mailbox.ExternalClashError`
   Raised when some mailbox-related condition beyond the control of the program causes it to be unable to proceed, such as when failing to acquire a lock that another program already holds a lock, or when a uniquely-generated file name already exists.

exception `mailbox.FormatError`
   Raised when the data in a file cannot be parsed, such as when an *MH* instance attempts to read a corrupted `.mh_sequences` file.

19.4.4 Examples

A simple example of printing the subjects of all messages in a mailbox that seem interesting:

```
import mailbox
for message in mailbox.mbox('~/mbox'):
    subject = message['subject']       # Could possibly be None.
    if subject and 'python' in subject.lower():
        print(subject)
```

To copy all mail from a Babyl mailbox to an MH mailbox, converting all of the format-specific information that can be converted:

```
import mailbox
destination = mailbox.MH('~/Mail')
destination.lock()
for message in mailbox.Babyl('~/RMAIL'):
    destination.add(mailbox.MHMessage(message))
destination.flush()
destination.unlock()
```

This example sorts mail from several mailing lists into different mailboxes, being careful to avoid mail corruption due to concurrent modification by other programs, mail loss due to interruption of the program, or premature termination due to malformed messages in the mailbox:

```
import mailbox
import email.errors

list_names = ('python-list', 'python-dev', 'python-bugs')

boxes = {name: mailbox.mbox('~/email/%s' % name) for name in list_names}
inbox = mailbox.Maildir('~/Maildir', factory=None)

for key in inbox.iterkeys():
    try:
        message = inbox[key]
    except email.errors.MessageParseError:
        continue                   # The message is malformed. Just leave it.

    for name in list_names:
```

```
                list_id = message['list-id']
                if list_id and name in list_id:
                    # Get mailbox to use
                    box = boxes[name]

                    # Write copy to disk before removing original.
                    # If there's a crash, you might duplicate a message, but
                    # that's better than losing a message completely.
                    box.lock()
                    box.add(message)
                    box.flush()
                    box.unlock()

                    # Remove original message
                    inbox.lock()
                    inbox.discard(key)
                    inbox.flush()
                    inbox.unlock()
                    break           # Found destination, so stop looking.

for box in boxes.itervalues():
    box.close()
```

19.5 mimetypes — Map filenames to MIME types

Source code: Lib/mimetypes.py

The *mimetypes* module converts between a filename or URL and the MIME type associated with the filename extension. Conversions are provided from filename to MIME type and from MIME type to filename extension; encodings are not supported for the latter conversion.

The module provides one class and a number of convenience functions. The functions are the normal interface to this module, but some applications may be interested in the class as well.

The functions described below provide the primary interface for this module. If the module has not been initialized, they will call *init()* if they rely on the information *init()* sets up.

mimetypes.**guess_type**(*url*, *strict=True*)

    Guess the type of a file based on its filename or URL, given by *url*. The return value is a tuple (`type, encoding`) where *type* is `None` if the type can't be guessed (missing or unknown suffix) or a string of the form `'type/subtype'`, usable for a MIME `content-type` header.

    encoding is `None` for no encoding or the name of the program used to encode (e.g. `compress` or `gzip`). The encoding is suitable for use as a `Content-Encoding` header, **not** as a `Content-Transfer-Encoding` header. The mappings are table driven. Encoding suffixes are case sensitive; type suffixes are first tried case sensitively, then case insensitively.

    The optional *strict* argument is a flag specifying whether the list of known MIME types is limited to only the official types registered with IANA. When *strict* is `True` (the default), only the IANA types are supported; when *strict* is `False`, some additional non-standard but commonly used MIME types are also recognized.

mimetypes.**guess_all_extensions**(*type*, *strict=True*)

    Guess the extensions for a file based on its MIME type, given by *type*. The return value is a list of strings giving all possible filename extensions, including the leading dot (`'.'`). The extensions are not guaranteed to have been associated with any particular data stream, but would be mapped to the MIME type *type* by *guess_type()*.

The optional *strict* argument has the same meaning as with the *guess_type()* function.

mimetypes.**guess_extension**(*type, strict=True*)
: Guess the extension for a file based on its MIME type, given by *type*. The return value is a string giving a filename extension, including the leading dot ('.'). The extension is not guaranteed to have been associated with any particular data stream, but would be mapped to the MIME type *type* by *guess_type()*. If no extension can be guessed for *type*, None is returned.

    The optional *strict* argument has the same meaning as with the *guess_type()* function.

Some additional functions and data items are available for controlling the behavior of the module.

mimetypes.**init**(*files=None*)
: Initialize the internal data structures. If given, *files* must be a sequence of file names which should be used to augment the default type map. If omitted, the file names to use are taken from *knownfiles*; on Windows, the current registry settings are loaded. Each file named in *files* or *knownfiles* takes precedence over those named before it. Calling *init()* repeatedly is allowed.

    Specifying an empty list for *files* will prevent the system defaults from being applied: only the well-known values will be present from a built-in list.

    Changed in version 3.2: Previously, Windows registry settings were ignored.

mimetypes.**read_mime_types**(*filename*)
: Load the type map given in the file *filename*, if it exists. The type map is returned as a dictionary mapping filename extensions, including the leading dot ('.'), to strings of the form 'type/subtype'. If the file *filename* does not exist or cannot be read, None is returned.

mimetypes.**add_type**(*type, ext, strict=True*)
: Add a mapping from the MIME type *type* to the extension *ext*. When the extension is already known, the new type will replace the old one. When the type is already known the extension will be added to the list of known extensions.

    When *strict* is True (the default), the mapping will be added to the official MIME types, otherwise to the non-standard ones.

mimetypes.**inited**
: Flag indicating whether or not the global data structures have been initialized. This is set to True by *init()*.

mimetypes.**knownfiles**
: List of type map file names commonly installed. These files are typically named `mime.types` and are installed in different locations by different packages.

mimetypes.**suffix_map**
: Dictionary mapping suffixes to suffixes. This is used to allow recognition of encoded files for which the encoding and the type are indicated by the same extension. For example, the `.tgz` extension is mapped to `.tar.gz` to allow the encoding and type to be recognized separately.

mimetypes.**encodings_map**
: Dictionary mapping filename extensions to encoding types.

mimetypes.**types_map**
: Dictionary mapping filename extensions to MIME types.

mimetypes.**common_types**
: Dictionary mapping filename extensions to non-standard, but commonly found MIME types.

An example usage of the module:

```
>>> import mimetypes
>>> mimetypes.init()
>>> mimetypes.knownfiles
['/etc/mime.types', '/etc/httpd/mime.types', ... ]
>>> mimetypes.suffix_map['.tgz']
'.tar.gz'
>>> mimetypes.encodings_map['.gz']
'gzip'
>>> mimetypes.types_map['.tgz']
'application/x-tar-gz'
```

19.5.1 MimeTypes Objects

The *MimeTypes* class may be useful for applications which may want more than one MIME-type database; it provides an interface similar to the one of the *mimetypes* module.

class mimetypes.MimeTypes(*filenames=()*, *strict=True*)

 This class represents a MIME-types database. By default, it provides access to the same database as the rest of this module. The initial database is a copy of that provided by the module, and may be extended by loading additional mime.types-style files into the database using the *read()* or *readfp()* methods. The mapping dictionaries may also be cleared before loading additional data if the default data is not desired.

 The optional *filenames* parameter can be used to cause additional files to be loaded "on top" of the default database.

 suffix_map

  Dictionary mapping suffixes to suffixes. This is used to allow recognition of encoded files for which the encoding and the type are indicated by the same extension. For example, the .tgz extension is mapped to .tar.gz to allow the encoding and type to be recognized separately. This is initially a copy of the global *suffix_map* defined in the module.

 encodings_map

  Dictionary mapping filename extensions to encoding types. This is initially a copy of the global *encodings_map* defined in the module.

 types_map

  Tuple containing two dictionaries, mapping filename extensions to MIME types: the first dictionary is for the non-standards types and the second one is for the standard types. They are initialized by *common_types* and *types_map*.

 types_map_inv

  Tuple containing two dictionaries, mapping MIME types to a list of filename extensions: the first dictionary is for the non-standards types and the second one is for the standard types. They are initialized by *common_types* and *types_map*.

 guess_extension(*type*, *strict=True*)

  Similar to the *guess_extension()* function, using the tables stored as part of the object.

 guess_type(*url*, *strict=True*)

  Similar to the *guess_type()* function, using the tables stored as part of the object.

 guess_all_extensions(*type*, *strict=True*)

  Similar to the *guess_all_extensions()* function, using the tables stored as part of the object.

 read(*filename*, *strict=True*)

  Load MIME information from a file named *filename*. This uses *readfp()* to parse the file.

If *strict* is `True`, information will be added to list of standard types, else to the list of non-standard types.

readfp(*fp, strict=True*)
Load MIME type information from an open file *fp*. The file must have the format of the standard `mime.types` files.

If *strict* is `True`, information will be added to the list of standard types, else to the list of non-standard types.

read_windows_registry(*strict=True*)
Load MIME type information from the Windows registry. Availability: Windows.

If *strict* is `True`, information will be added to the list of standard types, else to the list of non-standard types.

New in version 3.2.

19.6 `base64` — Base16, Base32, Base64, Base85 Data Encodings

Source code: Lib/base64.py

This module provides functions for encoding binary data to printable ASCII characters and decoding such encodings back to binary data. It provides encoding and decoding functions for the encodings specified in RFC 3548, which defines the Base16, Base32, and Base64 algorithms, and for the de-facto standard Ascii85 and Base85 encodings.

The RFC 3548 encodings are suitable for encoding binary data so that it can safely sent by email, used as parts of URLs, or included as part of an HTTP POST request. The encoding algorithm is not the same as the **uuencode** program.

There are two interfaces provided by this module. The modern interface supports encoding *bytes-like objects* to ASCII *bytes*, and decoding *bytes-like objects* or strings containing ASCII to *bytes*. Both base-64 alphabets defined in RFC 3548 (normal, and URL- and filesystem-safe) are supported.

The legacy interface does not support decoding from strings, but it does provide functions for encoding and decoding to and from *file objects*. It only supports the Base64 standard alphabet, and it adds newlines every 76 characters as per RFC 2045. Note that if you are looking for RFC 2045 support you probably want to be looking at the `email` package instead.

Changed in version 3.3: ASCII-only Unicode strings are now accepted by the decoding functions of the modern interface.

Changed in version 3.4: Any *bytes-like objects* are now accepted by all encoding and decoding functions in this module. Ascii85/Base85 support added.

The modern interface provides:

`base64.`**b64encode**(*s, altchars=None*)
Encode the *bytes-like object* *s* using Base64 and return the encoded *bytes*.

Optional *altchars* must be a *bytes-like object* of at least length 2 (additional characters are ignored) which specifies an alternative alphabet for the `+` and `/` characters. This allows an application to e.g. generate URL or filesystem safe Base64 strings. The default is `None`, for which the standard Base64 alphabet is used.

`base64.`**b64decode**(*s, altchars=None, validate=False*)
Decode the Base64 encoded *bytes-like object* or ASCII string *s* and return the decoded *bytes*.

Optional *altchars* must be a *bytes-like object* or ASCII string of at least length 2 (additional characters are ignored) which specifies the alternative alphabet used instead of the + and / characters.

A *binascii.Error* exception is raised if *s* is incorrectly padded.

If *validate* is `False` (the default), characters that are neither in the normal base-64 alphabet nor the alternative alphabet are discarded prior to the padding check. If *validate* is `True`, these non-alphabet characters in the input result in a *binascii.Error*.

base64.**standard_b64encode**(*s*)
: Encode *bytes-like object* *s* using the standard Base64 alphabet and return the encoded *bytes*.

base64.**standard_b64decode**(*s*)
: Decode *bytes-like object* or ASCII string *s* using the standard Base64 alphabet and return the decoded *bytes*.

base64.**urlsafe_b64encode**(*s*)
: Encode *bytes-like object* *s* using the URL- and filesystem-safe alphabet, which substitutes - instead of + and _ instead of / in the standard Base64 alphabet, and return the encoded *bytes*. The result can still contain =.

base64.**urlsafe_b64decode**(*s*)
: Decode *bytes-like object* or ASCII string *s* using the URL- and filesystem-safe alphabet, which substitutes - instead of + and _ instead of / in the standard Base64 alphabet, and return the decoded *bytes*.

base64.**b32encode**(*s*)
: Encode the *bytes-like object* *s* using Base32 and return the encoded *bytes*.

base64.**b32decode**(*s*, *casefold=False*, *map01=None*)
: Decode the Base32 encoded *bytes-like object* or ASCII string *s* and return the decoded *bytes*.

Optional *casefold* is a flag specifying whether a lowercase alphabet is acceptable as input. For security purposes, the default is `False`.

RFC 3548 allows for optional mapping of the digit 0 (zero) to the letter O (oh), and for optional mapping of the digit 1 (one) to either the letter I (eye) or letter L (el). The optional argument *map01* when not `None`, specifies which letter the digit 1 should be mapped to (when *map01* is not `None`, the digit 0 is always mapped to the letter O). For security purposes the default is `None`, so that 0 and 1 are not allowed in the input.

A *binascii.Error* is raised if *s* is incorrectly padded or if there are non-alphabet characters present in the input.

base64.**b16encode**(*s*)
: Encode the *bytes-like object* *s* using Base16 and return the encoded *bytes*.

base64.**b16decode**(*s*, *casefold=False*)
: Decode the Base16 encoded *bytes-like object* or ASCII string *s* and return the decoded *bytes*.

Optional *casefold* is a flag specifying whether a lowercase alphabet is acceptable as input. For security purposes, the default is `False`.

A *binascii.Error* is raised if *s* is incorrectly padded or if there are non-alphabet characters present in the input.

base64.**a85encode**(*b*, ***, *foldspaces=False*, *wrapcol=0*, *pad=False*, *adobe=False*)
: Encode the *bytes-like object* *b* using Ascii85 and return the encoded *bytes*.

foldspaces is an optional flag that uses the special short sequence 'y' instead of 4 consecutive spaces (ASCII 0x20) as supported by 'btoa'. This feature is not supported by the "standard" Ascii85 encoding.

wrapcol controls whether the output should have newline (`b'\n'`) characters added to it. If this is non-zero, each output line will be at most this many characters long.

pad controls whether the input is padded to a multiple of 4 before encoding. Note that the `btoa` implementation always pads.

adobe controls whether the encoded byte sequence is framed with `<~` and `~>`, which is used by the Adobe implementation.

New in version 3.4.

base64.a85decode(*b*, *, *foldspaces=False*, *adobe=False*, *ignorechars=b' \t\n\r\v'*)
Decode the Ascii85 encoded *bytes-like object* or ASCII string *b* and return the decoded *bytes*.

foldspaces is a flag that specifies whether the 'y' short sequence should be accepted as shorthand for 4 consecutive spaces (ASCII 0x20). This feature is not supported by the "standard" Ascii85 encoding.

adobe controls whether the input sequence is in Adobe Ascii85 format (i.e. is framed with `<~` and `~>`).

ignorechars should be a *bytes-like object* or ASCII string containing characters to ignore from the input. This should only contain whitespace characters, and by default contains all whitespace characters in ASCII.

New in version 3.4.

base64.b85encode(*b*, *pad=False*)
Encode the *bytes-like object* *b* using base85 (as used in e.g. git-style binary diffs) and return the encoded *bytes*.

If *pad* is true, the input is padded with `b'\0'` so its length is a multiple of 4 bytes before encoding.

New in version 3.4.

base64.b85decode(*b*)
Decode the base85-encoded *bytes-like object* or ASCII string *b* and return the decoded *bytes*. Padding is implicitly removed, if necessary.

New in version 3.4.

Note: Both Base85 and Ascii85 have an expansion factor of 5 to 4 (5 Base85 or Ascii85 characters can encode 4 binary bytes), while the better-known Base64 has an expansion factor of 6 to 4. They are therefore more efficient when space expensive. They differ by details such as the character map used for encoding.

The legacy interface:

base64.decode(*input*, *output*)
Decode the contents of the binary *input* file and write the resulting binary data to the *output* file. *input* and *output* must be *file objects*. *input* will be read until `input.readline()` returns an empty bytes object.

base64.decodebytes(*s*)
Decode the *bytes-like object* *s*, which must contain one or more lines of base64 encoded data, and return the decoded *bytes*.

New in version 3.1.

base64.decodestring(*s*)
Deprecated alias of `decodebytes()`.

Deprecated since version 3.1.

base64.encode(*input*, *output*)
Encode the contents of the binary *input* file and write the resulting base64 encoded data to the *output* file. *input* and *output* must be *file objects*. *input* will be read until `input.read()` returns an empty bytes object. `encode()` inserts a newline character (`b'\n'`) after every 76 bytes of the output, as well as ensuring that the output always ends with a newline, as per RFC 2045 (MIME).

base64.encodebytes(*s*)
 Encode the *bytes-like object* *s*, which can contain arbitrary binary data, and return *bytes* containing the base64-encoded data, with newlines (`b'\n'`) inserted after every 76 bytes of output, and ensuring that there is a trailing newline, as per RFC 2045 (MIME).

 New in version 3.1.

base64.encodestring(*s*)
 Deprecated alias of *encodebytes()*.

 Deprecated since version 3.1.

An example usage of the module:

```
>>> import base64
>>> encoded = base64.b64encode(b'data to be encoded')
>>> encoded
b'ZGF0YSB0byBiZSBlbmNvZGVk'
>>> data = base64.b64decode(encoded)
>>> data
b'data to be encoded'
```

See also:

Module *binascii* Support module containing ASCII-to-binary and binary-to-ASCII conversions.

 RFC 1521 **- MIME (Multipurpose Internet Mail Extensions) Part One: Mechanisms for Specifying**
  Section 5.2, "Base64 Content-Transfer-Encoding," provides the definition of the base64 encoding.

19.7 `binhex` — Encode and decode binhex4 files

Source code: Lib/binhex.py

This module encodes and decodes files in binhex4 format, a format allowing representation of Macintosh files in ASCII. Only the data fork is handled.

The *binhex* module defines the following functions:

binhex.binhex(*input*, *output*)
 Convert a binary file with filename *input* to binhex file *output*. The *output* parameter can either be a filename or a file-like object (any object supporting a `write()` and `close()` method).

binhex.hexbin(*input*, *output*)
 Decode a binhex file *input*. *input* may be a filename or a file-like object supporting `read()` and `close()` methods. The resulting file is written to a file named *output*, unless the argument is `None` in which case the output filename is read from the binhex file.

The following exception is also defined:

exception binhex.Error
 Exception raised when something can't be encoded using the binhex format (for example, a filename is too long to fit in the filename field), or when input is not properly encoded binhex data.

See also:

Module *binascii* Support module containing ASCII-to-binary and binary-to-ASCII conversions.

19.7.1 Notes

There is an alternative, more powerful interface to the coder and decoder, see the source for details.

If you code or decode textfiles on non-Macintosh platforms they will still use the old Macintosh newline convention (carriage-return as end of line).

19.8 `binascii` — Convert between binary and ASCII

The `binascii` module contains a number of methods to convert between binary and various ASCII-encoded binary representations. Normally, you will not use these functions directly but use wrapper modules like `uu`, `base64`, or `binhex` instead. The `binascii` module contains low-level functions written in C for greater speed that are used by the higher-level modules.

Note: a2b_* functions accept Unicode strings containing only ASCII characters. Other functions only accept *bytes-like objects* (such as `bytes`, `bytearray` and other objects that support the buffer protocol).

Changed in version 3.3: ASCII-only unicode strings are now accepted by the a2b_* functions.

The `binascii` module defines the following functions:

binascii.a2b_uu(*string*)
    Convert a single line of uuencoded data back to binary and return the binary data. Lines normally contain 45 (binary) bytes, except for the last line. Line data may be followed by whitespace.

binascii.b2a_uu(*data*)
    Convert binary data to a line of ASCII characters, the return value is the converted line, including a newline char. The length of *data* should be at most 45.

binascii.a2b_base64(*string*)
    Convert a block of base64 data back to binary and return the binary data. More than one line may be passed at a time.

binascii.b2a_base64(*data, *, newline=True*)
    Convert binary data to a line of ASCII characters in base64 coding. The return value is the converted line, including a newline char if *newline* is true. The output of this function conforms to RFC 3548.

Changed in version 3.6: Added the *newline* parameter.

binascii.a2b_qp(*data, header=False*)
    Convert a block of quoted-printable data back to binary and return the binary data. More than one line may be passed at a time. If the optional argument *header* is present and true, underscores will be decoded as spaces.

binascii.b2a_qp(*data, quotetabs=False, istext=True, header=False*)
    Convert binary data to a line(s) of ASCII characters in quoted-printable encoding. The return value is the converted line(s). If the optional argument *quotetabs* is present and true, all tabs and spaces will be encoded. If the optional argument *istext* is present and true, newlines are not encoded but trailing whitespace will be encoded. If the optional argument *header* is present and true, spaces will be encoded as underscores per RFC1522. If the optional argument *header* is present and false, newline characters will be encoded as well; otherwise linefeed conversion might corrupt the binary data stream.

binascii.a2b_hqx(*string*)
    Convert binhex4 formatted ASCII data to binary, without doing RLE-decompression. The string should contain a complete number of binary bytes, or (in case of the last portion of the binhex4 data) have the remaining bits zero.

binascii.rledecode_hqx(*data*)
> Perform RLE-decompression on the data, as per the binhex4 standard. The algorithm uses 0x90 after a byte as a repeat indicator, followed by a count. A count of 0 specifies a byte value of 0x90. The routine returns the decompressed data, unless data input data ends in an orphaned repeat indicator, in which case the *Incomplete* exception is raised.
>
> Changed in version 3.2: Accept only bytestring or bytearray objects as input.

binascii.rlecode_hqx(*data*)
> Perform binhex4 style RLE-compression on *data* and return the result.

binascii.b2a_hqx(*data*)
> Perform hexbin4 binary-to-ASCII translation and return the resulting string. The argument should already be RLE-coded, and have a length divisible by 3 (except possibly the last fragment).

binascii.crc_hqx(*data*, *value*)
> Compute a 16-bit CRC value of *data*, starting with *value* as the initial CRC, and return the result. This uses the CRC-CCITT polynomial $x^{16} + x^{12} + x^5 + 1$, often represented as 0x1021. This CRC is used in the binhex4 format.

binascii.crc32(*data*[, *value*])
> Compute CRC-32, the 32-bit checksum of *data*, starting with an initial CRC of *value*. The default initial CRC is zero. The algorithm is consistent with the ZIP file checksum. Since the algorithm is designed for use as a checksum algorithm, it is not suitable for use as a general hash algorithm. Use as follows:

```
print(binascii.crc32(b"hello world"))
# Or, in two pieces:
crc = binascii.crc32(b"hello")
crc = binascii.crc32(b" world", crc)
print('crc32 = {:#010x}'.format(crc))
```

> Changed in version 3.0: The result is always unsigned. To generate the same numeric value across all Python versions and platforms, use crc32(data) & 0xffffffff.

binascii.b2a_hex(*data*)
binascii.hexlify(*data*)
> Return the hexadecimal representation of the binary *data*. Every byte of *data* is converted into the corresponding 2-digit hex representation. The returned bytes object is therefore twice as long as the length of *data*.

binascii.a2b_hex(*hexstr*)
binascii.unhexlify(*hexstr*)
> Return the binary data represented by the hexadecimal string *hexstr*. This function is the inverse of *b2a_hex()*. *hexstr* must contain an even number of hexadecimal digits (which can be upper or lower case), otherwise an *Error* exception is raised.

exception binascii.Error
> Exception raised on errors. These are usually programming errors.

exception binascii.Incomplete
> Exception raised on incomplete data. These are usually not programming errors, but may be handled by reading a little more data and trying again.

See also:

Module *base64* Support for RFC compliant base64-style encoding in base 16, 32, 64, and 85.

Module *binhex* Support for the binhex format used on the Macintosh.

Module *uu* Support for UU encoding used on Unix.

Module *quopri* Support for quoted-printable encoding used in MIME email messages.

19.9 `quopri` — Encode and decode MIME quoted-printable data

Source code: Lib/quopri.py

This module performs quoted-printable transport encoding and decoding, as defined in RFC 1521: "MIME (Multipurpose Internet Mail Extensions) Part One: Mechanisms for Specifying and Describing the Format of Internet Message Bodies". The quoted-printable encoding is designed for data where there are relatively few nonprintable characters; the base64 encoding scheme available via the `base64` module is more compact if there are many such characters, as when sending a graphics file.

`quopri.decode(`*input, output, header=False*`)`
Decode the contents of the *input* file and write the resulting decoded binary data to the *output* file. *input* and *output* must be binary file objects. If the optional argument *header* is present and true, underscore will be decoded as space. This is used to decode "Q"-encoded headers as described in RFC 1522: "MIME (Multipurpose Internet Mail Extensions) Part Two: Message Header Extensions for Non-ASCII Text".

`quopri.encode(`*input, output, quotetabs, header=False*`)`
Encode the contents of the *input* file and write the resulting quoted-printable data to the *output* file. *input* and *output* must be binary file objects. *quotetabs*, a non-optional flag which controls whether to encode embedded spaces and tabs; when true it encodes such embedded whitespace, and when false it leaves them unencoded. Note that spaces and tabs appearing at the end of lines are always encoded, as per RFC 1521. *header* is a flag which controls if spaces are encoded as underscores as per RFC 1522.

`quopri.decodestring(`*s, header=False*`)`
Like `decode()`, except that it accepts a source `bytes` and returns the corresponding decoded `bytes`.

`quopri.encodestring(`*s, quotetabs=False, header=False*`)`
Like `encode()`, except that it accepts a source `bytes` and returns the corresponding encoded `bytes`. By default, it sends a `False` value to *quotetabs* parameter of the `encode()` function.

See also:

Module `base64` Encode and decode MIME base64 data

19.10 `uu` — Encode and decode uuencode files

Source code: Lib/uu.py

This module encodes and decodes files in uuencode format, allowing arbitrary binary data to be transferred over ASCII-only connections. Wherever a file argument is expected, the methods accept a file-like object. For backwards compatibility, a string containing a pathname is also accepted, and the corresponding file will be opened for reading and writing; the pathname `'-'` is understood to mean the standard input or output. However, this interface is deprecated; it's better for the caller to open the file itself, and be sure that, when required, the mode is `'rb'` or `'wb'` on Windows.

This code was contributed by Lance Ellinghouse, and modified by Jack Jansen.

The `uu` module defines the following functions:

`uu.encode(`*in_file, out_file, name=None, mode=None*`)`
Uuencode file *in_file* into file *out_file*. The uuencoded file will have the header specifying *name* and *mode* as the defaults for the results of decoding the file. The default defaults are taken from *in_file*, or `'-'` and `0o666` respectively.

uu.decode(*in_file, out_file=None, mode=None, quiet=False*)
This call decodes uuencoded file *in_file* placing the result on file *out_file*. If *out_file* is a pathname, *mode* is used to set the permission bits if the file must be created. Defaults for *out_file* and *mode* are taken from the uuencode header. However, if the file specified in the header already exists, a `uu.Error` is raised.

`decode()` may print a warning to standard error if the input was produced by an incorrect uuencoder and Python could recover from that error. Setting *quiet* to a true value silences this warning.

exception uu.Error
Subclass of `Exception`, this can be raised by `uu.decode()` under various situations, such as described above, but also including a badly formatted header, or truncated input file.

See also:

Module `binascii` Support module containing ASCII-to-binary and binary-to-ASCII conversions.

CHAPTER
TWENTY

STRUCTURED MARKUP PROCESSING TOOLS

Python supports a variety of modules to work with various forms of structured data markup. This includes modules to work with the Standard Generalized Markup Language (SGML) and the Hypertext Markup Language (HTML), and several interfaces for working with the Extensible Markup Language (XML).

20.1 `html` — HyperText Markup Language support

Source code: Lib/html/__init__.py

This module defines utilities to manipulate HTML.

`html.escape(s, quote=True)`
    Convert the characters `&`, `<` and `>` in string *s* to HTML-safe sequences. Use this if you need to display text that might contain such characters in HTML. If the optional flag *quote* is true, the characters (`"`) and (`'`) are also translated; this helps for inclusion in an HTML attribute value delimited by quotes, as in `<a href="...">`.

    New in version 3.2.

`html.unescape(s)`
    Convert all named and numeric character references (e.g. `&gt;`, `&#62;`, `&x3e;`) in the string *s* to the corresponding unicode characters. This function uses the rules defined by the HTML 5 standard for both valid and invalid character references, and the *list of HTML 5 named character references*.

    New in version 3.4.

Submodules in the `html` package are:

- *html.parser* – HTML/XHTML parser with lenient parsing mode
- *html.entities* – HTML entity definitions

20.2 `html.parser` — Simple HTML and XHTML parser

Source code: Lib/html/parser.py

This module defines a class *HTMLParser* which serves as the basis for parsing text files formatted in HTML (HyperText Mark-up Language) and XHTML.

1047

class html.parser.HTMLParser(*, *convert_charrefs=True*)

Create a parser instance able to parse invalid markup.

If *convert_charrefs* is `True` (the default), all character references (except the ones in `script/style` elements) are automatically converted to the corresponding Unicode characters.

An *HTMLParser* instance is fed HTML data and calls handler methods when start tags, end tags, text, comments, and other markup elements are encountered. The user should subclass *HTMLParser* and override its methods to implement the desired behavior.

This parser does not check that end tags match start tags or call the end-tag handler for elements which are closed implicitly by closing an outer element.

Changed in version 3.4: *convert_charrefs* keyword argument added.

Changed in version 3.5: The default value for argument *convert_charrefs* is now `True`.

20.2.1 Example HTML Parser Application

As a basic example, below is a simple HTML parser that uses the *HTMLParser* class to print out start tags, end tags, and data as they are encountered:

```
from html.parser import HTMLParser

class MyHTMLParser(HTMLParser):
    def handle_starttag(self, tag, attrs):
        print("Encountered a start tag:", tag)

    def handle_endtag(self, tag):
        print("Encountered an end tag :", tag)

    def handle_data(self, data):
        print("Encountered some data  :", data)

parser = MyHTMLParser()
parser.feed('<html><head><title>Test</title></head>'
            '<body><h1>Parse me!</h1></body></html>')
```

The output will then be:

```
Encountered a start tag: html
Encountered a start tag: head
Encountered a start tag: title
Encountered some data  : Test
Encountered an end tag : title
Encountered an end tag : head
Encountered a start tag: body
Encountered a start tag: h1
Encountered some data  : Parse me!
Encountered an end tag : h1
Encountered an end tag : body
Encountered an end tag : html
```

20.2.2 HTMLParser Methods

HTMLParser instances have the following methods:

HTMLParser.feed(*data*)
> Feed some text to the parser. It is processed insofar as it consists of complete elements; incomplete data is buffered until more data is fed or `close()` is called. *data* must be `str`.

HTMLParser.close()
> Force processing of all buffered data as if it were followed by an end-of-file mark. This method may be redefined by a derived class to define additional processing at the end of the input, but the redefined version should always call the *HTMLParser* base class method `close()`.

HTMLParser.reset()
> Reset the instance. Loses all unprocessed data. This is called implicitly at instantiation time.

HTMLParser.getpos()
> Return current line number and offset.

HTMLParser.get_starttag_text()
> Return the text of the most recently opened start tag. This should not normally be needed for structured processing, but may be useful in dealing with HTML "as deployed" or for re-generating input with minimal changes (whitespace between attributes can be preserved, etc.).

The following methods are called when data or markup elements are encountered and they are meant to be overridden in a subclass. The base class implementations do nothing (except for `handle_startendtag()`):

HTMLParser.handle_starttag(*tag, attrs*)
> This method is called to handle the start of a tag (e.g. `<div id="main">`).
>
> The *tag* argument is the name of the tag converted to lower case. The *attrs* argument is a list of (`name`, `value`) pairs containing the attributes found inside the tag's `<>` brackets. The *name* will be translated to lower case, and quotes in the *value* have been removed, and character and entity references have been replaced.
>
> For instance, for the tag `<A HREF="https://www.cwi.nl/">`, this method would be called as `handle_starttag('a', [('href', 'https://www.cwi.nl/')])`.
>
> All entity references from `html.entities` are replaced in the attribute values.

HTMLParser.handle_endtag(*tag*)
> This method is called to handle the end tag of an element (e.g. `</div>`).
>
> The *tag* argument is the name of the tag converted to lower case.

HTMLParser.handle_startendtag(*tag, attrs*)
> Similar to `handle_starttag()`, but called when the parser encounters an XHTML-style empty tag (`<img ... />`). This method may be overridden by subclasses which require this particular lexical information; the default implementation simply calls `handle_starttag()` and `handle_endtag()`.

HTMLParser.handle_data(*data*)
> This method is called to process arbitrary data (e.g. text nodes and the content of `<script>...</script>` and `<style>...</style>`).

HTMLParser.handle_entityref(*name*)
> This method is called to process a named character reference of the form `&name;` (e.g. `&gt;`), where *name* is a general entity reference (e.g. `'gt'`). This method is never called if *convert_charrefs* is `True`.

HTMLParser.handle_charref(*name*)
> This method is called to process decimal and hexadecimal numeric character references of the form `&#NNN;` and `&#xNNN;`. For example, the decimal equivalent for `&gt;` is `&#62;`, whereas the hexadecimal is `&#x3E;`; in this case the method will receive `'62'` or `'x3E'`. This method is never called if *convert_charrefs* is `True`.

HTMLParser.handle_comment(*data*)
> This method is called when a comment is encountered (e.g. `<!--comment-->`).

For example, the comment `<!-- comment -->` will cause this method to be called with the argument `' comment '`.

The content of Internet Explorer conditional comments (condcoms) will also be sent to this method, so, for `<!--[if IE 9]>IE9-specific content<![endif]-->`, this method will receive `'[if IE 9]>IE9-specific content<![endif]'`.

HTMLParser.handle_decl(*decl*)

This method is called to handle an HTML doctype declaration (e.g. `<!DOCTYPE html>`).

The *decl* parameter will be the entire contents of the declaration inside the `<!...>` markup (e.g. `'DOCTYPE html'`).

HTMLParser.handle_pi(*data*)

Method called when a processing instruction is encountered. The *data* parameter will contain the entire processing instruction. For example, for the processing instruction `<?proc color='red'>`, this method would be called as `handle_pi("proc color='red'")`. It is intended to be overridden by a derived class; the base class implementation does nothing.

> **Note:** The *HTMLParser* class uses the SGML syntactic rules for processing instructions. An XHTML processing instruction using the trailing `'?'` will cause the `'?'` to be included in *data*.

HTMLParser.unknown_decl(*data*)

This method is called when an unrecognized declaration is read by the parser.

The *data* parameter will be the entire contents of the declaration inside the `<![...]>` markup. It is sometimes useful to be overridden by a derived class. The base class implementation does nothing.

20.2.3 Examples

The following class implements a parser that will be used to illustrate more examples:

```
from html.parser import HTMLParser
from html.entities import name2codepoint

class MyHTMLParser(HTMLParser):
    def handle_starttag(self, tag, attrs):
        print("Start tag:", tag)
        for attr in attrs:
            print("     attr:", attr)

    def handle_endtag(self, tag):
        print("End tag  :", tag)

    def handle_data(self, data):
        print("Data     :", data)

    def handle_comment(self, data):
        print("Comment  :", data)

    def handle_entityref(self, name):
        c = chr(name2codepoint[name])
        print("Named ent:", c)

    def handle_charref(self, name):
        if name.startswith('x'):
            c = chr(int(name[1:], 16))
```

```
            else:
                c = chr(int(name))
            print("Num ent   :", c)

    def handle_decl(self, data):
        print("Decl     :", data)

parser = MyHTMLParser()
```

Parsing a doctype:

```
>>> parser.feed('<!DOCTYPE HTML PUBLIC "-//W3C//DTD HTML 4.01//EN" '
...             '"http://www.w3.org/TR/html4/strict.dtd">')
Decl     : DOCTYPE HTML PUBLIC "-//W3C//DTD HTML 4.01//EN" "http://www.w3.org/TR/html4/strict.dtd"
```

Parsing an element with a few attributes and a title:

```
>>> parser.feed('<img src="python-logo.png" alt="The Python logo">')
Start tag: img
     attr: ('src', 'python-logo.png')
     attr: ('alt', 'The Python logo')
>>>
>>> parser.feed('<h1>Python</h1>')
Start tag: h1
Data     : Python
End tag  : h1
```

The content of `script` and `style` elements is returned as is, without further parsing:

```
>>> parser.feed('<style type="text/css">#python { color: green }</style>')
Start tag: style
     attr: ('type', 'text/css')
Data     : #python { color: green }
End tag  : style

>>> parser.feed('<script type="text/javascript">'
...             'alert("<strong>hello!</strong>");</script>')
Start tag: script
     attr: ('type', 'text/javascript')
Data     : alert("<strong>hello!</strong>");
End tag  : script
```

Parsing comments:

```
>>> parser.feed('<!-- a comment -->'
...             '<!--[if IE 9]>IE-specific content<![endif]-->')
Comment  :  a comment 
Comment  : [if IE 9]>IE-specific content<![endif]
```

Parsing named and numeric character references and converting them to the correct char (note: these 3 references are all equivalent to `'>'`):

```
>>> parser.feed('&gt;&#62;&#x3E;')
Named ent: >
Num ent  : >
Num ent  : >
```

Feeding incomplete chunks to `feed()` works, but `handle_data()` might be called more than once (unless `convert_charrefs` is set to `True`):

```
>>> for chunk in ['<sp', 'an>buff', 'ered ', 'text</s', 'pan>']:
...     parser.feed(chunk)
...
Start tag: span
Data     : buff
Data     : ered
Data     : text
End tag  : span
```

Parsing invalid HTML (e.g. unquoted attributes) also works:

```
>>> parser.feed('<p><a class=link href=#main>tag soup</p ></a>')
Start tag: p
Start tag: a
    attr: ('class', 'link')
    attr: ('href', '#main')
Data     : tag soup
End tag  : p
End tag  : a
```

20.3 `html.entities` — Definitions of HTML general entities

Source code: Lib/html/entities.py

This module defines four dictionaries, `html5`, `name2codepoint`, `codepoint2name`, and `entitydefs`.

`html.entities.html5`
    A dictionary that maps HTML5 named character references[1] to the equivalent Unicode character(s), e.g. `html5['gt;'] == '>'`. Note that the trailing semicolon is included in the name (e.g. `'gt;'`), however some of the names are accepted by the standard even without the semicolon: in this case the name is present with and without the `';'`. See also `html.unescape()`.

    New in version 3.3.

`html.entities.entitydefs`
    A dictionary mapping XHTML 1.0 entity definitions to their replacement text in ISO Latin-1.

`html.entities.name2codepoint`
    A dictionary that maps HTML entity names to the Unicode code points.

`html.entities.codepoint2name`
    A dictionary that maps Unicode code points to HTML entity names.

20.4 XML Processing Modules

Source code: Lib/xml/

Python's interfaces for processing XML are grouped in the `xml` package.

---

[1] See https://www.w3.org/TR/html5/syntax.html#named-character-references

> **Warning:** The XML modules are not secure against erroneous or maliciously constructed data. If you need to parse untrusted or unauthenticated data see the *XML vulnerabilities* and *The defusedxml and defusedexpat Packages* sections.

It is important to note that modules in the `xml` package require that there be at least one SAX-compliant XML parser available. The Expat parser is included with Python, so the `xml.parsers.expat` module will always be available.

The documentation for the `xml.dom` and `xml.sax` packages are the definition of the Python bindings for the DOM and SAX interfaces.

The XML handling submodules are:

- `xml.etree.ElementTree`: the ElementTree API, a simple and lightweight XML processor
- `xml.dom`: the DOM API definition
- `xml.dom.minidom`: a minimal DOM implementation
- `xml.dom.pulldom`: support for building partial DOM trees
- `xml.sax`: SAX2 base classes and convenience functions
- `xml.parsers.expat`: the Expat parser binding

20.4.1 XML vulnerabilities

The XML processing modules are not secure against maliciously constructed data. An attacker can abuse XML features to carry out denial of service attacks, access local files, generate network connections to other machines, or circumvent firewalls.

The following table gives an overview of the known attacks and whether the various modules are vulnerable to them.

kind	sax	etree	minidom	pulldom	xmlrpc
billion laughs	**Vulnerable**	**Vulnerable**	**Vulnerable**	**Vulnerable**	**Vulnerable**
quadratic blowup	**Vulnerable**	**Vulnerable**	**Vulnerable**	**Vulnerable**	**Vulnerable**
external entity expansion	**Vulnerable**	Safe (1)	Safe (2)	**Vulnerable**	Safe (3)
DTD retrieval	**Vulnerable**	Safe	Safe	**Vulnerable**	Safe
decompression bomb	Safe	Safe	Safe	Safe	**Vulnerable**

1. `xml.etree.ElementTree` doesn't expand external entities and raises a `ParserError` when an entity occurs.
2. `xml.dom.minidom` doesn't expand external entities and simply returns the unexpanded entity verbatim.
3. `xmlrpclib` doesn't expand external entities and omits them.

billion laughs / exponential entity expansion The Billion Laughs attack – also known as exponential entity expansion – uses multiple levels of nested entities. Each entity refers to another entity several times, and the final entity definition contains a small string. The exponential expansion results in several gigabytes of text and consumes lots of memory and CPU time.

quadratic blowup entity expansion A quadratic blowup attack is similar to a Billion Laughs attack; it abuses entity expansion, too. Instead of nested entities it repeats one large entity with a couple of thousand chars over and over again. The attack isn't as efficient as the exponential case but it avoids triggering parser countermeasures that forbid deeply-nested entities.

external entity expansion Entity declarations can contain more than just text for replacement. They can also point to external resources or local files. The XML parser accesses the resource and embeds the content into the XML document.

DTD **retrieval** Some XML libraries like Python's *xml.dom.pulldom* retrieve document type definitions from remote or local locations. The feature has similar implications as the external entity expansion issue.

decompression bomb Decompression bombs (aka ZIP bomb) apply to all XML libraries that can parse compressed XML streams such as gzipped HTTP streams or LZMA-compressed files. For an attacker it can reduce the amount of transmitted data by three magnitudes or more.

The documentation for defusedxml on PyPI has further information about all known attack vectors with examples and references.

20.4.2 The `defusedxml` and `defusedexpat` Packages

defusedxml is a pure Python package with modified subclasses of all stdlib XML parsers that prevent any potentially malicious operation. Use of this package is recommended for any server code that parses untrusted XML data. The package also ships with example exploits and extended documentation on more XML exploits such as XPath injection.

defusedexpat provides a modified libexpat and a patched **pyexpat** module that have countermeasures against entity expansion DoS attacks. The **defusedexpat** module still allows a sane and configurable amount of entity expansions. The modifications may be included in some future release of Python, but will not be included in any bugfix releases of Python because they break backward compatibility.

20.5 `xml.etree.ElementTree` — The ElementTree XML API

Source code: Lib/xml/etree/ElementTree.py

The *xml.etree.ElementTree* module implements a simple and efficient API for parsing and creating XML data.

Changed in version 3.3: This module will use a fast implementation whenever available. The **xml.etree.cElementTree** module is deprecated.

> **Warning:** The *xml.etree.ElementTree* module is not secure against maliciously constructed data. If you need to parse untrusted or unauthenticated data see *XML vulnerabilities*.

20.5.1 Tutorial

This is a short tutorial for using *xml.etree.ElementTree* (**ET** in short). The goal is to demonstrate some of the building blocks and basic concepts of the module.

XML tree and elements

XML is an inherently hierarchical data format, and the most natural way to represent it is with a tree. ET has two classes for this purpose - *ElementTree* represents the whole XML document as a tree, and *Element* represents a single node in this tree. Interactions with the whole document (reading and writing to/from files) are usually done on the *ElementTree* level. Interactions with a single XML element and its sub-elements are done on the *Element* level.

Parsing XML

We'll be using the following XML document as the sample data for this section:

```xml
<?xml version="1.0"?>
<data>
    <country name="Liechtenstein">
        <rank>1</rank>
        <year>2008</year>
        <gdppc>141100</gdppc>
        <neighbor name="Austria" direction="E"/>
        <neighbor name="Switzerland" direction="W"/>
    </country>
    <country name="Singapore">
        <rank>4</rank>
        <year>2011</year>
        <gdppc>59900</gdppc>
        <neighbor name="Malaysia" direction="N"/>
    </country>
    <country name="Panama">
        <rank>68</rank>
        <year>2011</year>
        <gdppc>13600</gdppc>
        <neighbor name="Costa Rica" direction="W"/>
        <neighbor name="Colombia" direction="E"/>
    </country>
</data>
```

We can import this data by reading from a file:

```python
import xml.etree.ElementTree as ET
tree = ET.parse('country_data.xml')
root = tree.getroot()
```

Or directly from a string:

```python
root = ET.fromstring(country_data_as_string)
```

fromstring() parses XML from a string directly into an *Element*, which is the root element of the parsed tree. Other parsing functions may create an *ElementTree*. Check the documentation to be sure.

As an *Element*, `root` has a tag and a dictionary of attributes:

```python
>>> root.tag
'data'
>>> root.attrib
{}
```

It also has children nodes over which we can iterate:

```python
>>> for child in root:
...     print(child.tag, child.attrib)
...
country {'name': 'Liechtenstein'}
country {'name': 'Singapore'}
country {'name': 'Panama'}
```

Children are nested, and we can access specific child nodes by index:

```
>>> root[0][1].text
'2008'
```

Note: Not all elements of the XML input will end up as elements of the parsed tree. Currently, this module skips over any XML comments, processing instructions, and document type declarations in the input. Nevertheless, trees built using this module's API rather than parsing from XML text can have comments and processing instructions in them; they will be included when generating XML output. A document type declaration may be accessed by passing a custom *TreeBuilder* instance to the *XMLParser* constructor.

Pull API for non-blocking parsing

Most parsing functions provided by this module require the whole document to be read at once before returning any result. It is possible to use an *XMLParser* and feed data into it incrementally, but it is a push API that calls methods on a callback target, which is too low-level and inconvenient for most needs. Sometimes what the user really wants is to be able to parse XML incrementally, without blocking operations, while enjoying the convenience of fully constructed *Element* objects.

The most powerful tool for doing this is *XMLPullParser*. It does not require a blocking read to obtain the XML data, and is instead fed with data incrementally with *XMLPullParser.feed()* calls. To get the parsed XML elements, call *XMLPullParser.read_events()*. Here is an example:

```
>>> parser = ET.XMLPullParser(['start', 'end'])
>>> parser.feed('<mytag>sometext')
>>> list(parser.read_events())
[('start', <Element 'mytag' at 0x7fa66db2be58>)]
>>> parser.feed(' more text</mytag>')
>>> for event, elem in parser.read_events():
...     print(event)
...     print(elem.tag, 'text=', elem.text)
...
end
```

The obvious use case is applications that operate in a non-blocking fashion where the XML data is being received from a socket or read incrementally from some storage device. In such cases, blocking reads are unacceptable.

Because it's so flexible, *XMLPullParser* can be inconvenient to use for simpler use-cases. If you don't mind your application blocking on reading XML data but would still like to have incremental parsing capabilities, take a look at *iterparse()*. It can be useful when you're reading a large XML document and don't want to hold it wholly in memory.

Finding interesting elements

Element has some useful methods that help iterate recursively over all the sub-tree below it (its children, their children, and so on). For example, *Element.iter()*:

```
>>> for neighbor in root.iter('neighbor'):
...     print(neighbor.attrib)
...
{'name': 'Austria', 'direction': 'E'}
{'name': 'Switzerland', 'direction': 'W'}
{'name': 'Malaysia', 'direction': 'N'}
```

```
{'name': 'Costa Rica', 'direction': 'W'}
{'name': 'Colombia', 'direction': 'E'}
```

Element.findall() finds only elements with a tag which are direct children of the current element. *Element.find()* finds the *first* child with a particular tag, and *Element.text* accesses the element's text content. *Element.get()* accesses the element's attributes:

```
>>> for country in root.findall('country'):
...     rank = country.find('rank').text
...     name = country.get('name')
...     print(name, rank)
...
Liechtenstein 1
Singapore 4
Panama 68
```

More sophisticated specification of which elements to look for is possible by using *XPath*.

Modifying an XML File

ElementTree provides a simple way to build XML documents and write them to files. The *ElementTree.write()* method serves this purpose.

Once created, an *Element* object may be manipulated by directly changing its fields (such as *Element.text*), adding and modifying attributes (*Element.set()* method), as well as adding new children (for example with *Element.append()*).

Let's say we want to add one to each country's rank, and add an **updated** attribute to the rank element:

```
>>> for rank in root.iter('rank'):
...     new_rank = int(rank.text) + 1
...     rank.text = str(new_rank)
...     rank.set('updated', 'yes')
...
>>> tree.write('output.xml')
```

Our XML now looks like this:

```xml
<?xml version="1.0"?>
<data>
    <country name="Liechtenstein">
        <rank updated="yes">2</rank>
        <year>2008</year>
        <gdppc>141100</gdppc>
        <neighbor name="Austria" direction="E"/>
        <neighbor name="Switzerland" direction="W"/>
    </country>
    <country name="Singapore">
        <rank updated="yes">5</rank>
        <year>2011</year>
        <gdppc>59900</gdppc>
        <neighbor name="Malaysia" direction="N"/>
    </country>
    <country name="Panama">
        <rank updated="yes">69</rank>
        <year>2011</year>
        <gdppc>13600</gdppc>
        <neighbor name="Costa Rica" direction="W"/>
```

```
        <neighbor name="Colombia" direction="E"/>
    </country>
</data>
```

We can remove elements using *Element.remove()*. Let's say we want to remove all countries with a rank higher than 50:

```
>>> for country in root.findall('country'):
...     rank = int(country.find('rank').text)
...     if rank > 50:
...         root.remove(country)
...
>>> tree.write('output.xml')
```

Our XML now looks like this:

```
<?xml version="1.0"?>
<data>
    <country name="Liechtenstein">
        <rank updated="yes">2</rank>
        <year>2008</year>
        <gdppc>141100</gdppc>
        <neighbor name="Austria" direction="E"/>
        <neighbor name="Switzerland" direction="W"/>
    </country>
    <country name="Singapore">
        <rank updated="yes">5</rank>
        <year>2011</year>
        <gdppc>59900</gdppc>
        <neighbor name="Malaysia" direction="N"/>
    </country>
</data>
```

Building XML documents

The *SubElement()* function also provides a convenient way to create new sub-elements for a given element:

```
>>> a = ET.Element('a')
>>> b = ET.SubElement(a, 'b')
>>> c = ET.SubElement(a, 'c')
>>> d = ET.SubElement(c, 'd')
>>> ET.dump(a)
<a><b /><c><d /></c></a>
```

Parsing XML with Namespaces

If the XML input has namespaces, tags and attributes with prefixes in the form `prefix:sometag` get expanded to `{uri}sometag` where the *prefix* is replaced by the full URI. Also, if there is a default namespace, that full URI gets prepended to all of the non-prefixed tags.

Here is an XML example that incorporates two namespaces, one with the prefix "fictional" and the other serving as the default namespace:

```
<?xml version="1.0"?>
<actors xmlns:fictional="http://characters.example.com"
```

```
            xmlns="http://people.example.com">
    <actor>
        <name>John Cleese</name>
        <fictional:character>Lancelot</fictional:character>
        <fictional:character>Archie Leach</fictional:character>
    </actor>
    <actor>
        <name>Eric Idle</name>
        <fictional:character>Sir Robin</fictional:character>
        <fictional:character>Gunther</fictional:character>
        <fictional:character>Commander Clement</fictional:character>
    </actor>
</actors>
```

One way to search and explore this XML example is to manually add the URI to every tag or attribute in the xpath of a *find()* or *findall()*:

```
root = fromstring(xml_text)
for actor in root.findall('{http://people.example.com}actor'):
    name = actor.find('{http://people.example.com}name')
    print(name.text)
    for char in actor.findall('{http://characters.example.com}character'):
        print(' |-->', char.text)
```

A better way to search the namespaced XML example is to create a dictionary with your own prefixes and use those in the search functions:

```
ns = {'real_person': 'http://people.example.com',
      'role': 'http://characters.example.com'}

for actor in root.findall('real_person:actor', ns):
    name = actor.find('real_person:name', ns)
    print(name.text)
    for char in actor.findall('role:character', ns):
        print(' |-->', char.text)
```

These two approaches both output:

```
John Cleese
 |--> Lancelot
 |--> Archie Leach
Eric Idle
 |--> Sir Robin
 |--> Gunther
 |--> Commander Clement
```

Additional resources

See http://effbot.org/zone/element-index.htm for tutorials and links to other docs.

20.5.2 XPath support

This module provides limited support for XPath expressions for locating elements in a tree. The goal is to support a small subset of the abbreviated syntax; a full XPath engine is outside the scope of the module.

Example

Here's an example that demonstrates some of the XPath capabilities of the module. We'll be using the `countrydata` XML document from the *Parsing XML* section:

```
import xml.etree.ElementTree as ET

root = ET.fromstring(countrydata)

# Top-level elements
root.findall(".")

# All 'neighbor' grand-children of 'country' children of the top-level
# elements
root.findall("./country/neighbor")

# Nodes with name='Singapore' that have a 'year' child
root.findall(".//year/..[@name='Singapore']")

# 'year' nodes that are children of nodes with name='Singapore'
root.findall(".//*[@name='Singapore']/year")

# All 'neighbor' nodes that are the second child of their parent
root.findall(".//neighbor[2]")
```

Supported XPath syntax

Syntax	Meaning
`tag`	Selects all child elements with the given tag. For example, `spam` selects all child elements named `spam`, and `spam/egg` selects all grandchildren named `egg` in all children named `spam`.
`*`	Selects all child elements. For example, `*/egg` selects all grandchildren named `egg`.
`.`	Selects the current node. This is mostly useful at the beginning of the path, to indicate that it's a relative path.
`//`	Selects all subelements, on all levels beneath the current element. For example, `.//egg` selects all `egg` elements in the entire tree.
`..`	Selects the parent element. Returns `None` if the path attempts to reach the ancestors of the start element (the element `find` was called on).
`[@attrib]`	Selects all elements that have the given attribute.
`[@attrib='value']`	Selects all elements for which the given attribute has the given value. The value cannot contain quotes.
`[tag]`	Selects all elements that have a child named `tag`. Only immediate children are supported.
`[tag='text']`	Selects all elements that have a child named `tag` whose complete text content, including descendants, equals the given `text`.
`[position]`	Selects all elements that are located at the given position. The position can be either an integer (1 is the first position), the expression `last()` (for the last position), or a position relative to the last position (e.g. `last()-1`).

Predicates (expressions within square brackets) must be preceded by a tag name, an asterisk, or another predicate. `position` predicates must be preceded by a tag name.

20.5.3 Reference

Functions

`xml.etree.ElementTree.Comment(text=None)`
> Comment element factory. This factory function creates a special element that will be serialized as an XML comment by the standard serializer. The comment string can be either a bytestring or a Unicode string. *text* is a string containing the comment string. Returns an element instance representing a comment.
>
> Note that *XMLParser* skips over comments in the input instead of creating comment objects for them. An *ElementTree* will only contain comment nodes if they have been inserted into to the tree using one of the *Element* methods.

`xml.etree.ElementTree.dump(elem)`
> Writes an element tree or element structure to sys.stdout. This function should be used for debugging only.
>
> The exact output format is implementation dependent. In this version, it's written as an ordinary XML file.
>
> *elem* is an element tree or an individual element.

`xml.etree.ElementTree.fromstring(text)`
> Parses an XML section from a string constant. Same as *XML()*. *text* is a string containing XML data. Returns an *Element* instance.

`xml.etree.ElementTree.fromstringlist(sequence, parser=None)`
> Parses an XML document from a sequence of string fragments. *sequence* is a list or other sequence containing XML data fragments. *parser* is an optional parser instance. If not given, the standard *XMLParser* parser is used. Returns an *Element* instance.
>
> New in version 3.2.

`xml.etree.ElementTree.iselement(element)`
> Checks if an object appears to be a valid element object. *element* is an element instance. Returns a true value if this is an element object.

`xml.etree.ElementTree.iterparse(source, events=None, parser=None)`
> Parses an XML section into an element tree incrementally, and reports what's going on to the user. *source* is a filename or *file object* containing XML data. *events* is a sequence of events to report back. The supported events are the strings `"start"`, `"end"`, `"start-ns"` and `"end-ns"` (the "ns" events are used to get detailed namespace information). If *events* is omitted, only `"end"` events are reported. *parser* is an optional parser instance. If not given, the standard *XMLParser* parser is used. *parser* must be a subclass of *XMLParser* and can only use the default *TreeBuilder* as a target. Returns an *iterator* providing (`event, elem`) pairs.
>
> Note that while *iterparse()* builds the tree incrementally, it issues blocking reads on *source* (or the file it names). As such, it's unsuitable for applications where blocking reads can't be made. For fully non-blocking parsing, see *XMLPullParser*.
>
> **Note:** *iterparse()* only guarantees that it has seen the ">" character of a starting tag when it emits a "start" event, so the attributes are defined, but the contents of the text and tail attributes are undefined at that point. The same applies to the element children; they may or may not be present.
>
> If you need a fully populated element, look for "end" events instead.
>
> Deprecated since version 3.4: The *parser* argument.

xml.etree.ElementTree.parse(*source, parser=None*)
    Parses an XML section into an element tree. *source* is a filename or file object containing XML data. *parser* is an optional parser instance. If not given, the standard *XMLParser* parser is used. Returns an *ElementTree* instance.

xml.etree.ElementTree.ProcessingInstruction(*target, text=None*)
    PI element factory. This factory function creates a special element that will be serialized as an XML processing instruction. *target* is a string containing the PI target. *text* is a string containing the PI contents, if given. Returns an element instance, representing a processing instruction.

    Note that *XMLParser* skips over processing instructions in the input instead of creating comment objects for them. An *ElementTree* will only contain processing instruction nodes if they have been inserted into to the tree using one of the *Element* methods.

xml.etree.ElementTree.register_namespace(*prefix, uri*)
    Registers a namespace prefix. The registry is global, and any existing mapping for either the given prefix or the namespace URI will be removed. *prefix* is a namespace prefix. *uri* is a namespace uri. Tags and attributes in this namespace will be serialized with the given prefix, if at all possible.

    New in version 3.2.

xml.etree.ElementTree.SubElement(*parent, tag, attrib={}, **extra*)
    Subelement factory. This function creates an element instance, and appends it to an existing element.

    The element name, attribute names, and attribute values can be either bytestrings or Unicode strings. *parent* is the parent element. *tag* is the subelement name. *attrib* is an optional dictionary, containing element attributes. *extra* contains additional attributes, given as keyword arguments. Returns an element instance.

xml.etree.ElementTree.tostring(*element, encoding="us-ascii", method="xml", *, short_empty_elements=True*)
    Generates a string representation of an XML element, including all subelements. *element* is an *Element* instance. *encoding*[1] is the output encoding (default is US-ASCII). Use `encoding="unicode"` to generate a Unicode string (otherwise, a bytestring is generated). *method* is either `"xml"`, `"html"` or `"text"` (default is `"xml"`). *short_empty_elements* has the same meaning as in *ElementTree.write()*. Returns an (optionally) encoded string containing the XML data.

    New in version 3.4: The *short_empty_elements* parameter.

xml.etree.ElementTree.tostringlist(*element, encoding="us-ascii", method="xml", *, short_empty_elements=True*)
    Generates a string representation of an XML element, including all subelements. *element* is an *Element* instance. *encoding*[1] is the output encoding (default is US-ASCII). Use `encoding="unicode"` to generate a Unicode string (otherwise, a bytestring is generated). *method* is either `"xml"`, `"html"` or `"text"` (default is `"xml"`). *short_empty_elements* has the same meaning as in *ElementTree.write()*. Returns a list of (optionally) encoded strings containing the XML data. It does not guarantee any specific sequence, except that `b"".join(tostringlist(element)) == tostring(element)`.

    New in version 3.2.

    New in version 3.4: The *short_empty_elements* parameter.

xml.etree.ElementTree.XML(*text, parser=None*)
    Parses an XML section from a string constant. This function can be used to embed "XML literals" in Python code. *text* is a string containing XML data. *parser* is an optional parser instance. If not given, the standard *XMLParser* parser is used. Returns an *Element* instance.

xml.etree.ElementTree.XMLID(*text, parser=None*)
    Parses an XML section from a string constant, and also returns a dictionary which maps from element

---

[1] The encoding string included in XML output should conform to the appropriate standards. For example, "UTF-8" is valid, but "UTF8" is not. See https://www.w3.org/TR/2006/REC-xml11-20060816/#NT-EncodingDecl and https://www.iana.org/assignments/character-sets/character-sets.xhtml.

id:s to elements. *text* is a string containing XML data. *parser* is an optional parser instance. If not given, the standard *XMLParser* parser is used. Returns a tuple containing an *Element* instance and a dictionary.

Element Objects

class xml.etree.ElementTree.Element(*tag, attrib={}, **extra*)

Element class. This class defines the Element interface, and provides a reference implementation of this interface.

The element name, attribute names, and attribute values can be either bytestrings or Unicode strings. *tag* is the element name. *attrib* is an optional dictionary, containing element attributes. *extra* contains additional attributes, given as keyword arguments.

tag
A string identifying what kind of data this element represents (the element type, in other words).

text
tail
These attributes can be used to hold additional data associated with the element. Their values are usually strings but may be any application-specific object. If the element is created from an XML file, the *text* attribute holds either the text between the element's start tag and its first child or end tag, or None, and the *tail* attribute holds either the text between the element's end tag and the next tag, or None. For the XML data

```
<a><b>1<c>2<d/>3</c></b>4</a>
```

the *a* element has None for both *text* and *tail* attributes, the *b* element has *text* "1" and *tail* "4", the *c* element has *text* "2" and *tail* None, and the *d* element has *text* None and *tail* "3".

To collect the inner text of an element, see *itertext()*, for example "".join(element.itertext()).

Applications may store arbitrary objects in these attributes.

attrib
A dictionary containing the element's attributes. Note that while the *attrib* value is always a real mutable Python dictionary, an ElementTree implementation may choose to use another internal representation, and create the dictionary only if someone asks for it. To take advantage of such implementations, use the dictionary methods below whenever possible.

The following dictionary-like methods work on the element attributes.

clear()
Resets an element. This function removes all subelements, clears all attributes, and sets the text and tail attributes to None.

get(*key, default=None*)
Gets the element attribute named *key*.

Returns the attribute value, or *default* if the attribute was not found.

items()
Returns the element attributes as a sequence of (name, value) pairs. The attributes are returned in an arbitrary order.

keys()
Returns the elements attribute names as a list. The names are returned in an arbitrary order.

set(*key, value*)
Set the attribute *key* on the element to *value*.

The following methods work on the element's children (subelements).

append(*subelement*)
: Adds the element *subelement* to the end of this element's internal list of subelements. Raises `TypeError` if *subelement* is not an `Element`.

extend(*subelements*)
: Appends *subelements* from a sequence object with zero or more elements. Raises `TypeError` if a subelement is not an `Element`.

  New in version 3.2.

find(*match, namespaces=None*)
: Finds the first subelement matching *match*. *match* may be a tag name or a *path*. Returns an element instance or `None`. *namespaces* is an optional mapping from namespace prefix to full name.

findall(*match, namespaces=None*)
: Finds all matching subelements, by tag name or *path*. Returns a list containing all matching elements in document order. *namespaces* is an optional mapping from namespace prefix to full name.

findtext(*match, default=None, namespaces=None*)
: Finds text for the first subelement matching *match*. *match* may be a tag name or a *path*. Returns the text content of the first matching element, or *default* if no element was found. Note that if the matching element has no text content an empty string is returned. *namespaces* is an optional mapping from namespace prefix to full name.

getchildren()
: Deprecated since version 3.2: Use `list(elem)` or iteration.

getiterator(*tag=None*)
: Deprecated since version 3.2: Use method `Element.iter()` instead.

insert(*index, subelement*)
: Inserts *subelement* at the given position in this element. Raises `TypeError` if *subelement* is not an `Element`.

iter(*tag=None*)
: Creates a tree *iterator* with the current element as the root. The iterator iterates over this element and all elements below it, in document (depth first) order. If *tag* is not `None` or `'*'`, only elements whose tag equals *tag* are returned from the iterator. If the tree structure is modified during iteration, the result is undefined.

  New in version 3.2.

iterfind(*match, namespaces=None*)
: Finds all matching subelements, by tag name or *path*. Returns an iterable yielding all matching elements in document order. *namespaces* is an optional mapping from namespace prefix to full name.

  New in version 3.2.

itertext()
: Creates a text iterator. The iterator loops over this element and all subelements, in document order, and returns all inner text.

  New in version 3.2.

makeelement(*tag, attrib*)
: Creates a new element object of the same type as this element. Do not call this method, use the `SubElement()` factory function instead.

remove(*subelement*)

> Removes *subelement* from the element. Unlike the find* methods this method compares elements based on the instance identity, not on tag value or contents.

Element objects also support the following sequence type methods for working with subelements: `__delitem__()`, `__getitem__()`, `__setitem__()`, `__len__()`.

Caution: Elements with no subelements will test as `False`. This behavior will change in future versions. Use specific `len(elem)` or `elem is None` test instead.

```
element = root.find('foo')

if not element:  # careful!
    print("element not found, or element has no subelements")

if element is None:
    print("element not found")
```

ElementTree Objects

class xml.etree.ElementTree.ElementTree(*element=None, file=None*)

> ElementTree wrapper class. This class represents an entire element hierarchy, and adds some extra support for serialization to and from standard XML.
>
> *element* is the root element. The tree is initialized with the contents of the XML *file* if given.

_setroot(*element*)

> Replaces the root element for this tree. This discards the current contents of the tree, and replaces it with the given element. Use with care. *element* is an element instance.

find(*match, namespaces=None*)

> Same as *Element.find()*, starting at the root of the tree.

findall(*match, namespaces=None*)

> Same as *Element.findall()*, starting at the root of the tree.

findtext(*match, default=None, namespaces=None*)

> Same as *Element.findtext()*, starting at the root of the tree.

getiterator(*tag=None*)

> Deprecated since version 3.2: Use method *ElementTree.iter()* instead.

getroot()

> Returns the root element for this tree.

iter(*tag=None*)

> Creates and returns a tree iterator for the root element. The iterator loops over all elements in this tree, in section order. *tag* is the tag to look for (default is to return all elements).

iterfind(*match, namespaces=None*)

> Same as *Element.iterfind()*, starting at the root of the tree.
>
> New in version 3.2.

parse(*source, parser=None*)

> Loads an external XML section into this element tree. *source* is a file name or *file object*. *parser* is an optional parser instance. If not given, the standard *XMLParser* parser is used. Returns the section root element.

write(*file, encoding="us-ascii", xml_declaration=None, default_namespace=None, method="xml", *, short_empty_elements=True*)

> Writes the element tree to a file, as XML. *file* is a file name, or a *file object* opened for writing.

encoding[1] is the output encoding (default is US-ASCII). *xml_declaration* controls if an XML declaration should be added to the file. Use `False` for never, `True` for always, `None` for only if not US-ASCII or UTF-8 or Unicode (default is `None`). *default_namespace* sets the default XML namespace (for "xmlns"). *method* is either `"xml"`, `"html"` or `"text"` (default is `"xml"`). The keyword-only *short_empty_elements* parameter controls the formatting of elements that contain no content. If `True` (the default), they are emitted as a single self-closed tag, otherwise they are emitted as a pair of start/end tags.

The output is either a string (`str`) or binary (`bytes`). This is controlled by the *encoding* argument. If *encoding* is `"unicode"`, the output is a string; otherwise, it's binary. Note that this may conflict with the type of *file* if it's an open *file object*; make sure you do not try to write a string to a binary stream and vice versa.

New in version 3.4: The *short_empty_elements* parameter.

This is the XML file that is going to be manipulated:

```
<html>
    <head>
        <title>Example page</title>
    </head>
    <body>
        <p>Moved to <a href="http://example.org/">example.org</a>
        or <a href="http://example.com/">example.com</a>.</p>
    </body>
</html>
```

Example of changing the attribute "target" of every link in first paragraph:

```
>>> from xml.etree.ElementTree import ElementTree
>>> tree = ElementTree()
>>> tree.parse("index.xhtml")
<Element 'html' at 0xb77e6fac>
>>> p = tree.find("body/p")     # Finds first occurrence of tag p in body
>>> p
<Element 'p' at 0xb77ec26c>
>>> links = list(p.iter("a"))   # Returns list of all links
>>> links
[<Element 'a' at 0xb77ec2ac>, <Element 'a' at 0xb77ec1cc>]
>>> for i in links:             # Iterates through all found links
...     i.attrib["target"] = "blank"
>>> tree.write("output.xhtml")
```

QName Objects

class xml.etree.ElementTree.QName(*text_or_uri*, *tag=None*)

QName wrapper. This can be used to wrap a QName attribute value, in order to get proper namespace handling on output. *text_or_uri* is a string containing the QName value, in the form {uri}local, or, if the tag argument is given, the URI part of a QName. If *tag* is given, the first argument is interpreted as a URI, and this argument is interpreted as a local name. *QName* instances are opaque.

TreeBuilder Objects

class xml.etree.ElementTree.TreeBuilder(*element_factory=None*)

Generic element structure builder. This builder converts a sequence of start, data, and end method calls to a well-formed element structure. You can use this class to build an element structure using a custom XML parser, or a parser for some other XML-like format. *element_factory*, when given, must be a callable accepting two positional arguments: a tag and a dict of attributes. It is expected to return a new element instance.

close()
> Flushes the builder buffers, and returns the toplevel document element. Returns an *Element* instance.

data(*data*)
> Adds text to the current element. *data* is a string. This should be either a bytestring, or a Unicode string.

end(*tag*)
> Closes the current element. *tag* is the element name. Returns the closed element.

start(*tag, attrs*)
> Opens a new element. *tag* is the element name. *attrs* is a dictionary containing element attributes. Returns the opened element.

In addition, a custom *TreeBuilder* object can provide the following method:

doctype(*name, pubid, system*)
> Handles a doctype declaration. *name* is the doctype name. *pubid* is the public identifier. *system* is the system identifier. This method does not exist on the default *TreeBuilder* class.
>
> New in version 3.2.

XMLParser Objects

class xml.etree.ElementTree.XMLParser(*html=0, target=None, encoding=None*)
> This class is the low-level building block of the module. It uses *xml.parsers.expat* for efficient, event-based parsing of XML. It can be fed XML data incrementally with the *feed()* method, and parsing events are translated to a push API - by invoking callbacks on the *target* object. If *target* is omitted, the standard *TreeBuilder* is used. The *html* argument was historically used for backwards compatibility and is now deprecated. If *encoding*[1] is given, the value overrides the encoding specified in the XML file.
>
> Deprecated since version 3.4: The *html* argument. The remaining arguments should be passed via keyword to prepare for the removal of the *html* argument.
>
> **close()**
>> Finishes feeding data to the parser. Returns the result of calling the **close()** method of the *target* passed during construction; by default, this is the toplevel document element.
>
> **doctype**(*name, pubid, system*)
>> Deprecated since version 3.2: Define the *TreeBuilder.doctype()* method on a custom TreeBuilder target.
>
> **feed**(*data*)
>> Feeds data to the parser. *data* is encoded data.

XMLParser.feed() calls *target*'s **start(tag, attrs_dict)** method for each opening tag, its **end(tag)** method for each closing tag, and data is processed by method **data(data)**. *XMLParser.close()* calls *target*'s method **close()**. *XMLParser* can be used not only for building a tree structure. This is an example of counting the maximum depth of an XML file:

```
>>> from xml.etree.ElementTree import XMLParser
>>> class MaxDepth:                  # The target object of the parser
...     maxDepth = 0
...     depth = 0
...     def start(self, tag, attrib):   # Called for each opening tag.
```

```
...             self.depth += 1
...             if self.depth > self.maxDepth:
...                 self.maxDepth = self.depth
...     def end(self, tag):             # Called for each closing tag.
...         self.depth -= 1
...     def data(self, data):
...         pass            # We do not need to do anything with data.
...     def close(self):    # Called when all data has been parsed.
...         return self.maxDepth
...
>>> target = MaxDepth()
>>> parser = XMLParser(target=target)
>>> exampleXml = """
... <a>
...   <b>
...   </b>
...   <b>
...     <c>
...       <d>
...       </d>
...     </c>
...   </b>
... </a>"""
>>> parser.feed(exampleXml)
>>> parser.close()
4
```

XMLPullParser Objects

class xml.etree.ElementTree.XMLPullParser(*events=None*)

A pull parser suitable for non-blocking applications. Its input-side API is similar to that of *XMLParser*, but instead of pushing calls to a callback target, *XMLPullParser* collects an internal list of parsing events and lets the user read from it. *events* is a sequence of events to report back. The supported events are the strings `"start"`, `"end"`, `"start-ns"` and `"end-ns"` (the "ns" events are used to get detailed namespace information). If *events* is omitted, only `"end"` events are reported.

feed(*data*)
Feed the given bytes data to the parser.

close()
Signal the parser that the data stream is terminated. Unlike *XMLParser.close()*, this method always returns *None*. Any events not yet retrieved when the parser is closed can still be read with *read_events()*.

read_events()
Return an iterator over the events which have been encountered in the data fed to the parser. The iterator yields (`event`, `elem`) pairs, where *event* is a string representing the type of event (e.g. `"end"`) and *elem* is the encountered *Element* object.

Events provided in a previous call to *read_events()* will not be yielded again. Events are consumed from the internal queue only when they are retrieved from the iterator, so multiple readers iterating in parallel over iterators obtained from *read_events()* will have unpredictable results.

Note: *XMLPullParser* only guarantees that it has seen the ">" character of a starting tag when it emits a "start" event, so the attributes are defined, but the contents of the text and tail attributes are

undefined at that point. The same applies to the element children; they may or may not be present.
If you need a fully populated element, look for "end" events instead.

New in version 3.4.

Exceptions

class `xml.etree.ElementTree.ParseError`
XML parse error, raised by the various parsing methods in this module when parsing fails. The string representation of an instance of this exception will contain a user-friendly error message. In addition, it will have the following attributes available:

`code`
A numeric error code from the expat parser. See the documentation of *xml.parsers.expat* for the list of error codes and their meanings.

`position`
A tuple of *line*, *column* numbers, specifying where the error occurred.

20.6 `xml.dom` — The Document Object Model API

Source code: Lib/xml/dom/__init__.py

The Document Object Model, or "DOM," is a cross-language API from the World Wide Web Consortium (W3C) for accessing and modifying XML documents. A DOM implementation presents an XML document as a tree structure, or allows client code to build such a structure from scratch. It then gives access to the structure through a set of objects which provided well-known interfaces.

The DOM is extremely useful for random-access applications. SAX only allows you a view of one bit of the document at a time. If you are looking at one SAX element, you have no access to another. If you are looking at a text node, you have no access to a containing element. When you write a SAX application, you need to keep track of your program's position in the document somewhere in your own code. SAX does not do it for you. Also, if you need to look ahead in the XML document, you are just out of luck.

Some applications are simply impossible in an event driven model with no access to a tree. Of course you could build some sort of tree yourself in SAX events, but the DOM allows you to avoid writing that code. The DOM is a standard tree representation for XML data.

The Document Object Model is being defined by the W3C in stages, or "levels" in their terminology. The Python mapping of the API is substantially based on the DOM Level 2 recommendation.

DOM applications typically start by parsing some XML into a DOM. How this is accomplished is not covered at all by DOM Level 1, and Level 2 provides only limited improvements: There is a `DOMImplementation` object class which provides access to `Document` creation methods, but no way to access an XML reader/parser/Document builder in an implementation-independent way. There is also no well-defined way to access these methods without an existing `Document` object. In Python, each DOM implementation will provide a function *getDOMImplementation()*. DOM Level 3 adds a Load/Store specification, which defines an interface to the reader, but this is not yet available in the Python standard library.

Once you have a DOM document object, you can access the parts of your XML document through its properties and methods. These properties are defined in the DOM specification; this portion of the reference manual describes the interpretation of the specification in Python.

The specification provided by the W3C defines the DOM API for Java, ECMAScript, and OMG IDL. The Python mapping defined here is based in large part on the IDL version of the specification, but strict compliance is not required (though implementations are free to support the strict mapping from IDL). See section *Conformance* for a detailed discussion of mapping requirements.

See also:

Document Object Model (DOM) Level 2 Specification The W3C recommendation upon which the Python DOM API is based.

Document Object Model (DOM) Level 1 Specification The W3C recommendation for the DOM supported by `xml.dom.minidom`.

Python Language Mapping Specification This specifies the mapping from OMG IDL to Python.

20.6.1 Module Contents

The `xml.dom` contains the following functions:

`xml.dom.registerDOMImplementation(name, factory)`
    Register the *factory* function with the name *name*. The factory function should return an object which implements the `DOMImplementation` interface. The factory function can return the same object every time, or a new one for each call, as appropriate for the specific implementation (e.g. if that implementation supports some customization).

`xml.dom.getDOMImplementation(name=None, features=())`
    Return a suitable DOM implementation. The *name* is either well-known, the module name of a DOM implementation, or None. If it is not None, imports the corresponding module and returns a `DOMImplementation` object if the import succeeds. If no name is given, and if the environment variable `PYTHON_DOM` is set, this variable is used to find the implementation.

    If name is not given, this examines the available implementations to find one with the required feature set. If no implementation can be found, raise an *ImportError*. The features list must be a sequence of (`feature`, `version`) pairs which are passed to the `hasFeature()` method on available `DOMImplementation` objects.

Some convenience constants are also provided:

`xml.dom.EMPTY_NAMESPACE`
    The value used to indicate that no namespace is associated with a node in the DOM. This is typically found as the `namespaceURI` of a node, or used as the *namespaceURI* parameter to a namespaces-specific method.

`xml.dom.XML_NAMESPACE`
    The namespace URI associated with the reserved prefix `xml`, as defined by Namespaces in XML (section 4).

`xml.dom.XMLNS_NAMESPACE`
    The namespace URI for namespace declarations, as defined by Document Object Model (DOM) Level 2 Core Specification (section 1.1.8).

`xml.dom.XHTML_NAMESPACE`
    The URI of the XHTML namespace as defined by XHTML 1.0: The Extensible HyperText Markup Language (section 3.1.1).

In addition, `xml.dom` contains a base `Node` class and the DOM exception classes. The `Node` class provided by this module does not implement any of the methods or attributes defined by the DOM specification; concrete DOM implementations must provide those. The `Node` class provided as part of this module does provide the constants used for the `nodeType` attribute on concrete `Node` objects; they are located within the class rather than at the module level to conform with the DOM specifications.

20.6.2 Objects in the DOM

The definitive documentation for the DOM is the DOM specification from the W3C.

Note that DOM attributes may also be manipulated as nodes instead of as simple strings. It is fairly rare that you must do this, however, so this usage is not yet documented.

Interface	Section	Purpose
DOMImplementation	*DOMImplementation Objects*	Interface to the underlying implementation.
Node	*Node Objects*	Base interface for most objects in a document.
NodeList	*NodeList Objects*	Interface for a sequence of nodes.
DocumentType	*DocumentType Objects*	Information about the declarations needed to process a document.
Document	*Document Objects*	Object which represents an entire document.
Element	*Element Objects*	Element nodes in the document hierarchy.
Attr	*Attr Objects*	Attribute value nodes on element nodes.
Comment	*Comment Objects*	Representation of comments in the source document.
Text	*Text and CDATASection Objects*	Nodes containing textual content from the document.
ProcessingInstruction	*ProcessingInstruction Objects*	Processing instruction representation.

An additional section describes the exceptions defined for working with the DOM in Python.

DOMImplementation Objects

The DOMImplementation interface provides a way for applications to determine the availability of particular features in the DOM they are using. DOM Level 2 added the ability to create new Document and DocumentType objects using the DOMImplementation as well.

DOMImplementation.hasFeature(*feature*, *version*)
: Return true if the feature identified by the pair of strings *feature* and *version* is implemented.

DOMImplementation.createDocument(*namespaceUri*, *qualifiedName*, *doctype*)
: Return a new Document object (the root of the DOM), with a child Element object having the given *namespaceUri* and *qualifiedName*. The *doctype* must be a DocumentType object created by createDocumentType(), or None. In the Python DOM API, the first two arguments can also be None in order to indicate that no Element child is to be created.

DOMImplementation.createDocumentType(*qualifiedName*, *publicId*, *systemId*)
: Return a new DocumentType object that encapsulates the given *qualifiedName*, *publicId*, and *systemId* strings, representing the information contained in an XML document type declaration.

Node Objects

All of the components of an XML document are subclasses of Node.

Node.nodeType
: An integer representing the node type. Symbolic constants for the types are on the Node object: ELEMENT_NODE, ATTRIBUTE_NODE, TEXT_NODE, CDATA_SECTION_NODE, ENTITY_NODE, PROCESSING_INSTRUCTION_NODE, COMMENT_NODE, DOCUMENT_NODE, DOCUMENT_TYPE_NODE, NOTATION_NODE. This is a read-only attribute.

`Node.parentNode`
　　The parent of the current node, or `None` for the document node. The value is always a `Node` object or `None`. For `Element` nodes, this will be the parent element, except for the root element, in which case it will be the `Document` object. For `Attr` nodes, this is always `None`. This is a read-only attribute.

`Node.attributes`
　　A `NamedNodeMap` of attribute objects. Only elements have actual values for this; others provide `None` for this attribute. This is a read-only attribute.

`Node.previousSibling`
　　The node that immediately precedes this one with the same parent. For instance the element with an end-tag that comes just before the *self* element's start-tag. Of course, XML documents are made up of more than just elements so the previous sibling could be text, a comment, or something else. If this node is the first child of the parent, this attribute will be `None`. This is a read-only attribute.

`Ncde.nextSibling`
　　The node that immediately follows this one with the same parent. See also *previousSibling*. If this is the last child of the parent, this attribute will be `None`. This is a read-only attribute.

`Node.childNodes`
　　A list of nodes contained within this node. This is a read-only attribute.

`Node.firstChild`
　　The first child of the node, if there are any, or `None`. This is a read-only attribute.

`Node.lastChild`
　　The last child of the node, if there are any, or `None`. This is a read-only attribute.

`Node.localName`
　　The part of the `tagName` following the colon if there is one, else the entire `tagName`. The value is a string.

`Node.prefix`
　　The part of the `tagName` preceding the colon if there is one, else the empty string. The value is a string, or `None`.

`Node.namespaceURI`
　　The namespace associated with the element name. This will be a string or `None`. This is a read-only attribute.

`Node.nodeName`
　　This has a different meaning for each node type; see the DOM specification for details. You can always get the information you would get here from another property such as the `tagName` property for elements or the `name` property for attributes. For all node types, the value of this attribute will be either a string or `None`. This is a read-only attribute.

`Node.nodeValue`
　　This has a different meaning for each node type; see the DOM specification for details. The situation is similar to that with *nodeName*. The value is a string or `None`.

`Node.hasAttributes()`
　　Returns true if the node has any attributes.

`Node.hasChildNodes()`
　　Returns true if the node has any child nodes.

`Node.isSameNode(other)`
　　Returns true if *other* refers to the same node as this node. This is especially useful for DOM implementations which use any sort of proxy architecture (because more than one object can refer to the same node).

> **Note:** This is based on a proposed DOM Level 3 API which is still in the "working draft" stage, but this particular interface appears uncontroversial. Changes from the W3C will not necessarily affect this method in the Python DOM interface (though any new W3C API for this would also be supported).

Node.**appendChild**(*newChild*)
: Add a new child node to this node at the end of the list of children, returning *newChild*. If the node was already in the tree, it is removed first.

Node.**insertBefore**(*newChild, refChild*)
: Insert a new child node before an existing child. It must be the case that *refChild* is a child of this node; if not, `ValueError` is raised. *newChild* is returned. If *refChild* is `None`, it inserts *newChild* at the end of the children's list.

Node.**removeChild**(*oldChild*)
: Remove a child node. *oldChild* must be a child of this node; if not, `ValueError` is raised. *oldChild* is returned on success. If *oldChild* will not be used further, its **unlink()** method should be called.

Node.**replaceChild**(*newChild, oldChild*)
: Replace an existing node with a new node. It must be the case that *oldChild* is a child of this node; if not, `ValueError` is raised.

Node.**normalize**()
: Join adjacent text nodes so that all stretches of text are stored as single `Text` instances. This simplifies processing text from a DOM tree for many applications.

Node.**cloneNode**(*deep*)
: Clone this node. Setting *deep* means to clone all child nodes as well. This returns the clone.

NodeList Objects

A `NodeList` represents a sequence of nodes. These objects are used in two ways in the DOM Core recommendation: an `Element` object provides one as its list of child nodes, and the `getElementsByTagName()` and `getElementsByTagNameNS()` methods of `Node` return objects with this interface to represent query results.

The DOM Level 2 recommendation defines one method and one attribute for these objects:

NodeList.**item**(*i*)
: Return the *i*'th item from the sequence, if there is one, or `None`. The index *i* is not allowed to be less than zero or greater than or equal to the length of the sequence.

NodeList.**length**
: The number of nodes in the sequence.

In addition, the Python DOM interface requires that some additional support is provided to allow `NodeList` objects to be used as Python sequences. All `NodeList` implementations must include support for `__len__()` and `__getitem__()`; this allows iteration over the `NodeList` in `for` statements and proper support for the `len()` built-in function.

If a DOM implementation supports modification of the document, the `NodeList` implementation must also support the `__setitem__()` and `__delitem__()` methods.

DocumentType Objects

Information about the notations and entities declared by a document (including the external subset if the parser uses it and can provide the information) is available from a `DocumentType` object. The `DocumentType` for a document is available from the `Document` object's `doctype` attribute; if there is no `DOCTYPE` declaration for the document, the document's `doctype` attribute will be set to `None` instead of an instance of this interface.

`DocumentType` is a specialization of `Node`, and adds the following attributes:

DocumentType.publicId
　　The public identifier for the external subset of the document type definition. This will be a string or `None`.

DocumentType.systemId
　　The system identifier for the external subset of the document type definition. This will be a URI as a string, or `None`.

DocumentType.internalSubset
　　A string giving the complete internal subset from the document. This does not include the brackets which enclose the subset. If the document has no internal subset, this should be `None`.

DocumentType.name
　　The name of the root element as given in the `DOCTYPE` declaration, if present.

DocumentType.entities
　　This is a `NamedNodeMap` giving the definitions of external entities. For entity names defined more than once, only the first definition is provided (others are ignored as required by the XML recommendation). This may be `None` if the information is not provided by the parser, or if no entities are defined.

DocumentType.notations
　　This is a `NamedNodeMap` giving the definitions of notations. For notation names defined more than once, only the first definition is provided (others are ignored as required by the XML recommendation). This may be `None` if the information is not provided by the parser, or if no notations are defined.

Document Objects

A `Document` represents an entire XML document, including its constituent elements, attributes, processing instructions, comments etc. Remember that it inherits properties from `Node`.

Document.documentElement
　　The one and only root element of the document.

Document.createElement(*tagName*)
　　Create and return a new element node. The element is not inserted into the document when it is created. You need to explicitly insert it with one of the other methods such as `insertBefore()` or `appendChild()`.

Document.createElementNS(*namespaceURI*, *tagName*)
　　Create and return a new element with a namespace. The *tagName* may have a prefix. The element is not inserted into the document when it is created. You need to explicitly insert it with one of the other methods such as `insertBefore()` or `appendChild()`.

Document.createTextNode(*data*)
　　Create and return a text node containing the data passed as a parameter. As with the other creation methods, this one does not insert the node into the tree.

Document.createComment(*data*)
　　Create and return a comment node containing the data passed as a parameter. As with the other creation methods, this one does not insert the node into the tree.

Document.createProcessingInstruction(*target*, *data*)
　　Create and return a processing instruction node containing the *target* and *data* passed as parameters. As with the other creation methods, this one does not insert the node into the tree.

Document.createAttribute(*name*)
: Create and return an attribute node. This method does not associate the attribute node with any particular element. You must use setAttributeNode() on the appropriate Element object to use the newly created attribute instance.

Document.createAttributeNS(*namespaceURI*, *qualifiedName*)
: Create and return an attribute node with a namespace. The *tagName* may have a prefix. This method does not associate the attribute node with any particular element. You must use setAttributeNode() on the appropriate Element object to use the newly created attribute instance.

Document.getElementsByTagName(*tagName*)
: Search for all descendants (direct children, children's children, etc.) with a particular element type name.

Document.getElementsByTagNameNS(*namespaceURI*, *localName*)
: Search for all descendants (direct children, children's children, etc.) with a particular namespace URI and localname. The localname is the part of the namespace after the prefix.

Element Objects

Element is a subclass of Node, so inherits all the attributes of that class.

Element.tagName
: The element type name. In a namespace-using document it may have colons in it. The value is a string.

Element.getElementsByTagName(*tagName*)
: Same as equivalent method in the Document class.

Element.getElementsByTagNameNS(*namespaceURI*, *localName*)
: Same as equivalent method in the Document class.

Element.hasAttribute(*name*)
: Returns true if the element has an attribute named by *name*.

Element.hasAttributeNS(*namespaceURI*, *localName*)
: Returns true if the element has an attribute named by *namespaceURI* and *localName*.

Element.getAttribute(*name*)
: Return the value of the attribute named by *name* as a string. If no such attribute exists, an empty string is returned, as if the attribute had no value.

Element.getAttributeNode(*attrname*)
: Return the Attr node for the attribute named by *attrname*.

Element.getAttributeNS(*namespaceURI*, *localName*)
: Return the value of the attribute named by *namespaceURI* and *localName* as a string. If no such attribute exists, an empty string is returned, as if the attribute had no value.

Element.getAttributeNodeNS(*namespaceURI*, *localName*)
: Return an attribute value as a node, given a *namespaceURI* and *localName*.

Element.removeAttribute(*name*)
: Remove an attribute by name. If there is no matching attribute, a *NotFoundErr* is raised.

Element.removeAttributeNode(*oldAttr*)
: Remove and return *oldAttr* from the attribute list, if present. If *oldAttr* is not present, *NotFoundErr* is raised.

Element.removeAttributeNS(*namespaceURI*, *localName*)
: Remove an attribute by name. Note that it uses a localName, not a qname. No exception is raised if there is no matching attribute.

Element.setAttribute(*name, value*)
    Set an attribute value from a string.

Element.setAttributeNode(*newAttr*)
    Add a new attribute node to the element, replacing an existing attribute if necessary if the **name** attribute matches. If a replacement occurs, the old attribute node will be returned. If *newAttr* is already in use, *InuseAttributeErr* will be raised.

Element.setAttributeNodeNS(*newAttr*)
    Add a new attribute node to the element, replacing an existing attribute if necessary if the **namespaceURI** and **localName** attributes match. If a replacement occurs, the old attribute node will be returned. If *newAttr* is already in use, *InuseAttributeErr* will be raised.

Element.setAttributeNS(*namespaceURI, qname, value*)
    Set an attribute value from a string, given a *namespaceURI* and a *qname*. Note that a qname is the whole attribute name. This is different than above.

Attr Objects

Attr inherits from Node, so inherits all its attributes.

Attr.name
    The attribute name. In a namespace-using document it may include a colon.

Attr.localName
    The part of the name following the colon if there is one, else the entire name. This is a read-only attribute.

Attr.prefix
    The part of the name preceding the colon if there is one, else the empty string.

Attr.value
    The text value of the attribute. This is a synonym for the **nodeValue** attribute.

NamedNodeMap Objects

NamedNodeMap does *not* inherit from Node.

NamedNodeMap.length
    The length of the attribute list.

NamedNodeMap.item(*index*)
    Return an attribute with a particular index. The order you get the attributes in is arbitrary but will be consistent for the life of a DOM. Each item is an attribute node. Get its value with the **value** attribute.

There are also experimental methods that give this class more mapping behavior. You can use them or you can use the standardized **getAttribute***() family of methods on the **Element** objects.

Comment Objects

Comment represents a comment in the XML document. It is a subclass of Node, but cannot have child nodes.

Comment.data
    The content of the comment as a string. The attribute contains all characters between the leading `<!--` and trailing `-->`, but does not include them.

Text and CDATASection Objects

The `Text` interface represents text in the XML document. If the parser and DOM implementation support the DOM's XML extension, portions of the text enclosed in CDATA marked sections are stored in `CDATASection` objects. These two interfaces are identical, but provide different values for the `nodeType` attribute.

These interfaces extend the `Node` interface. They cannot have child nodes.

`Text.data`
    The content of the text node as a string.

Note: The use of a `CDATASection` node does not indicate that the node represents a complete CDATA marked section, only that the content of the node was part of a CDATA section. A single CDATA section may be represented by more than one node in the document tree. There is no way to determine whether two adjacent `CDATASection` nodes represent different CDATA marked sections.

ProcessingInstruction Objects

Represents a processing instruction in the XML document; this inherits from the `Node` interface and cannot have child nodes.

`ProcessingInstruction.target`
    The content of the processing instruction up to the first whitespace character. This is a read-only attribute.

`ProcessingInstruction.data`
    The content of the processing instruction following the first whitespace character.

Exceptions

The DOM Level 2 recommendation defines a single exception, *DOMException*, and a number of constants that allow applications to determine what sort of error occurred. *DOMException* instances carry a *code* attribute that provides the appropriate value for the specific exception.

The Python DOM interface provides the constants, but also expands the set of exceptions so that a specific exception exists for each of the exception codes defined by the DOM. The implementations must raise the appropriate specific exception, each of which carries the appropriate value for the *code* attribute.

exception xml.dom.DOMException
    Base exception class used for all specific DOM exceptions. This exception class cannot be directly instantiated.

exception xml.dom.DomstringSizeErr
    Raised when a specified range of text does not fit into a string. This is not known to be used in the Python DOM implementations, but may be received from DOM implementations not written in Python.

exception xml.dom.HierarchyRequestErr
    Raised when an attempt is made to insert a node where the node type is not allowed.

exception xml.dom.IndexSizeErr
    Raised when an index or size parameter to a method is negative or exceeds the allowed values.

exception xml.dom.InuseAttributeErr
    Raised when an attempt is made to insert an `Attr` node that is already present elsewhere in the document.

exception xml.dom.**InvalidAccessErr**

Raised if a parameter or an operation is not supported on the underlying object.

exception xml.dom.**InvalidCharacterErr**

This exception is raised when a string parameter contains a character that is not permitted in the context it's being used in by the XML 1.0 recommendation. For example, attempting to create an `Element` node with a space in the element type name will cause this error to be raised.

exception xml.dom.**InvalidModificationErr**

Raised when an attempt is made to modify the type of a node.

exception xml.dom.**InvalidStateErr**

Raised when an attempt is made to use an object that is not defined or is no longer usable.

exception xml.dom.**NamespaceErr**

If an attempt is made to change any object in a way that is not permitted with regard to the Namespaces in XML recommendation, this exception is raised.

exception xml.dom.**NotFoundErr**

Exception when a node does not exist in the referenced context. For example, `NamedNodeMap.removeNamedItem()` will raise this if the node passed in does not exist in the map.

exception xml.dom.**NotSupportedErr**

Raised when the implementation does not support the requested type of object or operation.

exception xml.dom.**NoDataAllowedErr**

This is raised if data is specified for a node which does not support data.

exception xml.dom.**NoModificationAllowedErr**

Raised on attempts to modify an object where modifications are not allowed (such as for read-only nodes).

exception xml.dom.**SyntaxErr**

Raised when an invalid or illegal string is specified.

exception xml.dom.**WrongDocumentErr**

Raised when a node is inserted in a different document than it currently belongs to, and the implementation does not support migrating the node from one document to the other.

The exception codes defined in the DOM recommendation map to the exceptions described above according to this table:

Constant	Exception
DOMSTRING_SIZE_ERR	*DomstringSizeErr*
HIERARCHY_REQUEST_ERR	*HierarchyRequestErr*
INDEX_SIZE_ERR	*IndexSizeErr*
INUSE_ATTRIBUTE_ERR	*InuseAttributeErr*
INVALID_ACCESS_ERR	*InvalidAccessErr*
INVALID_CHARACTER_ERR	*InvalidCharacterErr*
INVALID_MODIFICATION_ERR	*InvalidModificationErr*
INVALID_STATE_ERR	*InvalidStateErr*
NAMESPACE_ERR	*NamespaceErr*
NOT_FOUND_ERR	*NotFoundErr*
NOT_SUPPORTED_ERR	*NotSupportedErr*
NO_DATA_ALLOWED_ERR	*NoDataAllowedErr*
NO_MODIFICATION_ALLOWED_ERR	*NoModificationAllowedErr*
SYNTAX_ERR	*SyntaxErr*
WRONG_DOCUMENT_ERR	*WrongDocumentErr*

20.6.3 Conformance

This section describes the conformance requirements and relationships between the Python DOM API, the W3C DOM recommendations, and the OMG IDL mapping for Python.

Type Mapping

The IDL types used in the DOM specification are mapped to Python types according to the following table.

IDL Type	Python Type
boolean	bool or int
int	int
long int	int
unsigned int	int
DOMString	str or bytes
null	None

Accessor Methods

The mapping from OMG IDL to Python defines accessor functions for IDL `attribute` declarations in much the way the Java mapping does. Mapping the IDL declarations

```
readonly attribute string someValue;
         attribute string anotherValue;
```

yields three accessor functions: a "get" method for `someValue` (`_get_someValue()`), and "get" and "set" methods for `anotherValue` (`_get_anotherValue()` and `_set_anotherValue()`). The mapping, in particular, does not require that the IDL attributes are accessible as normal Python attributes: `object.someValue` is *not* required to work, and may raise an *AttributeError*.

The Python DOM API, however, *does* require that normal attribute access work. This means that the typical surrogates generated by Python IDL compilers are not likely to work, and wrapper objects may be needed on the client if the DOM objects are accessed via CORBA. While this does require some additional consideration for CORBA DOM clients, the implementers with experience using DOM over CORBA from Python do not consider this a problem. Attributes that are declared `readonly` may not restrict write access in all DOM implementations.

In the Python DOM API, accessor functions are not required. If provided, they should take the form defined by the Python IDL mapping, but these methods are considered unnecessary since the attributes are accessible directly from Python. "Set" accessors should never be provided for `readonly` attributes.

The IDL definitions do not fully embody the requirements of the W3C DOM API, such as the notion of certain objects, such as the return value of `getElementsByTagName()`, being "live". The Python DOM API does not require implementations to enforce such requirements.

20.7 `xml.dom.minidom` — Minimal DOM implementation

Source code: Lib/xml/dom/minidom.py

xml.dom.minidom is a minimal implementation of the Document Object Model interface, with an API similar to that in other languages. It is intended to be simpler than the full DOM and also significantly smaller.

Users who are not already proficient with the DOM should consider using the `xml.etree.ElementTree` module for their XML processing instead.

> **Warning:** The `xml.dom.minidom` module is not secure against maliciously constructed data. If you need to parse untrusted or unauthenticated data see *XML vulnerabilities*.

DOM applications typically start by parsing some XML into a DOM. With `xml.dom.minidom`, this is done through the parse functions:

```python
from xml.dom.minidom import parse, parseString

dom1 = parse('c:\\temp\\mydata.xml')  # parse an XML file by name

datasource = open('c:\\temp\\mydata.xml')
dom2 = parse(datasource)   # parse an open file

dom3 = parseString('<myxml>Some data<empty/> some more data</myxml>')
```

The `parse()` function can take either a filename or an open file object.

xml.dom.minidom.parse(*filename_or_file*, *parser=None*, *bufsize=None*)
    Return a `Document` from the given input. *filename_or_file* may be either a file name, or a file-like object. *parser*, if given, must be a SAX2 parser object. This function will change the document handler of the parser and activate namespace support; other parser configuration (like setting an entity resolver) must have been done in advance.

If you have XML in a string, you can use the `parseString()` function instead:

xml.dom.minidom.parseString(*string*, *parser=None*)
    Return a `Document` that represents the *string*. This method creates an `io.StringIO` object for the string and passes that on to `parse()`.

Both functions return a `Document` object representing the content of the document.

What the `parse()` and `parseString()` functions do is connect an XML parser with a "DOM builder" that can accept parse events from any SAX parser and convert them into a DOM tree. The name of the functions are perhaps misleading, but are easy to grasp when learning the interfaces. The parsing of the document will be completed before these functions return; it's simply that these functions do not provide a parser implementation themselves.

You can also create a `Document` by calling a method on a "DOM Implementation" object. You can get this object either by calling the `getDOMImplementation()` function in the `xml.dom` package or the `xml.dom.minidom` module. Once you have a `Document`, you can add child nodes to it to populate the DOM:

```python
from xml.dom.minidom import getDOMImplementation

impl = getDOMImplementation()

newdoc = impl.createDocument(None, "some_tag", None)
top_element = newdoc.documentElement
text = newdoc.createTextNode('Some textual content.')
top_element.appendChild(text)
```

Once you have a DOM document object, you can access the parts of your XML document through its properties and methods. These properties are defined in the DOM specification. The main property of the document object is the `documentElement` property. It gives you the main element in the XML document: the one that holds all others. Here is an example program:

```
dom3 = parseString("<myxml>Some data</myxml>")
assert dom3.documentElement.tagName == "myxml"
```

When you are finished with a DOM tree, you may optionally call the `unlink()` method to encourage early cleanup of the now-unneeded objects. `unlink()` is an *xml.dom.minidom*-specific extension to the DOM API that renders the node and its descendants are essentially useless. Otherwise, Python's garbage collector will eventually take care of the objects in the tree.

See also:

Document Object Model (DOM) Level 1 Specification The W3C recommendation for the DOM supported by *xml.dom.minidom*.

20.7.1 DOM Objects

The definition of the DOM API for Python is given as part of the *xml.dom* module documentation. This section lists the differences between the API and *xml.dom.minidom*.

`Node.unlink()`
> Break internal references within the DOM so that it will be garbage collected on versions of Python without cyclic GC. Even when cyclic GC is available, using this can make large amounts of memory available sooner, so calling this on DOM objects as soon as they are no longer needed is good practice. This only needs to be called on the `Document` object, but may be called on child nodes to discard children of that node.
>
> You can avoid calling this method explicitly by using the `with` statement. The following code will automatically unlink *dom* when the `with` block is exited:

```
with xml.dom.minidom.parse(datasource) as dom:
    ... # Work with dom.
```

`Node.writexml(writer, indent="", addindent="", newl="")`
> Write XML to the writer object. The writer should have a `write()` method which matches that of the file object interface. The *indent* parameter is the indentation of the current node. The *addindent* parameter is the incremental indentation to use for subnodes of the current one. The *newl* parameter specifies the string to use to terminate newlines.
>
> For the `Document` node, an additional keyword argument *encoding* can be used to specify the encoding field of the XML header.

`Node.toxml(encoding=None)`
> Return a string or byte string containing the XML represented by the DOM node.
>
> With an explicit *encoding*[1] argument, the result is a byte string in the specified encoding. With no *encoding* argument, the result is a Unicode string, and the XML declaration in the resulting string does not specify an encoding. Encoding this string in an encoding other than UTF-8 is likely incorrect, since UTF-8 is the default encoding of XML.

`Node.toprettyxml(indent="", newl="", encoding="")`
> Return a pretty-printed version of the document. *indent* specifies the indentation string and defaults to a tabulator; *newl* specifies the string emitted at the end of each line and defaults to \n.
>
> The *encoding* argument behaves like the corresponding argument of *toxml()*.

---

[1] The encoding name included in the XML output should conform to the appropriate standards. For example, "UTF-8" is valid, but "UTF8" is not valid in an XML document's declaration, even though Python accepts it as an encoding name. See https://www.w3.org/TR/2006/REC-xml11-20060816/#NT-EncodingDecl and https://www.iana.org/assignments/character-sets/character-sets.xhtml.

20.7.2 DOM Example

This example program is a fairly realistic example of a simple program. In this particular case, we do not take much advantage of the flexibility of the DOM.

```
import xml.dom.minidom

document = """\
<slideshow>
<title>Demo slideshow</title>
<slide><title>Slide title</title>
<point>This is a demo</point>
<point>Of a program for processing slides</point>
</slide>

<slide><title>Another demo slide</title>
<point>It is important</point>
<point>To have more than</point>
<point>one slide</point>
</slide>
</slideshow>
"""

dom = xml.dom.minidom.parseString(document)

def getText(nodelist):
    rc = []
    for node in nodelist:
        if node.nodeType == node.TEXT_NODE:
            rc.append(node.data)
    return ''.join(rc)

def handleSlideshow(slideshow):
    print("<html>")
    handleSlideshowTitle(slideshow.getElementsByTagName("title")[0])
    slides = slideshow.getElementsByTagName("slide")
    handleToc(slides)
    handleSlides(slides)
    print("</html>")

def handleSlides(slides):
    for slide in slides:
        handleSlide(slide)

def handleSlide(slide):
    handleSlideTitle(slide.getElementsByTagName("title")[0])
    handlePoints(slide.getElementsByTagName("point"))

def handleSlideshowTitle(title):
    print("<title>%s</title>" % getText(title.childNodes))

def handleSlideTitle(title):
    print("<h2>%s</h2>" % getText(title.childNodes))

def handlePoints(points):
    print("<ul>")
    for point in points:
        handlePoint(point)
```

```
        print("</ul>")
def handlePoint(point):
    print("<li>%s</li>" % getText(point.childNodes))
def handleToc(slides):
    for slide in slides:
        title = slide.getElementsByTagName("title")[0]
        print("<p>%s</p>" % getText(title.childNodes))

handleSlideshow(dom)
```

20.7.3 minidom and the DOM standard

The *xml.dom.minidom* module is essentially a DOM 1.0-compatible DOM with some DOM 2 features (primarily namespace features).

Usage of the DOM interface in Python is straight-forward. The following mapping rules apply:

- Interfaces are accessed through instance objects. Applications should not instantiate the classes themselves; they should use the creator functions available on the Document object. Derived interfaces support all operations (and attributes) from the base interfaces, plus any new operations.
- Operations are used as methods. Since the DOM uses only in parameters, the arguments are passed in normal order (from left to right). There are no optional arguments. void operations return None.
- IDL attributes map to instance attributes. For compatibility with the OMG IDL language mapping for Python, an attribute foo can also be accessed through accessor methods _get_foo() and _set_foo(). readonly attributes must not be changed; this is not enforced at runtime.
- The types short int, unsigned int, unsigned long long, and boolean all map to Python integer objects.
- The type DOMString maps to Python strings. *xml.dom.minidom* supports either bytes or strings, but will normally produce strings. Values of type DOMString may also be None where allowed to have the IDL null value by the DOM specification from the W3C.
- const declarations map to variables in their respective scope (e.g. xml.dom.minidom.Node.PROCESSING_INSTRUCTION_NODE); they must not be changed.
- DOMException is currently not supported in *xml.dom.minidom*. Instead, *xml.dom.minidom* uses standard Python exceptions such as *TypeError* and *AttributeError*.
- NodeList objects are implemented using Python's built-in list type. These objects provide the interface defined in the DOM specification, but with earlier versions of Python they do not support the official API. They are, however, much more "Pythonic" than the interface defined in the W3C recommendations.

The following interfaces have no implementation in *xml.dom.minidom*:

- DOMTimeStamp
- DocumentType
- DOMImplementation
- CharacterData
- CDATASection
- Notation
- Entity

- EntityReference
- DocumentFragment

Most of these reflect information in the XML document that is not of general utility to most DOM users.

20.8 `xml.dom.pulldom` — Support for building partial DOM trees

Source code: Lib/xml/dom/pulldom.py

The *xml.dom.pulldom* module provides a "pull parser" which can also be asked to produce DOM-accessible fragments of the document where necessary. The basic concept involves pulling "events" from a stream of incoming XML and processing them. In contrast to SAX which also employs an event-driven processing model together with callbacks, the user of a pull parser is responsible for explicitly pulling events from the stream, looping over those events until either processing is finished or an error condition occurs.

> **Warning:** The *xml.dom.pulldom* module is not secure against maliciously constructed data. If you need to parse untrusted or unauthenticated data see *XML vulnerabilities*.

Example:

```
from xml.dom import pulldom

doc = pulldom.parse('sales_items.xml')
for event, node in doc:
    if event == pulldom.START_ELEMENT and node.tagName == 'item':
        if int(node.getAttribute('price')) > 50:
            doc.expandNode(node)
            print(node.toxml())
```

event is a constant and can be one of:

- START_ELEMENT
- END_ELEMENT
- COMMENT
- START_DOCUMENT
- END_DOCUMENT
- CHARACTERS
- PROCESSING_INSTRUCTION
- IGNORABLE_WHITESPACE

node is an object of type xml.dom.minidom.Document, xml.dom.minidom.Element or xml.dom.minidom.Text.

Since the document is treated as a "flat" stream of events, the document "tree" is implicitly traversed and the desired elements are found regardless of their depth in the tree. In other words, one does not need to consider hierarchical issues such as recursive searching of the document nodes, although if the context of elements were important, one would either need to maintain some context-related state (i.e. remembering where one is in the document at any given point) or to make use of the *DOMEventStream.expandNode()* method and switch to DOM-related processing.

class xml.dom.pulldom.PullDom(*documentFactory=None*)
  Subclass of *xml.sax.handler.ContentHandler*.

class xml.dom.pulldom.SAX2DOM(*documentFactory=None*)
  Subclass of *xml.sax.handler.ContentHandler*.

xml.dom.pulldom.parse(*stream_or_string, parser=None, bufsize=None*)
  Return a *DOMEventStream* from the given input. *stream_or_string* may be either a file name, or a file-like object. *parser*, if given, must be an *XMLReader* object. This function will change the document handler of the parser and activate namespace support; other parser configuration (like setting an entity resolver) must have been done in advance.

If you have XML in a string, you can use the *parseString()* function instead:

xml.dom.pulldom.parseString(*string, parser=None*)
  Return a *DOMEventStream* that represents the (Unicode) *string*.

xml.dom.pulldom.default_bufsize
  Default value for the *bufsize* parameter to *parse()*.

  The value of this variable can be changed before calling *parse()* and the new value will take effect.

20.8.1 DOMEventStream Objects

class xml.dom.pulldom.DOMEventStream(*stream, parser, bufsize*)

  getEvent()
    Return a tuple containing *event* and the current *node* as xml.dom.minidom.Document if event equals START_DOCUMENT, xml.dom.minidom.Element if event equals START_ELEMENT or END_ELEMENT or xml.dom.minidom.Text if event equals CHARACTERS. The current node does not contain information about its children, unless *expandNode()* is called.

  expandNode(*node*)
    Expands all children of *node* into *node*. Example:

    ```
    from xml.dom import pulldom

    xml = '<html><title>Foo</title> <p>Some text <div>and more</div></p> </html>'
    doc = pulldom.parseString(xml)
    for event, node in doc:
        if event == pulldom.START_ELEMENT and node.tagName == 'p':
            # Following statement only prints '<p/>'
            print(node.toxml())
            doc.expandNode(node)
            # Following statement prints node with all its children '<p>Some text <div>and
    more</div></p>'
            print(node.toxml())
    ```

  reset()

20.9 xml.sax — Support for SAX2 parsers

Source code: Lib/xml/sax/__init__.py

The `xml.sax` package provides a number of modules which implement the Simple API for XML (SAX) interface for Python. The package itself provides the SAX exceptions and the convenience functions which will be most used by users of the SAX API.

> **Warning:** The `xml.sax` module is not secure against maliciously constructed data. If you need to parse untrusted or unauthenticated data see *XML vulnerabilities*.

The convenience functions are:

xml.sax.**make_parser**(*parser_list=[]*)
> Create and return a SAX *XMLReader* object. The first parser found will be used. If *parser_list* is provided, it must be a sequence of strings which name modules that have a function named **create_parser()**. Modules listed in *parser_list* will be used before modules in the default list of parsers.

xml.sax.**parse**(*filename_or_stream, handler, error_handler=handler.ErrorHandler()*)
> Create a SAX parser and use it to parse a document. The document, passed in as *filename_or_stream*, can be a filename or a file object. The *handler* parameter needs to be a SAX *ContentHandler* instance. If *error_handler* is given, it must be a SAX *ErrorHandler* instance; if omitted, *SAXParseException* will be raised on all errors. There is no return value; all work must be done by the *handler* passed in.

xml.sax.**parseString**(*string, handler, error_handler=handler.ErrorHandler()*)
> Similar to *parse()*, but parses from a buffer *string* received as a parameter. *string* must be a `str` instance or a *bytes-like object*.
>
> Changed in version 3.5: Added support of `str` instances.

A typical SAX application uses three kinds of objects: readers, handlers and input sources. "Reader" in this context is another term for parser, i.e. some piece of code that reads the bytes or characters from the input source, and produces a sequence of events. The events then get distributed to the handler objects, i.e. the reader invokes a method on the handler. A SAX application must therefore obtain a reader object, create or open the input sources, create the handlers, and connect these objects all together. As the final step of preparation, the reader is called to parse the input. During parsing, methods on the handler objects are called based on structural and syntactic events from the input data.

For these objects, only the interfaces are relevant; they are normally not instantiated by the application itself. Since Python does not have an explicit notion of interface, they are formally introduced as classes, but applications may use implementations which do not inherit from the provided classes. The *InputSource*, *Locator*, **Attributes**, **AttributesNS**, and *XMLReader* interfaces are defined in the module `xml.sax.xmlreader`. The handler interfaces are defined in `xml.sax.handler`. For convenience, *InputSource* (which is often instantiated directly) and the handler classes are also available from `xml.sax`. These interfaces are described below.

In addition to these classes, `xml.sax` provides the following exception classes.

exception xml.sax.**SAXException**(*msg, exception=None*)
> Encapsulate an XML error or warning. This class can contain basic error or warning information from either the XML parser or the application: it can be subclassed to provide additional functionality or to add localization. Note that although the handlers defined in the *ErrorHandler* interface receive instances of this exception, it is not required to actually raise the exception — it is also useful as a container for information.
>
> When instantiated, *msg* should be a human-readable description of the error. The optional *exception* parameter, if given, should be **None** or an exception that was caught by the parsing code and is being passed along as information.
>
> This is the base class for the other SAX exception classes.

exception xml.sax.SAXParseException(*msg, exception, locator*)
    Subclass of *SAXException* raised on parse errors. Instances of this class are passed to the methods of the SAX *ErrorHandler* interface to provide information about the parse error. This class supports the SAX *Locator* interface as well as the *SAXException* interface.

exception xml.sax.SAXNotRecognizedException(*msg, exception=None*)
    Subclass of *SAXException* raised when a SAX *XMLReader* is confronted with an unrecognized feature or property. SAX applications and extensions may use this class for similar purposes.

exception xml.sax.SAXNotSupportedException(*msg, exception=None*)
    Subclass of *SAXException* raised when a SAX *XMLReader* is asked to enable a feature that is not supported, or to set a property to a value that the implementation does not support. SAX applications and extensions may use this class for similar purposes.

See also:

SAX: The Simple API for XML This site is the focal point for the definition of the SAX API. It provides a Java implementation and online documentation. Links to implementations and historical information are also available.

Module *xml.sax.handler* Definitions of the interfaces for application-provided objects.

Module *xml.sax.saxutils* Convenience functions for use in SAX applications.

Module *xml.sax.xmlreader* Definitions of the interfaces for parser-provided objects.

20.9.1 SAXException Objects

The *SAXException* exception class supports the following methods:

SAXException.getMessage()
    Return a human-readable message describing the error condition.

SAXException.getException()
    Return an encapsulated exception object, or None.

20.10 xml.sax.handler — Base classes for SAX handlers

Source code: Lib/xml/sax/handler.py

The SAX API defines four kinds of handlers: content handlers, DTD handlers, error handlers, and entity resolvers. Applications normally only need to implement those interfaces whose events they are interested in; they can implement the interfaces in a single object or in multiple objects. Handler implementations should inherit from the base classes provided in the module *xml.sax.handler*, so that all methods get default implementations.

class xml.sax.handler.ContentHandler
    This is the main callback interface in SAX, and the one most important to applications. The order of events in this interface mirrors the order of the information in the document.

class xml.sax.handler.DTDHandler
    Handle DTD events.

    This interface specifies only those DTD events required for basic parsing (unparsed entities and attributes).

class xml.sax.handler.`EntityResolver`
    Basic interface for resolving entities. If you create an object implementing this interface, then register the object with your Parser, the parser will call the method in your object to resolve all external entities.

class xml.sax.handler.`ErrorHandler`
    Interface used by the parser to present error and warning messages to the application. The methods of this object control whether errors are immediately converted to exceptions or are handled in some other way.

In addition to these classes, *xml.sax.handler* provides symbolic constants for the feature and property names.

xml.sax.handler.`feature_namespaces`

> value: "http://xml.org/sax/features/namespaces"
> true: Perform Namespace processing.
> false: Optionally do not perform Namespace processing (implies namespace-prefixes; default).
> access: (parsing) read-only; (not parsing) read/write

xml.sax.handler.`feature_namespace_prefixes`

> value: "http://xml.org/sax/features/namespace-prefixes"
> true: Report the original prefixed names and attributes used for Namespace declarations.
> false: Do not report attributes used for Namespace declarations, and optionally do not report original prefixed names (default).
> access: (parsing) read-only; (not parsing) read/write

xml.sax.handler.`feature_string_interning`

> value: "http://xml.org/sax/features/string-interning"
> true: All element names, prefixes, attribute names, Namespace URIs, and local names are interned using the built-in intern function.
> false: Names are not necessarily interned, although they may be (default).
> access: (parsing) read-only; (not parsing) read/write

xml.sax.handler.`feature_validation`

> value: "http://xml.org/sax/features/validation"
> true: Report all validation errors (implies external-general-entities and external-parameter-entities).
> false: Do not report validation errors.
> access: (parsing) read-only; (not parsing) read/write

xml.sax.handler.`feature_external_ges`

> value: "http://xml.org/sax/features/external-general-entities"
> true: Include all external general (text) entities.
> false: Do not include external general entities.
> access: (parsing) read-only; (not parsing) read/write

xml.sax.handler.`feature_external_pes`

> value: "http://xml.org/sax/features/external-parameter-entities"
> true: Include all external parameter entities, including the external DTD subset.

false: Do not include any external parameter entities, even the external DTD subset.

access: (parsing) read-only; (not parsing) read/write

xml.sax.handler.all_features
List of all features.

xml.sax.handler.property_lexical_handler

value: `"http://xml.org/sax/properties/lexical-handler"`

data type: xml.sax.sax2lib.LexicalHandler (not supported in Python 2)

description: An optional extension handler for lexical events like comments.

access: read/write

xml.sax.handler.property_declaration_handler

value: `"http://xml.org/sax/properties/declaration-handler"`

data type: xml.sax.sax2lib.DeclHandler (not supported in Python 2)

description: An optional extension handler for DTD-related events other than notations and unparsed entities.

access: read/write

xml.sax.handler.property_dom_node

value: `"http://xml.org/sax/properties/dom-node"`

data type: org.w3c.dom.Node (not supported in Python 2)

description: When parsing, the current DOM node being visited if this is a DOM iterator; when not parsing, the root DOM node for iteration.

access: (parsing) read-only; (not parsing) read/write

xml.sax.handler.property_xml_string

value: `"http://xml.org/sax/properties/xml-string"`

data type: String

description: The literal string of characters that was the source for the current event.

access: read-only

xml.sax.handler.all_properties
List of all known property names.

20.10.1 ContentHandler Objects

Users are expected to subclass *ContentHandler* to support their application. The following methods are called by the parser on the appropriate events in the input document:

ContentHandler.setDocumentLocator(*locator*)
Called by the parser to give the application a locator for locating the origin of document events.

SAX parsers are strongly encouraged (though not absolutely required) to supply a locator: if it does so, it must supply the locator to the application by invoking this method before invoking any of the other methods in the DocumentHandler interface.

The locator allows the application to determine the end position of any document-related event, even if the parser is not reporting an error. Typically, the application will use this information for reporting its own errors (such as character content that does not match an application's business rules). The information returned by the locator is probably not sufficient for use with a search engine.

Note that the locator will return correct information only during the invocation of the events in this interface. The application should not attempt to use it at any other time.

ContentHandler.startDocument()
Receive notification of the beginning of a document.

The SAX parser will invoke this method only once, before any other methods in this interface or in DTDHandler (except for *setDocumentLocator()*).

ContentHandler.endDocument()
Receive notification of the end of a document.

The SAX parser will invoke this method only once, and it will be the last method invoked during the parse. The parser shall not invoke this method until it has either abandoned parsing (because of an unrecoverable error) or reached the end of input.

ContentHandler.startPrefixMapping(*prefix*, *uri***)**
Begin the scope of a prefix-URI Namespace mapping.

The information from this event is not necessary for normal Namespace processing: the SAX XML reader will automatically replace prefixes for element and attribute names when the **feature_namespaces** feature is enabled (the default).

There are cases, however, when applications need to use prefixes in character data or in attribute values, where they cannot safely be expanded automatically; the *startPrefixMapping()* and *endPrefixMapping()* events supply the information to the application to expand prefixes in those contexts itself, if necessary.

Note that *startPrefixMapping()* and *endPrefixMapping()* events are not guaranteed to be properly nested relative to each-other: all *startPrefixMapping()* events will occur before the corresponding *startElement()* event, and all *endPrefixMapping()* events will occur after the corresponding *endElement()* event, but their order is not guaranteed.

ContentHandler.endPrefixMapping(*prefix***)**
End the scope of a prefix-URI mapping.

See *startPrefixMapping()* for details. This event will always occur after the corresponding *endElement()* event, but the order of *endPrefixMapping()* events is not otherwise guaranteed.

ContentHandler.startElement(*name*, *attrs***)**
Signals the start of an element in non-namespace mode.

The *name* parameter contains the raw XML 1.0 name of the element type as a string and the *attrs* parameter holds an object of the **Attributes** interface (see *The Attributes Interface*) containing the attributes of the element. The object passed as *attrs* may be re-used by the parser; holding on to a reference to it is not a reliable way to keep a copy of the attributes. To keep a copy of the attributes, use the *copy()* method of the *attrs* object.

ContentHandler.endElement(*name***)**
Signals the end of an element in non-namespace mode.

The *name* parameter contains the name of the element type, just as with the *startElement()* event.

ContentHandler.startElementNS(*name*, *qname*, *attrs***)**
Signals the start of an element in namespace mode.

The *name* parameter contains the name of the element type as a (**uri**, **localname**) tuple, the *qname* parameter contains the raw XML 1.0 name used in the source document, and the *attrs* parameter holds an instance of the **AttributesNS** interface (see *The AttributesNS Interface*) containing the attributes of the element. If no namespace is associated with the element, the *uri* component of *name* will be **None**. The object passed as *attrs* may be re-used by the parser; holding on to a reference to it is not a reliable way to keep a copy of the attributes. To keep a copy of the attributes, use the *copy()* method of the *attrs* object.

Parsers may set the *qname* parameter to None, unless the `feature_namespace_prefixes` feature is activated.

ContentHandler.endElementNS(*name, qname*)
Signals the end of an element in namespace mode.

The *name* parameter contains the name of the element type, just as with the *startElementNS()* method, likewise the *qname* parameter.

ContentHandler.characters(*content*)
Receive notification of character data.

The Parser will call this method to report each chunk of character data. SAX parsers may return all contiguous character data in a single chunk, or they may split it into several chunks; however, all of the characters in any single event must come from the same external entity so that the Locator provides useful information.

content may be a string or bytes instance; the `expat` reader module always produces strings.

Note: The earlier SAX 1 interface provided by the Python XML Special Interest Group used a more Java-like interface for this method. Since most parsers used from Python did not take advantage of the older interface, the simpler signature was chosen to replace it. To convert old code to the new interface, use *content* instead of slicing content with the old *offset* and *length* parameters.

ContentHandler.ignorableWhitespace(*whitespace*)
Receive notification of ignorable whitespace in element content.

Validating Parsers must use this method to report each chunk of ignorable whitespace (see the W3C XML 1.0 recommendation, section 2.10): non-validating parsers may also use this method if they are capable of parsing and using content models.

SAX parsers may return all contiguous whitespace in a single chunk, or they may split it into several chunks; however, all of the characters in any single event must come from the same external entity, so that the Locator provides useful information.

ContentHandler.processingInstruction(*target, data*)
Receive notification of a processing instruction.

The Parser will invoke this method once for each processing instruction found: note that processing instructions may occur before or after the main document element.

A SAX parser should never report an XML declaration (XML 1.0, section 2.8) or a text declaration (XML 1.0, section 4.3.1) using this method.

ContentHandler.skippedEntity(*name*)
Receive notification of a skipped entity.

The Parser will invoke this method once for each entity skipped. Non-validating processors may skip entities if they have not seen the declarations (because, for example, the entity was declared in an external DTD subset). All processors may skip external entities, depending on the values of the `feature_external_ges` and the `feature_external_pes` properties.

20.10.2 DTDHandler Objects

DTDHandler instances provide the following methods:

DTDHandler.notationDecl(*name, publicId, systemId*)
Handle a notation declaration event.

DTDHandler.unparsedEntityDecl(*name, publicId, systemId, ndata*)
Handle an unparsed entity declaration event.

20.10.3 EntityResolver Objects

EntityResolver.resolveEntity(*publicId*, *systemId*)
    Resolve the system identifier of an entity and return either the system identifier to read from as a string, or an InputSource to read from. The default implementation returns *systemId*.

20.10.4 ErrorHandler Objects

Objects with this interface are used to receive error and warning information from the *XMLReader*. If you create an object that implements this interface, then register the object with your *XMLReader*, the parser will call the methods in your object to report all warnings and errors. There are three levels of errors available: warnings, (possibly) recoverable errors, and unrecoverable errors. All methods take a SAXParseException as the only parameter. Errors and warnings may be converted to an exception by raising the passed-in exception object.

ErrorHandler.error(*exception*)
    Called when the parser encounters a recoverable error. If this method does not raise an exception, parsing may continue, but further document information should not be expected by the application. Allowing the parser to continue may allow additional errors to be discovered in the input document.

ErrorHandler.fatalError(*exception*)
    Called when the parser encounters an error it cannot recover from; parsing is expected to terminate when this method returns.

ErrorHandler.warning(*exception*)
    Called when the parser presents minor warning information to the application. Parsing is expected to continue when this method returns, and document information will continue to be passed to the application. Raising an exception in this method will cause parsing to end.

20.11 `xml.sax.saxutils` — SAX Utilities

Source code: Lib/xml/sax/saxutils.py

The module *xml.sax.saxutils* contains a number of classes and functions that are commonly useful when creating SAX applications, either in direct use, or as base classes.

xml.sax.saxutils.escape(*data*, *entities={}*)
    Escape '&', '<', and '>' in a string of data.

    You can escape other strings of data by passing a dictionary as the optional *entities* parameter. The keys and values must all be strings; each key will be replaced with its corresponding value. The characters '&', '<' and '>' are always escaped, even if *entities* is provided.

xml.sax.saxutils.unescape(*data*, *entities={}*)
    Unescape '&', '<', and '>' in a string of data.

    You can unescape other strings of data by passing a dictionary as the optional *entities* parameter. The keys and values must all be strings; each key will be replaced with its corresponding value. '&', '<', and '>' are always unescaped, even if *entities* is provided.

xml.sax.saxutils.quoteattr(*data*, *entities={}*)
    Similar to *escape()*, but also prepares *data* to be used as an attribute value. The return value is a quoted version of *data* with any additional required replacements. *quoteattr()* will select a quote character based on the content of *data*, attempting to avoid encoding any quote characters in the string. If both single- and double-quote characters are already in *data*, the double-quote characters

will be encoded and *data* will be wrapped in double-quotes. The resulting string can be used directly as an attribute value:

```
>>> print("<element attr=%s>" % quoteattr("ab ' cd \" ef"))
<element attr="ab ' cd &quot; ef">
```

This function is useful when generating attribute values for HTML or any SGML using the reference concrete syntax.

class xml.sax.saxutils.XMLGenerator(*out=None, encoding='iso-8859-1', short_empty_elements=False*)

This class implements the *ContentHandler* interface by writing SAX events back into an XML document. In other words, using an *XMLGenerator* as the content handler will reproduce the original document being parsed. *out* should be a file-like object which will default to *sys.stdout*. *encoding* is the encoding of the output stream which defaults to `'iso-8859-1'`. *short_empty_elements* controls the formatting of elements that contain no content: if `False` (the default) they are emitted as a pair of start/end tags, if set to `True` they are emitted as a single self-closed tag.

New in version 3.2: The *short_empty_elements* parameter.

class xml.sax.saxutils.XMLFilterBase(*base*)

This class is designed to sit between an *XMLReader* and the client application's event handlers. By default, it does nothing but pass requests up to the reader and events on to the handlers unmodified, but subclasses can override specific methods to modify the event stream or the configuration requests as they pass through.

xml.sax.saxutils.prepare_input_source(*source, base=""*)

This function takes an input source and an optional base URL and returns a fully resolved *InputSource* object ready for reading. The input source can be given as a string, a file-like object, or an *InputSource* object; parsers will use this function to implement the polymorphic *source* argument to their **parse()** method.

20.12 xml.sax.xmlreader — Interface for XML parsers

Source code: Lib/xml/sax/xmlreader.py

SAX parsers implement the *XMLReader* interface. They are implemented in a Python module, which must provide a function **create_parser()**. This function is invoked by *xml.sax.make_parser()* with no arguments to create a new parser object.

class xml.sax.xmlreader.XMLReader

Base class which can be inherited by SAX parsers.

class xml.sax.xmlreader.IncrementalParser

In some cases, it is desirable not to parse an input source at once, but to feed chunks of the document as they get available. Note that the reader will normally not read the entire file, but read it in chunks as well; still **parse()** won't return until the entire document is processed. So these interfaces should be used if the blocking behaviour of **parse()** is not desirable.

When the parser is instantiated it is ready to begin accepting data from the feed method immediately. After parsing has been finished with a call to close the reset method must be called to make the parser ready to accept new data, either from feed or using the parse method.

Note that these methods must *not* be called during parsing, that is, after parse has been called and before it returns.

By default, the class also implements the parse method of the XMLReader interface using the feed, close and reset methods of the IncrementalParser interface as a convenience to SAX 2.0 driver writers.

class xml.sax.xmlreader.Locator
    Interface for associating a SAX event with a document location. A locator object will return valid results only during calls to DocumentHandler methods; at any other time, the results are unpredictable. If information is not available, methods may return None.

class xml.sax.xmlreader.InputSource(*system_id=None*)
    Encapsulation of the information needed by the *XMLReader* to read entities.

    This class may include information about the public identifier, system identifier, byte stream (possibly with character encoding information) and/or the character stream of an entity.

    Applications will create objects of this class for use in the *XMLReader.parse()* method and for returning from EntityResolver.resolveEntity.

    An *InputSource* belongs to the application, the *XMLReader* is not allowed to modify *InputSource* objects passed to it from the application, although it may make copies and modify those.

class xml.sax.xmlreader.AttributesImpl(*attrs*)
    This is an implementation of the **Attributes** interface (see section *The Attributes Interface*). This is a dictionary-like object which represents the element attributes in a **startElement()** call. In addition to the most useful dictionary operations, it supports a number of other methods as described by the interface. Objects of this class should be instantiated by readers; *attrs* must be a dictionary-like object containing a mapping from attribute names to attribute values.

class xml.sax.xmlreader.AttributesNSImpl(*attrs, qnames*)
    Namespace-aware variant of *AttributesImpl*, which will be passed to **startElementNS()**. It is derived from *AttributesImpl*, but understands attribute names as two-tuples of *namespaceURI* and *localname*. In addition, it provides a number of methods expecting qualified names as they appear in the original document. This class implements the **AttributesNS** interface (see section *The AttributesNS Interface*).

20.12.1 XMLReader Objects

The *XMLReader* interface supports the following methods:

XMLReader.parse(*source*)
    Process an input source, producing SAX events. The *source* object can be a system identifier (a string identifying the input source – typically a file name or a URL), a file-like object, or an *InputSource* object. When *parse()* returns, the input is completely processed, and the parser object can be discarded or reset.

    Changed in version 3.5: Added support of character streams.

XMLReader.getContentHandler()
    Return the current *ContentHandler*.

XMLReader.setContentHandler(*handler*)
    Set the current *ContentHandler*. If no *ContentHandler* is set, content events will be discarded.

XMLReader.getDTDHandler()
    Return the current *DTDHandler*.

XMLReader.setDTDHandler(*handler*)
    Set the current *DTDHandler*. If no *DTDHandler* is set, DTD events will be discarded.

XMLReader.getEntityResolver()
    Return the current *EntityResolver*.

XMLReader.setEntityResolver(*handler*)
    Set the current *EntityResolver*. If no *EntityResolver* is set, attempts to resolve an external entity will result in opening the system identifier for the entity, and fail if it is not available.

XMLReader.getErrorHandler()
    Return the current *ErrorHandler*.

XMLReader.setErrorHandler(*handler***)**
    Set the current error handler. If no *ErrorHandler* is set, errors will be raised as exceptions, and warnings will be printed.

XMLReader.setLocale(*locale***)**
    Allow an application to set the locale for errors and warnings.

    SAX parsers are not required to provide localization for errors and warnings; if they cannot support the requested locale, however, they must raise a SAX exception. Applications may request a locale change in the middle of a parse.

XMLReader.getFeature(*featurename***)**
    Return the current setting for feature *featurename*. If the feature is not recognized, SAXNotRecognizedException is raised. The well-known featurenames are listed in the module *xml.sax.handler*.

XMLReader.setFeature(*featurename*, *value***)**
    Set the *featurename* to *value*. If the feature is not recognized, SAXNotRecognizedException is raised. If the feature or its setting is not supported by the parser, *SAXNotSupportedException* is raised.

XMLReader.getProperty(*propertyname***)**
    Return the current setting for property *propertyname*. If the property is not recognized, a SAXNotRecognizedException is raised. The well-known propertynames are listed in the module *xml.sax.handler*.

XMLReader.setProperty(*propertyname*, *value***)**
    Set the *propertyname* to *value*. If the property is not recognized, SAXNotRecognizedException is raised. If the property or its setting is not supported by the parser, *SAXNotSupportedException* is raised.

20.12.2 IncrementalParser Objects

Instances of *IncrementalParser* offer the following additional methods:

IncrementalParser.feed(*data***)**
    Process a chunk of *data*.

IncrementalParser.close()
    Assume the end of the document. That will check well-formedness conditions that can be checked only at the end, invoke handlers, and may clean up resources allocated during parsing.

IncrementalParser.reset()
    This method is called after close has been called to reset the parser so that it is ready to parse new documents. The results of calling parse or feed after close without calling reset are undefined.

20.12.3 Locator Objects

Instances of *Locator* provide these methods:

Locator.getColumnNumber()
    Return the column number where the current event begins.

Locator.getLineNumber()
    Return the line number where the current event begins.

Locator.getPublicId()
    Return the public identifier for the current event.

`Locator.getSystemId()`
    Return the system identifier for the current event.

20.12.4 InputSource Objects

`InputSource.setPublicId(id)`
    Sets the public identifier of this *InputSource*.

`InputSource.getPublicId()`
    Returns the public identifier of this *InputSource*.

`InputSource.setSystemId(id)`
    Sets the system identifier of this *InputSource*.

`InputSource.getSystemId()`
    Returns the system identifier of this *InputSource*.

`InputSource.setEncoding(encoding)`
    Sets the character encoding of this *InputSource*.

    The encoding must be a string acceptable for an XML encoding declaration (see section 4.3.3 of the XML recommendation).

    The encoding attribute of the *InputSource* is ignored if the *InputSource* also contains a character stream.

`InputSource.getEncoding()`
    Get the character encoding of this InputSource.

`InputSource.setByteStream(bytefile)`
    Set the byte stream (a *binary file*) for this input source.

    The SAX parser will ignore this if there is also a character stream specified, but it will use a byte stream in preference to opening a URI connection itself.

    If the application knows the character encoding of the byte stream, it should set it with the setEncoding method.

`InputSource.getByteStream()`
    Get the byte stream for this input source.

    The getEncoding method will return the character encoding for this byte stream, or **None** if unknown.

`InputSource.setCharacterStream(charfile)`
    Set the character stream (a *text file*) for this input source.

    If there is a character stream specified, the SAX parser will ignore any byte stream and will not attempt to open a URI connection to the system identifier.

`InputSource.getCharacterStream()`
    Get the character stream for this input source.

20.12.5 The `Attributes` Interface

`Attributes` objects implement a portion of the *mapping protocol*, including the methods `copy()`, `get()`, `__contains__()`, `items()`, `keys()`, and `values()`. The following methods are also provided:

`Attributes.getLength()`
    Return the number of attributes.

`Attributes.getNames()`
    Return the names of the attributes.

Attributes.getType(*name*)
    Returns the type of the attribute *name*, which is normally `'CDATA'`.

Attributes.getValue(*name*)
    Return the value of attribute *name*.

20.12.6 The `AttributesNS` Interface

This interface is a subtype of the `Attributes` interface (see section *The Attributes Interface*). All methods supported by that interface are also available on `AttributesNS` objects.

The following methods are also available:

AttributesNS.getValueByQName(*name*)
    Return the value for a qualified name.

AttributesNS.getNameByQName(*name*)
    Return the `(namespace, localname)` pair for a qualified *name*.

AttributesNS.getQNameByName(*name*)
    Return the qualified name for a `(namespace, localname)` pair.

AttributesNS.getQNames()
    Return the qualified names of all attributes.

20.13 `xml.parsers.expat` — Fast XML parsing using Expat

> **Warning:** The `pyexpat` module is not secure against maliciously constructed data. If you need to parse untrusted or unauthenticated data see *XML vulnerabilities*.

The *xml.parsers.expat* module is a Python interface to the Expat non-validating XML parser. The module provides a single extension type, `xmlparser`, that represents the current state of an XML parser. After an `xmlparser` object has been created, various attributes of the object can be set to handler functions. When an XML document is then fed to the parser, the handler functions are called for the character data and markup in the XML document.

This module uses the `pyexpat` module to provide access to the Expat parser. Direct use of the `pyexpat` module is deprecated.

This module provides one exception and one type object:

exception xml.parsers.expat.ExpatError
    The exception raised when Expat reports an error. See section *ExpatError Exceptions* for more information on interpreting Expat errors.

exception xml.parsers.expat.error
    Alias for *ExpatError*.

xml.parsers.expat.XMLParserType
    The type of the return values from the *ParserCreate()* function.

The *xml.parsers.expat* module contains two functions:

xml.parsers.expat.ErrorString(*errno*)
    Returns an explanatory string for a given error number *errno*.

xml.parsers.expat.ParserCreate(*encoding=None, namespace_separator=None*)

Creates and returns a new xmlparser object. *encoding*, if specified, must be a string naming the encoding used by the XML data. Expat doesn't support as many encodings as Python does, and its repertoire of encodings can't be extended; it supports UTF-8, UTF-16, ISO-8859-1 (Latin1), and ASCII. If *encoding*[1] is given it will override the implicit or explicit encoding of the document.

Expat can optionally do XML namespace processing for you, enabled by providing a value for *namespace_separator*. The value must be a one-character string; a `ValueError` will be raised if the string has an illegal length (None is considered the same as omission). When namespace processing is enabled, element type names and attribute names that belong to a namespace will be expanded. The element name passed to the element handlers `StartElementHandler` and `EndElementHandler` will be the concatenation of the namespace URI, the namespace separator character, and the local part of the name. If the namespace separator is a zero byte (`chr(0)`) then the namespace URI and the local part will be concatenated without any separator.

For example, if *namespace_separator* is set to a space character (' ') and the following document is parsed:

```
<?xml version="1.0"?>
<root xmlns    = "http://default-namespace.org/"
      xmlns:py = "http://www.python.org/ns/">
  <py:elem1 />
  <elem2 xmlns="" />
</root>
```

`StartElementHandler` will receive the following strings for each element:

```
http://default-namespace.org/ root
http://www.python.org/ns/ elem1
elem2
```

Due to limitations in the Expat library used by pyexpat, the xmlparser instance returned can only be used to parse a single XML document. Call `ParserCreate` for each document to provide unique parser instances.

See also:

The Expat XML Parser Home page of the Expat project.

20.13.1 XMLParser Objects

xmlparser objects have the following methods:

xmlparser.Parse(*data*[, *isfinal*])

Parses the contents of the string *data*, calling the appropriate handler functions to process the parsed data. *isfinal* must be true on the final call to this method; it allows the parsing of a single file in fragments, not the submission of multiple files. *data* can be the empty string at any time.

xmlparser.ParseFile(*file*)

Parse XML data reading from the object *file*. *file* only needs to provide the `read(nbytes)` method, returning the empty string when there's no more data.

xmlparser.SetBase(*base*)

Sets the base to be used for resolving relative URIs in system identifiers in declarations. Resolving relative identifiers is left to the application: this value will be passed through as the *base* argument

---

[1] The encoding string included in XML output should conform to the appropriate standards. For example, "UTF-8" is valid, but "UTF8" is not. See https://www.w3.org/TR/2006/REC-xml11-20060816/#NT-EncodingDecl and https://www.iana.org/assignments/character-sets/character-sets.xhtml.

to the `ExternalEntityRefHandler()`, `NotationDeclHandler()`, and `UnparsedEntityDeclHandler()` functions.

`xmlparser.GetBase()`
> Returns a string containing the base set by a previous call to `SetBase()`, or **None** if `SetBase()` hasn't been called.

`xmlparser.GetInputContext()`
> Returns the input data that generated the current event as a string. The data is in the encoding of the entity which contains the text. When called while an event handler is not active, the return value is **None**.

`xmlparser.ExternalEntityParserCreate(context[, encoding])`
> Create a "child" parser which can be used to parse an external parsed entity referred to by content parsed by the parent parser. The *context* parameter should be the string passed to the `ExternalEntityRefHandler()` handler function, described below. The child parser is created with the `ordered_attributes` and `specified_attributes` set to the values of this parser.

`xmlparser.SetParamEntityParsing(flag)`
> Control parsing of parameter entities (including the external DTD subset). Possible *flag* values are `XML_PARAM_ENTITY_PARSING_NEVER`, `XML_PARAM_ENTITY_PARSING_UNLESS_STANDALONE` and `XML_PARAM_ENTITY_PARSING_ALWAYS`. Return true if setting the flag was successful.

`xmlparser.UseForeignDTD([flag])`
> Calling this with a true value for *flag* (the default) will cause Expat to call the `ExternalEntityRefHandler` with **None** for all arguments to allow an alternate DTD to be loaded. If the document does not contain a document type declaration, the `ExternalEntityRefHandler` will still be called, but the `StartDoctypeDeclHandler` and `EndDoctypeDeclHandler` will not be called.
>
> Passing a false value for *flag* will cancel a previous call that passed a true value, but otherwise has no effect.
>
> This method can only be called before the `Parse()` or `ParseFile()` methods are called; calling it after either of those have been called causes `ExpatError` to be raised with the `code` attribute set to `errors.codes[errors.XML_ERROR_CANT_CHANGE_FEATURE_ONCE_PARSING]`.

`xmlparser` objects have the following attributes:

`xmlparser.buffer_size`
> The size of the buffer used when `buffer_text` is true. A new buffer size can be set by assigning a new integer value to this attribute. When the size is changed, the buffer will be flushed.

`xmlparser.buffer_text`
> Setting this to true causes the `xmlparser` object to buffer textual content returned by Expat to avoid multiple calls to the `CharacterDataHandler()` callback whenever possible. This can improve performance substantially since Expat normally breaks character data into chunks at every line ending. This attribute is false by default, and may be changed at any time.

`xmlparser.buffer_used`
> If `buffer_text` is enabled, the number of bytes stored in the buffer. These bytes represent UTF-8 encoded text. This attribute has no meaningful interpretation when `buffer_text` is false.

`xmlparser.ordered_attributes`
> Setting this attribute to a non-zero integer causes the attributes to be reported as a list rather than a dictionary. The attributes are presented in the order found in the document text. For each attribute, two list entries are presented: the attribute name and the attribute value. (Older versions of this module also used this format.) By default, this attribute is false; it may be changed at any time.

`xmlparser.specified_attributes`
> If set to a non-zero integer, the parser will report only those attributes which were specified in the document instance and not those which were derived from attribute declarations. Applications which

set this need to be especially careful to use what additional information is available from the declarations as needed to comply with the standards for the behavior of XML processors. By default, this attribute is false; it may be changed at any time.

The following attributes contain values relating to the most recent error encountered by an **xmlparser** object, and will only have correct values once a call to `Parse()` or `ParseFile()` has raised an *xml.parsers.expat. ExpatError* exception.

xmlparser.ErrorByteIndex
Byte index at which an error occurred.

xmlparser.ErrorCode
Numeric code specifying the problem. This value can be passed to the *ErrorString()* function, or compared to one of the constants defined in the **errors** object.

xmlparser.ErrorColumnNumber
Column number at which an error occurred.

xmlparser.ErrorLineNumber
Line number at which an error occurred.

The following attributes contain values relating to the current parse location in an **xmlparser** object. During a callback reporting a parse event they indicate the location of the first of the sequence of characters that generated the event. When called outside of a callback, the position indicated will be just past the last parse event (regardless of whether there was an associated callback).

xmlparser.CurrentByteIndex
Current byte index in the parser input.

xmlparser.CurrentColumnNumber
Current column number in the parser input.

xmlparser.CurrentLineNumber
Current line number in the parser input.

Here is the list of handlers that can be set. To set a handler on an **xmlparser** object *o*, use `o.handlername = func`. *handlername* must be taken from the following list, and *func* must be a callable object accepting the correct number of arguments. The arguments are all strings, unless otherwise stated.

xmlparser.XmlDeclHandler(*version, encoding, standalone*)
Called when the XML declaration is parsed. The XML declaration is the (optional) declaration of the applicable version of the XML recommendation, the encoding of the document text, and an optional "standalone" declaration. *version* and *encoding* will be strings, and *standalone* will be 1 if the document is declared standalone, 0 if it is declared not to be standalone, or -1 if the standalone clause was omitted. This is only available with Expat version 1.95.0 or newer.

xmlparser.StartDoctypeDeclHandler(*doctypeName, systemId, publicId, has_internal_subset*)
Called when Expat begins parsing the document type declaration (`<!DOCTYPE ...`). The *doctypeName* is provided exactly as presented. The *systemId* and *publicId* parameters give the system and public identifiers if specified, or `None` if omitted. *has_internal_subset* will be true if the document contains and internal document declaration subset. This requires Expat version 1.2 or newer.

xmlparser.EndDoctypeDeclHandler()
Called when Expat is done parsing the document type declaration. This requires Expat version 1.2 or newer.

xmlparser.ElementDeclHandler(*name, model*)
Called once for each element type declaration. *name* is the name of the element type, and *model* is a representation of the content model.

xmlparser.AttlistDeclHandler(*elname, attname, type, default, required*)
Called for each declared attribute for an element type. If an attribute list declaration declares three attributes, this handler is called three times, once for each attribute. *elname* is the name of the element

to which the declaration applies and *attname* is the name of the attribute declared. The attribute type is a string passed as *type*; the possible values are `'CDATA'`, `'ID'`, `'IDREF'`, ... *default* gives the default value for the attribute used when the attribute is not specified by the document instance, or `None` if there is no default value (`#IMPLIED` values). If the attribute is required to be given in the document instance, *required* will be true. This requires Expat version 1.95.0 or newer.

xmlparser.StartElementHandler(*name, attributes*)
Called for the start of every element. *name* is a string containing the element name, and *attributes* is the element attributes. If *ordered_attributes* is true, this is a list (see *ordered_attributes* for a full description). Otherwise it's a dictionary mapping names to values.

xmlparser.EndElementHandler(*name*)
Called for the end of every element.

xmlparser.ProcessingInstructionHandler(*target, data*)
Called for every processing instruction.

xmlparser.CharacterDataHandler(*data*)
Called for character data. This will be called for normal character data, CDATA marked content, and ignorable whitespace. Applications which must distinguish these cases can use the *StartCdataSectionHandler*, *EndCdataSectionHandler*, and *ElementDeclHandler* callbacks to collect the required information.

xmlparser.UnparsedEntityDeclHandler(*entityName, base, systemId, publicId, notationName*)
Called for unparsed (NDATA) entity declarations. This is only present for version 1.2 of the Expat library; for more recent versions, use *EntityDeclHandler* instead. (The underlying function in the Expat library has been declared obsolete.)

xmlparser.EntityDeclHandler(*entityName, is_parameter_entity, value, base, systemId, publicId, notationName*)
Called for all entity declarations. For parameter and internal entities, *value* will be a string giving the declared contents of the entity; this will be `None` for external entities. The *notationName* parameter will be `None` for parsed entities, and the name of the notation for unparsed entities. *is_parameter_entity* will be true if the entity is a parameter entity or false for general entities (most applications only need to be concerned with general entities). This is only available starting with version 1.95.0 of the Expat library.

xmlparser.NotationDeclHandler(*notationName, base, systemId, publicId*)
Called for notation declarations. *notationName*, *base*, and *systemId*, and *publicId* are strings if given. If the public identifier is omitted, *publicId* will be `None`.

xmlparser.StartNamespaceDeclHandler(*prefix, uri*)
Called when an element contains a namespace declaration. Namespace declarations are processed before the *StartElementHandler* is called for the element on which declarations are placed.

xmlparser.EndNamespaceDeclHandler(*prefix*)
Called when the closing tag is reached for an element that contained a namespace declaration. This is called once for each namespace declaration on the element in the reverse of the order for which the *StartNamespaceDeclHandler* was called to indicate the start of each namespace declaration's scope. Calls to this handler are made after the corresponding *EndElementHandler* for the end of the element.

xmlparser.CommentHandler(*data*)
Called for comments. *data* is the text of the comment, excluding the leading `'<!--'` and trailing `'-->'`.

xmlparser.StartCdataSectionHandler()
Called at the start of a CDATA section. This and *EndCdataSectionHandler* are needed to be able to identify the syntactical start and end for CDATA sections.

xmlparser.EndCdataSectionHandler()
Called at the end of a CDATA section.

xmlparser.DefaultHandler(*data***)**
　　Called for any characters in the XML document for which no applicable handler has been specified. This means characters that are part of a construct which could be reported, but for which no handler has been supplied.

xmlparser.DefaultHandlerExpand(*data***)**
　　This is the same as the *DefaultHandler()*, but doesn't inhibit expansion of internal entities. The entity reference will not be passed to the default handler.

xmlparser.NotStandaloneHandler()
　　Called if the XML document hasn't been declared as being a standalone document. This happens when there is an external subset or a reference to a parameter entity, but the XML declaration does not set standalone to yes in an XML declaration. If this handler returns 0, then the parser will raise an XML_ERROR_NOT_STANDALONE error. If this handler is not set, no exception is raised by the parser for this condition.

xmlparser.ExternalEntityRefHandler(*context, base, systemId, publicId***)**
　　Called for references to external entities. *base* is the current base, as set by a previous call to *SetBase()*. The public and system identifiers, *systemId* and *publicId*, are strings if given; if the public identifier is not given, *publicId* will be None. The *context* value is opaque and should only be used as described below.

　　For external entities to be parsed, this handler must be implemented. It is responsible for creating the sub-parser using **ExternalEntityParserCreate(context)**, initializing it with the appropriate callbacks, and parsing the entity. This handler should return an integer; if it returns 0, the parser will raise an XML_ERROR_EXTERNAL_ENTITY_HANDLING error, otherwise parsing will continue.

　　If this handler is not provided, external entities are reported by the *DefaultHandler* callback, if provided.

20.13.2 ExpatError Exceptions

ExpatError exceptions have a number of interesting attributes:

ExpatError.code
　　Expat's internal error number for the specific error. The *errors.messages* dictionary maps these error numbers to Expat's error messages. For example:

```
from xml.parsers.expat import ParserCreate, ExpatError, errors

p = ParserCreate()
try:
    p.Parse(some_xml_document)
except ExpatError as err:
    print("Error:", errors.messages[err.code])
```

　　The *errors* module also provides error message constants and a dictionary *codes* mapping these messages back to the error codes, see below.

ExpatError.lineno
　　Line number on which the error was detected. The first line is numbered 1.

ExpatError.offset
　　Character offset into the line where the error occurred. The first column is numbered 0.

20.13.3 Example

The following program defines three handlers that just print out their arguments.

```python
import xml.parsers.expat

# 3 handler functions
def start_element(name, attrs):
    print('Start element:', name, attrs)
def end_element(name):
    print('End element:', name)
def char_data(data):
    print('Character data:', repr(data))

p = xml.parsers.expat.ParserCreate()

p.StartElementHandler = start_element
p.EndElementHandler = end_element
p.CharacterDataHandler = char_data

p.Parse("""<?xml version="1.0"?>
<parent id="top"><child1 name="paul">Text goes here</child1>
<child2 name="fred">More text</child2>
</parent>""", 1)
```

The output from this program is:

```
Start element: parent {'id': 'top'}
Start element: child1 {'name': 'paul'}
Character data: 'Text goes here'
End element: child1
Character data: '\n'
Start element: child2 {'name': 'fred'}
Character data: 'More text'
End element: child2
Character data: '\n'
End element: parent
```

20.13.4 Content Model Descriptions

Content models are described using nested tuples. Each tuple contains four values: the type, the quantifier, the name, and a tuple of children. Children are simply additional content model descriptions.

The values of the first two fields are constants defined in the *xml.parsers.expat.model* module. These constants can be collected in two groups: the model type group and the quantifier group.

The constants in the model type group are:

xml.parsers.expat.model.XML_CTYPE_ANY
    The element named by the model name was declared to have a content model of ANY.

xml.parsers.expat.model.XML_CTYPE_CHOICE
    The named element allows a choice from a number of options; this is used for content models such as (A | B | C).

xml.parsers.expat.model.XML_CTYPE_EMPTY
    Elements which are declared to be EMPTY have this model type.

xml.parsers.expat.model.XML_CTYPE_MIXED

xml.parsers.expat.model.XML_CTYPE_NAME

xml.parsers.expat.model.XML_CTYPE_SEQ
   Models which represent a series of models which follow one after the other are indicated with this model type. This is used for models such as (A, B, C).

The constants in the quantifier group are:

xml.parsers.expat.model.XML_CQUANT_NONE
   No modifier is given, so it can appear exactly once, as for A.

xml.parsers.expat.model.XML_CQUANT_OPT
   The model is optional: it can appear once or not at all, as for A?.

xml.parsers.expat.model.XML_CQUANT_PLUS
   The model must occur one or more times (like A+).

xml.parsers.expat.model.XML_CQUANT_REP
   The model must occur zero or more times, as for A*.

20.13.5 Expat error constants

The following constants are provided in the *xml.parsers.expat.errors* module. These constants are useful in interpreting some of the attributes of the **ExpatError** exception objects raised when an error has occurred. Since for backwards compatibility reasons, the constants' value is the error *message* and not the numeric error *code*, you do this by comparing its *code* attribute with **errors.codes[errors.XML_ERROR_*CONSTANT_NAME*]**.

The **errors** module has the following attributes:

xml.parsers.expat.errors.codes
   A dictionary mapping numeric error codes to their string descriptions.

   New in version 3.2.

xml.parsers.expat.errors.messages
   A dictionary mapping string descriptions to their error codes.

   New in version 3.2.

xml.parsers.expat.errors.XML_ERROR_ASYNC_ENTITY

xml.parsers.expat.errors.XML_ERROR_ATTRIBUTE_EXTERNAL_ENTITY_REF
   An entity reference in an attribute value referred to an external entity instead of an internal entity.

xml.parsers.expat.errors.XML_ERROR_BAD_CHAR_REF
   A character reference referred to a character which is illegal in XML (for example, character 0, or '&#0;').

xml.parsers.expat.errors.XML_ERROR_BINARY_ENTITY_REF
   An entity reference referred to an entity which was declared with a notation, so cannot be parsed.

xml.parsers.expat.errors.XML_ERROR_DUPLICATE_ATTRIBUTE
   An attribute was used more than once in a start tag.

xml.parsers.expat.errors.XML_ERROR_INCORRECT_ENCODING

xml.parsers.expat.errors.XML_ERROR_INVALID_TOKEN
   Raised when an input byte could not properly be assigned to a character; for example, a NUL byte (value 0) in a UTF-8 input stream.

xml.parsers.expat.errors.XML_ERROR_JUNK_AFTER_DOC_ELEMENT
   Something other than whitespace occurred after the document element.

xml.parsers.expat.errors.XML_ERROR_MISPLACED_XML_PI
   An XML declaration was found somewhere other than the start of the input data.

xml.parsers.expat.errors.XML_ERROR_NO_ELEMENTS
    The document contains no elements (XML requires all documents to contain exactly one top-level element)..

xml.parsers.expat.errors.XML_ERROR_NO_MEMORY
    Expat was not able to allocate memory internally.

xml.parsers.expat.errors.XML_ERROR_PARAM_ENTITY_REF
    A parameter entity reference was found where it was not allowed.

xml.parsers.expat.errors.XML_ERROR_PARTIAL_CHAR
    An incomplete character was found in the input.

xml.parsers.expat.errors.XML_ERROR_RECURSIVE_ENTITY_REF
    An entity reference contained another reference to the same entity; possibly via a different name, and possibly indirectly.

xml.parsers.expat.errors.XML_ERROR_SYNTAX
    Some unspecified syntax error was encountered.

xml.parsers.expat.errors.XML_ERROR_TAG_MISMATCH
    An end tag did not match the innermost open start tag.

xml.parsers.expat.errors.XML_ERROR_UNCLOSED_TOKEN
    Some token (such as a start tag) was not closed before the end of the stream or the next token was encountered.

xml.parsers.expat.errors.XML_ERROR_UNDEFINED_ENTITY
    A reference was made to an entity which was not defined.

xml.parsers.expat.errors.XML_ERROR_UNKNOWN_ENCODING
    The document encoding is not supported by Expat.

xml.parsers.expat.errors.XML_ERROR_UNCLOSED_CDATA_SECTION
    A CDATA marked section was not closed.

xml.parsers.expat.errors.XML_ERROR_EXTERNAL_ENTITY_HANDLING

xml.parsers.expat.errors.XML_ERROR_NOT_STANDALONE
    The parser determined that the document was not "standalone" though it declared itself to be in the XML declaration, and the NotStandaloneHandler was set and returned 0.

xml.parsers.expat.errors.XML_ERROR_UNEXPECTED_STATE

xml.parsers.expat.errors.XML_ERROR_ENTITY_DECLARED_IN_PE

xml.parsers.expat.errors.XML_ERROR_FEATURE_REQUIRES_XML_DTD
    An operation was requested that requires DTD support to be compiled in, but Expat was configured without DTD support. This should never be reported by a standard build of the *xml.parsers.expat* module.

xml.parsers.expat.errors.XML_ERROR_CANT_CHANGE_FEATURE_ONCE_PARSING
    A behavioral change was requested after parsing started that can only be changed before parsing has started. This is (currently) only raised by UseForeignDTD().

xml.parsers.expat.errors.XML_ERROR_UNBOUND_PREFIX
    An undeclared prefix was found when namespace processing was enabled.

xml.parsers.expat.errors.XML_ERROR_UNDECLARING_PREFIX
    The document attempted to remove the namespace declaration associated with a prefix.

xml.parsers.expat.errors.XML_ERROR_INCOMPLETE_PE
    A parameter entity contained incomplete markup.

xml.parsers.expat.errors.XML_ERROR_XML_DECL
    The document contained no document element at all.

xml.parsers.expat.errors.XML_ERROR_TEXT_DECL
    There was an error parsing a text declaration in an external entity.

xml.parsers.expat.errors.XML_ERROR_PUBLICID
    Characters were found in the public id that are not allowed.

xml.parsers.expat.errors.XML_ERROR_SUSPENDED
    The requested operation was made on a suspended parser, but isn't allowed. This includes attempts to provide additional input or to stop the parser.

xml.parsers.expat.errors.XML_ERROR_NOT_SUSPENDED
    An attempt to resume the parser was made when the parser had not been suspended.

xml.parsers.expat.errors.XML_ERROR_ABORTED
    This should not be reported to Python applications.

xml.parsers.expat.errors.XML_ERROR_FINISHED
    The requested operation was made on a parser which was finished parsing input, but isn't allowed. This includes attempts to provide additional input or to stop the parser.

xml.parsers.expat.errors.XML_ERROR_SUSPEND_PE

CHAPTER
TWENTYONE

INTERNET PROTOCOLS AND SUPPORT

The modules described in this chapter implement Internet protocols and support for related technology. They are all implemented in Python. Most of these modules require the presence of the system-dependent module `socket`, which is currently supported on most popular platforms. Here is an overview:

21.1 `webbrowser` — Convenient Web-browser controller

Source code: Lib/webbrowser.py

The `webbrowser` module provides a high-level interface to allow displaying Web-based documents to users. Under most circumstances, simply calling the `open()` function from this module will do the right thing.

Under Unix, graphical browsers are preferred under X11, but text-mode browsers will be used if graphical browsers are not available or an X11 display isn't available. If text-mode browsers are used, the calling process will block until the user exits the browser.

If the environment variable BROWSER exists, it is interpreted as the `os.pathsep`-separated list of browsers to try ahead of the platform defaults. When the value of a list part contains the string %s, then it is interpreted as a literal browser command line to be used with the argument URL substituted for %s; if the part does not contain %s, it is simply interpreted as the name of the browser to launch.[1]

For non-Unix platforms, or when a remote browser is available on Unix, the controlling process will not wait for the user to finish with the browser, but allow the remote browser to maintain its own windows on the display. If remote browsers are not available on Unix, the controlling process will launch a new browser and wait.

The script **webbrowser** can be used as a command-line interface for the module. It accepts a URL as the argument. It accepts the following optional parameters: -n opens the URL in a new browser window, if possible; -t opens the URL in a new browser page ("tab"). The options are, naturally, mutually exclusive. Usage example:

```
python -m webbrowser -t "http://www.python.org"
```

The following exception is defined:

exception `webbrowser.Error`
    Exception raised when a browser control error occurs.

The following functions are defined:

`webbrowser.open`(*url, new=0, autoraise=True*)
    Display *url* using the default browser. If *new* is 0, the *url* is opened in the same browser window if possible. If *new* is 1, a new browser window is opened if possible. If *new* is 2, a new browser page

---

[1] Executables named here without a full path will be searched in the directories given in the PATH environment variable.

("tab") is opened if possible. If *autoraise* is True, the window is raised if possible (note that under many window managers this will occur regardless of the setting of this variable).

Note that on some platforms, trying to open a filename using this function, may work and start the operating system's associated program. However, this is neither supported nor portable.

`webbrowser.open_new`(*url*)
Open *url* in a new window of the default browser, if possible, otherwise, open *url* in the only browser window.

`webbrowser.open_new_tab`(*url*)
Open *url* in a new page ("tab") of the default browser, if possible, otherwise equivalent to *open_new()*.

`webbrowser.get`(*using=None*)
Return a controller object for the browser type *using*. If *using* is None, return a controller for a default browser appropriate to the caller's environment.

`webbrowser.register`(*name, constructor, instance=None*)
Register the browser type *name*. Once a browser type is registered, the *get()* function can return a controller for that browser type. If *instance* is not provided, or is None, *constructor* will be called without parameters to create an instance when needed. If *instance* is provided, *constructor* will never be called, and may be None.

This entry point is only useful if you plan to either set the BROWSER variable or call *get()* with a nonempty argument matching the name of a handler you declare.

A number of browser types are predefined. This table gives the type names that may be passed to the *get()* function and the corresponding instantiations for the controller classes, all defined in this module.

Type Name	Class Name	Notes
'mozilla'	Mozilla('mozilla')	
'firefox'	Mozilla('mozilla')	
'netscape'	Mozilla('netscape')	
'galeon'	Galeon('galeon')	
'epiphany'	Galeon('epiphany')	
'skipstone'	BackgroundBrowser('skipstone')	
'kfmclient'	Konqueror()	(1)
'konqueror'	Konqueror()	(1)
'kfm'	Konqueror()	(1)
'mosaic'	BackgroundBrowser('mosaic')	
'opera'	Opera()	
'grail'	Grail()	
'links'	GenericBrowser('links')	
'elinks'	Elinks('elinks')	
'lynx'	GenericBrowser('lynx')	
'w3m'	GenericBrowser('w3m')	
'windows-default'	WindowsDefault	(2)
'macosx'	MacOSX('default')	(3)
'safari'	MacOSX('safari')	(3)
'google-chrome'	Chrome('google-chrome')	
'chrome'	Chrome('chrome')	
'chromium'	Chromium('chromium')	
'chromium-browser'	Chromium('chromium-browser')	

Notes:

1. "Konqueror" is the file manager for the KDE desktop environment for Unix, and only makes sense to use if KDE is running. Some way of reliably detecting KDE would be nice; the KDEDIR variable is not

sufficient. Note also that the name "kfm" is used even when using the **konqueror** command with KDE 2 — the implementation selects the best strategy for running Konqueror.

2. Only on Windows platforms.

3. Only on Mac OS X platform.

New in version 3.3: Support for Chrome/Chromium has been added.

Here are some simple examples:

```
url = 'http://docs.python.org/'

# Open URL in a new tab, if a browser window is already open.
webbrowser.open_new_tab(url)

# Open URL in new window, raising the window if possible.
webbrowser.open_new(url)
```

21.1.1 Browser Controller Objects

Browser controllers provide these methods which parallel three of the module-level convenience functions:

controller.open(*url*, *new=0*, *autoraise=True*)
> Display *url* using the browser handled by this controller. If *new* is 1, a new browser window is opened if possible. If *new* is 2, a new browser page ("tab") is opened if possible.

controller.open_new(*url*)
> Open *url* in a new window of the browser handled by this controller, if possible, otherwise, open *url* in the only browser window. Alias *open_new()*.

controller.open_new_tab(*url*)
> Open *url* in a new page ("tab") of the browser handled by this controller, if possible, otherwise equivalent to *open_new()*.

21.2 cgi — Common Gateway Interface support

Source code: Lib/cgi.py

Support module for Common Gateway Interface (CGI) scripts.

This module defines a number of utilities for use by CGI scripts written in Python.

21.2.1 Introduction

A CGI script is invoked by an HTTP server, usually to process user input submitted through an HTML <FORM> or <ISINDEX> element.

Most often, CGI scripts live in the server's special cgi-bin directory. The HTTP server places all sorts of information about the request (such as the client's hostname, the requested URL, the query string, and lots of other goodies) in the script's shell environment, executes the script, and sends the script's output back to the client.

The script's input is connected to the client too, and sometimes the form data is read this way; at other times the form data is passed via the "query string" part of the URL. This module is intended to take care of the different cases and provide a simpler interface to the Python script. It also provides a number of utilities that help in debugging scripts, and the latest addition is support for file uploads from a form (if your browser supports it).

The output of a CGI script should consist of two sections, separated by a blank line. The first section contains a number of headers, telling the client what kind of data is following. Python code to generate a minimal header section looks like this:

```
print("Content-Type: text/html")    # HTML is following
print()                             # blank line, end of headers
```

The second section is usually HTML, which allows the client software to display nicely formatted text with header, in-line images, etc. Here's Python code that prints a simple piece of HTML:

```
print("<TITLE>CGI script output</TITLE>")
print("<H1>This is my first CGI script</H1>")
print("Hello, world!")
```

21.2.2 Using the cgi module

Begin by writing `import cgi`.

When you write a new script, consider adding these lines:

```
import cgitb
cgitb.enable()
```

This activates a special exception handler that will display detailed reports in the Web browser if any errors occur. If you'd rather not show the guts of your program to users of your script, you can have the reports saved to files instead, with code like this:

```
import cgitb
cgitb.enable(display=0, logdir="/path/to/logdir")
```

It's very helpful to use this feature during script development. The reports produced by *cgitb* provide information that can save you a lot of time in tracking down bugs. You can always remove the **cgitb** line later when you have tested your script and are confident that it works correctly.

To get at submitted form data, use the **FieldStorage** class. If the form contains non-ASCII characters, use the *encoding* keyword parameter set to the value of the encoding defined for the document. It is usually contained in the META tag in the HEAD section of the HTML document or by the *Content-Type* header). This reads the form contents from the standard input or the environment (depending on the value of various environment variables set according to the CGI standard). Since it may consume standard input, it should be instantiated only once.

The **FieldStorage** instance can be indexed like a Python dictionary. It allows membership testing with the **in** operator, and also supports the standard dictionary method *keys()* and the built-in function *len()*. Form fields containing empty strings are ignored and do not appear in the dictionary; to keep such values, provide a true value for the optional *keep_blank_values* keyword parameter when creating the **FieldStorage** instance.

For instance, the following code (which assumes that the *Content-Type* header and blank line have already been printed) checks that the fields **name** and **addr** are both set to a non-empty string:

```
form = cgi.FieldStorage()
if "name" not in form or "addr" not in form:
    print("<H1>Error</H1>")
    print("Please fill in the name and addr fields.")
    return
```

```
print("<p>name:", form["name"].value)
print("<p>addr:", form["addr"].value)
...further form processing here...
```

Here the fields, accessed through `form[key]`, are themselves instances of `FieldStorage` (or `MiniFieldStorage`, depending on the form encoding). The `value` attribute of the instance yields the string value of the field. The `getvalue()` method returns this string value directly; it also accepts an optional second argument as a default to return if the requested key is not present.

If the submitted form data contains more than one field with the same name, the object retrieved by `form[key]` is not a `FieldStorage` or `MiniFieldStorage` instance but a list of such instances. Similarly, in this situation, `form.getvalue(key)` would return a list of strings. If you expect this possibility (when your HTML form contains multiple fields with the same name), use the `getlist()` method, which always returns a list of values (so that you do not need to special-case the single item case). For example, this code concatenates any number of username fields, separated by commas:

```
value = form.getlist("username")
usernames = ",".join(value)
```

If a field represents an uploaded file, accessing the value via the `value` attribute or the `getvalue()` method reads the entire file in memory as bytes. This may not be what you want. You can test for an uploaded file by testing either the `filename` attribute or the `file` attribute. You can then read the data from the `file` attribute before it is automatically closed as part of the garbage collection of the `FieldStorage` instance (the `read()` and `readline()` methods will return bytes):

```
fileitem = form["userfile"]
if fileitem.file:
    # It's an uploaded file; count lines
    linecount = 0
    while True:
        line = fileitem.file.readline()
        if not line: break
        linecount = linecount + 1
```

`FieldStorage` objects also support being used in a `with` statement, which will automatically close them when done.

If an error is encountered when obtaining the contents of an uploaded file (for example, when the user interrupts the form submission by clicking on a Back or Cancel button) the `done` attribute of the object for the field will be set to the value -1.

The file upload draft standard entertains the possibility of uploading multiple files from one field (using a recursive *multipart/** encoding). When this occurs, the item will be a dictionary-like `FieldStorage` item. This can be determined by testing its `type` attribute, which should be *multipart/form-data* (or perhaps another MIME type matching *multipart/**). In this case, it can be iterated over recursively just like the top-level form object.

When a form is submitted in the "old" format (as the query string or as a single data part of type *application/x-www-form-urlencoded*), the items will actually be instances of the class `MiniFieldStorage`. In this case, the `list`, `file`, and `filename` attributes are always None.

A form submitted via POST that also has a query string will contain both `FieldStorage` and `MiniFieldStorage` items.

Changed in version 3.4: The `file` attribute is automatically closed upon the garbage collection of the creating `FieldStorage` instance.

Changed in version 3.5: Added support for the context management protocol to the `FieldStorage` class.

21.2.3 Higher Level Interface

The previous section explains how to read CGI form data using the `FieldStorage` class. This section describes a higher level interface which was added to this class to allow one to do it in a more readable and intuitive way. The interface doesn't make the techniques described in previous sections obsolete — they are still useful to process file uploads efficiently, for example.

The interface consists of two simple methods. Using the methods you can process form data in a generic way, without the need to worry whether only one or more values were posted under one name.

In the previous section, you learned to write following code anytime you expected a user to post more than one value under one name:

```
item = form.getvalue("item")
if isinstance(item, list):
    # The user is requesting more than one item.
else:
    # The user is requesting only one item.
```

This situation is common for example when a form contains a group of multiple checkboxes with the same name:

```
<input type="checkbox" name="item" value="1" />
<input type="checkbox" name="item" value="2" />
```

In most situations, however, there's only one form control with a particular name in a form and then you expect and need only one value associated with this name. So you write a script containing for example this code:

```
user = form.getvalue("user").upper()
```

The problem with the code is that you should never expect that a client will provide valid input to your scripts. For example, if a curious user appends another `user=foo` pair to the query string, then the script would crash, because in this situation the `getvalue("user")` method call returns a list instead of a string. Calling the *upper()* method on a list is not valid (since lists do not have a method of this name) and results in an *AttributeError* exception.

Therefore, the appropriate way to read form data values was to always use the code which checks whether the obtained value is a single value or a list of values. That's annoying and leads to less readable scripts.

A more convenient approach is to use the methods *getfirst()* and *getlist()* provided by this higher level interface.

FieldStorage.getfirst(*name*, *default=None*)
  This method always returns only one value associated with form field *name*. The method returns only the first value in case that more values were posted under such name. Please note that the order in which the values are received may vary from browser to browser and should not be counted on.[1] If no such form field or value exists then the method returns the value specified by the optional parameter *default*. This parameter defaults to None if not specified.

FieldStorage.getlist(*name*)
  This method always returns a list of values associated with form field *name*. The method returns an empty list if no such form field or value exists for *name*. It returns a list consisting of one item if only one such value exists.

Using these methods you can write nice compact code:

---

[1] Note that some recent versions of the HTML specification do state what order the field values should be supplied in, but knowing whether a request was received from a conforming browser, or even from a browser at all, is tedious and error-prone.

```
import cgi
form = cgi.FieldStorage()
user = form.getfirst("user", "").upper()    # This way it's safe.
for item in form.getlist("item"):
    do_something(item)
```

21.2.4 Functions

These are useful if you want more control, or if you want to employ some of the algorithms implemented in this module in other circumstances.

cgi.parse(*fp=None, environ=os.environ, keep_blank_values=False, strict_parsing=False*)
    Parse a query in the environment or from a file (the file defaults to `sys.stdin`). The *keep_blank_values* and *strict_parsing* parameters are passed to `urllib.parse.parse_qs()` unchanged.

cgi.parse_qs(*qs, keep_blank_values=False, strict_parsing=False*)
    This function is deprecated in this module. Use `urllib.parse.parse_qs()` instead. It is maintained here only for backward compatibility.

cgi.parse_qsl(*qs, keep_blank_values=False, strict_parsing=False*)
    This function is deprecated in this module. Use `urllib.parse.parse_qsl()` instead. It is maintained here only for backward compatibility.

cgi.parse_multipart(*fp, pdict*)
    Parse input of type *multipart/form-data* (for file uploads). Arguments are *fp* for the input file and *pdict* for a dictionary containing other parameters in the `Content-Type` header.

    Returns a dictionary just like `urllib.parse.parse_qs()` keys are the field names, each value is a list of values for that field. This is easy to use but not much good if you are expecting megabytes to be uploaded — in that case, use the `FieldStorage` class instead which is much more flexible.

    Note that this does not parse nested multipart parts — use `FieldStorage` for that.

cgi.parse_header(*string*)
    Parse a MIME header (such as `Content-Type`) into a main value and a dictionary of parameters.

cgi.test()
    Robust test CGI script, usable as main program. Writes minimal HTTP headers and formats all information provided to the script in HTML form.

cgi.print_environ()
    Format the shell environment in HTML.

cgi.print_form(*form*)
    Format a form in HTML.

cgi.print_directory()
    Format the current directory in HTML.

cgi.print_environ_usage()
    Print a list of useful (used by CGI) environment variables in HTML.

cgi.escape(*s, quote=False*)
    Convert the characters '&', '<' and '>' in string *s* to HTML-safe sequences. Use this if you need to display text that might contain such characters in HTML. If the optional flag *quote* is true, the quotation mark character (") is also translated; this helps for inclusion in an HTML attribute value delimited by double quotes, as in `<a href="...">`. Note that single quotes are never translated.

    Deprecated since version 3.2: This function is unsafe because *quote* is false by default, and therefore deprecated. Use `html.escape()` instead.

21.2.5 Caring about security

There's one important rule: if you invoke an external program (via the *os.system()* or *os.popen()* functions, or others with similar functionality), make very sure you don't pass arbitrary strings received from the client to the shell. This is a well-known security hole whereby clever hackers anywhere on the Web can exploit a gullible CGI script to invoke arbitrary shell commands. Even parts of the URL or field names cannot be trusted, since the request doesn't have to come from your form!

To be on the safe side, if you must pass a string gotten from a form to a shell command, you should make sure the string contains only alphanumeric characters, dashes, underscores, and periods.

21.2.6 Installing your CGI script on a Unix system

Read the documentation for your HTTP server and check with your local system administrator to find the directory where CGI scripts should be installed; usually this is in a directory `cgi-bin` in the server tree.

Make sure that your script is readable and executable by "others"; the Unix file mode should be 0o755 octal (use `chmod 0755 filename`). Make sure that the first line of the script contains `#!` starting in column 1 followed by the pathname of the Python interpreter, for instance:

```
#!/usr/local/bin/python
```

Make sure the Python interpreter exists and is executable by "others".

Make sure that any files your script needs to read or write are readable or writable, respectively, by "others" — their mode should be 0o644 for readable and 0o666 for writable. This is because, for security reasons, the HTTP server executes your script as user "nobody", without any special privileges. It can only read (write, execute) files that everybody can read (write, execute). The current directory at execution time is also different (it is usually the server's cgi-bin directory) and the set of environment variables is also different from what you get when you log in. In particular, don't count on the shell's search path for executables (`PATH`) or the Python module search path (`PYTHONPATH`) to be set to anything interesting.

If you need to load modules from a directory which is not on Python's default module search path, you can change the path in your script, before importing other modules. For example:

```
import sys
sys.path.insert(0, "/usr/home/joe/lib/python")
sys.path.insert(0, "/usr/local/lib/python")
```

(This way, the directory inserted last will be searched first!)

Instructions for non-Unix systems will vary; check your HTTP server's documentation (it will usually have a section on CGI scripts).

21.2.7 Testing your CGI script

Unfortunately, a CGI script will generally not run when you try it from the command line, and a script that works perfectly from the command line may fail mysteriously when run from the server. There's one reason why you should still test your script from the command line: if it contains a syntax error, the Python interpreter won't execute it at all, and the HTTP server will most likely send a cryptic error to the client.

Assuming your script has no syntax errors, yet it does not work, you have no choice but to read the next section.

21.2.8 Debugging CGI scripts

First of all, check for trivial installation errors — reading the section above on installing your CGI script carefully can save you a lot of time. If you wonder whether you have understood the installation procedure correctly, try installing a copy of this module file (`cgi.py`) as a CGI script. When invoked as a script, the file will dump its environment and the contents of the form in HTML form. Give it the right mode etc, and send it a request. If it's installed in the standard `cgi-bin` directory, it should be possible to send it a request by entering a URL into your browser of the form:

```
http://yourhostname/cgi-bin/cgi.py?name=Joe+Blow&addr=At+Home
```

If this gives an error of type 404, the server cannot find the script – perhaps you need to install it in a different directory. If it gives another error, there's an installation problem that you should fix before trying to go any further. If you get a nicely formatted listing of the environment and form content (in this example, the fields should be listed as "addr" with value "At Home" and "name" with value "Joe Blow"), the `cgi.py` script has been installed correctly. If you follow the same procedure for your own script, you should now be able to debug it.

The next step could be to call the *cgi* module's *test()* function from your script: replace its main code with the single statement

```
cgi.test()
```

This should produce the same results as those gotten from installing the `cgi.py` file itself.

When an ordinary Python script raises an unhandled exception (for whatever reason: of a typo in a module name, a file that can't be opened, etc.), the Python interpreter prints a nice traceback and exits. While the Python interpreter will still do this when your CGI script raises an exception, most likely the traceback will end up in one of the HTTP server's log files, or be discarded altogether.

Fortunately, once you have managed to get your script to execute *some* code, you can easily send tracebacks to the Web browser using the *cgitb* module. If you haven't done so already, just add the lines:

```
import cgitb
cgitb.enable()
```

to the top of your script. Then try running it again; when a problem occurs, you should see a detailed report that will likely make apparent the cause of the crash.

If you suspect that there may be a problem in importing the *cgitb* module, you can use an even more robust approach (which only uses built-in modules):

```
import sys
sys.stderr = sys.stdout
print("Content-Type: text/plain")
print()
...your code here...
```

This relies on the Python interpreter to print the traceback. The content type of the output is set to plain text, which disables all HTML processing. If your script works, the raw HTML will be displayed by your client. If it raises an exception, most likely after the first two lines have been printed, a traceback will be displayed. Because no HTML interpretation is going on, the traceback will be readable.

21.2.9 Common problems and solutions

- Most HTTP servers buffer the output from CGI scripts until the script is completed. This means that it is not possible to display a progress report on the client's display while the script is running.

- Check the installation instructions above.
- Check the HTTP server's log files. (`tail -f logfile` in a separate window may be useful!)
- Always check a script for syntax errors first, by doing something like `python script.py`.
- If your script does not have any syntax errors, try adding `import cgitb; cgitb.enable()` to the top of the script.
- When invoking external programs, make sure they can be found. Usually, this means using absolute path names — `PATH` is usually not set to a very useful value in a CGI script.
- When reading or writing external files, make sure they can be read or written by the userid under which your CGI script will be running: this is typically the userid under which the web server is running, or some explicitly specified userid for a web server's `suexec` feature.
- Don't try to give a CGI script a set-uid mode. This doesn't work on most systems, and is a security liability as well.

21.3 `cgitb` — Traceback manager for CGI scripts

Source code: Lib/cgitb.py

The `cgitb` module provides a special exception handler for Python scripts. (Its name is a bit misleading. It was originally designed to display extensive traceback information in HTML for CGI scripts. It was later generalized to also display this information in plain text.) After this module is activated, if an uncaught exception occurs, a detailed, formatted report will be displayed. The report includes a traceback showing excerpts of the source code for each level, as well as the values of the arguments and local variables to currently running functions, to help you debug the problem. Optionally, you can save this information to a file instead of sending it to the browser.

To enable this feature, simply add this to the top of your CGI script:

```
import cgitb
cgitb.enable()
```

The options to the `enable()` function control whether the report is displayed in the browser and whether the report is logged to a file for later analysis.

`cgitb.enable(display=1, logdir=None, context=5, format="html")`

This function causes the `cgitb` module to take over the interpreter's default handling for exceptions by setting the value of `sys.excepthook`.

The optional argument *display* defaults to 1 and can be set to 0 to suppress sending the traceback to the browser. If the argument *logdir* is present, the traceback reports are written to files. The value of *logdir* should be a directory where these files will be placed. The optional argument *context* is the number of lines of context to display around the current line of source code in the traceback; this defaults to 5. If the optional argument *format* is `"html"`, the output is formatted as HTML. Any other value forces plain text output. The default value is `"html"`.

`cgitb.handler(info=None)`

This function handles an exception using the default settings (that is, show a report in the browser, but don't log to a file). This can be used when you've caught an exception and want to report it using `cgitb`. The optional *info* argument should be a 3-tuple containing an exception type, exception value, and traceback object, exactly like the tuple returned by `sys.exc_info()`. If the *info* argument is not supplied, the current exception is obtained from `sys.exc_info()`.

21.4 `wsgiref` — WSGI Utilities and Reference Implementation

The Web Server Gateway Interface (WSGI) is a standard interface between web server software and web applications written in Python. Having a standard interface makes it easy to use an application that supports WSGI with a number of different web servers.

Only authors of web servers and programming frameworks need to know every detail and corner case of the WSGI design. You don't need to understand every detail of WSGI just to install a WSGI application or to write a web application using an existing framework.

wsgiref is a reference implementation of the WSGI specification that can be used to add WSGI support to a web server or framework. It provides utilities for manipulating WSGI environment variables and response headers, base classes for implementing WSGI servers, a demo HTTP server that serves WSGI applications, and a validation tool that checks WSGI servers and applications for conformance to the WSGI specification (PEP 3333).

See https://wsgi.readthedocs.org/ for more information about WSGI, and links to tutorials and other resources.

21.4.1 `wsgiref.util` – WSGI environment utilities

This module provides a variety of utility functions for working with WSGI environments. A WSGI environment is a dictionary containing HTTP request variables as described in PEP 3333. All of the functions taking an *environ* parameter expect a WSGI-compliant dictionary to be supplied; please see PEP 3333 for a detailed specification.

wsgiref.util.guess_scheme(*environ*)

> Return a guess for whether `wsgi.url_scheme` should be "http" or "https", by checking for a `HTTPS` environment variable in the *environ* dictionary. The return value is a string.
>
> This function is useful when creating a gateway that wraps CGI or a CGI-like protocol such as FastCGI. Typically, servers providing such protocols will include a `HTTPS` variable with a value of "1" "yes", or "on" when a request is received via SSL. So, this function returns "https" if such a value is found, and "http" otherwise.

wsgiref.util.request_uri(*environ, include_query=True*)

> Return the full request URI, optionally including the query string, using the algorithm found in the "URL Reconstruction" section of PEP 3333. If *include_query* is false, the query string is not included in the resulting URI.

wsgiref.util.application_uri(*environ*)

> Similar to *request_uri()*, except that the `PATH_INFO` and `QUERY_STRING` variables are ignored. The result is the base URI of the application object addressed by the request.

wsgiref.util.shift_path_info(*environ*)

> Shift a single name from `PATH_INFO` to `SCRIPT_NAME` and return the name. The *environ* dictionary is *modified* in-place; use a copy if you need to keep the original `PATH_INFO` or `SCRIPT_NAME` intact.
>
> If there are no remaining path segments in `PATH_INFO`, `None` is returned.
>
> Typically, this routine is used to process each portion of a request URI path, for example to treat the path as a series of dictionary keys. This routine modifies the passed-in environment to make it suitable for invoking another WSGI application that is located at the target URI. For example, if there is a WSGI application at `/foo`, and the request URI path is `/foo/bar/baz`, and the WSGI application at `/foo` calls *shift_path_info()*, it will receive the string "bar", and the environment will be updated to be suitable for passing to a WSGI application at `/foo/bar`. That is, `SCRIPT_NAME` will change from `/foo` to `/foo/bar`, and `PATH_INFO` will change from `/bar/baz` to `/baz`.

When PATH_INFO is just a "/", this routine returns an empty string and appends a trailing slash to SCRIPT_NAME, even though empty path segments are normally ignored, and SCRIPT_NAME doesn't normally end in a slash. This is intentional behavior, to ensure that an application can tell the difference between URIs ending in /x from ones ending in /x/ when using this routine to do object traversal.

wsgiref.util.setup_testing_defaults(*environ*)
Update *environ* with trivial defaults for testing purposes.

This routine adds various parameters required for WSGI, including HTTP_HOST, SERVER_NAME, SERVER_PORT, REQUEST_METHOD, SCRIPT_NAME, PATH_INFO, and all of the PEP 3333-defined wsgi.* variables. It only supplies default values, and does not replace any existing settings for these variables.

This routine is intended to make it easier for unit tests of WSGI servers and applications to set up dummy environments. It should NOT be used by actual WSGI servers or applications, since the data is fake!

Example usage:

```python
from wsgiref.util import setup_testing_defaults
from wsgiref.simple_server import make_server

# A relatively simple WSGI application. It's going to print out the
# environment dictionary after being updated by setup_testing_defaults
def simple_app(environ, start_response):
    setup_testing_defaults(environ)

    status = '200 OK'
    headers = [('Content-type', 'text/plain; charset=utf-8')]

    start_response(status, headers)

    ret = [("%s: %s\n" % (key, value)).encode("utf-8")
           for key, value in environ.items()]
    return ret

with make_server('', 8000, simple_app) as httpd:
    print("Serving on port 8000...")
    httpd.serve_forever()
```

In addition to the environment functions above, the *wsgiref.util* module also provides these miscellaneous utilities:

wsgiref.util.is_hop_by_hop(*header_name*)
Return true if 'header_name' is an HTTP/1.1 "Hop-by-Hop" header, as defined by RFC 2616.

class wsgiref.util.FileWrapper(*filelike*, *blksize=8192*)
A wrapper to convert a file-like object to an *iterator*. The resulting objects support both __getitem__() and __iter__() iteration styles, for compatibility with Python 2.1 and Jython. As the object is iterated over, the optional *blksize* parameter will be repeatedly passed to the *filelike* object's read() method to obtain bytestrings to yield. When read() returns an empty bytestring, iteration is ended and is not resumable.

If *filelike* has a close() method, the returned object will also have a close() method, and it will invoke the *filelike* object's close() method when called.

Example usage:

```python
from io import StringIO
from wsgiref.util import FileWrapper

# We're using a StringIO-buffer for as the file-like object
```

```
filelike = StringIO("This is an example file-like object"*10)
wrapper = FileWrapper(filelike, blksize=5)

for chunk in wrapper:
    print(chunk)
```

21.4.2 wsgiref.headers – WSGI response header tools

This module provides a single class, *Headers*, for convenient manipulation of WSGI response headers using a mapping-like interface.

class wsgiref.headers.Headers([*headers*]**)**

Create a mapping-like object wrapping *headers*, which must be a list of header name/value tuples as described in PEP 3333. The default value of *headers* is an empty list.

Headers objects support typical mapping operations including __getitem__(), get(), __setitem__(), setdefault(), __delitem__() and __contains__(). For each of these methods, the key is the header name (treated case-insensitively), and the value is the first value associated with that header name. Setting a header deletes any existing values for that header, then adds a new value at the end of the wrapped header list. Headers' existing order is generally maintained, with new headers added to the end of the wrapped list.

Unlike a dictionary, *Headers* objects do not raise an error when you try to get or delete a key that isn't in the wrapped header list. Getting a nonexistent header just returns None, and deleting a nonexistent header does nothing.

Headers objects also support keys(), values(), and items() methods. The lists returned by keys() and items() can include the same key more than once if there is a multi-valued header. The len() of a *Headers* object is the same as the length of its items(), which is the same as the length of the wrapped header list. In fact, the items() method just returns a copy of the wrapped header list.

Calling bytes() on a *Headers* object returns a formatted bytestring suitable for transmission as HTTP response headers. Each header is placed on a line with its value, separated by a colon and a space. Each line is terminated by a carriage return and line feed, and the bytestring is terminated with a blank line.

In addition to their mapping interface and formatting features, *Headers* objects also have the following methods for querying and adding multi-valued headers, and for adding headers with MIME parameters:

get_all(*name***)**

Return a list of all the values for the named header.

The returned list will be sorted in the order they appeared in the original header list or were added to this instance, and may contain duplicates. Any fields deleted and re-inserted are always appended to the header list. If no fields exist with the given name, returns an empty list.

add_header(*name*, *value*, *******_params***)**

Add a (possibly multi-valued) header, with optional MIME parameters specified via keyword arguments.

name is the header field to add. Keyword arguments can be used to set MIME parameters for the header field. Each parameter must be a string or None. Underscores in parameter names are converted to dashes, since dashes are illegal in Python identifiers, but many MIME parameter names include dashes. If the parameter value is a string, it is added to the header value parameters in the form name="value". If it is None, only the parameter name is added. (This is used for MIME parameters without a value.) Example usage:

```
h.add_header('content-disposition', 'attachment', filename='bud.gif')
```

The above will add a header that looks like this:

```
Content-Disposition: attachment; filename="bud.gif"
```

Changed in version 3.5: *headers* parameter is optional.

21.4.3 wsgiref.simple_server – a simple WSGI HTTP server

This module implements a simple HTTP server (based on *http.server*) that serves WSGI applications. Each server instance serves a single WSGI application on a given host and port. If you want to serve multiple applications on a single host and port, you should create a WSGI application that parses **PATH_INFO** to select which application to invoke for each request. (E.g., using the **shift_path_info()** function from *wsgiref.util*.)

wsgiref.simple_server.**make_server**(*host, port, app, server_class=WSGIServer, handler_class=WSGIRequestHandler*)

Create a new WSGI server listening on *host* and *port*, accepting connections for *app*. The return value is an instance of the supplied *server_class*, and will process requests using the specified *handler_class*. *app* must be a WSGI application object, as defined by PEP 3333.

Example usage:

```
from wsgiref.simple_server import make_server, demo_app

with make_server('', 8000, demo_app) as httpd:
    print("Serving HTTP on port 8000...")

    # Respond to requests until process is killed
    httpd.serve_forever()

    # Alternative: serve one request, then exit
    httpd.handle_request()
```

wsgiref.simple_server.**demo_app**(*environ, start_response*)

This function is a small but complete WSGI application that returns a text page containing the message "Hello world!" and a list of the key/value pairs provided in the *environ* parameter. It's useful for verifying that a WSGI server (such as *wsgiref.simple_server*) is able to run a simple WSGI application correctly.

class wsgiref.simple_server.**WSGIServer**(*server_address, RequestHandlerClass*)

Create a *WSGIServer* instance. *server_address* should be a (**host**,**port**) tuple, and *RequestHandlerClass* should be the subclass of *http.server.BaseHTTPRequestHandler* that will be used to process requests.

You do not normally need to call this constructor, as the *make_server()* function can handle all the details for you.

WSGIServer is a subclass of *http.server.HTTPServer*, so all of its methods (such as **serve_forever()** and **handle_request()**) are available. *WSGIServer* also provides these WSGI-specific methods:

set_app(*application*)

Sets the callable *application* as the WSGI application that will receive requests.

get_app()

Returns the currently-set application callable.

Normally, however, you do not need to use these additional methods, as *set_app()* is normally called by *make_server()*, and the *get_app()* exists mainly for the benefit of request handler instances.

class wsgiref.simple_server.WSGIRequestHandler(*request, client_address, server*)
Create an HTTP handler for the given *request* (i.e. a socket), *client_address* (a (**host**,**port**) tuple), and *server* (*WSGIServer* instance).

You do not need to create instances of this class directly; they are automatically created as needed by *WSGIServer* objects. You can, however, subclass this class and supply it as a *handler_class* to the *make_server()* function. Some possibly relevant methods for overriding in subclasses:

get_environ()
Returns a dictionary containing the WSGI environment for a request. The default implementation copies the contents of the *WSGIServer* object's `base_environ` dictionary attribute and then adds various headers derived from the HTTP request. Each call to this method should return a new dictionary containing all of the relevant CGI environment variables as specified in PEP 3333.

get_stderr()
Return the object that should be used as the `wsgi.errors` stream. The default implementation just returns `sys.stderr`.

handle()
Process the HTTP request. The default implementation creates a handler instance using a *wsgiref.handlers* class to implement the actual WSGI application interface.

21.4.4 wsgiref.validate — WSGI conformance checker

When creating new WSGI application objects, frameworks, servers, or middleware, it can be useful to validate the new code's conformance using *wsgiref.validate*. This module provides a function that creates WSGI application objects that validate communications between a WSGI server or gateway and a WSGI application object, to check both sides for protocol conformance.

Note that this utility does not guarantee complete PEP 3333 compliance; an absence of errors from this module does not necessarily mean that errors do not exist. However, if this module does produce an error, then it is virtually certain that either the server or application is not 100% compliant.

This module is based on the `paste.lint` module from Ian Bicking's "Python Paste" library.

wsgiref.validate.validator(*application*)
Wrap *application* and return a new WSGI application object. The returned application will forward all requests to the original *application*, and will check that both the *application* and the server invoking it are conforming to the WSGI specification and to RFC 2616.

Any detected nonconformance results in an *AssertionError* being raised; note, however, that how these errors are handled is server-dependent. For example, *wsgiref.simple_server* and other servers based on *wsgiref.handlers* (that don't override the error handling methods to do something else) will simply output a message that an error has occurred, and dump the traceback to `sys.stderr` or some other error stream.

This wrapper may also generate output using the *warnings* module to indicate behaviors that are questionable but which may not actually be prohibited by PEP 3333. Unless they are suppressed using Python command-line options or the *warnings* API, any such warnings will be written to `sys.stderr` (*not* `wsgi.errors`, unless they happen to be the same object).

Example usage:

```
from wsgiref.validate import validator
from wsgiref.simple_server import make_server

# Our callable object which is intentionally not compliant to the
```

```
# standard, so the validator is going to break
def simple_app(environ, start_response):
    status = '200 OK'  # HTTP Status
    headers = [('Content-type', 'text/plain')]  # HTTP Headers
    start_response(status, headers)

    # This is going to break because we need to return a list, and
    # the validator is going to inform us
    return b"Hello World"

# This is the application wrapped in a validator
validator_app = validator(simple_app)

with make_server('', 8000, validator_app) as httpd:
    print("Listening on port 8000....")
    httpd.serve_forever()
```

21.4.5 wsgiref.handlers – server/gateway base classes

This module provides base handler classes for implementing WSGI servers and gateways. These base classes handle most of the work of communicating with a WSGI application, as long as they are given a CGI-like environment, along with input, output, and error streams.

class wsgiref.handlers.CGIHandler

CGI-based invocation via sys.stdin, sys.stdout, sys.stderr and os.environ. This is useful when you have a WSGI application and want to run it as a CGI script. Simply invoke CGIHandler().run(app), where app is the WSGI application object you wish to invoke.

This class is a subclass of *BaseCGIHandler* that sets wsgi.run_once to true, wsgi.multithread to false, and wsgi.multiprocess to true, and always uses *sys* and *os* to obtain the necessary CGI streams and environment.

class wsgiref.handlers.IISCGIHandler

A specialized alternative to *CGIHandler*, for use when deploying on Microsoft's IIS web server, without having set the config allowPathInfo option (IIS>=7) or metabase allowPathInfoForScriptMappings (IIS<7).

By default, IIS gives a PATH_INFO that duplicates the SCRIPT_NAME at the front, causing problems for WSGI applications that wish to implement routing. This handler strips any such duplicated path.

IIS can be configured to pass the correct PATH_INFO, but this causes another bug where PATH_TRANSLATED is wrong. Luckily this variable is rarely used and is not guaranteed by WSGI. On IIS<7, though, the setting can only be made on a vhost level, affecting all other script mappings, many of which break when exposed to the PATH_TRANSLATED bug. For this reason IIS<7 is almost never deployed with the fix. (Even IIS7 rarely uses it because there is still no UI for it.)

There is no way for CGI code to tell whether the option was set, so a separate handler class is provided. It is used in the same way as *CGIHandler*, i.e., by calling IISCGIHandler().run(app), where app is the WSGI application object you wish to invoke.

New in version 3.2.

class wsgiref.handlers.BaseCGIHandler(*stdin, stdout, stderr, environ, multithread=True, multiprocess=False*)

Similar to *CGIHandler*, but instead of using the *sys* and *os* modules, the CGI environment and I/O streams are specified explicitly. The *multithread* and *multiprocess* values are used to set the wsgi.multithread and wsgi.multiprocess flags for any applications run by the handler instance.

This class is a subclass of *SimpleHandler* intended for use with software other than HTTP "origin servers". If you are writing a gateway protocol implementation (such as CGI, FastCGI, SCGI, etc.) that uses a **Status:** header to send an HTTP status, you probably want to subclass this instead of *SimpleHandler*.

class wsgiref.handlers.SimpleHandler(*stdin, stdout, stderr, environ, multithread=True, multiprocess=False*)

Similar to *BaseCGIHandler*, but designed for use with HTTP origin servers. If you are writing an HTTP server implementation, you will probably want to subclass this instead of *BaseCGIHandler*.

This class is a subclass of *BaseHandler*. It overrides the **__init__()**, **get_stdin()**, **get_stderr()**, **add_cgi_vars()**, **_write()**, and **_flush()** methods to support explicitly setting the environment and streams via the constructor. The supplied environment and streams are stored in the **stdin**, **stdout**, **stderr**, and **environ** attributes.

The *write()* method of *stdout* should write each chunk in full, like *io.BufferedIOBase*.

class wsgiref.handlers.BaseHandler

This is an abstract base class for running WSGI applications. Each instance will handle a single HTTP request, although in principle you could create a subclass that was reusable for multiple requests.

BaseHandler instances have only one method intended for external use:

run(*app*)

Run the specified WSGI application, *app*.

All of the other *BaseHandler* methods are invoked by this method in the process of running the application, and thus exist primarily to allow customizing the process.

The following methods MUST be overridden in a subclass:

_write(*data*)

Buffer the bytes *data* for transmission to the client. It's okay if this method actually transmits the data; *BaseHandler* just separates write and flush operations for greater efficiency when the underlying system actually has such a distinction.

_flush()

Force buffered data to be transmitted to the client. It's okay if this method is a no-op (i.e., if *_write()* actually sends the data).

get_stdin()

Return an input stream object suitable for use as the **wsgi.input** of the request currently being processed.

get_stderr()

Return an output stream object suitable for use as the **wsgi.errors** of the request currently being processed.

add_cgi_vars()

Insert CGI variables for the current request into the **environ** attribute.

Here are some other methods and attributes you may wish to override. This list is only a summary, however, and does not include every method that can be overridden. You should consult the docstrings and source code for additional information before attempting to create a customized *BaseHandler* subclass.

Attributes and methods for customizing the WSGI environment:

wsgi_multithread

The value to be used for the **wsgi.multithread** environment variable. It defaults to true in *BaseHandler*, but may have a different default (or be set by the constructor) in the other subclasses.

wsgi_multiprocess

The value to be used for the `wsgi.multiprocess` environment variable. It defaults to true in *BaseHandler*, but may have a different default (or be set by the constructor) in the other subclasses.

wsgi_run_once

The value to be used for the `wsgi.run_once` environment variable. It defaults to false in *BaseHandler*, but *CGIHandler* sets it to true by default.

os_environ

The default environment variables to be included in every request's WSGI environment. By default, this is a copy of `os.environ` at the time that *wsgiref.handlers* was imported, but subclasses can either create their own at the class or instance level. Note that the dictionary should be considered read-only, since the default value is shared between multiple classes and instances.

server_software

If the *origin_server* attribute is set, this attribute's value is used to set the default `SERVER_SOFTWARE` WSGI environment variable, and also to set a default `Server:` header in HTTP responses. It is ignored for handlers (such as *BaseCGIHandler* and *CGIHandler*) that are not HTTP origin servers.

Changed in version 3.3: The term "Python" is replaced with implementation specific term like "CPython", "Jython" etc.

get_scheme()

Return the URL scheme being used for the current request. The default implementation uses the `guess_scheme()` function from *wsgiref.util* to guess whether the scheme should be "http" or "https", based on the current request's `environ` variables.

setup_environ()

Set the `environ` attribute to a fully-populated WSGI environment. The default implementation uses all of the above methods and attributes, plus the *get_stdin()*, *get_stderr()*, and *add_cgi_vars()* methods and the *wsgi_file_wrapper* attribute. It also inserts a `SERVER_SOFTWARE` key if not present, as long as the *origin_server* attribute is a true value and the *server_software* attribute is set.

Methods and attributes for customizing exception handling:

log_exception(*exc_info*)

Log the *exc_info* tuple in the server log. *exc_info* is a `(type, value, traceback)` tuple. The default implementation simply writes the traceback to the request's `wsgi.errors` stream and flushes it. Subclasses can override this method to change the format or retarget the output, mail the traceback to an administrator, or whatever other action may be deemed suitable.

traceback_limit

The maximum number of frames to include in tracebacks output by the default *log_exception()* method. If `None`, all frames are included.

error_output(*environ*, *start_response*)

This method is a WSGI application to generate an error page for the user. It is only invoked if an error occurs before headers are sent to the client.

This method can access the current error information using `sys.exc_info()`, and should pass that information to *start_response* when calling it (as described in the "Error Handling" section of PEP 3333).

The default implementation just uses the *error_status*, *error_headers*, and *error_body* attributes to generate an output page. Subclasses can override this to produce more dynamic error output.

error_status

The HTTP status used for error responses. This should be a status string as defined in PEP 3333; it defaults to a 500 code and message.

error_headers

The HTTP headers used for error responses. This should be a list of WSGI response headers ((name, value) tuples), as described in PEP 3333. The default list just sets the content type to text/plain.

error_body

The error response body. This should be an HTTP response body bytestring. It defaults to the plain text, "A server error occurred. Please contact the administrator."

Methods and attributes for PEP 3333's "Optional Platform-Specific File Handling" feature:

wsgi_file_wrapper

A wsgi.file_wrapper factory, or None. The default value of this attribute is the *wsgiref.util.FileWrapper* class.

sendfile()

Override to implement platform-specific file transmission. This method is called only if the application's return value is an instance of the class specified by the *wsgi_file_wrapper* attribute. It should return a true value if it was able to successfully transmit the file, so that the default transmission code will not be executed. The default implementation of this method just returns a false value.

Miscellaneous methods and attributes:

origin_server

This attribute should be set to a true value if the handler's *_write()* and *_flush()* are being used to communicate directly to the client, rather than via a CGI-like gateway protocol that wants the HTTP status in a special Status: header.

This attribute's default value is true in *BaseHandler*, but false in *BaseCGIHandler* and *CGIHandler*.

http_version

If *origin_server* is true, this string attribute is used to set the HTTP version of the response set to the client. It defaults to "1.0".

wsgiref.handlers.read_environ()

Transcode CGI variables from os.environ to PEP 3333 "bytes in unicode" strings, returning a new dictionary. This function is used by *CGIHandler* and *IISCGIHandler* in place of directly using os.environ, which is not necessarily WSGI-compliant on all platforms and web servers using Python 3 – specifically, ones where the OS's actual environment is Unicode (i.e. Windows), or ones where the environment is bytes, but the system encoding used by Python to decode it is anything other than ISO-8859-1 (e.g. Unix systems using UTF-8).

If you are implementing a CGI-based handler of your own, you probably want to use this routine instead of just copying values out of os.environ directly.

New in version 3.2.

21.4.6 Examples

This is a working "Hello World" WSGI application:

```python
from wsgiref.simple_server import make_server

# Every WSGI application must have an application object - a callable
# object that accepts two arguments. For that purpose, we're going to
# use a function (note that you're not limited to a function, you can
# use a class for example). The first argument passed to the function
# is a dictionary containing CGI-style environment variables and the
# second variable is the callable object (see PEP 333).
def hello_world_app(environ, start_response):
    status = '200 OK'  # HTTP Status
    headers = [('Content-type', 'text/plain; charset=utf-8')]  # HTTP Headers
    start_response(status, headers)

    # The returned object is going to be printed
    return [b"Hello World"]

with make_server('', 8000, hello_world_app) as httpd:
    print("Serving on port 8000...")

    # Serve until process is killed
    httpd.serve_forever()
```

21.5 `urllib` — URL handling modules

Source code: Lib/urllib/

`urllib` is a package that collects several modules for working with URLs:

- *urllib.request* for opening and reading URLs
- *urllib.error* containing the exceptions raised by *urllib.request*
- *urllib.parse* for parsing URLs
- *urllib.robotparser* for parsing `robots.txt` files

21.6 `urllib.request` — Extensible library for opening URLs

Source code: Lib/urllib/request.py

The *urllib.request* module defines functions and classes which help in opening URLs (mostly HTTP) in a complex world — basic and digest authentication, redirections, cookies and more.

See also:

The Requests package is recommended for a higher-level HTTP client interface.

The *urllib.request* module defines the following functions:

`urllib.request.urlopen`(*url, data=None*[, *timeout*], *, *cafile=None, capath=None, cadefault=False, context=None*)

   Open the URL *url*, which can be either a string or a *Request* object.

   data must be an object specifying additional data to be sent to the server, or `None` if no such data is needed. See *Request* for details.

urllib.request module uses HTTP/1.1 and includes `Connection:close` header in its HTTP requests.

The optional *timeout* parameter specifies a timeout in seconds for blocking operations like the connection attempt (if not specified, the global default timeout setting will be used). This actually only works for HTTP, HTTPS and FTP connections.

If *context* is specified, it must be a *ssl.SSLContext* instance describing the various SSL options. See *HTTPSConnection* for more details.

The optional *cafile* and *capath* parameters specify a set of trusted CA certificates for HTTPS requests. *cafile* should point to a single file containing a bundle of CA certificates, whereas *capath* should point to a directory of hashed certificate files. More information can be found in *ssl.SSLContext.load_verify_locations()*.

The *cadefault* parameter is ignored.

This function always returns an object which can work as a *context manager* and has methods such as

- `geturl()` — return the URL of the resource retrieved, commonly used to determine if a redirect was followed
- `info()` — return the meta-information of the page, such as headers, in the form of an *email.message_from_string()* instance (see Quick Reference to HTTP Headers)
- `getcode()` – return the HTTP status code of the response.

For HTTP and HTTPS URLs, this function returns a *http.client.HTTPResponse* object slightly modified. In addition to the three new methods above, the msg attribute contains the same information as the *reason* attribute — the reason phrase returned by server — instead of the response headers as it is specified in the documentation for *HTTPResponse*.

For FTP, file, and data URLs and requests explicitly handled by legacy *URLopener* and *FancyURLopener* classes, this function returns a `urllib.response.addinfourl` object.

Raises *URLError* on protocol errors.

Note that `None` may be returned if no handler handles the request (though the default installed global *OpenerDirector* uses *UnknownHandler* to ensure this never happens).

In addition, if proxy settings are detected (for example, when a `*_proxy` environment variable like `http_proxy` is set), *ProxyHandler* is default installed and makes sure the requests are handled through the proxy.

The legacy `urllib.urlopen` function from Python 2.6 and earlier has been discontinued; *urllib.request.urlopen()* corresponds to the old `urllib2.urlopen`. Proxy handling, which was done by passing a dictionary parameter to `urllib.urlopen`, can be obtained by using *ProxyHandler* objects.

Changed in version 3.2: *cafile* and *capath* were added.

Changed in version 3.2: HTTPS virtual hosts are now supported if possible (that is, if *ssl.HAS_SNI* is true).

New in version 3.2: *data* can be an iterable object.

Changed in version 3.3: *cadefault* was added.

Changed in version 3.4.3: *context* was added.

Deprecated since version 3.6: *cafile*, *capath* and *cadefault* are deprecated in favor of *context*. Please use *ssl.SSLContext.load_cert_chain()* instead, or let *ssl.create_default_context()* select the system's trusted CA certificates for you.

urllib.request.install_opener(*opener*)

Install an *OpenerDirector* instance as the default global opener. Installing an opener is only necessary if you want urlopen to use that opener; otherwise, simply call *OpenerDirector.open()* instead of *urlopen()*. The code does not check for a real *OpenerDirector*, and any class with the appropriate interface will work.

urllib.request.build_opener([*handler, ...*]**)**

Return an *OpenerDirector* instance, which chains the handlers in the order given. *handlers* can be either instances of *BaseHandler*, or subclasses of *BaseHandler* (in which case it must be possible to call the constructor without any parameters). Instances of the following classes will be in front of the *handlers*, unless the *handlers* contain them, instances of them or subclasses of them: *ProxyHandler* (if proxy settings are detected), *UnknownHandler*, *HTTPHandler*, *HTTPDefaultErrorHandler*, *HTTPRedirectHandler*, *FTPHandler*, *FileHandler*, *HTTPErrorProcessor*.

If the Python installation has SSL support (i.e., if the *ssl* module can be imported), *HTTPSHandler* will also be added.

A *BaseHandler* subclass may also change its **handler_order** attribute to modify its position in the handlers list.

urllib.request.pathname2url(*path***)**

Convert the pathname *path* from the local syntax for a path to the form used in the path component of a URL. This does not produce a complete URL. The return value will already be quoted using the *quote()* function.

urllib.request.url2pathname(*path***)**

Convert the path component *path* from a percent-encoded URL to the local syntax for a path. This does not accept a complete URL. This function uses *unquote()* to decode *path*.

urllib.request.getproxies()

This helper function returns a dictionary of scheme to proxy server URL mappings. It scans the environment for variables named **<scheme>_proxy**, in a case insensitive approach, for all operating systems first, and when it cannot find it, looks for proxy information from Mac OSX System Configuration for Mac OS X and Windows Systems Registry for Windows. If both lowercase and uppercase environment variables exist (and disagree), lowercase is preferred.

Note: If the environment variable **REQUEST_METHOD** is set, which usually indicates your script is running in a CGI environment, the environment variable **HTTP_PROXY** (uppercase **_PROXY**) will be ignored. This is because that variable can be injected by a client using the "Proxy:" HTTP header. If you need to use an HTTP proxy in a CGI environment, either use **ProxyHandler** explicitly, or make sure the variable name is in lowercase (or at least the **_proxy** suffix).

The following classes are provided:

class urllib.request.Request(*url, data=None, headers={}, origin_req_host=None, unverifiable=False, method=None***)**

This class is an abstraction of a URL request.

url should be a string containing a valid URL.

data must be an object specifying additional data to send to the server, or **None** if no such data is needed. Currently HTTP requests are the only ones that use *data*. The supported object types include bytes, file-like objects, and iterables. If no **Content-Length** nor **Transfer-Encoding** header field has been provided, *HTTPHandler* will set these headers according to the type of *data*. **Content-Length** will be used to send bytes objects, while **Transfer-Encoding: chunked** as specified in RFC 7230, Section 3.3.1 will be used to send files and other iterables.

For an HTTP POST request method, *data* should be a buffer in the standard *application/x-www-form-urlencoded* format. The *urllib.parse.urlencode()* function takes a mapping or sequence of 2-tuples and returns an ASCII string in this format. It should be encoded to bytes before being used as the *data* parameter.

headers should be a dictionary, and will be treated as if `add_header()` was called with each key and value as arguments. This is often used to "spoof" the `User-Agent` header value, which is used by a browser to identify itself – some HTTP servers only allow requests coming from common browsers as opposed to scripts. For example, Mozilla Firefox may identify itself as `"Mozilla/5.0 (X11; U; Linux i686) Gecko/20071127 Firefox/2.0.0.11"`, while *urllib*'s default user agent string is `"Python-urllib/2.6"` (on Python 2.6).

An appropriate `Content-Type` header should be included if the *data* argument is present. If this header has not been provided and *data* is not None, `Content-Type: application/x-www-form-urlencoded` will be added as a default.

The final two arguments are only of interest for correct handling of third-party HTTP cookies:

origin_req_host should be the request-host of the origin transaction, as defined by RFC 2965. It defaults to `http.cookiejar.request_host(self)`. This is the host name or IP address of the original request that was initiated by the user. For example, if the request is for an image in an HTML document, this should be the request-host of the request for the page containing the image.

unverifiable should indicate whether the request is unverifiable, as defined by RFC 2965. It defaults to False. An unverifiable request is one whose URL the user did not have the option to approve. For example, if the request is for an image in an HTML document, and the user had no option to approve the automatic fetching of the image, this should be true.

method should be a string that indicates the HTTP request method that will be used (e.g. `'HEAD'`). If provided, its value is stored in the *method* attribute and is used by *get_method()*. The default is `'GET'` if *data* is None or `'POST'` otherwise. Subclasses may indicate a different default method by setting the *method* attribute in the class itself.

Note: The request will not work as expected if the data object is unable to deliver its content more than once (e.g. a file or an iterable that can produce the content only once) and the request is retried for HTTP redirects or authentication. The *data* is sent to the HTTP server right away after the headers. There is no support for a 100-continue expectation in the library.

Changed in version 3.3: *Request.method* argument is added to the Request class.

Changed in version 3.4: Default *Request.method* may be indicated at the class level.

Changed in version 3.6: Do not raise an error if the `Content-Length` has not been provided and *data* is neither None nor a bytes object. Fall back to use chunked transfer encoding instead.

class urllib.request.OpenerDirector
    The *OpenerDirector* class opens URLs via *BaseHandler*s chained together. It manages the chaining of handlers, and recovery from errors.

class urllib.request.BaseHandler
    This is the base class for all registered handlers — and handles only the simple mechanics of registration.

class urllib.request.HTTPDefaultErrorHandler
    A class which defines a default handler for HTTP error responses; all responses are turned into *HTTPError* exceptions.

class urllib.request.HTTPRedirectHandler
    A class to handle redirections.

class urllib.request.HTTPCookieProcessor(*cookiejar=None*)
    A class to handle HTTP Cookies.

class urllib.request.ProxyHandler(*proxies=None*)
    Cause requests to go through a proxy. If *proxies* is given, it must be a dictionary mapping protocol names to URLs of proxies. The default is to read the list of proxies from the environment variables `<protocol>_proxy`. If no proxy environment variables are set, then in a Windows environment proxy

settings are obtained from the registry's Internet Settings section, and in a Mac OS X environment proxy information is retrieved from the OS X System Configuration Framework.

To disable autodetected proxy pass an empty dictionary.

The `no_proxy` environment variable can be used to specify hosts which shouldn't be reached via proxy; if set, it should be a comma-separated list of hostname suffixes, optionally with `:port` appended, for example `cern.ch,ncsa.uiuc.edu,some.host:8080`.

> **Note:** `HTTP_PROXY` will be ignored if a variable `REQUEST_METHOD` is set; see the documentation on *getproxies()*.

class urllib.request.HTTPPasswordMgr
Keep a database of `(realm, uri)` -> `(user, password)` mappings.

class urllib.request.HTTPPasswordMgrWithDefaultRealm
Keep a database of `(realm, uri)` -> `(user, password)` mappings. A realm of `None` is considered a catch-all realm, which is searched if no other realm fits.

class urllib.request.HTTPPasswordMgrWithPriorAuth
A variant of *HTTPPasswordMgrWithDefaultRealm* that also has a database of `uri` -> `is_authenticated` mappings. Can be used by a BasicAuth handler to determine when to send authentication credentials immediately instead of waiting for a 401 response first.

New in version 3.5.

class urllib.request.AbstractBasicAuthHandler(*password_mgr=None*)
This is a mixin class that helps with HTTP authentication, both to the remote host and to a proxy. *password_mgr*, if given, should be something that is compatible with *HTTPPasswordMgr*; refer to section *HTTPPasswordMgr Objects* for information on the interface that must be supported. If *passwd_mgr* also provides `is_authenticated` and `update_authenticated` methods (see *HTTPPasswordMgrWithPriorAuth Objects*), then the handler will use the `is_authenticated` result for a given URI to determine whether or not to send authentication credentials with the request. If `is_authenticated` returns `True` for the URI, credentials are sent. If `is_authenticated` is `False`, credentials are not sent, and then if a 401 response is received the request is re-sent with the authentication credentials. If authentication succeeds, `update_authenticated` is called to set `is_authenticated` `True` for the URI, so that subsequent requests to the URI or any of its super-URIs will automatically include the authentication credentials.

New in version 3.5: Added `is_authenticated` support.

class urllib.request.HTTPBasicAuthHandler(*password_mgr=None*)
Handle authentication with the remote host. *password_mgr*, if given, should be something that is compatible with *HTTPPasswordMgr*; refer to section *HTTPPasswordMgr Objects* for information on the interface that must be supported. HTTPBasicAuthHandler will raise a *ValueError* when presented with a wrong Authentication scheme.

class urllib.request.ProxyBasicAuthHandler(*password_mgr=None*)
Handle authentication with the proxy. *password_mgr*, if given, should be something that is compatible with *HTTPPasswordMgr*; refer to section *HTTPPasswordMgr Objects* for information on the interface that must be supported.

class urllib.request.AbstractDigestAuthHandler(*password_mgr=None*)
This is a mixin class that helps with HTTP authentication, both to the remote host and to a proxy. *password_mgr*, if given, should be something that is compatible with *HTTPPasswordMgr*; refer to section *HTTPPasswordMgr Objects* for information on the interface that must be supported.

class urllib.request.HTTPDigestAuthHandler(*password_mgr=None*)
Handle authentication with the remote host. *password_mgr*, if given, should be something that is

compatible with *HTTPPasswordMgr*; refer to section *HTTPPasswordMgr Objects* for information on the interface that must be supported. When both Digest Authentication Handler and Basic Authentication Handler are both added, Digest Authentication is always tried first. If the Digest Authentication returns a 40x response again, it is sent to Basic Authentication handler to Handle. This Handler method will raise a *ValueError* when presented with an authentication scheme other than Digest or Basic.

Changed in version 3.3: Raise *ValueError* on unsupported Authentication Scheme.

class urllib.request.ProxyDigestAuthHandler(*password_mgr=None*)

Handle authentication with the proxy. *password_mgr*, if given, should be something that is compatible with *HTTPPasswordMgr*; refer to section *HTTPPasswordMgr Objects* for information on the interface that must be supported.

class urllib.request.HTTPHandler

A class to handle opening of HTTP URLs.

class urllib.request.HTTPSHandler(*debuglevel=0*, *context=None*, *check_hostname=None*)

A class to handle opening of HTTPS URLs. *context* and *check_hostname* have the same meaning as in *http.client.HTTPSConnection*.

Changed in version 3.2: *context* and *check_hostname* were added.

class urllib.request.FileHandler

Open local files.

class urllib.request.DataHandler

Open data URLs.

New in version 3.4.

class urllib.request.FTPHandler

Open FTP URLs.

class urllib.request.CacheFTPHandler

Open FTP URLs, keeping a cache of open FTP connections to minimize delays.

class urllib.request.UnknownHandler

A catch-all class to handle unknown URLs.

class urllib.request.HTTPErrorProcessor

Process HTTP error responses.

21.6.1 Request Objects

The following methods describe *Request*'s public interface, and so all may be overridden in subclasses. It also defines several public attributes that can be used by clients to inspect the parsed request.

Request.full_url

The original URL passed to the constructor.

Changed in version 3.4.

Request.full_url is a property with setter, getter and a deleter. Getting *full_url* returns the original request URL with the fragment, if it was present.

Request.type

The URI scheme.

Request.host

The URI authority, typically a host, but may also contain a port separated by a colon.

Request.origin_req_host

The original host for the request, without port.

Request.selector
　　The URI path. If the *Request* uses a proxy, then selector will be the full URL that is passed to the proxy.

Request.data
　　The entity body for the request, or **None** if not specified.

　　Changed in version 3.4: Changing value of *Request.data* now deletes "Content-Length" header if it was previously set or calculated.

Request.unverifiable
　　boolean, indicates whether the request is unverifiable as defined by RFC 2965.

Request.method
　　The HTTP request method to use. By default its value is *None*, which means that *get_method()* will do its normal computation of the method to be used. Its value can be set (thus overriding the default computation in *get_method()*) either by providing a default value by setting it at the class level in a *Request* subclass, or by passing a value in to the *Request* constructor via the *method* argument.

　　New in version 3.3.

　　Changed in version 3.4: A default value can now be set in subclasses; previously it could only be set via the constructor argument.

Request.get_method()
　　Return a string indicating the HTTP request method. If *Request.method* is not **None**, return its value, otherwise return **'GET'** if *Request.data* is **None**, or **'POST'** if it's not. This is only meaningful for HTTP requests.

　　Changed in version 3.3: get_method now looks at the value of *Request.method*.

Request.add_header(key*, *val**)**
　　Add another header to the request. Headers are currently ignored by all handlers except HTTP handlers, where they are added to the list of headers sent to the server. Note that there cannot be more than one header with the same name, and later calls will overwrite previous calls in case the *key* collides. Currently, this is no loss of HTTP functionality, since all headers which have meaning when used more than once have a (header-specific) way of gaining the same functionality using only one header.

Request.add_unredirected_header(key*, *header**)**
　　Add a header that will not be added to a redirected request.

Request.has_header(header**)**
　　Return whether the instance has the named header (checks both regular and unredirected).

Request.remove_header(header**)**
　　Remove named header from the request instance (both from regular and unredirected headers).

　　New in version 3.4.

Request.get_full_url()
　　Return the URL given in the constructor.

　　Changed in version 3.4.

　　Returns *Request.full_url*

Request.set_proxy(host*, *type**)**
　　Prepare the request by connecting to a proxy server. The *host* and *type* will replace those of the instance, and the instance's selector will be the original URL given in the constructor.

Request.get_header(header_name*, *default=None**)**
　　Return the value of the given header. If the header is not present, return the default value.

`Request.header_items()`
   Return a list of tuples (header_name, header_value) of the Request headers.

Changed in version 3.4: The request methods add_data, has_data, get_data, get_type, get_host, get_selector, get_origin_req_host and is_unverifiable that were deprecated since 3.3 have been removed.

21.6.2 OpenerDirector Objects

OpenerDirector instances have the following methods:

`OpenerDirector.add_handler(handler)`
   handler should be an instance of *BaseHandler*. The following methods are searched, and added to the possible chains (note that HTTP errors are a special case).

   - `protocol_open()` — signal that the handler knows how to open *protocol* URLs.
   - `http_error_type()` — signal that the handler knows how to handle HTTP errors with HTTP error code *type*.
   - `protocol_error()` — signal that the handler knows how to handle errors from (non-`http`) *protocol*.
   - `protocol_request()` — signal that the handler knows how to pre-process *protocol* requests.
   - `protocol_response()` — signal that the handler knows how to post-process *protocol* responses.

`OpenerDirector.open(url, data=None[, timeout])`
   Open the given *url* (which can be a request object or a string), optionally passing the given *data*. Arguments, return values and exceptions raised are the same as those of *urlopen()* (which simply calls the *open()* method on the currently installed global *OpenerDirector*). The optional *timeout* parameter specifies a timeout in seconds for blocking operations like the connection attempt (if not specified, the global default timeout setting will be used). The timeout feature actually works only for HTTP, HTTPS and FTP connections).

`OpenerDirector.error(proto, *args)`
   Handle an error of the given protocol. This will call the registered error handlers for the given protocol with the given arguments (which are protocol specific). The HTTP protocol is a special case which uses the HTTP response code to determine the specific error handler; refer to the `http_error_*()` methods of the handler classes.

   Return values and exceptions raised are the same as those of *urlopen()*.

OpenerDirector objects open URLs in three stages:

The order in which these methods are called within each stage is determined by sorting the handler instances.

1. Every handler with a method named like `protocol_request()` has that method called to pre-process the request.

2. Handlers with a method named like `protocol_open()` are called to handle the request. This stage ends when a handler either returns a non-*None* value (ie. a response), or raises an exception (usually *URLError*). Exceptions are allowed to propagate.

   In fact, the above algorithm is first tried for methods named **default_open()**. If all such methods return *None*, the algorithm is repeated for methods named like **protocol_open()**. If all such methods return *None*, the algorithm is repeated for methods named **unknown_open()**.

   Note that the implementation of these methods may involve calls of the parent *OpenerDirector* instance's *open()* and *error()* methods.

3. Every handler with a method named like `protocol_response()` has that method called to post-process the response.

21.6.3 BaseHandler Objects

BaseHandler objects provide a couple of methods that are directly useful, and others that are meant to be used by derived classes. These are intended for direct use:

BaseHandler.add_parent(*director*)
: Add a director as parent.

BaseHandler.close()
: Remove any parents.

The following attribute and methods should only be used by classes derived from *BaseHandler*.

> **Note:** The convention has been adopted that subclasses defining protocol_request() or protocol_response() methods are named *Processor; all others are named *Handler.

BaseHandler.parent
: A valid *OpenerDirector*, which can be used to open using a different protocol, or handle errors.

BaseHandler.default_open(*req*)
: This method is *not* defined in *BaseHandler*, but subclasses should define it if they want to catch all URLs.

    This method, if implemented, will be called by the parent *OpenerDirector*. It should return a file-like object as described in the return value of the *open()* of *OpenerDirector*, or None. It should raise *URLError*, unless a truly exceptional thing happens (for example, *MemoryError* should not be mapped to URLError).

    This method will be called before any protocol-specific open method.

BaseHandler.protocol_open(*req*)
: This method is *not* defined in *BaseHandler*, but subclasses should define it if they want to handle URLs with the given protocol.

    This method, if defined, will be called by the parent *OpenerDirector*. Return values should be the same as for *default_open()*.

BaseHandler.unknown_open(*req*)
: This method is *not* defined in *BaseHandler*, but subclasses should define it if they want to catch all URLs with no specific registered handler to open it.

    This method, if implemented, will be called by the *parent OpenerDirector*. Return values should be the same as for *default_open()*.

BaseHandler.http_error_default(*req, fp, code, msg, hdrs*)
: This method is *not* defined in *BaseHandler*, but subclasses should override it if they intend to provide a catch-all for otherwise unhandled HTTP errors. It will be called automatically by the *OpenerDirector* getting the error, and should not normally be called in other circumstances.

    req will be a *Request* object, *fp* will be a file-like object with the HTTP error body, *code* will be the three-digit code of the error, *msg* will be the user-visible explanation of the code and *hdrs* will be a mapping object with the headers of the error.

    Return values and exceptions raised should be the same as those of *urlopen()*.

BaseHandler.http_error_nnn(*req, fp, code, msg, hdrs*)
: *nnn* should be a three-digit HTTP error code. This method is also not defined in *BaseHandler*, but will be called, if it exists, on an instance of a subclass, when an HTTP error with code *nnn* occurs.

    Subclasses should override this method to handle specific HTTP errors.

    Arguments, return values and exceptions raised should be the same as for *http_error_default()*.

BaseHandler.protocol_request(*req*)
    This method is *not* defined in `BaseHandler`, but subclasses should define it if they want to pre-process requests of the given protocol.

    This method, if defined, will be called by the parent `OpenerDirector`. *req* will be a `Request` object. The return value should be a `Request` object.

BaseHandler.protocol_response(*req, response*)
    This method is *not* defined in `BaseHandler`, but subclasses should define it if they want to post-process responses of the given protocol.

    This method, if defined, will be called by the parent `OpenerDirector`. *req* will be a `Request` object. *response* will be an object implementing the same interface as the return value of `urlopen()`. The return value should implement the same interface as the return value of `urlopen()`.

21.6.4 HTTPRedirectHandler Objects

> **Note:** Some HTTP redirections require action from this module's client code. If this is the case, `HTTPError` is raised. See RFC 2616 for details of the precise meanings of the various redirection codes.

> An HTTPError exception raised as a security consideration if the HTTPRedirectHandler is presented with a redirected URL which is not an HTTP, HTTPS or FTP URL.

HTTPRedirectHandler.redirect_request(*req, fp, code, msg, hdrs, newurl*)
    Return a `Request` or **None** in response to a redirect. This is called by the default implementations of the `http_error_30*()` methods when a redirection is received from the server. If a redirection should take place, return a new `Request` to allow `http_error_30*()` to perform the redirect to *newurl*. Otherwise, raise `HTTPError` if no other handler should try to handle this URL, or return **None** if you can't but another handler might.

> **Note:** The default implementation of this method does not strictly follow RFC 2616, which says that 301 and 302 responses to POST requests must not be automatically redirected without confirmation by the user. In reality, browsers do allow automatic redirection of these responses, changing the POST to a GET, and the default implementation reproduces this behavior.

HTTPRedirectHandler.http_error_301(*req, fp, code, msg, hdrs*)
    Redirect to the **Location:** or **URI:** URL. This method is called by the parent `OpenerDirector` when getting an HTTP 'moved permanently' response.

HTTPRedirectHandler.http_error_302(*req, fp, code, msg, hdrs*)
    The same as `http_error_301()`, but called for the 'found' response.

HTTPRedirectHandler.http_error_303(*req, fp, code, msg, hdrs*)
    The same as `http_error_301()`, but called for the 'see other' response.

HTTPRedirectHandler.http_error_307(*req, fp, code, msg, hdrs*)
    The same as `http_error_301()`, but called for the 'temporary redirect' response.

21.6.5 HTTPCookieProcessor Objects

HTTPCookieProcessor instances have one attribute:

HTTPCookieProcessor.cookiejar
    The *http.cookiejar.CookieJar* in which cookies are stored.

21.6.6 ProxyHandler Objects

ProxyHandler.protocol_open(*request*)
   The *ProxyHandler* will have a method `protocol_open()` for every *protocol* which has a proxy in the *proxies* dictionary given in the constructor. The method will modify requests to go through the proxy, by calling `request.set_proxy()`, and call the next handler in the chain to actually execute the protocol.

21.6.7 HTTPPasswordMgr Objects

These methods are available on *HTTPPasswordMgr* and *HTTPPasswordMgrWithDefaultRealm* objects.

HTTPPasswordMgr.add_password(*realm, uri, user, passwd*)
   uri can be either a single URI, or a sequence of URIs. *realm*, *user* and *passwd* must be strings. This causes `(user, passwd)` to be used as authentication tokens when authentication for *realm* and a super-URI of any of the given URIs is given.

HTTPPasswordMgr.find_user_password(*realm, authuri*)
   Get user/password for given realm and URI, if any. This method will return (`None`, `None`) if there is no matching user/password.

   For *HTTPPasswordMgrWithDefaultRealm* objects, the realm `None` will be searched if the given *realm* has no matching user/password.

21.6.8 HTTPPasswordMgrWithPriorAuth Objects

This password manager extends *HTTPPasswordMgrWithDefaultRealm* to support tracking URIs for which authentication credentials should always be sent.

HTTPPasswordMgrWithPriorAuth.add_password(*realm, uri, user, passwd, is_authenticated=False*)
   realm, uri, user, passwd are as for *HTTPPasswordMgr.add_password()*. *is_authenticated* sets the initial value of the `is_authenticated` flag for the given URI or list of URIs. If *is_authenticated* is specified as `True`, *realm* is ignored.

HTTPPasswordMgr.find_user_password(*realm, authuri*)
   Same as for *HTTPPasswordMgrWithDefaultRealm* objects

HTTPPasswordMgrWithPriorAuth.update_authenticated(*self, uri, is_authenticated=False*)
   Update the `is_authenticated` flag for the given *uri* or list of URIs.

HTTPPasswordMgrWithPriorAuth.is_authenticated(*self, authuri*)
   Returns the current state of the `is_authenticated` flag for the given URI.

21.6.9 AbstractBasicAuthHandler Objects

AbstractBasicAuthHandler.http_error_auth_reqed(*authreq, host, req, headers*)
   Handle an authentication request by getting a user/password pair, and re-trying the request. *authreq* should be the name of the header where the information about the realm is included in the request, *host* specifies the URL and path to authenticate for, *req* should be the (failed) *Request* object, and *headers* should be the error headers.

   host is either an authority (e.g. `"python.org"`) or a URL containing an authority component (e.g. `"http://python.org/"`). In either case, the authority must not contain a userinfo component (so, `"python.org"` and `"python.org:80"` are fine, `"joe:password@python.org"` is not).

21.6.10 HTTPBasicAuthHandler Objects

HTTPBasicAuthHandler.**http_error_401**(*req, fp, code, msg, hdrs*)
    Retry the request with authentication information, if available.

21.6.11 ProxyBasicAuthHandler Objects

ProxyBasicAuthHandler.**http_error_407**(*req, fp, code, msg, hdrs*)
    Retry the request with authentication information, if available.

21.6.12 AbstractDigestAuthHandler Objects

AbstractDigestAuthHandler.**http_error_auth_reqed**(*authreq, host, req, headers*)
    authreq should be the name of the header where the information about the realm is included in the request, *host* should be the host to authenticate to, *req* should be the (failed) *Request* object, and *headers* should be the error headers.

21.6.13 HTTPDigestAuthHandler Objects

HTTPDigestAuthHandler.**http_error_401**(*req, fp, code, msg, hdrs*)
    Retry the request with authentication information, if available.

21.6.14 ProxyDigestAuthHandler Objects

ProxyDigestAuthHandler.**http_error_407**(*req, fp, code, msg, hdrs*)
    Retry the request with authentication information, if available.

21.6.15 HTTPHandler Objects

HTTPHandler.**http_open**(*req*)
    Send an HTTP request, which can be either GET or POST, depending on req.has_data().

21.6.16 HTTPSHandler Objects

HTTPSHandler.**https_open**(*req*)
    Send an HTTPS request, which can be either GET or POST, depending on req.has_data().

21.6.17 FileHandler Objects

FileHandler.**file_open**(*req*)
    Open the file locally, if there is no host name, or the host name is 'localhost'.

    Changed in version 3.2: This method is applicable only for local hostnames. When a remote hostname is given, an *URLError* is raised.

21.6.18 DataHandler Objects

DataHandler.data_open(*req*)
> Read a data URL. This kind of URL contains the content encoded in the URL itself. The data URL syntax is specified in RFC 2397. This implementation ignores white spaces in base64 encoded data URLs so the URL may be wrapped in whatever source file it comes from. But even though some browsers don't mind about a missing padding at the end of a base64 encoded data URL, this implementation will raise an *ValueError* in that case.

21.6.19 FTPHandler Objects

FTPHandler.ftp_open(*req*)
> Open the FTP file indicated by *req*. The login is always done with empty username and password.

21.6.20 CacheFTPHandler Objects

CacheFTPHandler objects are *FTPHandler* objects with the following additional methods:

CacheFTPHandler.setTimeout(*t*)
> Set timeout of connections to *t* seconds.

CacheFTPHandler.setMaxConns(*m*)
> Set maximum number of cached connections to *m*.

21.6.21 UnknownHandler Objects

UnknownHandler.unknown_open()
> Raise a *URLError* exception.

21.6.22 HTTPErrorProcessor Objects

HTTPErrorProcessor.http_response()
> Process HTTP error responses.
>
> For 200 error codes, the response object is returned immediately.
>
> For non-200 error codes, this simply passes the job on to the **protocol_error_code**() handler methods, via *OpenerDirector.error()*. Eventually, *HTTPDefaultErrorHandler* will raise an *HTTPError* if no other handler handles the error.

HTTPErrorProcessor.https_response()
> Process HTTPS error responses.
>
> The behavior is same as *http_response()*.

21.6.23 Examples

In addition to the examples below, more examples are given in urllib-howto.

This example gets the python.org main page and displays the first 300 bytes of it.

```
>>> import urllib.request
>>> with urllib.request.urlopen('http://www.python.org/') as f:
...     print(f.read(300))
...
```

```
b'<!DOCTYPE html PUBLIC "-//W3C//DTD XHTML 1.0 Transitional//EN"
"http://www.w3.org/TR/xhtml1/DTD/xhtml1-transitional.dtd">\n\n\n<html
xmlns="http://www.w3.org/1999/xhtml" xml:lang="en" lang="en">\n\n<head>\n
<meta http-equiv="content-type" content="text/html; charset=utf-8" />\n
<title>Python Programming '
```

Note that urlopen returns a bytes object. This is because there is no way for urlopen to automatically determine the encoding of the byte stream it receives from the HTTP server. In general, a program will decode the returned bytes object to string once it determines or guesses the appropriate encoding.

The following W3C document, https://www.w3.org/International/O-charset, lists the various ways in which an (X)HTML or an XML document could have specified its encoding information.

As the python.org website uses *utf-8* encoding as specified in its meta tag, we will use the same for decoding the bytes object.

```
>>> with urllib.request.urlopen('http://www.python.org/') as f:
...     print(f.read(100).decode('utf-8'))
...
<!DOCTYPE html PUBLIC "-//W3C//DTD XHTML 1.0 Transitional//EN"
"http://www.w3.org/TR/xhtml1/DTD/xhtm
```

It is also possible to achieve the same result without using the *context manager* approach.

```
>>> import urllib.request
>>> f = urllib.request.urlopen('http://www.python.org/')
>>> print(f.read(100).decode('utf-8'))
<!DOCTYPE html PUBLIC "-//W3C//DTD XHTML 1.0 Transitional//EN"
"http://www.w3.org/TR/xhtml1/DTD/xhtm
```

In the following example, we are sending a data-stream to the stdin of a CGI and reading the data it returns to us. Note that this example will only work when the Python installation supports SSL.

```
>>> import urllib.request
>>> req = urllib.request.Request(url='https://localhost/cgi-bin/test.cgi',
...                     data=b'This data is passed to stdin of the CGI')
>>> with urllib.request.urlopen(req) as f:
...     print(f.read().decode('utf-8'))
...
Got Data: "This data is passed to stdin of the CGI"
```

The code for the sample CGI used in the above example is:

```
#!/usr/bin/env python
import sys
data = sys.stdin.read()
print('Content-type: text/plain\n\nGot Data: "%s"' % data)
```

Here is an example of doing a PUT request using *Request*:

```
import urllib.request
DATA = b'some data'
req = urllib.request.Request(url='http://localhost:8080', data=DATA,method='PUT')
with urllib.request.urlopen(req) as f:
    pass
print(f.status)
print(f.reason)
```

Use of Basic HTTP Authentication:

```python
import urllib.request
# Create an OpenerDirector with support for Basic HTTP Authentication...
auth_handler = urllib.request.HTTPBasicAuthHandler()
auth_handler.add_password(realm='PDQ Application',
                          uri='https://mahler:8092/site-updates.py',
                          user='klem',
                          passwd='kadidd!ehopper')
opener = urllib.request.build_opener(auth_handler)
# ...and install it globally so it can be used with urlopen.
urllib.request.install_opener(opener)
urllib.request.urlopen('http://www.example.com/login.html')
```

build_opener() provides many handlers by default, including a *ProxyHandler*. By default, *ProxyHandler* uses the environment variables named `<scheme>_proxy`, where `<scheme>` is the URL scheme involved. For example, the `http_proxy` environment variable is read to obtain the HTTP proxy's URL.

This example replaces the default *ProxyHandler* with one that uses programmatically-supplied proxy URLs, and adds proxy authorization support with *ProxyBasicAuthHandler*.

```python
proxy_handler = urllib.request.ProxyHandler({'http': 'http://www.example.com:3128/'})
proxy_auth_handler = urllib.request.ProxyBasicAuthHandler()
proxy_auth_handler.add_password('realm', 'host', 'username', 'password')

opener = urllib.request.build_opener(proxy_handler, proxy_auth_handler)
# This time, rather than install the OpenerDirector, we use it directly:
opener.open('http://www.example.com/login.html')
```

Adding HTTP headers:

Use the *headers* argument to the *Request* constructor, or:

```python
import urllib.request
req = urllib.request.Request('http://www.example.com/')
req.add_header('Referer', 'http://www.python.org/')
# Customize the default User-Agent header value:
req.add_header('User-Agent', 'urllib-example/0.1 (Contact: . . .)')
r = urllib.request.urlopen(req)
```

OpenerDirector automatically adds a **User-Agent** header to every *Request*. To change this:

```python
import urllib.request
opener = urllib.request.build_opener()
opener.addheaders = [('User-agent', 'Mozilla/5.0')]
opener.open('http://www.example.com/')
```

Also, remember that a few standard headers (*Content-Length*, *Content-Type* and *Host*) are added when the *Request* is passed to *urlopen()* (or *OpenerDirector.open()*). Here is an example session that uses the GET method to retrieve a URL containing parameters:

```python
>>> import urllib.request
>>> import urllib.parse
>>> params = urllib.parse.urlencode({'spam': 1, 'eggs': 2, 'bacon': 0})
>>> url = "http://www.musi-cal.com/cgi-bin/query?%s" % params
>>> with urllib.request.urlopen(url) as f:
...     print(f.read().decode('utf-8'))
...
```

The following example uses the POST method instead. Note that params output from urlencode is encoded to bytes before it is sent to urlopen as data:

```
>>> import urllib.request
>>> import urllib.parse
>>> data = urllib.parse.urlencode({'spam': 1, 'eggs': 2, 'bacon': 0})
>>> data = data.encode('ascii')
>>> with urllib.request.urlopen("http://requestb.in/xrb182xr", data) as f:
...     print(f.read().decode('utf-8'))
...
```

The following example uses an explicitly specified HTTP proxy, overriding environment settings:

```
>>> import urllib.request
>>> proxies = {'http': 'http://proxy.example.com:8080/'}
>>> opener = urllib.request.FancyURLopener(proxies)
>>> with opener.open("http://www.python.org") as f:
...     f.read().decode('utf-8')
...
```

The following example uses no proxies at all, overriding environment settings:

```
>>> import urllib.request
>>> opener = urllib.request.FancyURLopener({})
>>> with opener.open("http://www.python.org/") as f:
...     f.read().decode('utf-8')
...
```

21.6.24 Legacy interface

The following functions and classes are ported from the Python 2 module urllib (as opposed to urllib2). They might become deprecated at some point in the future.

urllib.request.urlretrieve(*url, filename=None, reporthook=None, data=None*)

> Copy a network object denoted by a URL to a local file. If the URL points to a local file, the object will not be copied unless filename is supplied. Return a tuple (`filename, headers`) where *filename* is the local file name under which the object can be found, and *headers* is whatever the `info()` method of the object returned by *urlopen()* returned (for a remote object). Exceptions are the same as for *urlopen()*.
>
> The second argument, if present, specifies the file location to copy to (if absent, the location will be a tempfile with a generated name). The third argument, if present, is a hook function that will be called once on establishment of the network connection and once after each block read thereafter. The hook will be passed three arguments; a count of blocks transferred so far, a block size in bytes, and the total size of the file. The third argument may be `-1` on older FTP servers which do not return a file size in response to a retrieval request.
>
> The following example illustrates the most common usage scenario:

```
>>> import urllib.request
>>> local_filename, headers = urllib.request.urlretrieve('http://python.org/')
>>> html = open(local_filename)
>>> html.close()
```

> If the *url* uses the `http:` scheme identifier, the optional *data* argument may be given to specify a POST request (normally the request type is GET). The *data* argument must be a bytes object in standard *application/x-www-form-urlencoded* format; see the *urllib.parse.urlencode()* function.
>
> *urlretrieve()* will raise `ContentTooShortError` when it detects that the amount of data available was less than the expected amount (which is the size reported by a *Content-Length* header). This can

occur, for example, when the download is interrupted.

The *Content-Length* is treated as a lower bound: if there's more data to read, urlretrieve reads more data, but if less data is available, it raises the exception.

You can still retrieve the downloaded data in this case, it is stored in the **content** attribute of the exception instance.

If no *Content-Length* header was supplied, urlretrieve can not check the size of the data it has downloaded, and just returns it. In this case you just have to assume that the download was successful.

urllib.request.urlcleanup()
Cleans up temporary files that may have been left behind by previous calls to *urlretrieve()*.

class urllib.request.URLopener(*proxies=None, **x509*)
Deprecated since version 3.3.

Base class for opening and reading URLs. Unless you need to support opening objects using schemes other than **http:**, **ftp:**, or **file:**, you probably want to use *FancyURLopener*.

By default, the *URLopener* class sends a *User-Agent* header of **urllib/VVV**, where *VVV* is the *urllib* version number. Applications can define their own *User-Agent* header by subclassing *URLopener* or *FancyURLopener* and setting the class attribute *version* to an appropriate string value in the subclass definition.

The optional *proxies* parameter should be a dictionary mapping scheme names to proxy URLs, where an empty dictionary turns proxies off completely. Its default value is **None**, in which case environmental proxy settings will be used if present, as discussed in the definition of *urlopen()*, above.

Additional keyword parameters, collected in *x509*, may be used for authentication of the client when using the **https:** scheme. The keywords *key_file* and *cert_file* are supported to provide an SSL key and certificate; both are needed to support client authentication.

URLopener objects will raise an *OSError* exception if the server returns an error code.

open(*fullurl, data=None*)
Open *fullurl* using the appropriate protocol. This method sets up cache and proxy information, then calls the appropriate open method with its input arguments. If the scheme is not recognized, *open_unknown()* is called. The *data* argument has the same meaning as the *data* argument of *urlopen()*.

open_unknown(*fullurl, data=None*)
Overridable interface to open unknown URL types.

retrieve(*url, filename=None, reporthook=None, data=None*)
Retrieves the contents of *url* and places it in *filename*. The return value is a tuple consisting of a local filename and either an *email.message.Message* object containing the response headers (for remote URLs) or **None** (for local URLs). The caller must then open and read the contents of *filename*. If *filename* is not given and the URL refers to a local file, the input filename is returned. If the URL is non-local and *filename* is not given, the filename is the output of *tempfile.mktemp()* with a suffix that matches the suffix of the last path component of the input URL. If *reporthook* is given, it must be a function accepting three numeric parameters: A chunk number, the maximum size chunks are read in and the total size of the download (-1 if unknown). It will be called once at the start and after each chunk of data is read from the network. *reporthook* is ignored for local URLs.

If the *url* uses the **http:** scheme identifier, the optional *data* argument may be given to specify a **POST** request (normally the request type is **GET**). The *data* argument must in standard **application/x-www-form-urlencoded** format; see the *urllib.parse.urlencode()* function.

version
Variable that specifies the user agent of the opener object. To get *urllib* to tell servers that it

is a particular user agent, set this in a subclass as a class variable or in the constructor before calling the base constructor.

class `urllib.request.FancyURLopener`(...)
Deprecated since version 3.3.

FancyURLopener subclasses *URLopener* providing default handling for the following HTTP response codes: 301, 302, 303, 307 and 401. For the 30x response codes listed above, the `Location` header is used to fetch the actual URL. For 401 response codes (authentication required), basic HTTP authentication is performed. For the 30x response codes, recursion is bounded by the value of the *maxtries* attribute, which defaults to 10.

For all other response codes, the method `http_error_default()` is called which you can override in subclasses to handle the error appropriately.

Note: According to the letter of RFC 2616, 301 and 302 responses to POST requests must not be automatically redirected without confirmation by the user. In reality, browsers do allow automatic redirection of these responses, changing the POST to a GET, and *urllib* reproduces this behaviour.

The parameters to the constructor are the same as those for *URLopener*.

Note: When performing basic authentication, a *FancyURLopener* instance calls its *prompt_user_passwd()* method. The default implementation asks the users for the required information on the controlling terminal. A subclass may override this method to support more appropriate behavior if needed.

The *FancyURLopener* class offers one additional method that should be overloaded to provide the appropriate behavior:

prompt_user_passwd(*host*, *realm*)
Return information needed to authenticate the user at the given host in the specified security realm. The return value should be a tuple, `(user, password)`, which can be used for basic authentication.

The implementation prompts for this information on the terminal; an application should override this method to use an appropriate interaction model in the local environment.

21.6.25 urllib.request Restrictions

- Currently, only the following protocols are supported: HTTP (versions 0.9 and 1.0), FTP, local files, and data URLs.

  Changed in version 3.4: Added support for data URLs.

- The caching feature of *urlretrieve()* has been disabled until someone finds the time to hack proper processing of Expiration time headers.

- There should be a function to query whether a particular URL is in the cache.

- For backward compatibility, if a URL appears to point to a local file but the file can't be opened, the URL is re-interpreted using the FTP protocol. This can sometimes cause confusing error messages.

- The *urlopen()* and *urlretrieve()* functions can cause arbitrarily long delays while waiting for a network connection to be set up. This means that it is difficult to build an interactive Web client using these functions without using threads.

- The data returned by *urlopen()* or *urlretrieve()* is the raw data returned by the server. This may be binary data (such as an image), plain text or (for example) HTML. The HTTP protocol provides type information in the reply header, which can be inspected by looking at the `Content-Type` header. If the returned data is HTML, you can use the module *html.parser* to parse it.
- The code handling the FTP protocol cannot differentiate between a file and a directory. This can lead to unexpected behavior when attempting to read a URL that points to a file that is not accessible. If the URL ends in a /, it is assumed to refer to a directory and will be handled accordingly. But if an attempt to read a file leads to a 550 error (meaning the URL cannot be found or is not accessible, often for permission reasons), then the path is treated as a directory in order to handle the case when a directory is specified by a URL but the trailing / has been left off. This can cause misleading results when you try to fetch a file whose read permissions make it inaccessible; the FTP code will try to read it, fail with a 550 error, and then perform a directory listing for the unreadable file. If fine-grained control is needed, consider using the *ftplib* module, subclassing *FancyURLopener*, or changing *_urlopener* to meet your needs.

21.7 urllib.response — Response classes used by urllib

The *urllib.response* module defines functions and classes which define a minimal file like interface, including **read()** and **readline()**. The typical response object is an addinfourl instance, which defines an **info()** method and that returns headers and a **geturl()** method that returns the url. Functions defined by this module are used internally by the *urllib.request* module.

21.8 urllib.parse — Parse URLs into components

Source code: Lib/urllib/parse.py

This module defines a standard interface to break Uniform Resource Locator (URL) strings up in components (addressing scheme, network location, path etc.), to combine the components back into a URL string, and to convert a "relative URL" to an absolute URL given a "base URL."

The module has been designed to match the Internet RFC on Relative Uniform Resource Locators. It supports the following URL schemes: `file`, `ftp`, `gopher`, `hdl`, `http`, `https`, `imap`, `mailto`, `mms`, `news`, `nntp`, `prospero`, `rsync`, `rtsp`, `rtspu`, `sftp`, `shttp`, `sip`, `sips`, `snews`, `svn`, `svn+ssh`, `telnet`, `wais`, `ws`, `wss`.

The *urllib.parse* module defines functions that fall into two broad categories: URL parsing and URL quoting. These are covered in detail in the following sections.

21.8.1 URL Parsing

The URL parsing functions focus on splitting a URL string into its components, or on combining URL components into a URL string.

urllib.parse.urlparse(*urlstring*, *scheme=''*, *allow_fragments=True*)
    Parse a URL into six components, returning a 6-tuple. This corresponds to the general structure of a URL: `scheme://netloc/path;parameters?query#fragment`. Each tuple item is a string, possibly empty. The components are not broken up in smaller parts (for example, the network location is a single string), and % escapes are not expanded. The delimiters as shown above are not part of the result, except for a leading slash in the *path* component, which is retained if present. For example:

```
>>> from urllib.parse import urlparse
>>> o = urlparse('http://www.cwi.nl:80/%7Eguido/Python.html')
>>> o
ParseResult(scheme='http', netloc='www.cwi.nl:80', path='/%7Eguido/Python.html',
            params='', query='', fragment='')
>>> o.scheme
'http'
>>> o.port
80
>>> o.geturl()
'http://www.cwi.nl:80/%7Eguido/Python.html'
```

Following the syntax specifications in RFC 1808, urlparse recognizes a netloc only if it is properly introduced by '//'. Otherwise the input is presumed to be a relative URL and thus to start with a path component.

```
>>> from urllib.parse import urlparse
>>> urlparse('//www.cwi.nl:80/%7Eguido/Python.html')
ParseResult(scheme='', netloc='www.cwi.nl:80', path='/%7Eguido/Python.html',
            params='', query='', fragment='')
>>> urlparse('www.cwi.nl/%7Eguido/Python.html')
ParseResult(scheme='', netloc='', path='www.cwi.nl/%7Eguido/Python.html',
            params='', query='', fragment='')
>>> urlparse('help/Python.html')
ParseResult(scheme='', netloc='', path='help/Python.html', params='',
            query='', fragment='')
```

The *scheme* argument gives the default addressing scheme, to be used only if the URL does not specify one. It should be the same type (text or bytes) as *urlstring*, except that the default value `''` is always allowed, and is automatically converted to `b''` if appropriate.

If the *allow_fragments* argument is false, fragment identifiers are not recognized. Instead, they are parsed as part of the path, parameters or query component, and `fragment` is set to the empty string in the return value.

The return value is actually an instance of a subclass of *tuple*. This class has the following additional read-only convenience attributes:

Attribute	Index	Value	Value if not present
scheme	0	URL scheme specifier	*scheme* parameter
netloc	1	Network location part	empty string
path	2	Hierarchical path	empty string
params	3	Parameters for last path element	empty string
query	4	Query component	empty string
fragment	5	Fragment identifier	empty string
username		User name	*None*
password		Password	*None*
hostname		Host name (lower case)	*None*
port		Port number as integer, if present	*None*

Reading the `port` attribute will raise a *ValueError* if an invalid port is specified in the URL. See section *Structured Parse Results* for more information on the result object.

Unmatched square brackets in the `netloc` attribute will raise a *ValueError*.

Changed in version 3.2: Added IPv6 URL parsing capabilities.

Changed in version 3.3: The fragment is now parsed for all URL schemes (unless *allow_fragment* is false), in accordance with RFC 3986. Previously, a whitelist of schemes that support fragments existed.

Changed in version 3.6: Out-of-range port numbers now raise `ValueError`, instead of returning `None`.

urllib.parse.**parse_qs**(*qs, keep_blank_values=False, strict_parsing=False, encoding='utf-8', errors='replace'*)

    Parse a query string given as a string argument (data of type `application/x-www-form-urlencoded`). Data are returned as a dictionary. The dictionary keys are the unique query variable names and the values are lists of values for each name.

    The optional argument *keep_blank_values* is a flag indicating whether blank values in percent-encoded queries should be treated as blank strings. A true value indicates that blanks should be retained as blank strings. The default false value indicates that blank values are to be ignored and treated as if they were not included.

    The optional argument *strict_parsing* is a flag indicating what to do with parsing errors. If false (the default), errors are silently ignored. If true, errors raise a `ValueError` exception.

    The optional *encoding* and *errors* parameters specify how to decode percent-encoded sequences into Unicode characters, as accepted by the `bytes.decode()` method.

    Use the `urllib.parse.urlencode()` function (with the `doseq` parameter set to `True`) to convert such dictionaries into query strings.

    Changed in version 3.2: Add *encoding* and *errors* parameters.

urllib.parse.**parse_qsl**(*qs, keep_blank_values=False, strict_parsing=False, encoding='utf-8', errors='replace'*)

    Parse a query string given as a string argument (data of type `application/x-www-form-urlencoded`). Data are returned as a list of name, value pairs.

    The optional argument *keep_blank_values* is a flag indicating whether blank values in percent-encoded queries should be treated as blank strings. A true value indicates that blanks should be retained as blank strings. The default false value indicates that blank values are to be ignored and treated as if they were not included.

    The optional argument *strict_parsing* is a flag indicating what to do with parsing errors. If false (the default), errors are silently ignored. If true, errors raise a `ValueError` exception.

    The optional *encoding* and *errors* parameters specify how to decode percent-encoded sequences into Unicode characters, as accepted by the `bytes.decode()` method.

    Use the `urllib.parse.urlencode()` function to convert such lists of pairs into query strings.

    Changed in version 3.2: Add *encoding* and *errors* parameters.

urllib.parse.**urlunparse**(*parts*)

    Construct a URL from a tuple as returned by **urlparse()**. The *parts* argument can be any six-item iterable. This may result in a slightly different, but equivalent URL, if the URL that was parsed originally had unnecessary delimiters (for example, a ? with an empty query; the RFC states that these are equivalent).

urllib.parse.**urlsplit**(*urlstring, scheme='', allow_fragments=True*)

    This is similar to `urlparse()`, but does not split the params from the URL. This should generally be used instead of `urlparse()` if the more recent URL syntax allowing parameters to be applied to each segment of the *path* portion of the URL (see RFC 2396) is wanted. A separate function is needed to separate the path segments and parameters. This function returns a 5-tuple: (addressing scheme, network location, path, query, fragment identifier).

    The return value is actually an instance of a subclass of `tuple`. This class has the following additional read-only convenience attributes:

Attribute	Index	Value	Value if not present
scheme	0	URL scheme specifier	*scheme* parameter
netloc	1	Network location part	empty string
path	2	Hierarchical path	empty string
query	3	Query component	empty string
fragment	4	Fragment identifier	empty string
username		User name	*None*
password		Password	*None*
hostname		Host name (lower case)	*None*
port		Port number as integer, if present	*None*

Reading the `port` attribute will raise a *ValueError* if an invalid port is specified in the URL. See section *Structured Parse Results* for more information on the result object.

Unmatched square brackets in the `netloc` attribute will raise a *ValueError*.

Changed in version 3.6: Out-of-range port numbers now raise *ValueError*, instead of returning *None*.

urllib.parse.urlunsplit(*parts*)

Combine the elements of a tuple as returned by *urlsplit()* into a complete URL as a string. The *parts* argument can be any five-item iterable. This may result in a slightly different, but equivalent URL, if the URL that was parsed originally had unnecessary delimiters (for example, a ? with an empty query; the RFC states that these are equivalent).

urllib.parse.urljoin(*base, url, allow_fragments=True*)

Construct a full ("absolute") URL by combining a "base URL" (*base*) with another URL (*url*). Informally, this uses components of the base URL, in particular the addressing scheme, the network location and (part of) the path, to provide missing components in the relative URL. For example:

```
>>> from urllib.parse import urljoin
>>> urljoin('http://www.cwi.nl/%7Eguido/Python.html', 'FAQ.html')
'http://www.cwi.nl/%7Eguido/FAQ.html'
```

The *allow_fragments* argument has the same meaning and default as for *urlparse()*.

Note: If *url* is an absolute URL (that is, starting with // or scheme://), the *url*'s host name and/or scheme will be present in the result. For example:

```
>>> urljoin('http://www.cwi.nl/%7Eguido/Python.html',
...         '//www.python.org/%7Eguido')
'http://www.python.org/%7Eguido'
```

If you do not want that behavior, preprocess the *url* with *urlsplit()* and *urlunsplit()*, removing possible *scheme* and *netloc* parts.

Changed in version 3.5: Behaviour updated to match the semantics defined in RFC 3986.

urllib.parse.urldefrag(*url*)

If *url* contains a fragment identifier, return a modified version of *url* with no fragment identifier, and the fragment identifier as a separate string. If there is no fragment identifier in *url*, return *url* unmodified and an empty string.

The return value is actually an instance of a subclass of *tuple*. This class has the following additional read-only convenience attributes:

Attribute	Index	Value	Value if not present
url	0	URL with no fragment	empty string
fragment	1	Fragment identifier	empty string

See section *Structured Parse Results* for more information on the result object.

Changed in version 3.2: Result is a structured object rather than a simple 2-tuple.

21.8.2 Parsing ASCII Encoded Bytes

The URL parsing functions were originally designed to operate on character strings only. In practice, it is useful to be able to manipulate properly quoted and encoded URLs as sequences of ASCII bytes. Accordingly, the URL parsing functions in this module all operate on *bytes* and *bytearray* objects in addition to *str* objects.

If *str* data is passed in, the result will also contain only *str* data. If *bytes* or *bytearray* data is passed in, the result will contain only *bytes* data.

Attempting to mix *str* data with *bytes* or *bytearray* in a single function call will result in a *TypeError* being raised, while attempting to pass in non-ASCII byte values will trigger *UnicodeDecodeError*.

To support easier conversion of result objects between *str* and *bytes*, all return values from URL parsing functions provide either an **encode()** method (when the result contains *str* data) or a **decode()** method (when the result contains *bytes* data). The signatures of these methods match those of the corresponding *str* and *bytes* methods (except that the default encoding is `'ascii'` rather than `'utf-8'`). Each produces a value of a corresponding type that contains either *bytes* data (for **encode()** methods) or *str* data (for **decode()** methods).

Applications that need to operate on potentially improperly quoted URLs that may contain non-ASCII data will need to do their own decoding from bytes to characters before invoking the URL parsing methods.

The behaviour described in this section applies only to the URL parsing functions. The URL quoting functions use their own rules when producing or consuming byte sequences as detailed in the documentation of the individual URL quoting functions.

Changed in version 3.2: URL parsing functions now accept ASCII encoded byte sequences

21.8.3 Structured Parse Results

The result objects from the *urlparse()*, *urlsplit()* and *urldefrag()* functions are subclasses of the *tuple* type. These subclasses add the attributes listed in the documentation for those functions, the encoding and decoding support described in the previous section, as well as an additional method:

urllib.parse.SplitResult.geturl()
    Return the re-combined version of the original URL as a string. This may differ from the original URL in that the scheme may be normalized to lower case and empty components may be dropped. Specifically, empty parameters, queries, and fragment identifiers will be removed.

    For *urldefrag()* results, only empty fragment identifiers will be removed. For *urlsplit()* and *urlparse()* results, all noted changes will be made to the URL returned by this method.

    The result of this method remains unchanged if passed back through the original parsing function:

```
>>> from urllib.parse import urlsplit
>>> url = 'HTTP://www.Python.org/doc/#'
>>> r1 = urlsplit(url)
>>> r1.geturl()
'http://www.Python.org/doc/'
```

```
>>> r2 = urlsplit(r1.geturl())
>>> r2.geturl()
'http://www.Python.org/doc/'
```

The following classes provide the implementations of the structured parse results when operating on *str* objects:

class urllib.parse.DefragResult(*url, fragment*)
   Concrete class for *urldefrag()* results containing *str* data. The **encode()** method returns a *DefragResultBytes* instance.

   New in version 3.2.

class urllib.parse.ParseResult(*scheme, netloc, path, params, query, fragment*)
   Concrete class for *urlparse()* results containing *str* data. The **encode()** method returns a *ParseResultBytes* instance.

class urllib.parse.SplitResult(*scheme, netloc, path, query, fragment*)
   Concrete class for *urlsplit()* results containing *str* data. The **encode()** method returns a *SplitResultBytes* instance.

The following classes provide the implementations of the parse results when operating on *bytes* or *bytearray* objects:

class urllib.parse.DefragResultBytes(*url, fragment*)
   Concrete class for *urldefrag()* results containing *bytes* data. The **decode()** method returns a *DefragResult* instance.

   New in version 3.2.

class urllib.parse.ParseResultBytes(*scheme, netloc, path, params, query, fragment*)
   Concrete class for *urlparse()* results containing *bytes* data. The **decode()** method returns a *ParseResult* instance.

   New in version 3.2.

class urllib.parse.SplitResultBytes(*scheme, netloc, path, query, fragment*)
   Concrete class for *urlsplit()* results containing *bytes* data. The **decode()** method returns a *SplitResult* instance.

   New in version 3.2.

21.8.4 URL Quoting

The URL quoting functions focus on taking program data and making it safe for use as URL components by quoting special characters and appropriately encoding non-ASCII text. They also support reversing these operations to recreate the original data from the contents of a URL component if that task isn't already covered by the URL parsing functions above.

urllib.parse.quote(*string, safe='/', encoding=None, errors=None*)
   Replace special characters in *string* using the %xx escape. Letters, digits, and the characters '_.-' are never quoted. By default, this function is intended for quoting the path section of URL. The optional *safe* parameter specifies additional ASCII characters that should not be quoted — its default value is '/'.

   string may be either a *str* or a *bytes*.

   The optional *encoding* and *errors* parameters specify how to deal with non-ASCII characters, as accepted by the *str.encode()* method. *encoding* defaults to 'utf-8'. *errors* defaults to 'strict', meaning unsupported characters raise a *UnicodeEncodeError*. *encoding* and *errors* must not be supplied if *string* is a *bytes*, or a *TypeError* is raised.

Note that `quote(string, safe, encoding, errors)` is equivalent to `quote_from_bytes(string.encode(encoding, errors), safe)`.

Example: `quote('/El Niño/')` yields `'/El%20Ni%C3%B1o/'`.

urllib.parse.quote_plus(*string, safe='', encoding=None, errors=None*)

Like `quote()`, but also replace spaces by plus signs, as required for quoting HTML form values when building up a query string to go into a URL. Plus signs in the original string are escaped unless they are included in *safe*. It also does not have *safe* default to `'/'`.

Example: `quote_plus('/El Niño/')` yields `'%2FEl+Ni%C3%B1o%2F'`.

urllib.parse.quote_from_bytes(*bytes, safe='/'*)

Like `quote()`, but accepts a `bytes` object rather than a `str`, and does not perform string-to-bytes encoding.

Example: `quote_from_bytes(b'a&\xef')` yields `'a%26%EF'`.

urllib.parse.unquote(*string, encoding='utf-8', errors='replace'*)

Replace %xx escapes by their single-character equivalent. The optional *encoding* and *errors* parameters specify how to decode percent-encoded sequences into Unicode characters, as accepted by the `bytes.decode()` method.

string must be a `str`.

encoding defaults to `'utf-8'`. *errors* defaults to `'replace'`, meaning invalid sequences are replaced by a placeholder character.

Example: `unquote('/El%20Ni%C3%B1o/')` yields `'/El Niño/'`.

urllib.parse.unquote_plus(*string, encoding='utf-8', errors='replace'*)

Like `unquote()`, but also replace plus signs by spaces, as required for unquoting HTML form values.

string must be a `str`.

Example: `unquote_plus('/El+Ni%C3%B1o/')` yields `'/El Niño/'`.

urllib.parse.unquote_to_bytes(*string*)

Replace %xx escapes by their single-octet equivalent, and return a `bytes` object.

string may be either a `str` or a `bytes`.

If it is a `str`, unescaped non-ASCII characters in *string* are encoded into UTF-8 bytes.

Example: `unquote_to_bytes('a%26%EF')` yields `b'a&\xef'`.

urllib.parse.urlencode(*query, doseq=False, safe='', encoding=None, errors=None, quote_via=quote_plus*)

Convert a mapping object or a sequence of two-element tuples, which may contain `str` or `bytes` objects, to a percent-encoded ASCII text string. If the resultant string is to be used as a *data* for POST operation with the `urlopen()` function, then it should be encoded to bytes, otherwise it would result in a `TypeError`.

The resulting string is a series of `key=value` pairs separated by `'&'` characters, where both *key* and *value* are quoted using the *quote_via* function. By default, `quote_plus()` is used to quote the values, which means spaces are quoted as a `'+'` character and `'/'` characters are encoded as %2F, which follows the standard for GET requests (`application/x-www-form-urlencoded`). An alternate function that can be passed as *quote_via* is `quote()`, which will encode spaces as %20 and not encode `'/'` characters. For maximum control of what is quoted, use `quote` and specify a value for *safe*.

When a sequence of two-element tuples is used as the *query* argument, the first element of each tuple is a key and the second is a value. The value element in itself can be a sequence and in that case, if the optional parameter *doseq* is evaluates to `True`, individual `key=value` pairs separated by `'&'` are generated for each element of the value sequence for the key. The order of parameters in the encoded string will match the order of parameter tuples in the sequence.

The *safe*, *encoding*, and *errors* parameters are passed down to *quote_via* (the *encoding* and *errors* parameters are only passed when a query element is a `str`).

To reverse this encoding process, `parse_qs()` and `parse_qsl()` are provided in this module to parse query strings into Python data structures.

Refer to *urllib examples* to find out how urlencode method can be used for generating query string for a URL or data for POST.

Changed in version 3.2: Query parameter supports bytes and string objects.

New in version 3.5: *quote_via* parameter.

See also:

RFC 3986 - **Uniform Resource Identifiers** This is the current standard (STD66). Any changes to urllib.parse module should conform to this. Certain deviations could be observed, which are mostly for backward compatibility purposes and for certain de-facto parsing requirements as commonly observed in major browsers.

RFC 2732 - **Format for Literal IPv6 Addresses in URL's.** This specifies the parsing requirements of IPv6 URLs.

RFC 2396 - **Uniform Resource Identifiers (URI): Generic Syntax** Document describing the generic syntactic requirements for both Uniform Resource Names (URNs) and Uniform Resource Locators (URLs).

RFC 2368 - **The mailto URL scheme.** Parsing requirements for mailto URL schemes.

RFC 1808 - **Relative Uniform Resource Locators** This Request For Comments includes the rules for joining an absolute and a relative URL, including a fair number of "Abnormal Examples" which govern the treatment of border cases.

RFC 1738 - **Uniform Resource Locators (URL)** This specifies the formal syntax and semantics of absolute URLs.

21.9 `urllib.error` — Exception classes raised by urllib.request

Source code: Lib/urllib/error.py

The `urllib.error` module defines the exception classes for exceptions raised by `urllib.request`. The base exception class is `URLError`.

The following exceptions are raised by `urllib.error` as appropriate:

exception urllib.error.URLError
    The handlers raise this exception (or derived exceptions) when they run into a problem. It is a subclass of `OSError`.

    reason
        The reason for this error. It can be a message string or another exception instance.

    Changed in version 3.3: `URLError` has been made a subclass of `OSError` instead of `IOError`.

exception urllib.error.HTTPError
    Though being an exception (a subclass of `URLError`), an `HTTPError` can also function as a non-exceptional file-like return value (the same thing that `urlopen()` returns). This is useful when handling exotic HTTP errors, such as requests for authentication.

code
> An HTTP status code as defined in RFC 2616. This numeric value corresponds to a value found in the dictionary of codes as found in *http.server.BaseHTTPRequestHandler.responses*.

reason
> This is usually a string explaining the reason for this error.

headers
> The HTTP response headers for the HTTP request that caused the *HTTPError*.
>
> New in version 3.4.

exception urllib.error.ContentTooShortError(*msg*, *content*)
> This exception is raised when the *urlretrieve()* function detects that the amount of the downloaded data is less than the expected amount (given by the *Content-Length* header). The **content** attribute stores the downloaded (and supposedly truncated) data.

21.10 urllib.robotparser — Parser for robots.txt

Source code: Lib/urllib/robotparser.py

This module provides a single class, *RobotFileParser*, which answers questions about whether or not a particular user agent can fetch a URL on the Web site that published the **robots.txt** file. For more details on the structure of **robots.txt** files, see http://www.robotstxt.org/orig.html.

class urllib.robotparser.RobotFileParser(*url=''*)
> This class provides methods to read, parse and answer questions about the **robots.txt** file at *url*.

> **set_url**(*url*)
>> Sets the URL referring to a **robots.txt** file.

> **read**()
>> Reads the **robots.txt** URL and feeds it to the parser.

> **parse**(*lines*)
>> Parses the lines argument.

> **can_fetch**(*useragent*, *url*)
>> Returns **True** if the *useragent* is allowed to fetch the *url* according to the rules contained in the parsed **robots.txt** file.

> **mtime**()
>> Returns the time the **robots.txt** file was last fetched. This is useful for long-running web spiders that need to check for new **robots.txt** files periodically.

> **modified**()
>> Sets the time the **robots.txt** file was last fetched to the current time.

> **crawl_delay**(*useragent*)
>> Returns the value of the **Crawl-delay** parameter from **robots.txt** for the *useragent* in question. If there is no such parameter or it doesn't apply to the *useragent* specified or the **robots.txt** entry for this parameter has invalid syntax, return **None**.
>>
>> New in version 3.6.

> **request_rate**(*useragent*)
>> Returns the contents of the **Request-rate** parameter from **robots.txt** as a *named tuple* **RequestRate(requests, seconds)**. If there is no such parameter or it doesn't apply to the *useragent* specified or the **robots.txt** entry for this parameter has invalid syntax, return **None**.

New in version 3.6.

The following example demonstrates basic use of the *RobotFileParser* class:

```
>>> import urllib.robotparser
>>> rp = urllib.robotparser.RobotFileParser()
>>> rp.set_url("http://www.musi-cal.com/robots.txt")
>>> rp.read()
>>> rrate = rp.request_rate("*")
>>> rrate.requests
3
>>> rrate.seconds
20
>>> rp.crawl_delay("*")
6
>>> rp.can_fetch("*", "http://www.musi-cal.com/cgi-bin/search?city=San+Francisco")
False
>>> rp.can_fetch("*", "http://www.musi-cal.com/")
True
```

21.11 `http` — HTTP modules

Source code: Lib/http/__init__.py

---

http is a package that collects several modules for working with the HyperText Transfer Protocol:

- *http.client* is a low-level HTTP protocol client; for high-level URL opening use *urllib.request*
- *http.server* contains basic HTTP server classes based on *socketserver*
- *http.cookies* has utilities for implementing state management with cookies
- *http.cookiejar* provides persistence of cookies

http is also a module that defines a number of HTTP status codes and associated messages through the *http.HTTPStatus* enum:

class http.HTTPStatus

New in version 3.5.

A subclass of *enum.IntEnum* that defines a set of HTTP status codes, reason phrases and long descriptions written in English.

Usage:

```
>>> from http import HTTPStatus
>>> HTTPStatus.OK
<HTTPStatus.OK: 200>
>>> HTTPStatus.OK == 200
True
>>> http.HTTPStatus.OK.value
200
>>> HTTPStatus.OK.phrase
'OK'
>>> HTTPStatus.OK.description
'Request fulfilled, document follows'
>>> list(HTTPStatus)
[<HTTPStatus.CONTINUE: 100>, <HTTPStatus.SWITCHING_PROTOCOLS: 101>, ...]
```

21.11.1 HTTP status codes

Supported, IANA-registered status codes available in `http.HTTPStatus` are:

Code	Enum Name	Details
100	CONTINUE	HTTP/1.1 RFC 7231, Section 6.2.1
101	SWITCHING_PROTOCOLS	HTTP/1.1 RFC 7231, Section 6.2.2
102	PROCESSING	WebDAV RFC 2518, Section 10.1
200	OK	HTTP/1.1 RFC 7231, Section 6.3.1
201	CREATED	HTTP/1.1 RFC 7231, Section 6.3.2
202	ACCEPTED	HTTP/1.1 RFC 7231, Section 6.3.3
203	NON_AUTHORITATIVE_INFORMATION	HTTP/1.1 RFC 7231, Section 6.3.4
204	NO_CONTENT	HTTP/1.1 RFC 7231, Section 6.3.5
205	RESET_CONTENT	HTTP/1.1 RFC 7231, Section 6.3.6
206	PARTIAL_CONTENT	HTTP/1.1 RFC 7233, Section 4.1
207	MULTI_STATUS	WebDAV RFC 4918, Section 11.1
208	ALREADY_REPORTED	WebDAV Binding Extensions RFC 5842, Section 7.1 (Experimen
226	IM_USED	Delta Encoding in HTTP RFC 3229, Section 10.4.1
300	MULTIPLE_CHOICES	HTTP/1.1 RFC 7231, Section 6.4.1
301	MOVED_PERMANENTLY	HTTP/1.1 RFC 7231, Section 6.4.2
302	FOUND	HTTP/1.1 RFC 7231, Section 6.4.3
303	SEE_OTHER	HTTP/1.1 RFC 7231, Section 6.4.4
304	NOT_MODIFIED	HTTP/1.1 RFC 7232, Section 4.1
305	USE_PROXY	HTTP/1.1 RFC 7231, Section 6.4.5
307	TEMPORARY_REDIRECT	HTTP/1.1 RFC 7231, Section 6.4.7
308	PERMANENT_REDIRECT	Permanent Redirect RFC 7238, Section 3 (Experimental)
400	BAD_REQUEST	HTTP/1.1 RFC 7231, Section 6.5.1
401	UNAUTHORIZED	HTTP/1.1 Authentication RFC 7235, Section 3.1
402	PAYMENT_REQUIRED	HTTP/1.1 RFC 7231, Section 6.5.2
403	FORBIDDEN	HTTP/1.1 RFC 7231, Section 6.5.3
404	NOT_FOUND	HTTP/1.1 RFC 7231, Section 6.5.4
405	METHOD_NOT_ALLOWED	HTTP/1.1 RFC 7231, Section 6.5.5
406	NOT_ACCEPTABLE	HTTP/1.1 RFC 7231, Section 6.5.6
407	PROXY_AUTHENTICATION_REQUIRED	HTTP/1.1 Authentication RFC 7235, Section 3.2
408	REQUEST_TIMEOUT	HTTP/1.1 RFC 7231, Section 6.5.7
409	CONFLICT	HTTP/1.1 RFC 7231, Section 6.5.8
410	GONE	HTTP/1.1 RFC 7231, Section 6.5.9
411	LENGTH_REQUIRED	HTTP/1.1 RFC 7231, Section 6.5.10
412	PRECONDITION_FAILED	HTTP/1.1 RFC 7232, Section 4.2
413	REQUEST_ENTITY_TOO_LARGE	HTTP/1.1 RFC 7231, Section 6.5.11
414	REQUEST_URI_TOO_LONG	HTTP/1.1 RFC 7231, Section 6.5.12
415	UNSUPPORTED_MEDIA_TYPE	HTTP/1.1 RFC 7231, Section 6.5.13
416	REQUEST_RANGE_NOT_SATISFIABLE	HTTP/1.1 Range Requests RFC 7233, Section 4.4
417	EXPECTATION_FAILED	HTTP/1.1 RFC 7231, Section 6.5.14
422	UNPROCESSABLE_ENTITY	WebDAV RFC 4918, Section 11.2
423	LOCKED	WebDAV RFC 4918, Section 11.3
424	FAILED_DEPENDENCY	WebDAV RFC 4918, Section 11.4
426	UPGRADE_REQUIRED	HTTP/1.1 RFC 7231, Section 6.5.15
428	PRECONDITION_REQUIRED	Additional HTTP Status Codes RFC 6585
429	TOO_MANY_REQUESTS	Additional HTTP Status Codes RFC 6585
431	REQUEST_HEADER_FIELDS_TOO_LARGE	Additional HTTP Status Codes RFC 6585

Table 21.1 – continued from previous page

Code	Enum Name	Details
500	`INTERNAL_SERVER_ERROR`	HTTP/1.1 RFC 7231, Section 6.6.1
501	`NOT_IMPLEMENTED`	HTTP/1.1 RFC 7231, Section 6.6.2
502	`BAD_GATEWAY`	HTTP/1.1 RFC 7231, Section 6.6.3
503	`SERVICE_UNAVAILABLE`	HTTP/1.1 RFC 7231, Section 6.6.4
504	`GATEWAY_TIMEOUT`	HTTP/1.1 RFC 7231, Section 6.6.5
505	`HTTP_VERSION_NOT_SUPPORTED`	HTTP/1.1 RFC 7231, Section 6.6.6
506	`VARIANT_ALSO_NEGOTIATES`	Transparent Content Negotiation in HTTP RFC 2295, Section
507	`INSUFFICIENT_STORAGE`	WebDAV RFC 4918, Section 11.5
508	`LOOP_DETECTED`	WebDAV Binding Extensions RFC 5842, Section 7.2 (Experime
510	`NOT_EXTENDED`	An HTTP Extension Framework RFC 2774, Section 7 (Experir
511	`NETWORK_AUTHENTICATION_REQUIRED`	Additional HTTP Status Codes RFC 6585, Section 6

In order to preserve backwards compatibility, enum values are also present in the `http.client` module in the form of constants. The enum name is equal to the constant name (i.e. `http.HTTPStatus.OK` is also available as `http.client.OK`).

21.12 `http.client` — HTTP protocol client

Source code: Lib/http/client.py

This module defines classes which implement the client side of the HTTP and HTTPS protocols. It is normally not used directly — the module `urllib.request` uses it to handle URLs that use HTTP and HTTPS.

See also:

The Requests package is recommended for a higher-level HTTP client interface.

Note: HTTPS support is only available if Python was compiled with SSL support (through the `ssl` module).

The module provides the following classes:

class `http.client.HTTPConnection`(*host, port=None*[, *timeout*], *source_address=None*)

An `HTTPConnection` instance represents one transaction with an HTTP server. It should be instantiated passing it a host and optional port number. If no port number is passed, the port is extracted from the host string if it has the form `host:port`, else the default HTTP port (80) is used. If the optional *timeout* parameter is given, blocking operations (like connection attempts) will timeout after that many seconds (if it is not given, the global default timeout setting is used). The optional *source_address* parameter may be a tuple of a (host, port) to use as the source address the HTTP connection is made from.

For example, the following calls all create instances that connect to the server at the same host and port:

```
>>> h1 = http.client.HTTPConnection('www.python.org')
>>> h2 = http.client.HTTPConnection('www.python.org:80')
>>> h3 = http.client.HTTPConnection('www.python.org', 80)
>>> h4 = http.client.HTTPConnection('www.python.org', 80, timeout=10)
```

Changed in version 3.2: *source_address* was added.

Changed in version 3.4: The *strict* parameter was removed. HTTP 0.9-style "Simple Responses" are not longer supported.

class http.client.HTTPSConnection(*host, port=None, key_file=None, cert_file=None[, timeout], source_address=None, *, context=None, check_hostname=None*)

A subclass of *HTTPConnection* that uses SSL for communication with secure servers. Default port is 443. If *context* is specified, it must be a *ssl.SSLContext* instance describing the various SSL options.

Please read *Security considerations* for more information on best practices.

Changed in version 3.2: *source_address*, *context* and *check_hostname* were added.

Changed in version 3.2: This class now supports HTTPS virtual hosts if possible (that is, if *ssl.HAS_SNI* is true).

Changed in version 3.4: The *strict* parameter was removed. HTTP 0.9-style "Simple Responses" are no longer supported.

Changed in version 3.4.3: This class now performs all the necessary certificate and hostname checks by default. To revert to the previous, unverified, behavior `ssl._create_unverified_context()` can be passed to the *context* parameter.

Deprecated since version 3.6: *key_file* and *cert_file* are deprecated in favor of *context*. Please use *ssl.SSLContext.load_cert_chain()* instead, or let *ssl.create_default_context()* select the system's trusted CA certificates for you.

The *check_hostname* parameter is also deprecated; the *ssl.SSLContext.check_hostname* attribute of *context* should be used instead.

class http.client.HTTPResponse(*sock, debuglevel=0, method=None, url=None*)

Class whose instances are returned upon successful connection. Not instantiated directly by user.

Changed in version 3.4: The *strict* parameter was removed. HTTP 0.9 style "Simple Responses" are no longer supported.

The following exceptions are raised as appropriate:

exception http.client.HTTPException
    The base class of the other exceptions in this module. It is a subclass of *Exception*.

exception http.client.NotConnected
    A subclass of *HTTPException*.

exception http.client.InvalidURL
    A subclass of *HTTPException*, raised if a port is given and is either non-numeric or empty.

exception http.client.UnknownProtocol
    A subclass of *HTTPException*.

exception http.client.UnknownTransferEncoding
    A subclass of *HTTPException*.

exception http.client.UnimplementedFileMode
    A subclass of *HTTPException*.

exception http.client.IncompleteRead
    A subclass of *HTTPException*.

exception http.client.ImproperConnectionState
    A subclass of *HTTPException*.

exception http.client.CannotSendRequest
    A subclass of *ImproperConnectionState*.

exception `http.client.CannotSendHeader`
   A subclass of *ImproperConnectionState*.

exception `http.client.ResponseNotReady`
   A subclass of *ImproperConnectionState*.

exception `http.client.BadStatusLine`
   A subclass of *HTTPException*. Raised if a server responds with a HTTP status code that we don't understand.

exception `http.client.LineTooLong`
   A subclass of *HTTPException*. Raised if an excessively long line is received in the HTTP protocol from the server.

exception `http.client.RemoteDisconnected`
   A subclass of *ConnectionResetError* and *BadStatusLine*. Raised by *HTTPConnection.getresponse()* when the attempt to read the response results in no data read from the connection, indicating that the remote end has closed the connection.

   New in version 3.5: Previously, *BadStatusLine*(`''`) was raised.

The constants defined in this module are:

`http.client.HTTP_PORT`
   The default port for the HTTP protocol (always `80`).

`http.client.HTTPS_PORT`
   The default port for the HTTPS protocol (always `443`).

`http.client.responses`
   This dictionary maps the HTTP 1.1 status codes to the W3C names.

   Example: `http.client.responses[http.client.NOT_FOUND]` is `'Not Found'`.

See *HTTP status codes* for a list of HTTP status codes that are available in this module as constants.

21.12.1 HTTPConnection Objects

HTTPConnection instances have the following methods:

`HTTPConnection.request`(*method, url, body=None, headers={}, *, encode_chunked=False*)
   This will send a request to the server using the HTTP request method *method* and the selector *url*.

   If *body* is specified, the specified data is sent after the headers are finished. It may be a *str*, a *bytes-like object*, an open *file object*, or an iterable of *bytes*. If *body* is a string, it is encoded as ISO-8859-1, the default for HTTP. If it is a bytes-like object, the bytes are sent as is. If it is a *file object*, the contents of the file is sent; this file object should support at least the `read()` method. If the file object is an instance of *io.TextIOBase*, the data returned by the `read()` method will be encoded as ISO-8859-1, otherwise the data returned by `read()` is sent as is. If *body* is an iterable, the elements of the iterable are sent as is until the iterable is exhausted.

   The *headers* argument should be a mapping of extra HTTP headers to send with the request.

   If *headers* contains neither Content-Length nor Transfer-Encoding, but there is a request body, one of those header fields will be added automatically. If *body* is `None`, the Content-Length header is set to 0 for methods that expect a body (`PUT`, `POST`, and `PATCH`). If *body* is a string or a bytes-like object that is not also a *file*, the Content-Length header is set to its length. Any other type of *body* (files and iterables in general) will be chunk-encoded, and the Transfer-Encoding header will automatically be set instead of Content-Length.

   The *encode_chunked* argument is only relevant if Transfer-Encoding is specified in *headers*. If *encode_chunked* is `False`, the HTTPConnection object assumes that all encoding is handled by the calling code. If it is `True`, the body will be chunk-encoded.

> **Note:** Chunked transfer encoding has been added to the HTTP protocol version 1.1. Unless the HTTP server is known to handle HTTP 1.1, the caller must either specify the Content-Length, or must pass a `str` or bytes-like object that is not also a file as the body representation.

New in version 3.2: *body* can now be an iterable.

Changed in version 3.6: If neither Content-Length nor Transfer-Encoding are set in *headers*, file and iterable *body* objects are now chunk-encoded. The *encode_chunked* argument was added. No attempt is made to determine the Content-Length for file objects.

`HTTPConnection.getresponse()`
　　Should be called after a request is sent to get the response from the server. Returns an *HTTPResponse* instance.

> **Note:** Note that you must have read the whole response before you can send a new request to the server.

Changed in version 3.5: If a `ConnectionError` or subclass is raised, the `HTTPConnection` object will be ready to reconnect when a new request is sent.

`HTTPConnection.set_debuglevel(level)`
　　Set the debugging level. The default debug level is 0, meaning no debugging output is printed. Any value greater than 0 will cause all currently defined debug output to be printed to stdout. The `debuglevel` is passed to any new *HTTPResponse* objects that are created.

New in version 3.1.

`HTTPConnection.set_tunnel(host, port=None, headers=None)`
　　Set the host and the port for HTTP Connect Tunnelling. This allows running the connection through a proxy server.

The host and port arguments specify the endpoint of the tunneled connection (i.e. the address included in the CONNECT request, *not* the address of the proxy server).

The headers argument should be a mapping of extra HTTP headers to send with the CONNECT request.

For example, to tunnel through a HTTPS proxy server running locally on port 8080, we would pass the address of the proxy to the *HTTPSConnection* constructor, and the address of the host that we eventually want to reach to the *set_tunnel()* method:

```
>>> import http.client
>>> conn = http.client.HTTPSConnection("localhost", 8080)
>>> conn.set_tunnel("www.python.org")
>>> conn.request("HEAD","/index.html")
```

New in version 3.2.

`HTTPConnection.connect()`
　　Connect to the server specified when the object was created. By default, this is called automatically when making a request if the client does not already have a connection.

`HTTPConnection.close()`
　　Close the connection to the server.

As an alternative to using the `request()` method described above, you can also send your request step by step, by using the four functions below.

HTTPConnection.putrequest(*method*, *url*, *skip_host=False*, *skip_accept_encoding=False*)
> This should be the first call after the connection to the server has been made. It sends a line to the server consisting of the *method* string, the *url* string, and the HTTP version (HTTP/1.1). To disable automatic sending of Host: or Accept-Encoding: headers (for example to accept additional content encodings), specify *skip_host* or *skip_accept_encoding* with non-False values.

HTTPConnection.putheader(*header*, *argument*[, ...])
> Send an RFC 822-style header to the server. It sends a line to the server consisting of the header, a colon and a space, and the first argument. If more arguments are given, continuation lines are sent, each consisting of a tab and an argument.

HTTPConnection.endheaders(*message_body=None*, ***, *encode_chunked=False*)
> Send a blank line to the server, signalling the end of the headers. The optional *message_body* argument can be used to pass a message body associated with the request.
>
> If *encode_chunked* is True, the result of each iteration of *message_body* will be chunk-encoded as specified in RFC 7230, Section 3.3.1. How the data is encoded is dependent on the type of *message_body*. If *message_body* implements the buffer interface the encoding will result in a single chunk. If *message_body* is a collections.Iterable, each iteration of *message_body* will result in a chunk. If *message_body* is a *file object*, each call to .read() will result in a chunk. The method automatically signals the end of the chunk-encoded data immediately after *message_body*.
>
> **Note:** Due to the chunked encoding specification, empty chunks yielded by an iterator body will be ignored by the chunk-encoder. This is to avoid premature termination of the read of the request by the target server due to malformed encoding.
>
> New in version 3.6: Chunked encoding support. The *encode_chunked* parameter was added.

HTTPConnection.send(*data*)
> Send data to the server. This should be used directly only after the *endheaders()* method has been called and before *getresponse()* is called.

21.12.2 HTTPResponse Objects

An *HTTPResponse* instance wraps the HTTP response from the server. It provides access to the request headers and the entity body. The response is an iterable object and can be used in a with statement.

Changed in version 3.5: The *io.BufferedIOBase* interface is now implemented and all of its reader operations are supported.

HTTPResponse.read([*amt*])
> Reads and returns the response body, or up to the next *amt* bytes.

HTTPResponse.readinto(*b*)
> Reads up to the next len(b) bytes of the response body into the buffer *b*. Returns the number of bytes read.
>
> New in version 3.3.

HTTPResponse.getheader(*name*, *default=None*)
> Return the value of the header *name*, or *default* if there is no header matching *name*. If there is more than one header with the name *name*, return all of the values joined by ', '. If 'default' is any iterable other than a single string, its elements are similarly returned joined by commas.

HTTPResponse.getheaders()
> Return a list of (header, value) tuples.

HTTPResponse.fileno()
    Return the fileno of the underlying socket.

HTTPResponse.msg
    A http.client.HTTPMessage instance containing the response headers. http.client.HTTPMessage is a subclass of *email.message.Message*.

HTTPResponse.version
    HTTP protocol version used by server. 10 for HTTP/1.0, 11 for HTTP/1.1.

HTTPResponse.status
    Status code returned by server.

HTTPResponse.reason
    Reason phrase returned by server.

HTTPResponse.debuglevel
    A debugging hook. If *debuglevel* is greater than zero, messages will be printed to stdout as the response is read and parsed.

HTTPResponse.closed
    Is True if the stream is closed.

21.12.3 Examples

Here is an example session that uses the GET method:

```
>>> import http.client
>>> conn = http.client.HTTPSConnection("www.python.org")
>>> conn.request("GET", "/")
>>> r1 = conn.getresponse()
>>> print(r1.status, r1.reason)
200 OK
>>> data1 = r1.read()  # This will return entire content.
>>> # The following example demonstrates reading data in chunks.
>>> conn.request("GET", "/")
>>> r1 = conn.getresponse()
>>> while not r1.closed:
...     print(r1.read(200))  # 200 bytes
b'<!doctype html>\n<!--[if"...
...
>>> # Example of an invalid request
>>> conn.request("GET", "/parrot.spam")
>>> r2 = conn.getresponse()
>>> print(r2.status, r2.reason)
404 Not Found
>>> data2 = r2.read()
>>> conn.close()
```

Here is an example session that uses the HEAD method. Note that the HEAD method never returns any data.

```
>>> import http.client
>>> conn = http.client.HTTPSConnection("www.python.org")
>>> conn.request("HEAD", "/")
>>> res = conn.getresponse()
>>> print(res.status, res.reason)
200 OK
>>> data = res.read()
>>> print(len(data))
```

```
0
>>> data == b''
True
```

Here is an example session that shows how to POST requests:

```
>>> import http.client, urllib.parse
>>> params = urllib.parse.urlencode({'@number': 12524, '@type': 'issue', '@action': 'show'})
>>> headers = {"Content-type": "application/x-www-form-urlencoded",
...            "Accept": "text/plain"}
>>> conn = http.client.HTTPConnection("bugs.python.org")
>>> conn.request("POST", "", params, headers)
>>> response = conn.getresponse()
>>> print(response.status, response.reason)
302 Found
>>> data = response.read()
>>> data
b'Redirecting to <a href="http://bugs.python.org/issue12524">http://bugs.python.org/issue12524</a>'
>>> conn.close()
```

Client side HTTP PUT requests are very similar to POST requests. The difference lies only the server side where HTTP server will allow resources to be created via PUT request. It should be noted that custom HTTP methods +are also handled in *urllib.request.Request* by sending the appropriate +method attribute.Here is an example session that shows how to do PUT request using http.client:

```
>>> # This creates an HTTP message
>>> # with the content of BODY as the enclosed representation
>>> # for the resource http://localhost:8080/file
...
>>> import http.client
>>> BODY = "***filecontents***"
>>> conn = http.client.HTTPConnection("localhost", 8080)
>>> conn.request("PUT", "/file", BODY)
>>> response = conn.getresponse()
>>> print(response.status, response.reason)
200, OK
```

21.12.4 HTTPMessage Objects

An `http.client.HTTPMessage` instance holds the headers from an HTTP response. It is implemented using the *email.message.Message* class.

21.13 `ftplib` — FTP protocol client

Source code: Lib/ftplib.py

This module defines the class *FTP* and a few related items. The *FTP* class implements the client side of the FTP protocol. You can use this to write Python programs that perform a variety of automated FTP jobs, such as mirroring other FTP servers. It is also used by the module *urllib.request* to handle URLs that use FTP. For more information on FTP (File Transfer Protocol), see Internet RFC 959.

Here's a sample session using the *ftplib* module:

```
>>> from ftplib import FTP
>>> ftp = FTP('ftp.debian.org')     # connect to host, default port
>>> ftp.login()                     # user anonymous, passwd anonymous@
'230 Login successful.'
>>> ftp.cwd('debian')               # change into "debian" directory
>>> ftp.retrlines('LIST')           # list directory contents
-rw-rw-r--    1 1176     1176         1063 Jun 15 10:18 README
...
drwxr-sr-x    5 1176     1176         4096 Dec 19  2000 pool
drwxr-sr-x    4 1176     1176         4096 Nov 17  2008 project
drwxr-xr-x    3 1176     1176         4096 Oct 10  2012 tools
'226 Directory send OK.'
>>> ftp.retrbinary('RETR README', open('README', 'wb').write)
'226 Transfer complete.'
>>> ftp.quit()
```

The module defines the following items:

class ftplib.FTP(*host=''*, *user=''*, *passwd=''*, *acct=''*, *timeout=None*, *source_address=None*)

Return a new instance of the *FTP* class. When *host* is given, the method call connect(host) is made. When *user* is given, additionally the method call login(user, passwd, acct) is made (where *passwd* and *acct* default to the empty string when not given). The optional *timeout* parameter specifies a timeout in seconds for blocking operations like the connection attempt (if is not specified, the global default timeout setting will be used). *source_address* is a 2-tuple (host, port) for the socket to bind to as its source address before connecting.

The *FTP* class supports the with statement, e.g.:

```
>>> from ftplib import FTP
>>> with FTP("ftp1.at.proftpd.org") as ftp:
...     ftp.login()
...     ftp.dir()
...
'230 Anonymous login ok, restrictions apply.'
dr-xr-xr-x   9 ftp      ftp           154 May  6 10:43 .
dr-xr-xr-x   9 ftp      ftp           154 May  6 10:43 ..
dr-xr-xr-x   5 ftp      ftp          4096 May  6 10:43 CentOS
dr-xr-xr-x   3 ftp      ftp            18 Jul 10  2008 Fedora
>>>
```

Changed in version 3.2: Support for the with statement was added.

Changed in version 3.3: *source_address* parameter was added.

class ftplib.FTP_TLS(*host=''*, *user=''*, *passwd=''*, *acct=''*, *keyfile=None*, *certfile=None*, *context=None*, *timeout=None*, *source_address=None*)

A *FTP* subclass which adds TLS support to FTP as described in RFC 4217. Connect as usual to port 21 implicitly securing the FTP control connection before authenticating. Securing the data connection requires the user to explicitly ask for it by calling the *prot_p()* method. *context* is a *ssl.SSLContext* object which allows bundling SSL configuration options, certificates and private keys into a single (potentially long-lived) structure. Please read *Security considerations* for best practices.

keyfile and *certfile* are a legacy alternative to *context* – they can point to PEM-formatted private key and certificate chain files (respectively) for the SSL connection.

New in version 3.2.

Changed in version 3.3: *source_address* parameter was added.

Changed in version 3.4: The class now supports hostname check with *ssl.SSLContext.check_hostname* and *Server Name Indication* (see *ssl.HAS_SNI*).

Deprecated since version 3.6: *keyfile* and *certfile* are deprecated in favor of *context*. Please use `ssl.SSLContext.load_cert_chain()` instead, or let `ssl.create_default_context()` select the system's trusted CA certificates for you.

Here's a sample session using the *FTP_TLS* class:

```
>>> ftps = FTP_TLS('ftp.pureftpd.org')
>>> ftps.login()
'230 Anonymous user logged in'
>>> ftps.prot_p()
'200 Data protection level set to "private"'
>>> ftps.nlst()
['6jack', 'OpenBSD', 'antilink', 'blogbench', 'bsdcam', 'clockspeed', 'djbdns-jedi', 'docs',
 'eaccelerator-jedi', 'favicon.ico', 'francotone', 'fugu', 'ignore', 'libpuzzle', 'metalog',
 'minidentd', 'misc', 'mysql-udf-global-user-variables', 'php-jenkins-hash', 'php-skein-hash
 ', 'php-webdav', 'phpaudit', 'phpbench', 'pincaster', 'ping', 'posto', 'pub', 'public',
 'public_keys', 'pure-ftpd', 'qscan', 'qtc', 'sharedance', 'skycache', 'sound', 'tmp', 'ucarp
 ']
```

exception ftplib.error_reply
Exception raised when an unexpected reply is received from the server.

exception ftplib.error_temp
Exception raised when an error code signifying a temporary error (response codes in the range 400–499) is received.

exception ftplib.error_perm
Exception raised when an error code signifying a permanent error (response codes in the range 500–599) is received.

exception ftplib.error_proto
Exception raised when a reply is received from the server that does not fit the response specifications of the File Transfer Protocol, i.e. begin with a digit in the range 1–5.

ftplib.all_errors
The set of all exceptions (as a tuple) that methods of *FTP* instances may raise as a result of problems with the FTP connection (as opposed to programming errors made by the caller). This set includes the four exceptions listed above as well as *OSError*.

See also:

Module `netrc` Parser for the .netrc file format. The file .netrc is typically used by FTP clients to load user authentication information before prompting the user.

21.13.1 FTP Objects

Several methods are available in two flavors: one for handling text files and another for binary files. These are named for the command which is used followed by `lines` for the text version or `binary` for the binary version.

FTP instances have the following methods:

FTP.set_debuglevel(*level*)
Set the instance's debugging level. This controls the amount of debugging output printed. The default, 0, produces no debugging output. A value of 1 produces a moderate amount of debugging output, generally a single line per request. A value of 2 or higher produces the maximum amount of debugging output, logging each line sent and received on the control connection.

FTP.connect(*host=''*, *port=0*, *timeout=None*, *source_address=None*)
Connect to the given host and port. The default port number is 21, as specified by the FTP protocol

specification. It is rarely needed to specify a different port number. This function should be called only once for each instance; it should not be called at all if a host was given when the instance was created. All other methods can only be used after a connection has been made. The optional *timeout* parameter specifies a timeout in seconds for the connection attempt. If no *timeout* is passed, the global default timeout setting will be used. *source_address* is a 2-tuple (`host, port`) for the socket to bind to as its source address before connecting.

Changed in version 3.3: *source_address* parameter was added.

FTP.getwelcome()
Return the welcome message sent by the server in reply to the initial connection. (This message sometimes contains disclaimers or help information that may be relevant to the user.)

FTP.login(*user='anonymous', passwd='', acct=''*)
Log in as the given *user*. The *passwd* and *acct* parameters are optional and default to the empty string. If no *user* is specified, it defaults to `'anonymous'`. If *user* is `'anonymous'`, the default *passwd* is `'anonymous@'`. This function should be called only once for each instance, after a connection has been established; it should not be called at all if a host and user were given when the instance was created. Most FTP commands are only allowed after the client has logged in. The *acct* parameter supplies "accounting information"; few systems implement this.

FTP.abort()
Abort a file transfer that is in progress. Using this does not always work, but it's worth a try.

FTP.sendcmd(*cmd*)
Send a simple command string to the server and return the response string.

FTP.voidcmd(*cmd*)
Send a simple command string to the server and handle the response. Return nothing if a response code corresponding to success (codes in the range 200–299) is received. Raise *error_reply* otherwise.

FTP.retrbinary(*cmd, callback, blocksize=8192, rest=None*)
Retrieve a file in binary transfer mode. *cmd* should be an appropriate RETR command: `'RETR filename'`. The *callback* function is called for each block of data received, with a single bytes argument giving the data block. The optional *blocksize* argument specifies the maximum chunk size to read on the low-level socket object created to do the actual transfer (which will also be the largest size of the data blocks passed to *callback*). A reasonable default is chosen. *rest* means the same thing as in the *transfercmd()* method.

FTP.retrlines(*cmd, callback=None*)
Retrieve a file or directory listing in ASCII transfer mode. *cmd* should be an appropriate RETR command (see *retrbinary()*) or a command such as LIST or NLST (usually just the string `'LIST'`). LIST retrieves a list of files and information about those files. NLST retrieves a list of file names. The *callback* function is called for each line with a string argument containing the line with the trailing CRLF stripped. The default *callback* prints the line to `sys.stdout`.

FTP.set_pasv(*val*)
Enable "passive" mode if *val* is true, otherwise disable passive mode. Passive mode is on by default.

FTP.storbinary(*cmd, fp, blocksize=8192, callback=None, rest=None*)
Store a file in binary transfer mode. *cmd* should be an appropriate STOR command: `"STOR filename"`. *fp* is a *file object* (opened in binary mode) which is read until EOF using its `read()` method in blocks of size *blocksize* to provide the data to be stored. The *blocksize* argument defaults to 8192. *callback* is an optional single parameter callable that is called on each block of data after it is sent. *rest* means the same thing as in the *transfercmd()* method.

Changed in version 3.2: *rest* parameter added.

FTP.storlines(*cmd, fp, callback=None*)
Store a file in ASCII transfer mode. *cmd* should be an appropriate STOR command (see *storbinary()*). Lines are read until EOF from the *file object* *fp* (opened in binary mode) using its *readline()* method

to provide the data to be stored. *callback* is an optional single parameter callable that is called on each line after it is sent.

FTP.transfercmd(*cmd, rest=None*)
Initiate a transfer over the data connection. If the transfer is active, send an EPRT or PORT command and the transfer command specified by *cmd*, and accept the connection. If the server is passive, send an EPSV or PASV command, connect to it, and start the transfer command. Either way, return the socket for the connection.

If optional *rest* is given, a REST command is sent to the server, passing *rest* as an argument. *rest* is usually a byte offset into the requested file, telling the server to restart sending the file's bytes at the requested offset, skipping over the initial bytes. Note however that RFC 959 requires only that *rest* be a string containing characters in the printable range from ASCII code 33 to ASCII code 126. The *transfercmd()* method, therefore, converts *rest* to a string, but no check is performed on the string's contents. If the server does not recognize the REST command, an *error_reply* exception will be raised. If this happens, simply call *transfercmd()* without a *rest* argument.

FTP.ntransfercmd(*cmd, rest=None*)
Like *transfercmd()*, but returns a tuple of the data connection and the expected size of the data. If the expected size could not be computed, None will be returned as the expected size. *cmd* and *rest* means the same thing as in *transfercmd()*.

FTP.mlsd(*path="", facts=[]*)
List a directory in a standardized format by using MLSD command (RFC 3659). If *path* is omitted the current directory is assumed. *facts* is a list of strings representing the type of information desired (e.g. ["type", "size", "perm"]). Return a generator object yielding a tuple of two elements for every file found in path. First element is the file name, the second one is a dictionary containing facts about the file name. Content of this dictionary might be limited by the *facts* argument but server is not guaranteed to return all requested facts.

New in version 3.3.

FTP.nlst(*argument[, ...]*)
Return a list of file names as returned by the NLST command. The optional *argument* is a directory to list (default is the current server directory). Multiple arguments can be used to pass non-standard options to the NLST command.

Note: If your server supports the command, *mlsd()* offers a better API.

FTP.dir(*argument[, ...]*)
Produce a directory listing as returned by the LIST command, printing it to standard output. The optional *argument* is a directory to list (default is the current server directory). Multiple arguments can be used to pass non-standard options to the LIST command. If the last argument is a function, it is used as a *callback* function as for *retrlines()*; the default prints to sys.stdout. This method returns None.

Note: If your server supports the command, *mlsd()* offers a better API.

FTP.rename(*fromname, toname*)
Rename file *fromname* on the server to *toname*.

FTP.delete(*filename*)
Remove the file named *filename* from the server. If successful, returns the text of the response, otherwise raises *error_perm* on permission errors or *error_reply* on other errors.

FTP.cwd(*pathname*)
Set the current directory on the server.

FTP.mkd(*pathname***)**
   Create a new directory on the server.

FTP.pwd()
   Return the pathname of the current directory on the server.

FTP.rmd(*dirname***)**
   Remove the directory named *dirname* on the server.

FTP.size(*filename***)**
   Request the size of the file named *filename* on the server. On success, the size of the file is returned as an integer, otherwise `None` is returned. Note that the `SIZE` command is not standardized, but is supported by many common server implementations.

FTP.quit()
   Send a `QUIT` command to the server and close the connection. This is the "polite" way to close a connection, but it may raise an exception if the server responds with an error to the `QUIT` command. This implies a call to the *close()* method which renders the *FTP* instance useless for subsequent calls (see below).

FTP.close()
   Close the connection unilaterally. This should not be applied to an already closed connection such as after a successful call to *quit()*. After this call the *FTP* instance should not be used any more (after a call to *close()* or *quit()* you cannot reopen the connection by issuing another *login()* method).

21.13.2 FTP_TLS Objects

FTP_TLS class inherits from *FTP*, defining these additional objects:

FTP_TLS.ssl_version
   The SSL version to use (defaults to *ssl.PROTOCOL_SSLv23*).

FTP_TLS.auth()
   Set up a secure control connection by using TLS or SSL, depending on what is specified in the *ssl_version* attribute.

   Changed in version 3.4: The method now supports hostname check with *ssl.SSLContext.check_hostname* and *Server Name Indication* (see *ssl.HAS_SNI*).

FTP_TLS.ccc()
   Revert control channel back to plaintext. This can be useful to take advantage of firewalls that know how to handle NAT with non-secure FTP without opening fixed ports.

   New in version 3.3.

FTP_TLS.prot_p()
   Set up secure data connection.

FTP_TLS.prot_c()
   Set up clear text data connection.

21.14 poplib — POP3 protocol client

Source code: Lib/poplib.py

This module defines a class, *POP3*, which encapsulates a connection to a POP3 server and implements the protocol as defined in RFC 1939. The *POP3* class supports both the minimal and optional command sets from RFC 1939. The *POP3* class also supports the STLS command introduced in RFC 2595 to enable encrypted communication on an already established connection.

Additionally, this module provides a class *POP3_SSL*, which provides support for connecting to POP3 servers that use SSL as an underlying protocol layer.

Note that POP3, though widely supported, is obsolescent. The implementation quality of POP3 servers varies widely, and too many are quite poor. If your mailserver supports IMAP, you would be better off using the *imaplib.IMAP4* class, as IMAP servers tend to be better implemented.

The *poplib* module provides two classes:

class poplib.POP3(*host, port=POP3_PORT[, timeout]*)

This class implements the actual POP3 protocol. The connection is created when the instance is initialized. If *port* is omitted, the standard POP3 port (110) is used. The optional *timeout* parameter specifies a timeout in seconds for the connection attempt (if not specified, the global default timeout setting will be used).

class poplib.POP3_SSL(*host, port=POP3_SSL_PORT, keyfile=None, certfile=None, timeout=None, context=None*)

This is a subclass of *POP3* that connects to the server over an SSL encrypted socket. If *port* is not specified, 995, the standard POP3-over-SSL port is used. *timeout* works as in the *POP3* constructor. *context* is an optional *ssl.SSLContext* object which allows bundling SSL configuration options, certificates and private keys into a single (potentially long-lived) structure. Please read *Security considerations* for best practices.

keyfile and *certfile* are a legacy alternative to *context* - they can point to PEM-formatted private key and certificate chain files, respectively, for the SSL connection.

Changed in version 3.2: *context* parameter added.

Changed in version 3.4: The class now supports hostname check with *ssl.SSLContext.check_hostname* and *Server Name Indication* (see *ssl.HAS_SNI*).

Deprecated since version 3.6: *keyfile* and *certfile* are deprecated in favor of *context*. Please use *ssl.SSLContext.load_cert_chain()* instead, or let *ssl.create_default_context()* select the system's trusted CA certificates for you.

One exception is defined as an attribute of the *poplib* module:

exception poplib.error_proto

Exception raised on any errors from this module (errors from *socket* module are not caught). The reason for the exception is passed to the constructor as a string.

See also:

Module *imaplib* The standard Python IMAP module.

Frequently Asked Questions About Fetchmail The FAQ for the **fetchmail** POP/IMAP client collects information on POP3 server variations and RFC noncompliance that may be useful if you need to write an application based on the POP protocol.

21.14.1 POP3 Objects

All POP3 commands are represented by methods of the same name, in lower-case; most return the response text sent by the server.

An *POP3* instance has the following methods:

POP3.set_debuglevel(*level*)

Set the instance's debugging level. This controls the amount of debugging output printed. The default, 0, produces no debugging output. A value of 1 produces a moderate amount of debugging output, generally a single line per request. A value of 2 or higher produces the maximum amount of debugging output, logging each line sent and received on the control connection.

POP3.getwelcome()
Returns the greeting string sent by the POP3 server.

POP3.capa()
Query the server's capabilities as specified in RFC 2449. Returns a dictionary in the form {'name': ['param'...]}.

New in version 3.4.

POP3.user(*username*)
Send user command, response should indicate that a password is required.

POP3.pass_(*password*)
Send password, response includes message count and mailbox size. Note: the mailbox on the server is locked until quit() is called.

POP3.apop(*user, secret*)
Use the more secure APOP authentication to log into the POP3 server.

POP3.rpop(*user*)
Use RPOP authentication (similar to UNIX r-commands) to log into POP3 server.

POP3.stat()
Get mailbox status. The result is a tuple of 2 integers: (message count, mailbox size).

POP3.list([*which*])
Request message list, result is in the form (response, ['mesg_num octets', ...], octets). If *which* is set, it is the message to list.

POP3.retr(*which*)
Retrieve whole message number *which*, and set its seen flag. Result is in form (response, ['line', ...], octets).

POP3.dele(*which*)
Flag message number *which* for deletion. On most servers deletions are not actually performed until QUIT (the major exception is Eudora QPOP, which deliberately violates the RFCs by doing pending deletes on any disconnect).

POP3.rset()
Remove any deletion marks for the mailbox.

POP3.noop()
Do nothing. Might be used as a keep-alive.

POP3.quit()
Signoff: commit changes, unlock mailbox, drop connection.

POP3.top(*which, howmuch*)
Retrieves the message header plus *howmuch* lines of the message after the header of message number *which*. Result is in form (response, ['line', ...], octets).

The POP3 TOP command this method uses, unlike the RETR command, doesn't set the message's seen flag; unfortunately, TOP is poorly specified in the RFCs and is frequently broken in off-brand servers. Test this method by hand against the POP3 servers you will use before trusting it.

POP3.uidl(*which=None*)
Return message digest (unique id) list. If *which* is specified, result contains the unique id for that message in the form 'response mesgnum uid, otherwise result is list (response, ['mesgnum uid', ...], octets).

POP3.`utf8()`
> Try to switch to UTF-8 mode. Returns the server response if successful, raises `error_proto` if not. Specified in RFC 6856.
>
> New in version 3.5.

POP3.`stls`(*context=None*)
> Start a TLS session on the active connection as specified in RFC 2595. This is only allowed before user authentication
>
> *context* parameter is a `ssl.SSLContext` object which allows bundling SSL configuration options, certificates and private keys into a single (potentially long-lived) structure. Please read *Security considerations* for best practices.
>
> This method supports hostname checking via `ssl.SSLContext.check_hostname` and *Server Name Indication* (see `ssl.HAS_SNI`).
>
> New in version 3.4.

Instances of *POP3_SSL* have no additional methods. The interface of this subclass is identical to its parent.

21.14.2 POP3 Example

Here is a minimal example (without error checking) that opens a mailbox and retrieves and prints all messages:

```
import getpass, poplib

M = poplib.POP3('localhost')
M.user(getpass.getuser())
M.pass_(getpass.getpass())
numMessages = len(M.list()[1])
for i in range(numMessages):
    for j in M.retr(i+1)[1]:
        print(j)
```

At the end of the module, there is a test section that contains a more extensive example of usage.

21.15 `imaplib` — IMAP4 protocol client

Source code: Lib/imaplib.py

This module defines three classes, *IMAP4*, *IMAP4_SSL* and *IMAP4_stream*, which encapsulate a connection to an IMAP4 server and implement a large subset of the IMAP4rev1 client protocol as defined in RFC 2060. It is backward compatible with IMAP4 (RFC 1730) servers, but note that the `STATUS` command is not supported in IMAP4.

Three classes are provided by the *imaplib* module, *IMAP4* is the base class:

class `imaplib.IMAP4`(*host=''*, *port=IMAP4_PORT*)
> This class implements the actual IMAP4 protocol. The connection is created and protocol version (IMAP4 or IMAP4rev1) is determined when the instance is initialized. If *host* is not specified, `''` (the local host) is used. If *port* is omitted, the standard IMAP4 port (143) is used.
>
> The *IMAP4* class supports the `with` statement. When used like this, the IMAP4 `LOGOUT` command is issued automatically when the `with` statement exits. E.g.:

```
>>> from imaplib import IMAP4
>>> with IMAP4("domain.org") as M:
...     M.noop()
...
('OK', [b'Nothing Accomplished. d25if65hy903weo.87'])
```

Changed in version 3.5: Support for the **with** statement was added.

Three exceptions are defined as attributes of the *IMAP4* class:

exception IMAP4.error
    Exception raised on any errors. The reason for the exception is passed to the constructor as a string.

exception IMAP4.abort
    IMAP4 server errors cause this exception to be raised. This is a sub-class of *IMAP4.error*. Note that closing the instance and instantiating a new one will usually allow recovery from this exception.

exception IMAP4.readonly
    This exception is raised when a writable mailbox has its status changed by the server. This is a subclass of *IMAP4.error*. Some other client now has write permission, and the mailbox will need to be re-opened to re-obtain write permission.

There's also a subclass for secure connections:

class imaplib.IMAP4_SSL(*host=''*, *port=IMAP4_SSL_PORT*, *keyfile=None*, *certfile=None*, *ssl_context=None*)
    This is a subclass derived from *IMAP4* that connects over an SSL encrypted socket (to use this class you need a socket module that was compiled with SSL support). If *host* is not specified, '' (the local host) is used. If *port* is omitted, the standard IMAP4-over-SSL port (993) is used. *ssl_context* is a *ssl.SSLContext* object which allows bundling SSL configuration options, certificates and private keys into a single (potentially long-lived) structure. Please read *Security considerations* for best practices.

    keyfile and *certfile* are a legacy alternative to *ssl_context* - they can point to PEM-formatted private key and certificate chain files for the SSL connection. Note that the *keyfile*/*certfile* parameters are mutually exclusive with *ssl_context*, a *ValueError* is raised if *keyfile*/*certfile* is provided along with *ssl_context*.

    Changed in version 3.3: *ssl_context* parameter added.

    Changed in version 3.4: The class now supports hostname check with *ssl.SSLContext.check_hostname* and Server Name Indication (see *ssl.HAS_SNI*).

    Deprecated since version 3.6: *keyfile* and *certfile* are deprecated in favor of *ssl_context*. Please use *ssl.SSLContext.load_cert_chain()* instead, or let *ssl.create_default_context()* select the system's trusted CA certificates for you.

The second subclass allows for connections created by a child process:

class imaplib.IMAP4_stream(*command*)
    This is a subclass derived from *IMAP4* that connects to the **stdin/stdout** file descriptors created by passing *command* to **subprocess.Popen()**.

The following utility functions are defined:

imaplib.Internaldate2tuple(*datestr*)
    Parse an IMAP4 INTERNALDATE string and return corresponding local time. The return value is a *time.struct_time* tuple or **None** if the string has wrong format.

imaplib.Int2AP(*num*)
    Converts an integer into a string representation using characters from the set [A .. P].

imaplib.ParseFlags(*flagstr*)
    Converts an IMAP4 FLAGS response to a tuple of individual flags.

`imaplib.Time2Internaldate`(*date_time*)

> Convert *date_time* to an IMAP4 INTERNALDATE representation. The return value is a string in the form: `"DD-Mmm-YYYY HH:MM:SS +HHMM"` (including double-quotes). The *date_time* argument can be a number (int or float) representing seconds since epoch (as returned by `time.time()`), a 9-tuple representing local time an instance of `time.struct_time` (as returned by `time.localtime()`), an aware instance of `datetime.datetime`, or a double-quoted string. In the last case, it is assumed to already be in the correct format.

Note that IMAP4 message numbers change as the mailbox changes; in particular, after an EXPUNGE command performs deletions the remaining messages are renumbered. So it is highly advisable to use UIDs instead, with the UID command.

At the end of the module, there is a test section that contains a more extensive example of usage.

See also:

Documents describing the protocol, and sources and binaries for servers implementing it, can all be found at the University of Washington's *IMAP Information Center* (https://www.washington.edu/imap/).

21.15.1 IMAP4 Objects

All IMAP4rev1 commands are represented by methods of the same name, either upper-case or lower-case.

All arguments to commands are converted to strings, except for AUTHENTICATE, and the last argument to APPEND which is passed as an IMAP4 literal. If necessary (the string contains IMAP4 protocol-sensitive characters and isn't enclosed with either parentheses or double quotes) each string is quoted. However, the *password* argument to the LOGIN command is always quoted. If you want to avoid having an argument string quoted (eg: the *flags* argument to STORE) then enclose the string in parentheses (eg: `r'(\Deleted)'`).

Each command returns a tuple: `(type, [data, ...])` where *type* is usually `'OK'` or `'NO'`, and *data* is either the text from the command response, or mandated results from the command. Each *data* is either a string, or a tuple. If a tuple, then the first part is the header of the response, and the second part contains the data (ie: 'literal' value).

The *message_set* options to commands below is a string specifying one or more messages to be acted upon. It may be a simple message number (`'1'`), a range of message numbers (`'2:4'`), or a group of non-contiguous ranges separated by commas (`'1:3,6:9'`). A range can contain an asterisk to indicate an infinite upper bound (`'3:*'`).

An *IMAP4* instance has the following methods:

`IMAP4.append`(*mailbox, flags, date_time, message*)
> Append *message* to named mailbox.

`IMAP4.authenticate`(*mechanism, authobject*)
> Authenticate command — requires response processing.
>
> *mechanism* specifies which authentication mechanism is to be used - it should appear in the instance variable `capabilities` in the form AUTH=mechanism.
>
> *authobject* must be a callable object:

```
data = authobject(response)
```

> It will be called to process server continuation responses; the *response* argument it is passed will be `bytes`. It should return `bytes` *data* that will be base64 encoded and sent to the server. It should return `None` if the client abort response * should be sent instead.
>
> Changed in version 3.5: string usernames and passwords are now encoded to `utf-8` instead of being limited to ASCII.

`IMAP4.check()`
    Checkpoint mailbox on server.

`IMAP4.close()`
    Close currently selected mailbox. Deleted messages are removed from writable mailbox. This is the recommended command before `LOGOUT`.

`IMAP4.copy(message_set, new_mailbox)`
    Copy *message_set* messages onto end of *new_mailbox*.

`IMAP4.create(mailbox)`
    Create new mailbox named *mailbox*.

`IMAP4.delete(mailbox)`
    Delete old mailbox named *mailbox*.

`IMAP4.deleteacl(mailbox, who)`
    Delete the ACLs (remove any rights) set for who on mailbox.

`IMAP4.enable(capability)`
    Enable *capability* (see RFC 5161). Most capabilities do not need to be enabled. Currently only the `UTF8=ACCEPT` capability is supported (see RFC 6855).

    New in version 3.5: The `enable()` method itself, and RFC 6855 support.

`IMAP4.expunge()`
    Permanently remove deleted items from selected mailbox. Generates an `EXPUNGE` response for each deleted message. Returned data contains a list of `EXPUNGE` message numbers in order received.

`IMAP4.fetch(message_set, message_parts)`
    Fetch (parts of) messages. *message_parts* should be a string of message part names enclosed within parentheses, eg: `"(UID BODY[TEXT])"`. Returned data are tuples of message part envelope and data.

`IMAP4.getacl(mailbox)`
    Get the `ACLs` for *mailbox*. The method is non-standard, but is supported by the `Cyrus` server.

`IMAP4.getannotation(mailbox, entry, attribute)`
    Retrieve the specified `ANNOTATION`s for *mailbox*. The method is non-standard, but is supported by the `Cyrus` server.

`IMAP4.getquota(root)`
    Get the `quota` *root*'s resource usage and limits. This method is part of the IMAP4 QUOTA extension defined in rfc2087.

`IMAP4.getquotaroot(mailbox)`
    Get the list of `quota roots` for the named *mailbox*. This method is part of the IMAP4 QUOTA extension defined in rfc2087.

`IMAP4.list([directory[, pattern]])`
    List mailbox names in *directory* matching *pattern*. *directory* defaults to the top-level mail folder, and *pattern* defaults to match anything. Returned data contains a list of `LIST` responses.

`IMAP4.login(user, password)`
    Identify the client using a plaintext password. The *password* will be quoted.

`IMAP4.login_cram_md5(user, password)`
    Force use of `CRAM-MD5` authentication when identifying the client to protect the password. Will only work if the server `CAPABILITY` response includes the phrase `AUTH=CRAM-MD5`.

`IMAP4.logout()`
    Shutdown connection to server. Returns server `BYE` response.

`IMAP4.lsub(directory='""', pattern='*')`
    List subscribed mailbox names in directory matching pattern. *directory* defaults to the top level

directory and *pattern* defaults to match any mailbox. Returned data are tuples of message part envelope and data.

IMAP4.**myrights**(*mailbox*)
> Show my ACLs for a mailbox (i.e. the rights that I have on mailbox).

IMAP4.**namespace**()
> Returns IMAP namespaces as defined in RFC2342.

IMAP4.**noop**()
> Send NOOP to server.

IMAP4.**open**(*host*, *port*)
> Opens socket to *port* at *host*. This method is implicitly called by the *IMAP4* constructor. The connection objects established by this method will be used in the *IMAP4.read()*, *IMAP4.readline()*, *IMAP4.send()*, and *IMAP4.shutdown()* methods. You may override this method.

IMAP4.**partial**(*message_num*, *message_part*, *start*, *length*)
> Fetch truncated part of a message. Returned data is a tuple of message part envelope and data.

IMAP4.**proxyauth**(*user*)
> Assume authentication as *user*. Allows an authorised administrator to proxy into any user's mailbox.

IMAP4.**read**(*size*)
> Reads *size* bytes from the remote server. You may override this method.

IMAP4.**readline**()
> Reads one line from the remote server. You may override this method.

IMAP4.**recent**()
> Prompt server for an update. Returned data is None if no new messages, else value of RECENT response.

IMAP4.**rename**(*oldmailbox*, *newmailbox*)
> Rename mailbox named *oldmailbox* to *newmailbox*.

IMAP4.**response**(*code*)
> Return data for response *code* if received, or None. Returns the given code, instead of the usual type.

IMAP4.**search**(*charset*, *criterion*[, ...])
> Search mailbox for matching messages. *charset* may be None, in which case no CHARSET will be specified in the request to the server. The IMAP protocol requires that at least one criterion be specified; an exception will be raised when the server returns an error. *charset* must be None if the UTF8=ACCEPT capability was enabled using the *enable()* command.
>
> Example:
> ```
> # M is a connected IMAP4 instance...
> typ, msgnums = M.search(None, 'FROM', '"LDJ"')
>
> # or:
> typ, msgnums = M.search(None, '(FROM "LDJ")')
> ```

IMAP4.**select**(*mailbox='INBOX'*, *readonly=False*)
> Select a mailbox. Returned data is the count of messages in *mailbox* (EXISTS response). The default *mailbox* is 'INBOX'. If the *readonly* flag is set, modifications to the mailbox are not allowed.

IMAP4.**send**(*data*)
> Sends data to the remote server. You may override this method.

IMAP4.**setacl**(*mailbox*, *who*, *what*)
> Set an ACL for *mailbox*. The method is non-standard, but is supported by the Cyrus server.

IMAP4.**setannotation**(*mailbox*, *entry*, *attribute*[, ...])
> Set ANNOTATIONs for *mailbox*. The method is non-standard, but is supported by the Cyrus server.

IMAP4.setquota(*root, limits*)
> Set the quota *root*'s resource *limits*. This method is part of the IMAP4 QUOTA extension defined in rfc2087.

IMAP4.shutdown()
> Close connection established in open. This method is implicitly called by *IMAP4.logout()*. You may override this method.

IMAP4.socket()
> Returns socket instance used to connect to server.

IMAP4.sort(*sort_criteria, charset, search_criterion*[, ...])
> The sort command is a variant of search with sorting semantics for the results. Returned data contains a space separated list of matching message numbers.
>
> Sort has two arguments before the *search_criterion* argument(s); a parenthesized list of *sort_criteria*, and the searching *charset*. Note that unlike search, the searching *charset* argument is mandatory. There is also a uid sort command which corresponds to sort the way that uid search corresponds to search. The sort command first searches the mailbox for messages that match the given searching criteria using the charset argument for the interpretation of strings in the searching criteria. It then returns the numbers of matching messages.
>
> This is an IMAP4rev1 extension command.

IMAP4.starttls(*ssl_context=None*)
> Send a STARTTLS command. The *ssl_context* argument is optional and should be a *ssl.SSLContext* object. This will enable encryption on the IMAP connection. Please read *Security considerations* for best practices.
>
> New in version 3.2.
>
> Changed in version 3.4: The method now supports hostname check with *ssl.SSLContext.check_hostname* and *Server Name Indication* (see *ssl.HAS_SNI*).

IMAP4.status(*mailbox, names*)
> Request named status conditions for *mailbox*.

IMAP4.store(*message_set, command, flag_list*)
> Alters flag dispositions for messages in mailbox. *command* is specified by section 6.4.6 of RFC 2060 as being one of "FLAGS", "+FLAGS", or "-FLAGS", optionally with a suffix of ".SILENT".
>
> For example, to set the delete flag on all messages:
>
> ```
> typ, data = M.search(None, 'ALL')
> for num in data[0].split():
>    M.store(num, '+FLAGS', '\\Deleted')
> M.expunge()
> ```
>
> ---
>
> **Note:** Creating flags containing ']' (for example: "[test]") violates RFC 3501 (the IMAP protocol). However, imaplib has historically allowed creation of such tags, and popular IMAP servers, such as Gmail, accept and produce such flags. There are non-Python programs which also create such tags. Although it is an RFC violation and IMAP clients and servers are supposed to be strict, imaplib nonetheless continues to allow such tags to be created for backward compatibility reasons, and as of python 3.6, handles them if they are sent from the server, since this improves real-world compatibility.
>
> ---

IMAP4.subscribe(*mailbox*)
> Subscribe to new mailbox.

IMAP4.thread(*threading_algorithm, charset, search_criterion*[, ...])
> The thread command is a variant of search with threading semantics for the results. Returned data

contains a space separated list of thread members.

Thread members consist of zero or more messages numbers, delimited by spaces, indicating successive parent and child.

Thread has two arguments before the *search_criterion* argument(s); a *threading_algorithm*, and the searching *charset*. Note that unlike `search`, the searching *charset* argument is mandatory. There is also a `uid thread` command which corresponds to `thread` the way that `uid search` corresponds to `search`. The `thread` command first searches the mailbox for messages that match the given searching criteria using the charset argument for the interpretation of strings in the searching criteria. It then returns the matching messages threaded according to the specified threading algorithm.

This is an IMAP4rev1 extension command.

IMAP4.uid(*command*, *arg*[, ...])

Execute command args with messages identified by UID, rather than message number. Returns response appropriate to command. At least one argument must be supplied; if none are provided, the server will return an error and an exception will be raised.

IMAP4.unsubscribe(*mailbox*)

Unsubscribe from old mailbox.

IMAP4.xatom(*name*[, ...])

Allow simple extension commands notified by server in CAPABILITY response.

The following attributes are defined on instances of *IMAP4*:

IMAP4.PROTOCOL_VERSION

The most recent supported protocol in the CAPABILITY response from the server.

IMAP4.debug

Integer value to control debugging output. The initialize value is taken from the module variable Debug. Values greater than three trace each command.

IMAP4.utf8_enabled

Boolean value that is normally `False`, but is set to `True` if an *enable()* command is successfully issued for the UTF8=ACCEPT capability.

New in version 3.5.

21.15.2 IMAP4 Example

Here is a minimal example (without error checking) that opens a mailbox and retrieves and prints all messages:

```
import getpass, imaplib

M = imaplib.IMAP4()
M.login(getpass.getuser(), getpass.getpass())
M.select()
typ, data = M.search(None, 'ALL')
for num in data[0].split():
    typ, data = M.fetch(num, '(RFC822)')
    print('Message %s\n%s\n' % (num, data[0][1]))
M.close()
M.logout()
```

21.16 `nntplib` — NNTP protocol client

Source code: Lib/nntplib.py

This module defines the class *NNTP* which implements the client side of the Network News Transfer Protocol. It can be used to implement a news reader or poster, or automated news processors. It is compatible with RFC 3977 as well as the older RFC 977 and RFC 2980.

Here are two small examples of how it can be used. To list some statistics about a newsgroup and print the subjects of the last 10 articles:

```
>>> s = nntplib.NNTP('news.gmane.org')
>>> resp, count, first, last, name = s.group('gmane.comp.python.committers')
>>> print('Group', name, 'has', count, 'articles, range', first, 'to', last)
Group gmane.comp.python.committers has 1096 articles, range 1 to 1096
>>> resp, overviews = s.over((last - 9, last))
>>> for id, over in overviews:
...     print(id, nntplib.decode_header(over['subject']))
...
1087 Re: Commit privileges for Łukasz Langa
1088 Re: 3.2 alpha 2 freeze
1089 Re: 3.2 alpha 2 freeze
1090 Re: Commit privileges for Łukasz Langa
1091 Re: Commit privileges for Łukasz Langa
1092 Updated ssh key
1093 Re: Updated ssh key
1094 Re: Updated ssh key
1095 Hello fellow committers!
1096 Re: Hello fellow committers!
>>> s.quit()
'205 Bye!'
```

To post an article from a binary file (this assumes that the article has valid headers, and that you have right to post on the particular newsgroup):

```
>>> s = nntplib.NNTP('news.gmane.org')
>>> f = open('article.txt', 'rb')
>>> s.post(f)
'240 Article posted successfully.'
>>> s.quit()
'205 Bye!'
```

The module itself defines the following classes:

class `nntplib.NNTP`(*host, port=119, user=None, password=None, readermode=None, usenetrc=False[, timeout]*)

Return a new *NNTP* object, representing a connection to the NNTP server running on host *host*, listening at port *port*. An optional *timeout* can be specified for the socket connection. If the optional *user* and *password* are provided, or if suitable credentials are present in /.netrc and the optional flag *usenetrc* is true, the `AUTHINFO USER` and `AUTHINFO PASS` commands are used to identify and authenticate the user to the server. If the optional flag *readermode* is true, then a `mode reader` command is sent before authentication is performed. Reader mode is sometimes necessary if you are connecting to an NNTP server on the local machine and intend to call reader-specific commands, such as `group`. If you get unexpected *NNTPPermanentError*s, you might need to set *readermode*. The *NNTP* class supports the **with** statement to unconditionally consume *OSError* exceptions and to close the NNTP connection when done, e.g.:

```
>>> from nntplib import NNTP
>>> with NNTP('news.gmane.org') as n:
...     n.group('gmane.comp.python.committers')
...
('211 1755 1 1755 gmane.comp.python.committers', 1755, 1, 1755, 'gmane.comp.python.committers
↪')
>>>
```

Changed in version 3.2: *usenetrc* is now `False` by default.

Changed in version 3.3: Support for the `with` statement was added.

class nntplib.NNTP_SSL(*host, port=563, user=None, password=None, ssl_context=None, readermode=None, usenetrc=False*[, *timeout*])

Return a new *NNTP_SSL* object, representing an encrypted connection to the NNTP server running on host *host*, listening at port *port*. *NNTP_SSL* objects have the same methods as *NNTP* objects. If *port* is omitted, port 563 (NNTPS) is used. *ssl_context* is also optional, and is a *SSLContext* object. Please read *Security considerations* for best practices. All other parameters behave the same as for *NNTP*.

Note that SSL-on-563 is discouraged per RFC 4642, in favor of STARTTLS as described below. However, some servers only support the former.

New in version 3.2.

Changed in version 3.4: The class now supports hostname check with *ssl.SSLContext.check_hostname* and *Server Name Indication* (see *ssl.HAS_SNI*).

exception nntplib.NNTPError

Derived from the standard exception *Exception*, this is the base class for all exceptions raised by the *nntplib* module. Instances of this class have the following attribute:

response

The response of the server if available, as a *str* object.

exception nntplib.NNTPReplyError

Exception raised when an unexpected reply is received from the server.

exception nntplib.NNTPTemporaryError

Exception raised when a response code in the range 400–499 is received.

exception nntplib.NNTPPermanentError

Exception raised when a response code in the range 500–599 is received.

exception nntplib.NNTPProtocolError

Exception raised when a reply is received from the server that does not begin with a digit in the range 1–5.

exception nntplib.NNTPDataError

Exception raised when there is some error in the response data.

21.16.1 NNTP Objects

When connected, *NNTP* and *NNTP_SSL* objects support the following methods and attributes.

Attributes

NNTP.nntp_version

An integer representing the version of the NNTP protocol supported by the server. In practice, this should be 2 for servers advertising RFC 3977 compliance and 1 for others.

New in version 3.2.

NNTP.nntp_implementation
    A string describing the software name and version of the NNTP server, or `None` if not advertised by the server.

    New in version 3.2.

Methods

The *response* that is returned as the first item in the return tuple of almost all methods is the server's response: a string beginning with a three-digit code. If the server's response indicates an error, the method raises one of the above exceptions.

Many of the following methods take an optional keyword-only argument *file*. When the *file* argument is supplied, it must be either a *file object* opened for binary writing, or the name of an on-disk file to be written to. The method will then write any data returned by the server (except for the response line and the terminating dot) to the file; any list of lines, tuples or objects that the method normally returns will be empty.

Changed in version 3.2: Many of the following methods have been reworked and fixed, which makes them incompatible with their 3.1 counterparts.

NNTP.quit()
    Send a `QUIT` command and close the connection. Once this method has been called, no other methods of the NNTP object should be called.

NNTP.getwelcome()
    Return the welcome message sent by the server in reply to the initial connection. (This message sometimes contains disclaimers or help information that may be relevant to the user.)

NNTP.getcapabilities()
    Return the RFC 3977 capabilities advertised by the server, as a *dict* instance mapping capability names to (possibly empty) lists of values. On legacy servers which don't understand the `CAPABILITIES` command, an empty dictionary is returned instead.

```
>>> s = NNTP('news.gmane.org')
>>> 'POST' in s.getcapabilities()
True
```

    New in version 3.2.

NNTP.login(user=None, password=None, usenetrc=True**)**
    Send `AUTHINFO` commands with the user name and password. If *user* and *password* are `None` and *usenetrc* is true, credentials from `~/.netrc` will be used if possible.

    Unless intentionally delayed, login is normally performed during the *NNTP* object initialization and separately calling this function is unnecessary. To force authentication to be delayed, you must not set *user* or *password* when creating the object, and must set *usenetrc* to False.

    New in version 3.2.

NNTP.starttls(ssl_context=None**)**
    Send a `STARTTLS` command. This will enable encryption on the NNTP connection. The *ssl_context* argument is optional and should be a *ssl.SSLContext* object. Please read *Security considerations* for best practices.

    Note that this may not be done after authentication information has been transmitted, and authentication occurs by default if possible during a *NNTP* object initialization. See *NNTP.login()* for information on suppressing this behavior.

    New in version 3.2.

Changed in version 3.4: The method now supports hostname check with `ssl.SSLContext.check_hostname` and *Server Name Indication* (see `ssl.HAS_SNI`).

NNTP.**newgroups**(*date, *, file=None*)
> Send a NEWGROUPS command. The *date* argument should be a `datetime.date` or `datetime.datetime` object. Return a pair (`response`, `groups`) where *groups* is a list representing the groups that are new since the given *date*. If *file* is supplied, though, then *groups* will be empty.
>
> ```
> >>> from datetime import date, timedelta
> >>> resp, groups = s.newgroups(date.today() - timedelta(days=3))
> >>> len(groups)
> 85
> >>> groups[0]
> GroupInfo(group='gmane.network.tor.devel', last='4', first='1', flag='m')
> ```

NNTP.**newnews**(*group, date, *, file=None*)
> Send a NEWNEWS command. Here, *group* is a group name or `'*'`, and *date* has the same meaning as for `newgroups()`. Return a pair (`response`, `articles`) where *articles* is a list of message ids.
>
> This command is frequently disabled by NNTP server administrators.

NNTP.**list**(*group_pattern=None, *, file=None*)
> Send a LIST or LIST ACTIVE command. Return a pair (`response`, `list`) where *list* is a list of tuples representing all the groups available from this NNTP server, optionally matching the pattern string *group_pattern*. Each tuple has the form (`group, last, first, flag`), where *group* is a group name, *last* and *first* are the last and first article numbers, and *flag* usually takes one of these values:
>
> - y: Local postings and articles from peers are allowed.
> - m: The group is moderated and all postings must be approved.
> - n: No local postings are allowed, only articles from peers.
> - j: Articles from peers are filed in the junk group instead.
> - x: No local postings, and articles from peers are ignored.
> - =foo.bar: Articles are filed in the `foo.bar` group instead.
>
> If *flag* has another value, then the status of the newsgroup should be considered unknown.
>
> This command can return very large results, especially if *group_pattern* is not specified. It is best to cache the results offline unless you really need to refresh them.
>
> Changed in version 3.2: *group_pattern* was added.

NNTP.**descriptions**(*grouppattern*)
> Send a LIST NEWSGROUPS command, where *grouppattern* is a wildmat string as specified in RFC 3977 (it's essentially the same as DOS or UNIX shell wildcard strings). Return a pair (`response`, `descriptions`), where *descriptions* is a dictionary mapping group names to textual descriptions.
>
> ```
> >>> resp, descs = s.descriptions('gmane.comp.python.*')
> >>> len(descs)
> 295
> >>> descs.popitem()
> ('gmane.comp.python.bio.general', 'BioPython discussion list (Moderated)')
> ```

NNTP.**description**(*group*)
> Get a description for a single group *group*. If more than one group matches (if 'group' is a real wildmat string), return the first match. If no group matches, return an empty string.
>
> This elides the response code from the server. If the response code is needed, use `descriptions()`.

`NNTP.group(name)`
    Send a GROUP command, where *name* is the group name. The group is selected as the current group, if it exists. Return a tuple (`response, count, first, last, name`) where *count* is the (estimated) number of articles in the group, *first* is the first article number in the group, *last* is the last article number in the group, and *name* is the group name.

`NNTP.over(message_spec, *, file=None)`
    Send an OVER command, or an XOVER command on legacy servers. *message_spec* can be either a string representing a message id, or a (`first, last`) tuple of numbers indicating a range of articles in the current group, or a (`first, None`) tuple indicating a range of articles starting from *first* to the last article in the current group, or *None* to select the current article in the current group.

    Return a pair (`response, overviews`). *overviews* is a list of (`article_number, overview`) tuples, one for each article selected by *message_spec*. Each *overview* is a dictionary with the same number of items, but this number depends on the server. These items are either message headers (the key is then the lower-cased header name) or metadata items (the key is then the metadata name prepended with `":"`). The following items are guaranteed to be present by the NNTP specification:

    - the `subject`, `from`, `date`, `message-id` and `references` headers
    - the `:bytes` metadata: the number of bytes in the entire raw article (including headers and body)
    - the `:lines` metadata: the number of lines in the article body

    The value of each item is either a string, or *None* if not present.

    It is advisable to use the `decode_header()` function on header values when they may contain non-ASCII characters:

    ```
    >>> _, _, first, last, _ = s.group('gmane.comp.python.devel')
    >>> resp, overviews = s.over((last, last))
    >>> art_num, over = overviews[0]
    >>> art_num
    117216
    >>> list(over.keys())
    ['xref', 'from', ':lines', ':bytes', 'references', 'date', 'message-id', 'subject']
    >>> over['from']
    '=?UTF-8?B?Ik1hcnRpbiB2LiBMw7Z3aXMi?= <martin@v.loewis.de>'
    >>> nntplib.decode_header(over['from'])
    '"Martin v. Löwis" <martin@v.loewis.de>'
    ```

    New in version 3.2.

`NNTP.help(*, file=None)`
    Send a HELP command. Return a pair (`response, list`) where *list* is a list of help strings.

`NNTP.stat(message_spec=None)`
    Send a STAT command, where *message_spec* is either a message id (enclosed in `'<'` and `'>'`) or an article number in the current group. If *message_spec* is omitted or *None*, the current article in the current group is considered. Return a triple (`response, number, id`) where *number* is the article number and *id* is the message id.

    ```
    >>> _, _, first, last, _ = s.group('gmane.comp.python.devel')
    >>> resp, number, message_id = s.stat(first)
    >>> number, message_id
    (9099, '<20030112190404.GE29873@epoch.metaslash.com>')
    ```

`NNTP.next()`
    Send a NEXT command. Return as for `stat()`.

`NNTP.last()`
    Send a LAST command. Return as for `stat()`.

NNTP.article(*message_spec=None*, *, *file=None*)

Send an `ARTICLE` command, where *message_spec* has the same meaning as for *stat()*. Return a tuple (`response, info`) where *info* is a *namedtuple* with three attributes *number*, *message_id* and *lines* (in that order). *number* is the article number in the group (or 0 if the information is not available), *message_id* the message id as a string, and *lines* a list of lines (without terminating newlines) comprising the raw message including headers and body.

```
>>> resp, info = s.article('<20030112190404.GE29873@epoch.metaslash.com>')
>>> info.number
0
>>> info.message_id
'<20030112190404.GE29873@epoch.metaslash.com>'
>>> len(info.lines)
65
>>> info.lines[0]
b'Path: main.gmane.org!not-for-mail'
>>> info.lines[1]
b'From: Neal Norwitz <neal@metaslash.com>'
>>> info.lines[-3:]
[b'There is a patch for 2.3 as well as 2.2.', b'', b'Neal']
```

NNTP.head(*message_spec=None*, *, *file=None*)

Same as *article()*, but sends a `HEAD` command. The *lines* returned (or written to *file*) will only contain the message headers, not the body.

NNTP.body(*message_spec=None*, *, *file=None*)

Same as *article()*, but sends a `BODY` command. The *lines* returned (or written to *file*) will only contain the message body, not the headers.

NNTP.post(*data*)

Post an article using the `POST` command. The *data* argument is either a *file object* opened for binary reading, or any iterable of bytes objects (representing raw lines of the article to be posted). It should represent a well-formed news article, including the required headers. The *post()* method automatically escapes lines beginning with . and appends the termination line.

If the method succeeds, the server's response is returned. If the server refuses posting, a *NNTPReplyError* is raised.

NNTP.ihave(*message_id*, *data*)

Send an `IHAVE` command. *message_id* is the id of the message to send to the server (enclosed in '<' and '>'). The *data* parameter and the return value are the same as for *post()*.

NNTP.date()

Return a pair (`response, date`). *date* is a *datetime* object containing the current date and time of the server.

NNTP.slave()

Send a `SLAVE` command. Return the server's *response*.

NNTP.set_debuglevel(*level*)

Set the instance's debugging level. This controls the amount of debugging output printed. The default, 0, produces no debugging output. A value of 1 produces a moderate amount of debugging output, generally a single line per request or response. A value of 2 or higher produces the maximum amount of debugging output, logging each line sent and received on the connection (including message text).

The following are optional NNTP extensions defined in RFC 2980. Some of them have been superseded by newer commands in RFC 3977.

NNTP.xhdr(*hdr*, *str*, *, *file=None*)

Send an `XHDR` command. The *hdr* argument is a header keyword, e.g. `'subject'`. The *str* argument should have the form `'first-last'` where *first* and *last* are the first and last article numbers to search.

Return a pair (`response, list`), where *list* is a list of pairs (`id, text`), where *id* is an article number (as a string) and *text* is the text of the requested header for that article. If the *file* parameter is supplied, then the output of the `XHDR` command is stored in a file. If *file* is a string, then the method will open a file with that name, write to it then close it. If *file* is a *file object*, then it will start calling `write()` on it to store the lines of the command output. If *file* is supplied, then the returned *list* is an empty list.

NNTP.**xover**(*start, end, *, file=None*)

Send an `XOVER` command. *start* and *end* are article numbers delimiting the range of articles to select. The return value is the same of for *over()*. It is recommended to use *over()* instead, since it will automatically use the newer `OVER` command if available.

NNTP.**xpath**(*id*)

Return a pair (`resp, path`), where *path* is the directory path to the article with message ID *id*. Most of the time, this extension is not enabled by NNTP server administrators.

Deprecated since version 3.3: The XPATH extension is not actively used.

21.16.2 Utility functions

The module also defines the following utility function:

nntplib.**decode_header**(*header_str*)

Decode a header value, un-escaping any escaped non-ASCII characters. *header_str* must be a `str` object. The unescaped value is returned. Using this function is recommended to display some headers in a human readable form:

```
>>> decode_header("Some subject")
'Some subject'
>>> decode_header("=?ISO-8859-15?Q?D=E9buter_en_Python?=")
'Débuter en Python'
>>> decode_header("Re: =?UTF-8?B?cHJvYmzDqG1lIGRlIG1hdHJpY2U=?=")
'Re: problème de matrice'
```

21.17 smtplib — SMTP protocol client

Source code: Lib/smtplib.py

The *smtplib* module defines an SMTP client session object that can be used to send mail to any Internet machine with an SMTP or ESMTP listener daemon. For details of SMTP and ESMTP operation, consult RFC 821 (Simple Mail Transfer Protocol) and RFC 1869 (SMTP Service Extensions).

class smtplib.**SMTP**(*host='', port=0, local_hostname=None*[, *timeout*], *source_address=None*)

An *SMTP* instance encapsulates an SMTP connection. It has methods that support a full repertoire of SMTP and ESMTP operations. If the optional host and port parameters are given, the SMTP *connect()* method is called with those parameters during initialization. If specified, *local_hostname* is used as the FQDN of the local host in the HELO/EHLO command. Otherwise, the local hostname is found using *socket.getfqdn()*. If the *connect()* call returns anything other than a success code, an *SMTPConnectError* is raised. The optional *timeout* parameter specifies a timeout in seconds for blocking operations like the connection attempt (if not specified, the global default timeout setting will be used). If the timeout expires, *socket.timeout* is raised. The optional source_address parameter allows binding to some specific source address in a machine with multiple network interfaces, and/or to some specific source TCP port. It takes a 2-tuple (host, port), for the socket to bind to as its source address before connecting. If omitted (or if host or port are '' and/or 0 respectively) the OS default behavior will be used.

For normal use, you should only require the initialization/connect, `sendmail()`, and `quit()` methods. An example is included below.

The *SMTP* class supports the `with` statement. When used like this, the SMTP `QUIT` command is issued automatically when the `with` statement exits. E.g.:

```
>>> from smtplib import SMTP
>>> with SMTP("domain.org") as smtp:
...     smtp.noop()
...
(250, b'Ok')
>>>
```

Changed in version 3.3: Support for the `with` statement was added.

Changed in version 3.3: source_address argument was added.

New in version 3.5: The SMTPUTF8 extension (RFC 6531) is now supported.

class smtplib.SMTP_SSL(*host=''*, *port=0*, *local_hostname=None*, *keyfile=None*, *certfile=None*[, *timeout*], *context=None*, *source_address=None*)

An *SMTP_SSL* instance behaves exactly the same as instances of *SMTP*. *SMTP_SSL* should be used for situations where SSL is required from the beginning of the connection and using `starttls()` is not appropriate. If *host* is not specified, the local host is used. If *port* is zero, the standard SMTP-over-SSL port (465) is used. The optional arguments *local_hostname*, *timeout* and *source_address* have the same meaning as they do in the *SMTP* class. *context*, also optional, can contain a *SSLContext* and allows configuring various aspects of the secure connection. Please read *Security considerations* for best practices.

keyfile and *certfile* are a legacy alternative to *context*, and can point to a PEM formatted private key and certificate chain file for the SSL connection.

Changed in version 3.3: *context* was added.

Changed in version 3.3: source_address argument was added.

Changed in version 3.4: The class now supports hostname check with `ssl.SSLContext.check_hostname` and *Server Name Indication* (see `ssl.HAS_SNI`).

Deprecated since version 3.6: *keyfile* and *certfile* are deprecated in favor of *context*. Please use `ssl.SSLContext.load_cert_chain()` instead, or let `ssl.create_default_context()` select the system's trusted CA certificates for you.

class smtplib.LMTP(*host=''*, *port=LMTP_PORT*, *local_hostname=None*, *source_address=None*)

The LMTP protocol, which is very similar to ESMTP, is heavily based on the standard SMTP client. It's common to use Unix sockets for LMTP, so our `connect()` method must support that as well as a regular host:port server. The optional arguments local_hostname and source_address have the same meaning as they do in the *SMTP* class. To specify a Unix socket, you must use an absolute path for *host*, starting with a '/'.

Authentication is supported, using the regular SMTP mechanism. When using a Unix socket, LMTP generally don't support or require any authentication, but your mileage might vary.

A nice selection of exceptions is defined as well:

exception smtplib.SMTPException

Subclass of *OSError* that is the base exception class for all the other exceptions provided by this module.

Changed in version 3.4: SMTPException became subclass of *OSError*

exception smtplib.**SMTPServerDisconnected**
> This exception is raised when the server unexpectedly disconnects, or when an attempt is made to use the *SMTP* instance before connecting it to a server.

exception smtplib.**SMTPResponseException**
> Base class for all exceptions that include an SMTP error code. These exceptions are generated in some instances when the SMTP server returns an error code. The error code is stored in the `smtp_code` attribute of the error, and the `smtp_error` attribute is set to the error message.

exception smtplib.**SMTPSenderRefused**
> Sender address refused. In addition to the attributes set by on all *SMTPResponseException* exceptions, this sets 'sender' to the string that the SMTP server refused.

exception smtplib.**SMTPRecipientsRefused**
> All recipient addresses refused. The errors for each recipient are accessible through the attribute `recipients`, which is a dictionary of exactly the same sort as *SMTP.sendmail()* returns.

exception smtplib.**SMTPDataError**
> The SMTP server refused to accept the message data.

exception smtplib.**SMTPConnectError**
> Error occurred during establishment of a connection with the server.

exception smtplib.**SMTPHeloError**
> The server refused our HELO message.

exception smtplib.**SMTPNotSupportedError**
> The command or option attempted is not supported by the server.
>
> New in version 3.5.

exception smtplib.**SMTPAuthenticationError**
> SMTP authentication went wrong. Most probably the server didn't accept the username/password combination provided.

See also:

RFC 821 - **Simple Mail Transfer Protocol** Protocol definition for SMTP. This document covers the model, operating procedure, and protocol details for SMTP.

RFC 1869 - **SMTP Service Extensions** Definition of the ESMTP extensions for SMTP. This describes a framework for extending SMTP with new commands, supporting dynamic discovery of the commands provided by the server, and defines a few additional commands.

21.17.1 SMTP Objects

An *SMTP* instance has the following methods:

SMTP.**set_debuglevel**(*level*)
> Set the debug output level. A value of 1 or `True` for *level* results in debug messages for connection and for all messages sent to and received from the server. A value of 2 for *level* results in these messages being timestamped.
>
> Changed in version 3.5: Added debuglevel 2.

SMTP.**docmd**(*cmd*, *args=''*)
> Send a command *cmd* to the server. The optional argument *args* is simply concatenated to the command, separated by a space.
>
> This returns a 2-tuple composed of a numeric response code and the actual response line (multiline responses are joined into one long line.)

In normal operation it should not be necessary to call this method explicitly. It is used to implement other methods and may be useful for testing private extensions.

If the connection to the server is lost while waiting for the reply, *SMTPServerDisconnected* will be raised.

SMTP.connect(*host='localhost'*, *port=0*)
Connect to a host on a given port. The defaults are to connect to the local host at the standard SMTP port (25). If the hostname ends with a colon (':') followed by a number, that suffix will be stripped off and the number interpreted as the port number to use. This method is automatically invoked by the constructor if a host is specified during instantiation. Returns a 2-tuple of the response code and message sent by the server in its connection response.

SMTP.helo(*name=''*)
Identify yourself to the SMTP server using HELO. The hostname argument defaults to the fully qualified domain name of the local host. The message returned by the server is stored as the `helo_resp` attribute of the object.

In normal operation it should not be necessary to call this method explicitly. It will be implicitly called by the *sendmail()* when necessary.

SMTP.ehlo(*name=''*)
Identify yourself to an ESMTP server using EHLO. The hostname argument defaults to the fully qualified domain name of the local host. Examine the response for ESMTP option and store them for use by *has_extn()*. Also sets several informational attributes: the message returned by the server is stored as the `ehlo_resp` attribute, `does_esmtp` is set to true or false depending on whether the server supports ESMTP, and `esmtp_features` will be a dictionary containing the names of the SMTP service extensions this server supports, and their parameters (if any).

Unless you wish to use *has_extn()* before sending mail, it should not be necessary to call this method explicitly. It will be implicitly called by *sendmail()* when necessary.

SMTP.ehlo_or_helo_if_needed()
This method call *ehlo()* and or *helo()* if there has been no previous EHLO or HELO command this session. It tries ESMTP EHLO first.

SMTPHeloError The server didn't reply properly to the HELO greeting.

SMTP.has_extn(*name*)
Return *True* if *name* is in the set of SMTP service extensions returned by the server, *False* otherwise. Case is ignored.

SMTP.verify(*address*)
Check the validity of an address on this server using SMTP VRFY. Returns a tuple consisting of code 250 and a full RFC 822 address (including human name) if the user address is valid. Otherwise returns an SMTP error code of 400 or greater and an error string.

Note: Many sites disable SMTP VRFY in order to foil spammers.

SMTP.login(*user*, *password*, ***, *initial_response_ok=True*)
Log in on an SMTP server that requires authentication. The arguments are the username and the password to authenticate with. If there has been no previous EHLO or HELO command this session, this method tries ESMTP EHLO first. This method will return normally if the authentication was successful, or may raise the following exceptions:

SMTPHeloError The server didn't reply properly to the HELO greeting.

SMTPAuthenticationError The server didn't accept the username/password combination.

SMTPNotSupportedError The AUTH command is not supported by the server.

21.17. smtplib — SMTP protocol client

SMTPException No suitable authentication method was found.

Each of the authentication methods supported by `smtplib` are tried in turn if they are advertised as supported by the server. See `auth()` for a list of supported authentication methods. *initial_response_ok* is passed through to `auth()`.

Optional keyword argument *initial_response_ok* specifies whether, for authentication methods that support it, an "initial response" as specified in RFC 4954 can be sent along with the `AUTH` command, rather than requiring a challenge/response.

Changed in version 3.5: `SMTPNotSupportedError` may be raised, and the *initial_response_ok* parameter was added.

SMTP.**auth**(*mechanism, authobject, *, initial_response_ok=True*)

Issue an SMTP `AUTH` command for the specified authentication *mechanism*, and handle the challenge response via *authobject*.

mechanism specifies which authentication mechanism is to be used as argument to the `AUTH` command; the valid values are those listed in the `auth` element of `esmtp_features`.

authobject must be a callable object taking an optional single argument:

> data = authobject(challenge=None)

If optional keyword argument *initial_response_ok* is true, `authobject()` will be called first with no argument. It can return the RFC 4954 "initial response" bytes which will be encoded and sent with the `AUTH` command as below. If the `authobject()` does not support an initial response (e.g. because it requires a challenge), it should return `None` when called with `challenge=None`. If *initial_response_ok* is false, then `authobject()` will not be called first with `None`.

If the initial response check returns `None`, or if *initial_response_ok* is false, `authobject()` will be called to process the server's challenge response; the *challenge* argument it is passed will be a `bytes`. It should return `bytes` *data* that will be base64 encoded and sent to the server.

The `SMTP` class provides `authobjects` for the `CRAM-MD5`, `PLAIN`, and `LOGIN` mechanisms; they are named `SMTP.auth_cram_md5`, `SMTP.auth_plain`, and `SMTP.auth_login` respectively. They all require that the `user` and `password` properties of the `SMTP` instance are set to appropriate values.

User code does not normally need to call `auth` directly, but can instead call the `login()` method, which will try each of the above mechanisms in turn, in the order listed. `auth` is exposed to facilitate the implementation of authentication methods not (or not yet) supported directly by `smtplib`.

New in version 3.5.

SMTP.**starttls**(*keyfile=None, certfile=None, context=None*)

Put the SMTP connection in TLS (Transport Layer Security) mode. All SMTP commands that follow will be encrypted. You should then call `ehlo()` again.

If *keyfile* and *certfile* are provided, these are passed to the `socket` module's `ssl()` function.

Optional *context* parameter is a `ssl.SSLContext` object; This is an alternative to using a keyfile and a certfile and if specified both *keyfile* and *certfile* should be `None`.

If there has been no previous `EHLO` or `HELO` command this session, this method tries ESMTP `EHLO` first.

`SMTPHeloError` The server didn't reply properly to the `HELO` greeting.

`SMTPNotSupportedError` The server does not support the STARTTLS extension.

`RuntimeError` SSL/TLS support is not available to your Python interpreter.

Changed in version 3.3: *context* was added.

Changed in version 3.4: The method now supports hostname check with `SSLContext.check_hostname` and *Server Name Indicator* (see `HAS_SNI`).

Changed in version 3.5: The error raised for lack of STARTTLS support is now the *SMTPNotSupportedError* subclass instead of the base *SMTPException*.

SMTP.**sendmail**(*from_addr*, *to_addrs*, *msg*, *mail_options=[]*, *rcpt_options=[]*)
Send mail. The required arguments are an RFC 822 from-address string, a list of RFC 822 to-address strings (a bare string will be treated as a list with 1 address), and a message string. The caller may pass a list of ESMTP options (such as `8bitmime`) to be used in `MAIL FROM` commands as *mail_options*. ESMTP options (such as `DSN` commands) that should be used with all `RCPT` commands can be passed as *rcpt_options*. (If you need to use different ESMTP options to different recipients you have to use the low-level methods such as `mail()`, `rcpt()` and `data()` to send the message.)

Note: The *from_addr* and *to_addrs* parameters are used to construct the message envelope used by the transport agents. `sendmail` does not modify the message headers in any way.

---

msg may be a string containing characters in the ASCII range, or a byte string. A string is encoded to bytes using the ascii codec, and lone `\r` and `\n` characters are converted to `\r\n` characters. A byte string is not modified.

If there has been no previous `EHLO` or `HELO` command this session, this method tries ESMTP `EHLO` first. If the server does ESMTP, message size and each of the specified options will be passed to it (if the option is in the feature set the server advertises). If `EHLO` fails, `HELO` will be tried and ESMTP options suppressed.

This method will return normally if the mail is accepted for at least one recipient. Otherwise it will raise an exception. That is, if this method does not raise an exception, then someone should get your mail. If this method does not raise an exception, it returns a dictionary, with one entry for each recipient that was refused. Each entry contains a tuple of the SMTP error code and the accompanying error message sent by the server.

If `SMTPUTF8` is included in *mail_options*, and the server supports it, *from_addr* and *to_addrs* may contain non-ASCII characters.

This method may raise the following exceptions:

SMTPRecipientsRefused All recipients were refused. Nobody got the mail. The `recipients` attribute of the exception object is a dictionary with information about the refused recipients (like the one returned when at least one recipient was accepted).

SMTPHeloError The server didn't reply properly to the HELO greeting.

SMTPSenderRefused The server didn't accept the *from_addr*.

SMTPDataError The server replied with an unexpected error code (other than a refusal of a recipient).

SMTPNotSupportedError `SMTPUTF8` was given in the *mail_options* but is not supported by the server.

Unless otherwise noted, the connection will be open even after an exception is raised.

Changed in version 3.2: *msg* may be a byte string.

Changed in version 3.5: `SMTPUTF8` support added, and *SMTPNotSupportedError* may be raised if `SMTPUTF8` is specified but the server does not support it.

SMTP.**send_message**(*msg*, *from_addr=None*, *to_addrs=None*, *mail_options=[]*, *rcpt_options=[]*)
This is a convenience method for calling *sendmail()* with the message represented by an *email.message.Message* object. The arguments have the same meaning as for *sendmail()*, except that *msg* is a `Message` object.

If *from_addr* is `None` or *to_addrs* is `None`, `send_message` fills those arguments with addresses extracted from the headers of *msg* as specified in RFC 5322: *from_addr* is set to the *Sender* field if it is present, and otherwise to the *From* field. *to_addrs* combines the values (if any) of the *To*, *Cc*, and *Bcc* fields from *msg*. If exactly one set of *Resent-** headers appear in the message, the regular headers are ignored and the *Resent-** headers are used instead. If the message contains more than one set of *Resent-** headers, a `ValueError` is raised, since there is no way to unambiguously detect the most recent set of *Resent-* headers.

send_message serializes *msg* using `BytesGenerator` with **\r\n** as the *linesep*, and calls `sendmail()` to transmit the resulting message. Regardless of the values of *from_addr* and *to_addrs*, **send_message** does not transmit any *Bcc* or *Resent-Bcc* headers that may appear in *msg*. If any of the addresses in *from_addr* and *to_addrs* contain non-ASCII characters and the server does not advertise **SMTPUTF8** support, an **SMTPNotSupported** error is raised. Otherwise the **Message** is serialized with a clone of its `policy` with the `utf8` attribute set to **True**, and **SMTPUTF8** and **BODY=8BITMIME** are added to *mail_options*.

New in version 3.2.

New in version 3.5: Support for internationalized addresses (**SMTPUTF8**).

SMTP.quit()

Terminate the SMTP session and close the connection. Return the result of the SMTP **QUIT** command.

Low-level methods corresponding to the standard SMTP/ESMTP commands **HELP**, **RSET**, **NOOP**, **MAIL**, **RCPT**, and **DATA** are also supported. Normally these do not need to be called directly, so they are not documented here. For details, consult the module code.

21.17.2 SMTP Example

This example prompts the user for addresses needed in the message envelope ('To' and 'From' addresses), and the message to be delivered. Note that the headers to be included with the message must be included in the message as entered; this example doesn't do any processing of the RFC 822 headers. In particular, the 'To' and 'From' addresses must be included in the message headers explicitly.

```
import smtplib

def prompt(prompt):
    return input(prompt).strip()

fromaddr = prompt("From: ")
toaddrs  = prompt("To: ").split()
print("Enter message, end with ^D (Unix) or ^Z (Windows):")

# Add the From: and To: headers at the start!
msg = ("From: %s\r\nTo: %s\r\n\r\n"
       % (fromaddr, ", ".join(toaddrs)))
while True:
    try:
        line = input()
    except EOFError:
        break
    if not line:
        break
    msg = msg + line

print("Message length is", len(msg))

server = smtplib.SMTP('localhost')
server.set_debuglevel(1)
server.sendmail(fromaddr, toaddrs, msg)
server.quit()
```

Note: In general, you will want to use the `email` package's features to construct an email message, which you can then send via `send_message()`; see *email: Examples*.

21.18 `smtpd` — SMTP Server

Source code: Lib/smtpd.py

This module offers several classes to implement SMTP (email) servers.

See also:

The aiosmtpd package is a recommended replacement for this module. It is based on `asyncio` and provides a more straightforward API. `smtpd` should be considered deprecated.

Several server implementations are present; one is a generic do-nothing implementation, which can be overridden, while the other two offer specific mail-sending strategies.

Additionally the SMTPChannel may be extended to implement very specific interaction behaviour with SMTP clients.

The code supports RFC 5321, plus the RFC 1870 SIZE and RFC 6531 SMTPUTF8 extensions.

21.18.1 SMTPServer Objects

class smtpd.SMTPServer(*localaddr, remoteaddr, data_size_limit=33554432, map=None, enable_SMTPUTF8=False, decode_data=False*)

Create a new *SMTPServer* object, which binds to local address *localaddr*. It will treat *remoteaddr* as an upstream SMTP relayer. Both *localaddr* and *remoteaddr* should be a *(host, port)* tuple. The object inherits from `asyncore.dispatcher`, and so will insert itself into `asyncore`'s event loop on instantiation.

data_size_limit specifies the maximum number of bytes that will be accepted in a `DATA` command. A value of `None` or `0` means no limit.

map is the socket map to use for connections (an initially empty dictionary is a suitable value). If not specified the `asyncore` global socket map is used.

enable_SMTPUTF8 determines whether the `SMTPUTF8` extension (as defined in RFC 6531) should be enabled. The default is `False`. When `True`, `SMTPUTF8` is accepted as a parameter to the `MAIL` command and when present is passed to `process_message()` in the `kwargs['mail_options']` list. *decode_data* and *enable_SMTPUTF8* cannot be set to `True` at the same time.

decode_data specifies whether the data portion of the SMTP transaction should be decoded using UTF-8. When *decode_data* is `False` (the default), the server advertises the `8BITMIME` extension (RFC 6152), accepts the `BODY=8BITMIME` parameter to the `MAIL` command, and when present passes it to `process_message()` in the `kwargs['mail_options']` list. *decode_data* and *enable_SMTPUTF8* cannot be set to `True` at the same time.

process_message(*peer, mailfrom, rcpttos, data, **kwargs*)

Raise a *NotImplementedError* exception. Override this in subclasses to do something useful with this message. Whatever was passed in the constructor as *remoteaddr* will be available as the *_remoteaddr* attribute. *peer* is the remote host's address, *mailfrom* is the envelope originator, *rcpttos* are the envelope recipients and *data* is a string containing the contents of the e-mail (which should be in RFC 5321 format).

If the *decode_data* constructor keyword is set to `True`, the *data* argument will be a unicode string. If it is set to `False`, it will be a bytes object.

kwargs is a dictionary containing additional information. It is empty if `decode_data=True` was given as an init argument, otherwise it contains the following keys:

> *mail_options*: a list of all received parameters to the `MAIL` command (the elements are uppercase strings; example: `['BODY=8BITMIME', 'SMTPUTF8']`).
>
> *rcpt_options*: same as *mail_options* but for the `RCPT` command. Currently no `RCPT TO` options are supported, so for now this will always be an empty list.

Implementations of `process_message` should use the `**kwargs` signature to accept arbitrary keyword arguments, since future feature enhancements may add keys to the kwargs dictionary.

Return `None` to request a normal `250 Ok` response; otherwise return the desired response string in RFC 5321 format.

channel_class
    Override this in subclasses to use a custom *SMTPChannel* for managing SMTP clients.

New in version 3.4: The *map* constructor argument.

Changed in version 3.5: *localaddr* and *remoteaddr* may now contain IPv6 addresses.

New in version 3.5: The *decode_data* and *enable_SMTPUTF8* constructor parameters, and the *kwargs* parameter to *process_message()* when *decode_data* is `False`.

Changed in version 3.6: *decode_data* is now `False` by default.

21.18.2 DebuggingServer Objects

class smtpd.DebuggingServer(*localaddr, remoteaddr*)
    Create a new debugging server. Arguments are as per *SMTPServer*. Messages will be discarded, and printed on stdout.

21.18.3 PureProxy Objects

class smtpd.PureProxy(*localaddr, remoteaddr*)
    Create a new pure proxy server. Arguments are as per *SMTPServer*. Everything will be relayed to *remoteaddr*. Note that running this has a good chance to make you into an open relay, so please be careful.

21.18.4 MailmanProxy Objects

class smtpd.MailmanProxy(*localaddr, remoteaddr*)
    Create a new pure proxy server. Arguments are as per *SMTPServer*. Everything will be relayed to *remoteaddr*, unless local mailman configurations knows about an address, in which case it will be handled via mailman. Note that running this has a good chance to make you into an open relay, so please be careful.

21.18.5 SMTPChannel Objects

class smtpd.SMTPChannel(*server, conn, addr, data_size_limit=33554432, map=None, enable_SMTPUTF8=False, decode_data=False*)
    Create a new *SMTPChannel* object which manages the communication between the server and a single SMTP client.

conn and *addr* are as per the instance variables described below.

data_size_limit specifies the maximum number of bytes that will be accepted in a DATA command. A value of None or 0 means no limit.

enable_SMTPUTF8 determines whether the SMTPUTF8 extension (as defined in RFC 6531) should be enabled. The default is False. *decode_data* and *enable_SMTPUTF8* cannot be set to True at the same time.

A dictionary can be specified in *map* to avoid using a global socket map.

decode_data specifies whether the data portion of the SMTP transaction should be decoded using UTF-8. The default is False. *decode_data* and *enable_SMTPUTF8* cannot be set to True at the same time.

To use a custom SMTPChannel implementation you need to override the *SMTPServer.channel_class* of your *SMTPServer*.

Changed in version 3.5: The *decode_data* and *enable_SMTPUTF8* parameters were added.

Changed in version 3.6: *decode_data* is now False by default.

The *SMTPChannel* has the following instance variables:

smtp_server
> Holds the *SMTPServer* that spawned this channel.

conn
> Holds the socket object connecting to the client.

addr
> Holds the address of the client, the second value returned by *socket.accept*

received_lines
> Holds a list of the line strings (decoded using UTF-8) received from the client. The lines have their "\r\n" line ending translated to "\n".

smtp_state
> Holds the current state of the channel. This will be either COMMAND initially and then DATA after the client sends a "DATA" line.

seen_greeting
> Holds a string containing the greeting sent by the client in its "HELO".

mailfrom
> Holds a string containing the address identified in the "MAIL FROM:" line from the client.

rcpttos
> Holds a list of strings containing the addresses identified in the "RCPT TO:" lines from the client.

received_data
> Holds a string containing all of the data sent by the client during the DATA state, up to but not including the terminating "\r\n.\r\n".

fqdn
> Holds the fully-qualified domain name of the server as returned by *socket.getfqdn()*.

peer
> Holds the name of the client peer as returned by conn.getpeername() where conn is *conn*.

The *SMTPChannel* operates by invoking methods named smtp_<command> upon reception of a command line from the client. Built into the base *SMTPChannel* class are methods for handling the following commands (and responding to them appropriately):

Command	Action taken
HELO	Accepts the greeting from the client and stores it in *seen_greeting*. Sets server to base command mode.
EHLO	Accepts the greeting from the client and stores it in *seen_greeting*. Sets server to extended command mode.
NOOP	Takes no action.
QUIT	Closes the connection cleanly.
MAIL	Accepts the "MAIL FROM:" syntax and stores the supplied address as *mailfrom*. In extended command mode, accepts the RFC 1870 SIZE attribute and responds appropriately based on the value of *data_size_limit*.
RCPT	Accepts the "RCPT TO:" syntax and stores the supplied addresses in the *rcpttos* list.
RSET	Resets the *mailfrom*, *rcpttos*, and *received_data*, but not the greeting.
DATA	Sets the internal state to DATA and stores remaining lines from the client in *received_data* until the terminator "\r\n.\r\n" is received.
HELP	Returns minimal information on command syntax
VRFY	Returns code 252 (the server doesn't know if the address is valid)
EXPN	Reports that the command is not implemented.

21.19 `telnetlib` — Telnet client

Source code: Lib/telnetlib.py

The *telnetlib* module provides a *Telnet* class that implements the Telnet protocol. See RFC 854 for details about the protocol. In addition, it provides symbolic constants for the protocol characters (see below), and for the telnet options. The symbolic names of the telnet options follow the definitions in `arpa/telnet.h`, with the leading `TELOPT_` removed. For symbolic names of options which are traditionally not included in `arpa/telnet.h`, see the module source itself.

The symbolic constants for the telnet commands are: IAC, DONT, DO, WONT, WILL, SE (Subnegotiation End), NOP (No Operation), DM (Data Mark), BRK (Break), IP (Interrupt process), AO (Abort output), AYT (Are You There), EC (Erase Character), EL (Erase Line), GA (Go Ahead), SB (Subnegotiation Begin).

class `telnetlib.Telnet`(*host=None, port=0[, timeout]*)

Telnet represents a connection to a Telnet server. The instance is initially not connected by default; the *open()* method must be used to establish a connection. Alternatively, the host name and optional port number can be passed to the constructor too, in which case the connection to the server will be established before the constructor returns. The optional *timeout* parameter specifies a timeout in seconds for blocking operations like the connection attempt (if not specified, the global default timeout setting will be used).

Do not reopen an already connected instance.

This class has many `read_*()` methods. Note that some of them raise *EOFError* when the end of the connection is read, because they can return an empty string for other reasons. See the individual descriptions below.

A *Telnet* object is a context manager and can be used in a `with` statement. When the `with` block ends, the *close()* method is called:

```
>>> from telnetlib import Telnet
>>> with Telnet('localhost', 23) as tn:
```

```
...     tn.interact()
...
```

Changed in version 3.6: Context manager support added

See also:

RFC 854 - **Telnet Protocol Specification** Definition of the Telnet protocol.

21.19.1 Telnet Objects

Telnet instances have the following methods:

Telnet.read_until(*expected, timeout=None*)
    Read until a given byte string, *expected*, is encountered or until *timeout* seconds have passed.

    When no match is found, return whatever is available instead, possibly empty bytes. Raise *EOFError* if the connection is closed and no cooked data is available.

Telnet.read_all()
    Read all data until EOF as bytes; block until connection closed.

Telnet.read_some()
    Read at least one byte of cooked data unless EOF is hit. Return b'' if EOF is hit. Block if no data is immediately available.

Telnet.read_very_eager()
    Read everything that can be without blocking in I/O (eager).

    Raise *EOFError* if connection closed and no cooked data available. Return b'' if no cooked data available otherwise. Do not block unless in the midst of an IAC sequence.

Telnet.read_eager()
    Read readily available data.

    Raise *EOFError* if connection closed and no cooked data available. Return b'' if no cooked data available otherwise. Do not block unless in the midst of an IAC sequence.

Telnet.read_lazy()
    Process and return data already in the queues (lazy).

    Raise *EOFError* if connection closed and no data available. Return b'' if no cooked data available otherwise. Do not block unless in the midst of an IAC sequence.

Telnet.read_very_lazy()
    Return any data available in the cooked queue (very lazy).

    Raise *EOFError* if connection closed and no data available. Return b'' if no cooked data available otherwise. This method never blocks.

Telnet.read_sb_data()
    Return the data collected between a SB/SE pair (suboption begin/end). The callback should access these data when it was invoked with a SE command. This method never blocks.

Telnet.open(*host, port=0[, timeout]*)
    Connect to a host. The optional second argument is the port number, which defaults to the standard Telnet port (23). The optional *timeout* parameter specifies a timeout in seconds for blocking operations like the connection attempt (if not specified, the global default timeout setting will be used).

    Do not try to reopen an already connected instance.

Telnet.msg(*msg, *args*)
> Print a debug message when the debug level is > 0. If extra arguments are present, they are substituted in the message using the standard string formatting operator.

Telnet.set_debuglevel(*debuglevel*)
> Set the debug level. The higher the value of *debuglevel*, the more debug output you get (on `sys.stdout`).

Telnet.close()
> Close the connection.

Telnet.get_socket()
> Return the socket object used internally.

Telnet.fileno()
> Return the file descriptor of the socket object used internally.

Telnet.write(*buffer*)
> Write a byte string to the socket, doubling any IAC characters. This can block if the connection is blocked. May raise `OSError` if the connection is closed.
>
> Changed in version 3.3: This method used to raise `socket.error`, which is now an alias of `OSError`.

Telnet.interact()
> Interaction function, emulates a very dumb Telnet client.

Telnet.mt_interact()
> Multithreaded version of `interact()`.

Telnet.expect(*list, timeout=None*)
> Read until one from a list of a regular expressions matches.
>
> The first argument is a list of regular expressions, either compiled (*regex objects*) or uncompiled (byte strings). The optional second argument is a timeout, in seconds; the default is to block indefinitely.
>
> Return a tuple of three items: the index in the list of the first regular expression that matches; the match object returned; and the bytes read up till and including the match.
>
> If end of file is found and no bytes were read, raise `EOFError`. Otherwise, when nothing matches, return `(-1, None, data)` where *data* is the bytes received so far (may be empty bytes if a timeout happened).
>
> If a regular expression ends with a greedy match (such as `.*`) or if more than one expression can match the same input, the results are non-deterministic, and may depend on the I/O timing.

Telnet.set_option_negotiation_callback(*callback*)
> Each time a telnet option is read on the input flow, this *callback* (if set) is called with the following parameters: callback(telnet socket, command (DO/DONT/WILL/WONT), option). No other action is done afterwards by telnetlib.

21.19.2 Telnet Example

A simple example illustrating typical use:

```
import getpass
import telnetlib

HOST = "localhost"
user = input("Enter your remote account: ")
password = getpass.getpass()

tn = telnetlib.Telnet(HOST)
```

```
tn.read_until(b"login: ")
tn.write(user.encode('ascii') + b"\n")
if password:
    tn.read_until(b"Password: ")
    tn.write(password.encode('ascii') + b"\n")

tn.write(b"ls\n")
tn.write(b"exit\n")

print(tn.read_all().decode('ascii'))
```

21.20 uuid — UUID objects according to RFC 4122

Source code: Lib/uuid.py

This module provides immutable *UUID* objects (the *UUID* class) and the functions *uuid1()*, *uuid3()*, *uuid4()*, *uuid5()* for generating version 1, 3, 4, and 5 UUIDs as specified in RFC 4122.

If all you want is a unique ID, you should probably call *uuid1()* or *uuid4()*. Note that *uuid1()* may compromise privacy since it creates a UUID containing the computer's network address. *uuid4()* creates a random UUID.

class uuid.UUID(*hex=None, bytes=None, bytes_le=None, fields=None, int=None, version=None*)

Create a UUID from either a string of 32 hexadecimal digits, a string of 16 bytes as the *bytes* argument, a string of 16 bytes in little-endian order as the *bytes_le* argument, a tuple of six integers (32-bit *time_low*, 16-bit *time_mid*, 16-bit *time_hi_version*, 8-bit *clock_seq_hi_variant*, 8-bit *clock_seq_low*, 48-bit *node*) as the *fields* argument, or a single 128-bit integer as the *int* argument. When a string of hex digits is given, curly braces, hyphens, and a URN prefix are all optional. For example, these expressions all yield the same UUID:

```
UUID('{12345678-1234-5678-1234-567812345678}')
UUID('12345678123456781234567812345678')
UUID('urn:uuid:12345678-1234-5678-1234-567812345678')
UUID(bytes=b'\x12\x34\x56\x78'*4)
UUID(bytes_le=b'\x78\x56\x34\x12\x34\x12\x78\x56' +
              b'\x12\x34\x56\x78\x12\x34\x56\x78')
UUID(fields=(0x12345678, 0x1234, 0x5678, 0x12, 0x34, 0x567812345678))
UUID(int=0x12345678123456781234567812345678)
```

Exactly one of *hex*, *bytes*, *bytes_le*, *fields*, or *int* must be given. The *version* argument is optional; if given, the resulting UUID will have its variant and version number set according to RFC 4122, overriding bits in the given *hex*, *bytes*, *bytes_le*, *fields*, or *int*.

Comparison of UUID objects are made by way of comparing their *UUID.int* attributes. Comparison with a non-UUID object raises a *TypeError*.

str(uuid) returns a string in the form 12345678-1234-5678-1234-567812345678 where the 32 hexadecimal digits represent the UUID.

UUID instances have these read-only attributes:

UUID.bytes

The UUID as a 16-byte string (containing the six integer fields in big-endian byte order).

UUID.bytes_le
　　The UUID as a 16-byte string (with *time_low*, *time_mid*, and *time_hi_version* in little-endian byte order).

UUID.fields
　　A tuple of the six integer fields of the UUID, which are also available as six individual attributes and two derived attributes:

Field	Meaning
time_low	the first 32 bits of the UUID
time_mid	the next 16 bits of the UUID
time_hi_version	the next 16 bits of the UUID
clock_seq_hi_variant	the next 8 bits of the UUID
clock_seq_low	the next 8 bits of the UUID
node	the last 48 bits of the UUID
time	the 60-bit timestamp
clock_seq	the 14-bit sequence number

UUID.hex
　　The UUID as a 32-character hexadecimal string.

UUID.int
　　The UUID as a 128-bit integer.

UUID.urn
　　The UUID as a URN as specified in RFC 4122.

UUID.variant
　　The UUID variant, which determines the internal layout of the UUID. This will be one of the constants *RESERVED_NCS*, *RFC_4122*, *RESERVED_MICROSOFT*, or *RESERVED_FUTURE*.

UUID.version
　　The UUID version number (1 through 5, meaningful only when the variant is *RFC_4122*).

The *uuid* module defines the following functions:

uuid.getnode()
　　Get the hardware address as a 48-bit positive integer. The first time this runs, it may launch a separate program, which could be quite slow. If all attempts to obtain the hardware address fail, we choose a random 48-bit number with its eighth bit set to 1 as recommended in RFC 4122. "Hardware address" means the MAC address of a network interface, and on a machine with multiple network interfaces the MAC address of any one of them may be returned.

uuid.uuid1(*node=None, clock_seq=None***)**
　　Generate a UUID from a host ID, sequence number, and the current time. If *node* is not given, *getnode()* is used to obtain the hardware address. If *clock_seq* is given, it is used as the sequence number; otherwise a random 14-bit sequence number is chosen.

uuid.uuid3(*namespace, name***)**
　　Generate a UUID based on the MD5 hash of a namespace identifier (which is a UUID) and a name (which is a string).

uuid.uuid4()
　　Generate a random UUID.

uuid.uuid5(*namespace, name***)**
　　Generate a UUID based on the SHA-1 hash of a namespace identifier (which is a UUID) and a name (which is a string).

The *uuid* module defines the following namespace identifiers for use with *uuid3()* or *uuid5()*.

uuid.NAMESPACE_DNS
When this namespace is specified, the *name* string is a fully-qualified domain name.

uuid.NAMESPACE_URL
When this namespace is specified, the *name* string is a URL.

uuid.NAMESPACE_OID
When this namespace is specified, the *name* string is an ISO OID.

uuid.NAMESPACE_X500
When this namespace is specified, the *name* string is an X.500 DN in DER or a text output format.

The *uuid* module defines the following constants for the possible values of the **variant** attribute:

uuid.RESERVED_NCS
Reserved for NCS compatibility.

uuid.RFC_4122
Specifies the UUID layout given in RFC 4122.

uuid.RESERVED_MICROSOFT
Reserved for Microsoft compatibility.

uuid.RESERVED_FUTURE
Reserved for future definition.

See also:

RFC 4122 - **A Universally Unique IDentifier (UUID) URN Namespace** This specification defines a Uniform Resource Name namespace for UUIDs, the internal format of UUIDs, and methods of generating UUIDs.

21.20.1 Example

Here are some examples of typical usage of the *uuid* module:

```
>>> import uuid

>>> # make a UUID based on the host ID and current time
>>> uuid.uuid1()
UUID('a8098c1a-f86e-11da-bd1a-00112444be1e')

>>> # make a UUID using an MD5 hash of a namespace UUID and a name
>>> uuid.uuid3(uuid.NAMESPACE_DNS, 'python.org')
UUID('6fa459ea-ee8a-3ca4-894e-db77e160355e')

>>> # make a random UUID
>>> uuid.uuid4()
UUID('16fd2706-8baf-433b-82eb-8c7fada847da')

>>> # make a UUID using a SHA-1 hash of a namespace UUID and a name
>>> uuid.uuid5(uuid.NAMESPACE_DNS, 'python.org')
UUID('886313e1-3b8a-5372-9b90-0c9aee199e5d')

>>> # make a UUID from a string of hex digits (braces and hyphens ignored)
>>> x = uuid.UUID('{00010203-0405-0607-0809-0a0b0c0d0e0f}')

>>> # convert a UUID to a string of hex digits in standard form
>>> str(x)
'00010203-0405-0607-0809-0a0b0c0d0e0f'
```

```
>>> # get the raw 16 bytes of the UUID
>>> x.bytes
b'\x00\x01\x02\x03\x04\x05\x06\x07\x08\t\n\x0b\x0c\r\x0e\x0f'

>>> # make a UUID from a 16-byte string
>>> uuid.UUID(bytes=x.bytes)
UUID('00010203-0405-0607-0809-0a0b0c0d0e0f')
```

21.21 socketserver — A framework for network servers

Source code: Lib/socketserver.py

The *socketserver* module simplifies the task of writing network servers.

There are four basic concrete server classes:

class socketserver.TCPServer(*server_address, RequestHandlerClass, bind_and_activate=True*)
This uses the Internet TCP protocol, which provides for continuous streams of data between the client and server. If *bind_and_activate* is true, the constructor automatically attempts to invoke *server_bind()* and *server_activate()*. The other parameters are passed to the *BaseServer* base class.

class socketserver.UDPServer(*server_address, RequestHandlerClass, bind_and_activate=True*)
This uses datagrams, which are discrete packets of information that may arrive out of order or be lost while in transit. The parameters are the same as for *TCPServer*.

class socketserver.UnixStreamServer(*server_address, RequestHandlerClass, bind_and_activate=True*)
class socketserver.UnixDatagramServer(*server_address, RequestHandlerClass, bind_and_activate=True*)
These more infrequently used classes are similar to the TCP and UDP classes, but use Unix domain sockets; they're not available on non-Unix platforms. The parameters are the same as for *TCPServer*.

These four classes process requests *synchronously*; each request must be completed before the next request can be started. This isn't suitable if each request takes a long time to complete, because it requires a lot of computation, or because it returns a lot of data which the client is slow to process. The solution is to create a separate process or thread to handle each request; the *ForkingMixIn* and *ThreadingMixIn* mix-in classes can be used to support asynchronous behaviour.

Creating a server requires several steps. First, you must create a request handler class by subclassing the *BaseRequestHandler* class and overriding its *handle()* method; this method will process incoming requests. Second, you must instantiate one of the server classes, passing it the server's address and the request handler class. It is recommended to use the server in a **with** statement. Then call the *handle_request()* or *serve_forever()* method of the server object to process one or many requests. Finally, call *server_close()* to close the socket (unless you used a **with** statement).

When inheriting from *ThreadingMixIn* for threaded connection behavior, you should explicitly declare how you want your threads to behave on an abrupt shutdown. The *ThreadingMixIn* class defines an attribute *daemon_threads*, which indicates whether or not the server should wait for thread termination. You should set the flag explicitly if you would like threads to behave autonomously; the default is *False*, meaning that Python will not exit until all threads created by *ThreadingMixIn* have exited.

Server classes have the same external methods and attributes, no matter what network protocol they use.

21.21.1 Server Creation Notes

There are five classes in an inheritance diagram, four of which represent synchronous servers of four types:

```
+------------+
| BaseServer |
+------------+
      |
      v
+------------+      +------------------+
| TCPServer  |----->| UnixStreamServer |
+------------+      +------------------+
      |
      v
+------------+      +-------------------+
| UDPServer  |----->| UnixDatagramServer |
+------------+      +-------------------+
```

Note that *UnixDatagramServer* derives from *UDPServer*, not from *UnixStreamServer* — the only difference between an IP and a Unix stream server is the address family, which is simply repeated in both Unix server classes.

class socketserver.**ForkingMixIn**
class socketserver.**ThreadingMixIn**

> Forking and threading versions of each type of server can be created using these mix-in classes. For instance, *ThreadingUDPServer* is created as follows:

```
class ThreadingUDPServer(ThreadingMixIn, UDPServer):
    pass
```

> The mix-in class comes first, since it overrides a method defined in *UDPServer*. Setting the various attributes also changes the behavior of the underlying server mechanism.
>
> *ForkingMixIn* and the Forking classes mentioned below are only available on POSIX platforms that support *fork()*.

class socketserver.**ForkingTCPServer**
class socketserver.**ForkingUDPServer**
class socketserver.**ThreadingTCPServer**
class socketserver.**ThreadingUDPServer**

> These classes are pre-defined using the mix-in classes.

To implement a service, you must derive a class from *BaseRequestHandler* and redefine its *handle()* method. You can then run various versions of the service by combining one of the server classes with your request handler class. The request handler class must be different for datagram or stream services. This can be hidden by using the handler subclasses *StreamRequestHandler* or *DatagramRequestHandler*.

Of course, you still have to use your head! For instance, it makes no sense to use a forking server if the service contains state in memory that can be modified by different requests, since the modifications in the child process would never reach the initial state kept in the parent process and passed to each child. In this case, you can use a threading server, but you will probably have to use locks to protect the integrity of the shared data.

On the other hand, if you are building an HTTP server where all data is stored externally (for instance, in the file system), a synchronous class will essentially render the service "deaf" while one request is being handled – which may be for a very long time if a client is slow to receive all the data it has requested. Here a threading or forking server is appropriate.

In some cases, it may be appropriate to process part of a request synchronously, but to finish processing in a forked child depending on the request data. This can be implemented by using a synchronous server and doing an explicit fork in the request handler class *handle()* method.

Another approach to handling multiple simultaneous requests in an environment that supports neither threads nor *fork()* (or where these are too expensive or inappropriate for the service) is to maintain an explicit table of partially finished requests and to use *selectors* to decide which request to work on next (or whether to handle a new incoming request). This is particularly important for stream services where each client can potentially be connected for a long time (if threads or subprocesses cannot be used). See *asyncore* for another way to manage this.

21.21.2 Server Objects

class socketserver.BaseServer(*server_address*, *RequestHandlerClass*)

This is the superclass of all Server objects in the module. It defines the interface, given below, but does not implement most of the methods, which is done in subclasses. The two parameters are stored in the respective *server_address* and *RequestHandlerClass* attributes.

fileno()

Return an integer file descriptor for the socket on which the server is listening. This function is most commonly passed to *selectors*, to allow monitoring multiple servers in the same process.

handle_request()

Process a single request. This function calls the following methods in order: *get_request()*, *verify_request()*, and *process_request()*. If the user-provided *handle()* method of the handler class raises an exception, the server's *handle_error()* method will be called. If no request is received within *timeout* seconds, *handle_timeout()* will be called and *handle_request()* will return.

serve_forever(*poll_interval=0.5*)

Handle requests until an explicit *shutdown()* request. Poll for shutdown every *poll_interval* seconds. Ignores the *timeout* attribute. It also calls *service_actions()*, which may be used by a subclass or mixin to provide actions specific to a given service. For example, the *ForkingMixIn* class uses *service_actions()* to clean up zombie child processes.

Changed in version 3.3: Added **service_actions** call to the **serve_forever** method.

service_actions()

This is called in the *serve_forever()* loop. This method can be overridden by subclasses or mixin classes to perform actions specific to a given service, such as cleanup actions.

New in version 3.3.

shutdown()

Tell the *serve_forever()* loop to stop and wait until it does.

server_close()

Clean up the server. May be overridden.

address_family

The family of protocols to which the server's socket belongs. Common examples are *socket.AF_INET* and *socket.AF_UNIX*.

RequestHandlerClass

The user-provided request handler class; an instance of this class is created for each request.

server_address

The address on which the server is listening. The format of addresses varies depending on the protocol family; see the documentation for the *socket* module for details. For Internet protocols, this is a tuple containing a string giving the address, and an integer port number: ('127.0.0.1', 80), for example.

socket
: The socket object on which the server will listen for incoming requests.

The server classes support the following class variables:

allow_reuse_address
: Whether the server will allow the reuse of an address. This defaults to *False*, and can be set in subclasses to change the policy.

request_queue_size
: The size of the request queue. If it takes a long time to process a single request, any requests that arrive while the server is busy are placed into a queue, up to *request_queue_size* requests. Once the queue is full, further requests from clients will get a "Connection denied" error. The default value is usually 5, but this can be overridden by subclasses.

socket_type
: The type of socket used by the server; *socket.SOCK_STREAM* and *socket.SOCK_DGRAM* are two common values.

timeout
: Timeout duration, measured in seconds, or *None* if no timeout is desired. If *handle_request()* receives no incoming requests within the timeout period, the *handle_timeout()* method is called.

There are various server methods that can be overridden by subclasses of base server classes like *TCPServer*; these methods aren't useful to external users of the server object.

finish_request(*request*, *client_address*)
: Actually processes the request by instantiating *RequestHandlerClass* and calling its *handle()* method.

get_request()
: Must accept a request from the socket, and return a 2-tuple containing the *new* socket object to be used to communicate with the client, and the client's address.

handle_error(*request*, *client_address*)
: This function is called if the *handle()* method of a *RequestHandlerClass* instance raises an exception. The default action is to print the traceback to standard error and continue handling further requests.

Changed in version 3.6: Now only called for exceptions derived from the *Exception* class.

handle_timeout()
: This function is called when the *timeout* attribute has been set to a value other than *None* and the timeout period has passed with no requests being received. The default action for forking servers is to collect the status of any child processes that have exited, while in threading servers this method does nothing.

process_request(*request*, *client_address*)
: Calls *finish_request()* to create an instance of the *RequestHandlerClass*. If desired, this function can create a new process or thread to handle the request; the *ForkingMixIn* and *ThreadingMixIn* classes do this.

server_activate()
: Called by the server's constructor to activate the server. The default behavior for a TCP server just invokes *listen()* on the server's socket. May be overridden.

server_bind()
: Called by the server's constructor to bind the socket to the desired address. May be overridden.

verify_request(*request*, *client_address*)
: Must return a Boolean value; if the value is *True*, the request will be processed, and if it's *False*, the request will be denied. This function can be overridden to implement access controls for a server. The default implementation always returns *True*.

Changed in version 3.6: Support for the *context manager* protocol was added. Exiting the context manager is equivalent to calling `server_close()`.

21.21.3 Request Handler Objects

class `socketserver.BaseRequestHandler`

This is the superclass of all request handler objects. It defines the interface, given below. A concrete request handler subclass must define a new `handle()` method, and can override any of the other methods. A new instance of the subclass is created for each request.

`setup()`

Called before the `handle()` method to perform any initialization actions required. The default implementation does nothing.

`handle()`

This function must do all the work required to service a request. The default implementation does nothing. Several instance attributes are available to it; the request is available as `self.request`; the client address as `self.client_address`; and the server instance as `self.server`, in case it needs access to per-server information.

The type of `self.request` is different for datagram or stream services. For stream services, `self.request` is a socket object; for datagram services, `self.request` is a pair of string and socket.

`finish()`

Called after the `handle()` method to perform any clean-up actions required. The default implementation does nothing. If `setup()` raises an exception, this function will not be called.

class `socketserver.StreamRequestHandler`
class `socketserver.DatagramRequestHandler`

These *BaseRequestHandler* subclasses override the `setup()` and `finish()` methods, and provide `self.rfile` and `self.wfile` attributes. The `self.rfile` and `self.wfile` attributes can be read or written, respectively, to get the request data or return data to the client.

The `rfile` attributes of both classes support the *io.BufferedIOBase* readable interface, and `DatagramRequestHandler.wfile` supports the *io.BufferedIOBase* writable interface.

Changed in version 3.6: `StreamRequestHandler.wfile` also supports the *io.BufferedIOBase* writable interface.

21.21.4 Examples

`socketserver.TCPServer` Example

This is the server side:

```
import socketserver

class MyTCPHandler(socketserver.BaseRequestHandler):
    """
    The request handler class for our server.

    It is instantiated once per connection to the server, and must
    override the handle() method to implement communication to the
    client.
    """
```

```python
    def handle(self):
        # self.request is the TCP socket connected to the client
        self.data = self.request.recv(1024).strip()
        print("{} wrote:".format(self.client_address[0]))
        print(self.data)
        # just send back the same data, but upper-cased
        self.request.sendall(self.data.upper())

if __name__ == "__main__":
    HOST, PORT = "localhost", 9999

    # Create the server, binding to localhost on port 9999
    with socketserver.TCPServer((HOST, PORT), MyTCPHandler) as server:
        # Activate the server; this will keep running until you
        # interrupt the program with Ctrl-C
        server.serve_forever()
```

An alternative request handler class that makes use of streams (file-like objects that simplify communication by providing the standard file interface):

```python
class MyTCPHandler(socketserver.StreamRequestHandler):

    def handle(self):
        # self.rfile is a file-like object created by the handler;
        # we can now use e.g. readline() instead of raw recv() calls
        self.data = self.rfile.readline().strip()
        print("{} wrote:".format(self.client_address[0]))
        print(self.data)
        # Likewise, self.wfile is a file-like object used to write back
        # to the client
        self.wfile.write(self.data.upper())
```

The difference is that the `readline()` call in the second handler will call `recv()` multiple times until it encounters a newline character, while the single `recv()` call in the first handler will just return what has been sent from the client in one `sendall()` call.

This is the client side:

```python
import socket
import sys

HOST, PORT = "localhost", 9999
data = " ".join(sys.argv[1:])

# Create a socket (SOCK_STREAM means a TCP socket)
with socket.socket(socket.AF_INET, socket.SOCK_STREAM) as sock:
    # Connect to server and send data
    sock.connect((HOST, PORT))
    sock.sendall(bytes(data + "\n", "utf-8"))

    # Receive data from the server and shut down
    received = str(sock.recv(1024), "utf-8")

print("Sent:     {}".format(data))
print("Received: {}".format(received))
```

The output of the example should look something like this:

Server:

```
$ python TCPServer.py
127.0.0.1 wrote:
b'hello world with TCP'
127.0.0.1 wrote:
b'python is nice'
```

Client:

```
$ python TCPClient.py hello world with TCP
Sent:     hello world with TCP
Received: HELLO WORLD WITH TCP
$ python TCPClient.py python is nice
Sent:     python is nice
Received: PYTHON IS NICE
```

socketserver.UDPServer Example

This is the server side:

```python
import socketserver

class MyUDPHandler(socketserver.BaseRequestHandler):
    """
    This class works similar to the TCP handler class, except that
    self.request consists of a pair of data and client socket, and since
    there is no connection the client address must be given explicitly
    when sending data back via sendto().
    """

    def handle(self):
        data = self.request[0].strip()
        socket = self.request[1]
        print("{} wrote:".format(self.client_address[0]))
        print(data)
        socket.sendto(data.upper(), self.client_address)

if __name__ == "__main__":
    HOST, PORT = "localhost", 9999
    with socketserver.UDPServer((HOST, PORT), MyUDPHandler) as server:
        server.serve_forever()
```

This is the client side:

```python
import socket
import sys

HOST, PORT = "localhost", 9999
data = " ".join(sys.argv[1:])

# SOCK_DGRAM is the socket type to use for UDP sockets
sock = socket.socket(socket.AF_INET, socket.SOCK_DGRAM)

# As you can see, there is no connect() call; UDP has no connections.
# Instead, data is directly sent to the recipient via sendto().
sock.sendto(bytes(data + "\n", "utf-8"), (HOST, PORT))
received = str(sock.recv(1024), "utf-8")
```

```
print("Sent:     {}".format(data))
print("Received: {}".format(received))
```

The output of the example should look exactly like for the TCP server example.

Asynchronous Mixins

To build asynchronous handlers, use the *ThreadingMixIn* and *ForkingMixIn* classes.

An example for the *ThreadingMixIn* class:

```
import socket
import threading
import socketserver

class ThreadedTCPRequestHandler(socketserver.BaseRequestHandler):

    def handle(self):
        data = str(self.request.recv(1024), 'ascii')
        cur_thread = threading.current_thread()
        response = bytes("{}: {}".format(cur_thread.name, data), 'ascii')
        self.request.sendall(response)

class ThreadedTCPServer(socketserver.ThreadingMixIn, socketserver.TCPServer):
    pass

def client(ip, port, message):
    with socket.socket(socket.AF_INET, socket.SOCK_STREAM) as sock:
        sock.connect((ip, port))
        sock.sendall(bytes(message, 'ascii'))
        response = str(sock.recv(1024), 'ascii')
        print("Received: {}".format(response))

if __name__ == "__main__":
    # Port 0 means to select an arbitrary unused port
    HOST, PORT = "localhost", 0

    server = ThreadedTCPServer((HOST, PORT), ThreadedTCPRequestHandler)
    with server:
        ip, port = server.server_address

        # Start a thread with the server -- that thread will then start one
        # more thread for each request
        server_thread = threading.Thread(target=server.serve_forever)
        # Exit the server thread when the main thread terminates
        server_thread.daemon = True
        server_thread.start()
        print("Server loop running in thread:", server_thread.name)

        client(ip, port, "Hello World 1")
        client(ip, port, "Hello World 2")
        client(ip, port, "Hello World 3")

        server.shutdown()
```

The output of the example should look something like this:

```
$ python ThreadedTCPServer.py
Server loop running in thread: Thread-1
Received: Thread-2: Hello World 1
Received: Thread-3: Hello World 2
Received: Thread-4: Hello World 3
```

The *ForkingMixIn* class is used in the same way, except that the server will spawn a new process for each request. Available only on POSIX platforms that support *fork()*.

21.22 `http.server` — HTTP servers

Source code: Lib/http/server.py

This module defines classes for implementing HTTP servers (Web servers).

One class, *HTTPServer*, is a *socketserver.TCPServer* subclass. It creates and listens at the HTTP socket, dispatching the requests to a handler. Code to create and run the server looks like this:

```
def run(server_class=HTTPServer, handler_class=BaseHTTPRequestHandler):
    server_address = ('', 8000)
    httpd = server_class(server_address, handler_class)
    httpd.serve_forever()
```

class http.server.HTTPServer(*server_address*, *RequestHandlerClass*)

    This class builds on the *TCPServer* class by storing the server address as instance variables named **server_name** and **server_port**. The server is accessible by the handler, typically through the handler's **server** instance variable.

The *HTTPServer* must be given a *RequestHandlerClass* on instantiation, of which this module provides three different variants:

class http.server.BaseHTTPRequestHandler(*request*, *client_address*, *server*)

    This class is used to handle the HTTP requests that arrive at the server. By itself, it cannot respond to any actual HTTP requests; it must be subclassed to handle each request method (e.g. GET or POST). *BaseHTTPRequestHandler* provides a number of class and instance variables, and methods for use by subclasses.

    The handler will parse the request and the headers, then call a method specific to the request type. The method name is constructed from the request. For example, for the request method SPAM, the do_SPAM() method will be called with no arguments. All of the relevant information is stored in instance variables of the handler. Subclasses should not need to override or extend the __init__() method.

    BaseHTTPRequestHandler has the following instance variables:

    client_address

        Contains a tuple of the form (host, port) referring to the client's address.

    server

        Contains the server instance.

    close_connection

        Boolean that should be set before *handle_one_request()* returns, indicating if another request may be expected, or if the connection should be shut down.

requestline
> Contains the string representation of the HTTP request line. The terminating CRLF is stripped. This attribute should be set by *handle_one_request()*. If no valid request line was processed, it should be set to the empty string.

command
> Contains the command (request type). For example, `'GET'`.

path
> Contains the request path.

request_version
> Contains the version string from the request. For example, `'HTTP/1.0'`.

headers
> Holds an instance of the class specified by the *MessageClass* class variable. This instance parses and manages the headers in the HTTP request. The `parse_headers()` function from *http.client* is used to parse the headers and it requires that the HTTP request provide a valid RFC 2822 style header.

rfile
> An *io.BufferedIOBase* input stream, ready to read from the start of the optional input data.

wfile
> Contains the output stream for writing a response back to the client. Proper adherence to the HTTP protocol must be used when writing to this stream in order to achieve successful interoperation with HTTP clients.
>
> Changed in version 3.6: This is an *io.BufferedIOBase* stream.

BaseHTTPRequestHandler has the following attributes:

server_version
> Specifies the server software version. You may want to override this. The format is multiple whitespace-separated strings, where each string is of the form name[/version]. For example, `'BaseHTTP/0.2'`.

sys_version
> Contains the Python system version, in a form usable by the *version_string* method and the *server_version* class variable. For example, `'Python/1.4'`.

error_message_format
> Specifies a format string that should be used by *send_error()* method for building an error response to the client. The string is filled by default with variables from *responses* based on the status code that passed to *send_error()*.

error_content_type
> Specifies the Content-Type HTTP header of error responses sent to the client. The default value is `'text/html'`.

protocol_version
> This specifies the HTTP protocol version used in responses. If set to `'HTTP/1.1'`, the server will permit HTTP persistent connections; however, your server *must* then include an accurate Content-Length header (using *send_header()*) in all of its responses to clients. For backwards compatibility, the setting defaults to `'HTTP/1.0'`.

MessageClass
> Specifies an *email.message.Message*-like class to parse HTTP headers. Typically, this is not overridden, and it defaults to `http.client.HTTPMessage`.

responses
> This attribute contains a mapping of error code integers to two-element tuples containing a short and long message. For example, `{code: (shortmessage, longmessage)}`. The *shortmessage* is

usually used as the *message* key in an error response, and *longmessage* as the *explain* key. It is used by `send_response_only()` and `send_error()` methods.

A `BaseHTTPRequestHandler` instance has the following methods:

handle()
    Calls `handle_one_request()` once (or, if persistent connections are enabled, multiple times) to handle incoming HTTP requests. You should never need to override it; instead, implement appropriate `do_*()` methods.

handle_one_request()
    This method will parse and dispatch the request to the appropriate `do_*()` method. You should never need to override it.

handle_expect_100()
    When a HTTP/1.1 compliant server receives an `Expect: 100-continue` request header it responds back with a `100 Continue` followed by `200 OK` headers. This method can be overridden to raise an error if the server does not want the client to continue. For e.g. server can chose to send `417 Expectation Failed` as a response header and `return False`.

    New in version 3.2.

send_error(code*, *message=None*, *explain=None***)**
    Sends and logs a complete error reply to the client. The numeric *code* specifies the HTTP error code, with *message* as an optional, short, human readable description of the error. The *explain* argument can be used to provide more detailed information about the error; it will be formatted using the `error_message_format` attribute and emitted, after a complete set of headers, as the response body. The `responses` attribute holds the default values for *message* and *explain* that will be used if no value is provided; for unknown codes the default value for both is the string ???. The body will be empty if the method is HEAD or the response code is one of the following: `1xx`, `204 No Content`, `205 Reset Content`, `304 Not Modified`.

    Changed in version 3.4: The error response includes a Content-Length header. Added the *explain* argument.

send_response(code*, *message=None***)**
    Adds a response header to the headers buffer and logs the accepted request. The HTTP response line is written to the internal buffer, followed by *Server* and *Date* headers. The values for these two headers are picked up from the `version_string()` and `date_time_string()` methods, respectively. If the server does not intend to send any other headers using the `send_header()` method, then `send_response()` should be followed by an `end_headers()` call.

    Changed in version 3.3: Headers are stored to an internal buffer and `end_headers()` needs to be called explicitly.

send_header(keyword*, *value***)**
    Adds the HTTP header to an internal buffer which will be written to the output stream when either `end_headers()` or `flush_headers()` is invoked. *keyword* should specify the header keyword, with *value* specifying its value. Note that, after the send_header calls are done, `end_headers()` MUST BE called in order to complete the operation.

    Changed in version 3.2: Headers are stored in an internal buffer.

send_response_only(code*, *message=None***)**
    Sends the response header only, used for the purposes when `100 Continue` response is sent by the server to the client. The headers not buffered and sent directly the output stream.If the *message* is not specified, the HTTP message corresponding the response *code* is sent.

    New in version 3.2.

end_headers()
    Adds a blank line (indicating the end of the HTTP headers in the response) to the headers buffer

and calls *flush_headers()*.

Changed in version 3.2: The buffered headers are written to the output stream.

flush_headers()
Finally send the headers to the output stream and flush the internal headers buffer.

New in version 3.3.

log_request(*code='-'*, *size='-'*)
Logs an accepted (successful) request. *code* should specify the numeric HTTP code associated with the response. If a size of the response is available, then it should be passed as the *size* parameter.

log_error(*...*)
Logs an error when a request cannot be fulfilled. By default, it passes the message to *log_message()*, so it takes the same arguments (*format* and additional values).

log_message(*format*, *...*)
Logs an arbitrary message to `sys.stderr`. This is typically overridden to create custom error logging mechanisms. The *format* argument is a standard printf-style format string, where the additional arguments to *log_message()* are applied as inputs to the formatting. The client ip address and current date and time are prefixed to every message logged.

version_string()
Returns the server software's version string. This is a combination of the *server_version* and *sys_version* attributes.

date_time_string(*timestamp=None*)
Returns the date and time given by *timestamp* (which must be `None` or in the format returned by *time.time()*), formatted for a message header. If *timestamp* is omitted, it uses the current date and time.

The result looks like `'Sun, 06 Nov 1994 08:49:37 GMT'`.

log_date_time_string()
Returns the current date and time, formatted for logging.

address_string()
Returns the client address.

Changed in version 3.3: Previously, a name lookup was performed. To avoid name resolution delays, it now always returns the IP address.

class http.server.SimpleHTTPRequestHandler(*request*, *client_address*, *server*)
This class serves files from the current directory and below, directly mapping the directory structure to HTTP requests.

A lot of the work, such as parsing the request, is done by the base class *BaseHTTPRequestHandler*. This class implements the *do_GET()* and *do_HEAD()* functions.

The following are defined as class-level attributes of *SimpleHTTPRequestHandler*:

server_version
This will be `"SimpleHTTP/"` + `__version__`, where `__version__` is defined at the module level.

extensions_map
A dictionary mapping suffixes into MIME types. The default is signified by an empty string, and is considered to be `application/octet-stream`. The mapping is used case-insensitively, and so should contain only lower-cased keys.

The *SimpleHTTPRequestHandler* class defines the following methods:

do_HEAD()
> This method serves the `'HEAD'` request type: it sends the headers it would send for the equivalent GET request. See the *do_GET()* method for a more complete explanation of the possible headers.

do_GET()
> The request is mapped to a local file by interpreting the request as a path relative to the current working directory.
>
> If the request was mapped to a directory, the directory is checked for a file named `index.html` or `index.htm` (in that order). If found, the file's contents are returned; otherwise a directory listing is generated by calling the `list_directory()` method. This method uses *os.listdir()* to scan the directory, and returns a 404 error response if the *listdir()* fails.
>
> If the request was mapped to a file, it is opened and the contents are returned. Any *OSError* exception in opening the requested file is mapped to a 404, `'File not found'` error. Otherwise, the content type is guessed by calling the `guess_type()` method, which in turn uses the *extensions_map* variable.
>
> A `'Content-type:'` header with the guessed content type is output, followed by a `'Content-Length:'` header with the file's size and a `'Last-Modified:'` header with the file's modification time.
>
> Then follows a blank line signifying the end of the headers, and then the contents of the file are output. If the file's MIME type starts with `text/` the file is opened in text mode; otherwise binary mode is used.
>
> For example usage, see the implementation of the *test()* function invocation in the *http.server* module.

The *SimpleHTTPRequestHandler* class can be used in the following manner in order to create a very basic webserver serving files relative to the current directory:

```python
import http.server
import socketserver

PORT = 8000

Handler = http.server.SimpleHTTPRequestHandler

with socketserver.TCPServer(("", PORT), Handler) as httpd:
    print("serving at port", PORT)
    httpd.serve_forever()
```

http.server can also be invoked directly using the `-m` switch of the interpreter with a `port number` argument. Similar to the previous example, this serves files relative to the current directory:

```
python -m http.server 8000
```

By default, server binds itself to all interfaces. The option `-b/--bind` specifies a specific address to which it should bind. For example, the following command causes the server to bind to localhost only:

```
python -m http.server 8000 --bind 127.0.0.1
```

New in version 3.4: `--bind` argument was introduced.

class http.server.CGIHTTPRequestHandler(*request*, *client_address*, *server*)
> This class is used to serve either files or output of CGI scripts from the current directory and below. Note that mapping HTTP hierarchic structure to local directory structure is exactly as in *SimpleHTTPRequestHandler*.

Note: CGI scripts run by the *CGIHTTPRequestHandler* class cannot execute redirects (HTTP code 302), because code 200 (script output follows) is sent prior to execution of the CGI script. This pre-empts the status code.

The class will however, run the CGI script, instead of serving it as a file, if it guesses it to be a CGI script. Only directory-based CGI are used — the other common server configuration is to treat special extensions as denoting CGI scripts.

The `do_GET()` and `do_HEAD()` functions are modified to run CGI scripts and serve the output, instead of serving files, if the request leads to somewhere below the `cgi_directories` path.

The *CGIHTTPRequestHandler* defines the following data member:

cgi_directories
    This defaults to `['/cgi-bin', '/htbin']` and describes directories to treat as containing CGI scripts.

The *CGIHTTPRequestHandler* defines the following method:

do_POST()
    This method serves the `'POST'` request type, only allowed for CGI scripts. Error 501, "Can only POST to CGI scripts", is output when trying to POST to a non-CGI url.

Note that CGI scripts will be run with UID of user nobody, for security reasons. Problems with the CGI script will be translated to error 403.

CGIHTTPRequestHandler can be enabled in the command line by passing the `--cgi` option:

```
python -m http.server --cgi 8000
```

21.23 `http.cookies` — HTTP state management

Source code: Lib/http/cookies.py

The *http.cookies* module defines classes for abstracting the concept of cookies, an HTTP state management mechanism. It supports both simple string-only cookies, and provides an abstraction for having any serializable data-type as cookie value.

The module formerly strictly applied the parsing rules described in the RFC 2109 and RFC 2068 specifications. It has since been discovered that MSIE 3.0x doesn't follow the character rules outlined in those specs and also many current day browsers and servers have relaxed parsing rules when comes to Cookie handling. As a result, the parsing rules used are a bit less strict.

The character set, *string.ascii_letters*, *string.digits* and `!#$%&'*+-.^_`|~:` denote the set of valid characters allowed by this module in Cookie name (as *key*).

Changed in version 3.3: Allowed ':' as a valid Cookie name character.

Note: On encountering an invalid cookie, *CookieError* is raised, so if your cookie data comes from a browser you should always prepare for invalid data and catch *CookieError* on parsing.

exception http.cookies.CookieError
    Exception failing because of RFC 2109 invalidity: incorrect attributes, incorrect *Set-Cookie* header, etc.

class http.cookies.BaseCookie([*input*]**)**
   This class is a dictionary-like object whose keys are strings and whose values are *Morsel* instances. Note that upon setting a key to a value, the value is first converted to a *Morsel* containing the key and the value.

   If *input* is given, it is passed to the *load()* method.

class http.cookies.SimpleCookie([*input*]**)**
   This class derives from *BaseCookie* and overrides `value_decode()` and `value_encode()` to be the identity and *str()* respectively.

See also:

Module *http.cookiejar* HTTP cookie handling for web *clients*. The *http.cookiejar* and *http.cookies* modules do not depend on each other.

RFC 2109 - **HTTP State Management Mechanism** This is the state management specification implemented by this module.

21.23.1 Cookie Objects

BaseCookie.value_decode(*val***)**
   Return a decoded value from a string representation. Return value can be any type. This method does nothing in *BaseCookie* — it exists so it can be overridden.

BaseCookie.value_encode(*val***)**
   Return an encoded value. *val* can be any type, but return value must be a string. This method does nothing in *BaseCookie* — it exists so it can be overridden.

   In general, it should be the case that *value_encode()* and *value_decode()* are inverses on the range of *value_decode*.

BaseCookie.output(*attrs=None, header='Set-Cookie:', sep='\r\n'***)**
   Return a string representation suitable to be sent as HTTP headers. *attrs* and *header* are sent to each *Morsel*'s *output()* method. *sep* is used to join the headers together, and is by default the combination `'\r\n'` (CRLF).

BaseCookie.js_output(*attrs=None***)**
   Return an embeddable JavaScript snippet, which, if run on a browser which supports JavaScript, will act the same as if the HTTP headers was sent.

   The meaning for *attrs* is the same as in *output()*.

BaseCookie.load(*rawdata***)**
   If *rawdata* is a string, parse it as an `HTTP_COOKIE` and add the values found there as *Morsel*s. If it is a dictionary, it is equivalent to:

```
for k, v in rawdata.items():
    cookie[k] = v
```

21.23.2 Morsel Objects

class http.cookies.Morsel
   Abstract a key/value pair, which has some RFC 2109 attributes.

   Morsels are dictionary-like objects, whose set of keys is constant — the valid RFC 2109 attributes, which are

   - expires

- path
- comment
- domain
- max-age
- secure
- version
- httponly

The attribute `httponly` specifies that the cookie is only transferred in HTTP requests, and is not accessible through JavaScript. This is intended to mitigate some forms of cross-site scripting.

The keys are case-insensitive and their default value is `''`.

Changed in version 3.5: `__eq__()` now takes *key* and *value* into account.

Morsel.value
The value of the cookie.

Deprecated since version 3.5: assigning to `value`; use `set()` instead.

Morsel.coded_value
The encoded value of the cookie — this is what should be sent.

Deprecated since version 3.5: assigning to `coded_value`; use `set()` instead.

Morsel.key
The name of the cookie.

Deprecated since version 3.5: assigning to `key`; use `set()` instead.

Morsel.set(*key, value, coded_value*)
Set the *key*, *value* and *coded_value* attributes.

Deprecated since version 3.5: The undocumented *LegalChars* parameter is ignored and will be removed in a future version.

Morsel.isReservedKey(*K*)
Whether *K* is a member of the set of keys of a *Morsel*.

Morsel.output(*attrs=None, header='Set-Cookie:'*)
Return a string representation of the Morsel, suitable to be sent as an HTTP header. By default, all the attributes are included, unless *attrs* is given, in which case it should be a list of attributes to use. *header* is by default `"Set-Cookie:"`.

Morsel.js_output(*attrs=None*)
Return an embeddable JavaScript snippet, which, if run on a browser which supports JavaScript, will act the same as if the HTTP header was sent.

The meaning for *attrs* is the same as in `output()`.

Morsel.OutputString(*attrs=None*)
Return a string representing the Morsel, without any surrounding HTTP or JavaScript.

The meaning for *attrs* is the same as in `output()`.

Morsel.update(*values*)
Update the values in the Morsel dictionary with the values in the dictionary *values*. Raise an error if any of the keys in the *values* dict is not a valid RFC 2109 attribute.

Changed in version 3.5: an error is raised for invalid keys.

Morsel.copy(*value*)
    Return a shallow copy of the Morsel object.

    Changed in version 3.5: return a Morsel object instead of a dict.

Morsel.setdefault(*key, value=None*)
    Raise an error if key is not a valid RFC 2109 attribute, otherwise behave the same as *dict.setdefault()*.

21.23.3 Example

The following example demonstrates how to use the *http.cookies* module.

```
>>> from http import cookies
>>> C = cookies.SimpleCookie()
>>> C["fig"] = "newton"
>>> C["sugar"] = "wafer"
>>> print(C) # generate HTTP headers
Set-Cookie: fig=newton
Set-Cookie: sugar=wafer
>>> print(C.output()) # same thing
Set-Cookie: fig=newton
Set-Cookie: sugar=wafer
>>> C = cookies.SimpleCookie()
>>> C["rocky"] = "road"
>>> C["rocky"]["path"] = "/cookie"
>>> print(C.output(header="Cookie:"))
Cookie: rocky=road; Path=/cookie
>>> print(C.output(attrs=[], header="Cookie:"))
Cookie: rocky=road
>>> C = cookies.SimpleCookie()
>>> C.load("chips=ahoy; vienna=finger") # load from a string (HTTP header)
>>> print(C)
Set-Cookie: chips=ahoy
Set-Cookie: vienna=finger
>>> C = cookies.SimpleCookie()
>>> C.load('keebler="E=everybody; L=\\"Loves\\"; fudge=\\012;";')
>>> print(C)
Set-Cookie: keebler="E=everybody; L=\"Loves\"; fudge=\012;"
>>> C = cookies.SimpleCookie()
>>> C["oreo"] = "doublestuff"
>>> C["oreo"]["path"] = "/"
>>> print(C)
Set-Cookie: oreo=doublestuff; Path=/
>>> C = cookies.SimpleCookie()
>>> C["twix"] = "none for you"
>>> C["twix"].value
'none for you'
>>> C = cookies.SimpleCookie()
>>> C["number"] = 7 # equivalent to C["number"] = str(7)
>>> C["string"] = "seven"
>>> C["number"].value
'7'
>>> C["string"].value
'seven'
>>> print(C)
Set-Cookie: number=7
Set-Cookie: string=seven
```

21.24 `http.cookiejar` — Cookie handling for HTTP clients

Source code: Lib/http/cookiejar.py

The `http.cookiejar` module defines classes for automatic handling of HTTP cookies. It is useful for accessing web sites that require small pieces of data – *cookies* – to be set on the client machine by an HTTP response from a web server, and then returned to the server in later HTTP requests.

Both the regular Netscape cookie protocol and the protocol defined by RFC 2965 are handled. RFC 2965 handling is switched off by default. RFC 2109 cookies are parsed as Netscape cookies and subsequently treated either as Netscape or RFC 2965 cookies according to the 'policy' in effect. Note that the great majority of cookies on the Internet are Netscape cookies. `http.cookiejar` attempts to follow the de-facto Netscape cookie protocol (which differs substantially from that set out in the original Netscape specification), including taking note of the `max-age` and `port` cookie-attributes introduced with RFC 2965.

Note: The various named parameters found in `Set-Cookie` and `Set-Cookie2` headers (eg. `domain` and `expires`) are conventionally referred to as *attributes*. To distinguish them from Python attributes, the documentation for this module uses the term *cookie-attribute* instead.

The module defines the following exception:

exception `http.cookiejar.LoadError`

Instances of `FileCookieJar` raise this exception on failure to load cookies from a file. `LoadError` is a subclass of `OSError`.

Changed in version 3.3: LoadError was made a subclass of `OSError` instead of `IOError`.

The following classes are provided:

class `http.cookiejar.CookieJar`(*policy=None*)

policy is an object implementing the `CookiePolicy` interface.

The `CookieJar` class stores HTTP cookies. It extracts cookies from HTTP requests, and returns them in HTTP responses. `CookieJar` instances automatically expire contained cookies when necessary. Subclasses are also responsible for storing and retrieving cookies from a file or database.

class `http.cookiejar.FileCookieJar`(*filename, delayload=None, policy=None*)

policy is an object implementing the `CookiePolicy` interface. For the other arguments, see the documentation for the corresponding attributes.

A `CookieJar` which can load cookies from, and perhaps save cookies to, a file on disk. Cookies are **NOT** loaded from the named file until either the `load()` or `revert()` method is called. Subclasses of this class are documented in section *FileCookieJar subclasses and co-operation with web browsers*.

class `http.cookiejar.CookiePolicy`

This class is responsible for deciding whether each cookie should be accepted from / returned to the server.

class `http.cookiejar.DefaultCookiePolicy`(*blocked_domains=None, allowed_domains=None, netscape=True, rfc2965=False, rfc2109_as_netscape=None, hide_cookie2=False, strict_domain=False, strict_rfc2965_unverifiable=True, strict_ns_unverifiable=False, strict_ns_domain=DefaultCookiePolicy.DomainLiberal, strict_ns_set_initial_dollar=False, strict_ns_set_path=False*)

Constructor arguments should be passed as keyword arguments only. *blocked_domains* is a sequence

of domain names that we never accept cookies from, nor return cookies to. *allowed_domains* if not
None, this is a sequence of the only domains for which we accept and return cookies. For all other
arguments, see the documentation for *CookiePolicy* and *DefaultCookiePolicy* objects.

DefaultCookiePolicy implements the standard accept / reject rules for Netscape and RFC 2965 cookies. By default, RFC 2109 cookies (ie. cookies received in a *Set-Cookie* header with a version cookie-attribute of 1) are treated according to the RFC 2965 rules. However, if RFC 2965 handling is turned off or *rfc2109_as_netscape* is True, RFC 2109 cookies are 'downgraded' by the *CookieJar* instance to Netscape cookies, by setting the **version** attribute of the *Cookie* instance to 0. *DefaultCookiePolicy* also provides some parameters to allow some fine-tuning of policy.

class http.cookiejar.Cookie
This class represents Netscape, RFC 2109 and RFC 2965 cookies. It is not expected that users of *http.cookiejar* construct their own *Cookie* instances. Instead, if necessary, call **make_cookies()** on a *CookieJar* instance.

See also:

Module *urllib.request* URL opening with automatic cookie handling.

Module *http.cookies* HTTP cookie classes, principally useful for server-side code. The *http.cookiejar* and *http.cookies* modules do not depend on each other.

https://curl.haxx.se/rfc/cookie_spec.html The specification of the original Netscape cookie protocol. Though this is still the dominant protocol, the 'Netscape cookie protocol' implemented by all the major browsers (and *http.cookiejar*) only bears a passing resemblance to the one sketched out in cookie_spec.html.

RFC 2109 - **HTTP State Management Mechanism** Obsoleted by RFC 2965. Uses *Set-Cookie* with version=1.

RFC 2965 - **HTTP State Management Mechanism** The Netscape protocol with the bugs fixed. Uses *Set-Cookie2* in place of *Set-Cookie*. Not widely used.

http://kristol.org/cookie/errata.html Unfinished errata to RFC 2965.

RFC 2964 - Use of HTTP State Management

21.24.1 CookieJar and FileCookieJar Objects

CookieJar objects support the *iterator* protocol for iterating over contained *Cookie* objects.

CookieJar has the following methods:

CookieJar.add_cookie_header(*request*)
Add correct *Cookie* header to *request*.

If policy allows (ie. the **rfc2965** and **hide_cookie2** attributes of the *CookieJar*'s *CookiePolicy* instance are true and false respectively), the *Cookie2* header is also added when appropriate.

The *request* object (usually a urllib.request..Request instance) must support the methods **get_full_url()**, **get_host()**, **get_type()**, **unverifiable()**, **has_header()**, **get_header()**, **header_items()**, **add_unredirected_header()** and **origin_req_host** attribute as documented by *urllib.request*.

Changed in version 3.3: *request* object needs **origin_req_host** attribute. Dependency on a deprecated method **get_origin_req_host()** has been removed.

CookieJar.extract_cookies(*response, request*)
Extract cookies from HTTP *response* and store them in the *CookieJar*, where allowed by policy.

The *CookieJar* will look for allowable *Set-Cookie* and *Set-Cookie2* headers in the *response* argument, and store cookies as appropriate (subject to the *CookiePolicy.set_ok()* method's approval).

The *response* object (usually the result of a call to `urllib.request.urlopen()`, or similar) should support an `info()` method, which returns an *email.message.Message* instance.

The *request* object (usually a *urllib.request.Request* instance) must support the methods `get_full_url()`, `get_host()`, `unverifiable()`, and `origin_req_host` attribute, as documented by *urllib.request*. The request is used to set default values for cookie-attributes as well as for checking that the cookie is allowed to be set.

Changed in version 3.3: *request* object needs `origin_req_host` attribute. Dependency on a deprecated method `get_origin_req_host()` has been removed.

CookieJar.set_policy(*policy*)
   Set the *CookiePolicy* instance to be used.

CookieJar.make_cookies(*response, request*)
   Return sequence of *Cookie* objects extracted from *response* object.

   See the documentation for *extract_cookies()* for the interfaces required of the *response* and *request* arguments.

CookieJar.set_cookie_if_ok(*cookie, request*)
   Set a *Cookie* if policy says it's OK to do so.

CookieJar.set_cookie(*cookie*)
   Set a *Cookie*, without checking with policy to see whether or not it should be set.

CookieJar.clear(*[domain[, path[, name]]]*)
   Clear some cookies.

   If invoked without arguments, clear all cookies. If given a single argument, only cookies belonging to that *domain* will be removed. If given two arguments, cookies belonging to the specified *domain* and URL *path* are removed. If given three arguments, then the cookie with the specified *domain*, *path* and *name* is removed.

   Raises *KeyError* if no matching cookie exists.

CookieJar.clear_session_cookies()
   Discard all session cookies.

   Discards all contained cookies that have a true `discard` attribute (usually because they had either no `max-age` or `expires` cookie-attribute, or an explicit `discard` cookie-attribute). For interactive browsers, the end of a session usually corresponds to closing the browser window.

   Note that the `save()` method won't save session cookies anyway, unless you ask otherwise by passing a true *ignore_discard* argument.

FileCookieJar implements the following additional methods:

FileCookieJar.save(*filename=None, ignore_discard=False, ignore_expires=False*)
   Save cookies to a file.

   This base class raises *NotImplementedError*. Subclasses may leave this method unimplemented.

   filename is the name of file in which to save cookies. If *filename* is not specified, `self.filename` is used (whose default is the value passed to the constructor, if any); if `self.filename` is *None*, *ValueError* is raised.

   ignore_discard: save even cookies set to be discarded. *ignore_expires*: save even cookies that have expired

   The file is overwritten if it already exists, thus wiping all the cookies it contains. Saved cookies can be restored later using the *load()* or *revert()* methods.

FileCookieJar.load(*filename=None, ignore_discard=False, ignore_expires=False*)
   Load cookies from a file.

Old cookies are kept unless overwritten by newly loaded ones.

Arguments are as for *save()*.

The named file must be in the format understood by the class, or *LoadError* will be raised. Also, *OSError* may be raised, for example if the file does not exist.

Changed in version 3.3: *IOError* used to be raised, it is now an alias of *OSError*.

FileCookieJar.revert(*filename=None, ignore_discard=False, ignore_expires=False*)
    Clear all cookies and reload cookies from a saved file.

    revert() can raise the same exceptions as *load()*. If there is a failure, the object's state will not be altered.

FileCookieJar instances have the following public attributes:

FileCookieJar.filename
    Filename of default file in which to keep cookies. This attribute may be assigned to.

FileCookieJar.delayload
    If true, load cookies lazily from disk. This attribute should not be assigned to. This is only a hint, since this only affects performance, not behaviour (unless the cookies on disk are changing). A *CookieJar* object may ignore it. None of the *FileCookieJar* classes included in the standard library lazily loads cookies.

21.24.2 FileCookieJar subclasses and co-operation with web browsers

The following *CookieJar* subclasses are provided for reading and writing.

class http.cookiejar.MozillaCookieJar(*filename, delayload=None, policy=None*)
    A *FileCookieJar* that can load from and save cookies to disk in the Mozilla `cookies.txt` file format (which is also used by the Lynx and Netscape browsers).

Note: This loses information about RFC 2965 cookies, and also about newer or non-standard cookie-attributes such as `port`.

Warning: Back up your cookies before saving if you have cookies whose loss / corruption would be inconvenient (there are some subtleties which may lead to slight changes in the file over a load / save round-trip).

Also note that cookies saved while Mozilla is running will get clobbered by Mozilla.

class http.cookiejar.LWPCookieJar(*filename, delayload=None, policy=None*)
    A *FileCookieJar* that can load from and save cookies to disk in format compatible with the libwww-perl library's `Set-Cookie3` file format. This is convenient if you want to store cookies in a human-readable file.

21.24.3 CookiePolicy Objects

Objects implementing the *CookiePolicy* interface have the following methods:

CookiePolicy.set_ok(*cookie, request*)
    Return boolean value indicating whether cookie should be accepted from server.

    cookie is a *Cookie* instance. *request* is an object implementing the interface defined by the documentation for *CookieJar.extract_cookies()*.

CookiePolicy.**return_ok**(*cookie*, *request*)
: Return boolean value indicating whether cookie should be returned to server.

    cookie is a *Cookie* instance. *request* is an object implementing the interface defined by the documentation for *CookieJar.add_cookie_header()*.

CookiePolicy.**domain_return_ok**(*domain*, *request*)
: Return false if cookies should not be returned, given cookie domain.

    This method is an optimization. It removes the need for checking every cookie with a particular domain (which might involve reading many files). Returning true from *domain_return_ok()* and *path_return_ok()* leaves all the work to *return_ok()*.

    If *domain_return_ok()* returns true for the cookie domain, *path_return_ok()* is called for the cookie path. Otherwise, *path_return_ok()* and *return_ok()* are never called for that cookie domain. If *path_return_ok()* returns true, *return_ok()* is called with the *Cookie* object itself for a full check. Otherwise, *return_ok()* is never called for that cookie path.

    Note that *domain_return_ok()* is called for every *cookie* domain, not just for the *request* domain. For example, the function might be called with both ".example.com" and "www.example.com" if the request domain is "www.example.com". The same goes for *path_return_ok()*.

    The *request* argument is as documented for *return_ok()*.

CookiePolicy.**path_return_ok**(*path*, *request*)
: Return false if cookies should not be returned, given cookie path.

    See the documentation for *domain_return_ok()*.

In addition to implementing the methods above, implementations of the *CookiePolicy* interface must also supply the following attributes, indicating which protocols should be used, and how. All of these attributes may be assigned to.

CookiePolicy.**netscape**
: Implement Netscape protocol.

CookiePolicy.**rfc2965**
: Implement RFC 2965 protocol.

CookiePolicy.**hide_cookie2**
: Don't add *Cookie2* header to requests (the presence of this header indicates to the server that we understand RFC 2965 cookies).

The most useful way to define a *CookiePolicy* class is by subclassing from *DefaultCookiePolicy* and overriding some or all of the methods above. *CookiePolicy* itself may be used as a 'null policy' to allow setting and receiving any and all cookies (this is unlikely to be useful).

21.24.4 DefaultCookiePolicy Objects

Implements the standard rules for accepting and returning cookies.

Both RFC 2965 and Netscape cookies are covered. RFC 2965 handling is switched off by default.

The easiest way to provide your own policy is to override this class and call its methods in your overridden implementations before adding your own additional checks:

```
import http.cookiejar
class MyCookiePolicy(http.cookiejar.DefaultCookiePolicy):
    def set_ok(self, cookie, request):
        if not http.cookiejar.DefaultCookiePolicy.set_ok(self, cookie, request):
            return False
        if i_dont_want_to_store_this_cookie(cookie):
```

The Python Library Reference, Release 3.6.4

```
        return False
    return True
```

In addition to the features required to implement the *CookiePolicy* interface, this class allows you to block and allow domains from setting and receiving cookies. There are also some strictness switches that allow you to tighten up the rather loose Netscape protocol rules a little bit (at the cost of blocking some benign cookies).

A domain blacklist and whitelist is provided (both off by default). Only domains not in the blacklist and present in the whitelist (if the whitelist is active) participate in cookie setting and returning. Use the *blocked_domains* constructor argument, and `blocked_domains()` and `set_blocked_domains()` methods (and the corresponding argument and methods for *allowed_domains*). If you set a whitelist, you can turn it off again by setting it to *None*.

Domains in block or allow lists that do not start with a dot must equal the cookie domain to be matched. For example, "example.com" matches a blacklist entry of "example.com", but "www.example.com" does not. Domains that do start with a dot are matched by more specific domains too. For example, both "www.example.com" and "www.coyote.example.com" match ".example.com" (but "example.com" itself does not). IP addresses are an exception, and must match exactly. For example, if blocked_domains contains "192.168.1.2" and ".168.1.2", 192.168.1.2 is blocked, but 193.168.1.2 is not.

DefaultCookiePolicy implements the following additional methods:

DefaultCookiePolicy.blocked_domains()
    Return the sequence of blocked domains (as a tuple).

DefaultCookiePolicy.set_blocked_domains(blocked_domains**)**
    Set the sequence of blocked domains.

DefaultCookiePolicy.is_blocked(domain**)**
    Return whether *domain* is on the blacklist for setting or receiving cookies.

DefaultCookiePolicy.allowed_domains()
    Return *None*, or the sequence of allowed domains (as a tuple).

DefaultCookiePolicy.set_allowed_domains(allowed_domains**)**
    Set the sequence of allowed domains, or *None*.

DefaultCookiePolicy.is_not_allowed(domain**)**
    Return whether *domain* is not on the whitelist for setting or receiving cookies.

DefaultCookiePolicy instances have the following attributes, which are all initialised from the constructor arguments of the same name, and which may all be assigned to.

DefaultCookiePolicy.rfc2109_as_netscape
    If true, request that the *CookieJar* instance downgrade RFC 2109 cookies (ie. cookies received in a *Set-Cookie* header with a version cookie-attribute of 1) to Netscape cookies by setting the version attribute of the *Cookie* instance to 0. The default value is *None*, in which case RFC 2109 cookies are downgraded if and only if RFC 2965 handling is turned off. Therefore, RFC 2109 cookies are downgraded by default.

General strictness switches:

DefaultCookiePolicy.strict_domain
    Don't allow sites to set two-component domains with country-code top-level domains like .co.uk, .gov.uk, .co.nz.etc. This is far from perfect and isn't guaranteed to work!

RFC 2965 protocol strictness switches:

DefaultCookiePolicy.strict_rfc2965_unverifiable
    Follow RFC 2965 rules on unverifiable transactions (usually, an unverifiable transaction is one resulting

from a redirect or a request for an image hosted on another site). If this is false, cookies are *never* blocked on the basis of verifiability

Netscape protocol strictness switches:

DefaultCookiePolicy.**strict_ns_unverifiable**
> Apply RFC 2965 rules on unverifiable transactions even to Netscape cookies.

DefaultCookiePolicy.**strict_ns_domain**
> Flags indicating how strict to be with domain-matching rules for Netscape cookies. See below for acceptable values.

DefaultCookiePolicy.**strict_ns_set_initial_dollar**
> Ignore cookies in Set-Cookie: headers that have names starting with '$'.

DefaultCookiePolicy.**strict_ns_set_path**
> Don't allow setting cookies whose path doesn't path-match request URI.

strict_ns_domain is a collection of flags. Its value is constructed by or-ing together (for example, DomainStrictNoDots|DomainStrictNonDomain means both flags are set).

DefaultCookiePolicy.**DomainStrictNoDots**
> When setting cookies, the 'host prefix' must not contain a dot (eg. www.foo.bar.com can't set a cookie for .bar.com, because www.foo contains a dot).

DefaultCookiePolicy.**DomainStrictNonDomain**
> Cookies that did not explicitly specify a domain cookie-attribute can only be returned to a domain equal to the domain that set the cookie (eg. spam.example.com won't be returned cookies from example.com that had no domain cookie-attribute).

DefaultCookiePolicy.**DomainRFC2965Match**
> When setting cookies, require a full RFC 2965 domain-match.

The following attributes are provided for convenience, and are the most useful combinations of the above flags:

DefaultCookiePolicy.**DomainLiberal**
> Equivalent to 0 (ie. all of the above Netscape domain strictness flags switched off).

DefaultCookiePolicy.**DomainStrict**
> Equivalent to DomainStrictNoDots|DomainStrictNonDomain.

21.24.5 Cookie Objects

Cookie instances have Python attributes roughly corresponding to the standard cookie-attributes specified in the various cookie standards. The correspondence is not one-to-one, because there are complicated rules for assigning default values, because the **max-age** and **expires** cookie-attributes contain equivalent information, and because RFC 2109 cookies may be 'downgraded' by *http.cookiejar* from version 1 to version 0 (Netscape) cookies.

Assignment to these attributes should not be necessary other than in rare circumstances in a *CookiePolicy* method. The class does not enforce internal consistency, so you should know what you're doing if you do that.

Cookie.**version**
> Integer or *None*. Netscape cookies have *version* 0. RFC 2965 and RFC 2109 cookies have a **version** cookie-attribute of 1. However, note that *http.cookiejar* may 'downgrade' RFC 2109 cookies to Netscape cookies, in which case *version* is 0.

Cookie.**name**
> Cookie name (a string).

Cookie.value
    Cookie value (a string), or `None`.

Cookie.port
    String representing a port or a set of ports (eg. '80', or '80,8080'), or `None`.

Cookie.path
    Cookie path (a string, eg. `'/acme/rocket_launchers'`).

Cookie.secure
    True if cookie should only be returned over a secure connection.

Cookie.expires
    Integer expiry date in seconds since epoch, or `None`. See also the `is_expired()` method.

Cookie.discard
    True if this is a session cookie.

Cookie.comment
    String comment from the server explaining the function of this cookie, or `None`.

Cookie.comment_url
    URL linking to a comment from the server explaining the function of this cookie, or `None`.

Cookie.rfc2109
    True if this cookie was received as an RFC 2109 cookie (ie. the cookie arrived in a `Set-Cookie` header, and the value of the Version cookie-attribute in that header was 1). This attribute is provided because `http.cookiejar` may 'downgrade' RFC 2109 cookies to Netscape cookies, in which case `version` is 0.

Cookie.port_specified
    True if a port or set of ports was explicitly specified by the server (in the `Set-Cookie` / `Set-Cookie2` header).

Cookie.domain_specified
    True if a domain was explicitly specified by the server.

Cookie.domain_initial_dot
    True if the domain explicitly specified by the server began with a dot (`'.'`).

Cookies may have additional non-standard cookie-attributes. These may be accessed using the following methods:

Cookie.has_nonstandard_attr(*name*)
    Return true if cookie has the named cookie-attribute.

Cookie.get_nonstandard_attr(*name*, *default=None*)
    If cookie has the named cookie-attribute, return its value. Otherwise, return *default*.

Cookie.set_nonstandard_attr(*name*, *value*)
    Set the value of the named cookie-attribute.

The `Cookie` class also defines the following method:

Cookie.is_expired(*now=None*)
    True if cookie has passed the time at which the server requested it should expire. If *now* is given (in seconds since the epoch), return whether the cookie has expired at the specified time.

21.24.6 Examples

The first example shows the most common usage of `http.cookiejar`:

```
import http.cookiejar, urllib.request
cj = http.cookiejar.CookieJar()
opener = urllib.request.build_opener(urllib.request.HTTPCookieProcessor(cj))
r = opener.open("http://example.com/")
```

This example illustrates how to open a URL using your Netscape, Mozilla, or Lynx cookies (assumes Unix/Netscape convention for location of the cookies file):

```
import os, http.cookiejar, urllib.request
cj = http.cookiejar.MozillaCookieJar()
cj.load(os.path.join(os.path.expanduser("~"), ".netscape", "cookies.txt"))
opener = urllib.request.build_opener(urllib.request.HTTPCookieProcessor(cj))
r = opener.open("http://example.com/")
```

The next example illustrates the use of *DefaultCookiePolicy*. Turn on RFC 2965 cookies, be more strict about domains when setting and returning Netscape cookies, and block some domains from setting cookies or having them returned:

```
import urllib.request
from http.cookiejar import CookieJar, DefaultCookiePolicy
policy = DefaultCookiePolicy(
    rfc2965=True, strict_ns_domain=Policy.DomainStrict,
    blocked_domains=["ads.net", ".ads.net"])
cj = CookieJar(policy)
opener = urllib.request.build_opener(urllib.request.HTTPCookieProcessor(cj))
r = opener.open("http://example.com/")
```

21.25 `xmlrpc` — XMLRPC server and client modules

XML-RPC is a Remote Procedure Call method that uses XML passed via HTTP as a transport. With it, a client can call methods with parameters on a remote server (the server is named by a URI) and get back structured data.

xmlrpc is a package that collects server and client modules implementing XML-RPC. The modules are:

- *xmlrpc.client*
- *xmlrpc.server*

21.26 `xmlrpc.client` — XML-RPC client access

Source code: Lib/xmlrpc/client.py

XML-RPC is a Remote Procedure Call method that uses XML passed via HTTP(S) as a transport. With it, a client can call methods with parameters on a remote server (the server is named by a URI) and get back structured data. This module supports writing XML-RPC client code; it handles all the details of translating between conformable Python objects and XML on the wire.

> **Warning:** The *xmlrpc.client* module is not secure against maliciously constructed data. If you need to parse untrusted or unauthenticated data see *XML vulnerabilities*.

Changed in version 3.5: For HTTPS URIs, *xmlrpc.client* now performs all the necessary certificate and hostname checks by default.

class xmlrpc.client.ServerProxy(*uri, transport=None, encoding=None, verbose=False, allow_none=False, use_datetime=False, use_builtin_types=False, *, context=None*)

Changed in version 3.3: The *use_builtin_types* flag was added.

A *ServerProxy* instance is an object that manages communication with a remote XML-RPC server. The required first argument is a URI (Uniform Resource Indicator), and will normally be the URL of the server. The optional second argument is a transport factory instance; by default it is an internal **SafeTransport** instance for https: URLs and an internal HTTP **Transport** instance otherwise. The optional third argument is an encoding, by default UTF-8. The optional fourth argument is a debugging flag.

The following parameters govern the use of the returned proxy instance. If *allow_none* is true, the Python constant **None** will be translated into XML; the default behaviour is for **None** to raise a *TypeError*. This is a commonly-used extension to the XML-RPC specification, but isn't supported by all clients and servers; see http://ontosys.com/xml-rpc/extensions.php for a description. The *use_builtin_types* flag can be used to cause date/time values to be presented as *datetime.datetime* objects and binary data to be presented as *bytes* objects; this flag is false by default. *datetime.datetime*, *bytes* and *bytearray* objects may be passed to calls. The obsolete *use_datetime* flag is similar to *use_builtin_types* but it applies only to date/time values.

Both the HTTP and HTTPS transports support the URL syntax extension for HTTP Basic Authentication: **http://user:pass@host:port/path**. The **user:pass** portion will be base64-encoded as an HTTP 'Authorization' header, and sent to the remote server as part of the connection process when invoking an XML-RPC method. You only need to use this if the remote server requires a Basic Authentication user and password. If an HTTPS URL is provided, *context* may be *ssl.SSLContext* and configures the SSL settings of the underlying HTTPS connection.

The returned instance is a proxy object with methods that can be used to invoke corresponding RPC calls on the remote server. If the remote server supports the introspection API, the proxy can also be used to query the remote server for the methods it supports (service discovery) and fetch other server-associated metadata.

Types that are conformable (e.g. that can be marshalled through XML), include the following (and except where noted, they are unmarshalled as the same Python type):

XML-RPC type	Python type
`boolean`	*bool*
`int`, `i1`, `i2`, `i4`, `i8` or `biginteger`	*int* in range from -2147483648 to 2147483647. Values get the `<int>` tag.
`double` or `float`	*float*. Values get the `<double>` tag.
`string`	*str*
`array`	*list* or *tuple* containing conformable elements. Arrays are returned as *lists*.
`struct`	*dict*. Keys must be strings, values may be any conformable type. Objects of user-defined classes can be passed in; only their *__dict__* attribute is transmitted.
`dateTime.iso8601`	*DateTime* or *datetime.datetime*. Returned type depends on values of *use_builtin_types* and *use_datetime* flags.
`base64`	*Binary*, *bytes* or *bytearray*. Returned type depends on the value of the *use_builtin_types* flag.
`nil`	The **None** constant. Passing is allowed only if *allow_none* is true.
`bigdecimal`	*decimal.Decimal*. Returned type only.

This is the full set of data types supported by XML-RPC. Method calls may also raise a special *Fault* instance, used to signal XML-RPC server errors, or *ProtocolError* used to signal an error in the HTTP/HTTPS transport layer. Both *Fault* and *ProtocolError* derive from a base class called **Error**. Note that the xmlrpc client module currently does not marshal instances of subclasses of built-in types.

When passing strings, characters special to XML such as <, >, and & will be automatically escaped. However, it's the caller's responsibility to ensure that the string is free of characters that aren't allowed in XML, such as the control characters with ASCII values between 0 and 31 (except, of course, tab, newline and carriage return); failing to do this will result in an XML-RPC request that isn't well-formed XML. If you have to pass arbitrary bytes via XML-RPC, use `bytes` or `bytearray` classes or the *Binary* wrapper class described below.

Server is retained as an alias for *ServerProxy* for backwards compatibility. New code should use *ServerProxy*.

Changed in version 3.5: Added the *context* argument.

Changed in version 3.6: Added support of type tags with prefixes (e.g. `ex:nil`). Added support of unmarshalling additional types used by Apache XML-RPC implementation for numerics: `i1`, `i2`, `i8`, `biginteger`, `float` and `bigdecimal`. See http://ws.apache.org/xmlrpc/types.html for a description.

See also:

XML-RPC HOWTO A good description of XML-RPC operation and client software in several languages. Contains pretty much everything an XML-RPC client developer needs to know.

XML-RPC Introspection Describes the XML-RPC protocol extension for introspection.

XML-RPC Specification The official specification.

Unofficial XML-RPC Errata Fredrik Lundh's "unofficial errata, intended to clarify certain details in the XML-RPC specification, as well as hint at 'best practices' to use when designing your own XML-RPC implementations."

21.26.1 ServerProxy Objects

A *ServerProxy* instance has a method corresponding to each remote procedure call accepted by the XML-RPC server. Calling the method performs an RPC, dispatched by both name and argument signature (e.g. the same method name can be overloaded with multiple argument signatures). The RPC finishes by returning a value, which may be either returned data in a conformant type or a *Fault* or *ProtocolError* object indicating an error.

Servers that support the XML introspection API support some common methods grouped under the reserved `system` attribute:

`ServerProxy.system.listMethods()`
    This method returns a list of strings, one for each (non-system) method supported by the XML-RPC server.

`ServerProxy.system.methodSignature(name)`
    This method takes one parameter, the name of a method implemented by the XML-RPC server. It returns an array of possible signatures for this method. A signature is an array of types. The first of these types is the return type of the method, the rest are parameters.

    Because multiple signatures (ie. overloading) is permitted, this method returns a list of signatures rather than a singleton.

    Signatures themselves are restricted to the top level parameters expected by a method. For instance if a method expects one array of structs as a parameter, and it returns a string, its signature is simply "string, array". If it expects three integers and returns a string, its signature is "string, int, int, int".

If no signature is defined for the method, a non-array value is returned. In Python this means that the type of the returned value will be something other than list.

ServerProxy.system.methodHelp(*name*)
> This method takes one parameter, the name of a method implemented by the XML-RPC server. It returns a documentation string describing the use of that method. If no such string is available, an empty string is returned. The documentation string may contain HTML markup.

Changed in version 3.5: Instances of *ServerProxy* support the *context manager* protocol for closing the underlying transport.

A working example follows. The server code:

```
from xmlrpc.server import SimpleXMLRPCServer

def is_even(n):
    return n % 2 == 0

server = SimpleXMLRPCServer(("localhost", 8000))
print("Listening on port 8000...")
server.register_function(is_even, "is_even")
server.serve_forever()
```

The client code for the preceding server:

```
import xmlrpc.client

with xmlrpc.client.ServerProxy("http://localhost:8000/") as proxy:
    print("3 is even: %s" % str(proxy.is_even(3)))
    print("100 is even: %s" % str(proxy.is_even(100)))
```

21.26.2 DateTime Objects

class xmlrpc.client.DateTime
> This class may be initialized with seconds since the epoch, a time tuple, an ISO 8601 time/date string, or a *datetime.datetime* instance. It has the following methods, supported mainly for internal use by the marshalling/unmarshalling code:
>
> **decode**(*string*)
> > Accept a string as the instance's new time value.
>
> **encode**(*out*)
> > Write the XML-RPC encoding of this *DateTime* item to the *out* stream object.
>
> It also supports certain of Python's built-in operators through rich comparison and **__repr__**() methods.

A working example follows. The server code:

```
import datetime
from xmlrpc.server import SimpleXMLRPCServer
import xmlrpc.client

def today():
    today = datetime.datetime.today()
    return xmlrpc.client.DateTime(today)

server = SimpleXMLRPCServer(("localhost", 8000))
print("Listening on port 8000...")
```

```
server.register_function(today, "today")
server.serve_forever()
```

The client code for the preceding server:

```
import xmlrpc.client
import datetime

proxy = xmlrpc.client.ServerProxy("http://localhost:8000/")

today = proxy.today()
# convert the ISO8601 string to a datetime object
converted = datetime.datetime.strptime(today.value, "%Y%m%dT%H:%M:%S")
print("Today: %s" % converted.strftime("%d.%m.%Y, %H:%M"))
```

21.26.3 Binary Objects

class `xmlrpc.client.Binary`

    This class may be initialized from bytes data (which may include NULs). The primary access to the content of a *Binary* object is provided by an attribute:

    data

        The binary data encapsulated by the *Binary* instance. The data is provided as a *bytes* object.

    Binary objects have the following methods, supported mainly for internal use by the marshalling/unmarshalling code:

    decode(bytes**)**

        Accept a base64 *bytes* object and decode it as the instance's new data.

    encode(out**)**

        Write the XML-RPC base 64 encoding of this binary item to the *out* stream object.

        The encoded data will have newlines every 76 characters as per RFC 2045 section 6.8, which was the de facto standard base64 specification when the XML-RPC spec was written.

    It also supports certain of Python's built-in operators through `__eq__()` and `__ne__()` methods.

Example usage of the binary objects. We're going to transfer an image over XMLRPC:

```
from xmlrpc.server import SimpleXMLRPCServer
import xmlrpc.client

def python_logo():
    with open("python_logo.jpg", "rb") as handle:
        return xmlrpc.client.Binary(handle.read())

server = SimpleXMLRPCServer(("localhost", 8000))
print("Listening on port 8000...")
server.register_function(python_logo, 'python_logo')

server.serve_forever()
```

The client gets the image and saves it to a file:

```
import xmlrpc.client

proxy = xmlrpc.client.ServerProxy("http://localhost:8000/")
```

```
with open("fetched_python_logo.jpg", "wb") as handle:
    handle.write(proxy.python_logo().data)
```

21.26.4 Fault Objects

class xmlrpc.client.Fault

A *Fault* object encapsulates the content of an XML-RPC fault tag. Fault objects have the following attributes:

faultCode

A string indicating the fault type.

faultString

A string containing a diagnostic message associated with the fault.

In the following example we're going to intentionally cause a *Fault* by returning a complex type object. The server code:

```
from xmlrpc.server import SimpleXMLRPCServer

# A marshalling error is going to occur because we're returning a
# complex number
def add(x, y):
    return x+y+0j

server = SimpleXMLRPCServer(("localhost", 8000))
print("Listening on port 8000...")
server.register_function(add, 'add')

server.serve_forever()
```

The client code for the preceding server:

```
import xmlrpc.client

proxy = xmlrpc.client.ServerProxy("http://localhost:8000/")
try:
    proxy.add(2, 5)
except xmlrpc.client.Fault as err:
    print("A fault occurred")
    print("Fault code: %d" % err.faultCode)
    print("Fault string: %s" % err.faultString)
```

21.26.5 ProtocolError Objects

class xmlrpc.client.ProtocolError

A *ProtocolError* object describes a protocol error in the underlying transport layer (such as a 404 'not found' error if the server named by the URI does not exist). It has the following attributes:

url

The URI or URL that triggered the error.

errcode

The error code.

errmsg

The error message or diagnostic string.

headers
A dict containing the headers of the HTTP/HTTPS request that triggered the error.

In the following example we're going to intentionally cause a *ProtocolError* by providing an invalid URI:

```
import xmlrpc.client

# create a ServerProxy with a URI that doesn't respond to XMLRPC requests
proxy = xmlrpc.client.ServerProxy("http://google.com/")

try:
    proxy.some_method()
except xmlrpc.client.ProtocolError as err:
    print("A protocol error occurred")
    print("URL: %s" % err.url)
    print("HTTP/HTTPS headers: %s" % err.headers)
    print("Error code: %d" % err.errcode)
    print("Error message: %s" % err.errmsg)
```

21.26.6 MultiCall Objects

The *MultiCall* object provides a way to encapsulate multiple calls to a remote server into a single request[1].

class xmlrpc.client.MultiCall(*server*)

Create an object used to boxcar method calls. *server* is the eventual target of the call. Calls can be made to the result object, but they will immediately return None, and only store the call name and parameters in the *MultiCall* object. Calling the object itself causes all stored calls to be transmitted as a single **system.multicall** request. The result of this call is a *generator*; iterating over this generator yields the individual results.

A usage example of this class follows. The server code:

```
from xmlrpc.server import SimpleXMLRPCServer

def add(x, y):
    return x + y

def subtract(x, y):
    return x - y

def multiply(x, y):
    return x * y

def divide(x, y):
    return x // y

# A simple server with simple arithmetic functions
server = SimpleXMLRPCServer(("localhost", 8000))
print("Listening on port 8000...")
server.register_multicall_functions()
server.register_function(add, 'add')
server.register_function(subtract, 'subtract')
server.register_function(multiply, 'multiply')
server.register_function(divide, 'divide')
server.serve_forever()
```

---

[1] This approach has been first presented in a discussion on xmlrpc.com.

The client code for the preceding server:

```
import xmlrpc.client

proxy = xmlrpc.client.ServerProxy("http://localhost:8000/")
multicall = xmlrpc.client.MultiCall(proxy)
multicall.add(7, 3)
multicall.subtract(7, 3)
multicall.multiply(7, 3)
multicall.divide(7, 3)
result = multicall()

print("7+3=%d, 7-3=%d, 7*3=%d, 7//3=%d" % tuple(result))
```

21.26.7 Convenience Functions

xmlrpc.client.dumps(*params, methodname=None, methodresponse=None, encoding=None, allow_none=False*)
   Convert *params* into an XML-RPC request. or into a response if *methodresponse* is true. *params* can be either a tuple of arguments or an instance of the Fault exception class. If *methodresponse* is true, only a single value can be returned, meaning that *params* must be of length 1. *encoding*, if supplied, is the encoding to use in the generated XML; the default is UTF-8. Python's None value cannot be used in standard XML-RPC; to allow using it via an extension, provide a true value for *allow_none*.

xmlrpc.client.loads(*data, use_datetime=False, use_builtin_types=False*)
   Convert an XML-RPC request or response into Python objects, a (**params, methodname**). *params* is a tuple of argument; *methodname* is a string, or None if no method name is present in the packet. If the XML-RPC packet represents a fault condition, this function will raise a Fault exception. The *use_builtin_types* flag can be used to cause date/time values to be presented as datetime.datetime objects and binary data to be presented as bytes objects; this flag is false by default.

   The obsolete *use_datetime* flag is similar to *use_builtin_types* but it applies only to date/time values.

   Changed in version 3.3: The *use_builtin_types* flag was added.

21.26.8 Example of Client Usage

```
# simple test program (from the XML-RPC specification)
from xmlrpc.client import ServerProxy, Error

# server = ServerProxy("http://localhost:8000") # local server
with ServerProxy("http://betty.userland.com") as proxy:

    print(proxy)

    try:
        print(proxy.examples.getStateName(41))
    except Error as v:
        print("ERROR", v)
```

To access an XML-RPC server through a HTTP proxy, you need to define a custom transport. The following example shows how:

```
import http.client
import xmlrpc.client
```

```
class ProxiedTransport(xmlrpc.client.Transport):

    def set_proxy(self, host, port=None, headers=None):
        self.proxy = host, port
        self.proxy_headers = headers

    def make_connection(self, host):
        connection = http.client.HTTPConnection(*self.proxy)
        connection.set_tunnel(host, headers=self.proxy_headers)
        self._connection = host, connection
        return connection

transport = ProxiedTransport()
transport.set_proxy('proxy-server', 8080)
server = xmlrpc.client.ServerProxy('http://betty.userland.com', transport=transport)
print(server.examples.getStateName(41))
```

21.26.9 Example of Client and Server Usage

See *SimpleXMLRPCServer Example*.

21.27 xmlrpc.server — Basic XML-RPC servers

Source code: Lib/xmlrpc/server.py

The *xmlrpc.server* module provides a basic server framework for XML-RPC servers written in Python. Servers can either be free standing, using *SimpleXMLRPCServer*, or embedded in a CGI environment, using *CGIXMLRPCRequestHandler*.

> **Warning:** The *xmlrpc.server* module is not secure against maliciously constructed data. If you need to parse untrusted or unauthenticated data see *XML vulnerabilities*.

class xmlrpc.server.SimpleXMLRPCServer(*addr, requestHandler=SimpleXMLRPCRequestHandler, logRequests=True, allow_none=False, encoding=None, bind_and_activate=True, use_builtin_types=False*)

Create a new server instance. This class provides methods for registration of functions that can be called by the XML-RPC protocol. The *requestHandler* parameter should be a factory for request handler instances; it defaults to *SimpleXMLRPCRequestHandler*. The *addr* and *requestHandler* parameters are passed to the *socketserver.TCPServer* constructor. If *logRequests* is true (the default), requests will be logged; setting this parameter to false will turn off logging. The *allow_none* and *encoding* parameters are passed on to *xmlrpc.client* and control the XML-RPC responses that will be returned from the server. The *bind_and_activate* parameter controls whether server_bind() and server_activate() are called immediately by the constructor; it defaults to true. Setting it to false allows code to manipulate the *allow_reuse_address* class variable before the address is bound. The *use_builtin_types* parameter is passed to the *loads()* function and controls which types are processed when date/times values or binary data are received; it defaults to false.

Changed in version 3.3: The *use_builtin_types* flag was added.

class `xmlrpc.server.CGIXMLRPCRequestHandler`(*allow_none=False*, *encoding=None*, *use_builtin_types=False*)

Create a new instance to handle XML-RPC requests in a CGI environment. The *allow_none* and *encoding* parameters are passed on to `xmlrpc.client` and control the XML-RPC responses that will be returned from the server. The *use_builtin_types* parameter is passed to the `loads()` function and controls which types are processed when date/times values or binary data are received; it defaults to false.

Changed in version 3.3: The *use_builtin_types* flag was added.

class `xmlrpc.server.SimpleXMLRPCRequestHandler`

Create a new request handler instance. This request handler supports `POST` requests and modifies logging so that the *logRequests* parameter to the `SimpleXMLRPCServer` constructor parameter is honored.

21.27.1 SimpleXMLRPCServer Objects

The `SimpleXMLRPCServer` class is based on `socketserver.TCPServer` and provides a means of creating simple, stand alone XML-RPC servers.

`SimpleXMLRPCServer.register_function`(*function*, *name=None*)

Register a function that can respond to XML-RPC requests. If *name* is given, it will be the method name associated with *function*, otherwise `function.__name__` will be used. *name* can be either a normal or Unicode string, and may contain characters not legal in Python identifiers, including the period character.

`SimpleXMLRPCServer.register_instance`(*instance*, *allow_dotted_names=False*)

Register an object which is used to expose method names which have not been registered using `register_function()`. If *instance* contains a `_dispatch()` method, it is called with the requested method name and the parameters from the request. Its API is `def _dispatch(self, method, params)` (note that *params* does not represent a variable argument list). If it calls an underlying function to perform its task, that function is called as `func(*params)`, expanding the parameter list. The return value from `_dispatch()` is returned to the client as the result. If *instance* does not have a `_dispatch()` method, it is searched for an attribute matching the name of the requested method.

If the optional *allow_dotted_names* argument is true and the instance does not have a `_dispatch()` method, then if the requested method name contains periods, each component of the method name is searched for individually, with the effect that a simple hierarchical search is performed. The value found from this search is then called with the parameters from the request, and the return value is passed back to the client.

> **Warning:** Enabling the *allow_dotted_names* option allows intruders to access your module's global variables and may allow intruders to execute arbitrary code on your machine. Only use this option on a secure, closed network.

`SimpleXMLRPCServer.register_introspection_functions`()

Registers the XML-RPC introspection functions `system.listMethods`, `system.methodHelp` and `system.methodSignature`.

`SimpleXMLRPCServer.register_multicall_functions`()

Registers the XML-RPC multicall function system.multicall.

`SimpleXMLRPCRequestHandler.rpc_paths`

An attribute value that must be a tuple listing valid path portions of the URL for receiving XML-RPC requests. Requests posted to other paths will result in a 404 "no such page" HTTP error. If this tuple is empty, all paths will be considered valid. The default value is (`'/'`, `'/RPC2'`).

SimpleXMLRPCServer Example

Server code:

```python
from xmlrpc.server import SimpleXMLRPCServer
from xmlrpc.server import SimpleXMLRPCRequestHandler

# Restrict to a particular path.
class RequestHandler(SimpleXMLRPCRequestHandler):
    rpc_paths = ('/RPC2',)

# Create server
with SimpleXMLRPCServer(("localhost", 8000),
                        requestHandler=RequestHandler) as server:
    server.register_introspection_functions()

    # Register pow() function; this will use the value of
    # pow.__name__ as the name, which is just 'pow'.
    server.register_function(pow)

    # Register a function under a different name
    def adder_function(x,y):
        return x + y
    server.register_function(adder_function, 'add')

    # Register an instance; all the methods of the instance are
    # published as XML-RPC methods (in this case, just 'mul').
    class MyFuncs:
        def mul(self, x, y):
            return x * y

    server.register_instance(MyFuncs())

    # Run the server's main loop
    server.serve_forever()
```

The following client code will call the methods made available by the preceding server:

```python
import xmlrpc.client

s = xmlrpc.client.ServerProxy('http://localhost:8000')
print(s.pow(2,3))  # Returns 2**3 = 8
print(s.add(2,3))  # Returns 5
print(s.mul(5,2))  # Returns 5*2 = 10

# Print list of available methods
print(s.system.listMethods())
```

The following example included in the `Lib/xmlrpc/server.py` module shows a server allowing dotted names and registering a multicall function.

> **Warning:** Enabling the *allow_dotted_names* option allows intruders to access your module's global variables and may allow intruders to execute arbitrary code on your machine. Only use this example only within a secure, closed network.

```
import datetime

class ExampleService:
    def getData(self):
        return '42'

    class currentTime:
        @staticmethod
        def getCurrentTime():
            return datetime.datetime.now()

with SimpleXMLRPCServer(("localhost", 8000)) as server:
    server.register_function(pow)
    server.register_function(lambda x,y: x+y, 'add')
    server.register_instance(ExampleService(), allow_dotted_names=True)
    server.register_multicall_functions()
    print('Serving XML-RPC on localhost port 8000')
    try:
        server.serve_forever()
    except KeyboardInterrupt:
        print("\nKeyboard interrupt received, exiting.")
        sys.exit(0)
```

This ExampleService demo can be invoked from the command line:

```
python -m xmlrpc.server
```

The client that interacts with the above server is included in *Lib/xmlrpc/client.py*:

```
server = ServerProxy("http://localhost:8000")

try:
    print(server.currentTime.getCurrentTime())
except Error as v:
    print("ERROR", v)

multi = MultiCall(server)
multi.getData()
multi.pow(2,9)
multi.add(1,2)
try:
    for response in multi():
        print(response)
except Error as v:
    print("ERROR", v)
```

This client which interacts with the demo XMLRPC server can be invoked as:

```
python -m xmlrpc.client
```

21.27.2 CGIXMLRPCRequestHandler

The *CGIXMLRPCRequestHandler* class can be used to handle XML-RPC requests sent to Python CGI scripts.

CGIXMLRPCRequestHandler.register_function(*function*, *name=None*)
    Register a function that can respond to XML-RPC requests. If *name* is given, it will be the method

name associated with function, otherwise *function.__name__* will be used. *name* can be either a normal or Unicode string, and may contain characters not legal in Python identifiers, including the period character.

CGIXMLRPCRequestHandler.register_instance(*instance*)
: Register an object which is used to expose method names which have not been registered using *register_function()*. If instance contains a _dispatch() method, it is called with the requested method name and the parameters from the request; the return value is returned to the client as the result. If instance does not have a _dispatch() method, it is searched for an attribute matching the name of the requested method; if the requested method name contains periods, each component of the method name is searched for individually, with the effect that a simple hierarchical search is performed. The value found from this search is then called with the parameters from the request, and the return value is passed back to the client.

CGIXMLRPCRequestHandler.register_introspection_functions()
: Register the XML-RPC introspection functions system.listMethods, system.methodHelp and system.methodSignature.

CGIXMLRPCRequestHandler.register_multicall_functions()
: Register the XML-RPC multicall function system.multicall.

CGIXMLRPCRequestHandler.handle_request(*request_text=None*)
: Handle an XML-RPC request. If *request_text* is given, it should be the POST data provided by the HTTP server, otherwise the contents of stdin will be used.

Example:

```
class MyFuncs:
    def mul(self, x, y):
        return x * y


handler = CGIXMLRPCRequestHandler()
handler.register_function(pow)
handler.register_function(lambda x,y: x+y, 'add')
handler.register_introspection_functions()
handler.register_instance(MyFuncs())
handler.handle_request()
```

21.27.3 Documenting XMLRPC server

These classes extend the above classes to serve HTML documentation in response to HTTP GET requests. Servers can either be free standing, using *DocXMLRPCServer*, or embedded in a CGI environment, using *DocCGIXMLRPCRequestHandler*.

class xmlrpc.server.DocXMLRPCServer(*addr, requestHandler=DocXMLRPCRequestHandler, logRequests=True, allow_none=False, encoding=None, bind_and_activate=True, use_builtin_types=True*)
: Create a new server instance. All parameters have the same meaning as for *SimpleXMLRPCServer*; *requestHandler* defaults to *DocXMLRPCRequestHandler*.

  Changed in version 3.3: The *use_builtin_types* flag was added.

class xmlrpc.server.DocCGIXMLRPCRequestHandler
: Create a new instance to handle XML-RPC requests in a CGI environment.

class xmlrpc.server.DocXMLRPCRequestHandler
: Create a new request handler instance. This request handler supports XML-RPC POST re-

quests, documentation GET requests, and modifies logging so that the *logRequests* parameter to the `DocXMLRPCServer` constructor parameter is honored.

21.27.4 DocXMLRPCServer Objects

The `DocXMLRPCServer` class is derived from `SimpleXMLRPCServer` and provides a means of creating self-documenting, stand alone XML-RPC servers. HTTP POST requests are handled as XML-RPC method calls. HTTP GET requests are handled by generating pydoc-style HTML documentation. This allows a server to provide its own web-based documentation.

DocXMLRPCServer.set_server_title(*server_title*)
: Set the title used in the generated HTML documentation. This title will be used inside the HTML "title" element.

DocXMLRPCServer.set_server_name(*server_name*)
: Set the name used in the generated HTML documentation. This name will appear at the top of the generated documentation inside a "h1" element.

DocXMLRPCServer.set_server_documentation(*server_documentation*)
: Set the description used in the generated HTML documentation. This description will appear as a paragraph, below the server name, in the documentation.

21.27.5 DocCGIXMLRPCRequestHandler

The `DocCGIXMLRPCRequestHandler` class is derived from `CGIXMLRPCRequestHandler` and provides a means of creating self-documenting, XML-RPC CGI scripts. HTTP POST requests are handled as XML-RPC method calls. HTTP GET requests are handled by generating pydoc-style HTML documentation. This allows a server to provide its own web-based documentation.

DocCGIXMLRPCRequestHandler.set_server_title(*server_title*)
: Set the title used in the generated HTML documentation. This title will be used inside the HTML "title" element.

DocCGIXMLRPCRequestHandler.set_server_name(*server_name*)
: Set the name used in the generated HTML documentation. This name will appear at the top of the generated documentation inside a "h1" element.

DocCGIXMLRPCRequestHandler.set_server_documentation(*server_documentation*)
: Set the description used in the generated HTML documentation. This description will appear as a paragraph, below the server name, in the documentation.

21.28 `ipaddress` — IPv4/IPv6 manipulation library

Source code: Lib/ipaddress.py

`ipaddress` provides the capabilities to create, manipulate and operate on IPv4 and IPv6 addresses and networks.

The functions and classes in this module make it straightforward to handle various tasks related to IP addresses, including checking whether or not two hosts are on the same subnet, iterating over all hosts in a particular subnet, checking whether or not a string represents a valid IP address or network definition, and so on.

This is the full module API reference—for an overview and introduction, see ipaddress-howto.

New in version 3.3.

21.28.1 Convenience factory functions

The *ipaddress* module provides factory functions to conveniently create IP addresses, networks and interfaces:

ipaddress.**ip_address**(*address*)

> Return an *IPv4Address* or *IPv6Address* object depending on the IP address passed as argument. Either IPv4 or IPv6 addresses may be supplied; integers less than 2**32 will be considered to be IPv4 by default. A *ValueError* is raised if *address* does not represent a valid IPv4 or IPv6 address.

```
>>> ipaddress.ip_address('192.168.0.1')
IPv4Address('192.168.0.1')
>>> ipaddress.ip_address('2001:db8::')
IPv6Address('2001:db8::')
```

ipaddress.**ip_network**(*address, strict=True*)

> Return an *IPv4Network* or *IPv6Network* object depending on the IP address passed as argument. *address* is a string or integer representing the IP network. Either IPv4 or IPv6 networks may be supplied; integers less than 2**32 will be considered to be IPv4 by default. *strict* is passed to *IPv4Network* or *IPv6Network* constructor. A *ValueError* is raised if *address* does not represent a valid IPv4 or IPv6 address, or if the network has host bits set.

```
>>> ipaddress.ip_network('192.168.0.0/28')
IPv4Network('192.168.0.0/28')
```

ipaddress.**ip_interface**(*address*)

> Return an *IPv4Interface* or *IPv6Interface* object depending on the IP address passed as argument. *address* is a string or integer representing the IP address. Either IPv4 or IPv6 addresses may be supplied; integers less than 2**32 will be considered to be IPv4 by default. A *ValueError* is raised if *address* does not represent a valid IPv4 or IPv6 address.

One downside of these convenience functions is that the need to handle both IPv4 and IPv6 formats means that error messages provide minimal information on the precise error, as the functions don't know whether the IPv4 or IPv6 format was intended. More detailed error reporting can be obtained by calling the appropriate version specific class constructors directly.

21.28.2 IP Addresses

Address objects

The *IPv4Address* and *IPv6Address* objects share a lot of common attributes. Some attributes that are only meaningful for IPv6 addresses are also implemented by *IPv4Address* objects, in order to make it easier to write code that handles both IP versions correctly.

class ipaddress.**IPv4Address**(*address*)

> Construct an IPv4 address. An *AddressValueError* is raised if *address* is not a valid IPv4 address.
>
> The following constitutes a valid IPv4 address:
>
> 1. A string in decimal-dot notation, consisting of four decimal integers in the inclusive range 0–255, separated by dots (e.g. 192.168.0.1). Each integer represents an octet (byte) in the address. Leading zeroes are tolerated only for values less than 8 (as there is no ambiguity between the decimal and octal interpretations of such strings).
> 2. An integer that fits into 32 bits.
> 3. An integer packed into a *bytes* object of length 4 (most significant octet first).

```
>>> ipaddress.IPv4Address('192.168.0.1')
IPv4Address('192.168.0.1')
>>> ipaddress.IPv4Address(3232235521)
IPv4Address('192.168.0.1')
>>> ipaddress.IPv4Address(b'\xC0\xA8\x00\x01')
IPv4Address('192.168.0.1')
```

version
> The appropriate version number: 4 for IPv4, 6 for IPv6.

max_prefixlen
> The total number of bits in the address representation for this version: 32 for IPv4, 128 for IPv6.
>
> The prefix defines the number of leading bits in an address that are compared to determine whether or not an address is part of a network.

compressed

exploded
> The string representation in dotted decimal notation. Leading zeroes are never included in the representation.
>
> As IPv4 does not define a shorthand notation for addresses with octets set to zero, these two attributes are always the same as str(addr) for IPv4 addresses. Exposing these attributes makes it easier to write display code that can handle both IPv4 and IPv6 addresses.

packed
> The binary representation of this address - a *bytes* object of the appropriate length (most significant octet first). This is 4 bytes for IPv4 and 16 bytes for IPv6.

reverse_pointer
> The name of the reverse DNS PTR record for the IP address, e.g.:

```
>>> ipaddress.ip_address("127.0.0.1").reverse_pointer
'1.0.0.127.in-addr.arpa'
>>> ipaddress.ip_address("2001:db8::1").reverse_pointer
'1.0.0.0.0.0.0.0.0.0.0.0.0.0.0.0.0.0.0.0.0.0.0.0.8.b.d.0.1.0.0.2.ip6.arpa'
```

> This is the name that could be used for performing a PTR lookup, not the resolved hostname itself.
>
> New in version 3.5.

is_multicast
> True if the address is reserved for multicast use. See RFC 3171 (for IPv4) or RFC 2373 (for IPv6).

is_private
> True if the address is allocated for private networks. See iana-ipv4-special-registry (for IPv4) or iana-ipv6-special-registry (for IPv6).

is_global
> True if the address is allocated for public networks. See iana-ipv4-special-registry (for IPv4) or iana-ipv6-special-registry (for IPv6).
>
> New in version 3.4.

is_unspecified
> True if the address is unspecified. See RFC 5735 (for IPv4) or RFC 2373 (for IPv6).

is_reserved
> True if the address is otherwise IETF reserved.

is_loopback
True if this is a loopback address. See RFC 3330 (for IPv4) or RFC 2373 (for IPv6).

is_link_local
True if the address is reserved for link-local usage. See RFC 3927.

class ipaddress.IPv6Address(*address*)

Construct an IPv6 address. An *AddressValueError* is raised if *address* is not a valid IPv6 address.

The following constitutes a valid IPv6 address:

1. A string consisting of eight groups of four hexadecimal digits, each group representing 16 bits. The groups are separated by colons. This describes an *exploded* (longhand) notation. The string can also be *compressed* (shorthand notation) by various means. See RFC 4291 for details. For example, `"0000:0000:0000:0000:0000:0abc:0007:0def"` can be compressed to `"::abc:7:def"`.
2. An integer that fits into 128 bits.
3. An integer packed into a *bytes* object of length 16, big-endian.

```
>>> ipaddress.IPv6Address('2001:db8::1000')
IPv6Address('2001:db8::1000')
```

compressed

The short form of the address representation, with leading zeroes in groups omitted and the longest sequence of groups consisting entirely of zeroes collapsed to a single empty group.

This is also the value returned by `str(addr)` for IPv6 addresses.

exploded

The long form of the address representation, with all leading zeroes and groups consisting entirely of zeroes included.

For the following attributes, see the corresponding documentation of the *IPv4Address* class:

packed

reverse_pointer

version

max_prefixlen

is_multicast

is_private

is_global

is_unspecified

is_reserved

is_loopback

is_link_local
New in version 3.4: is_global

is_site_local
True if the address is reserved for site-local usage. Note that the site-local address space has been deprecated by RFC 3879. Use *is_private* to test if this address is in the space of unique local addresses as defined by RFC 4193.

ipv4_mapped
For addresses that appear to be IPv4 mapped addresses (starting with `::FFFF/96`), this property will report the embedded IPv4 address. For any other address, this property will be **None**.

sixtofour

For addresses that appear to be 6to4 addresses (starting with 2002::/16) as defined by RFC 3056, this property will report the embedded IPv4 address. For any other address, this property will be None.

teredo

For addresses that appear to be Teredo addresses (starting with 2001::/32) as defined by RFC 4380, this property will report the embedded (server, client) IP address pair. For any other address, this property will be None.

Conversion to Strings and Integers

To interoperate with networking interfaces such as the socket module, addresses must be converted to strings or integers. This is handled using the *str()* and *int()* builtin functions:

```
>>> str(ipaddress.IPv4Address('192.168.0.1'))
'192.168.0.1'
>>> int(ipaddress.IPv4Address('192.168.0.1'))
3232235521
>>> str(ipaddress.IPv6Address('::1'))
'::1'
>>> int(ipaddress.IPv6Address('::1'))
1
```

Operators

Address objects support some operators. Unless stated otherwise, operators can only be applied between compatible objects (i.e. IPv4 with IPv4, IPv6 with IPv6).

Comparison operators

Address objects can be compared with the usual set of comparison operators. Some examples:

```
>>> IPv4Address('127.0.0.2') > IPv4Address('127.0.0.1')
True
>>> IPv4Address('127.0.0.2') == IPv4Address('127.0.0.1')
False
>>> IPv4Address('127.0.0.2') != IPv4Address('127.0.0.1')
True
```

Arithmetic operators

Integers can be added to or subtracted from address objects. Some examples:

```
>>> IPv4Address('127.0.0.2') + 3
IPv4Address('127.0.0.5')
>>> IPv4Address('127.0.0.2') - 3
IPv4Address('126.255.255.255')
>>> IPv4Address('255.255.255.255') + 1
Traceback (most recent call last):
  File "<stdin>", line 1, in <module>
ipaddress.AddressValueError: 4294967296 (>= 2**32) is not permitted as an IPv4 address
```

21.28.3 IP Network definitions

The *IPv4Network* and *IPv6Network* objects provide a mechanism for defining and inspecting IP network definitions. A network definition consists of a *mask* and a *network address*, and as such defines a range of IP addresses that equal the network address when masked (binary AND) with the mask. For example, a network definition with the mask 255.255.255.0 and the network address 192.168.1.0 consists of IP addresses in the inclusive range 192.168.1.0 to 192.168.1.255.

Prefix, net mask and host mask

There are several equivalent ways to specify IP network masks. A *prefix* /<nbits> is a notation that denotes how many high-order bits are set in the network mask. A *net mask* is an IP address with some number of high-order bits set. Thus the prefix /24 is equivalent to the net mask 255.255.255.0 in IPv4, or ffff:ff00:: in IPv6. In addition, a *host mask* is the logical inverse of a *net mask*, and is sometimes used (for example in Cisco access control lists) to denote a network mask. The host mask equivalent to /24 in IPv4 is 0.0.0.255.

Network objects

All attributes implemented by address objects are implemented by network objects as well. In addition, network objects implement additional attributes. All of these are common between *IPv4Network* and *IPv6Network*, so to avoid duplication they are only documented for *IPv4Network*.

class ipaddress.IPv4Network(*address*, *strict=True*)

Construct an IPv4 network definition. *address* can be one of the following:

1. A string consisting of an IP address and an optional mask, separated by a slash (/). The IP address is the network address, and the mask can be either a single number, which means it's a *prefix*, or a string representation of an IPv4 address. If it's the latter, the mask is interpreted as a *net mask* if it starts with a non-zero field, or as a *host mask* if it starts with a zero field. If no mask is provided, it's considered to be /32.

   For example, the following *address* specifications are equivalent: 192.168.1.0/24, 192.168.1.0/255.255.255.0 and 192.168.1.0/0.0.0.255.

2. An integer that fits into 32 bits. This is equivalent to a single-address network, with the network address being *address* and the mask being /32.

3. An integer packed into a *bytes* object of length 4, big-endian. The interpretation is similar to an integer *address*.

4. A two-tuple of an address description and a netmask, where the address description is either a string, a 32-bits integer, a 4-bytes packed integer, or an existing IPv4Address object; and the netmask is either an integer representing the prefix length (e.g. 24) or a string representing the prefix mask (e.g. 255.255.255.0).

An *AddressValueError* is raised if *address* is not a valid IPv4 address. A *NetmaskValueError* is raised if the mask is not valid for an IPv4 address.

If *strict* is True and host bits are set in the supplied address, then *ValueError* is raised. Otherwise, the host bits are masked out to determine the appropriate network address.

Unless stated otherwise, all network methods accepting other network/address objects will raise *TypeError* if the argument's IP version is incompatible to **self**

Changed in version 3.5: Added the two-tuple form for the *address* constructor parameter.

version

max_prefixlen

Refer to the corresponding attribute documentation in *IPv4Address*

is_multicast

is_private

is_unspecified

is_reserved

is_loopback

is_link_local
These attributes are true for the network as a whole if they are true for both the network address and the broadcast address

network_address
The network address for the network. The network address and the prefix length together uniquely define a network.

broadcast_address
The broadcast address for the network. Packets sent to the broadcast address should be received by every host on the network.

hostmask
The host mask, as a string.

with_prefixlen

compressed

exploded
A string representation of the network, with the mask in prefix notation.

with_prefixlen and compressed are always the same as str(network). exploded uses the exploded form the network address.

with_netmask
A string representation of the network, with the mask in net mask notation.

with_hostmask
A string representation of the network, with the mask in host mask notation.

num_addresses
The total number of addresses in the network.

prefixlen
Length of the network prefix, in bits.

hosts()
Returns an iterator over the usable hosts in the network. The usable hosts are all the IP addresses that belong to the network, except the network address itself and the network broadcast address.

```
>>> list(ip_network('192.0.2.0/29').hosts())
[IPv4Address('192.0.2.1'), IPv4Address('192.0.2.2'),
 IPv4Address('192.0.2.3'), IPv4Address('192.0.2.4'),
 IPv4Address('192.0.2.5'), IPv4Address('192.0.2.6')]
```

overlaps(*other*)
True if this network is partly or wholly contained in *other* or *other* is wholly contained in this network.

address_exclude(*network*)
Computes the network definitions resulting from removing the given *network* from this one. Returns an iterator of network objects. Raises ValueError if *network* is not completely contained in this network.

```
>>> n1 = ip_network('192.0.2.0/28')
>>> n2 = ip_network('192.0.2.1/32')
>>> list(n1.address_exclude(n2))
[IPv4Network('192.0.2.8/29'), IPv4Network('192.0.2.4/30'),
 IPv4Network('192.0.2.2/31'), IPv4Network('192.0.2.0/32')]
```

subnets(*prefixlen_diff=1, new_prefix=None*)

The subnets that join to make the current network definition, depending on the argument values. *prefixlen_diff* is the amount our prefix length should be increased by. *new_prefix* is the desired new prefix of the subnets; it must be larger than our prefix. One and only one of *prefixlen_diff* and *new_prefix* must be set. Returns an iterator of network objects.

```
>>> list(ip_network('192.0.2.0/24').subnets())
[IPv4Network('192.0.2.0/25'), IPv4Network('192.0.2.128/25')]
>>> list(ip_network('192.0.2.0/24').subnets(prefixlen_diff=2))
[IPv4Network('192.0.2.0/26'), IPv4Network('192.0.2.64/26'),
 IPv4Network('192.0.2.128/26'), IPv4Network('192.0.2.192/26')]
>>> list(ip_network('192.0.2.0/24').subnets(new_prefix=26))
[IPv4Network('192.0.2.0/26'), IPv4Network('192.0.2.64/26'),
 IPv4Network('192.0.2.128/26'), IPv4Network('192.0.2.192/26')]
>>> list(ip_network('192.0.2.0/24').subnets(new_prefix=23))
Traceback (most recent call last):
  File "<stdin>", line 1, in <module>
    raise ValueError('new prefix must be longer')
ValueError: new prefix must be longer
>>> list(ip_network('192.0.2.0/24').subnets(new_prefix=25))
[IPv4Network('192.0.2.0/25'), IPv4Network('192.0.2.128/25')]
```

supernet(*prefixlen_diff=1, new_prefix=None*)

The supernet containing this network definition, depending on the argument values. *prefixlen_diff* is the amount our prefix length should be decreased by. *new_prefix* is the desired new prefix of the supernet; it must be smaller than our prefix. One and only one of *prefixlen_diff* and *new_prefix* must be set. Returns a single network object.

```
>>> ip_network('192.0.2.0/24').supernet()
IPv4Network('192.0.2.0/23')
>>> ip_network('192.0.2.0/24').supernet(prefixlen_diff=2)
IPv4Network('192.0.0.0/22')
>>> ip_network('192.0.2.0/24').supernet(new_prefix=20)
IPv4Network('192.0.0.0/20')
```

compare_networks(*other*)

Compare this network to *other*. In this comparison only the network addresses are considered; host bits aren't. Returns either -1, 0 or 1.

```
>>> ip_network('192.0.2.1/32').compare_networks(ip_network('192.0.2.2/32'))
-1
>>> ip_network('192.0.2.1/32').compare_networks(ip_network('192.0.2.0/32'))
1
>>> ip_network('192.0.2.1/32').compare_networks(ip_network('192.0.2.1/32'))
0
```

class ipaddress.IPv6Network(*address, strict=True*)

Construct an IPv6 network definition. *address* can be one of the following:

1. A string consisting of an IP address and an optional mask, separated by a slash (/). The IP address is the network address, and the mask can be either a single number, which means it's a

prefix, or a string representation of an IPv6 address. If it's the latter, the mask is interpreted as a *net mask*. If no mask is provided, it's considered to be /128.

For example, the following *address* specifications are equivalent: 2001:db00::0/24 and 2001:db00::0/ffff:ff00::.

2. An integer that fits into 128 bits. This is equivalent to a single-address network, with the network address being *address* and the mask being /128.

3. An integer packed into a `bytes` object of length 16, big-endian. The interpretation is similar to an integer *address*.

4. A two-tuple of an address description and a netmask, where the address description is either a string, a 128-bits integer, a 16-bytes packed integer, or an existing IPv6Address object; and the netmask is an integer representing the prefix length.

An *AddressValueError* is raised if *address* is not a valid IPv6 address. A *NetmaskValueError* is raised if the mask is not valid for an IPv6 address.

If *strict* is True and host bits are set in the supplied address, then *ValueError* is raised. Otherwise, the host bits are masked out to determine the appropriate network address.

Changed in version 3.5: Added the two-tuple form for the *address* constructor parameter.

version

max_prefixlen

is_multicast

is_private

is_unspecified

is_reserved

is_loopback

is_link_local

network_address

broadcast_address

hostmask

with_prefixlen

compressed

exploded

with_netmask

with_hostmask

num_addresses

prefixlen

hosts()

overlaps(*other*)

address_exclude(*network*)

subnets(*prefixlen_diff=1*, *new_prefix=None*)

supernet(*prefixlen_diff=1*, *new_prefix=None*)

compare_networks(*other*)
    Refer to the corresponding attribute documentation in *IPv4Network*

is_site_local
   These attribute is true for the network as a whole if it is true for both the network address and the broadcast address

Operators

Network objects support some operators. Unless stated otherwise, operators can only be applied between compatible objects (i.e. IPv4 with IPv4, IPv6 with IPv6).

Logical operators

Network objects can be compared with the usual set of logical operators, similarly to address objects.

Iteration

Network objects can be iterated to list all the addresses belonging to the network. For iteration, *all* hosts are returned, including unusable hosts (for usable hosts, use the *hosts()* method). An example:

```
>>> for addr in IPv4Network('192.0.2.0/28'):
...     addr
...
IPv4Address('192.0.2.0')
IPv4Address('192.0.2.1')
IPv4Address('192.0.2.2')
IPv4Address('192.0.2.3')
IPv4Address('192.0.2.4')
IPv4Address('192.0.2.5')
IPv4Address('192.0.2.6')
IPv4Address('192.0.2.7')
IPv4Address('192.0.2.8')
IPv4Address('192.0.2.9')
IPv4Address('192.0.2.10')
IPv4Address('192.0.2.11')
IPv4Address('192.0.2.12')
IPv4Address('192.0.2.13')
IPv4Address('192.0.2.14')
IPv4Address('192.0.2.15')
```

Networks as containers of addresses

Network objects can act as containers of addresses. Some examples:

```
>>> IPv4Network('192.0.2.0/28')[0]
IPv4Address('192.0.2.0')
>>> IPv4Network('192.0.2.0/28')[15]
IPv4Address('192.0.2.15')
>>> IPv4Address('192.0.2.6') in IPv4Network('192.0.2.0/28')
True
>>> IPv4Address('192.0.3.6') in IPv4Network('192.0.2.0/28')
False
```

21.28.4 Interface objects

class ipaddress.IPv4Interface(*address*)

Construct an IPv4 interface. The meaning of *address* is as in the constructor of *IPv4Network*, except that arbitrary host addresses are always accepted.

IPv4Interface is a subclass of *IPv4Address*, so it inherits all the attributes from that class. In addition, the following attributes are available:

ip

The address (*IPv4Address*) without network information.

```
>>> interface = IPv4Interface('192.0.2.5/24')
>>> interface.ip
IPv4Address('192.0.2.5')
```

network

The network (*IPv4Network*) this interface belongs to.

```
>>> interface = IPv4Interface('192.0.2.5/24')
>>> interface.network
IPv4Network('192.0.2.0/24')
```

with_prefixlen

A string representation of the interface with the mask in prefix notation.

```
>>> interface = IPv4Interface('192.0.2.5/24')
>>> interface.with_prefixlen
'192.0.2.5/24'
```

with_netmask

A string representation of the interface with the network as a net mask.

```
>>> interface = IPv4Interface('192.0.2.5/24')
>>> interface.with_netmask
'192.0.2.5/255.255.255.0'
```

with_hostmask

A string representation of the interface with the network as a host mask.

```
>>> interface = IPv4Interface('192.0.2.5/24')
>>> interface.with_hostmask
'192.0.2.5/0.0.0.255'
```

class ipaddress.IPv6Interface(*address*)

Construct an IPv6 interface. The meaning of *address* is as in the constructor of *IPv6Network*, except that arbitrary host addresses are always accepted.

IPv6Interface is a subclass of *IPv6Address*, so it inherits all the attributes from that class. In addition, the following attributes are available:

ip

network

with_prefixlen

with_netmask

with_hostmask

Refer to the corresponding attribute documentation in *IPv4Interface*.

21.28.5 Other Module Level Functions

The module also provides the following module level functions:

ipaddress.v4_int_to_packed(*address*)
    Represent an address as 4 packed bytes in network (big-endian) order. *address* is an integer representation of an IPv4 IP address. A *ValueError* is raised if the integer is negative or too large to be an IPv4 IP address.

```
>>> ipaddress.ip_address(3221225985)
IPv4Address('192.0.2.1')
>>> ipaddress.v4_int_to_packed(3221225985)
b'\xc0\x00\x02\x01'
```

ipaddress.v6_int_to_packed(*address*)
    Represent an address as 16 packed bytes in network (big-endian) order. *address* is an integer representation of an IPv6 IP address. A *ValueError* is raised if the integer is negative or too large to be an IPv6 IP address.

ipaddress.summarize_address_range(*first, last*)
    Return an iterator of the summarized network range given the first and last IP addresses. *first* is the first *IPv4Address* or *IPv6Address* in the range and *last* is the last *IPv4Address* or *IPv6Address* in the range. A *TypeError* is raised if *first* or *last* are not IP addresses or are not of the same version. A *ValueError* is raised if *last* is not greater than *first* or if *first* address version is not 4 or 6.

```
>>> [ipaddr for ipaddr in ipaddress.summarize_address_range(
...     ipaddress.IPv4Address('192.0.2.0'),
...     ipaddress.IPv4Address('192.0.2.130'))]
[IPv4Network('192.0.2.0/25'), IPv4Network('192.0.2.128/31'), IPv4Network('192.0.2.130/32')]
```

ipaddress.collapse_addresses(*addresses*)
    Return an iterator of the collapsed *IPv4Network* or *IPv6Network* objects. *addresses* is an iterator of *IPv4Network* or *IPv6Network* objects. A *TypeError* is raised if *addresses* contains mixed version objects.

```
>>> [ipaddr for ipaddr in
... ipaddress.collapse_addresses([ipaddress.IPv4Network('192.0.2.0/25'),
... ipaddress.IPv4Network('192.0.2.128/25')])]
[IPv4Network('192.0.2.0/24')]
```

ipaddress.get_mixed_type_key(*obj*)
    Return a key suitable for sorting between networks and addresses. Address and Network objects are not sortable by default; they're fundamentally different, so the expression:

```
IPv4Address('192.0.2.0') <= IPv4Network('192.0.2.0/24')
```

    doesn't make sense. There are some times however, where you may wish to have *ipaddress* sort these anyway. If you need to do this, you can use this function as the **key** argument to *sorted()*.

    obj is either a network or address object.

21.28.6 Custom Exceptions

To support more specific error reporting from class constructors, the module defines the following exceptions:

exception ipaddress.AddressValueError(*ValueError*)
    Any value error related to the address.

exception ipaddress.`NetmaskValueError`(*ValueError*)
    Any value error related to the netmask.

CHAPTER

TWENTYTWO

MULTIMEDIA SERVICES

The modules described in this chapter implement various algorithms or interfaces that are mainly useful for multimedia applications. They are available at the discretion of the installation. Here's an overview:

22.1 audioop — Manipulate raw audio data

The *audioop* module contains some useful operations on sound fragments. It operates on sound fragments consisting of signed integer samples 8, 16, 24 or 32 bits wide, stored in *bytes-like objects*. All scalar items are integers, unless specified otherwise.

Changed in version 3.4: Support for 24-bit samples was added. All functions now accept any *bytes-like object*. String input now results in an immediate error.

This module provides support for a-LAW, u-LAW and Intel/DVI ADPCM encodings.

A few of the more complicated operations only take 16-bit samples, otherwise the sample size (in bytes) is always a parameter of the operation.

The module defines the following variables and functions:

exception audioop.**error**
    This exception is raised on all errors, such as unknown number of bytes per sample, etc.

audioop.**add**(*fragment1, fragment2, width*)
    Return a fragment which is the addition of the two samples passed as parameters. *width* is the sample width in bytes, either 1, 2, 3 or 4. Both fragments should have the same length. Samples are truncated in case of overflow.

audioop.**adpcm2lin**(*adpcmfragment, width, state*)
    Decode an Intel/DVI ADPCM coded fragment to a linear fragment. See the description of *lin2adpcm()* for details on ADPCM coding. Return a tuple (**sample, newstate**) where the sample has the width specified in *width*.

audioop.**alaw2lin**(*fragment, width*)
    Convert sound fragments in a-LAW encoding to linearly encoded sound fragments. a-LAW encoding always uses 8 bits samples, so *width* refers only to the sample width of the output fragment here.

audioop.**avg**(*fragment, width*)
    Return the average over all samples in the fragment.

audioop.**avgpp**(*fragment, width*)
    Return the average peak-peak value over all samples in the fragment. No filtering is done, so the usefulness of this routine is questionable.

audioop.bias(*fragment, width, bias*)
    Return a fragment that is the original fragment with a bias added to each sample. Samples wrap around in case of overflow.

audioop.byteswap(*fragment, width*)
    "Byteswap" all samples in a fragment and returns the modified fragment. Converts big-endian samples to little-endian and vice versa.

    New in version 3.4.

audioop.cross(*fragment, width*)
    Return the number of zero crossings in the fragment passed as an argument.

audioop.findfactor(*fragment, reference*)
    Return a factor F such that `rms(add(fragment, mul(reference, -F)))` is minimal, i.e., return the factor with which you should multiply *reference* to make it match as well as possible to *fragment*. The fragments should both contain 2-byte samples.

    The time taken by this routine is proportional to `len(fragment)`.

audioop.findfit(*fragment, reference*)
    Try to match *reference* as well as possible to a portion of *fragment* (which should be the longer fragment). This is (conceptually) done by taking slices out of *fragment*, using *findfactor()* to compute the best match, and minimizing the result. The fragments should both contain 2-byte samples. Return a tuple (`offset, factor`) where *offset* is the (integer) offset into *fragment* where the optimal match started and *factor* is the (floating-point) factor as per *findfactor()*.

audioop.findmax(*fragment, length*)
    Search *fragment* for a slice of length *length* samples (not bytes!) with maximum energy, i.e., return i for which `rms(fragment[i*2:(i+length)*2])` is maximal. The fragments should both contain 2-byte samples.

    The routine takes time proportional to `len(fragment)`.

audioop.getsample(*fragment, width, index*)
    Return the value of sample *index* from the fragment.

audioop.lin2adpcm(*fragment, width, state*)
    Convert samples to 4 bit Intel/DVI ADPCM encoding. ADPCM coding is an adaptive coding scheme, whereby each 4 bit number is the difference between one sample and the next, divided by a (varying) step. The Intel/DVI ADPCM algorithm has been selected for use by the IMA, so it may well become a standard.

    state is a tuple containing the state of the coder. The coder returns a tuple (`adpcmfrag, newstate`), and the *newstate* should be passed to the next call of *lin2adpcm()*. In the initial call, `None` can be passed as the state. *adpcmfrag* is the ADPCM coded fragment packed 2 4-bit values per byte.

audioop.lin2alaw(*fragment, width*)
    Convert samples in the audio fragment to a-LAW encoding and return this as a bytes object. a-LAW is an audio encoding format whereby you get a dynamic range of about 13 bits using only 8 bit samples. It is used by the Sun audio hardware, among others.

audioop.lin2lin(*fragment, width, newwidth*)
    Convert samples between 1-, 2-, 3- and 4-byte formats.

Note: In some audio formats, such as .WAV files, 16, 24 and 32 bit samples are signed, but 8 bit samples are unsigned. So when converting to 8 bit wide samples for these formats, you need to also add 128 to the result:

```
new_frames = audioop.lin2lin(frames, old_width, 1)
new_frames = audioop.bias(new_frames, 1, 128)
```

The same, in reverse, has to be applied when converting from 8 to 16, 24 or 32 bit width samples.

audioop.lin2ulaw(*fragment, width*)
    Convert samples in the audio fragment to u-LAW encoding and return this as a bytes object. u-LAW is an audio encoding format whereby you get a dynamic range of about 14 bits using only 8 bit samples. It is used by the Sun audio hardware, among others.

audioop.max(*fragment, width*)
    Return the maximum of the *absolute value* of all samples in a fragment.

audioop.maxpp(*fragment, width*)
    Return the maximum peak-peak value in the sound fragment.

audioop.minmax(*fragment, width*)
    Return a tuple consisting of the minimum and maximum values of all samples in the sound fragment.

audioop.mul(*fragment, width, factor*)
    Return a fragment that has all samples in the original fragment multiplied by the floating-point value *factor*. Samples are truncated in case of overflow.

audioop.ratecv(*fragment, width, nchannels, inrate, outrate, state*[, *weightA*[, *weightB*]])
    Convert the frame rate of the input fragment.

    state is a tuple containing the state of the converter. The converter returns a tuple (`newfragment, newstate`), and *newstate* should be passed to the next call of `ratecv()`. The initial call should pass `None` as the state.

    The *weightA* and *weightB* arguments are parameters for a simple digital filter and default to `1` and `0` respectively.

audioop.reverse(*fragment, width*)
    Reverse the samples in a fragment and returns the modified fragment.

audioop.rms(*fragment, width*)
    Return the root-mean-square of the fragment, i.e. `sqrt(sum(S_i^2)/n)`.

    This is a measure of the power in an audio signal.

audioop.tomono(*fragment, width, lfactor, rfactor*)
    Convert a stereo fragment to a mono fragment. The left channel is multiplied by *lfactor* and the right channel by *rfactor* before adding the two channels to give a mono signal.

audioop.tostereo(*fragment, width, lfactor, rfactor*)
    Generate a stereo fragment from a mono fragment. Each pair of samples in the stereo fragment are computed from the mono sample, whereby left channel samples are multiplied by *lfactor* and right channel samples by *rfactor*.

audioop.ulaw2lin(*fragment, width*)
    Convert sound fragments in u-LAW encoding to linearly encoded sound fragments. u-LAW encoding always uses 8 bits samples, so *width* refers only to the sample width of the output fragment here.

Note that operations such as *mul()* or *max()* make no distinction between mono and stereo fragments, i.e. all samples are treated equal. If this is a problem the stereo fragment should be split into two mono fragments first and recombined later. Here is an example of how to do that:

```
def mul_stereo(sample, width, lfactor, rfactor):
    lsample = audioop.tomono(sample, width, 1, 0)
    rsample = audioop.tomono(sample, width, 0, 1)
    lsample = audioop.mul(lsample, width, lfactor)
    rsample = audioop.mul(rsample, width, rfactor)
    lsample = audioop.tostereo(lsample, width, 1, 0)
```

```
    rsample = audioop.tostereo(rsample, width, 0, 1)
    return audioop.add(lsample, rsample, width)
```

If you use the ADPCM coder to build network packets and you want your protocol to be stateless (i.e. to be able to tolerate packet loss) you should not only transmit the data but also the state. Note that you should send the *initial* state (the one you passed to `lin2adpcm()`) along to the decoder, not the final state (as returned by the coder). If you want to use `struct.Struct` to store the state in binary you can code the first element (the predicted value) in 16 bits and the second (the delta index) in 8.

The ADPCM coders have never been tried against other ADPCM coders, only against themselves. It could well be that I misinterpreted the standards in which case they will not be interoperable with the respective standards.

The `find*()` routines might look a bit funny at first sight. They are primarily meant to do echo cancellation. A reasonably fast way to do this is to pick the most energetic piece of the output sample, locate that in the input sample and subtract the whole output sample from the input sample:

```
def echocancel(outputdata, inputdata):
    pos = audioop.findmax(outputdata, 800)    # one tenth second
    out_test = outputdata[pos*2:]
    in_test = inputdata[pos*2:]
    ipos, factor = audioop.findfit(in_test, out_test)
    # Optional (for better cancellation):
    # factor = audioop.findfactor(in_test[ipos*2:ipos*2+len(out_test)],
    #                             out_test)
    prefill = '\0'*(pos+ipos)*2
    postfill = '\0'*(len(inputdata)-len(prefill)-len(outputdata))
    outputdata = prefill + audioop.mul(outputdata, 2, -factor) + postfill
    return audioop.add(inputdata, outputdata, 2)
```

22.2 `aifc` — Read and write AIFF and AIFC files

Source code: Lib/aifc.py

This module provides support for reading and writing AIFF and AIFF-C files. AIFF is Audio Interchange File Format, a format for storing digital audio samples in a file. AIFF-C is a newer version of the format that includes the ability to compress the audio data.

Audio files have a number of parameters that describe the audio data. The sampling rate or frame rate is the number of times per second the sound is sampled. The number of channels indicate if the audio is mono, stereo, or quadro. Each frame consists of one sample per channel. The sample size is the size in bytes of each sample. Thus a frame consists of `nchannels * samplesize` bytes, and a second's worth of audio consists of `nchannels * samplesize * framerate` bytes.

For example, CD quality audio has a sample size of two bytes (16 bits), uses two channels (stereo) and has a frame rate of 44,100 frames/second. This gives a frame size of 4 bytes (2*2), and a second's worth occupies 2*2*44100 bytes (176,400 bytes).

Module `aifc` defines the following function:

`aifc.open`(*file*, *mode=None*)

Open an AIFF or AIFF-C file and return an object instance with methods that are described below. The argument *file* is either a string naming a file or a *file object*. *mode* must be `'r'` or `'rb'` when the file must be opened for reading, or `'w'` or `'wb'` when the file must be opened for writing. If omitted, `file.mode` is used if it exists, otherwise `'rb'` is used. When used for writing, the file object should be seekable, unless you know ahead of time how many samples you are going to write in total and use `writeframesraw()` and `setnframes()`. The *open()* function may be used in a `with` statement. When the `with` block completes, the *close()* method is called.

Changed in version 3.4: Support for the `with` statement was added.

Objects returned by *open()* when a file is opened for reading have the following methods:

aifc.**getnchannels()**
> Return the number of audio channels (1 for mono, 2 for stereo).

aifc.**getsampwidth()**
> Return the size in bytes of individual samples.

aifc.**getframerate()**
> Return the sampling rate (number of audio frames per second).

aifc.**getnframes()**
> Return the number of audio frames in the file.

aifc.**getcomptype()**
> Return a bytes array of length 4 describing the type of compression used in the audio file. For AIFF files, the returned value is `b'NONE'`.

aifc.**getcompname()**
> Return a bytes array convertible to a human-readable description of the type of compression used in the audio file. For AIFF files, the returned value is `b'not compressed'`.

aifc.**getparams()**
> Returns a *namedtuple()* (**nchannels, sampwidth, framerate, nframes, comptype, compname**), equivalent to output of the `get*()` methods.

aifc.**getmarkers()**
> Return a list of markers in the audio file. A marker consists of a tuple of three elements. The first is the mark ID (an integer), the second is the mark position in frames from the beginning of the data (an integer), the third is the name of the mark (a string).

aifc.**getmark(**id**)**
> Return the tuple as described in *getmarkers()* for the mark with the given *id*.

aifc.**readframes(**nframes**)**
> Read and return the next *nframes* frames from the audio file. The returned data is a string containing for each frame the uncompressed samples of all channels.

aifc.**rewind()**
> Rewind the read pointer. The next *readframes()* will start from the beginning.

aifc.**setpos(**pos**)**
> Seek to the specified frame number.

aifc.**tell()**
> Return the current frame number.

aifc.**close()**
> Close the AIFF file. After calling this method, the object can no longer be used.

Objects returned by *open()* when a file is opened for writing have all the above methods, except for `readframes()` and `setpos()`. In addition the following methods exist. The `get*()` methods can only be called after the corresponding `set*()` methods have been called. Before the first `writeframes()` or `writeframesraw()`, all parameters except for the number of frames must be filled in.

aifc.**aiff()**
> Create an AIFF file. The default is that an AIFF-C file is created, unless the name of the file ends in '.aiff' in which case the default is an AIFF file.

aifc.aifc()
    Create an AIFF-C file. The default is that an AIFF-C file is created, unless the name of the file ends in '.aiff' in which case the default is an AIFF file.

aifc.setnchannels(*nchannels***)**
    Specify the number of channels in the audio file.

aifc.setsampwidth(*width***)**
    Specify the size in bytes of audio samples.

aifc.setframerate(*rate***)**
    Specify the sampling frequency in frames per second.

aifc.setnframes(*nframes***)**
    Specify the number of frames that are to be written to the audio file. If this parameter is not set, or not set correctly, the file needs to support seeking.

aifc.setcomptype(*type, name***)**
    Specify the compression type. If not specified, the audio data will not be compressed. In AIFF files, compression is not possible. The name parameter should be a human-readable description of the compression type as a bytes array, the type parameter should be a bytes array of length 4. Currently the following compression types are supported: b'NONE', b'ULAW', b'ALAW', b'G722'.

aifc.setparams(*nchannels, sampwidth, framerate, comptype, compname***)**
    Set all the above parameters at once. The argument is a tuple consisting of the various parameters. This means that it is possible to use the result of a *getparams()* call as argument to *setparams()*.

aifc.setmark(*id, pos, name***)**
    Add a mark with the given id (larger than 0), and the given name at the given position. This method can be called at any time before *close()*.

aifc.tell()
    Return the current write position in the output file. Useful in combination with *setmark()*.

aifc.writeframes(*data***)**
    Write data to the output file. This method can only be called after the audio file parameters have been set.

    Changed in version 3.4: Any *bytes-like object* is now accepted.

aifc.writeframesraw(*data***)**
    Like *writeframes()*, except that the header of the audio file is not updated.

    Changed in version 3.4: Any *bytes-like object* is now accepted.

aifc.close()
    Close the AIFF file. The header of the file is updated to reflect the actual size of the audio data. After calling this method, the object can no longer be used.

22.3 sunau — Read and write Sun AU files

Source code: Lib/sunau.py

The *sunau* module provides a convenient interface to the Sun AU sound format. Note that this module is interface-compatible with the modules *aifc* and *wave*.

An audio file consists of a header followed by the data. The fields of the header are:

Field	Contents
magic word	The four bytes .snd.
header size	Size of the header, including info, in bytes.
data size	Physical size of the data, in bytes.
encoding	Indicates how the audio samples are encoded.
sample rate	The sampling rate.
# of channels	The number of channels in the samples.
info	ASCII string giving a description of the audio file (padded with null bytes).

Apart from the info field, all header fields are 4 bytes in size. They are all 32-bit unsigned integers encoded in big-endian byte order.

The *sunau* module defines the following functions:

sunau.open(*file*, *mode*)

If *file* is a string, open the file by that name, otherwise treat it as a seekable file-like object. *mode* can be any of

'r' Read only mode.

'w' Write only mode.

Note that it does not allow read/write files.

A *mode* of 'r' returns an AU_read object, while a *mode* of 'w' or 'wb' returns an AU_write object.

sunau.openfp(*file*, *mode*)

A synonym for *open()*, maintained for backwards compatibility.

The *sunau* module defines the following exception:

exception sunau.Error

An error raised when something is impossible because of Sun AU specs or implementation deficiency.

The *sunau* module defines the following data items:

sunau.AUDIO_FILE_MAGIC

An integer every valid Sun AU file begins with, stored in big-endian form. This is the string .snd interpreted as an integer.

sunau.AUDIO_FILE_ENCODING_MULAW_8
sunau.AUDIO_FILE_ENCODING_LINEAR_8
sunau.AUDIO_FILE_ENCODING_LINEAR_16
sunau.AUDIO_FILE_ENCODING_LINEAR_24
sunau.AUDIO_FILE_ENCODING_LINEAR_32
sunau.AUDIO_FILE_ENCODING_ALAW_8

Values of the encoding field from the AU header which are supported by this module.

sunau.AUDIO_FILE_ENCODING_FLOAT
sunau.AUDIO_FILE_ENCODING_DOUBLE
sunau.AUDIO_FILE_ENCODING_ADPCM_G721
sunau.AUDIO_FILE_ENCODING_ADPCM_G722
sunau.AUDIO_FILE_ENCODING_ADPCM_G723_3
sunau.AUDIO_FILE_ENCODING_ADPCM_G723_5

Additional known values of the encoding field from the AU header, but which are not supported by this module.

22.3.1 AU_read Objects

AU_read objects, as returned by *open()* above, have the following methods:

`AU_read.close()`
: Close the stream, and make the instance unusable. (This is called automatically on deletion.)

`AU_read.getnchannels()`
: Returns number of audio channels (1 for mono, 2 for stereo).

`AU_read.getsampwidth()`
: Returns sample width in bytes.

`AU_read.getframerate()`
: Returns sampling frequency.

`AU_read.getnframes()`
: Returns number of audio frames.

`AU_read.getcomptype()`
: Returns compression type. Supported compression types are `'ULAW'`, `'ALAW'` and `'NONE'`.

`AU_read.getcompname()`
: Human-readable version of `getcomptype()`. The supported types have the respective names `'CCITT G.711 u-law'`, `'CCITT G.711 A-law'` and `'not compressed'`.

`AU_read.getparams()`
: Returns a `namedtuple()` (nchannels, sampwidth, framerate, nframes, comptype, compname), equivalent to output of the `get*()` methods.

`AU_read.readframes(n)`
: Reads and returns at most *n* frames of audio, as a `bytes` object. The data will be returned in linear format. If the original data is in u-LAW format, it will be converted.

`AU_read.rewind()`
: Rewind the file pointer to the beginning of the audio stream.

The following two methods define a term "position" which is compatible between them, and is otherwise implementation dependent.

`AU_read.setpos(pos)`
: Set the file pointer to the specified position. Only values returned from `tell()` should be used for *pos*.

`AU_read.tell()`
: Return current file pointer position. Note that the returned value has nothing to do with the actual position in the file.

The following two functions are defined for compatibility with the `aifc`, and don't do anything interesting.

`AU_read.getmarkers()`
: Returns `None`.

`AU_read.getmark(id)`
: Raise an error.

22.3.2 AU_write Objects

AU_write objects, as returned by `open()` above, have the following methods:

`AU_write.setnchannels(n)`
: Set the number of channels.

`AU_write.setsampwidth(n)`
: Set the sample width (in bytes.)

    Changed in version 3.4: Added support for 24-bit samples.

AU_write.setframerate(*n*)
    Set the frame rate.

AU_write.setnframes(*n*)
    Set the number of frames. This can be later changed, when and if more frames are written.

AU_write.setcomptype(*type*, *name*)
    Set the compression type and description. Only 'NONE' and 'ULAW' are supported on output.

AU_write.setparams(*tuple*)
    The *tuple* should be (nchannels, sampwidth, framerate, nframes, comptype, compname), with values valid for the set*() methods. Set all parameters.

AU_write.tell()
    Return current position in the file, with the same disclaimer for the *AU_read.tell()* and *AU_read.setpos()* methods.

AU_write.writeframesraw(*data*)
    Write audio frames, without correcting *nframes*.

    Changed in version 3.4: Any *bytes-like object* is now accepted.

AU_write.writeframes(*data*)
    Write audio frames and make sure *nframes* is correct.

    Changed in version 3.4: Any *bytes-like object* is now accepted.

AU_write.close()
    Make sure *nframes* is correct, and close the file.

    This method is called upon deletion.

Note that it is invalid to set any parameters after calling **writeframes()** or **writeframesraw()**.

22.4 wave — Read and write WAV files

Source code: Lib/wave.py

The *wave* module provides a convenient interface to the WAV sound format. It does not support compression/decompression, but it does support mono/stereo.

The *wave* module defines the following function and exception:

wave.open(*file*, *mode=None*)
    If *file* is a string, open the file by that name, otherwise treat it as a file-like object. *mode* can be:

    'rb' Read only mode.

    'wb' Write only mode.

    Note that it does not allow read/write WAV files.

    A *mode* of 'rb' returns a Wave_read object, while a *mode* of 'wb' returns a Wave_write object. If *mode* is omitted and a file-like object is passed as *file*, **file.mode** is used as the default value for *mode*.

    If you pass in a file-like object, the wave object will not close it when its **close()** method is called; it is the caller's responsibility to close the file object.

    The *open()* function may be used in a **with** statement. When the **with** block completes, the *Wave_read.close()* or *Wave_write.close()* method is called.

    Changed in version 3.4: Added support for unseekable files.

wave.openfp(*file, mode*)
> A synonym for *open()*, maintained for backwards compatibility.

exception wave.Error
> An error raised when something is impossible because it violates the WAV specification or hits an implementation deficiency.

22.4.1 Wave_read Objects

Wave_read objects, as returned by *open()*, have the following methods:

Wave_read.close()
> Close the stream if it was opened by *wave*, and make the instance unusable. This is called automatically on object collection.

Wave_read.getnchannels()
> Returns number of audio channels (1 for mono, 2 for stereo).

Wave_read.getsampwidth()
> Returns sample width in bytes.

Wave_read.getframerate()
> Returns sampling frequency.

Wave_read.getnframes()
> Returns number of audio frames.

Wave_read.getcomptype()
> Returns compression type (`'NONE'` is the only supported type).

Wave_read.getcompname()
> Human-readable version of *getcomptype()*. Usually `'not compressed'` parallels `'NONE'`.

Wave_read.getparams()
> Returns a *namedtuple()* (nchannels, sampwidth, framerate, nframes, comptype, compname), equivalent to output of the **get*()** methods.

Wave_read.readframes(*n*)
> Reads and returns at most *n* frames of audio, as a *bytes* object.

Wave_read.rewind()
> Rewind the file pointer to the beginning of the audio stream.

The following two methods are defined for compatibility with the *aifc* module, and don't do anything interesting.

Wave_read.getmarkers()
> Returns None.

Wave_read.getmark(*id*)
> Raise an error.

The following two methods define a term "position" which is compatible between them, and is otherwise implementation dependent.

Wave_read.setpos(*pos*)
> Set the file pointer to the specified position.

Wave_read.tell()
> Return current file pointer position.

22.4.2 Wave_write Objects

For seekable output streams, the `wave` header will automatically be updated to reflect the number of frames actually written. For unseekable streams, the *nframes* value must be accurate when the first frame data is written. An accurate *nframes* value can be achieved either by calling *setnframes()* or *setparams()* with the number of frames that will be written before *close()* is called and then using *writeframesraw()* to write the frame data, or by calling *writeframes()* with all of the frame data to be written. In the latter case *writeframes()* will calculate the number of frames in the data and set *nframes* accordingly before writing the frame data.

Wave_write objects, as returned by *open()*, have the following methods:

Changed in version 3.4: Added support for unseekable files.

Wave_write.close()
Make sure *nframes* is correct, and close the file if it was opened by *wave*. This method is called upon object collection. It will raise an exception if the output stream is not seekable and *nframes* does not match the number of frames actually written.

Wave_write.setnchannels(n**)**
Set the number of channels.

Wave_write.setsampwidth(n**)**
Set the sample width to n bytes.

Wave_write.setframerate(n**)**
Set the frame rate to n.

Changed in version 3.2: A non-integral input to this method is rounded to the nearest integer.

Wave_write.setnframes(n**)**
Set the number of frames to n. This will be changed later if the number of frames actually written is different (this update attempt will raise an error if the output stream is not seekable).

Wave_write.setcomptype(type, name**)**
Set the compression type and description. At the moment, only compression type `NONE` is supported, meaning no compression.

Wave_write.setparams(tuple**)**
The *tuple* should be (`nchannels`, `sampwidth`, `framerate`, `nframes`, `comptype`, `compname`), with values valid for the `set*()` methods. Sets all parameters.

Wave_write.tell()
Return current position in the file, with the same disclaimer for the *Wave_read.tell()* and *Wave_read.setpos()* methods.

Wave_write.writeframesraw(data**)**
Write audio frames, without correcting *nframes*.

Changed in version 3.4: Any *bytes-like object* is now accepted.

Wave_write.writeframes(data**)**
Write audio frames and make sure *nframes* is correct. It will raise an error if the output stream is not seekable and the total number of frames that have been written after *data* has been written does not match the previously set value for *nframes*.

Changed in version 3.4: Any *bytes-like object* is now accepted.

Note that it is invalid to set any parameters after calling `writeframes()` or `writeframesraw()`, and any attempt to do so will raise *wave.Error*.

22.5 `chunk` — Read IFF chunked data

Source code: Lib/chunk.py

This module provides an interface for reading files that use EA IFF 85 chunks.[1] This format is used in at least the Audio Interchange File Format (AIFF/AIFF-C) and the Real Media File Format (RMFF). The WAVE audio file format is closely related and can also be read using this module.

A chunk has the following structure:

Offset	Length	Contents
0	4	Chunk ID
4	4	Size of chunk in big-endian byte order, not including the header
8	n	Data bytes, where n is the size given in the preceding field
$8 + n$	0 or 1	Pad byte needed if n is odd and chunk alignment is used

The ID is a 4-byte string which identifies the type of chunk.

The size field (a 32-bit value, encoded using big-endian byte order) gives the size of the chunk data, not including the 8-byte header.

Usually an IFF-type file consists of one or more chunks. The proposed usage of the *Chunk* class defined here is to instantiate an instance at the start of each chunk and read from the instance until it reaches the end, after which a new instance can be instantiated. At the end of the file, creating a new instance will fail with an *EOFError* exception.

class chunk.Chunk(*file, align=True, bigendian=True, inclheader=False*)

Class which represents a chunk. The *file* argument is expected to be a file-like object. An instance of this class is specifically allowed. The only method that is needed is `read()`. If the methods *seek()* and *tell()* are present and don't raise an exception, they are also used. If these methods are present and raise an exception, they are expected to not have altered the object. If the optional argument *align* is true, chunks are assumed to be aligned on 2-byte boundaries. If *align* is false, no alignment is assumed. The default value is true. If the optional argument *bigendian* is false, the chunk size is assumed to be in little-endian order. This is needed for WAVE audio files. The default value is true. If the optional argument *inclheader* is true, the size given in the chunk header includes the size of the header. The default value is false.

A *Chunk* object supports the following methods:

getname()
Returns the name (ID) of the chunk. This is the first 4 bytes of the chunk.

getsize()
Returns the size of the chunk.

close()
Close and skip to the end of the chunk. This does not close the underlying file.

The remaining methods will raise *OSError* if called after the *close()* method has been called. Before Python 3.3, they used to raise *IOError*, now an alias of *OSError*.

isatty()
Returns **False**.

seek(*pos, whence=0*)
Set the chunk's current position. The *whence* argument is optional and defaults to 0 (absolute file positioning); other values are 1 (seek relative to the current position) and 2 (seek relative to

---

[1] "EA IFF 85" Standard for Interchange Format Files, Jerry Morrison, Electronic Arts, January 1985.

the file's end). There is no return value. If the underlying file does not allow seek, only forward seeks are allowed.

tell()
Return the current position into the chunk.

read(*size=-1*)
Read at most *size* bytes from the chunk (less if the read hits the end of the chunk before obtaining *size* bytes). If the *size* argument is negative or omitted, read all data until the end of the chunk. An empty bytes object is returned when the end of the chunk is encountered immediately.

skip()
Skip to the end of the chunk. All further calls to read() for the chunk will return b''. If you are not interested in the contents of the chunk, this method should be called so that the file points to the start of the next chunk.

22.6 colorsys — Conversions between color systems

Source code: Lib/colorsys.py

The colorsys module defines bidirectional conversions of color values between colors expressed in the RGB (Red Green Blue) color space used in computer monitors and three other coordinate systems: YIQ, HLS (Hue Lightness Saturation) and HSV (Hue Saturation Value). Coordinates in all of these color spaces are floating point values. In the YIQ space, the Y coordinate is between 0 and 1, but the I and Q coordinates can be positive or negative. In all other spaces, the coordinates are all between 0 and 1.

See also:

More information about color spaces can be found at http://www.poynton.com/ColorFAQ.html and https://www.cambridgeincolour.com/tutorials/color-spaces.htm.

The colorsys module defines the following functions:

colorsys.rgb_to_yiq(*r, g, b*)
Convert the color from RGB coordinates to YIQ coordinates.

colorsys.yiq_to_rgb(*y, i, q*)
Convert the color from YIQ coordinates to RGB coordinates.

colorsys.rgb_to_hls(*r, g, b*)
Convert the color from RGB coordinates to HLS coordinates.

colorsys.hls_to_rgb(*h, l, s*)
Convert the color from HLS coordinates to RGB coordinates.

colorsys.rgb_to_hsv(*r, g, b*)
Convert the color from RGB coordinates to HSV coordinates.

colorsys.hsv_to_rgb(*h, s, v*)
Convert the color from HSV coordinates to RGB coordinates.

Example:

```
>>> import colorsys
>>> colorsys.rgb_to_hsv(0.2, 0.4, 0.4)
(0.5, 0.5, 0.4)
>>> colorsys.hsv_to_rgb(0.5, 0.5, 0.4)
(0.2, 0.4, 0.4)
```

22.7 `imghdr` — Determine the type of an image

Source code: Lib/imghdr.py

The *imghdr* module determines the type of image contained in a file or byte stream.

The *imghdr* module defines the following function:

imghdr.what(*filename*, *h=None*)
    Tests the image data contained in the file named by *filename*, and returns a string describing the image type. If optional *h* is provided, the *filename* is ignored and *h* is assumed to contain the byte stream to test.

    Changed in version 3.6: Accepts a *path-like object*.

The following image types are recognized, as listed below with the return value from *what()*:

Value	Image format
`'rgb'`	SGI ImgLib Files
`'gif'`	GIF 87a and 89a Files
`'pbm'`	Portable Bitmap Files
`'pgm'`	Portable Graymap Files
`'ppm'`	Portable Pixmap Files
`'tiff'`	TIFF Files
`'rast'`	Sun Raster Files
`'xbm'`	X Bitmap Files
`'jpeg'`	JPEG data in JFIF or Exif formats
`'bmp'`	BMP files
`'png'`	Portable Network Graphics
`'webp'`	WebP files
`'exr'`	OpenEXR Files

New in version 3.5: The *exr* and *webp* formats were added.

You can extend the list of file types *imghdr* can recognize by appending to this variable:

imghdr.tests
    A list of functions performing the individual tests. Each function takes two arguments: the byte-stream and an open file-like object. When *what()* is called with a byte-stream, the file-like object will be **None**.

    The test function should return a string describing the image type if the test succeeded, or **None** if it failed.

Example:

```
>>> import imghdr
>>> imghdr.what('bass.gif')
'gif'
```

22.8 `sndhdr` — Determine type of sound file

Source code: Lib/sndhdr.py

The `sndhdr` provides utility functions which attempt to determine the type of sound data which is in a file. When these functions are able to determine what type of sound data is stored in a file, they return a `namedtuple()`, containing five attributes: (`filetype, framerate, nchannels, nframes, sampwidth`). The value for *type* indicates the data type and will be one of the strings `'aifc'`, `'aiff'`, `'au'`, `'hcom'`, `'sndr'`, `'sndt'`, `'voc'`, `'wav'`, `'8svx'`, `'sb'`, `'ub'`, or `'ul'`. The *sampling_rate* will be either the actual value or 0 if unknown or difficult to decode. Similarly, *channels* will be either the number of channels or 0 if it cannot be determined or if the value is difficult to decode. The value for *frames* will be either the number of frames or -1. The last item in the tuple, *bits_per_sample*, will either be the sample size in bits or `'A'` for A-LAW or `'U'` for u-LAW.

sndhdr.what(*filename*)
> Determines the type of sound data stored in the file *filename* using `whathdr()`. If it succeeds, returns a namedtuple as described above, otherwise `None` is returned.
>
> Changed in version 3.5: Result changed from a tuple to a namedtuple.

sndhdr.whathdr(*filename*)
> Determines the type of sound data stored in a file based on the file header. The name of the file is given by *filename*. This function returns a namedtuple as described above on success, or `None`.
>
> Changed in version 3.5: Result changed from a tuple to a namedtuple.

22.9 ossaudiodev — Access to OSS-compatible audio devices

This module allows you to access the OSS (Open Sound System) audio interface. OSS is available for a wide range of open-source and commercial Unices, and is the standard audio interface for Linux and recent versions of FreeBSD.

Changed in version 3.3: Operations in this module now raise `OSError` where `IOError` was raised.

See also:

Open Sound System Programmer's Guide the official documentation for the OSS C API

The module defines a large number of constants supplied by the OSS device driver; see `<sys/soundcard.h>` on either Linux or FreeBSD for a listing.

`ossaudiodev` defines the following variables and functions:

exception ossaudiodev.OSSAudioError
> This exception is raised on certain errors. The argument is a string describing what went wrong.
>
> (If `ossaudiodev` receives an error from a system call such as `open()`, `write()`, or `ioctl()`, it raises `OSError`. Errors detected directly by `ossaudiodev` result in `OSSAudioError`.)
>
> (For backwards compatibility, the exception class is also available as `ossaudiodev.error`.)

ossaudiodev.open(*mode*)
ossaudiodev.open(*device, mode*)
> Open an audio device and return an OSS audio device object. This object supports many file-like methods, such as `read()`, `write()`, and `fileno()` (although there are subtle differences between conventional Unix read/write semantics and those of OSS audio devices). It also supports a number of audio-specific methods; see below for the complete list of methods.
>
> *device* is the audio device filename to use. If it is not specified, this module first looks in the environment variable `AUDIODEV` for a device to use. If not found, it falls back to `/dev/dsp`.
>
> *mode* is one of `'r'` for read-only (record) access, `'w'` for write-only (playback) access and `'rw'` for both. Since many sound cards only allow one process to have the recorder or player open at a time, it is

a good idea to open the device only for the activity needed. Further, some sound cards are half-duplex: they can be opened for reading or writing, but not both at once.

Note the unusual calling syntax: the *first* argument is optional, and the second is required. This is a historical artifact for compatibility with the older `linuxaudiodev` module which `ossaudiodev` supersedes.

`ossaudiodev.openmixer([device])`
Open a mixer device and return an OSS mixer device object. *device* is the mixer device filename to use. If it is not specified, this module first looks in the environment variable `MIXERDEV` for a device to use. If not found, it falls back to `/dev/mixer`.

22.9.1 Audio Device Objects

Before you can write to or read from an audio device, you must call three methods in the correct order:

1. `setfmt()` to set the output format
2. `channels()` to set the number of channels
3. `speed()` to set the sample rate

Alternately, you can use the `setparameters()` method to set all three audio parameters at once. This is more convenient, but may not be as flexible in all cases.

The audio device objects returned by `open()` define the following methods and (read-only) attributes:

`oss_audio_device.close()`
Explicitly close the audio device. When you are done writing to or reading from an audio device, you should explicitly close it. A closed device cannot be used again.

`oss_audio_device.fileno()`
Return the file descriptor associated with the device.

`oss_audio_device.read(size)`
Read *size* bytes from the audio input and return them as a Python string. Unlike most Unix device drivers, OSS audio devices in blocking mode (the default) will block `read()` until the entire requested amount of data is available.

`oss_audio_device.write(data)`
Write a *bytes-like object* data to the audio device and return the number of bytes written. If the audio device is in blocking mode (the default), the entire data is always written (again, this is different from usual Unix device semantics). If the device is in non-blocking mode, some data may not be written —see `writeall()`.

Changed in version 3.5: Writable *bytes-like object* is now accepted.

`oss_audio_device.writeall(data)`
Write a *bytes-like object* data to the audio device: waits until the audio device is able to accept data, writes as much data as it will accept, and repeats until *data* has been completely written. If the device is in blocking mode (the default), this has the same effect as `write()`; `writeall()` is only useful in non-blocking mode. Has no return value, since the amount of data written is always equal to the amount of data supplied.

Changed in version 3.5: Writable *bytes-like object* is now accepted.

Changed in version 3.2: Audio device objects also support the context management protocol, i.e. they can be used in a `with` statement.

The following methods each map to exactly one `ioctl()` system call. The correspondence is obvious: for example, `setfmt()` corresponds to the SNDCTL_DSP_SETFMT ioctl, and `sync()` to SNDCTL_DSP_SYNC (this can be useful when consulting the OSS documentation). If the underlying `ioctl()` fails, they all raise *OSError*.

oss_audio_device.nonblock()
> Put the device into non-blocking mode. Once in non-blocking mode, there is no way to return it to blocking mode.

oss_audio_device.getfmts()
> Return a bitmask of the audio output formats supported by the soundcard. Some of the formats supported by OSS are:

Format	Description
AFMT_MU_LAW	a logarithmic encoding (used by Sun `.au` files and `/dev/audio`)
AFMT_A_LAW	a logarithmic encoding
AFMT_IMA_ADPCM	a 4:1 compressed format defined by the Interactive Multimedia Association
AFMT_U8	Unsigned, 8-bit audio
AFMT_S16_LE	Signed, 16-bit audio, little-endian byte order (as used by Intel processors)
AFMT_S16_BE	Signed, 16-bit audio, big-endian byte order (as used by 68k, PowerPC, Sparc)
AFMT_S8	Signed, 8 bit audio
AFMT_U16_LE	Unsigned, 16-bit little-endian audio
AFMT_U16_BE	Unsigned, 16-bit big-endian audio

> Consult the OSS documentation for a full list of audio formats, and note that most devices support only a subset of these formats. Some older devices only support `AFMT_U8`; the most common format used today is `AFMT_S16_LE`.

oss_audio_device.setfmt(*format*)
> Try to set the current audio format to *format*—see *getfmts()* for a list. Returns the audio format that the device was set to, which may not be the requested format. May also be used to return the current audio format—do this by passing an "audio format" of `AFMT_QUERY`.

oss_audio_device.channels(*nchannels*)
> Set the number of output channels to *nchannels*. A value of 1 indicates monophonic sound, 2 stereophonic. Some devices may have more than 2 channels, and some high-end devices may not support mono. Returns the number of channels the device was set to.

oss_audio_device.speed(*samplerate*)
> Try to set the audio sampling rate to *samplerate* samples per second. Returns the rate actually set. Most sound devices don't support arbitrary sampling rates. Common rates are:

Rate	Description
8000	default rate for `/dev/audio`
11025	speech recording
22050	
44100	CD quality audio (at 16 bits/sample and 2 channels)
96000	DVD quality audio (at 24 bits/sample)

oss_audio_device.sync()
> Wait until the sound device has played every byte in its buffer. (This happens implicitly when the device is closed.) The OSS documentation recommends closing and re-opening the device rather than using *sync()*.

oss_audio_device.reset()
> Immediately stop playing or recording and return the device to a state where it can accept commands. The OSS documentation recommends closing and re-opening the device after calling *reset()*.

`oss_audio_device.post()`
> Tell the driver that there is likely to be a pause in the output, making it possible for the device to handle the pause more intelligently. You might use this after playing a spot sound effect, before waiting for user input, or before doing disk I/O.

The following convenience methods combine several ioctls, or one ioctl and some simple calculations.

`oss_audio_device.setparameters(`*format, nchannels, samplerate*[, *strict=False*]`)`
> Set the key audio sampling parameters—sample format, number of channels, and sampling rate—in one method call. *format*, *nchannels*, and *samplerate* should be as specified in the `setfmt()`, `channels()`, and `speed()` methods. If *strict* is true, `setparameters()` checks to see if each parameter was actually set to the requested value, and raises `OSSAudioError` if not. Returns a tuple (*format*, *nchannels*, *samplerate*) indicating the parameter values that were actually set by the device driver (i.e., the same as the return values of `setfmt()`, `channels()`, and `speed()`).
>
> For example,
>
> ```
> (fmt, channels, rate) = dsp.setparameters(fmt, channels, rate)
> ```
>
> is equivalent to
>
> ```
> fmt = dsp.setfmt(fmt)
> channels = dsp.channels(channels)
> rate = dsp.rate(rate)
> ```

`oss_audio_device.bufsize()`
> Returns the size of the hardware buffer, in samples.

`oss_audio_device.obufcount()`
> Returns the number of samples that are in the hardware buffer yet to be played.

`oss_audio_device.obuffree()`
> Returns the number of samples that could be queued into the hardware buffer to be played without blocking.

Audio device objects also support several read-only attributes:

`oss_audio_device.closed`
> Boolean indicating whether the device has been closed.

`oss_audio_device.name`
> String containing the name of the device file.

`oss_audio_device.mode`
> The I/O mode for the file, either `"r"`, `"rw"`, or `"w"`.

22.9.2 Mixer Device Objects

The mixer object provides two file-like methods:

`oss_mixer_device.close()`
> This method closes the open mixer device file. Any further attempts to use the mixer after this file is closed will raise an `OSError`.

`oss_mixer_device.fileno()`
> Returns the file handle number of the open mixer device file.

Changed in version 3.2: Mixer objects also support the context management protocol.

The remaining methods are specific to audio mixing:

`oss_mixer_device.controls()`
> This method returns a bitmask specifying the available mixer controls ("Control" being a specific mixable "channel", such as SOUND_MIXER_PCM or SOUND_MIXER_SYNTH). This bitmask indicates a subset of all available mixer controls—the SOUND_MIXER_* constants defined at module level. To determine if, for example, the current mixer object supports a PCM mixer, use the following Python code:
>
> ```
> mixer=ossaudiodev.openmixer()
> if mixer.controls() & (1 << ossaudiodev.SOUND_MIXER_PCM):
>     # PCM is supported
>     ... code ...
> ```
>
> For most purposes, the SOUND_MIXER_VOLUME (master volume) and SOUND_MIXER_PCM controls should suffice—but code that uses the mixer should be flexible when it comes to choosing mixer controls. On the Gravis Ultrasound, for example, SOUND_MIXER_VOLUME does not exist.

`oss_mixer_device.stereocontrols()`
> Returns a bitmask indicating stereo mixer controls. If a bit is set, the corresponding control is stereo; if it is unset, the control is either monophonic or not supported by the mixer (use in combination with *controls()* to determine which).
>
> See the code example for the *controls()* function for an example of getting data from a bitmask.

`oss_mixer_device.reccontrols()`
> Returns a bitmask specifying the mixer controls that may be used to record. See the code example for *controls()* for an example of reading from a bitmask.

`oss_mixer_device.get(control)`
> Returns the volume of a given mixer control. The returned volume is a 2-tuple (`left_volume`, `right_volume`). Volumes are specified as numbers from 0 (silent) to 100 (full volume). If the control is monophonic, a 2-tuple is still returned, but both volumes are the same.
>
> Raises *OSSAudioError* if an invalid control is specified, or *OSError* if an unsupported control is specified.

`oss_mixer_device.set(control, (left, right))`
> Sets the volume for a given mixer control to (`left`,`right`). `left` and `right` must be ints and between 0 (silent) and 100 (full volume). On success, the new volume is returned as a 2-tuple. Note that this may not be exactly the same as the volume specified, because of the limited resolution of some soundcard's mixers.
>
> Raises *OSSAudioError* if an invalid mixer control was specified, or if the specified volumes were out-of-range.

`oss_mixer_device.get_recsrc()`
> This method returns a bitmask indicating which control(s) are currently being used as a recording source.

`oss_mixer_device.set_recsrc(bitmask)`
> Call this function to specify a recording source. Returns a bitmask indicating the new recording source (or sources) if successful; raises *OSError* if an invalid source was specified. To set the current recording source to the microphone input:
>
> ```
> mixer.setrecsrc (1 << ossaudiodev.SOUND_MIXER_MIC)
> ```

CHAPTER
TWENTYTHREE

INTERNATIONALIZATION

The modules described in this chapter help you write software that is independent of language and locale by providing mechanisms for selecting a language to be used in program messages or by tailoring output to match local conventions.

The list of modules described in this chapter is:

23.1 gettext — Multilingual internationalization services

Source code: Lib/gettext.py

The *gettext* module provides internationalization (I18N) and localization (L10N) services for your Python modules and applications. It supports both the GNU **gettext** message catalog API and a higher level, class-based API that may be more appropriate for Python files. The interface described below allows you to write your module and application messages in one natural language, and provide a catalog of translated messages for running under different natural languages.

Some hints on localizing your Python modules and applications are also given.

23.1.1 GNU gettext API

The *gettext* module defines the following API, which is very similar to the GNU **gettext** API. If you use this API you will affect the translation of your entire application globally. Often this is what you want if your application is monolingual, with the choice of language dependent on the locale of your user. If you are localizing a Python module, or if your application needs to switch languages on the fly, you probably want to use the class-based API instead.

gettext.**bindtextdomain**(*domain*, *localedir=None*)

> Bind the *domain* to the locale directory *localedir*. More concretely, *gettext* will look for binary .mo files for the given domain using the path (on Unix): `localedir/language/LC_MESSAGES/domain.mo`, where *languages* is searched for in the environment variables **LANGUAGE**, **LC_ALL**, **LC_MESSAGES**, and **LANG** respectively.
>
> If *localedir* is omitted or **None**, then the current binding for *domain* is returned.[1]

gettext.**bind_textdomain_codeset**(*domain*, *codeset=None*)

> Bind the *domain* to *codeset*, changing the encoding of byte strings returned by the *lgettext()*, *ldgettext()*, *lngettext()* and *ldngettext()* functions. If *codeset* is omitted, then the current binding is returned.

---

[1] The default locale directory is system dependent; for example, on RedHat Linux it is /usr/share/locale, but on Solaris it is /usr/lib/locale. The *gettext* module does not try to support these system dependent defaults; instead its default is sys.prefix/share/locale. For this reason, it is always best to call *bindtextdomain()* with an explicit absolute path at the start of your application.

1269

gettext.textdomain(*domain=None*)
   Change or query the current global domain. If *domain* is None, then the current global domain is returned, otherwise the global domain is set to *domain*, which is returned.

gettext.gettext(*message*)
   Return the localized translation of *message*, based on the current global domain, language, and locale directory. This function is usually aliased as _() in the local namespace (see examples below).

gettext.dgettext(*domain, message*)
   Like *gettext()*, but look the message up in the specified *domain*.

gettext.ngettext(*singular, plural, n*)
   Like *gettext()*, but consider plural forms. If a translation is found, apply the plural formula to *n*, and return the resulting message (some languages have more than two plural forms). If no translation is found, return *singular* if *n* is 1; return *plural* otherwise.

   The Plural formula is taken from the catalog header. It is a C or Python expression that has a free variable *n*; the expression evaluates to the index of the plural in the catalog. See the GNU gettext documentation for the precise syntax to be used in .po files and the formulas for a variety of languages.

gettext.dngettext(*domain, singular, plural, n*)
   Like *ngettext()*, but look the message up in the specified *domain*.

gettext.lgettext(*message*)

gettext.ldgettext(*domain, message*)

gettext.lngettext(*singular, plural, n*)

gettext.ldngettext(*domain, singular, plural, n*)
   Equivalent to the corresponding functions without the l prefix (*gettext()*, *dgettext()*, *ngettext()* and *dngettext()*), but the translation is returned as a byte string encoded in the preferred system encoding if no other encoding was explicitly set with *bind_textdomain_codeset()*.

> **Warning:** These functions should be avoided in Python 3, because they return encoded bytes. It's much better to use alternatives which return Unicode strings instead, since most Python applications will want to manipulate human readable text as strings instead of bytes. Further, it's possible that you may get unexpected Unicode-related exceptions if there are encoding problems with the translated strings. It is possible that the l*() functions will be deprecated in future Python versions due to their inherent problems and limitations.

Note that GNU **gettext** also defines a dcgettext() method, but this was deemed not useful and so it is currently unimplemented.

Here's an example of typical usage for this API:

```
import gettext
gettext.bindtextdomain('myapplication', '/path/to/my/language/directory')
gettext.textdomain('myapplication')
_ = gettext.gettext
# ...
print(_('This is a translatable string.'))
```

23.1.2 Class-based API

The class-based API of the *gettext* module gives you more flexibility and greater convenience than the GNU **gettext** API. It is the recommended way of localizing your Python applications and modules. **gettext** defines a "translations" class which implements the parsing of GNU .mo format files, and has methods for returning strings. Instances of this "translations" class can also install themselves in the built-in namespace as the function _().

gettext.find(*domain, localedir=None, languages=None, all=False*)

This function implements the standard .mo file search algorithm. It takes a *domain*, identical to what `textdomain()` takes. Optional *localedir* is as in `bindtextdomain()` Optional *languages* is a list of strings, where each string is a language code.

If *localedir* is not given, then the default system locale directory is used.[2] If *languages* is not given, then the following environment variables are searched: LANGUAGE, LC_ALL, LC_MESSAGES, and LANG. The first one returning a non-empty value is used for the *languages* variable. The environment variables should contain a colon separated list of languages, which will be split on the colon to produce the expected list of language code strings.

`find()` then expands and normalizes the languages, and then iterates through them, searching for an existing file built of these components:

localedir/*language*/LC_MESSAGES/*domain*.mo

The first such file name that exists is returned by `find()`. If no such file is found, then None is returned. If *all* is given, it returns a list of all file names, in the order in which they appear in the languages list or the environment variables.

gettext.translation(*domain, localedir=None, languages=None, class_=None, fallback=False, codeset=None*)

Return a Translations instance based on the *domain*, *localedir*, and *languages*, which are first passed to `find()` to get a list of the associated .mo file paths. Instances with identical .mo file names are cached. The actual class instantiated is either *class_* if provided, otherwise *GNUTranslations*. The class's constructor must take a single *file object* argument. If provided, *codeset* will change the charset used to encode translated strings in the `lgettext()` and `lngettext()` methods.

If multiple files are found, later files are used as fallbacks for earlier ones. To allow setting the fallback, `copy.copy()` is used to clone each translation object from the cache; the actual instance data is still shared with the cache.

If no .mo file is found, this function raises *OSError* if *fallback* is false (which is the default), and returns a *NullTranslations* instance if *fallback* is true.

Changed in version 3.3: *IOError* used to be raised instead of *OSError*.

gettext.install(*domain, localedir=None, codeset=None, names=None*)

This installs the function _() in Python's builtins namespace, based on *domain*, *localedir*, and *codeset* which are passed to the function `translation()`.

For the *names* parameter, please see the description of the translation object's `install()` method.

As seen below, you usually mark the strings in your application that are candidates for translation, by wrapping them in a call to the _() function, like this:

```
print(_('This string will be translated.'))
```

For convenience, you want the _() function to be installed in Python's builtins namespace, so it is easily accessible in all modules of your application.

The NullTranslations class

Translation classes are what actually implement the translation of original source file message strings to translated message strings. The base class used by all translation classes is *NullTranslations*; this provides the basic interface you can use to write your own specialized translation classes. Here are the methods of NullTranslations:

---

[2] See the footnote for `bindtextdomain()` above.

class gettext.NullTranslations(*fp=None*)

Takes an optional *file object fp*, which is ignored by the base class. Initializes "protected" instance variables *_info* and *_charset* which are set by derived classes, as well as *_fallback*, which is set through `add_fallback()`. It then calls `self._parse(fp)` if *fp* is not None.

_parse(*fp*)

No-op'd in the base class, this method takes file object *fp*, and reads the data from the file, initializing its message catalog. If you have an unsupported message catalog file format, you should override this method to parse your format.

add_fallback(*fallback*)

Add *fallback* as the fallback object for the current translation object. A translation object should consult the fallback if it cannot provide a translation for a given message.

gettext(*message*)

If a fallback has been set, forward `gettext()` to the fallback. Otherwise, return *message*. Overridden in derived classes.

ngettext(*singular, plural, n*)

If a fallback has been set, forward `ngettext()` to the fallback. Otherwise, return *singular* if *n* is 1; return *plural* otherwise. Overridden in derived classes.

lgettext(*message*)

lngettext(*singular, plural, n*)

Equivalent to `gettext()` and `ngettext()`, but the translation is returned as a byte string encoded in the preferred system encoding if no encoding was explicitly set with `set_output_charset()`. Overridden in derived classes.

> **Warning:** These methods should be avoided in Python 3. See the warning for the `lgettext()` function.

info()

Return the "protected" _info variable.

charset()

Return the encoding of the message catalog file.

output_charset()

Return the encoding used to return translated messages in `lgettext()` and `lngettext()`.

set_output_charset(*charset*)

Change the encoding used to return translated messages.

install(*names=None*)

This method installs `gettext()` into the built-in namespace, binding it to _.

If the *names* parameter is given, it must be a sequence containing the names of functions you want to install in the builtins namespace in addition to _(). Supported names are `'gettext'`, `'ngettext'`, `'lgettext'` and `'lngettext'`.

Note that this is only one way, albeit the most convenient way, to make the _() function available to your application. Because it affects the entire application globally, and specifically the built-in namespace, localized modules should never install _(). Instead, they should use this code to make _() available to their module:

```
import gettext
t = gettext.translation('mymodule', ...)
_ = t.gettext
```

This puts _() only in the module's global namespace and so only affects calls within this module.

The GNUTranslations class

The *gettext* module provides one additional class derived from *NullTranslations*: *GNUTranslations*. This class overrides _parse() to enable reading GNU **gettext** format .mo files in both big-endian and little-endian format.

GNUTranslations parses optional meta-data out of the translation catalog. It is convention with GNU **gettext** to include meta-data as the translation for the empty string. This meta-data is in RFC 822-style key: value pairs, and should contain the Project-Id-Version key. If the key Content-Type is found, then the charset property is used to initialize the "protected" _charset instance variable, defaulting to None if not found. If the charset encoding is specified, then all message ids and message strings read from the catalog are converted to Unicode using this encoding, else ASCII encoding is assumed.

Since message ids are read as Unicode strings too, all *gettext() methods will assume message ids as Unicode strings, not byte strings.

The entire set of key/value pairs are placed into a dictionary and set as the "protected" _info instance variable.

If the .mo file's magic number is invalid, the major version number is unexpected, or if other problems occur while reading the file, instantiating a *GNUTranslations* class can raise *OSError*.

class gettext.GNUTranslations

> The following methods are overridden from the base class implementation:
>
> **gettext**(*message*)
>
>> Look up the *message* id in the catalog and return the corresponding message string, as a Unicode string. If there is no entry in the catalog for the *message* id, and a fallback has been set, the look up is forwarded to the fallback's *gettext()* method. Otherwise, the *message* id is returned.
>
> **ngettext**(*singular, plural, n*)
>
>> Do a plural-forms lookup of a message id. *singular* is used as the message id for purposes of lookup in the catalog, while *n* is used to determine which plural form to use. The returned message string is a Unicode string.
>>
>> If the message id is not found in the catalog, and a fallback is specified, the request is forwarded to the fallback's *ngettext()* method. Otherwise, when *n* is 1 *singular* is returned, and *plural* is returned in all other cases.
>>
>> Here is an example:
>>
>> ```
>> n = len(os.listdir('.'))
>> cat = GNUTranslations(somefile)
>> message = cat.ngettext(
>>     'There is %(num)d file in this directory',
>>     'There are %(num)d files in this directory',
>>     n) % {'num': n}
>> ```
>
> **lgettext**(*message*)
>
> **lngettext**(*singular, plural, n*)
>
>> Equivalent to *gettext()* and *ngettext()*, but the translation is returned as a byte string encoded in the preferred system encoding if no encoding was explicitly set with *set_output_charset()*.
>>
>> **Warning:** These methods should be avoided in Python 3. See the warning for the *lgettext()* function.

Solaris message catalog support

The Solaris operating system defines its own binary .mo file format, but since no documentation can be found on this format, it is not supported at this time.

The Catalog constructor

GNOME uses a version of the *gettext* module by James Henstridge, but this version has a slightly different API. Its documented usage was:

```
import gettext
cat = gettext.Catalog(domain, localedir)
_ = cat.gettext
print(_('hello world'))
```

For compatibility with this older module, the function `Catalog()` is an alias for the *translation()* function described above.

One difference between this module and Henstridge's: his catalog objects supported access through a mapping API, but this appears to be unused and so is not currently supported.

23.1.3 Internationalizing your programs and modules

Internationalization (I18N) refers to the operation by which a program is made aware of multiple languages. Localization (L10N) refers to the adaptation of your program, once internationalized, to the local language and cultural habits. In order to provide multilingual messages for your Python programs, you need to take the following steps:

1. prepare your program or module by specially marking translatable strings
2. run a suite of tools over your marked files to generate raw messages catalogs
3. create language specific translations of the message catalogs
4. use the *gettext* module so that message strings are properly translated

In order to prepare your code for I18N, you need to look at all the strings in your files. Any string that needs to be translated should be marked by wrapping it in _('...') — that is, a call to the function _(). For example:

```
filename = 'mylog.txt'
message = _('writing a log message')
fp = open(filename, 'w')
fp.write(message)
fp.close()
```

In this example, the string `'writing a log message'` is marked as a candidate for translation, while the strings `'mylog.txt'` and `'w'` are not.

There are a few tools to extract the strings meant for translation. The original GNU **gettext** only supported C or C++ source code but its extended version **xgettext** scans code written in a number of languages, including Python, to find strings marked as translatable. Babel is a Python internationalization library that includes a **pybabel** script to extract and compile message catalogs. François Pinard's program called **xpot** does a similar job and is available as part of his po-utils package.

(Python also includes pure-Python versions of these programs, called **pygettext.py** and **msgfmt.py**; some Python distributions will install them for you. **pygettext.py** is similar to **xgettext**, but only understands Python source code and cannot handle other programming languages such as C or C++. **pygettext.py** supports a command-line interface similar to **xgettext**; for details on its use, run pygettext.py --help.

msgfmt.py is binary compatible with GNU **msgfmt**. With these two programs, you may not need the GNU **gettext** package to internationalize your Python applications.)

xgettext, **pygettext**, and similar tools generate .po files that are message catalogs. They are structured human-readable files that contain every marked string in the source code, along with a placeholder for the translated versions of these strings.

Copies of these .po files are then handed over to the individual human translators who write translations for every supported natural language. They send back the completed language-specific versions as a <language-name>.po file that's compiled into a machine-readable .mo binary catalog file using the **msgfmt** program. The .mo files are used by the *gettext* module for the actual translation processing at run-time.

How you use the *gettext* module in your code depends on whether you are internationalizing a single module or your entire application. The next two sections will discuss each case.

Localizing your module

If you are localizing your module, you must take care not to make global changes, e.g. to the built-in namespace. You should not use the GNU **gettext** API but instead the class-based API.

Let's say your module is called "spam" and the module's various natural language translation .mo files reside in /usr/share/locale in GNU **gettext** format. Here's what you would put at the top of your module:

```
import gettext
t = gettext.translation('spam', '/usr/share/locale')
_ = t.gettext
```

Localizing your application

If you are localizing your application, you can install the _() function globally into the built-in namespace, usually in the main driver file of your application. This will let all your application-specific files just use _('...') without having to explicitly install it in each file.

In the simple case then, you need only add the following bit of code to the main driver file of your application:

```
import gettext
gettext.install('myapplication')
```

If you need to set the locale directory, you can pass it into the *install()* function:

```
import gettext
gettext.install('myapplication', '/usr/share/locale')
```

Changing languages on the fly

If your program needs to support many languages at the same time, you may want to create multiple translation instances and then switch between them explicitly, like so:

```
import gettext

lang1 = gettext.translation('myapplication', languages=['en'])
lang2 = gettext.translation('myapplication', languages=['fr'])
lang3 = gettext.translation('myapplication', languages=['de'])

# start by using language1
lang1.install()
```

```
# ... time goes by, user selects language 2
lang2.install()
# ... more time goes by, user selects language 3
lang3.install()
```

Deferred translations

In most coding situations, strings are translated where they are coded. Occasionally however, you need to mark strings for translation, but defer actual translation until later. A classic example is:

```
animals = ['mollusk',
           'albatross',
           'rat',
           'penguin',
           'python', ]
# ...
for a in animals:
    print(a)
```

Here, you want to mark the strings in the `animals` list as being translatable, but you don't actually want to translate them until they are printed.

Here is one way you can handle this situation:

```
def _(message): return message

animals = [_('mollusk'),
           _('albatross'),
           _('rat'),
           _('penguin'),
           _('python'), ]

del _

# ...
for a in animals:
    print(_(a))
```

This works because the dummy definition of _() simply returns the string unchanged. And this dummy definition will temporarily override any definition of _() in the built-in namespace (until the `del` command). Take care, though if you have a previous definition of _() in the local namespace.

Note that the second use of _() will not identify "a" as being translatable to the **gettext** program, because the parameter is not a string literal.

Another way to handle this is with the following example:

```
def N_(message): return message

animals = [N_('mollusk'),
           N_('albatross'),
           N_('rat'),
           N_('penguin'),
           N_('python'), ]

# ...
```

```
for a in animals:
    print(_(a))
```

In this case, you are marking translatable strings with the function `N_()`, which won't conflict with any definition of `_()`. However, you will need to teach your message extraction program to look for translatable strings marked with `N_()`. **xgettext**, **pygettext**, **pybabel extract**, and **xpot** all support this through the use of the `-k` command-line switch. The choice of `N_()` here is totally arbitrary; it could have just as easily been `MarkThisStringForTranslation()`.

23.1.4 Acknowledgements

The following people contributed code, feedback, design suggestions, previous implementations, and valuable experience to the creation of this module:

- Peter Funk
- James Henstridge
- Juan David Ibáñez Palomar
- Marc-André Lemburg
- Martin von Löwis
- François Pinard
- Barry Warsaw
- Gustavo Niemeyer

23.2 `locale` — Internationalization services

Source code: Lib/locale.py

The `locale` module opens access to the POSIX locale database and functionality. The POSIX locale mechanism allows programmers to deal with certain cultural issues in an application, without requiring the programmer to know all the specifics of each country where the software is executed.

The `locale` module is implemented on top of the `_locale` module, which in turn uses an ANSI C locale implementation if available.

The `locale` module defines the following exception and functions:

exception `locale.Error`
    Exception raised when the locale passed to *setlocale()* is not recognized.

`locale.setlocale`(*category, locale=None*)
    If *locale* is given and not `None`, *setlocale()* modifies the locale setting for the *category*. The available categories are listed in the data description below. *locale* may be a string, or an iterable of two strings (language code and encoding). If it's an iterable, it's converted to a locale name using the locale aliasing engine. An empty string specifies the user's default settings. If the modification of the locale fails, the exception *Error* is raised. If successful, the new locale setting is returned.

    If *locale* is omitted or `None`, the current setting for *category* is returned.

    setlocale() is not thread-safe on most systems. Applications typically start with a call of

```
import locale
locale.setlocale(locale.LC_ALL, '')
```

This sets the locale for all categories to the user's default setting (typically specified in the `LANG` environment variable). If the locale is not changed thereafter, using multithreading should not cause problems.

`locale.localeconv()`

Returns the database of the local conventions as a dictionary. This dictionary has the following strings as keys:

Category	Key	Meaning
LC_NUMERIC	`'decimal_point'`	Decimal point character.
	`'grouping'`	Sequence of numbers specifying which relative positions the `'thousands_sep'` is expected. If the sequence is terminated with CHAR_MAX, no further grouping is performed. If the sequence terminates with a 0, the last group size is repeatedly used.
	`'thousands_sep'`	Character used between groups.
LC_MONETARY	`'int_curr_symbol'`	International currency symbol.
	`'currency_symbol'`	Local currency symbol.
	`'p_cs_precedes/n_cs_precedes'`	Whether the currency symbol precedes the value (for positive resp. negative values).
	`'p_sep_by_space/n_sep_by_space'`	Whether the currency symbol is separated from the value by a space (for positive resp. negative values).
	`'mon_decimal_point'`	Decimal point used for monetary values.
	`'frac_digits'`	Number of fractional digits used in local formatting of monetary values.
	`'int_frac_digits'`	Number of fractional digits used in international formatting of monetary values.
	`'mon_thousands_sep'`	Group separator used for monetary values.
	`'mon_grouping'`	Equivalent to `'grouping'`, used for monetary values.
	`'positive_sign'`	Symbol used to annotate a positive monetary value.
	`'negative_sign'`	Symbol used to annotate a negative monetary value.
	`'p_sign_posn/n_sign_posn'`	The position of the sign (for positive resp. negative values), see below.

All numeric values can be set to CHAR_MAX to indicate that there is no value specified in this locale.

The possible values for `'p_sign_posn'` and `'n_sign_posn'` are given below.

Value	Explanation
0	Currency and value are surrounded by parentheses.
1	The sign should precede the value and currency symbol.
2	The sign should follow the value and currency symbol.
3	The sign should immediately precede the value.
4	The sign should immediately follow the value.
CHAR_MAX	Nothing is specified in this locale.

The function sets temporarily the LC_CTYPE locale to the LC_NUMERIC locale to decode `decimal_point` and `thousands_sep` byte strings if they are non-ASCII or longer than 1 byte, and the LC_NUMERIC locale is different than the LC_CTYPE locale. This temporary change affects other threads.

Changed in version 3.6.5: The function now sets temporarily the LC_CTYPE locale to the LC_NUMERIC locale in some cases.

`locale.nl_langinfo(option)`

Return some locale-specific information as a string. This function is not available on all systems, and the set of possible options might also vary across platforms. The possible argument values are numbers, for which symbolic constants are available in the locale module.

The *nl_langinfo()* function accepts one of the following keys. Most descriptions are taken from the corresponding description in the GNU C library.

`locale.CODESET`
  Get a string with the name of the character encoding used in the selected locale.

`locale.D_T_FMT`
  Get a string that can be used as a format string for *time.strftime()* to represent date and time in a locale-specific way.

`locale.D_FMT`
  Get a string that can be used as a format string for *time.strftime()* to represent a date in a locale-specific way.

`locale.T_FMT`
  Get a string that can be used as a format string for *time.strftime()* to represent a time in a locale-specific way.

`locale.T_FMT_AMPM`
  Get a format string for *time.strftime()* to represent time in the am/pm format.

`DAY_1 ... DAY_7`
  Get the name of the n-th day of the week.

  Note: This follows the US convention of DAY_1 being Sunday, not the international convention (ISO 8601) that Monday is the first day of the week.

`ABDAY_1 ... ABDAY_7`
  Get the abbreviated name of the n-th day of the week.

`MON_1 ... MON_12`
  Get the name of the n-th month.

`ABMON_1 ... ABMON_12`
  Get the abbreviated name of the n-th month.

`locale.RADIXCHAR`
  Get the radix character (decimal dot, decimal comma, etc.).

locale.THOUSEP
  Get the separator character for thousands (groups of three digits).

locale.YESEXPR
  Get a regular expression that can be used with the regex function to recognize a positive response to a yes/no question.

> **Note:** The expression is in the syntax suitable for the `regex()` function from the C library, which might differ from the syntax used in *re*.

locale.NOEXPR
  Get a regular expression that can be used with the regex(3) function to recognize a negative response to a yes/no question.

locale.CRNCYSTR
  Get the currency symbol, preceded by "-" if the symbol should appear before the value, "+" if the symbol should appear after the value, or "." if the symbol should replace the radix character.

locale.ERA
  Get a string that represents the era used in the current locale.

  Most locales do not define this value. An example of a locale which does define this value is the Japanese one. In Japan, the traditional representation of dates includes the name of the era corresponding to the then-emperor's reign.

  Normally it should not be necessary to use this value directly. Specifying the E modifier in their format strings causes the *time.strftime()* function to use this information. The format of the returned string is not specified, and therefore you should not assume knowledge of it on different systems.

locale.ERA_D_T_FMT
  Get a format string for *time.strftime()* to represent date and time in a locale-specific era-based way.

locale.ERA_D_FMT
  Get a format string for *time.strftime()* to represent a date in a locale-specific era-based way.

locale.ERA_T_FMT
  Get a format string for *time.strftime()* to represent a time in a locale-specific era-based way.

locale.ALT_DIGITS
  Get a representation of up to 100 values used to represent the values 0 to 99.

locale.getdefaultlocale([*envvars*]**)**
  Tries to determine the default locale settings and returns them as a tuple of the form (language code, encoding).

  According to POSIX, a program which has not called setlocale(LC_ALL, '') runs using the portable 'C' locale. Calling setlocale(LC_ALL, '') lets it use the default locale as defined by the LANG variable. Since we do not want to interfere with the current locale setting we thus emulate the behavior in the way described above.

  To maintain compatibility with other platforms, not only the LANG variable is tested, but a list of variables given as envvars parameter. The first found to be defined will be used. *envvars* defaults to the search path used in GNU gettext; it must always contain the variable name 'LANG'. The GNU gettext search path contains 'LC_ALL', 'LC_CTYPE', 'LANG' and 'LANGUAGE', in that order.

  Except for the code 'C', the language code corresponds to RFC 1766. *language code* and *encoding* may be None if their values cannot be determined.

locale.getlocale(*category=LC_CTYPE*)

Returns the current setting for the given locale category as sequence containing *language code, encoding*. *category* may be one of the LC_* values except *LC_ALL*. It defaults to *LC_CTYPE*.

Except for the code 'C', the language code corresponds to RFC 1766. *language code* and *encoding* may be None if their values cannot be determined.

locale.getpreferredencoding(*do_setlocale=True*)

Return the encoding used for text data, according to user preferences. User preferences are expressed differently on different systems, and might not be available programmatically on some systems, so this function only returns a guess.

On some systems, it is necessary to invoke *setlocale()* to obtain the user preferences, so this function is not thread-safe. If invoking setlocale is not necessary or desired, *do_setlocale* should be set to False.

locale.normalize(*localename*)

Returns a normalized locale code for the given locale name. The returned locale code is formatted for use with *setlocale()*. If normalization fails, the original name is returned unchanged.

If the given encoding is not known, the function defaults to the default encoding for the locale code just like *setlocale()*.

locale.resetlocale(*category=LC_ALL*)

Sets the locale for *category* to the default setting.

The default setting is determined by calling *getdefaultlocale()*. *category* defaults to *LC_ALL*.

locale.strcoll(*string1, string2*)

Compares two strings according to the current LC_COLLATE setting. As any other compare function, returns a negative, or a positive value, or 0, depending on whether *string1* collates before or after *string2* or is equal to it.

locale.strxfrm(*string*)

Transforms a string to one that can be used in locale-aware comparisons. For example, strxfrm(s1) < strxfrm(s2) is equivalent to strcoll(s1, s2) < 0. This function can be used when the same string is compared repeatedly, e.g. when collating a sequence of strings.

locale.format(*format, val, grouping=False, monetary=False*)

Formats a number *val* according to the current LC_NUMERIC setting. The format follows the conventions of the % operator. For floating point values, the decimal point is modified if appropriate. If *grouping* is true, also takes the grouping into account.

If *monetary* is true, the conversion uses monetary thousands separator and grouping strings.

Please note that this function will only work for exactly one %char specifier. For whole format strings, use *format_string()*.

locale.format_string(*format, val, grouping=False*)

Processes formatting specifiers as in format % val, but takes the current locale settings into account.

locale.currency(*val, symbol=True, grouping=False, international=False*)

Formats a number *val* according to the current LC_MONETARY settings.

The returned string includes the currency symbol if *symbol* is true, which is the default. If *grouping* is true (which is not the default), grouping is done with the value. If *international* is true (which is not the default), the international currency symbol is used.

Note that this function will not work with the 'C' locale, so you have to set a locale via *setlocale()* first.

locale.str(*float*)

Formats a floating point number using the same format as the built-in function str(float), but takes the decimal point into account.

locale.delocalize(*string*)
Converts a string into a normalized number string, following the *LC_NUMERIC* settings.

New in version 3.5.

locale.atof(*string*)
Converts a string to a floating point number, following the *LC_NUMERIC* settings.

locale.atoi(*string*)
Converts a string to an integer, following the *LC_NUMERIC* conventions.

locale.LC_CTYPE
Locale category for the character type functions. Depending on the settings of this category, the functions of module *string* dealing with case change their behaviour.

locale.LC_COLLATE
Locale category for sorting strings. The functions *strcoll()* and *strxfrm()* of the *locale* module are affected.

locale.LC_TIME
Locale category for the formatting of time. The function *time.strftime()* follows these conventions.

locale.LC_MONETARY
Locale category for formatting of monetary values. The available options are available from the *localeconv()* function.

locale.LC_MESSAGES
Locale category for message display. Python currently does not support application specific locale-aware messages. Messages displayed by the operating system, like those returned by *os.strerror()* might be affected by this category.

locale.LC_NUMERIC
Locale category for formatting numbers. The functions *format()*, *atoi()*, *atof()* and *str()* of the *locale* module are affected by that category. All other numeric formatting operations are not affected.

locale.LC_ALL
Combination of all locale settings. If this flag is used when the locale is changed, setting the locale for all categories is attempted. If that fails for any category, no category is changed at all. When the locale is retrieved using this flag, a string indicating the setting for all categories is returned. This string can be later used to restore the settings.

locale.CHAR_MAX
This is a symbolic constant used for different values returned by *localeconv()*.

Example:

```
>>> import locale
>>> loc = locale.getlocale()  # get current locale
# use German locale; name might vary with platform
>>> locale.setlocale(locale.LC_ALL, 'de_DE')
>>> locale.strcoll('f\xe4n', 'foo')  # compare a string containing an umlaut
>>> locale.setlocale(locale.LC_ALL, '')   # use user's preferred locale
>>> locale.setlocale(locale.LC_ALL, 'C')  # use default (C) locale
>>> locale.setlocale(locale.LC_ALL, loc)  # restore saved locale
```

23.2.1 Background, details, hints, tips and caveats

The C standard defines the locale as a program-wide property that may be relatively expensive to change. On top of that, some implementation are broken in such a way that frequent locale changes may cause core dumps. This makes the locale somewhat painful to use correctly.

Initially, when a program is started, the locale is the C locale, no matter what the user's preferred locale is. There is one exception: the *LC_CTYPE* category is changed at startup to set the current locale encoding to the user's preferred locale encoding. The program must explicitly say that it wants the user's preferred locale settings for other categories by calling `setlocale(LC_ALL, '')`.

It is generally a bad idea to call *setlocale()* in some library routine, since as a side effect it affects the entire program. Saving and restoring it is almost as bad: it is expensive and affects other threads that happen to run before the settings have been restored.

If, when coding a module for general use, you need a locale independent version of an operation that is affected by the locale (such as certain formats used with *time.strftime()*), you will have to find a way to do it without using the standard library routine. Even better is convincing yourself that using locale settings is okay. Only as a last resort should you document that your module is not compatible with non-C locale settings.

The only way to perform numeric operations according to the locale is to use the special functions defined by this module: *atof()*, *atoi()*, *format()*, *str()*.

There is no way to perform case conversions and character classifications according to the locale. For (Unicode) text strings these are done according to the character value only, while for byte strings, the conversions and classifications are done according to the ASCII value of the byte, and bytes whose high bit is set (i.e., non-ASCII bytes) are never converted or considered part of a character class such as letter or whitespace.

23.2.2 For extension writers and programs that embed Python

Extension modules should never call *setlocale()*, except to find out what the current locale is. But since the return value can only be used portably to restore it, that is not very useful (except perhaps to find out whether or not the locale is C).

When Python code uses the *locale* module to change the locale, this also affects the embedding application. If the embedding application doesn't want this to happen, it should remove the **_locale** extension module (which does all the work) from the table of built-in modules in the `config.c` file, and make sure that the **_locale** module is not accessible as a shared library.

23.2.3 Access to message catalogs

`locale.gettext(`*msg*`)`

`locale.dgettext(`*domain, msg*`)`

`locale.dcgettext(`*domain, msg, category*`)`

`locale.textdomain(`*domain*`)`

`locale.bindtextdomain(`*domain, dir*`)`

The locale module exposes the C library's gettext interface on systems that provide this interface. It consists of the functions `gettext()`, `dgettext()`, `dcgettext()`, `textdomain()`, `bindtextdomain()`, and `bind_textdomain_codeset()`. These are similar to the same functions in the *gettext* module, but use the C library's binary format for message catalogs, and the C library's search algorithms for locating message catalogs.

Python applications should normally find no need to invoke these functions, and should use *gettext* instead. A known exception to this rule are applications that link with additional C libraries which internally invoke `gettext()` or `dcgettext()`. For these applications, it may be necessary to bind the text domain, so that the libraries can properly locate their message catalogs.

CHAPTER
TWENTYFOUR

PROGRAM FRAMEWORKS

The modules described in this chapter are frameworks that will largely dictate the structure of your program. Currently the modules described here are all oriented toward writing command-line interfaces.

The full list of modules described in this chapter is:

24.1 `turtle` — Turtle graphics

Source code: Lib/turtle.py

24.1.1 Introduction

Turtle graphics is a popular way for introducing programming to kids. It was part of the original Logo programming language developed by Wally Feurzig and Seymour Papert in 1966.

Imagine a robotic turtle starting at (0, 0) in the x-y plane. After an `import turtle`, give it the command `turtle.forward(15)`, and it moves (on-screen!) 15 pixels in the direction it is facing, drawing a line as it moves. Give it the command `turtle.right(25)`, and it rotates in-place 25 degrees clockwise.

> **Turtle star**
>
> Turtle can draw intricate shapes using programs that repeat simple moves.

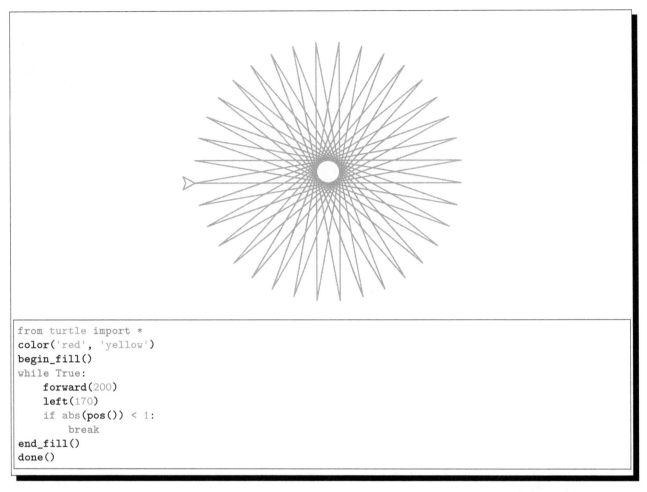

```
from turtle import *
color('red', 'yellow')
begin_fill()
while True:
    forward(200)
    left(170)
    if abs(pos()) < 1:
        break
end_fill()
done()
```

By combining together these and similar commands, intricate shapes and pictures can easily be drawn.

The *turtle* module is an extended reimplementation of the same-named module from the Python standard distribution up to version Python 2.5.

It tries to keep the merits of the old turtle module and to be (nearly) 100% compatible with it. This means in the first place to enable the learning programmer to use all the commands, classes and methods interactively when using the module from within IDLE run with the -n switch.

The turtle module provides turtle graphics primitives, in both object-oriented and procedure-oriented ways. Because it uses *tkinter* for the underlying graphics, it needs a version of Python installed with Tk support.

The object-oriented interface uses essentially two+two classes:

1. The *TurtleScreen* class defines graphics windows as a playground for the drawing turtles. Its constructor needs a **tkinter.Canvas** or a *ScrolledCanvas* as argument. It should be used when *turtle* is used as part of some application.

    The function *Screen()* returns a singleton object of a *TurtleScreen* subclass. This function should be used when *turtle* is used as a standalone tool for doing graphics. As a singleton object, inheriting from its class is not possible.

    All methods of TurtleScreen/Screen also exist as functions, i.e. as part of the procedure-oriented interface.

2. *RawTurtle* (alias: *RawPen*) defines Turtle objects which draw on a *TurtleScreen*. Its constructor needs a Canvas, ScrolledCanvas or TurtleScreen as argument, so the RawTurtle objects know where to

draw.

Derived from RawTurtle is the subclass *Turtle* (alias: **Pen**), which draws on "the" *Screen* instance which is automatically created, if not already present.

All methods of RawTurtle/Turtle also exist as functions, i.e. part of the procedure-oriented interface.

The procedural interface provides functions which are derived from the methods of the classes *Screen* and *Turtle*. They have the same names as the corresponding methods. A screen object is automatically created whenever a function derived from a Screen method is called. An (unnamed) turtle object is automatically created whenever any of the functions derived from a Turtle method is called.

To use multiple turtles on a screen one has to use the object-oriented interface.

Note: In the following documentation the argument list for functions is given. Methods, of course, have the additional first argument *self* which is omitted here.

24.1.2 Overview of available Turtle and Screen methods

Turtle methods

Turtle motion

    Move and draw

        forward() | fd()
        backward() | bk() | back()
        right() | rt()
        left() | lt()
        goto() | setpos() | setposition()
        setx()
        sety()
        setheading() | seth()
        home()
        circle()
        dot()
        stamp()
        clearstamp()
        clearstamps()
        undo()
        speed()

    Tell Turtle's state

        position() | pos()
        towards()
        xcor()
        ycor()
        heading()
        distance()

    Setting and measurement

        degrees()

- *radians()*

Pen control
Drawing state
- *pendown() | pd() | down()*
- *penup() | pu() | up()*
- *pensize() | width()*
- *pen()*
- *isdown()*

Color control
- *color()*
- *pencolor()*
- *fillcolor()*

Filling
- *filling()*
- *begin_fill()*
- *end_fill()*

More drawing control
- *reset()*
- *clear()*
- *write()*

Turtle state
Visibility
- *showturtle() | st()*
- *hideturtle() | ht()*
- *isvisible()*

Appearance
- *shape()*
- *resizemode()*
- *shapesize() | turtlesize()*
- *shearfactor()*
- *settiltangle()*
- *tiltangle()*
- *tilt()*
- *shapetransform()*
- *get_shapepoly()*

Using events
- *onclick()*
- *onrelease()*
- *ondrag()*

Special Turtle methods
- *begin_poly()*
- *end_poly()*
- *get_poly()*

clone()
getturtle() | getpen()
getscreen()
setundobuffer()
undobufferentries()

Methods of TurtleScreen/Screen

Window control
bgcolor()
bgpic()
clear() | clearscreen()
reset() | resetscreen()
screensize()
setworldcoordinates()

Animation control
delay()
tracer()
update()

Using screen events
listen()
onkey() | onkeyrelease()
onkeypress()
onclick() | onscreenclick()
ontimer()
mainloop() | done()

Settings and special methods
mode()
colormode()
getcanvas()
getshapes()
register_shape() | addshape()
turtles()
window_height()
window_width()

Input methods
textinput()
numinput()

Methods specific to Screen
bye()
exitonclick()
setup()
title()

24.1.3 Methods of RawTurtle/Turtle and corresponding functions

Most of the examples in this section refer to a Turtle instance called `turtle`.

Turtle motion

turtle.**forward**(*distance*)
turtle.**fd**(*distance*)

> **Parameters distance** – a number (integer or float)
>
> Move the turtle forward by the specified *distance*, in the direction the turtle is headed.
>
> ```
> >>> turtle.position()
> (0.00,0.00)
> >>> turtle.forward(25)
> >>> turtle.position()
> (25.00,0.00)
> >>> turtle.forward(-75)
> >>> turtle.position()
> (-50.00,0.00)
> ```

turtle.**back**(*distance*)
turtle.**bk**(*distance*)
turtle.**backward**(*distance*)

> **Parameters distance** – a number
>
> Move the turtle backward by *distance*, opposite to the direction the turtle is headed. Do not change the turtle's heading.
>
> ```
> >>> turtle.position()
> (0.00,0.00)
> >>> turtle.backward(30)
> >>> turtle.position()
> (-30.00,0.00)
> ```

turtle.**right**(*angle*)
turtle.**rt**(*angle*)

> **Parameters angle** – a number (integer or float)
>
> Turn turtle right by *angle* units. (Units are by default degrees, but can be set via the *degrees()* and *radians()* functions.) Angle orientation depends on the turtle mode, see *mode()*.
>
> ```
> >>> turtle.heading()
> 22.0
> >>> turtle.right(45)
> >>> turtle.heading()
> 337.0
> ```

turtle.**left**(*angle*)
turtle.**lt**(*angle*)

> **Parameters angle** – a number (integer or float)
>
> Turn turtle left by *angle* units. (Units are by default degrees, but can be set via the *degrees()* and *radians()* functions.) Angle orientation depends on the turtle mode, see *mode()*.

```
>>> turtle.heading()
22.0
>>> turtle.left(45)
>>> turtle.heading()
67.0
```

turtle.goto(*x, y=None*)
turtle.setpos(*x, y=None*)
turtle.setposition(*x, y=None*)

> Parameters
>
> - **x** – a number or a pair/vector of numbers
> - **y** – a number or None

If *y* is None, *x* must be a pair of coordinates or a *Vec2D* (e.g. as returned by *pos()*).

Move turtle to an absolute position. If the pen is down, draw line. Do not change the turtle's orientation.

```
>>> tp = turtle.pos()
>>> tp
(0.00,0.00)
>>> turtle.setpos(60,30)
>>> turtle.pos()
(60.00,30.00)
>>> turtle.setpos((20,80))
>>> turtle.pos()
(20.00,80.00)
>>> turtle.setpos(tp)
>>> turtle.pos()
(0.00,0.00)
```

turtle.setx(*x*)

> Parameters **x** – a number (integer or float)

Set the turtle's first coordinate to *x*, leave second coordinate unchanged.

```
>>> turtle.position()
(0.00,240.00)
>>> turtle.setx(10)
>>> turtle.position()
(10.00,240.00)
```

turtle.sety(*y*)

> Parameters **y** – a number (integer or float)

Set the turtle's second coordinate to *y*, leave first coordinate unchanged.

```
>>> turtle.position()
(0.00,40.00)
>>> turtle.sety(-10)
>>> turtle.position()
(0.00,-10.00)
```

turtle.setheading(*to_angle*)
turtle.seth(*to_angle*)

> Parameters **to_angle** – a number (integer or float)

Set the orientation of the turtle to *to_angle*. Here are some common directions in degrees:

standard mode	logo mode
0 - east	0 - north
90 - north	90 - east
180 - west	180 - south
270 - south	270 - west

```
>>> turtle.setheading(90)
>>> turtle.heading()
90.0
```

turtle.home()
> Move turtle to the origin – coordinates (0,0) – and set its heading to its start-orientation (which depends on the mode, see `mode()`).

```
>>> turtle.heading()
90.0
>>> turtle.position()
(0.00,-10.00)
>>> turtle.home()
>>> turtle.position()
(0.00,0.00)
>>> turtle.heading()
0.0
```

turtle.circle(*radius*, *extent=None*, *steps=None*)

> **Parameters**
> - **radius** – a number
> - **extent** – a number (or None)
> - **steps** – an integer (or None)

Draw a circle with given *radius*. The center is *radius* units left of the turtle; *extent* – an angle – determines which part of the circle is drawn. If *extent* is not given, draw the entire circle. If *extent* is not a full circle, one endpoint of the arc is the current pen position. Draw the arc in counterclockwise direction if *radius* is positive, otherwise in clockwise direction. Finally the direction of the turtle is changed by the amount of *extent*.

As the circle is approximated by an inscribed regular polygon, *steps* determines the number of steps to use. If not given, it will be calculated automatically. May be used to draw regular polygons.

```
>>> turtle.home()
>>> turtle.position()
(0.00,0.00)
>>> turtle.heading()
0.0
>>> turtle.circle(50)
>>> turtle.position()
(-0.00,0.00)
>>> turtle.heading()
0.0
>>> turtle.circle(120, 180)   # draw a semicircle
>>> turtle.position()
(0.00,240.00)
```

```
>>> turtle.heading()
180.0
```

turtle.dot(*size=None, *color*)

> Parameters
>
> - **size** – an integer >= 1 (if given)
> - **color** – a colorstring or a numeric color tuple
>
> Draw a circular dot with diameter *size*, using *color*. If *size* is not given, the maximum of pensize+4 and 2*pensize is used.
>
> ```
> >>> turtle.home()
> >>> turtle.dot()
> >>> turtle.fd(50); turtle.dot(20, "blue"); turtle.fd(50)
> >>> turtle.position()
> (100.00,-0.00)
> >>> turtle.heading()
> 0.0
> ```

turtle.stamp()

> Stamp a copy of the turtle shape onto the canvas at the current turtle position. Return a stamp_id for that stamp, which can be used to delete it by calling clearstamp(stamp_id).
>
> ```
> >>> turtle.color("blue")
> >>> turtle.stamp()
> 11
> >>> turtle.fd(50)
> ```

turtle.clearstamp(*stampid*)

> Parameters **stampid** – an integer, must be return value of previous *stamp()* call
>
> Delete stamp with given *stampid*.
>
> ```
> >>> turtle.position()
> (150.00,-0.00)
> >>> turtle.color("blue")
> >>> astamp = turtle.stamp()
> >>> turtle.fd(50)
> >>> turtle.position()
> (200.00,-0.00)
> >>> turtle.clearstamp(astamp)
> >>> turtle.position()
> (200.00,-0.00)
> ```

turtle.clearstamps(*n=None*)

> Parameters **n** – an integer (or None)
>
> Delete all or first/last *n* of turtle's stamps. If *n* is None, delete all stamps, if *n* > 0 delete first *n* stamps, else if *n* < 0 delete last *n* stamps.
>
> ```
> >>> for i in range(8):
> ...     turtle.stamp(); turtle.fd(30)
> 13
> 14
> 15
> 16
> ```

24.1. turtle — Turtle graphics

```
17
18
19
20
>>> turtle.clearstamps(2)
>>> turtle.clearstamps(-2)
>>> turtle.clearstamps()
```

`turtle.undo()`
> Undo (repeatedly) the last turtle action(s). Number of available undo actions is determined by the size of the undobuffer.

```
>>> for i in range(4):
...     turtle.fd(50); turtle.lt(80)
...
>>> for i in range(8):
...     turtle.undo()
```

`turtle.speed(speed=None)`
> **Parameters speed** – an integer in the range 0..10 or a speedstring (see below)

Set the turtle's speed to an integer value in the range 0..10. If no argument is given, return current speed.

If input is a number greater than 10 or smaller than 0.5, speed is set to 0. Speedstrings are mapped to speedvalues as follows:

- "fastest": 0
- "fast": 10
- "normal": 6
- "slow": 3
- "slowest": 1

Speeds from 1 to 10 enforce increasingly faster animation of line drawing and turtle turning.

Attention: *speed* = 0 means that *no* animation takes place. forward/back makes turtle jump and likewise left/right make the turtle turn instantly.

```
>>> turtle.speed()
3
>>> turtle.speed('normal')
>>> turtle.speed()
6
>>> turtle.speed(9)
>>> turtle.speed()
9
```

Tell Turtle's state

`turtle.position()`
`turtle.pos()`
> Return the turtle's current location (x,y) (as a *Vec2D* vector).

```
>>> turtle.pos()
(440.00,-0.00)
```

turtle.towards(*x, y=None*)

> Parameters
>
> > - **x** – a number or a pair/vector of numbers or a turtle instance
> > - **y** – a number if *x* is a number, else None
>
> Return the angle between the line from turtle position to position specified by (x,y), the vector or the other turtle. This depends on the turtle's start orientation which depends on the mode - "standard"/"world" or "logo").
>
> ```
> >>> turtle.goto(10, 10)
> >>> turtle.towards(0,0)
> 225.0
> ```

turtle.xcor()

> Return the turtle's x coordinate.
>
> ```
> >>> turtle.home()
> >>> turtle.left(50)
> >>> turtle.forward(100)
> >>> turtle.pos()
> (64.28,76.60)
> >>> print(round(turtle.xcor(), 5))
> 64.27876
> ```

turtle.ycor()

> Return the turtle's y coordinate.
>
> ```
> >>> turtle.home()
> >>> turtle.left(60)
> >>> turtle.forward(100)
> >>> print(turtle.pos())
> (50.00,86.60)
> >>> print(round(turtle.ycor(), 5))
> 86.60254
> ```

turtle.heading()

> Return the turtle's current heading (value depends on the turtle mode, see *mode()*).
>
> ```
> >>> turtle.home()
> >>> turtle.left(67)
> >>> turtle.heading()
> 67.0
> ```

turtle.distance(*x, y=None*)

> Parameters
>
> > - **x** – a number or a pair/vector of numbers or a turtle instance
> > - **y** – a number if *x* is a number, else None
>
> Return the distance from the turtle to (x,y), the given vector, or the given other turtle, in turtle step units.
>
> ```
> >>> turtle.home()
> >>> turtle.distance(30,40)
> 50.0
> >>> turtle.distance((30,40))
> 50.0
> ```

```
>>> joe = Turtle()
>>> joe.forward(77)
>>> turtle.distance(joe)
77.0
```

Settings for measurement

turtle.**degrees**(*fullcircle=360.0*)

> **Parameters fullcircle** – a number

Set angle measurement units, i.e. set number of "degrees" for a full circle. Default value is 360 degrees.

```
>>> turtle.home()
>>> turtle.left(90)
>>> turtle.heading()
90.0

Change angle measurement unit to grad (also known as gon,
grade, or gradian and equals 1/100-th of the right angle.)
>>> turtle.degrees(400.0)
>>> turtle.heading()
100.0
>>> turtle.degrees(360)
>>> turtle.heading()
90.0
```

turtle.**radians**()

Set the angle measurement units to radians. Equivalent to degrees(2*math.pi).

```
>>> turtle.home()
>>> turtle.left(90)
>>> turtle.heading()
90.0
>>> turtle.radians()
>>> turtle.heading()
1.5707963267948966
```

Pen control

Drawing state

turtle.**pendown**()
turtle.**pd**()
turtle.**down**()

> Pull the pen down – drawing when moving.

turtle.**penup**()
turtle.**pu**()
turtle.**up**()

> Pull the pen up – no drawing when moving.

turtle.**pensize**(*width=None*)
turtle.**width**(*width=None*)

> **Parameters width** – a positive number

Set the line thickness to *width* or return it. If resizemode is set to "auto" and turtleshape is a polygon, that polygon is drawn with the same line thickness. If no argument is given, the current pensize is returned.

```
>>> turtle.pensize()
1
>>> turtle.pensize(10)     # from here on lines of width 10 are drawn
```

turtle.**pen**(*pen=None, **pendict*)

> **Parameters**
>
> - **pen** – a dictionary with some or all of the below listed keys
> - **pendict** – one or more keyword-arguments with the below listed keys as keywords

Return or set the pen's attributes in a "pen-dictionary" with the following key/value pairs:

- "shown": True/False
- "pendown": True/False
- "pencolor": color-string or color-tuple
- "fillcolor": color-string or color-tuple
- "pensize": positive number
- "speed": number in range 0..10
- "resizemode": "auto" or "user" or "noresize"
- "stretchfactor": (positive number, positive number)
- "outline": positive number
- "tilt": number

This dictionary can be used as argument for a subsequent call to *pen()* to restore the former pen-state. Moreover one or more of these attributes can be provided as keyword-arguments. This can be used to set several pen attributes in one statement.

```
>>> turtle.pen(fillcolor="black", pencolor="red", pensize=10)
>>> sorted(turtle.pen().items())
[('fillcolor', 'black'), ('outline', 1), ('pencolor', 'red'),
 ('pendown', True), ('pensize', 10), ('resizemode', 'noresize'),
 ('shearfactor', 0.0), ('shown', True), ('speed', 9),
 ('stretchfactor', (1.0, 1.0)), ('tilt', 0.0)]
>>> penstate=turtle.pen()
>>> turtle.color("yellow", "")
>>> turtle.penup()
>>> sorted(turtle.pen().items())[:3]
[('fillcolor', ''), ('outline', 1), ('pencolor', 'yellow')]
>>> turtle.pen(penstate, fillcolor="green")
>>> sorted(turtle.pen().items())[:3]
[('fillcolor', 'green'), ('outline', 1), ('pencolor', 'red')]
```

turtle.**isdown**()

> Return True if pen is down, False if it's up.

```
>>> turtle.penup()
>>> turtle.isdown()
False
>>> turtle.pendown()
```

```
>>> turtle.isdown()
True
```

Color control

turtle.pencolor(*args*)
: Return or set the pencolor.

    Four input formats are allowed:

    pencolor() Return the current pencolor as color specification string or as a tuple (see example). May be used as input to another color/pencolor/fillcolor call.

    pencolor(colorstring) Set pencolor to *colorstring*, which is a Tk color specification string, such as "red", "yellow", or "#33cc8c".

    pencolor((r, g, b)) Set pencolor to the RGB color represented by the tuple of *r*, *g*, and *b*. Each of *r*, *g*, and *b* must be in the range 0..colormode, where colormode is either 1.0 or 255 (see *colormode()*).

    pencolor(r, g, b)

    :   Set pencolor to the RGB color represented by *r*, *g*, and *b*. Each of *r*, *g*, and *b* must be in the range 0..colormode.

    If turtleshape is a polygon, the outline of that polygon is drawn with the newly set pencolor.

    ```
    >>> colormode()
    1.0
    >>> turtle.pencolor()
    'red'
    >>> turtle.pencolor("brown")
    >>> turtle.pencolor()
    'brown'
    >>> tup = (0.2, 0.8, 0.55)
    >>> turtle.pencolor(tup)
    >>> turtle.pencolor()
    (0.2, 0.8, 0.5490196078431373)
    >>> colormode(255)
    >>> turtle.pencolor()
    (51.0, 204.0, 140.0)
    >>> turtle.pencolor('#32c18f')
    >>> turtle.pencolor()
    (50.0, 193.0, 143.0)
    ```

turtle.fillcolor(*args*)
: Return or set the fillcolor.

    Four input formats are allowed:

    fillcolor() Return the current fillcolor as color specification string, possibly in tuple format (see example). May be used as input to another color/pencolor/fillcolor call.

    fillcolor(colorstring) Set fillcolor to *colorstring*, which is a Tk color specification string, such as "red", "yellow", or "#33cc8c".

    fillcolor((r, g, b)) Set fillcolor to the RGB color represented by the tuple of *r*, *g*, and *b*. Each of *r*, *g*, and *b* must be in the range 0..colormode, where colormode is either 1.0 or 255 (see *colormode()*).

    fillcolor(r, g, b)

Set fillcolor to the RGB color represented by r, g, and b. Each of r, g, and b must be in the range 0..colormode.

If turtleshape is a polygon, the interior of that polygon is drawn with the newly set fillcolor.

```
>>> turtle.fillcolor("violet")
>>> turtle.fillcolor()
'violet'
>>> col = turtle.pencolor()
>>> col
(50.0, 193.0, 143.0)
>>> turtle.fillcolor(col)
>>> turtle.fillcolor()
(50.0, 193.0, 143.0)
>>> turtle.fillcolor('#ffffff')
>>> turtle.fillcolor()
(255.0, 255.0, 255.0)
```

turtle.color(*args*)
: Return or set pencolor and fillcolor.

    Several input formats are allowed. They use 0 to 3 arguments as follows:

    color()
    : Return the current pencolor and the current fillcolor as a pair of color specification strings or tuples as returned by *pencolor()* and *fillcolor()*.

    color(colorstring), color((r,g,b)), color(r,g,b)
    : Inputs as in *pencolor()*, set both, fillcolor and pencolor, to the given value.

    color(colorstring1, colorstring2), color((r1,g1,b1), (r2,g2,b2))
    : Equivalent to pencolor(colorstring1) and fillcolor(colorstring2) and analogously if the other input format is used.

    If turtleshape is a polygon, outline and interior of that polygon is drawn with the newly set colors.

```
>>> turtle.color("red", "green")
>>> turtle.color()
('red', 'green')
>>> color("#285078", "#a0c8f0")
>>> color()
((40.0, 80.0, 120.0), (160.0, 200.0, 240.0))
```

See also: Screen method *colormode()*.

Filling

turtle.filling()
: Return fillstate (**True** if filling, **False** else).

```
>>> turtle.begin_fill()
>>> if turtle.filling():
...     turtle.pensize(5)
... else:
...     turtle.pensize(3)
```

turtle.begin_fill()
: To be called just before drawing a shape to be filled.

turtle.end_fill()
: Fill the shape drawn after the last call to *begin_fill()*.

```
>>> turtle.color("black", "red")
>>> turtle.begin_fill()
>>> turtle.circle(80)
>>> turtle.end_fill()
```

More drawing control

`turtle.reset()`
   Delete the turtle's drawings from the screen, re-center the turtle and set variables to the default values.

```
>>> turtle.goto(0,-22)
>>> turtle.left(100)
>>> turtle.position()
(0.00,-22.00)
>>> turtle.heading()
100.0
>>> turtle.reset()
>>> turtle.position()
(0.00,0.00)
>>> turtle.heading()
0.0
```

`turtle.clear()`
   Delete the turtle's drawings from the screen. Do not move turtle. State and position of the turtle as well as drawings of other turtles are not affected.

`turtle.write`(*arg, move=False, align="left", font=("Arial", 8, "normal")*)

   Parameters
   - **arg** – object to be written to the TurtleScreen
   - **move** – True/False
   - **align** – one of the strings "left", "center" or right"
   - **font** – a triple (fontname, fontsize, fonttype)

   Write text - the string representation of *arg* - at the current turtle position according to *align* ("left", "center" or right") and with the given font. If *move* is true, the pen is moved to the bottom-right corner of the text. By default, *move* is **False**.

```
>>> turtle.write("Home = ", True, align="center")
>>> turtle.write((0,0), True)
```

Turtle state

Visibility

`turtle.hideturtle()`
`turtle.ht()`
   Make the turtle invisible. It's a good idea to do this while you're in the middle of doing some complex drawing, because hiding the turtle speeds up the drawing observably.

```
>>> turtle.hideturtle()
```

`turtle.showturtle()`

`turtle.st()`
> Make the turtle visible.

```
>>> turtle.showturtle()
```

`turtle.isvisible()`
> Return `True` if the Turtle is shown, `False` if it's hidden.

```
>>> turtle.hideturtle()
>>> turtle.isvisible()
False
>>> turtle.showturtle()
>>> turtle.isvisible()
True
```

Appearance

`turtle.shape(name=None)`
> **Parameters name** – a string which is a valid shapename

> Set turtle shape to shape with given *name* or, if name is not given, return name of current shape. Shape with *name* must exist in the TurtleScreen's shape dictionary. Initially there are the following polygon shapes: "arrow", "turtle", "circle", "square", "triangle", "classic". To learn about how to deal with shapes see Screen method *register_shape()*.

```
>>> turtle.shape()
'classic'
>>> turtle.shape("turtle")
>>> turtle.shape()
'turtle'
```

`turtle.resizemode(rmode=None)`
> **Parameters rmode** – one of the strings "auto", "user", "noresize"

> Set resizemode to one of the values: "auto", "user", "noresize". If *rmode* is not given, return current resizemode. Different resizemodes have the following effects:
> - "auto": adapts the appearance of the turtle corresponding to the value of pensize.
> - "user": adapts the appearance of the turtle according to the values of stretchfactor and outlinewidth (outline), which are set by *shapesize()*.
> - "noresize": no adaption of the turtle's appearance takes place.
>
> resizemode("user") is called by *shapesize()* when used with arguments.

```
>>> turtle.resizemode()
'noresize'
>>> turtle.resizemode("auto")
>>> turtle.resizemode()
'auto'
```

`turtle.shapesize(stretch_wid=None, stretch_len=None, outline=None)`
`turtle.turtlesize(stretch_wid=None, stretch_len=None, outline=None)`
> **Parameters**
> - **stretch_wid** – positive number
> - **stretch_len** – positive number

- **outline** – positive number

Return or set the pen's attributes x/y-stretchfactors and/or outline. Set resizemode to "user". If and only if resizemode is set to "user", the turtle will be displayed stretched according to its stretchfactors: *stretch_wid* is stretchfactor perpendicular to its orientation, *stretch_len* is stretchfactor in direction of its orientation, *outline* determines the width of the shapes's outline.

```
>>> turtle.shapesize()
(1.0, 1.0, 1)
>>> turtle.resizemode("user")
>>> turtle.shapesize(5, 5, 12)
>>> turtle.shapesize()
(5, 5, 12)
>>> turtle.shapesize(outline=8)
>>> turtle.shapesize()
(5, 5, 8)
```

turtle.**shearfactor**(*shear=None*)

    Parameters shear – number (optional)

Set or return the current shearfactor. Shear the turtleshape according to the given shearfactor shear, which is the tangent of the shear angle. Do *not* change the turtle's heading (direction of movement). If shear is not given: return the current shearfactor, i. e. the tangent of the shear angle, by which lines parallel to the heading of the turtle are sheared.

```
>>> turtle.shape("circle")
>>> turtle.shapesize(5,2)
>>> turtle.shearfactor(0.5)
>>> turtle.shearfactor()
0.5
```

turtle.**tilt**(*angle*)

    Parameters angle – a number

Rotate the turtleshape by *angle* from its current tilt-angle, but do *not* change the turtle's heading (direction of movement).

```
>>> turtle.reset()
>>> turtle.shape("circle")
>>> turtle.shapesize(5,2)
>>> turtle.tilt(30)
>>> turtle.fd(50)
>>> turtle.tilt(30)
>>> turtle.fd(50)
```

turtle.**settiltangle**(*angle*)

    Parameters angle – a number

Rotate the turtleshape to point in the direction specified by *angle*, regardless of its current tilt-angle. *Do not* change the turtle's heading (direction of movement).

```
>>> turtle.reset()
>>> turtle.shape("circle")
>>> turtle.shapesize(5,2)
>>> turtle.settiltangle(45)
>>> turtle.fd(50)
>>> turtle.settiltangle(-45)
>>> turtle.fd(50)
```

Deprecated since version 3.1.

turtle.**tiltangle**(*angle=None*)

> **Parameters angle** – a number (optional)

Set or return the current tilt-angle. If angle is given, rotate the turtleshape to point in the direction specified by angle, regardless of its current tilt-angle. Do *not* change the turtle's heading (direction of movement). If angle is not given: return the current tilt-angle, i. e. the angle between the orientation of the turtleshape and the heading of the turtle (its direction of movement).

```
>>> turtle.reset()
>>> turtle.shape("circle")
>>> turtle.shapesize(5,2)
>>> turtle.tilt(45)
>>> turtle.tiltangle()
45.0
```

turtle.**shapetransform**(*t11=None, t12=None, t21=None, t22=None*)

> **Parameters**
> - **t11** – a number (optional)
> - **t12** – a number (optional)
> - **t21** – a number (optional)
> - **t12** – a number (optional)

Set or return the current transformation matrix of the turtle shape.

If none of the matrix elements are given, return the transformation matrix as a tuple of 4 elements. Otherwise set the given elements and transform the turtleshape according to the matrix consisting of first row t11, t12 and second row t21, 22. The determinant t11 * t22 - t12 * t21 must not be zero, otherwise an error is raised. Modify stretchfactor, shearfactor and tiltangle according to the given matrix.

```
>>> turtle = Turtle()
>>> turtle.shape("square")
>>> turtle.shapesize(4,2)
>>> turtle.shearfactor(-0.5)
>>> turtle.shapetransform()
(4.0, -1.0, -0.0, 2.0)
```

turtle.**get_shapepoly**()

Return the current shape polygon as tuple of coordinate pairs. This can be used to define a new shape or components of a compound shape.

```
>>> turtle.shape("square")
>>> turtle.shapetransform(4, -1, 0, 2)
>>> turtle.get_shapepoly()
((50, -20), (30, 20), (-50, 20), (-30, -20))
```

Using events

turtle.**onclick**(*fun, btn=1, add=None*)

> **Parameters**
> - **fun** – a function with two arguments which will be called with the coordinates of the clicked point on the canvas

24.1. turtle — Turtle graphics

- **num** – number of the mouse-button, defaults to 1 (left mouse button)
- **add** – **True** or **False** – if **True**, a new binding will be added, otherwise it will replace a former binding

Bind *fun* to mouse-click events on this turtle. If *fun* is **None**, existing bindings are removed. Example for the anonymous turtle, i.e. the procedural way:

```
>>> def turn(x, y):
...     left(180)
...
>>> onclick(turn)  # Now clicking into the turtle will turn it.
>>> onclick(None)  # event-binding will be removed
```

turtle.onrelease(*fun*, *btn=1*, *add=None*)

> Parameters
>
> - **fun** – a function with two arguments which will be called with the coordinates of the clicked point on the canvas
> - **num** – number of the mouse-button, defaults to 1 (left mouse button)
> - **add** – **True** or **False** – if **True**, a new binding will be added, otherwise it will replace a former binding

Bind *fun* to mouse-button-release events on this turtle. If *fun* is **None**, existing bindings are removed.

```
>>> class MyTurtle(Turtle):
...     def glow(self,x,y):
...         self.fillcolor("red")
...     def unglow(self,x,y):
...         self.fillcolor("")
...
>>> turtle = MyTurtle()
>>> turtle.onclick(turtle.glow)     # clicking on turtle turns fillcolor red,
>>> turtle.onrelease(turtle.unglow) # releasing turns it to transparent.
```

turtle.ondrag(*fun*, *btn=1*, *add=None*)

> Parameters
>
> - **fun** – a function with two arguments which will be called with the coordinates of the clicked point on the canvas
> - **num** – number of the mouse-button, defaults to 1 (left mouse button)
> - **add** – **True** or **False** – if **True**, a new binding will be added, otherwise it will replace a former binding

Bind *fun* to mouse-move events on this turtle. If *fun* is **None**, existing bindings are removed.

Remark: Every sequence of mouse-move-events on a turtle is preceded by a mouse-click event on that turtle.

```
>>> turtle.ondrag(turtle.goto)
```

Subsequently, clicking and dragging the Turtle will move it across the screen thereby producing hand-drawings (if pen is down).

Special Turtle methods

turtle.**begin_poly**()
  Start recording the vertices of a polygon. Current turtle position is first vertex of polygon.

turtle.**end_poly**()
  Stop recording the vertices of a polygon. Current turtle position is last vertex of polygon. This will be connected with the first vertex.

turtle.**get_poly**()
  Return the last recorded polygon.

```
>>> turtle.home()
>>> turtle.begin_poly()
>>> turtle.fd(100)
>>> turtle.left(20)
>>> turtle.fd(30)
>>> turtle.left(60)
>>> turtle.fd(50)
>>> turtle.end_poly()
>>> p = turtle.get_poly()
>>> register_shape("myFavouriteShape", p)
```

turtle.**clone**()
  Create and return a clone of the turtle with same position, heading and turtle properties.

```
>>> mick = Turtle()
>>> joe = mick.clone()
```

turtle.**getturtle**()
turtle.**getpen**()
  Return the Turtle object itself. Only reasonable use: as a function to return the "anonymous turtle":

```
>>> pet = getturtle()
>>> pet.fd(50)
>>> pet
<turtle.Turtle object at 0x...>
```

turtle.**getscreen**()
  Return the *TurtleScreen* object the turtle is drawing on. TurtleScreen methods can then be called for that object.

```
>>> ts = turtle.getscreen()
>>> ts
<turtle._Screen object at 0x...>
>>> ts.bgcolor("pink")
```

turtle.**setundobuffer**(*size*)

> **Parameters size** – an integer or None

  Set or disable undobuffer. If *size* is an integer an empty undobuffer of given size is installed. *size* gives the maximum number of turtle actions that can be undone by the *undo()* method/function. If *size* is None, the undobuffer is disabled.

```
>>> turtle.setundobuffer(42)
```

turtle.**undobufferentries**()
  Return number of entries in the undobuffer.

```
>>> while undobufferentries():
...     undo()
```

Compound shapes

To use compound turtle shapes, which consist of several polygons of different color, you must use the helper class *Shape* explicitly as described below:

1. Create an empty Shape object of type "compound".
2. Add as many components to this object as desired, using the `addcomponent()` method.

   For example:

   ```
   >>> s = Shape("compound")
   >>> poly1 = ((0,0),(10,-5),(0,10),(-10,-5))
   >>> s.addcomponent(poly1, "red", "blue")
   >>> poly2 = ((0,0),(10,-5),(-10,-5))
   >>> s.addcomponent(poly2, "blue", "red")
   ```

3. Now add the Shape to the Screen's shapelist and use it:

   ```
   >>> register_shape("myshape", s)
   >>> shape("myshape")
   ```

Note: The *Shape* class is used internally by the *register_shape()* method in different ways. The application programmer has to deal with the Shape class *only* when using compound shapes like shown above!

24.1.4 Methods of TurtleScreen/Screen and corresponding functions

Most of the examples in this section refer to a TurtleScreen instance called `screen`.

Window control

turtle.bgcolor(*args*)

> **Parameters** `args` – a color string or three numbers in the range 0..colormode or a 3-tuple of such numbers

Set or return background color of the TurtleScreen.

```
>>> screen.bgcolor("orange")
>>> screen.bgcolor()
'orange'
>>> screen.bgcolor("#800080")
>>> screen.bgcolor()
(128.0, 0.0, 128.0)
```

turtle.bgpic(*picname=None*)

> **Parameters** `picname` – a string, name of a gif-file or `"nopic"`, or None

Set background image or return name of current backgroundimage. If *picname* is a filename, set the corresponding image as background. If *picname* is `"nopic"`, delete background image, if present. If *picname* is None, return the filename of the current backgroundimage.

```
>>> screen.bgpic()
'nopic'
>>> screen.bgpic("landscape.gif")
>>> screen.bgpic()
"landscape.gif"
```

turtle.clear()
turtle.clearscreen()

> Delete all drawings and all turtles from the TurtleScreen. Reset the now empty TurtleScreen to its initial state: white background, no background image, no event bindings and tracing on.
>
> **Note:** This TurtleScreen method is available as a global function only under the name clearscreen. The global function clear is a different one derived from the Turtle method clear.

turtle.reset()
turtle.resetscreen()

> Reset all Turtles on the Screen to their initial state.
>
> **Note:** This TurtleScreen method is available as a global function only under the name resetscreen. The global function reset is another one derived from the Turtle method reset.

turtle.screensize(*canvwidth=None, canvheight=None, bg=None*)

> **Parameters**
> - **canvwidth** – positive integer, new width of canvas in pixels
> - **canvheight** – positive integer, new height of canvas in pixels
> - **bg** – colorstring or color-tuple, new background color
>
> If no arguments are given, return current (canvaswidth, canvasheight). Else resize the canvas the turtles are drawing on. Do not alter the drawing window. To observe hidden parts of the canvas, use the scrollbars. With this method, one can make visible those parts of a drawing which were outside the canvas before.
>
> ```
> >>> screen.screensize()
> (400, 300)
> >>> screen.screensize(2000,1500)
> >>> screen.screensize()
> (2000, 1500)
> ```
>
> e.g. to search for an erroneously escaped turtle ;-)

turtle.setworldcoordinates(*llx, lly, urx, ury*)

> **Parameters**
> - **llx** – a number, x-coordinate of lower left corner of canvas
> - **lly** – a number, y-coordinate of lower left corner of canvas
> - **urx** – a number, x-coordinate of upper right corner of canvas
> - **ury** – a number, y-coordinate of upper right corner of canvas

24.1. turtle — Turtle graphics

Set up user-defined coordinate system and switch to mode "world" if necessary. This performs a
`screen.reset()`. If mode "world" is already active, all drawings are redrawn according to the new
coordinates.

ATTENTION: in user-defined coordinate systems angles may appear distorted.

```
>>> screen.reset()
>>> screen.setworldcoordinates(-50,-7.5,50,7.5)
>>> for _ in range(72):
...     left(10)
...
>>> for _ in range(8):
...     left(45); fd(2)    # a regular octagon
```

Animation control

turtle.delay(*delay=None*)

   Parameters delay – positive integer

   Set or return the drawing *delay* in milliseconds. (This is approximately the time interval between two
   consecutive canvas updates.) The longer the drawing delay, the slower the animation.

   Optional argument:

```
>>> screen.delay()
10
>>> screen.delay(5)
>>> screen.delay()
5
```

turtle.tracer(*n=None, delay=None*)

   Parameters

   - **n** – nonnegative integer
   - **delay** – nonnegative integer

   Turn turtle animation on/off and set delay for update drawings. If *n* is given, only each n-th regular
   screen update is really performed. (Can be used to accelerate the drawing of complex graphics.) When
   called without arguments, returns the currently stored value of n. Second argument sets delay value
   (see *delay()*).

```
>>> screen.tracer(8, 25)
>>> dist = 2
>>> for i in range(200):
...     fd(dist)
...     rt(90)
...     dist += 2
```

turtle.update()

   Perform a TurtleScreen update. To be used when tracer is turned off.

See also the RawTurtle/Turtle method *speed()*.

Using screen events

turtle.listen(*xdummy=None, ydummy=None*)

   Set focus on TurtleScreen (in order to collect key-events). Dummy arguments are provided in order to be able to pass `listen()` to the onclick method.

turtle.**onkey**(*fun, key*)
turtle.**onkeyrelease**(*fun, key*)

> **Parameters**
>
> - **fun** – a function with no arguments or `None`
> - **key** – a string: key (e.g. "a") or key-symbol (e.g. "space")
>
> Bind *fun* to key-release event of key. If *fun* is `None`, event bindings are removed. Remark: in order to be able to register key-events, TurtleScreen must have the focus. (See method `listen()`.)
>
> ```
> >>> def f():
> ...     fd(50)
> ...     lt(60)
> ...
> >>> screen.onkey(f, "Up")
> >>> screen.listen()
> ```

turtle.**onkeypress**(*fun, key=None*)

> **Parameters**
>
> - **fun** – a function with no arguments or `None`
> - **key** – a string: key (e.g. "a") or key-symbol (e.g. "space")
>
> Bind *fun* to key-press event of key if key is given, or to any key-press-event if no key is given. Remark: in order to be able to register key-events, TurtleScreen must have focus. (See method `listen()`.)
>
> ```
> >>> def f():
> ...     fd(50)
> ...
> >>> screen.onkey(f, "Up")
> >>> screen.listen()
> ```

turtle.**onclick**(*fun, btn=1, add=None*)
turtle.**onscreenclick**(*fun, btn=1, add=None*)

> **Parameters**
>
> - **fun** – a function with two arguments which will be called with the coordinates of the clicked point on the canvas
> - **num** – number of the mouse-button, defaults to 1 (left mouse button)
> - **add** – `True` or `False` – if `True`, a new binding will be added, otherwise it will replace a former binding
>
> Bind *fun* to mouse-click events on this screen. If *fun* is `None`, existing bindings are removed.
>
> Example for a TurtleScreen instance named `screen` and a Turtle instance named turtle:
>
> ```
> >>> screen.onclick(turtle.goto)  # Subsequently clicking into the TurtleScreen will
> >>>                              # make the turtle move to the clicked point.
> >>> screen.onclick(None)         # remove event binding again
> ```

> **Note:** This TurtleScreen method is available as a global function only under the name `onscreenclick`. The global function `onclick` is another one derived from the Turtle method `onclick`.

turtle.**ontimer**(*fun, t=0*)

24.1. turtle — Turtle graphics

Parameters

- **fun** – a function with no arguments
- **t** – a number $>= 0$

Install a timer that calls *fun* after *t* milliseconds.

```
>>> running = True
>>> def f():
...     if running:
...         fd(50)
...         lt(60)
...         screen.ontimer(f, 250)
>>> f()   ### makes the turtle march around
>>> running = False
```

`turtle.mainloop()`
`turtle.done()`

> Starts event loop - calling Tkinter's mainloop function. Must be the last statement in a turtle graphics program. Must *not* be used if a script is run from within IDLE in -n mode (No subprocess) - for interactive use of turtle graphics.

```
>>> screen.mainloop()
```

Input methods

`turtle.textinput(title, prompt)`

Parameters

- **title** – string
- **prompt** – string

Pop up a dialog window for input of a string. Parameter title is the title of the dialog window, prompt is a text mostly describing what information to input. Return the string input. If the dialog is canceled, return None.

```
>>> screen.textinput("NIM", "Name of first player:")
```

`turtle.numinput(title, prompt, default=None, minval=None, maxval=None)`

Parameters

- **title** – string
- **prompt** – string
- **default** – number (optional)
- **minval** – number (optional)
- **maxval** – number (optional)

Pop up a dialog window for input of a number. title is the title of the dialog window, prompt is a text mostly describing what numerical information to input. default: default value, minval: minimum value for input, maxval: maximum value for input The number input must be in the range minval .. maxval if these are given. If not, a hint is issued and the dialog remains open for correction. Return the number input. If the dialog is canceled, return None.

```
>>> screen.numinput("Poker", "Your stakes:", 1000, minval=10, maxval=10000)
```

Settings and special methods

turtle.**mode**(*mode=None*)

> **Parameters mode** – one of the strings "standard", "logo" or "world"

> Set turtle mode ("standard", "logo" or "world") and perform reset. If mode is not given, current mode is returned.

> Mode "standard" is compatible with old *turtle*. Mode "logo" is compatible with most Logo turtle graphics. Mode "world" uses user-defined "world coordinates". **Attention**: in this mode angles appear distorted if x/y unit-ratio doesn't equal 1.

Mode	Initial turtle heading	positive angles
"standard"	to the right (east)	counterclockwise
"logo"	upward (north)	clockwise

```
>>> mode("logo")    # resets turtle heading to north
>>> mode()
'logo'
```

turtle.**colormode**(*cmode=None*)

> **Parameters cmode** – one of the values 1.0 or 255

> Return the colormode or set it to 1.0 or 255. Subsequently r, g, b values of color triples have to be in the range 0..*cmode*.

```
>>> screen.colormode(1)
>>> turtle.pencolor(240, 160, 80)
Traceback (most recent call last):
   ...
TurtleGraphicsError: bad color sequence: (240, 160, 80)
>>> screen.colormode()
1.0
>>> screen.colormode(255)
>>> screen.colormode()
255
>>> turtle.pencolor(240,160,80)
```

turtle.**getcanvas**()

> Return the Canvas of this TurtleScreen. Useful for insiders who know what to do with a Tkinter Canvas.

```
>>> cv = screen.getcanvas()
>>> cv
<turtle.ScrolledCanvas object ...>
```

turtle.**getshapes**()

> Return a list of names of all currently available turtle shapes.

```
>>> screen.getshapes()
['arrow', 'blank', 'circle', ..., 'turtle']
```

turtle.**register_shape**(*name, shape=None*)
turtle.**addshape**(*name, shape=None*)

> There are three different ways to call this function:

> 1. *name* is the name of a gif-file and *shape* is None: Install the corresponding image shape.

24.1. turtle — Turtle graphics

```
>>> screen.register_shape("turtle.gif")
```

Note: Image shapes *do not* rotate when turning the turtle, so they do not display the heading of the turtle!

2. *name* is an arbitrary string and *shape* is a tuple of pairs of coordinates: Install the corresponding polygon shape.

```
>>> screen.register_shape("triangle", ((5,-3), (0,5), (-5,-3)))
```

3. *name* is an arbitrary string and shape is a (compound) *Shape* object: Install the corresponding compound shape.

Add a turtle shape to TurtleScreen's shapelist. Only thusly registered shapes can be used by issuing the command `shape(shapename)`.

turtle.turtles()
    Return the list of turtles on the screen.

```
>>> for turtle in screen.turtles():
...     turtle.color("red")
```

turtle.window_height()
    Return the height of the turtle window.

```
>>> screen.window_height()
480
```

turtle.window_width()
    Return the width of the turtle window.

```
>>> screen.window_width()
640
```

Methods specific to Screen, not inherited from TurtleScreen

turtle.bye()
    Shut the turtlegraphics window.

turtle.exitonclick()
    Bind bye() method to mouse clicks on the Screen.

    If the value "using_IDLE" in the configuration dictionary is **False** (default value), also enter mainloop. Remark: If IDLE with the **-n** switch (no subprocess) is used, this value should be set to **True** in `turtle.cfg`. In this case IDLE's own mainloop is active also for the client script.

turtle.setup(*width=_CFG["width"]*, *height=_CFG["height"]*, *startx=_CFG["leftright"]*, *starty=_CFG["topbottom"]*)
    Set the size and position of the main window. Default values of arguments are stored in the configuration dictionary and can be changed via a `turtle.cfg` file.

    Parameters

    - **width** – if an integer, a size in pixels, if a float, a fraction of the screen; default is 50% of screen
    - **height** – if an integer, the height in pixels, if a float, a fraction of the screen; default is 75% of screen

- **startx** – if positive, starting position in pixels from the left edge of the screen, if negative from the right edge, if None, center window horizontally
- **starty** – if positive, starting position in pixels from the top edge of the screen, if negative from the bottom edge, if None, center window vertically

```
>>> screen.setup (width=200, height=200, startx=0, starty=0)
>>>              # sets window to 200x200 pixels, in upper left of screen
>>> screen.setup(width=.75, height=0.5, startx=None, starty=None)
>>>              # sets window to 75% of screen by 50% of screen and centers
```

turtle.title(*titlestring*)

> **Parameters titlestring** – a string that is shown in the titlebar of the turtle graphics window

Set title of turtle window to *titlestring*.

```
>>> screen.title("Welcome to the turtle zoo!")
```

24.1.5 Public classes

class turtle.RawTurtle(*canvas*)
class turtle.RawPen(*canvas*)

> **Parameters canvas** – a tkinter.Canvas, a *ScrolledCanvas* or a *TurtleScreen*

Create a turtle. The turtle has all methods described above as "methods of Turtle/RawTurtle".

class turtle.Turtle
Subclass of RawTurtle, has the same interface but draws on a default *Screen* object created automatically when needed for the first time.

class turtle.TurtleScreen(*cv*)

> **Parameters cv** – a tkinter.Canvas

Provides screen oriented methods like setbg() etc. that are described above.

class turtle.Screen
Subclass of TurtleScreen, with *four methods added*.

class turtle.ScrolledCanvas(*master*)

> **Parameters master** – some Tkinter widget to contain the ScrolledCanvas, i.e. a Tkinter-canvas with scrollbars added

Used by class Screen, which thus automatically provides a ScrolledCanvas as playground for the turtles.

class turtle.Shape(*type_, data*)

> **Parameters type_** – one of the strings "polygon", "image", "compound"

Data structure modeling shapes. The pair (type_, data) must follow this specification:

type_	data
"polygon"	a polygon-tuple, i.e. a tuple of pairs of coordinates
"image"	an image (in this form only used internally!)
"compound"	None (a compound shape has to be constructed using the *addcomponent()* method)

addcomponent(*poly, fill, outline=None*)

Parameters
- **poly** – a polygon, i.e. a tuple of pairs of numbers
- **fill** – a color the *poly* will be filled with
- **outline** – a color for the poly's outline (if given)

Example:

```
>>> poly = ((0,0),(10,-5),(0,10),(-10,-5))
>>> s = Shape("compound")
>>> s.addcomponent(poly, "red", "blue")
>>> # ... add more components and then use register_shape()
```

See *Compound shapes*.

class turtle.Vec2D(*x*, *y*)

A two-dimensional vector class, used as a helper class for implementing turtle graphics. May be useful for turtle graphics programs too. Derived from tuple, so a vector is a tuple!

Provides (for *a*, *b* vectors, *k* number):

- **a + b** vector addition
- **a - b** vector subtraction
- **a * b** inner product
- **k * a** and **a * k** multiplication with scalar
- **abs(a)** absolute value of a
- **a.rotate(angle)** rotation

24.1.6 Help and configuration

How to use help

The public methods of the Screen and Turtle classes are documented extensively via docstrings. So these can be used as online-help via the Python help facilities:

- When using IDLE, tooltips show the signatures and first lines of the docstrings of typed in function-/method calls.
- Calling *help()* on methods or functions displays the docstrings:

```
>>> help(Screen.bgcolor)
Help on method bgcolor in module turtle:

bgcolor(self, *args) unbound turtle.Screen method
    Set or return backgroundcolor of the TurtleScreen.

    Arguments (if given): a color string or three numbers
    in the range 0..colormode or a 3-tuple of such numbers.


      >>> screen.bgcolor("orange")
      >>> screen.bgcolor()
      "orange"
      >>> screen.bgcolor(0.5,0,0.5)
      >>> screen.bgcolor()
      "#800080"
```

```
>>> help(Turtle.penup)
Help on method penup in module turtle:

penup(self) unbound turtle.Turtle method
    Pull the pen up -- no drawing when moving.

    Aliases: penup | pu | up

    No argument

    >>> turtle.penup()
```

- The docstrings of the functions which are derived from methods have a modified form:

```
>>> help(bgcolor)
Help on function bgcolor in module turtle:

bgcolor(*args)
    Set or return backgroundcolor of the TurtleScreen.

    Arguments (if given): a color string or three numbers
    in the range 0..colormode or a 3-tuple of such numbers.

    Example::

      >>> bgcolor("orange")
      >>> bgcolor()
      "orange"
      >>> bgcolor(0.5,0,0.5)
      >>> bgcolor()
      "#800080"

>>> help(penup)
Help on function penup in module turtle:

penup()
    Pull the pen up -- no drawing when moving.

    Aliases: penup | pu | up

    No argument

    Example:
    >>> penup()
```

These modified docstrings are created automatically together with the function definitions that are derived from the methods at import time.

Translation of docstrings into different languages

There is a utility to create a dictionary the keys of which are the method names and the values of which are the docstrings of the public methods of the classes Screen and Turtle.

turtle.**write_docstringdict**(*filename="turtle_docstringdict"*)

> **Parameters** `filename` – a string, used as filename

24.1. `turtle` — Turtle graphics 1315

Create and write docstring-dictionary to a Python script with the given filename. This function has to be called explicitly (it is not used by the turtle graphics classes). The docstring dictionary will be written to the Python script *filename*.py. It is intended to serve as a template for translation of the docstrings into different languages.

If you (or your students) want to use *turtle* with online help in your native language, you have to translate the docstrings and save the resulting file as e.g. `turtle_docstringdict_german.py`.

If you have an appropriate entry in your `turtle.cfg` file this dictionary will be read in at import time and will replace the original English docstrings.

At the time of this writing there are docstring dictionaries in German and in Italian. (Requests please to glingl@aon.at.)

How to configure Screen and Turtles

The built-in default configuration mimics the appearance and behaviour of the old turtle module in order to retain best possible compatibility with it.

If you want to use a different configuration which better reflects the features of this module or which better fits to your needs, e.g. for use in a classroom, you can prepare a configuration file `turtle.cfg` which will be read at import time and modify the configuration according to its settings.

The built in configuration would correspond to the following turtle.cfg:

```
width = 0.5
height = 0.75
leftright = None
topbottom = None
canvwidth = 400
canvheight = 300
mode = standard
colormode = 1.0
delay = 10
undobuffersize = 1000
shape = classic
pencolor = black
fillcolor = black
resizemode = noresize
visible = True
language = english
exampleturtle = turtle
examplescreen = screen
title = Python Turtle Graphics
using_IDLE = False
```

Short explanation of selected entries:

- The first four lines correspond to the arguments of the `Screen.setup()` method.
- Line 5 and 6 correspond to the arguments of the method `Screen.screensize()`.
- *shape* can be any of the built-in shapes, e.g: arrow, turtle, etc. For more info try `help(shape)`.
- If you want to use no fillcolor (i.e. make the turtle transparent), you have to write `fillcolor = ""` (but all nonempty strings must not have quotes in the cfg-file).
- If you want to reflect the turtle its state, you have to use `resizemode = auto`.
- If you set e.g. `language = italian` the docstringdict `turtle_docstringdict_italian.py` will be loaded at import time (if present on the import path, e.g. in the same directory as *turtle*.

- The entries *exampleturtle* and *examplescreen* define the names of these objects as they occur in the docstrings. The transformation of method-docstrings to function-docstrings will delete these names from the docstrings.
- *using_IDLE*: Set this to True if you regularly work with IDLE and its -n switch ("no subprocess"). This will prevent *exitonclick()* to enter the mainloop.

There can be a **turtle.cfg** file in the directory where *turtle* is stored and an additional one in the current working directory. The latter will override the settings of the first one.

The **Lib/turtledemo** directory contains a **turtle.cfg** file. You can study it as an example and see its effects when running the demos (preferably not from within the demo-viewer).

24.1.7 turtledemo — Demo scripts

The *turtledemo* package includes a set of demo scripts. These scripts can be run and viewed using the supplied demo viewer as follows:

```
python -m turtledemo
```

Alternatively, you can run the demo scripts individually. For example,

```
python -m turtledemo.bytedesign
```

The *turtledemo* package directory contains:

- A demo viewer **__main__.py** which can be used to view the sourcecode of the scripts and run them at the same time.
- Multiple scripts demonstrating different features of the *turtle* module. Examples can be accessed via the Examples menu. They can also be run standalone.
- A **turtle.cfg** file which serves as an example of how to write and use such files.

The demo scripts are:

Name	Description	Features
bytedesign	complex classical turtle graphics pattern	`tracer()`, delay, `update()`
chaos	graphs Verhulst dynamics, shows that computer's computations can generate results sometimes against the common sense expectations	world coordinates
clock	analog clock showing time of your computer	turtles as clock's hands, ontimer
colormixer	experiment with r, g, b	`ondrag()`
forest	3 breadth-first trees	randomization
fractalcurves	Hilbert & Koch curves	recursion
lindenmayer	ethnomathematics (indian kolams)	L-System
minimal_hanoi	Towers of Hanoi	Rectangular Turtles as Hanoi discs (shape, shapesize)
nim	play the classical nim game with three heaps of sticks against the computer.	turtles as nimsticks, event driven (mouse, keyboard)
paint	super minimalistic drawing program	`onclick()`
peace	elementary	turtle: appearance and animation
penrose	aperiodic tiling with kites and darts	`stamp()`
planet_and_moon	simulation of gravitational system	compound shapes, `Vec2D`
round_dance	dancing turtles rotating pairwise in opposite direction	compound shapes, clone shapesize, tilt, get_shapepoly, update
sorting_animate	visual demonstration of different sorting methods	simple alignment, randomization
tree	a (graphical) breadth first tree (using generators)	`clone()`
two_canvases	simple design	turtles on two canvases
wikipedia	a pattern from the wikipedia article on turtle graphics	`clone()`, `undo()`
yinyang	another elementary example	`circle()`

Have fun!

24.1.8 Changes since Python 2.6

- The methods `Turtle.tracer()`, `Turtle.window_width()` and `Turtle.window_height()` have been eliminated. Methods with these names and functionality are now available only as methods of `Screen`. The functions derived from these remain available. (In fact already in Python 2.6 these methods were merely duplications of the corresponding `TurtleScreen`/`Screen`-methods.)

- The method `Turtle.fill()` has been eliminated. The behaviour of `begin_fill()` and `end_fill()` have changed slightly: now every filling-process must be completed with an `end_fill()` call.

- A method `Turtle.filling()` has been added. It returns a boolean value: `True` if a filling process is under way, `False` otherwise. This behaviour corresponds to a `fill()` call without arguments in Python 2.6.

24.1.9 Changes since Python 3.0

- The methods `Turtle.shearfactor()`, `Turtle.shapetransform()` and `Turtle.get_shapepoly()` have been added. Thus the full range of regular linear transforms is now available for transforming turtle shapes. `Turtle.tiltangle()` has been enhanced in functionality: it now can be used to get or set the tiltangle. `Turtle.settiltangle()` has been deprecated.
- The method `Screen.onkeypress()` has been added as a complement to `Screen.onkey()` which in fact binds actions to the keyrelease event. Accordingly the latter has got an alias: `Screen.onkeyrelease()`.
- The method `Screen.mainloop()` has been added. So when working only with Screen and Turtle objects one must not additionally import `mainloop()` anymore.
- Two input methods has been added `Screen.textinput()` and `Screen.numinput()`. These popup input dialogs and return strings and numbers respectively.
- Two example scripts `tdemo_nim.py` and `tdemo_round_dance.py` have been added to the `Lib/turtledemo` directory.

24.2 cmd — Support for line-oriented command interpreters

Source code: Lib/cmd.py

The *Cmd* class provides a simple framework for writing line-oriented command interpreters. These are often useful for test harnesses, administrative tools, and prototypes that will later be wrapped in a more sophisticated interface.

class cmd.Cmd(*completekey='tab'*, *stdin=None*, *stdout=None*)

A *Cmd* instance or subclass instance is a line-oriented interpreter framework. There is no good reason to instantiate *Cmd* itself; rather, it's useful as a superclass of an interpreter class you define yourself in order to inherit *Cmd*'s methods and encapsulate action methods.

The optional argument *completekey* is the *readline* name of a completion key; it defaults to **Tab**. If *completekey* is not *None* and *readline* is available, command completion is done automatically.

The optional arguments *stdin* and *stdout* specify the input and output file objects that the Cmd instance or subclass instance will use for input and output. If not specified, they will default to *sys.stdin* and *sys.stdout*.

If you want a given *stdin* to be used, make sure to set the instance's *use_rawinput* attribute to **False**, otherwise *stdin* will be ignored.

24.2.1 Cmd Objects

A *Cmd* instance has the following methods:

Cmd.cmdloop(*intro=None*)

Repeatedly issue a prompt, accept input, parse an initial prefix off the received input, and dispatch to action methods, passing them the remainder of the line as argument.

The optional argument is a banner or intro string to be issued before the first prompt (this overrides the *intro* class attribute).

If the *readline* module is loaded, input will automatically inherit **bash**-like history-list editing (e.g. **Control-P** scrolls back to the last command, **Control-N** forward to the next one, **Control-F** moves the cursor to the right non-destructively, **Control-B** moves the cursor to the left non-destructively, etc.).

An end-of-file on input is passed back as the string `'EOF'`.

An interpreter instance will recognize a command name `foo` if and only if it has a method `do_foo()`. As a special case, a line beginning with the character `'?'` is dispatched to the method `do_help()`. As another special case, a line beginning with the character `'!'` is dispatched to the method `do_shell()` (if such a method is defined).

This method will return when the *postcmd()* method returns a true value. The *stop* argument to *postcmd()* is the return value from the command's corresponding `do_*()` method.

If completion is enabled, completing commands will be done automatically, and completing of commands args is done by calling `complete_foo()` with arguments *text*, *line*, *begidx*, and *endidx*. *text* is the string prefix we are attempting to match: all returned matches must begin with it. *line* is the current input line with leading whitespace removed, *begidx* and *endidx* are the beginning and ending indexes of the prefix text, which could be used to provide different completion depending upon which position the argument is in.

All subclasses of *Cmd* inherit a predefined `do_help()`. This method, called with an argument `'bar'`, invokes the corresponding method `help_bar()`, and if that is not present, prints the docstring of `do_bar()`, if available. With no argument, `do_help()` lists all available help topics (that is, all commands with corresponding `help_*()` methods or commands that have docstrings), and also lists any undocumented commands.

Cmd.onecmd(*str*)
: Interpret the argument as though it had been typed in response to the prompt. This may be overridden, but should not normally need to be; see the *precmd()* and *postcmd()* methods for useful execution hooks. The return value is a flag indicating whether interpretation of commands by the interpreter should stop. If there is a `do_*()` method for the command *str*, the return value of that method is returned, otherwise the return value from the *default()* method is returned.

Cmd.emptyline()
: Method called when an empty line is entered in response to the prompt. If this method is not overridden, it repeats the last nonempty command entered.

Cmd.default(*line*)
: Method called on an input line when the command prefix is not recognized. If this method is not overridden, it prints an error message and returns.

Cmd.completedefault(*text, line, begidx, endidx*)
: Method called to complete an input line when no command-specific `complete_*()` method is available. By default, it returns an empty list.

Cmd.precmd(*line*)
: Hook method executed just before the command line *line* is interpreted, but after the input prompt is generated and issued. This method is a stub in *Cmd*; it exists to be overridden by subclasses. The return value is used as the command which will be executed by the *onecmd()* method; the *precmd()* implementation may re-write the command or simply return *line* unchanged.

Cmd.postcmd(*stop, line*)
: Hook method executed just after a command dispatch is finished. This method is a stub in *Cmd*; it exists to be overridden by subclasses. *line* is the command line which was executed, and *stop* is a flag which indicates whether execution will be terminated after the call to *postcmd()*; this will be the return value of the *onecmd()* method. The return value of this method will be used as the new value for the internal flag which corresponds to *stop*; returning false will cause interpretation to continue.

Cmd.preloop()
: Hook method executed once when *cmdloop()* is called. This method is a stub in *Cmd*; it exists to be overridden by subclasses.

Cmd.postloop()
: Hook method executed once when *cmdloop()* is about to return. This method is a stub in *Cmd*; it

exists to be overridden by subclasses.

Instances of *Cmd* subclasses have some public instance variables:

Cmd.prompt
    The prompt issued to solicit input.

Cmd.identchars
    The string of characters accepted for the command prefix.

Cmd.lastcmd
    The last nonempty command prefix seen.

Cmd.cmdqueue
    A list of queued input lines. The cmdqueue list is checked in *cmdloop()* when new input is needed; if it is nonempty, its elements will be processed in order, as if entered at the prompt.

Cmd.intro
    A string to issue as an intro or banner. May be overridden by giving the *cmdloop()* method an argument.

Cmd.doc_header
    The header to issue if the help output has a section for documented commands.

Cmd.misc_header
    The header to issue if the help output has a section for miscellaneous help topics (that is, there are `help_*()` methods without corresponding `do_*()` methods).

Cmd.undoc_header
    The header to issue if the help output has a section for undocumented commands (that is, there are `do_*()` methods without corresponding `help_*()` methods).

Cmd.ruler
    The character used to draw separator lines under the help-message headers. If empty, no ruler line is drawn. It defaults to `'='`.

Cmd.use_rawinput
    A flag, defaulting to true. If true, *cmdloop()* uses *input()* to display a prompt and read the next command; if false, `sys.stdout.write()` and `sys.stdin.readline()` are used. (This means that by importing *readline*, on systems that support it, the interpreter will automatically support **Emacs**-like line editing and command-history keystrokes.)

24.2.2 Cmd Example

The *cmd* module is mainly useful for building custom shells that let a user work with a program interactively.

This section presents a simple example of how to build a shell around a few of the commands in the *turtle* module.

Basic turtle commands such as *forward()* are added to a *Cmd* subclass with method named `do_forward()`. The argument is converted to a number and dispatched to the turtle module. The docstring is used in the help utility provided by the shell.

The example also includes a basic record and playback facility implemented with the *precmd()* method which is responsible for converting the input to lowercase and writing the commands to a file. The `do_playback()` method reads the file and adds the recorded commands to the **cmdqueue** for immediate playback:

```
import cmd, sys
from turtle import *

class TurtleShell(cmd.Cmd):
    intro = 'Welcome to the turtle shell.   Type help or ? to list commands.\n'
```

```python
    prompt = '(turtle) '
    file = None

    # ----- basic turtle commands -----
    def do_forward(self, arg):
        'Move the turtle forward by the specified distance:  FORWARD 10'
        forward(*parse(arg))
    def do_right(self, arg):
        'Turn turtle right by given number of degrees:  RIGHT 20'
        right(*parse(arg))
    def do_left(self, arg):
        'Turn turtle left by given number of degrees:  LEFT 90'
        left(*parse(arg))
    def do_goto(self, arg):
        'Move turtle to an absolute position with changing orientation.  GOTO 100 200'
        goto(*parse(arg))
    def do_home(self, arg):
        'Return turtle to the home position:  HOME'
        home()
    def do_circle(self, arg):
        'Draw circle with given radius an options extent and steps:  CIRCLE 50'
        circle(*parse(arg))
    def do_position(self, arg):
        'Print the current turtle position:  POSITION'
        print('Current position is %d %d\n' % position())
    def do_heading(self, arg):
        'Print the current turtle heading in degrees:  HEADING'
        print('Current heading is %d\n' % (heading(),))
    def do_color(self, arg):
        'Set the color:  COLOR BLUE'
        color(arg.lower())
    def do_undo(self, arg):
        'Undo (repeatedly) the last turtle action(s):  UNDO'
    def do_reset(self, arg):
        'Clear the screen and return turtle to center:  RESET'
        reset()
    def do_bye(self, arg):
        'Stop recording, close the turtle window, and exit:  BYE'
        print('Thank you for using Turtle')
        self.close()
        bye()
        return True

    # ----- record and playback -----
    def do_record(self, arg):
        'Save future commands to filename:  RECORD rose.cmd'
        self.file = open(arg, 'w')
    def do_playback(self, arg):
        'Playback commands from a file:  PLAYBACK rose.cmd'
        self.close()
        with open(arg) as f:
            self.cmdqueue.extend(f.read().splitlines())
    def precmd(self, line):
        line = line.lower()
        if self.file and 'playback' not in line:
            print(line, file=self.file)
        return line
    def close(self):
```

```python
        if self.file:
            self.file.close()
            self.file = None

def parse(arg):
    'Convert a series of zero or more numbers to an argument tuple'
    return tuple(map(int, arg.split()))

if __name__ == '__main__':
    TurtleShell().cmdloop()
```

Here is a sample session with the turtle shell showing the help functions, using blank lines to repeat commands, and the simple record and playback facility:

```
Welcome to the turtle shell.   Type help or ? to list commands.

(turtle) ?

Documented commands (type help <topic>):
========================================
bye     color    goto     home    playback  record  right
circle  forward  heading  left    position  reset   undo

(turtle) help forward
Move the turtle forward by the specified distance:  FORWARD 10
(turtle) record spiral.cmd
(turtle) position
Current position is 0 0

(turtle) heading
Current heading is 0

(turtle) reset
(turtle) circle 20
(turtle) right 30
(turtle) circle 40
(turtle) right 30
(turtle) circle 60
(turtle) right 30
(turtle) circle 80
(turtle) right 30
(turtle) circle 100
(turtle) right 30
(turtle) circle 120
(turtle) right 30
(turtle) circle 120
(turtle) heading
Current heading is 180

(turtle) forward 100
(turtle)
(turtle) right 90
(turtle) forward 100
(turtle)
(turtle) right 90
(turtle) forward 400
(turtle) right 90
(turtle) forward 500
```

```
(turtle) right 90
(turtle) forward 400
(turtle) right 90
(turtle) forward 300
(turtle) playback spiral.cmd
Current position is 0 0

Current heading is 0

Current heading is 180

(turtle) bye
Thank you for using Turtle
```

24.3 `shlex` — Simple lexical analysis

Source code: Lib/shlex.py

The `shlex` class makes it easy to write lexical analyzers for simple syntaxes resembling that of the Unix shell. This will often be useful for writing minilanguages, (for example, in run control files for Python applications) or for parsing quoted strings.

The `shlex` module defines the following functions:

`shlex.split`(*s, comments=False, posix=True*)

Split the string *s* using shell-like syntax. If *comments* is `False` (the default), the parsing of comments in the given string will be disabled (setting the `commenters` attribute of the `shlex` instance to the empty string). This function operates in POSIX mode by default, but uses non-POSIX mode if the *posix* argument is false.

> **Note:** Since the `split()` function instantiates a `shlex` instance, passing `None` for *s* will read the string to split from standard input.

`shlex.quote`(*s*)

Return a shell-escaped version of the string *s*. The returned value is a string that can safely be used as one token in a shell command line, for cases where you cannot use a list.

This idiom would be unsafe:

```
>>> filename = 'somefile; rm -rf ~'
>>> command = 'ls -l {}'.format(filename)
>>> print(command)  # executed by a shell: boom!
ls -l somefile; rm -rf ~
```

`quote()` lets you plug the security hole:

```
>>> command = 'ls -l {}'.format(quote(filename))
>>> print(command)
ls -l 'somefile; rm -rf ~'
>>> remote_command = 'ssh home {}'.format(quote(command))
>>> print(remote_command)
ssh home 'ls -l '"'"'somefile; rm -rf ~'"'"''
```

The quoting is compatible with UNIX shells and with *split()*:

```
>>> remote_command = split(remote_command)
>>> remote_command
['ssh', 'home', "ls -l 'somefile; rm -rf ~'"]
>>> command = split(remote_command[-1])
>>> command
['ls', '-l', 'somefile; rm -rf ~']
```

New in version 3.3.

The *shlex* module defines the following class:

class shlex.shlex(*instream=None, infile=None, posix=False, punctuation_chars=False*)

A *shlex* instance or subclass instance is a lexical analyzer object. The initialization argument, if present, specifies where to read characters from. It must be a file-/stream-like object with *read()* and *readline()* methods, or a string. If no argument is given, input will be taken from `sys.stdin`. The second optional argument is a filename string, which sets the initial value of the *infile* attribute. If the *instream* argument is omitted or equal to `sys.stdin`, this second argument defaults to "stdin". The *posix* argument defines the operational mode: when *posix* is not true (default), the *shlex* instance will operate in compatibility mode. When operating in POSIX mode, *shlex* will try to be as close as possible to the POSIX shell parsing rules. The *punctuation_chars* argument provides a way to make the behaviour even closer to how real shells parse. This can take a number of values: the default value, `False`, preserves the behaviour seen under Python 3.5 and earlier. If set to `True`, then parsing of the characters `();<>|&` is changed: any run of these characters (considered punctuation characters) is returned as a single token. If set to a non-empty string of characters, those characters will be used as the punctuation characters. Any characters in the *wordchars* attribute that appear in *punctuation_chars* will be removed from *wordchars*. See *Improved Compatibility with Shells* for more information.

Changed in version 3.6: The *punctuation_chars* parameter was added.

See also:

Module *configparser* Parser for configuration files similar to the Windows `.ini` files.

24.3.1 shlex Objects

A *shlex* instance has the following methods:

shlex.get_token()
Return a token. If tokens have been stacked using *push_token()*, pop a token off the stack. Otherwise, read one from the input stream. If reading encounters an immediate end-of-file, *eof* is returned (the empty string (`''`) in non-POSIX mode, and `None` in POSIX mode).

shlex.push_token(*str*)
Push the argument onto the token stack.

shlex.read_token()
Read a raw token. Ignore the pushback stack, and do not interpret source requests. (This is not ordinarily a useful entry point, and is documented here only for the sake of completeness.)

shlex.sourcehook(*filename*)
When *shlex* detects a source request (see *source* below) this method is given the following token as argument, and expected to return a tuple consisting of a filename and an open file-like object.

Normally, this method first strips any quotes off the argument. If the result is an absolute pathname, or there was no previous source request in effect, or the previous source was a stream (such as `sys.stdin`), the result is left alone. Otherwise, if the result is a relative pathname, the directory part of the name of the file immediately before it on the source inclusion stack is prepended (this behavior is like the way the C preprocessor handles `#include "file.h"`).

The result of the manipulations is treated as a filename, and returned as the first component of the tuple, with *open()* called on it to yield the second component. (Note: this is the reverse of the order of arguments in instance initialization!)

This hook is exposed so that you can use it to implement directory search paths, addition of file extensions, and other namespace hacks. There is no corresponding 'close' hook, but a shlex instance will call the *close()* method of the sourced input stream when it returns EOF.

For more explicit control of source stacking, use the *push_source()* and *pop_source()* methods.

shlex.push_source(*newstream, newfile=None*)
Push an input source stream onto the input stack. If the filename argument is specified it will later be available for use in error messages. This is the same method used internally by the *sourcehook()* method.

shlex.pop_source()
Pop the last-pushed input source from the input stack. This is the same method used internally when the lexer reaches EOF on a stacked input stream.

shlex.error_leader(*infile=None, lineno=None*)
This method generates an error message leader in the format of a Unix C compiler error label; the format is '"%s", line %d: ', where the %s is replaced with the name of the current source file and the %d with the current input line number (the optional arguments can be used to override these).

This convenience is provided to encourage *shlex* users to generate error messages in the standard, parseable format understood by Emacs and other Unix tools.

Instances of *shlex* subclasses have some public instance variables which either control lexical analysis or can be used for debugging:

shlex.commenters
The string of characters that are recognized as comment beginners. All characters from the comment beginner to end of line are ignored. Includes just '#' by default.

shlex.wordchars
The string of characters that will accumulate into multi-character tokens. By default, includes all ASCII alphanumerics and underscore. In POSIX mode, the accented characters in the Latin-1 set are also included. If *punctuation_chars* is not empty, the characters ~-./*?=, which can appear in filename specifications and command line parameters, will also be included in this attribute, and any characters which appear in punctuation_chars will be removed from wordchars if they are present there.

shlex.whitespace
Characters that will be considered whitespace and skipped. Whitespace bounds tokens. By default, includes space, tab, linefeed and carriage-return.

shlex.escape
Characters that will be considered as escape. This will be only used in POSIX mode, and includes just '\' by default.

shlex.quotes
Characters that will be considered string quotes. The token accumulates until the same quote is encountered again (thus, different quote types protect each other as in the shell.) By default, includes ASCII single and double quotes.

shlex.escapedquotes
Characters in *quotes* that will interpret escape characters defined in *escape*. This is only used in POSIX mode, and includes just '"' by default.

shlex.whitespace_split
If True, tokens will only be split in whitespaces. This is useful, for example, for parsing command lines with *shlex*, getting tokens in a similar way to shell arguments. If this attribute is True,

punctuation_chars will have no effect, and splitting will happen only on whitespaces. When using *punctuation_chars*, which is intended to provide parsing closer to that implemented by shells, it is advisable to leave `whitespace_split` as `False` (the default value).

shlex.infile
   The name of the current input file, as initially set at class instantiation time or stacked by later source requests. It may be useful to examine this when constructing error messages.

shlex.instream
   The input stream from which this *shlex* instance is reading characters.

shlex.source
   This attribute is `None` by default. If you assign a string to it, that string will be recognized as a lexical-level inclusion request similar to the `source` keyword in various shells. That is, the immediately following token will be opened as a filename and input will be taken from that stream until EOF, at which point the *close()* method of that stream will be called and the input source will again become the original input stream. Source requests may be stacked any number of levels deep.

shlex.debug
   If this attribute is numeric and `1` or more, a *shlex* instance will print verbose progress output on its behavior. If you need to use this, you can read the module source code to learn the details.

shlex.lineno
   Source line number (count of newlines seen so far plus one).

shlex.token
   The token buffer. It may be useful to examine this when catching exceptions.

shlex.eof
   Token used to determine end of file. This will be set to the empty string (`''`), in non-POSIX mode, and to `None` in POSIX mode.

shlex.punctuation_chars
   Characters that will be considered punctuation. Runs of punctuation characters will be returned as a single token. However, note that no semantic validity checking will be performed: for example, '>>>' could be returned as a token, even though it may not be recognised as such by shells.

   New in version 3.6.

24.3.2 Parsing Rules

When operating in non-POSIX mode, *shlex* will try to obey to the following rules.

- Quote characters are not recognized within words (`Do"Not"Separate` is parsed as the single word `Do"Not"Separate`);
- Escape characters are not recognized;
- Enclosing characters in quotes preserve the literal value of all characters within the quotes;
- Closing quotes separate words (`"Do"Separate` is parsed as `"Do"` and `Separate`);
- If *whitespace_split* is `False`, any character not declared to be a word character, whitespace, or a quote will be returned as a single-character token. If it is `True`, *shlex* will only split words in whitespaces;
- EOF is signaled with an empty string (`''`);
- It's not possible to parse empty strings, even if quoted.

When operating in POSIX mode, *shlex* will try to obey to the following parsing rules.

- Quotes are stripped out, and do not separate words (`"Do"Not"Separate"` is parsed as the single word `DoNotSeparate`);

- Non-quoted escape characters (e.g. `'\'`) preserve the literal value of the next character that follows;
- Enclosing characters in quotes which are not part of *escapedquotes* (e.g. `"'"`) preserve the literal value of all characters within the quotes;
- Enclosing characters in quotes which are part of *escapedquotes* (e.g. `'"'`) preserves the literal value of all characters within the quotes, with the exception of the characters mentioned in *escape*. The escape characters retain its special meaning only when followed by the quote in use, or the escape character itself. Otherwise the escape character will be considered a normal character.
- EOF is signaled with a *None* value;
- Quoted empty strings (`''`) are allowed.

24.3.3 Improved Compatibility with Shells

New in version 3.6.

The *shlex* class provides compatibility with the parsing performed by common Unix shells like **bash**, **dash**, and **sh**. To take advantage of this compatibility, specify the **punctuation_chars** argument in the constructor. This defaults to **False**, which preserves pre-3.6 behaviour. However, if it is set to **True**, then parsing of the characters `();<>|&` is changed: any run of these characters is returned as a single token. While this is short of a full parser for shells (which would be out of scope for the standard library, given the multiplicity of shells out there), it does allow you to perform processing of command lines more easily than you could otherwise. To illustrate, you can see the difference in the following snippet:

```
>>> import shlex
>>> text = "a && b; c && d || e; f >'abc'; (def \"ghi\")"
>>> list(shlex.shlex(text))
['a', '&', '&', 'b', ';', 'c', '&', '&', 'd', '|', '|', 'e', ';', 'f', '>',
"'abc'", ';', '(', 'def', '"ghi"', ')']
>>> list(shlex.shlex(text, punctuation_chars=True))
['a', '&&', 'b', ';', 'c', '&&', 'd', '||', 'e', ';', 'f', '>', "'abc'",
';', '(', 'def', '"ghi"', ')']
```

Of course, tokens will be returned which are not valid for shells, and you'll need to implement your own error checks on the returned tokens.

Instead of passing **True** as the value for the punctuation_chars parameter, you can pass a string with specific characters, which will be used to determine which characters constitute punctuation. For example:

```
>>> import shlex
>>> s = shlex.shlex("a && b || c", punctuation_chars="|")
>>> list(s)
['a', '&', '&', 'b', '||', 'c']
```

Note: When **punctuation_chars** is specified, the *wordchars* attribute is augmented with the characters `~-./*?=`. That is because these characters can appear in file names (including wildcards) and command-line arguments (e.g. `--color=auto`). Hence:

```
>>> import shlex
>>> s = shlex.shlex('~/a && b-c --color=auto || d *.py?',
...                 punctuation_chars=True)
>>> list(s)
['~/a', '&&', 'b-c', '--color=auto', '||', 'd', '*.py?']
```

For best effect, `punctuation_chars` should be set in conjunction with `posix=True`. (Note that `posix=False` is the default for *shlex*.)

CHAPTER
TWENTYFIVE

GRAPHICAL USER INTERFACES WITH TK

Tk/Tcl has long been an integral part of Python. It provides a robust and platform independent windowing toolkit, that is available to Python programmers using the *tkinter* package, and its extension, the *tkinter.tix* and the *tkinter.ttk* modules.

The *tkinter* package is a thin object-oriented layer on top of Tcl/Tk. To use *tkinter*, you don't need to write Tcl code, but you will need to consult the Tk documentation, and occasionally the Tcl documentation. *tkinter* is a set of wrappers that implement the Tk widgets as Python classes. In addition, the internal module `_tkinter` provides a threadsafe mechanism which allows Python and Tcl to interact.

tkinter's chief virtues are that it is fast, and that it usually comes bundled with Python. Although its standard documentation is weak, good material is available, which includes: references, tutorials, a book and others. *tkinter* is also famous for having an outdated look and feel, which has been vastly improved in Tk 8.5. Nevertheless, there are many other GUI libraries that you could be interested in. For more information about alternatives, see the *Other Graphical User Interface Packages* section.

25.1 `tkinter` — Python interface to Tcl/Tk

Source code: Lib/tkinter/__init__.py

The *tkinter* package ("Tk interface") is the standard Python interface to the Tk GUI toolkit. Both Tk and *tkinter* are available on most Unix platforms, as well as on Windows systems. (Tk itself is not part of Python; it is maintained at ActiveState.) You can check that *tkinter* is properly installed on your system by running `python -m tkinter` from the command line; this should open a window demonstrating a simple Tk interface.

See also:

Python Tkinter Resources The Python Tkinter Topic Guide provides a great deal of information on using Tk from Python and links to other sources of information on Tk.

TKDocs Extensive tutorial plus friendlier widget pages for some of the widgets.

Tkinter reference: a GUI for Python On-line reference material.

Tkinter docs from effbot Online reference for tkinter supported by effbot.org.

Tcl/Tk manual Official manual for the latest tcl/tk version.

Programming Python Book by Mark Lutz, has excellent coverage of Tkinter.

Modern Tkinter for Busy Python Developers Book by Mark Rozerman about building attractive and modern graphical user interfaces with Python and Tkinter.

Python and Tkinter Programming The book by John Grayson (ISBN 1-884777-81-3).

25.1.1 Tkinter Modules

Most of the time, *tkinter* is all you really need, but a number of additional modules are available as well. The Tk interface is located in a binary module named `_tkinter`. This module contains the low-level interface to Tk, and should never be used directly by application programmers. It is usually a shared library (or DLL), but might in some cases be statically linked with the Python interpreter.

In addition to the Tk interface module, *tkinter* includes a number of Python modules, `tkinter.constants` being one of the most important. Importing *tkinter* will automatically import `tkinter.constants`, so, usually, to use Tkinter all you need is a simple import statement:

```
import tkinter
```

Or, more often:

```
from tkinter import *
```

class tkinter.Tk(*screenName=None, baseName=None, className='Tk', useTk=1*)
> The *Tk* class is instantiated without arguments. This creates a toplevel widget of Tk which usually is the main window of an application. Each instance has its own associated Tcl interpreter.

tkinter.Tcl(*screenName=None, baseName=None, className='Tk', useTk=0*)
> The *Tcl()* function is a factory function which creates an object much like that created by the *Tk* class, except that it does not initialize the Tk subsystem. This is most often useful when driving the Tcl interpreter in an environment where one doesn't want to create extraneous toplevel windows, or where one cannot (such as Unix/Linux systems without an X server). An object created by the *Tcl()* object can have a Toplevel window created (and the Tk subsystem initialized) by calling its `loadtk()` method.

Other modules that provide Tk support include:

tkinter.scrolledtext Text widget with a vertical scroll bar built in.

tkinter.colorchooser Dialog to let the user choose a color.

tkinter.commondialog Base class for the dialogs defined in the other modules listed here.

tkinter.filedialog Common dialogs to allow the user to specify a file to open or save.

tkinter.font Utilities to help work with fonts.

tkinter.messagebox Access to standard Tk dialog boxes.

tkinter.simpledialog Basic dialogs and convenience functions.

tkinter.dnd Drag-and-drop support for *tkinter*. This is experimental and should become deprecated when it is replaced with the Tk DND.

turtle Turtle graphics in a Tk window.

25.1.2 Tkinter Life Preserver

This section is not designed to be an exhaustive tutorial on either Tk or Tkinter. Rather, it is intended as a stop gap, providing some introductory orientation on the system.

Credits:

- Tk was written by John Ousterhout while at Berkeley.
- Tkinter was written by Steen Lumholt and Guido van Rossum.
- This Life Preserver was written by Matt Conway at the University of Virginia.

- The HTML rendering, and some liberal editing, was produced from a FrameMaker version by Ken Manheimer.
- Fredrik Lundh elaborated and revised the class interface descriptions, to get them current with Tk 4.2.
- Mike Clarkson converted the documentation to LaTeX, and compiled the User Interface chapter of the reference manual.

How To Use This Section

This section is designed in two parts: the first half (roughly) covers background material, while the second half can be taken to the keyboard as a handy reference.

When trying to answer questions of the form "how do I do blah", it is often best to find out how to do "blah" in straight Tk, and then convert this back into the corresponding *tkinter* call. Python programmers can often guess at the correct Python command by looking at the Tk documentation. This means that in order to use Tkinter, you will have to know a little bit about Tk. This document can't fulfill that role, so the best we can do is point you to the best documentation that exists. Here are some hints:

- The authors strongly suggest getting a copy of the Tk man pages. Specifically, the man pages in the **manN** directory are most useful. The **man3** man pages describe the C interface to the Tk library and thus are not especially helpful for script writers.
- Addison-Wesley publishes a book called Tcl and the Tk Toolkit by John Ousterhout (ISBN 0-201-63337-X) which is a good introduction to Tcl and Tk for the novice. The book is not exhaustive, and for many details it defers to the man pages.
- **tkinter/__init__.py** is a last resort for most, but can be a good place to go when nothing else makes sense.

See also:

Tcl/Tk 8.6 man pages The Tcl/Tk manual on www.tcl.tk.

ActiveState Tcl Home Page The Tk/Tcl development is largely taking place at ActiveState.

Tcl and the Tk Toolkit The book by John Ousterhout, the inventor of Tcl.

Practical Programming in Tcl and Tk Brent Welch's encyclopedic book.

A Simple Hello World Program

```
import tkinter as tk

class Application(tk.Frame):
    def __init__(self, master=None):
        super().__init__(master)
        self.pack()
        self.create_widgets()

    def create_widgets(self):
        self.hi_there = tk.Button(self)
        self.hi_there["text"] = "Hello World\n(click me)"
        self.hi_there["command"] = self.say_hi
        self.hi_there.pack(side="top")

        self.quit = tk.Button(self, text="QUIT", fg="red",
                              command=root.destroy)
        self.quit.pack(side="bottom")
```

```
    def say_hi(self):
        print("hi there, everyone!")
root = tk.Tk()
app = Application(master=root)
app.mainloop()
```

25.1.3 A (Very) Quick Look at Tcl/Tk

The class hierarchy looks complicated, but in actual practice, application programmers almost always refer to the classes at the very bottom of the hierarchy.

Notes:

- These classes are provided for the purposes of organizing certain functions under one namespace. They aren't meant to be instantiated independently.
- The *Tk* class is meant to be instantiated only once in an application. Application programmers need not instantiate one explicitly, the system creates one whenever any of the other classes are instantiated.
- The `Widget` class is not meant to be instantiated, it is meant only for subclassing to make "real" widgets (in C++, this is called an 'abstract class').

To make use of this reference material, there will be times when you will need to know how to read short passages of Tk and how to identify the various parts of a Tk command. (See section *Mapping Basic Tk into Tkinter* for the `tkinter` equivalents of what's below.)

Tk scripts are Tcl programs. Like all Tcl programs, Tk scripts are just lists of tokens separated by spaces. A Tk widget is just its *class*, the *options* that help configure it, and the *actions* that make it do useful things.

To make a widget in Tk, the command is always of the form:

```
classCommand newPathname options
```

classCommand denotes which kind of widget to make (a button, a label, a menu...)

newPathname is the new name for this widget. All names in Tk must be unique. To help enforce this, widgets in Tk are named with *pathnames*, just like files in a file system. The top level widget, the *root*, is called . (period) and children are delimited by more periods. For example, `.myApp.controlPanel.okButton` might be the name of a widget.

options configure the widget's appearance and in some cases, its behavior. The options come in the form of a list of flags and values. Flags are preceded by a '-', like Unix shell command flags, and values are put in quotes if they are more than one word.

For example:

```
button   .fred    -fg red -text "hi there"
   ^       ^         _____/
   |       |                    |
 class    new               options
command  widget     (-opt val -opt val ...)
```

Once created, the pathname to the widget becomes a new command. This new *widget command* is the programmer's handle for getting the new widget to perform some *action*. In C, you'd express this as someAction(fred, someOptions), in C++, you would express this as fred.someAction(someOptions), and in Tk, you say:

```
.fred someAction someOptions
```

Note that the object name, `.fred`, starts with a dot.

As you'd expect, the legal values for *someAction* will depend on the widget's class: `.fred disable` works if fred is a button (fred gets greyed out), but does not work if fred is a label (disabling of labels is not supported in Tk).

The legal values of *someOptions* is action dependent. Some actions, like `disable`, require no arguments, others, like a text-entry box's `delete` command, would need arguments to specify what range of text to delete.

25.1.4 Mapping Basic Tk into Tkinter

Class commands in Tk correspond to class constructors in Tkinter.

```
button .fred                    =====>    fred = Button()
```

The master of an object is implicit in the new name given to it at creation time. In Tkinter, masters are specified explicitly.

```
button .panel.fred              =====>    fred = Button(panel)
```

The configuration options in Tk are given in lists of hyphened tags followed by values. In Tkinter, options are specified as keyword-arguments in the instance constructor, and keyword-args for configure calls or as instance indices, in dictionary style, for established instances. See section *Setting Options* on setting options.

```
button .fred -fg red            =====>    fred = Button(panel, fg="red")
.fred configure -fg red         =====>    fred["fg"] = red
                                OR ==>    fred.config(fg="red")
```

In Tk, to perform an action on a widget, use the widget name as a command, and follow it with an action name, possibly with arguments (options). In Tkinter, you call methods on the class instance to invoke actions on the widget. The actions (methods) that a given widget can perform are listed in `tkinter/__init__.py`.

```
.fred invoke                    =====>    fred.invoke()
```

To give a widget to the packer (geometry manager), you call pack with optional arguments. In Tkinter, the Pack class holds all this functionality, and the various forms of the pack command are implemented as methods. All widgets in *tkinter* are subclassed from the Packer, and so inherit all the packing methods. See the *tkinter.tix* module documentation for additional information on the Form geometry manager.

```
pack .fred -side left           =====>    fred.pack(side="left")
```

25.1.5 How Tk and Tkinter are Related

From the top down:

Your App Here (Python) A Python application makes a *tkinter* call.

tkinter (Python Package) This call (say, for example, creating a button widget), is implemented in the *tkinter* package, which is written in Python. This Python function will parse the commands and the arguments and convert them into a form that makes them look as if they had come from a Tk script instead of a Python script.

_tkinter (C) These commands and their arguments will be passed to a C function in the _tkinter - note the underscore - extension module.

Tk Widgets (C and Tcl) This C function is able to make calls into other C modules, including the C functions that make up the Tk library. Tk is implemented in C and some Tcl. The Tcl part of the Tk widgets is used to bind certain default behaviors to widgets, and is executed once at the point where the Python *tkinter* package is imported. (The user never sees this stage).

Tk (C) The Tk part of the Tk Widgets implement the final mapping to ...

Xlib (C) the Xlib library to draw graphics on the screen.

25.1.6 Handy Reference

Setting Options

Options control things like the color and border width of a widget. Options can be set in three ways:

At object creation time, using keyword arguments

```
fred = Button(self, fg="red", bg="blue")
```

After object creation, treating the option name like a dictionary index

```
fred["fg"] = "red"
fred["bg"] = "blue"
```

Use the config() method to update multiple attrs subsequent to object creation

```
fred.config(fg="red", bg="blue")
```

For a complete explanation of a given option and its behavior, see the Tk man pages for the widget in question.

Note that the man pages list "STANDARD OPTIONS" and "WIDGET SPECIFIC OPTIONS" for each widget. The former is a list of options that are common to many widgets, the latter are the options that are idiosyncratic to that particular widget. The Standard Options are documented on the *options(3)* man page.

No distinction between standard and widget-specific options is made in this document. Some options don't apply to some kinds of widgets. Whether a given widget responds to a particular option depends on the class of the widget; buttons have a `command` option, labels do not.

The options supported by a given widget are listed in that widget's man page, or can be queried at runtime by calling the `config()` method without arguments, or by calling the `keys()` method on that widget. The return value of these calls is a dictionary whose key is the name of the option as a string (for example, `'relief'`) and whose values are 5-tuples.

Some options, like `bg` are synonyms for common options with long names (`bg` is shorthand for "background"). Passing the `config()` method the name of a shorthand option will return a 2-tuple, not 5-tuple. The 2-tuple passed back will contain the name of the synonym and the "real" option (such as `('bg', 'background')`).

Index	Meaning	Example
0	option name	`'relief'`
1	option name for database lookup	`'relief'`
2	option class for database lookup	`'Relief'`
3	default value	`'raised'`
4	current value	`'groove'`

Example:

```
>>> print(fred.config())
{'relief': ('relief', 'relief', 'Relief', 'raised', 'groove')}
```

Of course, the dictionary printed will include all the options available and their values. This is meant only as an example.

The Packer

The packer is one of Tk's geometry-management mechanisms. Geometry managers are used to specify the relative positioning of the positioning of widgets within their container - their mutual *master*. In contrast to the more cumbersome *placer* (which is used less commonly, and we do not cover here), the packer takes qualitative relationship specification - *above, to the left of, filling*, etc - and works everything out to determine the exact placement coordinates for you.

The size of any *master* widget is determined by the size of the "slave widgets" inside. The packer is used to control where slave widgets appear inside the master into which they are packed. You can pack widgets into frames, and frames into other frames, in order to achieve the kind of layout you desire. Additionally, the arrangement is dynamically adjusted to accommodate incremental changes to the configuration, once it is packed.

Note that widgets do not appear until they have had their geometry specified with a geometry manager. It's a common early mistake to leave out the geometry specification, and then be surprised when the widget is created but nothing appears. A widget will appear only after it has had, for example, the packer's `pack()` method applied to it.

The pack() method can be called with keyword-option/value pairs that control where the widget is to appear within its container, and how it is to behave when the main application window is resized. Here are some examples:

```
fred.pack()                    # defaults to side = "top"
fred.pack(side="left")
fred.pack(expand=1)
```

Packer Options

For more extensive information on the packer and the options that it can take, see the man pages and page 183 of John Ousterhout's book.

anchor Anchor type. Denotes where the packer is to place each slave in its parcel.

expand Boolean, 0 or 1.

fill Legal values: `'x'`, `'y'`, `'both'`, `'none'`.

ipadx and ipady A distance - designating internal padding on each side of the slave widget.

padx and pady A distance - designating external padding on each side of the slave widget.

side Legal values are: `'left'`, `'right'`, `'top'`, `'bottom'`.

Coupling Widget Variables

The current-value setting of some widgets (like text entry widgets) can be connected directly to application variables by using special options. These options are `variable`, `textvariable`, `onvalue`, `offvalue`, and `value`. This connection works both ways: if the variable changes for any reason, the widget it's connected to will be updated to reflect the new value.

Unfortunately, in the current implementation of *tkinter* it is not possible to hand over an arbitrary Python variable to a widget through a `variable` or `textvariable` option. The only kinds of variables for which this works are variables that are subclassed from a class called Variable, defined in *tkinter*.

There are many useful subclasses of Variable already defined: `StringVar`, `IntVar`, `DoubleVar`, and `BooleanVar`. To read the current value of such a variable, call the `get()` method on it, and to change its value you call the `set()` method. If you follow this protocol, the widget will always track the value of the variable, with no further intervention on your part.

For example:

```python
class App(Frame):
    def __init__(self, master=None):
        super().__init__(master)
        self.pack()

        self.entrythingy = Entry()
        self.entrythingy.pack()

        # here is the application variable
        self.contents = StringVar()
        # set it to some value
        self.contents.set("this is a variable")
        # tell the entry widget to watch this variable
        self.entrythingy["textvariable"] = self.contents

        # and here we get a callback when the user hits return.
        # we will have the program print out the value of the
        # application variable when the user hits return
        self.entrythingy.bind('<Key-Return>',
                             self.print_contents)

    def print_contents(self, event):
        print("hi. contents of entry is now ---->",
              self.contents.get())
```

The Window Manager

In Tk, there is a utility command, `wm`, for interacting with the window manager. Options to the `wm` command allow you to control things like titles, placement, icon bitmaps, and the like. In *tkinter*, these commands have been implemented as methods on the `Wm` class. Toplevel widgets are subclassed from the `Wm` class, and so can call the `Wm` methods directly.

To get at the toplevel window that contains a given widget, you can often just refer to the widget's master. Of course if the widget has been packed inside of a frame, the master won't represent a toplevel window. To get at the toplevel window that contains an arbitrary widget, you can call the `_root()` method. This method begins with an underscore to denote the fact that this function is part of the implementation, and not an interface to Tk functionality.

Here are some examples of typical usage:

```python
import tkinter as tk

class App(tk.Frame):
    def __init__(self, master=None):
        super().__init__(master)
        self.pack()
```

```python
# create the application
myapp = App()

#
# here are method calls to the window manager class
#
myapp.master.title("My Do-Nothing Application")
myapp.master.maxsize(1000, 400)

# start the program
myapp.mainloop()
```

Tk Option Data Types

anchor Legal values are points of the compass: `"n"`, `"ne"`, `"e"`, `"se"`, `"s"`, `"sw"`, `"w"`, `"nw"`, and also `"center"`.

bitmap There are eight built-in, named bitmaps: `'error'`, `'gray25'`, `'gray50'`, `'hourglass'`, `'info'`, `'questhead'`, `'question'`, `'warning'`. To specify an X bitmap filename, give the full path to the file, preceded with an @, as in `"@/usr/contrib/bitmap/gumby.bit"`.

boolean You can pass integers 0 or 1 or the strings `"yes"` or `"no"`.

callback This is any Python function that takes no arguments. For example:

```python
def print_it():
    print("hi there")
fred["command"] = print_it
```

color Colors can be given as the names of X colors in the rgb.txt file, or as strings representing RGB values in 4 bit: `"#RGB"`, 8 bit: `"#RRGGBB"`, 12 bit" `"#RRRGGGBBB"`, or 16 bit `"#RRRRGGGGBBBB"` ranges, where R,G,B here represent any legal hex digit. See page 160 of Ousterhout's book for details.

cursor The standard X cursor names from `cursorfont.h` can be used, without the `XC_` prefix. For example to get a hand cursor (`XC_hand2`), use the string `"hand2"`. You can also specify a bitmap and mask file of your own. See page 179 of Ousterhout's book.

distance Screen distances can be specified in either pixels or absolute distances. Pixels are given as numbers and absolute distances as strings, with the trailing character denoting units: `c` for centimetres, `i` for inches, `m` for millimetres, `p` for printer's points. For example, 3.5 inches is expressed as `"3.5i"`.

font Tk uses a list font name format, such as `{courier 10 bold}`. Font sizes with positive numbers are measured in points; sizes with negative numbers are measured in pixels.

geometry This is a string of the form `widthxheight`, where width and height are measured in pixels for most widgets (in characters for widgets displaying text). For example: `fred["geometry"] = "200x100"`.

justify Legal values are the strings: `"left"`, `"center"`, `"right"`, and `"fill"`.

region This is a string with four space-delimited elements, each of which is a legal distance (see above). For example: `"2 3 4 5"` and `"3i 2i 4.5i 2i"` and `"3c 2c 4c 10.43c"` are all legal regions.

relief Determines what the border style of a widget will be. Legal values are: `"raised"`, `"sunken"`, `"flat"`, `"groove"`, and `"ridge"`.

scrollcommand This is almost always the `set()` method of some scrollbar widget, but can be any widget method that takes a single argument.

wrap: Must be one of: `"none"`, `"char"`, or `"word"`.

Bindings and Events

The bind method from the widget command allows you to watch for certain events and to have a callback function trigger when that event type occurs. The form of the bind method is:

```
def bind(self, sequence, func, add=''):
```

where:

sequence is a string that denotes the target kind of event. (See the bind man page and page 201 of John Ousterhout's book for details).

func is a Python function, taking one argument, to be invoked when the event occurs. An Event instance will be passed as the argument. (Functions deployed this way are commonly known as *callbacks*.)

add is optional, either `''` or `'+'`. Passing an empty string denotes that this binding is to replace any other bindings that this event is associated with. Passing a `'+'` means that this function is to be added to the list of functions bound to this event type.

For example:

```
def turn_red(self, event):
    event.widget["activeforeground"] = "red"

self.button.bind("<Enter>", self.turn_red)
```

Notice how the widget field of the event is being accessed in the `turn_red()` callback. This field contains the widget that caught the X event. The following table lists the other event fields you can access, and how they are denoted in Tk, which can be useful when referring to the Tk man pages.

Tk	Tkinter Event Field	Tk	Tkinter Event Field
%f	focus	%A	char
%h	height	%E	send_event
%k	keycode	%K	keysym
%s	state	%N	keysym_num
%t	time	%T	type
%w	width	%W	widget
%x	x	%X	x_root
%y	y	%Y	y_root

The index Parameter

A number of widgets require "index" parameters to be passed. These are used to point at a specific place in a Text widget, or to particular characters in an Entry widget, or to particular menu items in a Menu widget.

Entry widget indexes (index, view index, etc.) Entry widgets have options that refer to character positions in the text being displayed. You can use these *tkinter* functions to access these special points in text widgets:

Text widget indexes The index notation for Text widgets is very rich and is best described in the Tk man pages.

Menu indexes (menu.invoke(), menu.entryconfig(), etc.) Some options and methods for menus manipulate specific menu entries. Anytime a menu index is needed for an option or a parameter, you may pass in:

- an integer which refers to the numeric position of the entry in the widget, counted from the top, starting with 0;

- the string "active", which refers to the menu position that is currently under the cursor;
- the string "last" which refers to the last menu item;
- An integer preceded by @, as in @6, where the integer is interpreted as a y pixel coordinate in the menu's coordinate system;
- the string "none", which indicates no menu entry at all, most often used with menu.activate() to deactivate all entries, and finally,
- a text string that is pattern matched against the label of the menu entry, as scanned from the top of the menu to the bottom. Note that this index type is considered after all the others, which means that matches for menu items labelled last, active, or none may be interpreted as the above literals, instead.

Images

Bitmap/Pixelmap images can be created through the subclasses of tkinter.Image:

- BitmapImage can be used for X11 bitmap data.
- PhotoImage can be used for GIF and PPM/PGM color bitmaps.

Either type of image is created through either the file or the data option (other options are available as well).

The image object can then be used wherever an image option is supported by some widget (e.g. labels, buttons, menus). In these cases, Tk will not keep a reference to the image. When the last Python reference to the image object is deleted, the image data is deleted as well, and Tk will display an empty box wherever the image was used.

25.1.7 File Handlers

Tk allows you to register and unregister a callback function which will be called from the Tk mainloop when I/O is possible on a file descriptor. Only one handler may be registered per file descriptor. Example code:

```
import tkinter
widget = tkinter.Tk()
mask = tkinter.READABLE | tkinter.WRITABLE
widget.tk.createfilehandler(file, mask, callback)
...
widget.tk.deletefilehandler(file)
```

This feature is not available on Windows.

Since you don't know how many bytes are available for reading, you may not want to use the *BufferedIOBase* or *TextIOBase read()* or *readline()* methods, since these will insist on reading a predefined number of bytes. For sockets, the *recv()* or *recvfrom()* methods will work fine; for other files, use raw reads or os.read(file.fileno(), maxbytecount).

Widget.tk.createfilehandler(*file, mask, func*)
> Registers the file handler callback function *func*. The *file* argument may either be an object with a *fileno()* method (such as a file or socket object), or an integer file descriptor. The *mask* argument is an ORed combination of any of the three constants below. The callback is called as follows:

```
callback(file, mask)
```

Widget.tk.deletefilehandler(*file*)
> Unregisters a file handler.

`tkinter.READABLE`
`tkinter.WRITABLE`
`tkinter.EXCEPTION`
Constants used in the *mask* arguments.

25.2 `tkinter.ttk` — Tk themed widgets

Source code: Lib/tkinter/ttk.py

The `tkinter.ttk` module provides access to the Tk themed widget set, introduced in Tk 8.5. If Python has not been compiled against Tk 8.5, this module can still be accessed if *Tile* has been installed. The former method using Tk 8.5 provides additional benefits including anti-aliased font rendering under X11 and window transparency (requiring a composition window manager on X11).

The basic idea for `tkinter.ttk` is to separate, to the extent possible, the code implementing a widget's behavior from the code implementing its appearance.

See also:

Tk Widget Styling Support A document introducing theming support for Tk

25.2.1 Using Ttk

To start using Ttk, import its module:

```
from tkinter import ttk
```

To override the basic Tk widgets, the import should follow the Tk import:

```
from tkinter import *
from tkinter.ttk import *
```

That code causes several `tkinter.ttk` widgets (`Button`, `Checkbutton`, `Entry`, `Frame`, `Label`, `LabelFrame`, `Menubutton`, `PanedWindow`, `Radiobutton`, `Scale` and `Scrollbar`) to automatically replace the Tk widgets.

This has the direct benefit of using the new widgets which gives a better look and feel across platforms; however, the replacement widgets are not completely compatible. The main difference is that widget options such as "fg", "bg" and others related to widget styling are no longer present in Ttk widgets. Instead, use the `ttk.Style` class for improved styling effects.

See also:

Converting existing applications to use Tile widgets A monograph (using Tcl terminology) about differences typically encountered when moving applications to use the new widgets.

25.2.2 Ttk Widgets

Ttk comes with 17 widgets, eleven of which already existed in tkinter: `Button`, `Checkbutton`, `Entry`, `Frame`, `Label`, `LabelFrame`, `Menubutton`, `PanedWindow`, `Radiobutton`, `Scale` and `Scrollbar`. The other six are new: *Combobox*, *Notebook*, *Progressbar*, `Separator`, `Sizegrip` and *Treeview*. And all them are subclasses of *Widget*.

Using the Ttk widgets gives the application an improved look and feel. As discussed above, there are differences in how the styling is coded.

Tk code:

```
l1 = tkinter.Label(text="Test", fg="black", bg="white")
l2 = tkinter.Label(text="Test", fg="black", bg="white")
```

Ttk code:

```
style = ttk.Style()
style.configure("BW.TLabel", foreground="black", background="white")

l1 = ttk.Label(text="Test", style="BW.TLabel")
l2 = ttk.Label(text="Test", style="BW.TLabel")
```

For more information about *TtkStyling*, see the *Style* class documentation.

25.2.3 Widget

`ttk.Widget` defines standard options and methods supported by Tk themed widgets and is not supposed to be directly instantiated.

Standard Options

All the `ttk` Widgets accepts the following options:

Option	Description
class	Specifies the window class. The class is used when querying the option database for the window's other options, to determine the default bindtags for the window, and to select the widget's default layout and style. This option is read-only, and may only be specified when the window is created.
cursor	Specifies the mouse cursor to be used for the widget. If set to the empty string (the default), the cursor is inherited for the parent widget.
takefocus	Determines whether the window accepts the focus during keyboard traversal. 0, 1 or an empty string is returned. If 0 is returned, it means that the window should be skipped entirely during keyboard traversal. If 1, it means that the window should receive the input focus as long as it is viewable. And an empty string means that the traversal scripts make the decision about whether or not to focus on the window.
style	May be used to specify a custom widget style.

Scrollable Widget Options

The following options are supported by widgets that are controlled by a scrollbar.

Option	Description
xscrollcommand	Used to communicate with horizontal scrollbars. When the view in the widget's window change, the widget will generate a Tcl command based on the scrollcommand. Usually this option consists of the method `Scrollbar.set()` of some scrollbar. This will cause the scrollbar to be updated whenever the view in the window changes.
yscrollcommand	Used to communicate with vertical scrollbars. For some more information, see above.

Label Options

The following options are supported by labels, buttons and other button-like widgets.

Option	Description
text	Specifies a text string to be displayed inside the widget.
textvariable	Specifies a name whose value will be used in place of the text option resource.
underline	If set, specifies the index (0-based) of a character to underline in the text string. The underline character is used for mnemonic activation.
image	Specifies an image to display. This is a list of 1 or more elements. The first element is the default image name. The rest of the list if a sequence of statespec/value pairs as defined by *Style.map()*, specifying different images to use when the widget is in a particular state or a combination of states. All images in the list should have the same size.
compound	Specifies how to display the image relative to the text, in the case both text and images options are present. Valid values are: • text: display text only • image: display image only • top, bottom, left, right: display image above, below, left of, or right of the text, respectively. • none: the default. display the image if present, otherwise the text.
width	If greater than zero, specifies how much space, in character widths, to allocate for the text label, if less than zero, specifies a minimum width. If zero or unspecified, the natural width of the text label is used.

Compatibility Options

Option	Description
state	May be set to "normal" or "disabled" to control the "disabled" state bit. This is a write-only option: setting it changes the widget state, but the *Widget.state()* method does not affect this option.

Widget States

The widget state is a bitmap of independent state flags.

Flag	Description
active	The mouse cursor is over the widget and pressing a mouse button will cause some action to occur
disabled	Widget is disabled under program control
focus	Widget has keyboard focus
pressed	Widget is being pressed
selected	"On", "true", or "current" for things like Checkbuttons and radiobuttons
background	Windows and Mac have a notion of an "active" or foreground window. The *background* state is set for widgets in a background window, and cleared for those in the foreground window
readonly	Widget should not allow user modification
alternate	A widget-specific alternate display format
invalid	The widget's value is invalid

A state specification is a sequence of state names, optionally prefixed with an exclamation point indicating that the bit is off.

ttk.Widget

Besides the methods described below, the `ttk.Widget` supports the methods `tkinter.Widget.cget()` and `tkinter.Widget.configure()`.

class tkinter.ttk.Widget

> **identify**(*x*, *y*)
>> Returns the name of the element at position *x* *y*, or the empty string if the point does not lie within any element.
>>
>> *x* and *y* are pixel coordinates relative to the widget.
>
> **instate**(*statespec*, *callback=None*, **args*, ***kw*)
>> Test the widget's state. If a callback is not specified, returns `True` if the widget state matches *statespec* and `False` otherwise. If callback is specified then it is called with args if widget state matches *statespec*.
>
> **state**(*statespec=None*)
>> Modify or inquire widget state. If *statespec* is specified, sets the widget state according to it and return a new *statespec* indicating which flags were changed. If *statespec* is not specified, returns the currently-enabled state flags.
>>
>> *statespec* will usually be a list or a tuple.

25.2.4 Combobox

The `ttk.Combobox` widget combines a text field with a pop-down list of values. This widget is a subclass of `Entry`.

Besides the methods inherited from `Widget`: `Widget.cget()`, `Widget.configure()`, `Widget.identify()`, `Widget.instate()` and `Widget.state()`, and the following inherited from `Entry`: `Entry.bbox()`, `Entry.delete()`, `Entry.icursor()`, `Entry.index()`, `Entry.insert()`, `Entry.selection()`, `Entry.xview()`, it has some other methods, described at `ttk.Combobox`.

Options

This widget accepts the following specific options:

Option	Description
exportselection	Boolean value. If set, the widget selection is linked to the Window Manager selection (which can be returned by invoking Misc.selection_get, for example).
justify	Specifies how the text is aligned within the widget. One of "left", "center", or "right".
height	Specifies the height of the pop-down listbox, in rows.
postcommand	A script (possibly registered with Misc.register) that is called immediately before displaying the values. It may specify which values to display.
state	One of "normal", "readonly", or "disabled". In the "readonly" state, the value may not be edited directly, and the user can only selection of the values from the dropdown list. In the "normal" state, the text field is directly editable. In the "disabled" state, no interaction is possible.
textvariable	Specifies a name whose value is linked to the widget value. Whenever the value associated with that name changes, the widget value is updated, and vice versa. See `tkinter.StringVar`.
values	Specifies the list of values to display in the drop-down listbox.
width	Specifies an integer value indicating the desired width of the entry window, in average-size characters of the widget's font.

Virtual events

The combobox widgets generates a <<**ComboboxSelected**>> virtual event when the user selects an element from the list of values.

ttk.Combobox

class `tkinter.ttk.Combobox`

> **current**(*newindex=None*)
> > If *newindex* is specified, sets the combobox value to the element position *newindex*. Otherwise, returns the index of the current value or -1 if the current value is not in the values list.
>
> **get**()
> > Returns the current value of the combobox.
>
> **set**(*value*)
> > Sets the value of the combobox to *value*.

25.2.5 Notebook

Ttk Notebook widget manages a collection of windows and displays a single one at a time. Each child window is associated with a tab, which the user may select to change the currently-displayed window.

Options

This widget accepts the following specific options:

Option	Description
height	If present and greater than zero, specifies the desired height of the pane area (not including internal padding or tabs). Otherwise, the maximum height of all panes is used.
padding	Specifies the amount of extra space to add around the outside of the notebook. The padding is a list up to four length specifications left top right bottom. If fewer than four elements are specified, bottom defaults to top, right defaults to left, and top defaults to left.
width	If present and greater than zero, specified the desired width of the pane area (not including internal padding). Otherwise, the maximum width of all panes is used.

Tab Options

There are also specific options for tabs:

Option	Description
state	Either "normal", "disabled" or "hidden". If "disabled", then the tab is not selectable. If "hidden", then the tab is not shown.
sticky	Specifies how the child window is positioned within the pane area. Value is a string containing zero or more of the characters "n", "s", "e" or "w". Each letter refers to a side (north, south, east or west) that the child window will stick to, as per the grid() geometry manager.
padding	Specifies the amount of extra space to add between the notebook and this pane. Syntax is the same as for the option padding used by this widget.
text	Specifies a text to be displayed in the tab.
image	Specifies an image to display in the tab. See the option image described in *Widget*.
compound	Specifies how to display the image relative to the text, in the case both options text and image are present. See *Label Options* for legal values.
underline	Specifies the index (0-based) of a character to underline in the text string. The underlined character is used for mnemonic activation if *Notebook.enable_traversal()* is called.

Tab Identifiers

The tab_id present in several methods of `ttk.Notebook` may take any of the following forms:

- An integer between zero and the number of tabs
- The name of a child window
- A positional specification of the form "@x,y", which identifies the tab
- The literal string "current", which identifies the currently-selected tab
- The literal string "end", which returns the number of tabs (only valid for *Notebook.index()*)

Virtual Events

This widget generates a **<<NotebookTabChanged>>** virtual event after a new tab is selected.

ttk.Notebook

class tkinter.ttk.Notebook

> **add**(*child*, ***kw*)
> > Adds a new tab to the notebook.
> >
> > If window is currently managed by the notebook but hidden, it is restored to its previous position.
> >
> > See *Tab Options* for the list of available options.
>
> **forget**(*tab_id*)
> > Removes the tab specified by *tab_id*, unmaps and unmanages the associated window.
>
> **hide**(*tab_id*)
> > Hides the tab specified by *tab_id*.
> >
> > The tab will not be displayed, but the associated window remains managed by the notebook and its configuration remembered. Hidden tabs may be restored with the *add()* command.
>
> **identify**(*x*, *y*)
> > Returns the name of the tab element at position *x*, *y*, or the empty string if none.
>
> **index**(*tab_id*)
> > Returns the numeric index of the tab specified by *tab_id*, or the total number of tabs if *tab_id* is the string "end".
>
> **insert**(*pos*, *child*, ***kw*)
> > Inserts a pane at the specified position.
> >
> > *pos* is either the string "end", an integer index, or the name of a managed child. If *child* is already managed by the notebook, moves it to the specified position.
> >
> > See *Tab Options* for the list of available options.
>
> **select**(*tab_id=None*)
> > Selects the specified *tab_id*.
> >
> > The associated child window will be displayed, and the previously-selected window (if different) is unmapped. If *tab_id* is omitted, returns the widget name of the currently selected pane.
>
> **tab**(*tab_id*, *option=None*, ***kw*)
> > Query or modify the options of the specific *tab_id*.
> >
> > If *kw* is not given, returns a dictionary of the tab option values. If *option* is specified, returns the value of that *option*. Otherwise, sets the options to the corresponding values.
>
> **tabs**()
> > Returns a list of windows managed by the notebook.
>
> **enable_traversal**()
> > Enable keyboard traversal for a toplevel window containing this notebook.
> >
> > This will extend the bindings for the toplevel window containing the notebook as follows:
> >
> > - `Control-Tab`: selects the tab following the currently selected one.
> > - `Shift-Control-Tab`: selects the tab preceding the currently selected one.
> > - `Alt-K`: where *K* is the mnemonic (underlined) character of any tab, will select that tab.
> >
> > Multiple notebooks in a single toplevel may be enabled for traversal, including nested notebooks. However, notebook traversal only works properly if all panes have the notebook they are in as master.

25.2.6 Progressbar

The `ttk.Progressbar` widget shows the status of a long-running operation. It can operate in two modes: 1) the determinate mode which shows the amount completed relative to the total amount of work to be done and 2) the indeterminate mode which provides an animated display to let the user know that work is progressing.

Options

This widget accepts the following specific options:

Option	Description
orient	One of "horizontal" or "vertical". Specifies the orientation of the progress bar.
length	Specifies the length of the long axis of the progress bar (width if horizontal, height if vertical).
mode	One of "determinate" or "indeterminate".
maximum	A number specifying the maximum value. Defaults to 100.
value	The current value of the progress bar. In "determinate" mode, this represents the amount of work completed. In "indeterminate" mode, it is interpreted as modulo *maximum*; that is, the progress bar completes one "cycle" when its value increases by *maximum*.
variable	A name which is linked to the option value. If specified, the value of the progress bar is automatically set to the value of this name whenever the latter is modified.
phase	Read-only option. The widget periodically increments the value of this option whenever its value is greater than 0 and, in determinate mode, less than maximum. This option may be used by the current theme to provide additional animation effects.

ttk.Progressbar

class tkinter.ttk.Progressbar

 start(*interval=None*)
    Begin autoincrement mode: schedules a recurring timer event that calls *Progressbar.step()* every *interval* milliseconds. If omitted, *interval* defaults to 50 milliseconds.

 step(*amount=None*)
    Increments the progress bar's value by *amount*.

    amount defaults to 1.0 if omitted.

 stop()
    Stop autoincrement mode: cancels any recurring timer event initiated by *Progressbar.start()* for this progress bar.

25.2.7 Separator

The `ttk.Separator` widget displays a horizontal or vertical separator bar.

It has no other methods besides the ones inherited from `ttk.Widget`.

Options

This widget accepts the following specific option:

Option	Description
orient	One of "horizontal" or "vertical". Specifies the orientation of the separator.

25.2.8 Sizegrip

The `ttk.Sizegrip` widget (also known as a grow box) allows the user to resize the containing toplevel window by pressing and dragging the grip.

This widget has neither specific options nor specific methods, besides the ones inherited from `ttk.Widget`.

Platform-specific notes

- On MacOS X, toplevel windows automatically include a built-in size grip by default. Adding a `Sizegrip` is harmless, since the built-in grip will just mask the widget.

Bugs

- If the containing toplevel's position was specified relative to the right or bottom of the screen (e.g. ….), the `Sizegrip` widget will not resize the window.
- This widget supports only "southeast" resizing.

25.2.9 Treeview

The `ttk.Treeview` widget displays a hierarchical collection of items. Each item has a textual label, an optional image, and an optional list of data values. The data values are displayed in successive columns after the tree label.

The order in which data values are displayed may be controlled by setting the widget option `displaycolumns`. The tree widget can also display column headings. Columns may be accessed by number or symbolic names listed in the widget option columns. See *Column Identifiers*.

Each item is identified by a unique name. The widget will generate item IDs if they are not supplied by the caller. There is a distinguished root item, named `{}`. The root item itself is not displayed; its children appear at the top level of the hierarchy.

Each item also has a list of tags, which can be used to associate event bindings with individual items and control the appearance of the item.

The Treeview widget supports horizontal and vertical scrolling, according to the options described in *Scrollable Widget Options* and the methods *Treeview.xview()* and *Treeview.yview()*.

Options

This widget accepts the following specific options:

Option	Description
columns	A list of column identifiers, specifying the number of columns and their names.
displaycolumns	A list of column identifiers (either symbolic or integer indices) specifying which data columns are displayed and the order in which they appear, or the string "#all".
height	Specifies the number of rows which should be visible. Note: the requested width is determined from the sum of the column widths.
padding	Specifies the internal padding for the widget. The padding is a list of up to four length specifications.
selectmode	Controls how the built-in class bindings manage the selection. One of "extended", "browse" or "none". If set to "extended" (the default), multiple items may be selected. If "browse", only a single item will be selected at a time. If "none", the selection will not be changed. Note that the application code and tag bindings can set the selection however they wish, regardless of the value of this option.
show	A list containing zero or more of the following values, specifying which elements of the tree to display. • tree: display tree labels in column #0. • headings: display the heading row. The default is "tree headings", i.e., show all elements. **Note:** Column #0 always refers to the tree column, even if show="tree" is not specified.

Item Options

The following item options may be specified for items in the insert and item widget commands.

Option	Description
text	The textual label to display for the item.
image	A Tk Image, displayed to the left of the label.
values	The list of values associated with the item. Each item should have the same number of values as the widget option columns. If there are fewer values than columns, the remaining values are assumed empty. If there are more values than columns, the extra values are ignored.
open	True/False value indicating whether the item's children should be displayed or hidden.
tags	A list of tags associated with this item.

Tag Options

The following options may be specified on tags:

Option	Description
foreground	Specifies the text foreground color.
background	Specifies the cell or item background color.
font	Specifies the font to use when drawing text.
image	Specifies the item image, in case the item's image option is empty.

Column Identifiers

Column identifiers take any of the following forms:
- A symbolic name from the list of columns option.
- An integer n, specifying the nth data column.
- A string of the form #n, where n is an integer, specifying the nth display column.

Notes:
- Item's option values may be displayed in a different order than the order in which they are stored.
- Column #0 always refers to the tree column, even if show="tree" is not specified.

A data column number is an index into an item's option values list; a display column number is the column number in the tree where the values are displayed. Tree labels are displayed in column #0. If option displaycolumns is not set, then data column n is displayed in column #n+1. Again, **column #0 always refers to the tree column**.

Virtual Events

The Treeview widget generates the following virtual events.

Event	Description
<<TreeviewSelect>>	Generated whenever the selection changes.
<<TreeviewOpen>>	Generated just before settings the focus item to open=True.
<<TreeviewClose>>	Generated just after setting the focus item to open=False.

The *Treeview.focus()* and *Treeview.selection()* methods can be used to determine the affected item or items.

ttk.Treeview

class tkinter.ttk.**Treeview**

>   **bbox**(*item, column=None*)
>   Returns the bounding box (relative to the treeview widget's window) of the specified *item* in the form (x, y, width, height).
>
>   If *column* is specified, returns the bounding box of that cell. If the *item* is not visible (i.e., if it is a descendant of a closed item or is scrolled offscreen), returns an empty string.
>
>   **get_children**(*item=None*)
>   Returns the list of children belonging to *item*.
>
>   If *item* is not specified, returns root children.
>
>   **set_children**(*item, *newchildren*)
>   Replaces *item*'s child with *newchildren*.
>
>   Children present in *item* that are not present in *newchildren* are detached from the tree. No items in *newchildren* may be an ancestor of *item*. Note that not specifying *newchildren* results in detaching *item*'s children.
>
>   **column**(*column, option=None, **kw*)
>   Query or modify the options for the specified *column*.

If *kw* is not given, returns a dict of the column option values. If *option* is specified then the value for that *option* is returned. Otherwise, sets the options to the corresponding values.

The valid options/values are:

- **id** Returns the column name. This is a read-only option.
- **anchor: One of the standard Tk anchor values.** Specifies how the text in this column should be aligned with respect to the cell.
- **minwidth: width** The minimum width of the column in pixels. The treeview widget will not make the column any smaller than specified by this option when the widget is resized or the user drags a column.
- **stretch: True/False** Specifies whether the column's width should be adjusted when the widget is resized.
- **width: width** The width of the column in pixels.

To configure the tree column, call this with column = "#0"

delete(**items*)
Delete all specified *items* and all their descendants.

The root item may not be deleted.

detach(**items*)
Unlinks all of the specified *items* from the tree.

The items and all of their descendants are still present, and may be reinserted at another point in the tree, but will not be displayed.

The root item may not be detached.

exists(*item*)
Returns True if the specified *item* is present in the tree.

focus(*item=None*)
If *item* is specified, sets the focus item to *item*. Otherwise, returns the current focus item, or '' if there is none.

heading(*column, option=None, **kw*)
Query or modify the heading options for the specified *column*.

If *kw* is not given, returns a dict of the heading option values. If *option* is specified then the value for that *option* is returned. Otherwise, sets the options to the corresponding values.

The valid options/values are:

- **text: text** The text to display in the column heading.
- **image: imageName** Specifies an image to display to the right of the column heading.
- **anchor: anchor** Specifies how the heading text should be aligned. One of the standard Tk anchor values.
- **command: callback** A callback to be invoked when the heading label is pressed.

To configure the tree column heading, call this with column = "#0".

identify(*component, x, y*)
Returns a description of the specified *component* under the point given by x and y, or the empty string if no such *component* is present at that position.

identify_row(*y*)
Returns the item ID of the item at position y.

identify_column(*x*)
> Returns the data column identifier of the cell at position *x*.
>
> The tree column has ID #0.

identify_region(*x, y*)
> Returns one of:
>
> | region | meaning |
> |---|---|
> | heading | Tree heading area. |
> | separator | Space between two columns headings. |
> | tree | The tree area. |
> | cell | A data cell. |
>
> Availability: Tk 8.6.

identify_element(*x, y*)
> Returns the element at position *x, y*.
>
> Availability: Tk 8.6.

index(*item*)
> Returns the integer index of *item* within its parent's list of children.

insert(*parent, index, iid=None, **kw*)
> Creates a new item and returns the item identifier of the newly created item.
>
> *parent* is the item ID of the parent item, or the empty string to create a new top-level item. *index* is an integer, or the value "end", specifying where in the list of parent's children to insert the new item. If *index* is less than or equal to zero, the new node is inserted at the beginning; if *index* is greater than or equal to the current number of children, it is inserted at the end. If *iid* is specified, it is used as the item identifier; *iid* must not already exist in the tree. Otherwise, a new unique identifier is generated.
>
> See *Item Options* for the list of available points.

item(*item, option=None, **kw*)
> Query or modify the options for the specified *item*.
>
> If no options are given, a dict with options/values for the item is returned. If *option* is specified then the value for that option is returned. Otherwise, sets the options to the corresponding values as given by *kw*.

move(*item, parent, index*)
> Moves *item* to position *index* in *parent*'s list of children.
>
> It is illegal to move an item under one of its descendants. If *index* is less than or equal to zero, *item* is moved to the beginning; if greater than or equal to the number of children, it is moved to the end. If *item* was detached it is reattached.

next(*item*)
> Returns the identifier of *item*'s next sibling, or '' if *item* is the last child of its parent.

parent(*item*)
> Returns the ID of the parent of *item*, or '' if *item* is at the top level of the hierarchy.

prev(*item*)
> Returns the identifier of *item*'s previous sibling, or '' if *item* is the first child of its parent.

reattach(*item, parent, index*)
> An alias for *Treeview.move()*.

see(*item*)
> Ensure that *item* is visible.
>
> Sets all of *item*'s ancestors open option to True, and scrolls the widget if necessary so that *item* is within the visible portion of the tree.

selection(*selop=None, items=None*)
> If *selop* is not specified, returns selected items. Otherwise, it will act according to the following selection methods.
>
> Deprecated since version 3.6, will be removed in version 3.8: Using selection() for changing the selection state is deprecated. Use the following selection methods instead.

selection_set(**items*)
> *items* becomes the new selection.
>
> Changed in version 3.6: *items* can be passed as separate arguments, not just as a single tuple.

selection_add(**items*)
> Add *items* to the selection.
>
> Changed in version 3.6: *items* can be passed as separate arguments, not just as a single tuple.

selection_remove(**items*)
> Remove *items* from the selection.
>
> Changed in version 3.6: *items* can be passed as separate arguments, not just as a single tuple.

selection_toggle(**items*)
> Toggle the selection state of each item in *items*.
>
> Changed in version 3.6: *items* can be passed as separate arguments, not just as a single tuple.

set(*item, column=None, value=None*)
> With one argument, returns a dictionary of column/value pairs for the specified *item*. With two arguments, returns the current value of the specified *column*. With three arguments, sets the value of given *column* in given *item* to the specified *value*.

tag_bind(*tagname, sequence=None, callback=None*)
> Bind a callback for the given event *sequence* to the tag *tagname*. When an event is delivered to an item, the callbacks for each of the item's tags option are called.

tag_configure(*tagname, option=None, **kw*)
> Query or modify the options for the specified *tagname*.
>
> If *kw* is not given, returns a dict of the option settings for *tagname*. If *option* is specified, returns the value for that *option* for the specified *tagname*. Otherwise, sets the options to the corresponding values for the given *tagname*.

tag_has(*tagname, item=None*)
> If *item* is specified, returns 1 or 0 depending on whether the specified *item* has the given *tagname*. Otherwise, returns a list of all items that have the specified tag.
>
> Availability: Tk 8.6

xview(**args*)
> Query or modify horizontal position of the treeview.

yview(**args*)
> Query or modify vertical position of the treeview.

25.2.10 Ttk Styling

Each widget in `ttk` is assigned a style, which specifies the set of elements making up the widget and how they are arranged, along with dynamic and default settings for element options. By default the style name is the same as the widget's class name, but it may be overridden by the widget's style option. If you don't know the class name of a widget, use the method `Misc.winfo_class()` (somewidget.winfo_class()).

See also:

Tcl'2004 conference presentation This document explains how the theme engine works

class tkinter.ttk.Style

This class is used to manipulate the style database.

configure(*style, query_opt=None, **kw*)

Query or set the default value of the specified option(s) in *style*.

Each key in *kw* is an option and each value is a string identifying the value for that option.

For example, to change every default button to be a flat button with some padding and a different background color:

```
from tkinter import ttk
import tkinter

root = tkinter.Tk()

ttk.Style().configure("TButton", padding=6, relief="flat",
    background="#ccc")

btn = ttk.Button(text="Sample")
btn.pack()

root.mainloop()
```

map(*style, query_opt=None, **kw*)

Query or sets dynamic values of the specified option(s) in *style*.

Each key in *kw* is an option and each value should be a list or a tuple (usually) containing statespecs grouped in tuples, lists, or some other preference. A statespec is a compound of one or more states and then a value.

An example may make it more understandable:

```
import tkinter
from tkinter import ttk

root = tkinter.Tk()

style = ttk.Style()
style.map("C.TButton",
    foreground=[('pressed', 'red'), ('active', 'blue')],
    background=[('pressed', '!disabled', 'black'), ('active', 'white')]
    )

colored_btn = ttk.Button(text="Test", style="C.TButton").pack()

root.mainloop()
```

Note that the order of the (states, value) sequences for an option does matter, if the order is changed to `[('active', 'blue'), ('pressed', 'red')]` in the foreground option, for example, the result would be a blue foreground when the widget were in active or pressed states.

lookup(*style, option, state=None, default=None*)
　　Returns the value specified for *option* in *style*.

　　If *state* is specified, it is expected to be a sequence of one or more states. If the *default* argument is set, it is used as a fallback value in case no specification for option is found.

　　To check what font a Button uses by default:

```
from tkinter import ttk
print(ttk.Style().lookup("TButton", "font"))
```

layout(*style, layoutspec=None*)
　　Define the widget layout for given *style*. If *layoutspec* is omitted, return the layout specification for given style.

　　layoutspec, if specified, is expected to be a list or some other sequence type (excluding strings), where each item should be a tuple and the first item is the layout name and the second item should have the format described in *Layouts*.

　　To understand the format, see the following example (it is not intended to do anything useful):

```
from tkinter import ttk
import tkinter

root = tkinter.Tk()

style = ttk.Style()
style.layout("TMenubutton", [
   ("Menubutton.background", None),
   ("Menubutton.button", {"children":
       [("Menubutton.focus", {"children":
           [("Menubutton.padding", {"children":
               [("Menubutton.label", {"side": "left", "expand": 1})]
           })]
       })]
   }),
])

mbtn = ttk.Menubutton(text='Text')
mbtn.pack()
root.mainloop()
```

element_create(*elementname, etype, *args, **kw*)
　　Create a new element in the current theme, of the given *etype* which is expected to be either "image", "from" or "vsapi". The latter is only available in Tk 8.6a for Windows XP and Vista and is not described here.

　　If "image" is used, *args* should contain the default image name followed by statespec/value pairs (this is the imagespec), and *kw* may have the following options:

- **border=padding** padding is a list of up to four integers, specifying the left, top, right, and bottom borders, respectively.
- **height=height** Specifies a minimum height for the element. If less than zero, the base image's height is used as a default.
- **padding=padding** Specifies the element's interior padding. Defaults to border's value if not specified.

- **sticky=spec** Specifies how the image is placed within the final parcel. spec contains zero or more characters "n", "s", "w", or "e".
- **width=width** Specifies a minimum width for the element. If less than zero, the base image's width is used as a default.

If "from" is used as the value of *etype*, *element_create()* will clone an existing element. *args* is expected to contain a themename, from which the element will be cloned, and optionally an element to clone from. If this element to clone from is not specified, an empty element will be used. *kw* is discarded.

element_names()
Returns the list of elements defined in the current theme.

element_options(*elementname*)
Returns the list of *elementname*'s options.

theme_create(*themename, parent=None, settings=None*)
Create a new theme.

It is an error if *themename* already exists. If *parent* is specified, the new theme will inherit styles, elements and layouts from the parent theme. If *settings* are present they are expected to have the same syntax used for *theme_settings()*.

theme_settings(*themename, settings*)
Temporarily sets the current theme to *themename*, apply specified *settings* and then restore the previous theme.

Each key in *settings* is a style and each value may contain the keys 'configure', 'map', 'layout' and 'element create' and they are expected to have the same format as specified by the methods *Style.configure()*, *Style.map()*, *Style.layout()* and *Style.element_create()* respectively.

As an example, let's change the Combobox for the default theme a bit:

```
from tkinter import ttk
import tkinter

root = tkinter.Tk()

style = ttk.Style()
style.theme_settings("default", {
    "TCombobox": {
        "configure": {"padding": 5},
        "map": {
            "background": [("active", "green2"),
                           ("!disabled", "green4")],
            "fieldbackground": [("!disabled", "green3")],
            "foreground": [("focus", "OliveDrab1"),
                           ("!disabled", "OliveDrab2")]
        }
    }
})

combo = ttk.Combobox().pack()

root.mainloop()
```

theme_names()
Returns a list of all known themes.

theme_use(*themename=None*)
If *themename* is not given, returns the theme in use. Otherwise, sets the current theme to

themename, refreshes all widgets and emits a <<ThemeChanged>> event.

Layouts

A layout can be just `None`, if it takes no options, or a dict of options specifying how to arrange the element. The layout mechanism uses a simplified version of the pack geometry manager: given an initial cavity, each element is allocated a parcel. Valid options/values are:

- **side: whichside** Specifies which side of the cavity to place the element; one of top, right, bottom or left. If omitted, the element occupies the entire cavity.
- **sticky: nswe** Specifies where the element is placed inside its allocated parcel.
- **unit: 0 or 1** If set to 1, causes the element and all of its descendants to be treated as a single element for the purposes of *Widget.identify()* et al. It's used for things like scrollbar thumbs with grips.
- **children: [sublayout...]** Specifies a list of elements to place inside the element. Each element is a tuple (or other sequence type) where the first item is the layout name, and the other is a *Layout*.

25.3 `tkinter.tix` — Extension widgets for Tk

Source code: Lib/tkinter/tix.py

Deprecated since version 3.6: This Tk extension is unmaintained and should not be used in new code. Use *tkinter.ttk* instead.

The *tkinter.tix* (Tk Interface Extension) module provides an additional rich set of widgets. Although the standard Tk library has many useful widgets, they are far from complete. The *tkinter.tix* library provides most of the commonly needed widgets that are missing from standard Tk: *HList*, *ComboBox*, *Control* (a.k.a. SpinBox) and an assortment of scrollable widgets. *tkinter.tix* also includes many more widgets that are generally useful in a wide range of applications: *NoteBook*, *FileEntry*, *PanedWindow*, etc; there are more than 40 of them.

With all these new widgets, you can introduce new interaction techniques into applications, creating more useful and more intuitive user interfaces. You can design your application by choosing the most appropriate widgets to match the special needs of your application and users.

See also:

Tix Homepage The home page for `Tix`. This includes links to additional documentation and downloads.

Tix Man Pages On-line version of the man pages and reference material.

Tix Programming Guide On-line version of the programmer's reference material.

Tix Development Applications Tix applications for development of Tix and Tkinter programs. Tide applications work under Tk or Tkinter, and include **TixInspect**, an inspector to remotely modify and debug Tix/Tk/Tkinter applications.

25.3.1 Using Tix

class `tkinter.tix.Tk`(*screenName=None, baseName=None, className='Tix'*)
　　Toplevel widget of Tix which represents mostly the main window of an application. It has an associated Tcl interpreter.

Classes in the *tkinter.tix* module subclasses the classes in the *tkinter*. The former imports the latter, so to use *tkinter.tix* with Tkinter, all you need to do is to import one module. In general, you can just import *tkinter.tix*, and replace the toplevel call to *tkinter.Tk* with **tix.Tk**:

```
from tkinter import tix
from tkinter.constants import *
root = tix.Tk()
```

To use *tkinter.tix*, you must have the Tix widgets installed, usually alongside your installation of the Tk widgets. To test your installation, try the following:

```
from tkinter import tix
root = tix.Tk()
root.tk.eval('package require Tix')
```

If this fails, you have a Tk installation problem which must be resolved before proceeding. Use the environment variable **TIX_LIBRARY** to point to the installed Tix library directory, and make sure you have the dynamic object library (`tix8183.dll` or `libtix8183.so`) in the same directory that contains your Tk dynamic object library (`tk8183.dll` or `libtk8183.so`). The directory with the dynamic object library should also have a file called `pkgIndex.tcl` (case sensitive), which contains the line:

```
package ifneeded Tix 8.1 [list load "[file join $dir tix8183.dll]" Tix]
```

25.3.2 Tix Widgets

Tix introduces over 40 widget classes to the *tkinter* repertoire.

Basic Widgets

class tkinter.tix.Balloon
 A Balloon that pops up over a widget to provide help. When the user moves the cursor inside a widget to which a Balloon widget has been bound, a small pop-up window with a descriptive message will be shown on the screen.

class tkinter.tix.ButtonBox
 The ButtonBox widget creates a box of buttons, such as is commonly used for Ok Cancel.

class tkinter.tix.ComboBox
 The ComboBox widget is similar to the combo box control in MS Windows. The user can select a choice by either typing in the entry subwidget or selecting from the listbox subwidget.

class tkinter.tix.Control
 The Control widget is also known as the **SpinBox** widget. The user can adjust the value by pressing the two arrow buttons or by entering the value directly into the entry. The new value will be checked against the user-defined upper and lower limits.

class tkinter.tix.LabelEntry
 The LabelEntry widget packages an entry widget and a label into one mega widget. It can be used to simplify the creation of "entry-form" type of interface.

class tkinter.tix.LabelFrame
 The LabelFrame widget packages a frame widget and a label into one mega widget. To create widgets inside a LabelFrame widget, one creates the new widgets relative to the **frame** subwidget and manage them inside the **frame** subwidget.

class tkinter.tix.Meter
   The Meter widget can be used to show the progress of a background job which may take a long time to execute.

class tkinter.tix.OptionMenu
   The OptionMenu creates a menu button of options.

class tkinter.tix.PopupMenu
   The PopupMenu widget can be used as a replacement of the `tk_popup` command. The advantage of the Tix *PopupMenu* widget is it requires less application code to manipulate.

class tkinter.tix.Select
   The Select widget is a container of button subwidgets. It can be used to provide radio-box or check-box style of selection options for the user.

class tkinter.tix.StdButtonBox
   The StdButtonBox widget is a group of standard buttons for Motif-like dialog boxes.

File Selectors

class tkinter.tix.DirList
   The DirList widget displays a list view of a directory, its previous directories and its sub-directories. The user can choose one of the directories displayed in the list or change to another directory.

class tkinter.tix.DirTree
   The DirTree widget displays a tree view of a directory, its previous directories and its sub-directories. The user can choose one of the directories displayed in the list or change to another directory.

class tkinter.tix.DirSelectDialog
   The DirSelectDialog widget presents the directories in the file system in a dialog window. The user can use this dialog window to navigate through the file system to select the desired directory.

class tkinter.tix.DirSelectBox
   The *DirSelectBox* is similar to the standard Motif(TM) directory-selection box. It is generally used for the user to choose a directory. DirSelectBox stores the directories mostly recently selected into a ComboBox widget so that they can be quickly selected again.

class tkinter.tix.ExFileSelectBox
   The ExFileSelectBox widget is usually embedded in a tixExFileSelectDialog widget. It provides a convenient method for the user to select files. The style of the *ExFileSelectBox* widget is very similar to the standard file dialog on MS Windows 3.1.

class tkinter.tix.FileSelectBox
   The FileSelectBox is similar to the standard Motif(TM) file-selection box. It is generally used for the user to choose a file. FileSelectBox stores the files mostly recently selected into a *ComboBox* widget so that they can be quickly selected again.

class tkinter.tix.FileEntry
   The FileEntry widget can be used to input a filename. The user can type in the filename manually. Alternatively, the user can press the button widget that sits next to the entry, which will bring up a file selection dialog.

Hierarchical ListBox

class tkinter.tix.HList
   The HList widget can be used to display any data that have a hierarchical structure, for example, file system directory trees. The list entries are indented and connected by branch lines according to their places in the hierarchy.

class tkinter.tix.CheckList
The CheckList widget displays a list of items to be selected by the user. CheckList acts similarly to the Tk checkbutton or radiobutton widgets, except it is capable of handling many more items than checkbuttons or radiobuttons.

class tkinter.tix.Tree
The Tree widget can be used to display hierarchical data in a tree form. The user can adjust the view of the tree by opening or closing parts of the tree.

Tabular ListBox

class tkinter.tix.TList
The TList widget can be used to display data in a tabular format. The list entries of a *TList* widget are similar to the entries in the Tk listbox widget. The main differences are (1) the *TList* widget can display the list entries in a two dimensional format and (2) you can use graphical images as well as multiple colors and fonts for the list entries.

Manager Widgets

class tkinter.tix.PanedWindow
The PanedWindow widget allows the user to interactively manipulate the sizes of several panes. The panes can be arranged either vertically or horizontally. The user changes the sizes of the panes by dragging the resize handle between two panes.

class tkinter.tix.ListNoteBook
The ListNoteBook widget is very similar to the `TixNoteBook` widget: it can be used to display many windows in a limited space using a notebook metaphor. The notebook is divided into a stack of pages (windows). At one time only one of these pages can be shown. The user can navigate through these pages by choosing the name of the desired page in the `hlist` subwidget.

class tkinter.tix.NoteBook
The NoteBook widget can be used to display many windows in a limited space using a notebook metaphor. The notebook is divided into a stack of pages. At one time only one of these pages can be shown. The user can navigate through these pages by choosing the visual "tabs" at the top of the NoteBook widget.

Image Types

The *tkinter.tix* module adds:

- pixmap capabilities to all *tkinter.tix* and *tkinter* widgets to create color images from XPM files.
- Compound image types can be used to create images that consists of multiple horizontal lines; each line is composed of a series of items (texts, bitmaps, images or spaces) arranged from left to right. For example, a compound image can be used to display a bitmap and a text string simultaneously in a Tk `Button` widget.

Miscellaneous Widgets

class tkinter.tix.InputOnly
The InputOnly widgets are to accept inputs from the user, which can be done with the **bind** command (Unix only).

Form Geometry Manager

In addition, `tkinter.tix` augments `tkinter` by providing:

class tkinter.tix.Form
　　The Form geometry manager based on attachment rules for all Tk widgets.

25.3.3 Tix Commands

class tkinter.tix.tixCommand
　　The tix commands provide access to miscellaneous elements of Tix's internal state and the Tix application context. Most of the information manipulated by these methods pertains to the application as a whole, or to a screen or display, rather than to a particular window.

　　To view the current settings, the common usage is:

```
from tkinter import tix
root = tix.Tk()
print(root.tix_configure())
```

tixCommand.tix_configure(cnf=None, **kw**)**
　　Query or modify the configuration options of the Tix application context. If no option is specified, returns a dictionary all of the available options. If option is specified with no value, then the method returns a list describing the one named option (this list will be identical to the corresponding sublist of the value returned if no option is specified). If one or more option-value pairs are specified, then the method modifies the given option(s) to have the given value(s); in this case the method returns an empty string. Option may be any of the configuration options.

tixCommand.tix_cget(option**)**
　　Returns the current value of the configuration option given by *option*. Option may be any of the configuration options.

tixCommand.tix_getbitmap(name**)**
　　Locates a bitmap file of the name `name.xpm` or `name` in one of the bitmap directories (see the `tix_addbitmapdir()` method). By using `tix_getbitmap()`, you can avoid hard coding the pathnames of the bitmap files in your application. When successful, it returns the complete pathname of the bitmap file, prefixed with the character @. The returned value can be used to configure the `bitmap` option of the Tk and Tix widgets.

tixCommand.tix_addbitmapdir(directory**)**
　　Tix maintains a list of directories under which the `tix_getimage()` and `tix_getbitmap()` methods will search for image files. The standard bitmap directory is `$TIX_LIBRARY/bitmaps`. The `tix_addbitmapdir()` method adds *directory* into this list. By using this method, the image files of an applications can also be located using the `tix_getimage()` or `tix_getbitmap()` method.

tixCommand.tix_filedialog([dlgclass]**)**
　　Returns the file selection dialog that may be shared among different calls from this application. This method will create a file selection dialog widget when it is called the first time. This dialog will be returned by all subsequent calls to `tix_filedialog()`. An optional dlgclass parameter can be passed as a string to specified what type of file selection dialog widget is desired. Possible options are `tix`, `FileSelectDialog` or `tixExFileSelectDialog`.

tixCommand.tix_getimage(self, name**)**
　　Locates an image file of the name `name.xpm`, `name.xbm` or `name.ppm` in one of the bitmap directories (see the `tix_addbitmapdir()` method above). If more than one file with the same name (but different extensions) exist, then the image type is chosen according to the depth of the X display: xbm images are chosen on monochrome displays and color images are chosen on color displays. By using `tix_getimage()`, you can avoid hard coding the pathnames of the image files in your application.

When successful, this method returns the name of the newly created image, which can be used to configure the image option of the Tk and Tix widgets.

tixCommand.**tix_option_get**(*name*)
Gets the options maintained by the Tix scheme mechanism.

tixCommand.**tix_resetoptions**(*newScheme*, *newFontSet*[, *newScmPrio*])
Resets the scheme and fontset of the Tix application to *newScheme* and *newFontSet*, respectively. This affects only those widgets created after this call. Therefore, it is best to call the resetoptions method before the creation of any widgets in a Tix application.

The optional parameter *newScmPrio* can be given to reset the priority level of the Tk options set by the Tix schemes.

Because of the way Tk handles the X option database, after Tix has been has imported and inited, it is not possible to reset the color schemes and font sets using the `tix_config()` method. Instead, the *tix_resetoptions()* method must be used.

25.4 `tkinter.scrolledtext` — Scrolled Text Widget

Source code: Lib/tkinter/scrolledtext.py

The *tkinter.scrolledtext* module provides a class of the same name which implements a basic text widget which has a vertical scroll bar configured to do the "right thing." Using the ScrolledText class is a lot easier than setting up a text widget and scroll bar directly. The constructor is the same as that of the tkinter.Text class.

The text widget and scrollbar are packed together in a Frame, and the methods of the Grid and Pack geometry managers are acquired from the Frame object. This allows the ScrolledText widget to be used directly to achieve most normal geometry management behavior.

Should more specific control be necessary, the following attributes are available:

ScrolledText.**frame**
    The frame which surrounds the text and scroll bar widgets.

ScrolledText.**vbar**
    The scroll bar widget.

25.5 IDLE

Source code: Lib/idlelib/

IDLE is Python's Integrated Development and Learning Environment.

IDLE has the following features:

- coded in 100% pure Python, using the *tkinter* GUI toolkit
- cross-platform: works mostly the same on Windows, Unix, and Mac OS X
- Python shell window (interactive interpreter) with colorizing of code input, output, and error messages
- multi-window text editor with multiple undo, Python colorizing, smart indent, call tips, auto completion, and other features
- search within any window, replace within editor windows, and search through multiple files (grep)

- debugger with persistent breakpoints, stepping, and viewing of global and local namespaces
- configuration, browsers, and other dialogs

25.5.1 Menus

IDLE has two main window types, the Shell window and the Editor window. It is possible to have multiple editor windows simultaneously. Output windows, such as used for Edit / Find in Files, are a subtype of edit window. They currently have the same top menu as Editor windows but a different default title and context menu.

IDLE's menus dynamically change based on which window is currently selected. Each menu documented below indicates which window type it is associated with.

File menu (Shell and Editor)

New File Create a new file editing window.

Open... Open an existing file with an Open dialog.

Recent Files Open a list of recent files. Click one to open it.

Open Module... Open an existing module (searches sys.path).

Class Browser Show functions, classes, and methods in the current Editor file in a tree structure. In the shell, open a module first.

Path Browser Show sys.path directories, modules, functions, classes and methods in a tree structure.

Save Save the current window to the associated file, if there is one. Windows that have been changed since being opened or last saved have a * before and after the window title. If there is no associated file, do Save As instead.

Save As... Save the current window with a Save As dialog. The file saved becomes the new associated file for the window.

Save Copy As... Save the current window to different file without changing the associated file.

Print Window Print the current window to the default printer.

Close Close the current window (ask to save if unsaved).

Exit Close all windows and quit IDLE (ask to save unsaved windows).

Edit menu (Shell and Editor)

Undo Undo the last change to the current window. A maximum of 1000 changes may be undone.

Redo Redo the last undone change to the current window.

Cut Copy selection into the system-wide clipboard; then delete the selection.

Copy Copy selection into the system-wide clipboard.

Paste Insert contents of the system-wide clipboard into the current window.

The clipboard functions are also available in context menus.

Select All Select the entire contents of the current window.

Find... Open a search dialog with many options

Find Again Repeat the last search, if there is one.

Find Selection Search for the currently selected string, if there is one.

Find in Files... Open a file search dialog. Put results in a new output window.

Replace... Open a search-and-replace dialog.

Go to Line Move cursor to the line number requested and make that line visible.

Show Completions Open a scrollable list allowing selection of keywords and attributes. See Completions in the Tips sections below.

Expand Word Expand a prefix you have typed to match a full word in the same window; repeat to get a different expansion.

Show call tip After an unclosed parenthesis for a function, open a small window with function parameter hints.

Show surrounding parens Highlight the surrounding parenthesis.

Format menu (Editor window only)

Indent Region Shift selected lines right by the indent width (default 4 spaces).

Dedent Region Shift selected lines left by the indent width (default 4 spaces).

Comment Out Region Insert ## in front of selected lines.

Uncomment Region Remove leading # or ## from selected lines.

Tabify Region Turn *leading* stretches of spaces into tabs. (Note: We recommend using 4 space blocks to indent Python code.)

Untabify Region Turn *all* tabs into the correct number of spaces.

Toggle Tabs Open a dialog to switch between indenting with spaces and tabs.

New Indent Width Open a dialog to change indent width. The accepted default by the Python community is 4 spaces.

Format Paragraph Reformat the current blank-line-delimited paragraph in comment block or multiline string or selected line in a string. All lines in the paragraph will be formatted to less than N columns, where N defaults to 72.

Strip trailing whitespace Remove trailing space and other whitespace characters after the last non-whitespace character of a line by applying str.rstrip to each line, including lines within multiline strings.

Run menu (Editor window only)

Python Shell Open or wake up the Python Shell window.

Check Module Check the syntax of the module currently open in the Editor window. If the module has not been saved IDLE will either prompt the user to save or autosave, as selected in the General tab of the Idle Settings dialog. If there is a syntax error, the approximate location is indicated in the Editor window.

Run Module Do Check Module (above). If no error, restart the shell to clean the environment, then execute the module. Output is displayed in the Shell window. Note that output requires use of `print` or `write`. When execution is complete, the Shell retains focus and displays a prompt. At this point, one may interactively explore the result of execution. This is similar to executing a file with `python -i file` at a command line.

Shell menu (Shell window only)

View Last Restart Scroll the shell window to the last Shell restart.

Restart Shell Restart the shell to clean the environment.

Interrupt Execution Stop a running program.

Debug menu (Shell window only)

Go to File/Line Look on the current line. with the cursor, and the line above for a filename and line number. If found, open the file if not already open, and show the line. Use this to view source lines referenced in an exception traceback and lines found by Find in Files. Also available in the context menu of the Shell window and Output windows.

Debugger (toggle) When activated, code entered in the Shell or run from an Editor will run under the debugger. In the Editor, breakpoints can be set with the context menu. This feature is still incomplete and somewhat experimental.

Stack Viewer Show the stack traceback of the last exception in a tree widget, with access to locals and globals.

Auto-open Stack Viewer Toggle automatically opening the stack viewer on an unhandled exception.

Options menu (Shell and Editor)

Configure IDLE Open a configuration dialog and change preferences for the following: fonts, indentation, keybindings, text color themes, startup windows and size, additional help sources, and extensions (see below). On OS X, open the configuration dialog by selecting Preferences in the application menu. To use a new built-in color theme (IDLE Dark) with older IDLEs, save it as a new custom theme.

Non-default user settings are saved in a .idlerc directory in the user's home directory. Problems caused by bad user configuration files are solved by editing or deleting one or more of the files in .idlerc.

Code Context (toggle)(Editor Window only) Open a pane at the top of the edit window which shows the block context of the code which has scrolled above the top of the window.

Window menu (Shell and Editor)

Zoom Height Toggles the window between normal size and maximum height. The initial size defaults to 40 lines by 80 chars unless changed on the General tab of the Configure IDLE dialog.

The rest of this menu lists the names of all open windows; select one to bring it to the foreground (deiconifying it if necessary).

Help menu (Shell and Editor)

About IDLE Display version, copyright, license, credits, and more.

IDLE Help Display a help file for IDLE detailing the menu options, basic editing and navigation, and other tips.

Python Docs Access local Python documentation, if installed, or start a web browser and open docs.python.org showing the latest Python documentation.

Turtle Demo Run the turtledemo module with example python code and turtle drawings.

Additional help sources may be added here with the Configure IDLE dialog under the General tab.

Context Menus

Open a context menu by right-clicking in a window (Control-click on OS X). Context menus have the standard clipboard functions also on the Edit menu.

Cut Copy selection into the system-wide clipboard; then delete the selection.

Copy Copy selection into the system-wide clipboard.

Paste Insert contents of the system-wide clipboard into the current window.

Editor windows also have breakpoint functions. Lines with a breakpoint set are specially marked. Breakpoints only have an effect when running under the debugger. Breakpoints for a file are saved in the user's .idlerc directory.

Set Breakpoint Set a breakpoint on the current line.

Clear Breakpoint Clear the breakpoint on that line.

Shell and Output windows have the following.

Go to file/line Same as in Debug menu.

25.5.2 Editing and navigation

In this section, 'C' refers to the `Control` key on Windows and Unix and the `Command` key on Mac OSX.

- `Backspace` deletes to the left; `Del` deletes to the right
- `C-Backspace` delete word left; `C-Del` delete word to the right
- Arrow keys and `Page Up`/`Page Down` to move around
- `C-LeftArrow` and `C-RightArrow` moves by words
- `Home`/`End` go to begin/end of line
- `C-Home`/`C-End` go to begin/end of file
- Some useful Emacs bindings are inherited from Tcl/Tk:
    - `C-a` beginning of line
    - `C-e` end of line
    - `C-k` kill line (but doesn't put it in clipboard)
    - `C-l` center window around the insertion point
    - `C-b` go backward one character without deleting (usually you can also use the cursor key for this)
    - `C-f` go forward one character without deleting (usually you can also use the cursor key for this)
    - `C-p` go up one line (usually you can also use the cursor key for this)
    - `C-d` delete next character

Standard keybindings (like `C-c` to copy and `C-v` to paste) may work. Keybindings are selected in the Configure IDLE dialog.

Automatic indentation

After a block-opening statement, the next line is indented by 4 spaces (in the Python Shell window by one tab). After certain keywords (break, return etc.) the next line is dedented. In leading indentation, `Backspace` deletes up to 4 spaces if they are there. `Tab` inserts spaces (in the Python Shell window one tab), number depends on Indent width. Currently, tabs are restricted to four spaces due to Tcl/Tk limitations.

See also the indent/dedent region commands in the edit menu.

Completions

Completions are supplied for functions, classes, and attributes of classes, both built-in and user-defined. Completions are also provided for filenames.

The AutoCompleteWindow (ACW) will open after a predefined delay (default is two seconds) after a '.' or (in a string) an os.sep is typed. If after one of those characters (plus zero or more other characters) a tab is typed the ACW will open immediately if a possible continuation is found.

If there is only one possible completion for the characters entered, a `Tab` will supply that completion without opening the ACW.

'Show Completions' will force open a completions window, by default the `C-space` will open a completions window. In an empty string, this will contain the files in the current directory. On a blank line, it will contain the built-in and user-defined functions and classes in the current namespaces, plus any modules imported. If some characters have been entered, the ACW will attempt to be more specific.

If a string of characters is typed, the ACW selection will jump to the entry most closely matching those characters. Entering a `tab` will cause the longest non-ambiguous match to be entered in the Editor window or Shell. Two `tab` in a row will supply the current ACW selection, as will return or a double click. Cursor keys, Page Up/Down, mouse selection, and the scroll wheel all operate on the ACW.

"Hidden" attributes can be accessed by typing the beginning of hidden name after a '.', e.g. '_'. This allows access to modules with `__all__` set, or to class-private attributes.

Completions and the 'Expand Word' facility can save a lot of typing!

Completions are currently limited to those in the namespaces. Names in an Editor window which are not via `__main__` and *sys.modules* will not be found. Run the module once with your imports to correct this situation. Note that IDLE itself places quite a few modules in sys.modules, so much can be found by default, e.g. the re module.

If you don't like the ACW popping up unbidden, simply make the delay longer or disable the extension.

Calltips

A calltip is shown when one types (after the name of an *accessible* function. A name expression may include dots and subscripts. A calltip remains until it is clicked, the cursor is moved out of the argument area, or) is typed. When the cursor is in the argument part of a definition, the menu or shortcut display a calltip.

A calltip consists of the function signature and the first line of the docstring. For builtins without an accessible signature, the calltip consists of all lines up the fifth line or the first blank line. These details may change.

The set of *accessible* functions depends on what modules have been imported into the user process, including those imported by Idle itself, and what definitions have been run, all since the last restart.

For example, restart the Shell and enter `itertools.count(`. A calltip appears because Idle imports itertools into the user process for its own use. (This could change.) Enter `turtle.write(` and nothing appears. Idle does not import turtle. The menu or shortcut do nothing either. Enter `import turtle` and then `turtle.write(` will work.

In an editor, import statements have no effect until one runs the file. One might want to run a file after writing the import statements at the top, or immediately run an existing file before editing.

Python Shell window

- `C-c` interrupts executing command
- `C-d` sends end-of-file; closes window if typed at a >>> prompt
- `Alt-/` (Expand word) is also useful to reduce typing

  Command history

  – `Alt-p` retrieves previous command matching what you have typed. On OS X use `C-p`.
  – `Alt-n` retrieves next. On OS X use `C-n`.
  – `Return` while on any previous command retrieves that command

Text colors

Idle defaults to black on white text, but colors text with special meanings. For the shell, these are shell output, shell error, user output, and user error. For Python code, at the shell prompt or in an editor, these are keywords, builtin class and function names, names following `class` and `def`, strings, and comments. For any text window, these are the cursor (when present), found text (when possible), and selected text.

Text coloring is done in the background, so uncolorized text is occasionally visible. To change the color scheme, use the Configure IDLE dialog Highlighting tab. The marking of debugger breakpoint lines in the editor and text in popups and dialogs is not user-configurable.

25.5.3 Startup and code execution

Upon startup with the `-s` option, IDLE will execute the file referenced by the environment variables `IDLESTARTUP` or `PYTHONSTARTUP`. IDLE first checks for `IDLESTARTUP`; if `IDLESTARTUP` is present the file referenced is run. If `IDLESTARTUP` is not present, IDLE checks for `PYTHONSTARTUP`. Files referenced by these environment variables are convenient places to store functions that are used frequently from the IDLE shell, or for executing import statements to import common modules.

In addition, Tk also loads a startup file if it is present. Note that the Tk file is loaded unconditionally. This additional file is `.Idle.py` and is looked for in the user's home directory. Statements in this file will be executed in the Tk namespace, so this file is not useful for importing functions to be used from IDLE's Python shell.

Command line usage

```
idle.py [-c command] [-d] [-e] [-h] [-i] [-r file] [-s] [-t title] [-] [arg] ...

-c command  run command in the shell window
-d          enable debugger and open shell window
-e          open editor window
-h          print help message with legal combinations and exit
-i          open shell window
-r file     run file in shell window
-s          run $IDLESTARTUP or $PYTHONSTARTUP first, in shell window
-t title    set title of shell window
-           run stdin in shell (- must be last option before args)
```

If there are arguments:

- If `-`, `-c`, or `r` is used, all arguments are placed in `sys.argv[1:...]` and `sys.argv[0]` is set to `''`, `'-c'`, or `'-r'`. No editor window is opened, even if that is the default set in the Options dialog.

- Otherwise, arguments are files opened for editing and `sys.argv` reflects the arguments passed to IDLE itself.

Startup failure

IDLE uses a socket to communicate between the IDLE GUI process and the user code execution process. A connection must be established whenever the Shell starts or restarts. (The latter is indicated by a divider line that says 'RESTART'). If the user process fails to connect to the GUI process, it displays a `Tk` error box with a 'cannot connect' message that directs the user here. It then exits.

A common cause of failure is a user-written file with the same name as a standard library module, such as *random.py* and *tkinter.py*. When such a file is located in the same directory as a file that is about to be run, IDLE cannot import the stdlib file. The current fix is to rename the user file.

Though less common than in the past, an antivirus or firewall program may stop the connection. If the program cannot be taught to allow the connection, then it must be turned off for IDLE to work. It is safe to allow this internal connection because no data is visible on external ports. A similar problem is a network mis-configuration that blocks connections.

Python installation issues occasionally stop IDLE: multiple versions can clash, or a single installation might need admin access. If one undo the clash, or cannot or does not want to run as admin, it might be easiest to completely remove Python and start over.

A zombie pythonw.exe process could be a problem. On Windows, use Task Manager to detect and stop one. Sometimes a restart initiated by a program crash or Keyboard Interrupt (control-C) may fail to connect. Dismissing the error box or Restart Shell on the Shell menu may fix a temporary problem.

When IDLE first starts, it attempts to read user configuration files in ~/.idlerc/ (~ is one's home directory). If there is a problem, an error message should be displayed. Leaving aside random disk glitches, this can be prevented by never editing the files by hand, using the configuration dialog, under Options, instead Options. Once it happens, the solution may be to delete one or more of the configuration files.

If IDLE quits with no message, and it was not started from a console, try starting from a console (`python -m idlelib`) and see if a message appears.

IDLE-console differences

With rare exceptions, the result of executing Python code with IDLE is intended to be the same as executing the same code in a console window. However, the different interface and operation occasionally affect visible results. For instance, `sys.modules` starts with more entries.

IDLE also replaces `sys.stdin`, `sys.stdout`, and `sys.stderr` with objects that get input from and send output to the Shell window. When Shell has the focus, it controls the keyboard and screen. This is normally transparent, but functions that directly access the keyboard and screen will not work. If `sys` is reset with `importlib.reload(sys)`, IDLE's changes are lost and things like `input`, `raw_input`, and `print` will not work correctly.

With IDLE's Shell, one enters, edits, and recalls complete statements. Some consoles only work with a single physical line at a time. IDLE uses `exec` to run each statement. As a result, `'__builtins__'` is always defined for each statement.

Developing tkinter applications

IDLE is intentionally different from standard Python in order to facilitate development of tkinter programs. Enter `import tkinter as tk; root = tk.Tk()` in standard Python and nothing appears. Enter the same in IDLE and a tk window appears. In standard Python, one must also enter `root.update()` to see the window. IDLE does the equivalent in the background, about 20 times a second, which is about every

50 milleseconds. Next enter `b = tk.Button(root, text='button'); b.pack()`. Again, nothing visibly changes in standard Python until one enters `root.update()`.

Most tkinter programs run `root.mainloop()`, which usually does not return until the tk app is destroyed. If the program is run with `python -i` or from an IDLE editor, a `>>>` shell prompt does not appear until `mainloop()` returns, at which time there is nothing left to interact with.

When running a tkinter program from an IDLE editor, one can comment out the mainloop call. One then gets a shell prompt immediately and can interact with the live application. One just has to remember to re-enable the mainloop call when running in standard Python.

Running without a subprocess

By default, IDLE executes user code in a separate subprocess via a socket, which uses the internal loopback interface. This connection is not externally visible and no data is sent to or received from the Internet. If firewall software complains anyway, you can ignore it.

If the attempt to make the socket connection fails, Idle will notify you. Such failures are sometimes transient, but if persistent, the problem may be either a firewall blocking the connection or misconfiguration of a particular system. Until the problem is fixed, one can run Idle with the -n command line switch.

If IDLE is started with the -n command line switch it will run in a single process and will not create the subprocess which runs the RPC Python execution server. This can be useful if Python cannot create the subprocess or the RPC socket interface on your platform. However, in this mode user code is not isolated from IDLE itself. Also, the environment is not restarted when Run/Run Module (F5) is selected. If your code has been modified, you must reload() the affected modules and re-import any specific items (e.g. from foo import baz) if the changes are to take effect. For these reasons, it is preferable to run IDLE with the default subprocess if at all possible.

Deprecated since version 3.4.

25.5.4 Help and preferences

Additional help sources

IDLE includes a help menu entry called "Python Docs" that will open the extensive sources of help, including tutorials, available at docs.python.org. Selected URLs can be added or removed from the help menu at any time using the Configure IDLE dialog. See the IDLE help option in the help menu of IDLE for more information.

Setting preferences

The font preferences, highlighting, keys, and general preferences can be changed via Configure IDLE on the Option menu. Keys can be user defined; IDLE ships with four built-in key sets. In addition, a user can create a custom key set in the Configure IDLE dialog under the keys tab.

Extensions

IDLE contains an extension facility. Preferences for extensions can be changed with the Extensions tab of the preferences dialog. See the beginning of config-extensions.def in the idlelib directory for further information. The only current default extension is zzdummy, an example also used for testing.

25.6 Other Graphical User Interface Packages

Major cross-platform (Windows, Mac OS X, Unix-like) GUI toolkits are available for Python:

See also:

PyGObject PyGObject provides introspection bindings for C libraries using GObject. One of these libraries is the GTK+ 3 widget set. GTK+ comes with many more widgets than Tkinter provides. An online Python GTK+ 3 Tutorial is available.

PyGTK PyGTK provides bindings for an older version of the library, GTK+ 2. It provides an object oriented interface that is slightly higher level than the C one. There are also bindings to GNOME. An online tutorial is available.

PyQt PyQt is a **sip**-wrapped binding to the Qt toolkit. Qt is an extensive C++ GUI application development framework that is available for Unix, Windows and Mac OS X. **sip** is a tool for generating bindings for C++ libraries as Python classes, and is specifically designed for Python.

PySide PySide is a newer binding to the Qt toolkit, provided by Nokia. Compared to PyQt, its licensing scheme is friendlier to non-open source applications.

wxPython wxPython is a cross-platform GUI toolkit for Python that is built around the popular wxWidgets (formerly wxWindows) C++ toolkit. It provides a native look and feel for applications on Windows, Mac OS X, and Unix systems by using each platform's native widgets where ever possible, (GTK+ on Unix-like systems). In addition to an extensive set of widgets, wxPython provides classes for online documentation and context sensitive help, printing, HTML viewing, low-level device context drawing, drag and drop, system clipboard access, an XML-based resource format and more, including an ever growing library of user-contributed modules.

PyGTK, PyQt, and wxPython, all have a modern look and feel and more widgets than Tkinter. In addition, there are many other GUI toolkits for Python, both cross-platform, and platform-specific. See the GUI Programming page in the Python Wiki for a much more complete list, and also for links to documents where the different GUI toolkits are compared.

CHAPTER
TWENTYSIX

DEVELOPMENT TOOLS

The modules described in this chapter help you write software. For example, the *pydoc* module takes a module and generates documentation based on the module's contents. The *doctest* and *unittest* modules contains frameworks for writing unit tests that automatically exercise code and verify that the expected output is produced. `2to3` can translate Python 2.x source code into valid Python 3.x code.

The list of modules described in this chapter is:

26.1 `typing` — Support for type hints

New in version 3.5.

Source code: Lib/typing.py

> **Note:** The typing module has been included in the standard library on a *provisional basis*. New features might be added and API may change even between minor releases if deemed necessary by the core developers.

This module supports type hints as specified by PEP 484 and PEP 526. The most fundamental support consists of the types *Any*, *Union*, *Tuple*, *Callable*, *TypeVar*, and *Generic*. For full specification please see PEP 484. For a simplified introduction to type hints see PEP 483.

The function below takes and returns a string and is annotated as follows:

```
def greeting(name: str) -> str:
    return 'Hello ' + name
```

In the function `greeting`, the argument `name` is expected to be of type *str* and the return type *str*. Subtypes are accepted as arguments.

26.1.1 Type aliases

A type alias is defined by assigning the type to the alias. In this example, `Vector` and `List[float]` will be treated as interchangeable synonyms:

```
from typing import List
Vector = List[float]

def scale(scalar: float, vector: Vector) -> Vector:
    return [scalar * num for num in vector]
```

```
# typechecks; a list of floats qualifies as a Vector.
new_vector = scale(2.0, [1.0, -4.2, 5.4])
```

Type aliases are useful for simplifying complex type signatures. For example:

```
from typing import Dict, Tuple, List

ConnectionOptions = Dict[str, str]
Address = Tuple[str, int]
Server = Tuple[Address, ConnectionOptions]

def broadcast_message(message: str, servers: List[Server]) -> None:
    ...

# The static type checker will treat the previous type signature as
# being exactly equivalent to this one.
def broadcast_message(
        message: str,
        servers: List[Tuple[Tuple[str, int], Dict[str, str]]]) -> None:
    ...
```

Note that `None` as a type hint is a special case and is replaced by `type(None)`.

26.1.2 NewType

Use the `NewType()` helper function to create distinct types:

```
from typing import NewType

UserId = NewType('UserId', int)
some_id = UserId(524313)
```

The static type checker will treat the new type as if it were a subclass of the original type. This is useful in helping catch logical errors:

```
def get_user_name(user_id: UserId) -> str:
    ...

# typechecks
user_a = get_user_name(UserId(42351))

# does not typecheck; an int is not a UserId
user_b = get_user_name(-1)
```

You may still perform all `int` operations on a variable of type `UserId`, but the result will always be of type `int`. This lets you pass in a `UserId` wherever an `int` might be expected, but will prevent you from accidentally creating a `UserId` in an invalid way:

```
# 'output' is of type 'int', not 'UserId'
output = UserId(23413) + UserId(54341)
```

Note that these checks are enforced only by the static type checker. At runtime the statement `Derived = NewType('Derived', Base)` will make `Derived` a function that immediately returns whatever parameter you pass it. That means the expression `Derived(some_value)` does not create a new class or introduce any overhead beyond that of a regular function call.

More precisely, the expression `some_value is Derived(some_value)` is always true at runtime.

This also means that it is not possible to create a subtype of `Derived` since it is an identity function at runtime, not an actual type:

```
from typing import NewType

UserId = NewType('UserId', int)

# Fails at runtime and does not typecheck
class AdminUserId(UserId): pass
```

However, it is possible to create a *NewType()* based on a 'derived' `NewType`:

```
from typing import NewType

UserId = NewType('UserId', int)

ProUserId = NewType('ProUserId', UserId)
```

and typechecking for `ProUserId` will work as expected.

See PEP 484 for more details.

Note: Recall that the use of a type alias declares two types to be *equivalent* to one another. Doing `Alias = Original` will make the static type checker treat `Alias` as being *exactly equivalent* to `Original` in all cases. This is useful when you want to simplify complex type signatures.

In contrast, `NewType` declares one type to be a *subtype* of another. Doing `Derived = NewType('Derived', Original)` will make the static type checker treat `Derived` as a *subclass* of `Original`, which means a value of type `Original` cannot be used in places where a value of type `Derived` is expected. This is useful when you want to prevent logic errors with minimal runtime cost.

New in version 3.5.2.

26.1.3 Callable

Frameworks expecting callback functions of specific signatures might be type hinted using `Callable[[Arg1Type, Arg2Type], ReturnType]`.

For example:

```
from typing import Callable

def feeder(get_next_item: Callable[[], str]) -> None:
    # Body

def async_query(on_success: Callable[[int], None],
                on_error: Callable[[int, Exception], None]) -> None:
    # Body
```

It is possible to declare the return type of a callable without specifying the call signature by substituting a literal ellipsis for the list of arguments in the type hint: `Callable[..., ReturnType]`.

26.1.4 Generics

Since type information about objects kept in containers cannot be statically inferred in a generic way, abstract base classes have been extended to support subscription to denote expected types for container elements.

```
from typing import Mapping, Sequence

def notify_by_email(employees: Sequence[Employee],
                    overrides: Mapping[str, str]) -> None: ...
```

Generics can be parametrized by using a new factory available in typing called *TypeVar*.

```
from typing import Sequence, TypeVar

T = TypeVar('T')      # Declare type variable

def first(l: Sequence[T]) -> T:   # Generic function
    return l[0]
```

26.1.5 User-defined generic types

A user-defined class can be defined as a generic class.

```
from typing import TypeVar, Generic
from logging import Logger

T = TypeVar('T')

class LoggedVar(Generic[T]):
    def __init__(self, value: T, name: str, logger: Logger) -> None:
        self.name = name
        self.logger = logger
        self.value = value

    def set(self, new: T) -> None:
        self.log('Set ' + repr(self.value))
        self.value = new

    def get(self) -> T:
        self.log('Get ' + repr(self.value))
        return self.value

    def log(self, message: str) -> None:
        self.logger.info('%s: %s', self.name, message)
```

Generic[T] as a base class defines that the class LoggedVar takes a single type parameter T . This also makes T valid as a type within the class body.

The *Generic* base class uses a metaclass that defines __getitem__() so that LoggedVar[t] is valid as a type:

```
from typing import Iterable

def zero_all_vars(vars: Iterable[LoggedVar[int]]) -> None:
    for var in vars:
        var.set(0)
```

A generic type can have any number of type variables, and type variables may be constrained:

```
from typing import TypeVar, Generic
...
```

```
T = TypeVar('T')
S = TypeVar('S', int, str)

class StrangePair(Generic[T, S]):
    ...
```

Each type variable argument to *Generic* must be distinct. This is thus invalid:

```
from typing import TypeVar, Generic
...

T = TypeVar('T')

class Pair(Generic[T, T]):   # INVALID
    ...
```

You can use multiple inheritance with *Generic*:

```
from typing import TypeVar, Generic, Sized

T = TypeVar('T')

class LinkedList(Sized, Generic[T]):
    ...
```

When inheriting from generic classes, some type variables could be fixed:

```
from typing import TypeVar, Mapping

T = TypeVar('T')

class MyDict(Mapping[str, T]):
    ...
```

In this case MyDict has a single parameter, T.

Using a generic class without specifying type parameters assumes *Any* for each position. In the following example, MyIterable is not generic but implicitly inherits from Iterable[Any]:

```
from typing import Iterable

class MyIterable(Iterable):  # Same as Iterable[Any]
```

User defined generic type aliases are also supported. Examples:

```
from typing import TypeVar, Iterable, Tuple, Union
S = TypeVar('S')
Response = Union[Iterable[S], int]

# Return type here is same as Union[Iterable[str], int]
def response(query: str) -> Response[str]:
    ...

T = TypeVar('T', int, float, complex)
Vec = Iterable[Tuple[T, T]]

def inproduct(v: Vec[T]) -> T: # Same as Iterable[Tuple[T, T]]
    return sum(x*y for x, y in v)
```

26.1. typing — Support for type hints

The metaclass used by *Generic* is a subclass of *abc.ABCMeta*. A generic class can be an ABC by including abstract methods or properties, and generic classes can also have ABCs as base classes without a metaclass conflict. Generic metaclasses are not supported. The outcome of parameterizing generics is cached, and most types in the typing module are hashable and comparable for equality.

26.1.6 The Any type

A special kind of type is *Any*. A static type checker will treat every type as being compatible with *Any* and *Any* as being compatible with every type.

This means that it is possible to perform any operation or method call on a value of type on *Any* and assign it to any variable:

```
from typing import Any

a = None        # type: Any
a = []          # OK
a = 2           # OK

s = ''          # type: str
s = a           # OK

def foo(item: Any) -> int:
    # Typechecks; 'item' could be any type,
    # and that type might have a 'bar' method
    item.bar()
    ...
```

Notice that no typechecking is performed when assigning a value of type *Any* to a more precise type. For example, the static type checker did not report an error when assigning a to s even though s was declared to be of type *str* and receives an *int* value at runtime!

Furthermore, all functions without a return type or parameter types will implicitly default to using *Any*:

```
def legacy_parser(text):
    ...
    return data

# A static type checker will treat the above
# as having the same signature as:
def legacy_parser(text: Any) -> Any:
    ...
    return data
```

This behavior allows *Any* to be used as an *escape hatch* when you need to mix dynamically and statically typed code.

Contrast the behavior of *Any* with the behavior of *object*. Similar to *Any*, every type is a subtype of *object*. However, unlike *Any*, the reverse is not true: *object* is *not* a subtype of every other type.

That means when the type of a value is *object*, a type checker will reject almost all operations on it, and assigning it to a variable (or using it as a return value) of a more specialized type is a type error. For example:

```
def hash_a(item: object) -> int:
    # Fails; an object does not have a 'magic' method.
    item.magic()
    ...
```

```
def hash_b(item: Any) -> int:
    # Typechecks
    item.magic()
    ...

# Typechecks, since ints and strs are subclasses of object
hash_a(42)
hash_a("foo")

# Typechecks, since Any is compatible with all types
hash_b(42)
hash_b("foo")
```

Use `object` to indicate that a value could be any type in a typesafe manner. Use `Any` to indicate that a value is dynamically typed.

26.1.7 Classes, functions, and decorators

The module defines the following classes, functions and decorators:

class typing.TypeVar

Type variable.

Usage:

```
T = TypeVar('T')  # Can be anything
A = TypeVar('A', str, bytes)  # Must be str or bytes
```

Type variables exist primarily for the benefit of static type checkers. They serve as the parameters for generic types as well as for generic function definitions. See class Generic for more information on generic types. Generic functions work as follows:

```
def repeat(x: T, n: int) -> Sequence[T]:
    """Return a list containing n references to x."""
    return [x]*n

def longest(x: A, y: A) -> A:
    """Return the longest of two strings."""
    return x if len(x) >= len(y) else y
```

The latter example's signature is essentially the overloading of (str, str) -> str and (bytes, bytes) -> bytes. Also note that if the arguments are instances of some subclass of `str`, the return type is still plain `str`.

At runtime, `isinstance(x, T)` will raise `TypeError`. In general, `isinstance()` and `issubclass()` should not be used with types.

Type variables may be marked covariant or contravariant by passing **covariant=True** or **contravariant=True**. See PEP 484 for more details. By default type variables are invariant. Alternatively, a type variable may specify an upper bound using **bound=<type>**. This means that an actual type substituted (explicitly or implicitly) for the type variable must be a subclass of the boundary type, see PEP 484.

class typing.Generic

Abstract base class for generic types.

A generic type is typically declared by inheriting from an instantiation of this class with one or more type variables. For example, a generic mapping type might be defined as:

```
class Mapping(Generic[KT, VT]):
    def __getitem__(self, key: KT) -> VT:
        ...
        # Etc.
```

This class can then be used as follows:

```
X = TypeVar('X')
Y = TypeVar('Y')

def lookup_name(mapping: Mapping[X, Y], key: X, default: Y) -> Y:
    try:
        return mapping[key]
    except KeyError:
        return default
```

class typing.Type(*Generic[CT_co]*)

A variable annotated with C may accept a value of type C. In contrast, a variable annotated with Type[C] may accept values that are classes themselves – specifically, it will accept the *class object* of C. For example:

```
a = 3           # Has type 'int'
b = int         # Has type 'Type[int]'
c = type(a)     # Also has type 'Type[int]'
```

Note that Type[C] is covariant:

```
class User: ...
class BasicUser(User): ...
class ProUser(User): ...
class TeamUser(User): ...

# Accepts User, BasicUser, ProUser, TeamUser, ...
def make_new_user(user_class: Type[User]) -> User:
    # ...
    return user_class()
```

The fact that Type[C] is covariant implies that all subclasses of C should implement the same constructor signature and class method signatures as C. The type checker should flag violations of this, but should also allow constructor calls in subclasses that match the constructor calls in the indicated base class. How the type checker is required to handle this particular case may change in future revisions of PEP 484.

The only legal parameters for *Type* are classes, unions of classes, and *Any*. For example:

```
def new_non_team_user(user_class: Type[Union[BaseUser, ProUser]]): ...
```

Type[Any] is equivalent to Type which in turn is equivalent to type, which is the root of Python's metaclass hierarchy.

New in version 3.5.2.

class typing.Iterable(*Generic[T_co]*)
    A generic version of *collections.abc.Iterable*.

class typing.Iterator(*Iterable[T_co]*)
    A generic version of *collections.abc.Iterator*.

class typing.Reversible(*Iterable[T_co]*)
    A generic version of *collections.abc.Reversible*.

class typing.SupportsInt
    An ABC with one abstract method `__int__`.

class typing.SupportsFloat
    An ABC with one abstract method `__float__`.

class typing.SupportsComplex
    An ABC with one abstract method `__complex__`.

class typing.SupportsBytes
    An ABC with one abstract method `__bytes__`.

class typing.SupportsAbs
    An ABC with one abstract method `__abs__` that is covariant in its return type.

class typing.SupportsRound
    An ABC with one abstract method `__round__` that is covariant in its return type.

class typing.Container(*Generic[T_co]*)
    A generic version of `collections.abc.Container`.

class typing.Hashable
    An alias to `collections.abc.Hashable`

class typing.Sized
    An alias to `collections.abc.Sized`

class typing.Collection(*Sized, Iterable[T_co], Container[T_co]*)
    A generic version of `collections.abc.Collection`

    New in version 3.6.

class typing.AbstractSet(*Sized, Collection[T_co]*)
    A generic version of `collections.abc.Set`.

class typing.MutableSet(*AbstractSet[T]*)
    A generic version of `collections.abc.MutableSet`.

class typing.Mapping(*Sized, Collection[KT], Generic[VT_co]*)
    A generic version of `collections.abc.Mapping`.

class typing.MutableMapping(*Mapping[KT, VT]*)
    A generic version of `collections.abc.MutableMapping`.

class typing.Sequence(*Reversible[T_co], Collection[T_co]*)
    A generic version of `collections.abc.Sequence`.

class typing.MutableSequence(*Sequence[T]*)
    A generic version of `collections.abc.MutableSequence`.

class typing.ByteString(*Sequence[int]*)
    A generic version of `collections.abc.ByteString`.

    This type represents the types `bytes`, `bytearray`, and `memoryview`.

    As a shorthand for this type, `bytes` can be used to annotate arguments of any of the types mentioned above.

class typing.Deque(*deque, MutableSequence[T]*)
    A generic version of `collections.deque`.

    New in version 3.6.1.

class typing.List(*list, MutableSequence[T]*)
    Generic version of `list`. Useful for annotating return types. To annotate arguments it is preferred to use abstract collection types such as `Mapping`, `Sequence`, or `AbstractSet`.

This type may be used as follows:

```
T = TypeVar('T', int, float)

def vec2(x: T, y: T) -> List[T]:
    return [x, y]

def keep_positives(vector: Sequence[T]) -> List[T]:
    return [item for item in vector if item > 0]
```

class typing.Set(*set, MutableSet[T]*)
    A generic version of `builtins.set`.

class typing.FrozenSet(*frozenset, AbstractSet[T_co]*)
    A generic version of `builtins.frozenset`.

class typing.MappingView(*Sized, Iterable[T_co]*)
    A generic version of `collections.abc.MappingView`.

class typing.KeysView(*MappingView[KT_co], AbstractSet[KT_co]*)
    A generic version of `collections.abc.KeysView`.

class typing.ItemsView(*MappingView, Generic[KT_co, VT_co]*)
    A generic version of `collections.abc.ItemsView`.

class typing.ValuesView(*MappingView[VT_co]*)
    A generic version of `collections.abc.ValuesView`.

class typing.Awaitable(*Generic[T_co]*)
    A generic version of `collections.abc.Awaitable`.

class typing.Coroutine(*Awaitable[V_co], Generic[T_co T_contra, V_co]*)
    A generic version of `collections.abc.Coroutine`. The variance and order of type variables correspond to those of `Generator`, for example:

```
from typing import List, Coroutine
c = None # type: Coroutine[List[str], str, int]
...
x = c.send('hi') # type: List[str]
async def bar() -> None:
    x = await c # type: int
```

class typing.AsyncIterable(*Generic[T_co]*)
    A generic version of `collections.abc.AsyncIterable`.

class typing.AsyncIterator(*AsyncIterable[T_co]*)
    A generic version of `collections.abc.AsyncIterator`.

class typing.ContextManager(*Generic[T_co]*)
    A generic version of `contextlib.AbstractContextManager`.

    New in version 3.6.

class typing.Dict(*dict, MutableMapping[KT, VT]*)
    A generic version of `dict`. The usage of this type is as follows:

```
def get_position_in_index(word_list: Dict[str, int], word: str) -> int:
    return word_list[word]
```

class typing.DefaultDict(*collections.defaultdict, MutableMapping[KT, VT]*)
    A generic version of `collections.defaultdict`.

    New in version 3.5.2.

class typing.Counter(*collections.Counter, Dict[T, int]*)
    A generic version of `collections.Counter`.

    New in version 3.6.1.

class typing.ChainMap(*collections.ChainMap, MutableMapping[KT, VT]*)
    A generic version of `collections.ChainMap`.

    New in version 3.6.1.

class typing.Generator(*Iterator[T_co], Generic[T_co, T_contra, V_co]*)
    A generator can be annotated by the generic type `Generator[YieldType, SendType, ReturnType]`. For example:

```
def echo_round() -> Generator[int, float, str]:
    sent = yield 0
    while sent >= 0:
        sent = yield round(sent)
    return 'Done'
```

   Note that unlike many other generics in the typing module, the `SendType` of *Generator* behaves contravariantly, not covariantly or invariantly.

   If your generator will only yield values, set the `SendType` and `ReturnType` to None:

```
def infinite_stream(start: int) -> Generator[int, None, None]:
    while True:
        yield start
        start += 1
```

   Alternatively, annotate your generator as having a return type of either `Iterable[YieldType]` or `Iterator[YieldType]`:

```
def infinite_stream(start: int) -> Iterator[int]:
    while True:
        yield start
        start += 1
```

class typing.AsyncGenerator(*AsyncIterator[T_co], Generic[T_co, T_contra]*)
    An async generator can be annotated by the generic type `AsyncGenerator[YieldType, SendType]`. For example:

```
async def echo_round() -> AsyncGenerator[int, float]:
    sent = yield 0
    while sent >= 0.0:
        rounded = await round(sent)
        sent = yield rounded
```

   Unlike normal generators, async generators cannot return a value, so there is no `ReturnType` type parameter. As with *Generator*, the `SendType` behaves contravariantly.

   If your generator will only yield values, set the `SendType` to None:

```
async def infinite_stream(start: int) -> AsyncGenerator[int, None]:
    while True:
        yield start
        start = await increment(start)
```

   Alternatively, annotate your generator as having a return type of either `AsyncIterable[YieldType]` or `AsyncIterator[YieldType]`:

26.1. typing — Support for type hints

```
async def infinite_stream(start: int) -> AsyncIterator[int]:
    while True:
        yield start
        start = await increment(start)
```

New in version 3.5.4.

class typing.Text

Text is an alias for str. It is provided to supply a forward compatible path for Python 2 code: in Python 2, Text is an alias for unicode.

Use Text to indicate that a value must contain a unicode string in a manner that is compatible with both Python 2 and Python 3:

```
def add_unicode_checkmark(text: Text) -> Text:
    return text + u' \u2713'
```

New in version 3.5.2.

class typing.io

Wrapper namespace for I/O stream types.

This defines the generic type IO[AnyStr] and subclasses TextIO and BinaryIO, deriving from IO[str] and IO[bytes], respectively. These represent the types of I/O streams such as returned by *open()*.

These types are also accessible directly as typing.IO, typing.TextIO, and typing.BinaryIO.

class typing.re

Wrapper namespace for regular expression matching types.

This defines the type aliases Pattern and Match which correspond to the return types from *re.compile()* and *re.match()*. These types (and the corresponding functions) are generic in AnyStr and can be made specific by writing Pattern[str], Pattern[bytes], Match[str], or Match[bytes].

These types are also accessible directly as typing.Pattern and typing.Match.

class typing.NamedTuple

Typed version of namedtuple.

Usage:

```
class Employee(NamedTuple):
    name: str
    id: int
```

This is equivalent to:

```
Employee = collections.namedtuple('Employee', ['name', 'id'])
```

To give a field a default value, you can assign to it in the class body:

```
class Employee(NamedTuple):
    name: str
    id: int = 3

employee = Employee('Guido')
assert employee.id == 3
```

Fields with a default value must come after any fields without a default.

The resulting class has two extra attributes: _field_types, giving a dict mapping field names to types, and _field_defaults, a dict mapping field names to default values. (The field names are in the _fields attribute, which is part of the namedtuple API.)

NamedTuple subclasses can also have docstrings and methods:

```
class Employee(NamedTuple):
    """Represents an employee."""
    name: str
    id: int = 3

    def __repr__(self) -> str:
        return f'<Employee {self.name}, id={self.id}>'
```

Backward-compatible usage:

```
Employee = NamedTuple('Employee', [('name', str), ('id', int)])
```

Changed in version 3.6: Added support for PEP 526 variable annotation syntax.

Changed in version 3.6.1: Added support for default values, methods, and docstrings.

typing.NewType(*typ*)

    A helper function to indicate a distinct types to a typechecker, see *NewType*. At runtime it returns a function that returns its argument. Usage:

```
UserId = NewType('UserId', int)
first_user = UserId(1)
```

New in version 3.5.2.

typing.cast(*typ*, *val*)

    Cast a value to a type.

    This returns the value unchanged. To the type checker this signals that the return value has the designated type, but at runtime we intentionally don't check anything (we want this to be as fast as possible).

typing.get_type_hints(*obj*[, *globals*[, *locals*]])

    Return a dictionary containing type hints for a function, method, module or class object.

    This is often the same as `obj.__annotations__`. In addition, forward references encoded as string literals are handled by evaluating them in `globals` and `locals` namespaces. If necessary, `Optional[t]` is added for function and method annotations if a default value equal to `None` is set. For a class C, return a dictionary constructed by merging all the `__annotations__` along `C.__mro__` in reverse order.

@typing.overload

    The @overload decorator allows describing functions and methods that support multiple different combinations of argument types. A series of @overload-decorated definitions must be followed by exactly one non-@overload-decorated definition (for the same function/method). The @overload-decorated definitions are for the benefit of the type checker only, since they will be overwritten by the non-@overload-decorated definition, while the latter is used at runtime but should be ignored by a type checker. At runtime, calling a @overload-decorated function directly will raise `NotImplementedError`. An example of overload that gives a more precise type than can be expressed using a union or a type variable:

```
@overload
def process(response: None) -> None:
    ...
@overload
def process(response: int) -> Tuple[int, str]:
    ...
@overload
def process(response: bytes) -> str:
```

```
    ...
def process(response):
    <actual implementation>
```

See PEP 484 for details and comparison with other typing semantics.

@typing.no_type_check
    Decorator to indicate that annotations are not type hints.

    This works as class or function *decorator*. With a class, it applies recursively to all methods defined in that class (but not to methods defined in its superclasses or subclasses).

    This mutates the function(s) in place.

@typing.no_type_check_decorator
    Decorator to give another decorator the *no_type_check()* effect.

    This wraps the decorator with something that wraps the decorated function in *no_type_check()*.

typing.Any
    Special type indicating an unconstrained type.

    - Every type is compatible with *Any*.
    - *Any* is compatible with every type.

typing.Union
    Union type; Union[X, Y] means either X or Y.

    To define a union, use e.g. Union[int, str]. Details:

    - The arguments must be types and there must be at least one.
    - Unions of unions are flattened, e.g.:

    ```
    Union[Union[int, str], float] == Union[int, str, float]
    ```

    - Unions of a single argument vanish, e.g.:

    ```
    Union[int] == int    # The constructor actually returns int
    ```

    - Redundant arguments are skipped, e.g.:

    ```
    Union[int, str, int] == Union[int, str]
    ```

    - When comparing unions, the argument order is ignored, e.g.:

    ```
    Union[int, str] == Union[str, int]
    ```

    - When a class and its subclass are present, the latter is skipped, e.g.:

    ```
    Union[int, object] == object
    ```

    - You cannot subclass or instantiate a union.
    - You cannot write Union[X][Y].
    - You can use Optional[X] as a shorthand for Union[X, None].

typing.Optional
    Optional type.

    Optional[X] is equivalent to Union[X, None].

    Note that this is not the same concept as an optional argument, which is one that has a default. An optional argument with a default needn't use the Optional qualifier on its type annotation (although it is inferred if the default is `None`). A mandatory argument may still have an `Optional` type if an explicit value of `None` is allowed.

typing.Tuple
Tuple type; `Tuple[X, Y]` is the type of a tuple of two items with the first item of type X and the second of type Y.

Example: `Tuple[T1, T2]` is a tuple of two elements corresponding to type variables T1 and T2. `Tuple[int, float, str]` is a tuple of an int, a float and a string.

To specify a variable-length tuple of homogeneous type, use literal ellipsis, e.g. `Tuple[int, ...]`. A plain *Tuple* is equivalent to `Tuple[Any, ...]`, and in turn to *tuple*.

typing.Callable
Callable type; `Callable[[int], str]` is a function of (int) -> str.

The subscription syntax must always be used with exactly two values: the argument list and the return type. The argument list must be a list of types or an ellipsis; the return type must be a single type.

There is no syntax to indicate optional or keyword arguments; such function types are rarely used as callback types. `Callable[..., ReturnType]` (literal ellipsis) can be used to type hint a callable taking any number of arguments and returning `ReturnType`. A plain *Callable* is equivalent to `Callable[..., Any]`, and in turn to *collections.abc.Callable*.

typing.ClassVar
Special type construct to mark class variables.

As introduced in PEP 526, a variable annotation wrapped in ClassVar indicates that a given attribute is intended to be used as a class variable and should not be set on instances of that class. Usage:

```
class Starship:
    stats: ClassVar[Dict[str, int]] = {} # class variable
    damage: int = 10                     # instance variable
```

ClassVar accepts only types and cannot be further subscribed.

ClassVar is not a class itself, and should not be used with *isinstance()* or *issubclass()*. *ClassVar* does not change Python runtime behavior, but it can be used by third-party type checkers. For example, a type checker might flag the following code as an error:

```
enterprise_d = Starship(3000)
enterprise_d.stats = {} # Error, setting class variable on instance
Starship.stats = {}     # This is OK
```

New in version 3.5.3.

typing.AnyStr
AnyStr is a type variable defined as `AnyStr = TypeVar('AnyStr', str, bytes)`.

It is meant to be used for functions that may accept any kind of string without allowing different kinds of strings to mix. For example:

```
def concat(a: AnyStr, b: AnyStr) -> AnyStr:
    return a + b

concat(u"foo", u"bar") # Ok, output has type 'unicode'
concat(b"foo", b"bar") # Ok, output has type 'bytes'
concat(u"foo", b"bar") # Error, cannot mix unicode and bytes
```

typing.TYPE_CHECKING
A special constant that is assumed to be `True` by 3rd party static type checkers. It is `False` at runtime. Usage:

```
if TYPE_CHECKING:
    import expensive_mod

def fun(arg: 'expensive_mod.SomeType') -> None:
    local_var: expensive_mod.AnotherType = other_fun()
```

Note that the first type annotation must be enclosed in quotes, making it a "forward reference", to hide the `expensive_mod` reference from the interpreter runtime. Type annotations for local variables are not evaluated, so the second annotation does not need to be enclosed in quotes.

New in version 3.5.2.

26.2 `pydoc` — Documentation generator and online help system

Source code: Lib/pydoc.py

The *pydoc* module automatically generates documentation from Python modules. The documentation can be presented as pages of text on the console, served to a Web browser, or saved to HTML files.

For modules, classes, functions and methods, the displayed documentation is derived from the docstring (i.e. the `__doc__` attribute) of the object, and recursively of its documentable members. If there is no docstring, *pydoc* tries to obtain a description from the block of comment lines just above the definition of the class, function or method in the source file, or at the top of the module (see `inspect.getcomments()`).

The built-in function `help()` invokes the online help system in the interactive interpreter, which uses *pydoc* to generate its documentation as text on the console. The same text documentation can also be viewed from outside the Python interpreter by running **pydoc** as a script at the operating system's command prompt. For example, running

```
pydoc sys
```

at a shell prompt will display documentation on the *sys* module, in a style similar to the manual pages shown by the Unix **man** command. The argument to **pydoc** can be the name of a function, module, or package, or a dotted reference to a class, method, or function within a module or module in a package. If the argument to **pydoc** looks like a path (that is, it contains the path separator for your operating system, such as a slash in Unix), and refers to an existing Python source file, then documentation is produced for that file.

Note: In order to find objects and their documentation, *pydoc* imports the module(s) to be documented. Therefore, any code on module level will be executed on that occasion. Use an `if __name__ == '__main__':` guard to only execute code when a file is invoked as a script and not just imported.

When printing output to the console, **pydoc** attempts to paginate the output for easier reading. If the `PAGER` environment variable is set, **pydoc** will use its value as a pagination program.

Specifying a `-w` flag before the argument will cause HTML documentation to be written out to a file in the current directory, instead of displaying text on the console.

Specifying a `-k` flag before the argument will search the synopsis lines of all available modules for the keyword given as the argument, again in a manner similar to the Unix **man** command. The synopsis line of a module is the first line of its documentation string.

You can also use **pydoc** to start an HTTP server on the local machine that will serve documentation to visiting Web browsers. **pydoc -p 1234** will start a HTTP server on port 1234, allowing you to browse the documentation at `http://localhost:1234/` in your preferred Web browser. Specifying 0 as the port number will select an arbitrary unused port.

`pydoc -b` will start the server and additionally open a web browser to a module index page. Each served page has a navigation bar at the top where you can *Get* help on an individual item, *Search* all modules with a keyword in their synopsis line, and go to the *Module index*, *Topics* and *Keywords* pages.

When `pydoc` generates documentation, it uses the current environment and path to locate modules. Thus, invoking `pydoc spam` documents precisely the version of the module you would get if you started the Python interpreter and typed `import spam`.

Module docs for core modules are assumed to reside in `https://docs.python.org/X.Y/library/` where X and Y are the major and minor version numbers of the Python interpreter. This can be overridden by setting the `PYTHONDOCS` environment variable to a different URL or to a local directory containing the Library Reference Manual pages.

Changed in version 3.2: Added the `-b` option.

Changed in version 3.3: The `-g` command line option was removed.

Changed in version 3.4: *pydoc* now uses *inspect.signature()* rather than *inspect.getfullargspec()* to extract signature information from callables.

26.3 `doctest` — Test interactive Python examples

Source code: Lib/doctest.py

The *doctest* module searches for pieces of text that look like interactive Python sessions, and then executes those sessions to verify that they work exactly as shown. There are several common ways to use doctest:

- To check that a module's docstrings are up-to-date by verifying that all interactive examples still work as documented.
- To perform regression testing by verifying that interactive examples from a test file or a test object work as expected.
- To write tutorial documentation for a package, liberally illustrated with input-output examples. Depending on whether the examples or the expository text are emphasized, this has the flavor of "literate testing" or "executable documentation".

Here's a complete but small example module:

```
"""
This is the "example" module.

The example module supplies one function, factorial().  For example,

>>> factorial(5)
120
"""

def factorial(n):
    """Return the factorial of n, an exact integer >= 0.

    >>> [factorial(n) for n in range(6)]
    [1, 1, 2, 6, 24, 120]
    >>> factorial(30)
    265252859812191058636308480000000
```

```
    >>> factorial(-1)
    Traceback (most recent call last):
        ...
    ValueError: n must be >= 0

    Factorials of floats are OK, but the float must be an exact integer:
    >>> factorial(30.1)
    Traceback (most recent call last):
        ...
    ValueError: n must be exact integer
    >>> factorial(30.0)
    265252859812191058636308480000000

    It must also not be ridiculously large:
    >>> factorial(1e100)
    Traceback (most recent call last):
        ...
    OverflowError: n too large
    """

    import math
    if not n >= 0:
        raise ValueError("n must be >= 0")
    if math.floor(n) != n:
        raise ValueError("n must be exact integer")
    if n+1 == n:  # catch a value like 1e300
        raise OverflowError("n too large")
    result = 1
    factor = 2
    while factor <= n:
        result *= factor
        factor += 1
    return result


if __name__ == "__main__":
    import doctest
    doctest.testmod()
```

If you run `example.py` directly from the command line, *doctest* works its magic:

```
$ python example.py
$
```

There's no output! That's normal, and it means all the examples worked. Pass -v to the script, and *doctest* prints a detailed log of what it's trying, and prints a summary at the end:

```
$ python example.py -v
Trying:
    factorial(5)
Expecting:
    120
ok
Trying:
    [factorial(n) for n in range(6)]
Expecting:
    [1, 1, 2, 6, 24, 120]
ok
```

And so on, eventually ending with:

```
Trying:
    factorial(1e100)
Expecting:
    Traceback (most recent call last):
        ...
    OverflowError: n too large
ok
2 items passed all tests:
   1 tests in __main__
   8 tests in __main__.factorial
9 tests in 2 items.
9 passed and 0 failed.
Test passed.
$
```

That's all you need to know to start making productive use of *doctest*! Jump in. The following sections provide full details. Note that there are many examples of doctests in the standard Python test suite and libraries. Especially useful examples can be found in the standard test file `Lib/test/test_doctest.py`.

26.3.1 Simple Usage: Checking Examples in Docstrings

The simplest way to start using doctest (but not necessarily the way you'll continue to do it) is to end each module M with:

```
if __name__ == "__main__":
    import doctest
    doctest.testmod()
```

doctest then examines docstrings in module M.

Running the module as a script causes the examples in the docstrings to get executed and verified:

```
python M.py
```

This won't display anything unless an example fails, in which case the failing example(s) and the cause(s) of the failure(s) are printed to stdout, and the final line of output is `***Test Failed*** N failures.`, where *N* is the number of examples that failed.

Run it with the -v switch instead:

```
python M.py -v
```

and a detailed report of all examples tried is printed to standard output, along with assorted summaries at the end.

You can force verbose mode by passing `verbose=True` to *testmod()*, or prohibit it by passing `verbose=False`. In either of those cases, `sys.argv` is not examined by *testmod()* (so passing -v or not has no effect).

There is also a command line shortcut for running *testmod()*. You can instruct the Python interpreter to run the doctest module directly from the standard library and pass the module name(s) on the command line:

```
python -m doctest -v example.py
```

This will import `example.py` as a standalone module and run *testmod()* on it. Note that this may not work correctly if the file is part of a package and imports other submodules from that package.

For more information on *testmod()*, see section *Basic API*.

26.3.2 Simple Usage: Checking Examples in a Text File

Another simple application of doctest is testing interactive examples in a text file. This can be done with the *testfile()* function:

```
import doctest
doctest.testfile("example.txt")
```

That short script executes and verifies any interactive Python examples contained in the file `example.txt`. The file content is treated as if it were a single giant docstring; the file doesn't need to contain a Python program! For example, perhaps `example.txt` contains this:

```
The ``example`` module
======================

Using ``factorial``
-------------------

This is an example text file in reStructuredText format.  First import
``factorial`` from the ``example`` module:

    >>> from example import factorial

Now use it:

    >>> factorial(6)
    120
```

Running `doctest.testfile("example.txt")` then finds the error in this documentation:

```
File "./example.txt", line 14, in example.txt
Failed example:
    factorial(6)
Expected:
    120
Got:
    720
```

As with *testmod()*, *testfile()* won't display anything unless an example fails. If an example does fail, then the failing example(s) and the cause(s) of the failure(s) are printed to stdout, using the same format as *testmod()*.

By default, *testfile()* looks for files in the calling module's directory. See section *Basic API* for a description of the optional arguments that can be used to tell it to look for files in other locations.

Like *testmod()*, *testfile()*'s verbosity can be set with the -v command-line switch or with the optional keyword argument *verbose*.

There is also a command line shortcut for running *testfile()*. You can instruct the Python interpreter to run the doctest module directly from the standard library and pass the file name(s) on the command line:

```
python -m doctest -v example.txt
```

Because the file name does not end with .py, *doctest* infers that it must be run with *testfile()*, not *testmod()*.

For more information on *testfile()*, see section *Basic API*.

26.3.3 How It Works

This section examines in detail how doctest works: which docstrings it looks at, how it finds interactive examples, what execution context it uses, how it handles exceptions, and how option flags can be used to control its behavior. This is the information that you need to know to write doctest examples; for information about actually running doctest on these examples, see the following sections.

Which Docstrings Are Examined?

The module docstring, and all function, class and method docstrings are searched. Objects imported into the module are not searched.

In addition, if `M.__test__` exists and "is true", it must be a dict, and each entry maps a (string) name to a function object, class object, or string. Function and class object docstrings found from `M.__test__` are searched, and strings are treated as if they were docstrings. In output, a key K in `M.__test__` appears with name

```
<name of M>.__test__.K
```

Any classes found are recursively searched similarly, to test docstrings in their contained methods and nested classes.

CPython implementation detail: Prior to version 3.4, extension modules written in C were not fully searched by doctest.

How are Docstring Examples Recognized?

In most cases a copy-and-paste of an interactive console session works fine, but doctest isn't trying to do an exact emulation of any specific Python shell.

```
>>> # comments are ignored
>>> x = 12
>>> x
12
>>> if x == 13:
...     print("yes")
... else:
...     print("no")
...     print("NO")
...     print("NO!!!")
...
no
NO
NO!!!
>>>
```

Any expected output must immediately follow the final '`>>> `' or '`... `' line containing the code, and the expected output (if any) extends to the next '`>>> `' or all-whitespace line.

The fine print:

- Expected output cannot contain an all-whitespace line, since such a line is taken to signal the end of expected output. If expected output does contain a blank line, put `<BLANKLINE>` in your doctest example each place a blank line is expected.
- All hard tab characters are expanded to spaces, using 8-column tab stops. Tabs in output generated by the tested code are not modified. Because any hard tabs in the sample output *are* expanded, this means that if the code output includes hard tabs, the only way the doctest can pass is if the

`NORMALIZE_WHITESPACE` option or *directive* is in effect. Alternatively, the test can be rewritten to capture the output and compare it to an expected value as part of the test. This handling of tabs in the source was arrived at through trial and error, and has proven to be the least error prone way of handling them. It is possible to use a different algorithm for handling tabs by writing a custom `DocTestParser` class.

- Output to stdout is captured, but not output to stderr (exception tracebacks are captured via a different means).
- If you continue a line via backslashing in an interactive session, or for any other reason use a backslash, you should use a raw docstring, which will preserve your backslashes exactly as you type them:

```
>>> def f(x):
...     r'''Backslashes in a raw docstring: m\n'''
>>> print(f.__doc__)
Backslashes in a raw docstring: m\n
```

Otherwise, the backslash will be interpreted as part of the string. For example, the `\n` above would be interpreted as a newline character. Alternatively, you can double each backslash in the doctest version (and not use a raw string):

```
>>> def f(x):
...     '''Backslashes in a raw docstring: m\\n'''
>>> print(f.__doc__)
Backslashes in a raw docstring: m\n
```

- The starting column doesn't matter:

```
>>> assert "Easy!"
      >>> import math
          >>> math.floor(1.9)
          1
```

and as many leading whitespace characters are stripped from the expected output as appeared in the initial '`>>> `' line that started the example.

What's the Execution Context?

By default, each time *doctest* finds a docstring to test, it uses a *shallow copy* of M's globals, so that running tests doesn't change the module's real globals, and so that one test in M can't leave behind crumbs that accidentally allow another test to work. This means examples can freely use any names defined at top-level in M, and names defined earlier in the docstring being run. Examples cannot see names defined in other docstrings.

You can force use of your own dict as the execution context by passing `globs=your_dict` to *testmod()* or *testfile()* instead.

What About Exceptions?

No problem, provided that the traceback is the only output produced by the example: just paste in the traceback.[1] Since tracebacks contain details that are likely to change rapidly (for example, exact file paths and line numbers), this is one case where doctest works hard to be flexible in what it accepts.

Simple example:

---

[1] Examples containing both expected output and an exception are not supported. Trying to guess where one ends and the other begins is too error-prone, and that also makes for a confusing test.

```
>>> [1, 2, 3].remove(42)
Traceback (most recent call last):
  File "<stdin>", line 1, in <module>
ValueError: list.remove(x): x not in list
```

That doctest succeeds if *ValueError* is raised, with the `list.remove(x): x not in list` detail as shown.

The expected output for an exception must start with a traceback header, which may be either of the following two lines, indented the same as the first line of the example:

```
Traceback (most recent call last):
Traceback (innermost last):
```

The traceback header is followed by an optional traceback stack, whose contents are ignored by doctest. The traceback stack is typically omitted, or copied verbatim from an interactive session.

The traceback stack is followed by the most interesting part: the line(s) containing the exception type and detail. This is usually the last line of a traceback, but can extend across multiple lines if the exception has a multi-line detail:

```
>>> raise ValueError('multi\n    line\ndetail')
Traceback (most recent call last):
  File "<stdin>", line 1, in <module>
ValueError: multi
    line
detail
```

The last three lines (starting with *ValueError*) are compared against the exception's type and detail, and the rest are ignored.

Best practice is to omit the traceback stack, unless it adds significant documentation value to the example. So the last example is probably better as:

```
>>> raise ValueError('multi\n    line\ndetail')
Traceback (most recent call last):
    ...
ValueError: multi
    line
detail
```

Note that tracebacks are treated very specially. In particular, in the rewritten example, the use of ... is independent of doctest's *ELLIPSIS* option. The ellipsis in that example could be left out, or could just as well be three (or three hundred) commas or digits, or an indented transcript of a Monty Python skit.

Some details you should read once, but won't need to remember:

- Doctest can't guess whether your expected output came from an exception traceback or from ordinary printing. So, e.g., an example that expects `ValueError: 42 is prime` will pass whether *ValueError* is actually raised or if the example merely prints that traceback text. In practice, ordinary output rarely begins with a traceback header line, so this doesn't create real problems.

- Each line of the traceback stack (if present) must be indented further than the first line of the example, *or* start with a non-alphanumeric character. The first line following the traceback header indented the same and starting with an alphanumeric is taken to be the start of the exception detail. Of course this does the right thing for genuine tracebacks.

- When the *IGNORE_EXCEPTION_DETAIL* doctest option is specified, everything following the leftmost colon and any module information in the exception name is ignored.

- The interactive shell omits the traceback header line for some *SyntaxError*s. But doctest uses the traceback header line to distinguish exceptions from non-exceptions. So in the rare case where you need to test a *SyntaxError* that omits the traceback header, you will need to manually add the traceback header line to your test example.

- For some *SyntaxError*s, Python displays the character position of the syntax error, using a ^ marker:

```
>>> 1 1
  File "<stdin>", line 1
    1 1
      ^
SyntaxError: invalid syntax
```

Since the lines showing the position of the error come before the exception type and detail, they are not checked by doctest. For example, the following test would pass, even though it puts the ^ marker in the wrong location:

```
>>> 1 1
  File "<stdin>", line 1
    1 1
     ^
SyntaxError: invalid syntax
```

Option Flags

A number of option flags control various aspects of doctest's behavior. Symbolic names for the flags are supplied as module constants, which can be bitwise ORed together and passed to various functions. The names can also be used in *doctest directives*, and may be passed to the doctest command line interface via the -o option.

New in version 3.4: The -o command line option.

The first group of options define test semantics, controlling aspects of how doctest decides whether actual output matches an example's expected output:

doctest.**DONT_ACCEPT_TRUE_FOR_1**
> By default, if an expected output block contains just 1, an actual output block containing just 1 or just **True** is considered to be a match, and similarly for 0 versus **False**. When *DONT_ACCEPT_TRUE_FOR_1* is specified, neither substitution is allowed. The default behavior caters to that Python changed the return type of many functions from integer to boolean; doctests expecting "little integer" output still work in these cases. This option will probably go away, but not for several years.

doctest.**DONT_ACCEPT_BLANKLINE**
> By default, if an expected output block contains a line containing only the string **<BLANKLINE>**, then that line will match a blank line in the actual output. Because a genuinely blank line delimits the expected output, this is the only way to communicate that a blank line is expected. When *DONT_ACCEPT_BLANKLINE* is specified, this substitution is not allowed.

doctest.**NORMALIZE_WHITESPACE**
> When specified, all sequences of whitespace (blanks and newlines) are treated as equal. Any sequence of whitespace within the expected output will match any sequence of whitespace within the actual output. By default, whitespace must match exactly. *NORMALIZE_WHITESPACE* is especially useful when a line of expected output is very long, and you want to wrap it across multiple lines in your source.

doctest.**ELLIPSIS**
> When specified, an ellipsis marker (...) in the expected output can match any substring in the actual output. This includes substrings that span line boundaries, and empty substrings, so it's best to keep usage of this simple. Complicated uses can lead to the same kinds of "oops, it matched too much!" surprises that .* is prone to in regular expressions.

`doctest.IGNORE_EXCEPTION_DETAIL`
> When specified, an example that expects an exception passes if an exception of the expected type is raised, even if the exception detail does not match. For example, an example expecting `ValueError: 42` will pass if the actual exception raised is `ValueError: 3*14`, but will fail, e.g., if `TypeError` is raised.
>
> It will also ignore the module name used in Python 3 doctest reports. Hence both of these variations will work with the flag specified, regardless of whether the test is run under Python 2.7 or Python 3.2 (or later versions):
>
> ```
> >>> raise CustomError('message')
> Traceback (most recent call last):
> CustomError: message
>
> >>> raise CustomError('message')
> Traceback (most recent call last):
> my_module.CustomError: message
> ```
>
> Note that `ELLIPSIS` can also be used to ignore the details of the exception message, but such a test may still fail based on whether or not the module details are printed as part of the exception name. Using `IGNORE_EXCEPTION_DETAIL` and the details from Python 2.3 is also the only clear way to write a doctest that doesn't care about the exception detail yet continues to pass under Python 2.3 or earlier (those releases do not support *doctest directives* and ignore them as irrelevant comments). For example:
>
> ```
> >>> (1, 2)[3] = 'moo'
> Traceback (most recent call last):
>   File "<stdin>", line 1, in <module>
> TypeError: object doesn't support item assignment
> ```
>
> passes under Python 2.3 and later Python versions with the flag specified, even though the detail changed in Python 2.4 to say "does not" instead of "doesn't".
>
> Changed in version 3.2: `IGNORE_EXCEPTION_DETAIL` now also ignores any information relating to the module containing the exception under test.

`doctest.SKIP`
> When specified, do not run the example at all. This can be useful in contexts where doctest examples serve as both documentation and test cases, and an example should be included for documentation purposes, but should not be checked. E.g., the example's output might be random; or the example might depend on resources which would be unavailable to the test driver.
>
> The SKIP flag can also be used for temporarily "commenting out" examples.

`doctest.COMPARISON_FLAGS`
> A bitmask or'ing together all the comparison flags above.

The second group of options controls how test failures are reported:

`doctest.REPORT_UDIFF`
> When specified, failures that involve multi-line expected and actual outputs are displayed using a unified diff.

`doctest.REPORT_CDIFF`
> When specified, failures that involve multi-line expected and actual outputs will be displayed using a context diff.

`doctest.REPORT_NDIFF`
> When specified, differences are computed by `difflib.Differ`, using the same algorithm as the popular `ndiff.py` utility. This is the only method that marks differences within lines as well as across lines. For example, if a line of expected output contains digit `1` where actual output contains letter `l`, a line is inserted with a caret marking the mismatching column positions.

`doctest.REPORT_ONLY_FIRST_FAILURE`
> When specified, display the first failing example in each doctest, but suppress output for all remaining examples. This will prevent doctest from reporting correct examples that break because of earlier failures; but it might also hide incorrect examples that fail independently of the first failure. When `REPORT_ONLY_FIRST_FAILURE` is specified, the remaining examples are still run, and still count towards the total number of failures reported; only the output is suppressed.

`doctest.FAIL_FAST`
> When specified, exit after the first failing example and don't attempt to run the remaining examples. Thus, the number of failures reported will be at most 1. This flag may be useful during debugging, since examples after the first failure won't even produce debugging output.
>
> The doctest command line accepts the option `-f` as a shorthand for `-o FAIL_FAST`.
>
> New in version 3.4.

`doctest.REPORTING_FLAGS`
> A bitmask or'ing together all the reporting flags above.

There is also a way to register new option flag names, though this isn't useful unless you intend to extend *doctest* internals via subclassing:

`doctest.register_optionflag(name)`
> Create a new option flag with a given name, and return the new flag's integer value. *register_optionflag()* can be used when subclassing *OutputChecker* or *DocTestRunner* to create new options that are supported by your subclasses. *register_optionflag()* should always be called using the following idiom:

```
MY_FLAG = register_optionflag('MY_FLAG')
```

Directives

Doctest directives may be used to modify the *option flags* for an individual example. Doctest directives are special Python comments following an example's source code:

```
directive              ::=  "#" "doctest:" directive_options
directive_options      ::=  directive_option ("," directive_option)\*
directive_option       ::=  on_or_off directive_option_name
on_or_off              ::=  "+" \| "-"
directive_option_name  ::=  "DONT_ACCEPT_BLANKLINE" \| "NORMALIZE_WHITESPACE" \| ...
```

Whitespace is not allowed between the + or - and the directive option name. The directive option name can be any of the option flag names explained above.

An example's doctest directives modify doctest's behavior for that single example. Use + to enable the named behavior, or - to disable it.

For example, this test passes:

```
>>> print(list(range(20)))
[0,   1,  2,  3,  4,  5,  6,  7,  8,  9,
10,  11, 12, 13, 14, 15, 16, 17, 18, 19]
```

Without the directive it would fail, both because the actual output doesn't have two blanks before the single-digit list elements, and because the actual output is on a single line. This test also passes, and also requires a directive to do so:

```
>>> print(list(range(20)))
[0, 1, ..., 18, 19]
```

Multiple directives can be used on a single physical line, separated by commas:

```
>>> print(list(range(20)))
[0,    1, ...,   18,    19]
```

If multiple directive comments are used for a single example, then they are combined:

```
>>> print(list(range(20)))
...
[0,    1, ...,   18,    19]
```

As the previous example shows, you can add ... lines to your example containing only directives. This can be useful when an example is too long for a directive to comfortably fit on the same line:

```
>>> print(list(range(5)) + list(range(10, 20)) + list(range(30, 40)))
...
[0, ..., 4, 10, ..., 19, 30, ..., 39]
```

Note that since all options are disabled by default, and directives apply only to the example they appear in, enabling options (via + in a directive) is usually the only meaningful choice. However, option flags can also be passed to functions that run doctests, establishing different defaults. In such cases, disabling an option via - in a directive can be useful.

Warnings

doctest is serious about requiring exact matches in expected output. If even a single character doesn't match, the test fails. This will probably surprise you a few times, as you learn exactly what Python does and doesn't guarantee about output. For example, when printing a dict, Python doesn't guarantee that the key-value pairs will be printed in any particular order, so a test like

```
>>> foo()
{"Hermione": "hippogryph", "Harry": "broomstick"}
```

is vulnerable! One workaround is to do

```
>>> foo() == {"Hermione": "hippogryph", "Harry": "broomstick"}
True
```

instead. Another is to do

```
>>> d = sorted(foo().items())
>>> d
[('Harry', 'broomstick'), ('Hermione', 'hippogryph')]
```

There are others, but you get the idea.

Another bad idea is to print things that embed an object address, like

```
>>> id(1.0)                 # certain to fail some of the time
7948648
>>> class C: pass
>>> C()                     # the default repr() for instances embeds an address
<__main__.C instance at 0x00AC18F0>
```

26.3. doctest — Test interactive Python examples

The *ELLIPSIS* directive gives a nice approach for the last example:

```
>>> C()
<__main__.C instance at 0x...>
```

Floating-point numbers are also subject to small output variations across platforms, because Python defers to the platform C library for float formatting, and C libraries vary widely in quality here.

```
>>> 1./7  # risky
0.14285714285714285
>>> print(1./7) # safer
0.142857142857
>>> print(round(1./7, 6))  # much safer
0.142857
```

Numbers of the form I/2.**J are safe across all platforms, and I often contrive doctest examples to produce numbers of that form:

```
>>> 3./4  # utterly safe
0.75
```

Simple fractions are also easier for people to understand, and that makes for better documentation.

26.3.4 Basic API

The functions *testmod()* and *testfile()* provide a simple interface to doctest that should be sufficient for most basic uses. For a less formal introduction to these two functions, see sections *Simple Usage: Checking Examples in Docstrings* and *Simple Usage: Checking Examples in a Text File*.

doctest.testfile(*filename*, *module_relative=True*, *name=None*, *package=None*, *globs=None*, *verbose=None*, *report=True*, *optionflags=0*, *extraglobs=None*, *raise_on_error=False*, *parser=DocTestParser()*, *encoding=None*)

All arguments except *filename* are optional, and should be specified in keyword form.

Test examples in the file named *filename*. Return `(failure_count, test_count)`.

Optional argument *module_relative* specifies how the filename should be interpreted:

- If *module_relative* is `True` (the default), then *filename* specifies an OS-independent module-relative path. By default, this path is relative to the calling module's directory; but if the *package* argument is specified, then it is relative to that package. To ensure OS-independence, *filename* should use / characters to separate path segments, and may not be an absolute path (i.e., it may not begin with /).

- If *module_relative* is `False`, then *filename* specifies an OS-specific path. The path may be absolute or relative; relative paths are resolved with respect to the current working directory.

Optional argument *name* gives the name of the test; by default, or if `None`, `os.path.basename(filename)` is used.

Optional argument *package* is a Python package or the name of a Python package whose directory should be used as the base directory for a module-relative filename. If no package is specified, then the calling module's directory is used as the base directory for module-relative filenames. It is an error to specify *package* if *module_relative* is `False`.

Optional argument *globs* gives a dict to be used as the globals when executing examples. A new shallow copy of this dict is created for the doctest, so its examples start with a clean slate. By default, or if `None`, a new empty dict is used.

Optional argument *extraglobs* gives a dict merged into the globals used to execute examples. This works like `dict.update()`: if *globs* and *extraglobs* have a common key, the associated value in *extraglobs* appears in the combined dict. By default, or if `None`, no extra globals are used. This is an advanced feature that allows parameterization of doctests. For example, a doctest can be written for a base class, using a generic name for the class, then reused to test any number of subclasses by passing an *extraglobs* dict mapping the generic name to the subclass to be tested.

Optional argument *verbose* prints lots of stuff if true, and prints only failures if false; by default, or if `None`, it's true if and only if `'-v'` is in `sys.argv`.

Optional argument *report* prints a summary at the end when true, else prints nothing at the end. In verbose mode, the summary is detailed, else the summary is very brief (in fact, empty if all tests passed).

Optional argument *optionflags* (default value 0) takes the bitwise OR of option flags. See section *Option Flags*.

Optional argument *raise_on_error* defaults to false. If true, an exception is raised upon the first failure or unexpected exception in an example. This allows failures to be post-mortem debugged. Default behavior is to continue running examples.

Optional argument *parser* specifies a `DocTestParser` (or subclass) that should be used to extract tests from the files. It defaults to a normal parser (i.e., `DocTestParser()`).

Optional argument *encoding* specifies an encoding that should be used to convert the file to unicode.

`doctest.testmod(`*m=None, name=None, globs=None, verbose=None, report=True, optionflags=0, extraglobs=None, raise_on_error=False, exclude_empty=False*`)`

All arguments are optional, and all except for *m* should be specified in keyword form.

Test examples in docstrings in functions and classes reachable from module *m* (or module `__main__` if *m* is not supplied or is `None`), starting with `m.__doc__`.

Also test examples reachable from dict `m.__test__`, if it exists and is not `None`. `m.__test__` maps names (strings) to functions, classes and strings; function and class docstrings are searched for examples; strings are searched directly, as if they were docstrings.

Only docstrings attached to objects belonging to module *m* are searched.

Return `(failure_count, test_count)`.

Optional argument *name* gives the name of the module; by default, or if `None`, `m.__name__` is used.

Optional argument *exclude_empty* defaults to false. If true, objects for which no doctests are found are excluded from consideration. The default is a backward compatibility hack, so that code still using `doctest.master.summarize()` in conjunction with `testmod()` continues to get output for objects with no tests. The *exclude_empty* argument to the newer `DocTestFinder` constructor defaults to true.

Optional arguments *extraglobs*, *verbose*, *report*, *optionflags*, *raise_on_error*, and *globs* are the same as for function `testfile()` above, except that *globs* defaults to `m.__dict__`.

`doctest.run_docstring_examples(`*f, globs, verbose=False, name="NoName", compileflags=None, optionflags=0*`)`

Test examples associated with object *f*; for example, *f* may be a string, a module, a function, or a class object.

A shallow copy of dictionary argument *globs* is used for the execution context.

Optional argument *name* is used in failure messages, and defaults to `"NoName"`.

If optional argument *verbose* is true, output is generated even if there are no failures. By default, output is generated only in case of an example failure.

Optional argument *compileflags* gives the set of flags that should be used by the Python compiler when running the examples. By default, or if `None`, flags are deduced corresponding to the set of future features found in *globs*.

Optional argument *optionflags* works as for function `testfile()` above.

26.3.5 Unittest API

As your collection of doctest'ed modules grows, you'll want a way to run all their doctests systematically. `doctest` provides two functions that can be used to create `unittest` test suites from modules and text files containing doctests. To integrate with `unittest` test discovery, include a `load_tests()` function in your test module:

```
import unittest
import doctest
import my_module_with_doctests

def load_tests(loader, tests, ignore):
    tests.addTests(doctest.DocTestSuite(my_module_with_doctests))
    return tests
```

There are two main functions for creating `unittest.TestSuite` instances from text files and modules with doctests:

`doctest.DocFileSuite(`*paths, module_relative=True, package=None, setUp=None, tearDown=None, globs=None, optionflags=0, parser=DocTestParser(), encoding=None`)`

Convert doctest tests from one or more text files to a `unittest.TestSuite`.

The returned `unittest.TestSuite` is to be run by the unittest framework and runs the interactive examples in each file. If an example in any file fails, then the synthesized unit test fails, and a `failureException` exception is raised showing the name of the file containing the test and a (sometimes approximate) line number.

Pass one or more paths (as strings) to text files to be examined.

Options may be provided as keyword arguments:

Optional argument *module_relative* specifies how the filenames in *paths* should be interpreted:

- If *module_relative* is `True` (the default), then each filename in *paths* specifies an OS-independent module-relative path. By default, this path is relative to the calling module's directory; but if the *package* argument is specified, then it is relative to that package. To ensure OS-independence, each filename should use / characters to separate path segments, and may not be an absolute path (i.e., it may not begin with /).

- If *module_relative* is `False`, then each filename in *paths* specifies an OS-specific path. The path may be absolute or relative; relative paths are resolved with respect to the current working directory.

Optional argument *package* is a Python package or the name of a Python package whose directory should be used as the base directory for module-relative filenames in *paths*. If no package is specified, then the calling module's directory is used as the base directory for module-relative filenames. It is an error to specify *package* if *module_relative* is `False`.

Optional argument *setUp* specifies a set-up function for the test suite. This is called before running the tests in each file. The *setUp* function will be passed a `DocTest` object. The setUp function can access the test globals as the *globs* attribute of the test passed.

Optional argument *tearDown* specifies a tear-down function for the test suite. This is called after running the tests in each file. The *tearDown* function will be passed a `DocTest` object. The setUp function can access the test globals as the *globs* attribute of the test passed.

Optional argument *globs* is a dictionary containing the initial global variables for the tests. A new copy of this dictionary is created for each test. By default, *globs* is a new empty dictionary.

Optional argument *optionflags* specifies the default doctest options for the tests, created by or-ing together individual option flags. See section `Option Flags`. See function `set_unittest_reportflags()` below for a better way to set reporting options.

Optional argument *parser* specifies a `DocTestParser` (or subclass) that should be used to extract tests from the files. It defaults to a normal parser (i.e., `DocTestParser()`).

Optional argument *encoding* specifies an encoding that should be used to convert the file to unicode.

The global `__file__` is added to the globals provided to doctests loaded from a text file using `DocFileSuite()`.

`doctest.DocTestSuite`(*module=None, globs=None, extraglobs=None, test_finder=None, setUp=None, tearDown=None, checker=None*)
Convert doctest tests for a module to a `unittest.TestSuite`.

The returned `unittest.TestSuite` is to be run by the unittest framework and runs each doctest in the module. If any of the doctests fail, then the synthesized unit test fails, and a `failureException` exception is raised showing the name of the file containing the test and a (sometimes approximate) line number.

Optional argument *module* provides the module to be tested. It can be a module object or a (possibly dotted) module name. If not specified, the module calling this function is used.

Optional argument *globs* is a dictionary containing the initial global variables for the tests. A new copy of this dictionary is created for each test. By default, *globs* is a new empty dictionary.

Optional argument *extraglobs* specifies an extra set of global variables, which is merged into *globs*. By default, no extra globals are used.

Optional argument *test_finder* is the `DocTestFinder` object (or a drop-in replacement) that is used to extract doctests from the module.

Optional arguments *setUp*, *tearDown*, and *optionflags* are the same as for function `DocFileSuite()` above.

This function uses the same search technique as `testmod()`.

Changed in version 3.5: `DocTestSuite()` returns an empty `unittest.TestSuite` if *module* contains no docstrings instead of raising `ValueError`.

Under the covers, `DocTestSuite()` creates a `unittest.TestSuite` out of `doctest.DocTestCase` instances, and `DocTestCase` is a subclass of `unittest.TestCase`. `DocTestCase` isn't documented here (it's an internal detail), but studying its code can answer questions about the exact details of `unittest` integration.

Similarly, `DocFileSuite()` creates a `unittest.TestSuite` out of `doctest.DocFileCase` instances, and `DocFileCase` is a subclass of `DocTestCase`.

So both ways of creating a `unittest.TestSuite` run instances of `DocTestCase`. This is important for a subtle reason: when you run `doctest` functions yourself, you can control the `doctest` options in use directly, by passing option flags to `doctest` functions. However, if you're writing a `unittest` framework, `unittest` ultimately controls when and how tests get run. The framework author typically wants to control `doctest` reporting options (perhaps, e.g., specified by command line options), but there's no way to pass options through `unittest` to `doctest` test runners.

For this reason, `doctest` also supports a notion of `doctest` reporting flags specific to `unittest` support, via this function:

doctest.set_unittest_reportflags(*flags*)
>   Set the *doctest* reporting flags to use.
>
>   Argument *flags* takes the bitwise OR of option flags. See section *Option Flags*. Only "reporting flags" can be used.
>
>   This is a module-global setting, and affects all future doctests run by module *unittest*: the `runTest()` method of `DocTestCase` looks at the option flags specified for the test case when the `DocTestCase` instance was constructed. If no reporting flags were specified (which is the typical and expected case), *doctest*'s *unittest* reporting flags are bitwise ORed into the option flags, and the option flags so augmented are passed to the *DocTestRunner* instance created to run the doctest. If any reporting flags were specified when the `DocTestCase` instance was constructed, *doctest*'s *unittest* reporting flags are ignored.
>
>   The value of the *unittest* reporting flags in effect before the function was called is returned by the function.

26.3.6 Advanced API

The basic API is a simple wrapper that's intended to make doctest easy to use. It is fairly flexible, and should meet most users' needs; however, if you require more fine-grained control over testing, or wish to extend doctest's capabilities, then you should use the advanced API.

The advanced API revolves around two container classes, which are used to store the interactive examples extracted from doctest cases:

- *Example*: A single Python *statement*, paired with its expected output.
- *DocTest*: A collection of *Example*s, typically extracted from a single docstring or text file.

Additional processing classes are defined to find, parse, and run, and check doctest examples:

- *DocTestFinder*: Finds all docstrings in a given module, and uses a *DocTestParser* to create a *DocTest* from every docstring that contains interactive examples.
- *DocTestParser*: Creates a *DocTest* object from a string (such as an object's docstring).
- *DocTestRunner*: Executes the examples in a *DocTest*, and uses an *OutputChecker* to verify their output.
- *OutputChecker*: Compares the actual output from a doctest example with the expected output, and decides whether they match.

The relationships among these processing classes are summarized in the following diagram:

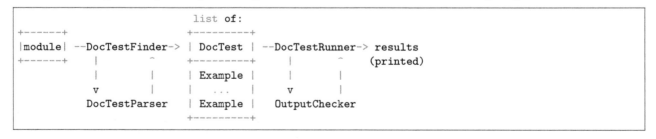

DocTest Objects

class doctest.DocTest(*examples, globs, name, filename, lineno, docstring*)
>   A collection of doctest examples that should be run in a single namespace. The constructor arguments are used to initialize the attributes of the same names.

DocTest defines the following attributes. They are initialized by the constructor, and should not be modified directly.

examples
> A list of *Example* objects encoding the individual interactive Python examples that should be run by this test.

globs
> The namespace (aka globals) that the examples should be run in. This is a dictionary mapping names to values. Any changes to the namespace made by the examples (such as binding new variables) will be reflected in *globs* after the test is run.

name
> A string name identifying the *DocTest*. Typically, this is the name of the object or file that the test was extracted from.

filename
> The name of the file that this *DocTest* was extracted from; or None if the filename is unknown, or if the *DocTest* was not extracted from a file.

lineno
> The line number within *filename* where this *DocTest* begins, or None if the line number is unavailable. This line number is zero-based with respect to the beginning of the file.

docstring
> The string that the test was extracted from, or None if the string is unavailable, or if the test was not extracted from a string.

Example Objects

class doctest.Example(*source, want, exc_msg=None, lineno=0, indent=0, options=None*)
> A single interactive example, consisting of a Python statement and its expected output. The constructor arguments are used to initialize the attributes of the same names.
>
> *Example* defines the following attributes. They are initialized by the constructor, and should not be modified directly.
>
> **source**
>> A string containing the example's source code. This source code consists of a single Python statement, and always ends with a newline; the constructor adds a newline when necessary.
>
> **want**
>> The expected output from running the example's source code (either from stdout, or a traceback in case of exception). *want* ends with a newline unless no output is expected, in which case it's an empty string. The constructor adds a newline when necessary.
>
> **exc_msg**
>> The exception message generated by the example, if the example is expected to generate an exception; or None if it is not expected to generate an exception. This exception message is compared against the return value of *traceback.format_exception_only()*. *exc_msg* ends with a newline unless it's None. The constructor adds a newline if needed.
>
> **lineno**
>> The line number within the string containing this example where the example begins. This line number is zero-based with respect to the beginning of the containing string.
>
> **indent**
>> The example's indentation in the containing string, i.e., the number of space characters that precede the example's first prompt.

options
    A dictionary mapping from option flags to `True` or `False`, which is used to override default options for this example. Any option flags not contained in this dictionary are left at their default value (as specified by the *DocTestRunner*'s `optionflags`). By default, no options are set.

DocTestFinder objects

class doctest.DocTestFinder(*verbose=False,   parser=DocTestParser(),   recurse=True,   exclude_empty=True*)

A processing class used to extract the *DocTest*s that are relevant to a given object, from its docstring and the docstrings of its contained objects. *DocTest*s can be extracted from modules, classes, functions, methods, staticmethods, classmethods, and properties.

The optional argument *verbose* can be used to display the objects searched by the finder. It defaults to `False` (no output).

The optional argument *parser* specifies the *DocTestParser* object (or a drop-in replacement) that is used to extract doctests from docstrings.

If the optional argument *recurse* is false, then *DocTestFinder.find()* will only examine the given object, and not any contained objects.

If the optional argument *exclude_empty* is false, then *DocTestFinder.find()* will include tests for objects with empty docstrings.

DocTestFinder defines the following method:

find(*obj[, name][, module][, globs][, extraglobs]*)
    Return a list of the *DocTest*s that are defined by *obj*'s docstring, or by any of its contained objects' docstrings.

   The optional argument *name* specifies the object's name; this name will be used to construct names for the returned *DocTest*s. If *name* is not specified, then `obj.__name__` is used.

   The optional parameter *module* is the module that contains the given object. If the module is not specified or is `None`, then the test finder will attempt to automatically determine the correct module. The object's module is used:

   - As a default namespace, if *globs* is not specified.
   - To prevent the DocTestFinder from extracting DocTests from objects that are imported from other modules. (Contained objects with modules other than *module* are ignored.)
   - To find the name of the file containing the object.
   - To help find the line number of the object within its file.

   If *module* is `False`, no attempt to find the module will be made. This is obscure, of use mostly in testing doctest itself: if *module* is `False`, or is `None` but cannot be found automatically, then all objects are considered to belong to the (non-existent) module, so all contained objects will (recursively) be searched for doctests.

   The globals for each *DocTest* is formed by combining *globs* and *extraglobs* (bindings in *extraglobs* override bindings in *globs*). A new shallow copy of the globals dictionary is created for each *DocTest*. If *globs* is not specified, then it defaults to the module's __dict__, if specified, or `{}` otherwise. If *extraglobs* is not specified, then it defaults to `{}`.

DocTestParser objects

class doctest.DocTestParser
    A processing class used to extract interactive examples from a string, and use them to create a *DocTest*

object.

DocTestParser defines the following methods:

get_doctest(*string, globs, name, filename, lineno*)
    Extract all doctest examples from the given string, and collect them into a *DocTest* object.

    globs, *name*, *filename*, and *lineno* are attributes for the new *DocTest* object. See the documentation for *DocTest* for more information.

get_examples(*string, name='<string>'*)
    Extract all doctest examples from the given string, and return them as a list of *Example* objects. Line numbers are 0-based. The optional argument *name* is a name identifying this string, and is only used for error messages.

parse(*string, name='<string>'*)
    Divide the given string into examples and intervening text, and return them as a list of alternating *Example*s and strings. Line numbers for the *Example*s are 0-based. The optional argument *name* is a name identifying this string, and is only used for error messages.

DocTestRunner objects

class doctest.DocTestRunner(*checker=None, verbose=None, optionflags=0*)
    A processing class used to execute and verify the interactive examples in a *DocTest*.

The comparison between expected outputs and actual outputs is done by an *OutputChecker*. This comparison may be customized with a number of option flags; see section *Option Flags* for more information. If the option flags are insufficient, then the comparison may also be customized by passing a subclass of *OutputChecker* to the constructor.

The test runner's display output can be controlled in two ways. First, an output function can be passed to **TestRunner.run()**; this function will be called with strings that should be displayed. It defaults to **sys.stdout.write**. If capturing the output is not sufficient, then the display output can be also customized by subclassing DocTestRunner, and overriding the methods *report_start()*, *report_success()*, *report_unexpected_exception()*, and *report_failure()*.

The optional keyword argument *checker* specifies the *OutputChecker* object (or drop-in replacement) that should be used to compare the expected outputs to the actual outputs of doctest examples.

The optional keyword argument *verbose* controls the *DocTestRunner*'s verbosity. If *verbose* is **True**, then information is printed about each example, as it is run. If *verbose* is **False**, then only failures are printed. If *verbose* is unspecified, or **None**, then verbose output is used iff the command-line switch -v is used.

The optional keyword argument *optionflags* can be used to control how the test runner compares expected output to actual output, and how it displays failures. For more information, see section *Option Flags*.

DocTestParser defines the following methods:

report_start(*out, test, example*)
    Report that the test runner is about to process the given example. This method is provided to allow subclasses of *DocTestRunner* to customize their output; it should not be called directly.

    example is the example about to be processed. *test* is the test *containing example*. *out* is the output function that was passed to *DocTestRunner.run()*.

report_success(*out, test, example, got*)
    Report that the given example ran successfully. This method is provided to allow subclasses of *DocTestRunner* to customize their output; it should not be called directly.

example is the example about to be processed. *got* is the actual output from the example. *test* is the test containing *example*. *out* is the output function that was passed to `DocTestRunner.run()`.

report_failure(*out, test, example, got*)
Report that the given example failed. This method is provided to allow subclasses of `DocTestRunner` to customize their output; it should not be called directly.

example is the example about to be processed. *got* is the actual output from the example. *test* is the test containing *example*. *out* is the output function that was passed to `DocTestRunner.run()`.

report_unexpected_exception(*out, test, example, exc_info*)
Report that the given example raised an unexpected exception. This method is provided to allow subclasses of `DocTestRunner` to customize their output; it should not be called directly.

example is the example about to be processed. *exc_info* is a tuple containing information about the unexpected exception (as returned by `sys.exc_info()`). *test* is the test containing *example*. *out* is the output function that was passed to `DocTestRunner.run()`.

run(*test, compileflags=None, out=None, clear_globs=True*)
Run the examples in *test* (a `DocTest` object), and display the results using the writer function *out*.

The examples are run in the namespace `test.globs`. If *clear_globs* is true (the default), then this namespace will be cleared after the test runs, to help with garbage collection. If you would like to examine the namespace after the test completes, then use *clear_globs=False*.

compileflags gives the set of flags that should be used by the Python compiler when running the examples. If not specified, then it will default to the set of future-import flags that apply to *globs*.

The output of each example is checked using the `DocTestRunner`'s output checker, and the results are formatted by the `DocTestRunner.report_*()` methods.

summarize(*verbose=None*)
Print a summary of all the test cases that have been run by this DocTestRunner, and return a *named tuple* `TestResults(failed, attempted)`.

The optional *verbose* argument controls how detailed the summary is. If the verbosity is not specified, then the `DocTestRunner`'s verbosity is used.

OutputChecker objects

class doctest.OutputChecker
A class used to check the whether the actual output from a doctest example matches the expected output. *OutputChecker* defines two methods: `check_output()`, which compares a given pair of outputs, and returns true if they match; and `output_difference()`, which returns a string describing the differences between two outputs.

OutputChecker defines the following methods:

check_output(*want, got, optionflags*)
Return `True` iff the actual output from an example (*got*) matches the expected output (*want*). These strings are always considered to match if they are identical; but depending on what option flags the test runner is using, several non-exact match types are also possible. See section *Option Flags* for more information about option flags.

output_difference(*example, got, optionflags*)
Return a string describing the differences between the expected output for a given example (*example*) and the actual output (*got*). *optionflags* is the set of option flags used to compare *want* and *got*.

26.3.7 Debugging

Doctest provides several mechanisms for debugging doctest examples:

- Several functions convert doctests to executable Python programs, which can be run under the Python debugger, *pdb*.
- The *DebugRunner* class is a subclass of *DocTestRunner* that raises an exception for the first failing example, containing information about that example. This information can be used to perform post-mortem debugging on the example.
- The *unittest* cases generated by *DocTestSuite()* support the *debug()* method defined by *unittest.TestCase*.
- You can add a call to *pdb.set_trace()* in a doctest example, and you'll drop into the Python debugger when that line is executed. Then you can inspect current values of variables, and so on. For example, suppose `a.py` contains just this module docstring:

```
"""
>>> def f(x):
...     g(x*2)
>>> def g(x):
...     print(x+3)
...     import pdb; pdb.set_trace()
>>> f(3)
9
"""
```

Then an interactive Python session may look like this:

```
>>> import a, doctest
>>> doctest.testmod(a)
--Return--
> <doctest a[1]>(3)g()->None
-> import pdb; pdb.set_trace()
(Pdb) list
  1     def g(x):
  2         print(x+3)
  3  ->     import pdb; pdb.set_trace()
[EOF]
(Pdb) p x
6
(Pdb) step
--Return--
> <doctest a[0]>(2)f()->None
-> g(x*2)
(Pdb) list
  1     def f(x):
  2  ->     g(x*2)
[EOF]
(Pdb) p x
3
(Pdb) step
--Return--
> <doctest a[2]>(1)?()->None
-> f(3)
(Pdb) cont
(0, 3)
>>>
```

Functions that convert doctests to Python code, and possibly run the synthesized code under the debugger:

doctest.script_from_examples(*s*)
> Convert text with examples to a script.
>
> Argument *s* is a string containing doctest examples. The string is converted to a Python script, where doctest examples in *s* are converted to regular code, and everything else is converted to Python comments. The generated script is returned as a string. For example,
>
> ```
> import doctest
> print(doctest.script_from_examples(r"""
>     Set x and y to 1 and 2.
>     >>> x, y = 1, 2
>
>     Print their sum:
>     >>> print(x+y)
>     3
> """))
> ```
>
> displays:
>
> ```
> # Set x and y to 1 and 2.
> x, y = 1, 2
> #
> # Print their sum:
> print(x+y)
> # Expected:
> ## 3
> ```
>
> This function is used internally by other functions (see below), but can also be useful when you want to transform an interactive Python session into a Python script.

doctest.testsource(*module*, *name*)
> Convert the doctest for an object to a script.
>
> Argument *module* is a module object, or dotted name of a module, containing the object whose doctests are of interest. Argument *name* is the name (within the module) of the object with the doctests of interest. The result is a string, containing the object's docstring converted to a Python script, as described for *script_from_examples()* above. For example, if module `a.py` contains a top-level function `f()`, then
>
> ```
> import a, doctest
> print(doctest.testsource(a, "a.f"))
> ```
>
> prints a script version of function `f()`'s docstring, with doctests converted to code, and the rest placed in comments.

doctest.debug(*module*, *name*, *pm=False*)
> Debug the doctests for an object.
>
> The *module* and *name* arguments are the same as for function *testsource()* above. The synthesized Python script for the named object's docstring is written to a temporary file, and then that file is run under the control of the Python debugger, *pdb*.
>
> A shallow copy of `module.__dict__` is used for both local and global execution context.
>
> Optional argument *pm* controls whether post-mortem debugging is used. If *pm* has a true value, the script file is run directly, and the debugger gets involved only if the script terminates via raising an unhandled exception. If it does, then post-mortem debugging is invoked, via *pdb.post_mortem()*,

passing the traceback object from the unhandled exception. If *pm* is not specified, or is false, the script is run under the debugger from the start, via passing an appropriate `exec()` call to `pdb.run()`.

doctest.debug_src(*src, pm=False, globs=None*)
Debug the doctests in a string.

This is like function `debug()` above, except that a string containing doctest examples is specified directly, via the *src* argument.

Optional argument *pm* has the same meaning as in function `debug()` above.

Optional argument *globs* gives a dictionary to use as both local and global execution context. If not specified, or `None`, an empty dictionary is used. If specified, a shallow copy of the dictionary is used.

The `DebugRunner` class, and the special exceptions it may raise, are of most interest to testing framework authors, and will only be sketched here. See the source code, and especially `DebugRunner`'s docstring (which is a doctest!) for more details:

class doctest.DebugRunner(*checker=None, verbose=None, optionflags=0*)

A subclass of `DocTestRunner` that raises an exception as soon as a failure is encountered. If an unexpected exception occurs, an `UnexpectedException` exception is raised, containing the test, the example, and the original exception. If the output doesn't match, then a `DocTestFailure` exception is raised, containing the test, the example, and the actual output.

For information about the constructor parameters and methods, see the documentation for `DocTestRunner` in section *Advanced API*.

There are two exceptions that may be raised by `DebugRunner` instances:

exception doctest.DocTestFailure(*test, example, got*)
An exception raised by `DocTestRunner` to signal that a doctest example's actual output did not match its expected output. The constructor arguments are used to initialize the attributes of the same names.

`DocTestFailure` defines the following attributes:

DocTestFailure.test
The `DocTest` object that was being run when the example failed.

DocTestFailure.example
The `Example` that failed.

DocTestFailure.got
The example's actual output.

exception doctest.UnexpectedException(*test, example, exc_info*)
An exception raised by `DocTestRunner` to signal that a doctest example raised an unexpected exception. The constructor arguments are used to initialize the attributes of the same names.

`UnexpectedException` defines the following attributes:

UnexpectedException.test
The `DocTest` object that was being run when the example failed.

UnexpectedException.example
The `Example` that failed.

UnexpectedException.exc_info
A tuple containing information about the unexpected exception, as returned by `sys.exc_info()`.

26.3.8 Soapbox

As mentioned in the introduction, `doctest` has grown to have three primary uses:

1. Checking examples in docstrings.

2. Regression testing.

3. Executable documentation / literate testing.

These uses have different requirements, and it is important to distinguish them. In particular, filling your docstrings with obscure test cases makes for bad documentation.

When writing a docstring, choose docstring examples with care. There's an art to this that needs to be learned—it may not be natural at first. Examples should add genuine value to the documentation. A good example can often be worth many words. If done with care, the examples will be invaluable for your users, and will pay back the time it takes to collect them many times over as the years go by and things change. I'm still amazed at how often one of my *doctest* examples stops working after a "harmless" change.

Doctest also makes an excellent tool for regression testing, especially if you don't skimp on explanatory text. By interleaving prose and examples, it becomes much easier to keep track of what's actually being tested, and why. When a test fails, good prose can make it much easier to figure out what the problem is, and how it should be fixed. It's true that you could write extensive comments in code-based testing, but few programmers do. Many have found that using doctest approaches instead leads to much clearer tests. Perhaps this is simply because doctest makes writing prose a little easier than writing code, while writing comments in code is a little harder. I think it goes deeper than just that: the natural attitude when writing a doctest-based test is that you want to explain the fine points of your software, and illustrate them with examples. This in turn naturally leads to test files that start with the simplest features, and logically progress to complications and edge cases. A coherent narrative is the result, instead of a collection of isolated functions that test isolated bits of functionality seemingly at random. It's a different attitude, and produces different results, blurring the distinction between testing and explaining.

Regression testing is best confined to dedicated objects or files. There are several options for organizing tests:

- Write text files containing test cases as interactive examples, and test the files using *testfile()* or *DocFileSuite()*. This is recommended, although is easiest to do for new projects, designed from the start to use doctest.

- Define functions named `_regrtest_topic` that consist of single docstrings, containing test cases for the named topics. These functions can be included in the same file as the module, or separated out into a separate test file.

- Define a `__test__` dictionary mapping from regression test topics to docstrings containing test cases.

When you have placed your tests in a module, the module can itself be the test runner. When a test fails, you can arrange for your test runner to re-run only the failing doctest while you debug the problem. Here is a minimal example of such a test runner:

```python
if __name__ == '__main__':
    import doctest
    flags = doctest.REPORT_NDIFF|doctest.FAIL_FAST
    if len(sys.argv) > 1:
        name = sys.argv[1]
        if name in globals():
            obj = globals()[name]
        else:
            obj = __test__[name]
        doctest.run_docstring_examples(obj, globals(), name=name,
                                       optionflags=flags)
    else:
        fail, total = doctest.testmod(optionflags=flags)
        print("{} failures out of {} tests".format(fail, total))
```

26.4 unittest — Unit testing framework

Source code: Lib/unittest/__init__.py

(If you are already familiar with the basic concepts of testing, you might want to skip to *the list of assert methods*.)

The *unittest* unit testing framework was originally inspired by JUnit and has a similar flavor as major unit testing frameworks in other languages. It supports test automation, sharing of setup and shutdown code for tests, aggregation of tests into collections, and independence of the tests from the reporting framework.

To achieve this, *unittest* supports some important concepts in an object-oriented way:

test fixture A *test fixture* represents the preparation needed to perform one or more tests, and any associate cleanup actions. This may involve, for example, creating temporary or proxy databases, directories, or starting a server process.

test case A *test case* is the individual unit of testing. It checks for a specific response to a particular set of inputs. *unittest* provides a base class, *TestCase*, which may be used to create new test cases.

test suite A *test suite* is a collection of test cases, test suites, or both. It is used to aggregate tests that should be executed together.

test runner A *test runner* is a component which orchestrates the execution of tests and provides the outcome to the user. The runner may use a graphical interface, a textual interface, or return a special value to indicate the results of executing the tests.

See also:

Module *doctest* Another test-support module with a very different flavor.

Simple Smalltalk Testing: With Patterns Kent Beck's original paper on testing frameworks using the pattern shared by *unittest*.

Nose and py.test Third-party unittest frameworks with a lighter-weight syntax for writing tests. For example, `assert func(10) == 42`.

The Python Testing Tools Taxonomy An extensive list of Python testing tools including functional testing frameworks and mock object libraries.

Testing in Python Mailing List A special-interest-group for discussion of testing, and testing tools, in Python.

The script `Tools/unittestgui/unittestgui.py` in the Python source distribution is a GUI tool for test discovery and execution. This is intended largely for ease of use for those new to unit testing. For production environments it is recommended that tests be driven by a continuous integration system such as Buildbot, Jenkins or Hudson.

26.4.1 Basic example

The *unittest* module provides a rich set of tools for constructing and running tests. This section demonstrates that a small subset of the tools suffice to meet the needs of most users.

Here is a short script to test three string methods:

```
import unittest

class TestStringMethods(unittest.TestCase):

    def test_upper(self):
```

```
        self.assertEqual('foo'.upper(), 'FOO')

    def test_isupper(self):
        self.assertTrue('FOO'.isupper())
        self.assertFalse('Foo'.isupper())

    def test_split(self):
        s = 'hello world'
        self.assertEqual(s.split(), ['hello', 'world'])
        # check that s.split fails when the separator is not a string
        with self.assertRaises(TypeError):
            s.split(2)

if __name__ == '__main__':
    unittest.main()
```

A testcase is created by subclassing *unittest.TestCase*. The three individual tests are defined with methods whose names start with the letters `test`. This naming convention informs the test runner about which methods represent tests.

The crux of each test is a call to *assertEqual()* to check for an expected result; *assertTrue()* or *assertFalse()* to verify a condition; or *assertRaises()* to verify that a specific exception gets raised. These methods are used instead of the `assert` statement so the test runner can accumulate all test results and produce a report.

The *setUp()* and *tearDown()* methods allow you to define instructions that will be executed before and after each test method. They are covered in more detail in the section *Organizing test code*.

The final block shows a simple way to run the tests. *unittest.main()* provides a command-line interface to the test script. When run from the command line, the above script produces an output that looks like this:

```
...
----------------------------------------------------------------------
Ran 3 tests in 0.000s

OK
```

Passing the -v option to your test script will instruct *unittest.main()* to enable a higher level of verbosity, and produce the following output:

```
test_isupper (__main__.TestStringMethods) ... ok
test_split (__main__.TestStringMethods) ... ok
test_upper (__main__.TestStringMethods) ... ok

----------------------------------------------------------------------
Ran 3 tests in 0.001s

OK
```

The above examples show the most commonly used *unittest* features which are sufficient to meet many everyday testing needs. The remainder of the documentation explores the full feature set from first principles.

26.4.2 Command-Line Interface

The unittest module can be used from the command line to run tests from modules, classes or even individual test methods:

```
python -m unittest test_module1 test_module2
python -m unittest test_module.TestClass
python -m unittest test_module.TestClass.test_method
```

You can pass in a list with any combination of module names, and fully qualified class or method names.

Test modules can be specified by file path as well:

```
python -m unittest tests/test_something.py
```

This allows you to use the shell filename completion to specify the test module. The file specified must still be importable as a module. The path is converted to a module name by removing the '.py' and converting path separators into '.'. If you want to execute a test file that isn't importable as a module you should execute the file directly instead.

You can run tests with more detail (higher verbosity) by passing in the -v flag:

```
python -m unittest -v test_module
```

When executed without arguments *Test Discovery* is started:

```
python -m unittest
```

For a list of all the command-line options:

```
python -m unittest -h
```

Changed in version 3.2: In earlier versions it was only possible to run individual test methods and not modules or classes.

Command-line options

unittest supports these command-line options:

-b, --buffer
: The standard output and standard error streams are buffered during the test run. Output during a passing test is discarded. Output is echoed normally on test fail or error and is added to the failure messages.

-c, --catch
: Control-C during the test run waits for the current test to end and then reports all the results so far. A second Control-C raises the normal *KeyboardInterrupt* exception.

  See *Signal Handling* for the functions that provide this functionality.

-f, --failfast
: Stop the test run on the first error or failure.

--locals
: Show local variables in tracebacks.

New in version 3.2: The command-line options -b, -c and -f were added.

New in version 3.5: The command-line option --locals.

The command line can also be used for test discovery, for running all of the tests in a project or just a subset.

26.4.3 Test Discovery

New in version 3.2.

Unittest supports simple test discovery. In order to be compatible with test discovery, all of the test files must be modules or packages (including *namespace packages*) importable from the top-level directory of the project (this means that their filenames must be valid identifiers).

Test discovery is implemented in `TestLoader.discover()`, but can also be used from the command line. The basic command-line usage is:

```
cd project_directory
python -m unittest discover
```

Note: As a shortcut, `python -m unittest` is the equivalent of `python -m unittest discover`. If you want to pass arguments to test discovery the `discover` sub-command must be used explicitly.

The `discover` sub-command has the following options:

-v, --verbose
: Verbose output

-s, --start-directory directory
: Directory to start discovery (. default)

-p, --pattern pattern
: Pattern to match test files (`test*.py` default)

-t, --top-level-directory directory
: Top level directory of project (defaults to start directory)

The -s, -p, and -t options can be passed in as positional arguments in that order. The following two command lines are equivalent:

```
python -m unittest discover -s project_directory -p "*_test.py"
python -m unittest discover project_directory "*_test.py"
```

As well as being a path it is possible to pass a package name, for example `myproject.subpackage.test`, as the start directory. The package name you supply will then be imported and its location on the filesystem will be used as the start directory.

> **Caution:** Test discovery loads tests by importing them. Once test discovery has found all the test files from the start directory you specify it turns the paths into package names to import. For example `foo/bar/baz.py` will be imported as `foo.bar.baz`.
>
> If you have a package installed globally and attempt test discovery on a different copy of the package then the import *could* happen from the wrong place. If this happens test discovery will warn you and exit.
>
> If you supply the start directory as a package name rather than a path to a directory then discover assumes that whichever location it imports from is the location you intended, so you will not get the warning.

Test modules and packages can customize test loading and discovery by through the *load_tests protocol*.

Changed in version 3.4: Test discovery supports *namespace packages*.

26.4.4 Organizing test code

The basic building blocks of unit testing are *test cases* — single scenarios that must be set up and checked for correctness. In `unittest`, test cases are represented by `unittest.TestCase` instances. To make your own test cases you must write subclasses of `TestCase` or use `FunctionTestCase`.

The testing code of a `TestCase` instance should be entirely self contained, such that it can be run either in isolation or in arbitrary combination with any number of other test cases.

The simplest `TestCase` subclass will simply implement a test method (i.e. a method whose name starts with `test`) in order to perform specific testing code:

```python
import unittest

class DefaultWidgetSizeTestCase(unittest.TestCase):
    def test_default_widget_size(self):
        widget = Widget('The widget')
        self.assertEqual(widget.size(), (50, 50))
```

Note that in order to test something, we use one of the `assert*()` methods provided by the `TestCase` base class. If the test fails, an exception will be raised, and `unittest` will identify the test case as a *failure*. Any other exceptions will be treated as *errors*.

Tests can be numerous, and their set-up can be repetitive. Luckily, we can factor out set-up code by implementing a method called `setUp()`, which the testing framework will automatically call for every single test we run:

```python
import unittest

class WidgetTestCase(unittest.TestCase):
    def setUp(self):
        self.widget = Widget('The widget')

    def test_default_widget_size(self):
        self.assertEqual(self.widget.size(), (50,50),
                         'incorrect default size')

    def test_widget_resize(self):
        self.widget.resize(100,150)
        self.assertEqual(self.widget.size(), (100,150),
                         'wrong size after resize')
```

Note: The order in which the various tests will be run is determined by sorting the test method names with respect to the built-in ordering for strings.

If the `setUp()` method raises an exception while the test is running, the framework will consider the test to have suffered an error, and the test method will not be executed.

Similarly, we can provide a `tearDown()` method that tidies up after the test method has been run:

```python
import unittest

class WidgetTestCase(unittest.TestCase):
    def setUp(self):
        self.widget = Widget('The widget')

    def tearDown(self):
        self.widget.dispose()
```

If *setUp()* succeeded, *tearDown()* will be run whether the test method succeeded or not.

Such a working environment for the testing code is called a *fixture*.

Test case instances are grouped together according to the features they test. *unittest* provides a mechanism for this: the *test suite*, represented by *unittest*'s *TestSuite* class. In most cases, calling *unittest.main()* will do the right thing and collect all the module's test cases for you, and then execute them.

However, should you want to customize the building of your test suite, you can do it yourself:

```
def suite():
    suite = unittest.TestSuite()
    suite.addTest(WidgetTestCase('test_default_widget_size'))
    suite.addTest(WidgetTestCase('test_widget_resize'))
    return suite

if __name__ == '__main__':
    runner = unittest.TextTestRunner()
    runner.run(suite())
```

You can place the definitions of test cases and test suites in the same modules as the code they are to test (such as `widget.py`), but there are several advantages to placing the test code in a separate module, such as `test_widget.py`:

- The test module can be run standalone from the command line.
- The test code can more easily be separated from shipped code.
- There is less temptation to change test code to fit the code it tests without a good reason.
- Test code should be modified much less frequently than the code it tests.
- Tested code can be refactored more easily.
- Tests for modules written in C must be in separate modules anyway, so why not be consistent?
- If the testing strategy changes, there is no need to change the source code.

26.4.5 Re-using old test code

Some users will find that they have existing test code that they would like to run from *unittest*, without converting every old test function to a *TestCase* subclass.

For this reason, *unittest* provides a *FunctionTestCase* class. This subclass of *TestCase* can be used to wrap an existing test function. Set-up and tear-down functions can also be provided.

Given the following test function:

```
def testSomething():
    something = makeSomething()
    assert something.name is not None
    # ...
```

one can create an equivalent test case instance as follows, with optional set-up and tear-down methods:

```
testcase = unittest.FunctionTestCase(testSomething,
                                     setUp=makeSomethingDB,
                                     tearDown=deleteSomethingDB)
```

Note: Even though `FunctionTestCase` can be used to quickly convert an existing test base over to a `unittest`-based system, this approach is not recommended. Taking the time to set up proper `TestCase` subclasses will make future test refactorings infinitely easier.

In some cases, the existing tests may have been written using the `doctest` module. If so, `doctest` provides a `DocTestSuite` class that can automatically build `unittest.TestSuite` instances from the existing `doctest`-based tests.

26.4.6 Skipping tests and expected failures

New in version 3.1.

Unittest supports skipping individual test methods and even whole classes of tests. In addition, it supports marking a test as an "expected failure," a test that is broken and will fail, but shouldn't be counted as a failure on a `TestResult`.

Skipping a test is simply a matter of using the `skip()` *decorator* or one of its conditional variants.

Basic skipping looks like this:

```python
class MyTestCase(unittest.TestCase):

    @unittest.skip("demonstrating skipping")
    def test_nothing(self):
        self.fail("shouldn't happen")

    @unittest.skipIf(mylib.__version__ < (1, 3),
                     "not supported in this library version")
    def test_format(self):
        # Tests that work for only a certain version of the library.
        pass

    @unittest.skipUnless(sys.platform.startswith("win"), "requires Windows")
    def test_windows_support(self):
        # windows specific testing code
        pass
```

This is the output of running the example above in verbose mode:

```
test_format (__main__.MyTestCase) ... skipped 'not supported in this library version'
test_nothing (__main__.MyTestCase) ... skipped 'demonstrating skipping'
test_windows_support (__main__.MyTestCase) ... skipped 'requires Windows'

----------------------------------------------------------------------
Ran 3 tests in 0.005s

OK (skipped=3)
```

Classes can be skipped just like methods:

```python
@unittest.skip("showing class skipping")
class MySkippedTestCase(unittest.TestCase):
    def test_not_run(self):
        pass
```

`TestCase.setUp()` can also skip the test. This is useful when a resource that needs to be set up is not available.

Expected failures use the *expectedFailure()* decorator.

```
class ExpectedFailureTestCase(unittest.TestCase):
    @unittest.expectedFailure
    def test_fail(self):
        self.assertEqual(1, 0, "broken")
```

It's easy to roll your own skipping decorators by making a decorator that calls *skip()* on the test when it wants it to be skipped. This decorator skips the test unless the passed object has a certain attribute:

```
def skipUnlessHasattr(obj, attr):
    if hasattr(obj, attr):
        return lambda func: func
    return unittest.skip("{!r} doesn't have {!r}".format(obj, attr))
```

The following decorators implement test skipping and expected failures:

@unittest.**skip**(*reason*)
: Unconditionally skip the decorated test. *reason* should describe why the test is being skipped.

@unittest.**skipIf**(*condition*, *reason*)
: Skip the decorated test if *condition* is true.

@unittest.**skipUnless**(*condition*, *reason*)
: Skip the decorated test unless *condition* is true.

@unittest.**expectedFailure**
: Mark the test as an expected failure. If the test fails when run, the test is not counted as a failure.

exception unittest.**SkipTest**(*reason*)
: This exception is raised to skip a test.

    Usually you can use *TestCase.skipTest()* or one of the skipping decorators instead of raising this directly.

Skipped tests will not have *setUp()* or *tearDown()* run around them. Skipped classes will not have *setUpClass()* or *tearDownClass()* run. Skipped modules will not have **setUpModule()** or **tearDownModule()** run.

26.4.7 Distinguishing test iterations using subtests

New in version 3.4.

When some of your tests differ only by a some very small differences, for instance some parameters, unittest allows you to distinguish them inside the body of a test method using the *subTest()* context manager.

For example, the following test:

```
class NumbersTest(unittest.TestCase):

    def test_even(self):
        """
        Test that numbers between 0 and 5 are all even.
        """
        for i in range(0, 6):
            with self.subTest(i=i):
                self.assertEqual(i % 2, 0)
```

will produce the following output:

```
======================================================================
FAIL: test_even (__main__.NumbersTest) (i=1)
----------------------------------------------------------------------
Traceback (most recent call last):
  File "subtests.py", line 32, in test_even
    self.assertEqual(i % 2, 0)
AssertionError: 1 != 0

======================================================================
FAIL: test_even (__main__.NumbersTest) (i=3)
----------------------------------------------------------------------
Traceback (most recent call last):
  File "subtests.py", line 32, in test_even
    self.assertEqual(i % 2, 0)
AssertionError: 1 != 0

======================================================================
FAIL: test_even (__main__.NumbersTest) (i=5)
----------------------------------------------------------------------
Traceback (most recent call last):
  File "subtests.py", line 32, in test_even
    self.assertEqual(i % 2, 0)
AssertionError: 1 != 0
```

Without using a subtest, execution would stop after the first failure, and the error would be less easy to diagnose because the value of i wouldn't be displayed:

```
======================================================================
FAIL: test_even (__main__.NumbersTest)
----------------------------------------------------------------------
Traceback (most recent call last):
  File "subtests.py", line 32, in test_even
    self.assertEqual(i % 2, 0)
AssertionError: 1 != 0
```

26.4.8 Classes and functions

This section describes in depth the API of *unittest*.

Test cases

class unittest.TestCase(*methodName='runTest'*)

Instances of the *TestCase* class represent the logical test units in the *unittest* universe. This class is intended to be used as a base class, with specific tests being implemented by concrete subclasses. This class implements the interface needed by the test runner to allow it to drive the tests, and methods that the test code can use to check for and report various kinds of failure.

Each instance of *TestCase* will run a single base method: the method named *methodName*. In most uses of *TestCase*, you will neither change the *methodName* nor reimplement the default runTest() method.

Changed in version 3.2: *TestCase* can be instantiated successfully without providing a *methodName*. This makes it easier to experiment with *TestCase* from the interactive interpreter.

TestCase instances provide three groups of methods: one group used to run the test, another used by the test implementation to check conditions and report failures, and some inquiry methods allowing information about the test itself to be gathered.

Methods in the first group (running the test) are:

setUp()
> Method called to prepare the test fixture. This is called immediately before calling the test method; other than *AssertionError* or *SkipTest*, any exception raised by this method will be considered an error rather than a test failure. The default implementation does nothing.

tearDown()
> Method called immediately after the test method has been called and the result recorded. This is called even if the test method raised an exception, so the implementation in subclasses may need to be particularly careful about checking internal state. Any exception, other than *AssertionError* or *SkipTest*, raised by this method will be considered an additional error rather than a test failure (thus increasing the total number of reported errors). This method will only be called if the *setUp()* succeeds, regardless of the outcome of the test method. The default implementation does nothing.

setUpClass()
> A class method called before tests in an individual class run. setUpClass is called with the class as the only argument and must be decorated as a *classmethod()*:
>
> ```
> @classmethod
> def setUpClass(cls):
>     ...
> ```
>
> See *Class and Module Fixtures* for more details.
>
> New in version 3.2.

tearDownClass()
> A class method called after tests in an individual class have run. tearDownClass is called with the class as the only argument and must be decorated as a *classmethod()*:
>
> ```
> @classmethod
> def tearDownClass(cls):
>     ...
> ```
>
> See *Class and Module Fixtures* for more details.
>
> New in version 3.2.

run(result=None**)**
> Run the test, collecting the result into the *TestResult* object passed as *result*. If *result* is omitted or None, a temporary result object is created (by calling the *defaultTestResult()* method) and used. The result object is returned to *run()*'s caller.
>
> The same effect may be had by simply calling the *TestCase* instance.
>
> Changed in version 3.3: Previous versions of **run** did not return the result. Neither did calling an instance.

skipTest(reason**)**
> Calling this during a test method or *setUp()* skips the current test. See *Skipping tests and expected failures* for more information.
>
> New in version 3.1.

subTest(msg=None, **params**)**
> Return a context manager which executes the enclosed code block as a subtest. *msg* and *params* are optional, arbitrary values which are displayed whenever a subtest fails, allowing you to identify them clearly.

A test case can contain any number of subtest declarations, and they can be arbitrarily nested.

See *Distinguishing test iterations using subtests* for more information.

New in version 3.4.

debug()
> Run the test without collecting the result. This allows exceptions raised by the test to be propagated to the caller, and can be used to support running tests under a debugger.

The `TestCase` class provides several assert methods to check for and report failures. The following table lists the most commonly used methods (see the tables below for more assert methods):

Method	Checks that	New in
`assertEqual(a, b)`	`a == b`	
`assertNotEqual(a, b)`	`a != b`	
`assertTrue(x)`	`bool(x) is True`	
`assertFalse(x)`	`bool(x) is False`	
`assertIs(a, b)`	`a is b`	3.1
`assertIsNot(a, b)`	`a is not b`	3.1
`assertIsNone(x)`	`x is None`	3.1
`assertIsNotNone(x)`	`x is not None`	3.1
`assertIn(a, b)`	`a in b`	3.1
`assertNotIn(a, b)`	`a not in b`	3.1
`assertIsInstance(a, b)`	`isinstance(a, b)`	3.2
`assertNotIsInstance(a, b)`	`not isinstance(a, b)`	3.2

All the assert methods accept a *msg* argument that, if specified, is used as the error message on failure (see also `longMessage`). Note that the *msg* keyword argument can be passed to `assertRaises()`, `assertRaisesRegex()`, `assertWarns()`, `assertWarnsRegex()` only when they are used as a context manager.

assertEqual(*first*, *second*, *msg=None*)
> Test that *first* and *second* are equal. If the values do not compare equal, the test will fail.
>
> In addition, if *first* and *second* are the exact same type and one of list, tuple, dict, set, frozenset or str or any type that a subclass registers with `addTypeEqualityFunc()` the type-specific equality function will be called in order to generate a more useful default error message (see also the *list of type-specific methods*).
>
> Changed in version 3.1: Added the automatic calling of type-specific equality function.
>
> Changed in version 3.2: `assertMultiLineEqual()` added as the default type equality function for comparing strings.

assertNotEqual(*first*, *second*, *msg=None*)
> Test that *first* and *second* are not equal. If the values do compare equal, the test will fail.

assertTrue(*expr*, *msg=None*)
assertFalse(*expr*, *msg=None*)
> Test that *expr* is true (or false).
>
> Note that this is equivalent to `bool(expr) is True` and not to `expr is True` (use `assertIs(expr, True)` for the latter). This method should also be avoided when more specific methods are available (e.g. `assertEqual(a, b)` instead of `assertTrue(a == b)`), because they provide a better error message in case of failure.

assertIs(*first*, *second*, *msg=None*)
assertIsNot(*first*, *second*, *msg=None*)
> Test that *first* and *second* evaluate (or don't evaluate) to the same object.

New in version 3.1.

assertIsNone(*expr, msg=None*)
assertIsNotNone(*expr, msg=None*)
   Test that *expr* is (or is not) None.

   New in version 3.1.

assertIn(*first, second, msg=None*)
assertNotIn(*first, second, msg=None*)
   Test that *first* is (or is not) in *second*.

   New in version 3.1.

assertIsInstance(*obj, cls, msg=None*)
assertNotIsInstance(*obj, cls, msg=None*)
   Test that *obj* is (or is not) an instance of *cls* (which can be a class or a tuple of classes, as supported by `isinstance()`). To check for the exact type, use `assertIs(type(obj), cls)`.

   New in version 3.2.

It is also possible to check the production of exceptions, warnings, and log messages using the following methods:

Method	Checks that	New in
`assertRaises(exc, fun, *args, **kwds)`	`fun(*args, **kwds)` raises *exc*	
`assertRaisesRegex(exc, r, fun, *args, **kwds)`	`fun(*args, **kwds)` raises *exc* and the message matches regex *r*	3.1
`assertWarns(warn, fun, *args, **kwds)`	`fun(*args, **kwds)` raises *warn*	3.2
`assertWarnsRegex(warn, r, fun, *args, **kwds)`	`fun(*args, **kwds)` raises *warn* and the message matches regex *r*	3.2
`assertLogs(logger, level)`	The `with` block logs on *logger* with minimum *level*	3.4

assertRaises(*exception, callable, *args, **kwds*)
assertRaises(*exception, msg=None*)
   Test that an exception is raised when *callable* is called with any positional or keyword arguments that are also passed to `assertRaises()`. The test passes if *exception* is raised, is an error if another exception is raised, or fails if no exception is raised. To catch any of a group of exceptions, a tuple containing the exception classes may be passed as *exception*.

   If only the *exception* and possibly the *msg* arguments are given, return a context manager so that the code under test can be written inline rather than as a function:

```
with self.assertRaises(SomeException):
    do_something()
```

   When used as a context manager, `assertRaises()` accepts the additional keyword argument *msg*.

   The context manager will store the caught exception object in its `exception` attribute. This can be useful if the intention is to perform additional checks on the exception raised:

```
with self.assertRaises(SomeException) as cm:
    do_something()

the_exception = cm.exception
self.assertEqual(the_exception.error_code, 3)
```

Changed in version 3.1: Added the ability to use *assertRaises()* as a context manager.

Changed in version 3.2: Added the `exception` attribute.

Changed in version 3.3: Added the *msg* keyword argument when used as a context manager.

assertRaisesRegex(*exception, regex, callable, *args, **kwds*)
assertRaisesRegex(*exception, regex, msg=None*)

    Like *assertRaises()* but also tests that *regex* matches on the string representation of the raised exception. *regex* may be a regular expression object or a string containing a regular expression suitable for use by *re.search()*. Examples:

```
self.assertRaisesRegex(ValueError, "invalid literal for.*XYZ'$",
                       int, 'XYZ')
```

or:

```
with self.assertRaisesRegex(ValueError, 'literal'):
   int('XYZ')
```

New in version 3.1: under the name **assertRaisesRegexp**.

Changed in version 3.2: Renamed to *assertRaisesRegex()*.

Changed in version 3.3: Added the *msg* keyword argument when used as a context manager.

assertWarns(*warning, callable, *args, **kwds*)
assertWarns(*warning, msg=None*)

    Test that a warning is triggered when *callable* is called with any positional or keyword arguments that are also passed to *assertWarns()*. The test passes if *warning* is triggered and fails if it isn't. Any exception is an error. To catch any of a group of warnings, a tuple containing the warning classes may be passed as *warnings*.

    If only the *warning* and possibly the *msg* arguments are given, return a context manager so that the code under test can be written inline rather than as a function:

```
with self.assertWarns(SomeWarning):
   do_something()
```

    When used as a context manager, *assertWarns()* accepts the additional keyword argument *msg*.

    The context manager will store the caught warning object in its `warning` attribute, and the source line which triggered the warnings in the `filename` and `lineno` attributes. This can be useful if the intention is to perform additional checks on the warning caught:

```
with self.assertWarns(SomeWarning) as cm:
   do_something()

self.assertIn('myfile.py', cm.filename)
self.assertEqual(320, cm.lineno)
```

    This method works regardless of the warning filters in place when it is called.

    New in version 3.2.

    Changed in version 3.3: Added the *msg* keyword argument when used as a context manager.

assertWarnsRegex(*warning, regex, callable, *args, **kwds*)
assertWarnsRegex(*warning, regex, msg=None*)

    Like *assertWarns()* but also tests that *regex* matches on the message of the triggered warning. *regex* may be a regular expression object or a string containing a regular expression suitable for use by *re.search()*. Example:

```
self.assertWarnsRegex(DeprecationWarning,
                      r'legacy_function\(\) is deprecated',
                      legacy_function, 'XYZ')
```

or:

```
with self.assertWarnsRegex(RuntimeWarning, 'unsafe frobnicating'):
    frobnicate('/etc/passwd')
```

New in version 3.2.

Changed in version 3.3: Added the *msg* keyword argument when used as a context manager.

assertLogs(*logger=None, level=None*)

A context manager to test that at least one message is logged on the *logger* or one of its children, with at least the given *level*.

If given, *logger* should be a `logging.Logger` object or a `str` giving the name of a logger. The default is the root logger, which will catch all messages.

If given, *level* should be either a numeric logging level or its string equivalent (for example either `"ERROR"` or `logging.ERROR`). The default is `logging.INFO`.

The test passes if at least one message emitted inside the `with` block matches the *logger* and *level* conditions, otherwise it fails.

The object returned by the context manager is a recording helper which keeps tracks of the matching log messages. It has two attributes:

records
   A list of `logging.LogRecord` objects of the matching log messages.

output
   A list of `str` objects with the formatted output of matching messages.

Example:

```
with self.assertLogs('foo', level='INFO') as cm:
    logging.getLogger('foo').info('first message')
    logging.getLogger('foo.bar').error('second message')
self.assertEqual(cm.output, ['INFO:foo:first message',
                             'ERROR:foo.bar:second message'])
```

New in version 3.4.

There are also other methods used to perform more specific checks, such as:

Method	Checks that	New in
assertAlmostEqual(a, b)	round(a-b, 7) == 0	
assertNotAlmostEqual(a, b)	round(a-b, 7) != 0	
assertGreater(a, b)	a > b	3.1
assertGreaterEqual(a, b)	a >= b	3.1
assertLess(a, b)	a < b	3.1
assertLessEqual(a, b)	a <= b	3.1
assertRegex(s, r)	r.search(s)	3.1
assertNotRegex(s, r)	not r.search(s)	3.2
assertCountEqual(a, b)	a and b have the same elements in the same number, regardless of their order	3.2

assertAlmostEqual(*first, second, places=7, msg=None, delta=None*)
assertNotAlmostEqual(*first, second, places=7, msg=None, delta=None*)

Test that *first* and *second* are approximately (or not approximately) equal by computing the difference, rounding to the given number of decimal *places* (default 7), and comparing to zero. Note that these methods round the values to the given number of *decimal places* (i.e. like the *round()* function) and not *significant digits*.

If *delta* is supplied instead of *places* then the difference between *first* and *second* must be less or equal to (or greater than) *delta*.

Supplying both *delta* and *places* raises a `TypeError`.

Changed in version 3.2: *assertAlmostEqual()* automatically considers almost equal objects that compare equal. *assertNotAlmostEqual()* automatically fails if the objects compare equal. Added the *delta* keyword argument.

assertGreater(*first, second, msg=None*)
assertGreaterEqual(*first, second, msg=None*)
assertLess(*first, second, msg=None*)
assertLessEqual(*first, second, msg=None*)

Test that *first* is respectively >, >=, < or <= than *second* depending on the method name. If not, the test will fail:

```
>>> self.assertGreaterEqual(3, 4)
AssertionError: "3" unexpectedly not greater than or equal to "4"
```

New in version 3.1.

assertRegex(*text, regex, msg=None*)
assertNotRegex(*text, regex, msg=None*)

Test that a *regex* search matches (or does not match) *text*. In case of failure, the error message will include the pattern and the *text* (or the pattern and the part of *text* that unexpectedly matched). *regex* may be a regular expression object or a string containing a regular expression suitable for use by *re.search()*.

New in version 3.1: under the name **assertRegexpMatches**.

Changed in version 3.2: The method **assertRegexpMatches()** has been renamed to *assertRegex()*.

New in version 3.2: *assertNotRegex()*.

New in version 3.5: The name `assertNotRegexpMatches` is a deprecated alias for `assertNotRegex()`.

assertCountEqual(*first, second, msg=None*)
   Test that sequence *first* contains the same elements as *second*, regardless of their order. When they don't, an error message listing the differences between the sequences will be generated.

   Duplicate elements are *not* ignored when comparing *first* and *second*. It verifies whether each element has the same count in both sequences. Equivalent to: `assertEqual(Counter(list(first)), Counter(list(second)))` but works with sequences of unhashable objects as well.

   New in version 3.2.

The `assertEqual()` method dispatches the equality check for objects of the same type to different type-specific methods. These methods are already implemented for most of the built-in types, but it's also possible to register new methods using `addTypeEqualityFunc()`:

addTypeEqualityFunc(*typeobj, function*)
   Registers a type-specific method called by `assertEqual()` to check if two objects of exactly the same *typeobj* (not subclasses) compare equal. *function* must take two positional arguments and a third msg=None keyword argument just as `assertEqual()` does. It must raise `self.failureException(msg)` when inequality between the first two parameters is detected – possibly providing useful information and explaining the inequalities in details in the error message.

   New in version 3.1.

The list of type-specific methods automatically used by `assertEqual()` are summarized in the following table. Note that it's usually not necessary to invoke these methods directly.

Method	Used to compare	New in
`assertMultiLineEqual(a, b)`	strings	3.1
`assertSequenceEqual(a, b)`	sequences	3.1
`assertListEqual(a, b)`	lists	3.1
`assertTupleEqual(a, b)`	tuples	3.1
`assertSetEqual(a, b)`	sets or frozensets	3.1
`assertDictEqual(a, b)`	dicts	3.1

assertMultiLineEqual(*first, second, msg=None*)
   Test that the multiline string *first* is equal to the string *second*. When not equal a diff of the two strings highlighting the differences will be included in the error message. This method is used by default when comparing strings with `assertEqual()`.

   New in version 3.1.

assertSequenceEqual(*first, second, msg=None, seq_type=None*)
   Tests that two sequences are equal. If a *seq_type* is supplied, both *first* and *second* must be instances of *seq_type* or a failure will be raised. If the sequences are different an error message is constructed that shows the difference between the two.

   This method is not called directly by `assertEqual()`, but it's used to implement `assertListEqual()` and `assertTupleEqual()`.

   New in version 3.1.

assertListEqual(*first, second, msg=None*)
assertTupleEqual(*first, second, msg=None*)
   Tests that two lists or tuples are equal. If not, an error message is constructed that shows only the differences between the two. An error is also raised if either of the parameters are of the wrong type. These methods are used by default when comparing lists or tuples with `assertEqual()`.

New in version 3.1.

assertSetEqual(*first, second, msg=None*)
> Tests that two sets are equal. If not, an error message is constructed that lists the differences between the sets. This method is used by default when comparing sets or frozensets with *assertEqual()*.
>
> Fails if either of *first* or *second* does not have a set.difference() method.
>
> New in version 3.1.

assertDictEqual(*first, second, msg=None*)
> Test that two dictionaries are equal. If not, an error message is constructed that shows the differences in the dictionaries. This method will be used by default to compare dictionaries in calls to *assertEqual()*.
>
> New in version 3.1.

Finally the *TestCase* provides the following methods and attributes:

fail(*msg=None*)
> Signals a test failure unconditionally, with *msg* or None for the error message.

failureException
> This class attribute gives the exception raised by the test method. If a test framework needs to use a specialized exception, possibly to carry additional information, it must subclass this exception in order to "play fair" with the framework. The initial value of this attribute is *AssertionError*.

longMessage
> This class attribute determines what happens when a custom failure message is passed as the msg argument to an assertXYY call that fails. True is the default value. In this case, the custom message is appended to the end of the standard failure message. When set to False, the custom message replaces the standard message.
>
> The class setting can be overridden in individual test methods by assigning an instance attribute, self.longMessage, to True or False before calling the assert methods.
>
> The class setting gets reset before each test call.
>
> New in version 3.1.

maxDiff
> This attribute controls the maximum length of diffs output by assert methods that report diffs on failure. It defaults to 80*8 characters. Assert methods affected by this attribute are *assertSequenceEqual()* (including all the sequence comparison methods that delegate to it), *assertDictEqual()* and *assertMultiLineEqual()*.
>
> Setting maxDiff to None means that there is no maximum length of diffs.
>
> New in version 3.2.

Testing frameworks can use the following methods to collect information on the test:

countTestCases()
> Return the number of tests represented by this test object. For *TestCase* instances, this will always be 1.

defaultTestResult()
> Return an instance of the test result class that should be used for this test case class (if no other result instance is provided to the *run()* method).
>
> For *TestCase* instances, this will always be an instance of *TestResult*; subclasses of *TestCase* should override this as necessary.

id()
> Return a string identifying the specific test case. This is usually the full name of the test method, including the module and class name.

shortDescription()
> Returns a description of the test, or None if no description has been provided. The default implementation of this method returns the first line of the test method's docstring, if available, or None.
>
> Changed in version 3.1: In 3.1 this was changed to add the test name to the short description even in the presence of a docstring. This caused compatibility issues with unittest extensions and adding the test name was moved to the *TextTestResult* in Python 3.2.

addCleanup(*function, *args, **kwargs*)
> Add a function to be called after *tearDown()* to cleanup resources used during the test. Functions will be called in reverse order to the order they are added (LIFO). They are called with any arguments and keyword arguments passed into *addCleanup()* when they are added.
>
> If *setUp()* fails, meaning that *tearDown()* is not called, then any cleanup functions added will still be called.
>
> New in version 3.1.

doCleanups()
> This method is called unconditionally after *tearDown()*, or after *setUp()* if *setUp()* raises an exception.
>
> It is responsible for calling all the cleanup functions added by *addCleanup()*. If you need cleanup functions to be called *prior* to *tearDown()* then you can call *doCleanups()* yourself.
>
> *doCleanups()* pops methods off the stack of cleanup functions one at a time, so it can be called at any time.
>
> New in version 3.1.

class unittest.FunctionTestCase(*testFunc, setUp=None, tearDown=None, description=None*)
> This class implements the portion of the *TestCase* interface which allows the test runner to drive the test, but does not provide the methods which test code can use to check and report errors. This is used to create test cases using legacy test code, allowing it to be integrated into a *unittest*-based test framework.

Deprecated aliases

For historical reasons, some of the *TestCase* methods had one or more aliases that are now deprecated. The following table lists the correct names along with their deprecated aliases:

Method Name	Deprecated alias	Deprecated alias
assertEqual()	failUnlessEqual	assertEquals
assertNotEqual()	failIfEqual	assertNotEquals
assertTrue()	failUnless	assert_
assertFalse()	failIf	
assertRaises()	failUnlessRaises	
assertAlmostEqual()	failUnlessAlmostEqual	assertAlmostEquals
assertNotAlmostEqual()	failIfAlmostEqual	assertNotAlmostEquals
assertRegex()		assertRegexpMatches
assertNotRegex()		assertNotRegexpMatches
assertRaisesRegex()		assertRaisesRegexp

Deprecated since version 3.1: the fail* aliases listed in the second column.

Deprecated since version 3.2: the assert* aliases listed in the third column.

Deprecated since version 3.2: `assertRegexpMatches` and `assertRaisesRegexp` have been renamed to *assertRegex()* and *assertRaisesRegex()*.

Deprecated since version 3.5: the `assertNotRegexpMatches` name in favor of *assertNotRegex()*.

Grouping tests

`class unittest.TestSuite`(*tests=()*)

This class represents an aggregation of individual test cases and test suites. The class presents the interface needed by the test runner to allow it to be run as any other test case. Running a *TestSuite* instance is the same as iterating over the suite, running each test individually.

If *tests* is given, it must be an iterable of individual test cases or other test suites that will be used to build the suite initially. Additional methods are provided to add test cases and suites to the collection later on.

TestSuite objects behave much like *TestCase* objects, except they do not actually implement a test. Instead, they are used to aggregate tests into groups of tests that should be run together. Some additional methods are available to add tests to *TestSuite* instances:

addTest(*test*)

Add a *TestCase* or *TestSuite* to the suite.

addTests(*tests*)

Add all the tests from an iterable of *TestCase* and *TestSuite* instances to this test suite.

This is equivalent to iterating over *tests*, calling *addTest()* for each element.

TestSuite shares the following methods with *TestCase*:

run(*result*)

Run the tests associated with this suite, collecting the result into the test result object passed as *result*. Note that unlike *TestCase.run()*, *TestSuite.run()* requires the result object to be passed in.

debug()

Run the tests associated with this suite without collecting the result. This allows exceptions raised by the test to be propagated to the caller and can be used to support running tests under a debugger.

countTestCases()

Return the number of tests represented by this test object, including all individual tests and sub-suites.

__iter__()

Tests grouped by a *TestSuite* are always accessed by iteration. Subclasses can lazily provide tests by overriding *__iter__()*. Note that this method may be called several times on a single suite (for example when counting tests or comparing for equality) so the tests returned by repeated iterations before *TestSuite.run()* must be the same for each call iteration. After *TestSuite.run()*, callers should not rely on the tests returned by this method unless the caller uses a subclass that overrides `TestSuite._removeTestAtIndex()` to preserve test references.

Changed in version 3.2: In earlier versions the *TestSuite* accessed tests directly rather than through iteration, so overriding *__iter__()* wasn't sufficient for providing tests.

Changed in version 3.4: In earlier versions the *TestSuite* held references to each *TestCase* after *TestSuite.run()*. Subclasses can restore that behavior by overriding `TestSuite._removeTestAtIndex()`.

In the typical usage of a *TestSuite* object, the *run()* method is invoked by a `TestRunner` rather than by the end-user test harness.

Loading and running tests

class unittest.TestLoader

The *TestLoader* class is used to create test suites from classes and modules. Normally, there is no need to create an instance of this class; the *unittest* module provides an instance that can be shared as *unittest.defaultTestLoader*. Using a subclass or instance, however, allows customization of some configurable properties.

TestLoader objects have the following attributes:

errors

A list of the non-fatal errors encountered while loading tests. Not reset by the loader at any point. Fatal errors are signalled by the relevant a method raising an exception to the caller. Non-fatal errors are also indicated by a synthetic test that will raise the original error when run.

New in version 3.5.

TestLoader objects have the following methods:

loadTestsFromTestCase(*testCaseClass*)

Return a suite of all test cases contained in the *TestCase*-derived `testCaseClass`.

A test case instance is created for each method named by *getTestCaseNames()*. By default these are the method names beginning with `test`. If *getTestCaseNames()* returns no methods, but the `runTest()` method is implemented, a single test case is created for that method instead.

loadTestsFromModule(*module, pattern=None*)

Return a suite of all test cases contained in the given module. This method searches *module* for classes derived from *TestCase* and creates an instance of the class for each test method defined for the class.

Note: While using a hierarchy of *TestCase*-derived classes can be convenient in sharing fixtures and helper functions, defining test methods on base classes that are not intended to be instantiated directly does not play well with this method. Doing so, however, can be useful when the fixtures are different and defined in subclasses.

If a module provides a `load_tests` function it will be called to load the tests. This allows modules to customize test loading. This is the *load_tests protocol*. The *pattern* argument is passed as the third argument to `load_tests`.

Changed in version 3.2: Support for `load_tests` added.

Changed in version 3.5: The undocumented and unofficial *use_load_tests* default argument is deprecated and ignored, although it is still accepted for backward compatibility. The method also now accepts a keyword-only argument *pattern* which is passed to `load_tests` as the third argument.

loadTestsFromName(*name, module=None*)

Return a suite of all test cases given a string specifier.

The specifier *name* is a "dotted name" that may resolve either to a module, a test case class, a test method within a test case class, a *TestSuite* instance, or a callable object which returns a *TestCase* or *TestSuite* instance. These checks are applied in the order listed here; that is, a method on a possible test case class will be picked up as "a test method within a test case class", rather than "a callable object".

For example, if you have a module `SampleTests` containing a *TestCase*-derived class `SampleTestCase` with three test methods (`test_one()`, `test_two()`, and `test_three()`), the specifier `'SampleTests.SampleTestCase'` would cause this method to return a suite which will run all three test methods. Using the specifier `'SampleTests.SampleTestCase.test_two'` would cause it to return a test suite which will run only the `test_two()` test method. The specifier can refer to modules and packages which have not been imported; they will be imported as a side-effect.

The method optionally resolves *name* relative to the given *module*.

Changed in version 3.5: If an *ImportError* or *AttributeError* occurs while traversing *name* then a synthetic test that raises that error when run will be returned. These errors are included in the errors accumulated by self.errors.

loadTestsFromNames(*names, module=None*)
Similar to *loadTestsFromName()*, but takes a sequence of names rather than a single name. The return value is a test suite which supports all the tests defined for each name.

getTestCaseNames(*testCaseClass*)
Return a sorted sequence of method names found within *testCaseClass*; this should be a subclass of *TestCase*.

discover(*start_dir, pattern='test*.py', top_level_dir=None*)
Find all the test modules by recursing into subdirectories from the specified start directory, and return a TestSuite object containing them. Only test files that match *pattern* will be loaded. (Using shell style pattern matching.) Only module names that are importable (i.e. are valid Python identifiers) will be loaded.

All test modules must be importable from the top level of the project. If the start directory is not the top level directory then the top level directory must be specified separately.

If importing a module fails, for example due to a syntax error, then this will be recorded as a single error and discovery will continue. If the import failure is due to *SkipTest* being raised, it will be recorded as a skip instead of an error.

If a package (a directory containing a file named `__init__.py`) is found, the package will be checked for a `load_tests` function. If this exists then it will be called `package.load_tests(loader, tests, pattern)`. Test discovery takes care to ensure that a package is only checked for tests once during an invocation, even if the load_tests function itself calls `loader.discover`.

If `load_tests` exists then discovery does *not* recurse into the package, `load_tests` is responsible for loading all tests in the package.

The pattern is deliberately not stored as a loader attribute so that packages can continue discovery themselves. *top_level_dir* is stored so `load_tests` does not need to pass this argument in to `loader.discover()`.

start_dir can be a dotted module name as well as a directory.

New in version 3.2.

Changed in version 3.4: Modules that raise *SkipTest* on import are recorded as skips, not errors. Discovery works for *namespace packages*. Paths are sorted before being imported so that execution order is the same even if the underlying file system's ordering is not dependent on file name.

Changed in version 3.5: Found packages are now checked for `load_tests` regardless of whether their path matches *pattern*, because it is impossible for a package name to match the default pattern.

The following attributes of a *TestLoader* can be configured either by subclassing or assignment on an instance:

testMethodPrefix
: String giving the prefix of method names which will be interpreted as test methods. The default value is `'test'`.

    This affects *getTestCaseNames()* and all the `loadTestsFrom*()` methods.

sortTestMethodsUsing
: Function to be used to compare method names when sorting them in *getTestCaseNames()* and all the `loadTestsFrom*()` methods.

suiteClass
: Callable object that constructs a test suite from a list of tests. No methods on the resulting object are needed. The default value is the *TestSuite* class.

    This affects all the `loadTestsFrom*()` methods.

class unittest.TestResult
: This class is used to compile information about which tests have succeeded and which have failed.

    A *TestResult* object stores the results of a set of tests. The *TestCase* and *TestSuite* classes ensure that results are properly recorded; test authors do not need to worry about recording the outcome of tests.

    Testing frameworks built on top of *unittest* may want access to the *TestResult* object generated by running a set of tests for reporting purposes; a *TestResult* instance is returned by the `TestRunner.run()` method for this purpose.

    TestResult instances have the following attributes that will be of interest when inspecting the results of running a set of tests:

    errors
    : A list containing 2-tuples of *TestCase* instances and strings holding formatted tracebacks. Each tuple represents a test which raised an unexpected exception.

    failures
    : A list containing 2-tuples of *TestCase* instances and strings holding formatted tracebacks. Each tuple represents a test where a failure was explicitly signalled using the `TestCase.assert*()` methods.

    skipped
    : A list containing 2-tuples of *TestCase* instances and strings holding the reason for skipping the test.

        New in version 3.1.

    expectedFailures
    : A list containing 2-tuples of *TestCase* instances and strings holding formatted tracebacks. Each tuple represents an expected failure of the test case.

    unexpectedSuccesses
    : A list containing *TestCase* instances that were marked as expected failures, but succeeded.

    shouldStop
    : Set to `True` when the execution of tests should stop by *stop()*.

    testsRun
    : The total number of tests run so far.

    buffer
    : If set to true, `sys.stdout` and `sys.stderr` will be buffered in between *startTest()* and *stopTest()* being called. Collected output will only be echoed onto the real `sys.stdout` and `sys.stderr` if the test fails or errors. Any output is also attached to the failure / error message.

        New in version 3.2.

failfast
>   If set to true *stop()* will be called on the first failure or error, halting the test run.
>
>   New in version 3.2.

tb_locals
>   If set to true then local variables will be shown in tracebacks.
>
>   New in version 3.5.

wasSuccessful()
>   Return `True` if all tests run so far have passed, otherwise returns `False`.
>
>   Changed in version 3.4: Returns `False` if there were any *unexpectedSuccesses* from tests marked with the *expectedFailure()* decorator.

stop()
>   This method can be called to signal that the set of tests being run should be aborted by setting the *shouldStop* attribute to `True`. TestRunner objects should respect this flag and return without running any additional tests.
>
>   For example, this feature is used by the *TextTestRunner* class to stop the test framework when the user signals an interrupt from the keyboard. Interactive tools which provide `TestRunner` implementations can use this in a similar manner.

The following methods of the *TestResult* class are used to maintain the internal data structures, and may be extended in subclasses to support additional reporting requirements. This is particularly useful in building tools which support interactive reporting while tests are being run.

startTest(*test*)
>   Called when the test case *test* is about to be run.

stopTest(*test*)
>   Called after the test case *test* has been executed, regardless of the outcome.

startTestRun()
>   Called once before any tests are executed.
>
>   New in version 3.1.

stopTestRun()
>   Called once after all tests are executed.
>
>   New in version 3.1.

addError(*test, err*)
>   Called when the test case *test* raises an unexpected exception. *err* is a tuple of the form returned by *sys.exc_info()*: (type, value, traceback).
>
>   The default implementation appends a tuple (test, formatted_err) to the instance's *errors* attribute, where *formatted_err* is a formatted traceback derived from *err*.

addFailure(*test, err*)
>   Called when the test case *test* signals a failure. *err* is a tuple of the form returned by *sys.exc_info()*: (type, value, traceback).
>
>   The default implementation appends a tuple (test, formatted_err) to the instance's *failures* attribute, where *formatted_err* is a formatted traceback derived from *err*.

addSuccess(*test*)
>   Called when the test case *test* succeeds.
>
>   The default implementation does nothing.

addSkip(*test, reason*)
>   Called when the test case *test* is skipped. *reason* is the reason the test gave for skipping.

The default implementation appends a tuple (`test`, `reason`) to the instance's *skipped* attribute.

addExpectedFailure(*test, err*)
Called when the test case *test* fails, but was marked with the *expectedFailure()* decorator.

The default implementation appends a tuple (`test`, `formatted_err`) to the instance's *expectedFailures* attribute, where *formatted_err* is a formatted traceback derived from *err*.

addUnexpectedSuccess(*test*)
Called when the test case *test* was marked with the *expectedFailure()* decorator, but succeeded.

The default implementation appends the test to the instance's *unexpectedSuccesses* attribute.

addSubTest(*test, subtest, outcome*)
Called when a subtest finishes. *test* is the test case corresponding to the test method. *subtest* is a custom *TestCase* instance describing the subtest.

If *outcome* is `None`, the subtest succeeded. Otherwise, it failed with an exception where *outcome* is a tuple of the form returned by *sys.exc_info()*: (`type`, `value`, `traceback`).

The default implementation does nothing when the outcome is a success, and records subtest failures as normal failures.

New in version 3.4.

class unittest.TextTestResult(*stream, descriptions, verbosity*)
A concrete implementation of *TestResult* used by the *TextTestRunner*.

New in version 3.2: This class was previously named **_TextTestResult**. The old name still exists as an alias but is deprecated.

unittest.defaultTestLoader
Instance of the *TestLoader* class intended to be shared. If no customization of the *TestLoader* is needed, this instance can be used instead of repeatedly creating new instances.

class unittest.TextTestRunner(*stream=None, descriptions=True, verbosity=1, failfast=False, buffer=False, resultclass=None, warnings=None, *, tb_locals=False*)
A basic test runner implementation that outputs results to a stream. If *stream* is `None`, the default, *sys.stderr* is used as the output stream. This class has a few configurable parameters, but is essentially very simple. Graphical applications which run test suites should provide alternate implementations. Such implementations should accept `**kwargs` as the interface to construct runners changes when features are added to unittest.

By default this runner shows *DeprecationWarning*, *PendingDeprecationWarning*, *ResourceWarning* and *ImportWarning* even if they are *ignored by default*. Deprecation warnings caused by *deprecated unittest methods* are also special-cased and, when the warning filters are `'default'` or `'always'`, they will appear only once per-module, in order to avoid too many warning messages. This behavior can be overridden using Python's `-Wd` or `-Wa` options (see Warning control) and leaving *warnings* to `None`.

Changed in version 3.2: Added the `warnings` argument.

Changed in version 3.2: The default stream is set to *sys.stderr* at instantiation time rather than import time.

Changed in version 3.5: Added the tb_locals parameter.

_makeResult()
This method returns the instance of TestResult used by *run()*. It is not intended to be called directly, but can be overridden in subclasses to provide a custom TestResult.

_makeResult() instantiates the class or callable passed in the **TextTestRunner** constructor as the **resultclass** argument. It defaults to *TextTestResult* if no **resultclass** is provided. The result class is instantiated with the following arguments:

```
stream, descriptions, verbosity
```

run(*test*)

> This method is the main public interface to the *TextTestRunner*. This method takes a *TestSuite* or *TestCase* instance. A *TestResult* is created by calling *_makeResult()* and the test(s) are run and the results printed to stdout.

unittest.main(*module='__main__', defaultTest=None, argv=None, testRunner=None, testLoader=unittest.defaultTestLoader, exit=True, verbosity=1, failfast=None, catchbreak=None, buffer=None, warnings=None*)

> A command-line program that loads a set of tests from *module* and runs them; this is primarily for making test modules conveniently executable. The simplest use for this function is to include the following line at the end of a test script:

```
if __name__ == '__main__':
    unittest.main()
```

You can run tests with more detailed information by passing in the verbosity argument:

```
if __name__ == '__main__':
    unittest.main(verbosity=2)
```

The *defaultTest* argument is either the name of a single test or an iterable of test names to run if no test names are specified via *argv*. If not specified or `None` and no test names are provided via *argv*, all tests found in *module* are run.

The *argv* argument can be a list of options passed to the program, with the first element being the program name. If not specified or `None`, the values of *sys.argv* are used.

The *testRunner* argument can either be a test runner class or an already created instance of it. By default **main** calls *sys.exit()* with an exit code indicating success or failure of the tests run.

The *testLoader* argument has to be a *TestLoader* instance, and defaults to *defaultTestLoader*.

main supports being used from the interactive interpreter by passing in the argument `exit=False`. This displays the result on standard output without calling *sys.exit()*:

```
>>> from unittest import main
>>> main(module='test_module', exit=False)
```

The *failfast, catchbreak* and *buffer* parameters have the same effect as the same-name *command-line options*.

The *warnings* argument specifies the *warning filter* that should be used while running the tests. If it's not specified, it will remain `None` if a `-W` option is passed to **python** (see Warning control), otherwise it will be set to `'default'`.

Calling **main** actually returns an instance of the `TestProgram` class. This stores the result of the tests run as the `result` attribute.

Changed in version 3.1: The *exit* parameter was added.

Changed in version 3.2: The *verbosity, failfast, catchbreak, buffer* and *warnings* parameters were added.

Changed in version 3.4: The *defaultTest* parameter was changed to also accept an iterable of test names.

load_tests Protocol

New in version 3.2.

Modules or packages can customize how tests are loaded from them during normal test runs or test discovery by implementing a function called `load_tests`.

If a test module defines `load_tests` it will be called by *TestLoader.loadTestsFromModule()* with the following arguments:

```
load_tests(loader, standard_tests, pattern)
```

where *pattern* is passed straight through from `loadTestsFromModule`. It defaults to None.

It should return a *TestSuite*.

loader is the instance of *TestLoader* doing the loading. *standard_tests* are the tests that would be loaded by default from the module. It is common for test modules to only want to add or remove tests from the standard set of tests. The third argument is used when loading packages as part of test discovery.

A typical `load_tests` function that loads tests from a specific set of *TestCase* classes may look like:

```
test_cases = (TestCase1, TestCase2, TestCase3)

def load_tests(loader, tests, pattern):
    suite = TestSuite()
    for test_class in test_cases:
        tests = loader.loadTestsFromTestCase(test_class)
        suite.addTests(tests)
    return suite
```

If discovery is started in a directory containing a package, either from the command line or by calling *TestLoader.discover()*, then the package `__init__.py` will be checked for `load_tests`. If that function does not exist, discovery will recurse into the package as though it were just another directory. Otherwise, discovery of the package's tests will be left up to `load_tests` which is called with the following arguments:

```
load_tests(loader, standard_tests, pattern)
```

This should return a *TestSuite* representing all the tests from the package. (`standard_tests` will only contain tests collected from `__init__.py`.)

Because the pattern is passed into `load_tests` the package is free to continue (and potentially modify) test discovery. A 'do nothing' `load_tests` function for a test package would look like:

```
def load_tests(loader, standard_tests, pattern):
    # top level directory cached on loader instance
    this_dir = os.path.dirname(__file__)
    package_tests = loader.discover(start_dir=this_dir, pattern=pattern)
    standard_tests.addTests(package_tests)
    return standard_tests
```

Changed in version 3.5: Discovery no longer checks package names for matching *pattern* due to the impossibility of package names matching the default pattern.

26.4.9 Class and Module Fixtures

Class and module level fixtures are implemented in *TestSuite*. When the test suite encounters a test from a new class then **tearDownClass()** from the previous class (if there is one) is called, followed by **setUpClass()** from the new class.

Similarly if a test is from a different module from the previous test then **tearDownModule** from the previous module is run, followed by **setUpModule** from the new module.

After all the tests have run the final **tearDownClass** and **tearDownModule** are run.

Note that shared fixtures do not play well with [potential] features like test parallelization and they break test isolation. They should be used with care.

The default ordering of tests created by the unittest test loaders is to group all tests from the same modules and classes together. This will lead to setUpClass / setUpModule (etc) being called exactly once per class and module. If you randomize the order, so that tests from different modules and classes are adjacent to each other, then these shared fixture functions may be called multiple times in a single test run.

Shared fixtures are not intended to work with suites with non-standard ordering. A `BaseTestSuite` still exists for frameworks that don't want to support shared fixtures.

If there are any exceptions raised during one of the shared fixture functions the test is reported as an error. Because there is no corresponding test instance an `_ErrorHolder` object (that has the same interface as a *TestCase*) is created to represent the error. If you are just using the standard unittest test runner then this detail doesn't matter, but if you are a framework author it may be relevant.

setUpClass and tearDownClass

These must be implemented as class methods:

```
import unittest

class Test(unittest.TestCase):
    @classmethod
    def setUpClass(cls):
        cls._connection = createExpensiveConnectionObject()

    @classmethod
    def tearDownClass(cls):
        cls._connection.destroy()
```

If you want the setUpClass and tearDownClass on base classes called then you must call up to them yourself. The implementations in *TestCase* are empty.

If an exception is raised during a setUpClass then the tests in the class are not run and the tearDownClass is not run. Skipped classes will not have setUpClass or tearDownClass run. If the exception is a *SkipTest* exception then the class will be reported as having been skipped instead of as an error.

setUpModule and tearDownModule

These should be implemented as functions:

```
def setUpModule():
    createConnection()

def tearDownModule():
    closeConnection()
```

If an exception is raised in a setUpModule then none of the tests in the module will be run and the tearDownModule will not be run. If the exception is a *SkipTest* exception then the module will be reported as having been skipped instead of as an error.

26.4.10 Signal Handling

New in version 3.2.

The -c/--catch command-line option to unittest, along with the **catchbreak** parameter to *unittest. main()*, provide more friendly handling of control-C during a test run. With catch break behavior enabled control-C will allow the currently running test to complete, and the test run will then end and report all the results so far. A second control-c will raise a *KeyboardInterrupt* in the usual way.

The control-c handling signal handler attempts to remain compatible with code or tests that install their own **signal.SIGINT** handler. If the **unittest** handler is called but *isn't* the installed **signal.SIGINT** handler, i.e. it has been replaced by the system under test and delegated to, then it calls the default handler. This will normally be the expected behavior by code that replaces an installed handler and delegates to it. For individual tests that need **unittest** control-c handling disabled the *removeHandler()* decorator can be used.

There are a few utility functions for framework authors to enable control-c handling functionality within test frameworks.

unittest.installHandler()
    Install the control-c handler. When a **signal.SIGINT** is received (usually in response to the user pressing control-c) all registered results have *stop()* called.

unittest.registerResult(*result*)
    Register a *TestResult* object for control-c handling. Registering a result stores a weak reference to it, so it doesn't prevent the result from being garbage collected.

    Registering a *TestResult* object has no side-effects if control-c handling is not enabled, so test frameworks can unconditionally register all results they create independently of whether or not handling is enabled.

unittest.removeResult(*result*)
    Remove a registered result. Once a result has been removed then *stop()* will no longer be called on that result object in response to a control-c.

unittest.removeHandler(*function=None*)
    When called without arguments this function removes the control-c handler if it has been installed. This function can also be used as a test decorator to temporarily remove the handler whilst the test is being executed:

```
@unittest.removeHandler
def test_signal_handling(self):
    ...
```

26.5 unittest.mock — mock object library

New in version 3.3.

Source code: Lib/unittest/mock.py

unittest.mock is a library for testing in Python. It allows you to replace parts of your system under test with mock objects and make assertions about how they have been used.

unittest.mock provides a core *Mock* class removing the need to create a host of stubs throughout your test suite. After performing an action, you can make assertions about which methods / attributes were used and arguments they were called with. You can also specify return values and set needed attributes in the normal way.

Additionally, mock provides a *patch()* decorator that handles patching module and class level attributes within the scope of a test, along with *sentinel* for creating unique objects. See the *quick guide* for some examples of how to use *Mock*, *MagicMock* and *patch()*.

Mock is very easy to use and is designed for use with *unittest*. Mock is based on the 'action -> assertion' pattern instead of 'record -> replay' used by many mocking frameworks.

There is a backport of *unittest.mock* for earlier versions of Python, available as mock on PyPI.

26.5.1 Quick Guide

Mock and *MagicMock* objects create all attributes and methods as you access them and store details of how they have been used. You can configure them, to specify return values or limit what attributes are available, and then make assertions about how they have been used:

```
>>> from unittest.mock import MagicMock
>>> thing = ProductionClass()
>>> thing.method = MagicMock(return_value=3)
>>> thing.method(3, 4, 5, key='value')
3
>>> thing.method.assert_called_with(3, 4, 5, key='value')
```

side_effect allows you to perform side effects, including raising an exception when a mock is called:

```
>>> mock = Mock(side_effect=KeyError('foo'))
>>> mock()
Traceback (most recent call last):
 ...
KeyError: 'foo'
```

```
>>> values = {'a': 1, 'b': 2, 'c': 3}
>>> def side_effect(arg):
...     return values[arg]
...
>>> mock.side_effect = side_effect
>>> mock('a'), mock('b'), mock('c')
(1, 2, 3)
>>> mock.side_effect = [5, 4, 3, 2, 1]
>>> mock(), mock(), mock()
(5, 4, 3)
```

Mock has many other ways you can configure it and control its behaviour. For example the *spec* argument configures the mock to take its specification from another object. Attempting to access attributes or methods on the mock that don't exist on the spec will fail with an *AttributeError*.

The *patch()* decorator / context manager makes it easy to mock classes or objects in a module under test. The object you specify will be replaced with a mock (or other object) during the test and restored when the test ends:

```
>>> from unittest.mock import patch
>>> @patch('module.ClassName2')
... @patch('module.ClassName1')
... def test(MockClass1, MockClass2):
...     module.ClassName1()
...     module.ClassName2()
...     assert MockClass1 is module.ClassName1
...     assert MockClass2 is module.ClassName2
...     assert MockClass1.called
...     assert MockClass2.called
...
>>> test()
```

Note: When you nest patch decorators the mocks are passed in to the decorated function in the same order they applied (the normal *python* order that decorators are applied). This means from the bottom up, so in the example above the mock for `module.ClassName1` is passed in first.

With *patch()* it matters that you patch objects in the namespace where they are looked up. This is normally straightforward, but for a quick guide read *where to patch*.

As well as a decorator *patch()* can be used as a context manager in a with statement:

```
>>> with patch.object(ProductionClass, 'method', return_value=None) as mock_method:
...     thing = ProductionClass()
...     thing.method(1, 2, 3)
...
>>> mock_method.assert_called_once_with(1, 2, 3)
```

There is also *patch.dict()* for setting values in a dictionary just during a scope and restoring the dictionary to its original state when the test ends:

```
>>> foo = {'key': 'value'}
>>> original = foo.copy()
>>> with patch.dict(foo, {'newkey': 'newvalue'}, clear=True):
...     assert foo == {'newkey': 'newvalue'}
...
>>> assert foo == original
```

Mock supports the mocking of Python *magic methods*. The easiest way of using magic methods is with the *MagicMock* class. It allows you to do things like:

```
>>> mock = MagicMock()
>>> mock.__str__.return_value = 'foobarbaz'
>>> str(mock)
'foobarbaz'
>>> mock.__str__.assert_called_with()
```

Mock allows you to assign functions (or other Mock instances) to magic methods and they will be called appropriately. The *MagicMock* class is just a Mock variant that has all of the magic methods pre-created for you (well, all the useful ones anyway).

The following is an example of using magic methods with the ordinary Mock class:

```
>>> mock = Mock()
>>> mock.__str__ = Mock(return_value='wheeeeee')
>>> str(mock)
'wheeeeee'
```

For ensuring that the mock objects in your tests have the same api as the objects they are replacing, you can use *auto-speccing*. Auto-speccing can be done through the *autospec* argument to patch, or the *create_autospec()* function. Auto-speccing creates mock objects that have the same attributes and methods as the objects they are replacing, and any functions and methods (including constructors) have the same call signature as the real object.

This ensures that your mocks will fail in the same way as your production code if they are used incorrectly:

```
>>> from unittest.mock import create_autospec
>>> def function(a, b, c):
...     pass
...
```

```
>>> mock_function = create_autospec(function, return_value='fishy')
>>> mock_function(1, 2, 3)
'fishy'
>>> mock_function.assert_called_once_with(1, 2, 3)
>>> mock_function('wrong arguments')
Traceback (most recent call last):
 ...
TypeError: <lambda>() takes exactly 3 arguments (1 given)
```

create_autospec() can also be used on classes, where it copies the signature of the `__init__` method, and on callable objects where it copies the signature of the `__call__` method.

26.5.2 The Mock Class

Mock is a flexible mock object intended to replace the use of stubs and test doubles throughout your code. Mocks are callable and create attributes as new mocks when you access them[1]. Accessing the same attribute will always return the same mock. Mocks record how you use them, allowing you to make assertions about what your code has done to them.

MagicMock is a subclass of *Mock* with all the magic methods pre-created and ready to use. There are also non-callable variants, useful when you are mocking out objects that aren't callable: *NonCallableMock* and *NonCallableMagicMock*

The *patch()* decorators makes it easy to temporarily replace classes in a particular module with a *Mock* object. By default *patch()* will create a *MagicMock* for you. You can specify an alternative class of *Mock* using the *new_callable* argument to *patch()*.

class unittest.mock.Mock(*spec=None, side_effect=None, return_value=DEFAULT, wraps=None, name=None, spec_set=None, unsafe=False, **kwargs*)

Create a new *Mock* object. *Mock* takes several optional arguments that specify the behaviour of the Mock object:

- *spec*: This can be either a list of strings or an existing object (a class or instance) that acts as the specification for the mock object. If you pass in an object then a list of strings is formed by calling dir on the object (excluding unsupported magic attributes and methods). Accessing any attribute not in this list will raise an *AttributeError*.

    If *spec* is an object (rather than a list of strings) then `__class__` returns the class of the spec object. This allows mocks to pass *isinstance()* tests.

- *spec_set*: A stricter variant of *spec*. If used, attempting to *set* or get an attribute on the mock that isn't on the object passed as *spec_set* will raise an *AttributeError*.

- *side_effect*: A function to be called whenever the Mock is called. See the *side_effect* attribute. Useful for raising exceptions or dynamically changing return values. The function is called with the same arguments as the mock, and unless it returns *DEFAULT*, the return value of this function is used as the return value.

    Alternatively *side_effect* can be an exception class or instance. In this case the exception will be raised when the mock is called.

    If *side_effect* is an iterable then each call to the mock will return the next value from the iterable.

    A *side_effect* can be cleared by setting it to None.

---

[1] The only exceptions are magic methods and attributes (those that have leading and trailing double underscores). Mock doesn't create these but instead raises an *AttributeError*. This is because the interpreter will often implicitly request these methods, and gets *very* confused to get a new Mock object when it expects a magic method. If you need magic method support see *magic methods*.

- *return_value*: The value returned when the mock is called. By default this is a new Mock (created on first access). See the `return_value` attribute.
- *unsafe*: By default if any attribute starts with *assert* or *assret* will raise an `AttributeError`. Passing unsafe=True will allow access to these attributes.

  New in version 3.5.
- *wraps*: Item for the mock object to wrap. If *wraps* is not None then calling the Mock will pass the call through to the wrapped object (returning the real result). Attribute access on the mock will return a Mock object that wraps the corresponding attribute of the wrapped object (so attempting to access an attribute that doesn't exist will raise an `AttributeError`).

  If the mock has an explicit *return_value* set then calls are not passed to the wrapped object and the *return_value* is returned instead.
- *name*: If the mock has a name then it will be used in the repr of the mock. This can be useful for debugging. The name is propagated to child mocks.

Mocks can also be called with arbitrary keyword arguments. These will be used to set attributes on the mock after it is created. See the `configure_mock()` method for details.

assert_called(*args, **kwargs*)

Assert that the mock was called at least once.

```
>>> mock = Mock()
>>> mock.method()
<Mock name='mock.method()' id='...'>
>>> mock.method.assert_called()
```

New in version 3.6.

assert_called_once(*args, **kwargs*)

Assert that the mock was called exactly once.

```
>>> mock = Mock()
>>> mock.method()
<Mock name='mock.method()' id='...'>
>>> mock.method.assert_called_once()
>>> mock.method()
<Mock name='mock.method()' id='...'>
>>> mock.method.assert_called_once()
Traceback (most recent call last):
...
AssertionError: Expected 'method' to have been called once. Called 2 times.
```

New in version 3.6.

assert_called_with(*args, **kwargs*)

This method is a convenient way of asserting that calls are made in a particular way:

```
>>> mock = Mock()
>>> mock.method(1, 2, 3, test='wow')
<Mock name='mock.method()' id='...'>
>>> mock.method.assert_called_with(1, 2, 3, test='wow')
```

assert_called_once_with(*args, **kwargs*)

Assert that the mock was called exactly once and that that call was with the specified arguments.

```
>>> mock = Mock(return_value=None)
>>> mock('foo', bar='baz')
>>> mock.assert_called_once_with('foo', bar='baz')
```

```
>>> mock('other', bar='values')
>>> mock.assert_called_once_with('other', bar='values')
Traceback (most recent call last):
  ...
AssertionError: Expected 'mock' to be called once. Called 2 times.
```

assert_any_call(*args, **kwargs)

assert the mock has been called with the specified arguments.

The assert passes if the mock has *ever* been called, unlike `assert_called_with()` and `assert_called_once_with()` that only pass if the call is the most recent one, and in the case of `assert_called_once_with()` it must also be the only call.

```
>>> mock = Mock(return_value=None)
>>> mock(1, 2, arg='thing')
>>> mock('some', 'thing', 'else')
>>> mock.assert_any_call(1, 2, arg='thing')
```

assert_has_calls(*calls, any_order=False*)

assert the mock has been called with the specified calls. The `mock_calls` list is checked for the calls.

If *any_order* is false (the default) then the calls must be sequential. There can be extra calls before or after the specified calls.

If *any_order* is true then the calls can be in any order, but they must all appear in `mock_calls`.

```
>>> mock = Mock(return_value=None)
>>> mock(1)
>>> mock(2)
>>> mock(3)
>>> mock(4)
>>> calls = [call(2), call(3)]
>>> mock.assert_has_calls(calls)
>>> calls = [call(4), call(2), call(3)]
>>> mock.assert_has_calls(calls, any_order=True)
```

assert_not_called()

Assert the mock was never called.

```
>>> m = Mock()
>>> m.hello.assert_not_called()
>>> obj = m.hello()
>>> m.hello.assert_not_called()
Traceback (most recent call last):
  ...
AssertionError: Expected 'hello' to not have been called. Called 1 times.
```

New in version 3.5.

reset_mock(**, return_value=False, side_effect=False*)

The reset_mock method resets all the call attributes on a mock object:

```
>>> mock = Mock(return_value=None)
>>> mock('hello')
>>> mock.called
True
>>> mock.reset_mock()
```

```
>>> mock.called
False
```

Changed in version 3.6: Added two keyword only argument to the reset_mock function.

This can be useful where you want to make a series of assertions that reuse the same object. Note that *reset_mock()* *doesn't* clear the return value, *side_effect* or any child attributes you have set using normal assignment by default. In case you want to reset *return_value* or *side_effect*, then pass the corresponding parameter as `True`. Child mocks and the return value mock (if any) are reset as well.

Note: *return_value*, and *side_effect* are keyword only argument.

mock_add_spec(*spec, spec_set=False*)
  Add a spec to a mock. *spec* can either be an object or a list of strings. Only attributes on the *spec* can be fetched as attributes from the mock.

  If *spec_set* is true then only attributes on the spec can be set.

attach_mock(*mock, attribute*)
  Attach a mock as an attribute of this one, replacing its name and parent. Calls to the attached mock will be recorded in the *method_calls* and *mock_calls* attributes of this one.

configure_mock(***kwargs*)
  Set attributes on the mock through keyword arguments.

  Attributes plus return values and side effects can be set on child mocks using standard dot notation and unpacking a dictionary in the method call:

```
>>> mock = Mock()
>>> attrs = {'method.return_value': 3, 'other.side_effect': KeyError}
>>> mock.configure_mock(**attrs)
>>> mock.method()
3
>>> mock.other()
Traceback (most recent call last):
  ...
KeyError
```

The same thing can be achieved in the constructor call to mocks:

```
>>> attrs = {'method.return_value': 3, 'other.side_effect': KeyError}
>>> mock = Mock(some_attribute='eggs', **attrs)
>>> mock.some_attribute
'eggs'
>>> mock.method()
3
>>> mock.other()
Traceback (most recent call last):
  ...
KeyError
```

configure_mock() exists to make it easier to do configuration after the mock has been created.

__dir__()
  Mock objects limit the results of dir(some_mock) to useful results. For mocks with a *spec* this includes all the permitted attributes for the mock.

  See *FILTER_DIR* for what this filtering does, and how to switch it off.

_get_child_mock(**kw*)

> Create the child mocks for attributes and return value. By default child mocks will be the same type as the parent. Subclasses of Mock may want to override this to customize the way child mocks are made.
>
> For non-callable mocks the callable variant will be used (rather than any custom subclass).

called

> A boolean representing whether or not the mock object has been called:

```
>>> mock = Mock(return_value=None)
>>> mock.called
False
>>> mock()
>>> mock.called
True
```

call_count

> An integer telling you how many times the mock object has been called:

```
>>> mock = Mock(return_value=None)
>>> mock.call_count
0
>>> mock()
>>> mock()
>>> mock.call_count
2
```

return_value

> Set this to configure the value returned by calling the mock:

```
>>> mock = Mock()
>>> mock.return_value = 'fish'
>>> mock()
'fish'
```

> The default return value is a mock object and you can configure it in the normal way:

```
>>> mock = Mock()
>>> mock.return_value.attribute = sentinel.Attribute
>>> mock.return_value()
<Mock name='mock()()' id='...'>
>>> mock.return_value.assert_called_with()
```

> *return_value* can also be set in the constructor:

```
>>> mock = Mock(return_value=3)
>>> mock.return_value
3
>>> mock()
3
```

side_effect

> This can either be a function to be called when the mock is called, an iterable or an exception (class or instance) to be raised.
>
> If you pass in a function it will be called with same arguments as the mock and unless the function returns the *DEFAULT* singleton the call to the mock will then return whatever the function returns. If the function returns *DEFAULT* then the mock will return its normal value (from the *return_value*).

If you pass in an iterable, it is used to retrieve an iterator which must yield a value on every call. This value can either be an exception instance to be raised, or a value to be returned from the call to the mock (*DEFAULT* handling is identical to the function case).

An example of a mock that raises an exception (to test exception handling of an API):

```
>>> mock = Mock()
>>> mock.side_effect = Exception('Boom!')
>>> mock()
Traceback (most recent call last):
  ...
Exception: Boom!
```

Using *side_effect* to return a sequence of values:

```
>>> mock = Mock()
>>> mock.side_effect = [3, 2, 1]
>>> mock(), mock(), mock()
(3, 2, 1)
```

Using a callable:

```
>>> mock = Mock(return_value=3)
>>> def side_effect(*args, **kwargs):
...     return DEFAULT
...
>>> mock.side_effect = side_effect
>>> mock()
3
```

side_effect can be set in the constructor. Here's an example that adds one to the value the mock is called with and returns it:

```
>>> side_effect = lambda value: value + 1
>>> mock = Mock(side_effect=side_effect)
>>> mock(3)
4
>>> mock(-8)
-7
```

Setting *side_effect* to **None** clears it:

```
>>> m = Mock(side_effect=KeyError, return_value=3)
>>> m()
Traceback (most recent call last):
  ...
KeyError
>>> m.side_effect = None
>>> m()
3
```

call_args

This is either **None** (if the mock hasn't been called), or the arguments that the mock was last called with. This will be in the form of a tuple: the first member is any ordered arguments the mock was called with (or an empty tuple) and the second member is any keyword arguments (or an empty dictionary).

```
>>> mock = Mock(return_value=None)
>>> print(mock.call_args)
```

```
None
>>> mock()
>>> mock.call_args
call()
>>> mock.call_args == ()
True
>>> mock(3, 4)
>>> mock.call_args
call(3, 4)
>>> mock.call_args == ((3, 4),)
True
>>> mock(3, 4, 5, key='fish', next='w00t!')
>>> mock.call_args
call(3, 4, 5, key='fish', next='w00t!')
```

call_args, along with members of the lists *call_args_list*, *method_calls* and *mock_calls* are *call* objects. These are tuples, so they can be unpacked to get at the individual arguments and make more complex assertions. See *calls as tuples*.

call_args_list

This is a list of all the calls made to the mock object in sequence (so the length of the list is the number of times it has been called). Before any calls have been made it is an empty list. The *call* object can be used for conveniently constructing lists of calls to compare with *call_args_list*.

```
>>> mock = Mock(return_value=None)
>>> mock()
>>> mock(3, 4)
>>> mock(key='fish', next='w00t!')
>>> mock.call_args_list
[call(), call(3, 4), call(key='fish', next='w00t!')]
>>> expected = [(), ((3, 4),), ({'key': 'fish', 'next': 'w00t!'},)]
>>> mock.call_args_list == expected
True
```

Members of *call_args_list* are *call* objects. These can be unpacked as tuples to get at the individual arguments. See *calls as tuples*.

method_calls

As well as tracking calls to themselves, mocks also track calls to methods and attributes, and *their* methods and attributes:

```
>>> mock = Mock()
>>> mock.method()
<Mock name='mock.method()' id='...'>
>>> mock.property.method.attribute()
<Mock name='mock.property.method.attribute()' id='...'>
>>> mock.method_calls
[call.method(), call.property.method.attribute()]
```

Members of *method_calls* are *call* objects. These can be unpacked as tuples to get at the individual arguments. See *calls as tuples*.

mock_calls

mock_calls records *all* calls to the mock object, its methods, magic methods *and* return value mocks.

```
>>> mock = MagicMock()
>>> result = mock(1, 2, 3)
>>> mock.first(a=3)
```

26.5. **unittest.mock** — mock object library

```
<MagicMock name='mock.first()' id='...'>
>>> mock.second()
<MagicMock name='mock.second()' id='...'>
>>> int(mock)
1
>>> result(1)
<MagicMock name='mock()()' id='...'>
>>> expected = [call(1, 2, 3), call.first(a=3), call.second(),
...             call.__int__(), call()(1)]
>>> mock.mock_calls == expected
True
```

Members of *mock_calls* are *call* objects. These can be unpacked as tuples to get at the individual arguments. See *calls as tuples*.

__class__

Normally the *__class__* attribute of an object will return its type. For a mock object with a spec, *__class__* returns the spec class instead. This allows mock objects to pass *isinstance()* tests for the object they are replacing / masquerading as:

```
>>> mock = Mock(spec=3)
>>> isinstance(mock, int)
True
```

__class__ is assignable to, this allows a mock to pass an *isinstance()* check without forcing you to use a spec:

```
>>> mock = Mock()
>>> mock.__class__ = dict
>>> isinstance(mock, dict)
True
```

class unittest.mock.NonCallableMock(*spec=None*, *wraps=None*, *name=None*, *spec_set=None*, ***kwargs*)

A non-callable version of *Mock*. The constructor parameters have the same meaning of *Mock*, with the exception of *return_value* and *side_effect* which have no meaning on a non-callable mock.

Mock objects that use a class or an instance as a spec or spec_set are able to pass *isinstance()* tests:

```
>>> mock = Mock(spec=SomeClass)
>>> isinstance(mock, SomeClass)
True
>>> mock = Mock(spec_set=SomeClass())
>>> isinstance(mock, SomeClass)
True
```

The *Mock* classes have support for mocking magic methods. See *magic methods* for the full details.

The mock classes and the *patch()* decorators all take arbitrary keyword arguments for configuration. For the *patch()* decorators the keywords are passed to the constructor of the mock being created. The keyword arguments are for configuring attributes of the mock:

```
>>> m = MagicMock(attribute=3, other='fish')
>>> m.attribute
3
>>> m.other
'fish'
```

The return value and side effect of child mocks can be set in the same way, using dotted notation. As you can't use dotted names directly in a call you have to create a dictionary and unpack it using **:

```
>>> attrs = {'method.return_value': 3, 'other.side_effect': KeyError}
>>> mock = Mock(some_attribute='eggs', **attrs)
>>> mock.some_attribute
'eggs'
>>> mock.method()
3
>>> mock.other()
Traceback (most recent call last):
 ...
KeyError
```

A callable mock which was created with a *spec* (or a *spec_set*) will introspect the specification object's signature when matching calls to the mock. Therefore, it can match the actual call's arguments regardless of whether they were passed positionally or by name:

```
>>> def f(a, b, c): pass
...
>>> mock = Mock(spec=f)
>>> mock(1, 2, c=3)
<Mock name='mock()' id='140161580456576'>
>>> mock.assert_called_with(1, 2, 3)
>>> mock.assert_called_with(a=1, b=2, c=3)
```

This applies to *assert_called_with()*, *assert_called_once_with()*, *assert_has_calls()* and *assert_any_call()*. When *Autospeccing*, it will also apply to method calls on the mock object.

Changed in version 3.4: Added signature introspection on specced and autospecced mock objects.

class unittest.mock.PropertyMock(*args, ***kwargs***)**

A mock intended to be used as a property, or other descriptor, on a class. *PropertyMock* provides __get__() and __set__() methods so you can specify a return value when it is fetched.

Fetching a *PropertyMock* instance from an object calls the mock, with no args. Setting it calls the mock with the value being set.

```
>>> class Foo:
...     @property
...     def foo(self):
...         return 'something'
...     @foo.setter
...     def foo(self, value):
...         pass
...
>>> with patch('__main__.Foo.foo', new_callable=PropertyMock) as mock_foo:
...     mock_foo.return_value = 'mockity-mock'
...     this_foo = Foo()
...     print(this_foo.foo)
...     this_foo.foo = 6
...
mockity-mock
>>> mock_foo.mock_calls
[call(), call(6)]
```

Because of the way mock attributes are stored you can't directly attach a *PropertyMock* to a mock object. Instead you can attach it to the mock type object:

```
>>> m = MagicMock()
>>> p = PropertyMock(return_value=3)
>>> type(m).foo = p
>>> m.foo
3
>>> p.assert_called_once_with()
```

Calling

Mock objects are callable. The call will return the value set as the *return_value* attribute. The default return value is a new Mock object; it is created the first time the return value is accessed (either explicitly or by calling the Mock) - but it is stored and the same one returned each time.

Calls made to the object will be recorded in the attributes like *call_args* and *call_args_list*.

If *side_effect* is set then it will be called after the call has been recorded, so if **side_effect** raises an exception the call is still recorded.

The simplest way to make a mock raise an exception when called is to make *side_effect* an exception class or instance:

```
>>> m = MagicMock(side_effect=IndexError)
>>> m(1, 2, 3)
Traceback (most recent call last):
 ...
IndexError
>>> m.mock_calls
[call(1, 2, 3)]
>>> m.side_effect = KeyError('Bang!')
>>> m('two', 'three', 'four')
Traceback (most recent call last):
 ...
KeyError: 'Bang!'
>>> m.mock_calls
[call(1, 2, 3), call('two', 'three', 'four')]
```

If **side_effect** is a function then whatever that function returns is what calls to the mock return. The **side_effect** function is called with the same arguments as the mock. This allows you to vary the return value of the call dynamically, based on the input:

```
>>> def side_effect(value):
...     return value + 1
...
>>> m = MagicMock(side_effect=side_effect)
>>> m(1)
2
>>> m(2)
3
>>> m.mock_calls
[call(1), call(2)]
```

If you want the mock to still return the default return value (a new mock), or any set return value, then there are two ways of doing this. Either return `mock.return_value` from inside **side_effect**, or return *DEFAULT*:

```
>>> m = MagicMock()
>>> def side_effect(*args, **kwargs):
```

```
...         return m.return_value
...
>>> m.side_effect = side_effect
>>> m.return_value = 3
>>> m()
3
>>> def side_effect(*args, **kwargs):
...         return DEFAULT
...
>>> m.side_effect = side_effect
>>> m()
3
```

To remove a `side_effect`, and return to the default behaviour, set the `side_effect` to None:

```
>>> m = MagicMock(return_value=6)
>>> def side_effect(*args, **kwargs):
...         return 3
...
>>> m.side_effect = side_effect
>>> m()
3
>>> m.side_effect = None
>>> m()
6
```

The `side_effect` can also be any iterable object. Repeated calls to the mock will return values from the iterable (until the iterable is exhausted and a *StopIteration* is raised):

```
>>> m = MagicMock(side_effect=[1, 2, 3])
>>> m()
1
>>> m()
2
>>> m()
3
>>> m()
Traceback (most recent call last):
  ...
StopIteration
```

If any members of the iterable are exceptions they will be raised instead of returned:

```
>>> iterable = (33, ValueError, 66)
>>> m = MagicMock(side_effect=iterable)
>>> m()
33
>>> m()
Traceback (most recent call last):
  ...
ValueError
>>> m()
66
```

Deleting Attributes

Mock objects create attributes on demand. This allows them to pretend to be objects of any type.

You may want a mock object to return `False` to a `hasattr()` call, or raise an `AttributeError` when an attribute is fetched. You can do this by providing an object as a `spec` for a mock, but that isn't always convenient.

You "block" attributes by deleting them. Once deleted, accessing an attribute will raise an `AttributeError`.

```
>>> mock = MagicMock()
>>> hasattr(mock, 'm')
True
>>> del mock.m
>>> hasattr(mock, 'm')
False
>>> del mock.f
>>> mock.f
Traceback (most recent call last):
    ...
AttributeError: f
```

Mock names and the name attribute

Since "name" is an argument to the *Mock* constructor, if you want your mock object to have a "name" attribute you can't just pass it in at creation time. There are two alternatives. One option is to use `configure_mock()`:

```
>>> mock = MagicMock()
>>> mock.configure_mock(name='my_name')
>>> mock.name
'my_name'
```

A simpler option is to simply set the "name" attribute after mock creation:

```
>>> mock = MagicMock()
>>> mock.name = "foo"
```

Attaching Mocks as Attributes

When you attach a mock as an attribute of another mock (or as the return value) it becomes a "child" of that mock. Calls to the child are recorded in the *method_calls* and *mock_calls* attributes of the parent. This is useful for configuring child mocks and then attaching them to the parent, or for attaching mocks to a parent that records all calls to the children and allows you to make assertions about the order of calls between mocks:

```
>>> parent = MagicMock()
>>> child1 = MagicMock(return_value=None)
>>> child2 = MagicMock(return_value=None)
>>> parent.child1 = child1
>>> parent.child2 = child2
>>> child1(1)
>>> child2(2)
>>> parent.mock_calls
[call.child1(1), call.child2(2)]
```

The exception to this is if the mock has a name. This allows you to prevent the "parenting" if for some reason you don't want it to happen.

```
>>> mock = MagicMock()
>>> not_a_child = MagicMock(name='not-a-child')
>>> mock.attribute = not_a_child
>>> mock.attribute()
<MagicMock name='not-a-child()' id='...'>
>>> mock.mock_calls
[]
```

Mocks created for you by *patch()* are automatically given names. To attach mocks that have names to a parent you use the *attach_mock()* method:

```
>>> thing1 = object()
>>> thing2 = object()
>>> parent = MagicMock()
>>> with patch('__main__.thing1', return_value=None) as child1:
...     with patch('__main__.thing2', return_value=None) as child2:
...         parent.attach_mock(child1, 'child1')
...         parent.attach_mock(child2, 'child2')
...         child1('one')
...         child2('two')
...
>>> parent.mock_calls
[call.child1('one'), call.child2('two')]
```

26.5.3 The patchers

The patch decorators are used for patching objects only within the scope of the function they decorate. They automatically handle the unpatching for you, even if exceptions are raised. All of these functions can also be used in with statements or as class decorators.

patch

Note: *patch()* is straightforward to use. The key is to do the patching in the right namespace. See the section *where to patch*.

---

unittest.mock.patch(*target, new=DEFAULT, spec=None, create=False, spec_set=None, autospec=None, new_callable=None, **kwargs*)

patch() acts as a function decorator, class decorator or a context manager. Inside the body of the function or with statement, the *target* is patched with a *new* object. When the function/with statement exits the patch is undone.

If *new* is omitted, then the target is replaced with a *MagicMock*. If *patch()* is used as a decorator and *new* is omitted, the created mock is passed in as an extra argument to the decorated function. If *patch()* is used as a context manager the created mock is returned by the context manager.

target should be a string in the form `'package.module.ClassName'`. The *target* is imported and the specified object replaced with the *new* object, so the *target* must be importable from the environment you are calling *patch()* from. The target is imported when the decorated function is executed, not at decoration time.

The *spec* and *spec_set* keyword arguments are passed to the *MagicMock* if patch is creating one for you.

In addition you can pass `spec=True` or `spec_set=True`, which causes patch to pass in the object being mocked as the spec/spec_set object.

new_callable allows you to specify a different class, or callable object, that will be called to create the *new* object. By default `MagicMock` is used.

A more powerful form of *spec* is *autospec*. If you set `autospec=True` then the mock will be created with a spec from the object being replaced. All attributes of the mock will also have the spec of the corresponding attribute of the object being replaced. Methods and functions being mocked will have their arguments checked and will raise a *TypeError* if they are called with the wrong signature. For mocks replacing a class, their return value (the 'instance') will have the same spec as the class. See the *create_autospec()* function and *Autospeccing*.

Instead of `autospec=True` you can pass `autospec=some_object` to use an arbitrary object as the spec instead of the one being replaced.

By default *patch()* will fail to replace attributes that don't exist. If you pass in `create=True`, and the attribute doesn't exist, patch will create the attribute for you when the patched function is called, and delete it again afterwards. This is useful for writing tests against attributes that your production code creates at runtime. It is off by default because it can be dangerous. With it switched on you can write passing tests against APIs that don't actually exist!

Note: Changed in version 3.5: If you are patching builtins in a module then you don't need to pass `create=True`, it will be added by default.

Patch can be used as a `TestCase` class decorator. It works by decorating each test method in the class. This reduces the boilerplate code when your test methods share a common patchings set. *patch()* finds tests by looking for method names that start with `patch.TEST_PREFIX`. By default this is `'test'`, which matches the way *unittest* finds tests. You can specify an alternative prefix by setting `patch.TEST_PREFIX`.

Patch can be used as a context manager, with the with statement. Here the patching applies to the indented block after the with statement. If you use "as" then the patched object will be bound to the name after the "as"; very useful if *patch()* is creating a mock object for you.

patch() takes arbitrary keyword arguments. These will be passed to the *Mock* (or *new_callable*) on construction.

`patch.dict(...)`, `patch.multiple(...)` and `patch.object(...)` are available for alternate use-cases.

patch() as function decorator, creating the mock for you and passing it into the decorated function:

```
>>> @patch('__main__.SomeClass')
... def function(normal_argument, mock_class):
...     print(mock_class is SomeClass)
...
>>> function(None)
True
```

Patching a class replaces the class with a *MagicMock* instance. If the class is instantiated in the code under test then it will be the *return_value* of the mock that will be used.

If the class is instantiated multiple times you could use *side_effect* to return a new mock each time. Alternatively you can set the *return_value* to be anything you want.

To configure return values on methods of *instances* on the patched class you must do this on the `return_value`. For example:

```
>>> class Class:
...     def method(self):
...         pass
```

1458 Chapter 26. Development Tools

```
...
>>> with patch('__main__.Class') as MockClass:
...     instance = MockClass.return_value
...     instance.method.return_value = 'foo'
...     assert Class() is instance
...     assert Class().method() == 'foo'
...
```

If you use *spec* or *spec_set* and *patch()* is replacing a *class*, then the return value of the created mock will have the same spec.

```
>>> Original = Class
>>> patcher = patch('__main__.Class', spec=True)
>>> MockClass = patcher.start()
>>> instance = MockClass()
>>> assert isinstance(instance, Original)
>>> patcher.stop()
```

The *new_callable* argument is useful where you want to use an alternative class to the default *MagicMock* for the created mock. For example, if you wanted a *NonCallableMock* to be used:

```
>>> thing = object()
>>> with patch('__main__.thing', new_callable=NonCallableMock) as mock_thing:
...     assert thing is mock_thing
...     thing()
...
Traceback (most recent call last):
  ...
TypeError: 'NonCallableMock' object is not callable
```

Another use case might be to replace an object with an *io.StringIO* instance:

```
>>> from io import StringIO
>>> def foo():
...     print('Something')
...
>>> @patch('sys.stdout', new_callable=StringIO)
... def test(mock_stdout):
...     foo()
...     assert mock_stdout.getvalue() == 'Something\n'
...
>>> test()
```

When *patch()* is creating a mock for you, it is common that the first thing you need to do is to configure the mock. Some of that configuration can be done in the call to patch. Any arbitrary keywords you pass into the call will be used to set attributes on the created mock:

```
>>> patcher = patch('__main__.thing', first='one', second='two')
>>> mock_thing = patcher.start()
>>> mock_thing.first
'one'
>>> mock_thing.second
'two'
```

As well as attributes on the created mock attributes, like the *return_value* and *side_effect*, of child mocks can also be configured. These aren't syntactically valid to pass in directly as keyword arguments, but a dictionary with these as keys can still be expanded into a *patch()* call using **:

```
>>> config = {'method.return_value': 3, 'other.side_effect': KeyError}
>>> patcher = patch('__main__.thing', **config)
>>> mock_thing = patcher.start()
>>> mock_thing.method()
3
>>> mock_thing.other()
Traceback (most recent call last):
  ...
KeyError
```

patch.object

patch.object(*target, attribute, new=DEFAULT, spec=None, create=False, spec_set=None, autospec=None, new_callable=None, **kwargs*)
patch the named member (*attribute*) on an object (*target*) with a mock object.

patch.object() can be used as a decorator, class decorator or a context manager. Arguments *new*, *spec*, *create*, *spec_set*, *autospec* and *new_callable* have the same meaning as for *patch()*. Like *patch()*, *patch.object()* takes arbitrary keyword arguments for configuring the mock object it creates.

When used as a class decorator *patch.object()* honours **patch.TEST_PREFIX** for choosing which methods to wrap.

You can either call *patch.object()* with three arguments or two arguments. The three argument form takes the object to be patched, the attribute name and the object to replace the attribute with.

When calling with the two argument form you omit the replacement object, and a mock is created for you and passed in as an extra argument to the decorated function:

```
>>> @patch.object(SomeClass, 'class_method')
... def test(mock_method):
...     SomeClass.class_method(3)
...     mock_method.assert_called_with(3)
...
>>> test()
```

spec, *create* and the other arguments to *patch.object()* have the same meaning as they do for *patch()*.

patch.dict

patch.dict(*in_dict, values=(), clear=False, **kwargs*)
Patch a dictionary, or dictionary like object, and restore the dictionary to its original state after the test.

in_dict can be a dictionary or a mapping like container. If it is a mapping then it must at least support getting, setting and deleting items plus iterating over keys.

in_dict can also be a string specifying the name of the dictionary, which will then be fetched by importing it.

values can be a dictionary of values to set in the dictionary. *values* can also be an iterable of (key, value) pairs.

If *clear* is true then the dictionary will be cleared before the new values are set.

patch.dict() can also be called with arbitrary keyword arguments to set values in the dictionary.

patch.dict() can be used as a context manager, decorator or class decorator. When used as a class decorator *patch.dict()* honours **patch.TEST_PREFIX** for choosing which methods to wrap.

`patch.dict()` can be used to add members to a dictionary, or simply let a test change a dictionary, and ensure the dictionary is restored when the test ends.

```
>>> foo = {}
>>> with patch.dict(foo, {'newkey': 'newvalue'}):
...     assert foo == {'newkey': 'newvalue'}
...
>>> assert foo == {}
```

```
>>> import os
>>> with patch.dict('os.environ', {'newkey': 'newvalue'}):
...     print(os.environ['newkey'])
...
newvalue
>>> assert 'newkey' not in os.environ
```

Keywords can be used in the `patch.dict()` call to set values in the dictionary:

```
>>> mymodule = MagicMock()
>>> mymodule.function.return_value = 'fish'
>>> with patch.dict('sys.modules', mymodule=mymodule):
...     import mymodule
...     mymodule.function('some', 'args')
...
'fish'
```

`patch.dict()` can be used with dictionary like objects that aren't actually dictionaries. At the very minimum they must support item getting, setting, deleting and either iteration or membership test. This corresponds to the magic methods __getitem__(), __setitem__(), __delitem__() and either __iter__() or __contains__().

```
>>> class Container:
...     def __init__(self):
...         self.values = {}
...     def __getitem__(self, name):
...         return self.values[name]
...     def __setitem__(self, name, value):
...         self.values[name] = value
...     def __delitem__(self, name):
...         del self.values[name]
...     def __iter__(self):
...         return iter(self.values)
...
>>> thing = Container()
>>> thing['one'] = 1
>>> with patch.dict(thing, one=2, two=3):
...     assert thing['one'] == 2
...     assert thing['two'] == 3
...
>>> assert thing['one'] == 1
>>> assert list(thing) == ['one']
```

patch.multiple

patch.**multiple**(*target*, *spec=None*, *create=False*, *spec_set=None*, *autospec=None*, *new_callable=None*, ***kwargs*)
    Perform multiple patches in a single call. It takes the object to be patched (either as an object or a

string to fetch the object by importing) and keyword arguments for the patches:

```
with patch.multiple(settings, FIRST_PATCH='one', SECOND_PATCH='two'):
    ...
```

Use *DEFAULT* as the value if you want *patch.multiple()* to create mocks for you. In this case the created mocks are passed into a decorated function by keyword, and a dictionary is returned when *patch.multiple()* is used as a context manager.

patch.multiple() can be used as a decorator, class decorator or a context manager. The arguments *spec*, *spec_set*, *create*, *autospec* and *new_callable* have the same meaning as for *patch()*. These arguments will be applied to *all* patches done by *patch.multiple()*.

When used as a class decorator *patch.multiple()* honours `patch.TEST_PREFIX` for choosing which methods to wrap.

If you want *patch.multiple()* to create mocks for you, then you can use *DEFAULT* as the value. If you use *patch.multiple()* as a decorator then the created mocks are passed into the decorated function by keyword.

```
>>> thing = object()
>>> other = object()
```

```
>>> @patch.multiple('__main__', thing=DEFAULT, other=DEFAULT)
... def test_function(thing, other):
...     assert isinstance(thing, MagicMock)
...     assert isinstance(other, MagicMock)
...
>>> test_function()
```

patch.multiple() can be nested with other **patch** decorators, but put arguments passed by keyword *after* any of the standard arguments created by *patch()*:

```
>>> @patch('sys.exit')
... @patch.multiple('__main__', thing=DEFAULT, other=DEFAULT)
... def test_function(mock_exit, other, thing):
...     assert 'other' in repr(other)
...     assert 'thing' in repr(thing)
...     assert 'exit' in repr(mock_exit)
...
>>> test_function()
```

If *patch.multiple()* is used as a context manager, the value returned by the context manger is a dictionary where created mocks are keyed by name:

```
>>> with patch.multiple('__main__', thing=DEFAULT, other=DEFAULT) as values:
...     assert 'other' in repr(values['other'])
...     assert 'thing' in repr(values['thing'])
...     assert values['thing'] is thing
...     assert values['other'] is other
...
```

patch methods: start and stop

All the patchers have `start()` and `stop()` methods. These make it simpler to do patching in `setUp` methods or where you want to do multiple patches without nesting decorators or with statements.

To use them call *patch()*, *patch.object()* or *patch.dict()* as normal and keep a reference to the returned `patcher` object. You can then call `start()` to put the patch in place and `stop()` to undo it.

If you are using *patch()* to create a mock for you then it will be returned by the call to `patcher.start`.

```
>>> patcher = patch('package.module.ClassName')
>>> from package import module
>>> original = module.ClassName
>>> new_mock = patcher.start()
>>> assert module.ClassName is not original
>>> assert module.ClassName is new_mock
>>> patcher.stop()
>>> assert module.ClassName is original
>>> assert module.ClassName is not new_mock
```

A typical use case for this might be for doing multiple patches in the `setUp` method of a `TestCase`:

```
>>> class MyTest(TestCase):
...     def setUp(self):
...         self.patcher1 = patch('package.module.Class1')
...         self.patcher2 = patch('package.module.Class2')
...         self.MockClass1 = self.patcher1.start()
...         self.MockClass2 = self.patcher2.start()
...
...     def tearDown(self):
...         self.patcher1.stop()
...         self.patcher2.stop()
...
...     def test_something(self):
...         assert package.module.Class1 is self.MockClass1
...         assert package.module.Class2 is self.MockClass2
...
>>> MyTest('test_something').run()
```

> **Caution:** If you use this technique you must ensure that the patching is "undone" by calling `stop`. This can be fiddlier than you might think, because if an exception is raised in the `setUp` then `tearDown` is not called. *unittest.TestCase.addCleanup()* makes this easier:
>
> ```
> >>> class MyTest(TestCase):
> ...     def setUp(self):
> ...         patcher = patch('package.module.Class')
> ...         self.MockClass = patcher.start()
> ...         self.addCleanup(patcher.stop)
> ...
> ...     def test_something(self):
> ...         assert package.module.Class is self.MockClass
> ...
> ```
>
> As an added bonus you no longer need to keep a reference to the `patcher` object.

It is also possible to stop all patches which have been started by using *patch.stopall()*.

`patch.stopall()`
    Stop all active patches. Only stops patches started with `start`.

patch builtins

You can patch any builtins within a module. The following example patches builtin *ord()*:

```
>>> @patch('__main__.ord')
... def test(mock_ord):
...     mock_ord.return_value = 101
...     print(ord('c'))
...
>>> test()
101
```

TEST_PREFIX

All of the patchers can be used as class decorators. When used in this way they wrap every test method on the class. The patchers recognise methods that start with `'test'` as being test methods. This is the same way that the *unittest.TestLoader* finds test methods by default.

It is possible that you want to use a different prefix for your tests. You can inform the patchers of the different prefix by setting `patch.TEST_PREFIX`:

```
>>> patch.TEST_PREFIX = 'foo'
>>> value = 3
>>>
>>> @patch('__main__.value', 'not three')
... class Thing:
...     def foo_one(self):
...         print(value)
...     def foo_two(self):
...         print(value)
...
>>>
>>> Thing().foo_one()
not three
>>> Thing().foo_two()
not three
>>> value
3
```

Nesting Patch Decorators

If you want to perform multiple patches then you can simply stack up the decorators.

You can stack up multiple patch decorators using this pattern:

```
>>> @patch.object(SomeClass, 'class_method')
... @patch.object(SomeClass, 'static_method')
... def test(mock1, mock2):
...     assert SomeClass.static_method is mock1
...     assert SomeClass.class_method is mock2
...     SomeClass.static_method('foo')
...     SomeClass.class_method('bar')
...     return mock1, mock2
...
>>> mock1, mock2 = test()
>>> mock1.assert_called_once_with('foo')
>>> mock2.assert_called_once_with('bar')
```

Note that the decorators are applied from the bottom upwards. This is the standard way that Python applies decorators. The order of the created mocks passed into your test function matches this order.

Where to patch

patch() works by (temporarily) changing the object that a *name* points to with another one. There can be many names pointing to any individual object, so for patching to work you must ensure that you patch the name used by the system under test.

The basic principle is that you patch where an object is *looked up*, which is not necessarily the same place as where it is defined. A couple of examples will help to clarify this.

Imagine we have a project that we want to test with the following structure:

```
a.py
    -> Defines SomeClass

b.py
    -> from a import SomeClass
    -> some_function instantiates SomeClass
```

Now we want to test `some_function` but we want to mock out `SomeClass` using *patch()*. The problem is that when we import module b, which we will have to do then it imports `SomeClass` from module a. If we use *patch()* to mock out `a.SomeClass` then it will have no effect on our test; module b already has a reference to the *real* `SomeClass` and it looks like our patching had no effect.

The key is to patch out `SomeClass` where it is used (or where it is looked up). In this case `some_function` will actually look up `SomeClass` in module b, where we have imported it. The patching should look like:

```
@patch('b.SomeClass')
```

However, consider the alternative scenario where instead of `from a import SomeClass` module b does `import a` and `some_function` uses `a.SomeClass`. Both of these import forms are common. In this case the class we want to patch is being looked up in the module and so we have to patch `a.SomeClass` instead:

```
@patch('a.SomeClass')
```

Patching Descriptors and Proxy Objects

Both *patch* and *patch.object* correctly patch and restore descriptors: class methods, static methods and properties. You should patch these on the *class* rather than an instance. They also work with *some* objects that proxy attribute access, like the django settings object.

26.5.4 MagicMock and magic method support

Mocking Magic Methods

Mock supports mocking the Python protocol methods, also known as "magic methods". This allows mock objects to replace containers or other objects that implement Python protocols.

Because magic methods are looked up differently from normal methods[2], this support has been specially implemented. This means that only specific magic methods are supported. The supported list includes

---

[2] Magic methods *should* be looked up on the class rather than the instance. Different versions of Python are inconsistent about applying this rule. The supported protocol methods should work with all supported versions of Python.

almost all of them. If there are any missing that you need please let us know.

You mock magic methods by setting the method you are interested in to a function or a mock instance. If you are using a function then it *must* take `self` as the first argument[3].

```
>>> def __str__(self):
...     return 'fooble'
...
>>> mock = Mock()
>>> mock.__str__ = __str__
>>> str(mock)
'fooble'
```

```
>>> mock = Mock()
>>> mock.__str__ = Mock()
>>> mock.__str__.return_value = 'fooble'
>>> str(mock)
'fooble'
```

```
>>> mock = Mock()
>>> mock.__iter__ = Mock(return_value=iter([]))
>>> list(mock)
[]
```

One use case for this is for mocking objects used as context managers in a `with` statement:

```
>>> mock = Mock()
>>> mock.__enter__ = Mock(return_value='foo')
>>> mock.__exit__ = Mock(return_value=False)
>>> with mock as m:
...     assert m == 'foo'
...
>>> mock.__enter__.assert_called_with()
>>> mock.__exit__.assert_called_with(None, None, None)
```

Calls to magic methods do not appear in `method_calls`, but they are recorded in `mock_calls`.

Note: If you use the *spec* keyword argument to create a mock then attempting to set a magic method that isn't in the spec will raise an `AttributeError`.

The full list of supported magic methods is:

- __hash__, __sizeof__, __repr__ and __str__
- __dir__, __format__ and __subclasses__
- __floor__, __trunc__ and __ceil__
- Comparisons: __lt__, __gt__, __le__, __ge__, __eq__ and __ne__
- Container methods: __getitem__, __setitem__, __delitem__, __contains__, __len__, __iter__, __reversed__ and __missing__
- Context manager: __enter__ and __exit__
- Unary numeric methods: __neg__, __pos__ and __invert__

---

[3] The function is basically hooked up to the class, but each `Mock` instance is kept isolated from the others.

- The numeric methods (including right hand and in-place variants): `__add__`, `__sub__`, `__mul__`, `__matmul__`, `__div__`, `__truediv__`, `__floordiv__`, `__mod__`, `__divmod__`, `__lshift__`, `__rshift__`, `__and__`, `__xor__`, `__or__`, and `__pow__`
- Numeric conversion methods: `__complex__`, `__int__`, `__float__` and `__index__`
- Descriptor methods: `__get__`, `__set__` and `__delete__`
- Pickling: `__reduce__`, `__reduce_ex__`, `__getinitargs__`, `__getnewargs__`, `__getstate__` and `__setstate__`

The following methods exist but are *not* supported as they are either in use by mock, can't be set dynamically, or can cause problems:

- `__getattr__`, `__setattr__`, `__init__` and `__new__`
- `__prepare__`, `__instancecheck__`, `__subclasscheck__`, `__del__`

Magic Mock

There are two `MagicMock` variants: *MagicMock* and *NonCallableMagicMock*.

class unittest.mock.MagicMock(**args*, ***kw*)

   `MagicMock` is a subclass of *Mock* with default implementations of most of the magic methods. You can use `MagicMock` without having to configure the magic methods yourself.

   The constructor parameters have the same meaning as for *Mock*.

   If you use the *spec* or *spec_set* arguments then *only* magic methods that exist in the spec will be created.

class unittest.mock.NonCallableMagicMock(**args*, ***kw*)

   A non-callable version of *MagicMock*.

   The constructor parameters have the same meaning as for *MagicMock*, with the exception of *return_value* and *side_effect* which have no meaning on a non-callable mock.

The magic methods are setup with *MagicMock* objects, so you can configure them and use them in the usual way:

```
>>> mock = MagicMock()
>>> mock[3] = 'fish'
>>> mock.__setitem__.assert_called_with(3, 'fish')
>>> mock.__getitem__.return_value = 'result'
>>> mock[2]
'result'
```

By default many of the protocol methods are required to return objects of a specific type. These methods are preconfigured with a default return value, so that they can be used without you having to do anything if you aren't interested in the return value. You can still *set* the return value manually if you want to change the default.

Methods and their defaults:

- `__lt__`: NotImplemented
- `__gt__`: NotImplemented
- `__le__`: NotImplemented
- `__ge__`: NotImplemented
- `__int__`: 1
- `__contains__`: False

- `__len__`: 0
- `__iter__`: iter([])
- `__exit__`: False
- `__complex__`: 1j
- `__float__`: 1.0
- `__bool__`: True
- `__index__`: 1
- `__hash__`: default hash for the mock
- `__str__`: default str for the mock
- `__sizeof__`: default sizeof for the mock

For example:

```
>>> mock = MagicMock()
>>> int(mock)
1
>>> len(mock)
0
>>> list(mock)
[]
>>> object() in mock
False
```

The two equality methods, `__eq__()` and `__ne__()`, are special. They do the default equality comparison on identity, using the *side_effect* attribute, unless you change their return value to return something else:

```
>>> MagicMock() == 3
False
>>> MagicMock() != 3
True
>>> mock = MagicMock()
>>> mock.__eq__.return_value = True
>>> mock == 3
True
```

The return value of `MagicMock.__iter__()` can be any iterable object and isn't required to be an iterator:

```
>>> mock = MagicMock()
>>> mock.__iter__.return_value = ['a', 'b', 'c']
>>> list(mock)
['a', 'b', 'c']
>>> list(mock)
['a', 'b', 'c']
```

If the return value *is* an iterator, then iterating over it once will consume it and subsequent iterations will result in an empty list:

```
>>> mock.__iter__.return_value = iter(['a', 'b', 'c'])
>>> list(mock)
['a', 'b', 'c']
>>> list(mock)
[]
```

`MagicMock` has all of the supported magic methods configured except for some of the obscure and obsolete ones. You can still set these up if you want.

Magic methods that are supported but not setup by default in `MagicMock` are:

- `__subclasses__`
- `__dir__`
- `__format__`
- `__get__`, `__set__` and `__delete__`
- `__reversed__` and `__missing__`
- `__reduce__`, `__reduce_ex__`, `__getinitargs__`, `__getnewargs__`, `__getstate__` and `__setstate__`
- `__getformat__` and `__setformat__`

26.5.5 Helpers

sentinel

`unittest.mock.sentinel`

> The `sentinel` object provides a convenient way of providing unique objects for your tests.
>
> Attributes are created on demand when you access them by name. Accessing the same attribute will always return the same object. The objects returned have a sensible repr so that test failure messages are readable.
>
> The `sentinel` attributes don't preserve their identity when they are *copied* or *pickled*.

Sometimes when testing you need to test that a specific object is passed as an argument to another method, or returned. It can be common to create named sentinel objects to test this. *sentinel* provides a convenient way of creating and testing the identity of objects like this.

In this example we monkey patch `method` to return `sentinel.some_object`:

```
>>> real = ProductionClass()
>>> real.method = Mock(name="method")
>>> real.method.return_value = sentinel.some_object
>>> result = real.method()
>>> assert result is sentinel.some_object
>>> sentinel.some_object
sentinel.some_object
```

DEFAULT

`unittest.mock.DEFAULT`

> The *DEFAULT* object is a pre-created sentinel (actually `sentinel.DEFAULT`). It can be used by *side_effect* functions to indicate that the normal return value should be used.

call

`unittest.mock.call(*args, **kwargs)`

> *call()* is a helper object for making simpler assertions, for comparing with *call_args*, *call_args_list*, *mock_calls* and *method_calls*. *call()* can also be used with *assert_has_calls()*.

```
>>> m = MagicMock(return_value=None)
>>> m(1, 2, a='foo', b='bar')
>>> m()
>>> m.call_args_list == [call(1, 2, a='foo', b='bar'), call()]
True
```

`call.call_list()`
    For a call object that represents multiple calls, `call_list()` returns a list of all the intermediate calls as well as the final call.

`call_list` is particularly useful for making assertions on "chained calls". A chained call is multiple calls on a single line of code. This results in multiple entries in `mock_calls` on a mock. Manually constructing the sequence of calls can be tedious.

`call_list()` can construct the sequence of calls from the same chained call:

```
>>> m = MagicMock()
>>> m(1).method(arg='foo').other('bar')(2.0)
<MagicMock name='mock().method().other()()' id='...'>
>>> kall = call(1).method(arg='foo').other('bar')(2.0)
>>> kall.call_list()
[call(1),
 call().method(arg='foo'),
 call().method().other('bar'),
 call().method().other()(2.0)]
>>> m.mock_calls == kall.call_list()
True
```

A `call` object is either a tuple of (positional args, keyword args) or (name, positional args, keyword args) depending on how it was constructed. When you construct them yourself this isn't particularly interesting, but the `call` objects that are in the `Mock.call_args`, `Mock.call_args_list` and `Mock.mock_calls` attributes can be introspected to get at the individual arguments they contain.

The `call` objects in `Mock.call_args` and `Mock.call_args_list` are two-tuples of (positional args, keyword args) whereas the `call` objects in `Mock.mock_calls`, along with ones you construct yourself, are three-tuples of (name, positional args, keyword args).

You can use their "tupleness" to pull out the individual arguments for more complex introspection and assertions. The positional arguments are a tuple (an empty tuple if there are no positional arguments) and the keyword arguments are a dictionary:

```
>>> m = MagicMock(return_value=None)
>>> m(1, 2, 3, arg='one', arg2='two')
>>> kall = m.call_args
>>> args, kwargs = kall
>>> args
(1, 2, 3)
>>> kwargs
{'arg2': 'two', 'arg': 'one'}
>>> args is kall[0]
True
>>> kwargs is kall[1]
True
```

```
>>> m = MagicMock()
>>> m.foo(4, 5, 6, arg='two', arg2='three')
<MagicMock name='mock.foo()' id='...'>
>>> kall = m.mock_calls[0]
>>> name, args, kwargs = kall
```

```
>>> name
'foo'
>>> args
(4, 5, 6)
>>> kwargs
{'arg2': 'three', 'arg': 'two'}
>>> name is m.mock_calls[0][0]
True
```

create_autospec

unittest.mock.create_autospec(*spec*, *spec_set=False*, *instance=False*, ***kwargs*)

Create a mock object using another object as a spec. Attributes on the mock will use the corresponding attribute on the *spec* object as their spec.

Functions or methods being mocked will have their arguments checked to ensure that they are called with the correct signature.

If *spec_set* is True then attempting to set attributes that don't exist on the spec object will raise an `AttributeError`.

If a class is used as a spec then the return value of the mock (the instance of the class) will have the same spec. You can use a class as the spec for an instance object by passing `instance=True`. The returned mock will only be callable if instances of the mock are callable.

`create_autospec()` also takes arbitrary keyword arguments that are passed to the constructor of the created mock.

See *Autospeccing* for examples of how to use auto-speccing with `create_autospec()` and the *autospec* argument to `patch()`.

ANY

unittest.mock.ANY

Sometimes you may need to make assertions about *some* of the arguments in a call to mock, but either not care about some of the arguments or want to pull them individually out of `call_args` and make more complex assertions on them.

To ignore certain arguments you can pass in objects that compare equal to *everything*. Calls to `assert_called_with()` and `assert_called_once_with()` will then succeed no matter what was passed in.

```
>>> mock = Mock(return_value=None)
>>> mock('foo', bar=object())
>>> mock.assert_called_once_with('foo', bar=ANY)
```

ANY can also be used in comparisons with call lists like `mock_calls`:

```
>>> m = MagicMock(return_value=None)
>>> m(1)
>>> m(1, 2)
>>> m(object())
>>> m.mock_calls == [call(1), call(1, 2), ANY]
True
```

FILTER_DIR

`unittest.mock.FILTER_DIR`

FILTER_DIR is a module level variable that controls the way mock objects respond to *dir()* (only for Python 2.6 or more recent). The default is `True`, which uses the filtering described below, to only show useful members. If you dislike this filtering, or need to switch it off for diagnostic purposes, then set `mock.FILTER_DIR = False`.

With filtering on, `dir(some_mock)` shows only useful attributes and will include any dynamically created attributes that wouldn't normally be shown. If the mock was created with a *spec* (or *autospec* of course) then all the attributes from the original are shown, even if they haven't been accessed yet:

```
>>> dir(Mock())
['assert_any_call',
 'assert_called_once_with',
 'assert_called_with',
 'assert_has_calls',
 'attach_mock',
 ...
>>> from urllib import request
>>> dir(Mock(spec=request))
['AbstractBasicAuthHandler',
 'AbstractDigestAuthHandler',
 'AbstractHTTPHandler',
 'BaseHandler',
 ...
```

Many of the not-very-useful (private to *Mock* rather than the thing being mocked) underscore and double underscore prefixed attributes have been filtered from the result of calling *dir()* on a *Mock*. If you dislike this behaviour you can switch it off by setting the module level switch *FILTER_DIR*:

```
>>> from unittest import mock
>>> mock.FILTER_DIR = False
>>> dir(mock.Mock())
['_NonCallableMock__get_return_value',
 '_NonCallableMock__get_side_effect',
 '_NonCallableMock__return_value_doc',
 '_NonCallableMock__set_return_value',
 '_NonCallableMock__set_side_effect',
 '__call__',
 '__class__',
 ...
```

Alternatively you can just use `vars(my_mock)` (instance members) and `dir(type(my_mock))` (type members) to bypass the filtering irrespective of `mock.FILTER_DIR`.

mock_open

`unittest.mock.mock_open(mock=None, read_data=None)`

> A helper function to create a mock to replace the use of *open()*. It works for *open()* called directly or used as a context manager.
>
> The *mock* argument is the mock object to configure. If `None` (the default) then a *MagicMock* will be created for you, with the API limited to methods or attributes available on standard file handles.

read_data is a string for the `read()`, *readline()*, and *readlines()* methods of the file handle to return. Calls to those methods will take data from *read_data* until it is depleted. The mock of these methods is pretty simplistic: every time the *mock* is called, the *read_data* is rewound to the start. If you need more control over the data that you are feeding to the tested code you will need to customize this mock for yourself. When that is insufficient, one of the in-memory filesystem packages on PyPI can offer a realistic filesystem for testing.

Changed in version 3.4: Added *readline()* and *readlines()* support. The mock of `read()` changed to consume *read_data* rather than returning it on each call.

Changed in version 3.5: *read_data* is now reset on each call to the *mock*.

Using *open()* as a context manager is a great way to ensure your file handles are closed properly and is becoming common:

```
with open('/some/path', 'w') as f:
    f.write('something')
```

The issue is that even if you mock out the call to *open()* it is the *returned object* that is used as a context manager (and has __enter__() and __exit__() called).

Mocking context managers with a *MagicMock* is common enough and fiddly enough that a helper function is useful.

```
>>> m = mock_open()
>>> with patch('__main__.open', m):
...     with open('foo', 'w') as h:
...         h.write('some stuff')
...
>>> m.mock_calls
[call('foo', 'w'),
 call().__enter__(),
 call().write('some stuff'),
 call().__exit__(None, None, None)]
>>> m.assert_called_once_with('foo', 'w')
>>> handle = m()
>>> handle.write.assert_called_once_with('some stuff')
```

And for reading files:

```
>>> with patch('__main__.open', mock_open(read_data='bibble')) as m:
...     with open('foo') as h:
...         result = h.read()
...
>>> m.assert_called_once_with('foo')
>>> assert result == 'bibble'
```

Autospeccing

Autospeccing is based on the existing `spec` feature of mock. It limits the api of mocks to the api of an original object (the spec), but it is recursive (implemented lazily) so that attributes of mocks only have the same api as the attributes of the spec. In addition mocked functions / methods have the same call signature as the original so they raise a *TypeError* if they are called incorrectly.

Before I explain how auto-speccing works, here's why it is needed.

Mock is a very powerful and flexible object, but it suffers from two flaws when used to mock out objects from a system under test. One of these flaws is specific to the *Mock* api and the other is a more general problem with using mock objects.

First the problem specific to *Mock*. *Mock* has two assert methods that are extremely handy: *assert_called_with()* and *assert_called_once_with()*.

```
>>> mock = Mock(name='Thing', return_value=None)
>>> mock(1, 2, 3)
>>> mock.assert_called_once_with(1, 2, 3)
>>> mock(1, 2, 3)
>>> mock.assert_called_once_with(1, 2, 3)
Traceback (most recent call last):
 ...
AssertionError: Expected 'mock' to be called once. Called 2 times.
```

Because mocks auto-create attributes on demand, and allow you to call them with arbitrary arguments, if you misspell one of these assert methods then your assertion is gone:

```
>>> mock = Mock(name='Thing', return_value=None)
>>> mock(1, 2, 3)
>>> mock.assret_called_once_with(4, 5, 6)
```

Your tests can pass silently and incorrectly because of the typo.

The second issue is more general to mocking. If you refactor some of your code, rename members and so on, any tests for code that is still using the *old api* but uses mocks instead of the real objects will still pass. This means your tests can all pass even though your code is broken.

Note that this is another reason why you need integration tests as well as unit tests. Testing everything in isolation is all fine and dandy, but if you don't test how your units are "wired together" there is still lots of room for bugs that tests might have caught.

mock already provides a feature to help with this, called speccing. If you use a class or instance as the **spec** for a mock then you can only access attributes on the mock that exist on the real class:

```
>>> from urllib import request
>>> mock = Mock(spec=request.Request)
>>> mock.assret_called_with
Traceback (most recent call last):
 ...
AttributeError: Mock object has no attribute 'assret_called_with'
```

The spec only applies to the mock itself, so we still have the same issue with any methods on the mock:

```
>>> mock.has_data()
<mock.Mock object at 0x...>
>>> mock.has_data.assret_called_with()
```

Auto-speccing solves this problem. You can either pass **autospec=True** to *patch()* / *patch.object()* or use the *create_autospec()* function to create a mock with a spec. If you use the **autospec=True** argument to *patch()* then the object that is being replaced will be used as the spec object. Because the speccing is done "lazily" (the spec is created as attributes on the mock are accessed) you can use it with very complex or deeply nested objects (like modules that import modules that import modules) without a big performance hit.

Here's an example of it in use:

```
>>> from urllib import request
>>> patcher = patch('__main__.request', autospec=True)
>>> mock_request = patcher.start()
>>> request is mock_request
True
```

```
>>> mock_request.Request
<MagicMock name='request.Request' spec='Request' id='...'>
```

You can see that `request.Request` has a spec. `request.Request` takes two arguments in the constructor (one of which is *self*). Here's what happens if we try to call it incorrectly:

```
>>> req = request.Request()
Traceback (most recent call last):
...
TypeError: <lambda>() takes at least 2 arguments (1 given)
```

The spec also applies to instantiated classes (i.e. the return value of specced mocks):

```
>>> req = request.Request('foo')
>>> req
<NonCallableMagicMock name='request.Request()' spec='Request' id='...'>
```

`Request` objects are not callable, so the return value of instantiating our mocked out `request.Request` is a non-callable mock. With the spec in place any typos in our asserts will raise the correct error:

```
>>> req.add_header('spam', 'eggs')
<MagicMock name='request.Request().add_header()' id='...'>
>>> req.add_header.assret_called_with
Traceback (most recent call last):
...
AttributeError: Mock object has no attribute 'assret_called_with'
>>> req.add_header.assert_called_with('spam', 'eggs')
```

In many cases you will just be able to add `autospec=True` to your existing *patch()* calls and then be protected against bugs due to typos and api changes.

As well as using *autospec* through *patch()* there is a *create_autospec()* for creating autospecced mocks directly:

```
>>> from urllib import request
>>> mock_request = create_autospec(request)
>>> mock_request.Request('foo', 'bar')
<NonCallableMagicMock name='mock.Request()' spec='Request' id='...'>
```

This isn't without caveats and limitations however, which is why it is not the default behaviour. In order to know what attributes are available on the spec object, autospec has to introspect (access attributes) the spec. As you traverse attributes on the mock a corresponding traversal of the original object is happening under the hood. If any of your specced objects have properties or descriptors that can trigger code execution then you may not be able to use autospec. On the other hand it is much better to design your objects so that introspection is safe[4].

A more serious problem is that it is common for instance attributes to be created in the `__init__()` method and not to exist on the class at all. *autospec* can't know about any dynamically created attributes and restricts the api to visible attributes.

```
>>> class Something:
...     def __init__(self):
...         self.a = 33
...
>>> with patch('__main__.Something', autospec=True):
...     thing = Something()
```

---

[4] This only applies to classes or already instantiated objects. Calling a mocked class to create a mock instance *does not* create a real instance. It is only attribute lookups - along with calls to *dir()* - that are done.

```
...     thing.a
...
Traceback (most recent call last):
   ...
AttributeError: Mock object has no attribute 'a'
```

There are a few different ways of resolving this problem. The easiest, but not necessarily the least annoying, way is to simply set the required attributes on the mock after creation. Just because *autospec* doesn't allow you to fetch attributes that don't exist on the spec it doesn't prevent you setting them:

```
>>> with patch('__main__.Something', autospec=True):
...     thing = Something()
...     thing.a = 33
...
```

There is a more aggressive version of both *spec* and *autospec* that *does* prevent you setting non-existent attributes. This is useful if you want to ensure your code only *sets* valid attributes too, but obviously it prevents this particular scenario:

```
>>> with patch('__main__.Something', autospec=True, spec_set=True):
...     thing = Something()
...     thing.a = 33
...
Traceback (most recent call last):
   ...
AttributeError: Mock object has no attribute 'a'
```

Probably the best way of solving the problem is to add class attributes as default values for instance members initialised in __init__(). Note that if you are only setting default attributes in __init__() then providing them via class attributes (shared between instances of course) is faster too. e.g.

```
class Something:
    a = 33
```

This brings up another issue. It is relatively common to provide a default value of None for members that will later be an object of a different type. None would be useless as a spec because it wouldn't let you access *any* attributes or methods on it. As None is *never* going to be useful as a spec, and probably indicates a member that will normally of some other type, autospec doesn't use a spec for members that are set to None. These will just be ordinary mocks (well - MagicMocks):

```
>>> class Something:
...         member = None
...
>>> mock = create_autospec(Something)
>>> mock.member.foo.bar.baz()
<MagicMock name='mock.member.foo.bar.baz()' id='...'>
```

If modifying your production classes to add defaults isn't to your liking then there are more options. One of these is simply to use an instance as the spec rather than the class. The other is to create a subclass of the production class and add the defaults to the subclass without affecting the production class. Both of these require you to use an alternative object as the spec. Thankfully *patch()* supports this - you can simply pass the alternative object as the *autospec* argument:

```
>>> class Something:
...     def __init__(self):
...         self.a = 33
...
```

```
>>> class SomethingForTest(Something):
...     a = 33
...
>>> p = patch('__main__.Something', autospec=SomethingForTest)
>>> mock = p.start()
>>> mock.a
<NonCallableMagicMock name='Something.a' spec='int' id='...'>
```

26.6 `unittest.mock` — getting started

New in version 3.3.

26.6.1 Using Mock

Mock Patching Methods

Common uses for *Mock* objects include:

- Patching methods
- Recording method calls on objects

You might want to replace a method on an object to check that it is called with the correct arguments by another part of the system:

```
>>> real = SomeClass()
>>> real.method = MagicMock(name='method')
>>> real.method(3, 4, 5, key='value')
<MagicMock name='method()' id='...'>
```

Once our mock has been used (`real.method` in this example) it has methods and attributes that allow you to make assertions about how it has been used.

Note: In most of these examples the *Mock* and *MagicMock* classes are interchangeable. As the `MagicMock` is the more capable class it makes a sensible one to use by default.

Once the mock has been called its *called* attribute is set to `True`. More importantly we can use the *assert_called_with()* or *assert_called_once_with()* method to check that it was called with the correct arguments.

This example tests that calling `ProductionClass().method` results in a call to the `something` method:

```
>>> class ProductionClass:
...     def method(self):
...         self.something(1, 2, 3)
...     def something(self, a, b, c):
...         pass
...
>>> real = ProductionClass()
>>> real.something = MagicMock()
>>> real.method()
>>> real.something.assert_called_once_with(1, 2, 3)
```

Mock for Method Calls on an Object

In the last example we patched a method directly on an object to check that it was called correctly. Another common use case is to pass an object into a method (or some part of the system under test) and then check that it is used in the correct way.

The simple `ProductionClass` below has a `closer` method. If it is called with an object then it calls `close` on it.

```
>>> class ProductionClass:
...     def closer(self, something):
...         something.close()
...
```

So to test it we need to pass in an object with a `close` method and check that it was called correctly.

```
>>> real = ProductionClass()
>>> mock = Mock()
>>> real.closer(mock)
>>> mock.close.assert_called_with()
```

We don't have to do any work to provide the 'close' method on our mock. Accessing close creates it. So, if 'close' hasn't already been called then accessing it in the test will create it, but `assert_called_with()` will raise a failure exception.

Mocking Classes

A common use case is to mock out classes instantiated by your code under test. When you patch a class, then that class is replaced with a mock. Instances are created by *calling the class*. This means you access the "mock instance" by looking at the return value of the mocked class.

In the example below we have a function `some_function` that instantiates `Foo` and calls a method on it. The call to `patch()` replaces the class `Foo` with a mock. The `Foo` instance is the result of calling the mock, so it is configured by modifying the mock *return_value*.

```
>>> def some_function():
...     instance = module.Foo()
...     return instance.method()
...
>>> with patch('module.Foo') as mock:
...     instance = mock.return_value
...     instance.method.return_value = 'the result'
...     result = some_function()
...     assert result == 'the result'
```

Naming your mocks

It can be useful to give your mocks a name. The name is shown in the repr of the mock and can be helpful when the mock appears in test failure messages. The name is also propagated to attributes or methods of the mock:

```
>>> mock = MagicMock(name='foo')
>>> mock
<MagicMock name='foo' id='...'>
>>> mock.method
<MagicMock name='foo.method' id='...'>
```

Tracking all Calls

Often you want to track more than a single call to a method. The *mock_calls* attribute records all calls to child attributes of the mock - and also to their children.

```
>>> mock = MagicMock()
>>> mock.method()
<MagicMock name='mock.method()' id='...'>
>>> mock.attribute.method(10, x=53)
<MagicMock name='mock.attribute.method()' id='...'>
>>> mock.mock_calls
[call.method(), call.attribute.method(10, x=53)]
```

If you make an assertion about `mock_calls` and any unexpected methods have been called, then the assertion will fail. This is useful because as well as asserting that the calls you expected have been made, you are also checking that they were made in the right order and with no additional calls:

You use the *call* object to construct lists for comparing with `mock_calls`:

```
>>> expected = [call.method(), call.attribute.method(10, x=53)]
>>> mock.mock_calls == expected
True
```

Setting Return Values and Attributes

Setting the return values on a mock object is trivially easy:

```
>>> mock = Mock()
>>> mock.return_value = 3
>>> mock()
3
```

Of course you can do the same for methods on the mock:

```
>>> mock = Mock()
>>> mock.method.return_value = 3
>>> mock.method()
3
```

The return value can also be set in the constructor:

```
>>> mock = Mock(return_value=3)
>>> mock()
3
```

If you need an attribute setting on your mock, just do it:

```
>>> mock = Mock()
>>> mock.x = 3
>>> mock.x
3
```

Sometimes you want to mock up a more complex situation, like for example `mock.connection.cursor().execute("SELECT 1")`. If we wanted this call to return a list, then we have to configure the result of the nested call.

We can use *call* to construct the set of calls in a "chained call" like this for easy assertion afterwards:

```
>>> mock = Mock()
>>> cursor = mock.connection.cursor.return_value
>>> cursor.execute.return_value = ['foo']
>>> mock.connection.cursor().execute("SELECT 1")
['foo']
>>> expected = call.connection.cursor().execute("SELECT 1").call_list()
>>> mock.mock_calls
[call.connection.cursor(), call.connection.cursor().execute('SELECT 1')]
>>> mock.mock_calls == expected
True
```

It is the call to `.call_list()` that turns our call object into a list of calls representing the chained calls.

Raising exceptions with mocks

A useful attribute is *side_effect*. If you set this to an exception class or instance then the exception will be raised when the mock is called.

```
>>> mock = Mock(side_effect=Exception('Boom!'))
>>> mock()
Traceback (most recent call last):
 ...
Exception: Boom!
```

Side effect functions and iterables

`side_effect` can also be set to a function or an iterable. The use case for `side_effect` as an iterable is where your mock is going to be called several times, and you want each call to return a different value. When you set `side_effect` to an iterable every call to the mock returns the next value from the iterable:

```
>>> mock = MagicMock(side_effect=[4, 5, 6])
>>> mock()
4
>>> mock()
5
>>> mock()
6
```

For more advanced use cases, like dynamically varying the return values depending on what the mock is called with, `side_effect` can be a function. The function will be called with the same arguments as the mock. Whatever the function returns is what the call returns:

```
>>> vals = {(1, 2): 1, (2, 3): 2}
>>> def side_effect(*args):
...     return vals[args]
...
>>> mock = MagicMock(side_effect=side_effect)
>>> mock(1, 2)
1
>>> mock(2, 3)
2
```

Creating a Mock from an Existing Object

One problem with over use of mocking is that it couples your tests to the implementation of your mocks rather than your real code. Suppose you have a class that implements `some_method`. In a test for another class, you provide a mock of this object that *also* provides `some_method`. If later you refactor the first class, so that it no longer has `some_method` - then your tests will continue to pass even though your code is now broken!

Mock allows you to provide an object as a specification for the mock, using the *spec* keyword argument. Accessing methods / attributes on the mock that don't exist on your specification object will immediately raise an attribute error. If you change the implementation of your specification, then tests that use that class will start failing immediately without you having to instantiate the class in those tests.

```
>>> mock = Mock(spec=SomeClass)
>>> mock.old_method()
Traceback (most recent call last):
 ...
AttributeError: object has no attribute 'old_method'
```

Using a specification also enables a smarter matching of calls made to the mock, regardless of whether some parameters were passed as positional or named arguments:

```
>>> def f(a, b, c): pass
...
>>> mock = Mock(spec=f)
>>> mock(1, 2, 3)
<Mock name='mock()' id='140161580456576'>
>>> mock.assert_called_with(a=1, b=2, c=3)
```

If you want this smarter matching to also work with method calls on the mock, you can use *auto-speccing*.

If you want a stronger form of specification that prevents the setting of arbitrary attributes as well as the getting of them then you can use *spec_set* instead of *spec*.

26.6.2 Patch Decorators

Note: With *patch()* it matters that you patch objects in the namespace where they are looked up. This is normally straightforward, but for a quick guide read *where to patch*.

A common need in tests is to patch a class attribute or a module attribute, for example patching a builtin or patching a class in a module to test that it is instantiated. Modules and classes are effectively global, so patching on them has to be undone after the test or the patch will persist into other tests and cause hard to diagnose problems.

mock provides three convenient decorators for this: *patch()*, *patch.object()* and *patch.dict()*. **patch** takes a single string, of the form `package.module.Class.attribute` to specify the attribute you are patching. It also optionally takes a value that you want the attribute (or class or whatever) to be replaced with. 'patch.object' takes an object and the name of the attribute you would like patched, plus optionally the value to patch it with.

patch.object:

```
>>> original = SomeClass.attribute
>>> @patch.object(SomeClass, 'attribute', sentinel.attribute)
... def test():
...     assert SomeClass.attribute == sentinel.attribute
```

```
>>> test()
>>> assert SomeClass.attribute == original
```

```
>>> @patch('package.module.attribute', sentinel.attribute)
... def test():
...     from package.module import attribute
...     assert attribute is sentinel.attribute
...
>>> test()
```

If you are patching a module (including *builtins*) then use *patch()* instead of *patch.object()*:

```
>>> mock = MagicMock(return_value=sentinel.file_handle)
>>> with patch('builtins.open', mock):
...     handle = open('filename', 'r')
...
>>> mock.assert_called_with('filename', 'r')
>>> assert handle == sentinel.file_handle, "incorrect file handle returned"
```

The module name can be 'dotted', in the form **package.module** if needed:

```
>>> @patch('package.module.ClassName.attribute', sentinel.attribute)
... def test():
...     from package.module import ClassName
...     assert ClassName.attribute == sentinel.attribute
...
>>> test()
```

A nice pattern is to actually decorate test methods themselves:

```
>>> class MyTest(unittest.TestCase):
...     @patch.object(SomeClass, 'attribute', sentinel.attribute)
...     def test_something(self):
...         self.assertEqual(SomeClass.attribute, sentinel.attribute)
...
>>> original = SomeClass.attribute
>>> MyTest('test_something').test_something()
>>> assert SomeClass.attribute == original
```

If you want to patch with a Mock, you can use *patch()* with only one argument (or *patch.object()* with two arguments). The mock will be created for you and passed into the test function / method:

```
>>> class MyTest(unittest.TestCase):
...     @patch.object(SomeClass, 'static_method')
...     def test_something(self, mock_method):
...         SomeClass.static_method()
...         mock_method.assert_called_with()
...
>>> MyTest('test_something').test_something()
```

You can stack up multiple patch decorators using this pattern:

```
>>> class MyTest(unittest.TestCase):
...     @patch('package.module.ClassName1')
...     @patch('package.module.ClassName2')
...     def test_something(self, MockClass2, MockClass1):
...         self.assertIs(package.module.ClassName1, MockClass1)
```

```
...             self.assertIs(package.module.ClassName2, MockClass2)
...
>>> MyTest('test_something').test_something()
```

When you nest patch decorators the mocks are passed in to the decorated function in the same order they applied (the normal *python* order that decorators are applied). This means from the bottom up, so in the example above the mock for `test_module.ClassName2` is passed in first.

There is also *patch.dict()* for setting values in a dictionary just during a scope and restoring the dictionary to its original state when the test ends:

```
>>> foo = {'key': 'value'}
>>> original = foo.copy()
>>> with patch.dict(foo, {'newkey': 'newvalue'}, clear=True):
...     assert foo == {'newkey': 'newvalue'}
...
>>> assert foo == original
```

`patch`, `patch.object` and `patch.dict` can all be used as context managers.

Where you use *patch()* to create a mock for you, you can get a reference to the mock using the "as" form of the with statement:

```
>>> class ProductionClass:
...     def method(self):
...         pass
...
>>> with patch.object(ProductionClass, 'method') as mock_method:
...     mock_method.return_value = None
...     real = ProductionClass()
...     real.method(1, 2, 3)
...
>>> mock_method.assert_called_with(1, 2, 3)
```

As an alternative `patch`, `patch.object` and `patch.dict` can be used as class decorators. When used in this way it is the same as applying the decorator individually to every method whose name starts with "test".

26.6.3 Further Examples

Here are some more examples for some slightly more advanced scenarios.

Mocking chained calls

Mocking chained calls is actually straightforward with mock once you understand the *return_value* attribute. When a mock is called for the first time, or you fetch its `return_value` before it has been called, a new *Mock* is created.

This means that you can see how the object returned from a call to a mocked object has been used by interrogating the `return_value` mock:

```
>>> mock = Mock()
>>> mock().foo(a=2, b=3)
<Mock name='mock().foo()' id='...'>
>>> mock.return_value.foo.assert_called_with(a=2, b=3)
```

From here it is a simple step to configure and then make assertions about chained calls. Of course another alternative is writing your code in a more testable way in the first place...

So, suppose we have some code that looks a little bit like this:

```
>>> class Something:
...     def __init__(self):
...         self.backend = BackendProvider()
...     def method(self):
...         response = self.backend.get_endpoint('foobar').create_call('spam', 'eggs').start_call()
...         # more code
```

Assuming that `BackendProvider` is already well tested, how do we test `method()`? Specifically, we want to test that the code section `# more code` uses the response object in the correct way.

As this chain of calls is made from an instance attribute we can monkey patch the `backend` attribute on a `Something` instance. In this particular case we are only interested in the return value from the final call to `start_call` so we don't have much configuration to do. Let's assume the object it returns is 'file-like', so we'll ensure that our response object uses the builtin *open()* as its `spec`.

To do this we create a mock instance as our mock backend and create a mock response object for it. To set the response as the return value for that final `start_call` we could do this:

```
mock_backend.get_endpoint.return_value.create_call.return_value.start_call.return_value = mock_response
```

We can do that in a slightly nicer way using the *configure_mock()* method to directly set the return value for us:

```
>>> something = Something()
>>> mock_response = Mock(spec=open)
>>> mock_backend = Mock()
>>> config = {'get_endpoint.return_value.create_call.return_value.start_call.return_value': mock_response}
>>> mock_backend.configure_mock(**config)
```

With these we monkey patch the "mock backend" in place and can make the real call:

```
>>> something.backend = mock_backend
>>> something.method()
```

Using *mock_calls* we can check the chained call with a single assert. A chained call is several calls in one line of code, so there will be several entries in `mock_calls`. We can use *call.call_list()* to create this list of calls for us:

```
>>> chained = call.get_endpoint('foobar').create_call('spam', 'eggs').start_call()
>>> call_list = chained.call_list()
>>> assert mock_backend.mock_calls == call_list
```

Partial mocking

In some tests I wanted to mock out a call to *datetime.date.today()* to return a known date, but I didn't want to prevent the code under test from creating new date objects. Unfortunately *datetime.date* is written in C, and so I couldn't just monkey-patch out the static `date.today()` method.

I found a simple way of doing this that involved effectively wrapping the date class with a mock, but passing through calls to the constructor to the real class (and returning real instances).

The *patch decorator* is used here to mock out the `date` class in the module under test. The `side_effect` attribute on the mock date class is then set to a lambda function that returns a real date. When the mock date class is called a real date will be constructed and returned by `side_effect`.

```
>>> from datetime import date
>>> with patch('mymodule.date') as mock_date:
...     mock_date.today.return_value = date(2010, 10, 8)
...     mock_date.side_effect = lambda *args, **kw: date(*args, **kw)
...
...     assert mymodule.date.today() == date(2010, 10, 8)
...     assert mymodule.date(2009, 6, 8) == date(2009, 6, 8)
...
```

Note that we don't patch *datetime.date* globally, we patch `date` in the module that *uses* it. See *where to patch*.

When `date.today()` is called a known date is returned, but calls to the `date(...)` constructor still return normal dates. Without this you can find yourself having to calculate an expected result using exactly the same algorithm as the code under test, which is a classic testing anti-pattern.

Calls to the date constructor are recorded in the `mock_date` attributes (`call_count` and friends) which may also be useful for your tests.

An alternative way of dealing with mocking dates, or other builtin classes, is discussed in this blog entry.

Mocking a Generator Method

A Python generator is a function or method that uses the `yield` statement to return a series of values when iterated over[1].

A generator method / function is called to return the generator object. It is the generator object that is then iterated over. The protocol method for iteration is *__iter__()*, so we can mock this using a *MagicMock*.

Here's an example class with an "iter" method implemented as a generator:

```
>>> class Foo:
...     def iter(self):
...         for i in [1, 2, 3]:
...             yield i
...
>>> foo = Foo()
>>> list(foo.iter())
[1, 2, 3]
```

How would we mock this class, and in particular its "iter" method?

To configure the values returned from the iteration (implicit in the call to *list*), we need to configure the object returned by the call to `foo.iter()`.

```
>>> mock_foo = MagicMock()
>>> mock_foo.iter.return_value = iter([1, 2, 3])
>>> list(mock_foo.iter())
[1, 2, 3]
```

Applying the same patch to every test method

If you want several patches in place for multiple test methods the obvious way is to apply the patch decorators to every method. This can feel like unnecessary repetition. For Python 2.6 or more recent you can use

---

[1] There are also generator expressions and more advanced uses of generators, but we aren't concerned about them here. A very good introduction to generators and how powerful they are is: Generator Tricks for Systems Programmers.

`patch()` (in all its various forms) as a class decorator. This applies the patches to all test methods on the class. A test method is identified by methods whose names start with `test`:

```
>>> @patch('mymodule.SomeClass')
... class MyTest(TestCase):
...
...     def test_one(self, MockSomeClass):
...         self.assertIs(mymodule.SomeClass, MockSomeClass)
...
...     def test_two(self, MockSomeClass):
...         self.assertIs(mymodule.SomeClass, MockSomeClass)
...
...     def not_a_test(self):
...         return 'something'
...
>>> MyTest('test_one').test_one()
>>> MyTest('test_two').test_two()
>>> MyTest('test_two').not_a_test()
'something'
```

An alternative way of managing patches is to use the *patch methods: start and stop*. These allow you to move the patching into your `setUp` and `tearDown` methods.

```
>>> class MyTest(TestCase):
...     def setUp(self):
...         self.patcher = patch('mymodule.foo')
...         self.mock_foo = self.patcher.start()
...
...     def test_foo(self):
...         self.assertIs(mymodule.foo, self.mock_foo)
...
...     def tearDown(self):
...         self.patcher.stop()
...
>>> MyTest('test_foo').run()
```

If you use this technique you must ensure that the patching is "undone" by calling `stop`. This can be fiddlier than you might think, because if an exception is raised in the setUp then tearDown is not called. *unittest.TestCase.addCleanup()* makes this easier:

```
>>> class MyTest(TestCase):
...     def setUp(self):
...         patcher = patch('mymodule.foo')
...         self.addCleanup(patcher.stop)
...         self.mock_foo = patcher.start()
...
...     def test_foo(self):
...         self.assertIs(mymodule.foo, self.mock_foo)
...
>>> MyTest('test_foo').run()
```

Mocking Unbound Methods

Whilst writing tests today I needed to patch an *unbound method* (patching the method on the class rather than on the instance). I needed self to be passed in as the first argument because I want to make asserts about which objects were calling this particular method. The issue is that you can't patch with a mock for this, because if you replace an unbound method with a mock it doesn't become a bound method when fetched from the instance, and so it doesn't get self passed in. The workaround is to patch the unbound method with a real function instead. The *patch()* decorator makes it so simple to patch out methods with a mock that having to create a real function becomes a nuisance.

If you pass `autospec=True` to patch then it does the patching with a *real* function object. This function object has the same signature as the one it is replacing, but delegates to a mock under the hood. You still get your mock auto-created in exactly the same way as before. What it means though, is that if you use it to patch out an unbound method on a class the mocked function will be turned into a bound method if it is fetched from an instance. It will have `self` passed in as the first argument, which is exactly what I wanted:

```
>>> class Foo:
...     def foo(self):
...         pass
...
>>> with patch.object(Foo, 'foo', autospec=True) as mock_foo:
...     mock_foo.return_value = 'foo'
...     foo = Foo()
...     foo.foo()
...
'foo'
>>> mock_foo.assert_called_once_with(foo)
```

If we don't use `autospec=True` then the unbound method is patched out with a Mock instance instead, and isn't called with `self`.

Checking multiple calls with mock

mock has a nice API for making assertions about how your mock objects are used.

```
>>> mock = Mock()
>>> mock.foo_bar.return_value = None
>>> mock.foo_bar('baz', spam='eggs')
>>> mock.foo_bar.assert_called_with('baz', spam='eggs')
```

If your mock is only being called once you can use the `assert_called_once_with()` method that also asserts that the `call_count` is one.

```
>>> mock.foo_bar.assert_called_once_with('baz', spam='eggs')
>>> mock.foo_bar()
>>> mock.foo_bar.assert_called_once_with('baz', spam='eggs')
Traceback (most recent call last):
    ...
AssertionError: Expected to be called once. Called 2 times.
```

Both `assert_called_with` and `assert_called_once_with` make assertions about the *most recent* call. If your mock is going to be called several times, and you want to make assertions about *all* those calls you can use *call_args_list*:

```
>>> mock = Mock(return_value=None)
>>> mock(1, 2, 3)
>>> mock(4, 5, 6)
>>> mock()
>>> mock.call_args_list
[call(1, 2, 3), call(4, 5, 6), call()]
```

The *call* helper makes it easy to make assertions about these calls. You can build up a list of expected calls and compare it to `call_args_list`. This looks remarkably similar to the repr of the `call_args_list`:

```
>>> expected = [call(1, 2, 3), call(4, 5, 6), call()]
>>> mock.call_args_list == expected
True
```

Coping with mutable arguments

Another situation is rare, but can bite you, is when your mock is called with mutable arguments. `call_args` and `call_args_list` store *references* to the arguments. If the arguments are mutated by the code under test then you can no longer make assertions about what the values were when the mock was called.

Here's some example code that shows the problem. Imagine the following functions defined in 'mymodule':

```
def frob(val):
    pass

def grob(val):
    "First frob and then clear val"
    frob(val)
    val.clear()
```

When we try to test that grob calls frob with the correct argument look what happens:

```
>>> with patch('mymodule.frob') as mock_frob:
...     val = {6}
...     mymodule.grob(val)
...
>>> val
set()
>>> mock_frob.assert_called_with({6})
Traceback (most recent call last):
    ...
AssertionError: Expected: (({6},), {})
Called with: ((set(),), {})
```

One possibility would be for mock to copy the arguments you pass in. This could then cause problems if you do assertions that rely on object identity for equality.

Here's one solution that uses the `side_effect` functionality. If you provide a `side_effect` function for a mock then `side_effect` will be called with the same args as the mock. This gives us an opportunity to copy the arguments and store them for later assertions. In this example I'm using *another* mock to store the arguments so that I can use the mock methods for doing the assertion. Again a helper function sets this up for me.

```
>>> from copy import deepcopy
>>> from unittest.mock import Mock, patch, DEFAULT
>>> def copy_call_args(mock):
...     new_mock = Mock()
...     def side_effect(*args, **kwargs):
...         args = deepcopy(args)
...         kwargs = deepcopy(kwargs)
...         new_mock(*args, **kwargs)
...         return DEFAULT
...     mock.side_effect = side_effect
...     return new_mock
...
>>> with patch('mymodule.frob') as mock_frob:
...     new_mock = copy_call_args(mock_frob)
```

```
...         val = {6}
...         mymodule.grob(val)
...
>>> new_mock.assert_called_with({6})
>>> new_mock.call_args
call({6})
```

`copy_call_args` is called with the mock that will be called. It returns a new mock that we do the assertion on. The `side_effect` function makes a copy of the args and calls our `new_mock` with the copy.

Note: If your mock is only going to be used once there is an easier way of checking arguments at the point they are called. You can simply do the checking inside a `side_effect` function.

```
>>> def side_effect(arg):
...     assert arg == {6}
...
>>> mock = Mock(side_effect=side_effect)
>>> mock({6})
>>> mock(set())
Traceback (most recent call last):
    ...
AssertionError
```

An alternative approach is to create a subclass of *Mock* or *MagicMock* that copies (using *copy.deepcopy()*) the arguments. Here's an example implementation:

```
>>> from copy import deepcopy
>>> class CopyingMock(MagicMock):
...     def __call__(self, *args, **kwargs):
...         args = deepcopy(args)
...         kwargs = deepcopy(kwargs)
...         return super(CopyingMock, self).__call__(*args, **kwargs)
...
>>> c = CopyingMock(return_value=None)
>>> arg = set()
>>> c(arg)
>>> arg.add(1)
>>> c.assert_called_with(set())
>>> c.assert_called_with(arg)
Traceback (most recent call last):
    ...
AssertionError: Expected call: mock({1})
Actual call: mock(set())
>>> c.foo
<CopyingMock name='mock.foo' id='...'>
```

When you subclass `Mock` or `MagicMock` all dynamically created attributes, and the `return_value` will use your subclass automatically. That means all children of a `CopyingMock` will also have the type `CopyingMock`.

Nesting Patches

Using patch as a context manager is nice, but if you do multiple patches you can end up with nested with statements indenting further and further to the right:

```
>>> class MyTest(TestCase):
...     def test_foo(self):
...         with patch('mymodule.Foo') as mock_foo:
...             with patch('mymodule.Bar') as mock_bar:
...                 with patch('mymodule.Spam') as mock_spam:
...                     assert mymodule.Foo is mock_foo
...                     assert mymodule.Bar is mock_bar
...                     assert mymodule.Spam is mock_spam
...
>>> original = mymodule.Foo
>>> MyTest('test_foo').test_foo()
>>> assert mymodule.Foo is original
```

With unittest `cleanup` functions and the *patch methods: start and stop* we can achieve the same effect without the nested indentation. A simple helper method, `create_patch`, puts the patch in place and returns the created mock for us:

```
>>> class MyTest(TestCase):
...     def create_patch(self, name):
...         patcher = patch(name)
...         thing = patcher.start()
...         self.addCleanup(patcher.stop)
...         return thing
...
...     def test_foo(self):
...         mock_foo = self.create_patch('mymodule.Foo')
...         mock_bar = self.create_patch('mymodule.Bar')
...         mock_spam = self.create_patch('mymodule.Spam')
...
...         assert mymodule.Foo is mock_foo
...         assert mymodule.Bar is mock_bar
...         assert mymodule.Spam is mock_spam
...
>>> original = mymodule.Foo
>>> MyTest('test_foo').run()
>>> assert mymodule.Foo is original
```

Mocking a dictionary with MagicMock

You may want to mock a dictionary, or other container object, recording all access to it whilst having it still behave like a dictionary.

We can do this with *MagicMock*, which will behave like a dictionary, and using *side_effect* to delegate dictionary access to a real underlying dictionary that is under our control.

When the `__getitem__()` and `__setitem__()` methods of our `MagicMock` are called (normal dictionary access) then `side_effect` is called with the key (and in the case of `__setitem__` the value too). We can also control what is returned.

After the `MagicMock` has been used we can use attributes like *call_args_list* to assert about how the dictionary was used:

```
>>> my_dict = {'a': 1, 'b': 2, 'c': 3}
>>> def getitem(name):
...     return my_dict[name]
```

```
...
>>> def setitem(name, val):
...     my_dict[name] = val
...
>>> mock = MagicMock()
>>> mock.__getitem__.side_effect = getitem
>>> mock.__setitem__.side_effect = setitem
```

Note: An alternative to using `MagicMock` is to use `Mock` and *only* provide the magic methods you specifically want:

```
>>> mock = Mock()
>>> mock.__getitem__ = Mock(side_effect=getitem)
>>> mock.__setitem__ = Mock(side_effect=setitem)
```

A *third* option is to use `MagicMock` but passing in `dict` as the *spec* (or *spec_set*) argument so that the `MagicMock` created only has dictionary magic methods available:

```
>>> mock = MagicMock(spec_set=dict)
>>> mock.__getitem__.side_effect = getitem
>>> mock.__setitem__.side_effect = setitem
```

With these side effect functions in place, the `mock` will behave like a normal dictionary but recording the access. It even raises a *KeyError* if you try to access a key that doesn't exist.

```
>>> mock['a']
1
>>> mock['c']
3
>>> mock['d']
Traceback (most recent call last):
    ...
KeyError: 'd'
>>> mock['b'] = 'fish'
>>> mock['d'] = 'eggs'
>>> mock['b']
'fish'
>>> mock['d']
'eggs'
```

After it has been used you can make assertions about the access using the normal mock methods and attributes:

```
>>> mock.__getitem__.call_args_list
[call('a'), call('c'), call('d'), call('b'), call('d')]
>>> mock.__setitem__.call_args_list
[call('b', 'fish'), call('d', 'eggs')]
>>> my_dict
{'a': 1, 'c': 3, 'b': 'fish', 'd': 'eggs'}
```

Mock subclasses and their attributes

There are various reasons why you might want to subclass *Mock*. One reason might be to add helper methods. Here's a silly example:

```
>>> class MyMock(MagicMock):
...     def has_been_called(self):
...         return self.called
...
>>> mymock = MyMock(return_value=None)
>>> mymock
<MyMock id='...'>
>>> mymock.has_been_called()
False
>>> mymock()
>>> mymock.has_been_called()
True
```

The standard behaviour for `Mock` instances is that attributes and the return value mocks are of the same type as the mock they are accessed on. This ensures that `Mock` attributes are `Mocks` and `MagicMock` attributes are `MagicMocks`[2]. So if you're subclassing to add helper methods then they'll also be available on the attributes and return value mock of instances of your subclass.

```
>>> mymock.foo
<MyMock name='mock.foo' id='...'>
>>> mymock.foo.has_been_called()
False
>>> mymock.foo()
<MyMock name='mock.foo()' id='...'>
>>> mymock.foo.has_been_called()
True
```

Sometimes this is inconvenient. For example, one user is subclassing mock to created a Twisted adaptor. Having this applied to attributes too actually causes errors.

`Mock` (in all its flavours) uses a method called `_get_child_mock` to create these "sub-mocks" for attributes and return values. You can prevent your subclass being used for attributes by overriding this method. The signature is that it takes arbitrary keyword arguments (`**kwargs`) which are then passed onto the mock constructor:

```
>>> class Subclass(MagicMock):
...     def _get_child_mock(self, **kwargs):
...         return MagicMock(**kwargs)
...
>>> mymock = Subclass()
>>> mymock.foo
<MagicMock name='mock.foo' id='...'>
>>> assert isinstance(mymock, Subclass)
>>> assert not isinstance(mymock.foo, Subclass)
>>> assert not isinstance(mymock(), Subclass)
```

Mocking imports with patch.dict

One situation where mocking can be hard is where you have a local import inside a function. These are harder to mock because they aren't using an object from the module namespace that we can patch out.

Generally local imports are to be avoided. They are sometimes done to prevent circular dependencies, for which there is *usually* a much better way to solve the problem (refactor the code) or to prevent "up front

---

[2] An exception to this rule are the non-callable mocks. Attributes use the callable variant because otherwise non-callable mocks couldn't have callable methods.

costs" by delaying the import. This can also be solved in better ways than an unconditional local import (store the module as a class or module attribute and only do the import on first use).

That aside there is a way to use `mock` to affect the results of an import. Importing fetches an *object* from the *sys.modules* dictionary. Note that it fetches an *object*, which need not be a module. Importing a module for the first time results in a module object being put in *sys.modules*, so usually when you import something you get a module back. This need not be the case however.

This means you can use *patch.dict()* to *temporarily* put a mock in place in *sys.modules*. Any imports whilst this patch is active will fetch the mock. When the patch is complete (the decorated function exits, the with statement body is complete or `patcher.stop()` is called) then whatever was there previously will be restored safely.

Here's an example that mocks out the 'fooble' module.

```
>>> mock = Mock()
>>> with patch.dict('sys.modules', {'fooble': mock}):
...     import fooble
...     fooble.blob()
...
<Mock name='mock.blob()' id='...'>
>>> assert 'fooble' not in sys.modules
>>> mock.blob.assert_called_once_with()
```

As you can see the `import fooble` succeeds, but on exit there is no 'fooble' left in *sys.modules*.

This also works for the `from module import name` form:

```
>>> mock = Mock()
>>> with patch.dict('sys.modules', {'fooble': mock}):
...     from fooble import blob
...     blob.blip()
...
<Mock name='mock.blob.blip()' id='...'>
>>> mock.blob.blip.assert_called_once_with()
```

With slightly more work you can also mock package imports:

```
>>> mock = Mock()
>>> modules = {'package': mock, 'package.module': mock.module}
>>> with patch.dict('sys.modules', modules):
...     from package.module import fooble
...     fooble()
...
<Mock name='mock.module.fooble()' id='...'>
>>> mock.module.fooble.assert_called_once_with()
```

Tracking order of calls and less verbose call assertions

The *Mock* class allows you to track the *order* of method calls on your mock objects through the *method_calls* attribute. This doesn't allow you to track the order of calls between separate mock objects, however we can use *mock_calls* to achieve the same effect.

Because mocks track calls to child mocks in `mock_calls`, and accessing an arbitrary attribute of a mock creates a child mock, we can create our separate mocks from a parent one. Calls to those child mock will then all be recorded, in order, in the `mock_calls` of the parent:

```
>>> manager = Mock()
>>> mock_foo = manager.foo
>>> mock_bar = manager.bar
```

```
>>> mock_foo.something()
<Mock name='mock.foo.something()' id='...'>
>>> mock_bar.other.thing()
<Mock name='mock.bar.other.thing()' id='...'>
```

```
>>> manager.mock_calls
[call.foo.something(), call.bar.other.thing()]
```

We can then assert about the calls, including the order, by comparing with the `mock_calls` attribute on the manager mock:

```
>>> expected_calls = [call.foo.something(), call.bar.other.thing()]
>>> manager.mock_calls == expected_calls
True
```

If `patch` is creating, and putting in place, your mocks then you can attach them to a manager mock using the *attach_mock()* method. After attaching calls will be recorded in `mock_calls` of the manager.

```
>>> manager = MagicMock()
>>> with patch('mymodule.Class1') as MockClass1:
...     with patch('mymodule.Class2') as MockClass2:
...         manager.attach_mock(MockClass1, 'MockClass1')
...         manager.attach_mock(MockClass2, 'MockClass2')
...         MockClass1().foo()
...         MockClass2().bar()
...
<MagicMock name='mock.MockClass1().foo()' id='...'>
<MagicMock name='mock.MockClass2().bar()' id='...'>
>>> manager.mock_calls
[call.MockClass1(),
 call.MockClass1().foo(),
 call.MockClass2(),
 call.MockClass2().bar()]
```

If many calls have been made, but you're only interested in a particular sequence of them then an alternative is to use the *assert_has_calls()* method. This takes a list of calls (constructed with the *call* object). If that sequence of calls are in *mock_calls* then the assert succeeds.

```
>>> m = MagicMock()
>>> m().foo().bar().baz()
<MagicMock name='mock().foo().bar().baz()' id='...'>
>>> m.one().two().three()
<MagicMock name='mock.one().two().three()' id='...'>
>>> calls = call.one().two().three().call_list()
>>> m.assert_has_calls(calls)
```

Even though the chained call `m.one().two().three()` aren't the only calls that have been made to the mock, the assert still succeeds.

Sometimes a mock may have several calls made to it, and you are only interested in asserting about *some* of those calls. You may not even care about the order. In this case you can pass `any_order=True` to `assert_has_calls`:

```
>>> m = MagicMock()
>>> m(1), m.two(2, 3), m.seven(7), m.fifty('50')
(...)
>>> calls = [call.fifty('50'), call(1), call.seven(7)]
>>> m.assert_has_calls(calls, any_order=True)
```

More complex argument matching

Using the same basic concept as *ANY* we can implement matchers to do more complex assertions on objects used as arguments to mocks.

Suppose we expect some object to be passed to a mock that by default compares equal based on object identity (which is the Python default for user defined classes). To use *assert_called_with()* we would need to pass in the exact same object. If we are only interested in some of the attributes of this object then we can create a matcher that will check these attributes for us.

You can see in this example how a 'standard' call to `assert_called_with` isn't sufficient:

```
>>> class Foo:
...     def __init__(self, a, b):
...         self.a, self.b = a, b
...
>>> mock = Mock(return_value=None)
>>> mock(Foo(1, 2))
>>> mock.assert_called_with(Foo(1, 2))
Traceback (most recent call last):
    ...
AssertionError: Expected: call(<__main__.Foo object at 0x...>)
Actual call: call(<__main__.Foo object at 0x...>)
```

A comparison function for our `Foo` class might look something like this:

```
>>> def compare(self, other):
...     if not type(self) == type(other):
...         return False
...     if self.a != other.a:
...         return False
...     if self.b != other.b:
...         return False
...     return True
...
```

And a matcher object that can use comparison functions like this for its equality operation would look something like this:

```
>>> class Matcher:
...     def __init__(self, compare, some_obj):
...         self.compare = compare
...         self.some_obj = some_obj
...     def __eq__(self, other):
...         return self.compare(self.some_obj, other)
...
```

Putting all this together:

```
>>> match_foo = Matcher(compare, Foo(1, 2))
>>> mock.assert_called_with(match_foo)
```

The Matcher is instantiated with our compare function and the Foo object we want to compare against. In `assert_called_with` the Matcher equality method will be called, which compares the object the mock was called with against the one we created our matcher with. If they match then `assert_called_with` passes, and if they don't an *AssertionError* is raised:

```
>>> match_wrong = Matcher(compare, Foo(3, 4))
>>> mock.assert_called_with(match_wrong)
Traceback (most recent call last):
    ...
AssertionError: Expected: ((<Matcher object at 0x...>,), {})
Called with: ((<Foo object at 0x...>,), {})
```

With a bit of tweaking you could have the comparison function raise the *AssertionError* directly and provide a more useful failure message.

As of version 1.5, the Python testing library PyHamcrest provides similar functionality, that may be useful here, in the form of its equality matcher (hamcrest.library.integration.match_equality).

26.7 2to3 - Automated Python 2 to 3 code translation

2to3 is a Python program that reads Python 2.x source code and applies a series of *fixers* to transform it into valid Python 3.x code. The standard library contains a rich set of fixers that will handle almost all code. 2to3 supporting library *lib2to3* is, however, a flexible and generic library, so it is possible to write your own fixers for 2to3. *lib2to3* could also be adapted to custom applications in which Python code needs to be edited automatically.

26.7.1 Using 2to3

2to3 will usually be installed with the Python interpreter as a script. It is also located in the `Tools/scripts` directory of the Python root.

2to3's basic arguments are a list of files or directories to transform. The directories are recursively traversed for Python sources.

Here is a sample Python 2.x source file, `example.py`:

```
def greet(name):
    print "Hello, {0}!".format(name)
print "What's your name?"
name = raw_input()
greet(name)
```

It can be converted to Python 3.x code via 2to3 on the command line:

```
$ 2to3 example.py
```

A diff against the original source file is printed. 2to3 can also write the needed modifications right back to the source file. (A backup of the original file is made unless `-n` is also given.) Writing the changes back is enabled with the `-w` flag:

```
$ 2to3 -w example.py
```

After transformation, `example.py` looks like this:

```
def greet(name):
    print("Hello, {0}!".format(name))
print("What's your name?")
name = input()
greet(name)
```

Comments and exact indentation are preserved throughout the translation process.

By default, 2to3 runs a set of *predefined fixers*. The -l flag lists all available fixers. An explicit set of fixers to run can be given with -f. Likewise the -x explicitly disables a fixer. The following example runs only the `imports` and `has_key` fixers:

```
$ 2to3 -f imports -f has_key example.py
```

This command runs every fixer except the `apply` fixer:

```
$ 2to3 -x apply example.py
```

Some fixers are *explicit*, meaning they aren't run by default and must be listed on the command line to be run. Here, in addition to the default fixers, the `idioms` fixer is run:

```
$ 2to3 -f all -f idioms example.py
```

Notice how passing `all` enables all default fixers.

Sometimes 2to3 will find a place in your source code that needs to be changed, but 2to3 cannot fix automatically. In this case, 2to3 will print a warning beneath the diff for a file. You should address the warning in order to have compliant 3.x code.

2to3 can also refactor doctests. To enable this mode, use the -d flag. Note that *only* doctests will be refactored. This also doesn't require the module to be valid Python. For example, doctest like examples in a reST document could also be refactored with this option.

The -v option enables output of more information on the translation process.

Since some print statements can be parsed as function calls or statements, 2to3 cannot always read files containing the print function. When 2to3 detects the presence of the `from __future__ import print_function` compiler directive, it modifies its internal grammar to interpret *print()* as a function. This change can also be enabled manually with the -p flag. Use -p to run fixers on code that already has had its print statements converted.

The -o or --output-dir option allows specification of an alternate directory for processed output files to be written to. The -n flag is required when using this as backup files do not make sense when not overwriting the input files.

New in version 3.2.3: The -o option was added.

The -W or --write-unchanged-files flag tells 2to3 to always write output files even if no changes were required to the file. This is most useful with -o so that an entire Python source tree is copied with translation from one directory to another. This option implies the -w flag as it would not make sense otherwise.

New in version 3.2.3: The -W flag was added.

The --add-suffix option specifies a string to append to all output filenames. The -n flag is required when specifying this as backups are not necessary when writing to different filenames. Example:

```
$ 2to3 -n -W --add-suffix=3 example.py
```

Will cause a converted file named `example.py3` to be written.

New in version 3.2.3: The --add-suffix option was added.

To translate an entire project from one directory tree to another use:

```
$ 2to3 --output-dir=python3-version/mycode -W -n python2-version/mycode
```

26.7.2 Fixers

Each step of transforming code is encapsulated in a fixer. The command `2to3 -l` lists them. As *documented above*, each can be turned on and off individually. They are described here in more detail.

apply
> Removes usage of `apply()`. For example `apply(function, *args, **kwargs)` is converted to `function(*args, **kwargs)`.

asserts
> Replaces deprecated *unittest* method names with the correct ones.

From	To
`failUnlessEqual(a, b)`	*assertEqual(a, b)*
`assertEquals(a, b)`	*assertEqual(a, b)*
`failIfEqual(a, b)`	*assertNotEqual(a, b)*
`assertNotEquals(a, b)`	*assertNotEqual(a, b)*
`failUnless(a)`	*assertTrue(a)*
`assert_(a)`	*assertTrue(a)*
`failIf(a)`	*assertFalse(a)*
`failUnlessRaises(exc, cal)`	*assertRaises(exc, cal)*
`failUnlessAlmostEqual(a, b)`	*assertAlmostEqual(a, b)*
`assertAlmostEquals(a, b)`	*assertAlmostEqual(a, b)*
`failIfAlmostEqual(a, b)`	*assertNotAlmostEqual(a, b)*
`assertNotAlmostEquals(a, b)`	*assertNotAlmostEqual(a, b)*

basestring
> Converts `basestring` to *str*.

buffer
> Converts `buffer` to *memoryview*. This fixer is optional because the *memoryview* API is similar but not exactly the same as that of `buffer`.

dict
> Fixes dictionary iteration methods. `dict.iteritems()` is converted to *dict.items()*, `dict.iterkeys()` to *dict.keys()*, and `dict.itervalues()` to *dict.values()*. Similarly, `dict.viewitems()`, `dict.viewkeys()` and `dict.viewvalues()` are converted respectively to *dict.items()*, *dict.keys()* and *dict.values()*. It also wraps existing usages of *dict.items()*, *dict.keys()*, and *dict.values()* in a call to *list*.

except
> Converts `except X, T` to `except X as T`.

exec
> Converts the `exec` statement to the *exec()* function.

execfile
> Removes usage of `execfile()`. The argument to `execfile()` is wrapped in calls to *open()*, *compile()*, and *exec()*.

exitfunc
> Changes assignment of `sys.exitfunc` to use of the *atexit* module.

filter
> Wraps *filter()* usage in a *list* call.

funcattrs
> Fixes function attributes that have been renamed. For example, `my_function.func_closure` is converted to `my_function.__closure__`.

future
> Removes `from __future__ import new_feature` statements.

getcwdu
> Renames `os.getcwdu()` to *os.getcwd()*.

has_key
> Changes `dict.has_key(key)` to `key in dict`.

idioms
> This optional fixer performs several transformations that make Python code more idiomatic. Type comparisons like `type(x) is SomeClass` and `type(x) == SomeClass` are converted to `isinstance(x, SomeClass)`. `while 1` becomes `while True`. This fixer also tries to make use of *sorted()* in appropriate places. For example, this block
>
> ```
> L = list(some_iterable)
> L.sort()
> ```
>
> is changed to
>
> ```
> L = sorted(some_iterable)
> ```

import
> Detects sibling imports and converts them to relative imports.

imports
> Handles module renames in the standard library.

imports2
> Handles other modules renames in the standard library. It is separate from the *imports* fixer only because of technical limitations.

input
> Converts `input(prompt)` to `eval(input(prompt))`.

intern
> Converts `intern()` to *sys.intern()*.

isinstance
> Fixes duplicate types in the second argument of *isinstance()*. For example, `isinstance(x, (int, int))` is converted to `isinstance(x, int)` and `isinstance(x, (int, float, int))` is converted to `isinstance(x, (int, float))`.

itertools_imports
> Removes imports of `itertools.ifilter()`, `itertools.izip()`, and `itertools.imap()`. Imports of `itertools.ifilterfalse()` are also changed to *itertools.filterfalse()*.

itertools
> Changes usage of `itertools.ifilter()`, `itertools.izip()`, and `itertools.imap()` to their built-in equivalents. `itertools.ifilterfalse()` is changed to *itertools.filterfalse()*.

long
> Renames `long` to *int*.

map
> Wraps *map()* in a *list* call. It also changes map(None, x) to list(x). Using from future_builtins import map disables this fixer.

metaclass
> Converts the old metaclass syntax (__metaclass__ = Meta in the class body) to the new (class X(metaclass=Meta)).

methodattrs
> Fixes old method attribute names. For example, meth.im_func is converted to meth.__func__.

ne
> Converts the old not-equal syntax, <>, to !=.

next
> Converts the use of iterator's next() methods to the *next()* function. It also renames *next()* methods to *__next__()*.

nonzero
> Renames __nonzero__() to __bool__().

numliterals
> Converts octal literals into the new syntax.

operator
> Converts calls to various functions in the *operator* module to other, but equivalent, function calls. When needed, the appropriate import statements are added, e.g. import collections. The following mapping are made:

From	To
operator.isCallable(obj)	hasattr(obj, '__call__')
operator.sequenceIncludes(obj)	operator.contains(obj)
operator.isSequenceType(obj)	isinstance(obj, collections.Sequence)
operator.isMappingType(obj)	isinstance(obj, collections.Mapping)
operator.isNumberType(obj)	isinstance(obj, numbers.Number)
operator.repeat(obj, n)	operator.mul(obj, n)
operator.irepeat(obj, n)	operator.imul(obj, n)

paren
> Add extra parenthesis where they are required in list comprehensions. For example, [x for x in 1, 2] becomes [x for x in (1, 2)].

print
> Converts the print statement to the *print()* function.

raise
> Converts raise E, V to raise E(V), and raise E, V, T to raise E(V).with_traceback(T). If E is a tuple, the translation will be incorrect because substituting tuples for exceptions has been removed in 3.0.

raw_input
> Converts raw_input() to *input()*.

reduce
> Handles the move of reduce() to *functools.reduce()*.

reload
> Converts reload() to *imp.reload()*.

renames
> Changes sys.maxint to *sys.maxsize*.

repr
    Replaces backtick repr with the *repr()* function.

set_literal
    Replaces use of the *set* constructor with set literals. This fixer is optional.

standarderror
    Renames StandardError to *Exception*.

sys_exc
    Changes the deprecated sys.exc_value, sys.exc_type, sys.exc_traceback to use *sys.exc_info()*.

throw
    Fixes the API change in generator's throw() method.

tuple_params
    Removes implicit tuple parameter unpacking. This fixer inserts temporary variables.

types
    Fixes code broken from the removal of some members in the *types* module.

unicode
    Renames unicode to *str*.

urllib
    Handles the rename of *urllib* and urllib2 to the *urllib* package.

ws_comma
    Removes excess whitespace from comma separated items. This fixer is optional.

xrange
    Renames xrange() to *range()* and wraps existing *range()* calls with *list*.

xreadlines
    Changes for x in file.xreadlines() to for x in file.

zip
    Wraps *zip()* usage in a *list* call. This is disabled when from future_builtins import zip appears.

26.7.3 lib2to3 - 2to3's library

Source code: Lib/lib2to3/

Note: The *lib2to3* API should be considered unstable and may change drastically in the future.

26.8 test — Regression tests package for Python

Note: The *test* package is meant for internal use by Python only. It is documented for the benefit of the core developers of Python. Any use of this package outside of Python's standard library is discouraged as code mentioned here can change or be removed without notice between releases of Python.

The *test* package contains all regression tests for Python as well as the modules *test.support* and **test.regrtest**. *test.support* is used to enhance your tests while **test.regrtest** drives the testing suite.

Each module in the *test* package whose name starts with `test_` is a testing suite for a specific module or feature. All new tests should be written using the *unittest* or *doctest* module. Some older tests are written using a "traditional" testing style that compares output printed to `sys.stdout`; this style of test is considered deprecated.

See also:

Module *unittest* Writing PyUnit regression tests.

Module *doctest* Tests embedded in documentation strings.

26.8.1 Writing Unit Tests for the `test` package

It is preferred that tests that use the *unittest* module follow a few guidelines. One is to name the test module by starting it with `test_` and end it with the name of the module being tested. The test methods in the test module should start with `test_` and end with a description of what the method is testing. This is needed so that the methods are recognized by the test driver as test methods. Also, no documentation string for the method should be included. A comment (such as `# Tests function returns only True or False`) should be used to provide documentation for test methods. This is done because documentation strings get printed out if they exist and thus what test is being run is not stated.

A basic boilerplate is often used:

```python
import unittest
from test import support

class MyTestCase1(unittest.TestCase):

    # Only use setUp() and tearDown() if necessary

    def setUp(self):
        ... code to execute in preparation for tests ...

    def tearDown(self):
        ... code to execute to clean up after tests ...

    def test_feature_one(self):
        # Test feature one.
        ... testing code ...

    def test_feature_two(self):
        # Test feature two.
        ... testing code ...

    ... more test methods ...

class MyTestCase2(unittest.TestCase):
    ... same structure as MyTestCase1 ...

... more test classes ...

if __name__ == '__main__':
    unittest.main()
```

This code pattern allows the testing suite to be run by `test.regrtest`, on its own as a script that supports the *unittest* CLI, or via the `python -m unittest` CLI.

The goal for regression testing is to try to break code. This leads to a few guidelines to be followed:

- The testing suite should exercise all classes, functions, and constants. This includes not just the external API that is to be presented to the outside world but also "private" code.
- Whitebox testing (examining the code being tested when the tests are being written) is preferred. Blackbox testing (testing only the published user interface) is not complete enough to make sure all boundary and edge cases are tested.
- Make sure all possible values are tested including invalid ones. This makes sure that not only all valid values are acceptable but also that improper values are handled correctly.
- Exhaust as many code paths as possible. Test where branching occurs and thus tailor input to make sure as many different paths through the code are taken.
- Add an explicit test for any bugs discovered for the tested code. This will make sure that the error does not crop up again if the code is changed in the future.
- Make sure to clean up after your tests (such as close and remove all temporary files).
- If a test is dependent on a specific condition of the operating system then verify the condition already exists before attempting the test.
- Import as few modules as possible and do it as soon as possible. This minimizes external dependencies of tests and also minimizes possible anomalous behavior from side-effects of importing a module.
- Try to maximize code reuse. On occasion, tests will vary by something as small as what type of input is used. Minimize code duplication by subclassing a basic test class with a class that specifies the input:

```
class TestFuncAcceptsSequencesMixin:

    func = mySuperWhammyFunction

    def test_func(self):
        self.func(self.arg)

class AcceptLists(TestFuncAcceptsSequencesMixin, unittest.TestCase):
    arg = [1, 2, 3]

class AcceptStrings(TestFuncAcceptsSequencesMixin, unittest.TestCase):
    arg = 'abc'

class AcceptTuples(TestFuncAcceptsSequencesMixin, unittest.TestCase):
    arg = (1, 2, 3)
```

When using this pattern, remember that all classes that inherit from *unittest.TestCase* are run as tests. The `Mixin` class in the example above does not have any data and so can't be run by itself, thus it does not inherit from *unittest.TestCase*.

See also:

Test Driven Development A book by Kent Beck on writing tests before code.

26.8.2 Running tests using the command-line interface

The `test` package can be run as a script to drive Python's regression test suite, thanks to the -m option: **python -m test**. Under the hood, it uses `test.regrtest`; the call **python -m test.regrtest** used in previous Python versions still works. Running the script by itself automatically starts running all regression tests in the `test` package. It does this by finding all modules in the package whose name starts with `test_`, importing them, and executing the function `test_main()` if present or loading the tests via unittest.TestLoader.loadTestsFromModule if `test_main` does not exist. The names of tests to execute may also be passed to the script. Specifying a single regression test (**python -m test test_spam**) will minimize output and only print whether the test passed or failed.

Running `test` directly allows what resources are available for tests to use to be set. You do this by using the -u command-line option. Specifying all as the value for the -u option enables all possible resources: **python -m test -uall**. If all but one resource is desired (a more common case), a comma-separated list of resources that are not desired may be listed after all. The command **python -m test -uall,-audio,-largefile** will run `test` with all resources except the audio and largefile resources. For a list of all resources and more command-line options, run **python -m test -h**.

Some other ways to execute the regression tests depend on what platform the tests are being executed on. On Unix, you can run **make test** at the top-level directory where Python was built. On Windows, executing **rt.bat** from your **PCBuild** directory will run all regression tests.

26.9 `test.support` — Utilities for the Python test suite

The `test.support` module provides support for Python's regression test suite.

Note: `test.support` is not a public module. It is documented here to help Python developers write tests. The API of this module is subject to change without backwards compatibility concerns between releases.

This module defines the following exceptions:

exception test.support.TestFailed
Exception to be raised when a test fails. This is deprecated in favor of *unittest*-based tests and *unittest.TestCase*'s assertion methods.

exception test.support.ResourceDenied
Subclass of *unittest.SkipTest*. Raised when a resource (such as a network connection) is not available. Raised by the *requires()* function.

The `test.support` module defines the following constants:

test.support.verbose
True when verbose output is enabled. Should be checked when more detailed information is desired about a running test. *verbose* is set by **test.regrtest**.

test.support.is_jython
True if the running interpreter is Jython.

test.support.TESTFN
Set to a name that is safe to use as the name of a temporary file. Any temporary file that is created should be closed and unlinked (removed).

The `test.support` module defines the following functions:

test.support.forget(*module_name*)
Remove the module named *module_name* from **sys.modules** and delete any byte-compiled files of the module.

test.support.is_resource_enabled(*resource*)
Return True if *resource* is enabled and available. The list of available resources is only set when **test.regrtest** is executing the tests.

test.support.requires(*resource, msg=None*)
Raise *ResourceDenied* if *resource* is not available. *msg* is the argument to *ResourceDenied* if it is raised. Always returns True if called by a function whose __name__ is '__main__'. Used when tests are executed by **test.regrtest**.

test.support.findfile(*filename, subdir=None*)
Return the path to the file named *filename*. If no match is found *filename* is returned. This does not equal a failure since it could be the path to the file.

Setting *subdir* indicates a relative path to use to find the file rather than looking directly in the path directories.

test.support.run_unittest(**classes*)

Execute *unittest.TestCase* subclasses passed to the function. The function scans the classes for methods starting with the prefix `test_` and executes the tests individually.

It is also legal to pass strings as parameters; these should be keys in `sys.modules`. Each associated module will be scanned by `unittest.TestLoader.loadTestsFromModule()`. This is usually seen in the following `test_main()` function:

```
def test_main():
    support.run_unittest(__name__)
```

This will run all tests defined in the named module.

test.support.run_doctest(*module, verbosity=None*)

Run *doctest.testmod()* on the given *module*. Return (`failure_count, test_count`).

If *verbosity* is `None`, *doctest.testmod()* is run with verbosity set to *verbose*. Otherwise, it is run with verbosity set to `None`.

test.support.check_warnings(**filters, quiet=True*)

A convenience wrapper for *warnings.catch_warnings()* that makes it easier to test that a warning was correctly raised. It is approximately equivalent to calling `warnings.catch_warnings(record=True)` with *warnings.simplefilter()* set to `always` and with the option to automatically validate the results that are recorded.

`check_warnings` accepts 2-tuples of the form (`"message regexp", WarningCategory`) as positional arguments. If one or more *filters* are provided, or if the optional keyword argument *quiet* is `False`, it checks to make sure the warnings are as expected: each specified filter must match at least one of the warnings raised by the enclosed code or the test fails, and if any warnings are raised that do not match any of the specified filters the test fails. To disable the first of these checks, set *quiet* to `True`.

If no arguments are specified, it defaults to:

```
check_warnings(("", Warning), quiet=True)
```

In this case all warnings are caught and no errors are raised.

On entry to the context manager, a `WarningRecorder` instance is returned. The underlying warnings list from *catch_warnings()* is available via the recorder object's *warnings* attribute. As a convenience, the attributes of the object representing the most recent warning can also be accessed directly through the recorder object (see example below). If no warning has been raised, then any of the attributes that would otherwise be expected on an object representing a warning will return `None`.

The recorder object also has a `reset()` method, which clears the warnings list.

The context manager is designed to be used like this:

```
with check_warnings(("assertion is always true", SyntaxWarning),
                    ("", UserWarning)):
    exec('assert(False, "Hey!")')
    warnings.warn(UserWarning("Hide me!"))
```

In this case if either warning was not raised, or some other warning was raised, *check_warnings()* would raise an error.

When a test needs to look more deeply into the warnings, rather than just checking whether or not they occurred, code like this can be used:

```
with check_warnings(quiet=True) as w:
    warnings.warn("foo")
    assert str(w.args[0]) == "foo"
    warnings.warn("bar")
    assert str(w.args[0]) == "bar"
    assert str(w.warnings[0].args[0]) == "foo"
    assert str(w.warnings[1].args[0]) == "bar"
    w.reset()
    assert len(w.warnings) == 0
```

Here all warnings will be caught, and the test code tests the captured warnings directly.

Changed in version 3.2: New optional arguments *filters* and *quiet*.

test.support.captured_stdin()
test.support.captured_stdout()
test.support.captured_stderr()

A context managers that temporarily replaces the named stream with *io.StringIO* object.

Example use with output streams:

```
with captured_stdout() as stdout, captured_stderr() as stderr:
    print("hello")
    print("error", file=sys.stderr)
assert stdout.getvalue() == "hello\n"
assert stderr.getvalue() == "error\n"
```

Example use with input stream:

```
with captured_stdin() as stdin:
    stdin.write('hello\n')
    stdin.seek(0)
    # call test code that consumes from sys.stdin
    captured = input()
self.assertEqual(captured, "hello")
```

test.support.temp_dir(*path=None, quiet=False*)

A context manager that creates a temporary directory at *path* and yields the directory.

If *path* is None, the temporary directory is created using *tempfile.mkdtemp()*. If *quiet* is False, the context manager raises an exception on error. Otherwise, if *path* is specified and cannot be created, only a warning is issued.

test.support.change_cwd(*path, quiet=False*)

A context manager that temporarily changes the current working directory to *path* and yields the directory.

If *quiet* is False, the context manager raises an exception on error. Otherwise, it issues only a warning and keeps the current working directory the same.

test.support.temp_cwd(*name='tempcwd', quiet=False*)

A context manager that temporarily creates a new directory and changes the current working directory (CWD).

The context manager creates a temporary directory in the current directory with name *name* before temporarily changing the current working directory. If *name* is None, the temporary directory is created using *tempfile.mkdtemp()*.

If *quiet* is False and it is not possible to create or change the CWD, an error is raised. Otherwise, only a warning is raised and the original CWD is used.

test.support.temp_umask(*umask*)
: A context manager that temporarily sets the process umask.

test.support.can_symlink()
: Return True if the OS supports symbolic links, False otherwise.

@test.support.skip_unless_symlink
: A decorator for running tests that require support for symbolic links.

@test.support.anticipate_failure(*condition*)
: A decorator to conditionally mark tests with *unittest.expectedFailure()*. Any use of this decorator should have an associated comment identifying the relevant tracker issue.

@test.support.run_with_locale(*catstr*, **locales*)
: A decorator for running a function in a different locale, correctly resetting it after it has finished. *catstr* is the locale category as a string (for example "LC_ALL"). The *locales* passed will be tried sequentially, and the first valid locale will be used.

test.support.make_bad_fd()
: Create an invalid file descriptor by opening and closing a temporary file, and returning its descriptor.

test.support.import_module(*name*, *deprecated=False*)
: This function imports and returns the named module. Unlike a normal import, this function raises *unittest.SkipTest* if the module cannot be imported.

   Module and package deprecation messages are suppressed during this import if *deprecated* is True.

   New in version 3.1.

test.support.import_fresh_module(*name*, *fresh=()*, *blocked=()*, *deprecated=False*)
: This function imports and returns a fresh copy of the named Python module by removing the named module from sys.modules before doing the import. Note that unlike reload(), the original module is not affected by this operation.

   fresh is an iterable of additional module names that are also removed from the sys.modules cache before doing the import.

   blocked is an iterable of module names that are replaced with None in the module cache during the import to ensure that attempts to import them raise *ImportError*.

   The named module and any modules named in the *fresh* and *blocked* parameters are saved before starting the import and then reinserted into sys.modules when the fresh import is complete.

   Module and package deprecation messages are suppressed during this import if *deprecated* is True.

   This function will raise *ImportError* if the named module cannot be imported.

   Example use:

   ```
   # Get copies of the warnings module for testing without affecting the
   # version being used by the rest of the test suite. One copy uses the
   # C implementation, the other is forced to use the pure Python fallback
   # implementation
   py_warnings = import_fresh_module('warnings', blocked=['_warnings'])
   c_warnings = import_fresh_module('warnings', fresh=['_warnings'])
   ```

   New in version 3.1.

test.support.bind_port(*sock*, *host=HOST*)
: Bind the socket to a free port and return the port number. Relies on ephemeral ports in order to ensure we are using an unbound port. This is important as many tests may be running simultaneously, especially in a buildbot environment. This method raises an exception if the sock.family is *AF_INET* and sock.type is *SOCK_STREAM*, and the socket has SO_REUSEADDR or SO_REUSEPORT set on it. Tests

should never set these socket options for TCP/IP sockets. The only case for setting these options is testing multicasting via multiple UDP sockets.

Additionally, if the `SO_EXCLUSIVEADDRUSE` socket option is available (i.e. on Windows), it will be set on the socket. This will prevent anyone else from binding to our host/port for the duration of the test.

`test.support.find_unused_port`(*family=socket.AF_INET, socktype=socket.SOCK_STREAM*)
Returns an unused port that should be suitable for binding. This is achieved by creating a temporary socket with the same family and type as the `sock` parameter (default is *AF_INET*, *SOCK_STREAM*), and binding it to the specified host address (defaults to `0.0.0.0`) with the port set to 0, eliciting an unused ephemeral port from the OS. The temporary socket is then closed and deleted, and the ephemeral port is returned.

Either this method or *bind_port()* should be used for any tests where a server socket needs to be bound to a particular port for the duration of the test. Which one to use depends on whether the calling code is creating a python socket, or if an unused port needs to be provided in a constructor or passed to an external program (i.e. the `-accept` argument to openssl's s_server mode). Always prefer *bind_port()* over *find_unused_port()* where possible. Using a hard coded port is discouraged since it can make multiple instances of the test impossible to run simultaneously, which is a problem for buildbots.

`test.support.load_package_tests`(*pkg_dir, loader, standard_tests, pattern*)
Generic implementation of the *unittest* `load_tests` protocol for use in test packages. *pkg_dir* is the root directory of the package; *loader*, *standard_tests*, and *pattern* are the arguments expected by `load_tests`. In simple cases, the test package's `__init__.py` can be the following:

```
import os
from test.support import load_package_tests

def load_tests(*args):
    return load_package_tests(os.path.dirname(__file__), *args)
```

`test.support.detect_api_mismatch`(*ref_api, other_api, *, ignore=()*)
Returns the set of attributes, functions or methods of *ref_api* not found on *other_api*, except for a defined list of items to be ignored in this check specified in *ignore*.

By default this skips private attributes beginning with '_' but includes all magic methods, i.e. those starting and ending in '__'.

New in version 3.5.

`test.support.check__all__`(*test_case, module, name_of_module=None, extra=(), blacklist=()*)
Assert that the `__all__` variable of *module* contains all public names.

The module's public names (its API) are detected automatically based on whether they match the public name convention and were defined in *module*.

The *name_of_module* argument can specify (as a string or tuple thereof) what module(s) an API could be defined in in order to be detected as a public API. One case for this is when *module* imports part of its public API from other modules, possibly a C backend (like `csv` and its `_csv`).

The *extra* argument can be a set of names that wouldn't otherwise be automatically detected as "public", like objects without a proper `__module__` attribute. If provided, it will be added to the automatically detected ones.

The *blacklist* argument can be a set of names that must not be treated as part of the public API even though their names indicate otherwise.

Example use:

```
import bar
import foo
```

```
import unittest
from test import support

class MiscTestCase(unittest.TestCase):
    def test__all__(self):
        support.check__all__(self, foo)

class OtherTestCase(unittest.TestCase):
    def test__all__(self):
        extra = {'BAR_CONST', 'FOO_CONST'}
        blacklist = {'baz'}  # Undocumented name.
        # bar imports part of its API from _bar.
        support.check__all__(self, bar, ('bar', '_bar'),
                             extra=extra, blacklist=blacklist)
```

New in version 3.6.

The *test.support* module defines the following classes:

class test.support.TransientResource(*exc*, ***kwargs*)

    Instances are a context manager that raises *ResourceDenied* if the specified exception type is raised. Any keyword arguments are treated as attribute/value pairs to be compared against any exception raised within the **with** statement. Only if all pairs match properly against attributes on the exception is *ResourceDenied* raised.

class test.support.EnvironmentVarGuard

    Class used to temporarily set or unset environment variables. Instances can be used as a context manager and have a complete dictionary interface for querying/modifying the underlying **os.environ**. After exit from the context manager all changes to environment variables done through this instance will be rolled back.

    Changed in version 3.1: Added dictionary interface.

EnvironmentVarGuard.set(*envvar*, *value*)

    Temporarily set the environment variable **envvar** to the value of **value**.

EnvironmentVarGuard.unset(*envvar*)

    Temporarily unset the environment variable **envvar**.

class test.support.SuppressCrashReport

    A context manager used to try to prevent crash dialog popups on tests that are expected to crash a subprocess.

    On Windows, it disables Windows Error Reporting dialogs using SetErrorMode.

    On UNIX, *resource.setrlimit()* is used to set *resource.RLIMIT_CORE*'s soft limit to 0 to prevent coredump file creation.

    On both platforms, the old value is restored by **__exit__**().

class test.support.WarningsRecorder

    Class used to record warnings for unit tests. See documentation of *check_warnings()* above for more details.

CHAPTER
TWENTYSEVEN

DEBUGGING AND PROFILING

These libraries help you with Python development: the debugger enables you to step through code, analyze stack frames and set breakpoints etc., and the profilers run code and give you a detailed breakdown of execution times, allowing you to identify bottlenecks in your programs.

27.1 bdb — Debugger framework

Source code: Lib/bdb.py

The *bdb* module handles basic debugger functions, like setting breakpoints or managing execution via the debugger.

The following exception is defined:

exception bdb.BdbQuit
    Exception raised by the *Bdb* class for quitting the debugger.

The *bdb* module also defines two classes:

class bdb.Breakpoint(*self*, *file*, *line*, *temporary=0*, *cond=None*, *funcname=None*)
    This class implements temporary breakpoints, ignore counts, disabling and (re-)enabling, and conditionals.

    Breakpoints are indexed by number through a list called **bpbynumber** and by **(file, line)** pairs through **bplist**. The former points to a single instance of class *Breakpoint*. The latter points to a list of such instances since there may be more than one breakpoint per line.

    When creating a breakpoint, its associated filename should be in canonical form. If a *funcname* is defined, a breakpoint hit will be counted when the first line of that function is executed. A conditional breakpoint always counts a hit.

    Breakpoint instances have the following methods:

    deleteMe()
        Delete the breakpoint from the list associated to a file/line. If it is the last breakpoint in that position, it also deletes the entry for the file/line.

    enable()
        Mark the breakpoint as enabled.

    disable()
        Mark the breakpoint as disabled.

    bpformat()
        Return a string with all the information about the breakpoint, nicely formatted:

        - The breakpoint number.

1511

- If it is temporary or not.
- Its file,line position.
- The condition that causes a break.
- If it must be ignored the next N times.
- The breakpoint hit count.

New in version 3.2.

bpprint(*out=None*)
   Print the output of *bpformat()* to the file *out*, or if it is None, to standard output.

class bdb.Bdb(*skip=None*)
   The *Bdb* class acts as a generic Python debugger base class.

   This class takes care of the details of the trace facility; a derived class should implement user interaction. The standard debugger class (*pdb.Pdb*) is an example.

   The *skip* argument, if given, must be an iterable of glob-style module name patterns. The debugger will not step into frames that originate in a module that matches one of these patterns. Whether a frame is considered to originate in a certain module is determined by the __name__ in the frame globals.

   New in version 3.1: The *skip* argument.

   The following methods of *Bdb* normally don't need to be overridden.

   canonic(*filename*)
      Auxiliary method for getting a filename in a canonical form, that is, as a case-normalized (on case-insensitive filesystems) absolute path, stripped of surrounding angle brackets.

   reset()
      Set the botframe, stopframe, returnframe and quitting attributes with values ready to start debugging.

   trace_dispatch(*frame, event, arg*)
      This function is installed as the trace function of debugged frames. Its return value is the new trace function (in most cases, that is, itself).

      The default implementation decides how to dispatch a frame, depending on the type of event (passed as a string) that is about to be executed. *event* can be one of the following:

      - "line": A new line of code is going to be executed.
      - "call": A function is about to be called, or another code block entered.
      - "return": A function or other code block is about to return.
      - "exception": An exception has occurred.
      - "c_call": A C function is about to be called.
      - "c_return": A C function has returned.
      - "c_exception": A C function has raised an exception.

      For the Python events, specialized functions (see below) are called. For the C events, no action is taken.

      The *arg* parameter depends on the previous event.

      See the documentation for *sys.settrace()* for more information on the trace function. For more information on code and frame objects, refer to types.

   dispatch_line(*frame*)
      If the debugger should stop on the current line, invoke the *user_line()* method (which should be overridden in subclasses). Raise a *BdbQuit* exception if the Bdb.quitting flag is set (which

can be set from *user_line()*). Return a reference to the *trace_dispatch()* method for further tracing in that scope.

dispatch_call(*frame*, *arg*)
If the debugger should stop on this function call, invoke the *user_call()* method (which should be overridden in subclasses). Raise a *BdbQuit* exception if the Bdb.quitting flag is set (which can be set from *user_call()*). Return a reference to the *trace_dispatch()* method for further tracing in that scope.

dispatch_return(*frame*, *arg*)
If the debugger should stop on this function return, invoke the *user_return()* method (which should be overridden in subclasses). Raise a *BdbQuit* exception if the Bdb.quitting flag is set (which can be set from *user_return()*). Return a reference to the *trace_dispatch()* method for further tracing in that scope.

dispatch_exception(*frame*, *arg*)
If the debugger should stop at this exception, invokes the *user_exception()* method (which should be overridden in subclasses). Raise a *BdbQuit* exception if the Bdb.quitting flag is set (which can be set from *user_exception()*). Return a reference to the *trace_dispatch()* method for further tracing in that scope.

Normally derived classes don't override the following methods, but they may if they want to redefine the definition of stopping and breakpoints.

stop_here(*frame*)
This method checks if the *frame* is somewhere below botframe in the call stack. botframe is the frame in which debugging started.

break_here(*frame*)
This method checks if there is a breakpoint in the filename and line belonging to *frame* or, at least, in the current function. If the breakpoint is a temporary one, this method deletes it.

break_anywhere(*frame*)
This method checks if there is a breakpoint in the filename of the current frame.

Derived classes should override these methods to gain control over debugger operation.

user_call(*frame*, *argument_list*)
This method is called from *dispatch_call()* when there is the possibility that a break might be necessary anywhere inside the called function.

user_line(*frame*)
This method is called from *dispatch_line()* when either *stop_here()* or *break_here()* yields True.

user_return(*frame*, *return_value*)
This method is called from *dispatch_return()* when *stop_here()* yields True.

user_exception(*frame*, *exc_info*)
This method is called from *dispatch_exception()* when *stop_here()* yields True.

do_clear(*arg*)
Handle how a breakpoint must be removed when it is a temporary one.

This method must be implemented by derived classes.

Derived classes and clients can call the following methods to affect the stepping state.

set_step()
Stop after one line of code.

set_next(*frame*)
Stop on the next line in or below the given frame.

set_return(*frame*)
> Stop when returning from the given frame.

set_until(*frame*)
> Stop when the line with the line no greater than the current one is reached or when returning from current frame.

set_trace([*frame*])
> Start debugging from *frame*. If *frame* is not specified, debugging starts from caller's frame.

set_continue()
> Stop only at breakpoints or when finished. If there are no breakpoints, set the system trace function to None.

set_quit()
> Set the quitting attribute to True. This raises *BdbQuit* in the next call to one of the dispatch_*() methods.

Derived classes and clients can call the following methods to manipulate breakpoints. These methods return a string containing an error message if something went wrong, or None if all is well.

set_break(*filename, lineno, temporary=0, cond, funcname*)
> Set a new breakpoint. If the *lineno* line doesn't exist for the *filename* passed as argument, return an error message. The *filename* should be in canonical form, as described in the *canonic()* method.

clear_break(*filename, lineno*)
> Delete the breakpoints in *filename* and *lineno*. If none were set, an error message is returned.

clear_bpbynumber(*arg*)
> Delete the breakpoint which has the index *arg* in the Breakpoint.bpbynumber. If *arg* is not numeric or out of range, return an error message.

clear_all_file_breaks(*filename*)
> Delete all breakpoints in *filename*. If none were set, an error message is returned.

clear_all_breaks()
> Delete all existing breakpoints.

get_bpbynumber(*arg*)
> Return a breakpoint specified by the given number. If *arg* is a string, it will be converted to a number. If *arg* is a non-numeric string, if the given breakpoint never existed or has been deleted, a *ValueError* is raised.
>
> New in version 3.2.

get_break(*filename, lineno*)
> Check if there is a breakpoint for *lineno* of *filename*.

get_breaks(*filename, lineno*)
> Return all breakpoints for *lineno* in *filename*, or an empty list if none are set.

get_file_breaks(*filename*)
> Return all breakpoints in *filename*, or an empty list if none are set.

get_all_breaks()
> Return all breakpoints that are set.

Derived classes and clients can call the following methods to get a data structure representing a stack trace.

get_stack(*f, t*)
> Get a list of records for a frame and all higher (calling) and lower frames, and the size of the higher part.

format_stack_entry(*frame_lineno*, *lprefix=': '*)
: Return a string with information about a stack entry, identified by a (**frame**, **lineno**) tuple:

  - The canonical form of the filename which contains the frame.
  - The function name, or "<lambda>".
  - The input arguments.
  - The return value.
  - The line of code (if it exists).

The following two methods can be called by clients to use a debugger to debug a *statement*, given as a string.

run(*cmd*, *globals=None*, *locals=None*)
: Debug a statement executed via the *exec()* function. *globals* defaults to `__main__.__dict__`, *locals* defaults to *globals*.

runeval(*expr*, *globals=None*, *locals=None*)
: Debug an expression executed via the *eval()* function. *globals* and *locals* have the same meaning as in *run()*.

runctx(*cmd*, *globals*, *locals*)
: For backwards compatibility. Calls the *run()* method.

runcall(*func*, **args*, ***kwds*)
: Debug a single function call, and return its result.

Finally, the module defines the following functions:

bdb.checkfuncname(*b*, *frame*)
: Check whether we should break here, depending on the way the breakpoint *b* was set.

  If it was set via line number, it checks if `b.line` is the same as the one in the frame also passed as argument. If the breakpoint was set via function name, we have to check we are in the right frame (the right function) and if we are in its first executable line.

bdb.effective(*file*, *line*, *frame*)
: Determine if there is an effective (active) breakpoint at this line of code. Return a tuple of the breakpoint and a boolean that indicates if it is ok to delete a temporary breakpoint. Return (**None**, **None**) if there is no matching breakpoint.

bdb.set_trace()
: Start debugging with a *Bdb* instance from caller's frame.

27.2 `faulthandler` — Dump the Python traceback

New in version 3.3.

This module contains functions to dump Python tracebacks explicitly, on a fault, after a timeout, or on a user signal. Call *faulthandler.enable()* to install fault handlers for the `SIGSEGV`, `SIGFPE`, `SIGABRT`, `SIGBUS`, and `SIGILL` signals. You can also enable them at startup by setting the `PYTHONFAULTHANDLER` environment variable or by using the `-X faulthandler` command line option.

The fault handler is compatible with system fault handlers like Apport or the Windows fault handler. The module uses an alternative stack for signal handlers if the `sigaltstack()` function is available. This allows it to dump the traceback even on a stack overflow.

The fault handler is called on catastrophic cases and therefore can only use signal-safe functions (e.g. it cannot allocate memory on the heap). Because of this limitation traceback dumping is minimal compared to normal Python tracebacks:

- Only ASCII is supported. The `backslashreplace` error handler is used on encoding.
- Each string is limited to 500 characters.
- Only the filename, the function name and the line number are displayed. (no source code)
- It is limited to 100 frames and 100 threads.
- The order is reversed: the most recent call is shown first.

By default, the Python traceback is written to *sys.stderr*. To see tracebacks, applications must be run in the terminal. A log file can alternatively be passed to *faulthandler.enable()*.

The module is implemented in C, so tracebacks can be dumped on a crash or when Python is deadlocked.

27.2.1 Dumping the traceback

faulthandler.dump_traceback(*file=sys.stderr, all_threads=True*)
   Dump the tracebacks of all threads into *file*. If *all_threads* is `False`, dump only the current thread.

   Changed in version 3.5: Added support for passing file descriptor to this function.

27.2.2 Fault handler state

faulthandler.enable(*file=sys.stderr, all_threads=True*)
   Enable the fault handler: install handlers for the `SIGSEGV`, `SIGFPE`, `SIGABRT`, `SIGBUS` and `SIGILL` signals to dump the Python traceback. If *all_threads* is `True`, produce tracebacks for every running thread. Otherwise, dump only the current thread.

   The *file* must be kept open until the fault handler is disabled: see *issue with file descriptors*.

   Changed in version 3.5: Added support for passing file descriptor to this function.

   Changed in version 3.6: On Windows, a handler for Windows exception is also installed.

faulthandler.disable()
   Disable the fault handler: uninstall the signal handlers installed by *enable()*.

faulthandler.is_enabled()
   Check if the fault handler is enabled.

27.2.3 Dumping the tracebacks after a timeout

faulthandler.dump_traceback_later(*timeout, repeat=False, file=sys.stderr, exit=False*)
   Dump the tracebacks of all threads, after a timeout of *timeout* seconds, or every *timeout* seconds if *repeat* is `True`. If *exit* is `True`, call *_exit()* with status=1 after dumping the tracebacks. (Note _exit() exits the process immediately, which means it doesn't do any cleanup like flushing file buffers.) If the function is called twice, the new call replaces previous parameters and resets the timeout. The timer has a sub-second resolution.

   The *file* must be kept open until the traceback is dumped or *cancel_dump_traceback_later()* is called: see *issue with file descriptors*.

   This function is implemented using a watchdog thread and therefore is not available if Python is compiled with threads disabled.

   Changed in version 3.5: Added support for passing file descriptor to this function.

faulthandler.cancel_dump_traceback_later()
    Cancel the last call to *dump_traceback_later()*.

27.2.4 Dumping the traceback on a user signal

faulthandler.register(*signum, file=sys.stderr, all_threads=True, chain=False*)
    Register a user signal: install a handler for the *signum* signal to dump the traceback of all threads, or of the current thread if *all_threads* is `False`, into *file*. Call the previous handler if chain is `True`.

    The *file* must be kept open until the signal is unregistered by *unregister()*: see *issue with file descriptors*.

    Not available on Windows.

    Changed in version 3.5: Added support for passing file descriptor to this function.

faulthandler.unregister(*signum*)
    Unregister a user signal: uninstall the handler of the *signum* signal installed by *register()*. Return `True` if the signal was registered, `False` otherwise.

    Not available on Windows.

27.2.5 Issue with file descriptors

enable(), *dump_traceback_later()* and *register()* keep the file descriptor of their *file* argument. If the file is closed and its file descriptor is reused by a new file, or if *os.dup2()* is used to replace the file descriptor, the traceback will be written into a different file. Call these functions again each time that the file is replaced.

27.2.6 Example

Example of a segmentation fault on Linux with and without enabling the fault handler:

```
$ python3 -c "import ctypes; ctypes.string_at(0)"
Segmentation fault

$ python3 -q -X faulthandler
>>> import ctypes
>>> ctypes.string_at(0)
Fatal Python error: Segmentation fault

Current thread 0x00007fb899f39700 (most recent call first):
  File "/home/python/cpython/Lib/ctypes/__init__.py", line 486 in string_at
  File "<stdin>", line 1 in <module>
Segmentation fault
```

27.3 pdb — The Python Debugger

Source code: Lib/pdb.py

The module *pdb* defines an interactive source code debugger for Python programs. It supports setting (conditional) breakpoints and single stepping at the source line level, inspection of stack frames, source code listing, and evaluation of arbitrary Python code in the context of any stack frame. It also supports post-mortem debugging and can be called under program control.

The debugger is extensible – it is actually defined as the class *Pdb*. This is currently undocumented but easily understood by reading the source. The extension interface uses the modules *bdb* and *cmd*.

The debugger's prompt is (Pdb). Typical usage to run a program under control of the debugger is:

```
>>> import pdb
>>> import mymodule
>>> pdb.run('mymodule.test()')
> <string>(0)?()
(Pdb) continue
> <string>(1)?()
(Pdb) continue
NameError: 'spam'
> <string>(1)?()
(Pdb)
```

Changed in version 3.3: Tab-completion via the *readline* module is available for commands and command arguments, e.g. the current global and local names are offered as arguments of the p command.

pdb.py can also be invoked as a script to debug other scripts. For example:

```
python3 -m pdb myscript.py
```

When invoked as a script, pdb will automatically enter post-mortem debugging if the program being debugged exits abnormally. After post-mortem debugging (or after normal exit of the program), pdb will restart the program. Automatic restarting preserves pdb's state (such as breakpoints) and in most cases is more useful than quitting the debugger upon program's exit.

New in version 3.2: **pdb.py** now accepts a -c option that executes commands as if given in a .pdbrc file, see *Debugger Commands*.

The typical usage to break into the debugger from a running program is to insert

```
import pdb; pdb.set_trace()
```

at the location you want to break into the debugger. You can then step through the code following this statement, and continue running without the debugger using the *continue* command.

The typical usage to inspect a crashed program is:

```
>>> import pdb
>>> import mymodule
>>> mymodule.test()
Traceback (most recent call last):
  File "<stdin>", line 1, in <module>
  File "./mymodule.py", line 4, in test
    test2()
  File "./mymodule.py", line 3, in test2
    print(spam)
NameError: spam
>>> pdb.pm()
> ./mymodule.py(3)test2()
-> print(spam)
(Pdb)
```

The module defines the following functions; each enters the debugger in a slightly different way:

pdb.run(*statement, globals=None, locals=None*)
    Execute the *statement* (given as a string or a code object) under debugger control. The debugger prompt appears before any code is executed; you can set breakpoints and type *continue*, or you can step through the statement using *step* or *next* (all these commands are explained below). The

1518 Chapter 27. Debugging and Profiling

optional *globals* and *locals* arguments specify the environment in which the code is executed; by default the dictionary of the module `__main__` is used. (See the explanation of the built-in `exec()` or `eval()` functions.)

pdb.runeval(*expression, globals=None, locals=None*)
    Evaluate the *expression* (given as a string or a code object) under debugger control. When `runeval()` returns, it returns the value of the expression. Otherwise this function is similar to `run()`.

pdb.runcall(*function, *args, **kwds*)
    Call the *function* (a function or method object, not a string) with the given arguments. When `runcall()` returns, it returns whatever the function call returned. The debugger prompt appears as soon as the function is entered.

pdb.set_trace()
    Enter the debugger at the calling stack frame. This is useful to hard-code a breakpoint at a given point in a program, even if the code is not otherwise being debugged (e.g. when an assertion fails).

pdb.post_mortem(*traceback=None*)
    Enter post-mortem debugging of the given *traceback* object. If no *traceback* is given, it uses the one of the exception that is currently being handled (an exception must be being handled if the default is to be used).

pdb.pm()
    Enter post-mortem debugging of the traceback found in `sys.last_traceback`.

The `run*` functions and `set_trace()` are aliases for instantiating the `Pdb` class and calling the method of the same name. If you want to access further features, you have to do this yourself:

class pdb.Pdb(*completekey='tab', stdin=None, stdout=None, skip=None, nosigint=False, readrc=True*)
    `Pdb` is the debugger class.

    The *completekey*, *stdin* and *stdout* arguments are passed to the underlying `cmd.Cmd` class; see the description there.

    The *skip* argument, if given, must be an iterable of glob-style module name patterns. The debugger will not step into frames that originate in a module that matches one of these patterns.[1]

    By default, Pdb sets a handler for the SIGINT signal (which is sent when the user presses `Ctrl-C` on the console) when you give a `continue` command. This allows you to break into the debugger again by pressing `Ctrl-C`. If you want Pdb not to touch the SIGINT handler, set *nosigint* to true.

    The *readrc* argument defaults to true and controls whether Pdb will load .pdbrc files from the filesystem.

    Example call to enable tracing with *skip*:

```
import pdb; pdb.Pdb(skip=['django.*']).set_trace()
```

    New in version 3.1: The *skip* argument.

    New in version 3.2: The *nosigint* argument. Previously, a SIGINT handler was never set by Pdb.

    Changed in version 3.6: The *readrc* argument.

    run(*statement, globals=None, locals=None*)
    runeval(*expression, globals=None, locals=None*)
    runcall(*function, *args, **kwds*)
    set_trace()
        See the documentation for the functions explained above.

---

[1] Whether a frame is considered to originate in a certain module is determined by the `__name__` in the frame globals.

27.3.1 Debugger Commands

The commands recognized by the debugger are listed below. Most commands can be abbreviated to one or two letters as indicated; e.g. `h(elp)` means that either `h` or `help` can be used to enter the help command (but not `he` or `hel`, nor `H` or `Help` or `HELP`). Arguments to commands must be separated by whitespace (spaces or tabs). Optional arguments are enclosed in square brackets (`[]`) in the command syntax; the square brackets must not be typed. Alternatives in the command syntax are separated by a vertical bar (`|`).

Entering a blank line repeats the last command entered. Exception: if the last command was a *list* command, the next 11 lines are listed.

Commands that the debugger doesn't recognize are assumed to be Python statements and are executed in the context of the program being debugged. Python statements can also be prefixed with an exclamation point (`!`). This is a powerful way to inspect the program being debugged; it is even possible to change a variable or call a function. When an exception occurs in such a statement, the exception name is printed but the debugger's state is not changed.

The debugger supports *aliases*. Aliases can have parameters which allows one a certain level of adaptability to the context under examination.

Multiple commands may be entered on a single line, separated by `;;`. (A single `;` is not used as it is the separator for multiple commands in a line that is passed to the Python parser.) No intelligence is applied to separating the commands; the input is split at the first `;;` pair, even if it is in the middle of a quoted string.

If a file `.pdbrc` exists in the user's home directory or in the current directory, it is read in and executed as if it had been typed at the debugger prompt. This is particularly useful for aliases. If both files exist, the one in the home directory is read first and aliases defined there can be overridden by the local file.

Changed in version 3.2: `.pdbrc` can now contain commands that continue debugging, such as *continue* or *next*. Previously, these commands had no effect.

h(elp) [command]
> Without argument, print the list of available commands. With a *command* as argument, print help about that command. `help pdb` displays the full documentation (the docstring of the *pdb* module). Since the *command* argument must be an identifier, `help exec` must be entered to get help on the `!` command.

w(here)
> Print a stack trace, with the most recent frame at the bottom. An arrow indicates the current frame, which determines the context of most commands.

d(own) [count]
> Move the current frame *count* (default one) levels down in the stack trace (to a newer frame).

u(p) [count]
> Move the current frame *count* (default one) levels up in the stack trace (to an older frame).

b(reak) [([filename:]lineno | function) [, condition]]
> With a *lineno* argument, set a break there in the current file. With a *function* argument, set a break at the first executable statement within that function. The line number may be prefixed with a filename and a colon, to specify a breakpoint in another file (probably one that hasn't been loaded yet). The file is searched on *sys.path*. Note that each breakpoint is assigned a number to which all the other breakpoint commands refer.
>
> If a second argument is present, it is an expression which must evaluate to true before the breakpoint is honored.
>
> Without argument, list all breaks, including for each breakpoint, the number of times that breakpoint has been hit, the current ignore count, and the associated condition if any.

tbreak [([filename:]lineno | function) [, condition]]
　　Temporary breakpoint, which is removed automatically when it is first hit. The arguments are the same as for *break*.

cl(ear) [filename:lineno | bpnumber [bpnumber ...]]
　　With a *filename:lineno* argument, clear all the breakpoints at this line. With a space separated list of breakpoint numbers, clear those breakpoints. Without argument, clear all breaks (but first ask confirmation).

disable [bpnumber [bpnumber ...]]
　　Disable the breakpoints given as a space separated list of breakpoint numbers. Disabling a breakpoint means it cannot cause the program to stop execution, but unlike clearing a breakpoint, it remains in the list of breakpoints and can be (re-)enabled.

enable [bpnumber [bpnumber ...]]
　　Enable the breakpoints specified.

ignore bpnumber [count]
　　Set the ignore count for the given breakpoint number. If count is omitted, the ignore count is set to 0. A breakpoint becomes active when the ignore count is zero. When non-zero, the count is decremented each time the breakpoint is reached and the breakpoint is not disabled and any associated condition evaluates to true.

condition bpnumber [condition]
　　Set a new *condition* for the breakpoint, an expression which must evaluate to true before the breakpoint is honored. If *condition* is absent, any existing condition is removed; i.e., the breakpoint is made unconditional.

commands [bpnumber]
　　Specify a list of commands for breakpoint number *bpnumber*. The commands themselves appear on the following lines. Type a line containing just **end** to terminate the commands. An example:

```
(Pdb) commands 1
(com) p some_variable
(com) end
(Pdb)
```

　　To remove all commands from a breakpoint, type commands and follow it immediately with **end**; that is, give no commands.

　　With no *bpnumber* argument, commands refers to the last breakpoint set.

　　You can use breakpoint commands to start your program up again. Simply use the continue command, or step, or any other command that resumes execution.

　　Specifying any command resuming execution (currently continue, step, next, return, jump, quit and their abbreviations) terminates the command list (as if that command was immediately followed by end). This is because any time you resume execution (even with a simple next or step), you may encounter another breakpoint—which could have its own command list, leading to ambiguities about which list to execute.

　　If you use the 'silent' command in the command list, the usual message about stopping at a breakpoint is not printed. This may be desirable for breakpoints that are to print a specific message and then continue. If none of the other commands print anything, you see no sign that the breakpoint was reached.

s(tep)
　　Execute the current line, stop at the first possible occasion (either in a function that is called or on the next line in the current function).

n(ext)
　　Continue execution until the next line in the current function is reached or it returns. (The difference

between *next* and *step* is that *step* stops inside a called function, while *next* executes called functions at (nearly) full speed, only stopping at the next line in the current function.)

unt(il) [lineno]
    Without argument, continue execution until the line with a number greater than the current one is reached.

    With a line number, continue execution until a line with a number greater or equal to that is reached. In both cases, also stop when the current frame returns.

    Changed in version 3.2: Allow giving an explicit line number.

r(eturn)
    Continue execution until the current function returns.

c(ont(inue))
    Continue execution, only stop when a breakpoint is encountered.

j(ump) lineno
    Set the next line that will be executed. Only available in the bottom-most frame. This lets you jump back and execute code again, or jump forward to skip code that you don't want to run.

    It should be noted that not all jumps are allowed – for instance it is not possible to jump into the middle of a `for` loop or out of a `finally` clause.

l(ist) [first[, last]]
    List source code for the current file. Without arguments, list 11 lines around the current line or continue the previous listing. With . as argument, list 11 lines around the current line. With one argument, list 11 lines around at that line. With two arguments, list the given range; if the second argument is less than the first, it is interpreted as a count.

    The current line in the current frame is indicated by ->. If an exception is being debugged, the line where the exception was originally raised or propagated is indicated by >>, if it differs from the current line.

    New in version 3.2: The >> marker.

ll | longlist
    List all source code for the current function or frame. Interesting lines are marked as for *list*.

    New in version 3.2.

a(rgs)
    Print the argument list of the current function.

p expression
    Evaluate the *expression* in the current context and print its value.

> **Note:** `print()` can also be used, but is not a debugger command — this executes the Python *print()* function.

pp expression
    Like the *p* command, except the value of the expression is pretty-printed using the *pprint* module.

whatis expression
    Print the type of the *expression*.

source expression
    Try to get source code for the given object and display it.

    New in version 3.2.

display [expression]
    Display the value of the expression if it changed, each time execution stops in the current frame.

    Without expression, list all display expressions for the current frame.

    New in version 3.2.

undisplay [expression]
    Do not display the expression any more in the current frame. Without expression, clear all display expressions for the current frame.

    New in version 3.2.

interact
    Start an interactive interpreter (using the `code` module) whose global namespace contains all the (global and local) names found in the current scope.

    New in version 3.2.

alias [name [command]]
    Create an alias called *name* that executes *command*. The command must *not* be enclosed in quotes. Replaceable parameters can be indicated by %1, %2, and so on, while %* is replaced by all the parameters. If no command is given, the current alias for *name* is shown. If no arguments are given, all aliases are listed.

    Aliases may be nested and can contain anything that can be legally typed at the pdb prompt. Note that internal pdb commands *can* be overridden by aliases. Such a command is then hidden until the alias is removed. Aliasing is recursively applied to the first word of the command line; all other words in the line are left alone.

    As an example, here are two useful aliases (especially when placed in the `.pdbrc` file):

```
# Print instance variables (usage "pi classInst")
alias pi for k in %1.__dict__.keys(): print("%1.",k,"=",%1.__dict__[k])
# Print instance variables in self
alias ps pi self
```

unalias name
    Delete the specified alias.

! statement
    Execute the (one-line) *statement* in the context of the current stack frame. The exclamation point can be omitted unless the first word of the statement resembles a debugger command. To set a global variable, you can prefix the assignment command with a `global` statement on the same line, e.g.:

```
(Pdb) global list_options; list_options = ['-l']
(Pdb)
```

run [args ...]
restart [args ...]
    Restart the debugged Python program. If an argument is supplied, it is split with `shlex` and the result is used as the new `sys.argv`. History, breakpoints, actions and debugger options are preserved. *restart* is an alias for *run*.

q(uit)
    Quit from the debugger. The program being executed is aborted.

27.4 The Python Profilers

Source code: Lib/profile.py and Lib/pstats.py

27.4.1 Introduction to the profilers

`cProfile` and `profile` provide *deterministic profiling* of Python programs. A *profile* is a set of statistics that describes how often and for how long various parts of the program executed. These statistics can be formatted into reports via the `pstats` module.

The Python standard library provides two different implementations of the same profiling interface:

1. `cProfile` is recommended for most users; it's a C extension with reasonable overhead that makes it suitable for profiling long-running programs. Based on `lsprof`, contributed by Brett Rosen and Ted Czotter.

2. `profile`, a pure Python module whose interface is imitated by `cProfile`, but which adds significant overhead to profiled programs. If you're trying to extend the profiler in some way, the task might be easier with this module. Originally designed and written by Jim Roskind.

Note: The profiler modules are designed to provide an execution profile for a given program, not for benchmarking purposes (for that, there is `timeit` for reasonably accurate results). This particularly applies to benchmarking Python code against C code: the profilers introduce overhead for Python code, but not for C-level functions, and so the C code would seem faster than any Python one.

27.4.2 Instant User's Manual

This section is provided for users that "don't want to read the manual." It provides a very brief overview, and allows a user to rapidly perform profiling on an existing application.

To profile a function that takes a single argument, you can do:

```
import cProfile
import re
cProfile.run('re.compile("foo|bar")')
```

(Use `profile` instead of `cProfile` if the latter is not available on your system.)

The above action would run `re.compile()` and print profile results like the following:

```
         197 function calls (192 primitive calls) in 0.002 seconds

   Ordered by: standard name

   ncalls  tottime  percall  cumtime  percall filename:lineno(function)
        1    0.000    0.000    0.001    0.001 <string>:1(<module>)
        1    0.000    0.000    0.001    0.001 re.py:212(compile)
        1    0.000    0.000    0.001    0.001 re.py:268(_compile)
        1    0.000    0.000    0.000    0.000 sre_compile.py:172(_compile_charset)
        1    0.000    0.000    0.000    0.000 sre_compile.py:201(_optimize_charset)
        4    0.000    0.000    0.000    0.000 sre_compile.py:25(_identityfunction)
      3/1    0.000    0.000    0.000    0.000 sre_compile.py:33(_compile)
```

The first line indicates that 197 calls were monitored. Of those calls, 192 were *primitive*, meaning that the call was not induced via recursion. The next line: `Ordered by: standard name`, indicates that the text string in the far right column was used to sort the output. The column headings include:

ncalls for the number of calls.

tottime for the total time spent in the given function (and excluding time made in calls to sub-functions)

percall is the quotient of `tottime` divided by `ncalls`

cumtime is the cumulative time spent in this and all subfunctions (from invocation till exit). This figure is accurate *even* for recursive functions.

percall is the quotient of `cumtime` divided by primitive calls

filename:lineno(function) provides the respective data of each function

When there are two numbers in the first column (for example 3/1), it means that the function recursed. The second value is the number of primitive calls and the former is the total number of calls. Note that when the function does not recurse, these two values are the same, and only the single figure is printed.

Instead of printing the output at the end of the profile run, you can save the results to a file by specifying a filename to the `run()` function:

```
import cProfile
import re
cProfile.run('re.compile("foo|bar")', 'restats')
```

The `pstats.Stats` class reads profile results from a file and formats them in various ways.

The file `cProfile` can also be invoked as a script to profile another script. For example:

```
python -m cProfile [-o output_file] [-s sort_order] myscript.py
```

`-o` writes the profile results to a file instead of to stdout

`-s` specifies one of the `sort_stats()` sort values to sort the output by. This only applies when `-o` is not supplied.

The `pstats` module's `Stats` class has a variety of methods for manipulating and printing the data saved into a profile results file:

```
import pstats
p = pstats.Stats('restats')
p.strip_dirs().sort_stats(-1).print_stats()
```

The `strip_dirs()` method removed the extraneous path from all the module names. The `sort_stats()` method sorted all the entries according to the standard module/line/name string that is printed. The `print_stats()` method printed out all the statistics. You might try the following sort calls:

```
p.sort_stats('name')
p.print_stats()
```

The first call will actually sort the list by function name, and the second call will print out the statistics. The following are some interesting calls to experiment with:

```
p.sort_stats('cumulative').print_stats(10)
```

This sorts the profile by cumulative time in a function, and then only prints the ten most significant lines. If you want to understand what algorithms are taking time, the above line is what you would use.

If you were looking to see what functions were looping a lot, and taking a lot of time, you would do:

```
p.sort_stats('time').print_stats(10)
```

to sort according to time spent within each function, and then print the statistics for the top ten functions.

You might also try:

```
p.sort_stats('file').print_stats('__init__')
```

This will sort all the statistics by file name, and then print out statistics for only the class init methods (since they are spelled with __init__ in them). As one final example, you could try:

```
p.sort_stats('time', 'cumulative').print_stats(.5, 'init')
```

This line sorts statistics with a primary key of time, and a secondary key of cumulative time, and then prints out some of the statistics. To be specific, the list is first culled down to 50% (re: .5) of its original size, then only lines containing init are maintained, and that sub-sub-list is printed.

If you wondered what functions called the above functions, you could now (p is still sorted according to the last criteria) do:

```
p.print_callers(.5, 'init')
```

and you would get a list of callers for each of the listed functions.

If you want more functionality, you're going to have to read the manual, or guess what the following functions do:

```
p.print_callees()
p.add('restats')
```

Invoked as a script, the *pstats* module is a statistics browser for reading and examining profile dumps. It has a simple line-oriented interface (implemented using *cmd*) and interactive help.

27.4.3 profile and cProfile Module Reference

Both the *profile* and *cProfile* modules provide the following functions:

profile.run(*command, filename=None, sort=-1*)
: This function takes a single argument that can be passed to the *exec()* function, and an optional file name. In all cases this routine executes:

    ```
    exec(command, __main__.__dict__, __main__.__dict__)
    ```

    and gathers profiling statistics from the execution. If no file name is present, then this function automatically creates a *Stats* instance and prints a simple profiling report. If the sort value is specified, it is passed to this *Stats* instance to control how the results are sorted.

profile.runctx(*command, globals, locals, filename=None, sort=-1*)
: This function is similar to *run()*, with added arguments to supply the globals and locals dictionaries for the *command* string. This routine executes:

    ```
    exec(command, globals, locals)
    ```

    and gathers profiling statistics as in the *run()* function above.

class profile.Profile(*timer=None, timeunit=0.0, subcalls=True, builtins=True*)
: This class is normally only used if more precise control over profiling is needed than what the cProfile.run() function provides.

    A custom timer can be supplied for measuring how long code takes to run via the *timer* argument. This must be a function that returns a single number representing the current time. If the number is an integer, the *timeunit* specifies a multiplier that specifies the duration of each unit of time. For example, if the timer returns times measured in thousands of seconds, the time unit would be .001.

Directly using the *Profile* class allows formatting profile results without writing the profile data to a file:

```
import cProfile, pstats, io
pr = cProfile.Profile()
pr.enable()
# ... do something ...
pr.disable()
s = io.StringIO()
sortby = 'cumulative'
ps = pstats.Stats(pr, stream=s).sort_stats(sortby)
ps.print_stats()
print(s.getvalue())
```

enable()
  Start collecting profiling data.

disable()
  Stop collecting profiling data.

create_stats()
  Stop collecting profiling data and record the results internally as the current profile.

print_stats(*sort=-1*)
  Create a *Stats* object based on the current profile and print the results to stdout.

dump_stats(*filename*)
  Write the results of the current profile to *filename*.

run(*cmd*)
  Profile the cmd via *exec()*.

runctx(*cmd, globals, locals*)
  Profile the cmd via *exec()* with the specified global and local environment.

runcall(*func, *args, **kwargs*)
  Profile `func(*args, **kwargs)`

27.4.4 The Stats Class

Analysis of the profiler data is done using the *Stats* class.

class pstats.Stats(**filenames or profile, stream=sys.stdout*)
  This class constructor creates an instance of a "statistics object" from a *filename* (or list of filenames) or from a `Profile` instance. Output will be printed to the stream specified by *stream*.

  The file selected by the above constructor must have been created by the corresponding version of *profile* or *cProfile*. To be specific, there is *no* file compatibility guaranteed with future versions of this profiler, and there is no compatibility with files produced by other profilers. If several files are provided, all the statistics for identical functions will be coalesced, so that an overall view of several processes can be considered in a single report. If additional files need to be combined with data in an existing *Stats* object, the *add()* method can be used.

  Instead of reading the profile data from a file, a `cProfile.Profile` or *profile.Profile* object can be used as the profile data source.

  Stats objects have the following methods:

  strip_dirs()
    This method for the *Stats* class removes all leading path information from file names. It is very useful in reducing the size of the printout to fit within (close to) 80 columns. This method modifies

the object, and the stripped information is lost. After performing a strip operation, the object is considered to have its entries in a "random" order, as it was just after object initialization and loading. If *strip_dirs()* causes two function names to be indistinguishable (they are on the same line of the same filename, and have the same function name), then the statistics for these two entries are accumulated into a single entry.

add(**filenames*)
This method of the *Stats* class accumulates additional profiling information into the current profiling object. Its arguments should refer to filenames created by the corresponding version of *profile.run()* or cProfile.run(). Statistics for identically named (re: file, line, name) functions are automatically accumulated into single function statistics.

dump_stats(*filename*)
Save the data loaded into the *Stats* object to a file named *filename*. The file is created if it does not exist, and is overwritten if it already exists. This is equivalent to the method of the same name on the *profile.Profile* and cProfile.Profile classes.

sort_stats(**keys*)
This method modifies the *Stats* object by sorting it according to the supplied criteria. The argument is typically a string identifying the basis of a sort (example: `'time'` or `'name'`).

When more than one key is provided, then additional keys are used as secondary criteria when there is equality in all keys selected before them. For example, `sort_stats('name', 'file')` will sort all the entries according to their function name, and resolve all ties (identical function names) by sorting by file name.

Abbreviations can be used for any key names, as long as the abbreviation is unambiguous. The following are the keys currently defined:

Valid Arg	Meaning
`'calls'`	call count
`'cumulative'`	cumulative time
`'cumtime'`	cumulative time
`'file'`	file name
`'filename'`	file name
`'module'`	file name
`'ncalls'`	call count
`'pcalls'`	primitive call count
`'line'`	line number
`'name'`	function name
`'nfl'`	name/file/line
`'stdname'`	standard name
`'time'`	internal time
`'tottime'`	internal time

Note that all sorts on statistics are in descending order (placing most time consuming items first), where as name, file, and line number searches are in ascending order (alphabetical). The subtle distinction between `'nfl'` and `'stdname'` is that the standard name is a sort of the name as printed, which means that the embedded line numbers get compared in an odd way. For example, lines 3, 20, and 40 would (if the file names were the same) appear in the string order 20, 3 and 40. In contrast, `'nfl'` does a numeric compare of the line numbers. In fact, `sort_stats('nfl')` is the same as `sort_stats('name', 'file', 'line')`.

For backward-compatibility reasons, the numeric arguments -1, 0, 1, and 2 are permitted. They are interpreted as `'stdname'`, `'calls'`, `'time'`, and `'cumulative'` respectively. If this old style format (numeric) is used, only one sort key (the numeric key) will be used, and additional arguments will be silently ignored.

reverse_order()
    This method for the *Stats* class reverses the ordering of the basic list within the object. Note that by default ascending vs descending order is properly selected based on the sort key of choice.

print_stats(**restrictions* **)**
    This method for the *Stats* class prints out a report as described in the *profile.run()* definition.

    The order of the printing is based on the last *sort_stats()* operation done on the object (subject to caveats in *add()* and *strip_dirs()*).

    The arguments provided (if any) can be used to limit the list down to the significant entries. Initially, the list is taken to be the complete set of profiled functions. Each restriction is either an integer (to select a count of lines), or a decimal fraction between 0.0 and 1.0 inclusive (to select a percentage of lines), or a string that will interpreted as a regular expression (to pattern match the standard name that is printed). If several restrictions are provided, then they are applied sequentially. For example:

```
print_stats(.1, 'foo:')
```

    would first limit the printing to first 10% of list, and then only print functions that were part of filename .*foo:. In contrast, the command:

```
print_stats('foo:', .1)
```

    would limit the list to all functions having file names .*foo:, and then proceed to only print the first 10% of them.

print_callers(**restrictions* **)**
    This method for the *Stats* class prints a list of all functions that called each function in the profiled database. The ordering is identical to that provided by *print_stats()*, and the definition of the restricting argument is also identical. Each caller is reported on its own line. The format differs slightly depending on the profiler that produced the stats:

    • With *profile*, a number is shown in parentheses after each caller to show how many times this specific call was made. For convenience, a second non-parenthesized number repeats the cumulative time spent in the function at the right.

    • With *cProfile*, each caller is preceded by three numbers: the number of times this specific call was made, and the total and cumulative times spent in the current function while it was invoked by this specific caller.

print_callees(**restrictions* **)**
    This method for the *Stats* class prints a list of all function that were called by the indicated function. Aside from this reversal of direction of calls (re: called vs was called by), the arguments and ordering are identical to the *print_callers()* method.

27.4.5 What Is Deterministic Profiling?

Deterministic profiling is meant to reflect the fact that all *function call*, *function return*, and *exception* events are monitored, and precise timings are made for the intervals between these events (during which time the user's code is executing). In contrast, *statistical profiling* (which is not done by this module) randomly samples the effective instruction pointer, and deduces where time is being spent. The latter technique traditionally involves less overhead (as the code does not need to be instrumented), but provides only relative indications of where time is being spent.

In Python, since there is an interpreter active during execution, the presence of instrumented code is not required to do deterministic profiling. Python automatically provides a *hook* (optional callback) for each event. In addition, the interpreted nature of Python tends to add so much overhead to execution, that deterministic profiling tends to only add small processing overhead in typical applications. The result is that deterministic profiling is not that expensive, yet provides extensive run time statistics about the execution of a Python program.

Call count statistics can be used to identify bugs in code (surprising counts), and to identify possible inline-expansion points (high call counts). Internal time statistics can be used to identify "hot loops" that should be carefully optimized. Cumulative time statistics should be used to identify high level errors in the selection of algorithms. Note that the unusual handling of cumulative times in this profiler allows statistics for recursive implementations of algorithms to be directly compared to iterative implementations.

27.4.6 Limitations

One limitation has to do with accuracy of timing information. There is a fundamental problem with deterministic profilers involving accuracy. The most obvious restriction is that the underlying "clock" is only ticking at a rate (typically) of about .001 seconds. Hence no measurements will be more accurate than the underlying clock. If enough measurements are taken, then the "error" will tend to average out. Unfortunately, removing this first error induces a second source of error.

The second problem is that it "takes a while" from when an event is dispatched until the profiler's call to get the time actually *gets* the state of the clock. Similarly, there is a certain lag when exiting the profiler event handler from the time that the clock's value was obtained (and then squirreled away), until the user's code is once again executing. As a result, functions that are called many times, or call many functions, will typically accumulate this error. The error that accumulates in this fashion is typically less than the accuracy of the clock (less than one clock tick), but it *can* accumulate and become very significant.

The problem is more important with *profile* than with the lower-overhead *cProfile*. For this reason, *profile* provides a means of calibrating itself for a given platform so that this error can be probabilistically (on the average) removed. After the profiler is calibrated, it will be more accurate (in a least square sense), but it will sometimes produce negative numbers (when call counts are exceptionally low, and the gods of probability work against you :-).) Do *not* be alarmed by negative numbers in the profile. They should *only* appear if you have calibrated your profiler, and the results are actually better than without calibration.

27.4.7 Calibration

The profiler of the *profile* module subtracts a constant from each event handling time to compensate for the overhead of calling the time function, and socking away the results. By default, the constant is 0. The following procedure can be used to obtain a better constant for a given platform (see *Limitations*).

```
import profile
pr = profile.Profile()
for i in range(5):
    print(pr.calibrate(10000))
```

The method executes the number of Python calls given by the argument, directly and again under the profiler, measuring the time for both. It then computes the hidden overhead per profiler event, and returns that as a float. For example, on a 1.8Ghz Intel Core i5 running Mac OS X, and using Python's time.clock() as the timer, the magical number is about 4.04e-6.

The object of this exercise is to get a fairly consistent result. If your computer is *very* fast, or your timer function has poor resolution, you might have to pass 100000, or even 1000000, to get consistent results.

When you have a consistent answer, there are three ways you can use it:

```
import profile

# 1. Apply computed bias to all Profile instances created hereafter.
profile.Profile.bias = your_computed_bias
```

```
# 2. Apply computed bias to a specific Profile instance.
pr = profile.Profile()
pr.bias = your_computed_bias

# 3. Specify computed bias in instance constructor.
pr = profile.Profile(bias=your_computed_bias)
```

If you have a choice, you are better off choosing a smaller constant, and then your results will "less often" show up as negative in profile statistics.

27.4.8 Using a custom timer

If you want to change how current time is determined (for example, to force use of wall-clock time or elapsed process time), pass the timing function you want to the `Profile` class constructor:

```
pr = profile.Profile(your_time_func)
```

The resulting profiler will then call `your_time_func`. Depending on whether you are using *profile.Profile* or `cProfile.Profile`, `your_time_func`'s return value will be interpreted differently:

profile.Profile `your_time_func` should return a single number, or a list of numbers whose sum is the current time (like what *os.times()* returns). If the function returns a single time number, or the list of returned numbers has length 2, then you will get an especially fast version of the dispatch routine.

> Be warned that you should calibrate the profiler class for the timer function that you choose (see *Calibration*). For most machines, a timer that returns a lone integer value will provide the best results in terms of low overhead during profiling. (*os.times()* is *pretty* bad, as it returns a tuple of floating point values). If you want to substitute a better timer in the cleanest fashion, derive a class and hardwire a replacement dispatch method that best handles your timer call, along with the appropriate calibration constant.

`cProfile.Profile` `your_time_func` should return a single number. If it returns integers, you can also invoke the class constructor with a second argument specifying the real duration of one unit of time. For example, if `your_integer_time_func` returns times measured in thousands of seconds, you would construct the `Profile` instance as follows:

```
pr = cProfile.Profile(your_integer_time_func, 0.001)
```

As the `cProfile.Profile` class cannot be calibrated, custom timer functions should be used with care and should be as fast as possible. For the best results with a custom timer, it might be necessary to hard-code it in the C source of the internal `_lsprof` module.

Python 3.3 adds several new functions in *time* that can be used to make precise measurements of process or wall-clock time. For example, see *time.perf_counter()*.

27.5 `timeit` — Measure execution time of small code snippets

Source code: Lib/timeit.py

This module provides a simple way to time small bits of Python code. It has both a *Command-Line Interface* as well as a *callable* one. It avoids a number of common traps for measuring execution times. See also Tim Peters' introduction to the "Algorithms" chapter in the *Python Cookbook*, published by O'Reilly.

27.5.1 Basic Examples

The following example shows how the *Command-Line Interface* can be used to compare three different expressions:

```
$ python3 -m timeit '"-".join(str(n) for n in range(100))'
10000 loops, best of 3: 30.2 usec per loop
$ python3 -m timeit '"-".join([str(n) for n in range(100)])'
10000 loops, best of 3: 27.5 usec per loop
$ python3 -m timeit '"-".join(map(str, range(100)))'
10000 loops, best of 3: 23.2 usec per loop
```

This can be achieved from the *Python Interface* with:

```
>>> import timeit
>>> timeit.timeit('"-".join(str(n) for n in range(100))', number=10000)
0.3018611848820001
>>> timeit.timeit('"-".join([str(n) for n in range(100)])', number=10000)
0.2727368790656328
>>> timeit.timeit('"-".join(map(str, range(100)))', number=10000)
0.23702679807320237
```

Note however that *timeit* will automatically determine the number of repetitions only when the command-line interface is used. In the *Examples* section you can find more advanced examples.

27.5.2 Python Interface

The module defines three convenience functions and a public class:

timeit.timeit(*stmt='pass'*, *setup='pass'*, *timer=<default timer>*, *number=1000000*, *globals=None*)
  Create a *Timer* instance with the given statement, *setup* code and *timer* function and run its *timeit()* method with *number* executions. The optional *globals* argument specifies a namespace in which to execute the code.

  Changed in version 3.5: The optional *globals* parameter was added.

timeit.repeat(*stmt='pass'*, *setup='pass'*, *timer=<default timer>*, *repeat=3*, *number=1000000*, *globals=None*)
  Create a *Timer* instance with the given statement, *setup* code and *timer* function and run its *repeat()* method with the given *repeat* count and *number* executions. The optional *globals* argument specifies a namespace in which to execute the code.

  Changed in version 3.5: The optional *globals* parameter was added.

timeit.default_timer()
  The default timer, which is always *time.perf_counter()*.

  Changed in version 3.3: *time.perf_counter()* is now the default timer.

class timeit.Timer(*stmt='pass'*, *setup='pass'*, *timer=<timer function>*, *globals=None*)
  Class for timing execution speed of small code snippets.

  The constructor takes a statement to be timed, an additional statement used for setup, and a timer function. Both statements default to `'pass'`; the timer function is platform-dependent (see the module doc string). *stmt* and *setup* may also contain multiple statements separated by ; or newlines, as long as they don't contain multi-line string literals. The statement will by default be executed within timeit's namespace; this behavior can be controlled by passing a namespace to *globals*.

  To measure the execution time of the first statement, use the *timeit()* method. The *repeat()* and *autorange()* methods are convenience methods to call *timeit()* multiple times.

The execution time of *setup* is excluded from the overall timed execution run.

The *stmt* and *setup* parameters can also take objects that are callable without arguments. This will embed calls to them in a timer function that will then be executed by `timeit()`. Note that the timing overhead is a little larger in this case because of the extra function calls.

Changed in version 3.5: The optional *globals* parameter was added.

timeit(*number=1000000*)

> Time *number* executions of the main statement. This executes the setup statement once, and then returns the time it takes to execute the main statement a number of times, measured in seconds as a float. The argument is the number of times through the loop, defaulting to one million. The main statement, the setup statement and the timer function to be used are passed to the constructor.
>
> ---
>
> **Note:** By default, `timeit()` temporarily turns off *garbage collection* during the timing. The advantage of this approach is that it makes independent timings more comparable. This disadvantage is that GC may be an important component of the performance of the function being measured. If so, GC can be re-enabled as the first statement in the *setup* string. For example:
>
> ```
> timeit.Timer('for i in range(10): oct(i)', 'gc.enable()').timeit()
> ```
>
> ---

autorange(*callback=None*)

> Automatically determine how many times to call `timeit()`.
>
> This is a convenience function that calls `timeit()` repeatedly so that the total time >= 0.2 second, returning the eventual (number of loops, time taken for that number of loops). It calls `timeit()` with *number* set to successive powers of ten (10, 100, 1000, ...) up to a maximum of one billion, until the time taken is at least 0.2 second, or the maximum is reached.
>
> If *callback* is given and is not `None`, it will be called after each trial with two arguments: `callback(number, time_taken)`.
>
> New in version 3.6.

repeat(*repeat=3, number=1000000*)

> Call `timeit()` a few times.
>
> This is a convenience function that calls the `timeit()` repeatedly, returning a list of results. The first argument specifies how many times to call `timeit()`. The second argument specifies the *number* argument for `timeit()`.
>
> ---
>
> **Note:** It's tempting to calculate mean and standard deviation from the result vector and report these. However, this is not very useful. In a typical case, the lowest value gives a lower bound for how fast your machine can run the given code snippet; higher values in the result vector are typically not caused by variability in Python's speed, but by other processes interfering with your timing accuracy. So the `min()` of the result is probably the only number you should be interested in. After that, you should look at the entire vector and apply common sense rather than statistics.
>
> ---

print_exc(*file=None*)

> Helper to print a traceback from the timed code.
>
> Typical use:
>
> ```
> t = Timer(...)    # outside the try/except
> try:
>     t.timeit(...) # or t.repeat(...)
> ```

```
except Exception:
    t.print_exc()
```

The advantage over the standard traceback is that source lines in the compiled template will be displayed. The optional *file* argument directs where the traceback is sent; it defaults to *sys.stderr*.

27.5.3 Command-Line Interface

When called as a program from the command line, the following form is used:

```
python -m timeit [-n N] [-r N] [-u U] [-s S] [-t] [-c] [-h] [statement ...]
```

Where the following options are understood:

-n N, --number=N
    how many times to execute 'statement'

-r N, --repeat=N
    how many times to repeat the timer (default 3)

-s S, --setup=S
    statement to be executed once initially (default **pass**)

-p, --process
    measure process time, not wallclock time, using *time.process_time()* instead of *time.perf_counter()*, which is the default

    New in version 3.3.

-t, --time
    use *time.time()* (deprecated)

-u, --unit=U
    specify a time unit for timer output; can select usec, msec, or sec

    New in version 3.5.

-c, --clock
    use *time.clock()* (deprecated)

-v, --verbose
    print raw timing results; repeat for more digits precision

-h, --help
    print a short usage message and exit

A multi-line statement may be given by specifying each line as a separate statement argument; indented lines are possible by enclosing an argument in quotes and using leading spaces. Multiple *-s* options are treated similarly.

If *-n* is not given, a suitable number of loops is calculated by trying successive powers of 10 until the total time is at least 0.2 seconds.

default_timer() measurements can be affected by other programs running on the same machine, so the best thing to do when accurate timing is necessary is to repeat the timing a few times and use the best time. The *-r* option is good for this; the default of 3 repetitions is probably enough in most cases. You can use *time.process_time()* to measure CPU time.

Note: There is a certain baseline overhead associated with executing a pass statement. The code here doesn't try to hide it, but you should be aware of it. The baseline overhead can be measured by invoking the program without arguments, and it might differ between Python versions.

27.5.4 Examples

It is possible to provide a setup statement that is executed only once at the beginning:

```
$ python -m timeit -s 'text = "sample string"; char = "g"' 'char in text'
10000000 loops, best of 3: 0.0877 usec per loop
$ python -m timeit -s 'text = "sample string"; char = "g"' 'text.find(char)'
1000000 loops, best of 3: 0.342 usec per loop
```

```
>>> import timeit
>>> timeit.timeit('char in text', setup='text = "sample string"; char = "g"')
0.41440500499993504
>>> timeit.timeit('text.find(char)', setup='text = "sample string"; char = "g"')
1.7246671520006203
```

The same can be done using the *Timer* class and its methods:

```
>>> import timeit
>>> t = timeit.Timer('char in text', setup='text = "sample string"; char = "g"')
>>> t.timeit()
0.3955516149999312
>>> t.repeat()
[0.40193588800002544, 0.3960157959998014, 0.39594301399984033]
```

The following examples show how to time expressions that contain multiple lines. Here we compare the cost of using *hasattr()* vs. **try/except** to test for missing and present object attributes:

```
$ python -m timeit 'try:' '  str.__bool__' 'except AttributeError:' '  pass'
100000 loops, best of 3: 15.7 usec per loop
$ python -m timeit 'if hasattr(str, "__bool__"): pass'
100000 loops, best of 3: 4.26 usec per loop

$ python -m timeit 'try:' '  int.__bool__' 'except AttributeError:' '  pass'
1000000 loops, best of 3: 1.43 usec per loop
$ python -m timeit 'if hasattr(int, "__bool__"): pass'
100000 loops, best of 3: 2.23 usec per loop
```

```
>>> import timeit
>>> # attribute is missing
>>> s = """\
... try:
...     str.__bool__
... except AttributeError:
...     pass
... """
>>> timeit.timeit(stmt=s, number=100000)
0.9138244460009446
>>> s = "if hasattr(str, '__bool__'): pass"
>>> timeit.timeit(stmt=s, number=100000)
0.5829014980008651
```

```
>>>
>>> # attribute is present
>>> s = """\
... try:
...     int.__bool__
... except AttributeError:
...     pass
... """
>>> timeit.timeit(stmt=s, number=100000)
0.04215312199994514
>>> s = "if hasattr(int, '__bool__'): pass"
>>> timeit.timeit(stmt=s, number=100000)
0.08588060699912603
```

To give the *timeit* module access to functions you define, you can pass a *setup* parameter which contains an import statement:

```
def test():
    """Stupid test function"""
    L = [i for i in range(100)]

if __name__ == '__main__':
    import timeit
    print(timeit.timeit("test()", setup="from __main__ import test"))
```

Another option is to pass *globals()* to the *globals* parameter, which will cause the code to be executed within your current global namespace. This can be more convenient than individually specifying imports:

```
def f(x):
    return x**2
def g(x):
    return x**4
def h(x):
    return x**8

import timeit
print(timeit.timeit('[func(42) for func in (f,g,h)]', globals=globals()))
```

27.6 `trace` — Trace or track Python statement execution

Source code: Lib/trace.py

The *trace* module allows you to trace program execution, generate annotated statement coverage listings, print caller/callee relationships and list functions executed during a program run. It can be used in another program or from the command line.

See also:

Coverage.py   A popular third-party coverage tool that provides HTML output along with advanced features such as branch coverage.

27.6.1 Command-Line Usage

The *trace* module can be invoked from the command line. It can be as simple as

```
python -m trace --count -C . somefile.py ...
```

The above will execute `somefile.py` and generate annotated listings of all Python modules imported during the execution into the current directory.

--help
    Display usage and exit.

--version
    Display the version of the module and exit.

Main options

At least one of the following options must be specified when invoking *trace*. The *--listfuncs* option is mutually exclusive with the *--trace* and *--count* options. When *--listfuncs* is provided, neither *--count* nor *--trace* are accepted, and vice versa.

-c, --count
    Produce a set of annotated listing files upon program completion that shows how many times each statement was executed. See also *--coverdir*, *--file* and *--no-report* below.

-t, --trace
    Display lines as they are executed.

-l, --listfuncs
    Display the functions executed by running the program.

-r, --report
    Produce an annotated list from an earlier program run that used the *--count* and *--file* option. This does not execute any code.

-T, --trackcalls
    Display the calling relationships exposed by running the program.

Modifiers

-f, --file=<file>
    Name of a file to accumulate counts over several tracing runs. Should be used with the *--count* option.

-C, --coverdir=<dir>
    Directory where the report files go. The coverage report for `package.module` is written to file *dir/package/module*.cover.

-m, --missing
    When generating annotated listings, mark lines which were not executed with >>>>>>.

-s, --summary
    When using *--count* or *--report*, write a brief summary to stdout for each file processed.

-R, --no-report
    Do not generate annotated listings. This is useful if you intend to make several runs with *--count*, and then produce a single set of annotated listings at the end.

-g, --timing
    Prefix each line with the time since the program started. Only used while tracing.

Filters

These options may be repeated multiple times.

--ignore-module=<mod>
    Ignore each of the given module names and its submodules (if it is a package). The argument can be a list of names separated by a comma.

--ignore-dir=<dir>
    Ignore all modules and packages in the named directory and subdirectories. The argument can be a list of directories separated by *os.pathsep*.

27.6.2 Programmatic Interface

class trace.Trace(*count=1, trace=1, countfuncs=0, countcallers=0, ignoremods=(), ignoredirs=(), infile=None, outfile=None, timing=False*)
    Create an object to trace execution of a single statement or expression. All parameters are optional. *count* enables counting of line numbers. *trace* enables line execution tracing. *countfuncs* enables listing of the functions called during the run. *countcallers* enables call relationship tracking. *ignoremods* is a list of modules or packages to ignore. *ignoredirs* is a list of directories whose modules or packages should be ignored. *infile* is the name of the file from which to read stored count information. *outfile* is the name of the file in which to write updated count information. *timing* enables a timestamp relative to when tracing was started to be displayed.

   run(*cmd*)
        Execute the command and gather statistics from the execution with the current tracing parameters. *cmd* must be a string or code object, suitable for passing into *exec()*.

   runctx(*cmd, globals=None, locals=None*)
        Execute the command and gather statistics from the execution with the current tracing parameters, in the defined global and local environments. If not defined, *globals* and *locals* default to empty dictionaries.

   runfunc(*func, *args, **kwds*)
        Call *func* with the given arguments under control of the *Trace* object with the current tracing parameters.

   results()
        Return a *CoverageResults* object that contains the cumulative results of all previous calls to **run**, **runctx** and **runfunc** for the given *Trace* instance. Does not reset the accumulated trace results.

class trace.CoverageResults
    A container for coverage results, created by *Trace.results()*. Should not be created directly by the user.

   update(*other*)
        Merge in data from another *CoverageResults* object.

   write_results(*show_missing=True, summary=False, coverdir=None*)
        Write coverage results. Set *show_missing* to show lines that had no hits. Set *summary* to include in the output the coverage summary per module. *coverdir* specifies the directory into which the coverage result files will be output. If None, the results for each source file are placed in its directory.

A simple example demonstrating the use of the programmatic interface:

```
import sys
import trace
```

```
# create a Trace object, telling it what to ignore, and whether to
# do tracing or line-counting or both.
tracer = trace.Trace(
    ignoredirs=[sys.prefix, sys.exec_prefix],
    trace=0,
    count=1)

# run the new command using the given tracer
tracer.run('main()')

# make a report, placing output in the current directory
r = tracer.results()
r.write_results(show_missing=True, coverdir=".")
```

27.7 `tracemalloc` — Trace memory allocations

New in version 3.4.

Source code: Lib/tracemalloc.py

The tracemalloc module is a debug tool to trace memory blocks allocated by Python. It provides the following information:

- Traceback where an object was allocated
- Statistics on allocated memory blocks per filename and per line number: total size, number and average size of allocated memory blocks
- Compute the differences between two snapshots to detect memory leaks

To trace most memory blocks allocated by Python, the module should be started as early as possible by setting the `PYTHONTRACEMALLOC` environment variable to 1, or by using `-X tracemalloc` command line option. The *tracemalloc.start()* function can be called at runtime to start tracing Python memory allocations.

By default, a trace of an allocated memory block only stores the most recent frame (1 frame). To store 25 frames at startup: set the `PYTHONTRACEMALLOC` environment variable to 25, or use the `-X tracemalloc=25` command line option.

27.7.1 Examples

Display the top 10

Display the 10 files allocating the most memory:

```
import tracemalloc

tracemalloc.start()

# ... run your application ...

snapshot = tracemalloc.take_snapshot()
top_stats = snapshot.statistics('lineno')

print("[ Top 10 ]")
```

```
for stat in top_stats[:10]:
    print(stat)
```

Example of output of the Python test suite:

```
[ Top 10 ]
<frozen importlib._bootstrap>:716: size=4855 KiB, count=39328, average=126 B
<frozen importlib._bootstrap>:284: size=521 KiB, count=3199, average=167 B
/usr/lib/python3.4/collections/__init__.py:368: size=244 KiB, count=2315, average=108 B
/usr/lib/python3.4/unittest/case.py:381: size=185 KiB, count=779, average=243 B
/usr/lib/python3.4/unittest/case.py:402: size=154 KiB, count=378, average=416 B
/usr/lib/python3.4/abc.py:133: size=88.7 KiB, count=347, average=262 B
<frozen importlib._bootstrap>:1446: size=70.4 KiB, count=911, average=79 B
<frozen importlib._bootstrap>:1454: size=52.0 KiB, count=25, average=2131 B
<string>:5: size=49.7 KiB, count=148, average=344 B
/usr/lib/python3.4/sysconfig.py:411: size=48.0 KiB, count=1, average=48.0 KiB
```

We can see that Python loaded 4855 KiB data (bytecode and constants) from modules and that the *collections* module allocated 244 KiB to build *namedtuple* types.

See *Snapshot.statistics()* for more options.

Compute differences

Take two snapshots and display the differences:

```
import tracemalloc
tracemalloc.start()
# ... start your application ...

snapshot1 = tracemalloc.take_snapshot()
# ... call the function leaking memory ...
snapshot2 = tracemalloc.take_snapshot()

top_stats = snapshot2.compare_to(snapshot1, 'lineno')

print("[ Top 10 differences ]")
for stat in top_stats[:10]:
    print(stat)
```

Example of output before/after running some tests of the Python test suite:

```
[ Top 10 differences ]
<frozen importlib._bootstrap>:716: size=8173 KiB (+4428 KiB), count=71332 (+39369), average=117 B
/usr/lib/python3.4/linecache.py:127: size=940 KiB (+940 KiB), count=8106 (+8106), average=119 B
/usr/lib/python3.4/unittest/case.py:571: size=298 KiB (+298 KiB), count=589 (+589), average=519 B
<frozen importlib._bootstrap>:284: size=1005 KiB (+166 KiB), count=7423 (+1526), average=139 B
/usr/lib/python3.4/mimetypes.py:217: size=112 KiB (+112 KiB), count=1334 (+1334), average=86 B
/usr/lib/python3.4/http/server.py:848: size=96.0 KiB (+96.0 KiB), count=1 (+1), average=96.0 KiB
/usr/lib/python3.4/inspect.py:1465: size=83.5 KiB (+83.5 KiB), count=109 (+109), average=784 B
/usr/lib/python3.4/unittest/mock.py:491: size=77.7 KiB (+77.7 KiB), count=143 (+143), average=557 B
/usr/lib/python3.4/urllib/parse.py:476: size=71.8 KiB (+71.8 KiB), count=969 (+969), average=76 B
/usr/lib/python3.4/contextlib.py:38: size=67.2 KiB (+67.2 KiB), count=126 (+126), average=546 B
```

We can see that Python has loaded 8173 KiB of module data (bytecode and constants), and that this is 4428 KiB more than had been loaded before the tests, when the previous snapshot was taken. Similarly, the *linecache* module has cached 940 KiB of Python source code to format tracebacks, all of it since the previous snapshot.

If the system has little free memory, snapshots can be written on disk using the `Snapshot.dump()` method to analyze the snapshot offline. Then use the `Snapshot.load()` method reload the snapshot.

Get the traceback of a memory block

Code to display the traceback of the biggest memory block:

```python
import tracemalloc

# Store 25 frames
tracemalloc.start(25)

# ... run your application ...

snapshot = tracemalloc.take_snapshot()
top_stats = snapshot.statistics('traceback')

# pick the biggest memory block
stat = top_stats[0]
print("%s memory blocks: %.1f KiB" % (stat.count, stat.size / 1024))
for line in stat.traceback.format():
    print(line)
```

Example of output of the Python test suite (traceback limited to 25 frames):

```
903 memory blocks: 870.1 KiB
  File "<frozen importlib._bootstrap>", line 716
  File "<frozen importlib._bootstrap>", line 1036
  File "<frozen importlib._bootstrap>", line 934
  File "<frozen importlib._bootstrap>", line 1068
  File "<frozen importlib._bootstrap>", line 619
  File "<frozen importlib._bootstrap>", line 1581
  File "<frozen importlib._bootstrap>", line 1614
  File "/usr/lib/python3.4/doctest.py", line 101
    import pdb
  File "<frozen importlib._bootstrap>", line 284
  File "<frozen importlib._bootstrap>", line 938
  File "<frozen importlib._bootstrap>", line 1068
  File "<frozen importlib._bootstrap>", line 619
  File "<frozen importlib._bootstrap>", line 1581
  File "<frozen importlib._bootstrap>", line 1614
  File "/usr/lib/python3.4/test/support/__init__.py", line 1728
    import doctest
  File "/usr/lib/python3.4/test/test_pickletools.py", line 21
    support.run_doctest(pickletools)
  File "/usr/lib/python3.4/test/regrtest.py", line 1276
    test_runner()
  File "/usr/lib/python3.4/test/regrtest.py", line 976
    display_failure=not verbose)
  File "/usr/lib/python3.4/test/regrtest.py", line 761
    match_tests=ns.match_tests)
  File "/usr/lib/python3.4/test/regrtest.py", line 1563
    main()
  File "/usr/lib/python3.4/test/__main__.py", line 3
    regrtest.main_in_temp_cwd()
  File "/usr/lib/python3.4/runpy.py", line 73
    exec(code, run_globals)
```

```
  File "/usr/lib/python3.4/runpy.py", line 160
    "__main__", fname, loader, pkg_name)
```

We can see that the most memory was allocated in the *importlib* module to load data (bytecode and constants) from modules: 870.1 KiB. The traceback is where the *importlib* loaded data most recently: on the `import pdb` line of the *doctest* module. The traceback may change if a new module is loaded.

Pretty top

Code to display the 10 lines allocating the most memory with a pretty output, ignoring `<frozen importlib._bootstrap>` and `<unknown>` files:

```python
import linecache
import os
import tracemalloc

def display_top(snapshot, key_type='lineno', limit=10):
    snapshot = snapshot.filter_traces((
        tracemalloc.Filter(False, "<frozen importlib._bootstrap>"),
        tracemalloc.Filter(False, "<unknown>"),
    ))
    top_stats = snapshot.statistics(key_type)

    print("Top %s lines" % limit)
    for index, stat in enumerate(top_stats[:limit], 1):
        frame = stat.traceback[0]
        # replace "/path/to/module/file.py" with "module/file.py"
        filename = os.sep.join(frame.filename.split(os.sep)[-2:])
        print("#%s: %s:%s: %.1f KiB"
              % (index, filename, frame.lineno, stat.size / 1024))
        line = linecache.getline(frame.filename, frame.lineno).strip()
        if line:
            print('    %s' % line)

    other = top_stats[limit:]
    if other:
        size = sum(stat.size for stat in other)
        print("%s other: %.1f KiB" % (len(other), size / 1024))
    total = sum(stat.size for stat in top_stats)
    print("Total allocated size: %.1f KiB" % (total / 1024))

tracemalloc.start()

# ... run your application ...

snapshot = tracemalloc.take_snapshot()
display_top(snapshot)
```

Example of output of the Python test suite:

```
Top 10 lines
#1: Lib/base64.py:414: 419.8 KiB
    _b85chars2 = [(a + b) for a in _b85chars for b in _b85chars]
#2: Lib/base64.py:306: 419.8 KiB
    _a85chars2 = [(a + b) for a in _a85chars for b in _a85chars]
#3: collections/__init__.py:368: 293.6 KiB
    exec(class_definition, namespace)
```

```
#4: Lib/abc.py:133: 115.2 KiB
    cls = super().__new__(mcls, name, bases, namespace)
#5: unittest/case.py:574: 103.1 KiB
    testMethod()
#6: Lib/linecache.py:127: 95.4 KiB
    lines = fp.readlines()
#7: urllib/parse.py:476: 71.8 KiB
    for a in _hexdig for b in _hexdig}
#8: <string>:5: 62.0 KiB
#9: Lib/_weakrefset.py:37: 60.0 KiB
    self.data = set()
#10: Lib/base64.py:142: 59.8 KiB
    _b32tab2 = [a + b for a in _b32tab for b in _b32tab]
6220 other: 3602.8 KiB
Total allocated size: 5303.1 KiB
```

See *Snapshot.statistics()* for more options.

27.7.2 API

Functions

tracemalloc.clear_traces()
> Clear traces of memory blocks allocated by Python.
>
> See also *stop()*.

tracemalloc.get_object_traceback(*obj***)**
> Get the traceback where the Python object *obj* was allocated. Return a *Traceback* instance, or **None** if the *tracemalloc* module is not tracing memory allocations or did not trace the allocation of the object.
>
> See also *gc.get_referrers()* and *sys.getsizeof()* functions.

tracemalloc.get_traceback_limit()
> Get the maximum number of frames stored in the traceback of a trace.
>
> The *tracemalloc* module must be tracing memory allocations to get the limit, otherwise an exception is raised.
>
> The limit is set by the *start()* function.

tracemalloc.get_traced_memory()
> Get the current size and peak size of memory blocks traced by the *tracemalloc* module as a tuple: (**current: int, peak: int**).

tracemalloc.get_tracemalloc_memory()
> Get the memory usage in bytes of the *tracemalloc* module used to store traces of memory blocks. Return an *int*.

tracemalloc.is_tracing()
> **True** if the *tracemalloc* module is tracing Python memory allocations, **False** otherwise.
>
> See also *start()* and *stop()* functions.

tracemalloc.start(*nframe: int=1***)**
> Start tracing Python memory allocations: install hooks on Python memory allocators. Collected tracebacks of traces will be limited to *nframe* frames. By default, a trace of a memory block only stores the most recent frame: the limit is 1. *nframe* must be greater or equal to 1.

Storing more than 1 frame is only useful to compute statistics grouped by `'traceback'` or to compute cumulative statistics: see the *Snapshot.compare_to()* and *Snapshot.statistics()* methods.

Storing more frames increases the memory and CPU overhead of the *tracemalloc* module. Use the *get_tracemalloc_memory()* function to measure how much memory is used by the *tracemalloc* module.

The **PYTHONTRACEMALLOC** environment variable (**PYTHONTRACEMALLOC=NFRAME**) and the **-X tracemalloc=NFRAME** command line option can be used to start tracing at startup.

See also *stop()*, *is_tracing()* and *get_traceback_limit()* functions.

tracemalloc.stop()
> Stop tracing Python memory allocations: uninstall hooks on Python memory allocators. Also clears all previously collected traces of memory blocks allocated by Python.
>
> Call *take_snapshot()* function to take a snapshot of traces before clearing them.
>
> See also *start()*, *is_tracing()* and *clear_traces()* functions.

tracemalloc.take_snapshot()
> Take a snapshot of traces of memory blocks allocated by Python. Return a new *Snapshot* instance.
>
> The snapshot does not include memory blocks allocated before the *tracemalloc* module started to trace memory allocations.
>
> Tracebacks of traces are limited to *get_traceback_limit()* frames. Use the *nframe* parameter of the *start()* function to store more frames.
>
> The *tracemalloc* module must be tracing memory allocations to take a snapshot, see the *start()* function.
>
> See also the *get_object_traceback()* function.

DomainFilter

class tracemalloc.DomainFilter(*inclusive: bool, domain: int*)
> Filter traces of memory blocks by their address space (domain).
>
> New in version 3.6.
>
> **inclusive**
> > If *inclusive* is `True` (include), match memory blocks allocated in the address space *domain*.
> >
> > If *inclusive* is `False` (exclude), match memory blocks not allocated in the address space *domain*.
>
> **domain**
> > Address space of a memory block (`int`). Read-only property.

Filter

class tracemalloc.Filter(*inclusive: bool, filename_pattern: str, lineno: int=None, all_frames: bool=False, domain: int=None*)
> Filter on traces of memory blocks.
>
> See the *fnmatch.fnmatch()* function for the syntax of *filename_pattern*. The `'.pyc'` file extension is replaced with `'.py'`.
>
> Examples:
> - `Filter(True, subprocess.__file__)` only includes traces of the *subprocess* module
> - `Filter(False, tracemalloc.__file__)` excludes traces of the *tracemalloc* module
> - `Filter(False, "<unknown>")` excludes empty tracebacks

Changed in version 3.5: The '.pyo' file extension is no longer replaced with '.py'.

Changed in version 3.6: Added the *domain* attribute.

domain
> Address space of a memory block (`int` or `None`).

inclusive
> If *inclusive* is `True` (include), only match memory blocks allocated in a file with a name matching *filename_pattern* at line number *lineno*.
>
> If *inclusive* is `False` (exclude), ignore memory blocks allocated in a file with a name matching *filename_pattern* at line number *lineno*.

lineno
> Line number (`int`) of the filter. If *lineno* is `None`, the filter matches any line number.

filename_pattern
> Filename pattern of the filter (`str`). Read-only property.

all_frames
> If *all_frames* is `True`, all frames of the traceback are checked. If *all_frames* is `False`, only the most recent frame is checked.
>
> This attribute has no effect if the traceback limit is 1. See the *get_traceback_limit()* function and *Snapshot.traceback_limit* attribute.

Frame

class tracemalloc.Frame
> Frame of a traceback.
>
> The *Traceback* class is a sequence of *Frame* instances.
>
> **filename**
> > Filename (`str`).
>
> **lineno**
> > Line number (`int`).

Snapshot

class tracemalloc.Snapshot
> Snapshot of traces of memory blocks allocated by Python.
>
> The *take_snapshot()* function creates a snapshot instance.
>
> **compare_to**(*old_snapshot: Snapshot, key_type: str, cumulative: bool=False*)
> > Compute the differences with an old snapshot. Get statistics as a sorted list of *StatisticDiff* instances grouped by *key_type*.
> >
> > See the *Snapshot.statistics()* method for *key_type* and *cumulative* parameters.
> >
> > The result is sorted from the biggest to the smallest by: absolute value of *StatisticDiff.size_diff*, *StatisticDiff.size*, absolute value of *StatisticDiff.count_diff*, *Statistic.count* and then by *StatisticDiff.traceback*.
>
> **dump**(*filename*)
> > Write the snapshot into a file.
> >
> > Use *load()* to reload the snapshot.

filter_traces(*filters*)
> Create a new *Snapshot* instance with a filtered *traces* sequence, *filters* is a list of *DomainFilter* and *Filter* instances. If *filters* is an empty list, return a new *Snapshot* instance with a copy of the traces.
>
> All inclusive filters are applied at once, a trace is ignored if no inclusive filters match it. A trace is ignored if at least one exclusive filter matches it.
>
> Changed in version 3.6: *DomainFilter* instances are now also accepted in *filters*.

classmethod load(*filename*)
> Load a snapshot from a file.
>
> See also *dump()*.

statistics(*key_type: str, cumulative: bool=False*)
> Get statistics as a sorted list of *Statistic* instances grouped by *key_type*:
>
> | key_type | description |
> |---|---|
> | 'filename' | filename |
> | 'lineno' | filename and line number |
> | 'traceback' | traceback |
>
> If *cumulative* is True, cumulate size and count of memory blocks of all frames of the traceback of a trace, not only the most recent frame. The cumulative mode can only be used with *key_type* equals to 'filename' and 'lineno'.
>
> The result is sorted from the biggest to the smallest by: *Statistic.size*, *Statistic.count* and then by *Statistic.traceback*.

traceback_limit
> Maximum number of frames stored in the traceback of *traces*: result of the *get_traceback_limit()* when the snapshot was taken.

traces
> Traces of all memory blocks allocated by Python: sequence of *Trace* instances.
>
> The sequence has an undefined order. Use the *Snapshot.statistics()* method to get a sorted list of statistics.

Statistic

class tracemalloc.Statistic
> Statistic on memory allocations.
>
> *Snapshot.statistics()* returns a list of *Statistic* instances.
>
> See also the *StatisticDiff* class.
>
> **count**
> > Number of memory blocks (int).
>
> **size**
> > Total size of memory blocks in bytes (int).
>
> **traceback**
> > Traceback where the memory block was allocated, *Traceback* instance.

StatisticDiff

class tracemalloc.StatisticDiff

Statistic difference on memory allocations between an old and a new *Snapshot* instance.

Snapshot.compare_to() returns a list of *StatisticDiff* instances. See also the *Statistic* class.

count

Number of memory blocks in the new snapshot (`int`): 0 if the memory blocks have been released in the new snapshot.

count_diff

Difference of number of memory blocks between the old and the new snapshots (`int`): 0 if the memory blocks have been allocated in the new snapshot.

size

Total size of memory blocks in bytes in the new snapshot (`int`): 0 if the memory blocks have been released in the new snapshot.

size_diff

Difference of total size of memory blocks in bytes between the old and the new snapshots (`int`): 0 if the memory blocks have been allocated in the new snapshot.

traceback

Traceback where the memory blocks were allocated, *Traceback* instance.

Trace

class tracemalloc.Trace

Trace of a memory block.

The *Snapshot.traces* attribute is a sequence of *Trace* instances.

size

Size of the memory block in bytes (`int`).

traceback

Traceback where the memory block was allocated, *Traceback* instance.

Traceback

class tracemalloc.Traceback

Sequence of *Frame* instances sorted from the most recent frame to the oldest frame.

A traceback contains at least 1 frame. If the `tracemalloc` module failed to get a frame, the filename `"<unknown>"` at line number 0 is used.

When a snapshot is taken, tracebacks of traces are limited to *get_traceback_limit()* frames. See the *take_snapshot()* function.

The *Trace.traceback* attribute is an instance of *Traceback* instance.

format(*limit=None*)

Format the traceback as a list of lines with newlines. Use the *linecache* module to retrieve lines from the source code. If *limit* is set, only format the *limit* most recent frames.

Similar to the *traceback.format_tb()* function, except that *format()* does not include newlines.

Example:

```
print("Traceback (most recent call first):")
for line in traceback:
    print(line)
```

Output:

```
Traceback (most recent call first):
  File "test.py", line 9
    obj = Object()
  File "test.py", line 12
    tb = tracemalloc.get_object_traceback(f())
```

CHAPTER
TWENTYEIGHT

SOFTWARE PACKAGING AND DISTRIBUTION

These libraries help you with publishing and installing Python software. While these modules are designed to work in conjunction with the Python Package Index, they can also be used with a local index server, or without any index server at all.

28.1 `distutils` — Building and installing Python modules

The *distutils* package provides support for building and installing additional modules into a Python installation. The new modules may be either 100%-pure Python, or may be extension modules written in C, or may be collections of Python packages which include modules coded in both Python and C.

Most Python users will *not* want to use this module directly, but instead use the cross-version tools maintained by the Python Packaging Authority. In particular, setuptools is an enhanced alternative to *distutils* that provides:

- support for declaring project dependencies
- additional mechanisms for configuring which files to include in source releases (including plugins for integration with version control systems)
- the ability to declare project "entry points", which can be used as the basis for application plugin systems
- the ability to automatically generate Windows command line executables at installation time rather than needing to prebuild them
- consistent behaviour across all supported Python versions

The recommended pip installer runs all `setup.py` scripts with `setuptools`, even if the script itself only imports `distutils`. Refer to the Python Packaging User Guide for more information.

For the benefits of packaging tool authors and users seeking a deeper understanding of the details of the current packaging and distribution system, the legacy *distutils* based user documentation and API reference remain available:

- install-index
- distutils-index

28.2 `ensurepip` — Bootstrapping the `pip` installer

New in version 3.4.

1549

The *ensurepip* package provides support for bootstrapping the `pip` installer into an existing Python installation or virtual environment. This bootstrapping approach reflects the fact that `pip` is an independent project with its own release cycle, and the latest available stable version is bundled with maintenance and feature releases of the CPython reference interpreter.

In most cases, end users of Python shouldn't need to invoke this module directly (as `pip` should be bootstrapped by default), but it may be needed if installing `pip` was skipped when installing Python (or when creating a virtual environment) or after explicitly uninstalling `pip`.

Note: This module *does not* access the internet. All of the components needed to bootstrap `pip` are included as internal parts of the package.

See also:

installing-index The end user guide for installing Python packages

PEP 453: **Explicit bootstrapping of pip in Python installations** The original rationale and specification for this module.

28.2.1 Command line interface

The command line interface is invoked using the interpreter's -m switch.

The simplest possible invocation is:

```
python -m ensurepip
```

This invocation will install `pip` if it is not already installed, but otherwise does nothing. To ensure the installed version of `pip` is at least as recent as the one bundled with `ensurepip`, pass the `--upgrade` option:

```
python -m ensurepip --upgrade
```

By default, `pip` is installed into the current virtual environment (if one is active) or into the system site packages (if there is no active virtual environment). The installation location can be controlled through two additional command line options:

- `--root <dir>`: Installs `pip` relative to the given root directory rather than the root of the currently active virtual environment (if any) or the default root for the current Python installation.
- `--user`: Installs `pip` into the user site packages directory rather than globally for the current Python installation (this option is not permitted inside an active virtual environment).

By default, the scripts `pipX` and `pipX.Y` will be installed (where X.Y stands for the version of Python used to invoke `ensurepip`). The scripts installed can be controlled through two additional command line options:

- `--altinstall`: if an alternate installation is requested, the `pipX` script will *not* be installed.
- `--default-pip`: **if a "default pip" installation is requested, the** `pip` script will be installed in addition to the two regular scripts.

Providing both of the script selection options will trigger an exception.

Changed in version 3.6.3: The exit status is non-zero if the command fails.

28.2.2 Module API

ensurepip exposes two functions for programmatic use:

ensurepip.version()
    Returns a string specifying the bundled version of pip that will be installed when bootstrapping an environment.

ensurepip.bootstrap(*root=None, upgrade=False, user=False, altinstall=False, default_pip=False, verbosity=0*)
    Bootstraps `pip` into the current or designated environment.

    root specifies an alternative root directory to install relative to. If *root* is `None`, then installation uses the default install location for the current environment.

    upgrade indicates whether or not to upgrade an existing installation of an earlier version of `pip` to the bundled version.

    user indicates whether to use the user scheme rather than installing globally.

    By default, the scripts `pipX` and `pipX.Y` will be installed (where X.Y stands for the current version of Python).

    If *altinstall* is set, then `pipX` will *not* be installed.

    If *default_pip* is set, then `pip` will be installed in addition to the two regular scripts.

    Setting both *altinstall* and *default_pip* will trigger `ValueError`.

    verbosity controls the level of output to `sys.stdout` from the bootstrapping operation.

> **Note:** The bootstrapping process has side effects on both `sys.path` and `os.environ`. Invoking the command line interface in a subprocess instead allows these side effects to be avoided.

> **Note:** The bootstrapping process may install additional modules required by `pip`, but other software should not assume those dependencies will always be present by default (as the dependencies may be removed in a future version of `pip`).

28.3 venv — Creation of virtual environments

New in version 3.3.

Source code: Lib/venv/

The *venv* module provides support for creating lightweight "virtual environments" with their own site directories, optionally isolated from system site directories. Each virtual environment has its own Python binary (allowing creation of environments with various Python versions) and can have its own independent set of installed Python packages in its site directories.

See PEP 405 for more information about Python virtual environments.

> **Note:** The `pyvenv` script has been deprecated as of Python 3.6 in favor of using `python3 -m venv` to help prevent any potential confusion as to which Python interpreter a virtual environment will be based on.

28.3.1 Creating virtual environments

Creation of *virtual environments* is done by executing the command venv:

```
python3 -m venv /path/to/new/virtual/environment
```

Running this command creates the target directory (creating any parent directories that don't exist already) and places a `pyvenv.cfg` file in it with a `home` key pointing to the Python installation from which the command was run. It also creates a `bin` (or `Scripts` on Windows) subdirectory containing a copy of the `python` binary (or binaries, in the case of Windows). It also creates an (initially empty) `lib/pythonX.Y/site-packages` subdirectory (on Windows, this is `Lib\site-packages`).

Deprecated since version 3.6: `pyvenv` was the recommended tool for creating virtual environments for Python 3.3 and 3.4, and is deprecated in Python 3.6.

Changed in version 3.5: The use of venv is now recommended for creating virtual environments.

See also:

Python Packaging User Guide: Creating and using virtual environments

On Windows, invoke the venv command as follows:

```
c:\>c:\Python35\python -m venv c:\path\to\myenv
```

Alternatively, if you configured the PATH and PATHEXT variables for your Python installation:

```
c:\>python -m venv c:\path\to\myenv
```

The command, if run with -h, will show the available options:

```
usage: venv [-h] [--system-site-packages] [--symlinks | --copies] [--clear]
            [--upgrade] [--without-pip]
            ENV_DIR [ENV_DIR ...]

Creates virtual Python environments in one or more target directories.

positional arguments:
  ENV_DIR               A directory to create the environment in.

optional arguments:
  -h, --help            show this help message and exit
  --system-site-packages
                        Give the virtual environment access to the system
                        site-packages dir.
  --symlinks            Try to use symlinks rather than copies, when symlinks
                        are not the default for the platform.
  --copies              Try to use copies rather than symlinks, even when
                        symlinks are the default for the platform.
  --clear               Delete the contents of the environment directory if it
                        already exists, before environment creation.
  --upgrade             Upgrade the environment directory to use this version
                        of Python, assuming Python has been upgraded in-place.
  --without-pip         Skips installing or upgrading pip in the virtual
                        environment (pip is bootstrapped by default)

Once an environment has been created, you may wish to activate it, e.g. by
sourcing an activate script in its bin directory.
```

Changed in version 3.4: Installs pip by default, added the `--without-pip` and `--copies` options

Changed in version 3.4: In earlier versions, if the target directory already existed, an error was raised, unless the `--clear` or `--upgrade` option was provided. Now, if an existing directory is specified, its contents are removed and the directory is processed as if it had been newly created.

The created `pyvenv.cfg` file also includes the `include-system-site-packages` key, set to `true` if `venv` is run with the `--system-site-packages` option, `false` otherwise.

Unless the `--without-pip` option is given, *ensurepip* will be invoked to bootstrap `pip` into the virtual environment.

Multiple paths can be given to `venv`, in which case an identical virtual environment will be created, according to the given options, at each provided path.

Once a virtual environment has been created, it can be "activated" using a script in the virtual environment's binary directory. The invocation of the script is platform-specific:

Platform	Shell	Command to activate virtual environment
Posix	bash/zsh	$ source <venv>/bin/activate
	fish	$. <venv>/bin/activate.fish
	csh/tcsh	$ source <venv>/bin/activate.csh
Windows	cmd.exe	C:\> <venv>\Scripts\activate.bat
	PowerShell	PS C:\> <venv>\Scripts\Activate.ps1

You don't specifically *need* to activate an environment; activation just prepends the virtual environment's binary directory to your path, so that "python" invokes the virtual environment's Python interpreter and you can run installed scripts without having to use their full path. However, all scripts installed in a virtual environment should be runnable without activating it, and run with the virtual environment's Python automatically.

You can deactivate a virtual environment by typing "deactivate" in your shell. The exact mechanism is platform-specific: for example, the Bash activation script defines a "deactivate" function, whereas on Windows there are separate scripts called `deactivate.bat` and `Deactivate.ps1` which are installed when the virtual environment is created.

New in version 3.4: `fish` and `csh` activation scripts.

Note: A virtual environment is a Python environment such that the Python interpreter, libraries and scripts installed into it are isolated from those installed in other virtual environments, and (by default) any libraries installed in a "system" Python, i.e., one which is installed as part of your operating system.

A virtual environment is a directory tree which contains Python executable files and other files which indicate that it is a virtual environment.

Common installation tools such as `Setuptools` and `pip` work as expected with virtual environments. In other words, when a virtual environment is active, they install Python packages into the virtual environment without needing to be told to do so explicitly.

When a virtual environment is active (i.e., the virtual environment's Python interpreter is running), the attributes *sys.prefix* and *sys.exec_prefix* point to the base directory of the virtual environment, whereas *sys.base_prefix* and *sys.base_exec_prefix* point to the non-virtual environment Python installation which was used to create the virtual environment. If a virtual environment is not active, then *sys.prefix* is the same as *sys.base_prefix* and *sys.exec_prefix* is the same as *sys.base_exec_prefix* (they all point to a non-virtual environment Python installation).

When a virtual environment is active, any options that change the installation path will be ignored from all distutils configuration files to prevent projects being inadvertently installed outside of the virtual environment.

When working in a command shell, users can make a virtual environment active by running an `activate` script in the virtual environment's executables directory (the precise filename is shell-dependent), which prepends the virtual environment's directory for executables to the `PATH` environment variable for the running shell. There should be no need in other circumstances to activate a virtual environment—scripts installed into virtual environments have a "shebang" line which points to the virtual environment's Python interpreter. This means that the script will run with that interpreter regardless of the value of `PATH`. On Windows, "shebang" line processing is supported if you have the Python Launcher for Windows installed (this was added to Python in 3.3 - see PEP 397 for more details). Thus, double-clicking an installed script in a Windows Explorer window should run the script with the correct interpreter without there needing to be any reference to its virtual environment in `PATH`.

28.3.2 API

The high-level method described above makes use of a simple API which provides mechanisms for third-party virtual environment creators to customize environment creation according to their needs, the *EnvBuilder* class.

class venv.EnvBuilder(*system_site_packages=False, clear=False, symlinks=False, upgrade=False, with_pip=False, prompt=None*)

The *EnvBuilder* class accepts the following keyword arguments on instantiation:

- `system_site_packages` – a Boolean value indicating that the system Python site-packages should be available to the environment (defaults to `False`).

- `clear` – a Boolean value which, if true, will delete the contents of any existing target directory, before creating the environment.

- `symlinks` – a Boolean value indicating whether to attempt to symlink the Python binary (and any necessary DLLs or other binaries, e.g. `pythonw.exe`), rather than copying. Defaults to `True` on Linux and Unix systems, but `False` on Windows.

- `upgrade` – a Boolean value which, if true, will upgrade an existing environment with the running Python - for use when that Python has been upgraded in-place (defaults to `False`).

- `with_pip` – a Boolean value which, if true, ensures pip is installed in the virtual environment. This uses *ensurepip* with the `--default-pip` option.

- `prompt` – a String to be used after virtual environment is activated (defaults to `None` which means directory name of the environment would be used).

Changed in version 3.4: Added the `with_pip` parameter

New in version 3.6: Added the `prompt` parameter

Creators of third-party virtual environment tools will be free to use the provided `EnvBuilder` class as a base class.

The returned env-builder is an object which has a method, `create`:

create(*env_dir*)

This method takes as required argument the path (absolute or relative to the current directory) of the target directory which is to contain the virtual environment. The `create` method will either create the environment in the specified directory, or raise an appropriate exception.

The `create` method of the `EnvBuilder` class illustrates the hooks available for subclass customization:

```
def create(self, env_dir):
    """
    Create a virtualized Python environment in a directory.
```

```
    env_dir is the target directory to create an environment in.
    """
    env_dir = os.path.abspath(env_dir)
    context = self.ensure_directories(env_dir)
    self.create_configuration(context)
    self.setup_python(context)
    self.setup_scripts(context)
    self.post_setup(context)
```

Each of the methods *ensure_directories()*, *create_configuration()*, *setup_python()*, *setup_scripts()* and *post_setup()* can be overridden.

ensure_directories(*env_dir*)
: Creates the environment directory and all necessary directories, and returns a context object. This is just a holder for attributes (such as paths), for use by the other methods. The directories are allowed to exist already, as long as either `clear` or `upgrade` were specified to allow operating on an existing environment directory.

create_configuration(*context*)
: Creates the `pyvenv.cfg` configuration file in the environment.

setup_python(*context*)
: Creates a copy of the Python executable (and, under Windows, DLLs) in the environment. On a POSIX system, if a specific executable `python3.x` was used, symlinks to `python` and `python3` will be created pointing to that executable, unless files with those names already exist.

setup_scripts(*context*)
: Installs activation scripts appropriate to the platform into the virtual environment.

post_setup(*context*)
: A placeholder method which can be overridden in third party implementations to pre-install packages in the virtual environment or perform other post-creation steps.

In addition, *EnvBuilder* provides this utility method that can be called from *setup_scripts()* or *post_setup()* in subclasses to assist in installing custom scripts into the virtual environment.

install_scripts(*context*, *path*)
: *path* is the path to a directory that should contain subdirectories "common", "posix", "nt", each containing scripts destined for the bin directory in the environment. The contents of "common" and the directory corresponding to *os.name* are copied after some text replacement of placeholders:

    - __VENV_DIR__ is replaced with the absolute path of the environment directory.
    - __VENV_NAME__ is replaced with the environment name (final path segment of environment directory).
    - __VENV_PROMPT__ is replaced with the prompt (the environment name surrounded by parentheses and with a following space)
    - __VENV_BIN_NAME__ is replaced with the name of the bin directory (either `bin` or `Scripts`).
    - __VENV_PYTHON__ is replaced with the absolute path of the environment's executable.

    The directories are allowed to exist (for when an existing environment is being upgraded).

There is also a module-level convenience function:

venv.create(*env_dir*, *system_site_packages=False*, *clear=False*, *symlinks=False*, *with_pip=False*)
: Create an *EnvBuilder* with the given keyword arguments, and call its *create()* method with the *env_dir* argument.

    Changed in version 3.4: Added the `with_pip` parameter

28.3.3 An example of extending EnvBuilder

The following script shows how to extend *EnvBuilder* by implementing a subclass which installs setuptools and pip into a created virtual environment:

```python
import os
import os.path
from subprocess import Popen, PIPE
import sys
from threading import Thread
from urllib.parse import urlparse
from urllib.request import urlretrieve
import venv

class ExtendedEnvBuilder(venv.EnvBuilder):
    """
    This builder installs setuptools and pip so that you can pip or
    easy_install other packages into the created virtual environment.

    :param nodist: If True, setuptools and pip are not installed into the
                   created virtual environment.
    :param nopip: If True, pip is not installed into the created
                  virtual environment.
    :param progress: If setuptools or pip are installed, the progress of the
                     installation can be monitored by passing a progress
                     callable. If specified, it is called with two
                     arguments: a string indicating some progress, and a
                     context indicating where the string is coming from.
                     The context argument can have one of three values:
                     'main', indicating that it is called from virtualize()
                     itself, and 'stdout' and 'stderr', which are obtained
                     by reading lines from the output streams of a subprocess
                     which is used to install the app.

                     If a callable is not specified, default progress
                     information is output to sys.stderr.
    """

    def __init__(self, *args, **kwargs):
        self.nodist = kwargs.pop('nodist', False)
        self.nopip = kwargs.pop('nopip', False)
        self.progress = kwargs.pop('progress', None)
        self.verbose = kwargs.pop('verbose', False)
        super().__init__(*args, **kwargs)

    def post_setup(self, context):
        """
        Set up any packages which need to be pre-installed into the
        virtual environment being created.

        :param context: The information for the virtual environment
                        creation request being processed.
        """
        os.environ['VIRTUAL_ENV'] = context.env_dir
        if not self.nodist:
            self.install_setuptools(context)
        # Can't install pip without setuptools
        if not self.nopip and not self.nodist:
```

```python
            self.install_pip(context)

    def reader(self, stream, context):
        """
        Read lines from a subprocess' output stream and either pass to a progress
        callable (if specified) or write progress information to sys.stderr.
        """
        progress = self.progress
        while True:
            s = stream.readline()
            if not s:
                break
            if progress is not None:
                progress(s, context)
            else:
                if not self.verbose:
                    sys.stderr.write('.')
                else:
                    sys.stderr.write(s.decode('utf-8'))
                sys.stderr.flush()
        stream.close()

    def install_script(self, context, name, url):
        _, _, path, _, _, _ = urlparse(url)
        fn = os.path.split(path)[-1]
        binpath = context.bin_path
        distpath = os.path.join(binpath, fn)
        # Download script into the virtual environment's binaries folder
        urlretrieve(url, distpath)
        progress = self.progress
        if self.verbose:
            term = '\n'
        else:
            term = ''
        if progress is not None:
            progress('Installing %s ...%s' % (name, term), 'main')
        else:
            sys.stderr.write('Installing %s ...%s' % (name, term))
            sys.stderr.flush()
        # Install in the virtual environment
        args = [context.env_exe, fn]
        p = Popen(args, stdout=PIPE, stderr=PIPE, cwd=binpath)
        t1 = Thread(target=self.reader, args=(p.stdout, 'stdout'))
        t1.start()
        t2 = Thread(target=self.reader, args=(p.stderr, 'stderr'))
        t2.start()
        p.wait()
        t1.join()
        t2.join()
        if progress is not None:
            progress('done.', 'main')
        else:
            sys.stderr.write('done.\n')
        # Clean up - no longer needed
        os.unlink(distpath)

    def install_setuptools(self, context):
        """
```

```python
        Install setuptools in the virtual environment.

        :param context: The information for the virtual environment
                        creation request being processed.
        """
        url = 'https://bitbucket.org/pypa/setuptools/downloads/ez_setup.py'
        self.install_script(context, 'setuptools', url)
        # clear up the setuptools archive which gets downloaded
        pred = lambda o: o.startswith('setuptools-') and o.endswith('.tar.gz')
        files = filter(pred, os.listdir(context.bin_path))
        for f in files:
            f = os.path.join(context.bin_path, f)
            os.unlink(f)

    def install_pip(self, context):
        """
        Install pip in the virtual environment.

        :param context: The information for the virtual environment
                        creation request being processed.
        """
        url = 'https://raw.github.com/pypa/pip/master/contrib/get-pip.py'
        self.install_script(context, 'pip', url)

def main(args=None):
    compatible = True
    if sys.version_info < (3, 3):
        compatible = False
    elif not hasattr(sys, 'base_prefix'):
        compatible = False
    if not compatible:
        raise ValueError('This script is only for use with '
                         'Python 3.3 or later')
    else:
        import argparse

        parser = argparse.ArgumentParser(prog=__name__,
                                         description='Creates virtual Python '
                                                     'environments in one or '
                                                     'more target '
                                                     'directories.')
        parser.add_argument('dirs', metavar='ENV_DIR', nargs='+',
                            help='A directory in which to create the '
                                 'virtual environment.')
        parser.add_argument('--no-setuptools', default=False,
                            action='store_true', dest='nodist',
                            help="Don't install setuptools or pip in the "
                                 "virtual environment.")
        parser.add_argument('--no-pip', default=False,
                            action='store_true', dest='nopip',
                            help="Don't install pip in the virtual "
                                 "environment.")
        parser.add_argument('--system-site-packages', default=False,
                            action='store_true', dest='system_site',
                            help='Give the virtual environment access to the '
                                 'system site-packages dir.')
        if os.name == 'nt':
            use_symlinks = False
```

```
            else:
                use_symlinks = True
            parser.add_argument('--symlinks', default=use_symlinks,
                                action='store_true', dest='symlinks',
                                help='Try to use symlinks rather than copies, '
                                     'when symlinks are not the default for '
                                     'the platform.')
            parser.add_argument('--clear', default=False, action='store_true',
                                dest='clear', help='Delete the contents of the '
                                                   'virtual environment '
                                                   'directory if it already '
                                                   'exists, before virtual '
                                                   'environment creation.')
            parser.add_argument('--upgrade', default=False, action='store_true',
                                dest='upgrade', help='Upgrade the virtual '
                                                     'environment directory to '
                                                     'use this version of '
                                                     'Python, assuming Python '
                                                     'has been upgraded '
                                                     'in-place.')
            parser.add_argument('--verbose', default=False, action='store_true',
                                dest='verbose', help='Display the output '
                                                     'from the scripts which '
                                                     'install setuptools and pip.')
            options = parser.parse_args(args)
            if options.upgrade and options.clear:
                raise ValueError('you cannot supply --upgrade and --clear together.')
            builder = ExtendedEnvBuilder(system_site_packages=options.system_site,
                                         clear=options.clear,
                                         symlinks=options.symlinks,
                                         upgrade=options.upgrade,
                                         nodist=options.nodist,
                                         nopip=options.nopip,
                                         verbose=options.verbose)
            for d in options.dirs:
                builder.create(d)

    if __name__ == '__main__':
        rc = 1
        try:
            main()
            rc = 0
        except Exception as e:
            print('Error: %s' % e, file=sys.stderr)
        sys.exit(rc)
```

This script is also available for download online.

28.4 zipapp — Manage executable python zip archives

New in version 3.5.

Source code: Lib/zipapp.py

This module provides tools to manage the creation of zip files containing Python code, which can be executed directly by the Python interpreter. The module provides both a *Command-Line Interface* and a *Python API*.

28.4.1 Basic Example

The following example shows how the *Command-Line Interface* can be used to create an executable archive from a directory containing Python code. When run, the archive will execute the `main` function from the module myapp in the archive.

```
$ python -m zipapp myapp -m "myapp:main"
$ python myapp.pyz
<output from myapp>
```

28.4.2 Command-Line Interface

When called as a program from the command line, the following form is used:

```
$ python -m zipapp source [options]
```

If *source* is a directory, this will create an archive from the contents of *source*. If *source* is a file, it should be an archive, and it will be copied to the target archive (or the contents of its shebang line will be displayed if the –info option is specified).

The following options are understood:

-o <output>, --output=<output>
> Write the output to a file named *output*. If this option is not specified, the output filename will be the same as the input *source*, with the extension .pyz added. If an explicit filename is given, it is used as is (so a .pyz extension should be included if required).
>
> An output filename must be specified if the *source* is an archive (and in that case, *output* must not be the same as *source*).

-p <interpreter>, --python=<interpreter>
> Add a #! line to the archive specifying *interpreter* as the command to run. Also, on POSIX, make the archive executable. The default is to write no #! line, and not make the file executable.

-m <mainfn>, --main=<mainfn>
> Write a __main__.py file to the archive that executes *mainfn*. The *mainfn* argument should have the form "pkg.mod:fn", where "pkg.mod" is a package/module in the archive, and "fn" is a callable in the given module. The __main__.py file will execute that callable.
>
> *--main* cannot be specified when copying an archive.

--info
> Display the interpreter embedded in the archive, for diagnostic purposes. In this case, any other options are ignored and SOURCE must be an archive, not a directory.

-h, --help
> Print a short usage message and exit.

28.4.3 Python API

The module defines two convenience functions:

zipapp.**create_archive**(*source*, *target=None*, *interpreter=None*, *main=None*)
> Create an application archive from *source*. The source can be any of the following:
>
> - The name of a directory, or a *pathlib.Path* object referring to a directory, in which case a new application archive will be created from the content of that directory.

- The name of an existing application archive file, or a *pathlib.Path* object referring to such a file, in which case the file is copied to the target (modifying it to reflect the value given for the *interpreter* argument). The file name should include the `.pyz` extension, if required.
- A file object open for reading in bytes mode. The content of the file should be an application archive, and the file object is assumed to be positioned at the start of the archive.

The *target* argument determines where the resulting archive will be written:

- If it is the name of a file, or a `pathlb.Path` object, the archive will be written to that file.
- If it is an open file object, the archive will be written to that file object, which must be open for writing in bytes mode.
- If the target is omitted (or `None`), the source must be a directory and the target will be a file with the same name as the source, with a `.pyz` extension added.

The *interpreter* argument specifies the name of the Python interpreter with which the archive will be executed. It is written as a "shebang" line at the start of the archive. On POSIX, this will be interpreted by the OS, and on Windows it will be handled by the Python launcher. Omitting the *interpreter* results in no shebang line being written. If an interpreter is specified, and the target is a filename, the executable bit of the target file will be set.

The *main* argument specifies the name of a callable which will be used as the main program for the archive. It can only be specified if the source is a directory, and the source does not already contain a `__main__.py` file. The *main* argument should take the form "pkg.module:callable" and the archive will be run by importing "pkg.module" and executing the given callable with no arguments. It is an error to omit *main* if the source is a directory and does not contain a `__main__.py` file, as otherwise the resulting archive would not be executable.

If a file object is specified for *source* or *target*, it is the caller's responsibility to close it after calling create_archive.

When copying an existing archive, file objects supplied only need `read` and `readline`, or `write` methods. When creating an archive from a directory, if the target is a file object it will be passed to the `zipfile.ZipFile` class, and must supply the methods needed by that class.

`zipapp.get_interpreter`(*archive*)

Return the interpreter specified in the `#!` line at the start of the archive. If there is no `#!` line, return *None*. The *archive* argument can be a filename or a file-like object open for reading in bytes mode. It is assumed to be at the start of the archive.

28.4.4 Examples

Pack up a directory into an archive, and run it.

```
$ python -m zipapp myapp
$ python myapp.pyz
<output from myapp>
```

The same can be done using the *create_archive()* functon:

```
>>> import zipapp
>>> zipapp.create_archive('myapp.pyz', 'myapp')
```

To make the application directly executable on POSIX, specify an interpreter to use.

```
$ python -m zipapp myapp -p "/usr/bin/env python"
$ ./myapp.pyz
<output from myapp>
```

To replace the shebang line on an existing archive, create a modified archive using the `create_archive()` function:

```
>>> import zipapp
>>> zipapp.create_archive('old_archive.pyz', 'new_archive.pyz', '/usr/bin/python3')
```

To update the file in place, do the replacement in memory using a `BytesIO` object, and then overwrite the source afterwards. Note that there is a risk when overwriting a file in place that an error will result in the loss of the original file. This code does not protect against such errors, but production code should do so. Also, this method will only work if the archive fits in memory:

```
>>> import zipapp
>>> import io
>>> temp = io.BytesIO()
>>> zipapp.create_archive('myapp.pyz', temp, '/usr/bin/python2')
>>> with open('myapp.pyz', 'wb') as f:
>>>     f.write(temp.getvalue())
```

Note that if you specify an interpreter and then distribute your application archive, you need to ensure that the interpreter used is portable. The Python launcher for Windows supports most common forms of POSIX #! line, but there are other issues to consider:

- If you use "/usr/bin/env python" (or other forms of the "python" command, such as "/usr/bin/python"), you need to consider that your users may have either Python 2 or Python 3 as their default, and write your code to work under both versions.
- If you use an explicit version, for example "/usr/bin/env python3" your application will not work for users who do not have that version. (This may be what you want if you have not made your code Python 2 compatible).
- There is no way to say "python X.Y or later", so be careful of using an exact version like "/usr/bin/env python3.4" as you will need to change your shebang line for users of Python 3.5, for example.

28.4.5 The Python Zip Application Archive Format

Python has been able to execute zip files which contain a `__main__.py` file since version 2.6. In order to be executed by Python, an application archive simply has to be a standard zip file containing a `__main__.py` file which will be run as the entry point for the application. As usual for any Python script, the parent of the script (in this case the zip file) will be placed on `sys.path` and thus further modules can be imported from the zip file.

The zip file format allows arbitrary data to be prepended to a zip file. The zip application format uses this ability to prepend a standard POSIX "shebang" line to the file (`#!/path/to/interpreter`).

Formally, the Python zip application format is therefore:

1. An optional shebang line, containing the characters `b'#!'` followed by an interpreter name, and then a newline (`b'\n'`) character. The interpreter name can be anything acceptable to the OS "shebang" processing, or the Python launcher on Windows. The interpreter should be encoded in UTF-8 on Windows, and in `sys.getfilesystemencoding()` on POSIX.
2. Standard zipfile data, as generated by the `zipfile` module. The zipfile content *must* include a file called `__main__.py` (which must be in the "root" of the zipfile - i.e., it cannot be in a subdirectory). The zipfile data can be compressed or uncompressed.

If an application archive has a shebang line, it may have the executable bit set on POSIX systems, to allow it to be executed directly.

There is no requirement that the tools in this module are used to create application archives - the module is a convenience, but archives in the above format created by any means are acceptable to Python.

CHAPTER
TWENTYNINE

PYTHON RUNTIME SERVICES

The modules described in this chapter provide a wide range of services related to the Python interpreter and its interaction with its environment. Here's an overview:

29.1 `sys` — System-specific parameters and functions

This module provides access to some variables used or maintained by the interpreter and to functions that interact strongly with the interpreter. It is always available.

sys.abiflags

> On POSIX systems where Python was built with the standard `configure` script, this contains the ABI flags as specified by PEP 3149.
>
> New in version 3.2.

sys.argv

> The list of command line arguments passed to a Python script. `argv[0]` is the script name (it is operating system dependent whether this is a full pathname or not). If the command was executed using the `-c` command line option to the interpreter, `argv[0]` is set to the string `'-c'`. If no script name was passed to the Python interpreter, `argv[0]` is the empty string.
>
> To loop over the standard input, or the list of files given on the command line, see the *fileinput* module.

sys.base_exec_prefix

> Set during Python startup, before `site.py` is run, to the same value as *exec_prefix*. If not running in a *virtual environment*, the values will stay the same; if `site.py` finds that a virtual environment is in use, the values of *prefix* and *exec_prefix* will be changed to point to the virtual environment, whereas *base_prefix* and *base_exec_prefix* will remain pointing to the base Python installation (the one which the virtual environment was created from).
>
> New in version 3.3.

sys.base_prefix

> Set during Python startup, before `site.py` is run, to the same value as *prefix*. If not running in a *virtual environment*, the values will stay the same; if `site.py` finds that a virtual environment is in use, the values of *prefix* and *exec_prefix* will be changed to point to the virtual environment, whereas *base_prefix* and *base_exec_prefix* will remain pointing to the base Python installation (the one which the virtual environment was created from).
>
> New in version 3.3.

sys.byteorder

> An indicator of the native byte order. This will have the value `'big'` on big-endian (most-significant byte first) platforms, and `'little'` on little-endian (least-significant byte first) platforms.

sys.builtin_module_names
A tuple of strings giving the names of all modules that are compiled into this Python interpreter. (This information is not available in any other way — `modules.keys()` only lists the imported modules.)

sys.call_tracing(*func, args*)
Call `func(*args)`, while tracing is enabled. The tracing state is saved, and restored afterwards. This is intended to be called from a debugger from a checkpoint, to recursively debug some other code.

sys.copyright
A string containing the copyright pertaining to the Python interpreter.

sys._clear_type_cache()
Clear the internal type cache. The type cache is used to speed up attribute and method lookups. Use the function *only* to drop unnecessary references during reference leak debugging.

This function should be used for internal and specialized purposes only.

sys._current_frames()
Return a dictionary mapping each thread's identifier to the topmost stack frame currently active in that thread at the time the function is called. Note that functions in the *traceback* module can build the call stack given such a frame.

This is most useful for debugging deadlock: this function does not require the deadlocked threads' cooperation, and such threads' call stacks are frozen for as long as they remain deadlocked. The frame returned for a non-deadlocked thread may bear no relationship to that thread's current activity by the time calling code examines the frame.

This function should be used for internal and specialized purposes only.

sys._debugmallocstats()
Print low-level information to stderr about the state of CPython's memory allocator.

If Python is configured –with-pydebug, it also performs some expensive internal consistency checks.

New in version 3.3.

CPython implementation detail: This function is specific to CPython. The exact output format is not defined here, and may change.

sys.dllhandle
Integer specifying the handle of the Python DLL. Availability: Windows.

sys.displayhook(*value*)
If *value* is not None, this function prints `repr(value)` to `sys.stdout`, and saves *value* in `builtins._`. If `repr(value)` is not encodable to `sys.stdout.encoding` with `sys.stdout.errors` error handler (which is probably `'strict'`), encode it to `sys.stdout.encoding` with `'backslashreplace'` error handler.

`sys.displayhook` is called on the result of evaluating an *expression* entered in an interactive Python session. The display of these values can be customized by assigning another one-argument function to `sys.displayhook`.

Pseudo-code:

```
def displayhook(value):
    if value is None:
        return
    # Set '_' to None to avoid recursion
    builtins._ = None
    text = repr(value)
    try:
        sys.stdout.write(text)
    except UnicodeEncodeError:
```

```
        bytes = text.encode(sys.stdout.encoding, 'backslashreplace')
        if hasattr(sys.stdout, 'buffer'):
            sys.stdout.buffer.write(bytes)
        else:
            text = bytes.decode(sys.stdout.encoding, 'strict')
            sys.stdout.write(text)
    sys.stdout.write("\n")
    builtins._ = value
```

Changed in version 3.2: Use `'backslashreplace'` error handler on *UnicodeEncodeError*.

sys.dont_write_bytecode

If this is true, Python won't try to write .pyc files on the import of source modules. This value is initially set to `True` or `False` depending on the -B command line option and the `PYTHONDONTWRITEBYTECODE` environment variable, but you can set it yourself to control bytecode file generation.

sys.excepthook(*type, value, traceback*)

This function prints out a given traceback and exception to `sys.stderr`.

When an exception is raised and uncaught, the interpreter calls `sys.excepthook` with three arguments, the exception class, exception instance, and a traceback object. In an interactive session this happens just before control is returned to the prompt; in a Python program this happens just before the program exits. The handling of such top-level exceptions can be customized by assigning another three-argument function to `sys.excepthook`.

sys.__displayhook__
sys.__excepthook__

These objects contain the original values of `displayhook` and `excepthook` at the start of the program. They are saved so that `displayhook` and `excepthook` can be restored in case they happen to get replaced with broken objects.

sys.exc_info()

This function returns a tuple of three values that give information about the exception that is currently being handled. The information returned is specific both to the current thread and to the current stack frame. If the current stack frame is not handling an exception, the information is taken from the calling stack frame, or its caller, and so on until a stack frame is found that is handling an exception. Here, "handling an exception" is defined as "executing an except clause." For any stack frame, only information about the exception being currently handled is accessible.

If no exception is being handled anywhere on the stack, a tuple containing three `None` values is returned. Otherwise, the values returned are `(type, value, traceback)`. Their meaning is: *type* gets the type of the exception being handled (a subclass of *BaseException*); *value* gets the exception instance (an instance of the exception type); *traceback* gets a traceback object (see the Reference Manual) which encapsulates the call stack at the point where the exception originally occurred.

sys.exec_prefix

A string giving the site-specific directory prefix where the platform-dependent Python files are installed; by default, this is also `'/usr/local'`. This can be set at build time with the `--exec-prefix` argument to the `configure` script. Specifically, all configuration files (e.g. the `pyconfig.h` header file) are installed in the directory *exec_prefix*/lib/python*X.Y*/config, and shared library modules are installed in *exec_prefix*/lib/python*X.Y*/lib-dynload, where *X.Y* is the version number of Python, for example 3.2.

Note: If a *virtual environment* is in effect, this value will be changed in `site.py` to point to the virtual environment. The value for the Python installation will still be available, via *base_exec_prefix*.

sys.executable
    A string giving the absolute path of the executable binary for the Python interpreter, on systems where this makes sense. If Python is unable to retrieve the real path to its executable, *sys.executable* will be an empty string or None.

sys.exit([*arg*]**)**
    Exit from Python. This is implemented by raising the *SystemExit* exception, so cleanup actions specified by finally clauses of try statements are honored, and it is possible to intercept the exit attempt at an outer level.

    The optional argument *arg* can be an integer giving the exit status (defaulting to zero), or another type of object. If it is an integer, zero is considered "successful termination" and any nonzero value is considered "abnormal termination" by shells and the like. Most systems require it to be in the range 0–127, and produce undefined results otherwise. Some systems have a convention for assigning specific meanings to specific exit codes, but these are generally underdeveloped; Unix programs generally use 2 for command line syntax errors and 1 for all other kind of errors. If another type of object is passed, None is equivalent to passing zero, and any other object is printed to *stderr* and results in an exit code of 1. In particular, sys.exit("some error message") is a quick way to exit a program when an error occurs.

    Since *exit()* ultimately "only" raises an exception, it will only exit the process when called from the main thread, and the exception is not intercepted.

    Changed in version 3.6: If an error occurs in the cleanup after the Python interpreter has caught *SystemExit* (such as an error flushing buffered data in the standard streams), the exit status is changed to 120.

sys.flags
    The *struct sequence* *flags* exposes the status of command line flags. The attributes are read only.

attribute	flag
debug	-d
inspect	-i
interactive	-i
optimize	-O or -OO
dont_write_bytecode	-B
no_user_site	-s
no_site	-S
ignore_environment	-E
verbose	-v
bytes_warning	-b
quiet	-q
hash_randomization	-R

    Changed in version 3.2: Added quiet attribute for the new -q flag.

    New in version 3.2.3: The hash_randomization attribute.

    Changed in version 3.3: Removed obsolete division_warning attribute.

sys.float_info
    A *struct sequence* holding information about the float type. It contains low level information about the precision and internal representation. The values correspond to the various floating-point constants defined in the standard header file float.h for the 'C' programming language; see section 5.2.4.2.2 of the 1999 ISO/IEC C standard *[C99]*, 'Characteristics of floating types', for details.

attribute	float.h macro	explanation
epsilon	DBL_EPSILON	difference between 1 and the least value greater than 1 that is representable as a float
dig	DBL_DIG	maximum number of decimal digits that can be faithfully represented in a float; see below
mant_dig	DBL_MANT_DIG	float precision: the number of base-`radix` digits in the significand of a float
max	DBL_MAX	maximum representable finite float
max_exp	DBL_MAX_EXP	maximum integer e such that `radix**(e-1)` is a representable finite float
max_10_exp	DBL_MAX_10_EXP	maximum integer e such that `10**e` is in the range of representable finite floats
min	DBL_MIN	minimum positive normalized float
min_exp	DBL_MIN_EXP	minimum integer e such that `radix**(e-1)` is a normalized float
min_10_exp	DBL_MIN_10_EXP	minimum integer e such that `10**e` is a normalized float
radix	FLT_RADIX	radix of exponent representation
rounds	FLT_ROUNDS	integer constant representing the rounding mode used for arithmetic operations. This reflects the value of the system FLT_ROUNDS macro at interpreter startup time. See section 5.2.4.2.2 of the C99 standard for an explanation of the possible values and their meanings.

The attribute `sys.float_info.dig` needs further explanation. If s is any string representing a decimal number with at most `sys.float_info.dig` significant digits, then converting s to a float and back again will recover a string representing the same decimal value:

```
>>> import sys
>>> sys.float_info.dig
15
>>> s = '3.14159265358979'    # decimal string with 15 significant digits
>>> format(float(s), '.15g')  # convert to float and back -> same value
'3.14159265358979'
```

But for strings with more than `sys.float_info.dig` significant digits, this isn't always true:

```
>>> s = '9876543211234567'    # 16 significant digits is too many!
>>> format(float(s), '.16g')  # conversion changes value
'9876543211234568'
```

sys.float_repr_style
A string indicating how the *repr()* function behaves for floats. If the string has value `'short'` then for a finite float x, `repr(x)` aims to produce a short string with the property that `float(repr(x)) == x`. This is the usual behaviour in Python 3.1 and later. Otherwise, `float_repr_style` has value `'legacy'` and `repr(x)` behaves in the same way as it did in versions of Python prior to 3.1.

New in version 3.1.

sys.getallocatedblocks()
Return the number of memory blocks currently allocated by the interpreter, regardless of their size. This function is mainly useful for tracking and debugging memory leaks. Because of the interpreter's internal caches, the result can vary from call to call; you may have to call `_clear_type_cache()` and `gc.collect()` to get more predictable results.

If a Python build or implementation cannot reasonably compute this information, `getallocatedblocks()` is allowed to return 0 instead.

New in version 3.4.

sys.getcheckinterval()
  Return the interpreter's "check interval"; see `setcheckinterval()`.

  Deprecated since version 3.2: Use `getswitchinterval()` instead.

sys.getdefaultencoding()
  Return the name of the current default string encoding used by the Unicode implementation.

sys.getdlopenflags()
  Return the current value of the flags that are used for `dlopen()` calls. Symbolic names for the flag values can be found in the `os` module (`RTLD_xxx` constants, e.g. `os.RTLD_LAZY`). Availability: Unix.

sys.getfilesystemencoding()
  Return the name of the encoding used to convert between Unicode filenames and bytes filenames. For best compatibility, str should be used for filenames in all cases, although representing filenames as bytes is also supported. Functions accepting or returning filenames should support either str or bytes and internally convert to the system's preferred representation.

  This encoding is always ASCII-compatible.

  `os.fsencode()` and `os.fsdecode()` should be used to ensure that the correct encoding and errors mode are used.

  - On Mac OS X, the encoding is `'utf-8'`.
  - On Unix, the encoding is the locale encoding.
  - On Windows, the encoding may be `'utf-8'` or `'mbcs'`, depending on user configuration.

  Changed in version 3.2: `getfilesystemencoding()` result cannot be **None** anymore.

  Changed in version 3.6: Windows is no longer guaranteed to return `'mbcs'`. See PEP 529 and `_enablelegacywindowsfsencoding()` for more information.

sys.getfilesystemencodeerrors()
  Return the name of the error mode used to convert between Unicode filenames and bytes filenames. The encoding name is returned from `getfilesystemencoding()`.

  `os.fsencode()` and `os.fsdecode()` should be used to ensure that the correct encoding and errors mode are used.

  New in version 3.6.

sys.getrefcount(*object*)
  Return the reference count of the *object*. The count returned is generally one higher than you might expect, because it includes the (temporary) reference as an argument to `getrefcount()`.

sys.getrecursionlimit()
  Return the current value of the recursion limit, the maximum depth of the Python interpreter stack. This limit prevents infinite recursion from causing an overflow of the C stack and crashing Python. It can be set by `setrecursionlimit()`.

sys.getsizeof(*object*[, *default*])
  Return the size of an object in bytes. The object can be any type of object. All built-in objects will return correct results, but this does not have to hold true for third-party extensions as it is implementation specific.

  Only the memory consumption directly attributed to the object is accounted for, not the memory consumption of objects it refers to.

  If given, *default* will be returned if the object does not provide means to retrieve the size. Otherwise a `TypeError` will be raised.

`getsizeof()` calls the object's `__sizeof__` method and adds an additional garbage collector overhead if the object is managed by the garbage collector.

See recursive sizeof recipe for an example of using `getsizeof()` recursively to find the size of containers and all their contents.

sys.getswitchinterval()
> Return the interpreter's "thread switch interval"; see `setswitchinterval()`.
>
> New in version 3.2.

sys._getframe([*depth*])
> Return a frame object from the call stack. If optional integer *depth* is given, return the frame object that many calls below the top of the stack. If that is deeper than the call stack, `ValueError` is raised. The default for *depth* is zero, returning the frame at the top of the call stack.
>
> **CPython implementation detail:** This function should be used for internal and specialized purposes only. It is not guaranteed to exist in all implementations of Python.

sys.getprofile()
> Get the profiler function as set by `setprofile()`.

sys.gettrace()
> Get the trace function as set by `settrace()`.
>
> **CPython implementation detail:** The `gettrace()` function is intended only for implementing debuggers, profilers, coverage tools and the like. Its behavior is part of the implementation platform, rather than part of the language definition, and thus may not be available in all Python implementations.

sys.getwindowsversion()
> Return a named tuple describing the Windows version currently running. The named elements are *major*, *minor*, *build*, *platform*, *service_pack*, *service_pack_minor*, *service_pack_major*, *suite_mask*, *product_type* and *platform_version*. *service_pack* contains a string, *platform_version* a 3-tuple and all other values are integers. The components can also be accessed by name, so `sys.getwindowsversion()[0]` is equivalent to `sys.getwindowsversion().major`. For compatibility with prior versions, only the first 5 elements are retrievable by indexing.
>
> *platform* will be 2 (VER_PLATFORM_WIN32_NT).
>
> *product_type* may be one of the following values:

Constant	Meaning
1 (VER_NT_WORKSTATION)	The system is a workstation.
2 (VER_NT_DOMAIN_CONTROLLER)	The system is a domain controller.
3 (VER_NT_SERVER)	The system is a server, but not a domain controller.

> This function wraps the Win32 `GetVersionEx()` function; see the Microsoft documentation on `OSVERSIONINFOEX()` for more information about these fields.
>
> *platform_version* returns the accurate major version, minor version and build number of the current operating system, rather than the version that is being emulated for the process. It is intended for use in logging rather than for feature detection.
>
> Availability: Windows.
>
> Changed in version 3.2: Changed to a named tuple and added *service_pack_minor*, *service_pack_major*, *suite_mask*, and *product_type*.
>
> Changed in version 3.6: Added *platform_version*

sys.get_asyncgen_hooks()
> Returns an *asyncgen_hooks* object, which is similar to a `namedtuple` of the form *(firstiter, finalizer)*,

where *firstiter* and *finalizer* are expected to be either None or functions which take an *asynchronous generator iterator* as an argument, and are used to schedule finalization of an asynchronous generator by an event loop.

New in version 3.6: See PEP 525 for more details.

Note: This function has been added on a provisional basis (see PEP 411 for details.)

`sys.get_coroutine_wrapper()`
Returns None, or a wrapper set by *set_coroutine_wrapper()*.

New in version 3.5: See PEP 492 for more details.

Note: This function has been added on a provisional basis (see PEP 411 for details.) Use it only for debugging purposes.

`sys.hash_info`
A *struct sequence* giving parameters of the numeric hash implementation. For more details about hashing of numeric types, see *Hashing of numeric types*.

attribute	explanation
width	width in bits used for hash values
modulus	prime modulus P used for numeric hash scheme
inf	hash value returned for a positive infinity
nan	hash value returned for a nan
imag	multiplier used for the imaginary part of a complex number
algorithm	name of the algorithm for hashing of str, bytes, and memoryview
hash_bits	internal output size of the hash algorithm
seed_bits	size of the seed key of the hash algorithm

New in version 3.2.

Changed in version 3.4: Added *algorithm*, *hash_bits* and *seed_bits*

`sys.hexversion`
The version number encoded as a single integer. This is guaranteed to increase with each version, including proper support for non-production releases. For example, to test that the Python interpreter is at least version 1.5.2, use:

```
if sys.hexversion >= 0x010502F0:
    # use some advanced feature
    ...
else:
    # use an alternative implementation or warn the user
    ...
```

This is called hexversion since it only really looks meaningful when viewed as the result of passing it to the built-in *hex()* function. The *struct sequence sys.version_info* may be used for a more human-friendly encoding of the same information.

More details of hexversion can be found at apiabiversion.

`sys.implementation`
An object containing information about the implementation of the currently running Python interpreter. The following attributes are required to exist in all Python implementations.

name is the implementation's identifier, e.g. `'cpython'`. The actual string is defined by the Python implementation, but it is guaranteed to be lower case.

version is a named tuple, in the same format as `sys.version_info`. It represents the version of the Python *implementation*. This has a distinct meaning from the specific version of the Python *language* to which the currently running interpreter conforms, which `sys.version_info` represents. For example, for PyPy 1.8 `sys.implementation.version` might be `sys.version_info(1, 8, 0, 'final', 0)`, whereas `sys.version_info` would be `sys.version_info(2, 7, 2, 'final', 0)`. For CPython they are the same value, since it is the reference implementation.

hexversion is the implementation version in hexadecimal format, like `sys.hexversion`.

cache_tag is the tag used by the import machinery in the filenames of cached modules. By convention, it would be a composite of the implementation's name and version, like `'cpython-33'`. However, a Python implementation may use some other value if appropriate. If `cache_tag` is set to `None`, it indicates that module caching should be disabled.

`sys.implementation` may contain additional attributes specific to the Python implementation. These non-standard attributes must start with an underscore, and are not described here. Regardless of its contents, `sys.implementation` will not change during a run of the interpreter, nor between implementation versions. (It may change between Python language versions, however.) See PEP 421 for more information.

New in version 3.3.

`sys.int_info`
    A *struct sequence* that holds information about Python's internal representation of integers. The attributes are read only.

Attribute	Explanation
`bits_per_digit`	number of bits held in each digit. Python integers are stored internally in base `2**int_info.bits_per_digit`
`sizeof_digit`	size in bytes of the C type used to represent a digit

New in version 3.1.

`sys.__interactivehook__`
    When this attribute exists, its value is automatically called (with no arguments) when the interpreter is launched in interactive mode. This is done after the `PYTHONSTARTUP` file is read, so that you can set this hook there. The *site* module *sets this*.

New in version 3.4.

`sys.intern(string)`
    Enter *string* in the table of "interned" strings and return the interned string – which is *string* itself or a copy. Interning strings is useful to gain a little performance on dictionary lookup – if the keys in a dictionary are interned, and the lookup key is interned, the key comparisons (after hashing) can be done by a pointer compare instead of a string compare. Normally, the names used in Python programs are automatically interned, and the dictionaries used to hold module, class or instance attributes have interned keys.

    Interned strings are not immortal; you must keep a reference to the return value of *intern()* around to benefit from it.

`sys.is_finalizing()`
    Return *True* if the Python interpreter is *shutting down*, *False* otherwise.

New in version 3.5.

`sys.last_type`
`sys.last_value`

sys.last_traceback
These three variables are not always defined; they are set when an exception is not handled and the interpreter prints an error message and a stack traceback. Their intended use is to allow an interactive user to import a debugger module and engage in post-mortem debugging without having to re-execute the command that caused the error. (Typical use is `import pdb; pdb.pm()` to enter the post-mortem debugger; see *pdb* module for more information.)

The meaning of the variables is the same as that of the return values from *exc_info()* above.

sys.maxsize
An integer giving the maximum value a variable of type `Py_ssize_t` can take. It's usually `2**31 - 1` on a 32-bit platform and `2**63 - 1` on a 64-bit platform.

sys.maxunicode
An integer giving the value of the largest Unicode code point, i.e. `1114111` (`0x10FFFF` in hexadecimal).

Changed in version 3.3: Before PEP 393, `sys.maxunicode` used to be either `0xFFFF` or `0x10FFFF`, depending on the configuration option that specified whether Unicode characters were stored as UCS-2 or UCS-4.

sys.meta_path
A list of *meta path finder* objects that have their *find_spec()* methods called to see if one of the objects can find the module to be imported. The *find_spec()* method is called with at least the absolute name of the module being imported. If the module to be imported is contained in a package, then the parent package's `__path__` attribute is passed in as a second argument. The method returns a *module spec*, or `None` if the module cannot be found.

See also:

importlib.abc.MetaPathFinder The abstract base class defining the interface of finder objects on *meta_path*.

importlib.machinery.ModuleSpec The concrete class which *find_spec()* should return instances of.

Changed in version 3.4: *Module specs* were introduced in Python 3.4, by PEP 451. Earlier versions of Python looked for a method called *find_module()*. This is still called as a fallback if a *meta_path* entry doesn't have a *find_spec()* method.

sys.modules
This is a dictionary that maps module names to modules which have already been loaded. This can be manipulated to force reloading of modules and other tricks. However, replacing the dictionary will not necessarily work as expected and deleting essential items from the dictionary may cause Python to fail.

sys.path
A list of strings that specifies the search path for modules. Initialized from the environment variable `PYTHONPATH`, plus an installation-dependent default.

As initialized upon program startup, the first item of this list, `path[0]`, is the directory containing the script that was used to invoke the Python interpreter. If the script directory is not available (e.g. if the interpreter is invoked interactively or if the script is read from standard input), `path[0]` is the empty string, which directs Python to search modules in the current directory first. Notice that the script directory is inserted *before* the entries inserted as a result of `PYTHONPATH`.

A program is free to modify this list for its own purposes. Only strings and bytes should be added to *sys.path*; all other data types are ignored during import.

See also:

Module *site* This describes how to use .pth files to extend *sys.path*.

`sys.path_hooks`
: A list of callables that take a path argument to try to create a *finder* for the path. If a finder can be created, it is to be returned by the callable, else raise `ImportError`.

    Originally specified in PEP 302.

`sys.path_importer_cache`
: A dictionary acting as a cache for *finder* objects. The keys are paths that have been passed to `sys.path_hooks` and the values are the finders that are found. If a path is a valid file system path but no finder is found on `sys.path_hooks` then `None` is stored.

    Originally specified in PEP 302.

    Changed in version 3.3: `None` is stored instead of `imp.NullImporter` when no finder is found.

`sys.platform`
: This string contains a platform identifier that can be used to append platform-specific components to `sys.path`, for instance.

    For Unix systems, except on Linux, this is the lowercased OS name as returned by `uname -s` with the first part of the version as returned by `uname -r` appended, e.g. `'sunos5'` or `'freebsd8'`, *at the time when Python was built*. Unless you want to test for a specific system version, it is therefore recommended to use the following idiom:

    ```
    if sys.platform.startswith('freebsd'):
        # FreeBSD-specific code here...
    elif sys.platform.startswith('linux'):
        # Linux-specific code here...
    ```

    For other systems, the values are:

System	platform value
Linux	`'linux'`
Windows	`'win32'`
Windows/Cygwin	`'cygwin'`
Mac OS X	`'darwin'`

    Changed in version 3.3: On Linux, `sys.platform` doesn't contain the major version anymore. It is always `'linux'`, instead of `'linux2'` or `'linux3'`. Since older Python versions include the version number, it is recommended to always use the `startswith` idiom presented above.

    See also:

    `os.name` has a coarser granularity. `os.uname()` gives system-dependent version information.

    The *platform* module provides detailed checks for the system's identity.

`sys.prefix`
: A string giving the site-specific directory prefix where the platform independent Python files are installed; by default, this is the string `'/usr/local'`. This can be set at build time with the `--prefix` argument to the **configure** script. The main collection of Python library modules is installed in the directory *prefix*`/lib/python`*X.Y* while the platform independent header files (all except `pyconfig.h`) are stored in *prefix*`/include/python`*X.Y*, where *X.Y* is the version number of Python, for example 3.2.

    Note: If a *virtual environment* is in effect, this value will be changed in `site.py` to point to the virtual environment. The value for the Python installation will still be available, via `base_prefix`.

`sys.ps1`

sys.ps2

Strings specifying the primary and secondary prompt of the interpreter. These are only defined if the interpreter is in interactive mode. Their initial values in this case are `'>>> '` and `'... '`. If a non-string object is assigned to either variable, its `str()` is re-evaluated each time the interpreter prepares to read a new interactive command; this can be used to implement a dynamic prompt.

sys.setcheckinterval(interval**)**

Set the interpreter's "check interval". This integer value determines how often the interpreter checks for periodic things such as thread switches and signal handlers. The default is 100, meaning the check is performed every 100 Python virtual instructions. Setting it to a larger value may increase performance for programs using threads. Setting it to a value <= 0 checks every virtual instruction, maximizing responsiveness as well as overhead.

Deprecated since version 3.2: This function doesn't have an effect anymore, as the internal logic for thread switching and asynchronous tasks has been rewritten. Use `setswitchinterval()` instead.

sys.setdlopenflags(n**)**

Set the flags used by the interpreter for `dlopen()` calls, such as when the interpreter loads extension modules. Among other things, this will enable a lazy resolving of symbols when importing a module, if called as `sys.setdlopenflags(0)`. To share symbols across extension modules, call as `sys.setdlopenflags(os.RTLD_GLOBAL)`. Symbolic names for the flag values can be found in the `os` module (`RTLD_xxx` constants, e.g. `os.RTLD_LAZY`).

Availability: Unix.

sys.setprofile(profilefunc**)**

Set the system's profile function, which allows you to implement a Python source code profiler in Python. See chapter *The Python Profilers* for more information on the Python profiler. The system's profile function is called similarly to the system's trace function (see `settrace()`), but it is called with different events, for example it isn't called for each executed line of code (only on call and return, but the return event is reported even when an exception has been set). The function is thread-specific, but there is no way for the profiler to know about context switches between threads, so it does not make sense to use this in the presence of multiple threads. Also, its return value is not used, so it can simply return None.

Profile functions should have three arguments: *frame*, *event*, and *arg*. *frame* is the current stack frame. *event* is a string: `'call'`, `'return'`, `'c_call'`, `'c_return'`, or `'c_exception'`. *arg* depends on the event type.

The events have the following meaning:

'call' A function is called (or some other code block entered). The profile function is called; *arg* is None.

'return' A function (or other code block) is about to return. The profile function is called; *arg* is the value that will be returned, or None if the event is caused by an exception being raised.

'c_call' A C function is about to be called. This may be an extension function or a built-in. *arg* is the C function object.

'c_return' A C function has returned. *arg* is the C function object.

'c_exception' A C function has raised an exception. *arg* is the C function object.

sys.setrecursionlimit(limit**)**

Set the maximum depth of the Python interpreter stack to *limit*. This limit prevents infinite recursion from causing an overflow of the C stack and crashing Python.

The highest possible limit is platform-dependent. A user may need to set the limit higher when they have a program that requires deep recursion and a platform that supports a higher limit. This should be done with care, because a too-high limit can lead to a crash.

If the new limit is too low at the current recursion depth, a `RecursionError` exception is raised.

Changed in version 3.5.1: A *RecursionError* exception is now raised if the new limit is too low at the current recursion depth.

sys.setswitchinterval(*interval*)
Set the interpreter's thread switch interval (in seconds). This floating-point value determines the ideal duration of the "timeslices" allocated to concurrently running Python threads. Please note that the actual value can be higher, especially if long-running internal functions or methods are used. Also, which thread becomes scheduled at the end of the interval is the operating system's decision. The interpreter doesn't have its own scheduler.

New in version 3.2.

sys.settrace(*tracefunc*)
Set the system's trace function, which allows you to implement a Python source code debugger in Python. The function is thread-specific; for a debugger to support multiple threads, it must be registered using *settrace()* for each thread being debugged.

Trace functions should have three arguments: *frame*, *event*, and *arg*. *frame* is the current stack frame. *event* is a string: `'call'`, `'line'`, `'return'` or `'exception'`. *arg* depends on the event type.

The trace function is invoked (with *event* set to `'call'`) whenever a new local scope is entered; it should return a reference to a local trace function to be used that scope, or `None` if the scope shouldn't be traced.

The local trace function should return a reference to itself (or to another function for further tracing in that scope), or `None` to turn off tracing in that scope.

The events have the following meaning:

`'call'` A function is called (or some other code block entered). The global trace function is called; *arg* is `None`; the return value specifies the local trace function.

`'line'` The interpreter is about to execute a new line of code or re-execute the condition of a loop. The local trace function is called; *arg* is `None`; the return value specifies the new local trace function. See `Objects/lnotab_notes.txt` for a detailed explanation of how this works.

`'return'` A function (or other code block) is about to return. The local trace function is called; *arg* is the value that will be returned, or `None` if the event is caused by an exception being raised. The trace function's return value is ignored.

`'exception'` An exception has occurred. The local trace function is called; *arg* is a tuple (`exception, value, traceback`); the return value specifies the new local trace function.

Note that as an exception is propagated down the chain of callers, an `'exception'` event is generated at each level.

For more information on code and frame objects, refer to types.

CPython implementation detail: The *settrace()* function is intended only for implementing debuggers, profilers, coverage tools and the like. Its behavior is part of the implementation platform, rather than part of the language definition, and thus may not be available in all Python implementations.

sys.set_asyncgen_hooks(*firstiter*, *finalizer*)
Accepts two optional keyword arguments which are callables that accept an *asynchronous generator iterator* as an argument. The *firstiter* callable will be called when an asynchronous generator is iterated for the first time. The *finalizer* will be called when an asynchronous generator is about to be garbage collected.

New in version 3.6: See PEP 525 for more details, and for a reference example of a *finalizer* method see the implementation of `asyncio.Loop.shutdown_asyncgens` in Lib/asyncio/base_events.py

Note: This function has been added on a provisional basis (see PEP 411 for details.)

`sys.set_coroutine_wrapper(`*wrapper*`)`
Allows intercepting creation of *coroutine* objects (only ones that are created by an `async def` function; generators decorated with *types.coroutine()* or *asyncio.coroutine()* will not be intercepted).

The *wrapper* argument must be either:

- a callable that accepts one argument (a coroutine object);
- `None`, to reset the wrapper.

If called twice, the new wrapper replaces the previous one. The function is thread-specific.

The *wrapper* callable cannot define new coroutines directly or indirectly:

```
def wrapper(coro):
    async def wrap(coro):
        return await coro
    return wrap(coro)
sys.set_coroutine_wrapper(wrapper)

async def foo():
    pass

# The following line will fail with a RuntimeError, because
# ``wrapper`` creates a ``wrap(coro)`` coroutine:
foo()
```

See also *get_coroutine_wrapper()*.

New in version 3.5: See PEP 492 for more details.

Note: This function has been added on a provisional basis (see PEP 411 for details.) Use it only for debugging purposes.

`sys._enablelegacywindowsfsencoding()`
Changes the default filesystem encoding and errors mode to 'mbcs' and 'replace' respectively, for consistency with versions of Python prior to 3.6.

This is equivalent to defining the `PYTHONLEGACYWINDOWSFSENCODING` environment variable before launching Python.

Availability: Windows

New in version 3.6: See PEP 529 for more details.

`sys.stdin`
`sys.stdout`
`sys.stderr`
File objects used by the interpreter for standard input, output and errors:

- `stdin` is used for all interactive input (including calls to *input()*);
- `stdout` is used for the output of *print()* and *expression* statements and for the prompts of *input()*;
- The interpreter's own prompts and its error messages go to `stderr`.

These streams are regular *text files* like those returned by the *open()* function. Their parameters are chosen as follows:

- The character encoding is platform-dependent. Under Windows, if the stream is interactive (that is, if its `isatty()` method returns `True`), the console codepage is used, otherwise the ANSI code page. Under other platforms, the locale encoding is used (see *locale.getpreferredencoding()*).

  Under all platforms though, you can override this value by setting the `PYTHONIOENCODING` environment variable before starting Python.

- When interactive, standard streams are line-buffered. Otherwise, they are block-buffered like regular text files. You can override this value with the `-u` command-line option.

Note: To write or read binary data from/to the standard streams, use the underlying binary *buffer* object. For example, to write bytes to *stdout*, use `sys.stdout.buffer.write(b'abc')`.

However, if you are writing a library (and do not control in which context its code will be executed), be aware that the standard streams may be replaced with file-like objects like *io.StringIO* which do not support the `buffer` attribute.

`sys.__stdin__`
`sys.__stdout__`
`sys.__stderr__`

> These objects contain the original values of `stdin`, `stderr` and `stdout` at the start of the program. They are used during finalization, and could be useful to print to the actual standard stream no matter if the `sys.std*` object has been redirected.
>
> It can also be used to restore the actual files to known working file objects in case they have been overwritten with a broken object. However, the preferred way to do this is to explicitly save the previous stream before replacing it, and restore the saved object.

Note: Under some conditions `stdin`, `stdout` and `stderr` as well as the original values `__stdin__`, `__stdout__` and `__stderr__` can be `None`. It is usually the case for Windows GUI apps that aren't connected to a console and Python apps started with **pythonw**.

`sys.thread_info`

> A *struct sequence* holding information about the thread implementation.

Attribute	Explanation
name	Name of the thread implementation: • `'nt'`: Windows threads • `'pthread'`: POSIX threads • `'solaris'`: Solaris threads
lock	Name of the lock implementation: • `'semaphore'`: a lock uses a semaphore • `'mutex+cond'`: a lock uses a mutex and a condition variable • `None` if this information is unknown
version	Name and version of the thread library. It is a string, or `None` if these informations are unknown.

New in version 3.3.

`sys.tracebacklimit`

> When this variable is set to an integer value, it determines the maximum number of levels of traceback information printed when an unhandled exception occurs. The default is `1000`. When set to 0 or less, all traceback information is suppressed and only the exception type and value are printed.

`sys.version`
> A string containing the version number of the Python interpreter plus additional information on the build number and compiler used. This string is displayed when the interactive interpreter is started. Do not extract version information out of it, rather, use *version_info* and the functions provided by the *platform* module.

`sys.api_version`
> The C API version for this interpreter. Programmers may find this useful when debugging version conflicts between Python and extension modules.

`sys.version_info`
> A tuple containing the five components of the version number: *major*, *minor*, *micro*, *releaselevel*, and *serial*. All values except *releaselevel* are integers; the release level is `'alpha'`, `'beta'`, `'candidate'`, or `'final'`. The version_info value corresponding to the Python version 2.0 is (2, 0, 0, 'final', 0). The components can also be accessed by name, so `sys.version_info[0]` is equivalent to `sys.version_info.major` and so on.
>
> Changed in version 3.1: Added named component attributes.

`sys.warnoptions`
> This is an implementation detail of the warnings framework; do not modify this value. Refer to the *warnings* module for more information on the warnings framework.

`sys.winver`
> The version number used to form registry keys on Windows platforms. This is stored as string resource 1000 in the Python DLL. The value is normally the first three characters of *version*. It is provided in the *sys* module for informational purposes; modifying this value has no effect on the registry keys used by Python. Availability: Windows.

`sys._xoptions`
> A dictionary of the various implementation-specific flags passed through the **-X** command-line option. Option names are either mapped to their values, if given explicitly, or to *True*. Example:
>
> ```
> $ ./python -Xa=b -Xc
> Python 3.2a3+ (py3k, Oct 16 2010, 20:14:50)
> [GCC 4.4.3] on linux2
> Type "help", "copyright", "credits" or "license" for more information.
> >>> import sys
> >>> sys._xoptions
> {'a': 'b', 'c': True}
> ```
>
> **CPython implementation detail:** This is a CPython-specific way of accessing options passed through **-X**. Other implementations may export them through other means, or not at all.
>
> New in version 3.2.

Citations

29.2 `sysconfig` — Provide access to Python's configuration information

New in version 3.2.

Source code: Lib/sysconfig.py

The *sysconfig* module provides access to Python's configuration information like the list of installation paths and the configuration variables relevant for the current platform.

29.2.1 Configuration variables

A Python distribution contains a `Makefile` and a `pyconfig.h` header file that are necessary to build both the Python binary itself and third-party C extensions compiled using *distutils*.

sysconfig puts all variables found in these files in a dictionary that can be accessed using *get_config_vars()* or *get_config_var()*.

Notice that on Windows, it's a much smaller set.

sysconfig.get_config_vars(**args*)
> With no arguments, return a dictionary of all configuration variables relevant for the current platform.
>
> With arguments, return a list of values that result from looking up each argument in the configuration variable dictionary.
>
> For each argument, if the value is not found, return `None`.

sysconfig.get_config_var(*name*)
> Return the value of a single variable *name*. Equivalent to `get_config_vars().get(name)`.
>
> If *name* is not found, return `None`.

Example of usage:

```
>>> import sysconfig
>>> sysconfig.get_config_var('Py_ENABLE_SHARED')
0
>>> sysconfig.get_config_var('LIBDIR')
'/usr/local/lib'
>>> sysconfig.get_config_vars('AR', 'CXX')
['ar', 'g++']
```

29.2.2 Installation paths

Python uses an installation scheme that differs depending on the platform and on the installation options. These schemes are stored in *sysconfig* under unique identifiers based on the value returned by *os.name*.

Every new component that is installed using *distutils* or a Distutils-based system will follow the same scheme to copy its file in the right places.

Python currently supports seven schemes:

- *posix_prefix*: scheme for Posix platforms like Linux or Mac OS X. This is the default scheme used when Python or a component is installed.
- *posix_home*: scheme for Posix platforms used when a *home* option is used upon installation. This scheme is used when a component is installed through Distutils with a specific home prefix.
- *posix_user*: scheme for Posix platforms used when a component is installed through Distutils and the *user* option is used. This scheme defines paths located under the user home directory.
- *nt*: scheme for NT platforms like Windows.
- *nt_user*: scheme for NT platforms, when the *user* option is used.

Each scheme is itself composed of a series of paths and each path has a unique identifier. Python currently uses eight paths:

- *stdlib*: directory containing the standard Python library files that are not platform-specific.
- *platstdlib*: directory containing the standard Python library files that are platform-specific.
- *platlib*: directory for site-specific, platform-specific files.

- *purelib*: directory for site-specific, non-platform-specific files.
- *include*: directory for non-platform-specific header files.
- *platinclude*: directory for platform-specific header files.
- *scripts*: directory for script files.
- *data*: directory for data files.

sysconfig provides some functions to determine these paths.

sysconfig.get_scheme_names()
Return a tuple containing all schemes currently supported in *sysconfig*.

sysconfig.get_path_names()
Return a tuple containing all path names currently supported in *sysconfig*.

sysconfig.get_path(*name*[, *scheme*[, *vars*[, *expand*]]]**)**
Return an installation path corresponding to the path *name*, from the install scheme named *scheme*.

name has to be a value from the list returned by *get_path_names()*.

sysconfig stores installation paths corresponding to each path name, for each platform, with variables to be expanded. For instance the *stdlib* path for the *nt* scheme is: {base}/Lib.

get_path() will use the variables returned by *get_config_vars()* to expand the path. All variables have default values for each platform so one may call this function and get the default value.

If *scheme* is provided, it must be a value from the list returned by *get_scheme_names()*. Otherwise, the default scheme for the current platform is used.

If *vars* is provided, it must be a dictionary of variables that will update the dictionary return by *get_config_vars()*.

If *expand* is set to False, the path will not be expanded using the variables.

If *name* is not found, return None.

sysconfig.get_paths([*scheme*[, *vars*[, *expand*]]]**)**
Return a dictionary containing all installation paths corresponding to an installation scheme. See *get_path()* for more information.

If *scheme* is not provided, will use the default scheme for the current platform.

If *vars* is provided, it must be a dictionary of variables that will update the dictionary used to expand the paths.

If *expand* is set to false, the paths will not be expanded.

If *scheme* is not an existing scheme, *get_paths()* will raise a *KeyError*.

29.2.3 Other functions

sysconfig.get_python_version()
Return the MAJOR.MINOR Python version number as a string. Similar to '%d.%d' % sys.version_info[:2].

sysconfig.get_platform()
Return a string that identifies the current platform.

This is used mainly to distinguish platform-specific build directories and platform-specific built distributions. Typically includes the OS name and version and the architecture (as supplied by *os.uname()*), although the exact information included depends on the OS; e.g. for IRIX the architecture isn't particularly important (IRIX only runs on SGI hardware), but for Linux the kernel version isn't particularly important.

Examples of returned values:

- linux-i586
- linux-alpha (?)
- solaris-2.6-sun4u
- irix-5.3
- irix64-6.2

Windows will return one of:

- win-amd64 (64bit Windows on AMD64 (aka x86_64, Intel64, EM64T, etc)
- win-ia64 (64bit Windows on Itanium)
- win32 (all others - specifically, sys.platform is returned)

Mac OS X can return:

- macosx-10.6-ppc
- macosx-10.4-ppc64
- macosx-10.3-i386
- macosx-10.4-fat

For other non-POSIX platforms, currently just returns *sys.platform*.

sysconfig.is_python_build()
    Return True if the running Python interpreter was built from source and is being run from its built location, and not from a location resulting from e.g. running **make install** or installing via a binary installer.

sysconfig.parse_config_h(*fp*[, *vars*])
    Parse a config.h-style file.

    fp is a file-like object pointing to the config.h-like file.

    A dictionary containing name/value pairs is returned. If an optional dictionary is passed in as the second argument, it is used instead of a new dictionary, and updated with the values read in the file.

sysconfig.get_config_h_filename()
    Return the path of pyconfig.h.

sysconfig.get_makefile_filename()
    Return the path of Makefile.

29.2.4 Using sysconfig as a script

You can use *sysconfig* as a script with Python's -*m* option:

```
$ python -m sysconfig
Platform: "macosx-10.4-i386"
Python version: "3.2"
Current installation scheme: "posix_prefix"

Paths:
        data = "/usr/local"
        include = "/Users/tarek/Dev/svn.python.org/py3k/Include"
        platinclude = "."
        platlib = "/usr/local/lib/python3.2/site-packages"
        platstdlib = "/usr/local/lib/python3.2"
```

```
            purelib = "/usr/local/lib/python3.2/site-packages"
            scripts = "/usr/local/bin"
            stdlib = "/usr/local/lib/python3.2"
Variables:
            AC_APPLE_UNIVERSAL_BUILD = "0"
            AIX_GENUINE_CPLUSPLUS = "0"
            AR = "ar"
            ARFLAGS = "rc"
            ...
```

This call will print in the standard output the information returned by *get_platform()*, *get_python_version()*, *get_path()* and *get_config_vars()*.

29.3 `builtins` — Built-in objects

This module provides direct access to all 'built-in' identifiers of Python; for example, `builtins.open` is the full name for the built-in function *open()*. See *Built-in Functions* and *Built-in Constants* for documentation.

This module is not normally accessed explicitly by most applications, but can be useful in modules that provide objects with the same name as a built-in value, but in which the built-in of that name is also needed. For example, in a module that wants to implement an *open()* function that wraps the built-in *open()*, this module can be used directly:

```
import builtins

def open(path):
    f = builtins.open(path, 'r')
    return UpperCaser(f)

class UpperCaser:
    '''Wrapper around a file that converts output to upper-case.'''

    def __init__(self, f):
        self._f = f

    def read(self, count=-1):
        return self._f.read(count).upper()

    # ...
```

As an implementation detail, most modules have the name `__builtins__` made available as part of their globals. The value of `__builtins__` is normally either this module or the value of this module's `__dict__` attribute. Since this is an implementation detail, it may not be used by alternate implementations of Python.

29.4 `__main__` — Top-level script environment

'`__main__`' is the name of the scope in which top-level code executes. A module's __name__ is set equal to '`__main__`' when read from standard input, a script, or from an interactive prompt.

A module can discover whether or not it is running in the main scope by checking its own `__name__`, which allows a common idiom for conditionally executing code in a module when it is run as a script or with `python -m` but not when it is imported:

```
if __name__ == "__main__":
    # execute only if run as a script
    main()
```

For a package, the same effect can be achieved by including a `__main__.py` module, the contents of which will be executed when the module is run with `-m`.

29.5 `warnings` — Warning control

Source code: Lib/warnings.py

Warning messages are typically issued in situations where it is useful to alert the user of some condition in a program, where that condition (normally) doesn't warrant raising an exception and terminating the program. For example, one might want to issue a warning when a program uses an obsolete module.

Python programmers issue warnings by calling the `warn()` function defined in this module. (C programmers use `PyErr_WarnEx()`; see exceptionhandling for details).

Warning messages are normally written to `sys.stderr`, but their disposition can be changed flexibly, from ignoring all warnings to turning them into exceptions. The disposition of warnings can vary based on the warning category (see below), the text of the warning message, and the source location where it is issued. Repetitions of a particular warning for the same source location are typically suppressed.

There are two stages in warning control: first, each time a warning is issued, a determination is made whether a message should be issued or not; next, if a message is to be issued, it is formatted and printed using a user-settable hook.

The determination whether to issue a warning message is controlled by the warning filter, which is a sequence of matching rules and actions. Rules can be added to the filter by calling `filterwarnings()` and reset to its default state by calling `resetwarnings()`.

The printing of warning messages is done by calling `showwarning()`, which may be overridden; the default implementation of this function formats the message by calling `formatwarning()`, which is also available for use by custom implementations.

See also:

`logging.captureWarnings()` allows you to handle all warnings with the standard logging infrastructure.

29.5.1 Warning Categories

There are a number of built-in exceptions that represent warning categories. This categorization is useful to be able to filter out groups of warnings. The following warnings category classes are currently defined:

Class	Description
`Warning`	This is the base class of all warning category classes. It is a subclass of `Exception`.
`UserWarning`	The default category for `warn()`.
`DeprecationWarning`	Base category for warnings about deprecated features (ignored by default).
`SyntaxWarning`	Base category for warnings about dubious syntactic features.
`RuntimeWarning`	Base category for warnings about dubious runtime features.
`FutureWarning`	Base category for warnings about constructs that will change semantically in the future.
`PendingDeprecationWarning`	Base category for warnings about features that will be deprecated in the future (ignored by default).
`ImportWarning`	Base category for warnings triggered during the process of importing a module (ignored by default).
`UnicodeWarning`	Base category for warnings related to Unicode.
`BytesWarning`	Base category for warnings related to `bytes` and `bytearray`.
`ResourceWarning`	Base category for warnings related to resource usage.

While these are technically built-in exceptions, they are documented here, because conceptually they belong to the warnings mechanism.

User code can define additional warning categories by subclassing one of the standard warning categories. A warning category must always be a subclass of the `Warning` class.

29.5.2 The Warnings Filter

The warnings filter controls whether warnings are ignored, displayed, or turned into errors (raising an exception).

Conceptually, the warnings filter maintains an ordered list of filter specifications; any specific warning is matched against each filter specification in the list in turn until a match is found; the match determines the disposition of the match. Each entry is a tuple of the form (*action*, *message*, *category*, *module*, *lineno*), where:

- *action* is one of the following strings:

Value	Disposition
`"error"`	turn matching warnings into exceptions
`"ignore"`	never print matching warnings
`"always"`	always print matching warnings
`"default"`	print the first occurrence of matching warnings for each location where the warning is issued
`"module"`	print the first occurrence of matching warnings for each module where the warning is issued
`"once"`	print only the first occurrence of matching warnings, regardless of location

- *message* is a string containing a regular expression that the start of the warning message must match. The expression is compiled to always be case-insensitive.
- *category* is a class (a subclass of `Warning`) of which the warning category must be a subclass in order to match.
- *module* is a string containing a regular expression that the module name must match. The expression is compiled to be case-sensitive.

- *lineno* is an integer that the line number where the warning occurred must match, or 0 to match all line numbers.

Since the *Warning* class is derived from the built-in *Exception* class, to turn a warning into an error we simply raise category(message).

The warnings filter is initialized by -W options passed to the Python interpreter command line. The interpreter saves the arguments for all -W options without interpretation in sys.warnoptions; the *warnings* module parses these when it is first imported (invalid options are ignored, after printing a message to sys.stderr).

Default Warning Filters

By default, Python installs several warning filters, which can be overridden by the command-line options passed to -W and calls to *filterwarnings()*.

- *DeprecationWarning* and *PendingDeprecationWarning*, and *ImportWarning* are ignored.
- *BytesWarning* is ignored unless the -b option is given once or twice; in this case this warning is either printed (-b) or turned into an exception (-bb).
- *ResourceWarning* is ignored unless Python was built in debug mode.

Changed in version 3.2: *DeprecationWarning* is now ignored by default in addition to *PendingDeprecationWarning*.

29.5.3 Temporarily Suppressing Warnings

If you are using code that you know will raise a warning, such as a deprecated function, but do not want to see the warning, then it is possible to suppress the warning using the *catch_warnings* context manager:

```
import warnings

def fxn():
    warnings.warn("deprecated", DeprecationWarning)

with warnings.catch_warnings():
    warnings.simplefilter("ignore")
    fxn()
```

While within the context manager all warnings will simply be ignored. This allows you to use known-deprecated code without having to see the warning while not suppressing the warning for other code that might not be aware of its use of deprecated code. Note: this can only be guaranteed in a single-threaded application. If two or more threads use the *catch_warnings* context manager at the same time, the behavior is undefined.

29.5.4 Testing Warnings

To test warnings raised by code, use the *catch_warnings* context manager. With it you can temporarily mutate the warnings filter to facilitate your testing. For instance, do the following to capture all raised warnings to check:

```
import warnings

def fxn():
    warnings.warn("deprecated", DeprecationWarning)
```

```python
with warnings.catch_warnings(record=True) as w:
    # Cause all warnings to always be triggered.
    warnings.simplefilter("always")
    # Trigger a warning.
    fxn()
    # Verify some things
    assert len(w) == 1
    assert issubclass(w[-1].category, DeprecationWarning)
    assert "deprecated" in str(w[-1].message)
```

One can also cause all warnings to be exceptions by using `error` instead of `always`. One thing to be aware of is that if a warning has already been raised because of a `once/default` rule, then no matter what filters are set the warning will not be seen again unless the warnings registry related to the warning has been cleared.

Once the context manager exits, the warnings filter is restored to its state when the context was entered. This prevents tests from changing the warnings filter in unexpected ways between tests and leading to indeterminate test results. The *showwarning()* function in the module is also restored to its original value. Note: this can only be guaranteed in a single-threaded application. If two or more threads use the *catch_warnings* context manager at the same time, the behavior is undefined.

When testing multiple operations that raise the same kind of warning, it is important to test them in a manner that confirms each operation is raising a new warning (e.g. set warnings to be raised as exceptions and check the operations raise exceptions, check that the length of the warning list continues to increase after each operation, or else delete the previous entries from the warnings list before each new operation).

29.5.5 Updating Code For New Versions of Python

Warnings that are only of interest to the developer are ignored by default. As such you should make sure to test your code with typically ignored warnings made visible. You can do this from the command-line by passing `-Wd` to the interpreter (this is shorthand for `-W default`). This enables default handling for all warnings, including those that are ignored by default. To change what action is taken for encountered warnings you simply change what argument is passed to `-W`, e.g. `-W error`. See the `-W` flag for more details on what is possible.

To programmatically do the same as `-Wd`, use:

```python
warnings.simplefilter('default')
```

Make sure to execute this code as soon as possible. This prevents the registering of what warnings have been raised from unexpectedly influencing how future warnings are treated.

Having certain warnings ignored by default is done to prevent a user from seeing warnings that are only of interest to the developer. As you do not necessarily have control over what interpreter a user uses to run their code, it is possible that a new version of Python will be released between your release cycles. The new interpreter release could trigger new warnings in your code that were not there in an older interpreter, e.g. *DeprecationWarning* for a module that you are using. While you as a developer want to be notified that your code is using a deprecated module, to a user this information is essentially noise and provides no benefit to them.

The *unittest* module has been also updated to use the `'default'` filter while running tests.

29.5.6 Available Functions

`warnings.warn(`*message, category=None, stacklevel=1, source=None*`)`
    Issue a warning, or maybe ignore it or raise an exception. The *category* argument, if given, must be a warning category class (see above); it defaults to *UserWarning*. Alternatively *message* can be a

Warning instance, in which case *category* will be ignored and `message.__class__` will be used. In this case the message text will be `str(message)`. This function raises an exception if the particular warning issued is changed into an error by the warnings filter see above. The *stacklevel* argument can be used by wrapper functions written in Python, like this:

```
def deprecation(message):
    warnings.warn(message, DeprecationWarning, stacklevel=2)
```

This makes the warning refer to `deprecation()`'s caller, rather than to the source of `deprecation()` itself (since the latter would defeat the purpose of the warning message).

source, if supplied, is the destroyed object which emitted a *ResourceWarning*.

Changed in version 3.6: Added *source* parameter.

`warnings.warn_explicit`(*message, category, filename, lineno, module=None, registry=None, module_globals=None, source=None*)

This is a low-level interface to the functionality of *warn()*, passing in explicitly the message, category, filename and line number, and optionally the module name and the registry (which should be the `__warningregistry__` dictionary of the module). The module name defaults to the filename with `.py` stripped; if no registry is passed, the warning is never suppressed. *message* must be a string and *category* a subclass of *Warning* or *message* may be a *Warning* instance, in which case *category* will be ignored.

module_globals, if supplied, should be the global namespace in use by the code for which the warning is issued. (This argument is used to support displaying source for modules found in zipfiles or other non-filesystem import sources).

source, if supplied, is the destroyed object which emitted a *ResourceWarning*.

Changed in version 3.6: Add the *source* parameter.

`warnings.showwarning`(*message, category, filename, lineno, file=None, line=None*)

Write a warning to a file. The default implementation calls `formatwarning(message, category, filename, lineno, line)` and writes the resulting string to *file*, which defaults to `sys.stderr`. You may replace this function with any callable by assigning to `warnings.showwarning`. *line* is a line of source code to be included in the warning message; if *line* is not supplied, *showwarning()* will try to read the line specified by *filename* and *lineno*.

`warnings.formatwarning`(*message, category, filename, lineno, line=None*)

Format a warning the standard way. This returns a string which may contain embedded newlines and ends in a newline. *line* is a line of source code to be included in the warning message; if *line* is not supplied, *formatwarning()* will try to read the line specified by *filename* and *lineno*.

`warnings.filterwarnings`(*action, message='', category=Warning, module='', lineno=0, append=False*)

Insert an entry into the list of *warnings filter specifications*. The entry is inserted at the front by default; if *append* is true, it is inserted at the end. This checks the types of the arguments, compiles the *message* and *module* regular expressions, and inserts them as a tuple in the list of warnings filters. Entries closer to the front of the list override entries later in the list, if both match a particular warning. Omitted arguments default to a value that matches everything.

`warnings.simplefilter`(*action, category=Warning, lineno=0, append=False*)

Insert a simple entry into the list of *warnings filter specifications*. The meaning of the function parameters is as for *filterwarnings()*, but regular expressions are not needed as the filter inserted always matches any message in any module as long as the category and line number match.

`warnings.resetwarnings()`

Reset the warnings filter. This discards the effect of all previous calls to *filterwarnings()*, including that of the `-W` command line options and calls to *simplefilter()*.

29.5.7 Available Context Managers

class warnings.catch_warnings(*, *record=False*, *module=None*)
    A context manager that copies and, upon exit, restores the warnings filter and the *showwarning()* function. If the *record* argument is *False* (the default) the context manager returns *None* on entry. If *record* is *True*, a list is returned that is progressively populated with objects as seen by a custom *showwarning()* function (which also suppresses output to `sys.stdout`). Each object in the list has attributes with the same names as the arguments to *showwarning()*.

    The *module* argument takes a module that will be used instead of the module returned when you import *warnings* whose filter will be protected. This argument exists primarily for testing the *warnings* module itself.

> **Note:** The *catch_warnings* manager works by replacing and then later restoring the module's *showwarning()* function and internal list of filter specifications. This means the context manager is modifying global state and therefore is not thread-safe.

29.6 `contextlib` — Utilities for `with`-statement contexts

Source code: Lib/contextlib.py

This module provides utilities for common tasks involving the `with` statement. For more information see also *Context Manager Types* and context-managers.

29.6.1 Utilities

Functions and classes provided:

class contextlib.AbstractContextManager
    An *abstract base class* for classes that implement `object.__enter__()` and `object.__exit__()`. A default implementation for `object.__enter__()` is provided which returns `self` while `object.__exit__()` is an abstract method which by default returns `None`. See also the definition of *Context Manager Types*.

    New in version 3.6.

@contextlib.contextmanager
    This function is a *decorator* that can be used to define a factory function for `with` statement context managers, without needing to create a class or separate `__enter__()` and `__exit__()` methods.

    A simple example (this is not recommended as a real way of generating HTML!):

```
from contextlib import contextmanager

@contextmanager
def tag(name):
    print("<%s>" % name)
    yield
    print("</%s>" % name)

>>> with tag("h1"):
...     print("foo")
...
```

```
<h1>
foo
</h1>
```

The function being decorated must return a *generator*-iterator when called. This iterator must yield exactly one value, which will be bound to the targets in the `with` statement's `as` clause, if any.

At the point where the generator yields, the block nested in the `with` statement is executed. The generator is then resumed after the block is exited. If an unhandled exception occurs in the block, it is reraised inside the generator at the point where the yield occurred. Thus, you can use a `try…except…finally` statement to trap the error (if any), or ensure that some cleanup takes place. If an exception is trapped merely in order to log it or to perform some action (rather than to suppress it entirely), the generator must reraise that exception. Otherwise the generator context manager will indicate to the `with` statement that the exception has been handled, and execution will resume with the statement immediately following the `with` statement.

contextmanager() uses *ContextDecorator* so the context managers it creates can be used as decorators as well as in `with` statements. When used as a decorator, a new generator instance is implicitly created on each function call (this allows the otherwise "one-shot" context managers created by *contextmanager()* to meet the requirement that context managers support multiple invocations in order to be used as decorators).

Changed in version 3.2: Use of *ContextDecorator*.

contextlib.closing(*thing*)

Return a context manager that closes *thing* upon completion of the block. This is basically equivalent to:

```
from contextlib import contextmanager

@contextmanager
def closing(thing):
    try:
        yield thing
    finally:
        thing.close()
```

And lets you write code like this:

```
from contextlib import closing
from urllib.request import urlopen

with closing(urlopen('http://www.python.org')) as page:
    for line in page:
        print(line)
```

without needing to explicitly close `page`. Even if an error occurs, `page.close()` will be called when the `with` block is exited.

contextlib.suppress(**exceptions*)

Return a context manager that suppresses any of the specified exceptions if they occur in the body of a with statement and then resumes execution with the first statement following the end of the with statement.

As with any other mechanism that completely suppresses exceptions, this context manager should be used only to cover very specific errors where silently continuing with program execution is known to be the right thing to do.

For example:

```
from contextlib import suppress

with suppress(FileNotFoundError):
    os.remove('somefile.tmp')

with suppress(FileNotFoundError):
    os.remove('someotherfile.tmp')
```

This code is equivalent to:

```
try:
    os.remove('somefile.tmp')
except FileNotFoundError:
    pass

try:
    os.remove('someotherfile.tmp')
except FileNotFoundError:
    pass
```

This context manager is *reentrant*.

New in version 3.4.

contextlib.redirect_stdout(*new_target*)

Context manager for temporarily redirecting *sys.stdout* to another file or file-like object.

This tool adds flexibility to existing functions or classes whose output is hardwired to stdout.

For example, the output of *help()* normally is sent to *sys.stdout*. You can capture that output in a string by redirecting the output to an *io.StringIO* object:

```
f = io.StringIO()
with redirect_stdout(f):
    help(pow)
s = f.getvalue()
```

To send the output of *help()* to a file on disk, redirect the output to a regular file:

```
with open('help.txt', 'w') as f:
    with redirect_stdout(f):
        help(pow)
```

To send the output of *help()* to *sys.stderr*:

```
with redirect_stdout(sys.stderr):
    help(pow)
```

Note that the global side effect on *sys.stdout* means that this context manager is not suitable for use in library code and most threaded applications. It also has no effect on the output of subprocesses. However, it is still a useful approach for many utility scripts.

This context manager is *reentrant*.

New in version 3.4.

contextlib.redirect_stderr(*new_target*)

Similar to *redirect_stdout()* but redirecting *sys.stderr* to another file or file-like object.

This context manager is *reentrant*.

New in version 3.5.

class contextlib.ContextDecorator

A base class that enables a context manager to also be used as a decorator.

Context managers inheriting from `ContextDecorator` have to implement `__enter__` and `__exit__` as normal. `__exit__` retains its optional exception handling even when used as a decorator.

`ContextDecorator` is used by *contextmanager()*, so you get this functionality automatically.

Example of `ContextDecorator`:

```
from contextlib import ContextDecorator

class mycontext(ContextDecorator):
    def __enter__(self):
        print('Starting')
        return self

    def __exit__(self, *exc):
        print('Finishing')
        return False

>>> @mycontext()
... def function():
...     print('The bit in the middle')
...
>>> function()
Starting
The bit in the middle
Finishing

>>> with mycontext():
...     print('The bit in the middle')
...
Starting
The bit in the middle
Finishing
```

This change is just syntactic sugar for any construct of the following form:

```
def f():
    with cm():
        # Do stuff
```

`ContextDecorator` lets you instead write:

```
@cm()
def f():
    # Do stuff
```

It makes it clear that the `cm` applies to the whole function, rather than just a piece of it (and saving an indentation level is nice, too).

Existing context managers that already have a base class can be extended by using `ContextDecorator` as a mixin class:

```
from contextlib import ContextDecorator

class mycontext(ContextBaseClass, ContextDecorator):
    def __enter__(self):
        return self
```

```
def __exit__(self, *exc):
    return False
```

Note: As the decorated function must be able to be called multiple times, the underlying context manager must support use in multiple `with` statements. If this is not the case, then the original construct with the explicit `with` statement inside the function should be used.

New in version 3.2.

class contextlib.ExitStack
A context manager that is designed to make it easy to programmatically combine other context managers and cleanup functions, especially those that are optional or otherwise driven by input data.

For example, a set of files may easily be handled in a single with statement as follows:

```
with ExitStack() as stack:
    files = [stack.enter_context(open(fname)) for fname in filenames]
    # All opened files will automatically be closed at the end of
    # the with statement, even if attempts to open files later
    # in the list raise an exception
```

Each instance maintains a stack of registered callbacks that are called in reverse order when the instance is closed (either explicitly or implicitly at the end of a `with` statement). Note that callbacks are *not* invoked implicitly when the context stack instance is garbage collected.

This stack model is used so that context managers that acquire their resources in their __init__ method (such as file objects) can be handled correctly.

Since registered callbacks are invoked in the reverse order of registration, this ends up behaving as if multiple nested `with` statements had been used with the registered set of callbacks. This even extends to exception handling - if an inner callback suppresses or replaces an exception, then outer callbacks will be passed arguments based on that updated state.

This is a relatively low level API that takes care of the details of correctly unwinding the stack of exit callbacks. It provides a suitable foundation for higher level context managers that manipulate the exit stack in application specific ways.

New in version 3.3.

enter_context(*cm*)
   Enters a new context manager and adds its __exit__() method to the callback stack. The return value is the result of the context manager's own __enter__() method.

   These context managers may suppress exceptions just as they normally would if used directly as part of a `with` statement.

push(*exit*)
   Adds a context manager's __exit__() method to the callback stack.

   As __enter__ is *not* invoked, this method can be used to cover part of an __enter__() implementation with a context manager's own __exit__() method.

   If passed an object that is not a context manager, this method assumes it is a callback with the same signature as a context manager's __exit__() method and adds it directly to the callback stack.

   By returning true values, these callbacks can suppress exceptions the same way context manager __exit__() methods can.

The passed in object is returned from the function, allowing this method to be used as a function decorator.

callback(*callback, *args, **kwds*)

Accepts an arbitrary callback function and arguments and adds it to the callback stack.

Unlike the other methods, callbacks added this way cannot suppress exceptions (as they are never passed the exception details).

The passed in callback is returned from the function, allowing this method to be used as a function decorator.

pop_all()

Transfers the callback stack to a fresh *ExitStack* instance and returns it. No callbacks are invoked by this operation - instead, they will now be invoked when the new stack is closed (either explicitly or implicitly at the end of a **with** statement).

For example, a group of files can be opened as an "all or nothing" operation as follows:

```
with ExitStack() as stack:
    files = [stack.enter_context(open(fname)) for fname in filenames]
    # Hold onto the close method, but don't call it yet.
    close_files = stack.pop_all().close
    # If opening any file fails, all previously opened files will be
    # closed automatically. If all files are opened successfully,
    # they will remain open even after the with statement ends.
    # close_files() can then be invoked explicitly to close them all.
```

close()

Immediately unwinds the callback stack, invoking callbacks in the reverse order of registration. For any context managers and exit callbacks registered, the arguments passed in will indicate that no exception occurred.

29.6.2 Examples and Recipes

This section describes some examples and recipes for making effective use of the tools provided by *contextlib*.

Supporting a variable number of context managers

The primary use case for *ExitStack* is the one given in the class documentation: supporting a variable number of context managers and other cleanup operations in a single **with** statement. The variability may come from the number of context managers needed being driven by user input (such as opening a user specified collection of files), or from some of the context managers being optional:

```
with ExitStack() as stack:
    for resource in resources:
        stack.enter_context(resource)
    if need_special_resource():
        special = acquire_special_resource()
        stack.callback(release_special_resource, special)
    # Perform operations that use the acquired resources
```

As shown, *ExitStack* also makes it quite easy to use **with** statements to manage arbitrary resources that don't natively support the context management protocol.

Simplifying support for single optional context managers

In the specific case of a single optional context manager, *ExitStack* instances can be used as a "do nothing" context manager, allowing a context manager to easily be omitted without affecting the overall structure of the source code:

```python
def debug_trace(details):
    if __debug__:
        return TraceContext(details)
    # Don't do anything special with the context in release mode
    return ExitStack()

with debug_trace():
    # Suite is traced in debug mode, but runs normally otherwise
```

Catching exceptions from __enter__ methods

It is occasionally desirable to catch exceptions from an __enter__ method implementation, *without* inadvertently catching exceptions from the `with` statement body or the context manager's __exit__ method. By using *ExitStack* the steps in the context management protocol can be separated slightly in order to allow this:

```python
stack = ExitStack()
try:
    x = stack.enter_context(cm)
except Exception:
    # handle __enter__ exception
else:
    with stack:
        # Handle normal case
```

Actually needing to do this is likely to indicate that the underlying API should be providing a direct resource management interface for use with `try/except/finally` statements, but not all APIs are well designed in that regard. When a context manager is the only resource management API provided, then *ExitStack* can make it easier to handle various situations that can't be handled directly in a `with` statement.

Cleaning up in an __enter__ implementation

As noted in the documentation of *ExitStack.push()*, this method can be useful in cleaning up an already allocated resource if later steps in the __enter__() implementation fail.

Here's an example of doing this for a context manager that accepts resource acquisition and release functions, along with an optional validation function, and maps them to the context management protocol:

```python
from contextlib import contextmanager, AbstractContextManager, ExitStack

class ResourceManager(AbstractContextManager):

    def __init__(self, acquire_resource, release_resource, check_resource_ok=None):
        self.acquire_resource = acquire_resource
        self.release_resource = release_resource
        if check_resource_ok is None:
            def check_resource_ok(resource):
                return True
        self.check_resource_ok = check_resource_ok
```

```
    @contextmanager
    def _cleanup_on_error(self):
        with ExitStack() as stack:
            stack.push(self)
            yield
            # The validation check passed and didn't raise an exception
            # Accordingly, we want to keep the resource, and pass it
            # back to our caller
            stack.pop_all()

    def __enter__(self):
        resource = self.acquire_resource()
        with self._cleanup_on_error():
            if not self.check_resource_ok(resource):
                msg = "Failed validation for {!r}"
                raise RuntimeError(msg.format(resource))
        return resource

    def __exit__(self, *exc_details):
        # We don't need to duplicate any of our resource release logic
        self.release_resource()
```

Replacing any use of try-finally and flag variables

A pattern you will sometimes see is a `try-finally` statement with a flag variable to indicate whether or not the body of the `finally` clause should be executed. In its simplest form (that can't already be handled just by using an `except` clause instead), it looks something like this:

```
cleanup_needed = True
try:
    result = perform_operation()
    if result:
        cleanup_needed = False
finally:
    if cleanup_needed:
        cleanup_resources()
```

As with any `try` statement based code, this can cause problems for development and review, because the setup code and the cleanup code can end up being separated by arbitrarily long sections of code.

ExitStack makes it possible to instead register a callback for execution at the end of a `with` statement, and then later decide to skip executing that callback:

```
from contextlib import ExitStack

with ExitStack() as stack:
    stack.callback(cleanup_resources)
    result = perform_operation()
    if result:
        stack.pop_all()
```

This allows the intended cleanup up behaviour to be made explicit up front, rather than requiring a separate flag variable.

If a particular application uses this pattern a lot, it can be simplified even further by means of a small helper class:

```python
from contextlib import ExitStack

class Callback(ExitStack):
    def __init__(self, callback, *args, **kwds):
        super(Callback, self).__init__()
        self.callback(callback, *args, **kwds)

    def cancel(self):
        self.pop_all()

with Callback(cleanup_resources) as cb:
    result = perform_operation()
    if result:
        cb.cancel()
```

If the resource cleanup isn't already neatly bundled into a standalone function, then it is still possible to use the decorator form of *ExitStack.callback()* to declare the resource cleanup in advance:

```python
from contextlib import ExitStack

with ExitStack() as stack:
    @stack.callback
    def cleanup_resources():
        ...

    result = perform_operation()
    if result:
        stack.pop_all()
```

Due to the way the decorator protocol works, a callback function declared this way cannot take any parameters. Instead, any resources to be released must be accessed as closure variables.

Using a context manager as a function decorator

ContextDecorator makes it possible to use a context manager in both an ordinary **with** statement and also as a function decorator.

For example, it is sometimes useful to wrap functions or groups of statements with a logger that can track the time of entry and time of exit. Rather than writing both a function decorator and a context manager for the task, inheriting from *ContextDecorator* provides both capabilities in a single definition:

```python
from contextlib import ContextDecorator
import logging

logging.basicConfig(level=logging.INFO)

class track_entry_and_exit(ContextDecorator):
    def __init__(self, name):
        self.name = name

    def __enter__(self):
        logging.info('Entering: %s', self.name)

    def __exit__(self, exc_type, exc, exc_tb):
        logging.info('Exiting: %s', self.name)
```

Instances of this class can be used as both a context manager:

```
with track_entry_and_exit('widget loader'):
    print('Some time consuming activity goes here')
    load_widget()
```

And also as a function decorator:

```
@track_entry_and_exit('widget loader')
def activity():
    print('Some time consuming activity goes here')
    load_widget()
```

Note that there is one additional limitation when using context managers as function decorators: there's no way to access the return value of __enter__(). If that value is needed, then it is still necessary to use an explicit with statement.

See also:

PEP 343 - The "with" statement The specification, background, and examples for the Python with statement.

29.6.3 Single use, reusable and reentrant context managers

Most context managers are written in a way that means they can only be used effectively in a with statement once. These single use context managers must be created afresh each time they're used - attempting to use them a second time will trigger an exception or otherwise not work correctly.

This common limitation means that it is generally advisable to create context managers directly in the header of the with statement where they are used (as shown in all of the usage examples above).

Files are an example of effectively single use context managers, since the first with statement will close the file, preventing any further IO operations using that file object.

Context managers created using *contextmanager()* are also single use context managers, and will complain about the underlying generator failing to yield if an attempt is made to use them a second time:

```
>>> from contextlib import contextmanager
>>> @contextmanager
... def singleuse():
...     print("Before")
...     yield
...     print("After")
...
>>> cm = singleuse()
>>> with cm:
...     pass
...
Before
After
>>> with cm:
...     pass
...
Traceback (most recent call last):
    ...
RuntimeError: generator didn't yield
```

Reentrant context managers

More sophisticated context managers may be "reentrant". These context managers can not only be used in multiple `with` statements, but may also be used *inside* a `with` statement that is already using the same context manager.

`threading.RLock` is an example of a reentrant context manager, as are `suppress()` and `redirect_stdout()`. Here's a very simple example of reentrant use:

```
>>> from contextlib import redirect_stdout
>>> from io import StringIO
>>> stream = StringIO()
>>> write_to_stream = redirect_stdout(stream)
>>> with write_to_stream:
...     print("This is written to the stream rather than stdout")
...     with write_to_stream:
...         print("This is also written to the stream")
...
>>> print("This is written directly to stdout")
This is written directly to stdout
>>> print(stream.getvalue())
This is written to the stream rather than stdout
This is also written to the stream
```

Real world examples of reentrancy are more likely to involve multiple functions calling each other and hence be far more complicated than this example.

Note also that being reentrant is *not* the same thing as being thread safe. `redirect_stdout()`, for example, is definitely not thread safe, as it makes a global modification to the system state by binding `sys.stdout` to a different stream.

Reusable context managers

Distinct from both single use and reentrant context managers are "reusable" context managers (or, to be completely explicit, "reusable, but not reentrant" context managers, since reentrant context managers are also reusable). These context managers support being used multiple times, but will fail (or otherwise not work correctly) if the specific context manager instance has already been used in a containing with statement.

`threading.Lock` is an example of a reusable, but not reentrant, context manager (for a reentrant lock, it is necessary to use `threading.RLock` instead).

Another example of a reusable, but not reentrant, context manager is `ExitStack`, as it invokes *all* currently registered callbacks when leaving any with statement, regardless of where those callbacks were added:

```
>>> from contextlib import ExitStack
>>> stack = ExitStack()
>>> with stack:
...     stack.callback(print, "Callback: from first context")
...     print("Leaving first context")
...
Leaving first context
Callback: from first context
>>> with stack:
...     stack.callback(print, "Callback: from second context")
...     print("Leaving second context")
...
Leaving second context
Callback: from second context
```

```
>>> with stack:
...     stack.callback(print, "Callback: from outer context")
...     with stack:
...         stack.callback(print, "Callback: from inner context")
...         print("Leaving inner context")
...     print("Leaving outer context")
...
Leaving inner context
Callback: from inner context
Callback: from outer context
Leaving outer context
```

As the output from the example shows, reusing a single stack object across multiple with statements works correctly, but attempting to nest them will cause the stack to be cleared at the end of the innermost with statement, which is unlikely to be desirable behaviour.

Using separate *ExitStack* instances instead of reusing a single instance avoids that problem:

```
>>> from contextlib import ExitStack
>>> with ExitStack() as outer_stack:
...     outer_stack.callback(print, "Callback: from outer context")
...     with ExitStack() as inner_stack:
...         inner_stack.callback(print, "Callback: from inner context")
...         print("Leaving inner context")
...     print("Leaving outer context")
...
Leaving inner context
Callback: from inner context
Leaving outer context
Callback: from outer context
```

29.7 abc — Abstract Base Classes

Source code: Lib/abc.py

This module provides the infrastructure for defining *abstract base classes* (ABCs) in Python, as outlined in PEP 3119; see the PEP for why this was added to Python. (See also PEP 3141 and the *numbers* module regarding a type hierarchy for numbers based on ABCs.)

The *collections* module has some concrete classes that derive from ABCs; these can, of course, be further derived. In addition the *collections.abc* submodule has some ABCs that can be used to test whether a class or instance provides a particular interface, for example, is it hashable or a mapping.

This module provides the metaclass *ABCMeta* for defining ABCs and a helper class *ABC* to alternatively define ABCs through inheritance:

class abc.ABC

A helper class that has *ABCMeta* as its metaclass. With this class, an abstract base class can be created by simply deriving from *ABC* avoiding sometimes confusing metaclass usage, for example:

```
from abc import ABC

class MyABC(ABC):
    pass
```

Note that the type of *ABC* is still *ABCMeta*, therefore inheriting from *ABC* requires the usual precautions regarding metaclass usage, as multiple inheritance may lead to metaclass conflicts. One may also define an abstract base class by passing the metaclass keyword and using *ABCMeta* directly, for example:

```
from abc import ABCMeta

class MyABC(metaclass=ABCMeta):
    pass
```

New in version 3.4.

class abc.**ABCMeta**

Metaclass for defining Abstract Base Classes (ABCs).

Use this metaclass to create an ABC. An ABC can be subclassed directly, and then acts as a mix-in class. You can also register unrelated concrete classes (even built-in classes) and unrelated ABCs as "virtual subclasses" – these and their descendants will be considered subclasses of the registering ABC by the built-in *issubclass()* function, but the registering ABC won't show up in their MRO (Method Resolution Order) nor will method implementations defined by the registering ABC be callable (not even via *super()*).[1]

Classes created with a metaclass of *ABCMeta* have the following method:

register(*subclass*)

Register *subclass* as a "virtual subclass" of this ABC. For example:

```
from abc import ABC

class MyABC(ABC):
    pass

MyABC.register(tuple)

assert issubclass(tuple, MyABC)
assert isinstance((), MyABC)
```

Changed in version 3.3: Returns the registered subclass, to allow usage as a class decorator.

Changed in version 3.4: To detect calls to *register()*, you can use the *get_cache_token()* function.

You can also override this method in an abstract base class:

__subclasshook__(*subclass*)

(Must be defined as a class method.)

Check whether *subclass* is considered a subclass of this ABC. This means that you can customize the behavior of **issubclass** further without the need to call *register()* on every class you want to consider a subclass of the ABC. (This class method is called from the **__subclasscheck__**() method of the ABC.)

This method should return **True**, **False** or **NotImplemented**. If it returns **True**, the *subclass* is considered a subclass of this ABC. If it returns **False**, the *subclass* is not considered a subclass of this ABC, even if it would normally be one. If it returns **NotImplemented**, the subclass check is continued with the usual mechanism.

For a demonstration of these concepts, look at this example ABC definition:

```
class Foo:
    def __getitem__(self, index):
```

---

[1] C++ programmers should note that Python's virtual base class concept is not the same as C++'s.

```
        ...
    def __len__(self):
        ...
    def get_iterator(self):
        return iter(self)

class MyIterable(ABC):

    @abstractmethod
    def __iter__(self):
        while False:
            yield None

    def get_iterator(self):
        return self.__iter__()

    @classmethod
    def __subclasshook__(cls, C):
        if cls is MyIterable:
            if any("__iter__" in B.__dict__ for B in C.__mro__):
                return True
        return NotImplemented

MyIterable.register(Foo)
```

The ABC `MyIterable` defines the standard iterable method, `__iter__()`, as an abstract method. The implementation given here can still be called from subclasses. The `get_iterator()` method is also part of the `MyIterable` abstract base class, but it does not have to be overridden in non-abstract derived classes.

The `__subclasshook__()` class method defined here says that any class that has an `__iter__()` method in its `__dict__` (or in that of one of its base classes, accessed via the `__mro__` list) is considered a `MyIterable` too.

Finally, the last line makes `Foo` a virtual subclass of `MyIterable`, even though it does not define an `__iter__()` method (it uses the old-style iterable protocol, defined in terms of `__len__()` and `__getitem__()`). Note that this will not make `get_iterator` available as a method of `Foo`, so it is provided separately.

The *abc* module also provides the following decorators:

@abc.abstractmethod

   A decorator indicating abstract methods.

   Using this decorator requires that the class's metaclass is *ABCMeta* or is derived from it. A class that has a metaclass derived from *ABCMeta* cannot be instantiated unless all of its abstract methods and properties are overridden. The abstract methods can be called using any of the normal 'super' call mechanisms. *abstractmethod()* may be used to declare abstract methods for properties and descriptors.

   Dynamically adding abstract methods to a class, or attempting to modify the abstraction status of a method or class once it is created, are not supported. The *abstractmethod()* only affects subclasses derived using regular inheritance; "virtual subclasses" registered with the ABC's `register()` method are not affected.

   When *abstractmethod()* is applied in combination with other method descriptors, it should be applied as the innermost decorator, as shown in the following usage examples:

```
class C(ABC):
    @abstractmethod
```

```
    def my_abstract_method(self, ...):
        ...
    @classmethod
    @abstractmethod
    def my_abstract_classmethod(cls, ...):
        ...
    @staticmethod
    @abstractmethod
    def my_abstract_staticmethod(...):
        ...

    @property
    @abstractmethod
    def my_abstract_property(self):
        ...
    @my_abstract_property.setter
    @abstractmethod
    def my_abstract_property(self, val):
        ...

    @abstractmethod
    def _get_x(self):
        ...
    @abstractmethod
    def _set_x(self, val):
        ...
    x = property(_get_x, _set_x)
```

In order to correctly interoperate with the abstract base class machinery, the descriptor must identify itself as abstract using `__isabstractmethod__`. In general, this attribute should be `True` if any of the methods used to compose the descriptor are abstract. For example, Python's built-in property does the equivalent of:

```
class Descriptor:
    ...
    @property
    def __isabstractmethod__(self):
        return any(getattr(f, '__isabstractmethod__', False) for
                   f in (self._fget, self._fset, self._fdel))
```

Note: Unlike Java abstract methods, these abstract methods may have an implementation. This implementation can be called via the *super()* mechanism from the class that overrides it. This could be useful as an end-point for a super-call in a framework that uses cooperative multiple-inheritance.

`@abc.abstractclassmethod`

A subclass of the built-in *classmethod()*, indicating an abstract classmethod. Otherwise it is similar to *abstractmethod()*.

This special case is deprecated, as the *classmethod()* decorator is now correctly identified as abstract when applied to an abstract method:

```
class C(ABC):
    @classmethod
    @abstractmethod
    def my_abstract_classmethod(cls, ...):
        ...
```

New in version 3.2.

Deprecated since version 3.3: It is now possible to use `classmethod` with `abstractmethod()`, making this decorator redundant.

@abc.abstractstaticmethod

A subclass of the built-in `staticmethod()`, indicating an abstract staticmethod. Otherwise it is similar to `abstractmethod()`.

This special case is deprecated, as the `staticmethod()` decorator is now correctly identified as abstract when applied to an abstract method:

```
class C(ABC):
    @staticmethod
    @abstractmethod
    def my_abstract_staticmethod(...):
        ...
```

New in version 3.2.

Deprecated since version 3.3: It is now possible to use `staticmethod` with `abstractmethod()`, making this decorator redundant.

@abc.abstractproperty

A subclass of the built-in `property()`, indicating an abstract property.

Using this function requires that the class's metaclass is `ABCMeta` or is derived from it. A class that has a metaclass derived from `ABCMeta` cannot be instantiated unless all of its abstract methods and properties are overridden. The abstract properties can be called using any of the normal 'super' call mechanisms.

This special case is deprecated, as the `property()` decorator is now correctly identified as abstract when applied to an abstract method:

```
class C(ABC):
    @property
    @abstractmethod
    def my_abstract_property(self):
        ...
```

The above example defines a read-only property; you can also define a read-write abstract property by appropriately marking one or more of the underlying methods as abstract:

```
class C(ABC):
    @property
    def x(self):
        ...

    @x.setter
    @abstractmethod
    def x(self, val):
        ...
```

If only some components are abstract, only those components need to be updated to create a concrete property in a subclass:

```
class D(C):
    @C.x.setter
    def x(self, val):
        ...
```

Deprecated since version 3.3: It is now possible to use *property*, `property.getter()`, `property.setter()` and `property.deleter()` with *abstractmethod()*, making this decorator redundant.

The *abc* module also provides the following functions:

abc.get_cache_token()
> Returns the current abstract base class cache token.
>
> The token is an opaque object (that supports equality testing) identifying the current version of the abstract base class cache for virtual subclasses. The token changes with every call to *ABCMeta.register()* on any ABC.
>
> New in version 3.4.

29.8 `atexit` — Exit handlers

The *atexit* module defines functions to register and unregister cleanup functions. Functions thus registered are automatically executed upon normal interpreter termination. *atexit* runs these functions in the *reverse* order in which they were registered; if you register A, B, and C, at interpreter termination time they will be run in the order C, B, A.

Note: The functions registered via this module are not called when the program is killed by a signal not handled by Python, when a Python fatal internal error is detected, or when *os._exit()* is called.

atexit.register(*func*, **args*, ***kwargs*)
> Register *func* as a function to be executed at termination. Any optional arguments that are to be passed to *func* must be passed as arguments to *register()*. It is possible to register the same function and arguments more than once.
>
> At normal program termination (for instance, if *sys.exit()* is called or the main module's execution completes), all functions registered are called in last in, first out order. The assumption is that lower level modules will normally be imported before higher level modules and thus must be cleaned up later.
>
> If an exception is raised during execution of the exit handlers, a traceback is printed (unless *SystemExit* is raised) and the exception information is saved. After all exit handlers have had a chance to run the last exception to be raised is re-raised.
>
> This function returns *func*, which makes it possible to use it as a decorator.

atexit.unregister(*func*)
> Remove *func* from the list of functions to be run at interpreter shutdown. After calling *unregister()*, *func* is guaranteed not to be called when the interpreter shuts down, even if it was registered more than once. *unregister()* silently does nothing if *func* was not previously registered.

See also:

Module *readline* Useful example of *atexit* to read and write *readline* history files.

29.8.1 `atexit` Example

The following simple example demonstrates how a module can initialize a counter from a file when it is imported and save the counter's updated value automatically when the program terminates without relying on the application making an explicit call into this module at termination.

```
try:
    with open("counterfile") as infile:
        _count = int(infile.read())
```

```
except FileNotFoundError:
    _count = 0

def incrcounter(n):
    global _count
    _count = _count + n

def savecounter():
    with open("counterfile", "w") as outfile:
        outfile.write("%d" % _count)

import atexit
atexit.register(savecounter)
```

Positional and keyword arguments may also be passed to *register()* to be passed along to the registered function when it is called:

```
def goodbye(name, adjective):
    print('Goodbye, %s, it was %s to meet you.' % (name, adjective))

import atexit
atexit.register(goodbye, 'Donny', 'nice')
# or:
atexit.register(goodbye, adjective='nice', name='Donny')
```

Usage as a *decorator*:

```
import atexit

@atexit.register
def goodbye():
    print("You are now leaving the Python sector.")
```

This only works with functions that can be called without arguments.

29.9 traceback — Print or retrieve a stack traceback

Source code: Lib/traceback.py

This module provides a standard interface to extract, format and print stack traces of Python programs. It exactly mimics the behavior of the Python interpreter when it prints a stack trace. This is useful when you want to print stack traces under program control, such as in a "wrapper" around the interpreter.

The module uses traceback objects — this is the object type that is stored in the *sys.last_traceback* variable and returned as the third item from *sys.exc_info()*.

The module defines the following functions:

traceback.print_tb(*tb*, *limit=None*, *file=None*)

Print up to *limit* stack trace entries from traceback object *tb* (starting from the caller's frame) if *limit* is positive. Otherwise, print the last `abs(limit)` entries. If *limit* is omitted or `None`, all entries are printed. If *file* is omitted or `None`, the output goes to `sys.stderr`; otherwise it should be an open file or file-like object to receive the output.

Changed in version 3.5: Added negative *limit* support.

traceback.print_exception(*etype, value, tb, limit=None, file=None, chain=True*)
   Print exception information and stack trace entries from traceback object *tb* to *file*. This differs from *print_tb()* in the following ways:

   - if *tb* is not None, it prints a header Traceback (most recent call last):
   - it prints the exception *etype* and *value* after the stack trace
   - if *type(value)* is *SyntaxError* and *value* has the appropriate format, it prints the line where the syntax error occurred with a caret indicating the approximate position of the error.

   The optional *limit* argument has the same meaning as for *print_tb()*. If *chain* is true (the default), then chained exceptions (the __cause__ or __context__ attributes of the exception) will be printed as well, like the interpreter itself does when printing an unhandled exception.

   Changed in version 3.5: The *etype* argument is ignored and inferred from the type of *value*.

traceback.print_exc(*limit=None, file=None, chain=True*)
   This is a shorthand for print_exception(*sys.exc_info(), limit, file, chain).

traceback.print_last(*limit=None, file=None, chain=True*)
   This is a shorthand for print_exception(sys.last_type, sys.last_value, sys.last_traceback, limit, file, chain). In general it will work only after an exception has reached an interactive prompt (see *sys.last_type*).

traceback.print_stack(*f=None, limit=None, file=None*)
   Print up to *limit* stack trace entries (starting from the invocation point) if *limit* is positive. Otherwise, print the last abs(limit) entries. If *limit* is omitted or None, all entries are printed. The optional *f* argument can be used to specify an alternate stack frame to start. The optional *file* argument has the same meaning as for *print_tb()*.

   Changed in version 3.5: Added negative *limit* support.

traceback.extract_tb(*tb, limit=None*)
   Return a list of "pre-processed" stack trace entries extracted from the traceback object *tb*. It is useful for alternate formatting of stack traces. The optional *limit* argument has the same meaning as for *print_tb()*. A "pre-processed" stack trace entry is a 4-tuple (*filename, line number, function name, text*) representing the information that is usually printed for a stack trace. The *text* is a string with leading and trailing whitespace stripped; if the source is not available it is None.

traceback.extract_stack(*f=None, limit=None*)
   Extract the raw traceback from the current stack frame. The return value has the same format as for *extract_tb()*. The optional *f* and *limit* arguments have the same meaning as for *print_stack()*.

traceback.format_list(*extracted_list*)
   Given a list of tuples as returned by *extract_tb()* or *extract_stack()*, return a list of strings ready for printing. Each string in the resulting list corresponds to the item with the same index in the argument list. Each string ends in a newline; the strings may contain internal newlines as well, for those items whose source text line is not None.

traceback.format_exception_only(*etype, value*)
   Format the exception part of a traceback. The arguments are the exception type and value such as given by sys.last_type and sys.last_value. The return value is a list of strings, each ending in a newline. Normally, the list contains a single string; however, for *SyntaxError* exceptions, it contains several lines that (when printed) display detailed information about where the syntax error occurred. The message indicating which exception occurred is the always last string in the list.

traceback.format_exception(*etype, value, tb, limit=None, chain=True*)
   Format a stack trace and the exception information. The arguments have the same meaning as the corresponding arguments to *print_exception()*. The return value is a list of strings, each ending in a newline and some containing internal newlines. When these lines are concatenated and printed, exactly the same text is printed as does *print_exception()*.

Changed in version 3.5: The *etype* argument is ignored and inferred from the type of *value*.

traceback.format_exc(*limit=None, chain=True*)
    This is like `print_exc(limit)` but returns a string instead of printing to a file.

traceback.format_tb(*tb, limit=None*)
    A shorthand for `format_list(extract_tb(tb, limit))`.

traceback.format_stack(*f=None, limit=None*)
    A shorthand for `format_list(extract_stack(f, limit))`.

traceback.clear_frames(*tb*)
    Clears the local variables of all the stack frames in a traceback *tb* by calling the `clear()` method of each frame object.

    New in version 3.4.

traceback.walk_stack(*f*)
    Walk a stack following `f.f_back` from the given frame, yielding the frame and line number for each frame. If *f* is `None`, the current stack is used. This helper is used with *StackSummary.extract()*.

    New in version 3.5.

traceback.walk_tb(*tb*)
    Walk a traceback following `tb_next` yielding the frame and line number for each frame. This helper is used with *StackSummary.extract()*.

    New in version 3.5.

The module also defines the following classes:

29.9.1 TracebackException Objects

New in version 3.5.

TracebackException objects are created from actual exceptions to capture data for later printing in a lightweight fashion.

class traceback.TracebackException(*exc_type, exc_value, exc_traceback, *, limit=None, lookup_lines=True, capture_locals=False*)
    Capture an exception for later rendering. *limit*, *lookup_lines* and *capture_locals* are as for the *StackSummary* class.

    Note that when locals are captured, they are also shown in the traceback.

    __cause__
        A *TracebackException* of the original `__cause__`.

    __context__
        A *TracebackException* of the original `__context__`.

    __suppress_context__
        The `__suppress_context__` value from the original exception.

    stack
        A *StackSummary* representing the traceback.

    exc_type
        The class of the original traceback.

    filename
        For syntax errors - the file name where the error occurred.

    lineno
        For syntax errors - the line number where the error occurred.

text
> For syntax errors - the text where the error occurred.

offset
> For syntax errors - the offset into the text where the error occurred.

msg
> For syntax errors - the compiler error message.

classmethod from_exception(*exc*, *, *limit=None*, *lookup_lines=True*, *capture_locals=False*)
> Capture an exception for later rendering. *limit*, *lookup_lines* and *capture_locals* are as for the *StackSummary* class.
>
> Note that when locals are captured, they are also shown in the traceback.

format(*, *chain=True*)
> Format the exception.
>
> If *chain* is not `True`, `__cause__` and `__context__` will not be formatted.
>
> The return value is a generator of strings, each ending in a newline and some containing internal newlines. *print_exception()* is a wrapper around this method which just prints the lines to a file.
>
> The message indicating which exception occurred is always the last string in the output.

format_exception_only()
> Format the exception part of the traceback.
>
> The return value is a generator of strings, each ending in a newline.
>
> Normally, the generator emits a single string; however, for *SyntaxError* exceptions, it emits several lines that (when printed) display detailed information about where the syntax error occurred.
>
> The message indicating which exception occurred is always the last string in the output.

29.9.2 StackSummary Objects

New in version 3.5.

StackSummary objects represent a call stack ready for formatting.

class traceback.StackSummary

> **classmethod extract**(*frame_gen*, *, *limit=None*, *lookup_lines=True*, *capture_locals=False*)
> > Construct a *StackSummary* object from a frame generator (such as is returned by *walk_stack()* or *walk_tb()*).
> >
> > If *limit* is supplied, only this many frames are taken from *frame_gen*. If *lookup_lines* is `False`, the returned *FrameSummary* objects will not have read their lines in yet, making the cost of creating the *StackSummary* cheaper (which may be valuable if it may not actually get formatted). If *capture_locals* is `True` the local variables in each *FrameSummary* are captured as object representations.
>
> **classmethod from_list**(*a_list*)
> > Construct a *StackSummary* object from a supplied old-style list of tuples. Each tuple should be a 4-tuple with filename, lineno, name, line as the elements.
>
> **format**()
> > Returns a list of strings ready for printing. Each string in the resulting list corresponds to a single frame from the stack. Each string ends in a newline; the strings may contain internal newlines as well, for those items with source text lines.

For long sequences of the same frame and line, the first few repetitions are shown, followed by a summary line stating the exact number of further repetitions.

Changed in version 3.6: Long sequences of repeated frames are now abbreviated.

29.9.3 FrameSummary Objects

New in version 3.5.

FrameSummary objects represent a single frame in a traceback.

class traceback.FrameSummary(*filename, lineno, name, lookup_line=True, locals=None, line=None*)

Represent a single frame in the traceback or stack that is being formatted or printed. It may optionally have a stringified version of the frames locals included in it. If *lookup_line* is False, the source code is not looked up until the *FrameSummary* has the line attribute accessed (which also happens when casting it to a tuple). line may be directly provided, and will prevent line lookups happening at all. *locals* is an optional local variable dictionary, and if supplied the variable representations are stored in the summary for later display.

29.9.4 Traceback Examples

This simple example implements a basic read-eval-print loop, similar to (but less useful than) the standard Python interactive interpreter loop. For a more complete implementation of the interpreter loop, refer to the *code* module.

```
import sys, traceback

def run_user_code(envdir):
    source = input(">>> ")
    try:
        exec(source, envdir)
    except Exception:
        print("Exception in user code:")
        print("-"*60)
        traceback.print_exc(file=sys.stdout)
        print("-"*60)

envdir = {}
while True:
    run_user_code(envdir)
```

The following example demonstrates the different ways to print and format the exception and traceback:

```
import sys, traceback

def lumberjack():
    bright_side_of_death()

def bright_side_of_death():
    return tuple()[0]

try:
    lumberjack()
except IndexError:
    exc_type, exc_value, exc_traceback = sys.exc_info()
    print("*** print_tb:")
```

```
    traceback.print_tb(exc_traceback, limit=1, file=sys.stdout)
    print("*** print_exception:")
    # exc_type below is ignored on 3.5 and later
    traceback.print_exception(exc_type, exc_value, exc_traceback,
                              limit=2, file=sys.stdout)
    print("*** print_exc:")
    traceback.print_exc(limit=2, file=sys.stdout)
    print("*** format_exc, first and last line:")
    formatted_lines = traceback.format_exc().splitlines()
    print(formatted_lines[0])
    print(formatted_lines[-1])
    print("*** format_exception:")
    # exc_type below is ignored on 3.5 and later
    print(repr(traceback.format_exception(exc_type, exc_value,
                                          exc_traceback)))
    print("*** extract_tb:")
    print(repr(traceback.extract_tb(exc_traceback)))
    print("*** format_tb:")
    print(repr(traceback.format_tb(exc_traceback)))
    print("*** tb_lineno:", exc_traceback.tb_lineno)
```

The output for the example would look similar to this:

```
*** print_tb:
  File "<doctest...>", line 10, in <module>
    lumberjack()
*** print_exception:
Traceback (most recent call last):
  File "<doctest...>", line 10, in <module>
    lumberjack()
  File "<doctest...>", line 4, in lumberjack
    bright_side_of_death()
IndexError: tuple index out of range
*** print_exc:
Traceback (most recent call last):
  File "<doctest...>", line 10, in <module>
    lumberjack()
  File "<doctest...>", line 4, in lumberjack
    bright_side_of_death()
IndexError: tuple index out of range
*** format_exc, first and last line:
Traceback (most recent call last):
IndexError: tuple index out of range
*** format_exception:
['Traceback (most recent call last):\n',
 '  File "<doctest...>", line 10, in <module>\n    lumberjack()\n',
 '  File "<doctest...>", line 4, in lumberjack\n    bright_side_of_death()\n',
 '  File "<doctest...>", line 7, in bright_side_of_death\n    return tuple()[0]\n',
 'IndexError: tuple index out of range\n']
*** extract_tb:
[<FrameSummary file <doctest...>, line 10 in <module>>,
 <FrameSummary file <doctest...>, line 4 in lumberjack>,
 <FrameSummary file <doctest...>, line 7 in bright_side_of_death>]
*** format_tb:
['  File "<doctest...>", line 10, in <module>\n    lumberjack()\n',
 '  File "<doctest...>", line 4, in lumberjack\n    bright_side_of_death()\n',
 '  File "<doctest...>", line 7, in bright_side_of_death\n    return tuple()[0]\n']
*** tb_lineno: 10
```

The following example shows the different ways to print and format the stack:

```
>>> import traceback
>>> def another_function():
...     lumberstack()
...
>>> def lumberstack():
...     traceback.print_stack()
...     print(repr(traceback.extract_stack()))
...     print(repr(traceback.format_stack()))
...
>>> another_function()
  File "<doctest>", line 10, in <module>
    another_function()
  File "<doctest>", line 3, in another_function
    lumberstack()
  File "<doctest>", line 6, in lumberstack
    traceback.print_stack()
[('<doctest>', 10, '<module>', 'another_function()'),
 ('<doctest>', 3, 'another_function', 'lumberstack()'),
 ('<doctest>', 7, 'lumberstack', 'print(repr(traceback.extract_stack()))')]
['  File "<doctest>", line 10, in <module>\n    another_function()\n',
 '  File "<doctest>", line 3, in another_function\n    lumberstack()\n',
 '  File "<doctest>", line 8, in lumberstack\n    print(repr(traceback.format_stack()))\n']
```

This last example demonstrates the final few formatting functions:

```
>>> import traceback
>>> traceback.format_list([('spam.py', 3, '<module>', 'spam.eggs()'),
...                        ('eggs.py', 42, 'eggs', 'return "bacon"')])
['  File "spam.py", line 3, in <module>\n    spam.eggs()\n',
 '  File "eggs.py", line 42, in eggs\n    return "bacon"\n']
>>> an_error = IndexError('tuple index out of range')
>>> traceback.format_exception_only(type(an_error), an_error)
['IndexError: tuple index out of range\n']
```

29.10 `__future__` — Future statement definitions

Source code: Lib/__future__.py

__future__ is a real module, and serves three purposes:

- To avoid confusing existing tools that analyze import statements and expect to find the modules they're importing.
- To ensure that future statements run under releases prior to 2.1 at least yield runtime exceptions (the import of __future__ will fail, because there was no module of that name prior to 2.1).
- To document when incompatible changes were introduced, and when they will be — or were — made mandatory. This is a form of executable documentation, and can be inspected programmatically via importing __future__ and examining its contents.

Each statement in __future__.py is of the form:

```
FeatureName = _Feature(OptionalRelease, MandatoryRelease,
                       CompilerFlag)
```

where, normally, *OptionalRelease* is less than *MandatoryRelease*, and both are 5-tuples of the same form as `sys.version_info`:

```
(PY_MAJOR_VERSION,  # the 2 in 2.1.0a3; an int
 PY_MINOR_VERSION,  # the 1; an int
 PY_MICRO_VERSION,  # the 0; an int
 PY_RELEASE_LEVEL,  # "alpha", "beta", "candidate" or "final"; string
 PY_RELEASE_SERIAL  # the 3; an int
)
```

OptionalRelease records the first release in which the feature was accepted.

In the case of a *MandatoryRelease* that has not yet occurred, *MandatoryRelease* predicts the release in which the feature will become part of the language.

Else *MandatoryRelease* records when the feature became part of the language; in releases at or after that, modules no longer need a future statement to use the feature in question, but may continue to use such imports.

MandatoryRelease may also be `None`, meaning that a planned feature got dropped.

Instances of class `_Feature` have two corresponding methods, `getOptionalRelease()` and `getMandatoryRelease()`.

CompilerFlag is the (bitfield) flag that should be passed in the fourth argument to the built-in function `compile()` to enable the feature in dynamically compiled code. This flag is stored in the `compiler_flag` attribute on `_Feature` instances.

No feature description will ever be deleted from `__future__`. Since its introduction in Python 2.1 the following features have found their way into the language using this mechanism:

feature	optional in	mandatory in	effect
nested_scopes	2.1.0b1	2.2	PEP 227: *Statically Nested Scopes*
generators	2.2.0a1	2.3	PEP 255: *Simple Generators*
division	2.2.0a2	3.0	PEP 238: *Changing the Division Operator*
absolute_import	2.5.0a1	3.0	PEP 328: *Imports: Multi-Line and Absolute/Relative*
with_statement	2.5.0a1	2.6	PEP 343: *The "with" Statement*
print_function	2.6.0a2	3.0	PEP 3105: *Make print a function*
unicode_literals	2.6.0a2	3.0	PEP 3112: *Bytes literals in Python 3000*
generator_stop	3.5.0b1	3.7	PEP 479: *StopIteration handling inside generators*

See also:

future How the compiler treats future imports.

29.11 gc — Garbage Collector interface

This module provides an interface to the optional garbage collector. It provides the ability to disable the collector, tune the collection frequency, and set debugging options. It also provides access to unreachable objects that the collector found but cannot free. Since the collector supplements the reference counting already used in Python, you can disable the collector if you are sure your program does not create reference cycles. Automatic collection can be disabled by calling `gc.disable()`. To debug a leaking program call `gc.set_debug(gc.DEBUG_LEAK)`. Notice that this includes `gc.DEBUG_SAVEALL`, causing garbage-collected objects to be saved in gc.garbage for inspection.

The `gc` module provides the following functions:

`gc.enable()`
:   Enable automatic garbage collection.

`gc.disable()`
:   Disable automatic garbage collection.

`gc.isenabled()`
:   Returns true if automatic collection is enabled.

`gc.collect(generation=2)`
:   With no arguments, run a full collection. The optional argument *generation* may be an integer specifying which generation to collect (from 0 to 2). A `ValueError` is raised if the generation number is invalid. The number of unreachable objects found is returned.

    The free lists maintained for a number of built-in types are cleared whenever a full collection or collection of the highest generation (2) is run. Not all items in some free lists may be freed due to the particular implementation, in particular `float`.

`gc.set_debug(flags)`
:   Set the garbage collection debugging flags. Debugging information will be written to `sys.stderr`. See below for a list of debugging flags which can be combined using bit operations to control debugging.

`gc.get_debug()`
:   Return the debugging flags currently set.

`gc.get_objects()`
:   Returns a list of all objects tracked by the collector, excluding the list returned.

`gc.get_stats()`
:   Return a list of three per-generation dictionaries containing collection statistics since interpreter start. The number of keys may change in the future, but currently each dictionary will contain the following items:

    - `collections` is the number of times this generation was collected;
    - `collected` is the total number of objects collected inside this generation;
    - `uncollectable` is the total number of objects which were found to be uncollectable (and were therefore moved to the `garbage` list) inside this generation.

    New in version 3.4.

`gc.set_threshold(threshold0[, threshold1[, threshold2]])`
:   Set the garbage collection thresholds (the collection frequency). Setting *threshold0* to zero disables collection.

    The GC classifies objects into three generations depending on how many collection sweeps they have survived. New objects are placed in the youngest generation (generation 0). If an object survives a collection it is moved into the next older generation. Since generation 2 is the oldest generation, objects in that generation remain there after a collection. In order to decide when to run, the collector keeps track of the number object allocations and deallocations since the last collection. When the number of allocations minus the number of deallocations exceeds *threshold0*, collection starts. Initially only generation 0 is examined. If generation 0 has been examined more than *threshold1* times since generation 1 has been examined, then generation 1 is examined as well. Similarly, *threshold2* controls the number of collections of generation 1 before collecting generation 2.

gc.get_count()
    Return the current collection counts as a tuple of (count0, count1, count2).

gc.get_threshold()
    Return the current collection thresholds as a tuple of (threshold0, threshold1, threshold2).

gc.get_referrers(*objs)
    Return the list of objects that directly refer to any of objs. This function will only locate those containers which support garbage collection; extension types which do refer to other objects but do not support garbage collection will not be found.

    Note that objects which have already been dereferenced, but which live in cycles and have not yet been collected by the garbage collector can be listed among the resulting referrers. To get only currently live objects, call *collect()* before calling *get_referrers()*.

    Care must be taken when using objects returned by *get_referrers()* because some of them could still be under construction and hence in a temporarily invalid state. Avoid using *get_referrers()* for any purpose other than debugging.

gc.get_referents(*objs)
    Return a list of objects directly referred to by any of the arguments. The referents returned are those objects visited by the arguments' C-level **tp_traverse** methods (if any), and may not be all objects actually directly reachable. **tp_traverse** methods are supported only by objects that support garbage collection, and are only required to visit objects that may be involved in a cycle. So, for example, if an integer is directly reachable from an argument, that integer object may or may not appear in the result list.

gc.is_tracked(obj)
    Returns **True** if the object is currently tracked by the garbage collector, **False** otherwise. As a general rule, instances of atomic types aren't tracked and instances of non-atomic types (containers, user-defined objects...) are. However, some type-specific optimizations can be present in order to suppress the garbage collector footprint of simple instances (e.g. dicts containing only atomic keys and values):

```
>>> gc.is_tracked(0)
False
>>> gc.is_tracked("a")
False
>>> gc.is_tracked([])
True
>>> gc.is_tracked({})
False
>>> gc.is_tracked({"a": 1})
False
>>> gc.is_tracked({"a": []})
True
```

    New in version 3.1.

The following variables are provided for read-only access (you can mutate the values but should not rebind them):

gc.garbage
    A list of objects which the collector found to be unreachable but could not be freed (uncollectable objects). Starting with Python 3.4, this list should be empty most of the time, except when using instances of C extension types with a non-NULL **tp_del** slot.

    If *DEBUG_SAVEALL* is set, then all unreachable objects will be added to this list rather than freed.

    Changed in version 3.2: If this list is non-empty at *interpreter shutdown*, a *ResourceWarning* is emitted, which is silent by default. If *DEBUG_UNCOLLECTABLE* is set, in addition all uncollectable objects are printed.

Changed in version 3.4: Following PEP 442, objects with a __del__() method don't end up in *gc.garbage* anymore.

gc.callbacks
A list of callbacks that will be invoked by the garbage collector before and after collection. The callbacks will be called with two arguments, *phase* and *info*.

phase can be one of two values:

"start": The garbage collection is about to start.

"stop": The garbage collection has finished.

info is a dict providing more information for the callback. The following keys are currently defined:

"generation": The oldest generation being collected.

"collected": When *phase* is "stop", the number of objects successfully collected.

"uncollectable": When *phase* is "stop", the number of objects that could not be collected and were put in *garbage*.

Applications can add their own callbacks to this list. The primary use cases are:

Gathering statistics about garbage collection, such as how often various generations are collected, and how long the collection takes.

Allowing applications to identify and clear their own uncollectable types when they appear in *garbage*.

New in version 3.3.

The following constants are provided for use with *set_debug()*:

gc.DEBUG_STATS
Print statistics during collection. This information can be useful when tuning the collection frequency.

gc.DEBUG_COLLECTABLE
Print information on collectable objects found.

gc.DEBUG_UNCOLLECTABLE
Print information of uncollectable objects found (objects which are not reachable but cannot be freed by the collector). These objects will be added to the **garbage** list.

Changed in version 3.2: Also print the contents of the *garbage* list at *interpreter shutdown*, if it isn't empty.

gc.DEBUG_SAVEALL
When set, all unreachable objects found will be appended to *garbage* rather than being freed. This can be useful for debugging a leaking program.

gc.DEBUG_LEAK
The debugging flags necessary for the collector to print information about a leaking program (equal to DEBUG_COLLECTABLE | DEBUG_UNCOLLECTABLE | DEBUG_SAVEALL).

29.12 inspect — Inspect live objects

Source code: Lib/inspect.py

The *inspect* module provides several useful functions to help get information about live objects such as modules, classes, methods, functions, tracebacks, frame objects, and code objects. For example, it can help you examine the contents of a class, retrieve the source code of a method, extract and format the argument list for a function, or get all the information you need to display a detailed traceback.

There are four main kinds of services provided by this module: type checking, getting source code, inspecting classes and functions, and examining the interpreter stack.

29.12.1 Types and members

The `getmembers()` function retrieves the members of an object such as a class or module. The functions whose names begin with "is" are mainly provided as convenient choices for the second argument to `getmembers()`. They also help you determine when you can expect to find the following special attributes:

Type	Attribute	Description
module	__doc__	documentation string
	__file__	filename (missing for built-in modules)
class	__doc__	documentation string
	__name__	name with which this class was defined
	__qualname__	qualified name
	__module__	name of module in which this class was defined
method	__doc__	documentation string
	__name__	name with which this method was defined
	__qualname__	qualified name
	__func__	function object containing implementation of method
	__self__	instance to which this method is bound, or `None`
function	__doc__	documentation string
	__name__	name with which this function was defined
	__qualname__	qualified name
	__code__	code object containing compiled function *bytecode*
	__defaults__	tuple of any default values for positional or keyword parameters
	__kwdefaults__	mapping of any default values for keyword-only parameters
	__globals__	global namespace in which this function was defined
	__annotations__	mapping of parameters names to annotations; `"return"` key is reserved for return
traceback	tb_frame	frame object at this level
	tb_lasti	index of last attempted instruction in bytecode
	tb_lineno	current line number in Python source code
	tb_next	next inner traceback object (called by this level)
frame	f_back	next outer frame object (this frame's caller)
	f_builtins	builtins namespace seen by this frame
	f_code	code object being executed in this frame
	f_globals	global namespace seen by this frame
	f_lasti	index of last attempted instruction in bytecode
	f_lineno	current line number in Python source code
	f_locals	local namespace seen by this frame
	f_restricted	0 or 1 if frame is in restricted execution mode
	f_trace	tracing function for this frame, or `None`
code	co_argcount	number of arguments (not including keyword only arguments, * or ** args)
	co_code	string of raw compiled bytecode
	co_cellvars	tuple of names of cell variables (referenced by containing scopes)
	co_consts	tuple of constants used in the bytecode
	co_filename	name of file in which this code object was created
	co_firstlineno	number of first line in Python source code

Continued

Table 29.1 – continued from previous page

Type	Attribute	Description
	co_flags	bitmap of CO_* flags, read more *here*
	co_lnotab	encoded mapping of line numbers to bytecode indices
	co_freevars	tuple of names of free variables (referenced via a function's closure)
	co_kwonlyargcount	number of keyword only arguments (not including ** arg)
	co_name	name with which this code object was defined
	co_names	tuple of names of local variables
	co_nlocals	number of local variables
	co_stacksize	virtual machine stack space required
	co_varnames	tuple of names of arguments and local variables
generator	__name__	name
	__qualname__	qualified name
	gi_frame	frame
	gi_running	is the generator running?
	gi_code	code
	gi_yieldfrom	object being iterated by `yield from`, or `None`
coroutine	__name__	name
	__qualname__	qualified name
	cr_await	object being awaited on, or `None`
	cr_frame	frame
	cr_running	is the coroutine running?
	cr_code	code
builtin	__doc__	documentation string
	__name__	original name of this function or method
	__qualname__	qualified name
	__self__	instance to which a method is bound, or `None`

Changed in version 3.5: Add `__qualname__` and `gi_yieldfrom` attributes to generators.

The `__name__` attribute of generators is now set from the function name, instead of the code name, and it can now be modified.

inspect.**getmembers**(*object*[, *predicate*])

    Return all the members of an object in a list of (name, value) pairs sorted by name. If the optional *predicate* argument is supplied, only members for which the predicate returns a true value are included.

Note: *getmembers()* will only return class attributes defined in the metaclass when the argument is a class and those attributes have been listed in the metaclass' custom `__dir__()`.

---

inspect.**getmodulename**(*path*)

    Return the name of the module named by the file *path*, without including the names of enclosing packages. The file extension is checked against all of the entries in *importlib.machinery.all_suffixes()*. If it matches, the final path component is returned with the extension removed. Otherwise, `None` is returned.

    Note that this function *only* returns a meaningful name for actual Python modules - paths that potentially refer to Python packages will still return `None`.

    Changed in version 3.3: The function is based directly on *importlib*.

inspect.**ismodule**(*object*)

    Return true if the object is a module.

inspect.**isclass**(*object*)

    Return true if the object is a class, whether built-in or created in Python code.

`inspect.ismethod(object)`
    Return true if the object is a bound method written in Python.

`inspect.isfunction(object)`
    Return true if the object is a Python function, which includes functions created by a *lambda* expression.

`inspect.isgeneratorfunction(object)`
    Return true if the object is a Python generator function.

`inspect.isgenerator(object)`
    Return true if the object is a generator.

`inspect.iscoroutinefunction(object)`
    Return true if the object is a *coroutine function* (a function defined with an `async def` syntax).

    New in version 3.5.

`inspect.iscoroutine(object)`
    Return true if the object is a *coroutine* created by an `async def` function.

    New in version 3.5.

`inspect.isawaitable(object)`
    Return true if the object can be used in `await` expression.

    Can also be used to distinguish generator-based coroutines from regular generators:

    ```
    def gen():
        yield
    @types.coroutine
    def gen_coro():
        yield

    assert not isawaitable(gen())
    assert isawaitable(gen_coro())
    ```

    New in version 3.5.

`inspect.isasyncgenfunction(object)`
    Return true if the object is an *asynchronous generator* function, for example:

    ```
    >>> async def agen():
    ...     yield 1
    ...
    >>> inspect.isasyncgenfunction(agen)
    True
    ```

    New in version 3.6.

`inspect.isasyncgen(object)`
    Return true if the object is an *asynchronous generator iterator* created by an *asynchronous generator* function.

    New in version 3.6.

`inspect.istraceback(object)`
    Return true if the object is a traceback.

`inspect.isframe(object)`
    Return true if the object is a frame.

`inspect.iscode(object)`
    Return true if the object is a code.

`inspect.isbuiltin(object)`
    Return true if the object is a built-in function or a bound built-in method.

`inspect.isroutine(object)`
    Return true if the object is a user-defined or built-in function or method.

`inspect.isabstract(object)`
    Return true if the object is an abstract base class.

`inspect.ismethoddescriptor(object)`
    Return true if the object is a method descriptor, but not if *ismethod()*, *isclass()*, *isfunction()* or *isbuiltin()* are true.

    This, for example, is true of `int.__add__`. An object passing this test has a `__get__()` method but not a `__set__()` method, but beyond that the set of attributes varies. A `__name__` attribute is usually sensible, and `__doc__` often is.

    Methods implemented via descriptors that also pass one of the other tests return false from the *ismethoddescriptor()* test, simply because the other tests promise more – you can, e.g., count on having the `__func__` attribute (etc) when an object passes *ismethod()*.

`inspect.isdatadescriptor(object)`
    Return true if the object is a data descriptor.

    Data descriptors have both a `__get__` and a `__set__` method. Examples are properties (defined in Python), getsets, and members. The latter two are defined in C and there are more specific tests available for those types, which is robust across Python implementations. Typically, data descriptors will also have `__name__` and `__doc__` attributes (properties, getsets, and members have both of these attributes), but this is not guaranteed.

`inspect.isgetsetdescriptor(object)`
    Return true if the object is a getset descriptor.

    CPython implementation detail: getsets are attributes defined in extension modules via `PyGetSetDef` structures. For Python implementations without such types, this method will always return `False`.

`inspect.ismemberdescriptor(object)`
    Return true if the object is a member descriptor.

    CPython implementation detail: Member descriptors are attributes defined in extension modules via `PyMemberDef` structures. For Python implementations without such types, this method will always return `False`.

29.12.2 Retrieving source code

`inspect.getdoc(object)`
    Get the documentation string for an object, cleaned up with *cleandoc()*. If the documentation string for an object is not provided and the object is a class, a method, a property or a descriptor, retrieve the documentation string from the inheritance hierarchy.

    Changed in version 3.5: Documentation strings are now inherited if not overridden.

`inspect.getcomments(object)`
    Return in a single string any lines of comments immediately preceding the object's source code (for a class, function, or method), or at the top of the Python source file (if the object is a module). If the object's source code is unavailable, return `None`. This could happen if the object has been defined in C or the interactive shell.

inspect.getfile(*object*)
  Return the name of the (text or binary) file in which an object was defined. This will fail with a *TypeError* if the object is a built-in module, class, or function.

inspect.getmodule(*object*)
  Try to guess which module an object was defined in.

inspect.getsourcefile(*object*)
  Return the name of the Python source file in which an object was defined. This will fail with a *TypeError* if the object is a built-in module, class, or function.

inspect.getsourcelines(*object*)
  Return a list of source lines and starting line number for an object. The argument may be a module, class, method, function, traceback, frame, or code object. The source code is returned as a list of the lines corresponding to the object and the line number indicates where in the original source file the first line of code was found. An *OSError* is raised if the source code cannot be retrieved.

  Changed in version 3.3: *OSError* is raised instead of *IOError*, now an alias of the former.

inspect.getsource(*object*)
  Return the text of the source code for an object. The argument may be a module, class, method, function, traceback, frame, or code object. The source code is returned as a single string. An *OSError* is raised if the source code cannot be retrieved.

  Changed in version 3.3: *OSError* is raised instead of *IOError*, now an alias of the former.

inspect.cleandoc(*doc*)
  Clean up indentation from docstrings that are indented to line up with blocks of code.

  All leading whitespace is removed from the first line. Any leading whitespace that can be uniformly removed from the second line onwards is removed. Empty lines at the beginning and end are subsequently removed. Also, all tabs are expanded to spaces.

29.12.3 Introspecting callables with the Signature object

New in version 3.3.

The Signature object represents the call signature of a callable object and its return annotation. To retrieve a Signature object, use the *signature()* function.

inspect.signature(*callable, *, follow_wrapped=True*)
  Return a *Signature* object for the given `callable`:

```
>>> from inspect import signature
>>> def foo(a, *, b:int, **kwargs):
...     pass

>>> sig = signature(foo)

>>> str(sig)
'(a, *, b:int, **kwargs)'

>>> str(sig.parameters['b'])
'b:int'

>>> sig.parameters['b'].annotation
<class 'int'>
```

Accepts a wide range of python callables, from plain functions and classes to *functools.partial()* objects.

Raises *ValueError* if no signature can be provided, and *TypeError* if that type of object is not supported.

New in version 3.5: `follow_wrapped` parameter. Pass `False` to get a signature of `callable` specifically (`callable.__wrapped__` will not be used to unwrap decorated callables.)

> **Note:** Some callables may not be introspectable in certain implementations of Python. For example, in CPython, some built-in functions defined in C provide no metadata about their arguments.

class `inspect.Signature`(*parameters=None, *, return_annotation=Signature.empty*)

A Signature object represents the call signature of a function and its return annotation. For each parameter accepted by the function it stores a *Parameter* object in its *parameters* collection.

The optional *parameters* argument is a sequence of *Parameter* objects, which is validated to check that there are no parameters with duplicate names, and that the parameters are in the right order, i.e. positional-only first, then positional-or-keyword, and that parameters with defaults follow parameters without defaults.

The optional *return_annotation* argument, can be an arbitrary Python object, is the "return" annotation of the callable.

Signature objects are *immutable*. Use *Signature.replace()* to make a modified copy.

Changed in version 3.5: Signature objects are picklable and hashable.

empty
   A special class-level marker to specify absence of a return annotation.

parameters
   An ordered mapping of parameters' names to the corresponding *Parameter* objects.

return_annotation
   The "return" annotation for the callable. If the callable has no "return" annotation, this attribute is set to *Signature.empty*.

bind(**args, **kwargs*)
   Create a mapping from positional and keyword arguments to parameters. Returns *BoundArguments* if **args* and ***kwargs* match the signature, or raises a *TypeError*.

bind_partial(**args, **kwargs*)
   Works the same way as *Signature.bind()*, but allows the omission of some required arguments (mimics *functools.partial()* behavior.) Returns *BoundArguments*, or raises a *TypeError* if the passed arguments do not match the signature.

replace(**[, parameters][, return_annotation]*)
   Create a new Signature instance based on the instance replace was invoked on. It is possible to pass different **parameters** and/or **return_annotation** to override the corresponding properties of the base signature. To remove return_annotation from the copied Signature, pass in *Signature.empty*.

```
>>> def test(a, b):
...     pass
>>> sig = signature(test)
>>> new_sig = sig.replace(return_annotation="new return anno")
>>> str(new_sig)
"(a, b) -> 'new return anno'"
```

classmethod `from_callable`(*obj, *, follow_wrapped=True*)
   Return a *Signature* (or its subclass) object for a given callable **obj**. Pass `follow_wrapped=False` to get a signature of **obj** without unwrapping its `__wrapped__` chain.

This method simplifies subclassing of *Signature*:

```
class MySignature(Signature):
    pass
sig = MySignature.from_callable(min)
assert isinstance(sig, MySignature)
```

New in version 3.5.

class inspect.Parameter(*name, kind, *, default=Parameter.empty, annotation=Parameter.empty*)

Parameter objects are *immutable*. Instead of modifying a Parameter object, you can use *Parameter.replace()* to create a modified copy.

Changed in version 3.5: Parameter objects are picklable and hashable.

empty
    A special class-level marker to specify absence of default values and annotations.

name
    The name of the parameter as a string. The name must be a valid Python identifier.

    CPython implementation detail: CPython generates implicit parameter names of the form .0 on the code objects used to implement comprehensions and generator expressions.

    Changed in version 3.6: These parameter names are exposed by this module as names like implicit0.

default
    The default value for the parameter. If the parameter has no default value, this attribute is set to *Parameter.empty*.

annotation
    The annotation for the parameter. If the parameter has no annotation, this attribute is set to *Parameter.empty*.

kind
    Describes how argument values are bound to the parameter. Possible values (accessible via *Parameter*, like `Parameter.KEYWORD_ONLY`):

Name	Meaning
POSITIONAL_ONLY	Value must be supplied as a positional argument. Python has no explicit syntax for defining positional-only parameters, but many built-in and extension module functions (especially those that accept only one or two parameters) accept them.
POSITIONAL_OR_KEYWORD	Value may be supplied as either a keyword or positional argument (this is the standard binding behaviour for functions implemented in Python.)
VAR_POSITIONAL	A tuple of positional arguments that aren't bound to any other parameter. This corresponds to a `*args` parameter in a Python function definition.
KEYWORD_ONLY	Value must be supplied as a keyword argument. Keyword only parameters are those which appear after a `*` or `*args` entry in a Python function definition.
VAR_KEYWORD	A dict of keyword arguments that aren't bound to any other parameter. This corresponds to a `**kwargs` parameter in a Python function definition.

Example: print all keyword-only arguments without default values:

```
>>> def foo(a, b, *, c, d=10):
...     pass

>>> sig = signature(foo)
>>> for param in sig.parameters.values():
...     if (param.kind == param.KEYWORD_ONLY and
...                        param.default is param.empty):
...         print('Parameter:', param)
Parameter: c
```

replace(*[, name][, kind][, default][, annotation]*)

    Create a new Parameter instance based on the instance replaced was invoked on. To override a *Parameter* attribute, pass the corresponding argument. To remove a default value or/and an annotation from a Parameter, pass *Parameter.empty*.

```
>>> from inspect import Parameter
>>> param = Parameter('foo', Parameter.KEYWORD_ONLY, default=42)
>>> str(param)
'foo=42'

>>> str(param.replace()) # Will create a shallow copy of 'param'
'foo=42'

>>> str(param.replace(default=Parameter.empty, annotation='spam'))
"foo:'spam'"
```

    Changed in version 3.4: In Python 3.3 Parameter objects were allowed to have **name** set to **None** if their **kind** was set to **POSITIONAL_ONLY**. This is no longer permitted.

class inspect.BoundArguments

    Result of a *Signature.bind()* or *Signature.bind_partial()* call. Holds the mapping of arguments to the function's parameters.

    arguments

        An ordered, mutable mapping (*collections.OrderedDict*) of parameters' names to arguments' values. Contains only explicitly bound arguments. Changes in *arguments* will reflect in *args* and *kwargs*.

        Should be used in conjunction with *Signature.parameters* for any argument processing purposes.

        Note: Arguments for which *Signature.bind()* or *Signature.bind_partial()* relied on a default value are skipped. However, if needed, use *BoundArguments.apply_defaults()* to add them.

    args

        A tuple of positional arguments values. Dynamically computed from the *arguments* attribute.

    kwargs

        A dict of keyword arguments values. Dynamically computed from the *arguments* attribute.

    signature

        A reference to the parent *Signature* object.

    apply_defaults()

        Set default values for missing arguments.

        For variable-positional arguments (**args*) the default is an empty tuple.

        For variable-keyword arguments (***kwargs*) the default is an empty dict.

```
>>> def foo(a, b='ham', *args): pass
>>> ba = inspect.signature(foo).bind('spam')
>>> ba.apply_defaults()
>>> ba.arguments
OrderedDict([('a', 'spam'), ('b', 'ham'), ('args', ())])
```

New in version 3.5.

The *args* and *kwargs* properties can be used to invoke functions:

```
def test(a, *, b):
    ...

sig = signature(test)
ba = sig.bind(10, b=20)
test(*ba.args, **ba.kwargs)
```

See also:

PEP 362 - **Function Signature Object.** The detailed specification, implementation details and examples.

29.12.4 Classes and functions

inspect.getclasstree(*classes, unique=False*)

Arrange the given list of classes into a hierarchy of nested lists. Where a nested list appears, it contains classes derived from the class whose entry immediately precedes the list. Each entry is a 2-tuple containing a class and a tuple of its base classes. If the *unique* argument is true, exactly one entry appears in the returned structure for each class in the given list. Otherwise, classes using multiple inheritance and their descendants will appear multiple times.

inspect.getargspec(*func*)

Get the names and default values of a Python function's parameters. A *named tuple* ArgSpec(args, varargs, keywords, defaults) is returned. *args* is a list of the parameter names. *varargs* and *keywords* are the names of the * and ** parameters or None. *defaults* is a tuple of default argument values or None if there are no default arguments; if this tuple has *n* elements, they correspond to the last *n* elements listed in *args*.

Deprecated since version 3.0: Use getfullargspec() for an updated API that is usually a drop-in replacement, but also correctly handles function annotations and keyword-only parameters.

Alternatively, use signature() and Signature Object, which provide a more structured introspection API for callables.

inspect.getfullargspec(*func*)

Get the names and default values of a Python function's parameters. A *named tuple* is returned:

FullArgSpec(args, varargs, varkw, defaults, kwonlyargs, kwonlydefaults, annotations)

args is a list of the positional parameter names. *varargs* is the name of the * parameter or None if arbitrary positional arguments are not accepted. *varkw* is the name of the ** parameter or None if arbitrary keyword arguments are not accepted. *defaults* is an *n*-tuple of default argument values corresponding to the last *n* positional parameters, or None if there are no such defaults defined. *kwonlyargs* is a list of keyword-only parameter names. *kwonlydefaults* is a dictionary mapping parameter names from *kwonlyargs* to the default values used if no argument is supplied. *annotations* is a dictionary mapping parameter names to annotations. The special key "return" is used to report the function return value annotation (if any).

Note that *signature()* and *Signature Object* provide the recommended API for callable introspection, and support additional behaviours (like positional-only arguments) that are sometimes encountered in extension module APIs. This function is retained primarily for use in code that needs to maintain compatibility with the Python 2 `inspect` module API.

Changed in version 3.4: This function is now based on *signature()*, but still ignores `__wrapped__` attributes and includes the already bound first parameter in the signature output for bound methods.

Changed in version 3.6: This method was previously documented as deprecated in favour of *signature()* in Python 3.5, but that decision has been reversed in order to restore a clearly supported standard interface for single-source Python 2/3 code migrating away from the legacy *getargspec()* API.

inspect.getargvalues(*frame*)

> Get information about arguments passed into a particular frame. A *named tuple* `ArgInfo(args, varargs, keywords, locals)` is returned. *args* is a list of the argument names. *varargs* and *keywords* are the names of the `*` and `**` arguments or `None`. *locals* is the locals dictionary of the given frame.

> Note: This function was inadvertently marked as deprecated in Python 3.5.

inspect.formatargspec(*args*[, *varargs, varkw, defaults, kwonlyargs, kwonlydefaults, annotations*[, *formatarg, formatvarargs, formatvarkw, formatvalue, formatreturns, formatannotations*]])

> Format a pretty argument spec from the values returned by *getfullargspec()*.

> The first seven arguments are (`args, varargs, varkw, defaults, kwonlyargs, kwonlydefaults, annotations`).

> The other six arguments are functions that are called to turn argument names, `*` argument name, `**` argument name, default values, return annotation and individual annotations into strings, respectively.

> For example:

```
>>> from inspect import formatargspec, getfullargspec
>>> def f(a: int, b: float):
...     pass
...
>>> formatargspec(*getfullargspec(f))
'(a: int, b: float)'
```

> Deprecated since version 3.5: Use *signature()* and *Signature Object*, which provide a better introspecting API for callables.

inspect.formatargvalues(*args*[, *varargs, varkw, locals, formatarg, formatvarargs, formatvarkw, formatvalue*])

> Format a pretty argument spec from the four values returned by *getargvalues()*. The format* arguments are the corresponding optional formatting functions that are called to turn names and values into strings.

> Note: This function was inadvertently marked as deprecated in Python 3.5.

inspect.getmro(*cls*)

> Return a tuple of class cls's base classes, including cls, in method resolution order. No class appears more than once in this tuple. Note that the method resolution order depends on cls's type. Unless a very peculiar user-defined metatype is in use, cls will be the first element of the tuple.

inspect.getcallargs(*func, *args, **kwds*)

Bind the *args* and *kwds* to the argument names of the Python function or method *func*, as if it was called with them. For bound methods, bind also the first argument (typically named `self`) to the associated instance. A dict is returned, mapping the argument names (including the names of the `*` and `**` arguments, if any) to their values from *args* and *kwds*. In case of invoking *func* incorrectly, i.e. whenever `func(*args, **kwds)` would raise an exception because of incompatible signature, an exception of the same type and the same or similar message is raised. For example:

```
>>> from inspect import getcallargs
>>> def f(a, b=1, *pos, **named):
...     pass
>>> getcallargs(f, 1, 2, 3) == {'a': 1, 'named': {}, 'b': 2, 'pos': (3,)}
True
>>> getcallargs(f, a=2, x=4) == {'a': 2, 'named': {'x': 4}, 'b': 1, 'pos': ()}
True
>>> getcallargs(f)
Traceback (most recent call last):
...
TypeError: f() missing 1 required positional argument: 'a'
```

New in version 3.2.

Deprecated since version 3.5: Use *Signature.bind()* and *Signature.bind_partial()* instead.

inspect.getclosurevars(*func*)

Get the mapping of external name references in a Python function or method *func* to their current values. A *named tuple* `ClosureVars(nonlocals, globals, builtins, unbound)` is returned. *nonlocals* maps referenced names to lexical closure variables, *globals* to the function's module globals and *builtins* to the builtins visible from the function body. *unbound* is the set of names referenced in the function that could not be resolved at all given the current module globals and builtins.

TypeError is raised if *func* is not a Python function or method.

New in version 3.3.

inspect.unwrap(*func, *, stop=None*)

Get the object wrapped by *func*. It follows the chain of `__wrapped__` attributes returning the last object in the chain.

stop is an optional callback accepting an object in the wrapper chain as its sole argument that allows the unwrapping to be terminated early if the callback returns a true value. If the callback never returns a true value, the last object in the chain is returned as usual. For example, *signature()* uses this to stop unwrapping if any object in the chain has a `__signature__` attribute defined.

ValueError is raised if a cycle is encountered.

New in version 3.4.

29.12.5 The interpreter stack

When the following functions return "frame records," each record is a *named tuple* `FrameInfo(frame, filename, lineno, function, code_context, index)`. The tuple contains the frame object, the filename, the line number of the current line, the function name, a list of lines of context from the source code, and the index of the current line within that list.

Changed in version 3.5: Return a named tuple instead of a tuple.

Note: Keeping references to frame objects, as found in the first element of the frame records these functions return, can cause your program to create reference cycles. Once a reference cycle has been created, the lifespan of all objects which can be accessed from the objects which form the cycle can become much longer even if Python's optional cycle detector is enabled. If such cycles must be created, it is important to ensure they are explicitly broken to avoid the delayed destruction of objects and increased memory consumption which occurs.

Though the cycle detector will catch these, destruction of the frames (and local variables) can be made deterministic by removing the cycle in a `finally` clause. This is also important if the cycle detector was disabled when Python was compiled or using *gc.disable()*. For example:

```
def handle_stackframe_without_leak():
    frame = inspect.currentframe()
    try:
        # do something with the frame
    finally:
        del frame
```

If you want to keep the frame around (for example to print a traceback later), you can also break reference cycles by using the `frame.clear()` method.

The optional *context* argument supported by most of these functions specifies the number of lines of context to return, which are centered around the current line.

inspect.**getframeinfo**(*frame, context=1*)

> Get information about a frame or traceback object. A *named tuple* `Traceback(filename, lineno, function, code_context, index)` is returned.

inspect.**getouterframes**(*frame, context=1*)

> Get a list of frame records for a frame and all outer frames. These frames represent the calls that lead to the creation of *frame*. The first entry in the returned list represents *frame*; the last entry represents the outermost call on *frame*'s stack.
>
> Changed in version 3.5: A list of *named tuples* `FrameInfo(frame, filename, lineno, function, code_context, index)` is returned.

inspect.**getinnerframes**(*traceback, context=1*)

> Get a list of frame records for a traceback's frame and all inner frames. These frames represent calls made as a consequence of *frame*. The first entry in the list represents *traceback*; the last entry represents where the exception was raised.
>
> Changed in version 3.5: A list of *named tuples* `FrameInfo(frame, filename, lineno, function, code_context, index)` is returned.

inspect.**currentframe**()

> Return the frame object for the caller's stack frame.
>
> **CPython implementation detail:** This function relies on Python stack frame support in the interpreter, which isn't guaranteed to exist in all implementations of Python. If running in an implementation without Python stack frame support this function returns `None`.

inspect.**stack**(*context=1*)

> Return a list of frame records for the caller's stack. The first entry in the returned list represents the caller; the last entry represents the outermost call on the stack.
>
> Changed in version 3.5: A list of *named tuples* `FrameInfo(frame, filename, lineno, function, code_context, index)` is returned.

inspect.**trace**(*context=1*)

> Return a list of frame records for the stack between the current frame and the frame in which an exception currently being handled was raised in. The first entry in the list represents the caller; the last entry represents where the exception was raised.

Changed in version 3.5: A list of *named tuples* `FrameInfo(frame, filename, lineno, function, code_context, index)` is returned.

29.12.6 Fetching attributes statically

Both `getattr()` and `hasattr()` can trigger code execution when fetching or checking for the existence of attributes. Descriptors, like properties, will be invoked and `__getattr__()` and `__getattribute__()` may be called.

For cases where you want passive introspection, like documentation tools, this can be inconvenient. `getattr_static()` has the same signature as `getattr()` but avoids executing code when it fetches attributes.

`inspect.getattr_static(obj, attr, default=None)`

Retrieve attributes without triggering dynamic lookup via the descriptor protocol, `__getattr__()` or `__getattribute__()`.

Note: this function may not be able to retrieve all attributes that getattr can fetch (like dynamically created attributes) and may find attributes that getattr can't (like descriptors that raise AttributeError). It can also return descriptors objects instead of instance members.

If the instance `__dict__` is shadowed by another member (for example a property) then this function will be unable to find instance members.

New in version 3.2.

`getattr_static()` does not resolve descriptors, for example slot descriptors or getset descriptors on objects implemented in C. The descriptor object is returned instead of the underlying attribute.

You can handle these with code like the following. Note that for arbitrary getset descriptors invoking these may trigger code execution:

```
# example code for resolving the builtin descriptor types
class _foo:
    __slots__ = ['foo']

slot_descriptor = type(_foo.foo)
getset_descriptor = type(type(open(__file__)).name)
wrapper_descriptor = type(str.__dict__['__add__'])
descriptor_types = (slot_descriptor, getset_descriptor, wrapper_descriptor)

result = getattr_static(some_object, 'foo')
if type(result) in descriptor_types:
    try:
        result = result.__get__()
    except AttributeError:
        # descriptors can raise AttributeError to
        # indicate there is no underlying value
        # in which case the descriptor itself will
        # have to do
        pass
```

29.12.7 Current State of Generators and Coroutines

When implementing coroutine schedulers and for other advanced uses of generators, it is useful to determine whether a generator is currently executing, is waiting to start or resume or execution, or has already terminated. `getgeneratorstate()` allows the current state of a generator to be determined easily.

inspect.getgeneratorstate(*generator*)
Get current state of a generator-iterator.

Possible states are:

- GEN_CREATED: Waiting to start execution.
- GEN_RUNNING: Currently being executed by the interpreter.
- GEN_SUSPENDED: Currently suspended at a yield expression.
- GEN_CLOSED: Execution has completed.

New in version 3.2.

inspect.getcoroutinestate(*coroutine*)
Get current state of a coroutine object. The function is intended to be used with coroutine objects created by `async def` functions, but will accept any coroutine-like object that has `cr_running` and `cr_frame` attributes.

Possible states are:

- CORO_CREATED: Waiting to start execution.
- CORO_RUNNING: Currently being executed by the interpreter.
- CORO_SUSPENDED: Currently suspended at an await expression.
- CORO_CLOSED: Execution has completed.

New in version 3.5.

The current internal state of the generator can also be queried. This is mostly useful for testing purposes, to ensure that internal state is being updated as expected:

inspect.getgeneratorlocals(*generator*)
Get the mapping of live local variables in *generator* to their current values. A dictionary is returned that maps from variable names to values. This is the equivalent of calling *locals()* in the body of the generator, and all the same caveats apply.

If *generator* is a *generator* with no currently associated frame, then an empty dictionary is returned. *TypeError* is raised if *generator* is not a Python generator object.

CPython implementation detail: This function relies on the generator exposing a Python stack frame for introspection, which isn't guaranteed to be the case in all implementations of Python. In such cases, this function will always return an empty dictionary.

New in version 3.3.

inspect.getcoroutinelocals(*coroutine*)
This function is analogous to *getgeneratorlocals()*, but works for coroutine objects created by `async def` functions.

New in version 3.5.

29.12.8 Code Objects Bit Flags

Python code objects have a `co_flags` attribute, which is a bitmap of the following flags:

inspect.CO_OPTIMIZED
The code object is optimized, using fast locals.

inspect.CO_NEWLOCALS
If set, a new dict will be created for the frame's `f_locals` when the code object is executed.

inspect.CO_VARARGS
The code object has a variable positional parameter (`*args`-like).

`inspect.CO_VARKEYWORDS`
   The code object has a variable keyword parameter (`**kwargs`-like).

`inspect.CO_NESTED`
   The flag is set when the code object is a nested function.

`inspect.CO_GENERATOR`
   The flag is set when the code object is a generator function, i.e. a generator object is returned when the code object is executed.

`inspect.CO_NOFREE`
   The flag is set if there are no free or cell variables.

`inspect.CO_COROUTINE`
   The flag is set when the code object is a coroutine function. When the code object is executed it returns a coroutine object. See PEP 492 for more details.

   New in version 3.5.

`inspect.CO_ITERABLE_COROUTINE`
   The flag is used to transform generators into generator-based coroutines. Generator objects with this flag can be used in `await` expression, and can `yield from` coroutine objects. See PEP 492 for more details.

   New in version 3.5.

`inspect.CO_ASYNC_GENERATOR`
   The flag is set when the code object is an asynchronous generator function. When the code object is executed it returns an asynchronous generator object. See PEP 525 for more details.

   New in version 3.6.

Note: The flags are specific to CPython, and may not be defined in other Python implementations. Furthermore, the flags are an implementation detail, and can be removed or deprecated in future Python releases. It's recommended to use public APIs from the *inspect* module for any introspection needs.

29.12.9 Command Line Interface

The *inspect* module also provides a basic introspection capability from the command line.

By default, accepts the name of a module and prints the source of that module. A class or function within the module can be printed instead by appended a colon and the qualified name of the target object.

`--details`
   Print information about the specified object rather than the source code

29.13 `site` — Site-specific configuration hook

Source code: Lib/site.py

This module is automatically imported during initialization. The automatic import can be suppressed using the interpreter's `-S` option.

Importing this module will append site-specific paths to the module search path and add a few builtins, unless `-S` was used. In that case, this module can be safely imported with no automatic modifications to the module search path or additions to the builtins. To explicitly trigger the usual site-specific additions, call the *site.main()* function.

Changed in version 3.3: Importing the module used to trigger paths manipulation even when using -S.

It starts by constructing up to four directories from a head and a tail part. For the head part, it uses `sys.prefix` and `sys.exec_prefix`; empty heads are skipped. For the tail part, it uses the empty string and then `lib/site-packages` (on Windows) or `lib/python`$X.Y$`/site-packages` (on Unix and Macintosh). For each of the distinct head-tail combinations, it sees if it refers to an existing directory, and if so, adds it to `sys.path` and also inspects the newly added path for configuration files.

Changed in version 3.5: Support for the "site-python" directory has been removed.

If a file named "pyvenv.cfg" exists one directory above sys.executable, sys.prefix and sys.exec_prefix are set to that directory and it is also checked for site-packages (sys.base_prefix and sys.base_exec_prefix will always be the "real" prefixes of the Python installation). If "pyvenv.cfg" (a bootstrap configuration file) contains the key "include-system-site-packages" set to anything other than "false" (case-insensitive), the system-level prefixes will still also be searched for site-packages; otherwise they won't.

A path configuration file is a file whose name has the form *name*.pth and exists in one of the four directories mentioned above; its contents are additional items (one per line) to be added to `sys.path`. Non-existing items are never added to `sys.path`, and no check is made that the item refers to a directory rather than a file. No item is added to `sys.path` more than once. Blank lines and lines beginning with # are skipped. Lines starting with `import` (followed by space or tab) are executed.

For example, suppose `sys.prefix` and `sys.exec_prefix` are set to /usr/local. The Python X.Y library is then installed in /usr/local/lib/python$X.Y$. Suppose this has a subdirectory /usr/local/lib/python$X.Y$/site-packages with three subsubdirectories, `foo`, `bar` and `spam`, and two path configuration files, `foo.pth` and `bar.pth`. Assume `foo.pth` contains the following:

```
# foo package configuration

foo
bar
bletch
```

and `bar.pth` contains:

```
# bar package configuration

bar
```

Then the following version-specific directories are added to `sys.path`, in this order:

```
/usr/local/lib/pythonX.Y/site-packages/bar
/usr/local/lib/pythonX.Y/site-packages/foo
```

Note that `bletch` is omitted because it doesn't exist; the `bar` directory precedes the `foo` directory because `bar.pth` comes alphabetically before `foo.pth`; and `spam` is omitted because it is not mentioned in either path configuration file.

After these path manipulations, an attempt is made to import a module named `sitecustomize`, which can perform arbitrary site-specific customizations. It is typically created by a system administrator in the site-packages directory. If this import fails with an *ImportError* exception, it is silently ignored. If Python is started without output streams available, as with `pythonw.exe` on Windows (which is used by default to start IDLE), attempted output from `sitecustomize` is ignored. Any exception other than *ImportError* causes a silent and perhaps mysterious failure of the process.

After this, an attempt is made to import a module named `usercustomize`, which can perform arbitrary user-specific customizations, if *ENABLE_USER_SITE* is true. This file is intended to be created in the user site-packages directory (see below), which is part of `sys.path` unless disabled by `-s`. An `ImportError` will be silently ignored.

Note that for some non-Unix systems, `sys.prefix` and `sys.exec_prefix` are empty, and the path manipulations are skipped; however the import of `sitecustomize` and `usercustomize` is still attempted.

29.13.1 Readline configuration

On systems that support `readline`, this module will also import and configure the `rlcompleter` module, if Python is started in interactive mode and without the `-S` option. The default behavior is enable tab-completion and to use `~/.python_history` as the history save file. To disable it, delete (or override) the `sys.__interactivehook__` attribute in your `sitecustomize` or `usercustomize` module or your `PYTHONSTARTUP` file.

Changed in version 3.4: Activation of rlcompleter and history was made automatic.

29.13.2 Module contents

site.PREFIXES
    A list of prefixes for site-packages directories.

site.ENABLE_USER_SITE
    Flag showing the status of the user site-packages directory. `True` means that it is enabled and was added to `sys.path`. `False` means that it was disabled by user request (with `-s` or `PYTHONNOUSERSITE`). `None` means it was disabled for security reasons (mismatch between user or group id and effective id) or by an administrator.

site.USER_SITE
    Path to the user site-packages for the running Python. Can be `None` if `getusersitepackages()` hasn't been called yet. Default value is `~/.local/lib/pythonX.Y/site-packages` for UNIX and non-framework Mac OS X builds, `~/Library/Python/X.Y/lib/python/site-packages` for Mac framework builds, and `%APPDATA%\Python\PythonXY\site-packages` on Windows. This directory is a site directory, which means that `.pth` files in it will be processed.

site.USER_BASE
    Path to the base directory for the user site-packages. Can be `None` if `getuserbase()` hasn't been called yet. Default value is `~/.local` for UNIX and Mac OS X non-framework builds, `~/Library/Python/X.Y` for Mac framework builds, and `%APPDATA%\Python` for Windows. This value is used by Distutils to compute the installation directories for scripts, data files, Python modules, etc. for the user installation scheme. See also `PYTHONUSERBASE`.

site.main()
    Adds all the standard site-specific directories to the module search path. This function is called automatically when this module is imported, unless the Python interpreter was started with the `-S` flag.

    Changed in version 3.3: This function used to be called unconditionally.

site.addsitedir(*sitedir, known_paths=None*)
    Add a directory to sys.path and process its `.pth` files. Typically used in `sitecustomize` or `usercustomize` (see above).

site.getsitepackages()
    Return a list containing all global site-packages directories.

    New in version 3.2.

site.getuserbase()
> Return the path of the user base directory, USER_BASE. If it is not initialized yet, this function will also set it, respecting PYTHONUSERBASE.
>
> New in version 3.2.

site.getusersitepackages()
> Return the path of the user-specific site-packages directory, USER_SITE. If it is not initialized yet, this function will also set it, respecting PYTHONNOUSERSITE and USER_BASE.
>
> New in version 3.2.

The *site* module also provides a way to get the user directories from the command line:

```
$ python3 -m site --user-site
/home/user/.local/lib/python3.3/site-packages
```

If it is called without arguments, it will print the contents of *sys.path* on the standard output, followed by the value of USER_BASE and whether the directory exists, then the same thing for USER_SITE, and finally the value of ENABLE_USER_SITE.

--user-base
> Print the path to the user base directory.

--user-site
> Print the path to the user site-packages directory.

If both options are given, user base and user site will be printed (always in this order), separated by *os.pathsep*.

If any option is given, the script will exit with one of these values: 0 if the user site-packages directory is enabled, 1 if it was disabled by the user, 2 if it is disabled for security reasons or by an administrator, and a value greater than 2 if there is an error.

See also:

PEP 370 – Per user site-packages directory

29.14 `fpectl` — Floating point exception control

Note: The *fpectl* module is not built by default, and its usage is discouraged and may be dangerous except in the hands of experts. See also the section *Limitations and other considerations* on limitations for more details.

Most computers carry out floating point operations in conformance with the so-called IEEE-754 standard. On any real computer, some floating point operations produce results that cannot be expressed as a normal floating point value. For example, try

```
>>> import math
>>> math.exp(1000)
inf
>>> math.exp(1000) / math.exp(1000)
nan
```

(The example above will work on many platforms. DEC Alpha may be one exception.) "Inf" is a special, non-numeric value in IEEE-754 that stands for "infinity", and "nan" means "not a number." Note that, other than the non-numeric results, nothing special happened when you asked Python to carry out those calculations. That is in fact the default behaviour prescribed in the IEEE-754 standard, and if it works for you, stop reading now.

In some circumstances, it would be better to raise an exception and stop processing at the point where the faulty operation was attempted. The *fpectl* module is for use in that situation. It provides control over floating point units from several hardware manufacturers, allowing the user to turn on the generation of SIGFPE whenever any of the IEEE-754 exceptions Division by Zero, Overflow, or Invalid Operation occurs. In tandem with a pair of wrapper macros that are inserted into the C code comprising your python system, SIGFPE is trapped and converted into the Python *FloatingPointError* exception.

The *fpectl* module defines the following functions and may raise the given exception:

fpectl.turnon_sigfpe()
    Turn on the generation of SIGFPE, and set up an appropriate signal handler.

fpectl.turnoff_sigfpe()
    Reset default handling of floating point exceptions.

exception fpectl.FloatingPointError
    After *turnon_sigfpe()* has been executed, a floating point operation that raises one of the IEEE-754 exceptions Division by Zero, Overflow, or Invalid operation will in turn raise this standard Python exception.

29.14.1 Example

The following example demonstrates how to start up and test operation of the *fpectl* module.

```
>>> import fpectl
>>> import fpetest
>>> fpectl.turnon_sigfpe()
>>> fpetest.test()
overflow        PASS
FloatingPointError: Overflow

div by 0        PASS
FloatingPointError: Division by zero
  [ more output from test elided ]
>>> import math
>>> math.exp(1000)
Traceback (most recent call last):
  File "<stdin>", line 1, in <module>
FloatingPointError: in math_1
```

29.14.2 Limitations and other considerations

Setting up a given processor to trap IEEE-754 floating point errors currently requires custom code on a per-architecture basis. You may have to modify *fpectl* to control your particular hardware.

Conversion of an IEEE-754 exception to a Python exception requires that the wrapper macros PyFPE_START_PROTECT and PyFPE_END_PROTECT be inserted into your code in an appropriate fashion. Python itself has been modified to support the *fpectl* module, but many other codes of interest to numerical analysts have not.

The *fpectl* module is not thread-safe.

See also:

Some files in the source distribution may be interesting in learning more about how this module operates. The include file `Include/pyfpe.h` discusses the implementation of this module at some length. `Modules/fpetestmodule.c` gives several examples of use. Many additional examples can be found in `Objects/floatobject.c`.

CHAPTER THIRTY

CUSTOM PYTHON INTERPRETERS

The modules described in this chapter allow writing interfaces similar to Python's interactive interpreter. If you want a Python interpreter that supports some special feature in addition to the Python language, you should look at the `code` module. (The `codeop` module is lower-level, used to support compiling a possibly-incomplete chunk of Python code.)

The full list of modules described in this chapter is:

30.1 code — Interpreter base classes

Source code: Lib/code.py

The `code` module provides facilities to implement read-eval-print loops in Python. Two classes and convenience functions are included which can be used to build applications which provide an interactive interpreter prompt.

class code.InteractiveInterpreter(*locals=None*)

This class deals with parsing and interpreter state (the user's namespace); it does not deal with input buffering or prompting or input file naming (the filename is always passed in explicitly). The optional *locals* argument specifies the dictionary in which code will be executed; it defaults to a newly created dictionary with key '`__name__`' set to '`__console__`' and key '`__doc__`' set to `None`.

class code.InteractiveConsole(*locals=None, filename="<console>"*)

Closely emulate the behavior of the interactive Python interpreter. This class builds on *InteractiveInterpreter* and adds prompting using the familiar `sys.ps1` and `sys.ps2`, and input buffering.

code.interact(*banner=None, readfunc=None, local=None, exitmsg=None*)

Convenience function to run a read-eval-print loop. This creates a new instance of *InteractiveConsole* and sets *readfunc* to be used as the *InteractiveConsole.raw_input()* method, if provided. If *local* is provided, it is passed to the *InteractiveConsole* constructor for use as the default namespace for the interpreter loop. The *interact()* method of the instance is then run with *banner* and *exitmsg* passed as the banner and exit message to use, if provided. The console object is discarded after use.

Changed in version 3.6: Added *exitmsg* parameter.

code.compile_command(*source, filename="<input>", symbol="single"*)

This function is useful for programs that want to emulate Python's interpreter main loop (a.k.a. the read-eval-print loop). The tricky part is to determine when the user has entered an incomplete command that can be completed by entering more text (as opposed to a complete command or a syntax error). This function *almost* always makes the same decision as the real interpreter main loop.

source is the source string; *filename* is the optional filename from which source was read, defaulting to `'<input>'`; and *symbol* is the optional grammar start symbol, which should be either `'single'` (the default) or `'eval'`.

Returns a code object (the same as `compile(source, filename, symbol)`) if the command is complete and valid; `None` if the command is incomplete; raises *SyntaxError* if the command is complete and contains a syntax error, or raises *OverflowError* or *ValueError* if the command contains an invalid literal.

30.1.1 Interactive Interpreter Objects

`InteractiveInterpreter.runsource(`*source, filename="<input>", symbol="single"*`)`

Compile and run some source in the interpreter. Arguments are the same as for *compile_command()*; the default for *filename* is `'<input>'`, and for *symbol* is `'single'`. One several things can happen:

- The input is incorrect; *compile_command()* raised an exception (*SyntaxError* or *OverflowError*). A syntax traceback will be printed by calling the *showsyntaxerror()* method. *runsource()* returns `False`.

- The input is incomplete, and more input is required; *compile_command()* returned `None`. *runsource()* returns `True`.

- The input is complete; *compile_command()* returned a code object. The code is executed by calling the *runcode()* (which also handles run-time exceptions, except for *SystemExit*). *runsource()* returns `False`.

The return value can be used to decide whether to use `sys.ps1` or `sys.ps2` to prompt the next line.

`InteractiveInterpreter.runcode(`*code*`)`

Execute a code object. When an exception occurs, *showtraceback()* is called to display a traceback. All exceptions are caught except *SystemExit*, which is allowed to propagate.

A note about *KeyboardInterrupt*: this exception may occur elsewhere in this code, and may not always be caught. The caller should be prepared to deal with it.

`InteractiveInterpreter.showsyntaxerror(`*filename=None*`)`

Display the syntax error that just occurred. This does not display a stack trace because there isn't one for syntax errors. If *filename* is given, it is stuffed into the exception instead of the default filename provided by Python's parser, because it always uses `'<string>'` when reading from a string. The output is written by the *write()* method.

`InteractiveInterpreter.showtraceback()`

Display the exception that just occurred. We remove the first stack item because it is within the interpreter object implementation. The output is written by the *write()* method.

Changed in version 3.5: The full chained traceback is displayed instead of just the primary traceback.

`InteractiveInterpreter.write(`*data*`)`

Write a string to the standard error stream (`sys.stderr`). Derived classes should override this to provide the appropriate output handling as needed.

30.1.2 Interactive Console Objects

The *InteractiveConsole* class is a subclass of *InteractiveInterpreter*, and so offers all the methods of the interpreter objects as well as the following additions.

`InteractiveConsole.interact(`*banner=None, exitmsg=None*`)`

Closely emulate the interactive Python console. The optional *banner* argument specify the banner to print before the first interaction; by default it prints a banner similar to the one printed by the standard Python interpreter, followed by the class name of the console object in parentheses (so as not to confuse this with the real interpreter – since it's so close!).

The optional *exitmsg* argument specifies an exit message printed when exiting. Pass the empty string to suppress the exit message. If *exitmsg* is not given or `None`, a default message is printed.

Changed in version 3.4: To suppress printing any banner, pass an empty string.

Changed in version 3.6: Print an exit message when exiting.

`InteractiveConsole.push(`*line*`)`
> Push a line of source text to the interpreter. The line should not have a trailing newline; it may have internal newlines. The line is appended to a buffer and the interpreter's `runsource()` method is called with the concatenated contents of the buffer as source. If this indicates that the command was executed or invalid, the buffer is reset; otherwise, the command is incomplete, and the buffer is left as it was after the line was appended. The return value is `True` if more input is required, `False` if the line was dealt with in some way (this is the same as `runsource()`).

`InteractiveConsole.resetbuffer()`
> Remove any unhandled source text from the input buffer.

`InteractiveConsole.raw_input(`*prompt=""*`)`
> Write a prompt and read a line. The returned line does not include the trailing newline. When the user enters the EOF key sequence, *EOFError* is raised. The base implementation reads from `sys.stdin`; a subclass may replace this with a different implementation.

30.2 `codeop` — Compile Python code

Source code: Lib/codeop.py

The *codeop* module provides utilities upon which the Python read-eval-print loop can be emulated, as is done in the *code* module. As a result, you probably don't want to use the module directly; if you want to include such a loop in your program you probably want to use the *code* module instead.

There are two parts to this job:

1. Being able to tell if a line of input completes a Python statement: in short, telling whether to print '>>>' or '...' next.

2. Remembering which future statements the user has entered, so subsequent input can be compiled with these in effect.

The *codeop* module provides a way of doing each of these things, and a way of doing them both.

To do just the former:

`codeop.compile_command(`*source, filename="<input>", symbol="single"*`)`
> Tries to compile *source*, which should be a string of Python code and return a code object if *source* is valid Python code. In that case, the filename attribute of the code object will be *filename*, which defaults to `'<input>'`. Returns `None` if *source* is *not* valid Python code, but is a prefix of valid Python code.
>
> If there is a problem with *source*, an exception will be raised. *SyntaxError* is raised if there is invalid Python syntax, and *OverflowError* or *ValueError* if there is an invalid literal.
>
> The *symbol* argument determines whether *source* is compiled as a statement (`'single'`, the default) or as an *expression* (`'eval'`). Any other value will cause *ValueError* to be raised.

> **Note:** It is possible (but not likely) that the parser stops parsing with a successful outcome before reaching the end of the source; in this case, trailing symbols may be ignored instead of causing an error. For example, a backslash followed by two newlines may be followed by arbitrary garbage. This will be fixed once the API for the parser is better.

class codeop.Compile
    Instances of this class have `__call__()` methods identical in signature to the built-in function *compile()*, but with the difference that if the instance compiles program text containing a *__future__* statement, the instance 'remembers' and compiles all subsequent program texts with the statement in force.

class codeop.CommandCompiler
    Instances of this class have `__call__()` methods identical in signature to *compile_command()*; the difference is that if the instance compiles program text containing a `__future__` statement, the instance 'remembers' and compiles all subsequent program texts with the statement in force.

CHAPTER
THIRTYONE

IMPORTING MODULES

The modules described in this chapter provide new ways to import other Python modules and hooks for customizing the import process.

The full list of modules described in this chapter is:

31.1 zipimport — Import modules from Zip archives

This module adds the ability to import Python modules (*.py, *.pyc) and packages from ZIP-format archives. It is usually not needed to use the *zipimport* module explicitly; it is automatically used by the built-in **import** mechanism for *sys.path* items that are paths to ZIP archives.

Typically, *sys.path* is a list of directory names as strings. This module also allows an item of *sys.path* to be a string naming a ZIP file archive. The ZIP archive can contain a subdirectory structure to support package imports, and a path within the archive can be specified to only import from a subdirectory. For example, the path **example.zip/lib/** would only import from the **lib/** subdirectory within the archive.

Any files may be present in the ZIP archive, but only files .py and .pyc are available for import. ZIP import of dynamic modules (.pyd, .so) is disallowed. Note that if an archive only contains .py files, Python will not attempt to modify the archive by adding the corresponding .pyc file, meaning that if a ZIP archive doesn't contain .pyc files, importing may be rather slow.

ZIP archives with an archive comment are currently not supported.

See also:

PKZIP Application Note Documentation on the ZIP file format by Phil Katz, the creator of the format and algorithms used.

PEP 273 - **Import Modules from Zip Archives** Written by James C. Ahlstrom, who also provided an implementation. Python 2.3 follows the specification in PEP 273, but uses an implementation written by Just van Rossum that uses the import hooks described in PEP 302.

PEP 302 - **New Import Hooks** The PEP to add the import hooks that help this module work.

This module defines an exception:

exception zipimport.ZipImportError
    Exception raised by zipimporter objects. It's a subclass of *ImportError*, so it can be caught as *ImportError*, too.

31.1.1 zipimporter Objects

zipimporter is the class for importing ZIP files.

class zipimport.zipimporter(*archivepath*)

Create a new zipimporter instance. *archivepath* must be a path to a ZIP file, or to a specific path within a ZIP file. For example, an *archivepath* of `foo/bar.zip/lib` will look for modules in the `lib` directory inside the ZIP file `foo/bar.zip` (provided that it exists).

ZipImportError is raised if *archivepath* doesn't point to a valid ZIP archive.

find_module(*fullname*[, *path*])

Search for a module specified by *fullname*. *fullname* must be the fully qualified (dotted) module name. It returns the zipimporter instance itself if the module was found, or *None* if it wasn't. The optional *path* argument is ignored—it's there for compatibility with the importer protocol.

get_code(*fullname*)

Return the code object for the specified module. Raise *ZipImportError* if the module couldn't be found.

get_data(*pathname*)

Return the data associated with *pathname*. Raise *OSError* if the file wasn't found.

Changed in version 3.3: *IOError* used to be raised instead of *OSError*.

get_filename(*fullname*)

Return the value `__file__` would be set to if the specified module was imported. Raise *ZipImportError* if the module couldn't be found.

New in version 3.1.

get_source(*fullname*)

Return the source code for the specified module. Raise *ZipImportError* if the module couldn't be found, return *None* if the archive does contain the module, but has no source for it.

is_package(*fullname*)

Return *True* if the module specified by *fullname* is a package. Raise *ZipImportError* if the module couldn't be found.

load_module(*fullname*)

Load the module specified by *fullname*. *fullname* must be the fully qualified (dotted) module name. It returns the imported module, or raises *ZipImportError* if it wasn't found.

archive

The file name of the importer's associated ZIP file, without a possible subpath.

prefix

The subpath within the ZIP file where modules are searched. This is the empty string for zipimporter objects which point to the root of the ZIP file.

The *archive* and *prefix* attributes, when combined with a slash, equal the original *archivepath* argument given to the *zipimporter* constructor.

31.1.2 Examples

Here is an example that imports a module from a ZIP archive - note that the *zipimport* module is not explicitly used.

```
$ unzip -l example.zip
Archive:  example.zip
  Length      Date    Time    Name
 --------    ----    ----    ----
```

```
     8467  11-26-02 22:30   jwzthreading.py
 --------                   -------
     8467                   1 file
$ ./python
Python 2.3 (#1, Aug 1 2003, 19:54:32)
>>> import sys
>>> sys.path.insert(0, 'example.zip')  # Add .zip file to front of path
>>> import jwzthreading
>>> jwzthreading.__file__
'example.zip/jwzthreading.py'
```

31.2 pkgutil — Package extension utility

Source code: Lib/pkgutil.py

This module provides utilities for the import system, in particular package support.

class pkgutil.ModuleInfo(*module_finder*, *name*, *ispkg*)

    A namedtuple that holds a brief summary of a module's info.

    New in version 3.6.

pkgutil.extend_path(*path*, *name*)

    Extend the search path for the modules which comprise a package. Intended use is to place the following code in a package's __init__.py:

```
from pkgutil import extend_path
__path__ = extend_path(__path__, __name__)
```

    This will add to the package's __path__ all subdirectories of directories on sys.path named after the package. This is useful if one wants to distribute different parts of a single logical package as multiple directories.

    It also looks for *.pkg files beginning where * matches the *name* argument. This feature is similar to *.pth files (see the *site* module for more information), except that it doesn't special-case lines starting with import. A *.pkg file is trusted at face value: apart from checking for duplicates, all entries found in a *.pkg file are added to the path, regardless of whether they exist on the filesystem. (This is a feature.)

    If the input path is not a list (as is the case for frozen packages) it is returned unchanged. The input path is not modified; an extended copy is returned. Items are only appended to the copy at the end.

    It is assumed that *sys.path* is a sequence. Items of *sys.path* that are not strings referring to existing directories are ignored. Unicode items on *sys.path* that cause errors when used as filenames may cause this function to raise an exception (in line with *os.path.isdir()* behavior).

class pkgutil.ImpImporter(*dirname=None*)

    PEP 302 Finder that wraps Python's "classic" import algorithm.

    If *dirname* is a string, a PEP 302 finder is created that searches that directory. If *dirname* is None, a PEP 302 finder is created that searches the current *sys.path*, plus any modules that are frozen or built-in.

    Note that *ImpImporter* does not currently support being used by placement on *sys.meta_path*.

    Deprecated since version 3.3: This emulation is no longer needed, as the standard import mechanism is now fully PEP 302 compliant and available in *importlib*.

class pkgutil.ImpLoader(*fullname, file, filename, etc*)
    Loader that wraps Python's "classic" import algorithm.

    Deprecated since version 3.3: This emulation is no longer needed, as the standard import mechanism is now fully PEP 302 compliant and available in *importlib*.

pkgutil.find_loader(*fullname*)
    Retrieve a module *loader* for the given *fullname*.

    This is a backwards compatibility wrapper around *importlib.util.find_spec()* that converts most failures to *ImportError* and only returns the loader rather than the full `ModuleSpec`.

    Changed in version 3.3: Updated to be based directly on *importlib* rather than relying on the package internal PEP 302 import emulation.

    Changed in version 3.4: Updated to be based on PEP 451

pkgutil.get_importer(*path_item*)
    Retrieve a *finder* for the given *path_item*.

    The returned finder is cached in *sys.path_importer_cache* if it was newly created by a path hook.

    The cache (or part of it) can be cleared manually if a rescan of *sys.path_hooks* is necessary.

    Changed in version 3.3: Updated to be based directly on *importlib* rather than relying on the package internal PEP 302 import emulation.

pkgutil.get_loader(*module_or_name*)
    Get a *loader* object for *module_or_name*.

    If the module or package is accessible via the normal import mechanism, a wrapper around the relevant part of that machinery is returned. Returns `None` if the module cannot be found or imported. If the named module is not already imported, its containing package (if any) is imported, in order to establish the package `__path__`.

    Changed in version 3.3: Updated to be based directly on *importlib* rather than relying on the package internal PEP 302 import emulation.

    Changed in version 3.4: Updated to be based on PEP 451

pkgutil.iter_importers(*fullname=""*)
    Yield *finder* objects for the given module name.

    If fullname contains a '.', the finders will be for the package containing fullname, otherwise they will be all registered top level finders (i.e. those on both sys.meta_path and sys.path_hooks).

    If the named module is in a package, that package is imported as a side effect of invoking this function.

    If no module name is specified, all top level finders are produced.

    Changed in version 3.3: Updated to be based directly on *importlib* rather than relying on the package internal PEP 302 import emulation.

pkgutil.iter_modules(*path=None, prefix=""*)
    Yields `ModuleInfo` for all submodules on *path*, or, if *path* is `None`, all top-level modules on `sys.path`.

    path should be either `None` or a list of paths to look for modules in.

    prefix is a string to output on the front of every module name on output.

    Note: Only works for a *finder* which defines an `iter_modules()` method. This interface is non-standard, so the module also provides implementations for *importlib.machinery.FileFinder* and *zipimport.zipimporter*.

Changed in version 3.3: Updated to be based directly on *importlib* rather than relying on the package internal PEP 302 import emulation.

pkgutil.**walk_packages**(*path=None, prefix='', onerror=None*)

Yields *ModuleInfo* for all modules recursively on *path*, or, if *path* is None, all accessible modules.

path should be either None or a list of paths to look for modules in.

prefix is a string to output on the front of every module name on output.

Note that this function must import all *packages* (*not* all modules!) on the given *path*, in order to access the __path__ attribute to find submodules.

onerror is a function which gets called with one argument (the name of the package which was being imported) if any exception occurs while trying to import a package. If no *onerror* function is supplied, *ImportError*s are caught and ignored, while all other exceptions are propagated, terminating the search.

Examples:

```
# list all modules python can access
walk_packages()

# list all submodules of ctypes
walk_packages(ctypes.__path__, ctypes.__name__ + '.')
```

Note: Only works for a *finder* which defines an iter_modules() method. This interface is non-standard, so the module also provides implementations for *importlib.machinery.FileFinder* and *zipimport.zipimporter*.

Changed in version 3.3: Updated to be based directly on *importlib* rather than relying on the package internal PEP 302 import emulation.

pkgutil.**get_data**(*package, resource*)

Get a resource from a package.

This is a wrapper for the *loader get_data* API. The *package* argument should be the name of a package, in standard module format (foo.bar). The *resource* argument should be in the form of a relative filename, using / as the path separator. The parent directory name .. is not allowed, and nor is a rooted name (starting with a /).

The function returns a binary string that is the contents of the specified resource.

For packages located in the filesystem, which have already been imported, this is the rough equivalent of:

```
d = os.path.dirname(sys.modules[package].__file__)
data = open(os.path.join(d, resource), 'rb').read()
```

If the package cannot be located or loaded, or it uses a *loader* which does not support *get_data*, then None is returned. In particular, the *loader* for *namespace packages* does not support *get_data*.

31.3 modulefinder — Find modules used by a script

Source code: Lib/modulefinder.py

This module provides a *ModuleFinder* class that can be used to determine the set of modules imported by a script. `modulefinder.py` can also be run as a script, giving the filename of a Python script as its argument, after which a report of the imported modules will be printed.

modulefinder.**AddPackagePath**(*pkg_name*, *path*)
> Record that the package named *pkg_name* can be found in the specified *path*.

modulefinder.**ReplacePackage**(*oldname*, *newname*)
> Allows specifying that the module named *oldname* is in fact the package named *newname*.

class modulefinder.**ModuleFinder**(*path=None*, *debug=0*, *excludes=[]*, *replace_paths=[]*)
> This class provides *run_script()* and *report()* methods to determine the set of modules imported by a script. *path* can be a list of directories to search for modules; if not specified, `sys.path` is used. *debug* sets the debugging level; higher values make the class print debugging messages about what it's doing. *excludes* is a list of module names to exclude from the analysis. *replace_paths* is a list of (`oldpath`, `newpath`) tuples that will be replaced in module paths.
>
> **report**()
> > Print a report to standard output that lists the modules imported by the script and their paths, as well as modules that are missing or seem to be missing.
>
> **run_script**(*pathname*)
> > Analyze the contents of the *pathname* file, which must contain Python code.
>
> **modules**
> > A dictionary mapping module names to modules. See *Example usage of ModuleFinder*.

31.3.1 Example usage of `ModuleFinder`

The script that is going to get analyzed later on (bacon.py):

```
import re, itertools

try:
    import baconhameggs
except ImportError:
    pass

try:
    import guido.python.ham
except ImportError:
    pass
```

The script that will output the report of bacon.py:

```
from modulefinder import ModuleFinder

finder = ModuleFinder()
finder.run_script('bacon.py')

print('Loaded modules:')
for name, mod in finder.modules.items():
    print('%s: ' % name, end='')
    print(','.join(list(mod.globalnames.keys())[:3]))

print('-'*50)
print('Modules not imported:')
print('\n'.join(finder.badmodules.keys()))
```

Sample output (may vary depending on the architecture):

```
Loaded modules:
_types:
copyreg:  _inverted_registry,_slotnames,__all__
sre_compile:  isstring,_sre,_optimize_unicode
_sre:
sre_constants:  REPEAT_ONE,makedict,AT_END_LINE
sys:
re:  __module__,finditer,_expand
itertools:
__main__:  re,itertools,baconhameggs
sre_parse:  _PATTERNENDERS,SRE_FLAG_UNICODE
array:
types:  __module__,IntType,TypeType
------------------------------------------------
Modules not imported:
guido.python.ham
baconhameggs
```

31.4 runpy — Locating and executing Python modules

Source code: Lib/runpy.py

The *runpy* module is used to locate and run Python modules without importing them first. Its main use is to implement the -m command line switch that allows scripts to be located using the Python module namespace rather than the filesystem.

Note that this is *not* a sandbox module - all code is executed in the current process, and any side effects (such as cached imports of other modules) will remain in place after the functions have returned.

Furthermore, any functions and classes defined by the executed code are not guaranteed to work correctly after a *runpy* function has returned. If that limitation is not acceptable for a given use case, *importlib* is likely to be a more suitable choice than this module.

The *runpy* module provides two functions:

runpy.run_module(*mod_name, init_globals=None, run_name=None, alter_sys=False*)

Execute the code of the specified module and return the resulting module globals dictionary. The module's code is first located using the standard import mechanism (refer to PEP 302 for details) and then executed in a fresh module namespace.

The *mod_name* argument should be an absolute module name. If the module name refers to a package rather than a normal module, then that package is imported and the __main__ submodule within that package is then executed and the resulting module globals dictionary returned.

The optional dictionary argument *init_globals* may be used to pre-populate the module's globals dictionary before the code is executed. The supplied dictionary will not be modified. If any of the special global variables below are defined in the supplied dictionary, those definitions are overridden by *run_module()*.

The special global variables __name__, __spec__, __file__, __cached__, __loader__ and __package__ are set in the globals dictionary before the module code is executed (Note that this is a minimal set of variables - other variables may be set implicitly as an interpreter implementation detail).

`__name__` is set to *run_name* if this optional argument is not *None*, to `mod_name + '.__main__'` if the named module is a package and to the *mod_name* argument otherwise.

`__spec__` will be set appropriately for the *actually* imported module (that is, `__spec__.name` will always be *mod_name* or `mod_name + '.__main__'`, never *run_name*).

`__file__`, `__cached__`, `__loader__` and `__package__` are set as normal based on the module spec.

If the argument *alter_sys* is supplied and evaluates to *True*, then `sys.argv[0]` is updated with the value of `__file__` and `sys.modules[__name__]` is updated with a temporary module object for the module being executed. Both `sys.argv[0]` and `sys.modules[__name__]` are restored to their original values before the function returns.

Note that this manipulation of *sys* is not thread-safe. Other threads may see the partially initialised module, as well as the altered list of arguments. It is recommended that the *sys* module be left alone when invoking this function from threaded code.

See also:

The -m option offering equivalent functionality from the command line.

Changed in version 3.1: Added ability to execute packages by looking for a `__main__` submodule.

Changed in version 3.2: Added `__cached__` global variable (see PEP 3147).

Changed in version 3.4: Updated to take advantage of the module spec feature added by PEP 451. This allows `__cached__` to be set correctly for modules run this way, as well as ensuring the real module name is always accessible as `__spec__.name`.

`runpy.run_path`(*file_path*, *init_globals=None*, *run_name=None*)

Execute the code at the named filesystem location and return the resulting module globals dictionary. As with a script name supplied to the CPython command line, the supplied path may refer to a Python source file, a compiled bytecode file or a valid sys.path entry containing a `__main__` module (e.g. a zipfile containing a top-level `__main__.py` file).

For a simple script, the specified code is simply executed in a fresh module namespace. For a valid sys.path entry (typically a zipfile or directory), the entry is first added to the beginning of `sys.path`. The function then looks for and executes a *__main__* module using the updated path. Note that there is no special protection against invoking an existing *__main__* entry located elsewhere on `sys.path` if there is no such module at the specified location.

The optional dictionary argument *init_globals* may be used to pre-populate the module's globals dictionary before the code is executed. The supplied dictionary will not be modified. If any of the special global variables below are defined in the supplied dictionary, those definitions are overridden by *run_path()*.

The special global variables `__name__`, `__spec__`, `__file__`, `__cached__`, `__loader__` and `__package__` are set in the globals dictionary before the module code is executed (Note that this is a minimal set of variables - other variables may be set implicitly as an interpreter implementation detail).

`__name__` is set to *run_name* if this optional argument is not *None* and to `'<run_path>'` otherwise.

If the supplied path directly references a script file (whether as source or as precompiled byte code), then `__file__` will be set to the supplied path, and `__spec__`, `__cached__`, `__loader__` and `__package__` will all be set to *None*.

If the supplied path is a reference to a valid sys.path entry, then `__spec__` will be set appropriately for the imported `__main__` module (that is, `__spec__.name` will always be `__main__`). `__file__`, `__cached__`, `__loader__` and `__package__` will be set as normal based on the module spec.

A number of alterations are also made to the *sys* module. Firstly, `sys.path` may be altered as described above. `sys.argv[0]` is updated with the value of `file_path` and `sys.modules[__name__]` is updated with a temporary module object for the module being executed. All modifications to items in *sys* are reverted before the function returns.

Note that, unlike *run_module()*, the alterations made to *sys* are not optional in this function as these adjustments are essential to allowing the execution of sys.path entries. As the thread-safety limitations still apply, use of this function in threaded code should be either serialised with the import lock or delegated to a separate process.

See also:

using-on-interface-options for equivalent functionality on the command line (`python path/to/script`).

New in version 3.2.

Changed in version 3.4: Updated to take advantage of the module spec feature added by PEP 451. This allows __cached__ to be set correctly in the case where __main__ is imported from a valid sys.path entry rather than being executed directly.

See also:

PEP 338 – **Executing modules as scripts** PEP written and implemented by Nick Coghlan.

PEP 366 – **Main module explicit relative imports** PEP written and implemented by Nick Coghlan.

PEP 451 – **A ModuleSpec Type for the Import System** PEP written and implemented by Eric Snow

using-on-general - CPython command line details

The *importlib.import_module()* function

31.5 `importlib` — The implementation of `import`

New in version 3.1.

Source code: Lib/importlib/__init__.py

31.5.1 Introduction

The purpose of the *importlib* package is two-fold. One is to provide the implementation of the `import` statement (and thus, by extension, the *__import__()* function) in Python source code. This provides an implementation of `import` which is portable to any Python interpreter. This also provides an implementation which is easier to comprehend than one implemented in a programming language other than Python.

Two, the components to implement `import` are exposed in this package, making it easier for users to create their own custom objects (known generically as an *importer*) to participate in the import process.

See also:

import The language reference for the `import` statement.

Packages specification Original specification of packages. Some semantics have changed since the writing of this document (e.g. redirecting based on `None` in *sys.modules*).

The *__import__()* **function** The `import` statement is syntactic sugar for this function.

PEP 235 Import on Case-Insensitive Platforms

PEP 263 Defining Python Source Code Encodings

PEP 302 New Import Hooks

PEP 328 Imports: Multi-Line and Absolute/Relative

PEP 366 Main module explicit relative imports

PEP 420 Implicit namespace packages

PEP 451 A ModuleSpec Type for the Import System

PEP 488 Elimination of PYO files

PEP 489 Multi-phase extension module initialization

PEP 3120 Using UTF-8 as the Default Source Encoding

PEP 3147 PYC Repository Directories

31.5.2 Functions

importlib.__import__(*name, globals=None, locals=None, fromlist=(), level=0*)
    An implementation of the built-in __import__() function.

> **Note:** Programmatic importing of modules should use import_module() instead of this function.

importlib.import_module(*name, package=None*)
    Import a module. The *name* argument specifies what module to import in absolute or relative terms (e.g. either pkg.mod or ..mod). If the name is specified in relative terms, then the *package* argument must be set to the name of the package which is to act as the anchor for resolving the package name (e.g. import_module('..mod', 'pkg.subpkg') will import pkg.mod).

    The import_module() function acts as a simplifying wrapper around importlib.__import__(). This means all semantics of the function are derived from importlib.__import__(). The most important difference between these two functions is that import_module() returns the specified package or module (e.g. pkg.mod), while __import__() returns the top-level package or module (e.g. pkg).

    If you are dynamically importing a module that was created since the interpreter began execution (e.g., created a Python source file), you may need to call invalidate_caches() in order for the new module to be noticed by the import system.

    Changed in version 3.3: Parent packages are automatically imported.

importlib.find_loader(*name, path=None*)
    Find the loader for a module, optionally within the specified *path*. If the module is in sys.modules, then sys.modules[name].__loader__ is returned (unless the loader would be None or is not set, in which case ValueError is raised). Otherwise a search using sys.meta_path is done. None is returned if no loader is found.

    A dotted name does not have its parents implicitly imported as that requires loading them and that may not be desired. To properly import a submodule you will need to import all parent packages of the submodule and use the correct argument to *path*.

    New in version 3.3.

    Changed in version 3.4: If __loader__ is not set, raise ValueError, just like when the attribute is set to None.

    Deprecated since version 3.4: Use importlib.util.find_spec() instead.

importlib.invalidate_caches()
    Invalidate the internal caches of finders stored at sys.meta_path. If a finder implements invalidate_caches() then it will be called to perform the invalidation. This function should be called if any modules are created/installed while your program is running to guarantee all finders will notice the new module's existence.

New in version 3.3.

importlib.reload(*module*)

Reload a previously imported *module*. The argument must be a module object, so it must have been successfully imported before. This is useful if you have edited the module source file using an external editor and want to try out the new version without leaving the Python interpreter. The return value is the module object (which can be different if re-importing causes a different object to be placed in *sys.modules*).

When *reload()* is executed:

- Python module's code is recompiled and the module-level code re-executed, defining a new set of objects which are bound to names in the module's dictionary by reusing the *loader* which originally loaded the module. The `init` function of extension modules is not called a second time.
- As with all other objects in Python the old objects are only reclaimed after their reference counts drop to zero.
- The names in the module namespace are updated to point to any new or changed objects.
- Other references to the old objects (such as names external to the module) are not rebound to refer to the new objects and must be updated in each namespace where they occur if that is desired.

There are a number of other caveats:

When a module is reloaded, its dictionary (containing the module's global variables) is retained. Redefinitions of names will override the old definitions, so this is generally not a problem. If the new version of a module does not define a name that was defined by the old version, the old definition remains. This feature can be used to the module's advantage if it maintains a global table or cache of objects — with a `try` statement it can test for the table's presence and skip its initialization if desired:

```
try:
    cache
except NameError:
    cache = {}
```

It is generally not very useful to reload built-in or dynamically loaded modules. Reloading *sys*, *__main__*, *builtins* and other key modules is not recommended. In many cases extension modules are not designed to be initialized more than once, and may fail in arbitrary ways when reloaded.

If a module imports objects from another module using **from** ... **import** ..., calling *reload()* for the other module does not redefine the objects imported from it — one way around this is to re-execute the **from** statement, another is to use **import** and qualified names (*module.name*) instead.

If a module instantiates instances of a class, reloading the module that defines the class does not affect the method definitions of the instances — they continue to use the old class definition. The same is true for derived classes.

New in version 3.4.

31.5.3 `importlib.abc` – Abstract base classes related to import

Source code: Lib/importlib/abc.py

The *importlib.abc* module contains all of the core abstract base classes used by **import**. Some subclasses of the core abstract base classes are also provided to help in implementing the core ABCs.

ABC hierarchy:

```
object
 +-- Finder (deprecated)
 |    +-- MetaPathFinder
 |    +-- PathEntryFinder
 +-- Loader
      +-- ResourceLoader --------+
      +-- InspectLoader          |
           +-- ExecutionLoader --+
                                 +-- FileLoader
                                 +-- SourceLoader
```

class importlib.abc.Finder

An abstract base class representing a *finder*.

Deprecated since version 3.3: Use `MetaPathFinder` or `PathEntryFinder` instead.

abstractmethod find_module(*fullname, path=None*)

An abstact method for finding a *loader* for the specified module. Originally specified in PEP 302, this method was meant for use in `sys.meta_path` and in the path-based import subsystem.

Changed in version 3.4: Returns `None` when called instead of raising `NotImplementedError`.

class importlib.abc.MetaPathFinder

An abstract base class representing a *meta path finder*. For compatibility, this is a subclass of `Finder`.

New in version 3.3.

find_spec(*fullname, path, target=None*)

An abstract method for finding a *spec* for the specified module. If this is a top-level import, *path* will be `None`. Otherwise, this is a search for a subpackage or module and *path* will be the value of `__path__` from the parent package. If a spec cannot be found, `None` is returned. When passed in, `target` is a module object that the finder may use to make a more educated guess about what spec to return.

New in version 3.4.

find_module(*fullname, path*)

A legacy method for finding a *loader* for the specified module. If this is a top-level import, *path* will be `None`. Otherwise, this is a search for a subpackage or module and *path* will be the value of `__path__` from the parent package. If a loader cannot be found, `None` is returned.

If `find_spec()` is defined, backwards-compatible functionality is provided.

Changed in version 3.4: Returns `None` when called instead of raising `NotImplementedError`. Can use `find_spec()` to provide functionality.

Deprecated since version 3.4: Use `find_spec()` instead.

invalidate_caches()

An optional method which, when called, should invalidate any internal cache used by the finder. Used by `importlib.invalidate_caches()` when invalidating the caches of all finders on `sys.meta_path`.

Changed in version 3.4: Returns `None` when called instead of `NotImplemented`.

class importlib.abc.PathEntryFinder

An abstract base class representing a *path entry finder*. Though it bears some similarities to `MetaPathFinder`, `PathEntryFinder` is meant for use only within the path-based import subsystem provided by `PathFinder`. This ABC is a subclass of `Finder` for compatibility reasons only.

New in version 3.3.

find_spec(*fullname, target=None*)

An abstract method for finding a *spec* for the specified module. The finder will search for the module only within the *path entry* to which it is assigned. If a spec cannot be found, None is returned. When passed in, target is a module object that the finder may use to make a more educated guess about what spec to return.

New in version 3.4.

find_loader(*fullname*)

A legacy method for finding a *loader* for the specified module. Returns a 2-tuple of (loader, portion) where portion is a sequence of file system locations contributing to part of a namespace package. The loader may be None while specifying portion to signify the contribution of the file system locations to a namespace package. An empty list can be used for portion to signify the loader is not part of a namespace package. If loader is None and portion is the empty list then no loader or location for a namespace package were found (i.e. failure to find anything for the module).

If *find_spec()* is defined then backwards-compatible functionality is provided.

Changed in version 3.4: Returns (None, []) instead of raising NotImplementedError. Uses *find_spec()* when available to provide functionality.

Deprecated since version 3.4: Use *find_spec()* instead.

find_module(*fullname*)

A concrete implementation of *Finder.find_module()* which is equivalent to self.find_loader(fullname)[0].

Deprecated since version 3.4: Use *find_spec()* instead.

invalidate_caches()

An optional method which, when called, should invalidate any internal cache used by the finder. Used by PathFinder.invalidate_caches() when invalidating the caches of all cached finders.

class importlib.abc.Loader

An abstract base class for a *loader*. See PEP 302 for the exact definition for a loader.

create_module(*spec*)

A method that returns the module object to use when importing a module. This method may return None, indicating that default module creation semantics should take place.

New in version 3.4.

Changed in version 3.5: Starting in Python 3.6, this method will not be optional when *exec_module()* is defined.

exec_module(*module*)

An abstract method that executes the module in its own namespace when a module is imported or reloaded. The module should already be initialized when exec_module() is called. When this method exists, *create_module()* must be defined.

New in version 3.4.

Changed in version 3.6: *create_module()* must also be defined.

load_module(*fullname*)

A legacy method for loading a module. If the module cannot be loaded, *ImportError* is raised, otherwise the loaded module is returned.

If the requested module already exists in *sys.modules*, that module should be used and reloaded. Otherwise the loader should create a new module and insert it into *sys.modules* before any loading begins, to prevent recursion from the import. If the loader inserted a module and the load fails, it must be removed by the loader from *sys.modules*; modules already in *sys.modules* before the loader began execution should be left alone (see *importlib.util.module_for_loader()*).

The loader should set several attributes on the module. (Note that some of these attributes can change when a module is reloaded):

- `__name__` The name of the module.
- `__file__` The path to where the module data is stored (not set for built-in modules).
- `__cached__` The path to where a compiled version of the module is/should be stored (not set when the attribute would be inappropriate).
- `__path__` A list of strings specifying the search path within a package. This attribute is not set on modules.
- `__package__` The parent package for the module/package. If the module is top-level then it has a value of the empty string. The *importlib.util.module_for_loader()* decorator can handle the details for `__package__`.
- `__loader__` The loader used to load the module. The *importlib.util.module_for_loader()* decorator can handle the details for `__package__`.

When *exec_module()* is available then backwards-compatible functionality is provided.

Changed in version 3.4: Raise *ImportError* when called instead of *NotImplementedError*. Functionality provided when *exec_module()* is available.

Deprecated since version 3.4: The recommended API for loading a module is *exec_module()* (and *create_module()*). Loaders should implement it instead of load_module(). The import machinery takes care of all the other responsibilities of load_module() when exec_module() is implemented.

module_repr(*module*)

A legacy method which when implemented calculates and returns the given module's repr, as a string. The module type's default repr() will use the result of this method as appropriate.

New in version 3.3.

Changed in version 3.4: Made optional instead of an abstractmethod.

Deprecated since version 3.4: The import machinery now takes care of this automatically.

class importlib.abc.ResourceLoader

An abstract base class for a *loader* which implements the optional PEP 302 protocol for loading arbitrary resources from the storage back-end.

abstractmethod get_data(*path*)

An abstract method to return the bytes for the data located at *path*. Loaders that have a file-like storage back-end that allows storing arbitrary data can implement this abstract method to give direct access to the data stored. *OSError* is to be raised if the *path* cannot be found. The *path* is expected to be constructed using a module's `__file__` attribute or an item from a package's `__path__`.

Changed in version 3.4: Raises *OSError* instead of *NotImplementedError*.

class importlib.abc.InspectLoader

An abstract base class for a *loader* which implements the optional PEP 302 protocol for loaders that inspect modules.

get_code(*fullname*)

Return the code object for a module, or **None** if the module does not have a code object (as would be the case, for example, for a built-in module). Raise an *ImportError* if loader cannot find the requested module.

> **Note:** While the method has a default implementation, it is suggested that it be overridden if possible for performance.

Changed in version 3.4: No longer abstract and a concrete implementation is provided.

abstractmethod get_source(*fullname*)
: An abstract method to return the source of a module. It is returned as a text string using *universal newlines*, translating all recognized line separators into `'\n'` characters. Returns `None` if no source is available (e.g. a built-in module). Raises `ImportError` if the loader cannot find the module specified.

    Changed in version 3.4: Raises `ImportError` instead of `NotImplementedError`.

is_package(*fullname*)
: An abstract method to return a true value if the module is a package, a false value otherwise. `ImportError` is raised if the *loader* cannot find the module.

    Changed in version 3.4: Raises `ImportError` instead of `NotImplementedError`.

static source_to_code(*data, path='<string>'*)
: Create a code object from Python source.

    The *data* argument can be whatever the `compile()` function supports (i.e. string or bytes). The *path* argument should be the "path" to where the source code originated from, which can be an abstract concept (e.g. location in a zip file).

    With the subsequent code object one can execute it in a module by running `exec(code, module.__dict__)`.

    New in version 3.4.

    Changed in version 3.5: Made the method static.

exec_module(*module*)
: Implementation of `Loader.exec_module()`.

    New in version 3.4.

load_module(*fullname*)
: Implementation of `Loader.load_module()`.

    Deprecated since version 3.4: use `exec_module()` instead.

class importlib.abc.ExecutionLoader
: An abstract base class which inherits from `InspectLoader` that, when implemented, helps a module to be executed as a script. The ABC represents an optional PEP 302 protocol.

    abstractmethod get_filename(*fullname*)
    : An abstract method that is to return the value of `__file__` for the specified module. If no path is available, `ImportError` is raised.

        If source code is available, then the method should return the path to the source file, regardless of whether a bytecode was used to load the module.

        Changed in version 3.4: Raises `ImportError` instead of `NotImplementedError`.

class importlib.abc.FileLoader(*fullname, path*)
: An abstract base class which inherits from `ResourceLoader` and `ExecutionLoader`, providing concrete implementations of `ResourceLoader.get_data()` and `ExecutionLoader.get_filename()`.

    The *fullname* argument is a fully resolved name of the module the loader is to handle. The *path* argument is the path to the file for the module.

    New in version 3.3.

name
    The name of the module the loader can handle.

path
    Path to the file of the module.

load_module(*fullname*)
    Calls super's `load_module()`.

    Deprecated since version 3.4: Use `Loader.exec_module()` instead.

abstractmethod get_filename(*fullname*)
    Returns *path*.

abstractmethod get_data(*path*)
    Reads *path* as a binary file and returns the bytes from it.

class importlib.abc.SourceLoader

An abstract base class for implementing source (and optionally bytecode) file loading. The class inherits from both `ResourceLoader` and `ExecutionLoader`, requiring the implementation of:

- `ResourceLoader.get_data()`
- `ExecutionLoader.get_filename()` Should only return the path to the source file; sourceless loading is not supported.

The abstract methods defined by this class are to add optional bytecode file support. Not implementing these optional methods (or causing them to raise `NotImplementedError`) causes the loader to only work with source code. Implementing the methods allows the loader to work with source *and* bytecode files; it does not allow for *sourceless* loading where only bytecode is provided. Bytecode files are an optimization to speed up loading by removing the parsing step of Python's compiler, and so no bytecode-specific API is exposed.

path_stats(*path*)
    Optional abstract method which returns a `dict` containing metadata about the specified path. Supported dictionary keys are:

- `'mtime'` (mandatory): an integer or floating-point number representing the modification time of the source code;
- `'size'` (optional): the size in bytes of the source code.

Any other keys in the dictionary are ignored, to allow for future extensions. If the path cannot be handled, `OSError` is raised.

New in version 3.3.

Changed in version 3.4: Raise `OSError` instead of `NotImplementedError`.

path_mtime(*path*)
    Optional abstract method which returns the modification time for the specified path.

Deprecated since version 3.3: This method is deprecated in favour of `path_stats()`. You don't have to implement it, but it is still available for compatibility purposes. Raise `OSError` if the path cannot be handled.

Changed in version 3.4: Raise `OSError` instead of `NotImplementedError`.

set_data(*path*, *data*)
    Optional abstract method which writes the specified bytes to a file path. Any intermediate directories which do not exist are to be created automatically.

When writing to the path fails because the path is read-only (`errno.EACCES`/`PermissionError`), do not propagate the exception.

Changed in version 3.4: No longer raises `NotImplementedError` when called.

get_code(*fullname*)
    Concrete implementation of `InspectLoader.get_code()`.

exec_module(*module*)
    Concrete implementation of `Loader.exec_module()`.

    New in version 3.4.

load_module(*fullname*)
    Concrete implementation of `Loader.load_module()`.

    Deprecated since version 3.4: Use `exec_module()` instead.

get_source(*fullname*)
    Concrete implementation of `InspectLoader.get_source()`.

is_package(*fullname*)
    Concrete implementation of `InspectLoader.is_package()`. A module is determined to be a package if its file path (as provided by `ExecutionLoader.get_filename()`) is a file named `__init__` when the file extension is removed **and** the module name itself does not end in `__init__`.

31.5.4 importlib.machinery – Importers and path hooks

Source code: Lib/importlib/machinery.py

This module contains the various objects that help `import` find and load modules.

importlib.machinery.SOURCE_SUFFIXES
    A list of strings representing the recognized file suffixes for source modules.

    New in version 3.3.

importlib.machinery.DEBUG_BYTECODE_SUFFIXES
    A list of strings representing the file suffixes for non-optimized bytecode modules.

    New in version 3.3.

    Deprecated since version 3.5: Use `BYTECODE_SUFFIXES` instead.

importlib.machinery.OPTIMIZED_BYTECODE_SUFFIXES
    A list of strings representing the file suffixes for optimized bytecode modules.

    New in version 3.3.

    Deprecated since version 3.5: Use `BYTECODE_SUFFIXES` instead.

importlib.machinery.BYTECODE_SUFFIXES
    A list of strings representing the recognized file suffixes for bytecode modules (including the leading dot).

    New in version 3.3.

    Changed in version 3.5: The value is no longer dependent on `__debug__`.

importlib.machinery.EXTENSION_SUFFIXES
    A list of strings representing the recognized file suffixes for extension modules.

    New in version 3.3.

importlib.machinery.all_suffixes()
    Returns a combined list of strings representing all file suffixes for modules recognized by the standard import machinery. This is a helper for code which simply needs to know if a filesystem path potentially refers to a module without needing any details on the kind of module (for example, `inspect.getmodulename()`).

New in version 3.3.

class importlib.machinery.BuiltinImporter
An *importer* for built-in modules. All known built-in modules are listed in `sys.builtin_module_names`. This class implements the *importlib.abc.MetaPathFinder* and *importlib.abc.InspectLoader* ABCs.

Only class methods are defined by this class to alleviate the need for instantiation.

Changed in version 3.5: As part of PEP 489, the builtin importer now implements `Loader.create_module()` and `Loader.exec_module()`

class importlib.machinery.FrozenImporter
An *importer* for frozen modules. This class implements the *importlib.abc.MetaPathFinder* and *importlib.abc.InspectLoader* ABCs.

Only class methods are defined by this class to alleviate the need for instantiation.

class importlib.machinery.WindowsRegistryFinder
Finder for modules declared in the Windows registry. This class implements the *importlib.abc.Finder* ABC.

Only class methods are defined by this class to alleviate the need for instantiation.

New in version 3.3.

Deprecated since version 3.6: Use `site` configuration instead. Future versions of Python may not enable this finder by default.

class importlib.machinery.PathFinder
A *Finder* for `sys.path` and package `__path__` attributes. This class implements the *importlib.abc.MetaPathFinder* ABC.

Only class methods are defined by this class to alleviate the need for instantiation.

classmethod find_spec(*fullname, path=None, target=None*)
Class method that attempts to find a *spec* for the module specified by *fullname* on `sys.path` or, if defined, on *path*. For each path entry that is searched, `sys.path_importer_cache` is checked. If a non-false object is found then it is used as the *path entry finder* to look for the module being searched for. If no entry is found in `sys.path_importer_cache`, then `sys.path_hooks` is searched for a finder for the path entry and, if found, is stored in `sys.path_importer_cache` along with being queried about the module. If no finder is ever found then **None** is both stored in the cache and returned.

New in version 3.4.

Changed in version 3.5: If the current working directory – represented by an empty string – is no longer valid then **None** is returned but no value is cached in `sys.path_importer_cache`.

classmethod find_module(*fullname, path=None*)
A legacy wrapper around `find_spec()`.

Deprecated since version 3.4: Use `find_spec()` instead.

classmethod invalidate_caches()
Calls *importlib.abc.PathEntryFinder.invalidate_caches()* on all finders stored in `sys.path_importer_cache`.

Changed in version 3.4: Calls objects in `sys.path_hooks` with the current working directory for `''` (i.e. the empty string).

class importlib.machinery.FileFinder(*path, *loader_details*)
A concrete implementation of *importlib.abc.PathEntryFinder* which caches results from the file system.

The *path* argument is the directory for which the finder is in charge of searching.

The *loader_details* argument is a variable number of 2-item tuples each containing a loader and a sequence of file suffixes the loader recognizes. The loaders are expected to be callables which accept two arguments of the module's name and the path to the file found.

The finder will cache the directory contents as necessary, making stat calls for each module search to verify the cache is not outdated. Because cache staleness relies upon the granularity of the operating system's state information of the file system, there is a potential race condition of searching for a module, creating a new file, and then searching for the module the new file represents. If the operations happen fast enough to fit within the granularity of stat calls, then the module search will fail. To prevent this from happening, when you create a module dynamically, make sure to call *importlib.invalidate_caches()*.

New in version 3.3.

path
: The path the finder will search in.

find_spec(*fullname, target=None*)
: Attempt to find the spec to handle *fullname* within *path*.

  New in version 3.4.

find_loader(*fullname*)
: Attempt to find the loader to handle *fullname* within *path*.

invalidate_caches()
: Clear out the internal cache.

classmethod path_hook(**loader_details*)
: A class method which returns a closure for use on *sys.path_hooks*. An instance of *FileFinder* is returned by the closure using the path argument given to the closure directly and *loader_details* indirectly.

  If the argument to the closure is not an existing directory, *ImportError* is raised.

class importlib.machinery.SourceFileLoader(*fullname, path*)
: A concrete implementation of *importlib.abc.SourceLoader* by subclassing *importlib.abc.FileLoader* and providing some concrete implementations of other methods.

  New in version 3.3.

  name
  : The name of the module that this loader will handle.

  path
  : The path to the source file.

  is_package(*fullname*)
  : Return true if *path* appears to be for a package.

  path_stats(*path*)
  : Concrete implementation of *importlib.abc.SourceLoader.path_stats()*.

  set_data(*path, data*)
  : Concrete implementation of *importlib.abc.SourceLoader.set_data()*.

  load_module(*name=None*)
  : Concrete implementation of *importlib.abc.Loader.load_module()* where specifying the name of the module to load is optional.

    Deprecated since version 3.6: Use *importlib.abc.Loader.exec_module()* instead.

class importlib.machinery.SourcelessFileLoader(*fullname, path*)
: A concrete implementation of *importlib.abc.FileLoader* which can import bytecode files (i.e. no source code files exist).

Please note that direct use of bytecode files (and thus not source code files) inhibits your modules from being usable by all Python implementations or new versions of Python which change the bytecode format.

New in version 3.3.

name
    The name of the module the loader will handle.

path
    The path to the bytecode file.

is_package(*fullname*)
    Determines if the module is a package based on *path*.

get_code(*fullname*)
    Returns the code object for *name* created from *path*.

get_source(*fullname*)
    Returns None as bytecode files have no source when this loader is used.

load_module(*name=None*)

Concrete implementation of *importlib.abc.Loader.load_module()* where specifying the name of the module to load is optional.

Deprecated since version 3.6: Use *importlib.abc.Loader.exec_module()* instead.

class importlib.machinery.ExtensionFileLoader(*fullname*, *path*)
    A concrete implementation of *importlib.abc.ExecutionLoader* for extension modules.

The *fullname* argument specifies the name of the module the loader is to support. The *path* argument is the path to the extension module's file.

New in version 3.3.

name
    Name of the module the loader supports.

path
    Path to the extension module.

create_module(*spec*)
    Creates the module object from the given specification in accordance with PEP 489.

    New in version 3.5.

exec_module(*module*)
    Initializes the given module object in accordance with PEP 489.

    New in version 3.5.

is_package(*fullname*)
    Returns True if the file path points to a package's __init__ module based on *EXTENSION_SUFFIXES*.

get_code(*fullname*)
    Returns None as extension modules lack a code object.

get_source(*fullname*)
    Returns None as extension modules do not have source code.

get_filename(*fullname*)
    Returns *path*.

    New in version 3.4.

class importlib.machinery.ModuleSpec(*name, loader, *, origin=None, loader_state=None, is_package=None*)

A specification for a module's import-system-related state. This is typically exposed as the module's `__spec__` attribute. In the descriptions below, the names in parentheses give the corresponding attribute available directly on the module object. E.g. `module.__spec__.origin == module.__file__`. Note however that while the *values* are usually equivalent, they can differ since there is no synchronization between the two objects. Thus it is possible to update the module's `__path__` at runtime, and this will not be automatically reflected in `__spec__.submodule_search_locations`.

New in version 3.4.

name

(`__name__`)

A string for the fully-qualified name of the module.

loader

(`__loader__`)

The loader to use for loading. For namespace packages this should be set to `None`.

origin

(`__file__`)

Name of the place from which the module is loaded, e.g. "builtin" for built-in modules and the filename for modules loaded from source. Normally "origin" should be set, but it may be `None` (the default) which indicates it is unspecified.

submodule_search_locations

(`__path__`)

List of strings for where to find submodules, if a package (`None` otherwise).

loader_state

Container of extra module-specific data for use during loading (or `None`).

cached

(`__cached__`)

String for where the compiled module should be stored (or `None`).

parent

(`__package__`)

(Read-only) Fully-qualified name of the package to which the module belongs as a submodule (or `None`).

has_location

Boolean indicating whether or not the module's "origin" attribute refers to a loadable location.

31.5.5 importlib.util – Utility code for importers

Source code: Lib/importlib/util.py

This module contains the various objects that help in the construction of an *importer*.

importlib.util.MAGIC_NUMBER
> The bytes which represent the bytecode version number. If you need help with loading/writing bytecode then consider *importlib.abc.SourceLoader*.
>
> New in version 3.4.

importlib.util.cache_from_source(*path*, *debug_override=None*, ***, *optimization=None*)
> Return the PEP 3147/PEP 488 path to the byte-compiled file associated with the source *path*. For example, if *path* is /foo/bar/baz.py the return value would be /foo/bar/__pycache__/baz.cpython-32.pyc for Python 3.2. The cpython-32 string comes from the current magic tag (see get_tag(); if sys.implementation.cache_tag is not defined then *NotImplementedError* will be raised).
>
> The *optimization* parameter is used to specify the optimization level of the bytecode file. An empty string represents no optimization, so /foo/bar/baz.py with an *optimization* of '' will result in a bytecode path of /foo/bar/__pycache__/baz.cpython-32.pyc. None causes the interpreter's optimization level to be used. Any other value's string representation being used, so /foo/bar/baz.py with an *optimization* of 2 will lead to the bytecode path of /foo/bar/__pycache__/baz.cpython-32.opt-2.pyc. The string representation of *optimization* can only be alphanumeric, else *ValueError* is raised.
>
> The *debug_override* parameter is deprecated and can be used to override the system's value for __debug__. A True value is the equivalent of setting *optimization* to the empty string. A False value is the same as setting *optimization* to 1. If both *debug_override* an *optimization* are not None then *TypeError* is raised.
>
> New in version 3.4.
>
> Changed in version 3.5: The *optimization* parameter was added and the *debug_override* parameter was deprecated.
>
> Changed in version 3.6: Accepts a *path-like object*.

importlib.util.source_from_cache(*path*)
> Given the *path* to a PEP 3147 file name, return the associated source code file path. For example, if *path* is /foo/bar/__pycache__/baz.cpython-32.pyc the returned path would be /foo/bar/baz.py. *path* need not exist, however if it does not conform to PEP 3147 or PEP 488 format, a ValueError is raised. If sys.implementation.cache_tag is not defined, *NotImplementedError* is raised.
>
> New in version 3.4.
>
> Changed in version 3.6: Accepts a *path-like object*.

importlib.util.decode_source(*source_bytes*)
> Decode the given bytes representing source code and return it as a string with universal newlines (as required by *importlib.abc.InspectLoader.get_source()*).
>
> New in version 3.4.

importlib.util.resolve_name(*name*, *package*)
> Resolve a relative module name to an absolute one.
>
> If **name** has no leading dots, then **name** is simply returned. This allows for usage such as importlib.util.resolve_name('sys', __package__) without doing a check to see if the **package** argument is needed.
>
> *ValueError* is raised if **name** is a relative module name but package is a false value (e.g. None or the empty string). *ValueError* is also raised a relative name would escape its containing package (e.g. requesting ..bacon from within the **spam** package).
>
> New in version 3.3.

importlib.util.find_spec(*name*, *package=None*)
> Find the *spec* for a module, optionally relative to the specified **package** name. If the module is in *sys.modules*, then sys.modules[name].__spec__ is returned (unless the spec would be None or is

not set, in which case *ValueError* is raised). Otherwise a search using *sys.meta_path* is done. None is returned if no spec is found.

If **name** is for a submodule (contains a dot), the parent module is automatically imported.

name and **package** work the same as for `import_module()`.

New in version 3.4.

importlib.util.**module_from_spec**(*spec*)

Create a new module based on **spec** and *spec.loader.create_module*.

If *spec.loader.create_module* does not return None, then any pre-existing attributes will not be reset. Also, no *AttributeError* will be raised if triggered while accessing **spec** or setting an attribute on the module.

This function is preferred over using *types.ModuleType* to create a new module as **spec** is used to set as many import-controlled attributes on the module as possible.

New in version 3.5.

@importlib.util.**module_for_loader**

A *decorator* for *importlib.abc.Loader.load_module()* to handle selecting the proper module object to load with. The decorated method is expected to have a call signature taking two positional arguments (e.g. `load_module(self, module)`) for which the second argument will be the module **object** to be used by the loader. Note that the decorator will not work on static methods because of the assumption of two arguments.

The decorated method will take in the **name** of the module to be loaded as expected for a *loader*. If the module is not found in *sys.modules* then a new one is constructed. Regardless of where the module came from, `__loader__` set to **self** and `__package__` is set based on what *importlib.abc.InspectLoader.is_package()* returns (if available). These attributes are set unconditionally to support reloading.

If an exception is raised by the decorated method and a module was added to *sys.modules*, then the module will be removed to prevent a partially initialized module from being in left in *sys.modules*. If the module was already in *sys.modules* then it is left alone.

Changed in version 3.3: `__loader__` and `__package__` are automatically set (when possible).

Changed in version 3.4: Set `__name__`, `__loader__` `__package__` unconditionally to support reloading.

Deprecated since version 3.4: The import machinery now directly performs all the functionality provided by this function.

@importlib.util.**set_loader**

A *decorator* for *importlib.abc.Loader.load_module()* to set the `__loader__` attribute on the returned module. If the attribute is already set the decorator does nothing. It is assumed that the first positional argument to the wrapped method (i.e. **self**) is what `__loader__` should be set to.

Changed in version 3.4: Set `__loader__` if set to None, as if the attribute does not exist.

Deprecated since version 3.4: The import machinery takes care of this automatically.

@importlib.util.**set_package**

A *decorator* for *importlib.abc.Loader.load_module()* to set the `__package__` attribute on the returned module. If `__package__` is set and has a value other than None it will not be changed.

Deprecated since version 3.4: The import machinery takes care of this automatically.

importlib.util.**spec_from_loader**(*name*, *loader*, ***, *origin=None*, *is_package=None*)

A factory function for creating a `ModuleSpec` instance based on a loader. The parameters have the same meaning as they do for ModuleSpec. The function uses available *loader* APIs, such as `InspectLoader.is_package()`, to fill in any missing information on the spec.

New in version 3.4.

importlib.util.spec_from_file_location(*name, location, *, loader=None, submodule_search_locations=None*)

A factory function for creating a `ModuleSpec` instance based on the path to a file. Missing information will be filled in on the spec by making use of loader APIs and by the implication that the module will be file-based.

New in version 3.4.

Changed in version 3.6: Accepts a *path-like object*.

class importlib.util.LazyLoader(*loader*)

A class which postpones the execution of the loader of a module until the module has an attribute accessed.

This class **only** works with loaders that define *exec_module()* as control over what module type is used for the module is required. For those same reasons, the loader's *create_module()* method must return `None` or a type for which its `__class__` attribute can be mutated along with not using *slots*. Finally, modules which substitute the object placed into *sys.modules* will not work as there is no way to properly replace the module references throughout the interpreter safely; *ValueError* is raised if such a substitution is detected.

> **Note:** For projects where startup time is critical, this class allows for potentially minimizing the cost of loading a module if it is never used. For projects where startup time is not essential then use of this class is **heavily** discouraged due to error messages created during loading being postponed and thus occurring out of context.

New in version 3.5.

Changed in version 3.6: Began calling *create_module()*, removing the compatibility warning for *importlib.machinery.BuiltinImporter* and *importlib.machinery.ExtensionFileLoader*.

classmethod factory(*loader*)

A static method which returns a callable that creates a lazy loader. This is meant to be used in situations where the loader is passed by class instead of by instance.

```
suffixes = importlib.machinery.SOURCE_SUFFIXES
loader = importlib.machinery.SourceFileLoader
lazy_loader = importlib.util.LazyLoader.factory(loader)
finder = importlib.machinery.FileFinder(path, (lazy_loader, suffixes))
```

31.5.6 Examples

Importing programmatically

To programmatically import a module, use *importlib.import_module()*.

```
import importlib

itertools = importlib.import_module('itertools')
```

Checking if a module can be imported

If you need to find out if a module can be imported without actually doing the import, then you should use *importlib.util.find_spec()*.

```python
import importlib.util
import sys

# For illustrative purposes.
name = 'itertools'

spec = importlib.util.find_spec(name)
if spec is None:
    print("can't find the itertools module")
else:
    # If you chose to perform the actual import ...
    module = importlib.util.module_from_spec(spec)
    spec.loader.exec_module(module)
    # Adding the module to sys.modules is optional.
    sys.modules[name] = module
```

Importing a source file directly

To import a Python source file directly, use the following recipe (Python 3.4 and newer only):

```python
import importlib.util
import sys

# For illustrative purposes.
import tokenize
file_path = tokenize.__file__
module_name = tokenize.__name__

spec = importlib.util.spec_from_file_location(module_name, file_path)
module = importlib.util.module_from_spec(spec)
spec.loader.exec_module(module)
# Optional; only necessary if you want to be able to import the module
# by name later.
sys.modules[module_name] = module
```

Setting up an importer

For deep customizations of import, you typically want to implement an *importer*. This means managing both the *finder* and *loader* side of things. For finders there are two flavours to choose from depending on your needs: a *meta path finder* or a *path entry finder*. The former is what you would put on `sys.meta_path` while the latter is what you create using a *path entry hook* on `sys.path_hooks` which works with `sys.path` entries to potentially create a finder. This example will show you how to register your own importers so that import will use them (for creating an importer for yourself, read the documentation for the appropriate classes defined within this package):

```python
import importlib.machinery
import sys

# For illustrative purposes only.
SpamMetaPathFinder = importlib.machinery.PathFinder
SpamPathEntryFinder = importlib.machinery.FileFinder
loader_details = (importlib.machinery.SourceFileLoader,
                  importlib.machinery.SOURCE_SUFFIXES)

# Setting up a meta path finder.
```

```
# Make sure to put the finder in the proper location in the list in terms of
# priority.
sys.meta_path.append(SpamMetaPathFinder)

# Setting up a path entry finder.
# Make sure to put the path hook in the proper location in the list in terms
# of priority.
sys.path_hooks.append(SpamPathEntryFinder.path_hook(loader_details))
```

Approximating `importlib.import_module()`

Import itself is implemented in Python code, making it possible to expose most of the import machinery through importlib. The following helps illustrate the various APIs that importlib exposes by providing an approximate implementation of *importlib.import_module()* (Python 3.4 and newer for the importlib usage, Python 3.6 and newer for other parts of the code).

```
import importlib.util
import sys

def import_module(name, package=None):
    """An approximate implementation of import."""
    absolute_name = importlib.util.resolve_name(name, package)
    try:
        return sys.modules[absolute_name]
    except KeyError:
        pass

    path = None
    if '.' in absolute_name:
        parent_name, _, child_name = absolute_name.rpartition('.')
        parent_module = import_module(parent_name)
        path = parent_module.spec.submodule_search_locations
    for finder in sys.meta_path:
        spec = finder.find_spec(absolute_name, path)
        if spec is not None:
            break
    else:
        raise ImportError(f'No module named {absolute_name!r}')
    module = importlib.util.module_from_spec(spec)
    spec.loader.exec_module(module)
    sys.modules[absolute_name] = module
    if path is not None:
        setattr(parent_module, child_name, module)
    return module
```

CHAPTER
THIRTYTWO

PYTHON LANGUAGE SERVICES

Python provides a number of modules to assist in working with the Python language. These modules support tokenizing, parsing, syntax analysis, bytecode disassembly, and various other facilities.

These modules include:

32.1 parser — Access Python parse trees

The *parser* module provides an interface to Python's internal parser and byte-code compiler. The primary purpose for this interface is to allow Python code to edit the parse tree of a Python expression and create executable code from this. This is better than trying to parse and modify an arbitrary Python code fragment as a string because parsing is performed in a manner identical to the code forming the application. It is also faster.

Note: From Python 2.5 onward, it's much more convenient to cut in at the Abstract Syntax Tree (AST) generation and compilation stage, using the *ast* module.

There are a few things to note about this module which are important to making use of the data structures created. This is not a tutorial on editing the parse trees for Python code, but some examples of using the *parser* module are presented.

Most importantly, a good understanding of the Python grammar processed by the internal parser is required. For full information on the language syntax, refer to reference-index. The parser itself is created from a grammar specification defined in the file **Grammar/Grammar** in the standard Python distribution. The parse trees stored in the ST objects created by this module are the actual output from the internal parser when created by the *expr()* or *suite()* functions, described below. The ST objects created by *sequence2st()* faithfully simulate those structures. Be aware that the values of the sequences which are considered "correct" will vary from one version of Python to another as the formal grammar for the language is revised. However, transporting code from one Python version to another as source text will always allow correct parse trees to be created in the target version, with the only restriction being that migrating to an older version of the interpreter will not support more recent language constructs. The parse trees are not typically compatible from one version to another, whereas source code has always been forward-compatible.

Each element of the sequences returned by *st2list()* or *st2tuple()* has a simple form. Sequences representing non-terminal elements in the grammar always have a length greater than one. The first element is an integer which identifies a production in the grammar. These integers are given symbolic names in the C header file **Include/graminit.h** and the Python module *symbol*. Each additional element of the sequence represents a component of the production as recognized in the input string: these are always sequences which have the same form as the parent. An important aspect of this structure which should be noted is that keywords used to identify the parent node type, such as the keyword **if** in an **if_stmt**, are included

in the node tree without any special treatment. For example, the `if` keyword is represented by the tuple
`(1, 'if')`, where `1` is the numeric value associated with all `NAME` tokens, including variable and function
names defined by the user. In an alternate form returned when line number information is requested, the
same token might be represented as `(1, 'if', 12)`, where the `12` represents the line number at which the
terminal symbol was found.

Terminal elements are represented in much the same way, but without any child elements and the addition
of the source text which was identified. The example of the `if` keyword above is representative. The various
types of terminal symbols are defined in the C header file `Include/token.h` and the Python module *token*.

The ST objects are not required to support the functionality of this module, but are provided for three
purposes: to allow an application to amortize the cost of processing complex parse trees, to provide a parse
tree representation which conserves memory space when compared to the Python list or tuple representation,
and to ease the creation of additional modules in C which manipulate parse trees. A simple "wrapper" class
may be created in Python to hide the use of ST objects.

The *parser* module defines functions for a few distinct purposes. The most important purposes are to create
ST objects and to convert ST objects to other representations such as parse trees and compiled code objects,
but there are also functions which serve to query the type of parse tree represented by an ST object.

See also:

Module *symbol* Useful constants representing internal nodes of the parse tree.

Module *token* Useful constants representing leaf nodes of the parse tree and functions for testing node
values.

32.1.1 Creating ST Objects

ST objects may be created from source code or from a parse tree. When creating an ST object from source,
different functions are used to create the `'eval'` and `'exec'` forms.

parser.expr(*source*)

The *expr()* function parses the parameter *source* as if it were an input to `compile(source, 'file.py', 'eval')`. If the parse succeeds, an ST object is created to hold the internal parse tree representation, otherwise an appropriate exception is raised.

parser.suite(*source*)

The *suite()* function parses the parameter *source* as if it were an input to `compile(source, 'file.py', 'exec')`. If the parse succeeds, an ST object is created to hold the internal parse tree representation, otherwise an appropriate exception is raised.

parser.sequence2st(*sequence*)

This function accepts a parse tree represented as a sequence and builds an internal representation if
possible. If it can validate that the tree conforms to the Python grammar and all nodes are valid
node types in the host version of Python, an ST object is created from the internal representation
and returned to the called. If there is a problem creating the internal representation, or if the tree
cannot be validated, a *ParserError* exception is raised. An ST object created this way should not
be assumed to compile correctly; normal exceptions raised by compilation may still be initiated when
the ST object is passed to *compilest()*. This may indicate problems not related to syntax (such as
a *MemoryError* exception), but may also be due to constructs such as the result of parsing `del f(0)`,
which escapes the Python parser but is checked by the bytecode compiler.

Sequences representing terminal tokens may be represented as either two-element lists of the form `(1, 'name')` or as three-element lists of the form `(1, 'name', 56)`. If the third element is present, it is
assumed to be a valid line number. The line number may be specified for any subset of the terminal
symbols in the input tree.

parser.tuple2st(*sequence*)

This is the same function as *sequence2st()*. This entry point is maintained for backward compatibility.

32.1.2 Converting ST Objects

ST objects, regardless of the input used to create them, may be converted to parse trees represented as list- or tuple- trees, or may be compiled into executable code objects. Parse trees may be extracted with or without line numbering information.

parser.st2list(*st, line_info=False, col_info=False*)
> This function accepts an ST object from the caller in *st* and returns a Python list representing the equivalent parse tree. The resulting list representation can be used for inspection or the creation of a new parse tree in list form. This function does not fail so long as memory is available to build the list representation. If the parse tree will only be used for inspection, *st2tuple()* should be used instead to reduce memory consumption and fragmentation. When the list representation is required, this function is significantly faster than retrieving a tuple representation and converting that to nested lists.
>
> If *line_info* is true, line number information will be included for all terminal tokens as a third element of the list representing the token. Note that the line number provided specifies the line on which the token *ends*. This information is omitted if the flag is false or omitted.

parser.st2tuple(*st, line_info=False, col_info=False*)
> This function accepts an ST object from the caller in *st* and returns a Python tuple representing the equivalent parse tree. Other than returning a tuple instead of a list, this function is identical to *st2list()*.
>
> If *line_info* is true, line number information will be included for all terminal tokens as a third element of the list representing the token. This information is omitted if the flag is false or omitted.

parser.compilest(*st, filename='<syntax-tree>'*)
> The Python byte compiler can be invoked on an ST object to produce code objects which can be used as part of a call to the built-in *exec()* or *eval()* functions. This function provides the interface to the compiler, passing the internal parse tree from *st* to the parser, using the source file name specified by the *filename* parameter. The default value supplied for *filename* indicates that the source was an ST object.
>
> Compiling an ST object may result in exceptions related to compilation; an example would be a *SyntaxError* caused by the parse tree for `del f(0)`: this statement is considered legal within the formal grammar for Python but is not a legal language construct. The *SyntaxError* raised for this condition is actually generated by the Python byte-compiler normally, which is why it can be raised at this point by the *parser* module. Most causes of compilation failure can be diagnosed programmatically by inspection of the parse tree.

32.1.3 Queries on ST Objects

Two functions are provided which allow an application to determine if an ST was created as an expression or a suite. Neither of these functions can be used to determine if an ST was created from source code via *expr()* or *suite()* or from a parse tree via *sequence2st()*.

parser.isexpr(*st*)
> When *st* represents an `'eval'` form, this function returns true, otherwise it returns false. This is useful, since code objects normally cannot be queried for this information using existing built-in functions. Note that the code objects created by *compilest()* cannot be queried like this either, and are identical to those created by the built-in *compile()* function.

parser.issuite(*st*)
> This function mirrors *isexpr()* in that it reports whether an ST object represents an `'exec'` form, commonly known as a "suite." It is not safe to assume that this function is equivalent to `not isexpr(st)`, as additional syntactic fragments may be supported in the future.

32.1.4 Exceptions and Error Handling

The parser module defines a single exception, but may also pass other built-in exceptions from other portions of the Python runtime environment. See each function for information about the exceptions it can raise.

exception `parser.ParserError`
> Exception raised when a failure occurs within the parser module. This is generally produced for validation failures rather than the built-in *SyntaxError* raised during normal parsing. The exception argument is either a string describing the reason of the failure or a tuple containing a sequence causing the failure from a parse tree passed to *sequence2st()* and an explanatory string. Calls to *sequence2st()* need to be able to handle either type of exception, while calls to other functions in the module will only need to be aware of the simple string values.

Note that the functions *compilest()*, *expr()*, and *suite()* may raise exceptions which are normally raised by the parsing and compilation process. These include the built in exceptions *MemoryError*, *OverflowError*, *SyntaxError*, and *SystemError*. In these cases, these exceptions carry all the meaning normally associated with them. Refer to the descriptions of each function for detailed information.

32.1.5 ST Objects

Ordered and equality comparisons are supported between ST objects. Pickling of ST objects (using the *pickle* module) is also supported.

parser.STType
> The type of the objects returned by *expr()*, *suite()* and *sequence2st()*.

ST objects have the following methods:

ST.compile(*filename='<syntax-tree>'*)
> Same as `compilest(st, filename)`.

ST.isexpr()
> Same as `isexpr(st)`.

ST.issuite()
> Same as `issuite(st)`.

ST.tolist(*line_info=False, col_info=False*)
> Same as `st2list(st, line_info, col_info)`.

ST.totuple(*line_info=False, col_info=False*)
> Same as `st2tuple(st, line_info, col_info)`.

32.1.6 Example: Emulation of `compile()`

While many useful operations may take place between parsing and bytecode generation, the simplest operation is to do nothing. For this purpose, using the *parser* module to produce an intermediate data structure is equivalent to the code

```
>>> code = compile('a + 5', 'file.py', 'eval')
>>> a = 5
>>> eval(code)
10
```

The equivalent operation using the *parser* module is somewhat longer, and allows the intermediate internal parse tree to be retained as an ST object:

```
>>> import parser
>>> st = parser.expr('a + 5')
>>> code = st.compile('file.py')
>>> a = 5
>>> eval(code)
10
```

An application which needs both ST and code objects can package this code into readily available functions:

```
import parser

def load_suite(source_string):
    st = parser.suite(source_string)
    return st, st.compile()

def load_expression(source_string):
    st = parser.expr(source_string)
    return st, st.compile()
```

32.2 ast — Abstract Syntax Trees

Source code: Lib/ast.py

The `ast` module helps Python applications to process trees of the Python abstract syntax grammar. The abstract syntax itself might change with each Python release; this module helps to find out programmatically what the current grammar looks like.

An abstract syntax tree can be generated by passing `ast.PyCF_ONLY_AST` as a flag to the *compile()* built-in function, or using the *parse()* helper provided in this module. The result will be a tree of objects whose classes all inherit from *ast.AST*. An abstract syntax tree can be compiled into a Python code object using the built-in *compile()* function.

32.2.1 Node classes

class ast.AST

This is the base of all AST node classes. The actual node classes are derived from the `Parser/Python.asdl` file, which is reproduced *below*. They are defined in the `_ast` C module and re-exported in *ast*.

There is one class defined for each left-hand side symbol in the abstract grammar (for example, `ast.stmt` or `ast.expr`). In addition, there is one class defined for each constructor on the right-hand side; these classes inherit from the classes for the left-hand side trees. For example, `ast.BinOp` inherits from `ast.expr`. For production rules with alternatives (aka "sums"), the left-hand side class is abstract: only instances of specific constructor nodes are ever created.

_fields

Each concrete class has an attribute *_fields* which gives the names of all child nodes.

Each instance of a concrete class has one attribute for each child node, of the type as defined in the grammar. For example, `ast.BinOp` instances have an attribute `left` of type `ast.expr`.

If these attributes are marked as optional in the grammar (using a question mark), the value might be `None`. If the attributes can have zero-or-more values (marked with an asterisk), the values are represented as Python lists. All possible attributes must be present and have valid values when compiling an AST with *compile()*.

lineno
col_offset

Instances of `ast.expr` and `ast.stmt` subclasses have *lineno* and *col_offset* attributes. The *lineno* is the line number of source text (1-indexed so the first line is line 1) and the *col_offset* is the UTF-8 byte offset of the first token that generated the node. The UTF-8 offset is recorded because the parser uses UTF-8 internally.

The constructor of a class `ast.T` parses its arguments as follows:

- If there are positional arguments, there must be as many as there are items in `T._fields`; they will be assigned as attributes of these names.
- If there are keyword arguments, they will set the attributes of the same names to the given values.

For example, to create and populate an `ast.UnaryOp` node, you could use

```
node = ast.UnaryOp()
node.op = ast.USub()
node.operand = ast.Num()
node.operand.n = 5
node.operand.lineno = 0
node.operand.col_offset = 0
node.lineno = 0
node.col_offset = 0
```

or the more compact

```
node = ast.UnaryOp(ast.USub(), ast.Num(5, lineno=0, col_offset=0),
                   lineno=0, col_offset=0)
```

32.2.2 Abstract Grammar

The abstract grammar is currently defined as follows:

```
-- ASDL's 7 builtin types are:
-- identifier, int, string, bytes, object, singleton, constant
--
-- singleton: None, True or False
-- constant can be None, whereas None means "no value" for object.

module Python
{
    mod = Module(stmt* body)
        | Interactive(stmt* body)
        | Expression(expr body)

        -- not really an actual node but useful in Jython's typesystem.
        | Suite(stmt* body)

    stmt = FunctionDef(identifier name, arguments args,
                       stmt* body, expr* decorator_list, expr? returns)
         | AsyncFunctionDef(identifier name, arguments args,
                            stmt* body, expr* decorator_list, expr? returns)

         | ClassDef(identifier name,
            expr* bases,
```

```
              keyword* keywords,
              stmt* body,
              expr* decorator_list)
        | Return(expr? value)

        | Delete(expr* targets)
        | Assign(expr* targets, expr value)
        | AugAssign(expr target, operator op, expr value)
        -- 'simple' indicates that we annotate simple name without parens
        | AnnAssign(expr target, expr annotation, expr? value, int simple)

        -- use 'orelse' because else is a keyword in target languages
        | For(expr target, expr iter, stmt* body, stmt* orelse)
        | AsyncFor(expr target, expr iter, stmt* body, stmt* orelse)
        | While(expr test, stmt* body, stmt* orelse)
        | If(expr test, stmt* body, stmt* orelse)
        | With(withitem* items, stmt* body)
        | AsyncWith(withitem* items, stmt* body)

        | Raise(expr? exc, expr? cause)
        | Try(stmt* body, excepthandler* handlers, stmt* orelse, stmt* finalbody)
        | Assert(expr test, expr? msg)

        | Import(alias* names)
        | ImportFrom(identifier? module, alias* names, int? level)

        | Global(identifier* names)
        | Nonlocal(identifier* names)
        | Expr(expr value)
        | Pass | Break | Continue

        -- XXX Jython will be different
        -- col_offset is the byte offset in the utf8 string the parser uses
        attributes (int lineno, int col_offset)

        -- BoolOp() can use left & right?
expr = BoolOp(boolop op, expr* values)
     | BinOp(expr left, operator op, expr right)
     | UnaryOp(unaryop op, expr operand)
     | Lambda(arguments args, expr body)
     | IfExp(expr test, expr body, expr orelse)
     | Dict(expr* keys, expr* values)
     | Set(expr* elts)
     | ListComp(expr elt, comprehension* generators)
     | SetComp(expr elt, comprehension* generators)
     | DictComp(expr key, expr value, comprehension* generators)
     | GeneratorExp(expr elt, comprehension* generators)
     -- the grammar constrains where yield expressions can occur
     | Await(expr value)
     | Yield(expr? value)
     | YieldFrom(expr value)
     -- need sequences for compare to distinguish between
     -- x < 4 < 3 and (x < 4) < 3
     | Compare(expr left, cmpop* ops, expr* comparators)
     | Call(expr func, expr* args, keyword* keywords)
     | Num(object n) -- a number as a PyObject.
     | Str(string s) -- need to specify raw, unicode, etc?
     | FormattedValue(expr value, int? conversion, expr? format_spec)
```

```
            | JoinedStr(expr* values)
            | Bytes(bytes s)
            | NameConstant(singleton value)
            | Ellipsis
            | Constant(constant value)

            -- the following expression can appear in assignment context
            | Attribute(expr value, identifier attr, expr_context ctx)
            | Subscript(expr value, slice slice, expr_context ctx)
            | Starred(expr value, expr_context ctx)
            | Name(identifier id, expr_context ctx)
            | List(expr* elts, expr_context ctx)
            | Tuple(expr* elts, expr_context ctx)

            -- col_offset is the byte offset in the utf8 string the parser uses
            attributes (int lineno, int col_offset)

    expr_context = Load | Store | Del | AugLoad | AugStore | Param

    slice = Slice(expr? lower, expr? upper, expr? step)
          | ExtSlice(slice* dims)
          | Index(expr value)

    boolop = And | Or

    operator = Add | Sub | Mult | MatMult | Div | Mod | Pow | LShift
             | RShift | BitOr | BitXor | BitAnd | FloorDiv

    unaryop = Invert | Not | UAdd | USub

    cmpop = Eq | NotEq | Lt | LtE | Gt | GtE | Is | IsNot | In | NotIn

    comprehension = (expr target, expr iter, expr* ifs, int is_async)

    excepthandler = ExceptHandler(expr? type, identifier? name, stmt* body)
                    attributes (int lineno, int col_offset)

    arguments = (arg* args, arg? vararg, arg* kwonlyargs, expr* kw_defaults,
                 arg? kwarg, expr* defaults)

    arg = (identifier arg, expr? annotation)
          attributes (int lineno, int col_offset)

    -- keyword arguments supplied to call (NULL identifier for **kwargs)
    keyword = (identifier? arg, expr value)

    -- import name with optional 'as' alias.
    alias = (identifier name, identifier? asname)

    withitem = (expr context_expr, expr? optional_vars)
}
```

32.2.3 ast Helpers

Apart from the node classes, the `ast` module defines these utility functions and classes for traversing abstract syntax trees:

ast.parse(*source, filename='<unknown>', mode='exec'*)

Parse the source into an AST node. Equivalent to `compile(source, filename, mode, ast.PyCF_ONLY_AST)`.

ast.literal_eval(*node_or_string*)

Safely evaluate an expression node or a string containing a Python literal or container display. The string or node provided may only consist of the following Python literal structures: strings, bytes, numbers, tuples, lists, dicts, sets, booleans, and `None`.

This can be used for safely evaluating strings containing Python values from untrusted sources without the need to parse the values oneself. It is not capable of evaluating arbitrarily complex expressions, for example involving operators or indexing.

Changed in version 3.2: Now allows bytes and set literals.

ast.get_docstring(*node, clean=True*)

Return the docstring of the given *node* (which must be a `FunctionDef`, `ClassDef` or `Module` node), or `None` if it has no docstring. If *clean* is true, clean up the docstring's indentation with *inspect.cleandoc()*.

ast.fix_missing_locations(*node*)

When you compile a node tree with *compile()*, the compiler expects `lineno` and `col_offset` attributes for every node that supports them. This is rather tedious to fill in for generated nodes, so this helper adds these attributes recursively where not already set, by setting them to the values of the parent node. It works recursively starting at *node*.

ast.increment_lineno(*node, n=1*)

Increment the line number of each node in the tree starting at *node* by *n*. This is useful to "move code" to a different location in a file.

ast.copy_location(*new_node, old_node*)

Copy source location (`lineno` and `col_offset`) from *old_node* to *new_node* if possible, and return *new_node*.

ast.iter_fields(*node*)

Yield a tuple of `(fieldname, value)` for each field in `node._fields` that is present on *node*.

ast.iter_child_nodes(*node*)

Yield all direct child nodes of *node*, that is, all fields that are nodes and all items of fields that are lists of nodes.

ast.walk(*node*)

Recursively yield all descendant nodes in the tree starting at *node* (including *node* itself), in no specified order. This is useful if you only want to modify nodes in place and don't care about the context.

class ast.NodeVisitor

A node visitor base class that walks the abstract syntax tree and calls a visitor function for every node found. This function may return a value which is forwarded by the *visit()* method.

This class is meant to be subclassed, with the subclass adding visitor methods.

visit(*node*)

Visit a node. The default implementation calls the method called **self.visit_***classname* where *classname* is the name of the node class, or *generic_visit()* if that method doesn't exist.

generic_visit(*node*)

This visitor calls *visit()* on all children of the node.

Note that child nodes of nodes that have a custom visitor method won't be visited unless the visitor calls *generic_visit()* or visits them itself.

Don't use the *NodeVisitor* if you want to apply changes to nodes during traversal. For this a special visitor exists (*NodeTransformer*) that allows modifications.

class ast.NodeTransformer

A *NodeVisitor* subclass that walks the abstract syntax tree and allows modification of nodes.

The *NodeTransformer* will walk the AST and use the return value of the visitor methods to replace or remove the old node. If the return value of the visitor method is None, the node will be removed from its location, otherwise it is replaced with the return value. The return value may be the original node in which case no replacement takes place.

Here is an example transformer that rewrites all occurrences of name lookups (foo) to data['foo']:

```
class RewriteName(NodeTransformer):

    def visit_Name(self, node):
        return copy_location(Subscript(
            value=Name(id='data', ctx=Load()),
            slice=Index(value=Str(s=node.id)),
            ctx=node.ctx
        ), node)
```

Keep in mind that if the node you're operating on has child nodes you must either transform the child nodes yourself or call the `generic_visit()` method for the node first.

For nodes that were part of a collection of statements (that applies to all statement nodes), the visitor may also return a list of nodes rather than just a single node.

Usually you use the transformer like this:

```
node = YourTransformer().visit(node)
```

ast.dump(*node, annotate_fields=True, include_attributes=False*)

Return a formatted dump of the tree in *node*. This is mainly useful for debugging purposes. The returned string will show the names and the values for fields. This makes the code impossible to evaluate, so if evaluation is wanted *annotate_fields* must be set to False. Attributes such as line numbers and column offsets are not dumped by default. If this is wanted, *include_attributes* can be set to True.

See also:

Green Tree Snakes, an external documentation resource, has good details on working with Python ASTs.

32.3 symtable — Access to the compiler's symbol tables

Source code: Lib/symtable.py

Symbol tables are generated by the compiler from AST just before bytecode is generated. The symbol table is responsible for calculating the scope of every identifier in the code. *symtable* provides an interface to examine these tables.

32.3.1 Generating Symbol Tables

symtable.symtable(*code, filename, compile_type*)

Return the toplevel *SymbolTable* for the Python source *code*. *filename* is the name of the file containing the code. *compile_type* is like the *mode* argument to *compile()*.

32.3.2 Examining Symbol Tables

class symtable.SymbolTable
> A namespace table for a block. The constructor is not public.
>
> **get_type()**
> > Return the type of the symbol table. Possible values are 'class', 'module', and 'function'.
>
> **get_id()**
> > Return the table's identifier.
>
> **get_name()**
> > Return the table's name. This is the name of the class if the table is for a class, the name of the function if the table is for a function, or 'top' if the table is global (*get_type()* returns 'module').
>
> **get_lineno()**
> > Return the number of the first line in the block this table represents.
>
> **is_optimized()**
> > Return True if the locals in this table can be optimized.
>
> **is_nested()**
> > Return True if the block is a nested class or function.
>
> **has_children()**
> > Return True if the block has nested namespaces within it. These can be obtained with *get_children()*.
>
> **has_exec()**
> > Return True if the block uses exec.
>
> **get_identifiers()**
> > Return a list of names of symbols in this table.
>
> **lookup(**name**)**
> > Lookup *name* in the table and return a *Symbol* instance.
>
> **get_symbols()**
> > Return a list of *Symbol* instances for names in the table.
>
> **get_children()**
> > Return a list of the nested symbol tables.

class symtable.Function
> A namespace for a function or method. This class inherits *SymbolTable*.
>
> **get_parameters()**
> > Return a tuple containing names of parameters to this function.
>
> **get_locals()**
> > Return a tuple containing names of locals in this function.
>
> **get_globals()**
> > Return a tuple containing names of globals in this function.
>
> **get_frees()**
> > Return a tuple containing names of free variables in this function.

class symtable.Class
> A namespace of a class. This class inherits *SymbolTable*.
>
> **get_methods()**
> > Return a tuple containing the names of methods declared in the class.

class symtable.Symbol
    An entry in a *SymbolTable* corresponding to an identifier in the source. The constructor is not public.

    get_name()
        Return the symbol's name.

    is_referenced()
        Return True if the symbol is used in its block.

    is_imported()
        Return True if the symbol is created from an import statement.

    is_parameter()
        Return True if the symbol is a parameter.

    is_global()
        Return True if the symbol is global.

    is_declared_global()
        Return True if the symbol is declared global with a global statement.

    is_local()
        Return True if the symbol is local to its block.

    is_free()
        Return True if the symbol is referenced in its block, but not assigned to.

    is_assigned()
        Return True if the symbol is assigned to in its block.

    is_namespace()
        Return True if name binding introduces new namespace.

        If the name is used as the target of a function or class statement, this will be true.

        For example:

        ```
        >>> table = symtable.symtable("def some_func(): pass", "string", "exec")
        >>> table.lookup("some_func").is_namespace()
        True
        ```

        Note that a single name can be bound to multiple objects. If the result is True, the name may also be bound to other objects, like an int or list, that does not introduce a new namespace.

    get_namespaces()
        Return a list of namespaces bound to this name.

    get_namespace()
        Return the namespace bound to this name. If more than one namespace is bound, *ValueError* is raised.

32.4 `symbol` — Constants used with Python parse trees

Source code: Lib/symbol.py

This module provides constants which represent the numeric values of internal nodes of the parse tree. Unlike most Python constants, these use lower-case names. Refer to the file `Grammar/Grammar` in the Python distribution for the definitions of the names in the context of the language grammar. The specific numeric values which the names map to may change between Python versions.

This module also provides one additional data object:

symbol.sym_name
    Dictionary mapping the numeric values of the constants defined in this module back to name strings, allowing more human-readable representation of parse trees to be generated.

32.5 `token` — Constants used with Python parse trees

Source code: Lib/token.py

This module provides constants which represent the numeric values of leaf nodes of the parse tree (terminal tokens). Refer to the file `Grammar/Grammar` in the Python distribution for the definitions of the names in the context of the language grammar. The specific numeric values which the names map to may change between Python versions.

The module also provides a mapping from numeric codes to names and some functions. The functions mirror definitions in the Python C header files.

token.tok_name
    Dictionary mapping the numeric values of the constants defined in this module back to name strings, allowing more human-readable representation of parse trees to be generated.

token.ISTERMINAL(*x***)**
    Return true for terminal token values.

token.ISNONTERMINAL(*x***)**
    Return true for non-terminal token values.

token.ISEOF(*x***)**
    Return true if x is the marker indicating the end of input.

The token constants are:

token.ENDMARKER
token.NAME
token.NUMBER
token.STRING
token.NEWLINE
token.INDENT
token.DEDENT
token.LPAR
token.RPAR
token.LSQB
token.RSQB
token.COLON
token.COMMA
token.SEMI
token.PLUS
token.MINUS
token.STAR
token.SLASH
token.VBAR
token.AMPER
token.LESS
token.GREATER
token.EQUAL

token.DOT
token.PERCENT
token.LBRACE
token.RBRACE
token.EQEQUAL
token.NOTEQUAL
token.LESSEQUAL
token.GREATEREQUAL
token.TILDE
token.CIRCUMFLEX
token.LEFTSHIFT
token.RIGHTSHIFT
token.DOUBLESTAR
token.PLUSEQUAL
token.MINEQUAL
token.STAREQUAL
token.SLASHEQUAL
token.PERCENTEQUAL
token.AMPEREQUAL
token.VBAREQUAL
token.CIRCUMFLEXEQUAL
token.LEFTSHIFTEQUAL
token.RIGHTSHIFTEQUAL
token.DOUBLESTAREQUAL
token.DOUBLESLASH
token.DOUBLESLASHEQUAL
token.AT
token.ATEQUAL
token.RARROW
token.ELLIPSIS
token.OP
token.AWAIT
token.ASYNC
token.ERRORTOKEN
token.N_TOKENS
token.NT_OFFSET

Changed in version 3.5: Added *AWAIT* and *ASYNC* tokens. Starting with Python 3.7, "async" and "await" will be tokenized as *NAME* tokens, and *AWAIT* and *ASYNC* will be removed.

32.6 keyword — Testing for Python keywords

Source code: Lib/keyword.py

This module allows a Python program to determine if a string is a keyword.

keyword.iskeyword(*s*)
    Return true if *s* is a Python keyword.

keyword.kwlist
    Sequence containing all the keywords defined for the interpreter. If any keywords are defined to only be active when particular *__future__* statements are in effect, these will be included as well.

32.7 `tokenize` — Tokenizer for Python source

Source code: Lib/tokenize.py

The *tokenize* module provides a lexical scanner for Python source code, implemented in Python. The scanner in this module returns comments as tokens as well, making it useful for implementing "pretty-printers," including colorizers for on-screen displays.

To simplify token stream handling, all operator and delimiter tokens and *Ellipsis* are returned using the generic *OP* token type. The exact type can be determined by checking the **exact_type** property on the *named tuple* returned from *tokenize.tokenize()*.

32.7.1 Tokenizing Input

The primary entry point is a *generator*:

tokenize.tokenize(*readline*)

> The *tokenize()* generator requires one argument, *readline*, which must be a callable object which provides the same interface as the *io.IOBase.readline()* method of file objects. Each call to the function should return one line of input as bytes.
>
> The generator produces 5-tuples with these members: the token type; the token string; a 2-tuple (srow, scol) of ints specifying the row and column where the token begins in the source; a 2-tuple (erow, ecol) of ints specifying the row and column where the token ends in the source; and the line on which the token was found. The line passed (the last tuple item) is the *logical* line; continuation lines are included. The 5 tuple is returned as a *named tuple* with the field names: **type string start end line**.
>
> The returned *named tuple* has an additional property named **exact_type** that contains the exact operator type for *token.OP* tokens. For all other token types **exact_type** equals the named tuple **type** field.
>
> Changed in version 3.1: Added support for named tuples.
>
> Changed in version 3.3: Added support for **exact_type**.
>
> *tokenize()* determines the source encoding of the file by looking for a UTF-8 BOM or encoding cookie, according to PEP 263.

All constants from the *token* module are also exported from *tokenize*, as are three additional token type values:

tokenize.COMMENT
> Token value used to indicate a comment.

tokenize.NL
> Token value used to indicate a non-terminating newline. The NEWLINE token indicates the end of a logical line of Python code; NL tokens are generated when a logical line of code is continued over multiple physical lines.

tokenize.ENCODING
> Token value that indicates the encoding used to decode the source bytes into text. The first token returned by *tokenize()* will always be an ENCODING token.

Another function is provided to reverse the tokenization process. This is useful for creating tools that tokenize a script, modify the token stream, and write back the modified script.

tokenize.untokenize(*iterable*)
> Converts tokens back into Python source code. The *iterable* must return sequences with at least two elements, the token type and the token string. Any additional sequence elements are ignored.
>
> The reconstructed script is returned as a single string. The result is guaranteed to tokenize back to match the input so that the conversion is lossless and round-trips are assured. The guarantee applies only to the token type and token string as the spacing between tokens (column positions) may change.
>
> It returns bytes, encoded using the ENCODING token, which is the first token sequence output by `tokenize()`.

`tokenize()` needs to detect the encoding of source files it tokenizes. The function it uses to do this is available:

tokenize.detect_encoding(*readline*)
> The `detect_encoding()` function is used to detect the encoding that should be used to decode a Python source file. It requires one argument, readline, in the same way as the `tokenize()` generator.
>
> It will call readline a maximum of twice, and return the encoding used (as a string) and a list of any lines (not decoded from bytes) it has read in.
>
> It detects the encoding from the presence of a UTF-8 BOM or an encoding cookie as specified in PEP 263. If both a BOM and a cookie are present, but disagree, a SyntaxError will be raised. Note that if the BOM is found, `'utf-8-sig'` will be returned as an encoding.
>
> If no encoding is specified, then the default of `'utf-8'` will be returned.
>
> Use `open()` to open Python source files: it uses `detect_encoding()` to detect the file encoding.

tokenize.open(*filename*)
> Open a file in read only mode using the encoding detected by `detect_encoding()`.
>
> New in version 3.2.

exception tokenize.TokenError
> Raised when either a docstring or expression that may be split over several lines is not completed anywhere in the file, for example:
>
> ```
> """Beginning of
> docstring
> ```
>
> or:
>
> ```
> [1,
> 2,
> 3
> ```

Note that unclosed single-quoted strings do not cause an error to be raised. They are tokenized as ERRORTOKEN, followed by the tokenization of their contents.

32.7.2 Command-Line Usage

New in version 3.3.

The `tokenize` module can be executed as a script from the command line. It is as simple as:

```
python -m tokenize [-e] [filename.py]
```

The following options are accepted:

-h, --help
> show this help message and exit

`-e, --exact`
> display token names using the exact type

If `filename.py` is specified its contents are tokenized to stdout. Otherwise, tokenization is performed on stdin.

32.7.3 Examples

Example of a script rewriter that transforms float literals into Decimal objects:

```
from tokenize import tokenize, untokenize, NUMBER, STRING, NAME, OP
from io import BytesIO

def decistmt(s):
    """Substitute Decimals for floats in a string of statements.

    >>> from decimal import Decimal
    >>> s = 'print(+21.3e-5*-.1234/81.7)'
    >>> decistmt(s)
    "print (+Decimal ('21.3e-5')*-Decimal ('.1234')/Decimal ('81.7'))"

    The format of the exponent is inherited from the platform C library.
    Known cases are "e-007" (Windows) and "e-07" (not Windows).  Since
    we're only showing 12 digits, and the 13th isn't close to 5, the
    rest of the output should be platform-independent.

    >>> exec(s)  #doctest: +ELLIPSIS
    -3.21716034272e-0...7

    Output from calculations with Decimal should be identical across all
    platforms.

    >>> exec(decistmt(s))
    -3.217160342717258261933904529E-7
    """
    result = []
    g = tokenize(BytesIO(s.encode('utf-8')).readline)  # tokenize the string
    for toknum, tokval, _, _, _ in g:
        if toknum == NUMBER and '.' in tokval:  # replace NUMBER tokens
            result.extend([
                (NAME, 'Decimal'),
                (OP, '('),
                (STRING, repr(tokval)),
                (OP, ')')
            ])
        else:
            result.append((toknum, tokval))
    return untokenize(result).decode('utf-8')
```

Example of tokenizing from the command line. The script:

```
def say_hello():
    print("Hello, World!")

say_hello()
```

will be tokenized to the following output where the first column is the range of the line/column coordinates where the token is found, the second column is the name of the token, and the final column is the value of the token (if any)

```
$ python -m tokenize hello.py
0,0-0,0:            ENCODING        'utf-8'
1,0-1,3:            NAME            'def'
1,4-1,13:           NAME            'say_hello'
1,13-1,14:          OP              '('
1,14-1,15:          OP              ')'
1,15-1,16:          OP              ':'
1,16-1,17:          NEWLINE         '\n'
2,0-2,4:            INDENT          '    '
2,4-2,9:            NAME            'print'
2,9-2,10:           OP              '('
2,10-2,25:          STRING          '"Hello, World!"'
2,25-2,26:          OP              ')'
2,26-2,27:          NEWLINE         '\n'
3,0-3,1:            NL              '\n'
4,0-4,0:            DEDENT          ''
4,0-4,9:            NAME            'say_hello'
4,9-4,10:           OP              '('
4,10-4,11:          OP              ')'
4,11-4,12:          NEWLINE         '\n'
5,0-5,0:            ENDMARKER       ''
```

The exact token type names can be displayed using the -e option:

```
$ python -m tokenize -e hello.py
0,0-0,0:            ENCODING        'utf-8'
1,0-1,3:            NAME            'def'
1,4-1,13:           NAME            'say_hello'
1,13-1,14:          LPAR            '('
1,14-1,15:          RPAR            ')'
1,15-1,16:          COLON           ':'
1,16-1,17:          NEWLINE         '\n'
2,0-2,4:            INDENT          '    '
2,4-2,9:            NAME            'print'
2,9-2,10:           LPAR            '('
2,10-2,25:          STRING          '"Hello, World!"'
2,25-2,26:          RPAR            ')'
2,26-2,27:          NEWLINE         '\n'
3,0-3,1:            NL              '\n'
4,0-4,0:            DEDENT          ''
4,0-4,9:            NAME            'say_hello'
4,9-4,10:           LPAR            '('
4,10-4,11:          RPAR            ')'
4,11-4,12:          NEWLINE         '\n'
5,0-5,0:            ENDMARKER       ''
```

32.8 tabnanny — Detection of ambiguous indentation

Source code: Lib/tabnanny.py

For the time being this module is intended to be called as a script. However it is possible to import it into an IDE and use the function *check()* described below.

Note: The API provided by this module is likely to change in future releases; such changes may not be backward compatible.

tabnanny.check(*file_or_dir*)
    If *file_or_dir* is a directory and not a symbolic link, then recursively descend the directory tree named by *file_or_dir*, checking all .py files along the way. If *file_or_dir* is an ordinary Python source file, it is checked for whitespace related problems. The diagnostic messages are written to standard output using the *print()* function.

tabnanny.verbose
    Flag indicating whether to print verbose messages. This is incremented by the -v option if called as a script.

tabnanny.filename_only
    Flag indicating whether to print only the filenames of files containing whitespace related problems. This is set to true by the -q option if called as a script.

exception tabnanny.NannyNag
    Raised by *process_tokens()* if detecting an ambiguous indent. Captured and handled in *check()*.

tabnanny.process_tokens(*tokens*)
    This function is used by *check()* to process tokens generated by the *tokenize* module.

See also:

Module *tokenize* Lexical scanner for Python source code.

32.9 pyclbr — Python class browser support

Source code: Lib/pyclbr.py

The *pyclbr* module can be used to determine some limited information about the classes, methods and top-level functions defined in a module. The information provided is sufficient to implement a traditional three-pane class browser. The information is extracted from the source code rather than by importing the module, so this module is safe to use with untrusted code. This restriction makes it impossible to use this module with modules not implemented in Python, including all standard and optional extension modules.

pyclbr.readmodule(*module, path=None*)
    Read a module and return a dictionary mapping class names to class descriptor objects. The parameter *module* should be the name of a module as a string; it may be the name of a module within a package. The *path* parameter should be a sequence, and is used to augment the value of sys.path, which is used to locate module source code.

pyclbr.readmodule_ex(*module, path=None*)
    Like *readmodule()*, but the returned dictionary, in addition to mapping class names to class descriptor objects, also maps top-level function names to function descriptor objects. Moreover, if the module being read is a package, the key '__path__' in the returned dictionary has as its value a list which contains the package search path.

32.9.1 Class Objects

The Class objects used as values in the dictionary returned by *readmodule()* and *readmodule_ex()* provide the following data attributes:

Class.module
    The name of the module defining the class described by the class descriptor.

Class.name
    The name of the class.

Class.super
    A list of `Class` objects which describe the immediate base classes of the class being described. Classes which are named as superclasses but which are not discoverable by `readmodule()` are listed as a string with the class name instead of as `Class` objects.

Class.methods
    A dictionary mapping method names to line numbers.

Class.file
    Name of the file containing the `class` statement defining the class.

Class.lineno
    The line number of the `class` statement within the file named by `file`.

32.9.2 Function Objects

The `Function` objects used as values in the dictionary returned by `readmodule_ex()` provide the following attributes:

Function.module
    The name of the module defining the function described by the function descriptor.

Function.name
    The name of the function.

Function.file
    Name of the file containing the `def` statement defining the function.

Function.lineno
    The line number of the `def` statement within the file named by `file`.

32.10 `py_compile` — Compile Python source files

Source code: Lib/py_compile.py

The `py_compile` module provides a function to generate a byte-code file from a source file, and another function used when the module source file is invoked as a script.

Though not often needed, this function can be useful when installing modules for shared use, especially if some of the users may not have permission to write the byte-code cache files in the directory containing the source code.

exception py_compile.PyCompileError
    Exception raised when an error occurs while attempting to compile the file.

py_compile.compile(*file, cfile=None, dfile=None, doraise=False, optimize=-1*)
    Compile a source file to byte-code and write out the byte-code cache file. The source code is loaded from the file named *file*. The byte-code is written to *cfile*, which defaults to the PEP 3147/PEP 488 path, ending in `.pyc`. For example, if *file* is `/foo/bar/baz.py` *cfile* will default to `/foo/bar/__pycache__/baz.cpython-32.pyc` for Python 3.2. If *dfile* is specified, it is used as the name of the source file in error messages when instead of *file*. If *doraise* is true, a `PyCompileError` is raised when an error is encountered while compiling *file*. If *doraise* is false (the default), an error string is written

to sys.stderr, but no exception is raised. This function returns the path to byte-compiled file, i.e. whatever *cfile* value was used.

If the path that *cfile* becomes (either explicitly specified or computed) is a symlink or non-regular file, *FileExistsError* will be raised. This is to act as a warning that import will turn those paths into regular files if it is allowed to write byte-compiled files to those paths. This is a side-effect of import using file renaming to place the final byte-compiled file into place to prevent concurrent file writing issues.

optimize controls the optimization level and is passed to the built-in *compile()* function. The default of -1 selects the optimization level of the current interpreter.

Changed in version 3.2: Changed default value of *cfile* to be PEP 3147-compliant. Previous default was *file* + 'c' ('o' if optimization was enabled). Also added the *optimize* parameter.

Changed in version 3.4: Changed code to use *importlib* for the byte-code cache file writing. This means file creation/writing semantics now match what *importlib* does, e.g. permissions, write-and-move semantics, etc. Also added the caveat that *FileExistsError* is raised if *cfile* is a symlink or non-regular file.

py_compile.main(*args=None*)

Compile several source files. The files named in *args* (or on the command line, if *args* is None) are compiled and the resulting byte-code is cached in the normal manner. This function does not search a directory structure to locate source files; it only compiles files named explicitly. If '-' is the only parameter in args, the list of files is taken from standard input.

Changed in version 3.2: Added support for '-'.

When this module is run as a script, the *main()* is used to compile all the files named on the command line. The exit status is nonzero if one of the files could not be compiled.

See also:

Module *compileall* Utilities to compile all Python source files in a directory tree.

32.11 compileall — Byte-compile Python libraries

Source code: Lib/compileall.py

This module provides some utility functions to support installing Python libraries. These functions compile Python source files in a directory tree. This module can be used to create the cached byte-code files at library installation time, which makes them available for use even by users who don't have write permission to the library directories.

32.11.1 Command-line use

This module can work as a script (using **python -m compileall**) to compile Python sources.

directory ...
file ...

Positional arguments are files to compile or directories that contain source files, traversed recursively. If no argument is given, behave as if the command line was -l <directories from sys.path>.

-l

Do not recurse into subdirectories, only compile source code files directly contained in the named or implied directories.

-f
>   Force rebuild even if timestamps are up-to-date.

-q
>   Do not print the list of files compiled. If passed once, error messages will still be printed. If passed twice (-qq), all output is suppressed.

-d destdir
>   Directory prepended to the path to each file being compiled. This will appear in compilation time tracebacks, and is also compiled in to the byte-code file, where it will be used in tracebacks and other messages in cases where the source file does not exist at the time the byte-code file is executed.

-x regex
>   regex is used to search the full path to each file considered for compilation, and if the regex produces a match, the file is skipped.

-i list
>   Read the file `list` and add each line that it contains to the list of files and directories to compile. If `list` is -, read lines from `stdin`.

-b
>   Write the byte-code files to their legacy locations and names, which may overwrite byte-code files created by another version of Python. The default is to write files to their PEP 3147 locations and names, which allows byte-code files from multiple versions of Python to coexist.

-r
>   Control the maximum recursion level for subdirectories. If this is given, then -l option will not be taken into account. `python -m compileall <directory> -r 0` is equivalent to `python -m compileall <directory> -l`.

-j N
>   Use *N* workers to compile the files within the given directory. If 0 is used, then the result of `os.cpu_count()` will be used.

Changed in version 3.2: Added the -i, -b and -h options.

Changed in version 3.5: Added the -j, -r, and -qq options. -q option was changed to a multilevel value. -b will always produce a byte-code file ending in .pyc, never .pyo.

There is no command-line option to control the optimization level used by the *compile()* function, because the Python interpreter itself already provides the option: `python -O -m compileall`.

32.11.2 Public functions

`compileall.compile_dir(`*dir, maxlevels=10, ddir=None, force=False, rx=None, quiet=0, legacy=False, optimize=-1, workers=1*`)`

>   Recursively descend the directory tree named by *dir*, compiling all .py files along the way. Return a true value if all the files compiled successfully, and a false value otherwise.
>
>   The *maxlevels* parameter is used to limit the depth of the recursion; it defaults to 10.
>
>   If *ddir* is given, it is prepended to the path to each file being compiled for use in compilation time tracebacks, and is also compiled in to the byte-code file, where it will be used in tracebacks and other messages in cases where the source file does not exist at the time the byte-code file is executed.
>
>   If *force* is true, modules are re-compiled even if the timestamps are up to date.
>
>   If *rx* is given, its search method is called on the complete path to each file considered for compilation, and if it returns a true value, the file is skipped.
>
>   If *quiet* is `False` or 0 (the default), the filenames and other information are printed to standard out. Set to 1, only errors are printed. Set to 2, all output is suppressed.

If *legacy* is true, byte-code files are written to their legacy locations and names, which may overwrite byte-code files created by another version of Python. The default is to write files to their PEP 3147 locations and names, which allows byte-code files from multiple versions of Python to coexist.

optimize specifies the optimization level for the compiler. It is passed to the built-in `compile()` function.

The argument *workers* specifies how many workers are used to compile files in parallel. The default is to not use multiple workers. If the platform can't use multiple workers and *workers* argument is given, then sequential compilation will be used as a fallback. If *workers* is lower than 0, a `ValueError` will be raised.

Changed in version 3.2: Added the *legacy* and *optimize* parameter.

Changed in version 3.5: Added the *workers* parameter.

Changed in version 3.5: *quiet* parameter was changed to a multilevel value.

Changed in version 3.5: The *legacy* parameter only writes out .pyc files, not .pyo files no matter what the value of *optimize* is.

Changed in version 3.6: Accepts a *path-like object*.

compileall.compile_file(*fullname, ddir=None, force=False, rx=None, quiet=0, legacy=False, optimize=-1*)

Compile the file with path *fullname*. Return a true value if the file compiled successfully, and a false value otherwise.

If *ddir* is given, it is prepended to the path to the file being compiled for use in compilation time tracebacks, and is also compiled in to the byte-code file, where it will be used in tracebacks and other messages in cases where the source file does not exist at the time the byte-code file is executed.

If *rx* is given, its search method is passed the full path name to the file being compiled, and if it returns a true value, the file is not compiled and `True` is returned.

If *quiet* is `False` or `0` (the default), the filenames and other information are printed to standard out. Set to `1`, only errors are printed. Set to `2`, all output is suppressed.

If *legacy* is true, byte-code files are written to their legacy locations and names, which may overwrite byte-code files created by another version of Python. The default is to write files to their PEP 3147 locations and names, which allows byte-code files from multiple versions of Python to coexist.

optimize specifies the optimization level for the compiler. It is passed to the built-in `compile()` function.

New in version 3.2.

Changed in version 3.5: *quiet* parameter was changed to a multilevel value.

Changed in version 3.5: The *legacy* parameter only writes out .pyc files, not .pyo files no matter what the value of *optimize* is.

compileall.compile_path(*skip_curdir=True, maxlevels=0, force=False, quiet=0, legacy=False, optimize=-1*)

Byte-compile all the .py files found along `sys.path`. Return a true value if all the files compiled successfully, and a false value otherwise.

If *skip_curdir* is true (the default), the current directory is not included in the search. All other parameters are passed to the `compile_dir()` function. Note that unlike the other compile functions, `maxlevels` defaults to 0.

Changed in version 3.2: Added the *legacy* and *optimize* parameter.

Changed in version 3.5: *quiet* parameter was changed to a multilevel value.

Changed in version 3.5: The *legacy* parameter only writes out .pyc files, not .pyo files no matter what the value of *optimize* is.

To force a recompile of all the .py files in the Lib/ subdirectory and all its subdirectories:

```
import compileall

compileall.compile_dir('Lib/', force=True)

# Perform same compilation, excluding files in .svn directories.
import re
compileall.compile_dir('Lib/', rx=re.compile(r'[/\\][.]svn'), force=True)

# pathlib.Path objects can also be used.
import pathlib
compileall.compile_dir(pathlib.Path('Lib/'), force=True)
```

See also:

Module `py_compile` Byte-compile a single source file.

32.12 `dis` — Disassembler for Python bytecode

Source code: Lib/dis.py

The `dis` module supports the analysis of CPython *bytecode* by disassembling it. The CPython bytecode which this module takes as an input is defined in the file **Include/opcode.h** and used by the compiler and the interpreter.

CPython implementation detail: Bytecode is an implementation detail of the CPython interpreter. No guarantees are made that bytecode will not be added, removed, or changed between versions of Python. Use of this module should not be considered to work across Python VMs or Python releases.

Changed in version 3.6: Use 2 bytes for each instruction. Previously the number of bytes varied by instruction.

Example: Given the function `myfunc()`:

```
def myfunc(alist):
    return len(alist)
```

the following command can be used to display the disassembly of `myfunc()`:

```
>>> dis.dis(myfunc)
 2           0 LOAD_GLOBAL              0 (len)
             2 LOAD_FAST                0 (alist)
             4 CALL_FUNCTION            1
             6 RETURN_VALUE
```

(The "2" is a line number).

32.12.1 Bytecode analysis

New in version 3.4.

The bytecode analysis API allows pieces of Python code to be wrapped in a *Bytecode* object that provides easy access to details of the compiled code.

class dis.Bytecode(*x*, ***, *first_line=None*, *current_offset=None*)

Analyse the bytecode corresponding to a function, generator, method, string of source code, or a code object (as returned by `compile()`).

This is a convenience wrapper around many of the functions listed below, most notably `get_instructions()`, as iterating over a `Bytecode` instance yields the bytecode operations as `Instruction` instances.

If *first_line* is not `None`, it indicates the line number that should be reported for the first source line in the disassembled code. Otherwise, the source line information (if any) is taken directly from the disassembled code object.

If *current_offset* is not `None`, it refers to an instruction offset in the disassembled code. Setting this means `dis()` will display a "current instruction" marker against the specified opcode.

classmethod from_traceback(*tb*)

Construct a `Bytecode` instance from the given traceback, setting *current_offset* to the instruction responsible for the exception.

codeobj

The compiled code object.

first_line

The first source line of the code object (if available)

dis()

Return a formatted view of the bytecode operations (the same as printed by `dis.dis()`, but returned as a multi-line string).

info()

Return a formatted multi-line string with detailed information about the code object, like `code_info()`.

Example:

```
>>> bytecode = dis.Bytecode(myfunc)
>>> for instr in bytecode:
...     print(instr.opname)
...
LOAD_GLOBAL
LOAD_FAST
CALL_FUNCTION
RETURN_VALUE
```

32.12.2 Analysis functions

The `dis` module also defines the following analysis functions that convert the input directly to the desired output. They can be useful if only a single operation is being performed, so the intermediate analysis object isn't useful:

dis.code_info(*x*)

Return a formatted multi-line string with detailed code object information for the supplied function, generator, method, source code string or code object.

Note that the exact contents of code info strings are highly implementation dependent and they may change arbitrarily across Python VMs or Python releases.

New in version 3.2.

dis.show_code(*x*, *, *file=None*)
> Print detailed code object information for the supplied function, method, source code string or code object to *file* (or `sys.stdout` if *file* is not specified).
>
> This is a convenient shorthand for `print(code_info(x), file=file)`, intended for interactive exploration at the interpreter prompt.
>
> New in version 3.2.
>
> Changed in version 3.4: Added *file* parameter.

dis.dis(*x=None*, *, *file=None*)
> Disassemble the *x* object. *x* can denote either a module, a class, a method, a function, a generator, a code object, a string of source code or a byte sequence of raw bytecode. For a module, it disassembles all functions. For a class, it disassembles all methods (including class and static methods). For a code object or sequence of raw bytecode, it prints one line per bytecode instruction. Strings are first compiled to code objects with the *compile()* built-in function before being disassembled. If no object is provided, this function disassembles the last traceback.
>
> The disassembly is written as text to the supplied *file* argument if provided and to `sys.stdout` otherwise.
>
> Changed in version 3.4: Added *file* parameter.

dis.distb(*tb=None*, *, *file=None*)
> Disassemble the top-of-stack function of a traceback, using the last traceback if none was passed. The instruction causing the exception is indicated.
>
> The disassembly is written as text to the supplied *file* argument if provided and to `sys.stdout` otherwise.
>
> Changed in version 3.4: Added *file* parameter.

dis.disassemble(*code*, *lasti=-1*, *, *file=None*)
dis.disco(*code*, *lasti=-1*, *, *file=None*)
> Disassemble a code object, indicating the last instruction if *lasti* was provided. The output is divided in the following columns:
>
> 1. the line number, for the first instruction of each line
> 2. the current instruction, indicated as `-->`,
> 3. a labelled instruction, indicated with `>>`,
> 4. the address of the instruction,
> 5. the operation code name,
> 6. operation parameters, and
> 7. interpretation of the parameters in parentheses.
>
> The parameter interpretation recognizes local and global variable names, constant values, branch targets, and compare operators.
>
> The disassembly is written as text to the supplied *file* argument if provided and to `sys.stdout` otherwise.
>
> Changed in version 3.4: Added *file* parameter.

dis.get_instructions(*x*, *, *first_line=None*)
> Return an iterator over the instructions in the supplied function, method, source code string or code object.
>
> The iterator generates a series of *Instruction* named tuples giving the details of each operation in the supplied code.

If *first_line* is not `None`, it indicates the line number that should be reported for the first source line in the disassembled code. Otherwise, the source line information (if any) is taken directly from the disassembled code object.

New in version 3.4.

dis.findlinestarts(*code*)

This generator function uses the `co_firstlineno` and `co_lnotab` attributes of the code object *code* to find the offsets which are starts of lines in the source code. They are generated as (`offset, lineno`) pairs. See Objects/lnotab_notes.txt for the `co_lnotab` format and how to decode it.

Changed in version 3.6: Line numbers can be decreasing. Before, they were always increasing.

dis.findlabels(*code*)

Detect all offsets in the code object *code* which are jump targets, and return a list of these offsets.

dis.stack_effect(*opcode*[, *oparg*])

Compute the stack effect of *opcode* with argument *oparg*.

New in version 3.4.

32.12.3 Python Bytecode Instructions

The `get_instructions()` function and `Bytecode` class provide details of bytecode instructions as `Instruction` instances:

class dis.Instruction

Details for a bytecode operation

opcode

numeric code for operation, corresponding to the opcode values listed below and the bytecode values in the *Opcode collections*.

opname

human readable name for operation

arg

numeric argument to operation (if any), otherwise `None`

argval

resolved arg value (if known), otherwise same as arg

argrepr

human readable description of operation argument

offset

start index of operation within bytecode sequence

starts_line

line started by this opcode (if any), otherwise `None`

is_jump_target

`True` if other code jumps to here, otherwise `False`

New in version 3.4.

The Python compiler currently generates the following bytecode instructions.

General instructions

NOP

Do nothing code. Used as a placeholder by the bytecode optimizer.

POP_TOP

Removes the top-of-stack (TOS) item.

ROT_TWO
    Swaps the two top-most stack items.

ROT_THREE
    Lifts second and third stack item one position up, moves top down to position three.

DUP_TOP
    Duplicates the reference on top of the stack.

    New in version 3.2.

DUP_TOP_TWO
    Duplicates the two references on top of the stack, leaving them in the same order.

    New in version 3.2.

Unary operations

Unary operations take the top of the stack, apply the operation, and push the result back on the stack.

UNARY_POSITIVE
    Implements TOS = +TOS.

UNARY_NEGATIVE
    Implements TOS = -TOS.

UNARY_NOT
    Implements TOS = not TOS.

UNARY_INVERT
    Implements TOS = ~TOS.

GET_ITER
    Implements TOS = iter(TOS).

GET_YIELD_FROM_ITER
    If TOS is a *generator iterator* or *coroutine* object it is left as is. Otherwise, implements TOS = iter(TOS).

    New in version 3.5.

Binary operations

Binary operations remove the top of the stack (TOS) and the second top-most stack item (TOS1) from the stack. They perform the operation, and put the result back on the stack.

BINARY_POWER
    Implements TOS = TOS1 ** TOS.

BINARY_MULTIPLY
    Implements TOS = TOS1 * TOS.

BINARY_MATRIX_MULTIPLY
    Implements TOS = TOS1 @ TOS.

    New in version 3.5.

BINARY_FLOOR_DIVIDE
    Implements TOS = TOS1 // TOS.

BINARY_TRUE_DIVIDE
    Implements TOS = TOS1 / TOS.

BINARY_MODULO
    Implements TOS = TOS1 % TOS.

BINARY_ADD
    Implements TOS = TOS1 + TOS.

BINARY_SUBTRACT
    Implements TOS = TOS1 - TOS.

BINARY_SUBSCR
    Implements TOS = TOS1[TOS].

BINARY_LSHIFT
    Implements TOS = TOS1 << TOS.

BINARY_RSHIFT
    Implements TOS = TOS1 >> TOS.

BINARY_AND
    Implements TOS = TOS1 & TOS.

BINARY_XOR
    Implements TOS = TOS1 ^ TOS.

BINARY_OR
    Implements TOS = TOS1 | TOS.

In-place operations

In-place operations are like binary operations, in that they remove TOS and TOS1, and push the result back on the stack, but the operation is done in-place when TOS1 supports it, and the resulting TOS may be (but does not have to be) the original TOS1.

INPLACE_POWER
    Implements in-place TOS = TOS1 ** TOS.

INPLACE_MULTIPLY
    Implements in-place TOS = TOS1 * TOS.

INPLACE_MATRIX_MULTIPLY
    Implements in-place TOS = TOS1 @ TOS.

    New in version 3.5.

INPLACE_FLOOR_DIVIDE
    Implements in-place TOS = TOS1 // TOS.

INPLACE_TRUE_DIVIDE
    Implements in-place TOS = TOS1 / TOS.

INPLACE_MODULO
    Implements in-place TOS = TOS1 % TOS.

INPLACE_ADD
    Implements in-place TOS = TOS1 + TOS.

INPLACE_SUBTRACT
    Implements in-place TOS = TOS1 - TOS.

INPLACE_LSHIFT
    Implements in-place TOS = TOS1 << TOS.

INPLACE_RSHIFT
    Implements in-place TOS = TOS1 >> TOS.

INPLACE_AND
    Implements in-place TOS = TOS1 & TOS.

INPLACE_XOR
    Implements in-place TOS = TOS1 ^ TOS.

INPLACE_OR
    Implements in-place TOS = TOS1 | TOS.

STORE_SUBSCR
    Implements TOS1[TOS] = TOS2.

DELETE_SUBSCR
    Implements del TOS1[TOS].

Coroutine opcodes

GET_AWAITABLE
    Implements TOS = get_awaitable(TOS), where get_awaitable(o) returns o if o is a coroutine object or a generator object with the CO_ITERABLE_COROUTINE flag, or resolves o.__await__.

    New in version 3.5.

GET_AITER
    Implements TOS = get_awaitable(TOS.__aiter__()). See GET_AWAITABLE for details about get_awaitable

    New in version 3.5.

GET_ANEXT
    Implements PUSH(get_awaitable(TOS.__anext__())). See GET_AWAITABLE for details about get_awaitable

    New in version 3.5.

BEFORE_ASYNC_WITH
    Resolves __aenter__ and __aexit__ from the object on top of the stack. Pushes __aexit__ and result of __aenter__() to the stack.

    New in version 3.5.

SETUP_ASYNC_WITH
    Creates a new frame object.

    New in version 3.5.

Miscellaneous opcodes

PRINT_EXPR
    Implements the expression statement for the interactive mode. TOS is removed from the stack and printed. In non-interactive mode, an expression statement is terminated with POP_TOP.

BREAK_LOOP
    Terminates a loop due to a break statement.

CONTINUE_LOOP(*target*)
    Continues a loop due to a continue statement. *target* is the address to jump to (which should be a FOR_ITER instruction).

SET_ADD(*i*)
    Calls set.add(TOS1[-i], TOS). Used to implement set comprehensions.

LIST_APPEND(*i*)
    Calls list.append(TOS[-i], TOS). Used to implement list comprehensions.

MAP_ADD(*i*)
    Calls dict.setitem(TOS1[-i], TOS, TOS1). Used to implement dict comprehensions.

    New in version 3.1.

For all of the SET_ADD, LIST_APPEND and MAP_ADD instructions, while the added value or key/value pair is popped off, the container object remains on the stack so that it is available for further iterations of the loop.

RETURN_VALUE
    Returns with TOS to the caller of the function.

YIELD_VALUE
　　Pops TOS and yields it from a *generator*.

YIELD_FROM
　　Pops TOS and delegates to it as a subiterator from a *generator*.

　　New in version 3.3.

SETUP_ANNOTATIONS
　　Checks whether `__annotations__` is defined in `locals()`, if not it is set up to an empty `dict`. This opcode is only emitted if a class or module body contains *variable annotations* statically.

　　New in version 3.6.

IMPORT_STAR
　　Loads all symbols not starting with `'_'` directly from the module TOS to the local namespace. The module is popped after loading all names. This opcode implements `from module import *`.

POP_BLOCK
　　Removes one block from the block stack. Per frame, there is a stack of blocks, denoting nested loops, try statements, and such.

POP_EXCEPT
　　Removes one block from the block stack. The popped block must be an exception handler block, as implicitly created when entering an except handler. In addition to popping extraneous values from the frame stack, the last three popped values are used to restore the exception state.

END_FINALLY
　　Terminates a `finally` clause. The interpreter recalls whether the exception has to be re-raised, or whether the function returns, and continues with the outer-next block.

LOAD_BUILD_CLASS
　　Pushes `builtins.__build_class__()` onto the stack. It is later called by *CALL_FUNCTION* to construct a class.

SETUP_WITH(*delta*)
　　This opcode performs several operations before a with block starts. First, it loads `__exit__()` from the context manager and pushes it onto the stack for later use by WITH_CLEANUP. Then, `__enter__()` is called, and a finally block pointing to *delta* is pushed. Finally, the result of calling the enter method is pushed onto the stack. The next opcode will either ignore it (*POP_TOP*), or store it in (a) variable(s) (*STORE_FAST*, *STORE_NAME*, or *UNPACK_SEQUENCE*).

　　New in version 3.2.

WITH_CLEANUP_START
　　Cleans up the stack when a `with` statement block exits. TOS is the context manager's `__exit__()` bound method. Below TOS are 1–3 values indicating how/why the finally clause was entered:

- SECOND = `None`
- (SECOND, THIRD) = (`WHY_{RETURN,CONTINUE}`), retval
- SECOND = `WHY_*`; no retval below it
- (SECOND, THIRD, FOURTH) = exc_info()

　　In the last case, `TOS(SECOND, THIRD, FOURTH)` is called, otherwise `TOS(None, None, None)`. Pushes SECOND and result of the call to the stack.

WITH_CLEANUP_FINISH
　　Pops exception type and result of 'exit' function call from the stack.

　　If the stack represents an exception, *and* the function call returns a 'true' value, this information is "zapped" and replaced with a single `WHY_SILENCED` to prevent *END_FINALLY* from re-raising the exception. (But non-local gotos will still be resumed.)

All of the following opcodes use their arguments.

STORE_NAME(*namei*)
> Implements `name = TOS`. *namei* is the index of *name* in the attribute `co_names` of the code object. The compiler tries to use `STORE_FAST` or `STORE_GLOBAL` if possible.

DELETE_NAME(*namei*)
> Implements `del name`, where *namei* is the index into `co_names` attribute of the code object.

UNPACK_SEQUENCE(*count*)
> Unpacks TOS into *count* individual values, which are put onto the stack right-to-left.

UNPACK_EX(*counts*)
> Implements assignment with a starred target: Unpacks an iterable in TOS into individual values, where the total number of values can be smaller than the number of items in the iterable: one of the new values will be a list of all leftover items.
>
> The low byte of *counts* is the number of values before the list value, the high byte of *counts* the number of values after it. The resulting values are put onto the stack right-to-left.

STORE_ATTR(*namei*)
> Implements `TOS.name = TOS1`, where *namei* is the index of name in `co_names`.

DELETE_ATTR(*namei*)
> Implements `del TOS.name`, using *namei* as index into `co_names`.

STORE_GLOBAL(*namei*)
> Works as `STORE_NAME`, but stores the name as a global.

DELETE_GLOBAL(*namei*)
> Works as `DELETE_NAME`, but deletes a global name.

LOAD_CONST(*consti*)
> Pushes `co_consts[consti]` onto the stack.

LOAD_NAME(*namei*)
> Pushes the value associated with `co_names[namei]` onto the stack.

BUILD_TUPLE(*count*)
> Creates a tuple consuming *count* items from the stack, and pushes the resulting tuple onto the stack.

BUILD_LIST(*count*)
> Works as `BUILD_TUPLE`, but creates a list.

BUILD_SET(*count*)
> Works as `BUILD_TUPLE`, but creates a set.

BUILD_MAP(*count*)
> Pushes a new dictionary object onto the stack. Pops `2 * count` items so that the dictionary holds *count* entries: `{..., TOS3: TOS2, TOS1: TOS}`.
>
> Changed in version 3.5: The dictionary is created from stack items instead of creating an empty dictionary pre-sized to hold *count* items.

BUILD_CONST_KEY_MAP(*count*)
> The version of `BUILD_MAP` specialized for constant keys. *count* values are consumed from the stack. The top element on the stack contains a tuple of keys.
>
> New in version 3.6.

BUILD_STRING(*count*)
> Concatenates *count* strings from the stack and pushes the resulting string onto the stack.
>
> New in version 3.6.

BUILD_TUPLE_UNPACK(*count*)
>   Pops *count* iterables from the stack, joins them in a single tuple, and pushes the result. Implements iterable unpacking in tuple displays (*x, *y, *z).
>
>   New in version 3.5.

BUILD_TUPLE_UNPACK_WITH_CALL(*count*)
>   This is similar to *BUILD_TUPLE_UNPACK*, but is used for f(*x, *y, *z) call syntax. The stack item at position count + 1 should be the corresponding callable f.
>
>   New in version 3.6.

BUILD_LIST_UNPACK(*count*)
>   This is similar to *BUILD_TUPLE_UNPACK*, but pushes a list instead of tuple. Implements iterable unpacking in list displays [*x, *y, *z].
>
>   New in version 3.5.

BUILD_SET_UNPACK(*count*)
>   This is similar to *BUILD_TUPLE_UNPACK*, but pushes a set instead of tuple. Implements iterable unpacking in set displays {*x, *y, *z}.
>
>   New in version 3.5.

BUILD_MAP_UNPACK(*count*)
>   Pops *count* mappings from the stack, merges them into a single dictionary, and pushes the result. Implements dictionary unpacking in dictionary displays {**x, **y, **z}.
>
>   New in version 3.5.

BUILD_MAP_UNPACK_WITH_CALL(*count*)
>   This is similar to *BUILD_MAP_UNPACK*, but is used for f(**x, **y, **z) call syntax. The stack item at position count + 2 should be the corresponding callable f.
>
>   New in version 3.5.
>
>   Changed in version 3.6: The position of the callable is determined by adding 2 to the opcode argument instead of encoding it in the second byte of the argument.

LOAD_ATTR(*namei*)
>   Replaces TOS with getattr(TOS, co_names[namei]).

COMPARE_OP(*opname*)
>   Performs a Boolean operation. The operation name can be found in cmp_op[opname].

IMPORT_NAME(*namei*)
>   Imports the module co_names[namei]. TOS and TOS1 are popped and provide the *fromlist* and *level* arguments of *__import__()*. The module object is pushed onto the stack. The current namespace is not affected: for a proper import statement, a subsequent *STORE_FAST* instruction modifies the namespace.

IMPORT_FROM(*namei*)
>   Loads the attribute co_names[namei] from the module found in TOS. The resulting object is pushed onto the stack, to be subsequently stored by a *STORE_FAST* instruction.

JUMP_FORWARD(*delta*)
>   Increments bytecode counter by *delta*.

POP_JUMP_IF_TRUE(*target*)
>   If TOS is true, sets the bytecode counter to *target*. TOS is popped.
>
>   New in version 3.1.

POP_JUMP_IF_FALSE(*target*)
>   If TOS is false, sets the bytecode counter to *target*. TOS is popped.

New in version 3.1.

JUMP_IF_TRUE_OR_POP(*target*)
    If TOS is true, sets the bytecode counter to *target* and leaves TOS on the stack. Otherwise (TOS is false), TOS is popped.

    New in version 3.1.

JUMP_IF_FALSE_OR_POP(*target*)
    If TOS is false, sets the bytecode counter to *target* and leaves TOS on the stack. Otherwise (TOS is true), TOS is popped.

    New in version 3.1.

JUMP_ABSOLUTE(*target*)
    Set bytecode counter to *target*.

FOR_ITER(*delta*)
    TOS is an *iterator*. Call its `__next__()` method. If this yields a new value, push it on the stack (leaving the iterator below it). If the iterator indicates it is exhausted TOS is popped, and the byte code counter is incremented by *delta*.

LOAD_GLOBAL(*namei*)
    Loads the global named `co_names[namei]` onto the stack.

SETUP_LOOP(*delta*)
    Pushes a block for a loop onto the block stack. The block spans from the current instruction with a size of *delta* bytes.

SETUP_EXCEPT(*delta*)
    Pushes a try block from a try-except clause onto the block stack. *delta* points to the first except block.

SETUP_FINALLY(*delta*)
    Pushes a try block from a try-except clause onto the block stack. *delta* points to the finally block.

LOAD_FAST(*var_num*)
    Pushes a reference to the local `co_varnames[var_num]` onto the stack.

STORE_FAST(*var_num*)
    Stores TOS into the local `co_varnames[var_num]`.

DELETE_FAST(*var_num*)
    Deletes local `co_varnames[var_num]`.

STORE_ANNOTATION(*namei*)
    Stores TOS as `locals()['__annotations__'][co_names[namei]] = TOS`.

    New in version 3.6.

LOAD_CLOSURE(*i*)
    Pushes a reference to the cell contained in slot *i* of the cell and free variable storage. The name of the variable is `co_cellvars[i]` if *i* is less than the length of *co_cellvars*. Otherwise it is `co_freevars[i - len(co_cellvars)]`.

LOAD_DEREF(*i*)
    Loads the cell contained in slot *i* of the cell and free variable storage. Pushes a reference to the object the cell contains on the stack.

LOAD_CLASSDEREF(*i*)
    Much like *LOAD_DEREF* but first checks the locals dictionary before consulting the cell. This is used for loading free variables in class bodies.

    New in version 3.4.

STORE_DEREF(*i*)
    Stores TOS into the cell contained in slot *i* of the cell and free variable storage.

DELETE_DEREF(*i*)

Empties the cell contained in slot *i* of the cell and free variable storage. Used by the `del` statement.

New in version 3.2.

RAISE_VARARGS(*argc*)

Raises an exception. *argc* indicates the number of parameters to the raise statement, ranging from 0 to 3. The handler will find the traceback as TOS2, the parameter as TOS1, and the exception as TOS.

CALL_FUNCTION(*argc*)

Calls a function. *argc* indicates the number of positional arguments. The positional arguments are on the stack, with the right-most argument on top. Below the arguments, the function object to call is on the stack. Pops all function arguments, and the function itself off the stack, and pushes the return value.

Changed in version 3.6: This opcode is used only for calls with positional arguments.

CALL_FUNCTION_KW(*argc*)

Calls a function. *argc* indicates the number of arguments (positional and keyword). The top element on the stack contains a tuple of keyword argument names. Below the tuple, keyword arguments are on the stack, in the order corresponding to the tuple. Below the keyword arguments, the positional arguments are on the stack, with the right-most parameter on top. Below the arguments, the function object to call is on the stack. Pops all function arguments, and the function itself off the stack, and pushes the return value.

Changed in version 3.6: Keyword arguments are packed in a tuple instead of a dictionary, *argc* indicates the total number of arguments

CALL_FUNCTION_EX(*flags*)

Calls a function. The lowest bit of *flags* indicates whether the var-keyword argument is placed at the top of the stack. Below the var-keyword argument, the var-positional argument is on the stack. Below the arguments, the function object to call is placed. Pops all function arguments, and the function itself off the stack, and pushes the return value. Note that this opcode pops at most three items from the stack. Var-positional and var-keyword arguments are packed by *BUILD_TUPLE_UNPACK_WITH_CALL* and *BUILD_MAP_UNPACK_WITH_CALL*.

New in version 3.6.

MAKE_FUNCTION(*argc*)

Pushes a new function object on the stack. From bottom to top, the consumed stack must consist of values if the argument carries a specified flag value

- 0x01 a tuple of default argument objects in positional order
- 0x02 a dictionary of keyword-only parameters' default values
- 0x04 an annotation dictionary
- 0x08 a tuple containing cells for free variables, making a closure
- the code associated with the function (at TOS1)
- the *qualified name* of the function (at TOS)

BUILD_SLICE(*argc*)

Pushes a slice object on the stack. *argc* must be 2 or 3. If it is 2, `slice(TOS1, TOS)` is pushed; if it is 3, `slice(TOS2, TOS1, TOS)` is pushed. See the *slice()* built-in function for more information.

EXTENDED_ARG(*ext*)

Prefixes any opcode which has an argument too big to fit into the default two bytes. *ext* holds two additional bytes which, taken together with the subsequent opcode's argument, comprise a four-byte argument, *ext* being the two most-significant bytes.

FORMAT_VALUE(*flags*)

Used for implementing formatted literal strings (f-strings). Pops an optional *fmt_spec* from the stack, then a required *value*. *flags* is interpreted as follows:

- (flags & 0x03) == 0x00: *value* is formatted as-is.
- (flags & 0x03) == 0x01: call str() on *value* before formatting it.
- (flags & 0x03) == 0x02: call repr() on *value* before formatting it.
- (flags & 0x03) == 0x03: call ascii() on *value* before formatting it.
- (flags & 0x04) == 0x04: pop *fmt_spec* from the stack and use it, else use an empty *fmt_spec*.

Formatting is performed using PyObject_Format(). The result is pushed on the stack.

New in version 3.6.

HAVE_ARGUMENT

This is not really an opcode. It identifies the dividing line between opcodes which don't use their argument and those that do (< HAVE_ARGUMENT and >= HAVE_ARGUMENT, respectively).

Changed in version 3.6: Now every instruction has an argument, but opcodes < HAVE_ARGUMENT ignore it. Before, only opcodes >= HAVE_ARGUMENT had an argument.

32.12.4 Opcode collections

These collections are provided for automatic introspection of bytecode instructions:

dis.**opname**
Sequence of operation names, indexable using the bytecode.

dis.**opmap**
Dictionary mapping operation names to bytecodes.

dis.**cmp_op**
Sequence of all compare operation names.

dis.**hasconst**
Sequence of bytecodes that have a constant parameter.

dis.**hasfree**
Sequence of bytecodes that access a free variable (note that 'free' in this context refers to names in the current scope that are referenced by inner scopes or names in outer scopes that are referenced from this scope. It does *not* include references to global or builtin scopes).

dis.**hasname**
Sequence of bytecodes that access an attribute by name.

dis.**hasjrel**
Sequence of bytecodes that have a relative jump target.

dis.**hasjabs**
Sequence of bytecodes that have an absolute jump target.

dis.**haslocal**
Sequence of bytecodes that access a local variable.

dis.**hascompare**
Sequence of bytecodes of Boolean operations.

32.13 `pickletools` — Tools for pickle developers

Source code: Lib/pickletools.py

This module contains various constants relating to the intimate details of the `pickle` module, some lengthy comments about the implementation, and a few useful functions for analyzing pickled data. The contents of this module are useful for Python core developers who are working on the `pickle`; ordinary users of the `pickle` module probably won't find the `pickletools` module relevant.

32.13.1 Command line usage

New in version 3.2.

When invoked from the command line, `python -m pickletools` will disassemble the contents of one or more pickle files. Note that if you want to see the Python object stored in the pickle rather than the details of pickle format, you may want to use `-m pickle` instead. However, when the pickle file that you want to examine comes from an untrusted source, `-m pickletools` is a safer option because it does not execute pickle bytecode.

For example, with a tuple `(1, 2)` pickled in file `x.pickle`:

```
$ python -m pickle x.pickle
(1, 2)

$ python -m pickletools x.pickle
    0: \x80 PROTO      3
    2: K    BININT1    1
    4: K    BININT1    2
    6: \x86 TUPLE2
    7: q    BINPUT     0
    9: .    STOP
highest protocol among opcodes = 2
```

Command line options

- `-a, --annotate`
    Annotate each line with a short opcode description.
- `-o, --output=<file>`
    Name of a file where the output should be written.
- `-l, --indentlevel=<num>`
    The number of blanks by which to indent a new MARK level.
- `-m, --memo`
    When multiple objects are disassembled, preserve memo between disassemblies.
- `-p, --preamble=<preamble>`
    When more than one pickle file are specified, print given preamble before each disassembly.

32.13.2 Programmatic Interface

`pickletools.dis`(*pickle, out=None, memo=None, indentlevel=4, annotate=0*)
    Outputs a symbolic disassembly of the pickle to the file-like object *out*, defaulting to `sys.stdout`.

pickle can be a string or a file-like object. *memo* can be a Python dictionary that will be used as the pickle's memo; it can be used to perform disassemblies across multiple pickles created by the same pickler. Successive levels, indicated by `MARK` opcodes in the stream, are indented by *indentlevel* spaces. If a nonzero value is given to *annotate*, each opcode in the output is annotated with a short description. The value of *annotate* is used as a hint for the column where annotation should start.

New in version 3.2: The *annotate* argument.

pickletools.genops(*pickle*)

Provides an *iterator* over all of the opcodes in a pickle, returning a sequence of (`opcode, arg, pos`) triples. *opcode* is an instance of an `OpcodeInfo` class; *arg* is the decoded value, as a Python object, of the opcode's argument; *pos* is the position at which this opcode is located. *pickle* can be a string or a file-like object.

pickletools.optimize(*picklestring*)

Returns a new equivalent pickle string after eliminating unused `PUT` opcodes. The optimized pickle is shorter, takes less transmission time, requires less storage space, and unpickles more efficiently.

CHAPTER
THIRTYTHREE

MISCELLANEOUS SERVICES

The modules described in this chapter provide miscellaneous services that are available in all Python versions. Here's an overview:

33.1 `formatter` — Generic output formatting

Deprecated since version 3.4: Due to lack of usage, the formatter module has been deprecated.

This module supports two interface definitions, each with multiple implementations: The *formatter* interface, and the *writer* interface which is required by the formatter interface.

Formatter objects transform an abstract flow of formatting events into specific output events on writer objects. Formatters manage several stack structures to allow various properties of a writer object to be changed and restored; writers need not be able to handle relative changes nor any sort of "change back" operation. Specific writer properties which may be controlled via formatter objects are horizontal alignment, font, and left margin indentations. A mechanism is provided which supports providing arbitrary, non-exclusive style settings to a writer as well. Additional interfaces facilitate formatting events which are not reversible, such as paragraph separation.

Writer objects encapsulate device interfaces. Abstract devices, such as file formats, are supported as well as physical devices. The provided implementations all work with abstract devices. The interface makes available mechanisms for setting the properties which formatter objects manage and inserting data into the output.

33.1.1 The Formatter Interface

Interfaces to create formatters are dependent on the specific formatter class being instantiated. The interfaces described below are the required interfaces which all formatters must support once initialized.

One data element is defined at the module level:

formatter.AS_IS
> Value which can be used in the font specification passed to the `push_font()` method described below, or as the new value to any other `push_property()` method. Pushing the `AS_IS` value allows the corresponding `pop_property()` method to be called without having to track whether the property was changed.

The following attributes are defined for formatter instance objects:

formatter.writer
> The writer instance with which the formatter interacts.

formatter.end_paragraph(*blanklines*)
   Close any open paragraphs and insert at least *blanklines* before the next paragraph.

formatter.add_line_break()
   Add a hard line break if one does not already exist. This does not break the logical paragraph.

formatter.add_hor_rule(**args*, ***kw*)
   Insert a horizontal rule in the output. A hard break is inserted if there is data in the current paragraph, but the logical paragraph is not broken. The arguments and keywords are passed on to the writer's **send_line_break**() method.

formatter.add_flowing_data(*data*)
   Provide data which should be formatted with collapsed whitespace. Whitespace from preceding and successive calls to *add_flowing_data()* is considered as well when the whitespace collapse is performed. The data which is passed to this method is expected to be word-wrapped by the output device. Note that any word-wrapping still must be performed by the writer object due to the need to rely on device and font information.

formatter.add_literal_data(*data*)
   Provide data which should be passed to the writer unchanged. Whitespace, including newline and tab characters, are considered legal in the value of *data*.

formatter.add_label_data(*format*, *counter*)
   Insert a label which should be placed to the left of the current left margin. This should be used for constructing bulleted or numbered lists. If the *format* value is a string, it is interpreted as a format specification for *counter*, which should be an integer. The result of this formatting becomes the value of the label; if *format* is not a string it is used as the label value directly. The label value is passed as the only argument to the writer's **send_label_data**() method. Interpretation of non-string label values is dependent on the associated writer.

   Format specifications are strings which, in combination with a counter value, are used to compute label values. Each character in the format string is copied to the label value, with some characters recognized to indicate a transform on the counter value. Specifically, the character '1' represents the counter value formatter as an Arabic number, the characters 'A' and 'a' represent alphabetic representations of the counter value in upper and lower case, respectively, and 'I' and 'i' represent the counter value in Roman numerals, in upper and lower case. Note that the alphabetic and roman transforms require that the counter value be greater than zero.

formatter.flush_softspace()
   Send any pending whitespace buffered from a previous call to *add_flowing_data()* to the associated writer object. This should be called before any direct manipulation of the writer object.

formatter.push_alignment(*align*)
   Push a new alignment setting onto the alignment stack. This may be AS_IS if no change is desired. If the alignment value is changed from the previous setting, the writer's **new_alignment**() method is called with the *align* value.

formatter.pop_alignment()
   Restore the previous alignment.

formatter.push_font((*size*, *italic*, *bold*, *teletype*))
   Change some or all font properties of the writer object. Properties which are not set to AS_IS are set to the values passed in while others are maintained at their current settings. The writer's **new_font**() method is called with the fully resolved font specification.

formatter.pop_font()
   Restore the previous font.

formatter.push_margin(*margin*)
   Increase the number of left margin indentations by one, associating the logical tag *margin* with the

new indentation. The initial margin level is 0. Changed values of the logical tag must be true values; false values other than `AS_IS` are not sufficient to change the margin.

formatter.**pop_margin**()
> Restore the previous margin.

formatter.**push_style**(*styles*)
> Push any number of arbitrary style specifications. All styles are pushed onto the styles stack in order. A tuple representing the entire stack, including `AS_IS` values, is passed to the writer's `new_styles()` method.

formatter.**pop_style**(*n=1*)
> Pop the last *n* style specifications passed to `push_style()`. A tuple representing the revised stack, including `AS_IS` values, is passed to the writer's `new_styles()` method.

formatter.**set_spacing**(*spacing*)
> Set the spacing style for the writer.

formatter.**assert_line_data**(*flag=1*)
> Inform the formatter that data has been added to the current paragraph out-of-band. This should be used when the writer has been manipulated directly. The optional *flag* argument can be set to false if the writer manipulations produced a hard line break at the end of the output.

33.1.2 Formatter Implementations

Two implementations of formatter objects are provided by this module. Most applications may use one of these classes without modification or subclassing.

class formatter.**NullFormatter**(*writer=None*)
> A formatter which does nothing. If *writer* is omitted, a `NullWriter` instance is created. No methods of the writer are called by `NullFormatter` instances. Implementations should inherit from this class if implementing a writer interface but don't need to inherit any implementation.

class formatter.**AbstractFormatter**(*writer*)
> The standard formatter. This implementation has demonstrated wide applicability to many writers, and may be used directly in most circumstances. It has been used to implement a full-featured World Wide Web browser.

33.1.3 The Writer Interface

Interfaces to create writers are dependent on the specific writer class being instantiated. The interfaces described below are the required interfaces which all writers must support once initialized. Note that while most applications can use the `AbstractFormatter` class as a formatter, the writer must typically be provided by the application.

writer.**flush**()
> Flush any buffered output or device control events.

writer.**new_alignment**(*align*)
> Set the alignment style. The *align* value can be any object, but by convention is a string or `None`, where `None` indicates that the writer's "preferred" alignment should be used. Conventional *align* values are `'left'`, `'center'`, `'right'`, and `'justify'`.

writer.**new_font**(*font*)
> Set the font style. The value of *font* will be `None`, indicating that the device's default font should be used, or a tuple of the form (`size`, `italic`, `bold`, `teletype`). Size will be a string indicating the size of font that should be used; specific strings and their interpretation must be defined by the application.

The *italic*, *bold*, and *teletype* values are Boolean values specifying which of those font attributes should be used.

writer.**new_margin**(*margin, level*)
: Set the margin level to the integer *level* and the logical tag to *margin*. Interpretation of the logical tag is at the writer's discretion; the only restriction on the value of the logical tag is that it not be a false value for non-zero values of *level*.

writer.**new_spacing**(*spacing*)
: Set the spacing style to *spacing*.

writer.**new_styles**(*styles*)
: Set additional styles. The *styles* value is a tuple of arbitrary values; the value AS_IS should be ignored. The *styles* tuple may be interpreted either as a set or as a stack depending on the requirements of the application and writer implementation.

writer.**send_line_break**()
: Break the current line.

writer.**send_paragraph**(*blankline*)
: Produce a paragraph separation of at least *blankline* blank lines, or the equivalent. The *blankline* value will be an integer. Note that the implementation will receive a call to *send_line_break()* before this call if a line break is needed; this method should not include ending the last line of the paragraph. It is only responsible for vertical spacing between paragraphs.

writer.**send_hor_rule**(**args, **kw*)
: Display a horizontal rule on the output device. The arguments to this method are entirely application- and writer-specific, and should be interpreted with care. The method implementation may assume that a line break has already been issued via *send_line_break()*.

writer.**send_flowing_data**(*data*)
: Output character data which may be word-wrapped and re-flowed as needed. Within any sequence of calls to this method, the writer may assume that spans of multiple whitespace characters have been collapsed to single space characters.

writer.**send_literal_data**(*data*)
: Output character data which has already been formatted for display. Generally, this should be interpreted to mean that line breaks indicated by newline characters should be preserved and no new line breaks should be introduced. The data may contain embedded newline and tab characters, unlike data provided to the **send_formatted_data()** interface.

writer.**send_label_data**(*data*)
: Set *data* to the left of the current left margin, if possible. The value of *data* is not restricted; treatment of non-string values is entirely application- and writer-dependent. This method will only be called at the beginning of a line.

33.1.4 Writer Implementations

Three implementations of the writer object interface are provided as examples by this module. Most applications will need to derive new writer classes from the *NullWriter* class.

class formatter.**NullWriter**
: A writer which only provides the interface definition; no actions are taken on any methods. This should be the base class for all writers which do not need to inherit any implementation methods.

class formatter.**AbstractWriter**
: A writer which can be used in debugging formatters, but not much else. Each method simply announces itself by printing its name and arguments on standard output.

class formatter.DumbWriter(*file=None, maxcol=72*)

Simple writer class which writes output on the *file object* passed in as *file* or, if *file* is omitted, on standard output. The output is simply word-wrapped to the number of columns specified by *maxcol*. This class is suitable for reflowing a sequence of paragraphs.

CHAPTER
THIRTYFOUR

MS WINDOWS SPECIFIC SERVICES

This chapter describes modules that are only available on MS Windows platforms.

34.1 `msilib` — Read and write Microsoft Installer files

Source code: Lib/msilib/__init__.py

The `msilib` supports the creation of Microsoft Installer (.msi) files. Because these files often contain an embedded "cabinet" file (.cab), it also exposes an API to create CAB files. Support for reading .cab files is currently not implemented; read support for the .msi database is possible.

This package aims to provide complete access to all tables in an .msi file, therefore, it is a fairly low-level API. Two primary applications of this package are the *distutils* command **bdist_msi**, and the creation of Python installer package itself (although that currently uses a different version of `msilib`).

The package contents can be roughly split into four parts: low-level CAB routines, low-level MSI routines, higher-level MSI routines, and standard table structures.

`msilib.FCICreate`(*cabname*, *files*)
: Create a new CAB file named *cabname*. *files* must be a list of tuples, each containing the name of the file on disk, and the name of the file inside the CAB file.

  The files are added to the CAB file in the order they appear in the list. All files are added into a single CAB file, using the MSZIP compression algorithm.

  Callbacks to Python for the various steps of MSI creation are currently not exposed.

`msilib.UuidCreate`()
: Return the string representation of a new unique identifier. This wraps the Windows API functions `UuidCreate()` and `UuidToString()`.

`msilib.OpenDatabase`(*path*, *persist*)
: Return a new database object by calling MsiOpenDatabase. *path* is the file name of the MSI file; *persist* can be one of the constants `MSIDBOPEN_CREATEDIRECT`, `MSIDBOPEN_CREATE`, `MSIDBOPEN_DIRECT`, `MSIDBOPEN_READONLY`, or `MSIDBOPEN_TRANSACT`, and may include the flag `MSIDBOPEN_PATCHFILE`. See the Microsoft documentation for the meaning of these flags; depending on the flags, an existing database is opened, or a new one created.

`msilib.CreateRecord`(*count*)
: Return a new record object by calling `MSICreateRecord()`. *count* is the number of fields of the record.

`msilib.init_database`(*name*, *schema*, *ProductName*, *ProductCode*, *ProductVersion*, *Manufacturer*)
: Create and return a new database *name*, initialize it with *schema*, and set the properties *ProductName*, *ProductCode*, *ProductVersion*, and *Manufacturer*.

schema must be a module object containing `tables` and `_Validation_records` attributes; typically, `msilib.schema` should be used.

The database will contain just the schema and the validation records when this function returns.

msilib.**add_data**(*database*, *table*, *records*)
: Add all *records* to the table named *table* in *database*.

    The *table* argument must be one of the predefined tables in the MSI schema, e.g. `'Feature'`, `'File'`, `'Component'`, `'Dialog'`, `'Control'`, etc.

    records should be a list of tuples, each one containing all fields of a record according to the schema of the table. For optional fields, `None` can be passed.

    Field values can be ints, strings, or instances of the Binary class.

class msilib.**Binary**(*filename*)
: Represents entries in the Binary table; inserting such an object using `add_data()` reads the file named *filename* into the table.

msilib.**add_tables**(*database*, *module*)
: Add all table content from *module* to *database*. *module* must contain an attribute *tables* listing all tables for which content should be added, and one attribute per table that has the actual content.

    This is typically used to install the sequence tables.

msilib.**add_stream**(*database*, *name*, *path*)
: Add the file *path* into the `_Stream` table of *database*, with the stream name *name*.

msilib.**gen_uuid**()
: Return a new UUID, in the format that MSI typically requires (i.e. in curly braces, and with all hexdigits in upper-case).

See also:

FCICreate UuidCreate UuidToString

34.1.1 Database Objects

Database.**OpenView**(*sql*)
: Return a view object, by calling `MSIDatabaseOpenView()`. *sql* is the SQL statement to execute.

Database.**Commit**()
: Commit the changes pending in the current transaction, by calling `MSIDatabaseCommit()`.

Database.**GetSummaryInformation**(*count*)
: Return a new summary information object, by calling `MsiGetSummaryInformation()`. *count* is the maximum number of updated values.

See also:

MSIDatabaseOpenView MSIDatabaseCommit MSIGetSummaryInformation

34.1.2 View Objects

View.**Execute**(*params*)
: Execute the SQL query of the view, through `MSIViewExecute()`. If *params* is not `None`, it is a record describing actual values of the parameter tokens in the query.

View.**GetColumnInfo**(*kind*)
: Return a record describing the columns of the view, through calling `MsiViewGetColumnInfo()`. *kind* can be either `MSICOLINFO_NAMES` or `MSICOLINFO_TYPES`.

`View.Fetch()`
    Return a result record of the query, through calling `MsiViewFetch()`.

`View.Modify(kind, data)`
    Modify the view, by calling `MsiViewModify()`. *kind* can be one of MSIMODIFY_SEEK, MSIMODIFY_REFRESH, MSIMODIFY_INSERT, MSIMODIFY_UPDATE, MSIMODIFY_ASSIGN, MSIMODIFY_REPLACE, MSIMODIFY_MERGE, MSIMODIFY_DELETE, MSIMODIFY_INSERT_TEMPORARY, MSIMODIFY_VALIDATE, MSIMODIFY_VALIDATE_NEW, MSIMODIFY_VALIDATE_FIELD, or MSIMODIFY_VALIDATE_DELETE.

    data must be a record describing the new data.

`View.Close()`
    Close the view, through `MsiViewClose()`.

See also:

MsiViewExecute MSIViewGetColumnInfo MsiViewFetch MsiViewModify MsiViewClose

34.1.3 Summary Information Objects

`SummaryInformation.GetProperty(field)`
    Return a property of the summary, through `MsiSummaryInfoGetProperty()`. *field* is the name of the property, and can be one of the constants PID_CODEPAGE, PID_TITLE, PID_SUBJECT, PID_AUTHOR, PID_KEYWORDS, PID_COMMENTS, PID_TEMPLATE, PID_LASTAUTHOR, PID_REVNUMBER, PID_LASTPRINTED, PID_CREATE_DTM, PID_LASTSAVE_DTM, PID_PAGECOUNT, PID_WORDCOUNT, PID_CHARCOUNT, PID_APPNAME, or PID_SECURITY.

`SummaryInformation.GetPropertyCount()`
    Return the number of summary properties, through `MsiSummaryInfoGetPropertyCount()`.

`SummaryInformation.SetProperty(field, value)`
    Set a property through `MsiSummaryInfoSetProperty()`. *field* can have the same values as in `GetProperty()`, *value* is the new value of the property. Possible value types are integer and string.

`SummaryInformation.Persist()`
    Write the modified properties to the summary information stream, using `MsiSummaryInfoPersist()`.

See also:

MsiSummaryInfoGetProperty MsiSummaryInfoGetPropertyCount MsiSummaryInfoSetProperty MsiSummaryInfoPersist

34.1.4 Record Objects

`Record.GetFieldCount()`
    Return the number of fields of the record, through `MsiRecordGetFieldCount()`.

`Record.GetInteger(field)`
    Return the value of *field* as an integer where possible. *field* must be an integer.

`Record.GetString(field)`
    Return the value of *field* as a string where possible. *field* must be an integer.

`Record.SetString(field, value)`
    Set *field* to *value* through `MsiRecordSetString()`. *field* must be an integer; *value* a string.

`Record.SetStream(field, value)`
    Set *field* to the contents of the file named *value*, through `MsiRecordSetStream()`. *field* must be an integer; *value* a string.

Record.SetInteger(*field, value*)
: Set *field* to *value* through `MsiRecordSetInteger()`. Both *field* and *value* must be an integer.

Record.ClearData()
: Set all fields of the record to 0, through `MsiRecordClearData()`.

See also:

MsiRecordGetFieldCount MsiRecordSetString MsiRecordSetStream MsiRecordSetInteger MsiRecordClearData

34.1.5 Errors

All wrappers around MSI functions raise `MSIError`; the string inside the exception will contain more detail.

34.1.6 CAB Objects

class msilib.CAB(*name*)
: The class *CAB* represents a CAB file. During MSI construction, files will be added simultaneously to the `Files` table, and to a CAB file. Then, when all files have been added, the CAB file can be written, then added to the MSI file.

    name is the name of the CAB file in the MSI file.

    append(*full, file, logical*)
    : Add the file with the pathname *full* to the CAB file, under the name *logical*. If there is already a file named *logical*, a new file name is created.

        Return the index of the file in the CAB file, and the new name of the file inside the CAB file.

    commit(*database*)
    : Generate a CAB file, add it as a stream to the MSI file, put it into the `Media` table, and remove the generated file from the disk.

34.1.7 Directory Objects

class msilib.Directory(*database, cab, basedir, physical, logical, default[, componentflags]*)
: Create a new directory in the Directory table. There is a current component at each point in time for the directory, which is either explicitly created through `start_component()`, or implicitly when files are added for the first time. Files are added into the current component, and into the cab file. To create a directory, a base directory object needs to be specified (can be `None`), the path to the physical directory, and a logical directory name. *default* specifies the DefaultDir slot in the directory table. *componentflags* specifies the default flags that new components get.

    start_component(*component=None, feature=None, flags=None, keyfile=None, uuid=None*)
    : Add an entry to the Component table, and make this component the current component for this directory. If no component name is given, the directory name is used. If no *feature* is given, the current feature is used. If no *flags* are given, the directory's default flags are used. If no *keyfile* is given, the KeyPath is left null in the Component table.

    add_file(*file, src=None, version=None, language=None*)
    : Add a file to the current component of the directory, starting a new one if there is no current component. By default, the file name in the source and the file table will be identical. If the *src* file is specified, it is interpreted relative to the current directory. Optionally, a *version* and a *language* can be specified for the entry in the File table.

glob(*pattern, exclude=None*)
: Add a list of files to the current component as specified in the glob pattern. Individual files can be excluded in the *exclude* list.

remove_pyc()
: Remove .pyc files on uninstall.

See also:

Directory Table File Table Component Table FeatureComponents Table

34.1.8 Features

class msilib.Feature(*db, id, title, desc, display, level=1, parent=None, directory=None, attributes=0*)
: Add a new record to the `Feature` table, using the values *id, parent.id, title, desc, display, level, directory*, and *attributes*. The resulting feature object can be passed to the `start_component()` method of *Directory*.

    set_current()
    : Make this feature the current feature of *msilib*. New components are automatically added to the default feature, unless a feature is explicitly specified.

See also:

Feature Table

34.1.9 GUI classes

msilib provides several classes that wrap the GUI tables in an MSI database. However, no standard user interface is provided; use `bdist_msi` to create MSI files with a user-interface for installing Python packages.

class msilib.Control(*dlg, name*)
: Base class of the dialog controls. *dlg* is the dialog object the control belongs to, and *name* is the control's name.

    event(*event, argument, condition=1, ordering=None*)
    : Make an entry into the `ControlEvent` table for this control.

    mapping(*event, attribute*)
    : Make an entry into the `EventMapping` table for this control.

    condition(*action, condition*)
    : Make an entry into the `ControlCondition` table for this control.

class msilib.RadioButtonGroup(*dlg, name, property*)
: Create a radio button control named *name*. *property* is the installer property that gets set when a radio button is selected.

    add(*name, x, y, width, height, text, value=None*)
    : Add a radio button named *name* to the group, at the coordinates *x, y, width, height*, and with the label *text*. If *value* is `None`, it defaults to *name*.

class msilib.Dialog(*db, name, x, y, w, h, attr, title, first, default, cancel*)
: Return a new *Dialog* object. An entry in the `Dialog` table is made, with the specified coordinates, dialog attributes, title, name of the first, default, and cancel controls.

    control(*name, type, x, y, width, height, attributes, property, text, control_next, help*)
    : Return a new *Control* object. An entry in the `Control` table is made with the specified parameters.

This is a generic method; for specific types, specialized methods are provided.

text(*name, x, y, width, height, attributes, text*)
    Add and return a `Text` control.

bitmap(*name, x, y, width, height, text*)
    Add and return a `Bitmap` control.

line(*name, x, y, width, height*)
    Add and return a `Line` control.

pushbutton(*name, x, y, width, height, attributes, text, next_control*)
    Add and return a `PushButton` control.

radiogroup(*name, x, y, width, height, attributes, property, text, next_control*)
    Add and return a `RadioButtonGroup` control.

checkbox(*name, x, y, width, height, attributes, property, text, next_control*)
    Add and return a `CheckBox` control.

See also:

Dialog Table Control Table Control Types ControlCondition Table ControlEvent Table EventMapping Table RadioButton Table

34.1.10 Precomputed tables

`msilib` provides a few subpackages that contain only schema and table definitions. Currently, these definitions are based on MSI version 2.0.

msilib.schema
    This is the standard MSI schema for MSI 2.0, with the *tables* variable providing a list of table definitions, and *_Validation_records* providing the data for MSI validation.

msilib.sequence
    This module contains table contents for the standard sequence tables: *AdminExecuteSequence*, *AdminUISequence*, *AdvtExecuteSequence*, *InstallExecuteSequence*, and *InstallUISequence*.

msilib.text
    This module contains definitions for the UIText and ActionText tables, for the standard installer actions.

34.2 `msvcrt` — Useful routines from the MS VC++ runtime

These functions provide access to some useful capabilities on Windows platforms. Some higher-level modules use these functions to build the Windows implementations of their services. For example, the `getpass` module uses this in the implementation of the `getpass()` function.

Further documentation on these functions can be found in the Platform API documentation.

The module implements both the normal and wide char variants of the console I/O api. The normal API deals only with ASCII characters and is of limited use for internationalized applications. The wide char API should be used where ever possible.

Changed in version 3.3: Operations in this module now raise `OSError` where `IOError` was raised.

34.2.1 File Operations

msvcrt.locking(*fd*, *mode*, *nbytes*)
    Lock part of a file based on file descriptor *fd* from the C runtime. Raises *OSError* on failure. The locked region of the file extends from the current file position for *nbytes* bytes, and may continue beyond the end of the file. *mode* must be one of the LK_* constants listed below. Multiple regions in a file may be locked at the same time, but may not overlap. Adjacent regions are not merged; they must be unlocked individually.

msvcrt.LK_LOCK
msvcrt.LK_RLCK
    Locks the specified bytes. If the bytes cannot be locked, the program immediately tries again after 1 second. If, after 10 attempts, the bytes cannot be locked, *OSError* is raised.

msvcrt.LK_NBLCK
msvcrt.LK_NBRLCK
    Locks the specified bytes. If the bytes cannot be locked, *OSError* is raised.

msvcrt.LK_UNLCK
    Unlocks the specified bytes, which must have been previously locked.

msvcrt.setmode(*fd*, *flags*)
    Set the line-end translation mode for the file descriptor *fd*. To set it to text mode, *flags* should be *os.O_TEXT*; for binary, it should be *os.O_BINARY*.

msvcrt.open_osfhandle(*handle*, *flags*)
    Create a C runtime file descriptor from the file handle *handle*. The *flags* parameter should be a bitwise OR of *os.O_APPEND*, *os.O_RDONLY*, and *os.O_TEXT*. The returned file descriptor may be used as a parameter to *os.fdopen()* to create a file object.

msvcrt.get_osfhandle(*fd*)
    Return the file handle for the file descriptor *fd*. Raises *OSError* if *fd* is not recognized.

34.2.2 Console I/O

msvcrt.kbhit()
    Return true if a keypress is waiting to be read.

msvcrt.getch()
    Read a keypress and return the resulting character as a byte string. Nothing is echoed to the console. This call will block if a keypress is not already available, but will not wait for **Enter** to be pressed. If the pressed key was a special function key, this will return '\000' or '\xe0'; the next call will return the keycode. The **Control-C** keypress cannot be read with this function.

msvcrt.getwch()
    Wide char variant of *getch()*, returning a Unicode value.

msvcrt.getche()
    Similar to *getch()*, but the keypress will be echoed if it represents a printable character.

msvcrt.getwche()
    Wide char variant of *getche()*, returning a Unicode value.

msvcrt.putch(*char*)
    Print the byte string *char* to the console without buffering.

msvcrt.putwch(*unicode_char*)
    Wide char variant of *putch()*, accepting a Unicode value.

msvcrt.ungetch(*char*)
  Cause the byte string *char* to be "pushed back" into the console buffer; it will be the next character read by *getch()* or *getche()*.

msvcrt.ungetwch(*unicode_char*)
  Wide char variant of *ungetch()*, accepting a Unicode value.

34.2.3 Other Functions

msvcrt.heapmin()
  Force the `malloc()` heap to clean itself up and return unused blocks to the operating system. On failure, this raises *OSError*.

34.3 `winreg` — Windows registry access

These functions expose the Windows registry API to Python. Instead of using an integer as the registry handle, a *handle object* is used to ensure that the handles are closed correctly, even if the programmer neglects to explicitly close them. Changed in version 3.3: Several functions in this module used to raise a *WindowsError*, which is now an alias of *OSError*.

34.3.1 Functions

This module offers the following functions:

winreg.CloseKey(*hkey*)
  Closes a previously opened registry key. The *hkey* argument specifies a previously opened key.

  Note: If *hkey* is not closed using this method (or via *hkey.Close()*), it is closed when the *hkey* object is destroyed by Python.

winreg.ConnectRegistry(*computer_name*, *key*)
  Establishes a connection to a predefined registry handle on another computer, and returns a *handle object*.

  computer_name is the name of the remote computer, of the form r"\\computername". If None, the local computer is used.

  key is the predefined handle to connect to.

  The return value is the handle of the opened key. If the function fails, an *OSError* exception is raised.

  Changed in version 3.3: See *above*.

winreg.CreateKey(*key*, *sub_key*)
  Creates or opens the specified key, returning a *handle object*.

  key is an already open key, or one of the predefined *HKEY_* constants*.

  sub_key is a string that names the key this method opens or creates.

  If *key* is one of the predefined keys, *sub_key* may be **None**. In that case, the handle returned is the same key handle passed in to the function.

  If the key already exists, this function opens the existing key.

The return value is the handle of the opened key. If the function fails, an *OSError* exception is raised.

Changed in version 3.3: See *above*.

winreg.CreateKeyEx(*key, sub_key, reserved=0, access=KEY_WRITE*)
Creates or opens the specified key, returning a *handle object*.

key is an already open key, or one of the predefined *HKEY_* constants*.

sub_key is a string that names the key this method opens or creates.

reserved is a reserved integer, and must be zero. The default is zero.

access is an integer that specifies an access mask that describes the desired security access for the key. Default is *KEY_WRITE*. See *Access Rights* for other allowed values.

If *key* is one of the predefined keys, *sub_key* may be **None**. In that case, the handle returned is the same key handle passed in to the function.

If the key already exists, this function opens the existing key.

The return value is the handle of the opened key. If the function fails, an *OSError* exception is raised.

New in version 3.2.

Changed in version 3.3: See *above*.

winreg.DeleteKey(*key, sub_key*)
Deletes the specified key.

key is an already open key, or one of the predefined *HKEY_* constants*.

sub_key is a string that must be a subkey of the key identified by the *key* parameter. This value must not be **None**, and the key may not have subkeys.

This method can not delete keys with subkeys.

If the method succeeds, the entire key, including all of its values, is removed. If the method fails, an *OSError* exception is raised.

Changed in version 3.3: See *above*.

winreg.DeleteKeyEx(*key, sub_key, access=KEY_WOW64_64KEY, reserved=0*)
Deletes the specified key.

Note: The *DeleteKeyEx()* function is implemented with the RegDeleteKeyEx Windows API function, which is specific to 64-bit versions of Windows. See the *RegDeleteKeyEx documentation*.

---

key is an already open key, or one of the predefined *HKEY_* constants*.

sub_key is a string that must be a subkey of the key identified by the *key* parameter. This value must not be **None**, and the key may not have subkeys.

reserved is a reserved integer, and must be zero. The default is zero.

access is an integer that specifies an access mask that describes the desired security access for the key. Default is *KEY_WOW64_64KEY*. See *Access Rights* for other allowed values.

This method can not delete keys with subkeys.

If the method succeeds, the entire key, including all of its values, is removed. If the method fails, an *OSError* exception is raised.

On unsupported Windows versions, *NotImplementedError* is raised.

New in version 3.2.

Changed in version 3.3: See *above*.

winreg.DeleteValue(*key, value*)
: Removes a named value from a registry key.

    key is an already open key, or one of the predefined *HKEY_* constants*.

    value is a string that identifies the value to remove.

winreg.EnumKey(*key, index*)
: Enumerates subkeys of an open registry key, returning a string.

    key is an already open key, or one of the predefined *HKEY_* constants*.

    index is an integer that identifies the index of the key to retrieve.

    The function retrieves the name of one subkey each time it is called. It is typically called repeatedly until an *OSError* exception is raised, indicating, no more values are available.

    Changed in version 3.3: See *above*.

winreg.EnumValue(*key, index*)
: Enumerates values of an open registry key, returning a tuple.

    key is an already open key, or one of the predefined *HKEY_* constants*.

    index is an integer that identifies the index of the value to retrieve.

    The function retrieves the name of one subkey each time it is called. It is typically called repeatedly, until an *OSError* exception is raised, indicating no more values.

    The result is a tuple of 3 items:

Index	Meaning
0	A string that identifies the value name
1	An object that holds the value data, and whose type depends on the underlying registry type
2	An integer that identifies the type of the value data (see table in docs for *SetValueEx()*)

    Changed in version 3.3: See *above*.

winreg.ExpandEnvironmentStrings(*str*)
: Expands environment variable placeholders %NAME% in strings like *REG_EXPAND_SZ*:

    ```
    >>> ExpandEnvironmentStrings('%windir%')
    'C:\\Windows'
    ```

winreg.FlushKey(*key*)
: Writes all the attributes of a key to the registry.

    key is an already open key, or one of the predefined *HKEY_* constants*.

    It is not necessary to call *FlushKey()* to change a key. Registry changes are flushed to disk by the registry using its lazy flusher. Registry changes are also flushed to disk at system shutdown. Unlike *CloseKey()*, the *FlushKey()* method returns only when all the data has been written to the registry. An application should only call *FlushKey()* if it requires absolute certainty that registry changes are on disk.

    Note: If you don't know whether a *FlushKey()* call is required, it probably isn't.

winreg.LoadKey(*key, sub_key, file_name*)
: Creates a subkey under the specified key and stores registration information from a specified file into that subkey.

key is a handle returned by `ConnectRegistry()` or one of the constants *HKEY_USERS* or *HKEY_LOCAL_MACHINE*.

sub_key is a string that identifies the subkey to load.

file_name is the name of the file to load registry data from. This file must have been created with the `SaveKey()` function. Under the file allocation table (FAT) file system, the filename may not have an extension.

A call to `LoadKey()` fails if the calling process does not have the **SE_RESTORE_PRIVILEGE** privilege. Note that privileges are different from permissions – see the RegLoadKey documentation for more details.

If *key* is a handle returned by `ConnectRegistry()`, then the path specified in *file_name* is relative to the remote computer.

winreg.OpenKey(*key, sub_key, reserved=0, access=KEY_READ*)
winreg.OpenKeyEx(*key, sub_key, reserved=0, access=KEY_READ*)
Opens the specified key, returning a handle object.

key is an already open key, or one of the predefined *HKEY_* constants*.

sub_key is a string that identifies the sub_key to open.

reserved is a reserved integer, and must be zero. The default is zero.

access is an integer that specifies an access mask that describes the desired security access for the key. Default is *KEY_READ*. See Access Rights for other allowed values.

The result is a new handle to the specified key.

If the function fails, `OSError` is raised.

Changed in version 3.2: Allow the use of named arguments.

Changed in version 3.3: See above.

winreg.QueryInfoKey(*key*)
Returns information about a key, as a tuple.

key is an already open key, or one of the predefined *HKEY_* constants*.

The result is a tuple of 3 items:

Index	Meaning
0	An integer giving the number of sub keys this key has.
1	An integer giving the number of values this key has.
2	An integer giving when the key was last modified (if available) as 100's of nanoseconds since Jan 1, 1601.

winreg.QueryValue(*key, sub_key*)
Retrieves the unnamed value for a key, as a string.

key is an already open key, or one of the predefined *HKEY_* constants*.

sub_key is a string that holds the name of the subkey with which the value is associated. If this parameter is **None** or empty, the function retrieves the value set by the `SetValue()` method for the key identified by *key*.

Values in the registry have name, type, and data components. This method retrieves the data for a key's first value that has a NULL name. But the underlying API call doesn't return the type, so always use `QueryValueEx()` if possible.

winreg.QueryValueEx(*key, value_name*)
Retrieves the type and data for a specified value name associated with an open registry key.

key is an already open key, or one of the predefined *HKEY_* constants*.

value_name is a string indicating the value to query.

The result is a tuple of 2 items:

Index	Meaning
0	The value of the registry item.
1	An integer giving the registry type for this value (see table in docs for *SetValueEx()*)

winreg.SaveKey(*key, file_name*)
Saves the specified key, and all its subkeys to the specified file.

key is an already open key, or one of the predefined *HKEY_* constants*.

file_name is the name of the file to save registry data to. This file cannot already exist. If this filename includes an extension, it cannot be used on file allocation table (FAT) file systems by the *LoadKey()* method.

If *key* represents a key on a remote computer, the path described by *file_name* is relative to the remote computer. The caller of this method must possess the **SeBackupPrivilege** security privilege. Note that privileges are different than permissions – see the Conflicts Between User Rights and Permissions documentation for more details.

This function passes NULL for *security_attributes* to the API.

winreg.SetValue(*key, sub_key, type, value*)
Associates a value with a specified key.

key is an already open key, or one of the predefined *HKEY_* constants*.

sub_key is a string that names the subkey with which the value is associated.

type is an integer that specifies the type of the data. Currently this must be *REG_SZ*, meaning only strings are supported. Use the *SetValueEx()* function for support for other data types.

value is a string that specifies the new value.

If the key specified by the *sub_key* parameter does not exist, the SetValue function creates it.

Value lengths are limited by available memory. Long values (more than 2048 bytes) should be stored as files with the filenames stored in the configuration registry. This helps the registry perform efficiently.

The key identified by the *key* parameter must have been opened with *KEY_SET_VALUE* access.

winreg.SetValueEx(*key, value_name, reserved, type, value*)
Stores data in the value field of an open registry key.

key is an already open key, or one of the predefined *HKEY_* constants*.

value_name is a string that names the subkey with which the value is associated.

reserved can be anything – zero is always passed to the API.

type is an integer that specifies the type of the data. See *Value Types* for the available types.

value is a string that specifies the new value.

This method can also set additional value and type information for the specified key. The key identified by the key parameter must have been opened with *KEY_SET_VALUE* access.

To open the key, use the *CreateKey()* or *OpenKey()* methods.

Value lengths are limited by available memory. Long values (more than 2048 bytes) should be stored as files with the filenames stored in the configuration registry. This helps the registry perform efficiently.

winreg.DisableReflectionKey(*key*)
    Disables registry reflection for 32-bit processes running on a 64-bit operating system.

    key is an already open key, or one of the predefined *HKEY_* constants*.

    Will generally raise *NotImplemented* if executed on a 32-bit operating system.

    If the key is not on the reflection list, the function succeeds but has no effect. Disabling reflection for a key does not affect reflection of any subkeys.

winreg.EnableReflectionKey(*key*)
    Restores registry reflection for the specified disabled key.

    key is an already open key, or one of the predefined *HKEY_* constants*.

    Will generally raise *NotImplemented* if executed on a 32-bit operating system.

    Restoring reflection for a key does not affect reflection of any subkeys.

winreg.QueryReflectionKey(*key*)
    Determines the reflection state for the specified key.

    key is an already open key, or one of the predefined *HKEY_* constants*.

    Returns `True` if reflection is disabled.

    Will generally raise *NotImplemented* if executed on a 32-bit operating system.

34.3.2 Constants

The following constants are defined for use in many `_winreg` functions.

HKEY_* Constants

winreg.HKEY_CLASSES_ROOT
    Registry entries subordinate to this key define types (or classes) of documents and the properties associated with those types. Shell and COM applications use the information stored under this key.

winreg.HKEY_CURRENT_USER
    Registry entries subordinate to this key define the preferences of the current user. These preferences include the settings of environment variables, data about program groups, colors, printers, network connections, and application preferences.

winreg.HKEY_LOCAL_MACHINE
    Registry entries subordinate to this key define the physical state of the computer, including data about the bus type, system memory, and installed hardware and software.

winreg.HKEY_USERS
    Registry entries subordinate to this key define the default user configuration for new users on the local computer and the user configuration for the current user.

winreg.HKEY_PERFORMANCE_DATA
    Registry entries subordinate to this key allow you to access performance data. The data is not actually stored in the registry; the registry functions cause the system to collect the data from its source.

winreg.HKEY_CURRENT_CONFIG
    Contains information about the current hardware profile of the local computer system.

winreg.HKEY_DYN_DATA
    This key is not used in versions of Windows after 98.

Access Rights

For more information, see Registry Key Security and Access.

`winreg.KEY_ALL_ACCESS`
    Combines the STANDARD_RIGHTS_REQUIRED, *KEY_QUERY_VALUE*, *KEY_SET_VALUE*, *KEY_CREATE_SUB_KEY*, *KEY_ENUMERATE_SUB_KEYS*, *KEY_NOTIFY*, and *KEY_CREATE_LINK* access rights.

`winreg.KEY_WRITE`
    Combines the STANDARD_RIGHTS_WRITE, *KEY_SET_VALUE*, and *KEY_CREATE_SUB_KEY* access rights.

`winreg.KEY_READ`
    Combines the STANDARD_RIGHTS_READ, *KEY_QUERY_VALUE*, *KEY_ENUMERATE_SUB_KEYS*, and *KEY_NOTIFY* values.

`winreg.KEY_EXECUTE`
    Equivalent to *KEY_READ*.

`winreg.KEY_QUERY_VALUE`
    Required to query the values of a registry key.

`winreg.KEY_SET_VALUE`
    Required to create, delete, or set a registry value.

`winreg.KEY_CREATE_SUB_KEY`
    Required to create a subkey of a registry key.

`winreg.KEY_ENUMERATE_SUB_KEYS`
    Required to enumerate the subkeys of a registry key.

`winreg.KEY_NOTIFY`
    Required to request change notifications for a registry key or for subkeys of a registry key.

`winreg.KEY_CREATE_LINK`
    Reserved for system use.

64-bit Specific

For more information, see Accessing an Alternate Registry View.

`winreg.KEY_WOW64_64KEY`
    Indicates that an application on 64-bit Windows should operate on the 64-bit registry view.

`winreg.KEY_WOW64_32KEY`
    Indicates that an application on 64-bit Windows should operate on the 32-bit registry view.

Value Types

For more information, see Registry Value Types.

`winreg.REG_BINARY`
    Binary data in any form.

`winreg.REG_DWORD`
    32-bit number.

`winreg.REG_DWORD_LITTLE_ENDIAN`
    A 32-bit number in little-endian format. Equivalent to *REG_DWORD*.

winreg.REG_DWORD_BIG_ENDIAN
　　A 32-bit number in big-endian format.

winreg.REG_EXPAND_SZ
　　Null-terminated string containing references to environment variables (%PATH%).

winreg.REG_LINK
　　A Unicode symbolic link.

winreg.REG_MULTI_SZ
　　A sequence of null-terminated strings, terminated by two null characters. (Python handles this termination automatically.)

winreg.REG_NONE
　　No defined value type.

winreg.REG_QWORD
　　A 64-bit number.

　　New in version 3.6.

winreg.REG_QWORD_LITTLE_ENDIAN
　　A 64-bit number in little-endian format. Equivalent to *REG_QWORD*.

　　New in version 3.6.

winreg.REG_RESOURCE_LIST
　　A device-driver resource list.

winreg.REG_FULL_RESOURCE_DESCRIPTOR
　　A hardware setting.

winreg.REG_RESOURCE_REQUIREMENTS_LIST
　　A hardware resource list.

winreg.REG_SZ
　　A null-terminated string.

34.3.3 Registry Handle Objects

This object wraps a Windows HKEY object, automatically closing it when the object is destroyed. To guarantee cleanup, you can call either the *Close()* method on the object, or the *CloseKey()* function.

All registry functions in this module return one of these objects.

All registry functions in this module which accept a handle object also accept an integer, however, use of the handle object is encouraged.

Handle objects provide semantics for `__bool__()` – thus

```
if handle:
    print("Yes")
```

will print **Yes** if the handle is currently valid (has not been closed or detached).

The object also support comparison semantics, so handle objects will compare true if they both reference the same underlying Windows handle value.

Handle objects can be converted to an integer (e.g., using the built-in *int()* function), in which case the underlying Windows handle value is returned. You can also use the *Detach()* method to return the integer handle, and also disconnect the Windows handle from the handle object.

PyHKEY.Close()
  Closes the underlying Windows handle.

  If the handle is already closed, no error is raised.

PyHKEY.Detach()
  Detaches the Windows handle from the handle object.

  The result is an integer that holds the value of the handle before it is detached. If the handle is already detached or closed, this will return zero.

  After calling this function, the handle is effectively invalidated, but the handle is not closed. You would call this function when you need the underlying Win32 handle to exist beyond the lifetime of the handle object.

PyHKEY.__enter__()
PyHKEY.__exit__(*exc_info)
  The HKEY object implements __enter__() and __exit__() and thus supports the context protocol for the `with` statement:

```
with OpenKey(HKEY_LOCAL_MACHINE, "foo") as key:
...    # work with key
```

  will automatically close *key* when control leaves the `with` block.

34.4 `winsound` — Sound-playing interface for Windows

The *winsound* module provides access to the basic sound-playing machinery provided by Windows platforms. It includes functions and several constants.

winsound.Beep(*frequency, duration*)
  Beep the PC's speaker. The *frequency* parameter specifies frequency, in hertz, of the sound, and must be in the range 37 through 32,767. The *duration* parameter specifies the number of milliseconds the sound should last. If the system is not able to beep the speaker, *RuntimeError* is raised.

winsound.PlaySound(*sound, flags*)
  Call the underlying PlaySound() function from the Platform API. The *sound* parameter may be a filename, a system sound alias, audio data as a *bytes-like object*, or None. Its interpretation depends on the value of *flags*, which can be a bitwise ORed combination of the constants described below. If the *sound* parameter is None, any currently playing waveform sound is stopped. If the system indicates an error, *RuntimeError* is raised.

winsound.MessageBeep(*type=MB_OK*)
  Call the underlying MessageBeep() function from the Platform API. This plays a sound as specified in the registry. The *type* argument specifies which sound to play; possible values are -1, MB_ICONASTERISK, MB_ICONEXCLAMATION, MB_ICONHAND, MB_ICONQUESTION, and MB_OK, all described below. The value -1 produces a "simple beep"; this is the final fallback if a sound cannot be played otherwise. If the system indicates an error, *RuntimeError* is raised.

winsound.SND_FILENAME
  The *sound* parameter is the name of a WAV file. Do not use with *SND_ALIAS*.

winsound.SND_ALIAS
  The *sound* parameter is a sound association name from the registry. If the registry contains no such name, play the system default sound unless *SND_NODEFAULT* is also specified. If no default sound is registered, raise *RuntimeError*. Do not use with *SND_FILENAME*.

All Win32 systems support at least the following; most systems support many more:

`PlaySound()` name	Corresponding Control Panel Sound name
`'SystemAsterisk'`	Asterisk
`'SystemExclamation'`	Exclamation
`'SystemExit'`	Exit Windows
`'SystemHand'`	Critical Stop
`'SystemQuestion'`	Question

For example:

```
import winsound
# Play Windows exit sound.
winsound.PlaySound("SystemExit", winsound.SND_ALIAS)

# Probably play Windows default sound, if any is registered (because
# "*" probably isn't the registered name of any sound).
winsound.PlaySound("*", winsound.SND_ALIAS)
```

winsound.SND_LOOP

    Play the sound repeatedly. The *SND_ASYNC* flag must also be used to avoid blocking. Cannot be used with *SND_MEMORY*.

winsound.SND_MEMORY

    The *sound* parameter to *PlaySound()* is a memory image of a WAV file, as a *bytes-like object*.

Note: This module does not support playing from a memory image asynchronously, so a combination of this flag and *SND_ASYNC* will raise *RuntimeError*.

---

winsound.SND_PURGE

    Stop playing all instances of the specified sound.

Note: This flag is not supported on modern Windows platforms.

---

winsound.SND_ASYNC

    Return immediately, allowing sounds to play asynchronously.

winsound.SND_NODEFAULT

    If the specified sound cannot be found, do not play the system default sound.

winsound.SND_NOSTOP

    Do not interrupt sounds currently playing.

winsound.SND_NOWAIT

    Return immediately if the sound driver is busy.

Note: This flag is not supported on modern Windows platforms.

---

winsound.MB_ICONASTERISK

    Play the `SystemDefault` sound.

winsound.MB_ICONEXCLAMATION

    Play the `SystemExclamation` sound.

winsound.MB_ICONHAND

    Play the `SystemHand` sound.

winsound.MB_ICONQUESTION
　　Play the `SystemQuestion` sound.

winsound.MB_OK
　　Play the `SystemDefault` sound.

CHAPTER
THIRTYFIVE

UNIX SPECIFIC SERVICES

The modules described in this chapter provide interfaces to features that are unique to the Unix operating system, or in some cases to some or many variants of it. Here's an overview:

35.1 posix — The most common POSIX system calls

This module provides access to operating system functionality that is standardized by the C Standard and the POSIX standard (a thinly disguised Unix interface).

Do not import this module directly. Instead, import the module *os*, which provides a *portable* version of this interface. On Unix, the *os* module provides a superset of the *posix* interface. On non-Unix operating systems the *posix* module is not available, but a subset is always available through the *os* interface. Once *os* is imported, there is *no* performance penalty in using it instead of *posix*. In addition, *os* provides some additional functionality, such as automatically calling *putenv()* when an entry in `os.environ` is changed.

Errors are reported as exceptions; the usual exceptions are given for type errors, while errors reported by the system calls raise *OSError*.

35.1.1 Large File Support

Several operating systems (including AIX, HP-UX, Irix and Solaris) provide support for files that are larger than 2 GiB from a C programming model where `int` and `long` are 32-bit values. This is typically accomplished by defining the relevant size and offset types as 64-bit values. Such files are sometimes referred to as *large files*.

Large file support is enabled in Python when the size of an `off_t` is larger than a `long` and the `long long` type is available and is at least as large as an `off_t`. It may be necessary to configure and compile Python with certain compiler flags to enable this mode. For example, it is enabled by default with recent versions of Irix, but with Solaris 2.6 and 2.7 you need to do something like:

```
CFLAGS="`getconf LFS_CFLAGS`" OPT="-g -O2 $CFLAGS" \
    ./configure
```

On large-file-capable Linux systems, this might work:

```
CFLAGS='-D_LARGEFILE64_SOURCE -D_FILE_OFFSET_BITS=64' OPT="-g -O2 $CFLAGS" \
    ./configure
```

35.1.2 Notable Module Contents

In addition to many functions described in the *os* module documentation, *posix* defines the following data item:

posix.environ
> A dictionary representing the string environment at the time the interpreter was started. Keys and values are bytes on Unix and str on Windows. For example, environ[b'HOME'] (environ['HOME'] on Windows) is the pathname of your home directory, equivalent to getenv("HOME") in C.
>
> Modifying this dictionary does not affect the string environment passed on by *execv()*, *popen()* or *system()*; if you need to change the environment, pass **environ** to *execve()* or add variable assignments and export statements to the command string for *system()* or *popen()*.
>
> Changed in version 3.2: On Unix, keys and values are bytes.

> **Note:** The *os* module provides an alternate implementation of **environ** which updates the environment on modification. Note also that updating *os.environ* will render this dictionary obsolete. Use of the *os* module version of this is recommended over direct access to the *posix* module.

35.2 pwd — The password database

This module provides access to the Unix user account and password database. It is available on all Unix versions.

Password database entries are reported as a tuple-like object, whose attributes correspond to the members of the **passwd** structure (Attribute field below, see <pwd.h>):

Index	Attribute	Meaning
0	pw_name	Login name
1	pw_passwd	Optional encrypted password
2	pw_uid	Numerical user ID
3	pw_gid	Numerical group ID
4	pw_gecos	User name or comment field
5	pw_dir	User home directory
6	pw_shell	User command interpreter

The uid and gid items are integers, all others are strings. *KeyError* is raised if the entry asked for cannot be found.

> **Note:** In traditional Unix the field pw_passwd usually contains a password encrypted with a DES derived algorithm (see module *crypt*). However most modern unices use a so-called *shadow password* system. On those unices the *pw_passwd* field only contains an asterisk ('*') or the letter 'x' where the encrypted password is stored in a file /etc/shadow which is not world readable. Whether the *pw_passwd* field contains anything useful is system-dependent. If available, the *spwd* module should be used where access to the encrypted password is required.

It defines the following items:

pwd.getpwuid(*uid*)
> Return the password database entry for the given numeric user ID.

pwd.getpwnam(*name*)
   Return the password database entry for the given user name.

pwd.getpwall()
   Return a list of all available password database entries, in arbitrary order.

See also:

Module *grp* An interface to the group database, similar to this.

Module *spwd* An interface to the shadow password database, similar to this.

35.3 `spwd` — The shadow password database

This module provides access to the Unix shadow password database. It is available on various Unix versions.

You must have enough privileges to access the shadow password database (this usually means you have to be root).

Shadow password database entries are reported as a tuple-like object, whose attributes correspond to the members of the `spwd` structure (Attribute field below, see `<shadow.h>`):

Index	Attribute	Meaning
0	sp_namp	Login name
1	sp_pwdp	Encrypted password
2	sp_lstchg	Date of last change
3	sp_min	Minimal number of days between changes
4	sp_max	Maximum number of days between changes
5	sp_warn	Number of days before password expires to warn user about it
6	sp_inact	Number of days after password expires until account is disabled
7	sp_expire	Number of days since 1970-01-01 when account expires
8	sp_flag	Reserved

The sp_namp and sp_pwdp items are strings, all others are integers. *KeyError* is raised if the entry asked for cannot be found.

The following functions are defined:

spwd.getspnam(*name*)
   Return the shadow password database entry for the given user name.

   Changed in version 3.6: Raises a *PermissionError* instead of *KeyError* if the user doesn't have privileges.

spwd.getspall()
   Return a list of all available shadow password database entries, in arbitrary order.

See also:

Module *grp* An interface to the group database, similar to this.

Module *pwd* An interface to the normal password database, similar to this.

35.4 `grp` — The group database

This module provides access to the Unix group database. It is available on all Unix versions.

Group database entries are reported as a tuple-like object, whose attributes correspond to the members of the `group` structure (Attribute field below, see `<pwd.h>`):

Index	Attribute	Meaning
0	gr_name	the name of the group
1	gr_passwd	the (encrypted) group password; often empty
2	gr_gid	the numerical group ID
3	gr_mem	all the group member's user names

The gid is an integer, name and password are strings, and the member list is a list of strings. (Note that most users are not explicitly listed as members of the group they are in according to the password database. Check both databases to get complete membership information. Also note that a `gr_name` that starts with a + or - is likely to be a YP/NIS reference and may not be accessible via *getgrnam()* or *getgrgid()*.)

It defines the following items:

grp.getgrgid(*gid*)
> Return the group database entry for the given numeric group ID. *KeyError* is raised if the entry asked for cannot be found.
>
> Deprecated since version 3.6: Since Python 3.6 the support of non-integer arguments like floats or strings in *getgrgid()* is deprecated.

grp.getgrnam(*name*)
> Return the group database entry for the given group name. *KeyError* is raised if the entry asked for cannot be found.

grp.getgrall()
> Return a list of all available group entries, in arbitrary order.

See also:

Module *pwd* An interface to the user database, similar to this.

Module *spwd* An interface to the shadow password database, similar to this.

35.5 `crypt` — Function to check Unix passwords

Source code: Lib/crypt.py

This module implements an interface to the *crypt(3)* routine, which is a one-way hash function based upon a modified DES algorithm; see the Unix man page for further details. Possible uses include storing hashed passwords so you can check passwords without storing the actual password, or attempting to crack Unix passwords with a dictionary.

Notice that the behavior of this module depends on the actual implementation of the *crypt(3)* routine in the running system. Therefore, any extensions available on the current implementation will also be available on this module.

35.5.1 Hashing Methods

New in version 3.3.

The *crypt* module defines the list of hashing methods (not all methods are available on all platforms):

crypt.METHOD_SHA512
    A Modular Crypt Format method with 16 character salt and 86 character hash. This is the strongest method.

crypt.METHOD_SHA256
    Another Modular Crypt Format method with 16 character salt and 43 character hash.

crypt.METHOD_MD5
    Another Modular Crypt Format method with 8 character salt and 22 character hash.

crypt.METHOD_CRYPT
    The traditional method with a 2 character salt and 13 characters of hash. This is the weakest method.

35.5.2 Module Attributes

New in version 3.3.

crypt.methods
    A list of available password hashing algorithms, as `crypt.METHOD_*` objects. This list is sorted from strongest to weakest.

35.5.3 Module Functions

The *crypt* module defines the following functions:

crypt.crypt(*word, salt=None*)
    word will usually be a user's password as typed at a prompt or in a graphical interface. The optional *salt* is either a string as returned from *mksalt()*, one of the `crypt.METHOD_*` values (though not all may be available on all platforms), or a full encrypted password including salt, as returned by this function. If *salt* is not provided, the strongest method will be used (as returned by *methods()*.

    Checking a password is usually done by passing the plain-text password as *word* and the full results of a previous *crypt()* call, which should be the same as the results of this call.

    salt (either a random 2 or 16 character string, possibly prefixed with `$digit$` to indicate the method) which will be used to perturb the encryption algorithm. The characters in *salt* must be in the set `[./a-zA-Z0-9]`, with the exception of Modular Crypt Format which prefixes a `$digit$`.

    Returns the hashed password as a string, which will be composed of characters from the same alphabet as the salt.

    Since a few *crypt(3)* extensions allow different values, with different sizes in the *salt*, it is recommended to use the full crypted password as salt when checking for a password.

    Changed in version 3.3: Accept `crypt.METHOD_*` values in addition to strings for *salt*.

crypt.mksalt(*method=None*)
    Return a randomly generated salt of the specified method. If no *method* is given, the strongest method available as returned by *methods()* is used.

    The return value is a string either of 2 characters in length for `crypt.METHOD_CRYPT`, or 19 characters starting with `$digit$` and 16 random characters from the set `[./a-zA-Z0-9]`, suitable for passing as the *salt* argument to *crypt()*.

    New in version 3.3.

35.5.4 Examples

A simple example illustrating typical use (a constant-time comparison operation is needed to limit exposure to timing attacks. `hmac.compare_digest()` is suitable for this purpose):

```
import pwd
import crypt
import getpass
from hmac import compare_digest as compare_hash

def login():
    username = input('Python login: ')
    cryptedpasswd = pwd.getpwnam(username)[1]
    if cryptedpasswd:
        if cryptedpasswd == 'x' or cryptedpasswd == '*':
            raise ValueError('no support for shadow passwords')
        cleartext = getpass.getpass()
        return compare_hash(crypt.crypt(cleartext, cryptedpasswd), cryptedpasswd)
    else:
        return True
```

To generate a hash of a password using the strongest available method and check it against the original:

```
import crypt
from hmac import compare_digest as compare_hash

hashed = crypt.crypt(plaintext)
if not compare_hash(hashed, crypt.crypt(plaintext, hashed)):
    raise ValueError("hashed version doesn't validate against original")
```

35.6 `termios` — POSIX style tty control

This module provides an interface to the POSIX calls for tty I/O control. For a complete description of these calls, see *termios(3)* Unix manual page. It is only available for those Unix versions that support POSIX *termios* style tty I/O control configured during installation.

All functions in this module take a file descriptor *fd* as their first argument. This can be an integer file descriptor, such as returned by `sys.stdin.fileno()`, or a *file object*, such as `sys.stdin` itself.

This module also defines all the constants needed to work with the functions provided here; these have the same name as their counterparts in C. Please refer to your system documentation for more information on using these terminal control interfaces.

The module defines the following functions:

`termios.tcgetattr(`*fd*`)`
> Return a list containing the tty attributes for file descriptor *fd*, as follows: `[iflag, oflag, cflag, lflag, ispeed, ospeed, cc]` where `cc` is a list of the tty special characters (each a string of length 1, except the items with indices `VMIN` and `VTIME`, which are integers when these fields are defined). The interpretation of the flags and the speeds as well as the indexing in the `cc` array must be done using the symbolic constants defined in the *termios* module.

`termios.tcsetattr(`*fd*, *when*, *attributes*`)`
> Set the tty attributes for file descriptor *fd* from the *attributes*, which is a list like the one returned by `tcgetattr()`. The *when* argument determines when the attributes are changed: `TCSANOW` to change

immediately, `TCSADRAIN` to change after transmitting all queued output, or `TCSAFLUSH` to change after transmitting all queued output and discarding all queued input.

termios.tcsendbreak(*fd, duration*)
   Send a break on file descriptor *fd*. A zero *duration* sends a break for 0.25 –0.5 seconds; a nonzero *duration* has a system dependent meaning.

termios.tcdrain(*fd*)
   Wait until all output written to file descriptor *fd* has been transmitted.

termios.tcflush(*fd, queue*)
   Discard queued data on file descriptor *fd*. The *queue* selector specifies which queue: `TCIFLUSH` for the input queue, `TCOFLUSH` for the output queue, or `TCIOFLUSH` for both queues.

termios.tcflow(*fd, action*)
   Suspend or resume input or output on file descriptor *fd*. The *action* argument can be `TCOOFF` to suspend output, `TCOON` to restart output, `TCIOFF` to suspend input, or `TCION` to restart input.

See also:

Module `tty` Convenience functions for common terminal control operations.

35.6.1 Example

Here's a function that prompts for a password with echoing turned off. Note the technique using a separate *tcgetattr()* call and a **try** ... **finally** statement to ensure that the old tty attributes are restored exactly no matter what happens:

```
def getpass(prompt="Password: "):
    import termios, sys
    fd = sys.stdin.fileno()
    old = termios.tcgetattr(fd)
    new = termios.tcgetattr(fd)
    new[3] = new[3] & ~termios.ECHO          # lflags
    try:
        termios.tcsetattr(fd, termios.TCSADRAIN, new)
        passwd = input(prompt)
    finally:
        termios.tcsetattr(fd, termios.TCSADRAIN, old)
    return passwd
```

35.7 `tty` — Terminal control functions

Source code: Lib/tty.py

The `tty` module defines functions for putting the tty into cbreak and raw modes.

Because it requires the `termios` module, it will work only on Unix.

The `tty` module defines the following functions:

tty.setraw(*fd, when=termios.TCSAFLUSH*)
   Change the mode of the file descriptor *fd* to raw. If *when* is omitted, it defaults to `termios.TCSAFLUSH`, and is passed to *termios.tcsetattr()*.

tty.setcbreak(*fd, when=termios.TCSAFLUSH*)
    Change the mode of file descriptor *fd* to cbreak. If *when* is omitted, it defaults to `termios.TCSAFLUSH`, and is passed to `termios.tcsetattr()`.

See also:

Module `termios` Low-level terminal control interface.

35.8 `pty` — Pseudo-terminal utilities

Source code: Lib/pty.py

The `pty` module defines operations for handling the pseudo-terminal concept: starting another process and being able to write to and read from its controlling terminal programmatically.

Because pseudo-terminal handling is highly platform dependent, there is code to do it only for Linux. (The Linux code is supposed to work on other platforms, but hasn't been tested yet.)

The `pty` module defines the following functions:

pty.fork()
    Fork. Connect the child's controlling terminal to a pseudo-terminal. Return value is (**pid, fd**). Note that the child gets *pid* 0, and the *fd* is *invalid*. The parent's return value is the *pid* of the child, and *fd* is a file descriptor connected to the child's controlling terminal (and also to the child's standard input and output).

pty.openpty()
    Open a new pseudo-terminal pair, using `os.openpty()` if possible, or emulation code for generic Unix systems. Return a pair of file descriptors (**master, slave**), for the master and the slave end, respectively.

pty.spawn(*argv*[, *master_read*[, *stdin_read*]])
    Spawn a process, and connect its controlling terminal with the current process's standard io. This is often used to baffle programs which insist on reading from the controlling terminal.

    The functions *master_read* and *stdin_read* should be functions which read from a file descriptor. The defaults try to read 1024 bytes each time they are called.

    Changed in version 3.4: `spawn()` now returns the status value from `os.waitpid()` on the child process.

35.8.1 Example

The following program acts like the Unix command *script(1)*, using a pseudo-terminal to record all input and output of a terminal session in a "typescript".

```
import argparse
import os
import pty
import sys
import time

parser = argparse.ArgumentParser()
parser.add_argument('-a', dest='append', action='store_true')
parser.add_argument('-p', dest='use_python', action='store_true')
parser.add_argument('filename', nargs='?', default='typescript')
options = parser.parse_args()
```

```python
shell = sys.executable if options.use_python else os.environ.get('SHELL', 'sh')
filename = options.filename
mode = 'ab' if options.append else 'wb'

with open(filename, mode) as script:
    def read(fd):
        data = os.read(fd, 1024)
        script.write(data)
        return data

    print('Script started, file is', filename)
    script.write(('Script started on %s\n' % time.asctime()).encode())

    pty.spawn(shell, read)

    script.write(('Script done on %s\n' % time.asctime()).encode())
    print('Script done, file is', filename)
```

35.9 fcntl — The fcntl and ioctl system calls

This module performs file control and I/O control on file descriptors. It is an interface to the fcntl() and ioctl() Unix routines. For a complete description of these calls, see *fcntl(2)* and *ioctl(2)* Unix manual pages.

All functions in this module take a file descriptor *fd* as their first argument. This can be an integer file descriptor, such as returned by sys.stdin.fileno(), or an *io.IOBase* object, such as sys.stdin itself, which provides a *fileno()* that returns a genuine file descriptor.

Changed in version 3.3: Operations in this module used to raise an *IOError* where they now raise an *OSError*.

The module defines the following functions:

fcntl.fcntl(*fd*, *cmd*, *arg=0*)
> Perform the operation *cmd* on file descriptor *fd* (file objects providing a *fileno()* method are accepted as well). The values used for *cmd* are operating system dependent, and are available as constants in the *fcntl* module, using the same names as used in the relevant C header files. The argument *arg* can either be an integer value, or a *bytes* object. With an integer value, the return value of this function is the integer return value of the C fcntl() call. When the argument is bytes it represents a binary structure, e.g. created by *struct.pack()*. The binary data is copied to a buffer whose address is passed to the C fcntl() call. The return value after a successful call is the contents of the buffer, converted to a *bytes* object. The length of the returned object will be the same as the length of the *arg* argument. This is limited to 1024 bytes. If the information returned in the buffer by the operating system is larger than 1024 bytes, this is most likely to result in a segmentation violation or a more subtle data corruption.
>
> If the fcntl() fails, an *OSError* is raised.

fcntl.ioctl(*fd*, *request*, *arg=0*, *mutate_flag=True*)
> This function is identical to the *fcntl()* function, except that the argument handling is even more complicated.
>
> The *request* parameter is limited to values that can fit in 32-bits. Additional constants of interest for use as the *request* argument can be found in the *termios* module, under the same names as used in the relevant C header files.

The parameter *arg* can be one of an integer, an object supporting the read-only buffer interface (like `bytes`) or an object supporting the read-write buffer interface (like `bytearray`).

In all but the last case, behaviour is as for the *fcntl()* function.

If a mutable buffer is passed, then the behaviour is determined by the value of the *mutate_flag* parameter.

If it is false, the buffer's mutability is ignored and behaviour is as for a read-only buffer, except that the 1024 byte limit mentioned above is avoided – so long as the buffer you pass is at least as long as what the operating system wants to put there, things should work.

If *mutate_flag* is true (the default), then the buffer is (in effect) passed to the underlying *ioctl()* system call, the latter's return code is passed back to the calling Python, and the buffer's new contents reflect the action of the *ioctl()*. This is a slight simplification, because if the supplied buffer is less than 1024 bytes long it is first copied into a static buffer 1024 bytes long which is then passed to *ioctl()* and copied back into the supplied buffer.

If the `ioctl()` fails, an *OSError* exception is raised.

An example:

```
>>> import array, fcntl, struct, termios, os
>>> os.getpgrp()
13341
>>> struct.unpack('h', fcntl.ioctl(0, termios.TIOCGPGRP, "  "))[0]
13341
>>> buf = array.array('h', [0])
>>> fcntl.ioctl(0, termios.TIOCGPGRP, buf, 1)
0
>>> buf
array('h', [13341])
```

fcntl.flock(*fd, operation*)

Perform the lock operation *operation* on file descriptor *fd* (file objects providing a *fileno()* method are accepted as well). See the Unix manual *flock(2)* for details. (On some systems, this function is emulated using `fcntl()`.)

If the `flock()` fails, an *OSError* exception is raised.

fcntl.lockf(*fd, cmd, len=0, start=0, whence=0*)

This is essentially a wrapper around the *fcntl()* locking calls. *fd* is the file descriptor of the file to lock or unlock, and *cmd* is one of the following values:

- LOCK_UN – unlock
- LOCK_SH – acquire a shared lock
- LOCK_EX – acquire an exclusive lock

When *cmd* is LOCK_SH or LOCK_EX, it can also be bitwise ORed with LOCK_NB to avoid blocking on lock acquisition. If LOCK_NB is used and the lock cannot be acquired, an *OSError* will be raised and the exception will have an *errno* attribute set to EACCES or EAGAIN (depending on the operating system; for portability, check for both values). On at least some systems, LOCK_EX can only be used if the file descriptor refers to a file opened for writing.

len is the number of bytes to lock, *start* is the byte offset at which the lock starts, relative to *whence*, and *whence* is as with *io.IOBase.seek()*, specifically:

- 0 – relative to the start of the file (*os.SEEK_SET*)
- 1 – relative to the current buffer position (*os.SEEK_CUR*)
- 2 – relative to the end of the file (*os.SEEK_END*)

The default for *start* is 0, which means to start at the beginning of the file. The default for *len* is 0 which means to lock to the end of the file. The default for *whence* is also 0.

Examples (all on a SVR4 compliant system):

```
import struct, fcntl, os

f = open(...)
rv = fcntl.fcntl(f, fcntl.F_SETFL, os.O_NDELAY)

lockdata = struct.pack('hhllhh', fcntl.F_WRLCK, 0, 0, 0, 0, 0)
rv = fcntl.fcntl(f, fcntl.F_SETLKW, lockdata)
```

Note that in the first example the return value variable *rv* will hold an integer value; in the second example it will hold a `bytes` object. The structure lay-out for the *lockdata* variable is system dependent — therefore using the `flock()` call may be better.

See also:

Module `os` If the locking flags `O_SHLOCK` and `O_EXLOCK` are present in the `os` module (on BSD only), the `os.open()` function provides an alternative to the `lockf()` and `flock()` functions.

35.10 pipes — Interface to shell pipelines

Source code: Lib/pipes.py

The `pipes` module defines a class to abstract the concept of a *pipeline* — a sequence of converters from one file to another.

Because the module uses **/bin/sh** command lines, a POSIX or compatible shell for `os.system()` and `os.popen()` is required.

The `pipes` module defines the following class:

class pipes.Template
   An abstraction of a pipeline.

Example:

```
>>> import pipes
>>> t = pipes.Template()
>>> t.append('tr a-z A-Z', '--')
>>> f = t.open('pipefile', 'w')
>>> f.write('hello world')
>>> f.close()
>>> open('pipefile').read()
'HELLO WORLD'
```

35.10.1 Template Objects

Template objects following methods:

Template.reset()
   Restore a pipeline template to its initial state.

Template.clone()
   Return a new, equivalent, pipeline template.

Template.debug(*flag*)
    If *flag* is true, turn debugging on. Otherwise, turn debugging off. When debugging is on, commands to be executed are printed, and the shell is given `set -x` command to be more verbose.

Template.append(*cmd, kind*)
    Append a new action at the end. The *cmd* variable must be a valid bourne shell command. The *kind* variable consists of two letters.

    The first letter can be either of '-' (which means the command reads its standard input), 'f' (which means the commands reads a given file on the command line) or '.' (which means the commands reads no input, and hence must be first.)

    Similarly, the second letter can be either of '-' (which means the command writes to standard output), 'f' (which means the command writes a file on the command line) or '.' (which means the command does not write anything, and hence must be last.)

Template.prepend(*cmd, kind*)
    Add a new action at the beginning. See `append()` for explanations of the arguments.

Template.open(*file, mode*)
    Return a file-like object, open to *file*, but read from or written to by the pipeline. Note that only one of 'r', 'w' may be given.

Template.copy(*infile, outfile*)
    Copy *infile* to *outfile* through the pipe.

35.11 resource — Resource usage information

This module provides basic mechanisms for measuring and controlling system resources utilized by a program.

Symbolic constants are used to specify particular system resources and to request usage information about either the current process or its children.

An *OSError* is raised on syscall failure.

exception resource.error
    A deprecated alias of *OSError*.

    Changed in version 3.3: Following PEP 3151, this class was made an alias of *OSError*.

35.11.1 Resource Limits

Resources usage can be limited using the `setrlimit()` function described below. Each resource is controlled by a pair of limits: a soft limit and a hard limit. The soft limit is the current limit, and may be lowered or raised by a process over time. The soft limit can never exceed the hard limit. The hard limit can be lowered to any value greater than the soft limit, but not raised. (Only processes with the effective UID of the super-user can raise a hard limit.)

The specific resources that can be limited are system dependent. They are described in the *getrlimit(2)* man page. The resources listed below are supported when the underlying operating system supports them; resources which cannot be checked or controlled by the operating system are not defined in this module for those platforms.

resource.RLIM_INFINITY
    Constant used to represent the limit for an unlimited resource.

`resource.getrlimit(resource)`
> Returns a tuple (`soft`, `hard`) with the current soft and hard limits of *resource*. Raises `ValueError` if an invalid resource is specified, or `error` if the underlying system call fails unexpectedly.

`resource.setrlimit(resource, limits)`
> Sets new limits of consumption of *resource*. The *limits* argument must be a tuple (`soft`, `hard`) of two integers describing the new limits. A value of `RLIM_INFINITY` can be used to request a limit that is unlimited.
>
> Raises `ValueError` if an invalid resource is specified, if the new soft limit exceeds the hard limit, or if a process tries to raise its hard limit. Specifying a limit of `RLIM_INFINITY` when the hard or system limit for that resource is not unlimited will result in a `ValueError`. A process with the effective UID of super-user can request any valid limit value, including unlimited, but `ValueError` will still be raised if the requested limit exceeds the system imposed limit.
>
> `setrlimit` may also raise `error` if the underlying system call fails.

`resource.prlimit(pid, resource[, limits])`
> Combines `setrlimit()` and `getrlimit()` in one function and supports to get and set the resources limits of an arbitrary process. If *pid* is 0, then the call applies to the current process. *resource* and *limits* have the same meaning as in `setrlimit()`, except that *limits* is optional.
>
> When *limits* is not given the function returns the *resource* limit of the process *pid*. When *limits* is given the *resource* limit of the process is set and the former resource limit is returned.
>
> Raises `ProcessLookupError` when *pid* can't be found and `PermissionError` when the user doesn't have `CAP_SYS_RESOURCE` for the process.
>
> Availability: Linux 2.6.36 or later with glibc 2.13 or later
>
> New in version 3.4.

These symbols define resources whose consumption can be controlled using the `setrlimit()` and `getrlimit()` functions described below. The values of these symbols are exactly the constants used by C programs.

The Unix man page for *getrlimit(2)* lists the available resources. Note that not all systems use the same symbol or same value to denote the same resource. This module does not attempt to mask platform differences — symbols not defined for a platform will not be available from this module on that platform.

`resource.RLIMIT_CORE`
> The maximum size (in bytes) of a core file that the current process can create. This may result in the creation of a partial core file if a larger core would be required to contain the entire process image.

`resource.RLIMIT_CPU`
> The maximum amount of processor time (in seconds) that a process can use. If this limit is exceeded, a `SIGXCPU` signal is sent to the process. (See the `signal` module documentation for information about how to catch this signal and do something useful, e.g. flush open files to disk.)

`resource.RLIMIT_FSIZE`
> The maximum size of a file which the process may create.

`resource.RLIMIT_DATA`
> The maximum size (in bytes) of the process's heap.

`resource.RLIMIT_STACK`
> The maximum size (in bytes) of the call stack for the current process. This only affects the stack of the main thread in a multi-threaded process.

`resource.RLIMIT_RSS`
> The maximum resident set size that should be made available to the process.

`resource.RLIMIT_NPROC`
> The maximum number of processes the current process may create.

`resource.RLIMIT_NOFILE`
   The maximum number of open file descriptors for the current process.

`resource.RLIMIT_OFILE`
   The BSD name for `RLIMIT_NOFILE`.

`resource.RLIMIT_MEMLOCK`
   The maximum address space which may be locked in memory.

`resource.RLIMIT_VMEM`
   The largest area of mapped memory which the process may occupy.

`resource.RLIMIT_AS`
   The maximum area (in bytes) of address space which may be taken by the process.

`resource.RLIMIT_MSGQUEUE`
   The number of bytes that can be allocated for POSIX message queues.

   Availability: Linux 2.6.8 or later.

   New in version 3.4.

`resource.RLIMIT_NICE`
   The ceiling for the process's nice level (calculated as 20 - rlim_cur).

   Availability: Linux 2.6.12 or later.

   New in version 3.4.

`resource.RLIMIT_RTPRIO`
   The ceiling of the real-time priority.

   Availability: Linux 2.6.12 or later.

   New in version 3.4.

`resource.RLIMIT_RTTIME`
   The time limit (in microseconds) on CPU time that a process can spend under real-time scheduling without making a blocking syscall.

   Availability: Linux 2.6.25 or later.

   New in version 3.4.

`resource.RLIMIT_SIGPENDING`
   The number of signals which the process may queue.

   Availability: Linux 2.6.8 or later.

   New in version 3.4.

`resource.RLIMIT_SBSIZE`
   The maximum size (in bytes) of socket buffer usage for this user. This limits the amount of network memory, and hence the amount of mbufs, that this user may hold at any time.

   Availability: FreeBSD 9 or later.

   New in version 3.4.

`resource.RLIMIT_SWAP`
   The maximum size (in bytes) of the swap space that may be reserved or used by all of this user id's processes. This limit is enforced only if bit 1 of the vm.overcommit sysctl is set. Please see *tuning(7)* for a complete description of this sysctl.

   Availability: FreeBSD 9 or later.

   New in version 3.4.

`resource.RLIMIT_NPTS`
>   The maximum number of pseudo-terminals created by this user id.
>
>   Availability: FreeBSD 9 or later.
>
>   New in version 3.4.

35.11.2 Resource Usage

These functions are used to retrieve resource usage information:

`resource.getrusage(who)`
>   This function returns an object that describes the resources consumed by either the current process or its children, as specified by the *who* parameter. The *who* parameter should be specified using one of the `RUSAGE_*` constants described below.
>
>   The fields of the return value each describe how a particular system resource has been used, e.g. amount of time spent running is user mode or number of times the process was swapped out of main memory. Some values are dependent on the clock tick internal, e.g. the amount of memory the process is using.
>
>   For backward compatibility, the return value is also accessible as a tuple of 16 elements.
>
>   The fields `ru_utime` and `ru_stime` of the return value are floating point values representing the amount of time spent executing in user mode and the amount of time spent executing in system mode, respectively. The remaining values are integers. Consult the *getrusage(2)* man page for detailed information about these values. A brief summary is presented here:

Index	Field	Resource
0	ru_utime	time in user mode (float)
1	ru_stime	time in system mode (float)
2	ru_maxrss	maximum resident set size
3	ru_ixrss	shared memory size
4	ru_idrss	unshared memory size
5	ru_isrss	unshared stack size
6	ru_minflt	page faults not requiring I/O
7	ru_majflt	page faults requiring I/O
8	ru_nswap	number of swap outs
9	ru_inblock	block input operations
10	ru_oublock	block output operations
11	ru_msgsnd	messages sent
12	ru_msgrcv	messages received
13	ru_nsignals	signals received
14	ru_nvcsw	voluntary context switches
15	ru_nivcsw	involuntary context switches

>   This function will raise a *ValueError* if an invalid *who* parameter is specified. It may also raise *error* exception in unusual circumstances.

`resource.getpagesize()`
>   Returns the number of bytes in a system page. (This need not be the same as the hardware page size.)

The following `RUSAGE_*` symbols are passed to the *getrusage()* function to specify which processes information should be provided for.

`resource.RUSAGE_SELF`
>   Pass to *getrusage()* to request resources consumed by the calling process, which is the sum of resources used by all threads in the process.

resource.RUSAGE_CHILDREN
   Pass to *getrusage()* to request resources consumed by child processes of the calling process which have been terminated and waited for.

resource.RUSAGE_BOTH
   Pass to *getrusage()* to request resources consumed by both the current process and child processes. May not be available on all systems.

resource.RUSAGE_THREAD
   Pass to *getrusage()* to request resources consumed by the current thread. May not be available on all systems.

   New in version 3.2.

35.12 `nis` — Interface to Sun's NIS (Yellow Pages)

The *nis* module gives a thin wrapper around the NIS library, useful for central administration of several hosts.

Because NIS exists only on Unix systems, this module is only available for Unix.

The *nis* module defines the following functions:

nis.match(*key, mapname, domain=default_domain*)
   Return the match for *key* in map *mapname*, or raise an error (*nis.error*) if there is none. Both should be strings, *key* is 8-bit clean. Return value is an arbitrary array of bytes (may contain **NULL** and other joys).

   Note that *mapname* is first checked if it is an alias to another name.

   The *domain* argument allows overriding the NIS domain used for the lookup. If unspecified, lookup is in the default NIS domain.

nis.cat(*mapname, domain=default_domain*)
   Return a dictionary mapping *key* to *value* such that `match(key, mapname)==value`. Note that both keys and values of the dictionary are arbitrary arrays of bytes.

   Note that *mapname* is first checked if it is an alias to another name.

   The *domain* argument allows overriding the NIS domain used for the lookup. If unspecified, lookup is in the default NIS domain.

nis.maps(*domain=default_domain*)
   Return a list of all valid maps.

   The *domain* argument allows overriding the NIS domain used for the lookup. If unspecified, lookup is in the default NIS domain.

nis.get_default_domain()
   Return the system default NIS domain.

The *nis* module defines the following exception:

exception nis.error
   An error raised when a NIS function returns an error code.

35.13 `syslog` — Unix syslog library routines

This module provides an interface to the Unix `syslog` library routines. Refer to the Unix manual pages for a detailed description of the `syslog` facility.

This module wraps the system `syslog` family of routines. A pure Python library that can speak to a syslog server is available in the *logging.handlers* module as `SysLogHandler`.

The module defines the following functions:

syslog.**syslog**(*message*)
syslog.**syslog**(*priority*, *message*)
> Send the string *message* to the system logger. A trailing newline is added if necessary. Each message is tagged with a priority composed of a *facility* and a *level*. The optional *priority* argument, which defaults to `LOG_INFO`, determines the message priority. If the facility is not encoded in *priority* using logical-or (`LOG_INFO | LOG_USER`), the value given in the *openlog()* call is used.
>
> If *openlog()* has not been called prior to the call to *syslog()*, `openlog()` will be called with no arguments.

syslog.**openlog**([*ident*[, *logoption*[, *facility*]]])
> Logging options of subsequent *syslog()* calls can be set by calling *openlog()*. *syslog()* will call *openlog()* with no arguments if the log is not currently open.
>
> The optional *ident* keyword argument is a string which is prepended to every message, and defaults to `sys.argv[0]` with leading path components stripped. The optional *logoption* keyword argument (default is 0) is a bit field – see below for possible values to combine. The optional *facility* keyword argument (default is `LOG_USER`) sets the default facility for messages which do not have a facility explicitly encoded.
>
> Changed in version 3.2: In previous versions, keyword arguments were not allowed, and *ident* was required. The default for *ident* was dependent on the system libraries, and often was `python` instead of the name of the python program file.

syslog.**closelog**()
> Reset the syslog module values and call the system library `closelog()`.
>
> This causes the module to behave as it does when initially imported. For example, *openlog()* will be called on the first *syslog()* call (if *openlog()* hasn't already been called), and *ident* and other *openlog()* parameters are reset to defaults.

syslog.**setlogmask**(*maskpri*)
> Set the priority mask to *maskpri* and return the previous mask value. Calls to *syslog()* with a priority level not set in *maskpri* are ignored. The default is to log all priorities. The function `LOG_MASK(pri)` calculates the mask for the individual priority *pri*. The function `LOG_UPTO(pri)` calculates the mask for all priorities up to and including *pri*.

The module defines the following constants:

Priority levels (high to low): `LOG_EMERG`, `LOG_ALERT`, `LOG_CRIT`, `LOG_ERR`, `LOG_WARNING`, `LOG_NOTICE`, `LOG_INFO`, `LOG_DEBUG`.

Facilities: `LOG_KERN`, `LOG_USER`, `LOG_MAIL`, `LOG_DAEMON`, `LOG_AUTH`, `LOG_LPR`, `LOG_NEWS`, `LOG_UUCP`, `LOG_CRON`, `LOG_SYSLOG`, `LOG_LOCAL0` to `LOG_LOCAL7`, and, if defined in <syslog.h>, `LOG_AUTHPRIV`.

Log options: `LOG_PID`, `LOG_CONS`, `LOG_NDELAY`, and, if defined in <syslog.h>, `LOG_ODELAY`, `LOG_NOWAIT`, and `LOG_PERROR`.

35.13.1 Examples

Simple example

A simple set of examples:

```
import syslog

syslog.syslog('Processing started')
if error:
    syslog.syslog(syslog.LOG_ERR, 'Processing started')
```

An example of setting some log options, these would include the process ID in logged messages, and write the messages to the destination facility used for mail logging:

```
syslog.openlog(logoption=syslog.LOG_PID, facility=syslog.LOG_MAIL)
syslog.syslog('E-mail processing initiated...')
```

CHAPTER
THIRTYSIX

SUPERSEDED MODULES

The modules described in this chapter are deprecated and only kept for backwards compatibility. They have been superseded by other modules.

36.1 `optparse` — Parser for command line options

Source code: Lib/optparse.py

Deprecated since version 3.2: The *optparse* module is deprecated and will not be developed further; development will continue with the *argparse* module.

---

optparse is a more convenient, flexible, and powerful library for parsing command-line options than the old *getopt* module. *optparse* uses a more declarative style of command-line parsing: you create an instance of *OptionParser*, populate it with options, and parse the command line. *optparse* allows users to specify options in the conventional GNU/POSIX syntax, and additionally generates usage and help messages for you.

Here's an example of using *optparse* in a simple script:

```
from optparse import OptionParser
...
parser = OptionParser()
parser.add_option("-f", "--file", dest="filename",
                  help="write report to FILE", metavar="FILE")
parser.add_option("-q", "--quiet",
                  action="store_false", dest="verbose", default=True,
                  help="don't print status messages to stdout")

(options, args) = parser.parse_args()
```

With these few lines of code, users of your script can now do the "usual thing" on the command-line, for example:

```
<yourscript> --file=outfile -q
```

As it parses the command line, *optparse* sets attributes of the **options** object returned by **parse_args()** based on user-supplied command-line values. When **parse_args()** returns from parsing this command line, **options.filename** will be `"outfile"` and **options.verbose** will be `False`. *optparse* supports both long and short options, allows short options to be merged together, and allows options to be associated with their arguments in a variety of ways. Thus, the following command lines are all equivalent to the above example:

```
<yourscript> -f outfile --quiet
<yourscript> --quiet --file outfile
<yourscript> -q -foutfile
<yourscript> -qfoutfile
```

Additionally, users can run one of

```
<yourscript> -h
<yourscript> --help
```

and *optparse* will print out a brief summary of your script's options:

```
Usage: <yourscript> [options]

Options:
  -h, --help            show this help message and exit
  -f FILE, --file=FILE  write report to FILE
  -q, --quiet           don't print status messages to stdout
```

where the value of *yourscript* is determined at runtime (normally from `sys.argv[0]`).

36.1.1 Background

optparse was explicitly designed to encourage the creation of programs with straightforward, conventional command-line interfaces. To that end, it supports only the most common command-line syntax and semantics conventionally used under Unix. If you are unfamiliar with these conventions, read this section to acquaint yourself with them.

Terminology

argument a string entered on the command-line, and passed by the shell to execl() or execv(). In Python, arguments are elements of `sys.argv[1:]` (`sys.argv[0]` is the name of the program being executed). Unix shells also use the term "word".

It is occasionally desirable to substitute an argument list other than `sys.argv[1:]`, so you should read "argument" as "an element of `sys.argv[1:]`, or of some other list provided as a substitute for `sys.argv[1:]`".

option an argument used to supply extra information to guide or customize the execution of a program. There are many different syntaxes for options; the traditional Unix syntax is a hyphen ("-") followed by a single letter, e.g. `-x` or `-F`. Also, traditional Unix syntax allows multiple options to be merged into a single argument, e.g. `-x -F` is equivalent to `-xF`. The GNU project introduced `--` followed by a series of hyphen-separated words, e.g. `--file` or `--dry-run`. These are the only two option syntaxes provided by *optparse*.

Some other option syntaxes that the world has seen include:

- a hyphen followed by a few letters, e.g. `-pf` (this is *not* the same as multiple options merged into a single argument)
- a hyphen followed by a whole word, e.g. `-file` (this is technically equivalent to the previous syntax, but they aren't usually seen in the same program)
- a plus sign followed by a single letter, or a few letters, or a word, e.g. `+f`, `+rgb`
- a slash followed by a letter, or a few letters, or a word, e.g. `/f`, `/file`

These option syntaxes are not supported by *optparse*, and they never will be. This is deliberate: the first three are non-standard on any environment, and the last only makes sense if you're exclusively targeting VMS, MS-DOS, and/or Windows.

option argument an argument that follows an option, is closely associated with that option, and is consumed from the argument list when that option is. With *optparse*, option arguments may either be in a separate argument from their option:

```
-f foo
--file foo
```

or included in the same argument:

```
-ffoo
--file=foo
```

Typically, a given option either takes an argument or it doesn't. Lots of people want an "optional option arguments" feature, meaning that some options will take an argument if they see it, and won't if they don't. This is somewhat controversial, because it makes parsing ambiguous: if -a takes an optional argument and -b is another option entirely, how do we interpret -ab? Because of this ambiguity, *optparse* does not support this feature.

positional argument something leftover in the argument list after options have been parsed, i.e. after options and their arguments have been parsed and removed from the argument list.

required option an option that must be supplied on the command-line; note that the phrase "required option" is self-contradictory in English. *optparse* doesn't prevent you from implementing required options, but doesn't give you much help at it either.

For example, consider this hypothetical command-line:

```
prog -v --report report.txt foo bar
```

-v and --report are both options. Assuming that --report takes one argument, report.txt is an option argument. foo and bar are positional arguments.

What are options for?

Options are used to provide extra information to tune or customize the execution of a program. In case it wasn't clear, options are usually *optional*. A program should be able to run just fine with no options whatsoever. (Pick a random program from the Unix or GNU toolsets. Can it run without any options at all and still make sense? The main exceptions are find, tar, and dd—all of which are mutant oddballs that have been rightly criticized for their non-standard syntax and confusing interfaces.)

Lots of people want their programs to have "required options". Think about it. If it's required, then it's *not optional*! If there is a piece of information that your program absolutely requires in order to run successfully, that's what positional arguments are for.

As an example of good command-line interface design, consider the humble cp utility, for copying files. It doesn't make much sense to try to copy files without supplying a destination and at least one source. Hence, cp fails if you run it with no arguments. However, it has a flexible, useful syntax that does not require any options at all:

```
cp SOURCE DEST
cp SOURCE ... DEST-DIR
```

You can get pretty far with just that. Most cp implementations provide a bunch of options to tweak exactly how the files are copied: you can preserve mode and modification time, avoid following symlinks, ask before clobbering existing files, etc. But none of this distracts from the core mission of cp, which is to copy either one file to another, or several files to another directory.

What are positional arguments for?

Positional arguments are for those pieces of information that your program absolutely, positively requires to run.

A good user interface should have as few absolute requirements as possible. If your program requires 17 distinct pieces of information in order to run successfully, it doesn't much matter *how* you get that information from the user—most people will give up and walk away before they successfully run the program. This applies whether the user interface is a command-line, a configuration file, or a GUI: if you make that many demands on your users, most of them will simply give up.

In short, try to minimize the amount of information that users are absolutely required to supply—use sensible defaults whenever possible. Of course, you also want to make your programs reasonably flexible. That's what options are for. Again, it doesn't matter if they are entries in a config file, widgets in the "Preferences" dialog of a GUI, or command-line options—the more options you implement, the more flexible your program is, and the more complicated its implementation becomes. Too much flexibility has drawbacks as well, of course; too many options can overwhelm users and make your code much harder to maintain.

36.1.2 Tutorial

While *optparse* is quite flexible and powerful, it's also straightforward to use in most cases. This section covers the code patterns that are common to any *optparse*-based program.

First, you need to import the OptionParser class; then, early in the main program, create an OptionParser instance:

```
from optparse import OptionParser
...
parser = OptionParser()
```

Then you can start defining options. The basic syntax is:

```
parser.add_option(opt_str, ...,
                  attr=value, ...)
```

Each option has one or more option strings, such as -f or --file, and several option attributes that tell *optparse* what to expect and what to do when it encounters that option on the command line.

Typically, each option will have one short option string and one long option string, e.g.:

```
parser.add_option("-f", "--file", ...)
```

You're free to define as many short option strings and as many long option strings as you like (including zero), as long as there is at least one option string overall.

The option strings passed to *OptionParser.add_option()* are effectively labels for the option defined by that call. For brevity, we will frequently refer to *encountering an option* on the command line; in reality, *optparse* encounters *option strings* and looks up options from them.

Once all of your options are defined, instruct *optparse* to parse your program's command line:

```
(options, args) = parser.parse_args()
```

(If you like, you can pass a custom argument list to parse_args(), but that's rarely necessary: by default it uses sys.argv[1:].)

`parse_args()` returns two values:

- `options`, an object containing values for all of your options—e.g. if `--file` takes a single string argument, then `options.file` will be the filename supplied by the user, or `None` if the user did not supply that option
- `args`, the list of positional arguments leftover after parsing options

This tutorial section only covers the four most important option attributes: *action*, *type*, *dest* (destination), and *help*. Of these, *action* is the most fundamental.

Understanding option actions

Actions tell *optparse* what to do when it encounters an option on the command line. There is a fixed set of actions hard-coded into *optparse*; adding new actions is an advanced topic covered in section *Extending optparse*. Most actions tell *optparse* to store a value in some variable—for example, take a string from the command line and store it in an attribute of `options`.

If you don't specify an option action, *optparse* defaults to `store`.

The store action

The most common option action is `store`, which tells *optparse* to take the next argument (or the remainder of the current argument), ensure that it is of the correct type, and store it to your chosen destination.

For example:

```
parser.add_option("-f", "--file",
                  action="store", type="string", dest="filename")
```

Now let's make up a fake command line and ask *optparse* to parse it:

```
args = ["-f", "foo.txt"]
(options, args) = parser.parse_args(args)
```

When *optparse* sees the option string `-f`, it consumes the next argument, `foo.txt`, and stores it in `options.filename`. So, after this call to `parse_args()`, `options.filename` is `"foo.txt"`.

Some other option types supported by *optparse* are `int` and `float`. Here's an option that expects an integer argument:

```
parser.add_option("-n", type="int", dest="num")
```

Note that this option has no long option string, which is perfectly acceptable. Also, there's no explicit action, since the default is `store`.

Let's parse another fake command-line. This time, we'll jam the option argument right up against the option: since `-n42` (one argument) is equivalent to `-n 42` (two arguments), the code

```
(options, args) = parser.parse_args(["-n42"])
print(options.num)
```

will print 42.

If you don't specify a type, *optparse* assumes `string`. Combined with the fact that the default action is `store`, that means our first example can be a lot shorter:

```
parser.add_option("-f", "--file", dest="filename")
```

If you don't supply a destination, *optparse* figures out a sensible default from the option strings: if the first long option string is `--foo-bar`, then the default destination is `foo_bar`. If there are no long option strings, *optparse* looks at the first short option string: the default destination for `-f` is `f`.

optparse also includes the built-in `complex` type. Adding types is covered in section *Extending optparse*.

Handling boolean (flag) options

Flag options—set a variable to true or false when a particular option is seen —are quite common. *optparse* supports them with two separate actions, `store_true` and `store_false`. For example, you might have a verbose flag that is turned on with `-v` and off with `-q`:

```
parser.add_option("-v", action="store_true", dest="verbose")
parser.add_option("-q", action="store_false", dest="verbose")
```

Here we have two different options with the same destination, which is perfectly OK. (It just means you have to be a bit careful when setting default values— see below.)

When *optparse* encounters `-v` on the command line, it sets `options.verbose` to `True`; when it encounters `-q`, `options.verbose` is set to `False`.

Other actions

Some other actions supported by *optparse* are:

`"store_const"` store a constant value

`"append"` append this option's argument to a list

`"count"` increment a counter by one

`"callback"` call a specified function

These are covered in section *Reference Guide*, Reference Guide and section *Option Callbacks*.

Default values

All of the above examples involve setting some variable (the "destination") when certain command-line options are seen. What happens if those options are never seen? Since we didn't supply any defaults, they are all set to `None`. This is usually fine, but sometimes you want more control. *optparse* lets you supply a default value for each destination, which is assigned before the command line is parsed.

First, consider the verbose/quiet example. If we want *optparse* to set verbose to `True` unless `-q` is seen, then we can do this:

```
parser.add_option("-v", action="store_true", dest="verbose", default=True)
parser.add_option("-q", action="store_false", dest="verbose")
```

Since default values apply to the *destination* rather than to any particular option, and these two options happen to have the same destination, this is exactly equivalent:

```
parser.add_option("-v", action="store_true", dest="verbose")
parser.add_option("-q", action="store_false", dest="verbose", default=True)
```

Consider this:

```
parser.add_option("-v", action="store_true", dest="verbose", default=False)
parser.add_option("-q", action="store_false", dest="verbose", default=True)
```

Again, the default value for verbose will be True: the last default value supplied for any particular destination is the one that counts.

A clearer way to specify default values is the set_defaults() method of OptionParser, which you can call at any time before calling parse_args():

```
parser.set_defaults(verbose=True)
parser.add_option(...)
(options, args) = parser.parse_args()
```

As before, the last value specified for a given option destination is the one that counts. For clarity, try to use one method or the other of setting default values, not both.

Generating help

optparse's ability to generate help and usage text automatically is useful for creating user-friendly command-line interfaces. All you have to do is supply a *help* value for each option, and optionally a short usage message for your whole program. Here's an OptionParser populated with user-friendly (documented) options:

```
usage = "usage: %prog [options] arg1 arg2"
parser = OptionParser(usage=usage)
parser.add_option("-v", "--verbose",
                  action="store_true", dest="verbose", default=True,
                  help="make lots of noise [default]")
parser.add_option("-q", "--quiet",
                  action="store_false", dest="verbose",
                  help="be vewwy quiet (I'm hunting wabbits)")
parser.add_option("-f", "--filename",
                  metavar="FILE", help="write output to FILE")
parser.add_option("-m", "--mode",
                  default="intermediate",
                  help="interaction mode: novice, intermediate, "
                       "or expert [default: %default]")
```

If *optparse* encounters either -h or --help on the command-line, or if you just call parser.print_help(), it prints the following to standard output:

```
Usage: <yourscript> [options] arg1 arg2

Options:
  -h, --help            show this help message and exit
  -v, --verbose         make lots of noise [default]
  -q, --quiet           be vewwy quiet (I'm hunting wabbits)
  -f FILE, --filename=FILE
                        write output to FILE
  -m MODE, --mode=MODE  interaction mode: novice, intermediate, or
                        expert [default: intermediate]
```

(If the help output is triggered by a help option, *optparse* exits after printing the help text.)

There's a lot going on here to help *optparse* generate the best possible help message:

- the script defines its own usage message:

  ```
  usage = "usage: %prog [options] arg1 arg2"
  ```

  optparse expands %prog in the usage string to the name of the current program, i.e. os.path.basename(sys.argv[0]). The expanded string is then printed before the detailed option help.

If you don't supply a usage string, *optparse* uses a bland but sensible default: `"Usage: %prog [options]"`, which is fine if your script doesn't take any positional arguments.

- every option defines a help string, and doesn't worry about line-wrapping— *optparse* takes care of wrapping lines and making the help output look good.
- options that take a value indicate this fact in their automatically-generated help message, e.g. for the "mode" option:

```
-m MODE, --mode=MODE
```

Here, "MODE" is called the meta-variable: it stands for the argument that the user is expected to supply to -m/--mode. By default, *optparse* converts the destination variable name to uppercase and uses that for the meta-variable. Sometimes, that's not what you want—for example, the **--filename** option explicitly sets `metavar="FILE"`, resulting in this automatically-generated option description:

```
-f FILE, --filename=FILE
```

This is important for more than just saving space, though: the manually written help text uses the meta-variable **FILE** to clue the user in that there's a connection between the semi-formal syntax **-f FILE** and the informal semantic description "write output to FILE". This is a simple but effective way to make your help text a lot clearer and more useful for end users.

- options that have a default value can include %default in the help string—*optparse* will replace it with *str()* of the option's default value. If an option has no default value (or the default value is None), %default expands to none.

Grouping Options

When dealing with many options, it is convenient to group these options for better help output. An *OptionParser* can contain several option groups, each of which can contain several options.

An option group is obtained using the class *OptionGroup*:

class optparse.**OptionGroup**(*parser, title, description=None*)
    where

- parser is the *OptionParser* instance the group will be insterted in to
- title is the group title
- description, optional, is a long description of the group

OptionGroup inherits from **OptionContainer** (like *OptionParser*) and so the **add_option()** method can be used to add an option to the group.

Once all the options are declared, using the *OptionParser* method **add_option_group()** the group is added to the previously defined parser.

Continuing with the parser defined in the previous section, adding an *OptionGroup* to a parser is easy:

```
group = OptionGroup(parser, "Dangerous Options",
                    "Caution: use these options at your own risk.  "
                    "It is believed that some of them bite.")
group.add_option("-g", action="store_true", help="Group option.")
parser.add_option_group(group)
```

This would result in the following help output:

```
Usage: <yourscript> [options] arg1 arg2

Options:
  -h, --help            show this help message and exit
  -v, --verbose         make lots of noise [default]
  -q, --quiet           be vewwy quiet (I'm hunting wabbits)
  -f FILE, --filename=FILE
                        write output to FILE
  -m MODE, --mode=MODE  interaction mode: novice, intermediate, or
                        expert [default: intermediate]

  Dangerous Options:
    Caution: use these options at your own risk.  It is believed that some
    of them bite.

    -g                  Group option.
```

A bit more complete example might involve using more than one group: still extending the previous example:

```
group = OptionGroup(parser, "Dangerous Options",
                    "Caution: use these options at your own risk.  "
                    "It is believed that some of them bite.")
group.add_option("-g", action="store_true", help="Group option.")
parser.add_option_group(group)

group = OptionGroup(parser, "Debug Options")
group.add_option("-d", "--debug", action="store_true",
                 help="Print debug information")
group.add_option("-s", "--sql", action="store_true",
                 help="Print all SQL statements executed")
group.add_option("-e", action="store_true", help="Print every action done")
parser.add_option_group(group)
```

that results in the following output:

```
Usage: <yourscript> [options] arg1 arg2

Options:
  -h, --help            show this help message and exit
  -v, --verbose         make lots of noise [default]
  -q, --quiet           be vewwy quiet (I'm hunting wabbits)
  -f FILE, --filename=FILE
                        write output to FILE
  -m MODE, --mode=MODE  interaction mode: novice, intermediate, or expert
                        [default: intermediate]

  Dangerous Options:
    Caution: use these options at your own risk.  It is believed that some
    of them bite.

    -g                  Group option.

  Debug Options:
    -d, --debug         Print debug information
    -s, --sql           Print all SQL statements executed
    -e                  Print every action done
```

Another interesting method, in particular when working programmatically with option groups is:

36.1. **optparse** — Parser for command line options

OptionParser.get_option_group(*opt_str*)
> Return the *OptionGroup* to which the short or long option string *opt_str* (e.g. `'-o'` or `'--option'`) belongs. If there's no such *OptionGroup*, return `None`.

Printing a version string

Similar to the brief usage string, *optparse* can also print a version string for your program. You have to supply the string as the `version` argument to OptionParser:

```
parser = OptionParser(usage="%prog [-f] [-q]", version="%prog 1.0")
```

`%prog` is expanded just like it is in `usage`. Apart from that, `version` can contain anything you like. When you supply it, *optparse* automatically adds a `--version` option to your parser. If it encounters this option on the command line, it expands your `version` string (by replacing `%prog`), prints it to stdout, and exits.

For example, if your script is called /usr/bin/foo:

```
$ /usr/bin/foo --version
foo 1.0
```

The following two methods can be used to print and get the `version` string:

OptionParser.print_version(*file=None*)
> Print the version message for the current program (`self.version`) to *file* (default stdout). As with *print_usage()*, any occurrence of `%prog` in `self.version` is replaced with the name of the current program. Does nothing if `self.version` is empty or undefined.

OptionParser.get_version()
> Same as *print_version()* but returns the version string instead of printing it.

How optparse handles errors

There are two broad classes of errors that *optparse* has to worry about: programmer errors and user errors. Programmer errors are usually erroneous calls to *OptionParser.add_option()*, e.g. invalid option strings, unknown option attributes, missing option attributes, etc. These are dealt with in the usual way: raise an exception (either `optparse.OptionError` or *TypeError*) and let the program crash.

Handling user errors is much more important, since they are guaranteed to happen no matter how stable your code is. *optparse* can automatically detect some user errors, such as bad option arguments (passing `-n 4x` where `-n` takes an integer argument), missing arguments (`-n` at the end of the command line, where `-n` takes an argument of any type). Also, you can call `OptionParser.error()` to signal an application-defined error condition:

```
(options, args) = parser.parse_args()
...
if options.a and options.b:
    parser.error("options -a and -b are mutually exclusive")
```

In either case, *optparse* handles the error the same way: it prints the program's usage message and an error message to standard error and exits with error status 2.

Consider the first example above, where the user passes `4x` to an option that takes an integer:

```
$ /usr/bin/foo -n 4x
Usage: foo [options]

foo: error: option -n: invalid integer value: '4x'
```

Or, where the user fails to pass a value at all:

```
$ /usr/bin/foo -n
Usage: foo [options]

foo: error: -n option requires an argument
```

optparse-generated error messages take care always to mention the option involved in the error; be sure to do the same when calling `OptionParser.error()` from your application code.

If *optparse*'s default error-handling behaviour does not suit your needs, you'll need to subclass OptionParser and override its `exit()` and/or `error()` methods.

Putting it all together

Here's what *optparse*-based scripts usually look like:

```
from optparse import OptionParser
...
def main():
    usage = "usage: %prog [options] arg"
    parser = OptionParser(usage)
    parser.add_option("-f", "--file", dest="filename",
                      help="read data from FILENAME")
    parser.add_option("-v", "--verbose",
                      action="store_true", dest="verbose")
    parser.add_option("-q", "--quiet",
                      action="store_false", dest="verbose")
    ...
    (options, args) = parser.parse_args()
    if len(args) != 1:
        parser.error("incorrect number of arguments")
    if options.verbose:
        print("reading %s..." % options.filename)
    ...

if __name__ == "__main__":
    main()
```

36.1.3 Reference Guide

Creating the parser

The first step in using *optparse* is to create an OptionParser instance.

class optparse.OptionParser(...)
    The OptionParser constructor has no required arguments, but a number of optional keyword arguments. You should always pass them as keyword arguments, i.e. do not rely on the order in which the arguments are declared.

usage (default: "%prog [options]") The usage summary to print when your program is run incorrectly or with a help option. When *optparse* prints the usage string, it expands %prog to os.path.basename(sys.argv[0]) (or to prog if you passed that keyword argument). To suppress a usage message, pass the special value optparse.SUPPRESS_USAGE.

option_list (default: []) A list of Option objects to populate the parser with. The options in option_list are added after any options in standard_option_list (a class attribute that may be set by OptionParser subclasses), but before any version or help options. Deprecated; use `add_option()` after creating the parser instead.

option_class (default: optparse.Option) Class to use when adding options to the parser in `add_option()`.

version (default: None) A version string to print when the user supplies a version option. If you supply a true value for **version**, *optparse* automatically adds a version option with the single option string --version. The substring %prog is expanded the same as for **usage**.

conflict_handler (default: "error") Specifies what to do when options with conflicting option strings are added to the parser; see section *Conflicts between options*.

description (default: None) A paragraph of text giving a brief overview of your program. *optparse* reformats this paragraph to fit the current terminal width and prints it when the user requests help (after **usage**, but before the list of options).

formatter (default: a new IndentedHelpFormatter) An instance of optparse.HelpFormatter that will be used for printing help text. *optparse* provides two concrete classes for this purpose: IndentedHelpFormatter and TitledHelpFormatter.

add_help_option (default: True) If true, *optparse* will add a help option (with option strings -h and --help) to the parser.

prog The string to use when expanding %prog in **usage** and **version** instead of os.path.basename(sys.argv[0]).

epilog (default: None) A paragraph of help text to print after the option help.

Populating the parser

There are several ways to populate the parser with options. The preferred way is by using *OptionParser.add_option()*, as shown in section *Tutorial*. `add_option()` can be called in one of two ways:

- pass it an Option instance (as returned by `make_option()`)
- pass it any combination of positional and keyword arguments that are acceptable to `make_option()` (i.e., to the Option constructor), and it will create the Option instance for you

The other alternative is to pass a list of pre-constructed Option instances to the OptionParser constructor, as in:

```
option_list = [
    make_option("-f", "--filename",
                action="store", type="string", dest="filename"),
    make_option("-q", "--quiet",
                action="store_false", dest="verbose"),
    ]
parser = OptionParser(option_list=option_list)
```

(`make_option()` is a factory function for creating Option instances; currently it is an alias for the Option constructor. A future version of *optparse* may split Option into several classes, and `make_option()` will pick the right class to instantiate. Do not instantiate Option directly.)

Defining options

Each Option instance represents a set of synonymous command-line option strings, e.g. -f and --file. You can specify any number of short or long option strings, but you must specify at least one overall option string.

The canonical way to create an Option instance is with the `add_option()` method of *OptionParser*.

OptionParser.**add_option**(*option*)
OptionParser.**add_option**(**opt_str, attr=value, ...*)
    To define an option with only a short option string:

```
parser.add_option("-f", attr=value, ...)
```

And to define an option with only a long option string:

```
parser.add_option("--foo", attr=value, ...)
```

The keyword arguments define attributes of the new Option object. The most important option attribute is *action*, and it largely determines which other attributes are relevant or required. If you pass irrelevant option attributes, or fail to pass required ones, *optparse* raises an `OptionError` exception explaining your mistake.

An option's *action* determines what *optparse* does when it encounters this option on the command-line. The standard option actions hard-coded into *optparse* are:

"store" store this option's argument (default)

"store_const" store a constant value

"store_true" store a true value

"store_false" store a false value

"append" append this option's argument to a list

"append_const" append a constant value to a list

"count" increment a counter by one

"callback" call a specified function

"help" print a usage message including all options and the documentation for them

(If you don't supply an action, the default is **"store"**. For this action, you may also supply *type* and *dest* option attributes; see *Standard option actions*.)

As you can see, most actions involve storing or updating a value somewhere. *optparse* always creates a special object for this, conventionally called **options** (it happens to be an instance of **optparse.Values**). Option arguments (and various other values) are stored as attributes of this object, according to the *dest* (destination) option attribute.

For example, when you call

```
parser.parse_args()
```

one of the first things *optparse* does is create the **options** object:

```
options = Values()
```

If one of the options in this parser is defined with

```
parser.add_option("-f", "--file", action="store", type="string", dest="filename")
```

and the command-line being parsed includes any of the following:

```
-ffoo
-f foo
--file=foo
--file foo
```

then *optparse*, on seeing this option, will do the equivalent of

```
options.filename = "foo"
```

The *type* and *dest* option attributes are almost as important as *action*, but *action* is the only one that makes sense for *all* options.

Option attributes

The following option attributes may be passed as keyword arguments to *OptionParser.add_option()*. If you pass an option attribute that is not relevant to a particular option, or fail to pass a required option attribute, *optparse* raises `OptionError`.

Option.action
>   (default: `"store"`)
>
>   Determines *optparse*'s behaviour when this option is seen on the command line; the available options are documented *here*.

Option.type
>   (default: `"string"`)
>
>   The argument type expected by this option (e.g., `"string"` or `"int"`); the available option types are documented *here*.

Option.dest
>   (default: derived from option strings)
>
>   If the option's action implies writing or modifying a value somewhere, this tells *optparse* where to write it: *dest* names an attribute of the **options** object that *optparse* builds as it parses the command line.

Option.default
>   The value to use for this option's destination if the option is not seen on the command line. See also *OptionParser.set_defaults()*.

Option.nargs
>   (default: 1)
>
>   How many arguments of type *type* should be consumed when this option is seen. If > 1, *optparse* will store a tuple of values to *dest*.

Option.const
>   For actions that store a constant value, the constant value to store.

Option.choices
>   For options of type `"choice"`, the list of strings the user may choose from.

Option.callback
>   For options with action `"callback"`, the callable to call when this option is seen. See section *Option Callbacks* for detail on the arguments passed to the callable.

Option.callback_args
Option.callback_kwargs
>   Additional positional and keyword arguments to pass to `callback` after the four standard callback arguments.

Option.help
>   Help text to print for this option when listing all available options after the user supplies a *help* option (such as `--help`). If no help text is supplied, the option will be listed without help text. To hide this option, use the special value `optparse.SUPPRESS_HELP`.

Option.`metavar`
   (default: derived from option strings)

   Stand-in for the option argument(s) to use when printing help text. See section *Tutorial* for an example.

Standard option actions

The various option actions all have slightly different requirements and effects. Most actions have several relevant option attributes which you may specify to guide *optparse*'s behaviour; a few have required attributes, which you must specify for any option using that action.

- `"store"` [relevant: *type*, *dest*, *nargs*, *choices*]

  The option must be followed by an argument, which is converted to a value according to *type* and stored in *dest*. If *nargs* > 1, multiple arguments will be consumed from the command line; all will be converted according to *type* and stored to *dest* as a tuple. See the *Standard option types* section.

  If *choices* is supplied (a list or tuple of strings), the type defaults to `"choice"`.

  If *type* is not supplied, it defaults to `"string"`.

  If *dest* is not supplied, *optparse* derives a destination from the first long option string (e.g., `--foo-bar` implies `foo_bar`). If there are no long option strings, *optparse* derives a destination from the first short option string (e.g., `-f` implies `f`).

  Example:

  ```
  parser.add_option("-f")
  parser.add_option("-p", type="float", nargs=3, dest="point")
  ```

  As it parses the command line

  ```
  -f foo.txt -p 1 -3.5 4 -fbar.txt
  ```

  optparse will set

  ```
  options.f = "foo.txt"
  options.point = (1.0, -3.5, 4.0)
  options.f = "bar.txt"
  ```

- `"store_const"` [required: *const*; relevant: *dest*]

  The value *const* is stored in *dest*.

  Example:

  ```
  parser.add_option("-q", "--quiet",
                    action="store_const", const=0, dest="verbose")
  parser.add_option("-v", "--verbose",
                    action="store_const", const=1, dest="verbose")
  parser.add_option("--noisy",
                    action="store_const", const=2, dest="verbose")
  ```

  If `--noisy` is seen, *optparse* will set

  ```
  options.verbose = 2
  ```

- `"store_true"` [relevant: *dest*]

  A special case of `"store_const"` that stores a true value to *dest*.

- "store_false" [relevant: *dest*]

  Like "store_true", but stores a false value.

  Example:

  ```
  parser.add_option("--clobber", action="store_true", dest="clobber")
  parser.add_option("--no-clobber", action="store_false", dest="clobber")
  ```

- "append" [relevant: *type*, *dest*, *nargs*, *choices*]

  The option must be followed by an argument, which is appended to the list in *dest*. If no default value for *dest* is supplied, an empty list is automatically created when *optparse* first encounters this option on the command-line. If *nargs* > 1, multiple arguments are consumed, and a tuple of length *nargs* is appended to *dest*.

  The defaults for *type* and *dest* are the same as for the "store" action.

  Example:

  ```
  parser.add_option("-t", "--tracks", action="append", type="int")
  ```

  If -t3 is seen on the command-line, *optparse* does the equivalent of:

  ```
  options.tracks = []
  options.tracks.append(int("3"))
  ```

  If, a little later on, --tracks=4 is seen, it does:

  ```
  options.tracks.append(int("4"))
  ```

  The **append** action calls the **append** method on the current value of the option. This means that any default value specified must have an **append** method. It also means that if the default value is non-empty, the default elements will be present in the parsed value for the option, with any values from the command line appended after those default values:

  ```
  >>> parser.add_option("--files", action="append", default=['~/.mypkg/defaults'])
  >>> opts, args = parser.parse_args(['--files', 'overrides.mypkg'])
  >>> opts.files
  ['~/.mypkg/defaults', 'overrides.mypkg']
  ```

- "append_const" [required: *const*; relevant: *dest*]

  Like "store_const", but the value *const* is appended to *dest*; as with "append", *dest* defaults to None, and an empty list is automatically created the first time the option is encountered.

- "count" [relevant: *dest*]

  Increment the integer stored at *dest*. If no default value is supplied, *dest* is set to zero before being incremented the first time.

  Example:

  ```
  parser.add_option("-v", action="count", dest="verbosity")
  ```

  The first time -v is seen on the command line, *optparse* does the equivalent of:

  ```
  options.verbosity = 0
  options.verbosity += 1
  ```

  Every subsequent occurrence of -v results in

```
options.verbosity += 1
```

- "callback" [required: *callback*; relevant: *type*, *nargs*, *callback_args*, *callback_kwargs*]

  Call the function specified by *callback*, which is called as

  ```
  func(option, opt_str, value, parser, *args, **kwargs)
  ```

  See section *Option Callbacks* for more detail.

- "help"

  Prints a complete help message for all the options in the current option parser. The help message is constructed from the **usage** string passed to OptionParser's constructor and the *help* string passed to every option.

  If no *help* string is supplied for an option, it will still be listed in the help message. To omit an option entirely, use the special value **optparse.SUPPRESS_HELP**.

  optparse automatically adds a *help* option to all OptionParsers, so you do not normally need to create one.

  Example:

  ```
  from optparse import OptionParser, SUPPRESS_HELP

  # usually, a help option is added automatically, but that can
  # be suppressed using the add_help_option argument
  parser = OptionParser(add_help_option=False)

  parser.add_option("-h", "--help", action="help")
  parser.add_option("-v", action="store_true", dest="verbose",
                    help="Be moderately verbose")
  parser.add_option("--file", dest="filename",
                    help="Input file to read data from")
  parser.add_option("--secret", help=SUPPRESS_HELP)
  ```

  If *optparse* sees either **-h** or **--help** on the command line, it will print something like the following help message to stdout (assuming **sys.argv[0]** is **"foo.py"**):

  ```
  Usage: foo.py [options]

  Options:
    -h, --help        Show this help message and exit
    -v                Be moderately verbose
    --file=FILENAME   Input file to read data from
  ```

  After printing the help message, *optparse* terminates your process with **sys.exit(0)**.

- "version"

  Prints the version number supplied to the OptionParser to stdout and exits. The version number is actually formatted and printed by the **print_version()** method of OptionParser. Generally only relevant if the **version** argument is supplied to the OptionParser constructor. As with *help* options, you will rarely create **version** options, since *optparse* automatically adds them when needed.

Standard option types

optparse has five built-in option types: **"string"**, **"int"**, **"choice"**, **"float"** and **"complex"**. If you need to add new option types, see section *Extending optparse*.

Arguments to string options are not checked or converted in any way: the text on the command line is stored in the destination (or passed to the callback) as-is.

Integer arguments (type `"int"`) are parsed as follows:

- if the number starts with `0x`, it is parsed as a hexadecimal number
- if the number starts with `0`, it is parsed as an octal number
- if the number starts with `0b`, it is parsed as a binary number
- otherwise, the number is parsed as a decimal number

The conversion is done by calling *int()* with the appropriate base (2, 8, 10, or 16). If this fails, so will *optparse*, although with a more useful error message.

`"float"` and `"complex"` option arguments are converted directly with *float()* and *complex()*, with similar error-handling.

`"choice"` options are a subtype of `"string"` options. The *choices* option attribute (a sequence of strings) defines the set of allowed option arguments. `optparse.check_choice()` compares user-supplied option arguments against this master list and raises `OptionValueError` if an invalid string is given.

Parsing arguments

The whole point of creating and populating an OptionParser is to call its **parse_args()** method:

```
(options, args) = parser.parse_args(args=None, values=None)
```

where the input parameters are

args the list of arguments to process (default: `sys.argv[1:]`)

values an `optparse.Values` object to store option arguments in (default: a new instance of `Values`) – if you give an existing object, the option defaults will not be initialized on it

and the return values are

options the same object that was passed in as **values**, or the optparse.Values instance created by *optparse*

args the leftover positional arguments after all options have been processed

The most common usage is to supply neither keyword argument. If you supply **values**, it will be modified with repeated *setattr()* calls (roughly one for every option argument stored to an option destination) and returned by **parse_args()**.

If **parse_args()** encounters any errors in the argument list, it calls the OptionParser's **error()** method with an appropriate end-user error message. This ultimately terminates your process with an exit status of 2 (the traditional Unix exit status for command-line errors).

Querying and manipulating your option parser

The default behavior of the option parser can be customized slightly, and you can also poke around your option parser and see what's there. OptionParser provides several methods to help you out:

OptionParser.disable_interspersed_args()
    Set parsing to stop on the first non-option. For example, if `-a` and `-b` are both simple options that take no arguments, *optparse* normally accepts this syntax:

```
prog -a arg1 -b arg2
```

and treats it as equivalent to

```
prog -a -b arg1 arg2
```

To disable this feature, call *disable_interspersed_args()*. This restores traditional Unix syntax, where option parsing stops with the first non-option argument.

Use this if you have a command processor which runs another command which has options of its own and you want to make sure these options don't get confused. For example, each command might have a different set of options.

OptionParser.**enable_interspersed_args**()
    Set parsing to not stop on the first non-option, allowing interspersing switches with command arguments. This is the default behavior.

OptionParser.**get_option**(*opt_str*)
    Returns the Option instance with the option string *opt_str*, or None if no options have that option string.

OptionParser.**has_option**(*opt_str*)
    Return true if the OptionParser has an option with option string *opt_str* (e.g., -q or --verbose).

OptionParser.**remove_option**(*opt_str*)
    If the *OptionParser* has an option corresponding to *opt_str*, that option is removed. If that option provided any other option strings, all of those option strings become invalid. If *opt_str* does not occur in any option belonging to this *OptionParser*, raises *ValueError*.

Conflicts between options

If you're not careful, it's easy to define options with conflicting option strings:

```
parser.add_option("-n", "--dry-run", ...)
...
parser.add_option("-n", "--noisy", ...)
```

(This is particularly true if you've defined your own OptionParser subclass with some standard options.)

Every time you add an option, *optparse* checks for conflicts with existing options. If it finds any, it invokes the current conflict-handling mechanism. You can set the conflict-handling mechanism either in the constructor:

```
parser = OptionParser(..., conflict_handler=handler)
```

or with a separate call:

```
parser.set_conflict_handler(handler)
```

The available conflict handlers are:

> **"error"** (default) assume option conflicts are a programming error and raise OptionConflictError
>
> **"resolve"** resolve option conflicts intelligently (see below)

As an example, let's define an *OptionParser* that resolves conflicts intelligently and add conflicting options to it:

```
parser = OptionParser(conflict_handler="resolve")
parser.add_option("-n", "--dry-run", ..., help="do no harm")
parser.add_option("-n", "--noisy", ..., help="be noisy")
```

36.1. optparse — Parser for command line options

At this point, *optparse* detects that a previously-added option is already using the `-n` option string. Since `conflict_handler` is `"resolve"`, it resolves the situation by removing `-n` from the earlier option's list of option strings. Now `--dry-run` is the only way for the user to activate that option. If the user asks for help, the help message will reflect that:

```
Options:
  --dry-run     do no harm
  ...
  -n, --noisy   be noisy
```

It's possible to whittle away the option strings for a previously-added option until there are none left, and the user has no way of invoking that option from the command-line. In that case, *optparse* removes that option completely, so it doesn't show up in help text or anywhere else. Carrying on with our existing OptionParser:

```
parser.add_option("--dry-run", ..., help="new dry-run option")
```

At this point, the original `-n`/`--dry-run` option is no longer accessible, so *optparse* removes it, leaving this help text:

```
Options:
  ...
  -n, --noisy   be noisy
  --dry-run     new dry-run option
```

Cleanup

OptionParser instances have several cyclic references. This should not be a problem for Python's garbage collector, but you may wish to break the cyclic references explicitly by calling **destroy()** on your OptionParser once you are done with it. This is particularly useful in long-running applications where large object graphs are reachable from your OptionParser.

Other methods

OptionParser supports several other public methods:

OptionParser.set_usage(*usage*)
    Set the usage string according to the rules described above for the **usage** constructor keyword argument. Passing **None** sets the default usage string; use **optparse.SUPPRESS_USAGE** to suppress a usage message.

OptionParser.print_usage(*file=None*)
    Print the usage message for the current program (`self.usage`) to *file* (default stdout). Any occurrence of the string %prog in `self.usage` is replaced with the name of the current program. Does nothing if `self.usage` is empty or not defined.

OptionParser.get_usage()
    Same as *print_usage()* but returns the usage string instead of printing it.

OptionParser.set_defaults(*dest=value, ...*)
    Set default values for several option destinations at once. Using *set_defaults()* is the preferred way to set default values for options, since multiple options can share the same destination. For example, if several "mode" options all set the same destination, any one of them can set the default, and the last one wins:

```
parser.add_option("--advanced", action="store_const",
                  dest="mode", const="advanced",
                  default="novice")    # overridden below
```

```
parser.add_option("--novice", action="store_const",
                  dest="mode", const="novice",
                  default="advanced")   # overrides above setting
```

To avoid this confusion, use *set_defaults()*:

```
parser.set_defaults(mode="advanced")
parser.add_option("--advanced", action="store_const",
                  dest="mode", const="advanced")
parser.add_option("--novice", action="store_const",
                  dest="mode", const="novice")
```

36.1.4 Option Callbacks

When *optparse*'s built-in actions and types aren't quite enough for your needs, you have two choices: extend *optparse* or define a callback option. Extending *optparse* is more general, but overkill for a lot of simple cases. Quite often a simple callback is all you need.

There are two steps to defining a callback option:

- define the option itself using the `"callback"` action
- write the callback; this is a function (or method) that takes at least four arguments, as described below

Defining a callback option

As always, the easiest way to define a callback option is by using the *OptionParser.add_option()* method. Apart from *action*, the only option attribute you must specify is `callback`, the function to call:

```
parser.add_option("-c", action="callback", callback=my_callback)
```

`callback` is a function (or other callable object), so you must have already defined `my_callback()` when you create this callback option. In this simple case, *optparse* doesn't even know if -c takes any arguments, which usually means that the option takes no arguments—the mere presence of -c on the command-line is all it needs to know. In some circumstances, though, you might want your callback to consume an arbitrary number of command-line arguments. This is where writing callbacks gets tricky; it's covered later in this section.

optparse always passes four particular arguments to your callback, and it will only pass additional arguments if you specify them via *callback_args* and *callback_kwargs*. Thus, the minimal callback function signature is:

```
def my_callback(option, opt, value, parser):
```

The four arguments to a callback are described below.

There are several other option attributes that you can supply when you define a callback option:

type has its usual meaning: as with the `"store"` or `"append"` actions, it instructs *optparse* to consume one argument and convert it to *type*. Rather than storing the converted value(s) anywhere, though, *optparse* passes it to your callback function.

nargs also has its usual meaning: if it is supplied and > 1, *optparse* will consume *nargs* arguments, each of which must be convertible to *type*. It then passes a tuple of converted values to your callback.

callback_args a tuple of extra positional arguments to pass to the callback

callback_kwargs a dictionary of extra keyword arguments to pass to the callback

How callbacks are called

All callbacks are called as follows:

```
func(option, opt_str, value, parser, *args, **kwargs)
```

where

option is the Option instance that's calling the callback

opt_str is the option string seen on the command-line that's triggering the callback. (If an abbreviated long option was used, opt_str will be the full, canonical option string—e.g. if the user puts --foo on the command-line as an abbreviation for --foobar, then opt_str will be "--foobar".)

value is the argument to this option seen on the command-line. *optparse* will only expect an argument if *type* is set; the type of value will be the type implied by the option's type. If *type* for this option is None (no argument expected), then value will be None. If *nargs* > 1, value will be a tuple of values of the appropriate type.

parser is the OptionParser instance driving the whole thing, mainly useful because you can access some other interesting data through its instance attributes:

> parser.largs the current list of leftover arguments, ie. arguments that have been consumed but are neither options nor option arguments. Feel free to modify parser.largs, e.g. by adding more arguments to it. (This list will become args, the second return value of parse_args().)
>
> parser.rargs the current list of remaining arguments, ie. with opt_str and value (if applicable) removed, and only the arguments following them still there. Feel free to modify parser.rargs, e.g. by consuming more arguments.
>
> parser.values the object where option values are by default stored (an instance of optparse.OptionValues). This lets callbacks use the same mechanism as the rest of *optparse* for storing option values; you don't need to mess around with globals or closures. You can also access or modify the value(s) of any options already encountered on the command-line.

args is a tuple of arbitrary positional arguments supplied via the *callback_args* option attribute.

kwargs is a dictionary of arbitrary keyword arguments supplied via *callback_kwargs*.

Raising errors in a callback

The callback function should raise `OptionValueError` if there are any problems with the option or its argument(s). *optparse* catches this and terminates the program, printing the error message you supply to stderr. Your message should be clear, concise, accurate, and mention the option at fault. Otherwise, the user will have a hard time figuring out what he did wrong.

Callback example 1: trivial callback

Here's an example of a callback option that takes no arguments, and simply records that the option was seen:

```
def record_foo_seen(option, opt_str, value, parser):
    parser.values.saw_foo = True

parser.add_option("--foo", action="callback", callback=record_foo_seen)
```

Of course, you could do that with the "store_true" action.

Callback example 2: check option order

Here's a slightly more interesting example: record the fact that -a is seen, but blow up if it comes after -b in the command-line.

```python
def check_order(option, opt_str, value, parser):
    if parser.values.b:
        raise OptionValueError("can't use -a after -b")
    parser.values.a = 1
...
parser.add_option("-a", action="callback", callback=check_order)
parser.add_option("-b", action="store_true", dest="b")
```

Callback example 3: check option order (generalized)

If you want to re-use this callback for several similar options (set a flag, but blow up if -b has already been seen), it needs a bit of work: the error message and the flag that it sets must be generalized.

```python
def check_order(option, opt_str, value, parser):
    if parser.values.b:
        raise OptionValueError("can't use %s after -b" % opt_str)
    setattr(parser.values, option.dest, 1)
...
parser.add_option("-a", action="callback", callback=check_order, dest='a')
parser.add_option("-b", action="store_true", dest="b")
parser.add_option("-c", action="callback", callback=check_order, dest='c')
```

Callback example 4: check arbitrary condition

Of course, you could put any condition in there—you're not limited to checking the values of already-defined options. For example, if you have options that should not be called when the moon is full, all you have to do is this:

```python
def check_moon(option, opt_str, value, parser):
    if is_moon_full():
        raise OptionValueError("%s option invalid when moon is full"
                               % opt_str)
    setattr(parser.values, option.dest, 1)
...
parser.add_option("--foo",
                  action="callback", callback=check_moon, dest="foo")
```

(The definition of `is_moon_full()` is left as an exercise for the reader.)

Callback example 5: fixed arguments

Things get slightly more interesting when you define callback options that take a fixed number of arguments. Specifying that a callback option takes arguments is similar to defining a `"store"` or `"append"` option: if you define *type*, then the option takes one argument that must be convertible to that type; if you further define *nargs*, then the option takes *nargs* arguments.

Here's an example that just emulates the standard `"store"` action:

```
def store_value(option, opt_str, value, parser):
    setattr(parser.values, option.dest, value)
...
parser.add_option("--foo",
                  action="callback", callback=store_value,
                  type="int", nargs=3, dest="foo")
```

Note that *optparse* takes care of consuming 3 arguments and converting them to integers for you; all you have to do is store them. (Or whatever; obviously you don't need a callback for this example.)

Callback example 6: variable arguments

Things get hairy when you want an option to take a variable number of arguments. For this case, you must write a callback, as *optparse* doesn't provide any built-in capabilities for it. And you have to deal with certain intricacies of conventional Unix command-line parsing that *optparse* normally handles for you. In particular, callbacks should implement the conventional rules for bare -- and - arguments:

- either -- or - can be option arguments
- bare -- (if not the argument to some option): halt command-line processing and discard the --
- bare - (if not the argument to some option): halt command-line processing but keep the - (append it to parser.largs)

If you want an option that takes a variable number of arguments, there are several subtle, tricky issues to worry about. The exact implementation you choose will be based on which trade-offs you're willing to make for your application (which is why *optparse* doesn't support this sort of thing directly).

Nevertheless, here's a stab at a callback for an option with variable arguments:

```
def vararg_callback(option, opt_str, value, parser):
    assert value is None
    value = []

    def floatable(str):
        try:
            float(str)
            return True
        except ValueError:
            return False

    for arg in parser.rargs:
        # stop on --foo like options
        if arg[:2] == "--" and len(arg) > 2:
            break
        # stop on -a, but not on -3 or -3.0
        if arg[:1] == "-" and len(arg) > 1 and not floatable(arg):
            break
        value.append(arg)

    del parser.rargs[:len(value)]
    setattr(parser.values, option.dest, value)

...
parser.add_option("-c", "--callback", dest="vararg_attr",
                  action="callback", callback=vararg_callback)
```

36.1.5 Extending optparse

Since the two major controlling factors in how *optparse* interprets command-line options are the action and type of each option, the most likely direction of extension is to add new actions and new types.

Adding new types

To add new types, you need to define your own subclass of *optparse*'s Option class. This class has a couple of attributes that define *optparse*'s types: *TYPES* and *TYPE_CHECKER*.

Option.TYPES
> A tuple of type names; in your subclass, simply define a new tuple *TYPES* that builds on the standard one.

Option.TYPE_CHECKER
> A dictionary mapping type names to type-checking functions. A type-checking function has the following signature:

```
def check_mytype(option, opt, value)
```

> where `option` is an Option instance, `opt` is an option string (e.g., `-f`), and `value` is the string from the command line that must be checked and converted to your desired type. `check_mytype()` should return an object of the hypothetical type `mytype`. The value returned by a type-checking function will wind up in the OptionValues instance returned by `OptionParser.parse_args()`, or be passed to a callback as the `value` parameter.
>
> Your type-checking function should raise `OptionValueError` if it encounters any problems. `OptionValueError` takes a single string argument, which is passed as-is to *OptionParser*'s `error()` method, which in turn prepends the program name and the string `"error:"` and prints everything to stderr before terminating the process.

Here's a silly example that demonstrates adding a `"complex"` option type to parse Python-style complex numbers on the command line. (This is even sillier than it used to be, because *optparse* 1.3 added built-in support for complex numbers, but never mind.)

First, the necessary imports:

```
from copy import copy
from optparse import Option, OptionValueError
```

You need to define your type-checker first, since it's referred to later (in the *TYPE_CHECKER* class attribute of your Option subclass):

```
def check_complex(option, opt, value):
    try:
        return complex(value)
    except ValueError:
        raise OptionValueError(
            "option %s: invalid complex value: %r" % (opt, value))
```

Finally, the Option subclass:

```
class MyOption (Option):
    TYPES = Option.TYPES + ("complex",)
    TYPE_CHECKER = copy(Option.TYPE_CHECKER)
    TYPE_CHECKER["complex"] = check_complex
```

(If we didn't make a *copy()* of *Option.TYPE_CHECKER*, we would end up modifying the *TYPE_CHECKER* attribute of *optparse*'s Option class. This being Python, nothing stops you from doing that except good manners and common sense.)

That's it! Now you can write a script that uses the new option type just like any other *optparse*-based script, except you have to instruct your OptionParser to use MyOption instead of Option:

```
parser = OptionParser(option_class=MyOption)
parser.add_option("-c", type="complex")
```

Alternately, you can build your own option list and pass it to OptionParser; if you don't use **add_option()** in the above way, you don't need to tell OptionParser which option class to use:

```
option_list = [MyOption("-c", action="store", type="complex", dest="c")]
parser = OptionParser(option_list=option_list)
```

Adding new actions

Adding new actions is a bit trickier, because you have to understand that *optparse* has a couple of classifications for actions:

"store" actions actions that result in *optparse* storing a value to an attribute of the current OptionValues instance; these options require a *dest* attribute to be supplied to the Option constructor.

"typed" actions actions that take a value from the command line and expect it to be of a certain type; or rather, a string that can be converted to a certain type. These options require a *type* attribute to the Option constructor.

These are overlapping sets: some default "store" actions are "store", "store_const", "append", and "count", while the default "typed" actions are "store", "append", and "callback".

When you add an action, you need to categorize it by listing it in at least one of the following class attributes of Option (all are lists of strings):

Option.**ACTIONS**
    All actions must be listed in ACTIONS.

Option.**STORE_ACTIONS**
    "store" actions are additionally listed here.

Option.**TYPED_ACTIONS**
    "typed" actions are additionally listed here.

Option.**ALWAYS_TYPED_ACTIONS**
    Actions that always take a type (i.e. whose options always take a value) are additionally listed here. The only effect of this is that *optparse* assigns the default type, "string", to options with no explicit type whose action is listed in *ALWAYS_TYPED_ACTIONS*.

In order to actually implement your new action, you must override Option's **take_action()** method and add a case that recognizes your action.

For example, let's add an "extend" action. This is similar to the standard "append" action, but instead of taking a single value from the command-line and appending it to an existing list, "extend" will take multiple values in a single comma-delimited string, and extend an existing list with them. That is, if --names is an "extend" option of type "string", the command line

```
--names=foo,bar --names blah --names ding,dong
```

would result in a list

```
["foo", "bar", "blah", "ding", "dong"]
```

Again we define a subclass of Option:

```
class MyOption(Option):

    ACTIONS = Option.ACTIONS + ("extend",)
    STORE_ACTIONS = Option.STORE_ACTIONS + ("extend",)
    TYPED_ACTIONS = Option.TYPED_ACTIONS + ("extend",)
    ALWAYS_TYPED_ACTIONS = Option.ALWAYS_TYPED_ACTIONS + ("extend",)

    def take_action(self, action, dest, opt, value, values, parser):
        if action == "extend":
            lvalue = value.split(",")
            values.ensure_value(dest, []).extend(lvalue)
        else:
            Option.take_action(
                self, action, dest, opt, value, values, parser)
```

Features of note:

- "extend" both expects a value on the command-line and stores that value somewhere, so it goes in both *STORE_ACTIONS* and *TYPED_ACTIONS*.
- to ensure that *optparse* assigns the default type of "string" to "extend" actions, we put the "extend" action in *ALWAYS_TYPED_ACTIONS* as well.
- MyOption.take_action() implements just this one new action, and passes control back to Option.take_action() for the standard *optparse* actions.
- values is an instance of the optparse_parser.Values class, which provides the very useful ensure_value() method. ensure_value() is essentially *getattr()* with a safety valve; it is called as

```
values.ensure_value(attr, value)
```

If the attr attribute of values doesn't exist or is None, then ensure_value() first sets it to value, and then returns 'value. This is very handy for actions like "extend", "append", and "count", all of which accumulate data in a variable and expect that variable to be of a certain type (a list for the first two, an integer for the latter). Using ensure_value() means that scripts using your action don't have to worry about setting a default value for the option destinations in question; they can just leave the default as None and ensure_value() will take care of getting it right when it's needed.

36.2 imp — Access the import internals

Source code: Lib/imp.py

Deprecated since version 3.4: The *imp* package is pending deprecation in favor of *importlib*.

This module provides an interface to the mechanisms used to implement the **import** statement. It defines the following constants and functions:

imp.get_magic()
    Return the magic string value used to recognize byte-compiled code files (.pyc files). (This value may be different for each Python version.)

    Deprecated since version 3.4: Use *importlib.util.MAGIC_NUMBER* instead.

imp.get_suffixes()
> Return a list of 3-element tuples, each describing a particular type of module. Each triple has the form (`suffix, mode, type`), where *suffix* is a string to be appended to the module name to form the filename to search for, *mode* is the mode string to pass to the built-in *open()* function to open the file (this can be `'r'` for text files or `'rb'` for binary files), and *type* is the file type, which has one of the values `PY_SOURCE`, `PY_COMPILED`, or `C_EXTENSION`, described below.
>
> Deprecated since version 3.3: Use the constants defined on *importlib.machinery* instead.

imp.find_module(*name*[, *path*]**)**
> Try to find the module *name*. If *path* is omitted or **None**, the list of directory names given by **sys.path** is searched, but first a few special places are searched: the function tries to find a built-in module with the given name (`C_BUILTIN`), then a frozen module (`PY_FROZEN`), and on some systems some other places are looked in as well (on Windows, it looks in the registry which may point to a specific file).
>
> Otherwise, *path* must be a list of directory names; each directory is searched for files with any of the suffixes returned by *get_suffixes()* above. Invalid names in the list are silently ignored (but all list items must be strings).
>
> If search is successful, the return value is a 3-element tuple (`file, pathname, description`):
>
> *file* is an open *file object* positioned at the beginning, *pathname* is the pathname of the file found, and *description* is a 3-element tuple as contained in the list returned by *get_suffixes()* describing the kind of module found.
>
> If the module does not live in a file, the returned *file* is **None**, *pathname* is the empty string, and the *description* tuple contains empty strings for its suffix and mode; the module type is indicated as given in parentheses above. If the search is unsuccessful, *ImportError* is raised. Other exceptions indicate problems with the arguments or environment.
>
> If the module is a package, *file* is **None**, *pathname* is the package path and the last item in the *description* tuple is `PKG_DIRECTORY`.
>
> This function does not handle hierarchical module names (names containing dots). In order to find *P.M*, that is, submodule *M* of package *P*, use *find_module()* and *load_module()* to find and load package *P*, and then use *find_module()* with the *path* argument set to `P.__path__`. When *P* itself has a dotted name, apply this recipe recursively.
>
> Deprecated since version 3.3: Use *importlib.util.find_spec()* instead unless Python 3.3 compatibility is required, in which case use *importlib.find_loader()*. For example usage of the former case, see the *Examples* section of the *importlib* documentation.

imp.load_module(*name, file, pathname, description***)**
> Load a module that was previously found by *find_module()* (or by an otherwise conducted search yielding compatible results). This function does more than importing the module: if the module was already imported, it will reload the module! The *name* argument indicates the full module name (including the package name, if this is a submodule of a package). The *file* argument is an open file, and *pathname* is the corresponding file name; these can be **None** and `''`, respectively, when the module is a package or not being loaded from a file. The *description* argument is a tuple, as would be returned by *get_suffixes()*, describing what kind of module must be loaded.
>
> If the load is successful, the return value is the module object; otherwise, an exception (usually *ImportError*) is raised.
>
> **Important:** the caller is responsible for closing the *file* argument, if it was not **None**, even when an exception is raised. This is best done using a `try ... finally` statement.
>
> Deprecated since version 3.3: If previously used in conjunction with *imp.find_module()* then consider using *importlib.import_module()*, otherwise use the loader returned by the replacement you chose for *imp.find_module()*. If you called *imp.load_module()* and related functions directly with file path

arguments then use a combination of *importlib.util.spec_from_file_location()* and *importlib.util.module_from_spec()*. See the *Examples* section of the *importlib* documentation for details of the various approaches.

imp.new_module(*name*)

Return a new empty module object called *name*. This object is *not* inserted in `sys.modules`.

Deprecated since version 3.4: Use *importlib.util.module_from_spec()* instead.

imp.reload(*module*)

Reload a previously imported *module*. The argument must be a module object, so it must have been successfully imported before. This is useful if you have edited the module source file using an external editor and want to try out the new version without leaving the Python interpreter. The return value is the module object (the same as the *module* argument).

When `reload(module)` is executed:

- Python modules' code is recompiled and the module-level code reexecuted, defining a new set of objects which are bound to names in the module's dictionary. The `init` function of extension modules is not called a second time.

- As with all other objects in Python the old objects are only reclaimed after their reference counts drop to zero.

- The names in the module namespace are updated to point to any new or changed objects.

- Other references to the old objects (such as names external to the module) are not rebound to refer to the new objects and must be updated in each namespace where they occur if that is desired.

There are a number of other caveats:

When a module is reloaded, its dictionary (containing the module's global variables) is retained. Redefinitions of names will override the old definitions, so this is generally not a problem. If the new version of a module does not define a name that was defined by the old version, the old definition remains. This feature can be used to the module's advantage if it maintains a global table or cache of objects — with a `try` statement it can test for the table's presence and skip its initialization if desired:

```
try:
    cache
except NameError:
    cache = {}
```

It is legal though generally not very useful to reload built-in or dynamically loaded modules, except for *sys*, *__main__* and *builtins*. In many cases, however, extension modules are not designed to be initialized more than once, and may fail in arbitrary ways when reloaded.

If a module imports objects from another module using `from ... import ...`, calling *reload()* for the other module does not redefine the objects imported from it — one way around this is to re-execute the `from` statement, another is to use `import` and qualified names (*module.*name*) instead.

If a module instantiates instances of a class, reloading the module that defines the class does not affect the method definitions of the instances — they continue to use the old class definition. The same is true for derived classes.

Changed in version 3.3: Relies on both `__name__` and `__loader__` being defined on the module being reloaded instead of just `__name__`.

Deprecated since version 3.4: Use *importlib.reload()* instead.

The following functions are conveniences for handling PEP 3147 byte-compiled file paths.

New in version 3.2.

imp.cache_from_source(*path, debug_override=None*)
Return the PEP 3147 path to the byte-compiled file associated with the source *path*. For example, if *path* is /foo/bar/baz.py the return value would be /foo/bar/__pycache__/baz.cpython-32.pyc for Python 3.2. The cpython-32 string comes from the current magic tag (see *get_tag()*; if sys.implementation.cache_tag is not defined then *NotImplementedError* will be raised). By passing in True or False for *debug_override* you can override the system's value for __debug__, leading to optimized bytecode.

path need not exist.

Changed in version 3.3: If sys.implementation.cache_tag is None, then *NotImplementedError* is raised.

Deprecated since version 3.4: Use *importlib.util.cache_from_source()* instead.

Changed in version 3.5: The *debug_override* parameter no longer creates a .pyo file.

imp.source_from_cache(*path*)
Given the *path* to a PEP 3147 file name, return the associated source code file path. For example, if *path* is /foo/bar/__pycache__/baz.cpython-32.pyc the returned path would be /foo/bar/baz.py. *path* need not exist, however if it does not conform to PEP 3147 format, a ValueError is raised. If sys.implementation.cache_tag is not defined, *NotImplementedError* is raised.

Changed in version 3.3: Raise *NotImplementedError* when sys.implementation.cache_tag is not defined.

Deprecated since version 3.4: Use *importlib.util.source_from_cache()* instead.

imp.get_tag()
Return the PEP 3147 magic tag string matching this version of Python's magic number, as returned by *get_magic()*.

Deprecated since version 3.4: Use sys.implementation.cache_tag directly starting in Python 3.3.

The following functions help interact with the import system's internal locking mechanism. Locking semantics of imports are an implementation detail which may vary from release to release. However, Python ensures that circular imports work without any deadlocks.

imp.lock_held()
Return True if the global import lock is currently held, else False. On platforms without threads, always return False.

On platforms with threads, a thread executing an import first holds a global import lock, then sets up a per-module lock for the rest of the import. This blocks other threads from importing the same module until the original import completes, preventing other threads from seeing incomplete module objects constructed by the original thread. An exception is made for circular imports, which by construction have to expose an incomplete module object at some point.

Changed in version 3.3: The locking scheme has changed to per-module locks for the most part. A global import lock is kept for some critical tasks, such as initializing the per-module locks.

Deprecated since version 3.4.

imp.acquire_lock()
Acquire the interpreter's global import lock for the current thread. This lock should be used by import hooks to ensure thread-safety when importing modules.

Once a thread has acquired the import lock, the same thread may acquire it again without blocking; the thread must release it once for each time it has acquired it.

On platforms without threads, this function does nothing.

Changed in version 3.3: The locking scheme has changed to per-module locks for the most part. A global import lock is kept for some critical tasks, such as initializing the per-module locks.

Deprecated since version 3.4.

imp.release_lock()
    Release the interpreter's global import lock. On platforms without threads, this function does nothing.

    Changed in version 3.3: The locking scheme has changed to per-module locks for the most part. A global import lock is kept for some critical tasks, such as initializing the per-module locks.

    Deprecated since version 3.4.

The following constants with integer values, defined in this module, are used to indicate the search result of *find_module()*.

imp.PY_SOURCE
    The module was found as a source file.

    Deprecated since version 3.3.

imp.PY_COMPILED
    The module was found as a compiled code object file.

    Deprecated since version 3.3.

imp.C_EXTENSION
    The module was found as dynamically loadable shared library.

    Deprecated since version 3.3.

imp.PKG_DIRECTORY
    The module was found as a package directory.

    Deprecated since version 3.3.

imp.C_BUILTIN
    The module was found as a built-in module.

    Deprecated since version 3.3.

imp.PY_FROZEN
    The module was found as a frozen module.

    Deprecated since version 3.3.

class imp.NullImporter(*path_string***)**
    The *NullImporter* type is a PEP 302 import hook that handles non-directory path strings by failing to find any modules. Calling this type with an existing directory or empty string raises *ImportError*. Otherwise, a *NullImporter* instance is returned.

    Instances have only one method:

    find_module(*fullname*[, *path*]**)**
        This method always returns None, indicating that the requested module could not be found.

    Changed in version 3.3: None is inserted into sys.path_importer_cache instead of an instance of *NullImporter*.

    Deprecated since version 3.4: Insert None into sys.path_importer_cache instead.

36.2.1 Examples

The following function emulates what was the standard import statement up to Python 1.4 (no hierarchical module names). (This *implementation* wouldn't work in that version, since *find_module()* has been extended and *load_module()* has been added in 1.4.)

```
import imp
import sys

def __import__(name, globals=None, locals=None, fromlist=None):
    # Fast path: see if the module has already been imported.
    try:
        return sys.modules[name]
    except KeyError:
        pass

    # If any of the following calls raises an exception,
    # there's a problem we can't handle -- let the caller handle it.

    fp, pathname, description = imp.find_module(name)

    try:
        return imp.load_module(name, fp, pathname, description)
    finally:
        # Since we may exit via an exception, close fp explicitly.
        if fp:
            fp.close()
```

CHAPTER
THIRTYSEVEN

UNDOCUMENTED MODULES

Here's a quick listing of modules that are currently undocumented, but that should be documented. Feel free to contribute documentation for them! (Send via email to docs@python.org.)

The idea and original contents for this chapter were taken from a posting by Fredrik Lundh; the specific contents of this chapter have been substantially revised.

37.1 Platform specific modules

These modules are used to implement the *os.path* module, and are not documented beyond this mention. There's little need to document these.

ntpath — Implementation of *os.path* on Win32 and Win64 platforms.

posixpath — Implementation of *os.path* on POSIX.

APPENDIX A

GLOSSARY

>>> The default Python prompt of the interactive shell. Often seen for code examples which can be executed interactively in the interpreter.

... The default Python prompt of the interactive shell when entering code for an indented code block or within a pair of matching left and right delimiters (parentheses, square brackets or curly braces).

2to3 A tool that tries to convert Python 2.x code to Python 3.x code by handling most of the incompatibilities which can be detected by parsing the source and traversing the parse tree.

2to3 is available in the standard library as *lib2to3*; a standalone entry point is provided as **Tools/scripts/2to3**. See *2to3 - Automated Python 2 to 3 code translation*.

abstract base class Abstract base classes complement *duck-typing* by providing a way to define interfaces when other techniques like *hasattr()* would be clumsy or subtly wrong (for example with magic methods). ABCs introduce virtual subclasses, which are classes that don't inherit from a class but are still recognized by *isinstance()* and *issubclass()*; see the *abc* module documentation. Python comes with many built-in ABCs for data structures (in the *collections.abc* module), numbers (in the *numbers* module), streams (in the *io* module), import finders and loaders (in the *importlib.abc* module). You can create your own ABCs with the *abc* module.

argument A value passed to a *function* (or *method*) when calling the function. There are two kinds of argument:

- *keyword argument*: an argument preceded by an identifier (e.g. **name=**) in a function call or passed as a value in a dictionary preceded by ******. For example, 3 and 5 are both keyword arguments in the following calls to *complex()*:

```
complex(real=3, imag=5)
complex(**{'real': 3, 'imag': 5})
```

- *positional argument*: an argument that is not a keyword argument. Positional arguments can appear at the beginning of an argument list and/or be passed as elements of an *iterable* preceded by *****. For example, 3 and 5 are both positional arguments in the following calls:

```
complex(3, 5)
complex(*(3, 5))
```

Arguments are assigned to the named local variables in a function body. See the calls section for the rules governing this assignment. Syntactically, any expression can be used to represent an argument; the evaluated value is assigned to the local variable.

See also the *parameter* glossary entry, the FAQ question on the difference between arguments and parameters, and PEP 362.

asynchronous context manager An object which controls the environment seen in an **async with** statement by defining **__aenter__()** and **__aexit__()** methods. Introduced by PEP 492.

asynchronous generator A function which returns an *asynchronous generator iterator*. It looks like a coroutine function defined with `async def` except that it contains `yield` expressions for producing a series of values usable in an `async for` loop.

Usually refers to a asynchronous generator function, but may refer to an *asynchronous generator iterator* in some contexts. In cases where the intended meaning isn't clear, using the full terms avoids ambiguity.

An asynchronous generator function may contain `await` expressions as well as `async for`, and `async with` statements.

asynchronous generator iterator An object created by a *asynchronous generator* function.

This is an *asynchronous iterator* which when called using the `__anext__()` method returns an awaitable object which will execute that the body of the asynchronous generator function until the next `yield` expression.

Each `yield` temporarily suspends processing, remembering the location execution state (including local variables and pending try-statements). When the *asynchronous generator iterator* effectively resumes with another awaitable returned by `__anext__()`, it picks-up where it left-off. See PEP 492 and PEP 525.

asynchronous iterable An object, that can be used in an `async for` statement. Must return an *asynchronous iterator* from its `__aiter__()` method. Introduced by PEP 492.

asynchronous iterator An object that implements `__aiter__()` and `__anext__()` methods. `__anext__` must return an *awaitable* object. `async for` resolves awaitable returned from asynchronous iterator's `__anext__()` method until it raises `StopAsyncIteration` exception. Introduced by PEP 492.

attribute A value associated with an object which is referenced by name using dotted expressions. For example, if an object *o* has an attribute *a* it would be referenced as *o.a*.

awaitable An object that can be used in an `await` expression. Can be a *coroutine* or an object with an `__await__()` method. See also PEP 492.

BDFL Benevolent Dictator For Life, a.k.a. Guido van Rossum, Python's creator.

binary file A *file object* able to read and write *bytes-like objects*. Examples of binary files are files opened in binary mode (`'rb'`, `'wb'` or `'rb+'`), `sys.stdin.buffer`, `sys.stdout.buffer`, and instances of `io.BytesIO` and `gzip.GzipFile`.

See also:

A *text file* reads and writes `str` objects.

bytes-like object An object that supports the bufferobjects and can export a C-*contiguous* buffer. This includes all `bytes`, `bytearray`, and `array.array` objects, as well as many common `memoryview` objects. Bytes-like objects can be used for various operations that work with binary data; these include compression, saving to a binary file, and sending over a socket.

Some operations need the binary data to be mutable. The documentation often refers to these as "read-write bytes-like objects". Example mutable buffer objects include `bytearray` and a `memoryview` of a `bytearray`. Other operations require the binary data to be stored in immutable objects ("read-only bytes-like objects"); examples of these include `bytes` and a `memoryview` of a `bytes` object.

bytecode Python source code is compiled into bytecode, the internal representation of a Python program in the CPython interpreter. The bytecode is also cached in `.pyc` files so that executing the same file is faster the second time (recompilation from source to bytecode can be avoided). This "intermediate language" is said to run on a *virtual machine* that executes the machine code corresponding to each bytecode. Do note that bytecodes are not expected to work between different Python virtual machines, nor to be stable between Python releases.

A list of bytecode instructions can be found in the documentation for *the dis module*.

class A template for creating user-defined objects. Class definitions normally contain method definitions which operate on instances of the class.

coercion The implicit conversion of an instance of one type to another during an operation which involves two arguments of the same type. For example, `int(3.15)` converts the floating point number to the integer 3, but in `3+4.5`, each argument is of a different type (one int, one float), and both must be converted to the same type before they can be added or it will raise a `TypeError`. Without coercion, all arguments of even compatible types would have to be normalized to the same value by the programmer, e.g., `float(3)+4.5` rather than just `3+4.5`.

complex number An extension of the familiar real number system in which all numbers are expressed as a sum of a real part and an imaginary part. Imaginary numbers are real multiples of the imaginary unit (the square root of `-1`), often written `i` in mathematics or `j` in engineering. Python has built-in support for complex numbers, which are written with this latter notation; the imaginary part is written with a `j` suffix, e.g., `3+1j`. To get access to complex equivalents of the *math* module, use *cmath*. Use of complex numbers is a fairly advanced mathematical feature. If you're not aware of a need for them, it's almost certain you can safely ignore them.

context manager An object which controls the environment seen in a `with` statement by defining `__enter__()` and `__exit__()` methods. See PEP 343.

contiguous A buffer is considered contiguous exactly if it is either *C-contiguous* or *Fortran contiguous*. Zero-dimensional buffers are C and Fortran contiguous. In one-dimensional arrays, the items must be laid out in memory next to each other, in order of increasing indexes starting from zero. In multidimensional C-contiguous arrays, the last index varies the fastest when visiting items in order of memory address. However, in Fortran contiguous arrays, the first index varies the fastest.

coroutine Coroutines is a more generalized form of subroutines. Subroutines are entered at one point and exited at another point. Coroutines can be entered, exited, and resumed at many different points. They can be implemented with the `async def` statement. See also PEP 492.

coroutine function A function which returns a *coroutine* object. A coroutine function may be defined with the `async def` statement, and may contain `await`, `async for`, and `async with` keywords. These were introduced by PEP 492.

CPython The canonical implementation of the Python programming language, as distributed on python.org. The term "CPython" is used when necessary to distinguish this implementation from others such as Jython or IronPython.

decorator A function returning another function, usually applied as a function transformation using the `@wrapper` syntax. Common examples for decorators are *classmethod()* and *staticmethod()*.

The decorator syntax is merely syntactic sugar, the following two function definitions are semantically equivalent:

```
def f(...):
    ...
f = staticmethod(f)

@staticmethod
def f(...):
    ...
```

The same concept exists for classes, but is less commonly used there. See the documentation for function definitions and class definitions for more about decorators.

descriptor Any object which defines the methods `__get__()`, `__set__()`, or `__delete__()`. When a class attribute is a descriptor, its special binding behavior is triggered upon attribute lookup. Normally, using *a.b* to get, set or delete an attribute looks up the object named *b* in the class dictionary for *a*, but if *b* is a descriptor, the respective descriptor method gets called. Understanding descriptors is a key to a deep understanding of Python because they are the basis for many features including functions, methods, properties, class methods, static methods, and reference to super classes.

For more information about descriptors' methods, see descriptors.

dictionary An associative array, where arbitrary keys are mapped to values. The keys can be any object with `__hash__()` and `__eq__()` methods. Called a hash in Perl.

dictionary view The objects returned from `dict.keys()`, `dict.values()`, and `dict.items()` are called dictionary views. They provide a dynamic view on the dictionary's entries, which means that when the dictionary changes, the view reflects these changes. To force the dictionary view to become a full list use `list(dictview)`. See *Dictionary view objects*.

docstring A string literal which appears as the first expression in a class, function or module. While ignored when the suite is executed, it is recognized by the compiler and put into the `__doc__` attribute of the enclosing class, function or module. Since it is available via introspection, it is the canonical place for documentation of the object.

duck-typing A programming style which does not look at an object's type to determine if it has the right interface; instead, the method or attribute is simply called or used ("If it looks like a duck and quacks like a duck, it must be a duck.") By emphasizing interfaces rather than specific types, well-designed code improves its flexibility by allowing polymorphic substitution. Duck-typing avoids tests using `type()` or `isinstance()`. (Note, however, that duck-typing can be complemented with *abstract base classes*.) Instead, it typically employs `hasattr()` tests or *EAFP* programming.

EAFP Easier to ask for forgiveness than permission. This common Python coding style assumes the existence of valid keys or attributes and catches exceptions if the assumption proves false. This clean and fast style is characterized by the presence of many `try` and `except` statements. The technique contrasts with the *LBYL* style common to many other languages such as C.

expression A piece of syntax which can be evaluated to some value. In other words, an expression is an accumulation of expression elements like literals, names, attribute access, operators or function calls which all return a value. In contrast to many other languages, not all language constructs are expressions. There are also *statement*s which cannot be used as expressions, such as `if`. Assignments are also statements, not expressions.

extension module A module written in C or C++, using Python's C API to interact with the core and with user code.

f-string String literals prefixed with `'f'` or `'F'` are commonly called "f-strings" which is short for formatted string literals. See also PEP 498.

file object An object exposing a file-oriented API (with methods such as `read()` or `write()`) to an underlying resource. Depending on the way it was created, a file object can mediate access to a real on-disk file or to another type of storage or communication device (for example standard input/output, in-memory buffers, sockets, pipes, etc.). File objects are also called *file-like objects* or *streams*.

There are actually three categories of file objects: raw *binary files*, buffered *binary files* and *text files*. Their interfaces are defined in the `io` module. The canonical way to create a file object is by using the `open()` function.

file-like object A synonym for *file object*.

finder An object that tries to find the *loader* for a module that is being imported.

Since Python 3.3, there are two types of finder: *meta path finders* for use with `sys.meta_path`, and *path entry finders* for use with `sys.path_hooks`.

See PEP 302, PEP 420 and PEP 451 for much more detail.

floor division Mathematical division that rounds down to nearest integer. The floor division operator is `//`. For example, the expression `11 // 4` evaluates to `2` in contrast to the `2.75` returned by float true division. Note that `(-11) // 4` is `-3` because that is `-2.75` rounded *downward*. See PEP 238.

function A series of statements which returns some value to a caller. It can also be passed zero or more *arguments* which may be used in the execution of the body. See also *parameter*, *method*, and the function section.

function annotation An arbitrary metadata value associated with a function parameter or return value. Its syntax is explained in section function. Annotations may be accessed via the __annotations__ special attribute of a function object.

Python itself does not assign any particular meaning to function annotations. They are intended to be interpreted by third-party libraries or tools. See PEP 3107, which describes some of their potential uses.

__future__ A pseudo-module which programmers can use to enable new language features which are not compatible with the current interpreter.

By importing the *__future__* module and evaluating its variables, you can see when a new feature was first added to the language and when it becomes the default:

```
>>> import __future__
>>> __future__.division
_Feature((2, 2, 0, 'alpha', 2), (3, 0, 0, 'alpha', 0), 8192)
```

garbage collection The process of freeing memory when it is not used anymore. Python performs garbage collection via reference counting and a cyclic garbage collector that is able to detect and break reference cycles. The garbage collector can be controlled using the *gc* module.

generator A function which returns a *generator iterator*. It looks like a normal function except that it contains `yield` expressions for producing a series of values usable in a for-loop or that can be retrieved one at a time with the *next()* function.

Usually refers to a generator function, but may refer to a *generator iterator* in some contexts. In cases where the intended meaning isn't clear, using the full terms avoids ambiguity.

generator iterator An object created by a *generator* function.

Each `yield` temporarily suspends processing, remembering the location execution state (including local variables and pending try-statements). When the *generator iterator* resumes, it picks-up where it left-off (in contrast to functions which start fresh on every invocation).

generator expression An expression that returns an iterator. It looks like a normal expression followed by a `for` expression defining a loop variable, range, and an optional `if` expression. The combined expression generates values for an enclosing function:

```
>>> sum(i*i for i in range(10))          # sum of squares 0, 1, 4, ... 81
285
```

generic function A function composed of multiple functions implementing the same operation for different types. Which implementation should be used during a call is determined by the dispatch algorithm.

See also the *single dispatch* glossary entry, the *functools.singledispatch()* decorator, and PEP 443.

GIL See *global interpreter lock*.

global interpreter lock The mechanism used by the *CPython* interpreter to assure that only one thread executes Python *bytecode* at a time. This simplifies the CPython implementation by making the object model (including critical built-in types such as *dict*) implicitly safe against concurrent access. Locking the entire interpreter makes it easier for the interpreter to be multi-threaded, at the expense of much of the parallelism afforded by multi-processor machines.

However, some extension modules, either standard or third-party, are designed so as to release the GIL when doing computationally-intensive tasks such as compression or hashing. Also, the GIL is always released when doing I/O.

Past efforts to create a "free-threaded" interpreter (one which locks shared data at a much finer granularity) have not been successful because performance suffered in the common single-processor case. It is believed that overcoming this performance issue would make the implementation much more complicated and therefore costlier to maintain.

hashable An object is *hashable* if it has a hash value which never changes during its lifetime (it needs a `__hash__()` method), and can be compared to other objects (it needs an `__eq__()` method). Hashable objects which compare equal must have the same hash value.

Hashability makes an object usable as a dictionary key and a set member, because these data structures use the hash value internally.

All of Python's immutable built-in objects are hashable; mutable containers (such as lists or dictionaries) are not. Objects which are instances of user-defined classes are hashable by default. They all compare unequal (except with themselves), and their hash value is derived from their *id()*.

IDLE An Integrated Development Environment for Python. IDLE is a basic editor and interpreter environment which ships with the standard distribution of Python.

immutable An object with a fixed value. Immutable objects include numbers, strings and tuples. Such an object cannot be altered. A new object has to be created if a different value has to be stored. They play an important role in places where a constant hash value is needed, for example as a key in a dictionary.

import path A list of locations (or *path entries*) that are searched by the *path based finder* for modules to import. During import, this list of locations usually comes from *sys.path*, but for subpackages it may also come from the parent package's `__path__` attribute.

importing The process by which Python code in one module is made available to Python code in another module.

importer An object that both finds and loads a module; both a *finder* and *loader* object.

interactive Python has an interactive interpreter which means you can enter statements and expressions at the interpreter prompt, immediately execute them and see their results. Just launch `python` with no arguments (possibly by selecting it from your computer's main menu). It is a very powerful way to test out new ideas or inspect modules and packages (remember `help(x)`).

interpreted Python is an interpreted language, as opposed to a compiled one, though the distinction can be blurry because of the presence of the bytecode compiler. This means that source files can be run directly without explicitly creating an executable which is then run. Interpreted languages typically have a shorter development/debug cycle than compiled ones, though their programs generally also run more slowly. See also *interactive*.

interpreter shutdown When asked to shut down, the Python interpreter enters a special phase where it gradually releases all allocated resources, such as modules and various critical internal structures. It also makes several calls to the *garbage collector*. This can trigger the execution of code in user-defined destructors or weakref callbacks. Code executed during the shutdown phase can encounter various exceptions as the resources it relies on may not function anymore (common examples are library modules or the warnings machinery).

The main reason for interpreter shutdown is that the `__main__` module or the script being run has finished executing.

iterable An object capable of returning its members one at a time. Examples of iterables include all sequence types (such as *list*, *str*, and *tuple*) and some non-sequence types like *dict*, *file objects*, and objects of any classes you define with an `__iter__()` method or with a `__getitem__()` method that implements *Sequence* semantics.

Iterables can be used in a `for` loop and in many other places where a sequence is needed (*zip()*, *map()*, ...). When an iterable object is passed as an argument to the built-in function *iter()*, it returns an iterator for the object. This iterator is good for one pass over the set of values. When using iterables, it is usually not necessary to call *iter()* or deal with iterator objects yourself. The `for` statement does that automatically for you, creating a temporary unnamed variable to hold the iterator for the duration of the loop. See also *iterator*, *sequence*, and *generator*.

iterator An object representing a stream of data. Repeated calls to the iterator's *__next__()* method (or passing it to the built-in function *next()*) return successive items in the stream. When no more data are available a *StopIteration* exception is raised instead. At this point, the iterator object is exhausted and any further calls to its *__next__()* method just raise *StopIteration* again. Iterators are required to have an *__iter__()* method that returns the iterator object itself so every iterator is also iterable and may be used in most places where other iterables are accepted. One notable exception is code which attempts multiple iteration passes. A container object (such as a *list*) produces a fresh new iterator each time you pass it to the *iter()* function or use it in a `for` loop. Attempting this with an iterator will just return the same exhausted iterator object used in the previous iteration pass, making it appear like an empty container.

More information can be found in *Iterator Types*.

key function A key function or collation function is a callable that returns a value used for sorting or ordering. For example, *locale.strxfrm()* is used to produce a sort key that is aware of locale specific sort conventions.

A number of tools in Python accept key functions to control how elements are ordered or grouped. They include *min()*, *max()*, *sorted()*, *list.sort()*, *heapq.merge()*, *heapq.nsmallest()*, *heapq.nlargest()*, and *itertools.groupby()*.

There are several ways to create a key function. For example. the *str.lower()* method can serve as a key function for case insensitive sorts. Alternatively, a key function can be built from a `lambda` expression such as `lambda r: (r[0], r[2])`. Also, the *operator* module provides three key function constructors: *attrgetter()*, *itemgetter()*, and *methodcaller()*. See the Sorting HOW TO for examples of how to create and use key functions.

keyword argument See *argument*.

lambda An anonymous inline function consisting of a single *expression* which is evaluated when the function is called. The syntax to create a lambda function is `lambda [arguments]: expression`

LBYL Look before you leap. This coding style explicitly tests for pre-conditions before making calls or lookups. This style contrasts with the *EAFP* approach and is characterized by the presence of many `if` statements.

In a multi-threaded environment, the LBYL approach can risk introducing a race condition between "the looking" and "the leaping". For example, the code, `if key in mapping: return mapping[key]` can fail if another thread removes *key* from *mapping* after the test, but before the lookup. This issue can be solved with locks or by using the EAFP approach.

list A built-in Python *sequence*. Despite its name it is more akin to an array in other languages than to a linked list since access to elements are O(1).

list comprehension A compact way to process all or part of the elements in a sequence and return a list with the results. `result = ['{:#04x}'.format(x) for x in range(256) if x % 2 == 0]` generates a list of strings containing even hex numbers (0x..) in the range from 0 to 255. The `if` clause is optional. If omitted, all elements in `range(256)` are processed.

loader An object that loads a module. It must define a method named `load_module()`. A loader is typically returned by a *finder*. See PEP 302 for details and *importlib.abc.Loader* for an *abstract base class*.

mapping A container object that supports arbitrary key lookups and implements the methods specified in the *Mapping* or *MutableMapping* *abstract base classes*. Examples include *dict*, *collections.defaultdict*, *collections.OrderedDict* and *collections.Counter*.

meta path finder A *finder* returned by a search of `sys.meta_path`. Meta path finders are related to, but different from *path entry finders*.

See `importlib.abc.MetaPathFinder` for the methods that meta path finders implement.

metaclass The class of a class. Class definitions create a class name, a class dictionary, and a list of base classes. The metaclass is responsible for taking those three arguments and creating the class. Most object oriented programming languages provide a default implementation. What makes Python special is that it is possible to create custom metaclasses. Most users never need this tool, but when the need arises, metaclasses can provide powerful, elegant solutions. They have been used for logging attribute access, adding thread-safety, tracking object creation, implementing singletons, and many other tasks.

More information can be found in metaclasses.

method A function which is defined inside a class body. If called as an attribute of an instance of that class, the method will get the instance object as its first *argument* (which is usually called `self`). See *function* and *nested scope*.

method resolution order Method Resolution Order is the order in which base classes are searched for a member during lookup. See The Python 2.3 Method Resolution Order for details of the algorithm used by the Python interpreter since the 2.3 release.

module An object that serves as an organizational unit of Python code. Modules have a namespace containing arbitrary Python objects. Modules are loaded into Python by the process of *importing*.

See also *package*.

module spec A namespace containing the import-related information used to load a module. An instance of `importlib.machinery.ModuleSpec`.

MRO See *method resolution order*.

mutable Mutable objects can change their value but keep their `id()`. See also *immutable*.

named tuple Any tuple-like class whose indexable elements are also accessible using named attributes (for example, `time.localtime()` returns a tuple-like object where the *year* is accessible either with an index such as `t[0]` or with a named attribute like `t.tm_year`).

A named tuple can be a built-in type such as `time.struct_time`, or it can be created with a regular class definition. A full featured named tuple can also be created with the factory function `collections.namedtuple()`. The latter approach automatically provides extra features such as a self-documenting representation like `Employee(name='jones', title='programmer')`.

namespace The place where a variable is stored. Namespaces are implemented as dictionaries. There are the local, global and built-in namespaces as well as nested namespaces in objects (in methods). Namespaces support modularity by preventing naming conflicts. For instance, the functions `builtins.open` and `os.open()` are distinguished by their namespaces. Namespaces also aid readability and maintainability by making it clear which module implements a function. For instance, writing `random.seed()` or `itertools.islice()` makes it clear that those functions are implemented by the *random* and *itertools* modules, respectively.

namespace package A PEP 420 *package* which serves only as a container for subpackages. Namespace packages may have no physical representation, and specifically are not like a *regular package* because they have no `__init__.py` file.

See also *module*.

nested scope The ability to refer to a variable in an enclosing definition. For instance, a function defined inside another function can refer to variables in the outer function. Note that nested scopes by default work only for reference and not for assignment. Local variables both read and write in the innermost scope. Likewise, global variables read and write to the global namespace. The `nonlocal` allows writing to outer scopes.

new-style class Old name for the flavor of classes now used for all class objects. In earlier Python versions, only new-style classes could use Python's newer, versatile features like `__slots__`, descriptors, properties, `__getattribute__()`, class methods, and static methods.

object Any data with state (attributes or value) and defined behavior (methods). Also the ultimate base class of any *new-style class*.

package A Python *module* which can contain submodules or recursively, subpackages. Technically, a package is a Python module with an `__path__` attribute.

See also *regular package* and *namespace package*.

parameter A named entity in a *function* (or method) definition that specifies an *argument* (or in some cases, arguments) that the function can accept. There are five kinds of parameter:

- *positional-or-keyword*: specifies an argument that can be passed either *positionally* or as a *keyword argument*. This is the default kind of parameter, for example *foo* and *bar* in the following:

    ```
    def func(foo, bar=None): ...
    ```

- *positional-only*: specifies an argument that can be supplied only by position. Python has no syntax for defining positional-only parameters. However, some built-in functions have positional-only parameters (e.g. `abs()`).

- *keyword-only*: specifies an argument that can be supplied only by keyword. Keyword-only parameters can be defined by including a single var-positional parameter or bare `*` in the parameter list of the function definition before them, for example *kw_only1* and *kw_only2* in the following:

    ```
    def func(arg, *, kw_only1, kw_only2): ...
    ```

- *var-positional*: specifies that an arbitrary sequence of positional arguments can be provided (in addition to any positional arguments already accepted by other parameters). Such a parameter can be defined by prepending the parameter name with `*`, for example *args* in the following:

    ```
    def func(*args, **kwargs): ...
    ```

- *var-keyword*: specifies that arbitrarily many keyword arguments can be provided (in addition to any keyword arguments already accepted by other parameters). Such a parameter can be defined by prepending the parameter name with `**`, for example *kwargs* in the example above.

Parameters can specify both optional and required arguments, as well as default values for some optional arguments.

See also the *argument* glossary entry, the FAQ question on the difference between arguments and parameters, the `inspect.Parameter` class, the function section, and PEP 362.

path entry A single location on the *import path* which the *path based finder* consults to find modules for importing.

path entry finder A *finder* returned by a callable on `sys.path_hooks` (i.e. a *path entry hook*) which knows how to locate modules given a *path entry*.

See `importlib.abc.PathEntryFinder` for the methods that path entry finders implement.

path entry hook A callable on the `sys.path_hook` list which returns a *path entry finder* if it knows how to find modules on a specific *path entry*.

path based finder One of the default *meta path finders* which searches an *import path* for modules.

path-like object An object representing a file system path. A path-like object is either a `str` or `bytes` object representing a path, or an object implementing the `os.PathLike` protocol. An object that supports the `os.PathLike` protocol can be converted to a `str` or `bytes` file system path by calling the *os.fspath()* function; *os.fsdecode()* and *os.fsencode()* can be used to guarantee a *str* or *bytes* result instead, respectively. Introduced by PEP 519.

portion A set of files in a single directory (possibly stored in a zip file) that contribute to a namespace package, as defined in PEP 420.

positional argument See *argument*.

provisional API A provisional API is one which has been deliberately excluded from the standard library's backwards compatibility guarantees. While major changes to such interfaces are not expected, as long as they are marked provisional, backwards incompatible changes (up to and including removal of the interface) may occur if deemed necessary by core developers. Such changes will not be made gratuitously – they will occur only if serious fundamental flaws are uncovered that were missed prior to the inclusion of the API.

Even for provisional APIs, backwards incompatible changes are seen as a "solution of last resort" - every attempt will still be made to find a backwards compatible resolution to any identified problems.

This process allows the standard library to continue to evolve over time, without locking in problematic design errors for extended periods of time. See PEP 411 for more details.

provisional package See *provisional API*.

Python 3000 Nickname for the Python 3.x release line (coined long ago when the release of version 3 was something in the distant future.) This is also abbreviated "Py3k".

Pythonic An idea or piece of code which closely follows the most common idioms of the Python language, rather than implementing code using concepts common to other languages. For example, a common idiom in Python is to loop over all elements of an iterable using a `for` statement. Many other languages don't have this type of construct, so people unfamiliar with Python sometimes use a numerical counter instead:

```
for i in range(len(food)):
    print(food[i])
```

As opposed to the cleaner, Pythonic method:

```
for piece in food:
    print(piece)
```

qualified name A dotted name showing the "path" from a module's global scope to a class, function or method defined in that module, as defined in PEP 3155. For top-level functions and classes, the qualified name is the same as the object's name:

```
>>> class C:
...     class D:
...         def meth(self):
...             pass
...
>>> C.__qualname__
'C'
>>> C.D.__qualname__
'C.D'
>>> C.D.meth.__qualname__
'C.D.meth'
```

When used to refer to modules, the *fully qualified name* means the entire dotted path to the module, including any parent packages, e.g. `email.mime.text`:

```
>>> import email.mime.text
>>> email.mime.text.__name__
'email.mime.text'
```

reference count The number of references to an object. When the reference count of an object drops to zero, it is deallocated. Reference counting is generally not visible to Python code, but it is a key element of the *CPython* implementation. The *sys* module defines a *getrefcount()* function that programmers can call to return the reference count for a particular object.

regular package A traditional *package*, such as a directory containing an `__init__.py` file.

See also *namespace package*.

__slots__ A declaration inside a class that saves memory by pre-declaring space for instance attributes and eliminating instance dictionaries. Though popular, the technique is somewhat tricky to get right and is best reserved for rare cases where there are large numbers of instances in a memory-critical application.

sequence An *iterable* which supports efficient element access using integer indices via the `__getitem__()` special method and defines a `__len__()` method that returns the length of the sequence. Some built-in sequence types are *list*, *str*, *tuple*, and *bytes*. Note that *dict* also supports `__getitem__()` and `__len__()`, but is considered a mapping rather than a sequence because the lookups use arbitrary *immutable* keys rather than integers.

The *collections.abc.Sequence* abstract base class defines a much richer interface that goes beyond just `__getitem__()` and `__len__()`, adding `count()`, `index()`, `__contains__()`, and `__reversed__()`. Types that implement this expanded interface can be registered explicitly using `register()`.

single dispatch A form of *generic function* dispatch where the implementation is chosen based on the type of a single argument.

slice An object usually containing a portion of a *sequence*. A slice is created using the subscript notation, `[]` with colons between numbers when several are given, such as in `variable_name[1:3:5]`. The bracket (subscript) notation uses *slice* objects internally.

special method A method that is called implicitly by Python to execute a certain operation on a type, such as addition. Such methods have names starting and ending with double underscores. Special methods are documented in specialnames.

statement A statement is part of a suite (a "block" of code). A statement is either an *expression* or one of several constructs with a keyword, such as `if`, `while` or `for`.

struct sequence A tuple with named elements. Struct sequences expose an interface similar to *named tuple* in that elements can either be accessed either by index or as an attribute. However, they do not have any of the named tuple methods like *_make()* or *_asdict()*. Examples of struct sequences include *sys.float_info* and the return value of *os.stat()*.

text encoding A codec which encodes Unicode strings to bytes.

text file A *file object* able to read and write *str* objects. Often, a text file actually accesses a byte-oriented datastream and handles the *text encoding* automatically. Examples of text files are files opened in text mode (`'r'` or `'w'`), *sys.stdin*, *sys.stdout*, and instances of *io.StringIO*.

See also:

A *binary file* reads and write *bytes* objects.

triple-quoted string A string which is bound by three instances of either a quotation mark (") or an apostrophe ('). While they don't provide any functionality not available with single-quoted strings, they are useful for a number of reasons. They allow you to include unescaped single and double quotes within a string and they can span multiple lines without the use of the continuation character, making them especially useful when writing docstrings.

type The type of a Python object determines what kind of object it is; every object has a type. An object's type is accessible as its `__class__` attribute or can be retrieved with `type(obj)`.

universal newlines A manner of interpreting text streams in which all of the following are recognized as ending a line: the Unix end-of-line convention `'\n'`, the Windows convention `'\r\n'`, and the old Macintosh convention `'\r'`. See PEP 278 and PEP 3116, as well as *bytes.splitlines()* for an additional use.

variable annotation A type metadata value associated with a module global variable or a class attribute. Its syntax is explained in section annassign. Annotations are stored in the `__annotations__` special attribute of a class or module object and can be accessed using *typing.get_type_hints()*.

Python itself does not assign any particular meaning to variable annotations. They are intended to be interpreted by third-party libraries or type checking tools. See PEP 526, PEP 484 which describe some of their potential uses.

virtual environment A cooperatively isolated runtime environment that allows Python users and applications to install and upgrade Python distribution packages without interfering with the behaviour of other Python applications running on the same system.

See also *venv*.

virtual machine A computer defined entirely in software. Python's virtual machine executes the *bytecode* emitted by the bytecode compiler.

Zen of Python Listing of Python design principles and philosophies that are helpful in understanding and using the language. The listing can be found by typing "`import this`" at the interactive prompt.

BIBLIOGRAPHY

[C99] ISO/IEC 9899:1999. "Programming languages – C." A public draft of this standard is available at http://www.open-std.org/jtc1/sc22/wg14/www/docs/n1256.pdf.

APPENDIX B

ABOUT THESE DOCUMENTS

These documents are generated from reStructuredText sources by Sphinx, a document processor specifically written for the Python documentation.

Development of the documentation and its toolchain is an entirely volunteer effort, just like Python itself. If you want to contribute, please take a look at the reporting-bugs page for information on how to do so. New volunteers are always welcome!

Many thanks go to:

- Fred L. Drake, Jr., the creator of the original Python documentation toolset and writer of much of the content;
- the Docutils project for creating reStructuredText and the Docutils suite;
- Fredrik Lundh for his Alternative Python Reference project from which Sphinx got many good ideas.

B.1 Contributors to the Python Documentation

Many people have contributed to the Python language, the Python standard library, and the Python documentation. See Misc/ACKS in the Python source distribution for a partial list of contributors.

It is only with the input and contributions of the Python community that Python has such wonderful documentation – Thank You!

APPENDIX C

HISTORY AND LICENSE

C.1 History of the software

Python was created in the early 1990s by Guido van Rossum at Stichting Mathematisch Centrum (CWI, see https://www.cwi.nl/) in the Netherlands as a successor of a language called ABC. Guido remains Python's principal author, although it includes many contributions from others.

In 1995, Guido continued his work on Python at the Corporation for National Research Initiatives (CNRI, see https://www.cnri.reston.va.us/) in Reston, Virginia where he released several versions of the software.

In May 2000, Guido and the Python core development team moved to BeOpen.com to form the BeOpen PythonLabs team. In October of the same year, the PythonLabs team moved to Digital Creations (now Zope Corporation; see http://www.zope.com/). In 2001, the Python Software Foundation (PSF, see https://www.python.org/psf/) was formed, a non-profit organization created specifically to own Python-related Intellectual Property. Zope Corporation is a sponsoring member of the PSF.

All Python releases are Open Source (see https://opensource.org/ for the Open Source Definition). Historically, most, but not all, Python releases have also been GPL-compatible; the table below summarizes the various releases.

Release	Derived from	Year	Owner	GPL compatible?
0.9.0 thru 1.2	n/a	1991-1995	CWI	yes
1.3 thru 1.5.2	1.2	1995-1999	CNRI	yes
1.6	1.5.2	2000	CNRI	no
2.0	1.6	2000	BeOpen.com	no
1.6.1	1.6	2001	CNRI	no
2.1	2.0+1.6.1	2001	PSF	no
2.0.1	2.0+1.6.1	2001	PSF	yes
2.1.1	2.1+2.0.1	2001	PSF	yes
2.1.2	2.1.1	2002	PSF	yes
2.1.3	2.1.2	2002	PSF	yes
2.2 and above	2.1.1	2001-now	PSF	yes

Note: GPL-compatible doesn't mean that we're distributing Python under the GPL. All Python licenses, unlike the GPL, let you distribute a modified version without making your changes open source. The GPL-compatible licenses make it possible to combine Python with other software that is released under the GPL; the others don't.

Thanks to the many outside volunteers who have worked under Guido's direction to make these releases possible.

C.2 Terms and conditions for accessing or otherwise using Python

C.2.1 PSF LICENSE AGREEMENT FOR PYTHON 3.6.4

1. This LICENSE AGREEMENT is between the Python Software Foundation ("PSF"), and the Individual or Organization ("Licensee") accessing and otherwise using Python 3.6.4 software in source or binary form and its associated documentation.

2. Subject to the terms and conditions of this License Agreement, PSF hereby grants Licensee a nonexclusive, royalty-free, world-wide license to reproduce, analyze, test, perform and/or display publicly, prepare derivative works, distribute, and otherwise use Python 3.6.4 alone or in any derivative version, provided, however, that PSF's License Agreement and PSF's notice of copyright, i.e., "Copyright © 2001-2018 Python Software Foundation; All Rights Reserved" are retained in Python 3.6.4 alone or in any derivative version prepared by Licensee.

3. In the event Licensee prepares a derivative work that is based on or incorporates Python 3.6.4 or any part thereof, and wants to make the derivative work available to others as provided herein, then Licensee hereby agrees to include in any such work a brief summary of the changes made to Python 3.6.4.

4. PSF is making Python 3.6.4 available to Licensee on an "AS IS" basis. PSF MAKES NO REPRESENTATIONS OR WARRANTIES, EXPRESS OR IMPLIED. BY WAY OF EXAMPLE, BUT NOT LIMITATION, PSF MAKES NO AND DISCLAIMS ANY REPRESENTATION OR WARRANTY OF MERCHANTABILITY OR FITNESS FOR ANY PARTICULAR PURPOSE OR THAT THE USE OF PYTHON 3.6.4 WILL NOT INFRINGE ANY THIRD PARTY RIGHTS.

5. PSF SHALL NOT BE LIABLE TO LICENSEE OR ANY OTHER USERS OF PYTHON 3.6.4 FOR ANY INCIDENTAL, SPECIAL, OR CONSEQUENTIAL DAMAGES OR LOSS AS A RESULT OF MODIFYING, DISTRIBUTING, OR OTHERWISE USING PYTHON 3.6.4, OR ANY DERIVATIVE THEREOF, EVEN IF ADVISED OF THE POSSIBILITY THEREOF.

6. This License Agreement will automatically terminate upon a material breach of its terms and conditions.

7. Nothing in this License Agreement shall be deemed to create any relationship of agency, partnership, or joint venture between PSF and Licensee. This License Agreement does not grant permission to use PSF trademarks or trade name in a trademark sense to endorse or promote products or services of Licensee, or any third party.

8. By copying, installing or otherwise using Python 3.6.4, Licensee agrees to be bound by the terms and conditions of this License Agreement.

C.2.2 BEOPEN.COM LICENSE AGREEMENT FOR PYTHON 2.0

BEOPEN PYTHON OPEN SOURCE LICENSE AGREEMENT VERSION 1

1. This LICENSE AGREEMENT is between BeOpen.com ("BeOpen"), having an office at 160 Saratoga Avenue, Santa Clara, CA 95051, and the Individual or Organization ("Licensee") accessing and otherwise using this software in source or binary

```
    form and its associated documentation ("the Software").

 2. Subject to the terms and conditions of this BeOpen Python License Agreement,
    BeOpen hereby grants Licensee a non-exclusive, royalty-free, world-wide license
    to reproduce, analyze, test, perform and/or display publicly, prepare derivative
    works, distribute, and otherwise use the Software alone or in any derivative
    version, provided, however, that the BeOpen Python License is retained in the
    Software, alone or in any derivative version prepared by Licensee.

 3. BeOpen is making the Software available to Licensee on an "AS IS" basis.
    BEOPEN MAKES NO REPRESENTATIONS OR WARRANTIES, EXPRESS OR IMPLIED.  BY WAY OF
    EXAMPLE, BUT NOT LIMITATION, BEOPEN MAKES NO AND DISCLAIMS ANY REPRESENTATION OR
    WARRANTY OF MERCHANTABILITY OR FITNESS FOR ANY PARTICULAR PURPOSE OR THAT THE
    USE OF THE SOFTWARE WILL NOT INFRINGE ANY THIRD PARTY RIGHTS.

 4. BEOPEN SHALL NOT BE LIABLE TO LICENSEE OR ANY OTHER USERS OF THE SOFTWARE FOR
    ANY INCIDENTAL, SPECIAL, OR CONSEQUENTIAL DAMAGES OR LOSS AS A RESULT OF USING,
    MODIFYING OR DISTRIBUTING THE SOFTWARE, OR ANY DERIVATIVE THEREOF, EVEN IF
    ADVISED OF THE POSSIBILITY THEREOF.

 5. This License Agreement will automatically terminate upon a material breach of
    its terms and conditions.

 6. This License Agreement shall be governed by and interpreted in all respects
    by the law of the State of California, excluding conflict of law provisions.
    Nothing in this License Agreement shall be deemed to create any relationship of
    agency, partnership, or joint venture between BeOpen and Licensee.  This License
    Agreement does not grant permission to use BeOpen trademarks or trade names in a
    trademark sense to endorse or promote products or services of Licensee, or any
    third party.  As an exception, the "BeOpen Python" logos available at
    http://www.pythonlabs.com/logos.html may be used according to the permissions
    granted on that web page.

 7. By copying, installing or otherwise using the software, Licensee agrees to be
    bound by the terms and conditions of this License Agreement.
```

C.2.3 CNRI LICENSE AGREEMENT FOR PYTHON 1.6.1

```
 1. This LICENSE AGREEMENT is between the Corporation for National Research
    Initiatives, having an office at 1895 Preston White Drive, Reston, VA 20191
    ("CNRI"), and the Individual or Organization ("Licensee") accessing and
    otherwise using Python 1.6.1 software in source or binary form and its
    associated documentation.

 2. Subject to the terms and conditions of this License Agreement, CNRI hereby
    grants Licensee a nonexclusive, royalty-free, world-wide license to reproduce,
    analyze, test, perform and/or display publicly, prepare derivative works,
    distribute, and otherwise use Python 1.6.1 alone or in any derivative version,
    provided, however, that CNRI's License Agreement and CNRI's notice of copyright,
    i.e., "Copyright © 1995-2001 Corporation for National Research Initiatives; All
    Rights Reserved" are retained in Python 1.6.1 alone or in any derivative version
    prepared by Licensee.  Alternately, in lieu of CNRI's License Agreement,
    Licensee may substitute the following text (omitting the quotes): "Python 1.6.1
    is made available subject to the terms and conditions in CNRI's License
    Agreement.  This Agreement together with Python 1.6.1 may be located on the
    Internet using the following unique, persistent identifier (known as a handle):
```

1895.22/1013. This Agreement may also be obtained from a proxy server on the
Internet using the following URL: http://hdl.handle.net/1895.22/1013."

3. In the event Licensee prepares a derivative work that is based on or
   incorporates Python 1.6.1 or any part thereof, and wants to make the derivative
   work available to others as provided herein, then Licensee hereby agrees to
   include in any such work a brief summary of the changes made to Python 1.6.1.

4. CNRI is making Python 1.6.1 available to Licensee on an "AS IS" basis. CNRI
   MAKES NO REPRESENTATIONS OR WARRANTIES, EXPRESS OR IMPLIED. BY WAY OF EXAMPLE,
   BUT NOT LIMITATION, CNRI MAKES NO AND DISCLAIMS ANY REPRESENTATION OR WARRANTY
   OF MERCHANTABILITY OR FITNESS FOR ANY PARTICULAR PURPOSE OR THAT THE USE OF
   PYTHON 1.6.1 WILL NOT INFRINGE ANY THIRD PARTY RIGHTS.

5. CNRI SHALL NOT BE LIABLE TO LICENSEE OR ANY OTHER USERS OF PYTHON 1.6.1 FOR
   ANY INCIDENTAL, SPECIAL, OR CONSEQUENTIAL DAMAGES OR LOSS AS A RESULT OF
   MODIFYING, DISTRIBUTING, OR OTHERWISE USING PYTHON 1.6.1, OR ANY DERIVATIVE
   THEREOF, EVEN IF ADVISED OF THE POSSIBILITY THEREOF.

6. This License Agreement will automatically terminate upon a material breach of
   its terms and conditions.

7. This License Agreement shall be governed by the federal intellectual property
   law of the United States, including without limitation the federal copyright
   law, and, to the extent such U.S. federal law does not apply, by the law of the
   Commonwealth of Virginia, excluding Virginia's conflict of law provisions.
   Notwithstanding the foregoing, with regard to derivative works based on Python
   1.6.1 that incorporate non-separable material that was previously distributed
   under the GNU General Public License (GPL), the law of the Commonwealth of
   Virginia shall govern this License Agreement only as to issues arising under or
   with respect to Paragraphs 4, 5, and 7 of this License Agreement. Nothing in
   this License Agreement shall be deemed to create any relationship of agency,
   partnership, or joint venture between CNRI and Licensee. This License Agreement
   does not grant permission to use CNRI trademarks or trade name in a trademark
   sense to endorse or promote products or services of Licensee, or any third
   party.

8. By clicking on the "ACCEPT" button where indicated, or by copying, installing
   or otherwise using Python 1.6.1, Licensee agrees to be bound by the terms and
   conditions of this License Agreement.

C.2.4 CWI LICENSE AGREEMENT FOR PYTHON 0.9.0 THROUGH 1.2

Copyright © 1991 - 1995, Stichting Mathematisch Centrum Amsterdam, The
Netherlands. All rights reserved.

Permission to use, copy, modify, and distribute this software and its
documentation for any purpose and without fee is hereby granted, provided that
the above copyright notice appear in all copies and that both that copyright
notice and this permission notice appear in supporting documentation, and that
the name of Stichting Mathematisch Centrum or CWI not be used in advertising or
publicity pertaining to distribution of the software without specific, written
prior permission.

STICHTING MATHEMATISCH CENTRUM DISCLAIMS ALL WARRANTIES WITH REGARD TO THIS
SOFTWARE, INCLUDING ALL IMPLIED WARRANTIES OF MERCHANTABILITY AND FITNESS, IN NO

```
EVENT SHALL STICHTING MATHEMATISCH CENTRUM BE LIABLE FOR ANY SPECIAL, INDIRECT
OR CONSEQUENTIAL DAMAGES OR ANY DAMAGES WHATSOEVER RESULTING FROM LOSS OF USE,
DATA OR PROFITS, WHETHER IN AN ACTION OF CONTRACT, NEGLIGENCE OR OTHER TORTIOUS
ACTION, ARISING OUT OF OR IN CONNECTION WITH THE USE OR PERFORMANCE OF THIS
SOFTWARE.
```

C.3 Licenses and Acknowledgements for Incorporated Software

This section is an incomplete, but growing list of licenses and acknowledgements for third-party software incorporated in the Python distribution.

C.3.1 Mersenne Twister

The `_random` module includes code based on a download from http://www.math.sci.hiroshima-u.ac.jp/~m-mat/MT/MT2002/emt19937ar.html. The following are the verbatim comments from the original code:

```
A C-program for MT19937, with initialization improved 2002/1/26.
Coded by Takuji Nishimura and Makoto Matsumoto.

Before using, initialize the state by using init_genrand(seed)
or init_by_array(init_key, key_length).

Copyright (C) 1997 - 2002, Makoto Matsumoto and Takuji Nishimura,
All rights reserved.

Redistribution and use in source and binary forms, with or without
modification, are permitted provided that the following conditions
are met:

  1. Redistributions of source code must retain the above copyright
     notice, this list of conditions and the following disclaimer.

  2. Redistributions in binary form must reproduce the above copyright
     notice, this list of conditions and the following disclaimer in the
     documentation and/or other materials provided with the distribution.

  3. The names of its contributors may not be used to endorse or promote
     products derived from this software without specific prior written
     permission.

THIS SOFTWARE IS PROVIDED BY THE COPYRIGHT HOLDERS AND CONTRIBUTORS
"AS IS" AND ANY EXPRESS OR IMPLIED WARRANTIES, INCLUDING, BUT NOT
LIMITED TO, THE IMPLIED WARRANTIES OF MERCHANTABILITY AND FITNESS FOR
A PARTICULAR PURPOSE ARE DISCLAIMED.  IN NO EVENT SHALL THE COPYRIGHT OWNER OR
CONTRIBUTORS BE LIABLE FOR ANY DIRECT, INDIRECT, INCIDENTAL, SPECIAL,
EXEMPLARY, OR CONSEQUENTIAL DAMAGES (INCLUDING, BUT NOT LIMITED TO,
PROCUREMENT OF SUBSTITUTE GOODS OR SERVICES; LOSS OF USE, DATA, OR
PROFITS; OR BUSINESS INTERRUPTION) HOWEVER CAUSED AND ON ANY THEORY OF
LIABILITY, WHETHER IN CONTRACT, STRICT LIABILITY, OR TORT (INCLUDING
NEGLIGENCE OR OTHERWISE) ARISING IN ANY WAY OUT OF THE USE OF THIS
SOFTWARE, EVEN IF ADVISED OF THE POSSIBILITY OF SUCH DAMAGE.


Any feedback is very welcome.
```

```
http://www.math.sci.hiroshima-u.ac.jp/~m-mat/MT/emt.html
email: m-mat @ math.sci.hiroshima-u.ac.jp (remove space)
```

C.3.2 Sockets

The *socket* module uses the functions, getaddrinfo(), and getnameinfo(), which are coded in separate source files from the WIDE Project, http://www.wide.ad.jp/.

```
Copyright (C) 1995, 1996, 1997, and 1998 WIDE Project.
All rights reserved.

Redistribution and use in source and binary forms, with or without
modification, are permitted provided that the following conditions
are met:
1. Redistributions of source code must retain the above copyright
   notice, this list of conditions and the following disclaimer.
2. Redistributions in binary form must reproduce the above copyright
   notice, this list of conditions and the following disclaimer in the
   documentation and/or other materials provided with the distribution.
3. Neither the name of the project nor the names of its contributors
   may be used to endorse or promote products derived from this software
   without specific prior written permission.

THIS SOFTWARE IS PROVIDED BY THE PROJECT AND CONTRIBUTORS ``AS IS'' AND
ANY EXPRESS OR IMPLIED WARRANTIES, INCLUDING, BUT NOT LIMITED TO, THE
IMPLIED WARRANTIES OF MERCHANTABILITY AND FITNESS FOR A PARTICULAR PURPOSE
ARE DISCLAIMED.  IN NO EVENT SHALL THE PROJECT OR CONTRIBUTORS BE LIABLE
FOR ANY DIRECT, INDIRECT, INCIDENTAL, SPECIAL, EXEMPLARY, OR CONSEQUENTIAL
DAMAGES (INCLUDING, BUT NOT LIMITED TO, PROCUREMENT OF SUBSTITUTE GOODS
OR SERVICES; LOSS OF USE, DATA, OR PROFITS; OR BUSINESS INTERRUPTION)
HOWEVER CAUSED AND ON ANY THEORY OF LIABILITY, WHETHER IN CONTRACT, STRICT
LIABILITY, OR TORT (INCLUDING NEGLIGENCE OR OTHERWISE) ARISING IN ANY WAY
OUT OF THE USE OF THIS SOFTWARE, EVEN IF ADVISED OF THE POSSIBILITY OF
SUCH DAMAGE.
```

C.3.3 Floating point exception control

The source for the *fpectl* module includes the following notice:

```
      ---------------------------------------------------------------------
     /                       Copyright (c) 1996.                          \
    |          The Regents of the University of California.                |
    |                        All rights reserved.                          |
    |                                                                      |
    |   Permission to use, copy, modify, and distribute this software for  |
    |   any purpose without fee is hereby granted, provided that this en-  |
    |   tire notice is included in all copies of any software which is or  |
    |   includes  a  copy  or  modification  of  this software and in all  |
    |   copies of the supporting documentation for such software.          |
    |                                                                      |
    |   This  work was produced at the University of California, Lawrence  |
    |   Livermore National Laboratory under  contract  no.  W-7405-ENG-48  |
    |   between  the  U.S.  Department  of  Energy and The Regents of the  |
    |   University of California for the operation of UC LLNL.             |
    |                                                                      |
```

```
|                          DISCLAIMER                                  |
|                                                                      |
|   This  software was prepared as an account of work sponsored by an  |
|   agency of the United States Government. Neither the United States  |
|   Government  nor the University of California nor any of their em-  |
|   ployees, makes any warranty, express or implied, or  assumes  any  |
|   liability  or  responsibility  for the accuracy, completeness, or  |
|   usefulness of any information, apparatus, product,  or  process    |
|   disclosed,   or  represents  that  its  use  would  not  infringe  |
|   privately-owned rights. Reference herein to any specific  commer-  |
|   cial  products,  process,  or  service  by trade name, trademark,  |
|   manufacturer, or otherwise, does not  necessarily  constitute  or  |
|   imply  its endorsement, recommendation, or favoring by the United  |
|   States Government or the University of California. The views  and  |
|   opinions  of authors expressed herein do not necessarily state or  |
|   reflect those of the United States Government or  the  University  |
|   of  California,  and shall not be used for advertising or product  |
 \  endorsement purposes.                                              /
  ---------------------------------------------------------------------
```

C.3.4 Asynchronous socket services

The *asynchat* and *asyncore* modules contain the following notice:

```
Copyright 1996 by Sam Rushing

                All Rights Reserved

Permission to use, copy, modify, and distribute this software and
its documentation for any purpose and without fee is hereby
granted, provided that the above copyright notice appear in all
copies and that both that copyright notice and this permission
notice appear in supporting documentation, and that the name of Sam
Rushing not be used in advertising or publicity pertaining to
distribution of the software without specific, written prior
permission.

SAM RUSHING DISCLAIMS ALL WARRANTIES WITH REGARD TO THIS SOFTWARE,
INCLUDING ALL IMPLIED WARRANTIES OF MERCHANTABILITY AND FITNESS, IN
NO EVENT SHALL SAM RUSHING BE LIABLE FOR ANY SPECIAL, INDIRECT OR
CONSEQUENTIAL DAMAGES OR ANY DAMAGES WHATSOEVER RESULTING FROM LOSS
OF USE, DATA OR PROFITS, WHETHER IN AN ACTION OF CONTRACT,
NEGLIGENCE OR OTHER TORTIOUS ACTION, ARISING OUT OF OR IN
CONNECTION WITH THE USE OR PERFORMANCE OF THIS SOFTWARE.
```

C.3.5 Cookie management

The *http.cookies* module contains the following notice:

```
Copyright 2000 by Timothy O'Malley <timo@alum.mit.edu>

                All Rights Reserved

Permission to use, copy, modify, and distribute this software
and its documentation for any purpose and without fee is hereby
```

```
granted, provided that the above copyright notice appear in all
copies and that both that copyright notice and this permission
notice appear in supporting documentation, and that the name of
Timothy O'Malley  not be used in advertising or publicity
pertaining to distribution of the software without specific, written
prior permission.

Timothy O'Malley DISCLAIMS ALL WARRANTIES WITH REGARD TO THIS
SOFTWARE, INCLUDING ALL IMPLIED WARRANTIES OF MERCHANTABILITY
AND FITNESS, IN NO EVENT SHALL Timothy O'Malley BE LIABLE FOR
ANY SPECIAL, INDIRECT OR CONSEQUENTIAL DAMAGES OR ANY DAMAGES
WHATSOEVER RESULTING FROM LOSS OF USE, DATA OR PROFITS,
WHETHER IN AN ACTION OF CONTRACT, NEGLIGENCE OR OTHER TORTIOUS
ACTION, ARISING OUT OF OR IN CONNECTION WITH THE USE OR
PERFORMANCE OF THIS SOFTWARE.
```

C.3.6 Execution tracing

The *trace* module contains the following notice:

```
portions copyright 2001, Autonomous Zones Industries, Inc., all rights...
err...   reserved and offered to the public under the terms of the
Python 2.2 license.
Author: Zooko O'Whielacronx
http://zooko.com/
mailto:zooko@zooko.com

Copyright 2000, Mojam Media, Inc., all rights reserved.
Author: Skip Montanaro

Copyright 1999, Bioreason, Inc., all rights reserved.
Author: Andrew Dalke

Copyright 1995-1997, Automatrix, Inc., all rights reserved.
Author: Skip Montanaro

Copyright 1991-1995, Stichting Mathematisch Centrum, all rights reserved.


Permission to use, copy, modify, and distribute this Python software and
its associated documentation for any purpose without fee is hereby
granted, provided that the above copyright notice appears in all copies,
and that both that copyright notice and this permission notice appear in
supporting documentation, and that the name of neither Automatrix,
Bioreason or Mojam Media be used in advertising or publicity pertaining to
distribution of the software without specific, written prior permission.
```

C.3.7 UUencode and UUdecode functions

The *uu* module contains the following notice:

```
Copyright 1994 by Lance Ellinghouse
Cathedral City, California Republic, United States of America.
                   All Rights Reserved
Permission to use, copy, modify, and distribute this software and its
```

```
documentation for any purpose and without fee is hereby granted,
provided that the above copyright notice appear in all copies and that
both that copyright notice and this permission notice appear in
supporting documentation, and that the name of Lance Ellinghouse
not be used in advertising or publicity pertaining to distribution
of the software without specific, written prior permission.
LANCE ELLINGHOUSE DISCLAIMS ALL WARRANTIES WITH REGARD TO
THIS SOFTWARE, INCLUDING ALL IMPLIED WARRANTIES OF MERCHANTABILITY AND
FITNESS, IN NO EVENT SHALL LANCE ELLINGHOUSE CENTRUM BE LIABLE
FOR ANY SPECIAL, INDIRECT OR CONSEQUENTIAL DAMAGES OR ANY DAMAGES
WHATSOEVER RESULTING FROM LOSS OF USE, DATA OR PROFITS, WHETHER IN AN
ACTION OF CONTRACT, NEGLIGENCE OR OTHER TORTIOUS ACTION, ARISING OUT
OF OR IN CONNECTION WITH THE USE OR PERFORMANCE OF THIS SOFTWARE.

Modified by Jack Jansen, CWI, July 1995:
- Use binascii module to do the actual line-by-line conversion
  between ascii and binary. This results in a 1000-fold speedup. The C
  version is still 5 times faster, though.
- Arguments more compliant with Python standard
```

C.3.8 XML Remote Procedure Calls

The *xmlrpc.client* module contains the following notice:

```
    The XML-RPC client interface is

Copyright (c) 1999-2002 by Secret Labs AB
Copyright (c) 1999-2002 by Fredrik Lundh

By obtaining, using, and/or copying this software and/or its
associated documentation, you agree that you have read, understood,
and will comply with the following terms and conditions:

Permission to use, copy, modify, and distribute this software and
its associated documentation for any purpose and without fee is
hereby granted, provided that the above copyright notice appears in
all copies, and that both that copyright notice and this permission
notice appear in supporting documentation, and that the name of
Secret Labs AB or the author not be used in advertising or publicity
pertaining to distribution of the software without specific, written
prior permission.

SECRET LABS AB AND THE AUTHOR DISCLAIMS ALL WARRANTIES WITH REGARD
TO THIS SOFTWARE, INCLUDING ALL IMPLIED WARRANTIES OF MERCHANT-
ABILITY AND FITNESS.  IN NO EVENT SHALL SECRET LABS AB OR THE AUTHOR
BE LIABLE FOR ANY SPECIAL, INDIRECT OR CONSEQUENTIAL DAMAGES OR ANY
DAMAGES WHATSOEVER RESULTING FROM LOSS OF USE, DATA OR PROFITS,
WHETHER IN AN ACTION OF CONTRACT, NEGLIGENCE OR OTHER TORTIOUS
ACTION, ARISING OUT OF OR IN CONNECTION WITH THE USE OR PERFORMANCE
OF THIS SOFTWARE.
```

C.3.9 test_epoll

The `test_epoll` module contains the following notice:

```
Copyright (c) 2001-2006 Twisted Matrix Laboratories.

Permission is hereby granted, free of charge, to any person obtaining
a copy of this software and associated documentation files (the
"Software"), to deal in the Software without restriction, including
without limitation the rights to use, copy, modify, merge, publish,
distribute, sublicense, and/or sell copies of the Software, and to
permit persons to whom the Software is furnished to do so, subject to
the following conditions:

The above copyright notice and this permission notice shall be
included in all copies or substantial portions of the Software.

THE SOFTWARE IS PROVIDED "AS IS", WITHOUT WARRANTY OF ANY KIND,
EXPRESS OR IMPLIED, INCLUDING BUT NOT LIMITED TO THE WARRANTIES OF
MERCHANTABILITY, FITNESS FOR A PARTICULAR PURPOSE AND
NONINFRINGEMENT. IN NO EVENT SHALL THE AUTHORS OR COPYRIGHT HOLDERS BE
LIABLE FOR ANY CLAIM, DAMAGES OR OTHER LIABILITY, WHETHER IN AN ACTION
OF CONTRACT, TORT OR OTHERWISE, ARISING FROM, OUT OF OR IN CONNECTION
WITH THE SOFTWARE OR THE USE OR OTHER DEALINGS IN THE SOFTWARE.
```

C.3.10 Select kqueue

The `select` module contains the following notice for the kqueue interface:

```
Copyright (c) 2000 Doug White, 2006 James Knight, 2007 Christian Heimes
All rights reserved.

Redistribution and use in source and binary forms, with or without
modification, are permitted provided that the following conditions
are met:
1. Redistributions of source code must retain the above copyright
   notice, this list of conditions and the following disclaimer.
2. Redistributions in binary form must reproduce the above copyright
   notice, this list of conditions and the following disclaimer in the
   documentation and/or other materials provided with the distribution.

THIS SOFTWARE IS PROVIDED BY THE AUTHOR AND CONTRIBUTORS ``AS IS'' AND
ANY EXPRESS OR IMPLIED WARRANTIES, INCLUDING, BUT NOT LIMITED TO, THE
IMPLIED WARRANTIES OF MERCHANTABILITY AND FITNESS FOR A PARTICULAR PURPOSE
ARE DISCLAIMED.  IN NO EVENT SHALL THE AUTHOR OR CONTRIBUTORS BE LIABLE
FOR ANY DIRECT, INDIRECT, INCIDENTAL, SPECIAL, EXEMPLARY, OR CONSEQUENTIAL
DAMAGES (INCLUDING, BUT NOT LIMITED TO, PROCUREMENT OF SUBSTITUTE GOODS
OR SERVICES; LOSS OF USE, DATA, OR PROFITS; OR BUSINESS INTERRUPTION)
HOWEVER CAUSED AND ON ANY THEORY OF LIABILITY, WHETHER IN CONTRACT, STRICT
LIABILITY, OR TORT (INCLUDING NEGLIGENCE OR OTHERWISE) ARISING IN ANY WAY
OUT OF THE USE OF THIS SOFTWARE, EVEN IF ADVISED OF THE POSSIBILITY OF
SUCH DAMAGE.
```

C.3.11 SipHash24

The file `Python/pyhash.c` contains Marek Majkowski' implementation of Dan Bernstein's SipHash24 algorithm. The contains the following note:

```
<MIT License>
Copyright (c) 2013  Marek Majkowski <marek@popcount.org>

Permission is hereby granted, free of charge, to any person obtaining a copy
of this software and associated documentation files (the "Software"), to deal
in the Software without restriction, including without limitation the rights
to use, copy, modify, merge, publish, distribute, sublicense, and/or sell
copies of the Software, and to permit persons to whom the Software is
furnished to do so, subject to the following conditions:

The above copyright notice and this permission notice shall be included in
all copies or substantial portions of the Software.
</MIT License>

Original location:
   https://github.com/majek/csiphash/

Solution inspired by code from:
   Samuel Neves (supercop/crypto_auth/siphash24/little)
   djb (supercop/crypto_auth/siphash24/little2)
   Jean-Philippe Aumasson (https://131002.net/siphash/siphash24.c)
```

C.3.12 strtod and dtoa

The file Python/dtoa.c, which supplies C functions dtoa and strtod for conversion of C doubles to and from strings, is derived from the file of the same name by David M. Gay, currently available from http://www.netlib.org/fp/. The original file, as retrieved on March 16, 2009, contains the following copyright and licensing notice:

```
/****************************************************************
 *
 * The author of this software is David M. Gay.
 *
 * Copyright (c) 1991, 2000, 2001 by Lucent Technologies.
 *
 * Permission to use, copy, modify, and distribute this software for any
 * purpose without fee is hereby granted, provided that this entire notice
 * is included in all copies of any software which is or includes a copy
 * or modification of this software and in all copies of the supporting
 * documentation for such software.
 *
 * THIS SOFTWARE IS BEING PROVIDED "AS IS", WITHOUT ANY EXPRESS OR IMPLIED
 * WARRANTY.  IN PARTICULAR, NEITHER THE AUTHOR NOR LUCENT MAKES ANY
 * REPRESENTATION OR WARRANTY OF ANY KIND CONCERNING THE MERCHANTABILITY
 * OF THIS SOFTWARE OR ITS FITNESS FOR ANY PARTICULAR PURPOSE.
 *
 ***************************************************************/
```

C.3.13 OpenSSL

The modules *hashlib*, *posix*, *ssl*, *crypt* use the OpenSSL library for added performance if made available by the operating system. Additionally, the Windows and Mac OS X installers for Python may include a copy of the OpenSSL libraries, so we include a copy of the OpenSSL license here:

```
LICENSE ISSUES
==============

The OpenSSL toolkit stays under a dual license, i.e. both the conditions of
the OpenSSL License and the original SSLeay license apply to the toolkit.
See below for the actual license texts. Actually both licenses are BSD-style
Open Source licenses. In case of any license issues related to OpenSSL
please contact openssl-core@openssl.org.

OpenSSL License
---------------

  /* ====================================================================
   * Copyright (c) 1998-2008 The OpenSSL Project.  All rights reserved.
   *
   * Redistribution and use in source and binary forms, with or without
   * modification, are permitted provided that the following conditions
   * are met:
   *
   * 1. Redistributions of source code must retain the above copyright
   *    notice, this list of conditions and the following disclaimer.
   *
   * 2. Redistributions in binary form must reproduce the above copyright
   *    notice, this list of conditions and the following disclaimer in
   *    the documentation and/or other materials provided with the
   *    distribution.
   *
   * 3. All advertising materials mentioning features or use of this
   *    software must display the following acknowledgment:
   *    "This product includes software developed by the OpenSSL Project
   *    for use in the OpenSSL Toolkit. (http://www.openssl.org/)"
   *
   * 4. The names "OpenSSL Toolkit" and "OpenSSL Project" must not be used to
   *    endorse or promote products derived from this software without
   *    prior written permission. For written permission, please contact
   *    openssl-core@openssl.org.
   *
   * 5. Products derived from this software may not be called "OpenSSL"
   *    nor may "OpenSSL" appear in their names without prior written
   *    permission of the OpenSSL Project.
   *
   * 6. Redistributions of any form whatsoever must retain the following
   *    acknowledgment:
   *    "This product includes software developed by the OpenSSL Project
   *    for use in the OpenSSL Toolkit (http://www.openssl.org/)"
   *
   * THIS SOFTWARE IS PROVIDED BY THE OpenSSL PROJECT ``AS IS'' AND ANY
   * EXPRESSED OR IMPLIED WARRANTIES, INCLUDING, BUT NOT LIMITED TO, THE
   * IMPLIED WARRANTIES OF MERCHANTABILITY AND FITNESS FOR A PARTICULAR
   * PURPOSE ARE DISCLAIMED.  IN NO EVENT SHALL THE OpenSSL PROJECT OR
   * ITS CONTRIBUTORS BE LIABLE FOR ANY DIRECT, INDIRECT, INCIDENTAL,
   * SPECIAL, EXEMPLARY, OR CONSEQUENTIAL DAMAGES (INCLUDING, BUT
   * NOT LIMITED TO, PROCUREMENT OF SUBSTITUTE GOODS OR SERVICES;
   * LOSS OF USE, DATA, OR PROFITS; OR BUSINESS INTERRUPTION)
   * HOWEVER CAUSED AND ON ANY THEORY OF LIABILITY, WHETHER IN CONTRACT,
   * STRICT LIABILITY, OR TORT (INCLUDING NEGLIGENCE OR OTHERWISE)
   * ARISING IN ANY WAY OUT OF THE USE OF THIS SOFTWARE, EVEN IF ADVISED
   * OF THE POSSIBILITY OF SUCH DAMAGE.
```

```
 *  ====================================================================
 *
 *  This product includes cryptographic software written by Eric Young
 *  (eay@cryptsoft.com).  This product includes software written by Tim
 *  Hudson (tjh@cryptsoft.com).
 *
 */

Original SSLeay License
-----------------------

  /* Copyright (C) 1995-1998 Eric Young (eay@cryptsoft.com)
   * All rights reserved.
   *
   * This package is an SSL implementation written
   * by Eric Young (eay@cryptsoft.com).
   * The implementation was written so as to conform with Netscapes SSL.
   *
   * This library is free for commercial and non-commercial use as long as
   * the following conditions are aheared to.  The following conditions
   * apply to all code found in this distribution, be it the RC4, RSA,
   * lhash, DES, etc., code; not just the SSL code.  The SSL documentation
   * included with this distribution is covered by the same copyright terms
   * except that the holder is Tim Hudson (tjh@cryptsoft.com).
   *
   * Copyright remains Eric Young's, and as such any Copyright notices in
   * the code are not to be removed.
   * If this package is used in a product, Eric Young should be given attribution
   * as the author of the parts of the library used.
   * This can be in the form of a textual message at program startup or
   * in documentation (online or textual) provided with the package.
   *
   * Redistribution and use in source and binary forms, with or without
   * modification, are permitted provided that the following conditions
   * are met:
   * 1. Redistributions of source code must retain the copyright
   *    notice, this list of conditions and the following disclaimer.
   * 2. Redistributions in binary form must reproduce the above copyright
   *    notice, this list of conditions and the following disclaimer in the
   *    documentation and/or other materials provided with the distribution.
   * 3. All advertising materials mentioning features or use of this software
   *    must display the following acknowledgement:
   *    "This product includes cryptographic software written by
   *     Eric Young (eay@cryptsoft.com)"
   *    The word 'cryptographic' can be left out if the rouines from the library
   *    being used are not cryptographic related :-).
   * 4. If you include any Windows specific code (or a derivative thereof) from
   *    the apps directory (application code) you must include an acknowledgement:
   *    "This product includes software written by Tim Hudson (tjh@cryptsoft.com)"
   *
   * THIS SOFTWARE IS PROVIDED BY ERIC YOUNG ``AS IS'' AND
   * ANY EXPRESS OR IMPLIED WARRANTIES, INCLUDING, BUT NOT LIMITED TO, THE
   * IMPLIED WARRANTIES OF MERCHANTABILITY AND FITNESS FOR A PARTICULAR PURPOSE
   * ARE DISCLAIMED.  IN NO EVENT SHALL THE AUTHOR OR CONTRIBUTORS BE LIABLE
   * FOR ANY DIRECT, INDIRECT, INCIDENTAL, SPECIAL, EXEMPLARY, OR CONSEQUENTIAL
   * DAMAGES (INCLUDING, BUT NOT LIMITED TO, PROCUREMENT OF SUBSTITUTE GOODS
   * OR SERVICES; LOSS OF USE, DATA, OR PROFITS; OR BUSINESS INTERRUPTION)
   * HOWEVER CAUSED AND ON ANY THEORY OF LIABILITY, WHETHER IN CONTRACT, STRICT
```

```
 *    LIABILITY, OR TORT (INCLUDING NEGLIGENCE OR OTHERWISE) ARISING IN ANY WAY
 *    OUT OF THE USE OF THIS SOFTWARE, EVEN IF ADVISED OF THE POSSIBILITY OF
 *    SUCH DAMAGE.
 *
 *    The licence and distribution terms for any publically available version or
 *    derivative of this code cannot be changed.   i.e. this code cannot simply be
 *    copied and put under another distribution licence
 *    [including the GNU Public Licence.]
 */
```

C.3.14 expat

The `pyexpat` extension is built using an included copy of the expat sources unless the build is configured `--with-system-expat`:

```
Copyright (c) 1998, 1999, 2000 Thai Open Source Software Center Ltd
                               and Clark Cooper

Permission is hereby granted, free of charge, to any person obtaining
a copy of this software and associated documentation files (the
"Software"), to deal in the Software without restriction, including
without limitation the rights to use, copy, modify, merge, publish,
distribute, sublicense, and/or sell copies of the Software, and to
permit persons to whom the Software is furnished to do so, subject to
the following conditions:

The above copyright notice and this permission notice shall be included
in all copies or substantial portions of the Software.

THE SOFTWARE IS PROVIDED "AS IS", WITHOUT WARRANTY OF ANY KIND,
EXPRESS OR IMPLIED, INCLUDING BUT NOT LIMITED TO THE WARRANTIES OF
MERCHANTABILITY, FITNESS FOR A PARTICULAR PURPOSE AND NONINFRINGEMENT.
IN NO EVENT SHALL THE AUTHORS OR COPYRIGHT HOLDERS BE LIABLE FOR ANY
CLAIM, DAMAGES OR OTHER LIABILITY, WHETHER IN AN ACTION OF CONTRACT,
TORT OR OTHERWISE, ARISING FROM, OUT OF OR IN CONNECTION WITH THE
SOFTWARE OR THE USE OR OTHER DEALINGS IN THE SOFTWARE.
```

C.3.15 libffi

The `_ctypes` extension is built using an included copy of the libffi sources unless the build is configured `--with-system-libffi`:

```
Copyright (c) 1996-2008  Red Hat, Inc and others.

Permission is hereby granted, free of charge, to any person obtaining
a copy of this software and associated documentation files (the
``Software''), to deal in the Software without restriction, including
without limitation the rights to use, copy, modify, merge, publish,
distribute, sublicense, and/or sell copies of the Software, and to
permit persons to whom the Software is furnished to do so, subject to
the following conditions:

The above copyright notice and this permission notice shall be included
in all copies or substantial portions of the Software.
```

```
THE SOFTWARE IS PROVIDED ``AS IS'', WITHOUT WARRANTY OF ANY KIND,
EXPRESS OR IMPLIED, INCLUDING BUT NOT LIMITED TO THE WARRANTIES OF
MERCHANTABILITY, FITNESS FOR A PARTICULAR PURPOSE AND
NONINFRINGEMENT.  IN NO EVENT SHALL THE AUTHORS OR COPYRIGHT
HOLDERS BE LIABLE FOR ANY CLAIM, DAMAGES OR OTHER LIABILITY,
WHETHER IN AN ACTION OF CONTRACT, TORT OR OTHERWISE, ARISING FROM,
OUT OF OR IN CONNECTION WITH THE SOFTWARE OR THE USE OR OTHER
DEALINGS IN THE SOFTWARE.
```

C.3.16 zlib

The `zlib` extension is built using an included copy of the zlib sources if the zlib version found on the system is too old to be used for the build:

```
Copyright (C) 1995-2011 Jean-loup Gailly and Mark Adler

This software is provided 'as-is', without any express or implied
warranty.  In no event will the authors be held liable for any damages
arising from the use of this software.

Permission is granted to anyone to use this software for any purpose,
including commercial applications, and to alter it and redistribute it
freely, subject to the following restrictions:

1. The origin of this software must not be misrepresented; you must not
   claim that you wrote the original software. If you use this software
   in a product, an acknowledgment in the product documentation would be
   appreciated but is not required.

2. Altered source versions must be plainly marked as such, and must not be
   misrepresented as being the original software.

3. This notice may not be removed or altered from any source distribution.

Jean-loup Gailly        Mark Adler
jloup@gzip.org          madler@alumni.caltech.edu
```

C.3.17 cfuhash

The implementation of the hash table used by the `tracemalloc` is based on the cfuhash project:

```
Copyright (c) 2005 Don Owens
All rights reserved.

This code is released under the BSD license:

Redistribution and use in source and binary forms, with or without
modification, are permitted provided that the following conditions
are met:

    * Redistributions of source code must retain the above copyright
      notice, this list of conditions and the following disclaimer.

    * Redistributions in binary form must reproduce the above
      copyright notice, this list of conditions and the following
```

```
    disclaimer in the documentation and/or other materials provided
    with the distribution.

  * Neither the name of the author nor the names of its
    contributors may be used to endorse or promote products derived
    from this software without specific prior written permission.

THIS SOFTWARE IS PROVIDED BY THE COPYRIGHT HOLDERS AND CONTRIBUTORS
"AS IS" AND ANY EXPRESS OR IMPLIED WARRANTIES, INCLUDING, BUT NOT
LIMITED TO, THE IMPLIED WARRANTIES OF MERCHANTABILITY AND FITNESS
FOR A PARTICULAR PURPOSE ARE DISCLAIMED. IN NO EVENT SHALL THE
COPYRIGHT OWNER OR CONTRIBUTORS BE LIABLE FOR ANY DIRECT, INDIRECT,
INCIDENTAL, SPECIAL, EXEMPLARY, OR CONSEQUENTIAL DAMAGES
(INCLUDING, BUT NOT LIMITED TO, PROCUREMENT OF SUBSTITUTE GOODS OR
SERVICES; LOSS OF USE, DATA, OR PROFITS; OR BUSINESS INTERRUPTION)
HOWEVER CAUSED AND ON ANY THEORY OF LIABILITY, WHETHER IN CONTRACT,
STRICT LIABILITY, OR TORT (INCLUDING NEGLIGENCE OR OTHERWISE)
ARISING IN ANY WAY OUT OF THE USE OF THIS SOFTWARE, EVEN IF ADVISED
OF THE POSSIBILITY OF SUCH DAMAGE.
```

C.3.18 libmpdec

The _decimal module is built using an included copy of the libmpdec library unless the build is configured --with-system-libmpdec:

```
Copyright (c) 2008-2016 Stefan Krah. All rights reserved.

Redistribution and use in source and binary forms, with or without
modification, are permitted provided that the following conditions
are met:

1. Redistributions of source code must retain the above copyright
   notice, this list of conditions and the following disclaimer.

2. Redistributions in binary form must reproduce the above copyright
   notice, this list of conditions and the following disclaimer in the
   documentation and/or other materials provided with the distribution.

THIS SOFTWARE IS PROVIDED BY THE AUTHOR AND CONTRIBUTORS "AS IS" AND
ANY EXPRESS OR IMPLIED WARRANTIES, INCLUDING, BUT NOT LIMITED TO, THE
IMPLIED WARRANTIES OF MERCHANTABILITY AND FITNESS FOR A PARTICULAR PURPOSE
ARE DISCLAIMED.  IN NO EVENT SHALL THE AUTHOR OR CONTRIBUTORS BE LIABLE
FOR ANY DIRECT, INDIRECT, INCIDENTAL, SPECIAL, EXEMPLARY, OR CONSEQUENTIAL
DAMAGES (INCLUDING, BUT NOT LIMITED TO, PROCUREMENT OF SUBSTITUTE GOODS
OR SERVICES; LOSS OF USE, DATA, OR PROFITS; OR BUSINESS INTERRUPTION)
HOWEVER CAUSED AND ON ANY THEORY OF LIABILITY, WHETHER IN CONTRACT, STRICT
LIABILITY, OR TORT (INCLUDING NEGLIGENCE OR OTHERWISE) ARISING IN ANY WAY
OUT OF THE USE OF THIS SOFTWARE, EVEN IF ADVISED OF THE POSSIBILITY OF
SUCH DAMAGE.
```

APPENDIX D

COPYRIGHT

Python and this documentation is:

Copyright © 2001-2018 Python Software Foundation. All rights reserved.

Copyright © 2000 BeOpen.com. All rights reserved.

Copyright © 1995-2000 Corporation for National Research Initiatives. All rights reserved.

Copyright © 1991-1995 Stichting Mathematisch Centrum. All rights reserved.

See *History and License* for complete license and permissions information.

PYTHON MODULE INDEX

—
__future__, 1611
__main__, 1582
_dummy_thread, 808
_thread, 807

a
abc, 1599
aifc, 1252
argparse, 590
array, 232
ast, 1671
asynchat, 936
asyncio, 872
asyncore, 932
atexit, 1604
audioop, 1249

b
base64, 1038
bdb, 1511
binascii, 1042
binhex, 1041
bisect, 230
builtins, 1582
bz2, 449

c
calendar, 203
cgi, 1109
cgitb, 1116
chunk, 1260
cmath, 281
cmd, 1319
code, 1637
codecs, 154
codeop, 1639
collections, 206
collections.abc, 222
colorsys, 1261
compileall, 1687
concurrent.futures, 781

configparser, 483
contextlib, 1588
copy, 246
copyreg, 414
cProfile, 1526
crypt *(Unix)*, 1732
csv, 477
ctypes, 694
curses *(Unix)*, 662
curses.ascii, 681
curses.panel, 684
curses.textpad, 680

d
datetime, 173
dbm, 418
dbm.dumb, 422
dbm.gnu *(Unix)*, 420
dbm.ndbm *(Unix)*, 421
decimal, 285
difflib, 125
dis, 1690
distutils, 1549
doctest, 1391
dummy_threading, 806

e
email, 949
email.charset, 1001
email.contentmanager, 978
email.encoders, 1003
email.errors, 972
email.generator, 962
email.header, 998
email.headerregistry, 973
email.iterators, 1006
email.message, 950
email.mime, 996
email.parser, 958
email.policy, 965
email.utils, 1004
encodings.idna, 170

encodings.mbcs, 171
encodings.utf_8_sig, 171
ensurepip, 1549
enum, 254
errno, 688

f
faulthandler, 1515
fcntl *(Unix)*, 1737
filecmp, 383
fileinput, 376
fnmatch, 390
formatter, 1705
fpectl *(Unix)*, 1633
fractions, 311
ftplib, 1161
functools, 341

g
gc, 1612
getopt, 621
getpass, 662
gettext, 1269
glob, 389
grp *(Unix)*, 1732
gzip, 446

h
hashlib, 509
heapq, 226
hmac, 519
html, 1047
html.entities, 1052
html.parser, 1047
http, 1153
http.client, 1155
http.cookiejar, 1215
http.cookies, 1211
http.server, 1206

i
imaplib, 1169
imghdr, 1262
imp, 1773
importlib, 1649
importlib.abc, 1651
importlib.machinery, 1657
importlib.util, 1661
inspect, 1615
io, 570
ipaddress, 1236
itertools, 327

j
json, 1007
json.tool, 1015

k
keyword, 1680

l
lib2to3, 1501
linecache, 391
locale, 1277
logging, 623
logging.config, 639
logging.handlers, 649
lzma, 452

m
macpath, 400
mailbox, 1017
mailcap, 1016
marshal, 417
math, 276
mimetypes, 1035
mmap, 943
modulefinder, 1645
msilib *(Windows)*, 1711
msvcrt *(Windows)*, 1716
multiprocessing, 739
multiprocessing.connection, 768
multiprocessing.dummy, 772
multiprocessing.managers, 759
multiprocessing.pool, 765
multiprocessing.sharedctypes, 757

n
netrc, 501
nis *(Unix)*, 1744
nntplib, 1176
numbers, 273

o
operator, 347
optparse, 1747
os, 525
os.path, 371
ossaudiodev *(Linux, FreeBSD)*, 1263

p
parser, 1667
pathlib, 355
pdb, 1517
pickle, 401
pickletools, 1703

pipes *(Unix)*, 1739
pkgutil, 1643
platform, 685
plistlib, 505
poplib, 1166
posix *(Unix)*, 1729
pprint, 247
profile, 1526
pstats, 1527
pty *(Linux)*, 1736
pwd *(Unix)*, 1730
py_compile, 1686
pyclbr, 1685
pydoc, 1390

q

queue, 804
quopri, 1044

r

random, 313
re, 105
readline *(Unix)*, 142
reprlib, 252
resource *(Unix)*, 1740
rlcompleter, 146
runpy, 1647

s

sched, 802
secrets, 520
select, 862
selectors, 869
shelve, 415
shlex, 1324
shutil, 392
signal, 938
site, 1630
smtpd, 1189
smtplib, 1182
sndhdr, 1262
socket, 811
socketserver, 1198
spwd *(Unix)*, 1731
sqlite3, 422
ssl, 832
stat, 378
statistics, 320
string, 95
stringprep, 141
struct, 149
subprocess, 787
sunau, 1254
symbol, 1678

symtable, 1676
sys, 1563
sysconfig, 1578
syslog *(Unix)*, 1745

t

tabnanny, 1684
tarfile, 465
telnetlib, 1192
tempfile, 385
termios *(Unix)*, 1734
test, 1501
test.support, 1504
textwrap, 135
threading, 727
time, 582
timeit, 1531
tkinter, 1331
tkinter.scrolledtext *(Tk)*, 1364
tkinter.tix, 1359
tkinter.ttk, 1342
token, 1679
tokenize, 1681
trace, 1536
traceback, 1605
tracemalloc, 1539
tty *(Unix)*, 1735
turtle, 1285
turtledemo, 1317
types, 242
typing, 1375

u

unicodedata, 139
unittest, 1415
unittest.mock, 1442
urllib, 1126
urllib.error, 1151
urllib.parse, 1144
urllib.request, 1126
urllib.response, 1144
urllib.robotparser, 1152
uu, 1044
uuid, 1195

v

venv, 1551

w

warnings, 1583
wave, 1257
weakref, 235
webbrowser, 1107
winreg *(Windows)*, 1718

winsound *(Windows)*, 1726
wsgiref, 1117
wsgiref.handlers, 1122
wsgiref.headers, 1119
wsgiref.simple_server, 1120
wsgiref.util, 1117
wsgiref.validate, 1121

X

xdrlib, 502
xml, 1052
xml.dom, 1069
xml.dom.minidom, 1079
xml.dom.pulldom, 1084
xml.etree.ElementTree, 1054
xml.parsers.expat, 1097
xml.parsers.expat.errors, 1104
xml.parsers.expat.model, 1103
xml.sax, 1085
xml.sax.handler, 1087
xml.sax.saxutils, 1092
xml.sax.xmlreader, 1093
xmlrpc.client, 1223
xmlrpc.server, 1231

Z

zipapp, 1559
zipfile, 457
zipimport, 1641
zlib, 443

INDEX

Symbols

*
    operator, 31
**
    operator, 31
+
    operator, 31
-
    operator, 31
--create <tarfile> <source1> ... <sourceN>
    tarfile command line option, 472
--details
    inspect command line option, 1630
--extract <tarfile> [<output_dir>]
    tarfile command line option, 472
--help
    trace command line option, 1537
--ignore-dir=<dir>
    trace command line option, 1538
--ignore-module=<mod>
    trace command line option, 1538
--info
    zipapp command line option, 1560
--list <tarfile>
    tarfile command line option, 472
--locals
    unittest command line option, 1417
--sort-keys
    command line option, 1016
--test <tarfile>
    tarfile command line option, 473
--user-base
    site command line option, 1633
--user-site
    site command line option, 1633
--version
    trace command line option, 1537
-C, --coverdir=<dir>
    trace command line option, 1537
-R, --no-report
    trace command line option, 1537
-T, --trackcalls
    trace command line option, 1537
-a, --annotate
    pickletools command line option, 1703
-b
    compileall command line option, 1688
-b, --buffer
    unittest command line option, 1417
-c <tarfile> <source1> ... <sourceN>
    tarfile command line option, 472
-c <zipfile> <source1> ... <sourceN>
    zipfile command line option, 465
-c, --catch
    unittest command line option, 1417
-c, --clock
    timeit command line option, 1534
-c, --count
    trace command line option, 1537
-d destdir
    compileall command line option, 1688
-e <tarfile> [<output_dir>]
    tarfile command line option, 472
-e <zipfile> <output_dir>
    zipfile command line option, 465
-e, --exact
    tokenize command line option, 1682
-f
    compileall command line option, 1687
-f, --failfast
    unittest command line option, 1417
-f, --file=<file>
    trace command line option, 1537
-g, --timing
    trace command line option, 1537
-h, --help
    command line option, 1016
    timeit command line option, 1534
    tokenize command line option, 1682
    zipapp command line option, 1560
-i list
    compileall command line option, 1688
-j N
    compileall command line option, 1688

1819

-l
    compileall command line option, 1687
-l <tarfile>
    tarfile command line option, 472
-l <zipfile>
    zipfile command line option, 465
-l, –indentlevel=<num>
    pickletools command line option, 1703
-l, –listfuncs
    trace command line option, 1537
-m <mainfn>, –main=<mainfn>
    zipapp command line option, 1560
-m, –memo
    pickletools command line option, 1703
-m, –missing
    trace command line option, 1537
-n N, –number=N
    timeit command line option, 1534
-o <output>, –output=<output>
    zipapp command line option, 1560
-o, –output=<file>
    pickletools command line option, 1703
-p <interpreter>, –python=<interpreter>
    zipapp command line option, 1560
-p, –pattern pattern
    unittest-discover command line option, 1418
-p, –preamble=<preamble>
    pickletools command line option, 1703
-p, –process
    timeit command line option, 1534
-q
    compileall command line option, 1688
-r
    compileall command line option, 1688
-r N, –repeat=N
    timeit command line option, 1534
-r, –report
    trace command line option, 1537
-s S, –setup=S
    timeit command line option, 1534
-s, –start-directory directory
    unittest-discover command line option, 1418
-s, –summary
    trace command line option, 1537
-t <tarfile>
    tarfile command line option, 473
-t <zipfile>
    zipfile command line option, 465
-t, –time
    timeit command line option, 1534
-t, –top-level-directory directory
    unittest-discover command line option, 1418
-t, –trace
    trace command line option, 1537

-u, –unit=U
    timeit command line option, 1534
-v, –verbose
    tarfile command line option, 473
    timeit command line option, 1534
    unittest-discover command line option, 1418
-x regex
    compileall command line option, 1688
..., 1781
.ini
    file, 483
.pdbrc
    file, 1520
/
    operator, 31
//
    operator, 31
==
    operator, 30
%
    operator, 31
% formatting, 51, 64
% interpolation, 51, 64
&
    operator, 32
__CData__ (class in ctypes), 720
__FuncPtr__ (class in ctypes), 715
__Pointer__ (class in ctypes), 725
__SimpleCData__ (class in ctypes), 721
__abs__() (in module operator), 348
__add__() (in module operator), 348
__and__() (in module operator), 348
__bases__ (class attribute), 82
__bytes__() (email.message.EmailMessage method), 951
__bytes__() (email.message.Message method), 989
__call__() (email.headerregistry.HeaderRegistry method), 977
__call__() (weakref.finalize method), 238
__callback__ (weakref.ref attribute), 236
__cause__ (traceback.TracebackException attribute), 1607
__ceil__() (fractions.Fraction method), 313
__class__ (instance attribute), 82
__class__ (unittest.mock.Mock attribute), 1452
__code__ (function object attribute), 81
__concat__() (in module operator), 349
__contains__() (email.message.EmailMessage method), 952
__contains__() (email.message.Message method), 991
__contains__() (in module operator), 350
__contains__() (mailbox.Mailbox method), 1020

__context__ (traceback.TracebackException attribute), 1607
__copy__() (copy protocol), 247
__debug__ (built-in variable), 27
__deepcopy__() (copy protocol), 247
__del__() (io.IOBase method), 574
__delitem__() (email.message.EmailMessage method), 953
__delitem__() (email.message.Message method), 991
__delitem__() (in module operator), 350
__delitem__() (mailbox.MH method), 1024
__delitem__() (mailbox.Mailbox method), 1018
__dict__ (object attribute), 82
__dir__() (unittest.mock.Mock method), 1448
__displayhook__ (in module sys), 1565
__doc__ (types.ModuleType attribute), 244
__enter__() (contextmanager method), 79
__enter__() (winreg.PyHKEY method), 1726
__eq__() (email.charset.Charset method), 1002
__eq__() (email.header.Header method), 1000
__eq__() (in module operator), 348
__eq__() (instance method), 30
__eq__() (memoryview method), 68
__excepthook__ (in module sys), 1565
__exit__() (contextmanager method), 79
__exit__() (winreg.PyHKEY method), 1726
__floor__() (fractions.Fraction method), 313
__floordiv__() (in module operator), 348
__format__, 12
__format__() (datetime.date method), 179
__format__() (datetime.datetime method), 187
__format__() (datetime.time method), 191
__fspath__() (os.PathLike method), 527
__future__, 1785
__future__ (module), 1611
__ge__() (in module operator), 348
__ge__() (instance method), 30
__getitem__() (email.headerregistry.HeaderRegistry method), 977
__getitem__() (email.message.EmailMessage method), 952
__getitem__() (email.message.Message method), 991
__getitem__() (in module operator), 350
__getitem__() (mailbox.Mailbox method), 1019
__getitem__() (re.match method), 118
__getnewargs__() (object method), 407
__getnewargs_ex__() (object method), 407
__getstate__() (copy protocol), 411
__getstate__() (object method), 407
__gt__() (in module operator), 348
__gt__() (instance method), 30
__iadd__() (in module operator), 353

__iand__() (in module operator), 353
__iconcat__() (in module operator), 353
__ifloordiv__() (in module operator), 353
__ilshift__() (in module operator), 353
__imatmul__() (in module operator), 353
__imod__() (in module operator), 353
__import__() (built-in function), 24
__import__() (in module importlib), 1650
__imul__() (in module operator), 353
__index__() (in module operator), 348
__init__() (difflib.HtmlDiff method), 126
__init__() (logging.Handler method), 628
__interactivehook__ (in module sys), 1571
__inv__() (in module operator), 349
__invert__() (in module operator), 349
__ior__() (in module operator), 353
__ipow__() (in module operator), 353
__irshift__() (in module operator), 353
__isub__() (in module operator), 354
__iter__() (container method), 36
__iter__() (iterator method), 36
__iter__() (mailbox.Mailbox method), 1019
__iter__() (unittest.TestSuite method), 1433
__itruediv__() (in module operator), 354
__ixor__() (in module operator), 354
__le__() (in module operator), 348
__le__() (instance method), 30
__len__() (email.message.EmailMessage method), 952
__len__() (email.message.Message method), 991
__len__() (mailbox.Mailbox method), 1020
__loader__ (types.ModuleType attribute), 244
__lshift__() (in module operator), 349
__lt__() (in module operator), 348
__lt__() (instance method), 30
__main__
    module, 1647, 1648
__main__ (module), 1582
__matmul__() (in module operator), 349
__missing__(), 76
__missing__() (collections.defaultdict method), 214
__mod__() (in module operator), 349
__mro__ (class attribute), 82
__mul__() (in module operator), 349
__name__ (definition attribute), 82
__name__ (types.ModuleType attribute), 244
__ne__() (email.charset.Charset method), 1002
__ne__() (email.header.Header method), 1000
__ne__() (in module operator), 348
__ne__() (instance method), 30
__neg__() (in module operator), 349
__next__() (csv.csvreader method), 481
__next__() (iterator method), 36

__not__() (in module operator), 348
__or__() (in module operator), 349
__package__ (types.ModuleType attribute), 244
__pos__() (in module operator), 349
__pow__() (in module operator), 349
__qualname__ (definition attribute), 82
__reduce__() (object method), 408
__reduce_ex__() (object method), 408
__repr__() (multiprocessing.managers.BaseProxy method), 765
__repr__() (netrc.netrc method), 501
__round__() (fractions.Fraction method), 313
__rshift__() (in module operator), 349
__setitem__() (email.message.EmailMessage method), 952
__setitem__() (email.message.Message method), 991
__setitem__() (in module operator), 350
__setitem__() (mailbox.Mailbox method), 1018
__setitem__() (mailbox.Maildir method), 1021
__setstate__() (copy protocol), 411
__setstate__() (object method), 407
__slots__, 1791
__stderr__ (in module sys), 1577
__stdin__ (in module sys), 1577
__stdout__ (in module sys), 1577
__str__() (datetime.date method), 179
__str__() (datetime.datetime method), 187
__str__() (datetime.time method), 191
__str__() (email.charset.Charset method), 1002
__str__() (email.header.Header method), 1000
__str__() (email.headerregistry.Address method), 978
__str__() (email.headerregistry.Group method), 978
__str__() (email.message.EmailMessage method), 951
__str__() (email.message.Message method), 988
__str__() (multiprocessing.managers.BaseProxy method), 765
__sub__() (in module operator), 349
__subclasses__() (class method), 82
__subclasshook__() (abc.ABCMeta method), 1600
__suppress_context__ (traceback.TracebackException attribute), 1607
__truediv__() (in module operator), 349
__xor__() (in module operator), 349
anonymous (ctypes.Structure attribute), 724
_asdict() (collections.somenamedtuple method), 217
_b_base_ (ctypes._CData attribute), 721
_b_needsfree_ (ctypes._CData attribute), 721
_callmethod() (multiprocessing.managers.BaseProxy method), 764

_clear_type_cache() (in module sys), 1564
_current_frames() (in module sys), 1564
_debugmallocstats() (in module sys), 1564
_dummy_thread (module), 808
_enablelegacywindowsfsencoding() (in module sys), 1576
_exit() (in module os), 559
_fields (ast.AST attribute), 1671
_fields (collections.somenamedtuple attribute), 218
fields (ctypes.Structure attribute), 724
_flush() (wsgiref.handlers.BaseHandler method), 1123
_get_child_mock() (unittest.mock.Mock method), 1448
_getframe() (in module sys), 1569
_getvalue() (multiprocessing.managers.BaseProxy method), 765
_handle (ctypes.PyDLL attribute), 714
length (ctypes.Array attribute), 725
_locale
    module, 1277
_make() (collections.somenamedtuple class method), 217
_makeResult() (unittest.TextTestRunner method), 1438
_name (ctypes.PyDLL attribute), 714
_objects (ctypes._CData attribute), 721
pack (ctypes.Structure attribute), 724
_parse() (gettext.NullTranslations method), 1272
_replace() (collections.somenamedtuple method), 217
_setroot() (xml.etree.ElementTree.ElementTree method), 1065
_source (collections.somenamedtuple attribute), 217
_structure() (in module email.iterators), 1007
_thread (module), 807
type (ctypes.Array attribute), 725
type (ctypes._Pointer attribute), 725
_write() (wsgiref.handlers.BaseHandler method), 1123
_xoptions (in module sys), 1578
^
    operator, 32
~
    operator, 32
|
    operator, 32
>>>, 1781
>
    operator, 30
>=
    operator, 30
>>
    operator, 32

A

<
    operator, 30
<=
    operator, 30
<<
    operator, 32
<protocol>_proxy, 1129
2to3, **1781**

A

A (in module re), 111
A-LAW, 1254, 1262
a-LAW, 1249
a2b_base64() (in module binascii), 1042
a2b_hex() (in module binascii), 1043
a2b_hqx() (in module binascii), 1042
a2b_qp() (in module binascii), 1042
a2b_uu() (in module binascii), 1042
a85decode() (in module base64), 1040
a85encode() (in module base64), 1039
ABC (class in abc), 1599
abc (module), 1599
ABCMeta (class in abc), 1600
abiflags (in module sys), 1563
abort() (asyncio.DatagramTransport method), 901
abort() (asyncio.WriteTransport method), 900
abort() (ftplib.FTP method), 1164
abort() (in module os), 558
abort() (threading.Barrier method), 738
above() (curses.panel.Panel method), 684
abs() (built-in function), 5
abs() (decimal.Context method), 299
abs() (in module operator), 348
abspath() (in module os.path), 371
abstract base class, **1781**
AbstractBasicAuthHandler (class in urllib.request), 1130
abstractclassmethod() (in module abc), 1602
AbstractContextManager (class in contextlib), 1588
AbstractDigestAuthHandler (class in urllib.request), 1130
AbstractEventLoop (class in asyncio), 873
AbstractEventLoopPolicy (class in asyncio), 887
AbstractFormatter (class in formatter), 1707
abstractmethod() (in module abc), 1601
abstractproperty() (in module abc), 1603
AbstractSet (class in typing), 1383
abstractstaticmethod() (in module abc), 1603
AbstractWriter (class in formatter), 1708
accept() (asyncore.dispatcher method), 934
accept() (multiprocessing.connection.Listener method), 769
accept() (socket.socket method), 821
access() (in module os), 540
accumulate() (in module itertools), 328
acos() (in module cmath), 282
acos() (in module math), 279
acosh() (in module cmath), 283
acosh() (in module math), 280
acquire() (_thread.lock method), 808
acquire() (asyncio.Condition method), 922
acquire() (asyncio.Lock method), 921
acquire() (asyncio.Semaphore method), 923
acquire() (logging.Handler method), 628
acquire() (multiprocessing.Lock method), 754
acquire() (multiprocessing.RLock method), 755
acquire() (threading.Condition method), 733
acquire() (threading.Lock method), 731
acquire() (threading.RLock method), 732
acquire() (threading.Semaphore method), 735
acquire_lock() (in module imp), 1776
Action (class in argparse), 610
action (optparse.Option attribute), 1760
ACTIONS (optparse.Option attribute), 1772
active_children() (in module multiprocessing), 750
active_count() (in module threading), 727
add() (decimal.Context method), 299
add() (frozenset method), 75
add() (in module audioop), 1249
add() (in module operator), 348
add() (mailbox.Mailbox method), 1018
add() (mailbox.Maildir method), 1021
add() (msilib.RadioButtonGroup method), 1715
add() (pstats.Stats method), 1528
add() (tarfile.TarFile method), 470
add() (tkinter.ttk.Notebook method), 1348
add_alias() (in module email.charset), 1003
add_alternative() (email.message.EmailMessage method), 957
add_argument() (argparse.ArgumentParser method), 600
add_argument_group() (argparse.ArgumentParser method), 617
add_attachment() (email.message.EmailMessage method), 957
add_cgi_vars() (wsgiref.handlers.BaseHandler method), 1123
add_charset() (in module email.charset), 1002
add_codec() (in module email.charset), 1003
add_cookie_header() (http.cookiejar.CookieJar method), 1216
add_data() (in module msilib), 1712
add_done_callback() (asyncio.Future method), 892
add_done_callback() (concurrent.futures.Future method), 785
add_fallback() (gettext.NullTranslations method), 1272
add_file() (msilib.Directory method), 1714

add_flag() (mailbox.MaildirMessage method), 1027
add_flag() (mailbox.mboxMessage method), 1028
add_flag() (mailbox.MMDFMessage method), 1032
add_flowing_data() (formatter.formatter method), 1706
add_folder() (mailbox.Maildir method), 1021
add_folder() (mailbox.MH method), 1023
add_get_handler() (email.contentmanager.ContentManager method), 979
add_handler() (urllib.request.OpenerDirector method), 1133
add_header() (email.message.EmailMessage method), 953
add_header() (email.message.Message method), 991
add_header() (urllib.request.Request method), 1132
add_header() (wsgiref.headers.Headers method), 1119
add_history() (in module readline), 144
add_hor_rule() (formatter.formatter method), 1706
add_label() (mailbox.BabylMessage method), 1031
add_label_data() (formatter.formatter method), 1706
add_line_break() (formatter.formatter method), 1706
add_literal_data() (formatter.formatter method), 1706
add_mutually_exclusive_group() (argparse.ArgumentParser method), 618
add_option() (optparse.OptionParser method), 1758
add_parent() (urllib.request.BaseHandler method), 1134
add_password() (urllib.request.HTTPPasswordMgr method), 1136
add_password() (urllib.request.HTTPPasswordMgrWithPriorAuth method), 1136
add_reader() (asyncio.AbstractEventLoop method), 879
add_related() (email.message.EmailMessage method), 957
add_section() (configparser.ConfigParser method), 497
add_section() (configparser.RawConfigParser method), 500
add_sequence() (mailbox.MHMessage method), 1030
add_set_handler() (email.contentmanager.ContentManager method), 979
add_signal_handler() (asyncio.AbstractEventLoop method), 881
add_stream() (in module msilib), 1712
add_subparsers() (argparse.ArgumentParser method), 613
add_tables() (in module msilib), 1712
add_type() (in module mimetypes), 1036
add_unredirected_header() (urllib.request.Request method), 1132
add_writer() (asyncio.AbstractEventLoop method), 879
addch() (curses.window method), 669
addCleanup() (unittest.TestCase method), 1432
addcomponent() (turtle.Shape method), 1313
addError() (unittest.TestResult method), 1437
addExpectedFailure() (unittest.TestResult method), 1438
addFailure() (unittest.TestResult method), 1437
addfile() (tarfile.TarFile method), 470
addFilter() (logging.Handler method), 628
addFilter() (logging.Logger method), 626
addHandler() (logging.Logger method), 627
addLevelName() (in module logging), 636
addnstr() (curses.window method), 670
AddPackagePath() (in module modulefinder), 1646
addr (smtpd.SMTPChannel attribute), 1191
addr_spec (email.headerregistry.Address attribute), 978
Address (class in email.headerregistry), 977
address (email.headerregistry.SingleAddressHeader attribute), 976
address (multiprocessing.connection.Listener attribute), 769
address (multiprocessing.managers.BaseManager attribute), 760
address_exclude() (ipaddress.IPv4Network method), 1242
address_exclude() (ipaddress.IPv6Network method), 1244
address_family (socketserver.BaseServer attribute), 1200
address_string() (http.server.BaseHTTPRequestHandler method), 1209
addresses (email.headerregistry.AddressHeader attribute), 975
addresses (email.headerregistry.Group attribute), 978
AddressHeader (class in email.headerregistry), 975
addressof() (in module ctypes), 718
AddressValueError, 1247
addshape() (in module turtle), 1311
addsitedir() (in module site), 1632
addSkip() (unittest.TestResult method), 1437
addstr() (curses.window method), 670
addSubTest() (unittest.TestResult method), 1438
addSuccess() (unittest.TestResult method), 1437
addTest() (unittest.TestSuite method), 1433
addTests() (unittest.TestSuite method), 1433
addTypeEqualityFunc() (unittest.TestCase method), 1430

addUnexpectedSuccess() (unittest.TestResult method), 1438
adjusted() (decimal.Decimal method), 290
adler32() (in module zlib), 443
ADPCM, Intel/DVI, 1249
adpcm2lin() (in module audioop), 1249
AF_ALG (in module socket), 815
AF_CAN (in module socket), 814
AF_INET (in module socket), 814
AF_INET6 (in module socket), 814
AF_LINK (in module socket), 815
AF_RDS (in module socket), 815
AF_UNIX (in module socket), 814
aifc (module), 1252
aifc() (aifc.aifc method), 1253
AIFF, 1252, 1260
aiff() (aifc.aifc method), 1253
AIFF-C, 1252, 1260
alarm() (in module signal), 940
alaw2lin() (in module audioop), 1249
ALERT_DESCRIPTION_HANDSHAKE_FAILURE (in module ssl), 843
ALERT_DESCRIPTION_INTERNAL_ERROR (in module ssl), 843
AlertDescription (class in ssl), 843
algorithms_available (in module hashlib), 510
algorithms_guaranteed (in module hashlib), 510
alias (pdb command), 1523
alignment() (in module ctypes), 718
alive (weakref.finalize attribute), 238
all() (built-in function), 5
all_errors (in module ftplib), 1163
all_features (in module xml.sax.handler), 1089
all_frames (tracemalloc.Filter attribute), 1545
all_properties (in module xml.sax.handler), 1089
all_suffixes() (in module importlib.machinery), 1657
all_tasks() (asyncio.Task class method), 894
allocate_lock() (in module _thread), 807
allow_reuse_address (socketserver.BaseServer attribute), 1201
allowed_domains() (http.cookiejar.DefaultCookiePolicy method), 1220
alt() (in module curses.ascii), 683
ALT_DIGITS (in module locale), 1280
altsep (in module os), 568
altzone (in module time), 590
ALWAYS_TYPED_ACTIONS (optparse.Option attribute), 1772
AMPER (in module token), 1679
AMPEREQUAL (in module token), 1679
and
    operator, 29
and_() (in module operator), 348
annotation (inspect.Parameter attribute), 1622

answer_challenge() (in module multiprocessing.connection), 768
anticipate_failure() (in module test.support), 1507
Any (in module typing), 1388
ANY (in module unittest.mock), 1471
any() (built-in function), 5
AnyStr (in module typing), 1389
api_version (in module sys), 1578
apop() (poplib.POP3 method), 1168
append() (array.array method), 233
append() (collections.deque method), 212
append() (email.header.Header method), 999
append() (imaplib.IMAP4 method), 1171
append() (msilib.CAB method), 1714
append() (pipes.Template method), 1740
append() (sequence method), 39
append() (xml.etree.ElementTree.Element method), 1064
append_history_file() (in module readline), 143
appendChild() (xml.dom.Node method), 1073
appendleft() (collections.deque method), 212
application_uri() (in module wsgiref.util), 1117
apply (2to3 fixer), 1498
apply() (multiprocessing.pool.Pool method), 766
apply_async() (multiprocessing.pool.Pool method), 766
apply_defaults() (inspect.BoundArguments method), 1623
architecture() (in module platform), 685
archive (zipimport.zipimporter attribute), 1642
aRepr (in module reprlib), 252
argparse (module), 590
args (BaseException attribute), 86
args (functools.partial attribute), 347
args (inspect.BoundArguments attribute), 1623
args (pdb command), 1522
args (subprocess.CompletedProcess attribute), 788
args (subprocess.Popen attribute), 795
argtypes (ctypes._FuncPtr attribute), 715
argument, 1781
ArgumentDefaultsHelpFormatter (class in argparse), 596
ArgumentError, 715
ArgumentParser (class in argparse), 592
arguments (inspect.BoundArguments attribute), 1623
argv (in module sys), 1563
arithmetic, 31
ArithmeticError, 86
array
    module, 53
array (class in array), 233
Array (class in ctypes), 725
array (module), 232

Array() (in module multiprocessing), 756
Array() (in module multiprocessing.sharedctypes), 757
Array() (multiprocessing.managers.SyncManager method), 761
arrays, 232
arraysize (sqlite3.Cursor attribute), 434
article() (nntplib.NNTP method), 1181
as_bytes() (email.message.EmailMessage method), 951
as_bytes() (email.message.Message method), 988
as_completed() (in module asyncio), 895
as_completed() (in module concurrent.futures), 786
as_integer_ratio() (decimal.Decimal method), 290
as_integer_ratio() (float method), 34
AS_IS (in module formatter), 1705
as_posix() (pathlib.PurePath method), 362
as_string() (email.message.EmailMessage method), 951
as_string() (email.message.Message method), 988
as_tuple() (decimal.Decimal method), 291
as_uri() (pathlib.PurePath method), 362
ASCII (in module re), 111
ascii() (built-in function), 5
ascii() (in module curses.ascii), 683
ascii_letters (in module string), 95
ascii_lowercase (in module string), 95
ascii_uppercase (in module string), 95
asctime() (in module time), 583
asin() (in module cmath), 282
asin() (in module math), 279
asinh() (in module cmath), 283
asinh() (in module math), 280
assert
    statement, 86
assert_any_call() (unittest.mock.Mock method), 1447
assert_called() (unittest.mock.Mock method), 1446
assert_called_once() (unittest.mock.Mock method), 1446
assert_called_once_with() (unittest.mock.Mock method), 1446
assert_called_with() (unittest.mock.Mock method), 1446
assert_has_calls() (unittest.mock.Mock method), 1447
assert_line_data() (formatter.formatter method), 1707
assert_not_called() (unittest.mock.Mock method), 1447
assertAlmostEqual() (unittest.TestCase method), 1429
assertCountEqual() (unittest.TestCase method), 1430

assertDictEqual() (unittest.TestCase method), 1431
assertEqual() (unittest.TestCase method), 1425
assertFalse() (unittest.TestCase method), 1425
assertGreater() (unittest.TestCase method), 1429
assertGreaterEqual() (unittest.TestCase method), 1429
assertIn() (unittest.TestCase method), 1426
AssertionError, 86
assertIs() (unittest.TestCase method), 1425
assertIsInstance() (unittest.TestCase method), 1426
assertIsNone() (unittest.TestCase method), 1426
assertIsNot() (unittest.TestCase method), 1425
assertIsNotNone() (unittest.TestCase method), 1426
assertLess() (unittest.TestCase method), 1429
assertLessEqual() (unittest.TestCase method), 1429
assertListEqual() (unittest.TestCase method), 1430
assertLogs() (unittest.TestCase method), 1428
assertMultiLineEqual() (unittest.TestCase method), 1430
assertNotAlmostEqual() (unittest.TestCase method), 1429
assertNotEqual() (unittest.TestCase method), 1425
assertNotIn() (unittest.TestCase method), 1426
assertNotIsInstance() (unittest.TestCase method), 1426
assertNotRegex() (unittest.TestCase method), 1429
assertRaises() (unittest.TestCase method), 1426
assertRaisesRegex() (unittest.TestCase method), 1427
assertRegex() (unittest.TestCase method), 1429
asserts (2to3 fixer), 1498
assertSequenceEqual() (unittest.TestCase method), 1430
assertSetEqual() (unittest.TestCase method), 1431
assertTrue() (unittest.TestCase method), 1425
assertTupleEqual() (unittest.TestCase method), 1430
assertWarns() (unittest.TestCase method), 1427
assertWarnsRegex() (unittest.TestCase method), 1427
assignment
    slice, 39
    subscript, 39
AST (class in ast), 1671
ast (module), 1671
astimezone() (datetime.datetime method), 184
ASYNC (in module token), 1679
async() (in module asyncio), 896
async_chat (class in asynchat), 936
async_chat.ac_in_buffer_size (in module asynchat), 936
async_chat.ac_out_buffer_size (in module asynchat), 936
AsyncGenerator (class in collections.abc), 225
AsyncGenerator (class in typing), 1385

AsyncGeneratorType (in module types), 243
asynchat (module), 936
asynchronous context manager, 1781
asynchronous generator, 1782
asynchronous generator iterator, 1782
asynchronous iterable, 1782
asynchronous iterator, 1782
asyncio (module), 872
asyncio.subprocess.DEVNULL (in module asyncio), 916
asyncio.subprocess.PIPE (in module asyncio), 916
asyncio.subprocess.Process (class in asyncio), 916
asyncio.subprocess.STDOUT (in module asyncio), 916
AsyncIterable (class in collections.abc), 225
AsyncIterable (class in typing), 1384
AsyncIterator (class in collections.abc), 225
AsyncIterator (class in typing), 1384
asyncore (module), 932
AsyncResult (class in multiprocessing.pool), 767
AT (in module token), 1679
at_eof() (asyncio.StreamReader method), 910
atan() (in module cmath), 282
atan() (in module math), 279
atan2() (in module math), 279
atanh() (in module cmath), 283
atanh() (in module math), 280
ATEQUAL (in module token), 1679
atexit (module), 1604
atexit (weakref.finalize attribute), 238
atof() (in module locale), 1282
atoi() (in module locale), 1282
attach() (email.message.Message method), 989
attach_mock() (unittest.mock.Mock method), 1448
AttlistDeclHandler() (xml.parsers.expat.xmlparser method), 1100
attrgetter() (in module operator), 350
attrib (xml.etree.ElementTree.Element attribute), 1063
attribute, 1782
AttributeError, 86
attributes (xml.dom.Node attribute), 1072
AttributesImpl (class in xml.sax.xmlreader), 1094
AttributesNSImpl (class in xml.sax.xmlreader), 1094
attroff() (curses.window method), 670
attron() (curses.window method), 670
attrset() (curses.window method), 670
Audio Interchange File Format, 1252, 1260
AUDIO_FILE_ENCODING_ADPCM_G721 (in module sunau), 1255
AUDIO_FILE_ENCODING_ADPCM_G722 (in module sunau), 1255
AUDIO_FILE_ENCODING_ADPCM_G723_3 (in module sunau), 1255
AUDIO_FILE_ENCODING_ADPCM_G723_5 (in module sunau), 1255
AUDIO_FILE_ENCODING_ALAW_8 (in module sunau), 1255
AUDIO_FILE_ENCODING_DOUBLE (in module sunau), 1255
AUDIO_FILE_ENCODING_FLOAT (in module sunau), 1255
AUDIO_FILE_ENCODING_LINEAR_16 (in module sunau), 1255
AUDIO_FILE_ENCODING_LINEAR_24 (in module sunau), 1255
AUDIO_FILE_ENCODING_LINEAR_32 (in module sunau), 1255
AUDIO_FILE_ENCODING_LINEAR_8 (in module sunau), 1255
AUDIO_FILE_ENCODING_MULAW_8 (in module sunau), 1255
AUDIO_FILE_MAGIC (in module sunau), 1255
AUDIODEV, 1263
audioop (module), 1249
auth() (ftplib.FTP_TLS method), 1166
auth() (smtplib.SMTP method), 1186
authenticate() (imaplib.IMAP4 method), 1171
AuthenticationError, 747
authenticators() (netrc.netrc method), 501
authkey (multiprocessing.Process attribute), 746
auto (class in enum), 254
autorange() (timeit.Timer method), 1533
avg() (in module audioop), 1249
avgpp() (in module audioop), 1249
avoids_symlink_attacks (shutil.rmtree attribute), 395
AWAIT (in module token), 1679
awaitable, 1782
Awaitable (class in collections.abc), 224
Awaitable (class in typing), 1384

B

b16decode() (in module base64), 1039
b16encode() (in module base64), 1039
b2a_base64() (in module binascii), 1042
b2a_hex() (in module binascii), 1043
b2a_hqx() (in module binascii), 1043
b2a_qp() (in module binascii), 1042
b2a_uu() (in module binascii), 1042
b32decode() (in module base64), 1039
b32encode() (in module base64), 1039
b64decode() (in module base64), 1038
b64encode() (in module base64), 1038
b85decode() (in module base64), 1040
b85encode() (in module base64), 1040
Babyl (class in mailbox), 1024
BabylMessage (class in mailbox), 1030

back() (in module turtle), 1290
backslashreplace_errors() (in module codecs), 159
backward() (in module turtle), 1290
BadStatusLine, 1157
BadZipFile, 458
BadZipfile, 458
Balloon (class in tkinter.tix), 1360
Barrier (class in multiprocessing), 754
Barrier (class in threading), 737
Barrier() (multiprocessing.managers.SyncManager method), 760
base64
    encoding, 1038
    module, 1042
base64 (module), 1038
base_exec_prefix (in module sys), 1563
base_prefix (in module sys), 1563
BaseCGIHandler (class in wsgiref.handlers), 1122
BaseCookie (class in http.cookies), 1211
BaseEventLoop (class in asyncio), 873
BaseException, 85
BaseHandler (class in urllib.request), 1129
BaseHandler (class in wsgiref.handlers), 1123
BaseHeader (class in email.headerregistry), 973
BaseHTTPRequestHandler (class in http.server), 1206
BaseManager (class in multiprocessing.managers), 759
basename() (in module os.path), 371
BaseProxy (class in multiprocessing.managers), 764
BaseRequestHandler (class in socketserver), 1202
BaseRotatingHandler (class in logging.handlers), 651
BaseSelector (class in selectors), 870
BaseServer (class in socketserver), 1200
basestring (2to3 fixer), 1498
BaseSubprocessTransport (class in asyncio), 901
BaseTransport (class in asyncio), 899
basicConfig() (in module logging), 637
BasicContext (class in decimal), 297
BasicInterpolation (class in configparser), 487
baudrate() (in module curses), 663
bbox() (tkinter.ttk.Treeview method), 1352
BDADDR_ANY (in module socket), 816
BDADDR_LOCAL (in module socket), 816
bdb
    module, 1517
Bdb (class in bdb), 1512
bdb (module), 1511
BdbQuit, 1511
BDFL, **1782**
beep() (in module curses), 663
Beep() (in module winsound), 1726
BEFORE_ASYNC_WITH (opcode), 1696
begin_fill() (in module turtle), 1299

begin_poly() (in module turtle), 1305
below() (curses.panel.Panel method), 684
Benchmarking, 1531
benchmarking, 583
betavariate() (in module random), 316
bgcolor() (in module turtle), 1306
bgpic() (in module turtle), 1306
bias() (in module audioop), 1249
bidirectional() (in module unicodedata), 139
BigEndianStructure (class in ctypes), 723
bin() (built-in function), 6
binary
    data, packing, 149
    literals, 31
Binary (class in msilib), 1712
Binary (class in xmlrpc.client), 1227
binary file, **1782**
binary mode, 18
binary semaphores, 807
BINARY_ADD (opcode), 1694
BINARY_AND (opcode), 1695
BINARY_FLOOR_DIVIDE (opcode), 1694
BINARY_LSHIFT (opcode), 1695
BINARY_MATRIX_MULTIPLY (opcode), 1694
BINARY_MODULO (opcode), 1694
BINARY_MULTIPLY (opcode), 1694
BINARY_OR (opcode), 1695
BINARY_POWER (opcode), 1694
BINARY_RSHIFT (opcode), 1695
BINARY_SUBSCR (opcode), 1695
BINARY_SUBTRACT (opcode), 1694
BINARY_TRUE_DIVIDE (opcode), 1694
BINARY_XOR (opcode), 1695
binascii (module), 1042
bind (widgets), 1340
bind() (asyncore.dispatcher method), 934
bind() (inspect.Signature method), 1621
bind() (socket.socket method), 821
bind_partial() (inspect.Signature method), 1621
bind_port() (in module test.support), 1507
bind_textdomain_codeset() (in module gettext), 1269
bindtextdomain() (in module gettext), 1269
bindtextdomain() (in module locale), 1283
binhex
    module, 1042
binhex (module), 1041
binhex() (in module binhex), 1041
bisect (module), 230
bisect() (in module bisect), 230
bisect_left() (in module bisect), 230
bisect_right() (in module bisect), 230
bit_length() (int method), 32
bitmap() (msilib.Dialog method), 1716

bitwise
    operations, 32
bk() (in module turtle), 1290
bkgd() (curses.window method), 670
bkgdset() (curses.window method), 670
blake2b() (in module hashlib), 512
blake2b, blake2s, 512
blake2b.MAX_DIGEST_SIZE (in module hashlib), 513
blake2b.MAX_KEY_SIZE (in module hashlib), 513
blake2b.PERSON_SIZE (in module hashlib), 513
blake2b.SALT_SIZE (in module hashlib), 513
blake2s() (in module hashlib), 512
blake2s.MAX_DIGEST_SIZE (in module hashlib), 513
blake2s.MAX_KEY_SIZE (in module hashlib), 513
blake2s.PERSON_SIZE (in module hashlib), 513
blake2s.SALT_SIZE (in module hashlib), 513
block_size (hmac.HMAC attribute), 520
blocked_domains() (http.cookiejar.DefaultCookiePolicy method), 1220
BlockingIOError, 90, 571
body() (nntplib.NNTP method), 1181
body_encode() (email.charset.Charset method), 1002
body_encoding (email.charset.Charset attribute), 1001
body_line_iterator() (in module email.iterators), 1006
BOM (in module codecs), 157
BOM_BE (in module codecs), 157
BOM_LE (in module codecs), 157
BOM_UTF16 (in module codecs), 157
BOM_UTF16_BE (in module codecs), 157
BOM_UTF16_LE (in module codecs), 157
BOM_UTF32 (in module codecs), 157
BOM_UTF32_BE (in module codecs), 157
BOM_UTF32_LE (in module codecs), 157
BOM_UTF8 (in module codecs), 157
bool (built-in class), 6
Boolean
    object, 30
    operations, 29
    type, 6
    values, 82
BOOLEAN_STATES (in module configparser), 493
bootstrap() (in module ensurepip), 1551
border() (curses.window method), 670
bottom() (curses.panel.Panel method), 684
bottom_panel() (in module curses.panel), 684
BoundArguments (class in inspect), 1623
BoundaryError, 972
BoundedSemaphore (class in asyncio), 923
BoundedSemaphore (class in multiprocessing), 754

BoundedSemaphore (class in threading), 735
BoundedSemaphore() (multiprocessing.managers.SyncManager method), 761
box() (curses.window method), 670
bpformat() (bdb.Breakpoint method), 1511
bpprint() (bdb.Breakpoint method), 1512
break (pdb command), 1520
break_anywhere() (bdb.Bdb method), 1513
break_here() (bdb.Bdb method), 1513
break_long_words (textwrap.TextWrapper attribute), 138
BREAK_LOOP (opcode), 1696
break_on_hyphens (textwrap.TextWrapper attribute), 138
Breakpoint (class in bdb), 1511
breakpoints, 1367
broadcast_address (ipaddress.IPv4Network attribute), 1242
broadcast_address (ipaddress.IPv6Network attribute), 1244
broken (threading.Barrier attribute), 738
BrokenBarrierError, 738
BrokenPipeError, 91
BrokenProcessPool, 787
BROWSER, 1107, 1108
BsdDbShelf (class in shelve), 416
buffer (2to3 fixer), 1498
buffer (io.TextIOBase attribute), 579
buffer (unittest.TestResult attribute), 1436
buffer protocol
    binary sequence types, 53
    str (built-in class), 43
buffer size, I/O, 18
buffer_info() (array.array method), 233
buffer_size (xml.parsers.expat.xmlparser attribute), 1099
buffer_text (xml.parsers.expat.xmlparser attribute), 1099
buffer_used (xml.parsers.expat.xmlparser attribute), 1099
BufferedIOBase (class in io), 575
BufferedRandom (class in io), 578
BufferedReader (class in io), 577
BufferedRWPair (class in io), 578
BufferedWriter (class in io), 578
BufferError, 86
BufferingHandler (class in logging.handlers), 659
BufferTooShort, 747
bufsize() (ossaudiodev.oss_audio_device method), 1266
BUILD_CONST_KEY_MAP (opcode), 1698
BUILD_LIST (opcode), 1698
BUILD_LIST_UNPACK (opcode), 1699

BUILD_MAP (opcode), 1698
BUILD_MAP_UNPACK (opcode), 1699
BUILD_MAP_UNPACK_WITH_CALL (opcode), 1699
build_opener() (in module urllib.request), 1128
BUILD_SET (opcode), 1698
BUILD_SET_UNPACK (opcode), 1699
BUILD_SLICE (opcode), 1701
BUILD_STRING (opcode), 1698
BUILD_TUPLE (opcode), 1698
BUILD_TUPLE_UNPACK (opcode), 1698
BUILD_TUPLE_UNPACK_WITH_CALL (opcode), 1699
built-in
    types, 29
built-in function
    compile, 81, 244, 1669
    complex, 31
    eval, 81, 248, 249, 1669
    exec, 10, 81, 1669
    float, 31
    hash, 39
    int, 31
    len, 37, 75
    max, 37
    min, 37
    slice, 1701
    type, 81
builtin_module_names (in module sys), 1564
BuiltinFunctionType (in module types), 244
BuiltinImporter (class in importlib.machinery), 1658
BuiltinMethodType (in module types), 244
builtins (module), 1582
ButtonBox (class in tkinter.tix), 1360
bye() (in module turtle), 1312
byref() (in module ctypes), 718
byte-code
    file, 1686, 1773
bytearray
    formatting, 64
    interpolation, 64
    methods, 55
    object, 39, 53, 54
bytearray (built-in class), 54
bytecode, **1782**
Bytecode (class in dis), 1690
Bytecode.codeobj (in module dis), 1691
Bytecode.first_line (in module dis), 1691
BYTECODE_SUFFIXES (in module importlib.machinery), 1657
byteorder (in module sys), 1563
bytes
    formatting, 64
    interpolation, 64
    methods, 55
    object, 53
    str (built-in class), 43
bytes (built-in class), 53
bytes (uuid.UUID attribute), 1195
bytes-like object, **1782**
bytes_le (uuid.UUID attribute), 1195
BytesFeedParser (class in email.parser), 959
BytesGenerator (class in email.generator), 962
BytesHeaderParser (class in email.parser), 960
BytesIO (class in io), 577
BytesParser (class in email.parser), 960
ByteString (class in collections.abc), 224
ByteString (class in typing), 1383
byteswap() (array.array method), 233
byteswap() (in module audioop), 1250
BytesWarning, 92
bz2 (module), 449
BZ2Compressor (class in bz2), 451
BZ2Decompressor (class in bz2), 451
BZ2File (class in bz2), 450

C

C
    language, 30, 31
    structures, 149
C-contiguous, 1783
c_bool (class in ctypes), 723
C_BUILTIN (in module imp), 1777
c_byte (class in ctypes), 721
c_char (class in ctypes), 721
c_char_p (class in ctypes), 721
c_contiguous (memoryview attribute), 73
c_double (class in ctypes), 722
C_EXTENSION (in module imp), 1777
c_float (class in ctypes), 722
c_int (class in ctypes), 722
c_int16 (class in ctypes), 722
c_int32 (class in ctypes), 722
c_int64 (class in ctypes), 722
c_int8 (class in ctypes), 722
c_long (class in ctypes), 722
c_longdouble (class in ctypes), 722
c_longlong (class in ctypes), 722
c_short (class in ctypes), 722
c_size_t (class in ctypes), 722
c_ssize_t (class in ctypes), 722
c_ubyte (class in ctypes), 722
c_uint (class in ctypes), 722
c_uint16 (class in ctypes), 722
c_uint32 (class in ctypes), 722
c_uint64 (class in ctypes), 723
c_uint8 (class in ctypes), 722
c_ulong (class in ctypes), 723

c_ulonglong (class in ctypes), 723
c_ushort (class in ctypes), 723
c_void_p (class in ctypes), 723
c_wchar (class in ctypes), 723
c_wchar_p (class in ctypes), 723
CAB (class in msilib), 1714
cache_from_source() (in module imp), 1775
cache_from_source() (in module importlib.util), 1662
cached (importlib.machinery.ModuleSpec attribute), 1661
CacheFTPHandler (class in urllib.request), 1131
calcsize() (in module struct), 150
Calendar (class in calendar), 203
calendar (module), 203
calendar() (in module calendar), 205
call() (in module subprocess), 797
call() (in module unittest.mock), 1469
call_args (unittest.mock.Mock attribute), 1450
call_args_list (unittest.mock.Mock attribute), 1451
call_at() (asyncio.AbstractEventLoop method), 875
call_count (unittest.mock.Mock attribute), 1449
call_exception_handler() (asyncio.AbstractEventLoop method), 882
CALL_FUNCTION (opcode), 1701
CALL_FUNCTION_EX (opcode), 1701
CALL_FUNCTION_KW (opcode), 1701
call_later() (asyncio.AbstractEventLoop method), 875
call_list() (unittest.mock.call method), 1470
call_soon() (asyncio.AbstractEventLoop method), 874
call_soon_threadsafe() (asyncio.AbstractEventLoop method), 874
call_tracing() (in module sys), 1564
Callable (class in collections.abc), 223
Callable (in module typing), 1389
callable() (built-in function), 7
CallableProxyType (in module weakref), 238
callback (optparse.Option attribute), 1760
callback() (contextlib.ExitStack method), 1593
callback_args (optparse.Option attribute), 1760
callback_kwargs (optparse.Option attribute), 1760
callbacks (in module gc), 1615
called (unittest.mock.Mock attribute), 1449
CalledProcessError, 789
CAN_BCM (in module socket), 815
can_change_color() (in module curses), 663
can_fetch() (urllib.robotparser.RobotFileParser method), 1152
CAN_RAW_FD_FRAMES (in module socket), 815
can_symlink() (in module test.support), 1507
can_write_eof() (asyncio.StreamWriter method), 910

can_write_eof() (asyncio.WriteTransport method), 900
cancel() (asyncio.Future method), 892
cancel() (asyncio.Handle method), 883
cancel() (asyncio.Task method), 894
cancel() (concurrent.futures.Future method), 785
cancel() (sched.scheduler method), 803
cancel() (threading.Timer method), 737
cancel_dump_traceback_later() (in module faulthandler), 1516
cancel_join_thread() (multiprocessing.Queue method), 750
cancelled() (asyncio.Future method), 892
cancelled() (concurrent.futures.Future method), 785
CancelledError, 786
CannotSendHeader, 1156
CannotSendRequest, 1156
canonic() (bdb.Bdb method), 1512
canonical() (decimal.Context method), 299
canonical() (decimal.Decimal method), 291
capa() (poplib.POP3 method), 1168
capitalize() (bytearray method), 60
capitalize() (bytes method), 60
capitalize() (str method), 44
captured_stderr() (in module test.support), 1506
captured_stdin() (in module test.support), 1506
captured_stdout() (in module test.support), 1506
captureWarnings() (in module logging), 638
capwords() (in module string), 105
casefold() (str method), 44
cast() (in module ctypes), 718
cast() (in module typing), 1387
cast() (memoryview method), 70
cat() (in module nis), 1744
catch_warnings (class in warnings), 1588
category() (in module unicodedata), 139
cbreak() (in module curses), 663
ccc() (ftplib.FTP_TLS method), 1166
CDLL (class in ctypes), 713
ceil() (in module math), 31, 276
center() (bytearray method), 58
center() (bytes method), 58
center() (str method), 44
CERT_NONE (in module ssl), 838
CERT_OPTIONAL (in module ssl), 838
CERT_REQUIRED (in module ssl), 838
cert_store_stats() (ssl.SSLContext method), 847
cert_time_to_seconds() (in module ssl), 837
CertificateError, 833
certificates, 853
CFUNCTYPE() (in module ctypes), 716
CGI
    debugging, 1115
    exceptions, 1116

protocol, 1109
security, 1114
tracebacks, 1116
cgi (module), 1109
cgi_directories (http.server.CGIHTTPRequestHandler attribute), 1211
CGIHandler (class in wsgiref.handlers), 1122
CGIHTTPRequestHandler (class in http.server), 1210
cgitb (module), 1116
CGIXMLRPCRequestHandler (class in xmlrpc.server), 1231
chain() (in module itertools), 329
chaining
    comparisons, 30
ChainMap (class in collections), 206
ChainMap (class in typing), 1385
change_cwd() (in module test.support), 1506
CHANNEL_BINDING_TYPES (in module ssl), 842
channel_class (smtpd.SMTPServer attribute), 1190
channels() (ossaudiodev.oss_audio_device method), 1265
CHAR_MAX (in module locale), 1282
character, 139
CharacterDataHandler() (xml.parsers.expat.xmlparser method), 1101
characters() (xml.sax.handler.ContentHandler method), 1091
characters_written (BlockingIOError attribute), 91
Charset (class in email.charset), 1001
charset() (gettext.NullTranslations method), 1272
chdir() (in module os), 541
check (lzma.LZMADecompressor attribute), 455
check() (imaplib.IMAP4 method), 1171
check() (in module tabnanny), 1685
check__all__() (in module test.support), 1508
check_call() (in module subprocess), 797
check_hostname (ssl.SSLContext attribute), 852
check_output() (doctest.OutputChecker method), 1410
check_output() (in module subprocess), 797
check_returncode() (subprocess.CompletedProcess method), 788
check_unused_args() (string.Formatter method), 97
check_warnings() (in module test.support), 1505
checkbox() (msilib.Dialog method), 1716
checkcache() (in module linecache), 392
checkfuncname() (in module bdb), 1515
CheckList (class in tkinter.tix), 1361
checksum
    Cyclic Redundancy Check, 444
chflags() (in module os), 541
chgat() (curses.window method), 671

childNodes (xml.dom.Node attribute), 1072
ChildProcessError, 91
chmod() (in module os), 541
chmod() (pathlib.Path method), 366
choice() (in module random), 315
choice() (in module secrets), 521
choices (optparse.Option attribute), 1760
choices() (in module random), 315
chown() (in module os), 542
chown() (in module shutil), 396
chr() (built-in function), 7
chroot() (in module os), 542
Chunk (class in chunk), 1260
chunk (module), 1260
cipher
    DES, 1732
cipher() (ssl.SSLSocket method), 845
circle() (in module turtle), 1292
CIRCUMFLEX (in module token), 1679
CIRCUMFLEXEQUAL (in module token), 1679
Clamped (class in decimal), 303
class, **1783**
Class (class in symtable), 1677
Class browser, 1365
classmethod() (built-in function), 7
ClassVar (in module typing), 1389
CLD_CONTINUED (in module os), 564
CLD_DUMPED (in module os), 564
CLD_EXITED (in module os), 564
CLD_TRAPPED (in module os), 564
clean() (mailbox.Maildir method), 1021
cleandoc() (in module inspect), 1620
clear (pdb command), 1521
Clear Breakpoint, 1367
clear() (asyncio.Event method), 921
clear() (collections.deque method), 212
clear() (curses.window method), 671
clear() (dict method), 77
clear() (email.message.EmailMessage method), 958
clear() (frozenset method), 75
clear() (http.cookiejar.CookieJar method), 1217
clear() (in module turtle), 1300, 1307
clear() (mailbox.Mailbox method), 1020
clear() (sequence method), 39
clear() (threading.Event method), 736
clear() (xml.etree.ElementTree.Element method), 1063
clear_all_breaks() (bdb.Bdb method), 1514
clear_all_file_breaks() (bdb.Bdb method), 1514
clear_bpbynumber() (bdb.Bdb method), 1514
clear_break() (bdb.Bdb method), 1514
clear_cache() (in module filecmp), 383
clear_content() (email.message.EmailMessage method), 958

clear_flags() (decimal.Context method), 298
clear_frames() (in module traceback), 1607
clear_history() (in module readline), 143
clear_session_cookies() (http.cookiejar.CookieJar method), 1217
clear_traces() (in module tracemalloc), 1543
clear_traps() (decimal.Context method), 298
clearcache() (in module linecache), 392
ClearData() (msilib.Record method), 1714
clearok() (curses.window method), 671
clearscreen() (in module turtle), 1307
clearstamp() (in module turtle), 1293
clearstamps() (in module turtle), 1293
Client() (in module multiprocessing.connection), 768
client_address (http.server.BaseHTTPRequestHandler attribute), 1206
clock() (in module time), 583
clock_getres() (in module time), 583
clock_gettime() (in module time), 583
CLOCK_HIGHRES (in module time), 589
CLOCK_MONOTONIC (in module time), 589
CLOCK_MONOTONIC_RAW (in module time), 589
CLOCK_PROCESS_CPUTIME_ID (in module time), 589
CLOCK_REALTIME (in module time), 590
clock_settime() (in module time), 584
CLOCK_THREAD_CPUTIME_ID (in module time), 589
clone() (email.generator.BytesGenerator method), 963
clone() (email.generator.Generator method), 964
clone() (email.policy.Policy method), 967
clone() (in module turtle), 1305
clone() (pipes.Template method), 1739
cloneNode() (xml.dom.Node method), 1073
close() (aifc.aifc method), 1253, 1254
close() (asyncio.AbstractEventLoop method), 874
close() (asyncio.BaseSubprocessTransport method), 902
close() (asyncio.BaseTransport method), 899
close() (asyncio.Server method), 882
close() (asyncio.StreamWriter method), 910
close() (asyncore.dispatcher method), 934
close() (chunk.Chunk method), 1260
close() (contextlib.ExitStack method), 1593
close() (dbm.dumb.dumbdbm method), 422
close() (dbm.gnu.gdbm method), 421
close() (dbm.ndbm.ndbm method), 422
close() (email.parser.BytesFeedParser method), 959
close() (ftplib.FTP method), 1166
close() (html.parser.HTMLParser method), 1049
close() (http.client.HTTPConnection method), 1158
close() (imaplib.IMAP4 method), 1172
close() (in module fileinput), 377
close() (in module os), 532
close() (io.IOBase method), 573
close() (logging.FileHandler method), 650
close() (logging.Handler method), 628
close() (logging.handlers.MemoryHandler method), 659
close() (logging.handlers.NTEventLogHandler method), 658
close() (logging.handlers.SocketHandler method), 654
close() (logging.handlers.SysLogHandler method), 656
close() (mailbox.Mailbox method), 1020
close() (mailbox.Maildir method), 1022
close() (mailbox.MH method), 1024
close() (mmap.mmap method), 945
Close() (msilib.View method), 1713
close() (multiprocessing.Connection method), 752
close() (multiprocessing.connection.Listener method), 769
close() (multiprocessing.pool.Pool method), 767
close() (multiprocessing.Queue method), 749
close() (os.scandir method), 547
close() (ossaudiodev.oss_audio_device method), 1264
close() (ossaudiodev.oss_mixer_device method), 1266
close() (select.devpoll method), 864
close() (select.epoll method), 865
close() (select.kqueue method), 867
close() (selectors.BaseSelector method), 871
close() (shelve.Shelf method), 415
close() (socket.socket method), 821
close() (sqlite3.Connection method), 427
close() (sqlite3.Cursor method), 434
close() (sunau.AU_read method), 1255
close() (sunau.AU_write method), 1257
close() (tarfile.TarFile method), 470
close() (telnetlib.Telnet method), 1194
close() (urllib.request.BaseHandler method), 1134
close() (wave.Wave_read method), 1258
close() (wave.Wave_write method), 1259
Close() (winreg.PyHKEY method), 1725
close() (xml.etree.ElementTree.TreeBuilder method), 1067
close() (xml.etree.ElementTree.XMLParser method), 1067
close() (xml.etree.ElementTree.XMLPullParser method), 1068
close() (xml.sax.xmlreader.IncrementalParser method), 1095
close() (zipfile.ZipFile method), 459

close_connection (http.server.BaseHTTPRequestHandler attribute), 1206
close_when_done() (asynchat.async_chat method), 937
closed (http.client.HTTPResponse attribute), 1160
closed (io.IOBase attribute), 573
closed (mmap.mmap attribute), 946
closed (ossaudiodev.oss_audio_device attribute), 1266
closed (select.devpoll attribute), 864
closed (select.epoll attribute), 865
closed (select.kqueue attribute), 867
CloseKey() (in module winreg), 1718
closelog() (in module syslog), 1745
closerange() (in module os), 532
closing() (in module contextlib), 1589
clrtobot() (curses.window method), 671
clrtoeol() (curses.window method), 671
cmath (module), 281
cmd
    module, 1517
Cmd (class in cmd), 1319
cmd (module), 1319
cmd (subprocess.CalledProcessError attribute), 789
cmd (subprocess.TimeoutExpired attribute), 789
cmdloop() (cmd.Cmd method), 1319
cmdqueue (cmd.Cmd attribute), 1321
cmp() (in module filecmp), 383
cmp_op (in module dis), 1702
cmp_to_key() (in module functools), 341
cmpfiles() (in module filecmp), 383
CMSG_LEN() (in module socket), 820
CMSG_SPACE() (in module socket), 820
CO_ASYNC_GENERATOR (in module inspect), 1630
CO_COROUTINE (in module inspect), 1630
CO_GENERATOR (in module inspect), 1630
CO_ITERABLE_COROUTINE (in module inspect), 1630
CO_NESTED (in module inspect), 1630
CO_NEWLOCALS (in module inspect), 1629
CO_NOFREE (in module inspect), 1630
CO_OPTIMIZED (in module inspect), 1629
CO_VARARGS (in module inspect), 1629
CO_VARKEYWORDS (in module inspect), 1630
code (module), 1637
code (SystemExit attribute), 89
code (urllib.error.HTTPError attribute), 1151
code (xml.etree.ElementTree.ParseError attribute), 1069
code (xml.parsers.expat.ExpatError attribute), 1102
code object, 81, 417
code_info() (in module dis), 1691
CodecInfo (class in codecs), 155

codecs, 154
    decode, 154
    encode, 154
codecs (module), 154
coded_value (http.cookies.Morsel attribute), 1213
codeop (module), 1639
codepoint2name (in module html.entities), 1052
codes (in module xml.parsers.expat.errors), 1104
CODESET (in module locale), 1279
CodeType (in module types), 243
coercion, 1783
col_offset (ast.AST attribute), 1672
collapse_addresses() (in module ipaddress), 1247
collapse_rfc2231_value() (in module email.utils), 1006
collect() (in module gc), 1613
collect_incoming_data() (asynchat.async_chat method), 937
Collection (class in collections.abc), 224
Collection (class in typing), 1383
collections (module), 206
collections.abc (module), 222
colno (json.JSONDecodeError attribute), 1014
colno (re.error attribute), 116
COLON (in module token), 1679
color() (in module turtle), 1299
color_content() (in module curses), 663
color_pair() (in module curses), 664
colormode() (in module turtle), 1311
colorsys (module), 1261
COLS, 669
column() (tkinter.ttk.Treeview method), 1352
COLUMNS, 669
columns (os.terminal_size attribute), 539
combinations() (in module itertools), 330
combinations_with_replacement() (in module itertools), 330
combine() (datetime.datetime class method), 182
combining() (in module unicodedata), 139
ComboBox (class in tkinter.tix), 1360
Combobox (class in tkinter.ttk), 1346
COMMA (in module token), 1679
command (http.server.BaseHTTPRequestHandler attribute), 1207
command line option
    --sort-keys, 1016
    -h, --help, 1016
    infile, 1016
    outfile, 1016
CommandCompiler (class in codeop), 1640
commands (pdb command), 1521
comment (http.cookiejar.Cookie attribute), 1222
COMMENT (in module tokenize), 1681
comment (zipfile.ZipFile attribute), 462

comment (zipfile.ZipInfo attribute), 464
Comment() (in module xml.etree.ElementTree), 1061
comment_url (http.cookiejar.Cookie attribute), 1222
commenters (shlex.shlex attribute), 1326
CommentHandler() (xml.parsers.expat.xmlparser method), 1101
commit() (msilib.CAB method), 1714
Commit() (msilib.Database method), 1712
commit() (sqlite3.Connection method), 426
common (filecmp.dircmp attribute), 384
Common Gateway Interface, 1109
common_dirs (filecmp.dircmp attribute), 384
common_files (filecmp.dircmp attribute), 384
common_funny (filecmp.dircmp attribute), 384
common_types (in module mimetypes), 1036
commonpath() (in module os.path), 372
commonprefix() (in module os.path), 372
communicate() (asyncio.asyncio.subprocess.Process method), 917
communicate() (subprocess.Popen method), 794
compare() (decimal.Context method), 299
compare() (decimal.Decimal method), 291
compare() (difflib.Differ method), 133
compare_digest() (in module hmac), 520
compare_digest() (in module secrets), 522
compare_networks() (ipaddress.IPv4Network method), 1243
compare_networks() (ipaddress.IPv6Network method), 1244
COMPARE_OP (opcode), 1699
compare_signal() (decimal.Context method), 299
compare_signal() (decimal.Decimal method), 291
compare_to() (tracemalloc.Snapshot method), 1545
compare_total() (decimal.Context method), 299
compare_total() (decimal.Decimal method), 291
compare_total_mag() (decimal.Context method), 299
compare_total_mag() (decimal.Decimal method), 291
comparing
    objects, 30
comparison
    operator, 30
COMPARISON_FLAGS (in module doctest), 1399
comparisons
    chaining, 30
Compat32 (class in email.policy), 971
compat32 (in module email.policy), 972
compile
    built-in function, 81, 244, 1669
Compile (class in codeop), 1640
compile() (built-in function), 7
compile() (in module py_compile), 1686
compile() (in module re), 111

compile() (parser.ST method), 1670
compile_command() (in module code), 1637
compile_command() (in module codeop), 1639
compile_dir() (in module compileall), 1688
compile_file() (in module compileall), 1689
compile_path() (in module compileall), 1689
compileall (module), 1687
compileall command line option
    -b, 1688
    -d destdir, 1688
    -f, 1687
    -i list, 1688
    -j N, 1688
    -l, 1687
    -q, 1688
    -r, 1688
    -x regex, 1688
    directory ..., 1687
    file ..., 1687
compilest() (in module parser), 1669
complete() (rlcompleter.Completer method), 147
complete_statement() (in module sqlite3), 425
completedefault() (cmd.Cmd method), 1320
CompletedProcess (class in subprocess), 788
complex
    built-in function, 31
complex (built-in class), 8
Complex (class in numbers), 273
complex number, **1783**
    literals, 31
    object, 30
compress() (bz2.BZ2Compressor method), 451
compress() (in module bz2), 452
compress() (in module gzip), 448
compress() (in module itertools), 331
compress() (in module lzma), 455
compress() (in module zlib), 443
compress() (lzma.LZMACompressor method), 454
compress() (zlib.Compress method), 445
compress_size (zipfile.ZipInfo attribute), 464
compress_type (zipfile.ZipInfo attribute), 464
compressed (ipaddress.IPv4Address attribute), 1238
compressed (ipaddress.IPv4Network attribute), 1242
compressed (ipaddress.IPv6Address attribute), 1239
compressed (ipaddress.IPv6Network attribute), 1244
compression() (ssl.SSLSocket method), 846
CompressionError, 467
compressobj() (in module zlib), 444
COMSPEC, 563, 791
concat() (in module operator), 349
concatenation
    operation, 37
concurrent.futures (module), 781
Condition (class in asyncio), 922

Condition (class in multiprocessing), 754
Condition (class in threading), 733
condition (pdb command), 1521
condition() (msilib.Control method), 1715
Condition() (multiprocessing.managers.SyncManager method), 761
ConfigParser (class in configparser), 496
configparser (module), 483
configuration
    file, 483
    file, debugger, 1520
    file, path, 1631
configuration information, 1578
configure() (tkinter.ttk.Style method), 1356
configure_mock() (unittest.mock.Mock method), 1448
confstr() (in module os), 567
confstr_names (in module os), 567
conjugate() (complex number method), 31
conjugate() (decimal.Decimal method), 291
conjugate() (numbers.Complex method), 273
conn (smtpd.SMTPChannel attribute), 1191
connect() (asyncore.dispatcher method), 934
connect() (ftplib.FTP method), 1163
connect() (http.client.HTTPConnection method), 1158
connect() (in module sqlite3), 425
connect() (multiprocessing.managers.BaseManager method), 759
connect() (smtplib.SMTP method), 1185
connect() (socket.socket method), 821
connect_accepted_socket() (asyncio.BaseEventLoop method), 878
connect_ex() (socket.socket method), 822
connect_read_pipe() (asyncio.AbstractEventLoop method), 880
connect_write_pipe() (asyncio.AbstractEventLoop method), 880
Connection (class in multiprocessing), 752
Connection (class in sqlite3), 426
connection (sqlite3.Cursor attribute), 434
connection_lost() (asyncio.BaseProtocol method), 902
connection_made() (asyncio.BaseProtocol method), 902
ConnectionAbortedError, 91
ConnectionError, 91
ConnectionRefusedError, 91
ConnectionResetError, 91
ConnectRegistry() (in module winreg), 1718
const (optparse.Option attribute), 1760
constructor() (in module copyreg), 414

consumed (asyncio.LimitOverrunError attribute), 911
container
    iteration over, 36
Container (class in collections.abc), 223
Container (class in typing), 1383
contains() (in module operator), 350
content type
    MIME, 1035
content_manager (email.policy.EmailPolicy attribute), 969
content_type (email.headerregistry.ContentTypeHeader attribute), 976
ContentDispositionHeader (class in email.headerregistry), 976
ContentHandler (class in xml.sax.handler), 1087
ContentManager (class in email.contentmanager), 978
contents (ctypes._Pointer attribute), 725
ContentTooShortError, 1152
ContentTransferEncoding (class in email.headerregistry), 976
ContentTypeHeader (class in email.headerregistry), 976
Context (class in decimal), 297
context (ssl.SSLSocket attribute), 846
context management protocol, 79
context manager, 79, **1783**
context_diff() (in module difflib), 126
ContextDecorator (class in contextlib), 1590
contextlib (module), 1588
ContextManager (class in typing), 1384
contextmanager() (in module contextlib), 1588
contiguous, **1783**
contiguous (memoryview attribute), 73
continue (pdb command), 1522
CONTINUE_LOOP (opcode), 1696
Control (class in msilib), 1715
Control (class in tkinter.tix), 1360
control() (msilib.Dialog method), 1715
control() (select.kqueue method), 867
controlnames (in module curses.ascii), 683
controls() (ossaudiodev.oss_mixer_device method), 1266
ConversionError, 504
conversions
    numeric, 31
convert_arg_line_to_args() (argparse.ArgumentParser method), 620
convert_field() (string.Formatter method), 97
Cookie (class in http.cookiejar), 1216
CookieError, 1211
CookieJar (class in http.cookiejar), 1215

cookiejar (urllib.request.HTTPCookieProcessor attribute), 1135
CookiePolicy (class in http.cookiejar), 1215
Coordinated Universal Time, 582
Copy, 1367
copy
    module, 414
    protocol, 407
copy (module), 246
copy() (collections.deque method), 212
copy() (decimal.Context method), 298
copy() (dict method), 77
copy() (frozenset method), 74
copy() (hashlib.hash method), 511
copy() (hmac.HMAC method), 520
copy() (http.cookies.Morsel method), 1213
copy() (imaplib.IMAP4 method), 1172
copy() (in module copy), 246
copy() (in module multiprocessing.sharedctypes), 758
copy() (in module shutil), 393
copy() (pipes.Template method), 1740
copy() (sequence method), 39
copy() (types.MappingProxyType method), 245
copy() (zlib.Compress method), 445
copy() (zlib.Decompress method), 446
copy2() (in module shutil), 394
copy_abs() (decimal.Context method), 299
copy_abs() (decimal.Decimal method), 292
copy_decimal() (decimal.Context method), 298
copy_location() (in module ast), 1675
copy_negate() (decimal.Context method), 299
copy_negate() (decimal.Decimal method), 292
copy_sign() (decimal.Context method), 299
copy_sign() (decimal.Decimal method), 292
copyfile() (in module shutil), 392
copyfileobj() (in module shutil), 392
copying files, 392
copymode() (in module shutil), 393
copyreg (module), 414
copyright (built-in variable), 28
copyright (in module sys), 1564
copysign() (in module math), 276
copystat() (in module shutil), 393
copytree() (in module shutil), 394
coroutine, 1783
Coroutine (class in collections.abc), 225
Coroutine (class in typing), 1384
coroutine function, 1783
coroutine() (in module asyncio), 889
coroutine() (in module types), 246
CoroutineType (in module types), 243
cos() (in module cmath), 283
cos() (in module math), 279
cosh() (in module cmath), 283

cosh() (in module math), 280
count (tracemalloc.Statistic attribute), 1546
count (tracemalloc.StatisticDiff attribute), 1547
count() (array.array method), 233
count() (bytearray method), 55
count() (bytes method), 55
count() (collections.deque method), 212
count() (in module itertools), 331
count() (sequence method), 37
count() (str method), 44
count_diff (tracemalloc.StatisticDiff attribute), 1547
Counter (class in collections), 209
Counter (class in typing), 1384
countOf() (in module operator), 350
countTestCases() (unittest.TestCase method), 1431
countTestCases() (unittest.TestSuite method), 1433
CoverageResults (class in trace), 1538
cProfile (module), 1526
CPU time, 583
cpu_count() (in module multiprocessing), 751
cpu_count() (in module os), 567
CPython, 1783
crawl_delay() (urllib.robotparser.RobotFileParser method), 1152
CRC (zipfile.ZipInfo attribute), 464
crc32() (in module binascii), 1043
crc32() (in module zlib), 444
crc_hqx() (in module binascii), 1043
create() (imaplib.IMAP4 method), 1172
create() (in module venv), 1555
create() (venv.EnvBuilder method), 1554
create_aggregate() (sqlite3.Connection method), 427
create_archive() (in module zipapp), 1560
create_autospec() (in module unittest.mock), 1471
create_collation() (sqlite3.Connection method), 428
create_configuration() (venv.EnvBuilder method), 1555
create_connection() (asyncio.AbstractEventLoop method), 876
create_connection() (in module socket), 816
create_datagram_endpoint() (asyncio.AbstractEventLoop method), 877
create_decimal() (decimal.Context method), 298
create_decimal_from_float() (decimal.Context method), 298
create_default_context() (in module ssl), 835
create_function() (sqlite3.Connection method), 427
create_future() (asyncio.AbstractEventLoop method), 875
create_module() (importlib.abc.Loader method), 1653
create_module() (importlib.machinery.ExtensionFileLoader method), 1660

CREATE_NEW_CONSOLE (in module subprocess), 796
CREATE_NEW_PROCESS_GROUP (in module subprocess), 797
create_server() (asyncio.AbstractEventLoop method), 878
create_socket() (asyncore.dispatcher method), 934
create_stats() (profile.Profile method), 1527
create_string_buffer() (in module ctypes), 718
create_subprocess_exec() (in module asyncio), 915
create_subprocess_shell() (in module asyncio), 915
create_system (zipfile.ZipInfo attribute), 464
create_task() (asyncio.AbstractEventLoop method), 875
create_unicode_buffer() (in module ctypes), 718
create_unix_connection() (asyncio.AbstractEventLoop method), 877
create_unix_server() (asyncio.AbstractEventLoop method), 878
create_version (zipfile.ZipInfo attribute), 464
createAttribute() (xml.dom.Document method), 1074
createAttributeNS() (xml.dom.Document method), 1075
createComment() (xml.dom.Document method), 1074
createDocument() (xml.dom.DOMImplementation method), 1071
createDocumentType() (xml.dom.DOMImplementation method), 1071
createElement() (xml.dom.Document method), 1074
createElementNS() (xml.dom.Document method), 1074
createfilehandler() (tkinter.Widget.tk method), 1341
CreateKey() (in module winreg), 1718
CreateKeyEx() (in module winreg), 1719
createLock() (logging.Handler method), 628
createLock() (logging.NullHandler method), 651
createProcessingInstruction() (xml.dom.Document method), 1074
CreateRecord() (in module msilib), 1711
createSocket() (logging.handlers.SocketHandler method), 655
createTextNode() (xml.dom.Document method), 1074
credits (built-in variable), 28
critical() (in module logging), 636
critical() (logging.Logger method), 626
CRNCYSTR (in module locale), 1280
cross() (in module audioop), 1250
crypt
    module, 1730
crypt (module), 1732
crypt() (in module crypt), 1733
crypt(3), 1732, 1733
cryptography, 509
csv, 477
csv (module), 477
cte (email.headerregistry.ContentTransferEncoding attribute), 976
cte_type (email.policy.Policy attribute), 967
ctermid() (in module os), 526
ctime() (datetime.date method), 179
ctime() (datetime.datetime method), 187
ctime() (in module time), 584
ctrl() (in module curses.ascii), 683
CTRL_BREAK_EVENT (in module signal), 939
CTRL_C_EVENT (in module signal), 939
ctypes (module), 694
curdir (in module os), 568
currency() (in module locale), 1281
current() (tkinter.ttk.Combobox method), 1346
current_process() (in module multiprocessing), 751
current_task() (asyncio.Task class method), 894
current_thread() (in module threading), 727
CurrentByteIndex (xml.parsers.expat.xmlparser attribute), 1100
CurrentColumnNumber (xml.parsers.expat.xmlparser attribute), 1100
currentframe() (in module inspect), 1627
CurrentLineNumber (xml.parsers.expat.xmlparser attribute), 1100
curs_set() (in module curses), 664
curses (module), 662
curses.ascii (module), 681
curses.panel (module), 684
curses.textpad (module), 680
Cursor (class in sqlite3), 431
cursor() (sqlite3.Connection method), 426
cursyncup() (curses.window method), 671
Cut, 1367
cwd() (ftplib.FTP method), 1165
cwd() (pathlib.Path class method), 365
cycle() (in module itertools), 332
Cyclic Redundancy Check, 444

D

D_FMT (in module locale), 1279
D_T_FMT (in module locale), 1279
daemon (multiprocessing.Process attribute), 746
daemon (threading.Thread attribute), 730
data
    packing binary, 149
    tabular, 477
Data (class in plistlib), 507
data (collections.UserDict attribute), 221

data (collections.UserList attribute), 221
data (select.kevent attribute), 868
data (selectors.SelectorKey attribute), 870
data (urllib.request.Request attribute), 1132
data (xml.dom.Comment attribute), 1076
data (xml.dom.ProcessingInstruction attribute), 1077
data (xml.dom.Text attribute), 1077
data (xmlrpc.client.Binary attribute), 1227
data() (xml.etree.ElementTree.TreeBuilder method), 1067
data_open() (urllib.request.DataHandler method), 1138
data_received() (asyncio.Protocol method), 903
database
    Unicode, 139
DatabaseError, 436
databases, 422
datagram_received() (asyncio.DatagramProtocol method), 903
DatagramHandler (class in logging.handlers), 655
DatagramProtocol (class in asyncio), 902
DatagramRequestHandler (class in socketserver), 1202
DataHandler (class in urllib.request), 1131
date (class in datetime), 177
date() (datetime.datetime method), 184
date() (nntplib.NNTP method), 1181
date_time (zipfile.ZipInfo attribute), 463
date_time_string() (http.server.BaseHTTPRequestHandler method), 1209
DateHeader (class in email.headerregistry), 975
datetime (class in datetime), 181
DateTime (class in xmlrpc.client), 1226
datetime (email.headerregistry.DateHeader attribute), 975
datetime (module), 173
day (datetime.date attribute), 178
day (datetime.datetime attribute), 183
day_abbr (in module calendar), 206
day_name (in module calendar), 205
daylight (in module time), 590
Daylight Saving Time, 582
DbfilenameShelf (class in shelve), 416
dbm (module), 418
dbm.dumb (module), 422
dbm.gnu
    module, 416
dbm.gnu (module), 420
dbm.ndbm
    module, 416
dbm.ndbm (module), 421
dcgettext() (in module locale), 1283
debug (imaplib.IMAP4 attribute), 1175

DEBUG (in module re), 111
debug (shlex.shlex attribute), 1327
debug (zipfile.ZipFile attribute), 462
debug() (in module doctest), 1412
debug() (in module logging), 635
debug() (logging.Logger method), 625
debug() (pipes.Template method), 1739
debug() (unittest.TestCase method), 1425
debug() (unittest.TestSuite method), 1433
DEBUG_BYTECODE_SUFFIXES (in module importlib.machinery), 1657
DEBUG_COLLECTABLE (in module gc), 1615
DEBUG_LEAK (in module gc), 1615
DEBUG_SAVEALL (in module gc), 1615
debug_src() (in module doctest), 1413
DEBUG_STATS (in module gc), 1615
DEBUG_UNCOLLECTABLE (in module gc), 1615
debugger, 1367, 1569, 1575
    configuration file, 1520
debugging, 1517
    CGI, 1115
DebuggingServer (class in smtpd), 1190
debuglevel (http.client.HTTPResponse attribute), 1160
DebugRunner (class in doctest), 1413
Decimal (class in decimal), 289
decimal (module), 285
decimal() (in module unicodedata), 139
DecimalException (class in decimal), 303
decode
    Codecs, 154
decode (codecs.CodecInfo attribute), 155
decode() (bytearray method), 55
decode() (bytes method), 55
decode() (codecs.Codec method), 159
decode() (codecs.IncrementalDecoder method), 161
decode() (in module base64), 1040
decode() (in module codecs), 154
decode() (in module quopri), 1044
decode() (in module uu), 1044
decode() (json.JSONDecoder method), 1012
decode() (xmlrpc.client.Binary method), 1227
decode() (xmlrpc.client.DateTime method), 1226
decode_header() (in module email.header), 1000
decode_header() (in module nntplib), 1182
decode_params() (in module email.utils), 1006
decode_rfc2231() (in module email.utils), 1006
decode_source() (in module importlib.util), 1662
decodebytes() (in module base64), 1040
DecodedGenerator (class in email.generator), 964
decodestring() (in module base64), 1040
decodestring() (in module quopri), 1044
decomposition() (in module unicodedata), 140
decompress() (bz2.BZ2Decompressor method), 451

decompress() (in module bz2), 452
decompress() (in module gzip), 448
decompress() (in module lzma), 455
decompress() (in module zlib), 444
decompress() (lzma.LZMADecompressor method), 455
decompress() (zlib.Decompress method), 446
decompressobj() (in module zlib), 445
decorator, **1783**
DEDENT (in module token), 1679
dedent() (in module textwrap), 136
deepcopy() (in module copy), 246
def_prog_mode() (in module curses), 664
def_shell_mode() (in module curses), 664
default (in module email.policy), 970
DEFAULT (in module unittest.mock), 1469
default (inspect.Parameter attribute), 1622
default (optparse.Option attribute), 1760
default() (cmd.Cmd method), 1320
default() (json.JSONEncoder method), 1013
DEFAULT_BUFFER_SIZE (in module io), 571
default_bufsize (in module xml.dom.pulldom), 1085
default_exception_handler() (asyncio.AbstractEventLoop method), 881
default_factory (collections.defaultdict attribute), 215
DEFAULT_FORMAT (in module tarfile), 467
DEFAULT_IGNORES (in module filecmp), 385
default_open() (urllib.request.BaseHandler method), 1134
DEFAULT_PROTOCOL (in module pickle), 403
default_timer() (in module timeit), 1532
DefaultContext (class in decimal), 297
DefaultCookiePolicy (class in http.cookiejar), 1215
defaultdict (class in collections), 214
DefaultDict (class in typing), 1384
DefaultHandler() (xml.parsers.expat.xmlparser method), 1101
DefaultHandlerExpand() (xml.parsers.expat.xmlparser method), 1102
defaults() (configparser.ConfigParser method), 497
DefaultSelector (class in selectors), 871
defaultTestLoader (in module unittest), 1438
defaultTestResult() (unittest.TestCase method), 1431
defects (email.headerregistry.BaseHeader attribute), 974
defects (email.message.EmailMessage attribute), 958
defects (email.message.Message attribute), 996
defpath (in module os), 568
DefragResult (class in urllib.parse), 1149
DefragResultBytes (class in urllib.parse), 1149
degrees() (in module math), 279

degrees() (in module turtle), 1296
del
    statement, 39, 75
del_param() (email.message.EmailMessage method), 954
del_param() (email.message.Message method), 993
delattr() (built-in function), 8
delay() (in module turtle), 1308
delay_output() (in module curses), 664
delayload (http.cookiejar.FileCookieJar attribute), 1218
delch() (curses.window method), 671
dele() (poplib.POP3 method), 1168
delete() (ftplib.FTP method), 1165
delete() (imaplib.IMAP4 method), 1172
delete() (tkinter.ttk.Treeview method), 1353
DELETE_ATTR (opcode), 1698
DELETE_DEREF (opcode), 1701
DELETE_FAST (opcode), 1700
DELETE_GLOBAL (opcode), 1698
DELETE_NAME (opcode), 1698
DELETE_SUBSCR (opcode), 1696
deleteacl() (imaplib.IMAP4 method), 1172
deletefilehandler() (tkinter.Widget.tk method), 1341
DeleteKey() (in module winreg), 1719
DeleteKeyEx() (in module winreg), 1719
deleteln() (curses.window method), 671
deleteMe() (bdb.Breakpoint method), 1511
DeleteValue() (in module winreg), 1719
delimiter (csv.Dialect attribute), 481
delitem() (in module operator), 350
deliver_challenge() (in module multiprocessing.connection), 768
delocalize() (in module locale), 1281
demo_app() (in module wsgiref.simple_server), 1120
denominator (fractions.Fraction attribute), 312
denominator (numbers.Rational attribute), 274
DeprecationWarning, 92
deque (class in collections), 211
Deque (class in typing), 1383
dequeue() (logging.handlers.QueueListener method), 661
DER_cert_to_PEM_cert() (in module ssl), 837
derwin() (curses.window method), 671
DES
    cipher, 1732
description (sqlite3.Cursor attribute), 434
description() (nntplib.NNTP method), 1179
descriptions() (nntplib.NNTP method), 1179
descriptor, **1783**
dest (optparse.Option attribute), 1760
detach() (io.BufferedIOBase method), 575
detach() (io.TextIOBase method), 579
detach() (socket.socket method), 822

detach() (tkinter.ttk.Treeview method), 1353
detach() (weakref.finalize method), 238
Detach() (winreg.PyHKEY method), 1726
detect_api_mismatch() (in module test.support), 1508
detect_encoding() (in module tokenize), 1682
deterministic profiling, 1524
device_encoding() (in module os), 532
devnull (in module os), 569
DEVNULL (in module subprocess), 788
devpoll() (in module select), 862
DevpollSelector (class in selectors), 871
dgettext() (in module gettext), 1270
dgettext() (in module locale), 1283
Dialect (class in csv), 479
dialect (csv.csvreader attribute), 481
dialect (csv.csvwriter attribute), 482
Dialog (class in msilib), 1715
dict (2to3 fixer), 1498
dict (built-in class), 76
Dict (class in typing), 1384
dict() (multiprocessing.managers.SyncManager method), 761
dictConfig() (in module logging.config), 639
dictionary, 1784
    object, 75
    type, operations on, 75
dictionary view, 1784
DictReader (class in csv), 479
DictWriter (class in csv), 479
diff_bytes() (in module difflib), 129
diff_files (filecmp.dircmp attribute), 384
Differ (class in difflib), 125, 133
difference() (frozenset method), 74
difference_update() (frozenset method), 75
difflib (module), 125
digest() (hashlib.hash method), 511
digest() (hashlib.shake method), 511
digest() (hmac.HMAC method), 519
digest_size (hmac.HMAC attribute), 520
digit() (in module unicodedata), 139
digits (in module string), 95
dir() (built-in function), 8
dir() (ftplib.FTP method), 1165
dircmp (class in filecmp), 384
directory
    changing, 541
    creating, 544
    deleting, 395, 546
    site-packages, 1631
    traversal, 555, 556
    walking, 555, 556
Directory (class in msilib), 1714
directory ...

compileall command line option, 1687
DirEntry (class in os), 548
DirList (class in tkinter.tix), 1361
dirname() (in module os.path), 372
DirSelectBox (class in tkinter.tix), 1361
DirSelectDialog (class in tkinter.tix), 1361
DirTree (class in tkinter.tix), 1361
dis (module), 1690
dis() (dis.Bytecode method), 1691
dis() (in module dis), 1692
dis() (in module pickletools), 1703
disable (pdb command), 1521
disable() (bdb.Breakpoint method), 1511
disable() (in module faulthandler), 1516
disable() (in module gc), 1613
disable() (in module logging), 636
disable() (profile.Profile method), 1527
disable_interspersed_args() (optparse.OptionParser method), 1764
DisableReflectionKey() (in module winreg), 1723
disassemble() (in module dis), 1692
discard (http.cookiejar.Cookie attribute), 1222
discard() (frozenset method), 75
discard() (mailbox.Mailbox method), 1018
discard() (mailbox.MH method), 1024
discard_buffers() (asynchat.async_chat method), 937
disco() (in module dis), 1692
discover() (unittest.TestLoader method), 1435
disk_usage() (in module shutil), 395
dispatch_call() (bdb.Bdb method), 1513
dispatch_exception() (bdb.Bdb method), 1513
dispatch_line() (bdb.Bdb method), 1512
dispatch_return() (bdb.Bdb method), 1513
dispatch_table (pickle.Pickler attribute), 404
dispatcher (class in asyncore), 932
dispatcher_with_send (class in asyncore), 934
display (pdb command), 1522
display_name (email.headerregistry.Address attribute), 977
display_name (email.headerregistry.Group attribute), 978
displayhook() (in module sys), 1564
dist() (in module platform), 688
distance() (in module turtle), 1295
distb() (in module dis), 1692
distutils (module), 1549
divide() (decimal.Context method), 299
divide_int() (decimal.Context method), 299
DivisionByZero (class in decimal), 303
divmod() (built-in function), 9
divmod() (decimal.Context method), 299
DllCanUnloadNow() (in module ctypes), 718
DllGetClassObject() (in module ctypes), 719

dllhandle (in module sys), 1564
dngettext() (in module gettext), 1270
do_clear() (bdb.Bdb method), 1513
do_command() (curses.textpad.Textbox method), 680
do_GET() (http.server.SimpleHTTPRequestHandler method), 1210
do_handshake() (ssl.SSLSocket method), 844
do_HEAD() (http.server.SimpleHTTPRequestHandler method), 1209
do_POST() (http.server.CGIHTTPRequestHandler method), 1211
doc (json.JSONDecodeError attribute), 1013
doc_header (cmd.Cmd attribute), 1321
DocCGIXMLRPCRequestHandler (class in xmlrpc.server), 1235
DocFileSuite() (in module doctest), 1404
doCleanups() (unittest.TestCase method), 1432
docmd() (smtplib.SMTP method), 1184
docstring, **1784**
docstring (doctest.DocTest attribute), 1407
DocTest (class in doctest), 1406
doctest (module), 1391
DocTestFailure, 1413
DocTestFinder (class in doctest), 1408
DocTestParser (class in doctest), 1408
DocTestRunner (class in doctest), 1409
DocTestSuite() (in module doctest), 1405
doctype() (xml.etree.ElementTree.TreeBuilder method), 1067
doctype() (xml.etree.ElementTree.XMLParser method), 1067
documentation
  generation, 1390
  online, 1390
documentElement (xml.dom.Document attribute), 1074
DocXMLRPCRequestHandler (class in xmlrpc.server), 1235
DocXMLRPCServer (class in xmlrpc.server), 1235
domain (email.headerregistry.Address attribute), 978
domain (tracemalloc.DomainFilter attribute), 1544
domain (tracemalloc.Filter attribute), 1545
domain_initial_dot (http.cookiejar.Cookie attribute), 1222
domain_return_ok() (http.cookiejar.CookiePolicy method), 1219
domain_specified (http.cookiejar.Cookie attribute), 1222
DomainFilter (class in tracemalloc), 1544
DomainLiberal (http.cookiejar.DefaultCookiePolicy attribute), 1221
DomainRFC2965Match (http.cookiejar.DefaultCookiePolicy attribute), 1221
DomainStrict (http.cookiejar.DefaultCookiePolicy attribute), 1221
DomainStrictNoDots (http.cookiejar.DefaultCookiePolicy attribute), 1221
DomainStrictNonDomain (http.cookiejar.DefaultCookiePolicy attribute), 1221
DOMEventStream (class in xml.dom.pulldom), 1085
DOMException, 1077
DomstringSizeErr, 1077
done() (asyncio.Future method), 892
done() (concurrent.futures.Future method), 785
done() (in module turtle), 1310
done() (xdrlib.Unpacker method), 504
DONT_ACCEPT_BLANKLINE (in module doctest), 1398
DONT_ACCEPT_TRUE_FOR_1 (in module doctest), 1398
dont_write_bytecode (in module sys), 1565
doRollover() (logging.handlers.RotatingFileHandler method), 653
doRollover() (logging.handlers.TimedRotatingFileHandler method), 654
DOT (in module token), 1679
dot() (in module turtle), 1293
DOTALL (in module re), 112
doublequote (csv.Dialect attribute), 481
DOUBLESLASH (in module token), 1679
DOUBLESLASHEQUAL (in module token), 1679
DOUBLESTAR (in module token), 1679
DOUBLESTAREQUAL (in module token), 1679
doupdate() (in module curses), 664
down (pdb command), 1520
down() (in module turtle), 1296
drain() (asyncio.StreamWriter method), 910
drop_whitespace (textwrap.TextWrapper attribute), 138
dropwhile() (in module itertools), 332
dst() (datetime.datetime method), 185
dst() (datetime.time method), 191
dst() (datetime.timezone method), 199
dst() (datetime.tzinfo method), 193
DTDHandler (class in xml.sax.handler), 1087
duck-typing, **1784**
DumbWriter (class in formatter), 1708
dummy_threading (module), 806
dump() (in module ast), 1676
dump() (in module json), 1009
dump() (in module marshal), 418
dump() (in module pickle), 403
dump() (in module plistlib), 506
dump() (in module xml.etree.ElementTree), 1061
dump() (pickle.Pickler method), 404

dump() (tracemalloc.Snapshot method), 1545
dump_stats() (profile.Profile method), 1527
dump_stats() (pstats.Stats method), 1528
dump_traceback() (in module faulthandler), 1516
dump_traceback_later() (in module faulthandler), 1516
dumps() (in module json), 1010
dumps() (in module marshal), 418
dumps() (in module pickle), 403
dumps() (in module plistlib), 506
dumps() (in module xmlrpc.client), 1230
dup() (in module os), 532
dup() (socket.socket method), 822
dup2() (in module os), 533
DUP_TOP (opcode), 1694
DUP_TOP_TWO (opcode), 1694
DuplicateOptionError, 500
DuplicateSectionError, 500
dwFlags (subprocess.STARTUPINFO attribute), 796
DynamicClassAttribute() (in module types), 245

E

e (in module cmath), 284
e (in module math), 280
E2BIG (in module errno), 689
EACCES (in module errno), 689
EADDRINUSE (in module errno), 693
EADDRNOTAVAIL (in module errno), 693
EADV (in module errno), 691
EAFNOSUPPORT (in module errno), 693
EAFP, 1784
EAGAIN (in module errno), 689
EALREADY (in module errno), 693
east_asian_width() (in module unicodedata), 139
EBADE (in module errno), 691
EBADF (in module errno), 689
EBADFD (in module errno), 692
EBADMSG (in module errno), 692
EBADR (in module errno), 691
EBADRQC (in module errno), 691
EBADSLT (in module errno), 691
EBFONT (in module errno), 691
EBUSY (in module errno), 689
ECHILD (in module errno), 689
echo() (in module curses), 664
echochar() (curses.window method), 671
ECHRNG (in module errno), 690
ECOMM (in module errno), 691
ECONNABORTED (in module errno), 693
ECONNREFUSED (in module errno), 693
ECONNRESET (in module errno), 693
EDEADLK (in module errno), 690
EDEADLOCK (in module errno), 691
EDESTADDRREQ (in module errno), 692

edit() (curses.textpad.Textbox method), 680
EDOM (in module errno), 690
EDOTDOT (in module errno), 692
EDQUOT (in module errno), 694
EEXIST (in module errno), 689
EFAULT (in module errno), 689
EFBIG (in module errno), 689
effective() (in module bdb), 1515
ehlo() (smtplib.SMTP method), 1185
ehlo_or_helo_if_needed() (smtplib.SMTP method), 1185
EHOSTDOWN (in module errno), 693
EHOSTUNREACH (in module errno), 693
EIDRM (in module errno), 690
EILSEQ (in module errno), 692
EINPROGRESS (in module errno), 693
EINTR (in module errno), 688
EINVAL (in module errno), 689
EIO (in module errno), 689
EISCONN (in module errno), 693
EISDIR (in module errno), 689
EISNAM (in module errno), 694
EL2HLT (in module errno), 691
EL2NSYNC (in module errno), 690
EL3HLT (in module errno), 690
EL3RST (in module errno), 690
Element (class in xml.etree.ElementTree), 1063
element_create() (tkinter.ttk.Style method), 1357
element_names() (tkinter.ttk.Style method), 1358
element_options() (tkinter.ttk.Style method), 1358
ElementDeclHandler() (xml.parsers.expat.xmlparser method), 1100
elements() (collections.Counter method), 209
ElementTree (class in xml.etree.ElementTree), 1065
ELIBACC (in module errno), 692
ELIBBAD (in module errno), 692
ELIBEXEC (in module errno), 692
ELIBMAX (in module errno), 692
ELIBSCN (in module errno), 692
Ellinghouse, Lance, 1044
Ellipsis (built-in variable), 27
ELLIPSIS (in module doctest), 1398
ELLIPSIS (in module token), 1679
ELNRNG (in module errno), 690
ELOOP (in module errno), 690
email (module), 949
email.charset (module), 1001
email.contentmanager (module), 978
email.encoders (module), 1003
email.errors (module), 972
email.generator (module), 962
email.header (module), 998
email.headerregistry (module), 973
email.iterators (module), 1006

email.message (module), 950, 987
email.mime (module), 996
email.parser (module), 958
email.policy (module), 965
email.utils (module), 1004
EmailMessage (class in email.message), 951
EmailPolicy (class in email.policy), 969
EMFILE (in module errno), 689
emit() (logging.FileHandler method), 650
emit() (logging.Handler method), 629
emit() (logging.handlers.BufferingHandler method), 659
emit() (logging.handlers.DatagramHandler method), 655
emit() (logging.handlers.HTTPHandler method), 660
emit() (logging.handlers.NTEventLogHandler method), 658
emit() (logging.handlers.QueueHandler method), 660
emit() (logging.handlers.RotatingFileHandler method), 653
emit() (logging.handlers.SMTPHandler method), 658
emit() (logging.handlers.SocketHandler method), 654
emit() (logging.handlers.SysLogHandler method), 656
emit() (logging.handlers.TimedRotatingFileHandler method), 654
emit() (logging.handlers.WatchedFileHandler method), 651
emit() (logging.NullHandler method), 651
emit() (logging.StreamHandler method), 650
EMLINK (in module errno), 690
Empty, 804
empty (inspect.Parameter attribute), 1622
empty (inspect.Signature attribute), 1621
empty() (asyncio.Queue method), 924
empty() (multiprocessing.Queue method), 749
empty() (multiprocessing.SimpleQueue method), 750
empty() (queue.Queue method), 805
empty() (sched.scheduler method), 803
EMPTY_NAMESPACE (in module xml.dom), 1070
emptyline() (cmd.Cmd method), 1320
EMSGSIZE (in module errno), 692
EMULTIHOP (in module errno), 692
enable (pdb command), 1521
enable() (bdb.Breakpoint method), 1511
enable() (imaplib.IMAP4 method), 1172
enable() (in module cgitb), 1116
enable() (in module faulthandler), 1516
enable() (in module gc), 1613
enable() (profile.Profile method), 1527
enable_callback_tracebacks() (in module sqlite3), 426
enable_interspersed_args() (optparse.OptionParser method), 1765

enable_load_extension() (sqlite3.Connection method), 429
enable_traversal() (tkinter.ttk.Notebook method), 1348
ENABLE_USER_SITE (in module site), 1632
EnableReflectionKey() (in module winreg), 1723
ENAMETOOLONG (in module errno), 690
ENAVAIL (in module errno), 694
enclose() (curses.window method), 671
encode
    Codecs, 154
encode (codecs.CodecInfo attribute), 155
encode() (codecs.Codec method), 159
encode() (codecs.IncrementalEncoder method), 160
encode() (email.header.Header method), 1000
encode() (in module base64), 1040
encode() (in module codecs), 154
encode() (in module quopri), 1044
encode() (in module uu), 1044
encode() (json.JSONEncoder method), 1013
encode() (str method), 44
encode() (xmlrpc.client.Binary method), 1227
encode() (xmlrpc.client.DateTime method), 1226
encode_7or8bit() (in module email.encoders), 1004
encode_base64() (in module email.encoders), 1003
encode_noop() (in module email.encoders), 1004
encode_quopri() (in module email.encoders), 1003
encode_rfc2231() (in module email.utils), 1006
encodebytes() (in module base64), 1040
EncodedFile() (in module codecs), 156
encodePriority() (logging.handlers.SysLogHandler method), 656
encodestring() (in module base64), 1041
encodestring() (in module quopri), 1044
encoding
    base64, 1038
    quoted-printable, 1044
encoding (curses.window attribute), 671
ENCODING (in module tarfile), 467
ENCODING (in module tokenize), 1681
encoding (io.TextIOBase attribute), 579
encoding (UnicodeError attribute), 90
encodings.idna (module), 170
encodings.mbcs (module), 171
encodings.utf_8_sig (module), 171
encodings_map (in module mimetypes), 1036
encodings_map (mimetypes.MimeTypes attribute), 1037
end (UnicodeError attribute), 90
end() (re.match method), 119
end() (xml.etree.ElementTree.TreeBuilder method), 1067
end_fill() (in module turtle), 1299
END_FINALLY (opcode), 1697

end_headers() (http.server.BaseHTTPRequestHandler method), 1208
end_paragraph() (formatter.formatter method), 1705
end_poly() (in module turtle), 1305
EndCdataSectionHandler() (xml.parsers.expat.xmlparser method), 1101
EndDoctypeDeclHandler() (xml.parsers.expat.xmlparser method), 1100
endDocument() (xml.sax.handler.ContentHandler method), 1090
endElement() (xml.sax.handler.ContentHandler method), 1090
EndElementHandler() (xml.parsers.expat.xmlparser method), 1101
endElementNS() (xml.sax.handler.ContentHandler method), 1091
endheaders() (http.client.HTTPConnection method), 1159
ENDMARKER (in module token), 1679
EndNamespaceDeclHandler() (xml.parsers.expat.xmlparser method), 1101
endpos (re.match attribute), 119
endPrefixMapping() (xml.sax.handler.ContentHandler method), 1090
endswith() (bytearray method), 56
endswith() (bytes method), 56
endswith() (str method), 44
endwin() (in module curses), 664
ENETDOWN (in module errno), 693
ENETRESET (in module errno), 693
ENETUNREACH (in module errno), 693
ENFILE (in module errno), 689
ENOANO (in module errno), 691
ENOBUFS (in module errno), 693
ENOCSI (in module errno), 691
ENODATA (in module errno), 691
ENODEV (in module errno), 689
ENOENT (in module errno), 688
ENOEXEC (in module errno), 689
ENOLCK (in module errno), 690
ENOLINK (in module errno), 691
ENOMEM (in module errno), 689
ENOMSG (in module errno), 690
ENONET (in module errno), 691
ENOPKG (in module errno), 691
ENOPROTOOPT (in module errno), 692
ENOSPC (in module errno), 690
ENOSR (in module errno), 691
ENOSTR (in module errno), 691
ENOSYS (in module errno), 690
ENOTBLK (in module errno), 689
ENOTCONN (in module errno), 693
ENOTDIR (in module errno), 689
ENOTEMPTY (in module errno), 690
ENOTNAM (in module errno), 694
ENOTSOCK (in module errno), 692
ENOTTY (in module errno), 689
ENOTUNIQ (in module errno), 692
enqueue() (logging.handlers.QueueHandler method), 660
enqueue_sentinel() (logging.handlers.QueueListener method), 661
ensure_directories() (venv.EnvBuilder method), 1555
ensure_future() (in module asyncio), 895
ensurepip (module), 1549
enter() (sched.scheduler method), 803
enter_context() (contextlib.ExitStack method), 1592
enterabs() (sched.scheduler method), 803
entities (xml.dom.DocumentType attribute), 1074
EntityDeclHandler() (xml.parsers.expat.xmlparser method), 1101
entitydefs (in module html.entities), 1052
EntityResolver (class in xml.sax.handler), 1087
Enum (class in enum), 254
enum (module), 254
enum_certificates() (in module ssl), 838
enum_crls() (in module ssl), 838
enumerate() (built-in function), 9
enumerate() (in module threading), 727
EnumKey() (in module winreg), 1720
EnumValue() (in module winreg), 1720
EnvBuilder (class in venv), 1554
environ (in module os), 526
environ (in module posix), 1730
environb (in module os), 526
environment variable
    <protocol>_proxy, 1129
    AUDIODEV, 1263
    BROWSER, 1107, 1108
    COLS, 669
    COLUMNS, 669
    COMSPEC, 563, 791
    HOME, 372
    HOMEDRIVE, 372
    HOMEPATH, 372
    http_proxy, 1127, 1140
    IDLESTARTUP, 1370
    KDEDIR, 1108
    LANG, 1269, 1271, 1278, 1280
    LANGUAGE, 1269, 1271
    LC_ALL, 1269, 1271
    LC_MESSAGES, 1269, 1271
    LINES, 664, 669

LNAME, 662
LOGNAME, 528, 662
MIXERDEV, 1264
no_proxy, 1130
PAGER, 1390
PATH, 558, 562, 568, 1107, 1114, 1116
POSIXLY_CORRECT, 622
PYTHON_DOM, 1070
PYTHONASYNCIODEBUG, 882, 926
PYTHONDOCS, 1391
PYTHONDONTWRITEBYTECODE, 1565
PYTHONFAULTHANDLER, 1515
PYTHONIOENCODING, 1577
PYTHONLEGACYWINDOWSFSENCODING, 1576
PYTHONNOUSERSITE, 1632, 1633
PYTHONPATH, 1114, 1572
PYTHONSTARTUP, 145, 1370, 1571, 1632
PYTHONTRACEMALLOC, 1539, 1544
PYTHONUSERBASE, 1632, 1633
SystemRoot, 793
TEMP, 387
TERM, 668
TIX_LIBRARY, 1360
TMP, 387
TMPDIR, 387
TZ, 588, 589
USER, 662
USERNAME, 528, 662
USERPROFILE, 372
environment variables
    deleting, 532
    setting, 529
EnvironmentError, 90
Environments
    virtual, 1551
EnvironmentVarGuard (class in test.support), 1509
ENXIO (in module errno), 689
eof (bz2.BZ2Decompressor attribute), 451
eof (lzma.LZMADecompressor attribute), 455
eof (shlex.shlex attribute), 1327
eof (ssl.MemoryBIO attribute), 859
eof (zlib.Decompress attribute), 446
eof_received() (asyncio.Protocol method), 903
EOFError, 86
EOPNOTSUPP (in module errno), 693
EOVERFLOW (in module errno), 692
EPERM (in module errno), 688
EPFNOSUPPORT (in module errno), 693
epilogue (email.message.EmailMessage attribute), 958
epilogue (email.message.Message attribute), 996
EPIPE (in module errno), 690
epoch, 582

epoll() (in module select), 862
EpollSelector (class in selectors), 871
EPROTO (in module errno), 691
EPROTONOSUPPORT (in module errno), 692
EPROTOTYPE (in module errno), 692
eq() (in module operator), 348
EQEQUAL (in module token), 1679
EQUAL (in module token), 1679
ERA (in module locale), 1280
ERA_D_FMT (in module locale), 1280
ERA_D_T_FMT (in module locale), 1280
ERA_T_FMT (in module locale), 1280
ERANGE (in module errno), 690
erase() (curses.window method), 671
erasechar() (in module curses), 664
EREMCHG (in module errno), 692
EREMOTE (in module errno), 691
EREMOTEIO (in module errno), 694
ERESTART (in module errno), 692
erf() (in module math), 280
erfc() (in module math), 280
EROFS (in module errno), 690
ERR (in module curses), 675
errcheck (ctypes._FuncPtr attribute), 715
errcode (xmlrpc.client.ProtocolError attribute), 1228
errmsg (xmlrpc.client.ProtocolError attribute), 1228
errno
    module, 87
errno (module), 688
errno (OSError attribute), 88
Error, 396, 436, 480, 500, 504, 1033, 1041, 1043, 1045, 1107, 1255, 1258, 1277
error, 115, 149, 246, 418, 420–422, 443, 525, 622, 663, 807, 813, 862, 1097, 1249, 1740, 1744
error() (argparse.ArgumentParser method), 620
error() (in module logging), 636
error() (logging.Logger method), 626
error() (urllib.request.OpenerDirector method), 1133
error() (xml.sax.handler.ErrorHandler method), 1092
error_body (wsgiref.handlers.BaseHandler attribute), 1125
error_content_type (http.server.BaseHTTPRequestHandler attribute), 1207
error_headers (wsgiref.handlers.BaseHandler attribute), 1125
error_leader() (shlex.shlex method), 1326
error_message_format (http.server.BaseHTTPRequestHandler attribute), 1207
error_output() (wsgiref.handlers.BaseHandler method), 1124
error_perm, 1163
error_proto, 1163, 1167

error_received() (asyncio.DatagramProtocol method), 903
error_reply, 1163
error_status (wsgiref.handlers.BaseHandler attribute), 1125
error_temp, 1163
ErrorByteIndex (xml.parsers.expat.xmlparser attribute), 1100
errorcode (in module errno), 688
ErrorCode (xml.parsers.expat.xmlparser attribute), 1100
ErrorColumnNumber (xml.parsers.expat.xmlparser attribute), 1100
ErrorHandler (class in xml.sax.handler), 1088
ErrorLineNumber (xml.parsers.expat.xmlparser attribute), 1100
Errors
    logging, 623
errors (io.TextIOBase attribute), 579
errors (unittest.TestLoader attribute), 1434
errors (unittest.TestResult attribute), 1436
ErrorString() (in module xml.parsers.expat), 1097
ERRORTOKEN (in module token), 1679
escape (shlex.shlex attribute), 1326
escape() (in module cgi), 1113
escape() (in module glob), 390
escape() (in module html), 1047
escape() (in module re), 115
escape() (in module xml.sax.saxutils), 1092
escapechar (csv.Dialect attribute), 481
escapedquotes (shlex.shlex attribute), 1326
ESHUTDOWN (in module errno), 693
ESOCKTNOSUPPORT (in module errno), 693
ESPIPE (in module errno), 690
ESRCH (in module errno), 688
ESRMNT (in module errno), 691
ESTALE (in module errno), 694
ESTRPIPE (in module errno), 692
ETIME (in module errno), 691
ETIMEDOUT (in module errno), 693
Etiny() (decimal.Context method), 298
ETOOMANYREFS (in module errno), 693
Etop() (decimal.Context method), 299
ETXTBSY (in module errno), 689
EUCLEAN (in module errno), 694
EUNATCH (in module errno), 690
EUSERS (in module errno), 692
eval
    built-in function, 81, 248, 249, 1669
eval() (built-in function), 10
Event (class in asyncio), 921
Event (class in multiprocessing), 754
Event (class in threading), 736
event scheduling, 802

event() (msilib.Control method), 1715
Event() (multiprocessing.managers.SyncManager method), 761
events (selectors.SelectorKey attribute), 870
events (widgets), 1340
EWOULDBLOCK (in module errno), 690
EX_CANTCREAT (in module os), 560
EX_CONFIG (in module os), 560
EX_DATAERR (in module os), 559
EX_IOERR (in module os), 560
EX_NOHOST (in module os), 559
EX_NOINPUT (in module os), 559
EX_NOPERM (in module os), 560
EX_NOTFOUND (in module os), 560
EX_NOUSER (in module os), 559
EX_OK (in module os), 559
EX_OSERR (in module os), 560
EX_OSFILE (in module os), 560
EX_PROTOCOL (in module os), 560
EX_SOFTWARE (in module os), 559
EX_TEMPFAIL (in module os), 560
EX_UNAVAILABLE (in module os), 559
EX_USAGE (in module os), 559
Example (class in doctest), 1407
example (doctest.DocTestFailure attribute), 1413
example (doctest.UnexpectedException attribute), 1413
examples (doctest.DocTest attribute), 1407
exc_info (doctest.UnexpectedException attribute), 1413
exc_info() (in module sys), 1565
exc_msg (doctest.Example attribute), 1407
exc_type (traceback.TracebackException attribute), 1607
excel (class in csv), 480
excel_tab (class in csv), 480
except
    statement, 85
except (2to3 fixer), 1498
excepthook() (in module sys), 1116, 1565
Exception, 86
EXCEPTION (in module tkinter), 1341
exception() (asyncio.Future method), 892
exception() (asyncio.StreamReader method), 909
exception() (concurrent.futures.Future method), 785
exception() (in module logging), 636
exception() (logging.Logger method), 626
exceptions
    in CGI scripts, 1116
EXDEV (in module errno), 689
exec
    built-in function, 10, 81, 1669
exec (2to3 fixer), 1498
exec() (built-in function), 10

exec_module() (importlib.abc.InspectLoader method), 1655
exec_module() (importlib.abc.Loader method), 1653
exec_module() (importlib.abc.SourceLoader method), 1657
exec_module() (importlib.machinery.ExtensionFileLoader method), 1660
exec_prefix (in module sys), 1565
execfile (2to3 fixer), 1498
execl() (in module os), 558
execle() (in module os), 558
execlp() (in module os), 558
execlpe() (in module os), 558
executable (in module sys), 1565
Executable Zip Files, 1559
Execute() (msilib.View method), 1712
execute() (sqlite3.Connection method), 427
execute() (sqlite3.Cursor method), 431
executemany() (sqlite3.Connection method), 427
executemany() (sqlite3.Cursor method), 432
executescript() (sqlite3.Connection method), 427
executescript() (sqlite3.Cursor method), 433
ExecutionLoader (class in importlib.abc), 1655
Executor (class in concurrent.futures), 781
execv() (in module os), 558
execve() (in module os), 558
execvp() (in module os), 558
execvpe() (in module os), 558
ExFileSelectBox (class in tkinter.tix), 1361
EXFULL (in module errno), 691
exists() (in module os.path), 372
exists() (pathlib.Path method), 366
exists() (tkinter.ttk.Treeview method), 1353
exit (built-in variable), 28
exit() (argparse.ArgumentParser method), 620
exit() (in module _thread), 807
exit() (in module sys), 1566
exitcode (multiprocessing.Process attribute), 746
exitfunc (2to3 fixer), 1498
exitonclick() (in module turtle), 1312
ExitStack (class in contextlib), 1592
exp() (decimal.Context method), 299
exp() (decimal.Decimal method), 292
exp() (in module cmath), 282
exp() (in module math), 278
expand() (re.match method), 117
expand_tabs (textwrap.TextWrapper attribute), 137
ExpandEnvironmentStrings() (in module winreg), 1720
expandNode() (xml.dom.pulldom.DOMEventStream method), 1085
expandtabs() (bytearray method), 60
expandtabs() (bytes method), 60
expandtabs() (str method), 44

expanduser() (in module os.path), 372
expanduser() (pathlib.Path method), 366
expandvars() (in module os.path), 373
Expat, 1097
ExpatError, 1097
expect() (telnetlib.Telnet method), 1194
expected (asyncio.IncompleteReadError attribute), 911
expectedFailure() (in module unittest), 1422
expectedFailures (unittest.TestResult attribute), 1436
expires (http.cookiejar.Cookie attribute), 1222
exploded (ipaddress.IPv4Address attribute), 1238
exploded (ipaddress.IPv4Network attribute), 1242
exploded (ipaddress.IPv6Address attribute), 1239
exploded (ipaddress.IPv6Network attribute), 1244
expm1() (in module math), 278
expovariate() (in module random), 316
expr() (in module parser), 1668
expression, **1784**
expunge() (imaplib.IMAP4 method), 1172
extend() (array.array method), 233
extend() (collections.deque method), 212
extend() (sequence method), 39
extend() (xml.etree.ElementTree.Element method), 1064
extend_path() (in module pkgutil), 1643
EXTENDED_ARG (opcode), 1701
ExtendedContext (class in decimal), 297
ExtendedInterpolation (class in configparser), 488
extendleft() (collections.deque method), 212
extension module, **1784**
EXTENSION_SUFFIXES (in module importlib.machinery), 1657
ExtensionFileLoader (class in importlib.machinery), 1660
extensions_map (http.server.SimpleHTTPRequestHandler attribute), 1209
External Data Representation, 402, 502
external_attr (zipfile.ZipInfo attribute), 464
ExternalClashError, 1034
ExternalEntityParserCreate() (xml.parsers.expat.xmlparser method), 1099
ExternalEntityRefHandler() (xml.parsers.expat.xmlparser method), 1102
extra (zipfile.ZipInfo attribute), 464
extract() (tarfile.TarFile method), 469
extract() (traceback.StackSummary class method), 1608
extract() (zipfile.ZipFile method), 460
extract_cookies() (http.cookiejar.CookieJar method), 1216

extract_stack() (in module traceback), 1606
extract_tb() (in module traceback), 1606
extract_version (zipfile.ZipInfo attribute), 464
extractall() (tarfile.TarFile method), 469
extractall() (zipfile.ZipFile method), 460
ExtractError, 467
extractfile() (tarfile.TarFile method), 470
extsep (in module os), 568

F

f-string, 1784
f_contiguous (memoryview attribute), 73
F_LOCK (in module os), 534
F_OK (in module os), 541
F_TEST (in module os), 534
F_TLOCK (in module os), 534
F_ULOCK (in module os), 534
fabs() (in module math), 276
factorial() (in module math), 276
factory() (importlib.util.LazyLoader class method), 1664
fail() (unittest.TestCase method), 1431
FAIL_FAST (in module doctest), 1400
failfast (unittest.TestResult attribute), 1436
failureException (unittest.TestCase attribute), 1431
failures (unittest.TestResult attribute), 1436
False, 29, 82
false, 29
False (Built-in object), 29
False (built-in variable), 27
family (socket.socket attribute), 827
FancyURLopener (class in urllib.request), 1143
fast (pickle.Pickler attribute), 405
fatalError() (xml.sax.handler.ErrorHandler method), 1092
Fault (class in xmlrpc.client), 1228
faultCode (xmlrpc.client.Fault attribute), 1228
faulthandler (module), 1515
faultString (xmlrpc.client.Fault attribute), 1228
fchdir() (in module os), 542
fchmod() (in module os), 533
fchown() (in module os), 533
FCICreate() (in module msilib), 1711
fcntl (module), 1737
fcntl() (in module fcntl), 1737
fd (selectors.SelectorKey attribute), 870
fd() (in module turtle), 1290
fdatasync() (in module os), 533
fdopen() (in module os), 532
Feature (class in msilib), 1715
feature_external_ges (in module xml.sax.handler), 1088
feature_external_pes (in module xml.sax.handler), 1088

feature_namespace_prefixes (in module xml.sax.handler), 1088
feature_namespaces (in module xml.sax.handler), 1088
feature_string_interning (in module xml.sax.handler), 1088
feature_validation (in module xml.sax.handler), 1088
feed() (email.parser.BytesFeedParser method), 959
feed() (html.parser.HTMLParser method), 1048
feed() (xml.etree.ElementTree.XMLParser method), 1067
feed() (xml.etree.ElementTree.XMLPullParser method), 1068
feed() (xml.sax.xmlreader.IncrementalParser method), 1095
feed_data() (asyncio.StreamReader method), 909
feed_eof() (asyncio.StreamReader method), 909
FeedParser (class in email.parser), 960
fetch() (imaplib.IMAP4 method), 1172
Fetch() (msilib.View method), 1712
fetchall() (sqlite3.Cursor method), 434
fetchmany() (sqlite3.Cursor method), 433
fetchone() (sqlite3.Cursor method), 433
fflags (select.kevent attribute), 868
field_size_limit() (in module csv), 478
fieldnames (csv.csvreader attribute), 482
fields (uuid.UUID attribute), 1196
file
    .ini, 483
    .pdbrc, 1520
    byte-code, 1686, 1773
    configuration, 483
    copying, 392
    debugger configuration, 1520
    large files, 1729
    mime.types, 1036
    path configuration, 1631
    plist, 505
    temporary, 385
file (pyclbr.Class attribute), 1686
file (pyclbr.Function attribute), 1686
file ...
    compileall command line option, 1687
file control
    UNIX, 1737
file name
    temporary, 385
file object, 1784
    io module, 570
    open() built-in function, 16
file-like object, 1784
FILE_ATTRIBUTE_ARCHIVE (in module stat), 382

FILE_ATTRIBUTE_COMPRESSED (in module stat), 382
FILE_ATTRIBUTE_DEVICE (in module stat), 382
FILE_ATTRIBUTE_DIRECTORY (in module stat), 382
FILE_ATTRIBUTE_ENCRYPTED (in module stat), 382
FILE_ATTRIBUTE_HIDDEN (in module stat), 382
FILE_ATTRIBUTE_INTEGRITY_STREAM (in module stat), 382
FILE_ATTRIBUTE_NO_SCRUB_DATA (in module stat), 382
FILE_ATTRIBUTE_NORMAL (in module stat), 382
FILE_ATTRIBUTE_NOT_CONTENT_INDEXED (in module stat), 382
FILE_ATTRIBUTE_OFFLINE (in module stat), 382
FILE_ATTRIBUTE_READONLY (in module stat), 382
FILE_ATTRIBUTE_REPARSE_POINT (in module stat), 382
FILE_ATTRIBUTE_SPARSE_FILE (in module stat), 382
FILE_ATTRIBUTE_SYSTEM (in module stat), 382
FILE_ATTRIBUTE_TEMPORARY (in module stat), 382
FILE_ATTRIBUTE_VIRTUAL (in module stat), 382
file_dispatcher (class in asyncore), 934
file_open() (urllib.request.FileHandler method), 1137
file_size (zipfile.ZipInfo attribute), 464
file_wrapper (class in asyncore), 934
filecmp (module), 383
fileConfig() (in module logging.config), 640
FileCookieJar (class in http.cookiejar), 1215
FileEntry (class in tkinter.tix), 1361
FileExistsError, 91
FileFinder (class in importlib.machinery), 1658
FileHandler (class in logging), 650
FileHandler (class in urllib.request), 1131
FileInput (class in fileinput), 377
fileinput (module), 376
FileIO (class in io), 576
filelineno() (in module fileinput), 377
FileLoader (class in importlib.abc), 1655
filemode() (in module stat), 379
filename (doctest.DocTest attribute), 1407
filename (http.cookiejar.FileCookieJar attribute), 1218
filename (OSError attribute), 88
filename (traceback.TracebackException attribute), 1607
filename (tracemalloc.Frame attribute), 1545
filename (zipfile.ZipFile attribute), 462
filename (zipfile.ZipInfo attribute), 463
filename() (in module fileinput), 376
filename2 (OSError attribute), 88
filename_only (in module tabnanny), 1685
filename_pattern (tracemalloc.Filter attribute), 1545
filenames
    pathname expansion, 389
    wildcard expansion, 390
fileno() (http.client.HTTPResponse method), 1159
fileno() (in module fileinput), 377
fileno() (io.IOBase method), 573
fileno() (multiprocessing.Connection method), 752
fileno() (ossaudiodev.oss_audio_device method), 1264
fileno() (ossaudiodev.oss_mixer_device method), 1266
fileno() (select.devpoll method), 864
fileno() (select.epoll method), 865
fileno() (select.kqueue method), 867
fileno() (selectors.DevpollSelector method), 871
fileno() (selectors.EpollSelector method), 871
fileno() (selectors.KqueueSelector method), 871
fileno() (socket.socket method), 822
fileno() (socketserver.BaseServer method), 1200
fileno() (telnetlib.Telnet method), 1194
FileNotFoundError, 91
fileobj (selectors.SelectorKey attribute), 869
FileSelectBox (class in tkinter.tix), 1361
FileType (class in argparse), 616
FileWrapper (class in wsgiref.util), 1118
fill() (in module textwrap), 135
fill() (textwrap.TextWrapper method), 139
fillcolor() (in module turtle), 1298
filling() (in module turtle), 1299
filter (2to3 fixer), 1498
Filter (class in logging), 630
Filter (class in tracemalloc), 1544
filter (select.kevent attribute), 867
filter() (built-in function), 11
filter() (in module curses), 664
filter() (in module fnmatch), 391
filter() (logging.Filter method), 630
filter() (logging.Handler method), 628
filter() (logging.Logger method), 627
FILTER_DIR (in module unittest.mock), 1472
filter_traces() (tracemalloc.Snapshot method), 1545
filterfalse() (in module itertools), 332
filterwarnings() (in module warnings), 1587
finalize (class in weakref), 238

find() (bytearray method), 56
find() (bytes method), 56
find() (doctest.DocTestFinder method), 1408
find() (in module gettext), 1271
find() (mmap.mmap method), 946
find() (str method), 45
find() (xml.etree.ElementTree.Element method), 1064
find() (xml.etree.ElementTree.ElementTree method), 1065
find_class() (pickle protocol), 412
find_class() (pickle.Unpickler method), 405
find_library() (in module ctypes.util), 719
find_loader() (importlib.abc.PathEntryFinder method), 1653
find_loader() (importlib.machinery.FileFinder method), 1659
find_loader() (in module importlib), 1650
find_loader() (in module pkgutil), 1644
find_longest_match() (difflib.SequenceMatcher method), 130
find_module() (imp.NullImporter method), 1777
find_module() (importlib.abc.Finder method), 1652
find_module() (importlib.abc.MetaPathFinder method), 1652
find_module() (importlib.abc.PathEntryFinder method), 1653
find_module() (importlib.machinery.PathFinder class method), 1658
find_module() (in module imp), 1774
find_module() (zipimport.zipimporter method), 1642
find_msvcrt() (in module ctypes.util), 719
find_spec() (importlib.abc.MetaPathFinder method), 1652
find_spec() (importlib.abc.PathEntryFinder method), 1652
find_spec() (importlib.machinery.FileFinder method), 1659
find_spec() (importlib.machinery.PathFinder class method), 1658
find_spec() (in module importlib.util), 1662
find_unused_port() (in module test.support), 1508
find_user_password() (urllib.request.HTTPPasswordMgr method), 1136
findall() (in module re), 114
findall() (re.regex method), 117
findall() (xml.etree.ElementTree.Element method), 1064
findall() (xml.etree.ElementTree.ElementTree method), 1065
findCaller() (logging.Logger method), 627
finder, **1784**

Finder (class in importlib.abc), 1652
findfactor() (in module audioop), 1250
findfile() (in module test.support), 1504
findfit() (in module audioop), 1250
finditer() (in module re), 114
finditer() (re.regex method), 117
findlabels() (in module dis), 1693
findlinestarts() (in module dis), 1693
findmatch() (in module mailcap), 1017
findmax() (in module audioop), 1250
findtext() (xml.etree.ElementTree.Element method), 1064
findtext() (xml.etree.ElementTree.ElementTree method), 1065
finish() (socketserver.BaseRequestHandler method), 1202
finish_request() (socketserver.BaseServer method), 1201
firstChild (xml.dom.Node attribute), 1072
firstkey() (dbm.gnu.gdbm method), 420
firstweekday() (in module calendar), 205
fix_missing_locations() (in module ast), 1675
fix_sentence_endings (textwrap.TextWrapper attribute), 138
Flag (class in enum), 254
flag_bits (zipfile.ZipInfo attribute), 464
flags (in module sys), 1566
flags (re.regex attribute), 117
flags (select.kevent attribute), 867
flash() (in module curses), 664
flatten() (email.generator.BytesGenerator method), 963
flatten() (email.generator.Generator method), 964
flattening
    objects, 401
float
    built-in function, 31
float (built-in class), 11
float_info (in module sys), 1566
float_repr_style (in module sys), 1567
floating point
    literals, 31
    object, 30
FloatingPointError, 86, 1634
FloatOperation (class in decimal), 304
flock() (in module fcntl), 1738
floor division, **1784**
floor() (in module math), 31, 276
floordiv() (in module operator), 348
flush() (bz2.BZ2Compressor method), 451
flush() (formatter.writer method), 1707
flush() (io.BufferedWriter method), 578
flush() (io.IOBase method), 573
flush() (logging.Handler method), 628

flush() (logging.handlers.BufferingHandler method), 659
flush() (logging.handlers.MemoryHandler method), 659
flush() (logging.StreamHandler method), 650
flush() (lzma.LZMACompressor method), 454
flush() (mailbox.Mailbox method), 1020
flush() (mailbox.Maildir method), 1022
flush() (mailbox.MH method), 1024
flush() (mmap.mmap method), 946
flush() (zlib.Compress method), 445
flush() (zlib.Decompress method), 446
flush_headers() (http.server.BaseHTTPRequestHandler method), 1209
flush_softspace() (formatter.formatter method), 1706
flushinp() (in module curses), 664
FlushKey() (in module winreg), 1720
fma() (decimal.Context method), 299
fma() (decimal.Decimal method), 292
fmod() (in module math), 276
FMT_BINARY (in module plistlib), 507
FMT_XML (in module plistlib), 507
fnmatch (module), 390
fnmatch() (in module fnmatch), 391
fnmatchcase() (in module fnmatch), 391
focus() (tkinter.ttk.Treeview method), 1353
fold (datetime.datetime attribute), 183
fold (datetime.time attribute), 190
fold() (email.headerregistry.BaseHeader method), 974
fold() (email.policy.Compat32 method), 971
fold() (email.policy.EmailPolicy method), 970
fold() (email.policy.Policy method), 969
fold_binary() (email.policy.Compat32 method), 972
fold_binary() (email.policy.EmailPolicy method), 970
fold_binary() (email.policy.Policy method), 969
FOR_ITER (opcode), 1700
forget() (in module test.support), 1504
forget() (tkinter.ttk.Notebook method), 1348
fork() (in module os), 560
fork() (in module pty), 1736
ForkingMixIn (class in socketserver), 1199
ForkingTCPServer (class in socketserver), 1199
ForkingUDPServer (class in socketserver), 1199
forkpty() (in module os), 560
Form (class in tkinter.tix), 1363
format (memoryview attribute), 72
format (struct.Struct attribute), 154
format() (built-in function), 12
format() (in module locale), 1281
format() (logging.Formatter method), 629
format() (logging.Handler method), 629

format() (pprint.PrettyPrinter method), 249
format() (str method), 45
format() (string.Formatter method), 96
format() (traceback.StackSummary method), 1608
format() (traceback.TracebackException method), 1608
format() (tracemalloc.Traceback method), 1547
format_datetime() (in module email.utils), 1006
format_exc() (in module traceback), 1607
format_exception() (in module traceback), 1606
format_exception_only() (in module traceback), 1606
format_exception_only() (traceback.TracebackException method), 1608
format_field() (string.Formatter method), 97
format_help() (argparse.ArgumentParser method), 619
format_list() (in module traceback), 1606
format_map() (str method), 45
format_stack() (in module traceback), 1607
format_stack_entry() (bdb.Bdb method), 1514
format_string() (in module locale), 1281
format_tb() (in module traceback), 1607
format_usage() (argparse.ArgumentParser method), 619
FORMAT_VALUE (opcode), 1701
formataddr() (in module email.utils), 1004
formatargspec() (in module inspect), 1625
formatargvalues() (in module inspect), 1625
formatdate() (in module email.utils), 1005
FormatError, 1034
FormatError() (in module ctypes), 719
formatException() (logging.Formatter method), 630
formatmonth() (calendar.HTMLCalendar method), 204
formatmonth() (calendar.TextCalendar method), 204
formatStack() (logging.Formatter method), 630
Formatter (class in logging), 629
Formatter (class in string), 96
formatter (module), 1705
formatTime() (logging.Formatter method), 629
formatting, bytearray (%), 64
formatting, bytes (%), 64
formatting, string (%), 51
formatwarning() (in module warnings), 1587
formatyear() (calendar.HTMLCalendar method), 204
formatyear() (calendar.TextCalendar method), 204
formatyearpage() (calendar.HTMLCalendar method), 204
Fortran contiguous, 1783
forward() (in module turtle), 1290
found_terminator() (asynchat.async_chat method), 937
fpathconf() (in module os), 533

fpectl (module), 1633
fqdn (smtpd.SMTPChannel attribute), 1191
Fraction (class in fractions), 311
fractions (module), 311
Frame (class in tracemalloc), 1545
frame (tkinter.scrolledtext.ScrolledText attribute), 1364
FrameSummary (class in traceback), 1609
FrameType (in module types), 244
freeze_support() (in module multiprocessing), 751
frexp() (in module math), 277
from_address() (ctypes._CData method), 720
from_buffer() (ctypes._CData method), 720
from_buffer_copy() (ctypes._CData method), 720
from_bytes() (int class method), 33
from_callable() (inspect.Signature class method), 1621
from_decimal() (fractions.Fraction method), 312
from_exception() (traceback.TracebackException class method), 1608
from_file() (zipfile.ZipInfo class method), 463
from_float() (decimal.Decimal method), 292
from_float() (fractions.Fraction method), 312
from_iterable() (itertools.chain class method), 330
from_list() (traceback.StackSummary class method), 1608
from_param() (ctypes._CData method), 720
from_traceback() (dis.Bytecode class method), 1691
frombuf() (tarfile.TarInfo class method), 471
frombytes() (array.array method), 234
fromfd() (in module socket), 817
fromfd() (select.epoll method), 865
fromfd() (select.kqueue method), 867
fromfile() (array.array method), 234
fromhex() (bytearray class method), 54
fromhex() (bytes class method), 53
fromhex() (float class method), 34
fromkeys() (collections.Counter method), 210
fromkeys() (dict class method), 77
fromlist() (array.array method), 234
fromordinal() (datetime.date class method), 178
fromordinal() (datetime.datetime class method), 182
fromshare() (in module socket), 817
fromstring() (array.array method), 234
fromstring() (in module xml.etree.ElementTree), 1061
fromstringlist() (in module xml.etree.ElementTree), 1061
fromtarfile() (tarfile.TarInfo class method), 471
fromtimestamp() (datetime.date class method), 177
fromtimestamp() (datetime.datetime class method), 181
fromunicode() (array.array method), 234
fromutc() (datetime.timezone method), 199

fromutc() (datetime.tzinfo method), 194
FrozenImporter (class in importlib.machinery), 1658
frozenset (built-in class), 73
FrozenSet (class in typing), 1384
fsdecode() (in module os), 527
fsencode() (in module os), 527
fspath() (in module os), 527
fstat() (in module os), 533
fstatvfs() (in module os), 533
fsum() (in module math), 277
fsync() (in module os), 533
FTP, 1144
    ftplib (standard module), 1161
    protocol, 1143, 1161
FTP (class in ftplib), 1162
ftp_open() (urllib.request.FTPHandler method), 1138
FTP_TLS (class in ftplib), 1162
FTPHandler (class in urllib.request), 1131
ftplib (module), 1161
ftruncate() (in module os), 534
Full, 804
full() (asyncio.Queue method), 924
full() (multiprocessing.Queue method), 749
full() (queue.Queue method), 805
full_url (urllib.request.Request attribute), 1131
fullmatch() (in module re), 113
fullmatch() (re.regex method), 116
func (functools.partial attribute), 347
funcattrs (2to3 fixer), 1499
function, **1785**
Function (class in symtable), 1677
function annotation, **1785**
FunctionTestCase (class in unittest), 1432
FunctionType (in module types), 243
functools (module), 341
funny_files (filecmp.dircmp attribute), 384
future (2to3 fixer), 1499
Future (class in asyncio), 891
Future (class in concurrent.futures), 785
FutureWarning, 92
fwalk() (in module os), 556

G

G.722, 1254
gaierror, 813
gamma() (in module math), 280
gammavariate() (in module random), 316
garbage (in module gc), 1614
garbage collection, **1785**
gather() (curses.textpad.Textbox method), 681
gather() (in module asyncio), 896
gauss() (in module random), 316
gc (module), 1612

gcd() (in module fractions), 313
gcd() (in module math), 277
ge() (in module operator), 348
gen_uuid() (in module msilib), 1712
generator, **1785**, 1785
Generator (class in collections.abc), 224
Generator (class in email.generator), 963
Generator (class in typing), 1385
generator expression, **1785**, 1785
generator iterator, **1785**
GeneratorExit, 86
GeneratorType (in module types), 243
Generic (class in typing), 1381
generic function, **1785**
generic_visit() (ast.NodeVisitor method), 1675
genops() (in module pickletools), 1704
get() (asyncio.Queue method), 924
get() (configparser.ConfigParser method), 498
get() (dict method), 77
get() (email.message.EmailMessage method), 953
get() (email.message.Message method), 991
get() (in module webbrowser), 1108
get() (mailbox.Mailbox method), 1019
get() (multiprocessing.pool.AsyncResult method), 767
get() (multiprocessing.Queue method), 749
get() (multiprocessing.SimpleQueue method), 750
get() (ossaudiodev.oss_mixer_device method), 1267
get() (queue.Queue method), 805
get() (tkinter.ttk.Combobox method), 1346
get() (types.MappingProxyType method), 245
get() (xml.etree.ElementTree.Element method), 1063
GET_AITER (opcode), 1696
get_all() (email.message.EmailMessage method), 953
get_all() (email.message.Message method), 991
get_all() (wsgiref.headers.Headers method), 1119
get_all_breaks() (bdb.Bdb method), 1514
get_all_start_methods() (in module multiprocessing), 751
GET_ANEXT (opcode), 1696
get_app() (wsgiref.simple_server.WSGIServer method), 1120
get_archive_formats() (in module shutil), 398
get_asyncgen_hooks() (in module sys), 1569
GET_AWAITABLE (opcode), 1696
get_begidx() (in module readline), 145
get_blocking() (in module os), 534
get_body() (email.message.EmailMessage method), 956
get_body_encoding() (email.charset.Charset method), 1002
get_boundary() (email.message.EmailMessage method), 955

get_boundary() (email.message.Message method), 994
get_bpbynumber() (bdb.Bdb method), 1514
get_break() (bdb.Bdb method), 1514
get_breaks() (bdb.Bdb method), 1514
get_buffer() (xdrlib.Packer method), 502
get_buffer() (xdrlib.Unpacker method), 503
get_bytes() (mailbox.Mailbox method), 1019
get_ca_certs() (ssl.SSLContext method), 848
get_cache_token() (in module abc), 1604
get_channel_binding() (ssl.SSLSocket method), 846
get_charset() (email.message.Message method), 990
get_charsets() (email.message.EmailMessage method), 955
get_charsets() (email.message.Message method), 994
get_children() (symtable.SymbolTable method), 1677
get_children() (tkinter.ttk.Treeview method), 1352
get_ciphers() (ssl.SSLContext method), 848
get_clock_info() (in module time), 584
get_close_matches() (in module difflib), 127
get_code() (importlib.abc.InspectLoader method), 1654
get_code() (importlib.abc.SourceLoader method), 1656
get_code() (importlib.machinery.ExtensionFileLoader method), 1660
get_code() (importlib.machinery.SourcelessFileLoader method), 1660
get_code() (zipimport.zipimporter method), 1642
get_completer() (in module readline), 144
get_completer_delims() (in module readline), 145
get_completion_type() (in module readline), 145
get_config_h_filename() (in module sysconfig), 1581
get_config_var() (in module sysconfig), 1579
get_config_vars() (in module sysconfig), 1579
get_content() (email.contentmanager.ContentManager method), 978
get_content() (email.message.EmailMessage method), 957
get_content() (in module email.contentmanager), 979
get_content_charset() (email.message.EmailMessage method), 955
get_content_charset() (email.message.Message method), 994
get_content_disposition() (email.message.EmailMessage method), 955
get_content_disposition() (email.message.Message method), 994
get_content_maintype() (email.message.EmailMessage method), 954

get_content_maintype() (email.message.Message method), 992
get_content_subtype() (email.message.EmailMessage method), 954
get_content_subtype() (email.message.Message method), 992
get_content_type() (email.message.EmailMessage method), 954
get_content_type() (email.message.Message method), 992
get_context() (in module multiprocessing), 751
get_coroutine_wrapper() (in module sys), 1570
get_count() (in module gc), 1613
get_current_history_length() (in module readline), 143
get_data() (importlib.abc.FileLoader method), 1656
get_data() (importlib.abc.ResourceLoader method), 1654
get_data() (in module pkgutil), 1645
get_data() (zipimport.zipimporter method), 1642
get_date() (mailbox.MaildirMessage method), 1027
get_debug() (asyncio.AbstractEventLoop method), 882
get_debug() (in module gc), 1613
get_default() (argparse.ArgumentParser method), 619
get_default_domain() (in module nis), 1744
get_default_type() (email.message.EmailMessage method), 954
get_default_type() (email.message.Message method), 992
get_default_verify_paths() (in module ssl), 837
get_dialect() (in module csv), 478
get_docstring() (in module ast), 1675
get_doctest() (doctest.DocTestParser method), 1409
get_endidx() (in module readline), 145
get_environ() (wsgiref.simple_server.WSGIRequestHandler method), 1121
get_errno() (in module ctypes), 719
get_event_loop() (asyncio.AbstractEventLoopPolicy method), 887
get_event_loop() (in module asyncio), 885
get_event_loop_policy() (in module asyncio), 888
get_examples() (doctest.DocTestParser method), 1409
get_exception_handler() (asyncio.AbstractEventLoop method), 881
get_exec_path() (in module os), 528
get_extra_info() (asyncio.BaseTransport method), 899
get_extra_info() (asyncio.StreamWriter method), 911

get_field() (string.Formatter method), 96
get_file() (mailbox.Babyl method), 1025
get_file() (mailbox.Mailbox method), 1019
get_file() (mailbox.Maildir method), 1022
get_file() (mailbox.mbox method), 1022
get_file() (mailbox.MH method), 1024
get_file() (mailbox.MMDF method), 1025
get_file_breaks() (bdb.Bdb method), 1514
get_filename() (email.message.EmailMessage method), 954
get_filename() (email.message.Message method), 994
get_filename() (importlib.abc.ExecutionLoader method), 1655
get_filename() (importlib.abc.FileLoader method), 1656
get_filename() (importlib.machinery.ExtensionFileLoader method), 1660
get_filename() (zipimport.zipimporter method), 1642
get_flags() (mailbox.MaildirMessage method), 1027
get_flags() (mailbox.mboxMessage method), 1028
get_flags() (mailbox.MMDFMessage method), 1032
get_folder() (mailbox.Maildir method), 1021
get_folder() (mailbox.MH method), 1023
get_frees() (symtable.Function method), 1677
get_from() (mailbox.mboxMessage method), 1028
get_from() (mailbox.MMDFMessage method), 1032
get_full_url() (urllib.request.Request method), 1132
get_globals() (symtable.Function method), 1677
get_grouped_opcodes() (difflib.SequenceMatcher method), 131
get_handle_inheritable() (in module os), 539
get_header() (urllib.request.Request method), 1132
get_history_item() (in module readline), 143
get_history_length() (in module readline), 143
get_id() (symtable.SymbolTable method), 1677
get_ident() (in module _thread), 807
get_ident() (in module threading), 727
get_identifiers() (symtable.SymbolTable method), 1677
get_importer() (in module pkgutil), 1644
get_info() (mailbox.MaildirMessage method), 1027
get_inheritable() (in module os), 539
get_inheritable() (socket.socket method), 822
get_instructions() (in module dis), 1692
get_interpreter() (in module zipapp), 1561
GET_ITER (opcode), 1694
get_key() (selectors.BaseSelector method), 871
get_labels() (mailbox.Babyl method), 1024
get_labels() (mailbox.BabylMessage method), 1031
get_last_error() (in module ctypes), 719
get_line_buffer() (in module readline), 143
get_lineno() (symtable.SymbolTable method), 1677

get_loader() (in module pkgutil), 1644
get_locals() (symtable.Function method), 1677
get_logger() (in module multiprocessing), 771
get_magic() (in module imp), 1773
get_makefile_filename() (in module sysconfig), 1581
get_map() (selectors.BaseSelector method), 871
get_matching_blocks() (difflib.SequenceMatcher method), 130
get_message() (mailbox.Mailbox method), 1019
get_method() (urllib.request.Request method), 1132
get_methods() (symtable.Class method), 1677
get_mixed_type_key() (in module ipaddress), 1247
get_name() (symtable.Symbol method), 1678
get_name() (symtable.SymbolTable method), 1677
get_namespace() (symtable.Symbol method), 1678
get_namespaces() (symtable.Symbol method), 1678
get_nonstandard_attr() (http.cookiejar.Cookie method), 1222
get_nowait() (asyncio.Queue method), 924
get_nowait() (multiprocessing.Queue method), 749
get_nowait() (queue.Queue method), 805
get_object_traceback() (in module tracemalloc), 1543
get_objects() (in module gc), 1613
get_opcodes() (difflib.SequenceMatcher method), 131
get_option() (optparse.OptionParser method), 1765
get_option_group() (optparse.OptionParser method), 1755
get_osfhandle() (in module msvcrt), 1717
get_output_charset() (email.charset.Charset method), 1002
get_param() (email.message.Message method), 993
get_parameters() (symtable.Function method), 1677
get_params() (email.message.Message method), 992
get_path() (in module sysconfig), 1580
get_path_names() (in module sysconfig), 1580
get_paths() (in module sysconfig), 1580
get_payload() (email.message.Message method), 989
get_pid() (asyncio.BaseSubprocessTransport method), 901
get_pipe_transport() (asyncio.BaseSubprocessTransport method), 901
get_platform() (in module sysconfig), 1580
get_poly() (in module turtle), 1305
get_position() (xdrlib.Unpacker method), 503
get_protocol() (asyncio.BaseTransport method), 899
get_python_version() (in module sysconfig), 1580
get_recsrc() (ossaudiodev.oss_mixer_device method), 1267
get_referents() (in module gc), 1614
get_referrers() (in module gc), 1614

get_request() (socketserver.BaseServer method), 1201
get_returncode() (asyncio.BaseSubprocessTransport method), 901
get_scheme() (wsgiref.handlers.BaseHandler method), 1124
get_scheme_names() (in module sysconfig), 1580
get_sequences() (mailbox.MH method), 1023
get_sequences() (mailbox.MHMessage method), 1030
get_server() (multiprocessing.managers.BaseManager method), 759
get_server_certificate() (in module ssl), 837
get_shapepoly() (in module turtle), 1303
get_socket() (telnetlib.Telnet method), 1194
get_source() (importlib.abc.InspectLoader method), 1655
get_source() (importlib.abc.SourceLoader method), 1657
get_source() (importlib.machinery.ExtensionFileLoader method), 1660
get_source() (importlib.machinery.SourcelessFileLoader method), 1660
get_source() (zipimport.zipimporter method), 1642
get_stack() (asyncio.Task method), 894
get_stack() (bdb.Bdb method), 1514
get_start_method() (in module multiprocessing), 751
get_starttag_text() (html.parser.HTMLParser method), 1049
get_stats() (in module gc), 1613
get_stderr() (wsgiref.handlers.BaseHandler method), 1123
get_stderr() (wsgiref.simple_server.WSGIRequestHandler method), 1121
get_stdin() (wsgiref.handlers.BaseHandler method), 1123
get_string() (mailbox.Mailbox method), 1019
get_subdir() (mailbox.MaildirMessage method), 1026
get_suffixes() (in module imp), 1773
get_symbols() (symtable.SymbolTable method), 1677
get_tag() (in module imp), 1776
get_task_factory() (asyncio.AbstractEventLoop method), 876
get_terminal_size() (in module os), 539
get_terminal_size() (in module shutil), 400
get_terminator() (asynchat.async_chat method), 937
get_threshold() (in module gc), 1614
get_token() (shlex.shlex method), 1325
get_traceback_limit() (in module tracemalloc), 1543

get_traced_memory() (in module tracemalloc), 1543
get_tracemalloc_memory() (in module tracemalloc), 1543
get_type() (symtable.SymbolTable method), 1677
get_type_hints() (in module typing), 1387
get_unixfrom() (email.message.EmailMessage method), 952
get_unixfrom() (email.message.Message method), 989
get_unpack_formats() (in module shutil), 399
get_usage() (optparse.OptionParser method), 1766
get_value() (string.Formatter method), 96
get_version() (optparse.OptionParser method), 1756
get_visible() (mailbox.BabylMessage method), 1031
get_wch() (curses.window method), 672
get_write_buffer_limits() (asyncio.WriteTransport method), 900
get_write_buffer_size() (asyncio.WriteTransport method), 900
GET_YIELD_FROM_ITER (opcode), 1694
getacl() (imaplib.IMAP4 method), 1172
getaddresses() (in module email.utils), 1005
getaddrinfo() (asyncio.AbstractEventLoop method), 880
getaddrinfo() (in module socket), 817
getallocatedblocks() (in module sys), 1567
getannotation() (imaplib.IMAP4 method), 1172
getargspec() (in module inspect), 1624
getargvalues() (in module inspect), 1625
getatime() (in module os.path), 373
getattr() (built-in function), 12
getattr_static() (in module inspect), 1628
getAttribute() (xml.dom.Element method), 1075
getAttributeNode() (xml.dom.Element method), 1075
getAttributeNodeNS() (xml.dom.Element method), 1075
getAttributeNS() (xml.dom.Element method), 1075
GetBase() (xml.parsers.expat.xmlparser method), 1099
getbegyx() (curses.window method), 671
getbkgd() (curses.window method), 671
getboolean() (configparser.ConfigParser method), 498
getbuffer() (io.BytesIO method), 577
getByteStream() (xml.sax.xmlreader.InputSource method), 1096
getcallargs() (in module inspect), 1625
getcanvas() (in module turtle), 1311
getcapabilities() (nntplib.NNTP method), 1178
getcaps() (in module mailcap), 1017
getch() (curses.window method), 672
getch() (in module msvcrt), 1717

getCharacterStream() (xml.sax.xmlreader.InputSource method), 1096
getche() (in module msvcrt), 1717
getcheckinterval() (in module sys), 1568
getChild() (logging.Logger method), 625
getchildren() (xml.etree.ElementTree.Element method), 1064
getclasstree() (in module inspect), 1624
getclosurevars() (in module inspect), 1626
GetColumnInfo() (msilib.View method), 1712
getColumnNumber() (xml.sax.xmlreader.Locator method), 1095
getcomments() (in module inspect), 1619
getcompname() (aifc.aifc method), 1253
getcompname() (sunau.AU_read method), 1256
getcompname() (wave.Wave_read method), 1258
getcomptype() (aifc.aifc method), 1253
getcomptype() (sunau.AU_read method), 1256
getcomptype() (wave.Wave_read method), 1258
getContentHandler() (xml.sax.xmlreader.XMLReader method), 1094
getcontext() (in module decimal), 296
getcoroutinelocals() (in module inspect), 1629
getcoroutinestate() (in module inspect), 1629
getctime() (in module os.path), 373
getcwd() (in module os), 543
getcwdb() (in module os), 543
getcwdu (2to3 fixer), 1499
getdecoder() (in module codecs), 155
getdefaultencoding() (in module sys), 1568
getdefaultlocale() (in module locale), 1280
getdefaulttimeout() (in module socket), 820
getdlopenflags() (in module sys), 1568
getdoc() (in module inspect), 1619
getDOMImplementation() (in module xml.dom), 1070
getDTDHandler() (xml.sax.xmlreader.XMLReader method), 1094
getEffectiveLevel() (logging.Logger method), 625
getegid() (in module os), 528
getElementsByTagName() (xml.dom.Document method), 1075
getElementsByTagName() (xml.dom.Element method), 1075
getElementsByTagNameNS() (xml.dom.Document method), 1075
getElementsByTagNameNS() (xml.dom.Element method), 1075
getencoder() (in module codecs), 155
getEncoding() (xml.sax.xmlreader.InputSource method), 1096
getEntityResolver() (xml.sax.xmlreader.XMLReader method), 1094
getenv() (in module os), 527

getenvb() (in module os), 527
getErrorHandler() (xml.sax.xmlreader.XMLReader method), 1094
geteuid() (in module os), 528
getEvent() (xml.dom.pulldom.DOMEventStream method), 1085
getEventCategory() (logging.handlers.NTEventLogHandler method), 658
getEventType() (logging.handlers.NTEventLogHandler method), 658
getException() (xml.sax.SAXException method), 1087
getFeature() (xml.sax.xmlreader.XMLReader method), 1095
GetFieldCount() (msilib.Record method), 1713
getfile() (in module inspect), 1619
getfilesystemencodeerrors() (in module sys), 1568
getfilesystemencoding() (in module sys), 1568
getfirst() (cgi.FieldStorage method), 1112
getfloat() (configparser.ConfigParser method), 498
getfmts() (ossaudiodev.oss_audio_device method), 1265
getfqdn() (in module socket), 818
getframeinfo() (in module inspect), 1627
getframerate() (aifc.aifc method), 1253
getframerate() (sunau.AU_read method), 1256
getframerate() (wave.Wave_read method), 1258
getfullargspec() (in module inspect), 1624
getgeneratorlocals() (in module inspect), 1629
getgeneratorstate() (in module inspect), 1628
getgid() (in module os), 528
getgrall() (in module grp), 1732
getgrgid() (in module grp), 1732
getgrnam() (in module grp), 1732
getgrouplist() (in module os), 528
getgroups() (in module os), 528
getheader() (http.client.HTTPResponse method), 1159
getheaders() (http.client.HTTPResponse method), 1159
gethostbyaddr() (in module socket), 531, 818
gethostbyname() (in module socket), 818
gethostbyname_ex() (in module socket), 818
gethostname() (in module socket), 531, 818
getincrementaldecoder() (in module codecs), 155
getincrementalencoder() (in module codecs), 155
getinfo() (zipfile.ZipFile method), 459
getinnerframes() (in module inspect), 1627
GetInputContext() (xml.parsers.expat.xmlparser method), 1099
getint() (configparser.ConfigParser method), 498
GetInteger() (msilib.Record method), 1713
getitem() (in module operator), 350
getiterator() (xml.etree.ElementTree.Element method), 1064
getiterator() (xml.etree.ElementTree.ElementTree method), 1065
getitimer() (in module signal), 941
getkey() (curses.window method), 672
GetLastError() (in module ctypes), 719
getLength() (xml.sax.xmlreader.Attributes method), 1096
getLevelName() (in module logging), 636
getline() (in module linecache), 391
getLineNumber() (xml.sax.xmlreader.Locator method), 1095
getlist() (cgi.FieldStorage method), 1112
getloadavg() (in module os), 568
getlocale() (in module locale), 1280
getLogger() (in module logging), 634
getLoggerClass() (in module logging), 634
getlogin() (in module os), 528
getLogRecordFactory() (in module logging), 634
getmark() (aifc.aifc method), 1253
getmark() (sunau.AU_read method), 1256
getmark() (wave.Wave_read method), 1258
getmarkers() (aifc.aifc method), 1253
getmarkers() (sunau.AU_read method), 1256
getmarkers() (wave.Wave_read method), 1258
getmaxyx() (curses.window method), 672
getmember() (tarfile.TarFile method), 469
getmembers() (in module inspect), 1617
getmembers() (tarfile.TarFile method), 469
getMessage() (logging.LogRecord method), 631
getMessage() (xml.sax.SAXException method), 1087
getMessageID() (logging.handlers.NTEventLogHandler method), 658
getmodule() (in module inspect), 1620
getmodulename() (in module inspect), 1617
getmouse() (in module curses), 665
getmro() (in module inspect), 1625
getmtime() (in module os.path), 373
getname() (chunk.Chunk method), 1260
getName() (threading.Thread method), 730
getNameByQName() (xml.sax.xmlreader.AttributesNS method), 1097
getnameinfo() (asyncio.AbstractEventLoop method), 880
getnameinfo() (in module socket), 818
getnames() (tarfile.TarFile method), 469
getNames() (xml.sax.xmlreader.Attributes method), 1096
getnchannels() (aifc.aifc method), 1253
getnchannels() (sunau.AU_read method), 1256
getnchannels() (wave.Wave_read method), 1258
getnframes() (aifc.aifc method), 1253

getnframes() (sunau.AU_read method), 1256
getnframes() (wave.Wave_read method), 1258
getnode, 1196
getnode() (in module uuid), 1196
getopt (module), 621
getopt() (in module getopt), 621
GetoptError, 622
getouterframes() (in module inspect), 1627
getoutput() (in module subprocess), 801
getpagesize() (in module resource), 1743
getparams() (aifc.aifc method), 1253
getparams() (sunau.AU_read method), 1256
getparams() (wave.Wave_read method), 1258
getparyx() (curses.window method), 672
getpass (module), 662
getpass() (in module getpass), 662
GetPassWarning, 662
getpeercert() (ssl.SSLSocket method), 844
getpeername() (socket.socket method), 822
getpen() (in module turtle), 1305
getpgid() (in module os), 528
getpgrp() (in module os), 528
getpid() (in module os), 529
getpos() (html.parser.HTMLParser method), 1049
getppid() (in module os), 529
getpreferredencoding() (in module locale), 1281
getpriority() (in module os), 529
getprofile() (in module sys), 1569
GetProperty() (msilib.SummaryInformation method), 1713
getProperty() (xml.sax.xmlreader.XMLReader method), 1095
GetPropertyCount() (msilib.SummaryInformation method), 1713
getprotobyname() (in module socket), 818
getproxies() (in module urllib.request), 1128
getPublicId() (xml.sax.xmlreader.InputSource method), 1096
getPublicId() (xml.sax.xmlreader.Locator method), 1095
getpwall() (in module pwd), 1731
getpwnam() (in module pwd), 1731
getpwuid() (in module pwd), 1730
getQNameByName() (xml.sax.xmlreader.AttributesNS method), 1097
getQNames() (xml.sax.xmlreader.AttributesNS method), 1097
getquota() (imaplib.IMAP4 method), 1172
getquotaroot() (imaplib.IMAP4 method), 1172
getrandbits() (in module random), 315
getrandom() (in module os), 569
getreader() (in module codecs), 155
getrecursionlimit() (in module sys), 1568
getrefcount() (in module sys), 1568

getresgid() (in module os), 529
getresponse() (http.client.HTTPConnection method), 1158
getresuid() (in module os), 529
getrlimit() (in module resource), 1740
getroot() (xml.etree.ElementTree.ElementTree method), 1065
getrusage() (in module resource), 1743
getsample() (in module audioop), 1250
getsampwidth() (aifc.aifc method), 1253
getsampwidth() (sunau.AU_read method), 1256
getsampwidth() (wave.Wave_read method), 1258
getscreen() (in module turtle), 1305
getservbyname() (in module socket), 818
getservbyport() (in module socket), 818
GetSetDescriptorType (in module types), 244
getshapes() (in module turtle), 1311
getsid() (in module os), 531
getsignal() (in module signal), 940
getsitepackages() (in module site), 1632
getsize() (chunk.Chunk method), 1260
getsize() (in module os.path), 373
getsizeof() (in module sys), 1568
getsockname() (socket.socket method), 822
getsockopt() (socket.socket method), 822
getsource() (in module inspect), 1620
getsourcefile() (in module inspect), 1620
getsourcelines() (in module inspect), 1620
getspall() (in module spwd), 1731
getspnam() (in module spwd), 1731
getstate() (codecs.IncrementalDecoder method), 161
getstate() (codecs.IncrementalEncoder method), 160
getstate() (in module random), 314
getstatusoutput() (in module subprocess), 801
getstr() (curses.window method), 672
GetString() (msilib.Record method), 1713
getSubject() (logging.handlers.SMTPHandler method), 659
GetSummaryInformation() (msilib.Database method), 1712
getswitchinterval() (in module sys), 1569
getSystemId() (xml.sax.xmlreader.InputSource method), 1096
getSystemId() (xml.sax.xmlreader.Locator method), 1095
getsyx() (in module curses), 665
gettarinfo() (tarfile.TarFile method), 470
gettempdir() (in module tempfile), 387
gettempdirb() (in module tempfile), 387
gettempprefix() (in module tempfile), 387
gettempprefixb() (in module tempfile), 388
getTestCaseNames() (unittest.TestLoader method), 1435
gettext (module), 1269

gettext() (gettext.GNUTranslations method), 1273
gettext() (gettext.NullTranslations method), 1272
gettext() (in module gettext), 1270
gettext() (in module locale), 1283
gettimeout() (socket.socket method), 822
gettrace() (in module sys), 1569
getturtle() (in module turtle), 1305
getType() (xml.sax.xmlreader.Attributes method), 1096
getuid() (in module os), 529
geturl() (urllib.parse.urllib.parse.SplitResult method), 1148
getuser() (in module getpass), 662
getuserbase() (in module site), 1632
getusersitepackages() (in module site), 1633
getvalue() (io.BytesIO method), 577
getvalue() (io.StringIO method), 581
getValue() (xml.sax.xmlreader.Attributes method), 1097
getValueByQName() (xml.sax.xmlreader.AttributesNS method), 1097
getwch() (in module msvcrt), 1717
getwche() (in module msvcrt), 1717
getweakrefcount() (in module weakref), 236
getweakrefs() (in module weakref), 236
getwelcome() (ftplib.FTP method), 1164
getwelcome() (nntplib.NNTP method), 1178
getwelcome() (poplib.POP3 method), 1168
getwin() (in module curses), 665
getwindowsversion() (in module sys), 1569
getwriter() (in module codecs), 155
getxattr() (in module os), 557
getyx() (curses.window method), 672
gid (tarfile.TarInfo attribute), 471
GIL, 1785
glob
    module, 390
glob (module), 389
glob() (in module glob), 389
glob() (msilib.Directory method), 1714
glob() (pathlib.Path method), 366
global interpreter lock, 1785
globals() (built-in function), 12
globs (doctest.DocTest attribute), 1407
gmtime() (in module time), 584
gname (tarfile.TarInfo attribute), 471
GNOME, 1274
GNU_FORMAT (in module tarfile), 467
gnu_getopt() (in module getopt), 622
GNUTranslations (class in gettext), 1273
got (doctest.DocTestFailure attribute), 1413
goto() (in module turtle), 1291
Graphical User Interface, 1331
GREATER (in module token), 1679

GREATEREQUAL (in module token), 1679
Greenwich Mean Time, 582
GRND_NONBLOCK (in module os), 570
GRND_RANDOM (in module os), 570
Group (class in email.headerregistry), 978
group() (nntplib.NNTP method), 1179
group() (pathlib.Path method), 367
group() (re.match method), 117
groupby() (in module itertools), 332
groupdict() (re.match method), 119
groupindex (re.regex attribute), 117
groups (email.headerregistry.AddressHeader attribute), 975
groups (re.regex attribute), 117
groups() (re.match method), 118
grp (module), 1732
gt() (in module operator), 348
guess_all_extensions() (in module mimetypes), 1035
guess_all_extensions() (mimetypes.MimeTypes method), 1037
guess_extension() (in module mimetypes), 1036
guess_extension() (mimetypes.MimeTypes method), 1037
guess_scheme() (in module wsgiref.util), 1117
guess_type() (in module mimetypes), 1035
guess_type() (mimetypes.MimeTypes method), 1037
GUI, 1331
gzip (module), 446
GzipFile (class in gzip), 447

H

halfdelay() (in module curses), 665
Handle (class in asyncio), 883
handle() (http.server.BaseHTTPRequestHandler method), 1208
handle() (logging.Handler method), 628
handle() (logging.handlers.QueueListener method), 661
handle() (logging.Logger method), 627
handle() (logging.NullHandler method), 651
handle() (socketserver.BaseRequestHandler method), 1202
handle() (wsgiref.simple_server.WSGIRequestHandler method), 1121
handle_accept() (asyncore.dispatcher method), 933
handle_accepted() (asyncore.dispatcher method), 933
handle_charref() (html.parser.HTMLParser method), 1049
handle_close() (asyncore.dispatcher method), 933
handle_comment() (html.parser.HTMLParser method), 1049
handle_connect() (asyncore.dispatcher method), 933

handle_data() (html.parser.HTMLParser method), 1049
handle_decl() (html.parser.HTMLParser method), 1050
handle_defect() (email.policy.Policy method), 967
handle_endtag() (html.parser.HTMLParser method), 1049
handle_entityref() (html.parser.HTMLParser method), 1049
handle_error() (asyncore.dispatcher method), 933
handle_error() (socketserver.BaseServer method), 1201
handle_expect_100() (http.server.BaseHTTPRequestHandler method), 1208
handle_expt() (asyncore.dispatcher method), 933
handle_one_request() (http.server.BaseHTTPRequestHandler method), 1208
handle_pi() (html.parser.HTMLParser method), 1050
handle_read() (asyncore.dispatcher method), 933
handle_request() (socketserver.BaseServer method), 1200
handle_request() (xmlrpc.server.CGIXMLRPCRequestHandler method), 1235
handle_startendtag() (html.parser.HTMLParser method), 1049
handle_starttag() (html.parser.HTMLParser method), 1049
handle_timeout() (socketserver.BaseServer method), 1201
handle_write() (asyncore.dispatcher method), 933
handleError() (logging.Handler method), 628
handleError() (logging.handlers.SocketHandler method), 654
Handler (class in logging), 628
handler() (in module cgitb), 1116
harmonic_mean() (in module statistics), 321
HAS_ALPN (in module ssl), 842
has_children() (symtable.SymbolTable method), 1677
has_colors() (in module curses), 665
HAS_ECDH (in module ssl), 842
has_exec() (symtable.SymbolTable method), 1677
has_extn() (smtplib.SMTP method), 1185
has_header() (csv.Sniffer method), 480
has_header() (urllib.request.Request method), 1132
has_ic() (in module curses), 665
has_il() (in module curses), 665
has_ipv6 (in module socket), 815
has_key (2to3 fixer), 1499
has_key() (in module curses), 665
has_location (importlib.machinery.ModuleSpec attribute), 1661
has_nonstandard_attr() (http.cookiejar.Cookie method), 1222
HAS_NPN (in module ssl), 842
has_option() (configparser.ConfigParser method), 497
has_option() (optparse.OptionParser method), 1765
has_section() (configparser.ConfigParser method), 497
HAS_SNI (in module ssl), 842
has_ticket (ssl.SSLSession attribute), 860
HAS_TLSv1_3 (in module ssl), 842
hasattr() (built-in function), 12
hasAttribute() (xml.dom.Element method), 1075
hasAttributeNS() (xml.dom.Element method), 1075
hasAttributes() (xml.dom.Node method), 1072
hasChildNodes() (xml.dom.Node method), 1072
hascompare (in module dis), 1702
hasconst (in module dis), 1702
hasFeature() (xml.dom.DOMImplementation method), 1071
hasfree (in module dis), 1702
hash
    built-in function, 39
hash() (built-in function), 12
hash.block_size (in module hashlib), 510
hash.digest_size (in module hashlib), 510
hash_info (in module sys), 1570
hashable, 1786
Hashable (class in collections.abc), 223
Hashable (class in typing), 1383
hasHandlers() (logging.Logger method), 627
hashlib (module), 509
hasjabs (in module dis), 1702
hasjrel (in module dis), 1702
haslocal (in module dis), 1702
hasname (in module dis), 1702
HAVE_ARGUMENT (opcode), 1702
HAVE_THREADS (in module decimal), 302
HCI_DATA_DIR (in module socket), 816
HCI_FILTER (in module socket), 816
HCI_TIME_STAMP (in module socket), 816
head() (nntplib.NNTP method), 1181
Header (class in email.header), 999
header_encode() (email.charset.Charset method), 1002
header_encode_lines() (email.charset.Charset method), 1002
header_encoding (email.charset.Charset attribute), 1001
header_factory (email.policy.EmailPolicy attribute), 969
header_fetch_parse() (email.policy.Compat32 method), 971

header_fetch_parse() (email.policy.EmailPolicy method), 970
header_fetch_parse() (email.policy.Policy method), 968
header_items() (urllib.request.Request method), 1132
header_max_count() (email.policy.EmailPolicy method), 970
header_max_count() (email.policy.Policy method), 968
header_offset (zipfile.ZipInfo attribute), 464
header_source_parse() (email.policy.Compat32 method), 971
header_source_parse() (email.policy.EmailPolicy method), 970
header_source_parse() (email.policy.Policy method), 968
header_store_parse() (email.policy.Compat32 method), 971
header_store_parse() (email.policy.EmailPolicy method), 970
header_store_parse() (email.policy.Policy method), 968
HeaderError, 467
HeaderParseError, 972
HeaderParser (class in email.parser), 961
HeaderRegistry (class in email.headerregistry), 976
headers
    MIME, 1035, 1109
Headers (class in wsgiref.headers), 1119
headers (http.server.BaseHTTPRequestHandler attribute), 1207
headers (urllib.error.HTTPError attribute), 1152
headers (xmlrpc.client.ProtocolError attribute), 1228
heading() (in module turtle), 1295
heading() (tkinter.ttk.Treeview method), 1353
heapify() (in module heapq), 227
heapmin() (in module msvcrt), 1718
heappop() (in module heapq), 226
heappush() (in module heapq), 226
heappushpop() (in module heapq), 226
heapq (module), 226
heapreplace() (in module heapq), 227
helo() (smtplib.SMTP method), 1185
help
    online, 1390
help (optparse.Option attribute), 1760
help (pdb command), 1520
help() (built-in function), 12
help() (nntplib.NNTP method), 1180
herror, 813
hex (uuid.UUID attribute), 1196
hex() (built-in function), 13
hex() (bytearray method), 55
hex() (bytes method), 54
hex() (float method), 34
hex() (memoryview method), 69
hexadecimal
    literals, 31
hexbin() (in module binhex), 1041
hexdigest() (hashlib.hash method), 511
hexdigest() (hashlib.shake method), 511
hexdigest() (hmac.HMAC method), 520
hexdigits (in module string), 95
hexlify() (in module binascii), 1043
hexversion (in module sys), 1570
hidden() (curses.panel.Panel method), 684
hide() (curses.panel.Panel method), 684
hide() (tkinter.ttk.Notebook method), 1348
hide_cookie2 (http.cookiejar.CookiePolicy attribute), 1219
hideturtle() (in module turtle), 1300
HierarchyRequestErr, 1077
HIGHEST_PROTOCOL (in module pickle), 403
HKEY_CLASSES_ROOT (in module winreg), 1723
HKEY_CURRENT_CONFIG (in module winreg), 1723
HKEY_CURRENT_USER (in module winreg), 1723
HKEY_DYN_DATA (in module winreg), 1723
HKEY_LOCAL_MACHINE (in module winreg), 1723
HKEY_PERFORMANCE_DATA (in module winreg), 1723
HKEY_USERS (in module winreg), 1723
hline() (curses.window method), 672
HList (class in tkinter.tix), 1361
hls_to_rgb() (in module colorsys), 1261
hmac (module), 519
HOME, 372
home() (in module turtle), 1292
home() (pathlib.Path class method), 365
HOMEDRIVE, 372
HOMEPATH, 372
hook_compressed() (in module fileinput), 378
hook_encoded() (in module fileinput), 378
host (urllib.request.Request attribute), 1131
hostmask (ipaddress.IPv4Network attribute), 1242
hostmask (ipaddress.IPv6Network attribute), 1244
hosts (netrc.netrc attribute), 502
hosts() (ipaddress.IPv4Network method), 1242
hosts() (ipaddress.IPv6Network method), 1244
hour (datetime.datetime attribute), 183
hour (datetime.time attribute), 190
HRESULT (class in ctypes), 723
hStdError (subprocess.STARTUPINFO attribute), 796

hStdInput (subprocess.STARTUPINFO attribute), 796
hStdOutput (subprocess.STARTUPINFO attribute), 796
hsv_to_rgb() (in module colorsys), 1261
ht() (in module turtle), 1300
HTML, 1047, 1143
html (module), 1047
html.entities (module), 1052
html.parser (module), 1047
html5 (in module html.entities), 1052
HTMLCalendar (class in calendar), 204
HtmlDiff (class in difflib), 126
HTMLParser (class in html.parser), 1047
htonl() (in module socket), 819
htons() (in module socket), 819
HTTP
    http (standard module), 1153
    http.client (standard module), 1155
    protocol, 1109, 1143, 1153, 1155, 1206
HTTP (in module email.policy), 971
http (module), 1153
http.client (module), 1155
http.cookiejar (module), 1215
http.cookies (module), 1211
http.server (module), 1206
http_error_301() (urllib.request.HTTPRedirectHandler method), 1135
http_error_302() (urllib.request.HTTPRedirectHandler method), 1135
http_error_303() (urllib.request.HTTPRedirectHandler method), 1135
http_error_307() (urllib.request.HTTPRedirectHandler method), 1135
http_error_401() (urllib.request.HTTPBasicAuthHandler method), 1137
http_error_401() (urllib.request.HTTPDigestAuthHandler method), 1137
http_error_407() (urllib.request.ProxyBasicAuthHandler method), 1137
http_error_407() (urllib.request.ProxyDigestAuthHandler method), 1137
http_error_auth_reqed() (urllib.request.AbstractBasicAuthHandler method), 1136
http_error_auth_reqed() (urllib.request.AbstractDigestAuthHandler method), 1137
http_error_default() (urllib.request.BaseHandler method), 1134
http_error_nnn() (urllib.request.BaseHandler method), 1134
http_open() (urllib.request.HTTPHandler method), 1137
HTTP_PORT (in module http.client), 1157
http_proxy, 1127, 1140
http_response() (urllib.request.HTTPErrorProcessor method), 1138
http_version (wsgiref.handlers.BaseHandler attribute), 1125
HTTPBasicAuthHandler (class in urllib.request), 1130
HTTPConnection (class in http.client), 1155
HTTPCookieProcessor (class in urllib.request), 1129
httpd, 1206
HTTPDefaultErrorHandler (class in urllib.request), 1129
HTTPDigestAuthHandler (class in urllib.request), 1130
HTTPError, 1151
HTTPErrorProcessor (class in urllib.request), 1131
HTTPException, 1156
HTTPHandler (class in logging.handlers), 659
HTTPHandler (class in urllib.request), 1131
HTTPPasswordMgr (class in urllib.request), 1130
HTTPPasswordMgrWithDefaultRealm (class in urllib.request), 1130
HTTPPasswordMgrWithPriorAuth (class in urllib.request), 1130
HTTPRedirectHandler (class in urllib.request), 1129
HTTPResponse (class in http.client), 1156
https_open() (urllib.request.HTTPSHandler method), 1137
HTTPS_PORT (in module http.client), 1157
https_response() (urllib.request.HTTPErrorProcessor method), 1138
HTTPSConnection (class in http.client), 1156
HTTPServer (class in http.server), 1206
HTTPSHandler (class in urllib.request), 1131
HTTPStatus (class in http), 1153
hypot() (in module math), 279

I

I (in module re), 112
I/O control
    buffering, 18, 823
    POSIX, 1734
    tty, 1734

UNIX, 1737
iadd() (in module operator), 353
iand() (in module operator), 353
iconcat() (in module operator), 353
id (ssl.SSLSession attribute), 860
id() (built-in function), 13
id() (unittest.TestCase method), 1431
idcok() (curses.window method), 672
ident (select.kevent attribute), 867
ident (threading.Thread attribute), 730
identchars (cmd.Cmd attribute), 1321
identify() (tkinter.ttk.Notebook method), 1348
identify() (tkinter.ttk.Treeview method), 1353
identify() (tkinter.ttk.Widget method), 1345
identify_column() (tkinter.ttk.Treeview method), 1353
identify_element() (tkinter.ttk.Treeview method), 1354
identify_region() (tkinter.ttk.Treeview method), 1354
identify_row() (tkinter.ttk.Treeview method), 1353
idioms (2to3 fixer), 1499
IDLE, 1364, **1786**
IDLESTARTUP, 1370
idlok() (curses.window method), 672
IEEE-754, 1633
if
    statement, 29
if_indextoname() (in module socket), 821
if_nameindex() (in module socket), 820
if_nametoindex() (in module socket), 820
ifloordiv() (in module operator), 353
iglob() (in module glob), 389
ignorableWhitespace() (xml.sax.handler.ContentHandler method), 1091
ignore (pdb command), 1521
ignore_errors() (in module codecs), 159
IGNORE_EXCEPTION_DETAIL (in module doctest), 1398
ignore_patterns() (in module shutil), 394
IGNORECASE (in module re), 112
ihave() (nntplib.NNTP method), 1181
IISCGIHandler (class in wsgiref.handlers), 1122
ilshift() (in module operator), 353
imag (numbers.Complex attribute), 273
imap() (multiprocessing.pool.Pool method), 766
IMAP4
    protocol, 1169
IMAP4 (class in imaplib), 1169
IMAP4.abort, 1170
IMAP4.error, 1170
IMAP4.readonly, 1170
IMAP4_SSL
    protocol, 1169

IMAP4_SSL (class in imaplib), 1170
IMAP4_stream
    protocol, 1169
IMAP4_stream (class in imaplib), 1170
imap_unordered() (multiprocessing.pool.Pool method), 767
imaplib (module), 1169
imatmul() (in module operator), 353
imghdr (module), 1262
immedok() (curses.window method), 672
immutable, **1786**
    sequence types, 39
imod() (in module operator), 353
imp
    module, 24
imp (module), 1773
ImpImporter (class in pkgutil), 1643
implementation (in module sys), 1570
ImpLoader (class in pkgutil), 1643
import
    statement, 24, 1773
import (2to3 fixer), 1499
import path, **1786**
import_fresh_module() (in module test.support), 1507
IMPORT_FROM (opcode), 1699
import_module() (in module importlib), 1650
import_module() (in module test.support), 1507
IMPORT_NAME (opcode), 1699
IMPORT_STAR (opcode), 1697
importer, **1786**
ImportError, 86
importing, **1786**
importlib (module), 1649
importlib.abc (module), 1651
importlib.machinery (module), 1657
importlib.util (module), 1661
imports (2to3 fixer), 1499
imports2 (2to3 fixer), 1499
ImportWarning, 92
ImproperConnectionState, 1156
imul() (in module operator), 353
in
    operator, 30, 37
in_dll() (ctypes._CData method), 720
in_table_a1() (in module stringprep), 141
in_table_b1() (in module stringprep), 141
in_table_c11() (in module stringprep), 141
in_table_c11_c12() (in module stringprep), 141
in_table_c12() (in module stringprep), 141
in_table_c21() (in module stringprep), 141
in_table_c21_c22() (in module stringprep), 141
in_table_c22() (in module stringprep), 141
in_table_c3() (in module stringprep), 141

in_table_c4() (in module stringprep), 142
in_table_c5() (in module stringprep), 142
in_table_c6() (in module stringprep), 142
in_table_c7() (in module stringprep), 142
in_table_c8() (in module stringprep), 142
in_table_c9() (in module stringprep), 142
in_table_d1() (in module stringprep), 142
in_table_d2() (in module stringprep), 142
in_transaction (sqlite3.Connection attribute), 426
inch() (curses.window method), 672
inclusive (tracemalloc.DomainFilter attribute), 1544
inclusive (tracemalloc.Filter attribute), 1545
Incomplete, 1043
IncompleteRead, 1156
IncompleteReadError, 911
increment_lineno() (in module ast), 1675
IncrementalDecoder (class in codecs), 160
incrementaldecoder (codecs.CodecInfo attribute), 155
IncrementalEncoder (class in codecs), 160
incrementalencoder (codecs.CodecInfo attribute), 155
IncrementalNewlineDecoder (class in io), 581
IncrementalParser (class in xml.sax.xmlreader), 1093
indent (doctest.Example attribute), 1407
INDENT (in module token), 1679
indent() (in module textwrap), 136
IndentationError, 89
index() (array.array method), 234
index() (bytearray method), 56
index() (bytes method), 56
index() (collections.deque method), 212
index() (in module operator), 348
index() (sequence method), 37
index() (str method), 45
index() (tkinter.ttk.Notebook method), 1348
index() (tkinter.ttk.Treeview method), 1354
IndexError, 87
indexOf() (in module operator), 350
IndexSizeErr, 1077
inet_aton() (in module socket), 819
inet_ntoa() (in module socket), 819
inet_ntop() (in module socket), 819
inet_pton() (in module socket), 819
Inexact (class in decimal), 303
inf (in module cmath), 284
inf (in module math), 281
infile
    command line option, 1016
infile (shlex.shlex attribute), 1327
Infinity, 11
infj (in module cmath), 284
info() (dis.Bytecode method), 1691
info() (gettext.NullTranslations method), 1272

info() (in module logging), 635
info() (logging.Logger method), 626
infolist() (zipfile.ZipFile method), 459
ini file, 483
init() (in module mimetypes), 1036
init_color() (in module curses), 665
init_database() (in module msilib), 1711
init_pair() (in module curses), 665
inited (in module mimetypes), 1036
initgroups() (in module os), 529
initial_indent (textwrap.TextWrapper attribute), 138
initscr() (in module curses), 665
inode() (os.DirEntry method), 548
INPLACE_ADD (opcode), 1695
INPLACE_AND (opcode), 1695
INPLACE_FLOOR_DIVIDE (opcode), 1695
INPLACE_LSHIFT (opcode), 1695
INPLACE_MATRIX_MULTIPLY (opcode), 1695
INPLACE_MODULO (opcode), 1695
INPLACE_MULTIPLY (opcode), 1695
INPLACE_OR (opcode), 1695
INPLACE_POWER (opcode), 1695
INPLACE_RSHIFT (opcode), 1695
INPLACE_SUBTRACT (opcode), 1695
INPLACE_TRUE_DIVIDE (opcode), 1695
INPLACE_XOR (opcode), 1695
input (2to3 fixer), 1499
input() (built-in function), 13
input() (in module fileinput), 376
input_charset (email.charset.Charset attribute), 1001
input_codec (email.charset.Charset attribute), 1002
InputOnly (class in tkinter.tix), 1362
InputSource (class in xml.sax.xmlreader), 1094
insch() (curses.window method), 672
insdelln() (curses.window method), 672
insert() (array.array method), 234
insert() (collections.deque method), 212
insert() (sequence method), 39
insert() (tkinter.ttk.Notebook method), 1348
insert() (tkinter.ttk.Treeview method), 1354
insert() (xml.etree.ElementTree.Element method), 1064
insert_text() (in module readline), 143
insertBefore() (xml.dom.Node method), 1073
insertln() (curses.window method), 673
insnstr() (curses.window method), 673
insort() (in module bisect), 230
insort_left() (in module bisect), 230
insort_right() (in module bisect), 230
inspect (module), 1615
inspect command line option
    –details, 1630

InspectLoader (class in importlib.abc), 1654
insstr() (curses.window method), 673
install() (gettext.NullTranslations method), 1272
install() (in module gettext), 1271
install_opener() (in module urllib.request), 1127
install_scripts() (venv.EnvBuilder method), 1555
installHandler() (in module unittest), 1442
instate() (tkinter.ttk.Widget method), 1345
instr() (curses.window method), 673
instream (shlex.shlex attribute), 1327
Instruction (class in dis), 1693
Instruction.arg (in module dis), 1693
Instruction.argrepr (in module dis), 1693
Instruction.argval (in module dis), 1693
Instruction.is_jump_target (in module dis), 1693
Instruction.offset (in module dis), 1693
Instruction.opcode (in module dis), 1693
Instruction.opname (in module dis), 1693
Instruction.starts_line (in module dis), 1693
int
    built-in function, 31
int (built-in class), 13
int (uuid.UUID attribute), 1196
Int2AP() (in module imaplib), 1170
int_info (in module sys), 1571
integer
    literals, 31
    object, 30
    types, operations on, 32
Integral (class in numbers), 274
Integrated Development Environment, 1364
IntegrityError, 436
Intel/DVI ADPCM, 1249
IntEnum (class in enum), 254
interact (pdb command), 1523
interact() (code.InteractiveConsole method), 1638
interact() (in module code), 1637
interact() (telnetlib.Telnet method), 1194
interactive, 1786
InteractiveConsole (class in code), 1637
InteractiveInterpreter (class in code), 1637
intern (2to3 fixer), 1499
intern() (in module sys), 1571
internal_attr (zipfile.ZipInfo attribute), 464
Internaldate2tuple() (in module imaplib), 1170
internalSubset (xml.dom.DocumentType attribute), 1074
Internet, 1107
interpolation, bytearray (%), 64
interpolation, bytes (%), 64
interpolation, string (%), 51
InterpolationDepthError, 500
InterpolationError, 500
InterpolationMissingOptionError, 501

InterpolationSyntaxError, 501
interpreted, **1786**
interpreter prompts, 1574
interpreter shutdown, **1786**
interrupt() (sqlite3.Connection method), 428
interrupt_main() (in module _thread), 807
InterruptedError, 91
intersection() (frozenset method), 74
intersection_update() (frozenset method), 75
IntFlag (class in enum), 254
intro (cmd.Cmd attribute), 1321
InuseAttributeErr, 1077
inv() (in module operator), 349
InvalidAccessErr, 1077
invalidate_caches() (importlib.abc.MetaPathFinder method), 1652
invalidate_caches() (importlib.abc.PathEntryFinder method), 1653
invalidate_caches() (importlib.machinery.FileFinder method), 1659
invalidate_caches() (importlib.machinery.PathFinder class method), 1658
invalidate_caches() (in module importlib), 1650
InvalidCharacterErr, 1078
InvalidModificationErr, 1078
InvalidOperation (class in decimal), 303
InvalidStateErr, 1078
InvalidStateError, 891
InvalidURL, 1156
invert() (in module operator), 349
io (class in typing), 1386
io (module), 570
io.StringIO
    object, 43
IOBase (class in io), 573
ioctl() (in module fcntl), 1737
ioctl() (socket.socket method), 822
IOError, 90
ior() (in module operator), 353
ip (ipaddress.IPv4Interface attribute), 1246
ip (ipaddress.IPv6Interface attribute), 1246
ip_address() (in module ipaddress), 1237
ip_interface() (in module ipaddress), 1237
ip_network() (in module ipaddress), 1237
ipaddress (module), 1236
ipow() (in module operator), 353
ipv4_mapped (ipaddress.IPv6Address attribute), 1239
IPv4Address (class in ipaddress), 1237
IPv4Interface (class in ipaddress), 1246
IPv4Network (class in ipaddress), 1241
IPv6Address (class in ipaddress), 1239
IPv6Interface (class in ipaddress), 1246

IPv6Network (class in ipaddress), 1243
irshift() (in module operator), 353
is
    operator, 30
is not
    operator, 30
is_() (in module operator), 348
is_absolute() (pathlib.PurePath method), 362
is_alive() (multiprocessing.Process method), 746
is_alive() (threading.Thread method), 730
is_assigned() (symtable.Symbol method), 1678
is_attachment() (email.message.EmailMessage method), 955
is_authenticated() (urllib.request.HTTPPasswordMgrWithPriorAuth method), 1136
is_block_device() (pathlib.Path method), 367
is_blocked() (http.cookiejar.DefaultCookiePolicy method), 1220
is_canonical() (decimal.Context method), 299
is_canonical() (decimal.Decimal method), 292
is_char_device() (pathlib.Path method), 367
IS_CHARACTER_JUNK() (in module difflib), 129
is_check_supported() (in module lzma), 455
is_closed() (asyncio.AbstractEventLoop method), 873
is_closing() (asyncio.BaseTransport method), 899
is_declared_global() (symtable.Symbol method), 1678
is_dir() (os.DirEntry method), 548
is_dir() (pathlib.Path method), 367
is_dir() (zipfile.ZipInfo method), 463
is_enabled() (in module faulthandler), 1516
is_expired() (http.cookiejar.Cookie method), 1222
is_fifo() (pathlib.Path method), 367
is_file() (os.DirEntry method), 549
is_file() (pathlib.Path method), 367
is_finalizing() (in module sys), 1571
is_finite() (decimal.Context method), 299
is_finite() (decimal.Decimal method), 293
is_free() (symtable.Symbol method), 1678
is_global (ipaddress.IPv4Address attribute), 1238
is_global (ipaddress.IPv6Address attribute), 1239
is_global() (symtable.Symbol method), 1678
is_hop_by_hop() (in module wsgiref.util), 1118
is_imported() (symtable.Symbol method), 1678
is_infinite() (decimal.Context method), 299
is_infinite() (decimal.Decimal method), 293
is_integer() (float method), 34
is_jython (in module test.support), 1504
IS_LINE_JUNK() (in module difflib), 129
is_linetouched() (curses.window method), 673
is_link_local (ipaddress.IPv4Address attribute), 1239
is_link_local (ipaddress.IPv4Network attribute), 1242
is_link_local (ipaddress.IPv6Address attribute), 1239
is_link_local (ipaddress.IPv6Network attribute), 1244
is_local() (symtable.Symbol method), 1678
is_loopback (ipaddress.IPv4Address attribute), 1238
is_loopback (ipaddress.IPv4Network attribute), 1242
is_loopback (ipaddress.IPv6Address attribute), 1239
is_loopback (ipaddress.IPv6Network attribute), 1244
is_multicast (ipaddress.IPv4Address attribute), 1238
is_multicast (ipaddress.IPv4Network attribute), 1241
is_multicast (ipaddress.IPv6Address attribute), 1239
is_multicast (ipaddress.IPv6Network attribute), 1244
is_multipart() (email.message.EmailMessage method), 951
is_multipart() (email.message.Message method), 989
is_namespace() (symtable.Symbol method), 1678
is_nan() (decimal.Context method), 299
is_nan() (decimal.Decimal method), 293
is_nested() (symtable.SymbolTable method), 1677
is_normal() (decimal.Context method), 300
is_normal() (decimal.Decimal method), 293
is_not() (in module operator), 348
is_not_allowed() (http.cookiejar.DefaultCookiePolicy method), 1220
is_optimized() (symtable.SymbolTable method), 1677
is_package() (importlib.abc.InspectLoader method), 1655
is_package() (importlib.abc.SourceLoader method), 1657
is_package() (importlib.machinery.ExtensionFileLoader method), 1660
is_package() (importlib.machinery.SourceFileLoader method), 1659
is_package() (importlib.machinery.SourcelessFileLoader method), 1660
is_package() (zipimport.zipimporter method), 1642
is_parameter() (symtable.Symbol method), 1678
is_private (ipaddress.IPv4Address attribute), 1238
is_private (ipaddress.IPv4Network attribute), 1242
is_private (ipaddress.IPv6Address attribute), 1239
is_private (ipaddress.IPv6Network attribute), 1244
is_python_build() (in module sysconfig), 1581
is_qnan() (decimal.Context method), 300
is_qnan() (decimal.Decimal method), 293
is_referenced() (symtable.Symbol method), 1678
is_reserved (ipaddress.IPv4Address attribute), 1238

is_reserved (ipaddress.IPv4Network attribute), 1242
is_reserved (ipaddress.IPv6Address attribute), 1239
is_reserved (ipaddress.IPv6Network attribute), 1244
is_reserved() (pathlib.PurePath method), 363
is_resource_enabled() (in module test.support), 1504
is_running() (asyncio.AbstractEventLoop method), 873
is_set() (asyncio.Event method), 922
is_set() (threading.Event method), 736
is_signed() (decimal.Context method), 300
is_signed() (decimal.Decimal method), 293
is_site_local (ipaddress.IPv6Address attribute), 1239
is_site_local (ipaddress.IPv6Network attribute), 1244
is_snan() (decimal.Context method), 300
is_snan() (decimal.Decimal method), 293
is_socket() (pathlib.Path method), 367
is_subnormal() (decimal.Context method), 300
is_subnormal() (decimal.Decimal method), 293
is_symlink() (os.DirEntry method), 549
is_symlink() (pathlib.Path method), 367
is_tarfile() (in module tarfile), 467
is_term_resized() (in module curses), 666
is_tracing() (in module tracemalloc), 1543
is_tracked() (in module gc), 1614
is_unspecified (ipaddress.IPv4Address attribute), 1238
is_unspecified (ipaddress.IPv4Network attribute), 1242
is_unspecified (ipaddress.IPv6Address attribute), 1239
is_unspecified (ipaddress.IPv6Network attribute), 1244
is_wintouched() (curses.window method), 673
is_zero() (decimal.Context method), 300
is_zero() (decimal.Decimal method), 293
is_zipfile() (in module zipfile), 458
isabs() (in module os.path), 373
isabstract() (in module inspect), 1619
IsADirectoryError, 91
isalnum() (bytearray method), 61
isalnum() (bytes method), 61
isalnum() (in module curses.ascii), 682
isalnum() (str method), 45
isalpha() (bytearray method), 61
isalpha() (bytes method), 61
isalpha() (in module curses.ascii), 682
isalpha() (str method), 46
isascii() (in module curses.ascii), 682
isasyncgen() (in module inspect), 1618
isasyncgenfunction() (in module inspect), 1618
isatty() (chunk.Chunk method), 1260

isatty() (in module os), 534
isatty() (io.IOBase method), 573
isawaitable() (in module inspect), 1618
isblank() (in module curses.ascii), 682
isblk() (tarfile.TarInfo method), 472
isbuiltin() (in module inspect), 1618
ischr() (tarfile.TarInfo method), 472
isclass() (in module inspect), 1617
isclose() (in module cmath), 283
isclose() (in module math), 277
iscntrl() (in module curses.ascii), 682
iscode() (in module inspect), 1618
iscoroutine() (in module asyncio), 896
iscoroutine() (in module inspect), 1618
iscoroutinefunction() (in module asyncio), 896
iscoroutinefunction() (in module inspect), 1618
isctrl() (in module curses.ascii), 683
isDaemon() (threading.Thread method), 730
isdatadescriptor() (in module inspect), 1619
isdecimal() (str method), 46
isdev() (tarfile.TarInfo method), 472
isdigit() (bytearray method), 61
isdigit() (bytes method), 61
isdigit() (in module curses.ascii), 682
isdigit() (str method), 46
isdir() (in module os.path), 373
isdir() (tarfile.TarInfo method), 472
isdisjoint() (frozenset method), 74
isdown() (in module turtle), 1297
iselement() (in module xml.etree.ElementTree), 1061
isenabled() (in module gc), 1613
isEnabledFor() (logging.Logger method), 625
isendwin() (in module curses), 666
ISEOF() (in module token), 1679
isexpr() (in module parser), 1669
isexpr() (parser.ST method), 1670
isfifo() (tarfile.TarInfo method), 472
isfile() (in module os.path), 373
isfile() (tarfile.TarInfo method), 471
isfinite() (in module cmath), 283
isfinite() (in module math), 278
isfirstline() (in module fileinput), 377
isframe() (in module inspect), 1618
isfunction() (in module inspect), 1618
isgenerator() (in module inspect), 1618
isgeneratorfunction() (in module inspect), 1618
isgetsetdescriptor() (in module inspect), 1619
isgraph() (in module curses.ascii), 682
isidentifier() (str method), 46
isinf() (in module cmath), 283
isinf() (in module math), 278
isinstance (2to3 fixer), 1499
isinstance() (built-in function), 14
iskeyword() (in module keyword), 1680

isleap() (in module calendar), 205
islice() (in module itertools), 333
islink() (in module os.path), 373
islnk() (tarfile.TarInfo method), 472
islower() (bytearray method), 61
islower() (bytes method), 61
islower() (in module curses.ascii), 683
islower() (str method), 46
ismemberdescriptor() (in module inspect), 1619
ismeta() (in module curses.ascii), 683
ismethod() (in module inspect), 1618
ismethoddescriptor() (in module inspect), 1619
ismodule() (in module inspect), 1617
ismount() (in module os.path), 373
isnan() (in module cmath), 283
isnan() (in module math), 278
ISNONTERMINAL() (in module token), 1679
isnumeric() (str method), 46
isocalendar() (datetime.date method), 179
isocalendar() (datetime.datetime method), 186
isoformat() (datetime.date method), 179
isoformat() (datetime.datetime method), 186
isoformat() (datetime.time method), 190
isolation_level (sqlite3.Connection attribute), 426
isoweekday() (datetime.date method), 179
isoweekday() (datetime.datetime method), 186
isprint() (in module curses.ascii), 683
isprintable() (str method), 46
ispunct() (in module curses.ascii), 683
isreadable() (in module pprint), 248
isreadable() (pprint.PrettyPrinter method), 249
isrecursive() (in module pprint), 249
isrecursive() (pprint.PrettyPrinter method), 249
isreg() (tarfile.TarInfo method), 471
isReservedKey() (http.cookies.Morsel method), 1213
isroutine() (in module inspect), 1619
isSameNode() (xml.dom.Node method), 1072
isspace() (bytearray method), 62
isspace() (bytes method), 62
isspace() (in module curses.ascii), 683
isspace() (str method), 46
isstdin() (in module fileinput), 377
issubclass() (built-in function), 14
issubset() (frozenset method), 74
issuite() (in module parser), 1669
issuite() (parser.ST method), 1670
issuperset() (frozenset method), 74
issym() (tarfile.TarInfo method), 472
ISTERMINAL() (in module token), 1679
istitle() (bytearray method), 62
istitle() (bytes method), 62
istitle() (str method), 46
istraceback() (in module inspect), 1618
isub() (in module operator), 354

isupper() (bytearray method), 62
isupper() (bytes method), 62
isupper() (in module curses.ascii), 683
isupper() (str method), 46
isvisible() (in module turtle), 1301
isxdigit() (in module curses.ascii), 683
item() (tkinter.ttk.Treeview method), 1354
item() (xml.dom.NamedNodeMap method), 1076
item() (xml.dom.NodeList method), 1073
itemgetter() (in module operator), 351
items() (configparser.ConfigParser method), 498
items() (dict method), 77
items() (email.message.EmailMessage method), 953
items() (email.message.Message method), 991
items() (mailbox.Mailbox method), 1019
items() (types.MappingProxyType method), 245
items() (xml.etree.ElementTree.Element method), 1063
itemsize (array.array attribute), 233
itemsize (memoryview attribute), 72
ItemsView (class in collections.abc), 224
ItemsView (class in typing), 1384
iter() (built-in function), 14
iter() (xml.etree.ElementTree.Element method), 1064
iter() (xml.etree.ElementTree.ElementTree method), 1065
iter_attachments() (email.message.EmailMessage method), 956
iter_child_nodes() (in module ast), 1675
iter_fields() (in module ast), 1675
iter_importers() (in module pkgutil), 1644
iter_modules() (in module pkgutil), 1644
iter_parts() (email.message.EmailMessage method), 957
iter_unpack() (in module struct), 150
iter_unpack() (struct.Struct method), 154
iterable, **1786**
Iterable (class in collections.abc), 223
Iterable (class in typing), 1382
iterator, **1787**
Iterator (class in collections.abc), 224
Iterator (class in typing), 1382
iterator protocol, 36
iterdecode() (in module codecs), 156
iterdir() (pathlib.Path method), 367
iterdump() (sqlite3.Connection method), 431
iterencode() (in module codecs), 156
iterencode() (json.JSONEncoder method), 1013
iterfind() (xml.etree.ElementTree.Element method), 1064
iterfind() (xml.etree.ElementTree.ElementTree method), 1065
iteritems() (mailbox.Mailbox method), 1019

iterkeys() (mailbox.Mailbox method), 1019
itermonthdates() (calendar.Calendar method), 203
itermonthdays() (calendar.Calendar method), 203
itermonthdays2() (calendar.Calendar method), 203
iterparse() (in module xml.etree.ElementTree), 1061
itertext() (xml.etree.ElementTree.Element method), 1064
itertools (2to3 fixer), 1499
itertools (module), 327
itertools_imports (2to3 fixer), 1499
itervalues() (mailbox.Mailbox method), 1019
iterweekdays() (calendar.Calendar method), 203
ITIMER_PROF (in module signal), 940
ITIMER_REAL (in module signal), 940
ITIMER_VIRTUAL (in module signal), 940
ItimerError, 940
itruediv() (in module operator), 354
ixor() (in module operator), 354

J

Jansen, Jack, 1044
java_ver() (in module platform), 687
join() (asyncio.Queue method), 924
join() (bytearray method), 56
join() (bytes method), 56
join() (in module os.path), 374
join() (multiprocessing.JoinableQueue method), 750
join() (multiprocessing.pool.Pool method), 767
join() (multiprocessing.Process method), 746
join() (queue.Queue method), 805
join() (str method), 46
join() (threading.Thread method), 730
join_thread() (multiprocessing.Queue method), 749
JoinableQueue (class in multiprocessing), 750
joinpath() (pathlib.PurePath method), 363
js_output() (http.cookies.BaseCookie method), 1212
js_output() (http.cookies.Morsel method), 1213
json (module), 1007
json.tool (module), 1015
JSONDecodeError, 1013
JSONDecoder (class in json), 1011
JSONEncoder (class in json), 1012
jump (pdb command), 1522
JUMP_ABSOLUTE (opcode), 1700
JUMP_FORWARD (opcode), 1699
JUMP_IF_FALSE_OR_POP (opcode), 1700
JUMP_IF_TRUE_OR_POP (opcode), 1700

K

kbhit() (in module msvcrt), 1717
KDEDIR, 1108
kevent() (in module select), 863
key (http.cookies.Morsel attribute), 1213
key function, **1787**

KEY_ALL_ACCESS (in module winreg), 1724
KEY_CREATE_LINK (in module winreg), 1724
KEY_CREATE_SUB_KEY (in module winreg), 1724
KEY_ENUMERATE_SUB_KEYS (in module winreg), 1724
KEY_EXECUTE (in module winreg), 1724
KEY_NOTIFY (in module winreg), 1724
KEY_QUERY_VALUE (in module winreg), 1724
KEY_READ (in module winreg), 1724
KEY_SET_VALUE (in module winreg), 1724
KEY_WOW64_32KEY (in module winreg), 1724
KEY_WOW64_64KEY (in module winreg), 1724
KEY_WRITE (in module winreg), 1724
KeyboardInterrupt, 87
KeyError, 87
keyname() (in module curses), 666
keypad() (curses.window method), 673
keyrefs() (weakref.WeakKeyDictionary method), 237
keys() (dict method), 77
keys() (email.message.EmailMessage method), 953
keys() (email.message.Message method), 991
keys() (mailbox.Mailbox method), 1019
keys() (sqlite3.Row method), 435
keys() (types.MappingProxyType method), 245
keys() (xml.etree.ElementTree.Element method), 1063
KeysView (class in collections.abc), 224
KeysView (class in typing), 1384
keyword (module), 1680
keyword argument, **1787**
keywords (functools.partial attribute), 347
kill() (asyncio.asyncio.subprocess.Process method), 917
kill() (asyncio.BaseSubprocessTransport method), 901
kill() (in module os), 561
kill() (subprocess.Popen method), 795
killchar() (in module curses), 666
killpg() (in module os), 561
kind (inspect.Parameter attribute), 1622
knownfiles (in module mimetypes), 1036
kqueue() (in module select), 863
KqueueSelector (class in selectors), 871
kwargs (inspect.BoundArguments attribute), 1623
kwlist (in module keyword), 1680

L

L (in module re), 112
LabelEntry (class in tkinter.tix), 1360
LabelFrame (class in tkinter.tix), 1360
lambda, **1787**
LambdaType (in module types), 243
LANG, 1269, 1271, 1278, 1280

LANGUAGE, 1269, 1271
language
    C, 30, 31
large files, 1729
LargeZipFile, 458
last() (nntplib.NNTP method), 1180
last_accepted (multiprocessing.connection.Listener attribute), 769
last_traceback (in module sys), 1571
last_type (in module sys), 1571
last_value (in module sys), 1571
lastChild (xml.dom.Node attribute), 1072
lastcmd (cmd.Cmd attribute), 1321
lastgroup (re.match attribute), 119
lastindex (re.match attribute), 119
lastResort (in module logging), 638
lastrowid (sqlite3.Cursor attribute), 434
layout() (tkinter.ttk.Style method), 1357
lazycache() (in module linecache), 392
LazyLoader (class in importlib.util), 1664
LBRACE (in module token), 1679
LBYL, 1787
LC_ALL, 1269, 1271
LC_ALL (in module locale), 1282
LC_COLLATE (in module locale), 1282
LC_CTYPE (in module locale), 1282
LC_MESSAGES, 1269, 1271
LC_MESSAGES (in module locale), 1282
LC_MONETARY (in module locale), 1282
LC_NUMERIC (in module locale), 1282
LC_TIME (in module locale), 1282
lchflags() (in module os), 543
lchmod() (in module os), 543
lchmod() (pathlib.Path method), 368
lchown() (in module os), 543
ldexp() (in module math), 278
ldgettext() (in module gettext), 1270
ldngettext() (in module gettext), 1270
le() (in module operator), 348
leapdays() (in module calendar), 205
leaveok() (curses.window method), 673
left (filecmp.dircmp attribute), 384
left() (in module turtle), 1290
left_list (filecmp.dircmp attribute), 384
left_only (filecmp.dircmp attribute), 384
LEFTSHIFT (in module token), 1679
LEFTSHIFTEQUAL (in module token), 1679
len
    built-in function, 37, 75
len() (built-in function), 14
length (xml.dom.NamedNodeMap attribute), 1076
length (xml.dom.NodeList attribute), 1073
length_hint() (in module operator), 350
LESS (in module token), 1679

LESSEQUAL (in module token), 1679
lexists() (in module os.path), 372
lgamma() (in module math), 280
lgettext() (gettext.GNUTranslations method), 1273
lgettext() (gettext.NullTranslations method), 1272
lgettext() (in module gettext), 1270
lib2to3 (module), 1501
libc_ver() (in module platform), 688
library (in module dbm.ndbm), 421
library (ssl.SSLError attribute), 833
LibraryLoader (class in ctypes), 714
license (built-in variable), 28
LifoQueue (class in asyncio), 925
LifoQueue (class in queue), 804
light-weight processes, 807
limit_denominator() (fractions.Fraction method), 313
LimitOverrunError, 911
lin2adpcm() (in module audioop), 1250
lin2alaw() (in module audioop), 1250
lin2lin() (in module audioop), 1250
lin2ulaw() (in module audioop), 1251
line() (msilib.Dialog method), 1716
line-buffered I/O, 18
line_buffering (io.TextIOWrapper attribute), 580
line_num (csv.csvreader attribute), 482
linecache (module), 391
lineno (ast.AST attribute), 1672
lineno (doctest.DocTest attribute), 1407
lineno (doctest.Example attribute), 1407
lineno (json.JSONDecodeError attribute), 1014
lineno (pyclbr.Class attribute), 1686
lineno (pyclbr.Function attribute), 1686
lineno (re.error attribute), 116
lineno (shlex.shlex attribute), 1327
lineno (traceback.TracebackException attribute), 1607
lineno (tracemalloc.Filter attribute), 1545
lineno (tracemalloc.Frame attribute), 1545
lineno (xml.parsers.expat.ExpatError attribute), 1102
lineno() (in module fileinput), 377
LINES, 664, 669
lines (os.terminal_size attribute), 539
linesep (email.policy.Policy attribute), 967
linesep (in module os), 568
lineterminator (csv.Dialect attribute), 481
LineTooLong, 1157
link() (in module os), 543
linkname (tarfile.TarInfo attribute), 471
linux_distribution() (in module platform), 688
list, 1787
    object, 39, 40
    type, operations on, 39

list (built-in class), 40
List (class in typing), 1383
list (pdb command), 1522
list comprehension, 1787
list() (imaplib.IMAP4 method), 1172
list() (multiprocessing.managers.SyncManager method), 761
list() (nntplib.NNTP method), 1179
list() (poplib.POP3 method), 1168
list() (tarfile.TarFile method), 469
LIST_APPEND (opcode), 1696
list_dialects() (in module csv), 478
list_folders() (mailbox.Maildir method), 1021
list_folders() (mailbox.MH method), 1023
listdir() (in module os), 543
listen() (asyncore.dispatcher method), 934
listen() (in module logging.config), 640
listen() (in module turtle), 1308
listen() (socket.socket method), 823
Listener (class in multiprocessing.connection), 768
listMethods() (xmlrpc.client.ServerProxy.system method), 1225
ListNoteBook (class in tkinter.tix), 1362
listxattr() (in module os), 557
literal_eval() (in module ast), 1675
literals
    binary, 31
    complex number, 31
    floating point, 31
    hexadecimal, 31
    integer, 31
    numeric, 31
    octal, 31
LittleEndianStructure (class in ctypes), 723
ljust() (bytearray method), 58
ljust() (bytes method), 58
ljust() (str method), 47
LK_LOCK (in module msvcrt), 1717
LK_NBLCK (in module msvcrt), 1717
LK_NBRLCK (in module msvcrt), 1717
LK_RLCK (in module msvcrt), 1717
LK_UNLCK (in module msvcrt), 1717
ll (pdb command), 1522
LMTP (class in smtplib), 1183
ln() (decimal.Context method), 300
ln() (decimal.Decimal method), 293
LNAME, 662
lngettext() (gettext.GNUTranslations method), 1273
lngettext() (gettext.NullTranslations method), 1272
lngettext() (in module gettext), 1270
load() (http.cookiejar.FileCookieJar method), 1217
load() (http.cookies.BaseCookie method), 1212
load() (in module json), 1010
load() (in module marshal), 418

load() (in module pickle), 403
load() (in module plistlib), 505
load() (pickle.Unpickler method), 405
load() (tracemalloc.Snapshot class method), 1546
LOAD_ATTR (opcode), 1699
LOAD_BUILD_CLASS (opcode), 1697
load_cert_chain() (ssl.SSLContext method), 847
LOAD_CLASSDEREF (opcode), 1700
LOAD_CLOSURE (opcode), 1700
LOAD_CONST (opcode), 1698
load_default_certs() (ssl.SSLContext method), 848
LOAD_DEREF (opcode), 1700
load_dh_params() (ssl.SSLContext method), 851
load_extension() (sqlite3.Connection method), 430
LOAD_FAST (opcode), 1700
LOAD_GLOBAL (opcode), 1700
load_module() (importlib.abc.FileLoader method), 1656
load_module() (importlib.abc.InspectLoader method), 1655
load_module() (importlib.abc.Loader method), 1653
load_module() (importlib.abc.SourceLoader method), 1657
load_module() (importlib.machinery.SourceFileLoader method), 1659
load_module() (importlib.machinery.SourcelessFileLoader method), 1660
load_module() (in module imp), 1774
load_module() (zipimport.zipimporter method), 1642
LOAD_NAME (opcode), 1698
load_package_tests() (in module test.support), 1508
load_verify_locations() (ssl.SSLContext method), 848
loader, 1787
Loader (class in importlib.abc), 1653
loader (importlib.machinery.ModuleSpec attribute), 1661
loader_state (importlib.machinery.ModuleSpec attribute), 1661
LoadError, 1215
LoadKey() (in module winreg), 1720
LoadLibrary() (ctypes.LibraryLoader method), 714
loads() (in module json), 1011
loads() (in module marshal), 418
loads() (in module pickle), 404
loads() (in module plistlib), 505
loads() (in module xmlrpc.client), 1230
loadTestsFromModule() (unittest.TestLoader method), 1434
loadTestsFromName() (unittest.TestLoader method), 1434
loadTestsFromNames() (unittest.TestLoader method), 1435

loadTestsFromTestCase() (unittest.TestLoader method), 1434
local (class in threading), 728
localcontext() (in module decimal), 296
LOCALE (in module re), 112
locale (module), 1277
localeconv() (in module locale), 1278
LocaleHTMLCalendar (class in calendar), 204
LocaleTextCalendar (class in calendar), 204
localName (xml.dom.Attr attribute), 1076
localName (xml.dom.Node attribute), 1072
locals() (built-in function), 14
localtime() (in module email.utils), 1004
localtime() (in module time), 584
Locator (class in xml.sax.xmlreader), 1094
Lock (class in asyncio), 920
Lock (class in multiprocessing), 754
Lock (class in threading), 731
lock() (mailbox.Babyl method), 1025
lock() (mailbox.Mailbox method), 1020
lock() (mailbox.Maildir method), 1022
lock() (mailbox.mbox method), 1022
lock() (mailbox.MH method), 1024
lock() (mailbox.MMDF method), 1025
Lock() (multiprocessing.managers.SyncManager method), 761
lock_held() (in module imp), 1776
locked() (_thread.lock method), 808
locked() (asyncio.Condition method), 922
locked() (asyncio.Lock method), 921
locked() (asyncio.Semaphore method), 923
lockf() (in module fcntl), 1738
lockf() (in module os), 534
locking() (in module msvcrt), 1717
LockType (in module _thread), 807
log() (in module cmath), 282
log() (in module logging), 636
log() (in module math), 278
log() (logging.Logger method), 626
log10() (decimal.Context method), 300
log10() (decimal.Decimal method), 293
log10() (in module cmath), 282
log10() (in module math), 279
log1p() (in module math), 278
log2() (in module math), 278
log_date_time_string() (http.server.BaseHTTPRequestHandler method), 1209
log_error() (http.server.BaseHTTPRequestHandler method), 1209
log_exception() (wsgiref.handlers.BaseHandler method), 1124
log_message() (http.server.BaseHTTPRequestHandler method), 1209

log_request() (http.server.BaseHTTPRequestHandler method), 1209
log_to_stderr() (in module multiprocessing), 771
logb() (decimal.Context method), 300
logb() (decimal.Decimal method), 293
Logger (class in logging), 624
LoggerAdapter (class in logging), 634
logging
    Errors, 623
logging (module), 623
logging.config (module), 639
logging.handlers (module), 649
logical_and() (decimal.Context method), 300
logical_and() (decimal.Decimal method), 293
logical_invert() (decimal.Context method), 300
logical_invert() (decimal.Decimal method), 293
logical_or() (decimal.Context method), 300
logical_or() (decimal.Decimal method), 293
logical_xor() (decimal.Context method), 300
logical_xor() (decimal.Decimal method), 293
login() (ftplib.FTP method), 1164
login() (imaplib.IMAP4 method), 1172
login() (nntplib.NNTP method), 1178
login() (smtplib.SMTP method), 1185
login_cram_md5() (imaplib.IMAP4 method), 1172
LOGNAME, 528, 662
lognormvariate() (in module random), 317
logout() (imaplib.IMAP4 method), 1172
LogRecord (class in logging), 631
long (2to3 fixer), 1499
longMessage (unittest.TestCase attribute), 1431
longname() (in module curses), 666
lookup() (in module codecs), 154
lookup() (in module unicodedata), 139
lookup() (symtable.SymbolTable method), 1677
lookup() (tkinter.ttk.Style method), 1357
lookup_error() (in module codecs), 158
LookupError, 86
loop() (in module asyncore), 932
lower() (bytearray method), 62
lower() (bytes method), 62
lower() (str method), 47
LPAR (in module token), 1679
lru_cache() (in module functools), 341
lseek() (in module os), 534
lshift() (in module operator), 349
LSQB (in module token), 1679
lstat() (in module os), 544
lstat() (pathlib.Path method), 368
lstrip() (bytearray method), 58
lstrip() (bytes method), 58
lstrip() (str method), 47
lsub() (imaplib.IMAP4 method), 1172
lt() (in module operator), 348

lt() (in module turtle), 1290
LWPCookieJar (class in http.cookiejar), 1218
lzma (module), 452
LZMACompressor (class in lzma), 453
LZMADecompressor (class in lzma), 454
LZMAError, 452
LZMAFile (class in lzma), 453

M

M (in module re), 112
mac_ver() (in module platform), 687
machine() (in module platform), 685
macpath (module), 400
macros (netrc.netrc attribute), 502
MAGIC_NUMBER (in module importlib.util), 1661
MagicMock (class in unittest.mock), 1467
Mailbox (class in mailbox), 1018
mailbox (module), 1017
mailcap (module), 1016
Maildir (class in mailbox), 1021
MaildirMessage (class in mailbox), 1026
mailfrom (smtpd.SMTPChannel attribute), 1191
MailmanProxy (class in smtpd), 1190
main() (in module py_compile), 1687
main() (in module site), 1632
main() (in module unittest), 1439
main_thread() (in module threading), 727
mainloop() (in module turtle), 1310
maintype (email.headerregistry.ContentTypeHeader attribute), 976
major (email.headerregistry.MIMEVersionHeader attribute), 976
major() (in module os), 545
make_alternative() (email.message.EmailMessage method), 957
make_archive() (in module shutil), 397
make_bad_fd() (in module test.support), 1507
make_cookies() (http.cookiejar.CookieJar method), 1217
make_file() (difflib.HtmlDiff method), 126
MAKE_FUNCTION (opcode), 1701
make_header() (in module email.header), 1001
make_mixed() (email.message.EmailMessage method), 957
make_msgid() (in module email.utils), 1004
make_parser() (in module xml.sax), 1086
make_related() (email.message.EmailMessage method), 957
make_server() (in module wsgiref.simple_server), 1120
make_table() (difflib.HtmlDiff method), 126
makedev() (in module os), 545
makedirs() (in module os), 544

makeelement() (xml.etree.ElementTree.Element method), 1064
makefile() (socket.socket method), 823
makeLogRecord() (in module logging), 637
makePickle() (logging.handlers.SocketHandler method), 655
makeRecord() (logging.Logger method), 627
makeSocket() (logging.handlers.DatagramHandler method), 655
makeSocket() (logging.handlers.SocketHandler method), 655
maketrans() (bytearray static method), 56
maketrans() (bytes static method), 56
maketrans() (str static method), 47
mangle_from_ (email.policy.Compat32 attribute), 971
mangle_from_ (email.policy.Policy attribute), 967
map (2to3 fixer), 1499
map() (built-in function), 14
map() (concurrent.futures.Executor method), 782
map() (multiprocessing.pool.Pool method), 766
map() (tkinter.ttk.Style method), 1356
MAP_ADD (opcode), 1696
map_async() (multiprocessing.pool.Pool method), 766
map_table_b2() (in module stringprep), 141
map_table_b3() (in module stringprep), 141
map_to_type() (email.headerregistry.HeaderRegistry method), 977
mapLogRecord() (logging.handlers.HTTPHandler method), 660
mapping, **1787**
    object, 75
    types, operations on, 75
Mapping (class in collections.abc), 224
Mapping (class in typing), 1383
mapping() (msilib.Control method), 1715
MappingProxyType (class in types), 244
MappingView (class in collections.abc), 224
MappingView (class in typing), 1384
mapPriority() (logging.handlers.SysLogHandler method), 657
maps (collections.ChainMap attribute), 207
maps() (in module nis), 1744
marshal (module), 417
marshalling
    objects, 401
masking
    operations, 32
match() (in module nis), 1744
match() (in module re), 113
match() (pathlib.PurePath method), 363
match() (re.regex method), 116
match_hostname() (in module ssl), 836

math
    module, 31, 284
math (module), 276
matmul() (in module operator), 349
max
    built-in function, 37
max (datetime.date attribute), 178
max (datetime.datetime attribute), 182
max (datetime.time attribute), 189
max (datetime.timedelta attribute), 175
max() (built-in function), 15
max() (decimal.Context method), 300
max() (decimal.Decimal method), 293
max() (in module audioop), 1251
max_count (email.headerregistry.BaseHeader attribute), 974
MAX_EMAX (in module decimal), 302
MAX_INTERPOLATION_DEPTH (in module configparser), 499
max_line_length (email.policy.Policy attribute), 967
max_lines (textwrap.TextWrapper attribute), 138
max_mag() (decimal.Context method), 300
max_mag() (decimal.Decimal method), 294
MAX_PREC (in module decimal), 302
max_prefixlen (ipaddress.IPv4Address attribute), 1238
max_prefixlen (ipaddress.IPv4Network attribute), 1241
max_prefixlen (ipaddress.IPv6Address attribute), 1239
max_prefixlen (ipaddress.IPv6Network attribute), 1244
maxarray (reprlib.Repr attribute), 253
maxdeque (reprlib.Repr attribute), 253
maxdict (reprlib.Repr attribute), 253
maxDiff (unittest.TestCase attribute), 1431
maxfrozenset (reprlib.Repr attribute), 253
maxlen (collections.deque attribute), 212
maxlevel (reprlib.Repr attribute), 253
maxlist (reprlib.Repr attribute), 253
maxlong (reprlib.Repr attribute), 253
maxother (reprlib.Repr attribute), 253
maxpp() (in module audioop), 1251
maxset (reprlib.Repr attribute), 253
maxsize (asyncio.Queue attribute), 925
maxsize (in module sys), 1572
maxstring (reprlib.Repr attribute), 253
maxtuple (reprlib.Repr attribute), 253
maxunicode (in module sys), 1572
MAXYEAR (in module datetime), 173
MB_ICONASTERISK (in module winsound), 1727
MB_ICONEXCLAMATION (in module winsound), 1727
MB_ICONHAND (in module winsound), 1727

MB_ICONQUESTION (in module winsound), 1727
MB_OK (in module winsound), 1728
mbox (class in mailbox), 1022
mboxMessage (class in mailbox), 1028
mean() (in module statistics), 320
median() (in module statistics), 321
median_grouped() (in module statistics), 322
median_high() (in module statistics), 322
median_low() (in module statistics), 322
MemberDescriptorType (in module types), 244
memmove() (in module ctypes), 719
MemoryBIO (class in ssl), 859
MemoryError, 87
MemoryHandler (class in logging.handlers), 659
memoryview
    object, 53
memoryview (built-in class), 67
memset() (in module ctypes), 719
merge() (in module heapq), 227
Message (class in email.message), 988
Message (class in mailbox), 1026
message digest, MD5, 509
message_factory (email.policy.Policy attribute), 967
message_from_bytes() (in module email), 961
message_from_file() (in module email), 961
message_from_string() (in module email), 961
MessageBeep() (in module winsound), 1726
MessageClass (http.server.BaseHTTPRequestHandler attribute), 1207
MessageError, 972
MessageParseError, 972
messages (in module xml.parsers.expat.errors), 1104
meta path finder, **1788**
meta() (in module curses), 666
meta_path (in module sys), 1572
metaclass, **1788**
metaclass (2to3 fixer), 1500
MetaPathFinder (class in importlib.abc), 1652
metavar (optparse.Option attribute), 1760
MetavarTypeHelpFormatter (class in argparse), 596
Meter (class in tkinter.tix), 1360
method, **1788**
    object, 80
method (urllib.request.Request attribute), 1132
method resolution order, **1788**
method_calls (unittest.mock.Mock attribute), 1451
METHOD_CRYPT (in module crypt), 1733
METHOD_MD5 (in module crypt), 1733
METHOD_SHA256 (in module crypt), 1733
METHOD_SHA512 (in module crypt), 1733
methodattrs (2to3 fixer), 1500
methodcaller() (in module operator), 351
methodHelp() (xmlrpc.client.ServerProxy.system method), 1226

methods
    bytearray, 55
    bytes, 55
    string, 43
methods (in module crypt), 1733
methods (pyclbr.Class attribute), 1686
methodSignature() (xmlrpc.client.ServerProxy.system method), 1225
MethodType (in module types), 244
MH (class in mailbox), 1023
MHMessage (class in mailbox), 1029
microsecond (datetime.datetime attribute), 183
microsecond (datetime.time attribute), 190
MIME
    base64 encoding, 1038
    content type, 1035
    headers, 1035, 1109
    quoted-printable encoding, 1044
MIMEApplication (class in email.mime.application), 997
MIMEAudio (class in email.mime.audio), 997
MIMEBase (class in email.mime.base), 996
MIMEImage (class in email.mime.image), 997
MIMEMessage (class in email.mime.message), 998
MIMEMultipart (class in email.mime.multipart), 996
MIMENonMultipart (class in email.mime.nonmultipart), 996
MIMEPart (class in email.message), 958
MIMEText (class in email.mime.text), 998
MimeTypes (class in mimetypes), 1037
mimetypes (module), 1035
MIMEVersionHeader (class in email.headerregistry), 976
min
    built-in function, 37
min (datetime.date attribute), 178
min (datetime.datetime attribute), 182
min (datetime.time attribute), 189
min (datetime.timedelta attribute), 175
min() (built-in function), 15
min() (decimal.Context method), 300
min() (decimal.Decimal method), 294
MIN_EMIN (in module decimal), 302
MIN_ETINY (in module decimal), 302
min_mag() (decimal.Context method), 300
min_mag() (decimal.Decimal method), 294
MINEQUAL (in module token), 1679
minmax() (in module audioop), 1251
minor (email.headerregistry.MIMEVersionHeader attribute), 976
minor() (in module os), 545
MINUS (in module token), 1679
minus() (decimal.Context method), 300

minute (datetime.datetime attribute), 183
minute (datetime.time attribute), 190
MINYEAR (in module datetime), 173
mirrored() (in module unicodedata), 139
misc_header (cmd.Cmd attribute), 1321
MissingSectionHeaderError, 501
MIXERDEV, 1264
mkd() (ftplib.FTP method), 1165
mkdir() (in module os), 544
mkdir() (pathlib.Path method), 368
mkdtemp() (in module tempfile), 387
mkfifo() (in module os), 545
mknod() (in module os), 545
mksalt() (in module crypt), 1733
mkstemp() (in module tempfile), 386
mktemp() (in module tempfile), 389
mktime() (in module time), 584
mktime_tz() (in module email.utils), 1005
mlsd() (ftplib.FTP method), 1165
mmap (class in mmap), 944
mmap (module), 943
MMDF (class in mailbox), 1025
MMDFMessage (class in mailbox), 1032
Mock (class in unittest.mock), 1445
mock_add_spec() (unittest.mock.Mock method), 1448
mock_calls (unittest.mock.Mock attribute), 1451
mock_open() (in module unittest.mock), 1472
mod() (in module operator), 349
mode (io.FileIO attribute), 577
mode (ossaudiodev.oss_audio_device attribute), 1266
mode (tarfile.TarInfo attribute), 471
mode() (in module statistics), 323
mode() (in module turtle), 1311
modf() (in module math), 278
modified() (urllib.robotparser.RobotFileParser method), 1152
Modify() (msilib.View method), 1713
modify() (select.devpoll method), 864
modify() (select.epoll method), 865
modify() (select.poll method), 866
modify() (selectors.BaseSelector method), 870
module, 1788
    __main__, 1647, 1648
    _locale, 1277
    array, 53
    base64, 1042
    bdb, 1517
    binhex, 1042
    cmd, 1517
    copy, 414
    crypt, 1730
    dbm.gnu, 416

dbm.ndbm, 416
errno, 87
glob, 390
imp, 24
math, 31, 284
os, 1729
pickle, 247, 414, 415, 417
pty, 536
pwd, 372
pyexpat, 1097
re, 44, 390
search path, 392, 1572, 1630
shelve, 417
signal, 808
sitecustomize, 1631
socket, 1107
stat, 549
string, 1282
struct, 827
sys, 18
types, 81
urllib.request, 1155
usercustomize, 1631
uu, 1042
module (pyclbr.Class attribute), 1685
module (pyclbr.Function attribute), 1686
module spec, **1788**
module_for_loader() (in module importlib.util), 1663
module_from_spec() (in module importlib.util), 1663
module_repr() (importlib.abc.Loader method), 1654
ModuleFinder (class in modulefinder), 1646
modulefinder (module), 1645
ModuleInfo (class in pkgutil), 1643
ModuleNotFoundError, 87
modules (in module sys), 1572
modules (modulefinder.ModuleFinder attribute), 1646
ModuleSpec (class in importlib.machinery), 1660
ModuleType (class in types), 244
monotonic() (in module time), 584
month (datetime.date attribute), 178
month (datetime.datetime attribute), 183
month() (in module calendar), 205
month_abbr (in module calendar), 206
month_name (in module calendar), 206
monthcalendar() (in module calendar), 205
monthdatescalendar() (calendar.Calendar method), 203
monthdays2calendar() (calendar.Calendar method), 203
monthdayscalendar() (calendar.Calendar method), 203

monthrange() (in module calendar), 205
Morsel (class in http.cookies), 1212
most_common() (collections.Counter method), 209
mouseinterval() (in module curses), 666
mousemask() (in module curses), 666
move() (curses.panel.Panel method), 684
move() (curses.window method), 673
move() (in module shutil), 395
move() (mmap.mmap method), 946
move() (tkinter.ttk.Treeview method), 1354
move_to_end() (collections.OrderedDict method), 219
MozillaCookieJar (class in http.cookiejar), 1218
MRO, **1788**
mro() (class method), 82
msg (http.client.HTTPResponse attribute), 1160
msg (json.JSONDecodeError attribute), 1013
msg (re.error attribute), 115
msg (traceback.TracebackException attribute), 1608
msg() (telnetlib.Telnet method), 1193
msi, 1711
msilib (module), 1711
msvcrt (module), 1716
mt_interact() (telnetlib.Telnet method), 1194
mtime (gzip.GzipFile attribute), 448
mtime (tarfile.TarInfo attribute), 471
mtime() (urllib.robotparser.RobotFileParser method), 1152
mul() (in module audioop), 1251
mul() (in module operator), 349
MultiCall (class in xmlrpc.client), 1229
MULTILINE (in module re), 112
MultipartConversionError, 972
multiply() (decimal.Context method), 300
multiprocessing (module), 739
multiprocessing.connection (module), 768
multiprocessing.dummy (module), 772
multiprocessing.Manager() (in module multiprocessing.sharedctypes), 759
multiprocessing.managers (module), 759
multiprocessing.pool (module), 765
multiprocessing.sharedctypes (module), 757
mutable, **1788**
    sequence types, 39
MutableMapping (class in collections.abc), 224
MutableMapping (class in typing), 1383
MutableSequence (class in collections.abc), 224
MutableSequence (class in typing), 1383
MutableSet (class in collections.abc), 224
MutableSet (class in typing), 1383
mvderwin() (curses.window method), 673
mvwin() (curses.window method), 673
myrights() (imaplib.IMAP4 method), 1173

N

N_TOKENS (in module token), 1679
n_waiting (threading.Barrier attribute), 738
name (codecs.CodecInfo attribute), 155
name (doctest.DocTest attribute), 1407
name (email.headerregistry.BaseHeader attribute), 974
name (hashlib.hash attribute), 511
name (hmac.HMAC attribute), 520
name (http.cookiejar.Cookie attribute), 1221
name (importlib.abc.FileLoader attribute), 1655
name (importlib.machinery.ExtensionFileLoader attribute), 1660
name (importlib.machinery.ModuleSpec attribute), 1661
name (importlib.machinery.SourceFileLoader attribute), 1659
name (importlib.machinery.SourcelessFileLoader attribute), 1660
name (in module os), 525
NAME (in module token), 1679
name (inspect.Parameter attribute), 1622
name (io.FileIO attribute), 577
name (multiprocessing.Process attribute), 746
name (os.DirEntry attribute), 548
name (ossaudiodev.oss_audio_device attribute), 1266
name (pyclbr.Class attribute), 1686
name (pyclbr.Function attribute), 1686
name (tarfile.TarInfo attribute), 471
name (threading.Thread attribute), 730
name (xml.dom.Attr attribute), 1076
name (xml.dom.DocumentType attribute), 1074
name() (in module unicodedata), 139
name2codepoint (in module html.entities), 1052
named tuple, 1788
NamedTemporaryFile() (in module tempfile), 386
NamedTuple (class in typing), 1386
namedtuple() (in module collections), 216
NameError, 87
namelist() (zipfile.ZipFile method), 459
nameprep() (in module encodings.idna), 171
namer (logging.handlers.BaseRotatingHandler attribute), 651
namereplace_errors() (in module codecs), 159
namespace, 1788
Namespace (class in argparse), 613
Namespace (class in multiprocessing.managers), 761
namespace package, 1788
namespace() (imaplib.IMAP4 method), 1173
Namespace() (multiprocessing.managers.SyncManager method), 761
NAMESPACE_DNS (in module uuid), 1196
NAMESPACE_OID (in module uuid), 1197
NAMESPACE_URL (in module uuid), 1197
NAMESPACE_X500 (in module uuid), 1197
NamespaceErr, 1078
namespaceURI (xml.dom.Node attribute), 1072
NaN, 11
nan (in module cmath), 284
nan (in module math), 281
nanj (in module cmath), 284
NannyNag, 1685
napms() (in module curses), 666
nargs (optparse.Option attribute), 1760
nbytes (memoryview attribute), 72
ndiff() (in module difflib), 127
ndim (memoryview attribute), 72
ne (2to3 fixer), 1500
ne() (in module operator), 348
needs_input (bz2.BZ2Decompressor attribute), 451
needs_input (lzma.LZMADecompressor attribute), 455
neg() (in module operator), 349
nested scope, 1788
NetmaskValueError, 1247
netrc (class in netrc), 501
netrc (module), 501
NetrcParseError, 501
netscape (http.cookiejar.CookiePolicy attribute), 1219
network (ipaddress.IPv4Interface attribute), 1246
network (ipaddress.IPv6Interface attribute), 1246
Network News Transfer Protocol, 1176
network_address (ipaddress.IPv4Network attribute), 1242
network_address (ipaddress.IPv6Network attribute), 1244
new() (in module hashlib), 510
new() (in module hmac), 519
new-style class, 1789
new_alignment() (formatter.writer method), 1707
new_child() (collections.ChainMap method), 207
new_class() (in module types), 243
new_event_loop() (asyncio.AbstractEventLoopPolicy method), 887
new_event_loop() (in module asyncio), 885
new_font() (formatter.writer method), 1707
new_margin() (formatter.writer method), 1708
new_module() (in module imp), 1775
new_panel() (in module curses.panel), 684
new_spacing() (formatter.writer method), 1708
new_styles() (formatter.writer method), 1708
newgroups() (nntplib.NNTP method), 1179
NEWLINE (in module token), 1679
newlines (io.TextIOBase attribute), 579

newnews() (nntplib.NNTP method), 1179
newpad() (in module curses), 666
NewType() (in module typing), 1387
newwin() (in module curses), 666
next (2to3 fixer), 1500
next (pdb command), 1521
next() (built-in function), 15
next() (nntplib.NNTP method), 1180
next() (tarfile.TarFile method), 469
next() (tkinter.ttk.Treeview method), 1354
next_minus() (decimal.Context method), 300
next_minus() (decimal.Decimal method), 294
next_plus() (decimal.Context method), 300
next_plus() (decimal.Decimal method), 294
next_toward() (decimal.Context method), 300
next_toward() (decimal.Decimal method), 294
nextfile() (in module fileinput), 377
nextkey() (dbm.gnu.gdbm method), 421
nextSibling (xml.dom.Node attribute), 1072
ngettext() (gettext.GNUTranslations method), 1273
ngettext() (gettext.NullTranslations method), 1272
ngettext() (in module gettext), 1270
nice() (in module os), 561
nis (module), 1744
NL (in module tokenize), 1681
nl() (in module curses), 667
nl_langinfo() (in module locale), 1279
nlargest() (in module heapq), 227
nlst() (ftplib.FTP method), 1165
NNTP
    protocol, 1176
NNTP (class in nntplib), 1176
nntp_implementation (nntplib.NNTP attribute), 1178
NNTP_SSL (class in nntplib), 1177
nntp_version (nntplib.NNTP attribute), 1177
NNTPDataError, 1177
NNTPError, 1177
nntplib (module), 1176
NNTPPermanentError, 1177
NNTPProtocolError, 1177
NNTPReplyError, 1177
NNTPTemporaryError, 1177
no_proxy, 1130
no_type_check() (in module typing), 1388
no_type_check_decorator() (in module typing), 1388
nocbreak() (in module curses), 667
NoDataAllowedErr, 1078
node() (in module platform), 685
nodelay() (curses.window method), 673
nodeName (xml.dom.Node attribute), 1072
NodeTransformer (class in ast), 1675
nodeType (xml.dom.Node attribute), 1071

nodeValue (xml.dom.Node attribute), 1072
NodeVisitor (class in ast), 1675
noecho() (in module curses), 667
NOEXPR (in module locale), 1280
NoModificationAllowedErr, 1078
nonblock() (ossaudiodev.oss_audio_device method), 1265
NonCallableMagicMock (class in unittest.mock), 1467
NonCallableMock (class in unittest.mock), 1452
None (Built-in object), 29
None (built-in variable), 27
nonl() (in module curses), 667
nonzero (2to3 fixer), 1500
noop() (imaplib.IMAP4 method), 1173
noop() (poplib.POP3 method), 1168
NoOptionError, 500
NOP (opcode), 1693
noqiflush() (in module curses), 667
noraw() (in module curses), 667
normalize() (decimal.Context method), 301
normalize() (decimal.Decimal method), 294
normalize() (in module locale), 1281
normalize() (in module unicodedata), 140
normalize() (xml.dom.Node method), 1073
NORMALIZE_WHITESPACE (in module doctest), 1398
normalvariate() (in module random), 317
normcase() (in module os.path), 374
normpath() (in module os.path), 374
NoSectionError, 500
NoSuchMailboxError, 1033
not
    operator, 29
not in
    operator, 30, 37
not_() (in module operator), 348
NotADirectoryError, 91
notationDecl() (xml.sax.handler.DTDHandler method), 1091
NotationDeclHandler() (xml.parsers.expat.xmlparser method), 1101
notations (xml.dom.DocumentType attribute), 1074
NotConnected, 1156
NoteBook (class in tkinter.tix), 1362
Notebook (class in tkinter.ttk), 1348
NotEmptyError, 1034
NOTEQUAL (in module token), 1679
NotFoundErr, 1078
notify() (asyncio.Condition method), 922
notify() (threading.Condition method), 734
notify_all() (asyncio.Condition method), 922
notify_all() (threading.Condition method), 734
notimeout() (curses.window method), 673

NotImplemented (built-in variable), 27
NotImplementedError, 87
NotStandaloneHandler() (xml.parsers.expat.xmlparser method), 1102
NotSupportedErr, 1078
noutrefresh() (curses.window method), 674
now() (datetime.datetime class method), 181
NSIG (in module signal), 940
nsmallest() (in module heapq), 227
NT_OFFSET (in module token), 1679
NTEventLogHandler (class in logging.handlers), 657
ntohl() (in module socket), 819
ntohs() (in module socket), 819
ntransfercmd() (ftplib.FTP method), 1165
NullFormatter (class in formatter), 1707
NullHandler (class in logging), 651
NullImporter (class in imp), 1777
NullTranslations (class in gettext), 1271
NullWriter (class in formatter), 1708
num_addresses (ipaddress.IPv4Network attribute), 1242
num_addresses (ipaddress.IPv6Network attribute), 1244
Number (class in numbers), 273
NUMBER (in module token), 1679
number_class() (decimal.Context method), 301
number_class() (decimal.Decimal method), 294
numbers (module), 273
numerator (fractions.Fraction attribute), 312
numerator (numbers.Rational attribute), 274
numeric
    conversions, 31
    literals, 31
    object, 30
    types, operations on, 31
numeric() (in module unicodedata), 139
Numerical Python, 21
numinput() (in module turtle), 1310
numliterals (2to3 fixer), 1500

O

O_APPEND (in module os), 535
O_ASYNC (in module os), 535
O_BINARY (in module os), 535
O_CLOEXEC (in module os), 535
O_CREAT (in module os), 535
O_DIRECT (in module os), 535
O_DIRECTORY (in module os), 535
O_DSYNC (in module os), 535
O_EXCL (in module os), 535
O_EXLOCK (in module os), 535
O_NDELAY (in module os), 535
O_NOATIME (in module os), 535
O_NOCTTY (in module os), 535
O_NOFOLLOW (in module os), 535
O_NOINHERIT (in module os), 535
O_NONBLOCK (in module os), 535
O_PATH (in module os), 535
O_RANDOM (in module os), 535
O_RDONLY (in module os), 535
O_RDWR (in module os), 535
O_RSYNC (in module os), 535
O_SEQUENTIAL (in module os), 535
O_SHLOCK (in module os), 535
O_SHORT_LIVED (in module os), 535
O_SYNC (in module os), 535
O_TEMPORARY (in module os), 535
O_TEXT (in module os), 535
O_TMPFILE (in module os), 535
O_TRUNC (in module os), 535
O_WRONLY (in module os), 535
obj (memoryview attribute), 71
object, **1789**
    Boolean, 30
    bytearray, 39, 53, 54
    bytes, 53
    code, 81, 417
    complex number, 30
    dictionary, 75
    floating point, 30
    integer, 30
    io.StringIO, 43
    list, 39, 40
    mapping, 75
    memoryview, 53
    method, 80
    numeric, 30
    range, 41
    sequence, 37
    set, 73
    socket, 811
    string, 43
    traceback, 1565, 1605
    tuple, 39, 41
    type, 23
object (built-in class), 15
object (UnicodeError attribute), 90
objects
    comparing, 30
    flattening, 401
    marshalling, 401
    persistent, 401
    pickling, 401
    serializing, 401
obufcount() (ossaudiodev.oss_audio_device method), 1266

obuffree() (ossaudiodev.oss_audio_device method), 1266
oct() (built-in function), 15
octal
    literals, 31
octdigits (in module string), 95
offset (traceback.TracebackException attribute), 1608
offset (xml.parsers.expat.ExpatError attribute), 1102
OK (in module curses), 675
OleDLL (class in ctypes), 713
onclick() (in module turtle), 1303, 1309
ondrag() (in module turtle), 1304
onecmd() (cmd.Cmd method), 1320
onkey() (in module turtle), 1309
onkeypress() (in module turtle), 1309
onkeyrelease() (in module turtle), 1309
onrelease() (in module turtle), 1304
onscreenclick() (in module turtle), 1309
ontimer() (in module turtle), 1309
OP (in module token), 1679
OP_ALL (in module ssl), 840
OP_CIPHER_SERVER_PREFERENCE (in module ssl), 841
OP_NO_COMPRESSION (in module ssl), 841
OP_NO_SSLv2 (in module ssl), 840
OP_NO_SSLv3 (in module ssl), 840
OP_NO_TICKET (in module ssl), 841
OP_NO_TLSv1 (in module ssl), 841
OP_NO_TLSv1_1 (in module ssl), 841
OP_NO_TLSv1_2 (in module ssl), 841
OP_NO_TLSv1_3 (in module ssl), 841
OP_SINGLE_DH_USE (in module ssl), 841
OP_SINGLE_ECDH_USE (in module ssl), 841
open() (built-in function), 16
open() (imaplib.IMAP4 method), 1173
open() (in module aifc), 1252
open() (in module bz2), 449
open() (in module codecs), 156
open() (in module dbm), 419
open() (in module dbm.dumb), 422
open() (in module dbm.gnu), 420
open() (in module dbm.ndbm), 421
open() (in module gzip), 447
open() (in module io), 571
open() (in module lzma), 452
open() (in module os), 534
open() (in module ossaudiodev), 1263
open() (in module shelve), 415
open() (in module sunau), 1255
open() (in module tarfile), 465
open() (in module tokenize), 1682
open() (in module wave), 1257
open() (in module webbrowser), 1107
open() (pathlib.Path method), 368
open() (pipes.Template method), 1740
open() (tarfile.TarFile class method), 469
open() (telnetlib.Telnet method), 1193
open() (urllib.request.OpenerDirector method), 1133
open() (urllib.request.URLopener method), 1142
open() (webbrowser.controller method), 1109
open() (zipfile.ZipFile method), 460
open_connection() (in module asyncio), 908
open_new() (in module webbrowser), 1108
open_new() (webbrowser.controller method), 1109
open_new_tab() (in module webbrowser), 1108
open_new_tab() (webbrowser.controller method), 1109
open_osfhandle() (in module msvcrt), 1717
open_unix_connection() (in module asyncio), 909
open_unknown() (urllib.request.URLopener method), 1142
OpenDatabase() (in module msilib), 1711
OpenerDirector (class in urllib.request), 1129
openfp() (in module sunau), 1255
openfp() (in module wave), 1257
OpenKey() (in module winreg), 1721
OpenKeyEx() (in module winreg), 1721
openlog() (in module syslog), 1745
openmixer() (in module ossaudiodev), 1264
openpty() (in module os), 536
openpty() (in module pty), 1736
OpenSSL
    (use in module hashlib), 509
    (use in module ssl), 832
OPENSSL_VERSION (in module ssl), 842
OPENSSL_VERSION_INFO (in module ssl), 842
OPENSSL_VERSION_NUMBER (in module ssl), 842
OpenView() (msilib.Database method), 1712
operation
    concatenation, 37
    repetition, 37
    slice, 37
    subscript, 37
operations
    bitwise, 32
    Boolean, 29
    masking, 32
    shifting, 32
operations on
    dictionary type, 75
    integer types, 32
    list type, 39
    mapping types, 75
    numeric types, 31
    sequence types, 37, 39
operator

*, 31
**, 31
+, 31
-, 31
/, 31
//, 31
==, 30
%, 31
&, 32
^, 32
~, 32
|, 32
>, 30
>=, 30
>>, 32
<, 30
<=, 30
<<, 32
and, 29
comparison, 30
in, 30, 37
is, 30
is not, 30
not, 29
not in, 30, 37
or, 29
operator (2to3 fixer), 1500
operator (module), 347
opmap (in module dis), 1702
opname (in module dis), 1702
optimize() (in module pickletools), 1704
OPTIMIZED_BYTECODE_SUFFIXES (in module importlib.machinery), 1657
Optional (in module typing), 1388
OptionGroup (class in optparse), 1754
OptionMenu (class in tkinter.tix), 1361
OptionParser (class in optparse), 1757
Options (class in ssl), 841
options (doctest.Example attribute), 1407
options (ssl.SSLContext attribute), 852
options() (configparser.ConfigParser method), 497
optionxform() (configparser.ConfigParser method), 499
optionxform() (in module configparser), 493
optparse (module), 1747
or
    operator, 29
or_() (in module operator), 349
ord() (built-in function), 19
ordered_attributes (xml.parsers.expat.xmlparser attribute), 1099
OrderedDict (class in collections), 219
origin (importlib.machinery.ModuleSpec attribute), 1661

origin_req_host (urllib.request.Request attribute), 1131
origin_server (wsgiref.handlers.BaseHandler attribute), 1125
os
    module, 1729
os (module), 525
os.path (module), 371
os_environ (wsgiref.handlers.BaseHandler attribute), 1124
OSError, 87
ossaudiodev (module), 1263
OSSAudioError, 1263
outfile
    command line option, 1016
output (subprocess.CalledProcessError attribute), 789
output (subprocess.TimeoutExpired attribute), 789
output (unittest.TestCase attribute), 1428
output() (http.cookies.BaseCookie method), 1212
output() (http.cookies.Morsel method), 1213
output_charset (email.charset.Charset attribute), 1002
output_charset() (gettext.NullTranslations method), 1272
output_codec (email.charset.Charset attribute), 1002
output_difference() (doctest.OutputChecker method), 1410
OutputChecker (class in doctest), 1410
OutputString() (http.cookies.Morsel method), 1213
over() (nntplib.NNTP method), 1180
Overflow (class in decimal), 303
OverflowError, 88
overlaps() (ipaddress.IPv4Network method), 1242
overlaps() (ipaddress.IPv6Network method), 1244
overlay() (curses.window method), 674
overload() (in module typing), 1387
overwrite() (curses.window method), 674
owner() (pathlib.Path method), 368

P

p (pdb command), 1522
P_ALL (in module os), 564
P_DETACH (in module os), 562
P_NOWAIT (in module os), 562
P_NOWAITO (in module os), 562
P_OVERLAY (in module os), 562
P_PGID (in module os), 564
P_PID (in module os), 564
P_WAIT (in module os), 562
pack() (in module struct), 149
pack() (mailbox.MH method), 1023
pack() (struct.Struct method), 154

pack_array() (xdrlib.Packer method), 503
pack_bytes() (xdrlib.Packer method), 503
pack_double() (xdrlib.Packer method), 503
pack_farray() (xdrlib.Packer method), 503
pack_float() (xdrlib.Packer method), 502
pack_fopaque() (xdrlib.Packer method), 503
pack_fstring() (xdrlib.Packer method), 503
pack_into() (in module struct), 150
pack_into() (struct.Struct method), 154
pack_list() (xdrlib.Packer method), 503
pack_opaque() (xdrlib.Packer method), 503
pack_string() (xdrlib.Packer method), 503
package, 1631, **1789**
packed (ipaddress.IPv4Address attribute), 1238
packed (ipaddress.IPv6Address attribute), 1239
Packer (class in xdrlib), 502
packing
    binary data, 149
packing (widgets), 1337
PAGER, 1390
pair_content() (in module curses), 667
pair_number() (in module curses), 667
PanedWindow (class in tkinter.tix), 1362
parameter, **1789**
Parameter (class in inspect), 1622
ParameterizedMIMEHeader (class in email.headerregistry), 976
parameters (inspect.Signature attribute), 1621
params (email.headerregistry.ParameterizedMIMEHeader attribute), 976
pardir (in module os), 568
paren (2to3 fixer), 1500
parent (importlib.machinery.ModuleSpec attribute), 1661
parent (urllib.request.BaseHandler attribute), 1134
parent() (tkinter.ttk.Treeview method), 1354
parentNode (xml.dom.Node attribute), 1071
parents (collections.ChainMap attribute), 207
paretovariate() (in module random), 317
parse() (doctest.DocTestParser method), 1409
parse() (email.parser.BytesParser method), 960
parse() (email.parser.Parser method), 961
parse() (in module ast), 1674
parse() (in module cgi), 1113
parse() (in module xml.dom.minidom), 1080
parse() (in module xml.dom.pulldom), 1085
parse() (in module xml.etree.ElementTree), 1061
parse() (in module xml.sax), 1086
parse() (string.Formatter method), 96
parse() (urllib.robotparser.RobotFileParser method), 1152
parse() (xml.etree.ElementTree.ElementTree method), 1065
Parse() (xml.parsers.expat.xmlparser method), 1098

parse() (xml.sax.xmlreader.XMLReader method), 1094
parse_and_bind() (in module readline), 142
parse_args() (argparse.ArgumentParser method), 610
PARSE_COLNAMES (in module sqlite3), 424
parse_config_h() (in module sysconfig), 1581
PARSE_DECLTYPES (in module sqlite3), 424
parse_header() (in module cgi), 1113
parse_known_args() (argparse.ArgumentParser method), 619
parse_multipart() (in module cgi), 1113
parse_qs() (in module cgi), 1113
parse_qs() (in module urllib.parse), 1146
parse_qsl() (in module cgi), 1113
parse_qsl() (in module urllib.parse), 1146
parseaddr() (in module email.utils), 1004
parsebytes() (email.parser.BytesParser method), 960
parsedate() (in module email.utils), 1005
parsedate_to_datetime() (in module email.utils), 1005
parsedate_tz() (in module email.utils), 1005
ParseError (class in xml.etree.ElementTree), 1069
ParseFile() (xml.parsers.expat.xmlparser method), 1098
ParseFlags() (in module imaplib), 1170
Parser (class in email.parser), 960
parser (module), 1667
ParserCreate() (in module xml.parsers.expat), 1097
ParserError, 1670
ParseResult (class in urllib.parse), 1149
ParseResultBytes (class in urllib.parse), 1149
parsestr() (email.parser.Parser method), 961
parseString() (in module xml.dom.minidom), 1080
parseString() (in module xml.dom.pulldom), 1085
parseString() (in module xml.sax), 1086
parsing
    Python source code, 1667
    URL, 1144
ParsingError, 501
partial (asyncio.IncompleteReadError attribute), 911
partial() (imaplib.IMAP4 method), 1173
partial() (in module functools), 343
partialmethod (class in functools), 343
parties (threading.Barrier attribute), 738
partition() (bytearray method), 57
partition() (bytes method), 57
partition() (str method), 47
pass_() (poplib.POP3 method), 1168
Paste, 1367
patch() (in module unittest.mock), 1457
patch.dict() (in module unittest.mock), 1460
patch.multiple() (in module unittest.mock), 1461
patch.object() (in module unittest.mock), 1460

Index 1883

patch.stopall() (in module unittest.mock), 1463
PATH, 558, 562, 568, 1107, 1114, 1116
path
    configuration file, 1631
    module search, 392, 1572, 1630
    operations, 355, 371
Path (class in pathlib), 364
path (http.cookiejar.Cookie attribute), 1222
path (http.server.BaseHTTPRequestHandler attribute), 1207
path (importlib.abc.FileLoader attribute), 1656
path (importlib.machinery.ExtensionFileLoader attribute), 1660
path (importlib.machinery.FileFinder attribute), 1659
path (importlib.machinery.SourceFileLoader attribute), 1659
path (importlib.machinery.SourcelessFileLoader attribute), 1660
path (in module sys), 1572
path (os.DirEntry attribute), 548
path based finder, 1789
Path browser, 1365
path entry, 1789
path entry finder, 1789
path entry hook, 1789
path-like object, 1789
path_hook() (importlib.machinery.FileFinder class method), 1659
path_hooks (in module sys), 1572
path_importer_cache (in module sys), 1573
path_mtime() (importlib.abc.SourceLoader method), 1656
path_return_ok() (http.cookiejar.CookiePolicy method), 1219
path_stats() (importlib.abc.SourceLoader method), 1656
path_stats() (importlib.machinery.SourceFileLoader method), 1659
pathconf() (in module os), 545
pathconf_names (in module os), 545
PathEntryFinder (class in importlib.abc), 1652
PathFinder (class in importlib.machinery), 1658
pathlib (module), 355
PathLike (class in os), 527
pathname2url() (in module urllib.request), 1128
pathsep (in module os), 568
pattern (re.error attribute), 115
pattern (re.regex attribute), 117
pause() (in module signal), 940
pause_reading() (asyncio.ReadTransport method), 900
pause_writing() (asyncio.BaseProtocol method), 904
PAX_FORMAT (in module tarfile), 467

pax_headers (tarfile.TarFile attribute), 470
pax_headers (tarfile.TarInfo attribute), 471
pbkdf2_hmac() (in module hashlib), 511
pd() (in module turtle), 1296
Pdb (class in pdb), 1517, 1519
pdb (module), 1517
peek() (bz2.BZ2File method), 450
peek() (gzip.GzipFile method), 448
peek() (io.BufferedReader method), 578
peek() (lzma.LZMAFile method), 453
peek() (weakref.finalize method), 238
peer (smtpd.SMTPChannel attribute), 1191
PEM_cert_to_DER_cert() (in module ssl), 837
pen() (in module turtle), 1297
pencolor() (in module turtle), 1298
pending (ssl.MemoryBIO attribute), 859
pending() (ssl.SSLSocket method), 846
PendingDeprecationWarning, 92
pendown() (in module turtle), 1296
pensize() (in module turtle), 1296
penup() (in module turtle), 1296
PERCENT (in module token), 1679
PERCENTEQUAL (in module token), 1679
perf_counter() (in module time), 585
Performance, 1531
PermissionError, 91
permutations() (in module itertools), 334
Persist() (msilib.SummaryInformation method), 1713
persistence, 401
persistent
    objects, 401
persistent_id (pickle protocol), 408
persistent_id() (pickle.Pickler method), 404
persistent_load (pickle protocol), 408
persistent_load() (pickle.Unpickler method), 405
PF_CAN (in module socket), 814
PF_RDS (in module socket), 815
pformat() (in module pprint), 248
pformat() (pprint.PrettyPrinter method), 249
phase() (in module cmath), 282
pi (in module cmath), 284
pi (in module math), 280
pickle
    module, 247, 414, 415, 417
pickle (module), 401
pickle() (in module copyreg), 414
PickleError, 404
Pickler (class in pickle), 404
pickletools (module), 1703
pickletools command line option
    -a, –annotate, 1703
    -l, –indentlevel=<num>, 1703
    -m, –memo, 1703

-o, –output=<file>, 1703
-p, –preamble=<preamble>, 1703
pickling
    objects, 401
PicklingError, 404
pid (asyncio.asyncio.subprocess.Process attribute), 918
pid (multiprocessing.Process attribute), 746
pid (subprocess.Popen attribute), 795
PIPE (in module subprocess), 788
Pipe() (in module multiprocessing), 749
pipe() (in module os), 536
pipe2() (in module os), 536
PIPE_BUF (in module select), 864
pipe_connection_lost() (asyncio.SubprocessProtocol method), 902
pipe_data_received() (asyncio.SubprocessProtocol method), 902
pipes (module), 1739
PKG_DIRECTORY (in module imp), 1777
pkgutil (module), 1643
placeholder (textwrap.TextWrapper attribute), 138
platform (in module sys), 1573
platform (module), 685
platform() (in module platform), 685
PlaySound() (in module winsound), 1726
plist
    file, 505
plistlib (module), 505
plock() (in module os), 561
PLUS (in module token), 1679
plus() (decimal.Context method), 301
PLUSEQUAL (in module token), 1679
pm() (in module pdb), 1519
POINTER() (in module ctypes), 719
pointer() (in module ctypes), 719
polar() (in module cmath), 282
Policy (class in email.policy), 966
poll() (in module select), 863
poll() (multiprocessing.Connection method), 752
poll() (select.devpoll method), 864
poll() (select.epoll method), 865
poll() (select.poll method), 866
poll() (subprocess.Popen method), 794
PollSelector (class in selectors), 871
Pool (class in multiprocessing.pool), 765
pop() (array.array method), 234
pop() (collections.deque method), 212
pop() (dict method), 77
pop() (frozenset method), 75
pop() (mailbox.Mailbox method), 1020
pop() (sequence method), 39
POP3
    protocol, 1166

POP3 (class in poplib), 1167
POP3_SSL (class in poplib), 1167
pop_alignment() (formatter.formatter method), 1706
pop_all() (contextlib.ExitStack method), 1593
POP_BLOCK (opcode), 1697
POP_EXCEPT (opcode), 1697
pop_font() (formatter.formatter method), 1706
POP_JUMP_IF_FALSE (opcode), 1699
POP_JUMP_IF_TRUE (opcode), 1699
pop_margin() (formatter.formatter method), 1707
pop_source() (shlex.shlex method), 1326
pop_style() (formatter.formatter method), 1707
POP_TOP (opcode), 1693
Popen (class in subprocess), 790
popen() (in module os), 561, 863
popen() (in module platform), 687
popitem() (collections.OrderedDict method), 219
popitem() (dict method), 77
popitem() (mailbox.Mailbox method), 1020
popleft() (collections.deque method), 212
poplib (module), 1166
PopupMenu (class in tkinter.tix), 1361
port (http.cookiejar.Cookie attribute), 1222
port_specified (http.cookiejar.Cookie attribute), 1222
portion, 1790
pos (json.JSONDecodeError attribute), 1013
pos (re.error attribute), 115
pos (re.match attribute), 119
pos() (in module operator), 349
pos() (in module turtle), 1294
position (xml.etree.ElementTree.ParseError attribute), 1069
position() (in module turtle), 1294
positional argument, 1790
POSIX
    I/O control, 1734
    threads, 807
posix (module), 1729
POSIX_FADV_DONTNEED (in module os), 536
POSIX_FADV_NOREUSE (in module os), 536
POSIX_FADV_NORMAL (in module os), 536
POSIX_FADV_RANDOM (in module os), 536
POSIX_FADV_SEQUENTIAL (in module os), 536
POSIX_FADV_WILLNEED (in module os), 536
posix_fadvise() (in module os), 536
posix_fallocate() (in module os), 536
POSIXLY_CORRECT, 622
PosixPath (class in pathlib), 365
post() (nntplib.NNTP method), 1181
post() (ossaudiodev.oss_audio_device method), 1265
post_mortem() (in module pdb), 1519

post_setup() (venv.EnvBuilder method), 1555
postcmd() (cmd.Cmd method), 1320
postloop() (cmd.Cmd method), 1320
pow() (built-in function), 19
pow() (in module math), 279
pow() (in module operator), 349
power() (decimal.Context method), 301
pp (pdb command), 1522
pprint (module), 247
pprint() (in module pprint), 248
pprint() (pprint.PrettyPrinter method), 249
prcal() (in module calendar), 205
pread() (in module os), 537
preamble (email.message.EmailMessage attribute), 958
preamble (email.message.Message attribute), 995
precmd() (cmd.Cmd method), 1320
prefix (in module sys), 1573
prefix (xml.dom.Attr attribute), 1076
prefix (xml.dom.Node attribute), 1072
prefix (zipimport.zipimporter attribute), 1642
PREFIXES (in module site), 1632
prefixlen (ipaddress.IPv4Network attribute), 1242
prefixlen (ipaddress.IPv6Network attribute), 1244
preloop() (cmd.Cmd method), 1320
prepare() (logging.handlers.QueueHandler method), 660
prepare() (logging.handlers.QueueListener method), 661
prepare_class() (in module types), 243
prepare_input_source() (in module xml.sax.saxutils), 1093
prepend() (pipes.Template method), 1740
PrettyPrinter (class in pprint), 247
prev() (tkinter.ttk.Treeview method), 1354
previousSibling (xml.dom.Node attribute), 1072
print (2to3 fixer), 1500
print() (built-in function), 19
print_callees() (pstats.Stats method), 1529
print_callers() (pstats.Stats method), 1529
print_directory() (in module cgi), 1113
print_environ() (in module cgi), 1113
print_environ_usage() (in module cgi), 1113
print_exc() (in module traceback), 1606
print_exc() (timeit.Timer method), 1533
print_exception() (in module traceback), 1605
PRINT_EXPR (opcode), 1696
print_form() (in module cgi), 1113
print_help() (argparse.ArgumentParser method), 619
print_last() (in module traceback), 1606
print_stack() (asyncio.Task method), 894
print_stack() (in module traceback), 1606
print_stats() (profile.Profile method), 1527

print_stats() (pstats.Stats method), 1529
print_tb() (in module traceback), 1605
print_usage() (argparse.ArgumentParser method), 619
print_usage() (optparse.OptionParser method), 1766
print_version() (optparse.OptionParser method), 1756
printable (in module string), 95
printdir() (zipfile.ZipFile method), 461
printf-style formatting, 51, 64
PRIO_PGRP (in module os), 529
PRIO_PROCESS (in module os), 529
PRIO_USER (in module os), 529
PriorityQueue (class in asyncio), 925
PriorityQueue (class in queue), 804
prlimit() (in module resource), 1741
prmonth() (calendar.TextCalendar method), 204
prmonth() (in module calendar), 205
ProactorEventLoop (class in asyncio), 886
process
    group, 528, 529
    id, 529
    id of parent, 529
    killing, 561
    scheduling priority, 529, 530
    signalling, 561
Process (class in multiprocessing), 745
process() (logging.LoggerAdapter method), 634
process_exited() (asyncio.SubprocessProtocol method), 903
process_message() (smtpd.SMTPServer method), 1189
process_request() (socketserver.BaseServer method), 1201
process_time() (in module time), 585
process_tokens() (in module tabnanny), 1685
ProcessError, 747
processes, light-weight, 807
ProcessingInstruction() (in module xml.etree.ElementTree), 1062
processingInstruction() (xml.sax.handler.ContentHandler method), 1091
ProcessingInstructionHandler() (xml.parsers.expat.xmlparser method), 1101
ProcessLookupError, 91
processor time, 583
processor() (in module platform), 686
ProcessPoolExecutor (class in concurrent.futures), 784
product() (in module itertools), 335
Profile (class in profile), 1526
profile (module), 1526

profile function, 728, 1569, 1574
profiler, 1569, 1574
profiling, deterministic, 1524
ProgrammingError, 436
Progressbar (class in tkinter.ttk), 1349
prompt (cmd.Cmd attribute), 1321
prompt_user_passwd() (urllib.request.FancyURLopener method), 1143
prompts, interpreter, 1574
propagate (logging.Logger attribute), 624
property (built-in class), 19
property list, 505
property_declaration_handler (in module xml.sax.handler), 1089
property_dom_node (in module xml.sax.handler), 1089
property_lexical_handler (in module xml.sax.handler), 1089
property_xml_string (in module xml.sax.handler), 1089
PropertyMock (class in unittest.mock), 1453
prot_c() (ftplib.FTP_TLS method), 1166
prot_p() (ftplib.FTP_TLS method), 1166
proto (socket.socket attribute), 827
protocol
    CGI, 1109
    context management, 79
    copy, 407
    FTP, 1143, 1161
    HTTP, 1109, 1143, 1153, 1155, 1206
    IMAP4, 1169
    IMAP4_SSL, 1169
    IMAP4_stream, 1169
    iterator, 36
    NNTP, 1176
    POP3, 1166
    SMTP, 1182
    Telnet, 1192
Protocol (class in asyncio), 902
protocol (ssl.SSLContext attribute), 852
PROTOCOL_SSLv2 (in module ssl), 840
PROTOCOL_SSLv23 (in module ssl), 839
PROTOCOL_SSLv3 (in module ssl), 840
PROTOCOL_TLS (in module ssl), 839
PROTOCOL_TLS_CLIENT (in module ssl), 839
PROTOCOL_TLS_SERVER (in module ssl), 839
PROTOCOL_TLSv1 (in module ssl), 840
PROTOCOL_TLSv1_1 (in module ssl), 840
PROTOCOL_TLSv1_2 (in module ssl), 840
protocol_version (http.server.BaseHTTPRequestHandler attribute), 1207
PROTOCOL_VERSION (imaplib.IMAP4 attribute), 1175

ProtocolError (class in xmlrpc.client), 1228
provisional API, 1790
provisional package, 1790
proxy() (in module weakref), 236
proxyauth() (imaplib.IMAP4 method), 1173
ProxyBasicAuthHandler (class in urllib.request), 1130
ProxyDigestAuthHandler (class in urllib.request), 1131
ProxyHandler (class in urllib.request), 1129
ProxyType (in module weakref), 238
ProxyTypes (in module weakref), 238
pryear() (calendar.TextCalendar method), 204
ps1 (in module sys), 1573
ps2 (in module sys), 1573
pstats (module), 1527
pstdev() (in module statistics), 323
pthread_kill() (in module signal), 941
pthread_sigmask() (in module signal), 941
pthreads, 807
pty
    module, 536
pty (module), 1736
pu() (in module turtle), 1296
publicId (xml.dom.DocumentType attribute), 1074
PullDom (class in xml.dom.pulldom), 1084
punctuation (in module string), 95
punctuation_chars (shlex.shlex attribute), 1327
PurePath (class in pathlib), 357
PurePath.anchor (in module pathlib), 361
PurePath.drive (in module pathlib), 360
PurePath.name (in module pathlib), 361
PurePath.parent (in module pathlib), 361
PurePath.parents (in module pathlib), 361
PurePath.parts (in module pathlib), 360
PurePath.root (in module pathlib), 360
PurePath.stem (in module pathlib), 362
PurePath.suffix (in module pathlib), 362
PurePath.suffixes (in module pathlib), 362
PurePosixPath (class in pathlib), 358
PureProxy (class in smtpd), 1190
PureWindowsPath (class in pathlib), 358
purge() (in module re), 115
Purpose.CLIENT_AUTH (in module ssl), 843
Purpose.SERVER_AUTH (in module ssl), 843
push() (asynchat.async_chat method), 937
push() (code.InteractiveConsole method), 1639
push() (contextlib.ExitStack method), 1592
push_alignment() (formatter.formatter method), 1706
push_font() (formatter.formatter method), 1706
push_margin() (formatter.formatter method), 1706
push_source() (shlex.shlex method), 1326
push_style() (formatter.formatter method), 1707

push_token() (shlex.shlex method), 1325
push_with_producer() (asynchat.async_chat method), 937
pushbutton() (msilib.Dialog method), 1716
put() (asyncio.Queue method), 925
put() (multiprocessing.Queue method), 749
put() (multiprocessing.SimpleQueue method), 750
put() (queue.Queue method), 805
put_nowait() (asyncio.Queue method), 925
put_nowait() (multiprocessing.Queue method), 749
put_nowait() (queue.Queue method), 805
putch() (in module msvcrt), 1717
putenv() (in module os), 529
putheader() (http.client.HTTPConnection method), 1159
putp() (in module curses), 667
putrequest() (http.client.HTTPConnection method), 1158
putwch() (in module msvcrt), 1717
putwin() (curses.window method), 674
pvariance() (in module statistics), 323
pwd
    module, 372
pwd (module), 1730
pwd() (ftplib.FTP method), 1166
pwrite() (in module os), 537
py_compile (module), 1686
PY_COMPILED (in module imp), 1777
PY_FROZEN (in module imp), 1777
py_object (class in ctypes), 723
PY_SOURCE (in module imp), 1777
pyclbr (module), 1685
PyCompileError, 1686
PyDLL (class in ctypes), 713
pydoc (module), 1390
pyexpat
    module, 1097
PYFUNCTYPE() (in module ctypes), 716
Python 3000, 1790
Python Editor, 1364
Python Enhancement Proposals
    PEP 205, 239
    PEP 227, 1612
    PEP 235, 1649
    PEP 236, 7
    PEP 237, 52, 66
    PEP 238, 1612, 1784
    PEP 249, 423, 424
    PEP 255, 1612
    PEP 263, 1649, 1681, 1682
    PEP 273, 1641
    PEP 278, 1792
    PEP 282, 398, 639
    PEP 292, 103
    PEP 302, 24, 392, 1573, 1641, 1643, 1647, 1649, 1652–1655, 1777, 1784, 1787
    PEP 305, 477
    PEP 307, 402
    PEP 3101, 96
    PEP 3105, 1612
    PEP 3107, 1785
    PEP 3112, 1612
    PEP 3115, 243
    PEP 3116, 1792
    PEP 3118, 68
    PEP 3119, 226, 1599
    PEP 3120, 1650
    PEP 3141, 273, 1599
    PEP 3147, 1648, 1650, 1662, 1686–1689, 1775, 1776
    PEP 3148, 786
    PEP 3149, 1563
    PEP 3151, 92, 813, 862, 1740
    PEP 3153, 931
    PEP 3154, 402
    PEP 3155, 1790
    PEP 3156, 931
    PEP 324, 787
    PEP 328, 25, 1612, 1650
    PEP 3333, 1117–1121, 1124, 1125
    PEP 338, 1649
    PEP 342, 224
    PEP 343, 1597, 1612, 1783
    PEP 362, 1624, 1781, 1789
    PEP 366, 1649, 1650
    PEP 370, 1633
    PEP 378, 99
    PEP 380, 872, 888
    PEP 383, 158, 811
    PEP 393, 164, 169, 1572
    PEP 397, 1554
    PEP 405, 1551
    PEP 411, 1570, 1576, 1790
    PEP 420, 1650, 1784, 1788, 1790
    PEP 421, 1571
    PEP 428, 356
    PEP 442, 1615
    PEP 443, 1785
    PEP 451, 1572, 1644, 1648–1650, 1784
    PEP 453, 1550
    PEP 461, 66
    PEP 468, 220
    PEP 475, 18, 91, 535, 537, 538, 565, 585, 821–826, 864–867, 871, 943
    PEP 479, 1612
    PEP 483, 1375
    PEP 484, 1375, 1377, 1381, 1382, 1388, 1792
    PEP 485, 277, 284

PEP 488, 1650, 1662, 1686
PEP 489, 1650, 1658, 1660
PEP 492, 225, 1570, 1576, 1630, 1781–1783
PEP 498, 1784
PEP 506, 521
PEP 515, 100
PEP 519, 1790
PEP 524, 569
PEP 525, 225, 1570, 1575, 1630, 1782
PEP 526, 1375, 1387, 1389, 1792
PEP 529, 1568, 1576
python_branch() (in module platform), 686
python_build() (in module platform), 686
python_compiler() (in module platform), 686
PYTHON_DOM, 1070
python_implementation() (in module platform), 686
python_revision() (in module platform), 686
python_version() (in module platform), 686
python_version_tuple() (in module platform), 686
PYTHONASYNCIODEBUG, 882, 926
PYTHONDOCS, 1391
PYTHONDONTWRITEBYTECODE, 1565
PYTHONFAULTHANDLER, 1515
Pythonic, 1790
PYTHONIOENCODING, 1577
PYTHONLEGACYWINDOWSFSENCODING, 1576
PYTHONNOUSERSITE, 1632, 1633
PYTHONPATH, 1114, 1572
PYTHONSTARTUP, 145, 1370, 1571, 1632
PYTHONTRACEMALLOC, 1539, 1544
PYTHONUSERBASE, 1632, 1633
PyZipFile (class in zipfile), 462

Q

qiflush() (in module curses), 667
QName (class in xml.etree.ElementTree), 1066
qsize() (asyncio.Queue method), 925
qsize() (multiprocessing.Queue method), 749
qsize() (queue.Queue method), 805
qualified name, 1790
quantize() (decimal.Context method), 301
quantize() (decimal.Decimal method), 294
QueryInfoKey() (in module winreg), 1721
QueryReflectionKey() (in module winreg), 1723
QueryValue() (in module winreg), 1721
QueryValueEx() (in module winreg), 1721
Queue (class in asyncio), 924
Queue (class in multiprocessing), 749
Queue (class in queue), 804
queue (module), 804
queue (sched.scheduler attribute), 804
Queue() (multiprocessing.managers.SyncManager method), 761

QueueEmpty, 925
QueueFull, 925
QueueHandler (class in logging.handlers), 660
QueueListener (class in logging.handlers), 661
quick_ratio() (difflib.SequenceMatcher method), 131
quit (built-in variable), 28
quit (pdb command), 1523
quit() (ftplib.FTP method), 1166
quit() (nntplib.NNTP method), 1178
quit() (poplib.POP3 method), 1168
quit() (smtplib.SMTP method), 1188
quopri (module), 1044
quote() (in module email.utils), 1004
quote() (in module shlex), 1324
quote() (in module urllib.parse), 1149
QUOTE_ALL (in module csv), 480
quote_from_bytes() (in module urllib.parse), 1150
QUOTE_MINIMAL (in module csv), 480
QUOTE_NONE (in module csv), 480
QUOTE_NONNUMERIC (in module csv), 480
quote_plus() (in module urllib.parse), 1150
quoteattr() (in module xml.sax.saxutils), 1092
quotechar (csv.Dialect attribute), 481
quoted-printable
    encoding, 1044
quotes (shlex.shlex attribute), 1326
quoting (csv.Dialect attribute), 481

R

R_OK (in module os), 541
radians() (in module math), 279
radians() (in module turtle), 1296
RadioButtonGroup (class in msilib), 1715
radiogroup() (msilib.Dialog method), 1716
radix() (decimal.Context method), 301
radix() (decimal.Decimal method), 295
RADIXCHAR (in module locale), 1279
raise
    statement, 85
raise (2to3 fixer), 1500
raise_on_defect (email.policy.Policy attribute), 967
RAISE_VARARGS (opcode), 1701
RAND_add() (in module ssl), 836
RAND_bytes() (in module ssl), 835
RAND_egd() (in module ssl), 836
RAND_pseudo_bytes() (in module ssl), 836
RAND_status() (in module ssl), 836
randbelow() (in module secrets), 521
randbits() (in module secrets), 521
randint() (in module random), 315
random (module), 313
random() (in module random), 316
randrange() (in module random), 315
range

object, 41
range (built-in class), 41
RARROW (in module token), 1679
ratecv() (in module audioop), 1251
ratio() (difflib.SequenceMatcher method), 131
Rational (class in numbers), 273
raw (io.BufferedIOBase attribute), 575
raw() (in module curses), 667
raw_data_manager (in module email.contentmanager), 979
raw_decode() (json.JSONDecoder method), 1012
raw_input (2to3 fixer), 1500
raw_input() (code.InteractiveConsole method), 1639
RawArray() (in module multiprocessing.sharedctypes), 757
RawConfigParser (class in configparser), 500
RawDescriptionHelpFormatter (class in argparse), 596
RawIOBase (class in io), 574
RawPen (class in turtle), 1313
RawTextHelpFormatter (class in argparse), 596
RawTurtle (class in turtle), 1313
RawValue() (in module multiprocessing.sharedctypes), 757
RBRACE (in module token), 1679
rcpttos (smtpd.SMTPChannel attribute), 1191
re
    module, 44, 390
re (class in typing), 1386
re (module), 105
re (re.match attribute), 120
read() (asyncio.StreamReader method), 909
read() (chunk.Chunk method), 1261
read() (codecs.StreamReader method), 162
read() (configparser.ConfigParser method), 497
read() (http.client.HTTPResponse method), 1159
read() (imaplib.IMAP4 method), 1173
read() (in module os), 537
read() (io.BufferedIOBase method), 575
read() (io.BufferedReader method), 578
read() (io.RawIOBase method), 574
read() (io.TextIOBase method), 579
read() (mimetypes.MimeTypes method), 1037
read() (mmap.mmap method), 946
read() (ossaudiodev.oss_audio_device method), 1264
read() (ssl.MemoryBIO method), 860
read() (ssl.SSLSocket method), 844
read() (urllib.robotparser.RobotFileParser method), 1152
read() (zipfile.ZipFile method), 461
read1() (io.BufferedIOBase method), 576
read1() (io.BufferedReader method), 578
read1() (io.BytesIO method), 577

read_all() (telnetlib.Telnet method), 1193
read_byte() (mmap.mmap method), 946
read_bytes() (pathlib.Path method), 368
read_dict() (configparser.ConfigParser method), 498
read_eager() (telnetlib.Telnet method), 1193
read_environ() (in module wsgiref.handlers), 1125
read_events() (xml.etree.ElementTree.XMLPullParser method), 1068
read_file() (configparser.ConfigParser method), 497
read_history_file() (in module readline), 143
read_init_file() (in module readline), 142
read_lazy() (telnetlib.Telnet method), 1193
read_mime_types() (in module mimetypes), 1036
read_sb_data() (telnetlib.Telnet method), 1193
read_some() (telnetlib.Telnet method), 1193
read_string() (configparser.ConfigParser method), 498
read_text() (pathlib.Path method), 368
read_token() (shlex.shlex method), 1325
read_until() (telnetlib.Telnet method), 1193
read_very_eager() (telnetlib.Telnet method), 1193
read_very_lazy() (telnetlib.Telnet method), 1193
read_windows_registry() (mimetypes.MimeTypes method), 1038
READABLE (in module tkinter), 1341
readable() (asyncore.dispatcher method), 933
readable() (io.IOBase method), 573
readall() (io.RawIOBase method), 575
reader() (in module csv), 477
ReadError, 467
readexactly() (asyncio.StreamReader method), 909
readfp() (configparser.ConfigParser method), 499
readfp() (mimetypes.MimeTypes method), 1038
readframes() (aifc.aifc method), 1253
readframes() (sunau.AU_read method), 1256
readframes() (wave.Wave_read method), 1258
readinto() (http.client.HTTPResponse method), 1159
readinto() (io.BufferedIOBase method), 576
readinto() (io.RawIOBase method), 575
readinto1() (io.BufferedIOBase method), 576
readinto1() (io.BytesIO method), 577
readline (module), 142
readline() (asyncio.StreamReader method), 909
readline() (codecs.StreamReader method), 162
readline() (imaplib.IMAP4 method), 1173
readline() (io.IOBase method), 573
readline() (io.TextIOBase method), 579
readline() (mmap.mmap method), 946
readlines() (codecs.StreamReader method), 162
readlines() (io.IOBase method), 573
readlink() (in module os), 546
readmodule() (in module pyclbr), 1685
readmodule_ex() (in module pyclbr), 1685

readonly (memoryview attribute), 72
readPlist() (in module plistlib), 506
readPlistFromBytes() (in module plistlib), 506
ReadTransport (class in asyncio), 900
readuntil() (asyncio.StreamReader method), 910
readv() (in module os), 538
ready() (multiprocessing.pool.AsyncResult method), 767
Real (class in numbers), 273
real (numbers.Complex attribute), 273
Real Media File Format, 1260
real_quick_ratio() (difflib.SequenceMatcher method), 131
realpath() (in module os.path), 374
reason (http.client.HTTPResponse attribute), 1160
reason (ssl.SSLError attribute), 833
reason (UnicodeError attribute), 90
reason (urllib.error.HTTPError attribute), 1152
reason (urllib.error.URLError attribute), 1151
reattach() (tkinter.ttk.Treeview method), 1354
reccontrols() (ossaudiodev.oss_mixer_device method), 1267
received_data (smtpd.SMTPChannel attribute), 1191
received_lines (smtpd.SMTPChannel attribute), 1191
recent() (imaplib.IMAP4 method), 1173
records (unittest.TestCase attribute), 1428
rect() (in module cmath), 282
rectangle() (in module curses.textpad), 680
RecursionError, 88
recursive_repr() (in module reprlib), 252
recv() (asyncore.dispatcher method), 934
recv() (multiprocessing.Connection method), 752
recv() (socket.socket method), 823
recv_bytes() (multiprocessing.Connection method), 753
recv_bytes_into() (multiprocessing.Connection method), 753
recv_into() (socket.socket method), 825
recvfrom() (socket.socket method), 823
recvfrom_into() (socket.socket method), 825
recvmsg() (socket.socket method), 823
recvmsg_into() (socket.socket method), 824
redirect_request() (urllib.request.HTTPRedirectHandler method), 1135
redirect_stderr() (in module contextlib), 1590
redirect_stdout() (in module contextlib), 1590
redisplay() (in module readline), 143
redrawln() (curses.window method), 674
redrawwin() (curses.window method), 674
reduce (2to3 fixer), 1500
reduce() (in module functools), 344

ref (class in weakref), 236
reference count, 1791
ReferenceError, 88, 239
ReferenceType (in module weakref), 238
refold_source (email.policy.EmailPolicy attribute), 969
refresh() (curses.window method), 674
REG_BINARY (in module winreg), 1724
REG_DWORD (in module winreg), 1724
REG_DWORD_BIG_ENDIAN (in module winreg), 1724
REG_DWORD_LITTLE_ENDIAN (in module winreg), 1724
REG_EXPAND_SZ (in module winreg), 1725
REG_FULL_RESOURCE_DESCRIPTOR (in module winreg), 1725
REG_LINK (in module winreg), 1725
REG_MULTI_SZ (in module winreg), 1725
REG_NONE (in module winreg), 1725
REG_QWORD (in module winreg), 1725
REG_QWORD_LITTLE_ENDIAN (in module winreg), 1725
REG_RESOURCE_LIST (in module winreg), 1725
REG_RESOURCE_REQUIREMENTS_LIST (in module winreg), 1725
REG_SZ (in module winreg), 1725
register() (abc.ABCMeta method), 1600
register() (in module atexit), 1604
register() (in module codecs), 156
register() (in module faulthandler), 1517
register() (in module webbrowser), 1108
register() (multiprocessing.managers.BaseManager method), 760
register() (select.devpoll method), 864
register() (select.epoll method), 865
register() (select.poll method), 866
register() (selectors.BaseSelector method), 870
register_adapter() (in module sqlite3), 425
register_archive_format() (in module shutil), 398
register_converter() (in module sqlite3), 425
register_defect() (email.policy.Policy method), 968
register_dialect() (in module csv), 478
register_error() (in module codecs), 158
register_function() (xmlrpc.server.CGIXMLRPCRequestHandler method), 1234
register_function() (xmlrpc.server.SimpleXMLRPCServer method), 1232
register_instance() (xmlrpc.server.CGIXMLRPCRequestHandler method), 1235
register_instance() (xmlrpc.server.SimpleXMLRPCServer method),

register_introspection_functions() (xmlrpc.server.CGIXMLRPCRequestHandler method), 1235
register_introspection_functions() (xmlrpc.server.SimpleXMLRPCServer method), 1232
register_multicall_functions() (xmlrpc.server.CGIXMLRPCRequestHandler method), 1235
register_multicall_functions() (xmlrpc.server.SimpleXMLRPCServer method), 1232
register_namespace() (in module xml.etree.ElementTree), 1062
register_optionflag() (in module doctest), 1400
register_shape() (in module turtle), 1311
register_unpack_format() (in module shutil), 399
registerDOMImplementation() (in module xml.dom), 1070
registerResult() (in module unittest), 1442
regular package, 1791
relative
    URL, 1144
relative_to() (pathlib.PurePath method), 364
release() (_thread.lock method), 808
release() (asyncio.Condition method), 922
release() (asyncio.Lock method), 921
release() (asyncio.Semaphore method), 923
release() (in module platform), 686
release() (logging.Handler method), 628
release() (memoryview method), 69
release() (multiprocessing.Lock method), 755
release() (multiprocessing.RLock method), 755
release() (threading.Condition method), 733
release() (threading.Lock method), 731
release() (threading.RLock method), 732
release() (threading.Semaphore method), 735
release_lock() (in module imp), 1777
reload (2to3 fixer), 1500
reload() (in module imp), 1775
reload() (in module importlib), 1651
relpath() (in module os.path), 374
remainder() (decimal.Context method), 301
remainder_near() (decimal.Context method), 301
remainder_near() (decimal.Decimal method), 295
RemoteDisconnected, 1157
remove() (array.array method), 234
remove() (collections.deque method), 212
remove() (frozenset method), 75
remove() (in module os), 546
remove() (mailbox.Mailbox method), 1018
remove() (mailbox.MH method), 1024
remove() (sequence method), 39
remove() (xml.etree.ElementTree.Element method), 1064
remove_done_callback() (asyncio.Future method), 892
remove_flag() (mailbox.MaildirMessage method), 1027
remove_flag() (mailbox.mboxMessage method), 1029
remove_flag() (mailbox.MMDFMessage method), 1033
remove_folder() (mailbox.Maildir method), 1021
remove_folder() (mailbox.MH method), 1023
remove_header() (urllib.request.Request method), 1132
remove_history_item() (in module readline), 144
remove_label() (mailbox.BabylMessage method), 1031
remove_option() (configparser.ConfigParser method), 499
remove_option() (optparse.OptionParser method), 1765
remove_pyc() (msilib.Directory method), 1715
remove_reader() (asyncio.AbstractEventLoop method), 879
remove_section() (configparser.ConfigParser method), 499
remove_sequence() (mailbox.MHMessage method), 1030
remove_signal_handler() (asyncio.AbstractEventLoop method), 881
remove_writer() (asyncio.AbstractEventLoop method), 879
removeAttribute() (xml.dom.Element method), 1075
removeAttributeNode() (xml.dom.Element method), 1075
removeAttributeNS() (xml.dom.Element method), 1075
removeChild() (xml.dom.Node method), 1073
removedirs() (in module os), 546
removeFilter() (logging.Handler method), 628
removeFilter() (logging.Logger method), 626
removeHandler() (in module unittest), 1442
removeHandler() (logging.Logger method), 627
removeResult() (in module unittest), 1442
removexattr() (in module os), 557
rename() (ftplib.FTP method), 1165
rename() (imaplib.IMAP4 method), 1173
rename() (in module os), 546
rename() (pathlib.Path method), 369
renames (2to3 fixer), 1500
renames() (in module os), 546
reopenIfNeeded() (logging.handlers.WatchedFileHandler method), 651
reorganize() (dbm.gnu.gdbm method), 421

repeat() (in module itertools), 335
repeat() (in module timeit), 1532
repeat() (timeit.Timer method), 1533
repetition
    operation, 37
replace() (bytearray method), 57
replace() (bytes method), 57
replace() (curses.panel.Panel method), 684
replace() (datetime.date method), 179
replace() (datetime.datetime method), 184
replace() (datetime.time method), 190
replace() (in module os), 547
replace() (inspect.Parameter method), 1623
replace() (inspect.Signature method), 1621
replace() (pathlib.Path method), 369
replace() (str method), 47
replace_errors() (in module codecs), 158
replace_header() (email.message.EmailMessage method), 953
replace_header() (email.message.Message method), 992
replace_history_item() (in module readline), 144
replace_whitespace (textwrap.TextWrapper attribute), 137
replaceChild() (xml.dom.Node method), 1073
ReplacePackage() (in module modulefinder), 1646
report() (filecmp.dircmp method), 384
report() (modulefinder.ModuleFinder method), 1646
REPORT_CDIFF (in module doctest), 1399
report_failure() (doctest.DocTestRunner method), 1410
report_full_closure() (filecmp.dircmp method), 384
REPORT_NDIFF (in module doctest), 1399
REPORT_ONLY_FIRST_FAILURE (in module doctest), 1400
report_partial_closure() (filecmp.dircmp method), 384
report_start() (doctest.DocTestRunner method), 1409
report_success() (doctest.DocTestRunner method), 1409
REPORT_UDIFF (in module doctest), 1399
report_unexpected_exception() (doctest.DocTestRunner method), 1410
REPORTING_FLAGS (in module doctest), 1400
repr (2to3 fixer), 1500
Repr (class in reprlib), 252
repr() (built-in function), 20
repr() (in module reprlib), 252
repr() (reprlib.Repr method), 253
repr1() (reprlib.Repr method), 253
reprlib (module), 252
Request (class in urllib.request), 1128

request() (http.client.HTTPConnection method), 1157
request_queue_size (socketserver.BaseServer attribute), 1201
request_rate() (urllib.robotparser.RobotFileParser method), 1152
request_uri() (in module wsgiref.util), 1117
request_version (http.server.BaseHTTPRequestHandler attribute), 1207
RequestHandlerClass (socketserver.BaseServer attribute), 1200
requestline (http.server.BaseHTTPRequestHandler attribute), 1206
requires() (in module test.support), 1504
reserved (zipfile.ZipInfo attribute), 464
RESERVED_FUTURE (in module uuid), 1197
RESERVED_MICROSOFT (in module uuid), 1197
RESERVED_NCS (in module uuid), 1197
reset() (bdb.Bdb method), 1512
reset() (codecs.IncrementalDecoder method), 161
reset() (codecs.IncrementalEncoder method), 160
reset() (codecs.StreamReader method), 163
reset() (codecs.StreamWriter method), 162
reset() (html.parser.HTMLParser method), 1049
reset() (in module turtle), 1300, 1307
reset() (ossaudiodev.oss_audio_device method), 1265
reset() (pipes.Template method), 1739
reset() (threading.Barrier method), 738
reset() (xdrlib.Packer method), 502
reset() (xdrlib.Unpacker method), 503
reset() (xml.dom.pulldom.DOMEventStream method), 1085
reset() (xml.sax.xmlreader.IncrementalParser method), 1095
reset_mock() (unittest.mock.Mock method), 1447
reset_prog_mode() (in module curses), 667
reset_shell_mode() (in module curses), 667
resetbuffer() (code.InteractiveConsole method), 1639
resetlocale() (in module locale), 1281
resetscreen() (in module turtle), 1307
resetty() (in module curses), 667
resetwarnings() (in module warnings), 1587
resize() (curses.window method), 674
resize() (in module ctypes), 719
resize() (mmap.mmap method), 946
resize_term() (in module curses), 667
resizemode() (in module turtle), 1301
resizeterm() (in module curses), 668
resolution (datetime.date attribute), 178
resolution (datetime.datetime attribute), 182
resolution (datetime.time attribute), 189
resolution (datetime.timedelta attribute), 175
resolve() (pathlib.Path method), 369

resolve_name() (in module importlib.util), 1662
resolveEntity() (xml.sax.handler.EntityResolver method), 1092
resource (module), 1740
ResourceDenied, 1504
ResourceLoader (class in importlib.abc), 1654
ResourceWarning, 92
response (nntplib.NNTPError attribute), 1177
response() (imaplib.IMAP4 method), 1173
ResponseNotReady, 1157
responses (http.server.BaseHTTPRequestHandler attribute), 1207
responses (in module http.client), 1157
restart (pdb command), 1523
restore() (in module difflib), 128
restype (ctypes._FuncPtr attribute), 715
result() (asyncio.Future method), 892
result() (concurrent.futures.Future method), 785
results() (trace.Trace method), 1538
resume_reading() (asyncio.ReadTransport method), 900
resume_writing() (asyncio.BaseProtocol method), 904
retr() (poplib.POP3 method), 1168
retrbinary() (ftplib.FTP method), 1164
retrieve() (urllib.request.URLopener method), 1142
retrlines() (ftplib.FTP method), 1164
return (pdb command), 1522
return_annotation (inspect.Signature attribute), 1621
return_ok() (http.cookiejar.CookiePolicy method), 1218
RETURN_VALUE (opcode), 1696
return_value (unittest.mock.Mock attribute), 1449
returncode (asyncio.asyncio.subprocess.Process attribute), 918
returncode (subprocess.CalledProcessError attribute), 789
returncode (subprocess.CompletedProcess attribute), 788
returncode (subprocess.Popen attribute), 795
reverse() (array.array method), 234
reverse() (collections.deque method), 212
reverse() (in module audioop), 1251
reverse() (sequence method), 39
reverse_order() (pstats.Stats method), 1529
reverse_pointer (ipaddress.IPv4Address attribute), 1238
reverse_pointer (ipaddress.IPv6Address attribute), 1239
reversed() (built-in function), 20
Reversible (class in collections.abc), 224
Reversible (class in typing), 1382
revert() (http.cookiejar.FileCookieJar method), 1218
rewind() (aifc.aifc method), 1253
rewind() (sunau.AU_read method), 1256
rewind() (wave.Wave_read method), 1258
RFC
    RFC 1014, 502
    RFC 1123, 586
    RFC 1321, 509
    RFC 1422, 853
    RFC 1521, 1041, 1044
    RFC 1522, 1044
    RFC 1524, 1017
    RFC 1730, 1169
    RFC 1738, 1151
    RFC 1750, 836
    RFC 1766, 1280, 1281
    RFC 1808, 1145, 1151
    RFC 1832, 502
    RFC 1869, 1182, 1184
    RFC 1870, 1189, 1192
    RFC 1939, 1166, 1167
    RFC 2045, 949, 954, 976, 992, 993, 999, 1038, 1040, 1041
    RFC 2046, 949, 980, 999
    RFC 2047, 949, 969, 974, 999, 1000, 1005
    RFC 2060, 1169, 1174
    RFC 2068, 1211
    RFC 2104, 519
    RFC 2109, 1211–1216
    RFC 2183, 949, 955, 994
    RFC 2231, 949, 953, 954, 992, 993, 999, 1006
    RFC 2295, 1155
    RFC 2368, 1151
    RFC 2373, 1238, 1239
    RFC 2396, 1146, 1151
    RFC 2397, 1138
    RFC 2449, 1168
    RFC 2518, 1154
    RFC 2595, 1167, 1169
    RFC 2616, 1118, 1135, 1143
    RFC 2732, 1151
    RFC 2774, 1155
    RFC 2818, 836
    RFC 2821, 949
    RFC 2822, 586, 990, 999, 1000, 1004, 1005, 1026, 1207
    RFC 2964, 1216
    RFC 2965, 1129, 1215, 1216
    RFC 2980, 1176, 1181
    RFC 3056, 1240
    RFC 3171, 1238
    RFC 3229, 1154
    RFC 3280, 845
    RFC 3330, 1239
    RFC 3454, 141

RFC 3490, 169–171
RFC 3492, 169, 170
RFC 3493, 832
RFC 3501, 1174
RFC 3542, 820
RFC 3548, 1038, 1039, 1042
RFC 3659, 1165
RFC 3879, 1239
RFC 3927, 1239
RFC 3977, 1176–1179, 1181
RFC 3986, 1146, 1147, 1151
RFC 4122, 1195, 1197
RFC 4180, 477
RFC 4193, 1239
RFC 4217, 1162
RFC 4291, 1239
RFC 4380, 1240
RFC 4627, 1007, 1015
RFC 4642, 1177
RFC 4918, 1154, 1155
RFC 4954, 1186
RFC 5161, 1172
RFC 5233, 949, 987
RFC 5246, 843
RFC 5280, 836, 837
RFC 5321, 978, 1189, 1190
RFC 5322, 950, 960, 963, 964, 967, 969, 972–975, 977, 978, 1187
RFC 5735, 1238
RFC 5842, 1154, 1155
RFC 5929, 846
RFC 6066, 842, 850
RFC 6125, 836, 837
RFC 6152, 1189
RFC 6531, 951, 969, 1183, 1189, 1191
RFC 6532, 949, 950, 960, 969
RFC 6585, 1154, 1155
RFC 6855, 1172
RFC 6856, 1169
RFC 7159, 1007, 1014, 1015
RFC 7230, 1128, 1159
RFC 7231, 1154, 1155
RFC 7232, 1154
RFC 7233, 1154
RFC 7235, 1154
RFC 7238, 1154
RFC 7301, 842, 850
RFC 7914, 512
RFC 821, 1182, 1184
RFC 822, 586, 999, 1159, 1185, 1187, 1188, 1273
RFC 854, 1192, 1193
RFC 959, 1161
RFC 977, 1176
rfc2109 (http.cookiejar.Cookie attribute), 1222
rfc2109_as_netscape (http.cookiejar.DefaultCookiePolicy attribute), 1220
rfc2965 (http.cookiejar.CookiePolicy attribute), 1219
RFC_4122 (in module uuid), 1197
rfile (http.server.BaseHTTPRequestHandler attribute), 1207
rfind() (bytearray method), 57
rfind() (bytes method), 57
rfind() (mmap.mmap method), 946
rfind() (str method), 47
rgb_to_hls() (in module colorsys), 1261
rgb_to_hsv() (in module colorsys), 1261
rgb_to_yiq() (in module colorsys), 1261
rglob() (pathlib.Path method), 369
right (filecmp.dircmp attribute), 384
right() (in module turtle), 1290
right_list (filecmp.dircmp attribute), 384
right_only (filecmp.dircmp attribute), 384
RIGHTSHIFT (in module token), 1679
RIGHTSHIFTEQUAL (in module token), 1679
rindex() (bytearray method), 57
rindex() (bytes method), 57
rindex() (str method), 47
rjust() (bytearray method), 58
rjust() (bytes method), 58
rjust() (str method), 47
rlcompleter (module), 146
rlecode_hqx() (in module binascii), 1043
rledecode_hqx() (in module binascii), 1043
RLIM_INFINITY (in module resource), 1740
RLIMIT_AS (in module resource), 1742
RLIMIT_CORE (in module resource), 1741
RLIMIT_CPU (in module resource), 1741
RLIMIT_DATA (in module resource), 1741
RLIMIT_FSIZE (in module resource), 1741
RLIMIT_MEMLOCK (in module resource), 1742
RLIMIT_MSGQUEUE (in module resource), 1742
RLIMIT_NICE (in module resource), 1742
RLIMIT_NOFILE (in module resource), 1742
RLIMIT_NPROC (in module resource), 1741
RLIMIT_NPTS (in module resource), 1742
RLIMIT_OFILE (in module resource), 1742
RLIMIT_RSS (in module resource), 1741
RLIMIT_RTPRIO (in module resource), 1742
RLIMIT_RTTIME (in module resource), 1742
RLIMIT_SBSIZE (in module resource), 1742
RLIMIT_SIGPENDING (in module resource), 1742
RLIMIT_STACK (in module resource), 1741
RLIMIT_SWAP (in module resource), 1742
RLIMIT_VMEM (in module resource), 1742
RLock (class in multiprocessing), 755
RLock (class in threading), 732
RLock() (multiprocessing.managers.SyncManager method), 761

rmd() (ftplib.FTP method), 1166
rmdir() (in module os), 547
rmdir() (pathlib.Path method), 369
RMFF, 1260
rms() (in module audioop), 1251
rmtree() (in module shutil), 395
RobotFileParser (class in urllib.robotparser), 1152
robots.txt, 1152
rollback() (sqlite3.Connection method), 427
ROT_THREE (opcode), 1694
ROT_TWO (opcode), 1694
rotate() (collections.deque method), 212
rotate() (decimal.Context method), 301
rotate() (decimal.Decimal method), 295
rotate() (logging.handlers.BaseRotatingHandler method), 652
RotatingFileHandler (class in logging.handlers), 652
rotation_filename() (logging.handlers.BaseRotatingHandler method), 652
rotator (logging.handlers.BaseRotatingHandler attribute), 652
round() (built-in function), 21
ROUND_05UP (in module decimal), 303
ROUND_CEILING (in module decimal), 302
ROUND_DOWN (in module decimal), 302
ROUND_FLOOR (in module decimal), 302
ROUND_HALF_DOWN (in module decimal), 302
ROUND_HALF_EVEN (in module decimal), 302
ROUND_HALF_UP (in module decimal), 302
ROUND_UP (in module decimal), 302
Rounded (class in decimal), 304
Row (class in sqlite3), 435
row_factory (sqlite3.Connection attribute), 430
rowcount (sqlite3.Cursor attribute), 434
RPAR (in module token), 1679
rpartition() (bytearray method), 57
rpartition() (bytes method), 57
rpartition() (str method), 47
rpc_paths (xmlrpc.server.SimpleXMLRPCRequestHandler attribute), 1232
rpop() (poplib.POP3 method), 1168
rset() (poplib.POP3 method), 1168
rshift() (in module operator), 349
rsplit() (bytearray method), 59
rsplit() (bytes method), 59
rsplit() (str method), 47
RSQB (in module token), 1679
rstrip() (bytearray method), 59
rstrip() (bytes method), 59
rstrip() (str method), 48
rt() (in module turtle), 1290
RTLD_DEEPBIND (in module os), 569
RTLD_GLOBAL (in module os), 569

RTLD_LAZY (in module os), 569
RTLD_LOCAL (in module os), 569
RTLD_NODELETE (in module os), 569
RTLD_NOLOAD (in module os), 569
RTLD_NOW (in module os), 569
ruler (cmd.Cmd attribute), 1321
run (pdb command), 1523
Run script, 1366
run() (bdb.Bdb method), 1515
run() (doctest.DocTestRunner method), 1410
run() (in module pdb), 1518
run() (in module profile), 1526
run() (in module subprocess), 787
run() (multiprocessing.Process method), 746
run() (pdb.Pdb method), 1519
run() (profile.Profile method), 1527
run() (sched.scheduler method), 803
run() (threading.Thread method), 730
run() (trace.Trace method), 1538
run() (unittest.TestCase method), 1424
run() (unittest.TestSuite method), 1433
run() (unittest.TextTestRunner method), 1439
run() (wsgiref.handlers.BaseHandler method), 1123
run_coroutine_threadsafe() (in module asyncio), 896
run_docstring_examples() (in module doctest), 1403
run_doctest() (in module test.support), 1505
run_forever() (asyncio.AbstractEventLoop method), 873
run_in_executor() (asyncio.AbstractEventLoop method), 881
run_module() (in module runpy), 1647
run_path() (in module runpy), 1648
run_script() (modulefinder.ModuleFinder method), 1646
run_unittest() (in module test.support), 1505
run_until_complete() (asyncio.AbstractEventLoop method), 873
run_with_locale() (in module test.support), 1507
runcall() (bdb.Bdb method), 1515
runcall() (in module pdb), 1519
runcall() (pdb.Pdb method), 1519
runcall() (profile.Profile method), 1527
runcode() (code.InteractiveInterpreter method), 1638
runctx() (bdb.Bdb method), 1515
runctx() (in module profile), 1526
runctx() (profile.Profile method), 1527
runctx() (trace.Trace method), 1538
runeval() (bdb.Bdb method), 1515
runeval() (in module pdb), 1519
runeval() (pdb.Pdb method), 1519
runfunc() (trace.Trace method), 1538
running() (concurrent.futures.Future method), 785
runpy (module), 1647

runsource() (code.InteractiveInterpreter method), 1638
RuntimeError, 88
RuntimeWarning, 92
RUSAGE_BOTH (in module resource), 1744
RUSAGE_CHILDREN (in module resource), 1743
RUSAGE_SELF (in module resource), 1743
RUSAGE_THREAD (in module resource), 1744

S

S (in module re), 112
S_ENFMT (in module stat), 382
S_IEXEC (in module stat), 382
S_IFBLK (in module stat), 380
S_IFCHR (in module stat), 380
S_IFDIR (in module stat), 380
S_IFDOOR (in module stat), 380
S_IFIFO (in module stat), 380
S_IFLNK (in module stat), 380
S_IFMT() (in module stat), 379
S_IFPORT (in module stat), 381
S_IFREG (in module stat), 380
S_IFSOCK (in module stat), 380
S_IFWHT (in module stat), 381
S_IMODE() (in module stat), 379
S_IREAD (in module stat), 382
S_IRGRP (in module stat), 381
S_IROTH (in module stat), 381
S_IRUSR (in module stat), 381
S_IRWXG (in module stat), 381
S_IRWXO (in module stat), 381
S_IRWXU (in module stat), 381
S_ISBLK() (in module stat), 378
S_ISCHR() (in module stat), 378
S_ISDIR() (in module stat), 378
S_ISDOOR() (in module stat), 378
S_ISFIFO() (in module stat), 378
S_ISGID (in module stat), 381
S_ISLNK() (in module stat), 378
S_ISPORT() (in module stat), 378
S_ISREG() (in module stat), 378
S_ISSOCK() (in module stat), 378
S_ISUID (in module stat), 381
S_ISVTX (in module stat), 381
S_ISWHT() (in module stat), 379
S_IWGRP (in module stat), 381
S_IWOTH (in module stat), 381
S_IWRITE (in module stat), 382
S_IWUSR (in module stat), 381
S_IXGRP (in module stat), 381
S_IXOTH (in module stat), 382
S_IXUSR (in module stat), 381
safe_substitute() (string.Template method), 104
saferepr() (in module pprint), 249

same_files (filecmp.dircmp attribute), 384
same_quantum() (decimal.Context method), 301
same_quantum() (decimal.Decimal method), 295
samefile() (in module os.path), 374
samefile() (pathlib.Path method), 370
SameFileError, 393
sameopenfile() (in module os.path), 375
samestat() (in module os.path), 375
sample() (in module random), 316
save() (http.cookiejar.FileCookieJar method), 1217
SaveKey() (in module winreg), 1722
savetty() (in module curses), 668
SAX2DOM (class in xml.dom.pulldom), 1085
SAXException, 1086
SAXNotRecognizedException, 1087
SAXNotSupportedException, 1087
SAXParseException, 1086
scaleb() (decimal.Context method), 301
scaleb() (decimal.Decimal method), 295
scandir() (in module os), 547
scanf(), 121
sched (module), 802
SCHED_BATCH (in module os), 566
SCHED_FIFO (in module os), 566
sched_get_priority_max() (in module os), 567
sched_get_priority_min() (in module os), 567
sched_getaffinity() (in module os), 567
sched_getparam() (in module os), 567
sched_getscheduler() (in module os), 567
SCHED_IDLE (in module os), 566
SCHED_OTHER (in module os), 566
sched_param (class in os), 566
sched_priority (os.sched_param attribute), 566
SCHED_RESET_ON_FORK (in module os), 566
SCHED_RR (in module os), 566
sched_rr_get_interval() (in module os), 567
sched_setaffinity() (in module os), 567
sched_setparam() (in module os), 567
sched_setscheduler() (in module os), 567
SCHED_SPORADIC (in module os), 566
sched_yield() (in module os), 567
scheduler (class in sched), 802
schema (in module msilib), 1716
Screen (class in turtle), 1313
screensize() (in module turtle), 1307
script_from_examples() (in module doctest), 1412
scroll() (curses.window method), 674
ScrolledCanvas (class in turtle), 1313
scrollok() (curses.window method), 674
scrypt() (in module hashlib), 512
search
    path, module, 392, 1572, 1630
search() (imaplib.IMAP4 method), 1173
search() (in module re), 112

search() (re.regex method), 116
second (datetime.datetime attribute), 183
second (datetime.time attribute), 190
seconds since the epoch, 582
secrets (module), 520
SECTCRE (in module configparser), 494
sections() (configparser.ConfigParser method), 497
secure (http.cookiejar.Cookie attribute), 1222
secure hash algorithm, SHA1, SHA224, SHA256, SHA384, SHA512, 509
Secure Sockets Layer, 832
security
    CGI, 1114
see() (tkinter.ttk.Treeview method), 1354
seed() (in module random), 314
seek() (chunk.Chunk method), 1260
seek() (io.IOBase method), 574
seek() (io.TextIOBase method), 579
seek() (mmap.mmap method), 946
SEEK_CUR (in module os), 534
SEEK_END (in module os), 534
SEEK_SET (in module os), 534
seekable() (io.IOBase method), 574
seen_greeting (smtpd.SMTPChannel attribute), 1191
Select (class in tkinter.tix), 1361
select (module), 862
select() (imaplib.IMAP4 method), 1173
select() (in module select), 863
select() (selectors.BaseSelector method), 870
select() (tkinter.ttk.Notebook method), 1348
selected_alpn_protocol() (ssl.SSLSocket method), 846
selected_npn_protocol() (ssl.SSLSocket method), 846
selection() (tkinter.ttk.Treeview method), 1355
selection_add() (tkinter.ttk.Treeview method), 1355
selection_remove() (tkinter.ttk.Treeview method), 1355
selection_set() (tkinter.ttk.Treeview method), 1355
selection_toggle() (tkinter.ttk.Treeview method), 1355
selector (urllib.request.Request attribute), 1131
SelectorEventLoop (class in asyncio), 885
SelectorKey (class in selectors), 869
selectors (module), 869
SelectSelector (class in selectors), 871
Semaphore (class in asyncio), 923
Semaphore (class in multiprocessing), 755
Semaphore (class in threading), 735
Semaphore() (multiprocessing.managers.SyncManager method), 761
semaphores, binary, 807

SEMI (in module token), 1679
send() (asyncore.dispatcher method), 934
send() (http.client.HTTPConnection method), 1159
send() (imaplib.IMAP4 method), 1173
send() (logging.handlers.DatagramHandler method), 655
send() (logging.handlers.SocketHandler method), 655
send() (multiprocessing.Connection method), 752
send() (socket.socket method), 825
send_bytes() (multiprocessing.Connection method), 753
send_error() (http.server.BaseHTTPRequestHandler method), 1208
send_flowing_data() (formatter.writer method), 1708
send_header() (http.server.BaseHTTPRequestHandler method), 1208
send_hor_rule() (formatter.writer method), 1708
send_label_data() (formatter.writer method), 1708
send_line_break() (formatter.writer method), 1708
send_literal_data() (formatter.writer method), 1708
send_message() (smtplib.SMTP method), 1187
send_paragraph() (formatter.writer method), 1708
send_response() (http.server.BaseHTTPRequestHandler method), 1208
send_response_only() (http.server.BaseHTTPRequestHandler method), 1208
send_signal() (asyncio.asyncio.subprocess.Process method), 917
send_signal() (asyncio.BaseSubprocessTransport method), 901
send_signal() (subprocess.Popen method), 795
sendall() (socket.socket method), 825
sendcmd() (ftplib.FTP method), 1164
sendfile() (in module os), 537
sendfile() (socket.socket method), 826
sendfile() (wsgiref.handlers.BaseHandler method), 1125
sendmail() (smtplib.SMTP method), 1187
sendmsg() (socket.socket method), 826
sendmsg_afalg() (socket.socket method), 826
sendto() (asyncio.DatagramTransport method), 901
sendto() (socket.socket method), 825
sentinel (in module unittest.mock), 1469
sentinel (multiprocessing.Process attribute), 747
sep (in module os), 568
sequence, 1791
    iteration, 36
    object, 37
    types, immutable, 39
    types, mutable, 39
    types, operations on, 37, 39
Sequence (class in collections.abc), 224
Sequence (class in typing), 1383

sequence (in module msilib), 1716
sequence2st() (in module parser), 1668
SequenceMatcher (class in difflib), 125, 129
serializing
    objects, 401
serve_forever() (socketserver.BaseServer method), 1200
server
    WWW, 1109, 1206
Server (class in asyncio), 882
server (http.server.BaseHTTPRequestHandler attribute), 1206
server_activate() (socketserver.BaseServer method), 1201
server_address (socketserver.BaseServer attribute), 1200
server_bind() (socketserver.BaseServer method), 1201
server_close() (socketserver.BaseServer method), 1200
server_hostname (ssl.SSLSocket attribute), 847
server_side (ssl.SSLSocket attribute), 846
server_software (wsgiref.handlers.BaseHandler attribute), 1124
server_version (http.server.BaseHTTPRequestHandler attribute), 1207
server_version (http.server.SimpleHTTPRequestHandler attribute), 1209
ServerProxy (class in xmlrpc.client), 1224
service_actions() (socketserver.BaseServer method), 1200
session (ssl.SSLSocket attribute), 847
session_reused (ssl.SSLSocket attribute), 847
session_stats() (ssl.SSLContext method), 851
set
    object, 73
set (built-in class), 73
Set (class in collections.abc), 224
Set (class in typing), 1384
Set Breakpoint, 1367
set() (asyncio.Event method), 922
set() (configparser.ConfigParser method), 498
set() (configparser.RawConfigParser method), 500
set() (http.cookies.Morsel method), 1213
set() (ossaudiodev.oss_mixer_device method), 1267
set() (test.support.EnvironmentVarGuard method), 1509
set() (threading.Event method), 736
set() (tkinter.ttk.Combobox method), 1346
set() (tkinter.ttk.Treeview method), 1355
set() (xml.etree.ElementTree.Element method), 1063
SET_ADD (opcode), 1696
set_allowed_domains() (http.cookiejar.DefaultCookiePolicy method), 1220
set_alpn_protocols() (ssl.SSLContext method), 850
set_app() (wsgiref.simple_server.WSGIServer method), 1120
set_asyncgen_hooks() (in module sys), 1575
set_authorizer() (sqlite3.Connection method), 428
set_auto_history() (in module readline), 144
set_blocked_domains() (http.cookiejar.DefaultCookiePolicy method), 1220
set_blocking() (in module os), 537
set_boundary() (email.message.EmailMessage method), 955
set_boundary() (email.message.Message method), 994
set_break() (bdb.Bdb method), 1514
set_charset() (email.message.Message method), 990
set_children() (tkinter.ttk.Treeview method), 1352
set_ciphers() (ssl.SSLContext method), 849
set_completer() (in module readline), 144
set_completer_delims() (in module readline), 145
set_completion_display_matches_hook() (in module readline), 145
set_content() (email.contentmanager.ContentManager method), 979
set_content() (email.message.EmailMessage method), 957
set_content() (in module email.contentmanager), 980
set_continue() (bdb.Bdb method), 1514
set_cookie() (http.cookiejar.CookieJar method), 1217
set_cookie_if_ok() (http.cookiejar.CookieJar method), 1217
set_coroutine_wrapper() (in module sys), 1576
set_current() (msilib.Feature method), 1715
set_data() (importlib.abc.SourceLoader method), 1656
set_data() (importlib.machinery.SourceFileLoader method), 1659
set_date() (mailbox.MaildirMessage method), 1027
set_debug() (asyncio.AbstractEventLoop method), 882
set_debug() (in module gc), 1613
set_debuglevel() (ftplib.FTP method), 1163
set_debuglevel() (http.client.HTTPConnection method), 1158
set_debuglevel() (nntplib.NNTP method), 1181
set_debuglevel() (poplib.POP3 method), 1167
set_debuglevel() (smtplib.SMTP method), 1184
set_debuglevel() (telnetlib.Telnet method), 1194
set_default_executor() (asyncio.AbstractEventLoop method), 881
set_default_type() (email.message.EmailMessage

method), 954
set_default_type() (email.message.Message method), 992
set_default_verify_paths() (ssl.SSLContext method), 849
set_defaults() (argparse.ArgumentParser method), 618
set_defaults() (optparse.OptionParser method), 1766
set_ecdh_curve() (ssl.SSLContext method), 851
set_errno() (in module ctypes), 719
set_event_loop() (asyncio.AbstractEventLoopPolicy method), 887
set_event_loop() (in module asyncio), 885
set_event_loop_policy() (in module asyncio), 888
set_exception() (asyncio.Future method), 892
set_exception() (asyncio.StreamReader method), 909
set_exception() (concurrent.futures.Future method), 786
set_exception_handler() (asyncio.AbstractEventLoop method), 881
set_executable() (in module multiprocessing), 752
set_flags() (mailbox.MaildirMessage method), 1027
set_flags() (mailbox.mboxMessage method), 1028
set_flags() (mailbox.MMDFMessage method), 1032
set_from() (mailbox.mboxMessage method), 1028
set_from() (mailbox.MMDFMessage method), 1032
set_handle_inheritable() (in module os), 539
set_history_length() (in module readline), 143
set_info() (mailbox.MaildirMessage method), 1027
set_inheritable() (in module os), 539
set_inheritable() (socket.socket method), 826
set_labels() (mailbox.BabylMessage method), 1031
set_last_error() (in module ctypes), 719
set_literal (2to3 fixer), 1501
set_loader() (in module importlib.util), 1663
set_next() (bdb.Bdb method), 1513
set_nonstandard_attr() (http.cookiejar.Cookie method), 1222
set_npn_protocols() (ssl.SSLContext method), 850
set_ok() (http.cookiejar.CookiePolicy method), 1218
set_option_negotiation_callback() (telnetlib.Telnet method), 1194
set_output_charset() (gettext.NullTranslations method), 1272
set_package() (in module importlib.util), 1663
set_param() (email.message.EmailMessage method), 954
set_param() (email.message.Message method), 993
set_pasv() (ftplib.FTP method), 1164
set_payload() (email.message.Message method), 990

set_policy() (http.cookiejar.CookieJar method), 1217
set_position() (xdrlib.Unpacker method), 503
set_pre_input_hook() (in module readline), 144
set_progress_handler() (sqlite3.Connection method), 429
set_protocol() (asyncio.BaseTransport method), 899
set_proxy() (urllib.request.Request method), 1132
set_quit() (bdb.Bdb method), 1514
set_recsrc() (ossaudiodev.oss_mixer_device method), 1267
set_result() (asyncio.Future method), 892
set_result() (concurrent.futures.Future method), 786
set_return() (bdb.Bdb method), 1513
set_running_or_notify_cancel() (concurrent.futures.Future method), 785
set_seq1() (difflib.SequenceMatcher method), 130
set_seq2() (difflib.SequenceMatcher method), 130
set_seqs() (difflib.SequenceMatcher method), 130
set_sequences() (mailbox.MH method), 1023
set_sequences() (mailbox.MHMessage method), 1030
set_server_documentation() (xmlrpc.server.DocCGIXMLRPCRequestHandler method), 1236
set_server_documentation() (xmlrpc.server.DocXMLRPCServer method), 1236
set_server_name() (xmlrpc.server.DocCGIXMLRPCRequestHandler method), 1236
set_server_name() (xmlrpc.server.DocXMLRPCServer method), 1236
set_server_title() (xmlrpc.server.DocCGIXMLRPCRequestHandler method), 1236
set_server_title() (xmlrpc.server.DocXMLRPCServer method), 1236
set_servername_callback() (ssl.SSLContext method), 850
set_spacing() (formatter.formatter method), 1707
set_start_method() (in module multiprocessing), 752
set_startup_hook() (in module readline), 144
set_step() (bdb.Bdb method), 1513
set_subdir() (mailbox.MaildirMessage method), 1026
set_task_factory() (asyncio.AbstractEventLoop method), 875
set_terminator() (asynchat.async_chat method), 937
set_threshold() (in module gc), 1613

set_trace() (bdb.Bdb method), 1514
set_trace() (in module bdb), 1515
set_trace() (in module pdb), 1519
set_trace() (pdb.Pdb method), 1519
set_trace_callback() (sqlite3.Connection method), 429
set_transport() (asyncio.StreamReader method), 909
set_tunnel() (http.client.HTTPConnection method), 1158
set_type() (email.message.Message method), 994
set_unittest_reportflags() (in module doctest), 1405
set_unixfrom() (email.message.EmailMessage method), 952
set_unixfrom() (email.message.Message method), 989
set_until() (bdb.Bdb method), 1514
set_url() (urllib.robotparser.RobotFileParser method), 1152
set_usage() (optparse.OptionParser method), 1766
set_userptr() (curses.panel.Panel method), 684
set_visible() (mailbox.BabylMessage method), 1031
set_wakeup_fd() (in module signal), 941
set_write_buffer_limits() (asyncio.WriteTransport method), 900
setacl() (imaplib.IMAP4 method), 1173
setannotation() (imaplib.IMAP4 method), 1173
setattr() (built-in function), 21
setAttribute() (xml.dom.Element method), 1075
setAttributeNode() (xml.dom.Element method), 1076
setAttributeNodeNS() (xml.dom.Element method), 1076
setAttributeNS() (xml.dom.Element method), 1076
SetBase() (xml.parsers.expat.xmlparser method), 1098
setblocking() (socket.socket method), 826
setByteStream() (xml.sax.xmlreader.InputSource method), 1096
setcbreak() (in module tty), 1735
setCharacterStream() (xml.sax.xmlreader.InputSource method), 1096
setcheckinterval() (in module sys), 1574
setcomptype() (aifc.aifc method), 1254
setcomptype() (sunau.AU_write method), 1257
setcomptype() (wave.Wave_write method), 1259
setContentHandler() (xml.sax.xmlreader.XMLReader method), 1094
setcontext() (in module decimal), 296
setDaemon() (threading.Thread method), 730
setdefault() (dict method), 77
setdefault() (http.cookies.Morsel method), 1214
setdefaulttimeout() (in module socket), 820
setdlopenflags() (in module sys), 1574

setDocumentLocator() (xml.sax.handler.ContentHandler method), 1089
setDTDHandler() (xml.sax.xmlreader.XMLReader method), 1094
setegid() (in module os), 530
setEncoding() (xml.sax.xmlreader.InputSource method), 1096
setEntityResolver() (xml.sax.xmlreader.XMLReader method), 1094
setErrorHandler() (xml.sax.xmlreader.XMLReader method), 1095
seteuid() (in module os), 530
setFeature() (xml.sax.xmlreader.XMLReader method), 1095
setfirstweekday() (in module calendar), 205
setfmt() (ossaudiodev.oss_audio_device method), 1265
setFormatter() (logging.Handler method), 628
setframerate() (aifc.aifc method), 1254
setframerate() (sunau.AU_write method), 1256
setframerate() (wave.Wave_write method), 1259
setgid() (in module os), 530
setgroups() (in module os), 530
seth() (in module turtle), 1291
setheading() (in module turtle), 1291
sethostname() (in module socket), 820
SetInteger() (msilib.Record method), 1713
setitem() (in module operator), 350
setitimer() (in module signal), 941
setLevel() (logging.Handler method), 628
setLevel() (logging.Logger method), 624
setlocale() (in module locale), 1277
setLocale() (xml.sax.xmlreader.XMLReader method), 1095
setLoggerClass() (in module logging), 638
setlogmask() (in module syslog), 1745
setLogRecordFactory() (in module logging), 638
setmark() (aifc.aifc method), 1254
setMaxConns() (urllib.request.CacheFTPHandler method), 1138
setmode() (in module msvcrt), 1717
setName() (threading.Thread method), 730
setnchannels() (aifc.aifc method), 1254
setnchannels() (sunau.AU_write method), 1256
setnchannels() (wave.Wave_write method), 1259
setnframes() (aifc.aifc method), 1254
setnframes() (sunau.AU_write method), 1257
setnframes() (wave.Wave_write method), 1259
SetParamEntityParsing() (xml.parsers.expat.xmlparser method), 1099
setparameters() (ossaudiodev.oss_audio_device method), 1266
setparams() (aifc.aifc method), 1254

setparams() (sunau.AU_write method), 1257
setparams() (wave.Wave_write method), 1259
setpassword() (zipfile.ZipFile method), 461
setpgid() (in module os), 530
setpgrp() (in module os), 530
setpos() (aifc.aifc method), 1253
setpos() (in module turtle), 1291
setpos() (sunau.AU_read method), 1256
setpos() (wave.Wave_read method), 1258
setposition() (in module turtle), 1291
setpriority() (in module os), 530
setprofile() (in module sys), 1574
setprofile() (in module threading), 728
SetProperty() (msilib.SummaryInformation method), 1713
setProperty() (xml.sax.xmlreader.XMLReader method), 1095
setPublicId() (xml.sax.xmlreader.InputSource method), 1096
setquota() (imaplib.IMAP4 method), 1174
setraw() (in module tty), 1735
setrecursionlimit() (in module sys), 1574
setregid() (in module os), 530
setresgid() (in module os), 530
setresuid() (in module os), 531
setreuid() (in module os), 531
setrlimit() (in module resource), 1741
setsampwidth() (aifc.aifc method), 1254
setsampwidth() (sunau.AU_write method), 1256
setsampwidth() (wave.Wave_write method), 1259
setscrreg() (curses.window method), 675
setsid() (in module os), 531
setsockopt() (socket.socket method), 827
setstate() (codecs.IncrementalDecoder method), 161
setstate() (codecs.IncrementalEncoder method), 160
setstate() (in module random), 315
SetStream() (msilib.Record method), 1713
SetString() (msilib.Record method), 1713
setswitchinterval() (in module sys), 1575
setSystemId() (xml.sax.xmlreader.InputSource method), 1096
setsyx() (in module curses), 668
setTarget() (logging.handlers.MemoryHandler method), 659
settiltangle() (in module turtle), 1302
settimeout() (socket.socket method), 827
setTimeout() (urllib.request.CacheFTPHandler method), 1138
settrace() (in module sys), 1575
settrace() (in module threading), 728
setuid() (in module os), 531
setundobuffer() (in module turtle), 1305
setup() (in module turtle), 1312
setup() (socketserver.BaseRequestHandler method), 1202
setUp() (unittest.TestCase method), 1424
SETUP_ANNOTATIONS (opcode), 1697
SETUP_ASYNC_WITH (opcode), 1696
setup_environ() (wsgiref.handlers.BaseHandler method), 1124
SETUP_EXCEPT (opcode), 1700
SETUP_FINALLY (opcode), 1700
SETUP_LOOP (opcode), 1700
setup_python() (venv.EnvBuilder method), 1555
setup_scripts() (venv.EnvBuilder method), 1555
setup_testing_defaults() (in module wsgiref.util), 1118
SETUP_WITH (opcode), 1697
setUpClass() (unittest.TestCase method), 1424
setupterm() (in module curses), 668
SetValue() (in module winreg), 1722
SetValueEx() (in module winreg), 1722
setworldcoordinates() (in module turtle), 1307
setx() (in module turtle), 1291
setxattr() (in module os), 557
sety() (in module turtle), 1291
SF_APPEND (in module stat), 382
SF_ARCHIVED (in module stat), 382
SF_IMMUTABLE (in module stat), 382
SF_MNOWAIT (in module os), 538
SF_NODISKIO (in module os), 538
SF_NOUNLINK (in module stat), 382
SF_SNAPSHOT (in module stat), 382
SF_SYNC (in module os), 538
Shape (class in turtle), 1313
shape (memoryview attribute), 72
shape() (in module turtle), 1301
shapesize() (in module turtle), 1301
shapetransform() (in module turtle), 1303
share() (socket.socket method), 827
shared_ciphers() (ssl.SSLSocket method), 845
shearfactor() (in module turtle), 1302
Shelf (class in shelve), 416
shelve
    module, 417
shelve (module), 415
shield() (in module asyncio), 897
shift() (decimal.Context method), 301
shift() (decimal.Decimal method), 295
shift_path_info() (in module wsgiref.util), 1117
shifting
    operations, 32
shlex (class in shlex), 1325
shlex (module), 1324
shortDescription() (unittest.TestCase method), 1432
shorten() (in module textwrap), 136

shouldFlush() (logging.handlers.BufferingHandler method), 659
shouldFlush() (logging.handlers.MemoryHandler method), 659
shouldStop (unittest.TestResult attribute), 1436
show() (curses.panel.Panel method), 684
show_code() (in module dis), 1691
showsyntaxerror() (code.InteractiveInterpreter method), 1638
showtraceback() (code.InteractiveInterpreter method), 1638
showturtle() (in module turtle), 1300
showwarning() (in module warnings), 1587
shuffle() (in module random), 315
shutdown() (concurrent.futures.Executor method), 782
shutdown() (imaplib.IMAP4 method), 1174
shutdown() (in module logging), 638
shutdown() (multiprocessing.managers.BaseManager method), 760
shutdown() (socket.socket method), 827
shutdown() (socketserver.BaseServer method), 1200
shutdown_asyncgens() (asyncio.AbstractEventLoop method), 874
shutil (module), 392
side_effect (unittest.mock.Mock attribute), 1449
SIG_BLOCK (in module signal), 940
SIG_DFL (in module signal), 939
SIG_IGN (in module signal), 939
SIG_SETMASK (in module signal), 940
SIG_UNBLOCK (in module signal), 940
siginterrupt() (in module signal), 942
signal
    module, 808
signal (module), 938
signal() (in module signal), 942
Signature (class in inspect), 1621
signature (inspect.BoundArguments attribute), 1623
signature() (in module inspect), 1620
sigpending() (in module signal), 942
sigtimedwait() (in module signal), 943
sigwait() (in module signal), 942
sigwaitinfo() (in module signal), 942
Simple Mail Transfer Protocol, 1182
SimpleCookie (class in http.cookies), 1212
simplefilter() (in module warnings), 1587
SimpleHandler (class in wsgiref.handlers), 1123
SimpleHTTPRequestHandler (class in http.server), 1209
SimpleNamespace (class in types), 245
SimpleQueue (class in multiprocessing), 750
SimpleXMLRPCRequestHandler (class in xmlrpc.server), 1232
SimpleXMLRPCServer (class in xmlrpc.server), 1231

sin() (in module cmath), 283
sin() (in module math), 279
single dispatch, **1791**
SingleAddressHeader (class in email.headerregistry), 975
singledispatch() (in module functools), 344
sinh() (in module cmath), 283
sinh() (in module math), 280
SIO_KEEPALIVE_VALS (in module socket), 815
SIO_LOOPBACK_FAST_PATH (in module socket), 815
SIO_RCVALL (in module socket), 815
site (module), 1630
site command line option
    --user-base, 1633
    --user-site, 1633
site-packages
    directory, 1631
sitecustomize
    module, 1631
sixtofour (ipaddress.IPv6Address attribute), 1239
size (struct.Struct attribute), 154
size (tarfile.TarInfo attribute), 471
size (tracemalloc.Statistic attribute), 1546
size (tracemalloc.StatisticDiff attribute), 1547
size (tracemalloc.Trace attribute), 1547
size() (ftplib.FTP method), 1166
size() (mmap.mmap method), 946
size_diff (tracemalloc.StatisticDiff attribute), 1547
Sized (class in collections.abc), 223
Sized (class in typing), 1383
sizeof() (in module ctypes), 720
SKIP (in module doctest), 1399
skip() (chunk.Chunk method), 1261
skip() (in module unittest), 1422
skip_unless_symlink() (in module test.support), 1507
skipIf() (in module unittest), 1422
skipinitialspace (csv.Dialect attribute), 481
skipped (unittest.TestResult attribute), 1436
skippedEntity() (xml.sax.handler.ContentHandler method), 1091
SkipTest, 1422
skipTest() (unittest.TestCase method), 1424
skipUnless() (in module unittest), 1422
SLASH (in module token), 1679
SLASHEQUAL (in module token), 1679
slave() (nntplib.NNTP method), 1181
sleep() (in module asyncio), 897
sleep() (in module time), 585
slice, **1791**
    assignment, 39
    built-in function, 1701
    operation, 37

slice (built-in class), 21
SMTP
    protocol, 1182
SMTP (class in smtplib), 1182
SMTP (in module email.policy), 970
smtp_server (smtpd.SMTPChannel attribute), 1191
SMTP_SSL (class in smtplib), 1183
smtp_state (smtpd.SMTPChannel attribute), 1191
SMTPAuthenticationError, 1184
SMTPChannel (class in smtpd), 1190
SMTPConnectError, 1184
smtpd (module), 1189
SMTPDataError, 1184
SMTPException, 1183
SMTPHandler (class in logging.handlers), 658
SMTPHeloError, 1184
smtplib (module), 1182
SMTPNotSupportedError, 1184
SMTPRecipientsRefused, 1184
SMTPResponseException, 1184
SMTPSenderRefused, 1184
SMTPServer (class in smtpd), 1189
SMTPServerDisconnected, 1183
SMTPUTF8 (in module email.policy), 970
Snapshot (class in tracemalloc), 1545
SND_ALIAS (in module winsound), 1726
SND_ASYNC (in module winsound), 1727
SND_FILENAME (in module winsound), 1726
SND_LOOP (in module winsound), 1727
SND_MEMORY (in module winsound), 1727
SND_NODEFAULT (in module winsound), 1727
SND_NOSTOP (in module winsound), 1727
SND_NOWAIT (in module winsound), 1727
SND_PURGE (in module winsound), 1727
sndhdr (module), 1262
sniff() (csv.Sniffer method), 480
Sniffer (class in csv), 480
sock_accept() (asyncio.AbstractEventLoop method), 880
SOCK_CLOEXEC (in module socket), 814
sock_connect() (asyncio.AbstractEventLoop method), 879
SOCK_DGRAM (in module socket), 814
SOCK_NONBLOCK (in module socket), 814
SOCK_RAW (in module socket), 814
SOCK_RDM (in module socket), 814
sock_recv() (asyncio.AbstractEventLoop method), 879
sock_sendall() (asyncio.AbstractEventLoop method), 879
SOCK_SEQPACKET (in module socket), 814
SOCK_STREAM (in module socket), 814
socket
    module, 1107

object, 811
socket (module), 811
socket (socketserver.BaseServer attribute), 1200
socket() (imaplib.IMAP4 method), 1174
socket() (in module socket), 816, 863
socket_type (socketserver.BaseServer attribute), 1201
SocketHandler (class in logging.handlers), 654
socketpair() (in module socket), 816
sockets (asyncio.Server attribute), 883
socketserver (module), 1198
SocketType (in module socket), 817
SOL_ALG (in module socket), 815
SOL_RDS (in module socket), 815
SOMAXCONN (in module socket), 814
sort() (imaplib.IMAP4 method), 1174
sort() (list method), 40
sort_stats() (pstats.Stats method), 1528
sorted() (built-in function), 21
sortTestMethodsUsing (unittest.TestLoader attribute), 1436
source (doctest.Example attribute), 1407
source (pdb command), 1522
source (shlex.shlex attribute), 1327
source_from_cache() (in module imp), 1776
source_from_cache() (in module importlib.util), 1662
SOURCE_SUFFIXES (in module importlib.machinery), 1657
source_to_code() (importlib.abc.InspectLoader static method), 1655
SourceFileLoader (class in importlib.machinery), 1659
sourcehook() (shlex.shlex method), 1325
SourcelessFileLoader (class in importlib.machinery), 1659
SourceLoader (class in importlib.abc), 1656
span() (re.match method), 119
spawn() (in module pty), 1736
spawnl() (in module os), 561
spawnle() (in module os), 561
spawnlp() (in module os), 561
spawnlpe() (in module os), 561
spawnv() (in module os), 561
spawnve() (in module os), 561
spawnvp() (in module os), 561
spawnvpe() (in module os), 561
spec_from_file_location() (in module importlib.util), 1663
spec_from_loader() (in module importlib.util), 1663
special method, **1791**
specified_attributes (xml.parsers.expat.xmlparser attribute), 1099
speed() (in module turtle), 1294

speed() (ossaudiodev.oss_audio_device method), 1265
split() (bytearray method), 59
split() (bytes method), 59
split() (in module os.path), 375
split() (in module re), 113
split() (in module shlex), 1324
split() (re.regex method), 117
split() (str method), 48
splitdrive() (in module os.path), 375
splitext() (in module os.path), 375
splitlines() (bytearray method), 62
splitlines() (bytes method), 62
splitlines() (str method), 48
SplitResult (class in urllib.parse), 1149
SplitResultBytes (class in urllib.parse), 1149
splitunc() (in module os.path), 375
SpooledTemporaryFile() (in module tempfile), 386
sprintf-style formatting, 51, 64
spwd (module), 1731
sqlite3 (module), 422
sqlite_version (in module sqlite3), 424
sqlite_version_info (in module sqlite3), 424
sqrt() (decimal.Context method), 301
sqrt() (decimal.Decimal method), 295
sqrt() (in module cmath), 282
sqrt() (in module math), 279
SSL, 832
ssl (module), 832
ssl_version (ftplib.FTP_TLS attribute), 1166
SSLContext (class in ssl), 847
SSLEOFError, 833
SSLError, 832
SSLErrorNumber (class in ssl), 843
SSLObject (class in ssl), 858
SSLSession (class in ssl), 860
SSLSocket (class in ssl), 843
SSLSyscallError, 833
SSLWantReadError, 833
SSLWantWriteError, 833
SSLZeroReturnError, 833
st() (in module turtle), 1300
st2list() (in module parser), 1669
st2tuple() (in module parser), 1669
ST_ATIME (in module stat), 380
st_atime (os.stat_result attribute), 550
st_atime_ns (os.stat_result attribute), 550
st_birthtime (os.stat_result attribute), 551
st_blksize (os.stat_result attribute), 551
st_blocks (os.stat_result attribute), 551
st_creator (os.stat_result attribute), 551
ST_CTIME (in module stat), 380
st_ctime (os.stat_result attribute), 550
st_ctime_ns (os.stat_result attribute), 550
ST_DEV (in module stat), 380
st_dev (os.stat_result attribute), 550
st_file_attributes (os.stat_result attribute), 551
st_flags (os.stat_result attribute), 551
st_gen (os.stat_result attribute), 551
ST_GID (in module stat), 380
st_gid (os.stat_result attribute), 550
ST_INO (in module stat), 380
st_ino (os.stat_result attribute), 550
ST_MODE (in module stat), 379
st_mode (os.stat_result attribute), 550
ST_MTIME (in module stat), 380
st_mtime (os.stat_result attribute), 550
st_mtime_ns (os.stat_result attribute), 550
ST_NLINK (in module stat), 380
st_nlink (os.stat_result attribute), 550
st_rdev (os.stat_result attribute), 551
st_rsize (os.stat_result attribute), 551
ST_SIZE (in module stat), 380
st_size (os.stat_result attribute), 550
st_type (os.stat_result attribute), 551
ST_UID (in module stat), 380
st_uid (os.stat_result attribute), 550
stack (traceback.TracebackException attribute), 1607
stack viewer, 1367
stack() (in module inspect), 1627
stack_effect() (in module dis), 1693
stack_size() (in module _thread), 807
stack_size() (in module threading), 728
stackable streams, 154
StackSummary (class in traceback), 1608
stamp() (in module turtle), 1293
standard_b64decode() (in module base64), 1039
standard_b64encode() (in module base64), 1039
standarderror (2to3 fixer), 1501
standend() (curses.window method), 675
standout() (curses.window method), 675
STAR (in module token), 1679
STAREQUAL (in module token), 1679
starmap() (in module itertools), 335
starmap() (multiprocessing.pool.Pool method), 767
starmap_async() (multiprocessing.pool.Pool method), 767
start (range attribute), 42
start (UnicodeError attribute), 90
start() (in module tracemalloc), 1543
start() (logging.handlers.QueueListener method), 661
start() (multiprocessing.managers.BaseManager method), 759
start() (multiprocessing.Process method), 746
start() (re.match method), 119

start() (threading.Thread method), 729
start() (tkinter.ttk.Progressbar method), 1349
start() (xml.etree.ElementTree.TreeBuilder method), 1067
start_color() (in module curses), 668
start_component() (msilib.Directory method), 1714
start_new_thread() (in module _thread), 807
start_server() (in module asyncio), 908
start_unix_server() (in module asyncio), 909
StartCdataSectionHandler() (xml.parsers.expat.xmlparser method), 1101
StartDoctypeDeclHandler() (xml.parsers.expat.xmlparser method), 1100
startDocument() (xml.sax.handler.ContentHandler method), 1090
startElement() (xml.sax.handler.ContentHandler method), 1090
StartElementHandler() (xml.parsers.expat.xmlparser method), 1101
startElementNS() (xml.sax.handler.ContentHandler method), 1090
STARTF_USESHOWWINDOW (in module subprocess), 796
STARTF_USESTDHANDLES (in module subprocess), 796
startfile() (in module os), 563
StartNamespaceDeclHandler() (xml.parsers.expat.xmlparser method), 1101
startPrefixMapping() (xml.sax.handler.ContentHandler method), 1090
startswith() (bytearray method), 57
startswith() (bytes method), 57
startswith() (str method), 49
startTest() (unittest.TestResult method), 1437
startTestRun() (unittest.TestResult method), 1437
starttls() (imaplib.IMAP4 method), 1174
starttls() (nntplib.NNTP method), 1178
starttls() (smtplib.SMTP method), 1186
STARTUPINFO (class in subprocess), 796
stat
    module, 549
stat (module), 378
stat() (in module os), 549
stat() (nntplib.NNTP method), 1180
stat() (os.DirEntry method), 549
stat() (pathlib.Path method), 365
stat() (poplib.POP3 method), 1168
stat_float_times() (in module os), 552
stat_result (class in os), 550
state() (tkinter.ttk.Widget method), 1345
statement, 1791

assert, 86
del, 39, 75
except, 85
if, 29
import, 24, 1773
raise, 85
try, 85
while, 29
staticmethod() (built-in function), 22
Statistic (class in tracemalloc), 1546
StatisticDiff (class in tracemalloc), 1547
statistics (module), 320
statistics() (tracemalloc.Snapshot method), 1546
StatisticsError, 325
Stats (class in pstats), 1527
status (http.client.HTTPResponse attribute), 1160
status() (imaplib.IMAP4 method), 1174
statvfs() (in module os), 552
STD_ERROR_HANDLE (in module subprocess), 796
STD_INPUT_HANDLE (in module subprocess), 796
STD_OUTPUT_HANDLE (in module subprocess), 796
StdButtonBox (class in tkinter.tix), 1361
stderr (asyncio.asyncio.subprocess.Process attribute), 918
stderr (in module sys), 1576
stderr (subprocess.CalledProcessError attribute), 789
stderr (subprocess.CompletedProcess attribute), 788
stderr (subprocess.Popen attribute), 795
stderr (subprocess.TimeoutExpired attribute), 789
stdev() (in module statistics), 324
stdin (asyncio.asyncio.subprocess.Process attribute), 917
stdin (in module sys), 1576
stdin (subprocess.Popen attribute), 795
stdout (asyncio.asyncio.subprocess.Process attribute), 918
STDOUT (in module subprocess), 788
stdout (in module sys), 1576
stdout (subprocess.CalledProcessError attribute), 789
stdout (subprocess.CompletedProcess attribute), 788
stdout (subprocess.Popen attribute), 795
stdout (subprocess.TimeoutExpired attribute), 789
step (pdb command), 1521
step (range attribute), 42
step() (tkinter.ttk.Progressbar method), 1349
stereocontrols() (ossaudiodev.oss_mixer_device method), 1267
stls() (poplib.POP3 method), 1169
stop (range attribute), 42

stop() (asyncio.AbstractEventLoop method), 873
stop() (in module tracemalloc), 1544
stop() (logging.handlers.QueueListener method), 661
stop() (tkinter.ttk.Progressbar method), 1349
stop() (unittest.TestResult method), 1437
stop_here() (bdb.Bdb method), 1513
StopAsyncIteration, 89
StopIteration, 88
stopListening() (in module logging.config), 641
stopTest() (unittest.TestResult method), 1437
stopTestRun() (unittest.TestResult method), 1437
storbinary() (ftplib.FTP method), 1164
store() (imaplib.IMAP4 method), 1174
STORE_ACTIONS (optparse.Option attribute), 1772
STORE_ANNOTATION (opcode), 1700
STORE_ATTR (opcode), 1698
STORE_DEREF (opcode), 1700
STORE_FAST (opcode), 1700
STORE_GLOBAL (opcode), 1698
STORE_NAME (opcode), 1698
STORE_SUBSCR (opcode), 1695
storlines() (ftplib.FTP method), 1164
str (built-in class), 43
    (see also string), 43
str() (in module locale), 1281
strcoll() (in module locale), 1281
StreamError, 467
StreamHandler (class in logging), 650
StreamReader (class in asyncio), 909
StreamReader (class in codecs), 162
streamreader (codecs.CodecInfo attribute), 155
StreamReaderProtocol (class in asyncio), 911
StreamReaderWriter (class in codecs), 163
StreamRecoder (class in codecs), 163
StreamRequestHandler (class in socketserver), 1202
streams, 154
    stackable, 154
StreamWriter (class in asyncio), 910
StreamWriter (class in codecs), 161
streamwriter (codecs.CodecInfo attribute), 155
strerror (OSError attribute), 88
strerror() (in module os), 531
strftime() (datetime.date method), 179
strftime() (datetime.datetime method), 187
strftime() (datetime.time method), 191
strftime() (in module time), 585
strict (csv.Dialect attribute), 481
strict (in module email.policy), 971
strict_domain (http.cookiejar.DefaultCookiePolicy attribute), 1220
strict_errors() (in module codecs), 158
strict_ns_domain (http.cookiejar.DefaultCookiePolicy attribute), 1221
strict_ns_set_initial_dollar (http.cookiejar.DefaultCookiePolicy attribute), 1221
strict_ns_set_path (http.cookiejar.DefaultCookiePolicy attribute), 1221
strict_ns_unverifiable (http.cookiejar.DefaultCookiePolicy attribute), 1221
strict_rfc2965_unverifiable (http.cookiejar.DefaultCookiePolicy attribute), 1220
strides (memoryview attribute), 73
string
    format() (built-in function), 12
    formatting, printf, 51
    interpolation, printf, 51
    methods, 43
    module, 1282
    object, 43
    str (built-in class), 43
    str() (built-in function), 22
    text sequence type, 43
STRING (in module token), 1679
string (module), 95
string (re.match attribute), 120
string_at() (in module ctypes), 720
StringIO (class in io), 580
stringprep (module), 141
strip() (bytearray method), 60
strip() (bytes method), 60
strip() (str method), 49
strip_dirs() (pstats.Stats method), 1527
stripspaces (curses.textpad.Textbox attribute), 681
strptime() (datetime.datetime class method), 182
strptime() (in module time), 587
struct
    module, 827
Struct (class in struct), 153
struct (module), 149
struct sequence, **1791**
struct_time (class in time), 587
Structure (class in ctypes), 723
structures
    C, 149
strxfrm() (in module locale), 1281
STType (in module parser), 1670
Style (class in tkinter.ttk), 1356
sub() (in module operator), 349
sub() (in module re), 114
sub() (re.regex method), 117
subdirs (filecmp.dircmp attribute), 385
SubElement() (in module xml.etree.ElementTree), 1062
submit() (concurrent.futures.Executor method), 781

submodule_search_locations (importlib.machinery.ModuleSpec attribute), 1661
subn() (in module re), 115
subn() (re.regex method), 117
subnets() (ipaddress.IPv4Network method), 1243
subnets() (ipaddress.IPv6Network method), 1244
Subnormal (class in decimal), 304
suboffsets (memoryview attribute), 73
subpad() (curses.window method), 675
subprocess (module), 787
subprocess_exec() (asyncio.AbstractEventLoop method), 915
subprocess_shell() (asyncio.AbstractEventLoop method), 916
SubprocessError, 788
SubprocessProtocol (class in asyncio), 902
subscribe() (imaplib.IMAP4 method), 1174
subscript
    assignment, 39
    operation, 37
subsequent_indent (textwrap.TextWrapper attribute), 138
substitute() (string.Template method), 104
subTest() (unittest.TestCase method), 1424
subtract() (collections.Counter method), 209
subtract() (decimal.Context method), 302
subtype (email.headerregistry.ContentTypeHeader attribute), 976
subwin() (curses.window method), 675
successful() (multiprocessing.pool.AsyncResult method), 767
suffix_map (in module mimetypes), 1036
suffix_map (mimetypes.MimeTypes attribute), 1037
suite() (in module parser), 1668
suiteClass (unittest.TestLoader attribute), 1436
sum() (built-in function), 22
summarize() (doctest.DocTestRunner method), 1410
summarize_address_range() (in module ipaddress), 1247
sunau (module), 1254
super (pyclbr.Class attribute), 1686
super() (built-in function), 22
supernet() (ipaddress.IPv4Network method), 1243
supernet() (ipaddress.IPv6Network method), 1244
supports_bytes_environ (in module os), 531
supports_dir_fd (in module os), 552
supports_effective_ids (in module os), 553
supports_fd (in module os), 553
supports_follow_symlinks (in module os), 553
supports_unicode_filenames (in module os.path), 375
SupportsAbs (class in typing), 1383
SupportsBytes (class in typing), 1383
SupportsComplex (class in typing), 1383
SupportsFloat (class in typing), 1383
SupportsInt (class in typing), 1383
SupportsRound (class in typing), 1383
suppress() (in module contextlib), 1589
SuppressCrashReport (class in test.support), 1509
SW_HIDE (in module subprocess), 796
swapcase() (bytearray method), 63
swapcase() (bytes method), 63
swapcase() (str method), 50
sym_name (in module symbol), 1679
Symbol (class in symtable), 1677
symbol (module), 1678
SymbolTable (class in symtable), 1677
symlink() (in module os), 553
symlink_to() (pathlib.Path method), 370
symmetric_difference() (frozenset method), 74
symmetric_difference_update() (frozenset method), 75
symtable (module), 1676
symtable() (in module symtable), 1676
sync() (dbm.dumb.dumbdbm method), 422
sync() (dbm.gnu.gdbm method), 421
sync() (in module os), 554
sync() (ossaudiodev.oss_audio_device method), 1265
sync() (shelve.Shelf method), 415
syncdown() (curses.window method), 675
synchronized() (in module multiprocessing.sharedctypes), 758
SyncManager (class in multiprocessing.managers), 760
syncok() (curses.window method), 675
syncup() (curses.window method), 675
SyntaxErr, 1078
SyntaxError, 89
SyntaxWarning, 92
sys
    module, 18
sys (module), 1563
sys_exc (2to3 fixer), 1501
sys_version (http.server.BaseHTTPRequestHandler attribute), 1207
sysconf() (in module os), 568
sysconf_names (in module os), 568
sysconfig (module), 1578
syslog (module), 1745
syslog() (in module syslog), 1745
SysLogHandler (class in logging.handlers), 656
system() (in module os), 563
system() (in module platform), 686
system_alias() (in module platform), 686
SystemError, 89
SystemExit, 89

systemId (xml.dom.DocumentType attribute), 1074
SystemRandom (class in random), 317
SystemRandom (class in secrets), 521
SystemRoot, 793

T

T_FMT (in module locale), 1279
T_FMT_AMPM (in module locale), 1279
tab() (tkinter.ttk.Notebook method), 1348
TabError, 89
tabnanny (module), 1684
tabs() (tkinter.ttk.Notebook method), 1348
tabsize (textwrap.TextWrapper attribute), 137
tabular
    data, 477
tag (xml.etree.ElementTree.Element attribute), 1063
tag_bind() (tkinter.ttk.Treeview method), 1355
tag_configure() (tkinter.ttk.Treeview method), 1355
tag_has() (tkinter.ttk.Treeview method), 1355
tagName (xml.dom.Element attribute), 1075
tail (xml.etree.ElementTree.Element attribute), 1063
take_snapshot() (in module tracemalloc), 1544
takewhile() (in module itertools), 336
tan() (in module cmath), 283
tan() (in module math), 279
tanh() (in module cmath), 283
tanh() (in module math), 280
TarError, 467
TarFile (class in tarfile), 467, 468
tarfile (module), 465
tarfile command line option
    --create <tarfile> <source1> ... <sourceN>, 472
    --extract <tarfile> [<output_dir>], 472
    --list <tarfile>, 472
    --test <tarfile>, 473
    -c <tarfile> <source1> ... <sourceN>, 472
    -e <tarfile> [<output_dir>], 472
    -l <tarfile>, 472
    -t <tarfile>, 473
    -v, --verbose, 473
target (xml.dom.ProcessingInstruction attribute), 1077
TarInfo (class in tarfile), 471
Task (class in asyncio), 893
task_done() (asyncio.Queue method), 925
task_done() (multiprocessing.JoinableQueue method), 750
task_done() (queue.Queue method), 805
tau (in module cmath), 284
tau (in module math), 280
tb_locals (unittest.TestResult attribute), 1437
tbreak (pdb command), 1520
tcdrain() (in module termios), 1735
tcflow() (in module termios), 1735
tcflush() (in module termios), 1735
tcgetattr() (in module termios), 1734
tcgetpgrp() (in module os), 538
Tcl() (in module tkinter), 1332
TCPServer (class in socketserver), 1198
tcsendbreak() (in module termios), 1735
tcsetattr() (in module termios), 1734
tcsetpgrp() (in module os), 538
tearDown() (unittest.TestCase method), 1424
tearDownClass() (unittest.TestCase method), 1424
tee() (in module itertools), 336
tell() (aifc.aifc method), 1253, 1254
tell() (chunk.Chunk method), 1261
tell() (io.IOBase method), 574
tell() (io.TextIOBase method), 580
tell() (mmap.mmap method), 946
tell() (sunau.AU_read method), 1256
tell() (sunau.AU_write method), 1257
tell() (wave.Wave_read method), 1258
tell() (wave.Wave_write method), 1259
Telnet (class in telnetlib), 1192
telnetlib (module), 1192
TEMP, 387
temp_cwd() (in module test.support), 1506
temp_dir() (in module test.support), 1506
temp_umask() (in module test.support), 1506
tempdir (in module tempfile), 388
tempfile (module), 385
Template (class in pipes), 1739
Template (class in string), 104
template (string.Template attribute), 104
temporary
    file, 385
    file name, 385
TemporaryDirectory() (in module tempfile), 386
TemporaryFile() (in module tempfile), 385
teredo (ipaddress.IPv6Address attribute), 1240
TERM, 668
termattrs() (in module curses), 668
terminal_size (class in os), 539
terminate() (asyncio.asyncio.subprocess.Process method), 917
terminate() (asyncio.BaseSubprocessTransport method), 901
terminate() (multiprocessing.pool.Pool method), 767
terminate() (multiprocessing.Process method), 747
terminate() (subprocess.Popen method), 795
termios (module), 1734
termname() (in module curses), 668
test (doctest.DocTestFailure attribute), 1413
test (doctest.UnexpectedException attribute), 1413
test (module), 1501
test() (in module cgi), 1113
test.support (module), 1504

TestCase (class in unittest), 1423
TestFailed, 1504
testfile() (in module doctest), 1402
TESTFN (in module test.support), 1504
TestLoader (class in unittest), 1434
testMethodPrefix (unittest.TestLoader attribute), 1435
testmod() (in module doctest), 1403
TestResult (class in unittest), 1436
tests (in module imghdr), 1262
testsource() (in module doctest), 1412
testsRun (unittest.TestResult attribute), 1436
TestSuite (class in unittest), 1433
testzip() (zipfile.ZipFile method), 461
Text (class in typing), 1386
text (in module msilib), 1716
text (traceback.TracebackException attribute), 1607
text (xml.etree.ElementTree.Element attribute), 1063
text encoding, **1791**
text file, **1791**
text mode, 18
text() (msilib.Dialog method), 1716
text_factory (sqlite3.Connection attribute), 430
Textbox (class in curses.textpad), 680
TextCalendar (class in calendar), 204
textdomain() (in module gettext), 1270
textdomain() (in module locale), 1283
textinput() (in module turtle), 1310
TextIOBase (class in io), 579
TextIOWrapper (class in io), 580
TextTestResult (class in unittest), 1438
TextTestRunner (class in unittest), 1438
textwrap (module), 135
TextWrapper (class in textwrap), 137
theme_create() (tkinter.ttk.Style method), 1358
theme_names() (tkinter.ttk.Style method), 1358
theme_settings() (tkinter.ttk.Style method), 1358
theme_use() (tkinter.ttk.Style method), 1358
THOUSEP (in module locale), 1279
Thread (class in threading), 729
thread() (imaplib.IMAP4 method), 1174
thread_info (in module sys), 1577
threading (module), 727
ThreadingMixIn (class in socketserver), 1199
ThreadingTCPServer (class in socketserver), 1199
ThreadingUDPServer (class in socketserver), 1199
ThreadPoolExecutor (class in concurrent.futures), 783
threads
    POSIX, 807
throw (2to3 fixer), 1501
ticket_lifetime_hint (ssl.SSLSession attribute), 860
tigetflag() (in module curses), 668

tigetnum() (in module curses), 668
tigetstr() (in module curses), 668
TILDE (in module token), 1679
tilt() (in module turtle), 1302
tiltangle() (in module turtle), 1303
time (class in datetime), 189
time (module), 582
time (ssl.SSLSession attribute), 860
time() (asyncio.AbstractEventLoop method), 875
time() (datetime.datetime method), 184
time() (in module time), 588
Time2Internaldate() (in module imaplib), 1170
timedelta (class in datetime), 175
TimedRotatingFileHandler (class in logging.handlers), 653
timegm() (in module calendar), 205
timeit (module), 1531
timeit command line option
    -c, --clock, 1534
    -h, --help, 1534
    -n N, --number=N, 1534
    -p, --process, 1534
    -r N, --repeat=N, 1534
    -s S, --setup=S, 1534
    -t, --time, 1534
    -u, --unit=U, 1534
    -v, --verbose, 1534
timeit() (in module timeit), 1532
timeit() (timeit.Timer method), 1533
timeout, 813
timeout (socketserver.BaseServer attribute), 1201
timeout (ssl.SSLSession attribute), 860
timeout (subprocess.TimeoutExpired attribute), 789
timeout() (curses.window method), 675
TIMEOUT_MAX (in module _thread), 807
TIMEOUT_MAX (in module threading), 728
TimeoutError, 91, 748, 786, 891
TimeoutExpired, 789
Timer (class in threading), 737
Timer (class in timeit), 1532
times() (in module os), 563
timestamp() (datetime.datetime method), 185
timetuple() (datetime.date method), 179
timetuple() (datetime.datetime method), 185
timetz() (datetime.datetime method), 184
timezone (class in datetime), 199
timezone (in module time), 590
title() (bytearray method), 63
title() (bytes method), 63
title() (in module turtle), 1313
title() (str method), 50
Tix, 1359
tix_addbitmapdir() (tkinter.tix.tixCommand method), 1363

tix_cget() (tkinter.tix.tixCommand method), 1363
tix_configure() (tkinter.tix.tixCommand method), 1363
tix_filedialog() (tkinter.tix.tixCommand method), 1363
tix_getbitmap() (tkinter.tix.tixCommand method), 1363
tix_getimage() (tkinter.tix.tixCommand method), 1363
TIX_LIBRARY, 1360
tix_option_get() (tkinter.tix.tixCommand method), 1364
tix_resetoptions() (tkinter.tix.tixCommand method), 1364
tixCommand (class in tkinter.tix), 1363
Tk, 1331
Tk (class in tkinter), 1332
Tk (class in tkinter.tix), 1359
Tk Option Data Types, 1339
Tkinter, 1331
tkinter (module), 1331
tkinter.scrolledtext (module), 1364
tkinter.tix (module), 1359
tkinter.ttk (module), 1342
TList (class in tkinter.tix), 1362
TLS, 832
TMP, 387
TMPDIR, 387
to_bytes() (int method), 33
to_eng_string() (decimal.Context method), 302
to_eng_string() (decimal.Decimal method), 295
to_integral() (decimal.Decimal method), 296
to_integral_exact() (decimal.Context method), 302
to_integral_exact() (decimal.Decimal method), 296
to_integral_value() (decimal.Decimal method), 296
to_sci_string() (decimal.Context method), 302
ToASCII() (in module encodings.idna), 171
tobuf() (tarfile.TarInfo method), 471
tobytes() (array.array method), 234
tobytes() (memoryview method), 69
today() (datetime.date class method), 177
today() (datetime.datetime class method), 181
tofile() (array.array method), 234
tok_name (in module token), 1679
token (module), 1679
token (shlex.shlex attribute), 1327
token_bytes() (in module secrets), 521
token_hex() (in module secrets), 521
token_urlsafe() (in module secrets), 521
TokenError, 1682
tokenize (module), 1681
tokenize command line option
    -e, --exact, 1682
    -h, --help, 1682
tokenize() (in module tokenize), 1681
tolist() (array.array method), 234
tolist() (memoryview method), 69
tolist() (parser.ST method), 1670
tomono() (in module audioop), 1251
toordinal() (datetime.date method), 179
toordinal() (datetime.datetime method), 185
top() (curses.panel.Panel method), 685
top() (poplib.POP3 method), 1168
top_panel() (in module curses.panel), 684
toprettyxml() (xml.dom.minidom.Node method), 1081
tostereo() (in module audioop), 1251
tostring() (array.array method), 234
tostring() (in module xml.etree.ElementTree), 1062
tostringlist() (in module xml.etree.ElementTree), 1062
total_changes (sqlite3.Connection attribute), 431
total_ordering() (in module functools), 342
total_seconds() (datetime.timedelta method), 177
totuple() (parser.ST method), 1670
touch() (pathlib.Path method), 370
touchline() (curses.window method), 675
touchwin() (curses.window method), 675
tounicode() (array.array method), 234
ToUnicode() (in module encodings.idna), 171
towards() (in module turtle), 1294
toxml() (xml.dom.minidom.Node method), 1081
tparm() (in module curses), 668
Trace (class in trace), 1538
Trace (class in tracemalloc), 1547
trace (module), 1536
trace command line option
    --help, 1537
    --ignore-dir=<dir>, 1538
    --ignore-module=<mod>, 1538
    --version, 1537
    -C, --coverdir=<dir>, 1537
    -R, --no-report, 1537
    -T, --trackcalls, 1537
    -c, --count, 1537
    -f, --file=<file>, 1537
    -g, --timing, 1537
    -l, --listfuncs, 1537
    -m, --missing, 1537
    -r, --report, 1537
    -s, --summary, 1537
    -t, --trace, 1537
trace function, 728, 1569, 1575
trace() (in module inspect), 1627
trace_dispatch() (bdb.Bdb method), 1512
traceback
    object, 1565, 1605
Traceback (class in tracemalloc), 1547

traceback (module), 1605
traceback (tracemalloc.Statistic attribute), 1546
traceback (tracemalloc.StatisticDiff attribute), 1547
traceback (tracemalloc.Trace attribute), 1547
traceback_limit (tracemalloc.Snapshot attribute), 1546
traceback_limit (wsgiref.handlers.BaseHandler attribute), 1124
TracebackException (class in traceback), 1607
tracebacklimit (in module sys), 1577
tracebacks
    in CGI scripts, 1116
TracebackType (in module types), 244
tracemalloc (module), 1539
tracer() (in module turtle), 1308
traces (tracemalloc.Snapshot attribute), 1546
transfercmd() (ftplib.FTP method), 1165
TransientResource (class in test.support), 1509
translate() (bytearray method), 57
translate() (bytes method), 57
translate() (in module fnmatch), 391
translate() (str method), 50
translation() (in module gettext), 1271
transport (asyncio.StreamWriter attribute), 910
Transport Layer Security, 832
Tree (class in tkinter.tix), 1362
TreeBuilder (class in xml.etree.ElementTree), 1066
Treeview (class in tkinter.ttk), 1352
triangular() (in module random), 316
triple-quoted string, **1791**
True, 29, 82
true, 29
True (built-in variable), 27
truediv() (in module operator), 349
trunc() (in module math), 31, 278
truncate() (in module os), 554
truncate() (io.IOBase method), 574
truth
    value, 29
truth() (in module operator), 348
try
    statement, 85
ttk, 1342
tty
    I/O control, 1734
tty (module), 1735
ttyname() (in module os), 538
tuple
    object, 39, 41
tuple (built-in class), 41
Tuple (in module typing), 1389
tuple2st() (in module parser), 1668
tuple_params (2to3 fixer), 1501
turnoff_sigfpe() (in module fpectl), 1634

turnon_sigfpe() (in module fpectl), 1634
Turtle (class in turtle), 1313
turtle (module), 1285
turtledemo (module), 1317
turtles() (in module turtle), 1312
TurtleScreen (class in turtle), 1313
turtlesize() (in module turtle), 1301
type, **1792**
    Boolean, 6
    built-in function, 81
    object, 23
    operations on dictionary, 75
    operations on list, 39
type (built-in class), 23
Type (class in typing), 1382
type (optparse.Option attribute), 1760
type (socket.socket attribute), 827
type (tarfile.TarInfo attribute), 471
type (urllib.request.Request attribute), 1131
TYPE_CHECKER (optparse.Option attribute), 1771
TYPE_CHECKING (in module typing), 1389
typeahead() (in module curses), 668
typecode (array.array attribute), 233
typecodes (in module array), 233
TYPED_ACTIONS (optparse.Option attribute), 1772
typed_subpart_iterator() (in module email.iterators), 1006
TypeError, 89
types
    built-in, 29
    immutable sequence, 39
    module, 81
    mutable sequence, 39
    operations on integer, 32
    operations on mapping, 75
    operations on numeric, 31
    operations on sequence, 37, 39
types (2to3 fixer), 1501
types (module), 242
TYPES (optparse.Option attribute), 1771
types_map (in module mimetypes), 1036
types_map (mimetypes.MimeTypes attribute), 1037
types_map_inv (mimetypes.MimeTypes attribute), 1037
TypeVar (class in typing), 1381
typing (module), 1375
TZ, 588, 589
tzinfo (class in datetime), 192
tzinfo (datetime.datetime attribute), 183
tzinfo (datetime.time attribute), 190
tzname (in module time), 590
tzname() (datetime.datetime method), 185

tzname() (datetime.time method), 191
tzname() (datetime.timezone method), 199
tzname() (datetime.tzinfo method), 193
tzset() (in module time), 588

U

u-LAW, 1249, 1254, 1262
ucd_3_2_0 (in module unicodedata), 140
udata (select.kevent attribute), 869
UDPServer (class in socketserver), 1198
UF_APPEND (in module stat), 382
UF_COMPRESSED (in module stat), 382
UF_HIDDEN (in module stat), 382
UF_IMMUTABLE (in module stat), 382
UF_NODUMP (in module stat), 382
UF_NOUNLINK (in module stat), 382
UF_OPAQUE (in module stat), 382
uid (tarfile.TarInfo attribute), 471
uid() (imaplib.IMAP4 method), 1175
uidl() (poplib.POP3 method), 1168
ulaw2lin() (in module audioop), 1251
umask() (in module os), 531
unalias (pdb command), 1523
uname (tarfile.TarInfo attribute), 471
uname() (in module os), 531
uname() (in module platform), 686
UNARY_INVERT (opcode), 1694
UNARY_NEGATIVE (opcode), 1694
UNARY_NOT (opcode), 1694
UNARY_POSITIVE (opcode), 1694
UnboundLocalError, 90
unbuffered I/O, 18
UNC paths
    and os.makedirs(), 544
unconsumed_tail (zlib.Decompress attribute), 445
unctrl() (in module curses), 669
unctrl() (in module curses.ascii), 683
Underflow (class in decimal), 304
undisplay (pdb command), 1523
undo() (in module turtle), 1294
undobufferentries() (in module turtle), 1305
undoc_header (cmd.Cmd attribute), 1321
unescape() (in module html), 1047
unescape() (in module xml.sax.saxutils), 1092
UnexpectedException, 1413
unexpectedSuccesses (unittest.TestResult attribute), 1436
unget_wch() (in module curses), 669
ungetch() (in module curses), 669
ungetch() (in module msvcrt), 1717
ungetmouse() (in module curses), 669
ungetwch() (in module msvcrt), 1718
unhexlify() (in module binascii), 1043
Unicode, 139, 154

database, 139
unicode (2to3 fixer), 1501
unicodedata (module), 139
UnicodeDecodeError, 90
UnicodeEncodeError, 90
UnicodeError, 90
UnicodeTranslateError, 90
UnicodeWarning, 92
unidata_version (in module unicodedata), 140
unified_diff() (in module difflib), 128
uniform() (in module random), 316
UnimplementedFileMode, 1156
Union (class in ctypes), 723
Union (in module typing), 1388
union() (frozenset method), 74
unique() (in module enum), 254, 257
unittest (module), 1415
unittest command line option
    --locals, 1417
    -b, --buffer, 1417
    -c, --catch, 1417
    -f, --failfast, 1417
unittest-discover command line option
    -p, --pattern pattern, 1418
    -s, --start-directory directory, 1418
    -t, --top-level-directory directory, 1418
    -v, --verbose, 1418
unittest.mock (module), 1442
universal newlines, **1792**
    bytearray.splitlines method, 62
    bytes.splitlines method, 62
    csv.reader function, 477
    importlib.abc.InspectLoader.get_source
        method, 1655
    io.IncrementalNewlineDecoder class, 581
    io.TextIOWrapper class, 580
    open() built-in function, 17
    str.splitlines method, 48
    subprocess module, 790
UNIX
    file control, 1737
    I/O control, 1737
unix_dialect (class in csv), 480
UnixDatagramServer (class in socketserver), 1198
UnixStreamServer (class in socketserver), 1198
unknown_decl() (html.parser.HTMLParser method), 1050
unknown_open() (urllib.request.BaseHandler method), 1134
unknown_open() (urllib.request.UnknownHandler method), 1138
UnknownHandler (class in urllib.request), 1131
UnknownProtocol, 1156
UnknownTransferEncoding, 1156

unlink() (in module os), 554
unlink() (pathlib.Path method), 370
unlink() (xml.dom.minidom.Node method), 1081
unlock() (mailbox.Babyl method), 1025
unlock() (mailbox.Mailbox method), 1020
unlock() (mailbox.Maildir method), 1022
unlock() (mailbox.mbox method), 1022
unlock() (mailbox.MH method), 1024
unlock() (mailbox.MMDF method), 1025
unpack() (in module struct), 150
unpack() (struct.Struct method), 154
unpack_archive() (in module shutil), 398
unpack_array() (xdrlib.Unpacker method), 504
unpack_bytes() (xdrlib.Unpacker method), 504
unpack_double() (xdrlib.Unpacker method), 504
UNPACK_EX (opcode), 1698
unpack_farray() (xdrlib.Unpacker method), 504
unpack_float() (xdrlib.Unpacker method), 504
unpack_fopaque() (xdrlib.Unpacker method), 504
unpack_from() (in module struct), 150
unpack_from() (struct.Struct method), 154
unpack_fstring() (xdrlib.Unpacker method), 504
unpack_list() (xdrlib.Unpacker method), 504
unpack_opaque() (xdrlib.Unpacker method), 504
UNPACK_SEQUENCE (opcode), 1698
unpack_string() (xdrlib.Unpacker method), 504
Unpacker (class in xdrlib), 502
unparsedEntityDecl() (xml.sax.handler.DTDHandler method), 1091
UnparsedEntityDeclHandler() (xml.parsers.expat.xmlparser method), 1101
Unpickler (class in pickle), 405
UnpicklingError, 404
unquote() (in module email.utils), 1004
unquote() (in module urllib.parse), 1150
unquote_plus() (in module urllib.parse), 1150
unquote_to_bytes() (in module urllib.parse), 1150
unregister() (in module atexit), 1604
unregister() (in module faulthandler), 1517
unregister() (select.devpoll method), 864
unregister() (select.epoll method), 865
unregister() (select.poll method), 866
unregister() (selectors.BaseSelector method), 870
unregister_archive_format() (in module shutil), 398
unregister_dialect() (in module csv), 478
unregister_unpack_format() (in module shutil), 399
unset() (test.support.EnvironmentVarGuard method), 1509
unsetenv() (in module os), 531
UnstructuredHeader (class in email.headerregistry), 974
unsubscribe() (imaplib.IMAP4 method), 1175
UnsupportedOperation, 571

until (pdb command), 1522
untokenize() (in module tokenize), 1681
untouchwin() (curses.window method), 675
unused_data (bz2.BZ2Decompressor attribute), 451
unused_data (lzma.LZMADecompressor attribute), 455
unused_data (zlib.Decompress attribute), 445
unverifiable (urllib.request.Request attribute), 1132
unwrap() (in module inspect), 1626
unwrap() (ssl.SSLSocket method), 846
up (pdb command), 1520
up() (in module turtle), 1296
update() (collections.Counter method), 210
update() (dict method), 77
update() (frozenset method), 75
update() (hashlib.hash method), 511
update() (hmac.HMAC method), 519
update() (http.cookies.Morsel method), 1213
update() (in module turtle), 1308
update() (mailbox.Mailbox method), 1020
update() (mailbox.Maildir method), 1021
update() (trace.CoverageResults method), 1538
update_authenticated() (urllib.request.HTTPPasswordMgrWithPriorAuth method), 1136
update_lines_cols() (in module curses), 669
update_panels() (in module curses.panel), 684
update_visible() (mailbox.BabylMessage method), 1031
update_wrapper() (in module functools), 346
upper() (bytearray method), 64
upper() (bytes method), 64
upper() (str method), 50
urandom() (in module os), 569
URL, 1109, 1144, 1152, 1206
    parsing, 1144
    relative, 1144
url (xmlrpc.client.ProtocolError attribute), 1228
url2pathname() (in module urllib.request), 1128
urlcleanup() (in module urllib.request), 1142
urldefrag() (in module urllib.parse), 1147
urlencode() (in module urllib.parse), 1150
URLError, 1151
urljoin() (in module urllib.parse), 1147
urllib (2to3 fixer), 1501
urllib (module), 1126
urllib.error (module), 1151
urllib.parse (module), 1144
urllib.request
    module, 1155
urllib.request (module), 1126
urllib.response (module), 1144
urllib.robotparser (module), 1152
urlopen() (in module urllib.request), 1126

URLopener (class in urllib.request), 1142
urlparse() (in module urllib.parse), 1144
urlretrieve() (in module urllib.request), 1141
urlsafe_b64decode() (in module base64), 1039
urlsafe_b64encode() (in module base64), 1039
urlsplit() (in module urllib.parse), 1146
urlunparse() (in module urllib.parse), 1146
urlunsplit() (in module urllib.parse), 1147
urn (uuid.UUID attribute), 1196
use_default_colors() (in module curses), 669
use_env() (in module curses), 669
use_rawinput (cmd.Cmd attribute), 1321
UseForeignDTD() (xml.parsers.expat.xmlparser method), 1099
USER, 662
user
    effective id, 528
    id, 529
    id, setting, 531
user() (poplib.POP3 method), 1168
USER_BASE (in module site), 1632
user_call() (bdb.Bdb method), 1513
user_exception() (bdb.Bdb method), 1513
user_line() (bdb.Bdb method), 1513
user_return() (bdb.Bdb method), 1513
USER_SITE (in module site), 1632
usercustomize
    module, 1631
UserDict (class in collections), 221
UserList (class in collections), 221
USERNAME, 528, 662
username (email.headerregistry.Address attribute), 978
USERPROFILE, 372
userptr() (curses.panel.Panel method), 685
UserString (class in collections), 221
UserWarning, 92
USTAR_FORMAT (in module tarfile), 467
UTC, 582
utc (datetime.timezone attribute), 199
utcfromtimestamp() (datetime.datetime class method), 182
utcnow() (datetime.datetime class method), 181
utcoffset() (datetime.datetime method), 185
utcoffset() (datetime.time method), 191
utcoffset() (datetime.timezone method), 199
utcoffset() (datetime.tzinfo method), 192
utctimetuple() (datetime.datetime method), 185
utf8 (email.policy.EmailPolicy attribute), 969
utf8() (poplib.POP3 method), 1168
utf8_enabled (imaplib.IMAP4 attribute), 1175
utime() (in module os), 554
uu
    module, 1042

uu (module), 1044
UUID (class in uuid), 1195
uuid (module), 1195
uuid1, 1196
uuid1() (in module uuid), 1196
uuid3, 1196
uuid3() (in module uuid), 1196
uuid4, 1196
uuid4() (in module uuid), 1196
uuid5, 1196
uuid5() (in module uuid), 1196
UuidCreate() (in module msilib), 1711

V

v4_int_to_packed() (in module ipaddress), 1247
v6_int_to_packed() (in module ipaddress), 1247
validator() (in module wsgiref.validate), 1121
value
    truth, 29
value (ctypes._SimpleCData attribute), 721
value (http.cookiejar.Cookie attribute), 1221
value (http.cookies.Morsel attribute), 1213
value (xml.dom.Attr attribute), 1076
Value() (in module multiprocessing), 756
Value() (in module multiprocessing.sharedctypes), 758
Value() (multiprocessing.managers.SyncManager method), 761
value_decode() (http.cookies.BaseCookie method), 1212
value_encode() (http.cookies.BaseCookie method), 1212
ValueError, 90
valuerefs() (weakref.WeakValueDictionary method), 237
values
    Boolean, 82
values() (dict method), 77
values() (email.message.EmailMessage method), 953
values() (email.message.Message method), 991
values() (mailbox.Mailbox method), 1019
values() (types.MappingProxyType method), 245
ValuesView (class in collections.abc), 224
ValuesView (class in typing), 1384
variable annotation, **1792**
variance() (in module statistics), 324
variant (uuid.UUID attribute), 1196
vars() (built-in function), 23
VBAR (in module token), 1679
vbar (tkinter.scrolledtext.ScrolledText attribute), 1364
VBAREQUAL (in module token), 1679
Vec2D (class in turtle), 1314
venv (module), 1551

VERBOSE (in module re), 112
verbose (in module tabnanny), 1685
verbose (in module test.support), 1504
verify() (smtplib.SMTP method), 1185
VERIFY_CRL_CHECK_CHAIN (in module ssl), 839
VERIFY_CRL_CHECK_LEAF (in module ssl), 839
VERIFY_DEFAULT (in module ssl), 839
verify_flags (ssl.SSLContext attribute), 852
verify_mode (ssl.SSLContext attribute), 852
verify_request() (socketserver.BaseServer method), 1201
VERIFY_X509_STRICT (in module ssl), 839
VERIFY_X509_TRUSTED_FIRST (in module ssl), 839
VerifyFlags (class in ssl), 839
VerifyMode (class in ssl), 839
version (email.headerregistry.MIMEVersionHeader attribute), 976
version (http.client.HTTPResponse attribute), 1160
version (http.cookiejar.Cookie attribute), 1221
version (in module curses), 676
version (in module marshal), 418
version (in module sqlite3), 424
version (in module sys), 1577
version (ipaddress.IPv4Address attribute), 1238
version (ipaddress.IPv4Network attribute), 1241
version (ipaddress.IPv6Address attribute), 1239
version (ipaddress.IPv6Network attribute), 1244
version (urllib.request.URLopener attribute), 1142
version (uuid.UUID attribute), 1196
version() (in module ensurepip), 1550
version() (in module platform), 686
version() (ssl.SSLSocket method), 846
version_info (in module sqlite3), 424
version_info (in module sys), 1578
version_string() (http.server.BaseHTTPRequestHandler method), 1209
vformat() (string.Formatter method), 96
virtual
    Environments, 1551
virtual environment, **1792**
virtual machine, **1792**
visit() (ast.NodeVisitor method), 1675
vline() (curses.window method), 675
voidcmd() (ftplib.FTP method), 1164
volume (zipfile.ZipInfo attribute), 464
vonmisesvariate() (in module random), 317

W

W_OK (in module os), 541
wait() (asyncio.asyncio.subprocess.Process method), 917
wait() (asyncio.Condition method), 923
wait() (asyncio.Event method), 922
wait() (in module asyncio), 897
wait() (in module concurrent.futures), 786
wait() (in module multiprocessing.connection), 769
wait() (in module os), 564
wait() (multiprocessing.pool.AsyncResult method), 767
wait() (subprocess.Popen method), 794
wait() (threading.Barrier method), 737
wait() (threading.Condition method), 734
wait() (threading.Event method), 736
wait3() (in module os), 565
wait4() (in module os), 565
wait_closed() (asyncio.Server method), 882
wait_for() (asyncio.Condition method), 923
wait_for() (in module asyncio), 898
wait_for() (threading.Condition method), 734
waitid() (in module os), 564
waitpid() (in module os), 564
walk() (email.message.EmailMessage method), 955
walk() (email.message.Message method), 994
walk() (in module ast), 1675
walk() (in module os), 555
walk_packages() (in module pkgutil), 1645
walk_stack() (in module traceback), 1607
walk_tb() (in module traceback), 1607
want (doctest.Example attribute), 1407
warn() (in module warnings), 1586
warn_explicit() (in module warnings), 1587
Warning, 92, 436
warning() (in module logging), 636
warning() (logging.Logger method), 626
warning() (xml.sax.handler.ErrorHandler method), 1092
warnings, 1583
warnings (module), 1583
WarningsRecorder (class in test.support), 1509
warnoptions (in module sys), 1578
wasSuccessful() (unittest.TestResult method), 1437
WatchedFileHandler (class in logging.handlers), 651
wave (module), 1257
WCONTINUED (in module os), 565
WCOREDUMP() (in module os), 565
WeakKeyDictionary (class in weakref), 236
WeakMethod (class in weakref), 237
weakref (module), 235
WeakSet (class in weakref), 237
WeakValueDictionary (class in weakref), 237
webbrowser (module), 1107
weekday() (datetime.date method), 179
weekday() (datetime.datetime method), 186
weekday() (in module calendar), 205
weekheader() (in module calendar), 205

weibullvariate() (in module random), 317
WEXITED (in module os), 564
WEXITSTATUS() (in module os), 566
wfile (http.server.BaseHTTPRequestHandler attribute), 1207
what() (in module imghdr), 1262
what() (in module sndhdr), 1263
whathdr() (in module sndhdr), 1263
whatis (pdb command), 1522
where (pdb command), 1520
which() (in module shutil), 396
whichdb() (in module dbm), 418
while
    statement, 29
whitespace (in module string), 96
whitespace (shlex.shlex attribute), 1326
whitespace_split (shlex.shlex attribute), 1326
Widget (class in tkinter.ttk), 1345
width (textwrap.TextWrapper attribute), 137
width() (in module turtle), 1296
WIFCONTINUED() (in module os), 565
WIFEXITED() (in module os), 566
WIFSIGNALED() (in module os), 566
WIFSTOPPED() (in module os), 565
win32_ver() (in module platform), 687
WinDLL (class in ctypes), 713
window manager (widgets), 1338
window() (curses.panel.Panel method), 685
window_height() (in module turtle), 1312
window_width() (in module turtle), 1312
Windows ini file, 483
WindowsError, 90
WindowsPath (class in pathlib), 365
WindowsRegistryFinder (class in importlib.machinery), 1658
winerror (OSError attribute), 88
WinError() (in module ctypes), 720
WINFUNCTYPE() (in module ctypes), 716
winreg (module), 1718
WinSock, 863
winsound (module), 1726
winver (in module sys), 1578
WITH_CLEANUP_FINISH (opcode), 1697
WITH_CLEANUP_START (opcode), 1697
with_hostmask (ipaddress.IPv4Interface attribute), 1246
with_hostmask (ipaddress.IPv4Network attribute), 1242
with_hostmask (ipaddress.IPv6Interface attribute), 1246
with_hostmask (ipaddress.IPv6Network attribute), 1244
with_name() (pathlib.PurePath method), 364
with_netmask (ipaddress.IPv4Interface attribute), 1246
with_netmask (ipaddress.IPv4Network attribute), 1242
with_netmask (ipaddress.IPv6Interface attribute), 1246
with_netmask (ipaddress.IPv6Network attribute), 1244
with_prefixlen (ipaddress.IPv4Interface attribute), 1246
with_prefixlen (ipaddress.IPv4Network attribute), 1242
with_prefixlen (ipaddress.IPv6Interface attribute), 1246
with_prefixlen (ipaddress.IPv6Network attribute), 1244
with_suffix() (pathlib.PurePath method), 364
with_traceback() (BaseException method), 86
WNOHANG (in module os), 565
WNOWAIT (in module os), 564
wordchars (shlex.shlex attribute), 1326
World Wide Web, 1107, 1144, 1152
wrap() (in module textwrap), 135
wrap() (textwrap.TextWrapper method), 139
wrap_bio() (ssl.SSLContext method), 851
wrap_future() (in module asyncio), 896
wrap_socket() (in module ssl), 833
wrap_socket() (ssl.SSLContext method), 851
wrapper() (in module curses), 669
wraps() (in module functools), 346
WRITABLE (in module tkinter), 1341
writable() (asyncore.dispatcher method), 933
writable() (io.IOBase method), 574
write() (asyncio.StreamWriter method), 911
write() (asyncio.WriteTransport method), 900
write() (code.InteractiveInterpreter method), 1638
write() (codecs.StreamWriter method), 161
write() (configparser.ConfigParser method), 499
write() (email.generator.BytesGenerator method), 963
write() (email.generator.Generator method), 964
write() (in module os), 538
write() (in module turtle), 1300
write() (io.BufferedIOBase method), 576
write() (io.BufferedWriter method), 578
write() (io.RawIOBase method), 575
write() (io.TextIOBase method), 580
write() (mmap.mmap method), 946
write() (ossaudiodev.oss_audio_device method), 1264
write() (ssl.MemoryBIO method), 860
write() (ssl.SSLSocket method), 844
write() (telnetlib.Telnet method), 1194

write() (xml.etree.ElementTree.ElementTree method), 1065
write() (zipfile.ZipFile method), 461
write_byte() (mmap.mmap method), 947
write_bytes() (pathlib.Path method), 370
write_docstringdict() (in module turtle), 1315
write_eof() (asyncio.StreamWriter method), 911
write_eof() (asyncio.WriteTransport method), 901
write_eof() (ssl.MemoryBIO method), 860
write_history_file() (in module readline), 143
write_results() (trace.CoverageResults method), 1538
write_text() (pathlib.Path method), 370
writeall() (ossaudiodev.oss_audio_device method), 1264
writeframes() (aifc.aifc method), 1254
writeframes() (sunau.AU_write method), 1257
writeframes() (wave.Wave_write method), 1259
writeframesraw() (aifc.aifc method), 1254
writeframesraw() (sunau.AU_write method), 1257
writeframesraw() (wave.Wave_write method), 1259
writeheader() (csv.DictWriter method), 482
writelines() (asyncio.StreamWriter method), 911
writelines() (asyncio.WriteTransport method), 900
writelines() (codecs.StreamWriter method), 161
writelines() (io.IOBase method), 574
writePlist() (in module plistlib), 506
writePlistToBytes() (in module plistlib), 506
writepy() (zipfile.PyZipFile method), 462
writer (formatter.formatter attribute), 1705
writer() (in module csv), 478
writerow() (csv.csvwriter method), 482
writerows() (csv.csvwriter method), 482
writestr() (zipfile.ZipFile method), 462
WriteTransport (class in asyncio), 900
writev() (in module os), 538
writexml() (xml.dom.minidom.Node method), 1081
WrongDocumentErr, 1078
ws_comma (2to3 fixer), 1501
wsgi_file_wrapper (wsgiref.handlers.BaseHandler attribute), 1125
wsgi_multiprocess (wsgiref.handlers.BaseHandler attribute), 1123
wsgi_multithread (wsgiref.handlers.BaseHandler attribute), 1123
wsgi_run_once (wsgiref.handlers.BaseHandler attribute), 1124
wsgiref (module), 1117
wsgiref.handlers (module), 1122
wsgiref.headers (module), 1119
wsgiref.simple_server (module), 1120
wsgiref.util (module), 1117
wsgiref.validate (module), 1121
WSGIRequestHandler (class in wsgiref.simple_server), 1121
WSGIServer (class in wsgiref.simple_server), 1120
wShowWindow (subprocess.STARTUPINFO attribute), 796
WSTOPPED (in module os), 564
WSTOPSIG() (in module os), 566
wstring_at() (in module ctypes), 720
WTERMSIG() (in module os), 566
WUNTRACED (in module os), 565
WWW, 1107, 1144, 1152
    server, 1109, 1206

X

X (in module re), 112
X509 certificate, 853
X_OK (in module os), 541
xatom() (imaplib.IMAP4 method), 1175
XATTR_CREATE (in module os), 558
XATTR_REPLACE (in module os), 558
XATTR_SIZE_MAX (in module os), 557
xcor() (in module turtle), 1295
XDR, 502
xdrlib (module), 502
xhdr() (nntplib.NNTP method), 1181
XHTML, 1047
XHTML_NAMESPACE (in module xml.dom), 1070
xml (module), 1052
XML() (in module xml.etree.ElementTree), 1062
xml.dom (module), 1069
xml.dom.minidom (module), 1079
xml.dom.pulldom (module), 1084
xml.etree.ElementTree (module), 1054
xml.parsers.expat (module), 1097
xml.parsers.expat.errors (module), 1104
xml.parsers.expat.model (module), 1103
xml.sax (module), 1085
xml.sax.handler (module), 1087
xml.sax.saxutils (module), 1092
xml.sax.xmlreader (module), 1093
XML_ERROR_ABORTED (in module xml.parsers.expat.errors), 1106
XML_ERROR_ASYNC_ENTITY (in module xml.parsers.expat.errors), 1104
XML_ERROR_ATTRIBUTE_EXTERNAL_ENTITY_REF (in module xml.parsers.expat.errors), 1104
XML_ERROR_BAD_CHAR_REF (in module xml.parsers.expat.errors), 1104
XML_ERROR_BINARY_ENTITY_REF (in module xml.parsers.expat.errors), 1104
XML_ERROR_CANT_CHANGE_FEATURE_ONCE_PA (in module xml.parsers.expat.errors), 1105
XML_ERROR_DUPLICATE_ATTRIBUTE (in module xml.parsers.expat.errors), 1104

XML_ERROR_ENTITY_DECLARED_IN_PE
    (in module xml.parsers.expat.errors), 1105
XML_ERROR_EXTERNAL_ENTITY_HANDLING
    (in module xml.parsers.expat.errors), 1105
XML_ERROR_FEATURE_REQUIRES_XML_DTD
    (in module xml.parsers.expat.errors), 1105
XML_ERROR_FINISHED (in module xml.parsers.expat.errors), 1106
XML_ERROR_INCOMPLETE_PE (in module xml.parsers.expat.errors), 1105
XML_ERROR_INCORRECT_ENCODING (in module xml.parsers.expat.errors), 1104
XML_ERROR_INVALID_TOKEN (in module xml.parsers.expat.errors), 1104
XML_ERROR_JUNK_AFTER_DOC_ELEMENT (in module xml.parsers.expat.errors), 1104
XML_ERROR_MISPLACED_XML_PI (in module xml.parsers.expat.errors), 1104
XML_ERROR_NO_ELEMENTS (in module xml.parsers.expat.errors), 1104
XML_ERROR_NO_MEMORY (in module xml.parsers.expat.errors), 1105
XML_ERROR_NOT_STANDALONE (in module xml.parsers.expat.errors), 1105
XML_ERROR_NOT_SUSPENDED (in module xml.parsers.expat.errors), 1106
XML_ERROR_PARAM_ENTITY_REF (in module xml.parsers.expat.errors), 1105
XML_ERROR_PARTIAL_CHAR (in module xml.parsers.expat.errors), 1105
XML_ERROR_PUBLICID (in module xml.parsers.expat.errors), 1106
XML_ERROR_RECURSIVE_ENTITY_REF (in module xml.parsers.expat.errors), 1105
XML_ERROR_SUSPEND_PE (in module xml.parsers.expat.errors), 1106
XML_ERROR_SUSPENDED (in module xml.parsers.expat.errors), 1106
XML_ERROR_SYNTAX (in module xml.parsers.expat.errors), 1105
XML_ERROR_TAG_MISMATCH (in module xml.parsers.expat.errors), 1105
XML_ERROR_TEXT_DECL (in module xml.parsers.expat.errors), 1105
XML_ERROR_UNBOUND_PREFIX (in module xml.parsers.expat.errors), 1105
XML_ERROR_UNCLOSED_CDATA_SECTION (in module xml.parsers.expat.errors), 1105
XML_ERROR_UNCLOSED_TOKEN (in module xml.parsers.expat.errors), 1105
XML_ERROR_UNDECLARING_PREFIX (in module xml.parsers.expat.errors), 1105
XML_ERROR_UNDEFINED_ENTITY (in module xml.parsers.expat.errors), 1105
XML_ERROR_UNEXPECTED_STATE (in module xml.parsers.expat.errors), 1105
XML_ERROR_UNKNOWN_ENCODING (in module xml.parsers.expat.errors), 1105
XML_ERROR_XML_DECL (in module xml.parsers.expat.errors), 1105
XML_NAMESPACE (in module xml.dom), 1070
xmlcharrefreplace_errors() (in module codecs), 159
XmlDeclHandler() (xml.parsers.expat.xmlparser method), 1100
XMLFilterBase (class in xml.sax.saxutils), 1093
XMLGenerator (class in xml.sax.saxutils), 1093
XMLID() (in module xml.etree.ElementTree), 1062
XMLNS_NAMESPACE (in module xml.dom), 1070
XMLParser (class in xml.etree.ElementTree), 1067
XMLParserType (in module xml.parsers.expat), 1097
XMLPullParser (class in xml.etree.ElementTree), 1068
XMLReader (class in xml.sax.xmlreader), 1093
xmlrpc.client (module), 1223
xmlrpc.server (module), 1231
xor() (in module operator), 349
xover() (nntplib.NNTP method), 1182
xpath() (nntplib.NNTP method), 1182
xrange (2to3 fixer), 1501
xreadlines (2to3 fixer), 1501
xview() (tkinter.ttk.Treeview method), 1355

Y

Y2K, 582
ycor() (in module turtle), 1295
year (datetime.date attribute), 178
year (datetime.datetime attribute), 183
Year 2000, 582
Year 2038, 582
yeardatescalendar() (calendar.Calendar method), 203
yeardays2calendar() (calendar.Calendar method), 203
yeardayscalendar() (calendar.Calendar method), 204
YESEXPR (in module locale), 1280
YIELD_FROM (opcode), 1697
YIELD_VALUE (opcode), 1696
yiq_to_rgb() (in module colorsys), 1261
yview() (tkinter.ttk.Treeview method), 1355

Z

Zen of Python, 1792
ZeroDivisionError, 90
zfill() (bytearray method), 64
zfill() (bytes method), 64
zfill() (str method), 50
zip (2to3 fixer), 1501

zip() (built-in function), 24
ZIP_BZIP2 (in module zipfile), 458
ZIP_DEFLATED (in module zipfile), 458
zip_longest() (in module itertools), 336
ZIP_LZMA (in module zipfile), 458
ZIP_STORED (in module zipfile), 458
zipapp (module), 1559
zipapp command line option
    –info, 1560
    -h, –help, 1560
    -m <mainfn>, –main=<mainfn>, 1560
    -o <output>, –output=<output>, 1560
    -p <interpreter>, –python=<interpreter>, 1560
ZipFile (class in zipfile), 459
zipfile (module), 457
zipfile command line option
    -c <zipfile> <source1> ... <sourceN>, 465
    -e <zipfile> <output_dir>, 465
    -l <zipfile>, 465
    -t <zipfile>, 465
zipimport (module), 1641
zipimporter (class in zipimport), 1642
ZipImportError, 1641
ZipInfo (class in zipfile), 458
zlib (module), 443
ZLIB_RUNTIME_VERSION (in module zlib), 446
ZLIB_VERSION (in module zlib), 446

CPSIA information can be obtained
at www.ICGtesting.com
Printed in the USA
LVHW061522040523
746089LV00023B/91